9th Edition

THEORY OF STRATEGIC MANAGEMENT

WITH CASES

9th Edition

THEORY OF STRATEGIC MANAGEMENT

WITH CASES

Gareth R. Jones
Texas A&M University

Charles W. L. Hill
University of Washington

SOUTH-WESTERN
CENGAGE Learning

Australia • Brazil • Japan • Korea • Mexico • Singapore • Spain • United Kingdom • United States

TH-WESTERN
GAGE Learning

...ory of Strategic Management: ...ith Cases
Gareth R. Jones and Charles W. L. Hill

Vice President of Editorial, Business:
Jack W. Calhoun

Vice President/Editor-in-Chief:
Melissa Acuna

Sr. Acquisitions Editor: Michele Rhoades

Sr. Editorial Assistant: Ruth Belanger

Developmental Editor:
Suzanna Bainbridge

Marketing Manager: Nathan Anderson

Marketing Coordinator: Suellen Ruttkay

Marketing Communications Manager:
Jim Overly

Assoc. Content Project Manager:
Jana Lewis

Assoc. Media Editor: Danny Bolan

Sr. Manufacturing Buyer:
Sandee Milewski

Production Service: S4Carlisle
Publishing Services

Sr. Art Director: Tippy McIntosh

Internal Designer:

Cover Image: Shutterstock

For product information and technology assistance, contact us at
Cengage Learning Customer & Sales Support, 1-800-354-9706

For permission to use material from this text or product,
submit all requests online at **www.cengage.com/permissions**.
Further permissions questions can be e-mailed to
permissionrequest@cengage.com

ExamView® is a registered trademark of eInstruction Corp. Windows is a registered trademark of the Microsoft Corporation used herein under license. Macintosh and Power Macintosh are registered trademarks of Apple Computer, Inc. used herein under license.
© 2008 Cengage Learning. All Rights Reserved.

Cengage Learning WebTutor™ is a trademark of Cengage Learning.

Library of Congress Control Number: 2009934262
International Student Edition ISBN-13: 978-0-538-75250-3
International Student Edition ISBN-10: 0-538-75250-5

Cengage Learning International Offices

Asia
cengageasia.com
tel: (65) 6410 1200

Australia/New Zealand
cengage.com.au
tel: (61) 3 9685 4111

Brazil
cengage.com.br
tel: (011) 3665 9900

India
cengage.co.in
tel: (91) 11 30484837/38

Latin America
cengage.com.mx
tel: +52 (55) 1500 6000

UK/Europe/Middle East/Africa
cengage.co.uk
tel: (44) 207 067 2500

Represented in Canada by Nelson Education, Ltd.
nelson.com
tel: (416) 752 9100 / (800) 668 0671
Cengage Learning products are represented in Canada by
Nelson Education, Ltd.

For product information: **www.cengage.com/international**
Visit your local offi ce: **www.cengage.com/global**
Visit our corporate website: **www.cengage.com**

Printed in China by China Translation & Printing Services Limited
1 2 3 4 5 6 7 12 11 10 09

BRIEF CONTENTS

CONTENTS

PART FOUR   IMPLEMENTING STRATEGY

Chapter 11   **Performance and Governance**   **345**

PART FIVE   CASES IN STRATEGIC MANAGEMENT

PREFACE

Since the eighth edition was published, this book has strengthened its position as a market leader in the Strategic Management market. This tells us that we continue to meet the expectations of existing users and attract many new users to our book. It is clear that most strategy instructors share with us a concern for our currency in the text and its examples to ensure that cutting-edge issues and new developments in strategic management are continually addressed.

Just as in the last edition, our objective in writing the ninth edition has been to maintain all that was good about prior editions. As we move steadily into the second decade of the 21st Century, we continue to refine our approach by expanding our discussion of established strategic management issues and adding new material as management trends develop to present a more complete, clear, and current account of strategic management. We believe that the result is a book that is more closely aligned with the needs of today's professors and students and with the realities of competition in the global environment.

COMPREHENSIVE AND UP-TO-DATE COVERAGE

We have updated many of the features running throughout the chapters, including all new Opening Cases and Running Cases. For the Running Cases, Walmart is the focus corporation. In this edition, we have made no changes to the number or sequencing of our chapters. However, we have made many significant changes inside each chapter to refine and update our presentation of strategic management. Continuing real-world changes in strategic management practices such as the increased use of cost reduction strategies like global outsourcing, ethical issues, and lean production, and a continued emphasis on the business model as the driver of differentiation and competitive advantage, have led to many changes in our approach. To emphasize the importance of ethical decision making in strategic management, we have included a new marginal feature—Ethical Dilemma—that asks students to make sound management decisions while considering ethical ramifications in business.

Throughout the revision process, we have been careful to preserve the *balanced and integrated* nature of our account of strategic management. As we have continued to add new material, we have also shortened or deleted coverage of out-of-date or less important models and concepts to help students identify and focus on the core concepts and issues in the field. We have also paid close attention to retaining the book's readability.

Finally, it is important to emphasize that we have overhauled the case selection. The cases are all either new to this edition, or revised and updated versions of cases that appeared in prior editions. As always, we have used a tight screen to filter out irrelevant cases, and we believe that the selection we offer is the best on the market. We would like to extend our gratitude to the case authors who have contributed to this edition: Isaac Cohen (*San Jose State University*), Alan N. Hoffman (Bentley College), Frank C. Barnes (*University of North Carolina–Charlotte*), and Beverly B. Tyler (*North Carolina State University.*)

PRACTICING STRATEGIC MANAGEMENT: AN INTERACTIVE APPROACH

We have received a lot of positive feedback about the usefulness of the end-of-chapter exercises and assignments in the Practicing Strategic Management sections in our book. They offer a wide range of hands-on learning experiences for students. Following the Chapter Summary and Discussion Questions, each chapter contains the following exercises and assignments:

- **Small group exercise.** This short (20-minute) experiential exercise asks students to divide into groups and discuss a scenario concerning some aspect of strategic management. For example, the scenario in Chapter 11 asks students to identify the stakeholders of their educational institution and evaluate how stakeholders' claims are being and should be met.
- **Article file.** As in the last edition, this exercise requires students to search business magazines to identify a company that is facing a particular strategic management problem. For instance, students are asked to locate and research a company pursuing a low-cost or a differentiation strategy, and to describe this company's strategy, its advantages and disadvantages, and the core competencies required to pursue it. Students' presentations of their findings lead to lively class discussions.
- **Strategic management project.** In small groups, students choose a company to study for the whole semester and then analyze the company using the series of questions provided at the end of every chapter. For example, students might select Ford Motor Co. and, using the series of chapter questions, collect information on Ford's top managers, mission, ethical position, domestic and global strategy and structure, and so on. Students write a case study of their company and present it to the class at the end of the semester. In the past, we also had students present one or more of the cases in the book early in the semester, but now in our classes, we treat the students' own projects as the major class assignment and their case presentations as the climax of the semester's learning experience.
- **Closing case study.** A short closing case provides an opportunity for a short class discussion of a chapter-related theme.

In creating these exercises, it is not our intention to suggest that they should *all* be used for *every* chapter. For example, over a semester, an instructor might combine a group Strategic Management Project with five to six Article File assignments, while incorporating eight to ten Small Group Exercises in class.

We have found that our interactive approach to teaching strategic management appeals to students. It also greatly improves the quality of their learning experience. Our approach is more fully discussed in the *Instructor's Resource Manual*.

STRATEGIC MANAGEMENT CASES

The twenty-two cases that we have selected for this edition will appeal, we are certain, to students and professors alike, both because these cases are intrinsically interesting and because of the number of strategic management issues they illuminate. The organizations discussed in the cases range from large, well-known companies, for which students can do research to update the information, to small, entrepreneurial businesses that illustrate the uncertainty and challenge of the strategic management process. In addition, the selections include many international cases, and most of the other cases contain some element of global strategy. Refer to the Contents for a complete listing of the cases with brief descriptions.

To help students learn how to effectively analyze and write a case study, we continue to include a special section on this subject. It has a checklist and an explanation of areas to consider, suggested research tools, and tips on financial analysis. We feel that our entire selection of cases is unrivaled in breadth and depth, and we are grateful to the other case authors who have contributed to this edition.

TEACHING AND LEARNING AIDS

Taken together, the teaching and learning features of *Strategic Management* provide a package that is unsurpassed in its coverage and that supports the integrated approach that we have taken throughout the book.

For the Instructor

- **The Instructor's Resource Manual:** Theory has been completely revised. For each chapter, we provide a clearly focused synopsis, a list of teaching objectives, a comprehensive lecture outline, teaching notes for the *Ethical Dilemma* feature, suggested answers to discussion questions, and comments on the end-of-chapter activities. Each Opening Case, Strategy in Action boxed feature, and Closing Case has a synopsis and a corresponding teaching note to help guide class discussion.
- **ExamView Test Bank** offers a set of comprehensive true/false, multiple-choice, and essay questions for each chapter in the book. The mix of questions has been adjusted to provide fewer fact-based of simple memorization items and to provide more items that rely on synthesis or application. Also, more items now reflect real or hypothetical situations in organizations. Every question is keyed to the Learning Objectives outlined in the text and includes an answer and text page reference.
- **Case Teaching Notes** include a complete list of case discussion questions as well as a comprehensive teaching note for each case, which gives a complete analysis of case issues.
- **DVD program** highlights many issues of interest and can be used to spark class discussion. It offers a compilation of footage from the Videos for Humanities video series.
- **Companion website** contains many features to aid instructors, including instructor-based PowerPoint, a DVD guide, and access to the student website.
- **WebTutor** is a web platform containing premium content such as unique web quizzes, audio summary and quiz files, lecture PowerPoint slides, and crossword puzzles for key terms from the text.

For the Student

- **Companion Website** includes chapter summaries, learning objectives, web quizzes, glossary, and flashcards.

ACKNOWLEDGMENTS

This book is the product of far more than two authors. We are grateful to our Acquisitions Editor, Michele Rhoades; our developmental editor, Suzanna Bainbridge; and our Marketing Manager, Nathan Anderson, for their help in developing and promoting the book and for providing us with timely feedback and information from professors and reviewers, which allowed us to shape the book to meet the needs of its intended market. We are also grateful to Jana Lewis and Tiffany Timmerman, project editors, for their adept handling of production. We are also grateful to the case authors for allowing us to use their materials. We also want to thank the departments of management at the University of Washington and Texas A&M University for providing the setting and atmosphere in which the book could be written, and the students of these universities who react to and provide input for many of our ideas. In addition, the following reviewers of this and earlier editions gave us valuable suggestions for improving the manuscript from its original version to its current form:

Ken Armstrong, *Anderson University*
Richard Babcock, *University of San Francisco*
Kunal Banerji, *West Virginia University*
Kevin Banning, *Auburn University – Montgomery*
Glenn Bassett, *University of Bridgeport*
Thomas H. Berliner, *The University of Texas at Dallas*
Bonnie Bollinger, *Ivy Technical Community College*
Richard G. Brandenburg, *University of Vermont*
Steven Braund, *University of Hull*
Philip Bromiley, *University of Minnesota*
Geoffrey Brooks, *Western Oregon State College*
Amanda Budde, *University of Hawaii*
Lowell Busenitz, *University of Houston*
Charles J. Capps III, *Sam Houston State University*
Don Caruth, *Texas A&M Commerce*
Gene R. Conaster, *Golden State University*
Steven W. Congden, *University of Hartford*
Catherine M. Daily, *Ohio State University*
Robert DeFillippi, *Suffolk University Sawyer School of Management*
Helen Deresky, *SUNY – Plattsburgh*
Fred J. Dorn, *University of Mississippi*
Gerald E. Evans, *The University of Montana*
John Fahy, *Trinity College, Dublin*
Patricia Feltes, *Southwest Missouri State University*
Bruce Fern, *New York University*
Mark Fiegener, *Oregon State University*
Chuck Foley, *Columbus State Community College*
Isaac Fox, *Washington State University*
Craig Galbraith, *University of North Carolina at Wilmington*
Scott R. Gallagher, *Rutgers University*
Eliezer Geisler, *Northeastern Illinois University*
Gretchen Gemeinhardt, *University of Houston*
Lynn Godkin, *Lamar University*

Sanjay Goel, *University of Minnesota – Duluth*
Robert L. Goldberg, *Northeastern University*
James Grinnell, *Merrimack College*
Russ Hagberg, *Northern Illinois University*
Allen Harmon, *University of Minnesota – Duluth*
David Hoopes, *California State University – Dominguez Hills*
Todd Hostager, *University of Wisconsin – Eau Claire*
Graham L. Hubbard, *University of Minnesota*
Tammy G. Hunt, *University of North Carolina at Wilmington*
James Gaius Ibe, *Morris College*
W. Grahm Irwin, *Miami University*
Homer Johnson, *Loyola University – Chicago*
Jonathan L. Johnson, *University of Arkansas – Walton College
  of Business Administration*
Marios Katsioloudes, *St. Joseph's University*
Robert Keating, *University of North Carolina at Wilmington*
Geoffrey King, *California State University – Fullerton*
Rico Lam, *University of Oregon*
Robert J. Litschert, *Virginia Polytechnic Institute and State University*
Franz T. Lohrke, *Louisiana State University*
Paul Mallette, *Colorado State University*
Daniel Marrone, *SUNY Farmingdale*
Lance A. Masters, *California State University – San Bernardino*
Robert N. McGrath, *Embry-Riddle Aeronautical University*
Charles Mercer, *Drury College*
Van Miller, *University of Dayton*
Tom Morris, *University of San Diego*
Joanna Mulholland, *West Chester University of Pennsylvania*
James Muraski, *Marquette University*
John Nebeck, *Viterbo University*
Francine Newth, *Providence College*
Don Okhomina, *Fayetteville State University*
Phaedon P. Papadopoulos, *Houston Baptist University*
John Pappalardo, *Keene State College*
Paul R. Reed, *Sam Houston State University*
Rhonda K. Reger, *Arizona State University*
Malika Richards, *Indiana University*
Simon Rodan, *San Jose State*
Stuart Rosenberg, *Dowling College*
Douglas Ross, *Towson University*
Ronald Sanchez, *University of Illinois*
Joseph A. Schenk, *University of Dayton*
Brian Shaffer, *University of Kentucky*
Leonard Sholtis, *Eastern Michigan University*
Pradip K. Shukla, *Chapman University*
Mel Sillmon, *University of Michigan – Dearborn*
Dennis L. Smart, *University of Nebraska at Omaha*
Barbara Spencer, *Clemson University*
Lawrence Steenberg, *University of Evansville*
Kim A. Stewart, *University of Denver*

Ted Takamura, *Warner Pacific College*
Scott Taylor, *Florida Metropolitan University*
Thuhang Tran, *Middle Tennessee University*
Bobby Vaught, *Southwest Missouri State*
Robert P. Vichas, *Florida Atlantic University*
John Vitton, *University of North Dakota*
Edward Ward, *St. Cloud State University*
Kenneth Wendeln, *Indiana University*
Daniel L. White, *Drexel University*
Edgar L. Williams, Jr., *Norfolk State University*
Jun Zhao, *Governors State University*

Gareth R. Jones
Charles W.L. Hill

9th Edition

THEORY OF STRATEGIC MANAGEMENT

WITH CASES

LEADERSHIP, STRATEGY, AND COMPETITIVE ADVANTAGE

LEARNING OBJECTIVES

After reading this chapter, you should be able to

- Explain what is meant by "competitive advantage"
- Discuss the strategic role of managers at different levels in an organization
- Identify the main steps in a strategic planning process
- Discuss the main pitfalls of planning and how those pitfalls can be avoided

- Outline the cognitive biases that might lead to poor strategic decisions and explain how these biases can be overcome
- Discuss the role played by strategic leaders in the strategy-making process

Walmart's Competitive Advantage   Walmart is one of the most extraordinary success stories in business history.

Started in 1962 by Sam Walton, Walmart has grown to become the world's largest corporation. In 2008, the discount retailer whose mantra is "everyday low prices" had sales of $410 billion, 7,400 stores in 15 countries and 2 million employees. Some 8% of all retail sales in the United States are made at a Walmart store. Walmart is not only large; it is also very profitable. In 2008, the company earned a return on invested capital of 14.5%, better than its well-managed rivals Costco and Target, which earned 11.7% and 9.5%, respectively. As shown in Figure 1.1, Walmart has been consistently more profitable than its rivals for years, although of late its rivals have been closing the gap.

Walmart's consistently superior profitability reflects a competitive advantage that is based on a number of strategies. Back in 1962, Walmart was one of the first companies to apply the self-service supermarket business model developed by grocery chains to general merchandise. Unlike its rivals such as Kmart and Target who focused on urban and suburban locations, Sam Walton's Walmart concentrated on small southern towns that were ignored by its rivals. Walmart grew quickly by pricing lower than local retailers, often putting them out of business. By the time its rivals realized that small towns could support large discount, general merchandise stores, Walmart had already preempted them. These towns, which were large enough to support one discount retailer—but not two—provided a secure profit base for Walmart.

The company was also an innovator in information systems, logistics, and human resource practices. These strategies resulted in higher productivity and lower costs than its rivals, which enabled the company to earn a high profit while charging low prices. Walmart led the way among American retailers in developing and implementing sophisticated product tracking systems by using bar code technology and checkout scanners. This information technology enabled Walmart to track what was selling and adjust its inventory accordingly so that the products found in a store matched local demand. By avoiding overstocking, Walmart did not have to hold periodic sales to shift unsold inventory. Over time, Walmart linked this information system to a nationwide network of distribution centers where inventory was stored and then shipped to stores within a 250-mile radius on a daily basis. The combination of distribution centers and information centers enabled Walmart to reduce the amount of inventory it held in stores, thereby devoting more of that valuable space to selling and reducing the amount of capital it had tied up in inventory.

With regard to human resources, the tone was set by Sam Walton. He had a strong belief that employees should be respected and rewarded for helping to improve the profitability of the company. Underpinning this belief, Walton referred to employees as associates.

He established a profit-sharing plan for all employees and, after the company went public in 1970, a program that allowed employees to purchase Walmart stock at a discount to its market value. Walmart was rewarded for this approach by high employee productivity, which translated into lower operating costs and higher profitability.

As Walmart grew larger, the sheer size and purchasing power of the company enabled it to drive down the prices that it paid suppliers, passing on those saving to customers in the form of lower prices, which enabled Walmart to gain more market share and hence demand even lower prices. To take the sting out of the persistent demands for lower prices, Walmart shared its sales information with suppliers on a daily basis, enabling them to gain efficiencies by configuring their own production schedules to sales at Walmart.

By the 1990s, Walmart was already the largest general seller of general merchandise in America. To keep its growth going, Walmart started to diversify into the grocery business, opening 200,000-square-foot supercenter stores that sold groceries and general merchandise under one roof. Walmart also diversified into the warehouse club business with the establishment of Sam's Club. The company began expanding internationally in 1991 with its entry into Mexico.

For all its success, however, Walmart is now encountering very real limits to profitable growth. The U.S. market is approaching saturation, and growth overseas has proved more difficult than the company hoped. The company was forced to exit Germany and South Korea after losing money there and has found it tough going into several other developed nations, such as Britain. Moreover, rivals Target and Costco have continued to improve their performances and are now snapping at Walmart's heels.[1]

Figure 1.1   Profitability of Walmart and Competitors

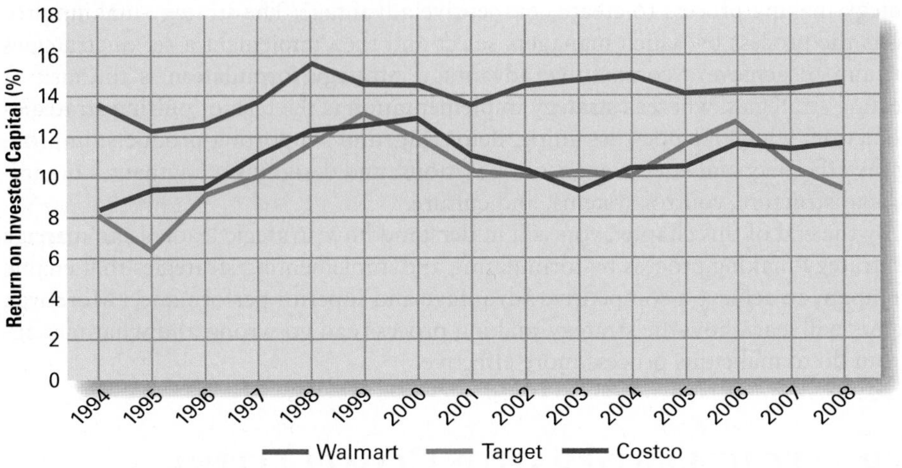

Source: Value Line Calculations. Data for 2008 are estimates based on three quarters.

Overview

Why do some companies succeed while others fail? Why has Walmart been able to consistently outperform its well-managed rivals? In the airline industry, how is it that Southwest Airlines has managed to keep increasing its revenues and profits through both good times and bad, while rivals such as US Airways and United Airlines have had to seek bankruptcy protection? What explains the consistent growth and profitability of Nucor Steel, now the largest steelmaker in America, during a period when many of its once larger rivals disappeared into bankruptcy?

In this book, we argue that the strategies that a company's managers pursue have a major impact on its performance relative to its competitors. A **strategy** is a set of related actions that managers take to increase their company's performance. For most, if not all, companies, achieving superior performance relative to rivals is the ultimate challenge. If a company's strategies result in superior performance, it is said to have a competitive advantage. Walmart's strategies produced superior performance from 1994 to 2008; as a result, Walmart has enjoyed a competitive advantage over its rivals. How did Walmart achieve this competitive advantage? As explained in the opening case, it was due to the successful pursuit of a number of strategies by Walmart's managers, most notably the company's founder, Sam Walton. These strategies enabled the company to lower its cost structure, charge low prices, gain market share, and become more profitable than its rivals. (We will return to the example of Walmart several times throughout this book in a running case that examines various aspects of Walmart's strategy and performance.)

This book identifies and describes the strategies that managers can pursue to achieve superior performance and provide their company with a competitive advantage. One of its central aims is to give you a thorough understanding of the analytical techniques and skills necessary to identify and implement strategies successfully. The first step toward achieving this objective is to describe in detail what superior performance and competitive advantage mean and to explain the pivotal roles that managers play in leading the strategy-making process.

Strategic leadership is about how to most effectively manage a company's strategy-making process to create competitive advantage. The strategy-making process is the process by which managers select and then implement a set of strategies that aim to achieve a competitive advantage. **Strategy formulation** is the task of selecting strategies, whereas **strategy implementation** is the task of putting strategies into action, which includes designing, delivering, and supporting products; improving the efficiency and effectiveness of operations; and designing a company's organizational structure, control systems, and culture.

By the end of this chapter, you will understand how strategic leaders can manage the strategy-making process by formulating and implementing strategies that enable a company to achieve a competitive advantage and superior performance. Moreover, readers will learn how the strategy-making process can go wrong and what managers can do to make this process more effective.

STRATEGIC LEADERSHIP, COMPETITIVE ADVANTAGE, AND SUPERIOR PERFORMANCE

Strategic leadership is concerned with managing the strategy-making process to increase the performance of a company, thereby increasing the value of the enterprise to its owners and shareholders. As shown in Figure 1.2, to increase shareholder value, managers must pursue strategies that increase the profitability of the company and ensure that profits grow. (For more details please see the Appendix to Chapter 1 on the text companion website.) To do this, a company must be able to outperform its rivals; it must have a competitive advantage.

Superior Performance

Maximizing shareholder value is the ultimate goal of profit-making companies for two reasons. First, shareholders provide a company with the risk capital that enables managers to buy the resources needed to produce and sell goods and services.

Figure 1.2 Determinants of Shareholder Value

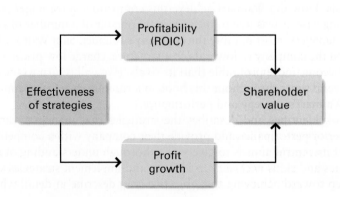

Risk capital is capital that cannot be recovered if a company fails and goes bankrupt. In the case of Walmart, for example, shareholders provided Sam Walton's company with the capital it used to build stores and distribution centers, invest in information systems, purchase inventory to sell to customers, and so on. Had Walmart failed, its shareholders would have lost their money; their shares would have been worthless. Thus, shareholders will not provide risk capital unless they believe that managers are committed to pursuing strategies that give them a good return on their capital investment. Second, shareholders are the legal owners of a corporation, and their shares represent a claim on the profits generated by a company. Thus, managers have an obligation to invest those profits in ways that maximize shareholder value. Of course, as explained later in this book, managers must behave in a legal, ethical, and socially responsible manner while at the same time working to maximize shareholder value.

By **shareholder value** we mean the returns that shareholders earn from purchasing shares in a company. These returns come from two sources: (1) capital appreciation in the value of a company's shares and (2) dividend payments. For example, between January 2 and December 31, 2008, the value of one share in Walmart increased from $46.90 to $56.06, which represents a capital appreciation of $9.16. In addition, Walmart paid out a dividend of $0.95 per share during 2008. Thus, if an investor had bought one share of Walmart on January 2 and held onto it for the entire year, his or her return would have been $10.11 ($9.16 + $0.95), an impressive 21.6% return on investment in a year when the stock market as a whole was down 35%! One reason Walmart's shareholders did so well during 2008 was that investors believed that managers were pursuing strategies that would both increase the long-term profitability of the company and significantly grow its profits in the future.

One way of measuring the **profitability** of a company is by the return that it makes on the capital invested in the enterprise.[2] The return on invested capital (ROIC) that a company earns is defined as its net profit over the capital invested in the firm (profit/capital invested). By net profit we mean net income after tax. By capital we mean the sum of money invested in the company: that is, stockholders' equity plus debt owed to creditors. Thus, profitability is the result of how efficiently and effectively managers use the capital at their disposal to produce goods and services that satisfy customer needs. A company that uses its capital efficiently and effectively makes a positive return on invested capital.

The **profit growth** of a company can be measured by the increase in net profit over time. A company can grow its profits if it sells products in markets that are growing rapidly, gains market share from rivals, increases the amount it sells to existing customers, expands overseas, or diversifies profitably into new lines of business. For example, between 1994 and 2008 Walmart increased its net profit from $2.68 billion to $13.8 billion. It was able to do this because the company (1) took market share from rivals, (2) established stores in nine foreign nations that collectively generated $70 billion in sales by 2008, and (3) entered the grocery business. Due to the increase in net profit, Walmart's earnings per share increased from $0.59 to $3.50, making each share more valuable, and leading, in turn, to appreciation in the value of Walmart's shares.

Together, profitability and profit growth are the principal drivers of shareholder value (see the Appendix to Chapter 1 on the text companion website). To boost profitability and grow profits over time, managers must formulate and implement strategies that give their companies a competitive advantage over their rivals. Walmart's strategies have enabled the company to maintain a high level of profitability and to simultaneously grow its profits over time. As a result, investors who purchased Walmart's stock in January 1994 when the shares were trading at $11 would have made a return of more than 500% if they had held onto them through December 2008. By pursuing strategies that lead to high and sustained profitability and profit growth, Walmart's managers have thus rewarded shareholders for their decisions to invest in the company.

One of the key challenges managers face is to simultaneously generate high profitability and increase the profits of the company. Companies that have high profitability but whose profits are not growing will not be as highly valued by shareholders as a company that has both high profitability and rapid profit growth (see Appendix to Chapter 1 on the text companion website). At the same time, managers need to be aware that if they grow profits but profitability declines, that too will not be as highly valued by shareholders. What shareholders want to see, and what managers must try to deliver through strategic leadership, is *profitable growth*: that is, high profitability and sustainable profit growth. This is not easy, but some of the most successful enterprises of our era have achieved it, companies such as Microsoft, Google, Intel, and Walmart.

Competitive Advantage and a Company's Business Model

Managers do not make strategic decisions in a competitive vacuum. Their company is competing against other companies for customers. Competition is a rough-and-tumble process in which only the most efficient and effective companies win out. It is a race without end. To maximize shareholder value, managers must formulate and implement strategies that enable their companies to outperform rivals and give them a competitive advantage. A company is said to have a **competitive advantage** over its rivals when its profitability is greater than the average profitability and profit growth of other companies competing for the same set of customers. The higher its profitability relative to rivals, the greater its competitive advantage will be. A company has a **sustained competitive advantage** when its strategies enable it to maintain above-average profitability for a number of years. As discussed in the opening case, Walmart had a significant and sustained competitive advantage over rivals such as Target, Costco, and Kmart between 1994 and 2008.

If a company has a sustained competitive advantage, it is likely to gain market share from its rivals and thus grow its profits more rapidly than those of rivals. In turn, competitive advantage will also lead to higher profit growth than that shown by rivals.

The key to understanding competitive advantage is appreciating how the different strategies managers pursue over time can create activities that fit together to make a company unique or different from its rivals and able to consistently outperform them. A **business model** is a manager's conception of how the set of strategies his company pursues should mesh together into a congruent whole, enabling the company to gain a competitive advantage and achieve superior profitability and profit growth. In essence, a business model is a kind of mental model, or gestalt, of how the various strategies and capital investments made by a company should fit together to generate above-average profitability and profit growth. A business model encompasses the totality of how a company will

- Select its customers.
- Define and differentiate its product offerings.
- Create value for its customers.

- Acquire and keep customers.
- Produce goods or services.
- Lower costs.
- Deliver those goods and services to the market.
- Organize activities within the company.
- Configure its resources.
- Achieve and sustain a high level of profitability.
- Grow the business over time.

The business model at discount stores such as Walmart, for example, is based on the idea that costs can be lowered by replacing a full-service retail format with a self-service format and a wider selection of products sold in a large footprint store that contains minimal fixtures and fittings. These savings are passed on to consumers in the form of lower prices, which in turn grow revenues and help the company to achieve further cost reductions from economies of scale. Over time, this business model has proved superior to the business models adopted by smaller, full-service mom and pop stores and traditional high service department stores such as Sears Roebuck and Co. The business model—known as the self-service supermarket business model—was first developed by grocery retailers in the 1950s and later refined and improved on by general merchandisers such as Walmart. More recently, the same basic business model has been applied to toys (Toys"R"Us), office supplies (Staples, Office Depot), and home improvement supplies (Home Depot and Lowes).

Walmart outperformed close rivals who adopted the same basic business model as Kmart because of key differences in strategies and because they implemented the business model more effectively. As a result, over time Walmart created unique activities that have become the foundation of its competitive advantage. For example, Walmart was one of the first retailers to make strategic investments in distribution centers and information systems, which lowered the costs of managing inventory (see the opening case). This gave Walmart a competitive advantage over rivals such as Kmart, which suffered from poor inventory controls and thus higher costs. So although Walmart and Kmart pursued similar business models, they were not identical. Key differences in the choice of strategies and the effectiveness of implementation created two unique organizations: one that attained a competitive advantage, and one that ended up with a competitive disadvantage.

The business model that managers develop may not only lead to higher profitability and thus competitive advantage at a certain point in time, but it may also help the firm to grow its profits over time, thereby maximizing shareholder value while maintaining or even increasing profitability. Thus, Walmart's business model was so efficient and effective that it enabled the company to take market share from rivals such as Kmart, thereby growing profits over time. In addition, as alluded to earlier, Walmart was able to grow profits by applying its business model to new international markets, opening stores in nine different countries, and adding groceries to its product mix in large Walmart supercenters.

Industry Differences in Performance

It is important to recognize that in addition to its business model and associated strategies, a company's performance is also determined by the characteristics of the industry in which it competes. Different industries are characterized by different competitive conditions. In some, demand is growing rapidly; in others, it is contracting.

Some might be beset by excess capacity and persistent price wars, others by strong demand and rising prices. In some, technological change might be revolutionizing competition. Others might be characterized by stable technology. In some industries, high profitability among incumbent companies might induce new companies to enter the industry, and these new entrants might subsequently depress prices and profits in the industry. In other industries, new entry might be difficult, and periods of high profitability might persist for a considerable period of time. Thus, the different competitive conditions prevailing in different industries might lead to differences in profitability and profit growth. For example, average profitability might be higher in some industries and lower in other industries because competitive conditions vary from industry to industry.

Figure 1.3 shows the average profitability, measured by ROIC, among companies in several different industries between 2004 and 2008. The drug industry had a favorable competitive environment: demand for drugs was high and competition was generally not based on price. Just the opposite occured in the air transport industry, which was extremely price competitive. Exactly how industries differ is discussed in detail in Chapter 2. For now, the important point to remember is that the profitability and profit growth of a company are determined by two main factors: its relative success in its industry and the overall performance of its industry relative to other industries.[3]

Performance in Nonprofit Enterprises

A final point concerns the concept of superior performance in the nonprofit sector. By definition, nonprofit enterprises such as government agencies, universities, and charities are not in "business" to make profits. Nevertheless, they are expected to use their resources efficiently and operate effectively, and their managers set goals to

Figure 1.3 Return on Invested Capital in Selected Industries, 2004–2008

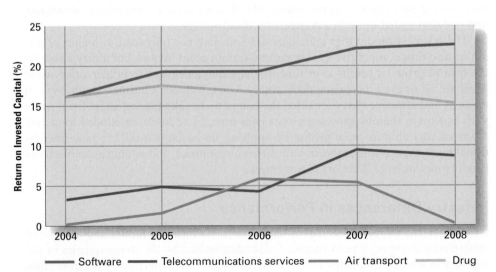

Source: Value Line Investment Survey.

measure their performance. The performance goal for a business school might be to get its programs ranked among the best in the nation. The performance goal for a charity might be to prevent childhood illnesses in poor countries. The performance goal for a government agency might be to improve its services while not exceeding its budget. The managers of nonprofits need to map out strategies to attain these goals. They also need to understand that nonprofits compete with each other for scarce resources, just as businesses do. For example, charities compete for scarce donations, and their managers must plan and develop strategies that lead to high performance and demonstrate a track record of meeting performance goals. A successful strategy gives potential donors a compelling message about why they should contribute additional donations. Thus, planning and thinking strategically are as important for managers in the nonprofit sector as they are for managers in profit-seeking firms.

STRATEGIC MANAGERS

Managers are the linchpins in the strategy-making process. Individual managers must take responsibility for formulating strategies to attain a competitive advantage and for putting those strategies into effect. They must lead the strategy-making process. The strategies that made Walmart so successful were not chosen by some abstract entity known as "the company"; they were chosen by the company's founder, Sam Walton, and the managers he hired.

Walmart's success was based in large part on how well the company's managers performed their strategic roles. In this section, we look at the strategic roles of different managers. Later in the chapter, we discuss strategic leadership, which is how managers can effectively lead the strategy-making process.

In most companies, there are two main types of managers: **general managers** who bear responsibility for the overall performance of the company or for one of its major self-contained subunits or divisions and **functional managers** who are responsible for supervising a particular function, that is, a task, an activity, or an operation, such as accounting, marketing, research and development (R&D), information technology, or logistics.

A company is a collection of functions or departments that work together to bring a particular good or service to the market. If a company provides several different kinds of goods or services, it often duplicates these functions and creates a series of self-contained divisions (each of which contains its own set of functions) to manage each different good or service. The general managers of these divisions then become responsible for their particular product line. The overriding concern of general managers is for the health of the whole company or division under their direction; they are responsible for deciding how to create a competitive advantage and achieve high profitability with the resources and capital they have at their disposal. Figure 1.4 shows the organization of a **multidivisional company,** that is, a company that competes in several different businesses and has created a separate, self-contained division to manage each. There are three main levels of management: corporate, business, and functional. General managers are found at the first two of these levels, but their strategic roles differ depending on their spheres of responsibility.

Figure 1.4   Levels of Strategic Management

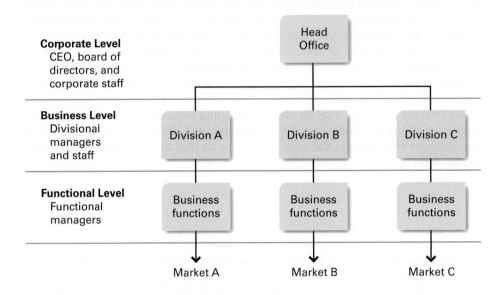

Corporate Level
CEO, board of directors, and corporate staff

Business Level
Divisional managers and staff

Functional Level
Functional managers

Head Office

Division A   Division B   Division C

Business functions   Business functions   Business functions

Market A   Market B   Market C

Corporate-Level Managers

The corporate level of management consists of the chief executive officer (CEO), other senior executives, and corporate staff. These individuals occupy the apex of decision making within the organization. The CEO is the principal general manager. In consultation with other senior executives, the role of corporate-level managers is to oversee the development of strategies for the whole organization. This role includes defining the goals of the organization, determining what businesses it should be in, allocating resources among the different businesses, formulating and implementing strategies that span individual businesses, and providing leadership for the entire organization.

Consider General Electric as an example. GE is active in a wide range of businesses, including lighting equipment, major appliances, motor and transportation equipment, turbine generators, construction and engineering services, industrial electronics, medical systems, aerospace, aircraft engines, and financial services. The main strategic responsibilities of its CEO, Jeffrey Immelt, are setting overall strategic goals, allocating resources among the different business areas, deciding whether the firm should divest itself of any of its businesses, and determining whether it should acquire any new ones. In other words, it is up to Immelt to develop strategies that span individual businesses; his concern is with building and managing the corporate portfolio of businesses to maximize corporate profitability.

It is not Immelt's specific responsibility to develop strategies for competing in the individual business areas, such as financial services. The development of such strategies is the responsibility of the general managers in these different businesses, known as business-level managers. It is, however, Immelt's responsibility to probe the strategic thinking of business-level managers to make sure that they are pursuing robust business models and strategies that will contribute toward the maximization of GE's long-run profitability, to coach and motivate those managers, to reward them for attaining or exceeding goals, and to hold them accountable for poor performance.

Corporate-level managers also provide a link between the people who oversee the strategic development of a firm and those who own it (the shareholders). Corporate-level managers, and particularly the CEO, can be viewed as the agents of shareholders.[4] It is their responsibility to ensure that the corporate and business strategies that the company pursues are consistent with maximizing profitability and profit growth. If they are not, then ultimately the CEO is likely to be called to account by the shareholders.

Business-Level Managers

A **business unit** is a self-contained division (with its own functions, for example, finance, purchasing, production, and marketing departments) that provides a product or service for a particular market. The principal general manager at the business level, or the business-level manager, is the head of the division. The strategic role of these managers is to translate the general statements of direction and intent that come from the corporate level into concrete strategies for individual businesses. Whereas corporate-level general managers are concerned with strategies that span individual businesses, business-level managers are concerned with strategies that are specific to a particular business. At GE, a major corporate goal is to be first or second in every business in which the corporation competes. The general managers in each division work out for their business the details of a business model that is consistent with this objective.

Functional-Level Managers

Functional-level managers are responsible for the specific business functions or operations (human resources, purchasing, product development, customer service, and so on) that constitute a company or one of its divisions. Thus, a functional manager's sphere of responsibility is generally confined to one organizational activity, whereas general managers oversee the operation of a whole company or division. Although they are not responsible for the overall performance of the organization, functional managers nevertheless have a major strategic role: to develop functional strategies in their area that help fulfill the strategic objectives set by business- and corporate-level managers.

In GE's aerospace business, for instance, manufacturing managers are responsible for developing manufacturing strategies consistent with corporate objectives. Moreover, functional managers provide most of the information that makes it possible for business- and corporate-level managers to formulate realistic and attainable strategies. Indeed, because they are closer to the customer than is the typical general manager, functional managers themselves may generate important ideas that subsequently become major strategies for the company. Thus, it is important for general managers to listen closely to the ideas of their functional managers. An equally great responsibility for managers at the operational level is strategy implementation: the execution of corporate- and business-level plans.

THE STRATEGY-MAKING PROCESS

We can now turn our attention to the process by which managers formulate and implement strategies. Many writers have emphasized that strategy is the outcome of a formal planning process and that top management plays the most important role in this process.[5] Although this view has some basis in reality, it is not the whole story.

As we shall see later in the chapter, valuable strategies often emerge from deep within the organization without prior planning. Nevertheless, a consideration of formal, rational planning is a useful starting point for our journey into the world of strategy. Accordingly, we consider what might be described as a typical formal strategic planning model for making strategy.

A Model of the Strategic Planning Process

The formal strategic planning process has five main steps:

1. Select the corporate mission and major corporate goals.
2. Analyze the organization's external competitive environment to identify opportunities and threats.
3. Analyze the organization's internal operating environment to identify the organization's strengths and weaknesses.
4. Select strategies that build on the organization's strengths and correct its weaknesses in order to take advantage of external opportunities and counter external threats. These strategies should be consistent with the mission and major goals of the organization. They should be congruent and constitute a viable business model.
5. Implement the strategies.

The task of analyzing the organization's external and internal environments and then selecting appropriate strategies constitutes strategy formulation. In contrast, as noted earlier, strategy implementation involves putting the strategies (or plan) into action. This includes taking actions consistent with the selected strategies of the company at the corporate, business, and functional levels; allocating roles and responsibilities among managers (typically through the design of organizational structure); allocating resources (including capital and money); setting short-term objectives; and designing the organization's control and reward systems. These steps are illustrated in Figure 1.5 (which can also be viewed as a plan for the rest of this book).

Each step in Figure 1.5 constitutes a sequential step in the strategic planning process. At step 1, each round or cycle of the planning process begins with a statement of the corporate mission and major corporate goals. This statement is shaped by the existing business model of the company. The mission statement is followed by the foundation of strategic thinking: external analysis, internal analysis, and strategic choice. The strategy-making process ends with the design of the organizational structure and the culture and control systems necessary to implement the organization's chosen strategy. This chapter discusses how to select a corporate mission and choose major goals. Other parts of strategic planning are reserved for later chapters, as indicated in Figure 1.5.

Some organizations go through a new cycle of the strategic planning process every year. This does not necessarily mean that managers choose a new strategy each year. In many instances, the result is simply to modify or reaffirm a strategy and structure already in place. The strategic plans generated by the planning process generally look at a period of one to five years, with the plan being updated, or rolled forward, every year. In most organizations, the results of the annual strategic planning process are used as input into the budgetary process for the coming year so that strategic planning is used to shape resource allocation within the organization.

Figure 1.5   Main Components of the Strategic Planning Process

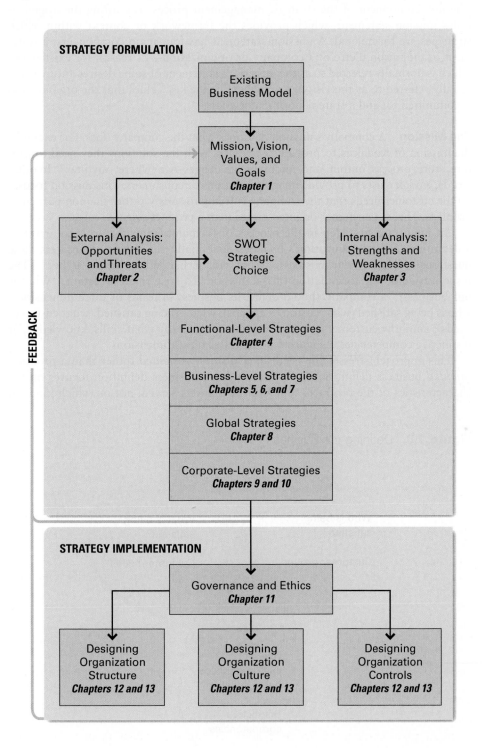

Mission Statement

The first component of the strategic management process is crafting the organization's mission statement, which provides the framework or context within which strategies are formulated. A mission statement has four main components: a statement of the raison d'être of a company or organization—its reason for existence—which is normally referred to as the mission; a statement of some desired future state, usually referred to as the vision; a statement of the key values that the organization is committed to; and a statement of major goals.

The Mission A company's **mission** describes what the company does. For example, the mission of Kodak is to provide "customers with the solutions they need to capture, store, process, output, and communicate images—anywhere, anytime."[6] In other words, Kodak exists to provide imaging solutions to consumers. This mission focuses on the customer needs that the company is trying to satisfy rather than on particular products. This is a customer-oriented rather than a product-oriented mission.

An important first step in the process of formulating a mission is to arrive at a definition of the organization's business. Essentially, the definition answers these questions: "What is our business? What will it be? What should it be?"[7] The responses guide the formulation of the mission. To answer the question, "What is our business?" a company should define its business in terms of three dimensions: who is being satisfied (what customer groups); what is being satisfied (what customer needs); and how customers' needs are being satisfied (by what skills, knowledge, or distinctive competencies).[8] Figure 1.6 illustrates these dimensions.

This approach stresses the need for a *customer-oriented* rather than a *product-oriented* business definition. A product-oriented business definition focuses on the characteristics of the products sold and the markets served, not on which kinds of

Figure 1.6 Defining the Business

customer needs the products are satisfying. Such an approach obscures the company's true mission because a product is only the physical manifestation of applying a particular skill to satisfy a particular need for a particular customer group. In practice, that need may be served in many different ways, and a broad customer-oriented business definition that identifies these ways can safeguard companies from being caught unaware by major shifts in demand.

By helping anticipate demand shifts, a customer-oriented mission statement can also assist companies in capitalizing on changes in their environments. It can help answer the question, "What will our business be?" Kodak's mission statement—to provide "customers with the solutions they need to capture, store, process, output, and communicate images"—is a customer-oriented statement that focuses on customer needs rather than a particular product (or solution) for satisfying those needs, such as chemical film processing. For this reason, from the early 1990s on, it drove Kodak's investments in digital imaging technologies, which have replaced much of Kodak's traditional business based on chemical film processing.

The need to take a customer-oriented view of a company's business has often been ignored. History is littered with the wreckage of once-great corporations that did not define their businesses or defined them incorrectly so that ultimately they declined. In the 1950s and 1960s, many office equipment companies such as Smith Corona and Underwood defined their businesses as the production of typewriters. This product-oriented definition ignored the fact that they were really in the business of satisfying customers' information-processing needs. Unfortunately for those companies, when new technology arrived that better served customer needs for information processing (computers), demand for typewriters plummeted. The last great typewriter company, Smith Corona, went bankrupt in 1996, a victim of the success of computer-based word-processing technology.

In contrast, IBM correctly foresaw what its business would be. In the 1950s, IBM was a leader in the manufacture of typewriters and mechanical tabulating equipment using punch-card technology. However, unlike many of its competitors, IBM defined its business as providing a means for *information processing and storage*, rather than just supplying mechanical tabulating equipment and typewriters.[9] Given this definition, the company's subsequent move into computers, software systems, office systems, and printers was logical.

Vision　　The **vision** of a company lays out some desired future state; it articulates, often in bold terms, what the company would like to achieve. Nokia, the world's largest manufacturer of mobile (wireless) phones, has been operating with a very simple but powerful vision for some time: "If it can go mobile, it will!" This vision implied that not only would voice technology go mobile but also a host of other services based on data, such as imaging and Internet browsing. This vision led Nokia to become a leader in developing mobile handsets that not only can be used for voice communication but also take pictures, browse the Internet, play games, and manipulate personal and corporate information.

Values　　The **values** of a company state how managers and employees should conduct themselves, how they should do business, and what kind of organization they should build to help a company achieve its mission. Insofar as they help drive and shape behavior within a company, values are commonly seen as the bedrock of a company's organizational culture: the set of values, norms, and standards that control how employees work to achieve an organization's mission and goals. An organization's culture is commonly seen as an important source of its competitive advantage.[10] (We discuss the issue of organization culture in depth in Chapter 12.) For example, Nucor Steel is one of the most productive and profitable steel firms in the world. Its competitive advantage is based in part on the extremely high productivity of its workforce, which the company maintains is a direct result of its cultural values, which in turn determine how it treats its employees. These values are as follows:

- "Management is obligated to manage Nucor in such a way that employees will have the opportunity to earn according to their productivity."
- "Employees should be able to feel confident that if they do their jobs properly, they will have a job tomorrow."
- "Employees have the right to be treated fairly and must believe that they will be."
- "Employees must have an avenue of appeal when they believe they are being treated unfairly."[11]

At Nucor, values emphasizing pay for performance, job security, and fair treatment for employees help to create an atmosphere within the company that leads to high employee productivity. In turn, this has helped to give Nucor one of the lowest cost structures in its industry, which helps to explain the company's profitability in a very price-competitive business.

In one study of organizational values, researchers identified a set of values associated with high-performing organizations that help companies achieve superior financial performance through their impact on employee behavior.[12] These values included respect for the interests of key organizational **stakeholders:** individuals or groups that have an interest, claim, or stake in the company, in what it does, and in how well it performs.[13] They include stockholders, bondholders, employees, customers, the communities in which the company does business, and the general public. The study found that deep respect for the interests of customers, employees, suppliers, and shareholders was associated with high performance. The study also noted that the encouragement of leadership and entrepreneurial behavior by mid- and lower-level managers and a willingness to support change efforts within the organization contributed to high performance. Companies that emphasize such values consistently throughout their organization include Hewlett-Packard, Walmart, and PepsiCo. The same study identified the values of poorly performing companies, values that, as might be expected, are not articulated in company mission statements: (1) arrogance, particularly to ideas from outside the company; (2) a lack of respect for key stakeholders; and (3) a history of resisting change efforts and "punishing" mid- and lower-level managers who showed "too much leadership." General Motors was held up as an example of one such organization. According to the research, mid- or lower-level managers who showed too much leadership and initiative at GM were not promoted!

Ethical Dilemma

You are the general manager of a home mortgage lender within a large diversified financial services firm. The firm's mission statement emphasizes the importance of acting with integrity at all times. The CEO describes this as "doing the right thing rather than trying to do all things right." This same CEO has presented you with "nonnegotiable" challenging profitability and growth goals for the coming year. Achieving these goals may result in cash and promotion payoffs. Missing the goals may hurt your career. Hitting those goals will require you to lower lending standards and lend money to people who are unable to meet their mortgage payments. If people default on their loans, however, your company can seize their homes and resell them, mitigating the risk. What should you do?

MAJOR GOALS

Having stated the mission, vision, and key values, strategic managers can take the next step in the formulation of a mission statement: establishing major goals. A **goal** is a precise and measurable desired future state that a company attempts to realize. In this context, the purpose of goals is to specify with precision what must be done if the company is to attain its mission or vision.

Well-constructed goals have four main characteristics:[14]

1. They are precise and measurable. Measurable goals give managers a yardstick or standard against which they can judge their performance.
2. They address crucial issues. To maintain focus, managers should select a limited number of major goals to assess the performance of the company. The goals that are selected should be crucial or important ones.
3. They are challenging but realistic. They give all employees an incentive to look for ways of improving the operations of an organization. If a goal is unrealistic in the challenges it poses, employees may give up; a goal that is too easy may fail to motivate managers and other employees.[15]
4. They specify a time period in which the goals should be achieved, when that is appropriate. Time constraints tell employees that success requires a goal to be attained by a given date, not after that date. Deadlines can inject a sense of urgency into goal attainment and act as a motivator. However, not all goals require time constraints.

Well-constructed goals also provide a means by which the performance of managers can be evaluated.

As noted earlier, although most companies operate with a variety of goals, the central goal of most corporations is to maximize shareholder returns; doing this requires both high profitability and sustained profit growth. Thus, most companies operate with goals for profitability and profit growth. However, it is important that top managers do not make the mistake of overemphasizing current profitability to the detriment of long-term profitability and profit growth.[16] The overzealous pursuit of current profitability to maximize short-term ROIC can encourage such misguided managerial actions as cutting expenditures judged to be nonessential in the short run, for instance, expenditures for research and development, marketing, and new capital investments. Although cutting current expenditures increases current profitability, the resulting underinvestment, lack of innovation, and diminished marketing can jeopardize long-run profitability and profit growth.

To guard against short-run behavior, managers need to ensure that they adopt goals whose attainment will increase the long-run performance and competitiveness of their enterprises. Long-term goals are related to such issues as product development, customer satisfaction, and efficiency, and they emphasize specific objectives or targets concerning such details as employee and capital productivity, product quality, innovation, customer satisfaction, and customer service.

External Analysis

The second component of the strategic management process is an analysis of the organization's external operating environment. The essential purpose of the external analysis is to identify strategic opportunities and threats in the organization's operating environment that will affect how it pursues its mission. Strategy in Action 1.1 describes how an analysis of opportunities and threats in the external environment led to a strategic shift at Time Inc.

Three interrelated environments should be examined when undertaking an external analysis: the industry environment in which the company operates; the country or national environment; and the wider socioeconomic or macroenvironment. Analyzing the industry environment requires an assessment of the competitive structure of the company's industry, including the competitive position of the company and its

1.1 STRATEGY IN ACTION

Strategic Analysis at Time Inc.

Time Inc., the magazine publishing division of media conglomerate Time Warner, has a venerable history. Its magazine titles include *Time, Fortune, Sports Illustrated*, and *People*, all long-time leaders in their respective categories. By the mid–2000s, however, Time Inc. recognized that it needed to change its strategy. By 2005, circulation at *Time* was down by 12%; *Fortune*, by 10%; and *Sports Illustrated*, by 17%.

An external analysis revealed what was going on. The readership of Time's magazines was aging. Increasingly, younger readers were getting what they wanted from the Web. This was both a *threat* for Time Inc., because its Web offerings were not strong, and an *opportunity*, because with the right offerings Time Inc. could capture this audience. Time also realized that advertising dollars were migrating rapidly to the Web. If the company was going to hold onto its share, its Web offerings had to be every bit as good as its print offerings.

An internal analysis revealed why, despite multiple attempts, Time had failed to capitalize on the opportunities offered by the emergence of the Web. Although Time had tremendous *strengths*, including powerful brands and strong reporting, development of its Web offerings had been hindered by a serious *weakness*—an editorial culture that regarded Web publishing as a backwater. At *People*, for example, the online operation was "like a distant moon" according to managing editor Martha Nelson. Managers at Time Inc. had also been worried that Web offerings would cannibalize print offerings and help accelerate the decline of magazine circulation, with dire financial consequences for the company. As a result of this culture, efforts to move publications onto the Web underfunded or stymied by a lack of management attention and commitment.

It was Martha Nelson at *People* who, in 2003, showed the way forward for the company. Her *strategy* for overcoming the *weakness* at Time Inc. and better exploiting

opportunities on the Web started with merging the print and online newsrooms at *People*, thus removing the distinction between them. Then she relaunched the magazine's online site, made major editorial commitments to Web publishing, stated that original content should appear on the Web, and emphasized the importance of driving traffic to the site and earning advertising revenues. Over the next two years, page views at People.com increased fivefold.

Ann Moore, the CEO at Time Inc., formalized this strategy in 2005, mandating that all print offerings should follow the lead of People.com, integrating print and online newsrooms and investing significantly more resources in Web publishing. To drive this home, Time hired several well-known bloggers to write for its online publications. Moore's goal was to neutralize the cultural *weakness* that had hindered online efforts in the past at Time Inc. and to direct resources toward Web publishing.

In 2006, Time made another strategic move designed to exploit the opportunities associated with the Web when it started a partnership with the 24-hour news channel, CNN, putting all of its financial magazines onto a site that is jointly owned, CNNMoney.com. The site, which offers free access to *Fortune, Money*, and *Business 2.0*, quickly took the third spot in online financial Web sites behind Yahoo finance and MSN. This was followed with a redesigned Web site for *Sports Illustrated* that has rolled out video downloads for iPods and mobile phones.

To drive home the shift to Web-centric publishing, in 2007 Time announced another change in strategy—it would sell off 18 magazine titles that, while good performers, did not appear to have much traction on the Web. Ann Moore stated that going forward Time would be focusing its energy, resources, and investments on the company's largest and most profitable brands, brands that have demonstrated an ability to draw large audiences in digital form.

Sources: A. Van Duyn, "Time Inc. Revamp to Include Sale of 18 Titles," *Financial Times*, September 13, 2006, 24. M. Karnitsching, "Time Inc. Makes New Bid to Be Big Web Player," *Wall Street Journal*, March 29, 2006, B1. M. Flamm, "Time Tries the Web Again," *Crain's New York Business*, January 16, 2006, 3.

major rivals. It also requires analysis of the nature, stage, dynamics, and history of the industry. Because many markets are now global markets, analyzing the industry environment also means assessing the impact of globalization on competition within an industry. Such an analysis may reveal that a company should move some production facilities to another nation, that it should aggressively expand in emerging markets such as China, or that it should beware of new competition from emerging nations. Analyzing the macroenvironment consists of examining macroeconomic, social, government, legal, international, and technological factors that may affect the company and its industry. We look at external analysis in Chapter 2.

Internal Analysis

Internal analysis, the third component of the strategic planning process, focuses on reviewing the resources, capabilities, and competencies of a company. The goal is to identify the strengths and weaknesses of the company. For example, as described in Strategy in Action 1.1, an internal analysis at Time Inc. revealed that while the company had strong well-known brands such as *Fortune, Money, Sports Illustrated,* and *People* (a strength), and strong reporting capabilities (another strength), it suffered from a lack of editorial commitment to online publishing (a weaknesses). We consider internal analysis in Chapter 3.

SWOT Analysis and the Business Model

The next component of strategic thinking requires the generation of a series of strategic alternatives, or choices of future strategies to pursue, given the company's internal strengths and weaknesses and its external opportunities and threats. The comparison of strengths, weaknesses, opportunities, and threats is normally referred to as a **SWOT analysis.**[17] The central purpose is to identify the strategies to exploit external opportunities, counter threats, build on and protect company strengths, and eradicate weaknesses.

At Time Inc., managers saw the move of readership to the Web as both an *opportunity* that they must exploit and a *threat* to Time's established print magazines. They recognized that Time's well-known brands and strong reporting capabilities were *strengths* that would serve it well online, but an editorial culture that marginalized online publishing was a *weakness* that had to be fixed. The *strategies* that managers at Time Inc. used included merging the print and online newsrooms to remove distinctions between them; investing significant financial resources in online sites; and entering into a partnership with CNN, which already had a strong online presence.

More generally, the goal of a SWOT analysis is to create, affirm, or fine-tune a company-specific business model that will best align, fit, or match a company's resources and capabilities to the demands of the environment in which it operates. Managers compare and contrast the various alternative possible strategies against each other and then identify the set of strategies that will create and sustain a competitive advantage. These strategies can be divided into four main categories:

1. *Functional-level strategies* are directed at improving the effectiveness of operations within a company, such as manufacturing, marketing, materials management, product development, and customer service. We review functional-level strategies in Chapter 4.

2. *Business-level strategies* encompass the business's overall competitive theme, the way it positions itself in the marketplace to gain a competitive advantage, and the different positioning strategies that can be used in different industry settings, for example, cost leadership, differentiation, focusing on a particular niche or segment of the industry, or some combination of these. We review business-level strategies in Chapters 5, 6 and 7.

3. *Global strategies* address how to expand operations outside the home country to grow and prosper in a world where competitive advantage is determined at a global level. We review global strategies in Chapter 8.

4. *Corporate-level strategies* answer the primary questions: What business or businesses should we be in to maximize the long-run profitability and profit growth of the organization. How should we enter and increase our presence in these businesses to gain a competitive advantage? We review corporate-level strategies in Chapters 9 and 10.

The strategies identified through a SWOT analysis should be congruent with each other. Thus, functional-level strategies should be consistent with, or support, the company's business-level strategy and global strategy. Moreover, as we explain later in this book, corporate-level strategies should support business-level strategies. When taken together, the various strategies pursued by a company constitute a viable business model. In essence, a SWOT analysis is a methodology for choosing between competing business models and for fine-tuning the business model that managers choose. For example, when Microsoft entered the video game market with its Xbox offering, it had to settle on the best business model for competing in this market. Microsoft used a SWOT analysis to compare alternatives and settled on a "razor and razor blades" business model in which the Xbox console is priced below cost to build sales (the "razor"), while profits are made from royalties on the sale of games for the Xbox (the "blades").

Strategy Implementation

Having chosen a set of congruent strategies to achieve a competitive advantage and increase performance, managers must put those strategies into action: strategy has to be implemented. Strategy implementation involves taking actions at the functional, business, and corporate levels to execute a strategic plan. Implementation can include, for example, putting quality improvement programs into place, changing the way a product is designed, positioning the product differently in the marketplace, segmenting the marketing and offering different versions of the product to different consumer groups, implementing price increases or decreases, expanding through mergers and acquisitions, or downsizing the company by closing down or selling off parts of the company. These and other topics are discussed in detail in Chapters 4 through 10.

Strategy implementation also entails designing the best organizational structure and the best culture and control systems to put a chosen strategy into action. In addition, senior managers need to put a governance system in place to make sure that all within the organization act in a manner that is not only consistent with maximizing profitability and profit growth but also legal and ethical. In this book, we look at the topic of governance and ethics in Chapter 11; we discuss the organizational structure, culture, and controls required to implement business-level strategies in Chapter 12;

and we present the structure, culture, and controls required to implement corporate-level strategies in Chapter 13.

The Feedback Loop

The feedback loop in Figure 1.5 indicates that strategic planning is ongoing; it never ends. Once a strategy has been implemented, its execution must be monitored to determine the extent to which strategic goals and objectives are actually being achieved and to what degree competitive advantage is being created and sustained. This information and knowledge is passed back to the corporate level through feedback loops and becomes the input for the next round of strategy formulation and implementation. Top managers can then decide whether to reaffirm the existing business model and the existing strategies and goals or suggest changes for the future. For example, if a strategic goal proves to be too optimistic, the next time a more conservative goal is set. Or feedback may reveal that the business model is not working, so managers may seek ways to change it. In essence, this is what happened at Time Inc. (see Strategy in Action 1.1).

STRATEGY AS AN EMERGENT PROCESS

The planning model suggests that a company's strategies are the result of a plan, the strategic planning process itself is rational and highly structured, and the process is orchestrated by top management. Several scholars have criticized the formal planning model for three main reasons: the unpredictability of the real world; the role that lower-level managers can play in the strategic management process; and the fact that many successful strategies are often the result of serendipity, not rational strategizing. They have advocated an alternative view of strategy making.[18]

Strategy Making in an Unpredictable World

Critics of formal planning systems argue that we live in a world in which uncertainty, complexity, and ambiguity dominate, and in which small chance events can have a large and unpredictable impact on outcomes.[19] In such circumstances, they claim, even the most carefully thought-out strategic plans are prone to being rendered useless by rapid and unforeseen change. In an unpredictable world, there is a premium on being able to respond quickly to changing circumstances and to alter the strategies of the organization accordingly. The dramatic rise of Google, for example, with its business-model-based revenues earned from advertising links associated with search results (the so-called pay-per-click business model), disrupted the business models of companies that made money from online advertising. Nobody foresaw this development or planned for it, but they had to respond to it rapidly. Companies with strong online advertising presences, including Yahoo.com and Microsoft's MSN network, rapidly changed their strategies to adapt to the threat posed by Google. Specifically, both developed their own search engines and copied Google's pay-per-click business model. According to critics of formal systems, such a flexible approach to strategy making is not possible within the framework of a traditional strategic planning process, with its implicit assumption that an organization's strategies need to be reviewed only during the annual strategic planning exercise.

Autonomous Action:
Strategy Making by Lower-Level Managers

Another criticism leveled at the rational planning model of strategy is that too much importance is attached to the role of top management, particularly the CEO.[20] An alternative view is that individual managers deep within an organization can and often do exert a profound influence over the strategic direction of the firm.[21] Writing with Robert Burgelman of Stanford University, Andy Grove, the former CEO of Intel, noted that many important strategic decisions at Intel were initiated not by top managers but by the autonomous action of lower-level managers deep within Intel who, on their own initiative, formulated new strategies and worked to persuade top-level managers to alter the strategic priorities of the firm.[22] These strategic decisions included the decision to exit an important market (the DRAM memory chip market) and develop a certain class of microprocessors (RISC-based microprocessors) in direct contrast to the stated strategy of Intel's top managers. Another example of autonomous action, this one at Starbucks, is given in Strategy in Action 1.2.

Autonomous action may be particularly important in helping established companies deal with the uncertainty created by the arrival of a radical new technology that changes the dominant paradigm in an industry.[23] Top managers usually rise to preeminence by successfully executing the established strategy of the firm. Therefore, they may have an emotional commitment to the status quo and are often unable to see things from a different perspective. In this sense, they can be a conservative force that promotes inertia. Lower-level managers, however, are less likely to have the same commitment to the status quo and have more to gain from promoting new technologies and strategies. They may be the first ones to recognize new strategic opportunities and lobby for strategic change. As described in Strategy in Action 1.3, this seems to have been the case at a discount stockbroker Charles Schwab, that had to adjust to the arrival of the Web in the 1990s.

1.2 STRATEGY IN ACTION

Starbucks's Music Business

Anyone who has walked into a Starbucks cannot help but notice that, in addition to various coffee beverages and food, the company also sells music CDs. Most Starbucks stores now have racks displaying about 20 CDs. Reports suggest that when Starbucks decides to carry a CD, it typically ranks among the top four retailers selling it. The interesting thing about Starbucks's entry into music retailing is that it was not the result of a formal planning process. The company's journey into music retailing started in the late 1980s when Tim Jones, then the manager of a Starbucks in Seattle's University Village, started to bring his own tapes of music compilations into the store to play. Soon Jones was getting requests for copies from customers. Jones told this to Starbucks's CEO, Howard Schultz, and suggested that Starbucks start to sell its own music. At first, Schultz was skeptical, but, after repeated lobbying efforts by Jones, he eventually took up the suggestion. Today, Starbucks not only sells CDs, it is also moving into music downloading with its "Hear Music" Starbucks stores, where customers can listen to and burn music from Starbucks's 200,000-song online music library while sipping their coffee.

Source: S. Gray and E. Smith. "Coffee and Music Create a Potent Mix at Starbucks," *Wall Street Journal*, July 19, 2005, A1.

1.3 STRATEGY IN ACTION

A Strategic Shift at Charles Schwab

In the mid-1990s, Charles Schwab was the most successful discount stockbroker in the world. Over 20 years, it had gained share from full-service brokers like Merrill Lynch by offering deep discounts on the commissions charged for stock trades. Although Schwab had a nationwide network of branches, most customers executed their trades through a telephone system called Telebroker. Others used online proprietary software, Street Smart, which had to be purchased from Schwab. It was a business model that worked well; then along came E*Trade.

E*Trade was a discount brokerage started in 1994 by Bill Porter, a physicist and an inventor, to take advantage of the opportunity created by the rapid emergence of the World Wide Web. E*Trade launched the first dedicated Web site for online trading. E*Trade had no branches, no brokers, and no telephone system for taking orders; thus it had a very low-cost structure. Customers traded stocks over the company's Web site. Due to its low-cost structure, E*Trade was able to announce a flat $14.95 commission on stock trades, a figure significantly below Schwab's average commission, which at the time was $65. It was clear from the outset that E*Trade and other online brokers, such as Ameritrade, which soon followed, offered a direct threat to Schwab. Not only were their cost structures and commission rates considerably below Schwab's, but the ease, speed, and flexibility of trading stocks over the Web suddenly made Schwab's Street Smart trading software seem limited and its telephone system antiquated.

Deep within Schwab, William Pearson, a young software specialist who had worked on the development of Street Smart, immediately saw the transformational power of the Web. Pearson believed that Schwab needed to develop its own Web-based software, and quickly. Try as he might, though, Pearson could not get the attention of his supervisor. He tried a number of other executives but found support hard to come by. Eventually he approached Anne Hennegar, a former Schwab manager who worked as a consultant to the company. Hennegar suggested that Pearson meet with Tom Seip, an executive vice president at Schwab who was known for his ability to think outside the box. Hennegar approached Seip on Pearson's behalf, and Seip responded positively, asking her to set up a meeting. Hennegar and Pearson turned up expecting to meet with just Seip, but to their surprise, in walked Charles Schwab; the chief operating officer, David Pottruck; and the vice presidents in charge of strategic planning and the electronic brokerage arena.

As the group watched Pearson's demo of how a Web-based system would look and work, they became increasingly excited. It was clear to those in the room that a Web-based system using real-time information, personalization, customization, and interactivity all advanced Schwab's commitment to empowering customers. By the end of the meeting, Pearson had received a green light to start work on the project. A year later, Schwab launched its own Web-based offering, eSchwab, which enabled Schwab clients to execute stock trades for a low flat-rate commission. eSchwab went on to become the core of the company's offering, enabling it to stave off competition from deep discount brokers like E*Trade.

Sources: John Kador, *Charles Schwab: How One Company Beat Wall Street and Reinvented the Brokerage Industry*, New York: John Wiley & Sons, 2002; Erick Schonfeld, "Schwab Puts It All Online," *Fortune*, December 7, 1998, 94–99.

Serendipity and Strategy

Business history is replete with examples of accidental events that help to push companies in new and profitable directions. What these examples suggest is that many successful strategies are not the result of well-thought-out plans but of serendipity, that is, of stumbling across good things unexpectedly. One such example occurred at 3M in the 1960s. At that time, 3M was producing fluorocarbons for sale as coolant liquid in air conditioning equipment. One day, a researcher working with fluorocarbons in a 3M lab spilled some of the liquid on her shoes. Later that day, when she spilled coffee over her shoes, she watched with interest as the coffee formed into little beads of liquid and then ran off her shoes without leaving a stain. Reflecting on this phenomenon, she realized that a fluorocarbon-based liquid might turn out to be useful for protecting fabrics from liquid stains, and so the idea for Scotchgard was born. Subsequently, Scotchgard became one of 3M's most profitable products and took the company into the fabric protection business, an area it had never planned to participate in.[24]

Serendipitous discoveries and events can open all sorts of profitable avenues for a company. But some companies have missed profitable opportunities because serendipitous discoveries or events were inconsistent with their prior (planned) conception of what their strategy should be. In one of the classic examples of such myopia, a century ago, the telegraph company Western Union turned down an opportunity to purchase the rights to an invention made by Alexander Graham Bell. The invention was the telephone, a technology that subsequently made the telegraph obsolete.

Intended and Emergent Strategies

Henry Mintzberg's model of strategy development provides a more encompassing view of what strategy actually is. According to this model, illustrated in Figure 1.7, a company's realized strategy is the product of whatever planned strategies are actually put into action (the company's deliberate strategies) and of any unplanned, or emergent, strategies. In Mintzberg's view, many planned strategies are not implemented because of unpredicted changes in the environment (they are unrealized). Emergent strategies are the unplanned responses to unforeseen circumstances. They arise from autonomous action by individual managers deep within the organization, serendipitous discoveries or events, or an unplanned strategic shift by top-level managers in response to changed circumstances. They are not the product of formal top-down planning mechanisms.

Figure 1.7 Emergent and Deliberate Strategies

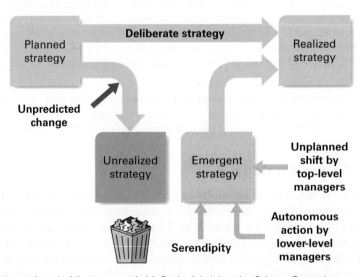

Source: Adapted from H. Mintzberg and A. McGugh, *Administrative Science Quarterly*, Vol. 30. No 2, June 1985.

Mintzberg maintains that emergent strategies are often successful and may be more appropriate than intended strategies. In the classic description of this process, Richard Pascale described how this was the case for the entry of Honda Motor Co. into the United States motorcycle market.[25] When a number of Honda executives arrived in Los Angeles from Japan in 1959 to establish a United States operation, their original aim (intended strategy) was to focus on selling 250 cc and 350 cc machines to confirmed motorcycle enthusiasts rather than 50 cc Honda Cubs, which were a big hit in Japan. Their instinct told them that the Honda 50s were not suitable for the United States market, where everything was bigger and more luxurious than in Japan.

However, sales of the 250 cc and 350 cc bikes were sluggish, and the bikes themselves were plagued by mechanical failure. It looked as if Honda's strategy was going to fail. At the same time, the Japanese executives who were using the Honda 50s to run errands around Los Angeles were attracting a lot of attention. One day, they got a call from a Sears Roebuck and Co. buyer who wanted to sell the 50 cc bikes to a broad market of Americans who were not necessarily motorcycle enthusiasts. The Honda executives were hesitant to sell the small bikes for fear of alienating serious bikers who might then associate Honda with "wimpy" machines. In the end, however, they were pushed into doing so by the failure of the 250 cc and 350 cc models.

Honda had stumbled onto a previously untouched market segment that was to prove huge: the average American who had never owned a motorcycle. Honda had also found an untried channel of distribution: general retailers rather than specialty motorcycle stores. By 1964, nearly one out of every two motorcycles sold in the United States was a Honda.

The conventional explanation for Honda's success is that the company redefined the United States motorcycle industry with a brilliantly conceived intended strategy. The fact was that Honda's intended strategy was a near disaster. The strategy that emerged did so not through planning but through unplanned action in response to unforeseen circumstances. Nevertheless, credit should be given to the Japanese management for recognizing the strength of the emergent strategy and for pursuing it with vigor.

The critical point demonstrated by the Honda example is that successful strategies can often emerge within an organization without prior planning and in response to unforeseen circumstances. As Mintzberg has noted, strategies can take root wherever people have the capacity to learn and the resources to support that capacity.

In practice, the strategies of most organizations are probably a combination of the intended (planned) and the emergent. The message for management is that it needs to recognize the process of emergence and intervene when appropriate, killing off bad emergent strategies but nurturing potentially good ones.[26] To make such decisions, managers must be able to judge the worth of emergent strategies. They must be able to think strategically. Although emergent strategies arise from within the organization without prior planning—that is, without going through the steps illustrated in Figure 1.5 in a sequential fashion—top management still has to evaluate emergent strategies. Such evaluation involves comparing each emergent strategy with the organization's goals, external environmental opportunities and threats, and internal strengths and weaknesses. The objective is to assess whether the emergent strategy fits the company's needs and capabilities. In addition, Mintzberg stresses that an organization's capability to produce emergent strategies is a function of the kind of corporate culture that the organization's structure and control systems foster. In other words, the different components of the strategic management process are just as important from the perspective of emergent strategies as they are from the perspective of intended strategies.

STRATEGIC PLANNING IN PRACTICE

Despite criticisms, research suggests that formal planning systems do help managers make better strategic decisions. A study that analyzed the results of 26 previously published studies came to the conclusion that, on average, strategic planning has a positive impact on company performance.[27] Another study of strategic planning in 656 firms found that formal planning methodologies and emergent strategies both form part of a good strategy formulation process, particularly in an unstable environment.[28] For strategic planning to work, it is important that top-level managers plan not just in the context of the current competitive environment but also in the context of the future competitive environment. To try to forecast what that future will look like, managers can use scenario planning techniques to plan for different possible futures. They can also involve operating managers in the planning process and seek to shape the future competitive environment by emphasizing strategic intent.

Scenario Planning

One reason that strategic planning may fail over the long run is that strategic managers, in their initial enthusiasm for planning techniques, may forget that the future is inherently unpredictable. Even the best-laid plans can fall apart if unforeseen contingencies occur, and that happens all the time in the real world. The recognition that uncertainty makes it difficult to forecast the future accurately led planners at Royal Dutch Shell to pioneer the scenario approach to planning.[29] **Scenario planning** involves formulating plans that are based on what-if scenarios about the future. In the typical scenario planning exercise, some scenarios are optimistic, and some are pessimistic. Teams of managers are asked to develop specific strategies to cope with each scenario. A set of indicators is chosen as signposts to track trends and identify the probability that any particular scenario is coming to pass. The idea is to get managers to understand the dynamic and complex nature of their environment, to think through problems in a strategic fashion, and to generate a range of strategic options that might be pursued under different circumstances.[30] The scenario approach to planning has spread rapidly among large companies. One survey found that more than 50% of the Fortune 500 companies use some form of scenario-planning methods.[31]

The oil company Royal Dutch Shell has perhaps done more than most to pioneer the concept of scenario planning, and its experience demonstrates the power of the approach.[32] Shell has been using scenario planning since the 1980s. Today, it uses two main scenarios to refine its strategic planning. The scenarios relate to the future demand for oil. One, called "Dynamics as Usual," sees a gradual shift from carbon fuels such as oil to natural gas to renewable energy. The second scenario, "The Spirit of the Coming Age," looks at the possibility that a technological revolution will lead to a rapid shift to new energy sources.[33] Shell is making investments that will ensure the profitability of the company whichever scenario comes to pass, and it is carefully tracking technological and market trends for signs of which scenario is becoming more likely over time.

The great virtue of the scenario approach to planning is that it can push managers to think outside the box, to anticipate what they might have to do in different situations, and to learn that the world is a complex and unpredictable place that places a premium on flexibility rather than on inflexible plans based on assumptions about the future that may turn out to be incorrect. As a result of scenario planning, organizations might pursue one dominant strategy related to the scenario that is judged to be most likely, but they make some investments that will pay off if other scenarios come to the fore (see Figure 1.8). Thus, the current strategy of Shell is based on the assumption that the world will only gradually shift away from carbon-based fuels (its "Dynamics as Usual" scenario), but the company is also hedging its bets by investing in new energy technologies and mapping out a strategy to pursue should its second scenario come to pass.

Decentralized Planning

A mistake that some companies have made in constructing their strategic planning process has been to treat planning as an exclusively top management responsibility. This ivory tower approach can result in strategic plans formulated in a vacuum by top managers who have little understanding or appreciation of current operating realities. Consequently, top managers may formulate strategies that do more harm than good. For example, when demographic data indicated that houses and families were shrinking, planners at GE's appliance group concluded that smaller appliances were the wave of the future. Because they had little contact with home builders and retailers, they did not realize that kitchens and bathrooms were the two rooms that were not shrinking. Nor did they appreciate that when couples both worked, they wanted big refrigerators to cut down on trips to the supermarket. GE ended up wasting a lot of time designing small appliances with limited demand.

The ivory tower concept of planning can also lead to tensions between corporate-, business-, and functional-level managers. The experience of GE's appliance group is again illuminating. Many of the corporate managers in the planning group were recruited from consulting firms or top-flight business schools. Many of the functional-level managers took this pattern of recruitment to mean that corporate managers did not think they were smart enough to think through strategic problems for themselves.

Figure 1.8 Scenario Planning

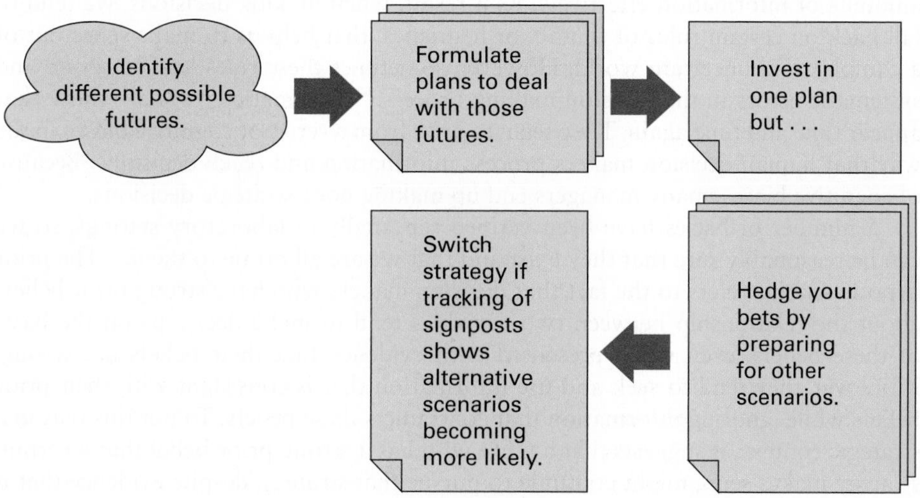

They felt shut out of the decision-making process, which they believed to be unfairly constituted. Out of this perceived lack of procedural justice grew an "us-versus-them" mindset that quickly escalated into hostility. As a result, even when the planners were right, operating managers would not listen to them. For example, the planners correctly recognized the importance of the globalization of the appliance market and the emerging Japanese threat; however, operating managers, who then saw Sears Roebuck as the competition, paid them little heed. Finally, ivory tower planning ignores the important strategic role of autonomous action by lower-level managers and serendipity.

Correcting the ivory tower approach to planning requires recognizing that successful strategic planning encompasses managers at all levels of the corporation. Much of the best planning can and should be done by business- and functional-level managers who are closest to the facts; in other words, planning should be decentralized. The role of corporate-level planners should be that of facilitators who help business- and functional-level managers do the planning by setting the broad strategic goals of the organization and providing the resources required to identify the strategies that might be required to attain those goals.

STRATEGIC DECISION MAKING

Even the best-designed strategic planning systems will fail to produce the desired results if managers do not use the information at their disposal effectively. Consequently, it is important that strategic managers learn to make better use of the information they have and understand why they sometimes make poor decisions. One important way in which managers can make better use of their knowledge and information is to understand how common cognitive biases can result in good managers making bad decisions.[34]

Cognitive Biases and Strategic Decision Making

The rationality of human decision makers is bounded by our own cognitive capabilities.[35] We are not supercomputers, and it is difficult for us to absorb and process large amounts of information effectively. As a result, when making decisions, we tend to fall back on certain rules of thumb, or heuristics, that help us to make sense out of a complex and uncertain world. However, sometimes these rules lead to severe and systematic errors in the decision-making process.[36] Systematic errors are those that appear time and time again. They seem to arise from a series of **cognitive biases** in the way that human decision makers process information and reach decisions. Because of cognitive biases, many managers end up making poor strategic decisions.

A number of biases have been verified repeatedly in laboratory settings, so we can be reasonably sure that they exist and that we are all prone to them.[37] The **prior hypothesis bias** refers to the fact that decision makers who have strong prior beliefs about the relationship between two variables tend to make decisions on the basis of these beliefs, even when presented with evidence that their beliefs are wrong. Moreover, they tend to seek and use information that is consistent with their prior beliefs while ignoring information that contradicts these beliefs. To put this bias in a strategic context, it suggests that a CEO who has a strong prior belief that a certain strategy makes sense might continue to pursue that strategy, despite evidence that it is inappropriate or failing.

Another well-known cognitive bias, **escalating commitment,** occurs when decision makers, having already committed significant resources to a project, commit even more resources even if they receive feedback that the project is failing.[38] This may be an irrational response; a more logical response would be to abandon the project and move on (that is, to cut your losses and run), rather than escalate commitment. Feelings of personal responsibility for a project apparently induce decision makers to stick with a project despite evidence that it is failing.

A third bias, **reasoning by analogy,** involves the use of simple analogies to make sense out of complex problems. The problem with this heuristic is that the analogy may not be valid. A fourth bias, **representativeness,** is rooted in the tendency to generalize from a small sample or even a single vivid anecdote. This bias violates the statistical law of large numbers that says that it is inappropriate to generalize from a small sample, let alone from a single case. In many respects, the dot-com boom of the late 1990s was based on reasoning by analogy and representativeness. Prospective entrepreneurs saw some of the early dot-com companies, such as Amazon and Yahoo!, achieve rapid success, at least judged by some metrics. Reasoning by analogy from a very small sample, they assumed that any dot-com could achieve similar success. Many investors reached similar conclusions. The result was a massive wave of start-ups that jumped into the Internet space in an attempt to capitalize on the perceived opportunities. That the vast majority of these companies subsequently went bankrupt is testament to the fact that the analogy was wrong and that the success of the small sample of early entrants was no guarantee that all dot-coms would succeed.

A fifth cognitive bias is referred to as **the illusion of control**: the tendency to overestimate one's ability to control events. General or top managers seem to be particularly prone to this bias: having risen to the top of an organization, they tend to be overconfident about their ability to succeed. According to Richard Roll, such overconfidence leads to what he has termed the hubris hypothesis of takeovers.[39] Roll argues that top managers are typically overconfident about their ability to create value by acquiring other companies. Hence, they end up making poor acquisition decisions, often paying far too much for the companies they acquire. Subsequently, servicing the debt taken on to finance such an acquisition makes it all but impossible to make money from the acquisition.

The **availability error** is yet another common bias. The availability error arises from our predisposition to estimate the probability of an outcome based on how easy the outcome is to imagine. For example, more people seem to fear a plane crash than a car accident, and yet statistically one is far more likely to be killed in a car on the way to the airport than in a plane crash. They overweigh the probability of a plane crash because the outcome is easier to imagine, and because plane crashes are more vivid events than car crashes, which affect only small numbers of people at a time. As a result of the availability error, managers might allocate resources to a project whose outcome is easier to imagine than to one that might have the highest return.

Techniques for Improving Decision Making

The existence of cognitive biases raises the issue of how to bring critical information to bear on the decision-making mechanism so that a company's strategic decisions are realistic and based on thorough evaluation. Two techniques known to enhance strategic thinking and counteract cognitive biases are devil's advocacy and dialectic inquiry.[40]

Devil's advocacy requires the generation of both a plan and a critical analysis of the plan. One member of the decision-making group acts as the devil's advocate, bringing out all the reasons that might make the proposal unacceptable. In this way, decision makers can become aware of the possible perils of recommended courses of action.

Dialectic inquiry is more complex because it requires the generation of a plan (a thesis) and a counterplan (an antithesis) that reflect plausible but conflicting courses of action.[41] Strategic managers listen to a debate between advocates of the plan and counterplan and then decide which plan will lead to the higher performance. The purpose of the debate is to reveal the problems with definitions, recommended courses of action, and assumptions of both plans. As a result of this exercise, strategic managers are able to form a new and more encompassing conceptualization of the problem, which then becomes the final plan (a synthesis). Dialectic inquiry can promote strategic thinking.

Another technique for countering cognitive biases is the outside view, which has been championed by Nobel Prize winner Daniel Kahneman and his associates.[42] The **outside view** requires planners to identify a reference class of analogous past strategic initiatives, determine whether those initiatives succeeded or failed, and evaluate the project at hand against those prior initiatives. According to Kahneman, this technique is particularly useful for countering biases, such as the illusion of control (hubris), reasoning by analogy, and representativeness. For example, when considering a potential acquisition, planners should look at the track record of acquisitions made by other enterprises (the reference class), determine if they succeeded or failed, and objectively evaluate the potential acquisition against that reference class. Kahneman argues that such a reality check against a large sample of prior events tends to constrain the inherent optimism of planners and produce more realistic assessments and plans.

STRATEGIC LEADERSHIP

One of the key strategic roles of both general and functional managers is to use all their knowledge, energy, and enthusiasm to provide strategic leadership for their subordinates and develop a high-performing organization. Several authors have identified a few key characteristics of good strategic leaders that lead to high performance: (1) vision, eloquence, and consistency; (2) articulation of the business model; (3) commitment; (4) being well informed; (5) willingness to delegate and empower; (6) astute use of power; and (7) emotional intelligence.[43]

Vision, Eloquence, and Consistency

One of the key tasks of leadership is to give an organization a sense of direction. Strong leaders seem to have clear and compelling visions of where their organizations should go, are eloquent enough to communicate these visions to others within the organization in terms that energize people, and consistently articulate their visions until they become part of the organization's culture.[44]

In the political arena, John F. Kennedy, Winston Churchill, Martin Luther King Jr., and Margaret Thatcher have all been described as examples of visionary leaders. Think of the impact of Kennedy's sentence, "Ask not what your country can do for you—ask what you can do for your country"; of King's "I have a dream" speech; and of Churchill's "we will never surrender." Kennedy and Thatcher were able to use their political office to push for governmental actions that were consistent with their vision. Churchill's speech galvanized a nation to defend itself against an aggressor, and King was able to pressure the government from outside to make changes in society.

Examples of strong business leaders include Microsoft's Bill Gates; Jack Welch, the former CEO of General Electric; and Sam Walton, Walmart's founder. For years, Bill Gates' vision of a world in which there would be a Windows-based personal computer on every desk was a driving force at Microsoft. More recently, the vision has evolved into one of a world in which Windows-based software can be found on any computing device, from PCs and servers to video game consoles (Xbox), cell phones, and handheld computers. At GE, Jack Welch was responsible for articulating the simple but powerful vision that GE should be first or second in every business in which it competed or it should exit from that business. Similarly, it was Walmart founder Sam Walton who established and articulated the vision that has been central to Walmart's success: passing on cost savings from suppliers and operating efficiencies to customers in the form of everyday low prices.

Articulation of the Business Model

Another key characteristic of good strategic leaders is their ability to identify and articulate the business model the company will use to attain its vision. A business model is a manager's conception of how the various strategies that the company pursues fit together into a congruent whole. At Dell Computer, for example, it was Michael Dell who identified and articulated the basic business model of the company: the direct sales business model. The various strategies that Dell has pursued over the years have refined this basic model, creating one that is very robust in terms of its efficiency and effectiveness. Although individual strategies can take root in many different places in an organization, and their identification is not the exclusive preserve of top management, only strategic leaders have the perspective required to make sure that the various strategies fit together into a congruent whole and form a valid and compelling business model. If strategic leaders lack clear conception of what the business model of the company is or should be, it is likely that the strategies the firm pursues will not fit together, and the result will be lack of focus and poor performance.

Commitment

Strong leaders demonstrate their commitment to their vision and business model by actions and words, and they often lead by example. Consider Nucor's former CEO. Ken Iverson. Nucor is a very efficient steelmaker with perhaps the lowest cost structure in the steel industry. It has turned in 30 years of profitable performance in an industry where most other companies have lost money because of a relentless focus on cost minimization. In his tenure as CEO, Iverson set the example: he answered his own phone, employed only one secretary, drove an old car, flew coach class, and was proud of the fact that his base salary was the lowest of the Fortune 500 CEOs. (Iverson made most of his money from performance-based pay bonuses.) This commitment was a powerful signal to employees that Iverson was serious about doing everything possible to minimize costs. It earned him the respect of Nucor employees and made them more willing to work hard. Although Iverson has retired, his legacy lives on in the cost-conscious organizational culture that has been built at Nucor, and like all other great leaders, his impact will last beyond his tenure.

Being Well Informed

Effective strategic leaders develop a network of formal and informal sources who keep them well informed about what is going on within their company. At Starbucks, for example, the first thing that former CEO Jim Donald did every morning was call up to 10 stores to talk to the managers and other employees and get a sense for how their stores were performing. Donald also stopped at a local Starbucks every morning on the way to work to buy his morning coffee. This allowed him to get to know individual employees very well. Donald found these informal contacts to be a very useful source of information about how the company was performing.[45]

Similarly, Herb Kelleher, the founder of Southwest Airlines, was able to find out much about the health of his company by dropping in unannounced on aircraft maintenance facilities and helping workers perform their tasks. Herb Kelleher would also often help airline attendants on Southwest flights, distributing refreshments and talking to customers. One frequent flyer on Southwest Airlines reported sitting next to Kelleher three times in 10 years. Each time, Kelleher asked him and others sitting nearby how Southwest Airlines was doing in a number of areas, looking for trends and spotting inconsistencies.[46]

Using informal and unconventional ways to gather information is wise because formal channels can be captured by special interests within the organization or by gatekeepers, managers who may misrepresent the true state of affairs to the leader. People like Donald and Kelleher who constantly interact with employees at all levels are better able to build informal information networks than leaders who closet themselves and never interact with lower-level employees.

Willingness to Delegate and Empower

High-performance leaders are skilled at delegation. They recognize that unless they learn how to delegate effectively, they can quickly become overloaded with responsibilities. They also recognize that empowering subordinates to make decisions is a good motivation tool and often results in decisions being made by those who must implement them. At the same time, astute leaders recognize that they need to maintain control over certain key decisions. Thus, although they will delegate many important decisions to lower-level employees, they will not delegate those that they judge to be of critical importance to the future success of the organization, such as articulating the company's vision and business model.

The Astute Use of Power

In a now classic article on leadership, Edward Wrapp noted that effective leaders tend to be very astute in their use of power.[47] He argued that strategic leaders must often play the power game with skill and attempt to build consensus for their ideas rather than use their authority to force ideas through; they must act as members of a coalition, or its democratic leaders, rather than as dictators. Jeffery Pfeffer has articulated a similar vision of the politically astute manager who gets things done in organizations through the intelligent use of power.[48] In Pfeffer's view, power comes from control over resources that are important to the organization: budgets, capital, positions, information, and knowledge. Politically astute managers use these resources to acquire another critical resource: critically placed allies who can help them attain their strategic objectives. Pfeffer stresses that one does not need to be a CEO to assemble power in an organization. Sometimes junior functional managers can build surprisingly effective power bases and use them to influence organizational outcomes.

Emotional Intelligence

Emotional intelligence is a term that Daniel Goldman coined to describe a bundle of psychological attributes that many strong and effective leaders exhibit:[49]

- **Self-awareness:** the ability to understand one's own moods, emotions, and drives, as well as their effect on others
- **Self-regulation:** the ability to control or redirect disruptive impulses or moods, that is, to think before acting
- **Motivation:** a passion for work that goes beyond money or status and a propensity to pursue goals with energy and persistence
- **Empathy:** the ability to understand the feelings and viewpoints of subordinates and to take those into account when making decisions
- **Social skills:** friendliness with a purpose

According to Goldman, leaders who possess these attributes—who exhibit a high degree of emotional intelligence—tend to be more effective than those who lack these attributes. Their self-awareness and self-regulation help to elicit the trust and confidence of subordinates. In Goldman's view, people respect leaders who, because they are self-aware, recognize their own limitations and, because they are self-regulating, consider decisions carefully. Goldman also argues that self-aware and self-regulating individuals tend to be more self-confident and therefore better able to cope with ambiguity and more open to change. A strong motivation exhibited in a passion for work can also be infectious, helping to persuade others to join together in pursuit of a common goal or organizational mission. Finally, strong empathy and social skills can help leaders earn the loyalty of subordinates. Empathetic and socially adept individuals tend to be skilled at managing disputes between managers, better able to find common ground and purpose among diverse constituencies, and better able to move people in a desired direction compared to leaders who lack these skills. In short, Goldman argues that the psychological makeup of a leader matters.

SUMMARY OF CHAPTER

1. A strategy is a set of related actions that managers take to increase their company's performance goals.

2. The major goal of a company is to maximize the returns that shareholders get from holding shares in the company. To maximize shareholder value, managers must pursue strategies that result in high and sustained profitability and also in profit growth.

3. The profitability of a company can be measured by the return that it makes on the capital invested in the enterprise. The profit growth of a company can be measured by the growth in earnings per share. Profitability and profit growth are determined by the strategies managers adopt.

4. A company has a competitive advantage over its rivals when it is more profitable than the average for all firms in its industry. It has a sustained competitive advantage when it is able to maintain above-average profitability over a number of years. In general, a company with a competitive advantage will grow its profits more rapidly than its rivals will.

5. General managers are responsible for the overall performance of the organization or for one of its major self-contained divisions. Their overriding strategic concern is for the health of the total organization under their direction.

6. Functional managers are responsible for a particular business function or operation. Although

they lack general management responsibilities, they play a very important strategic role.

7. Formal strategic planning models stress that an organization's strategy is the outcome of a rational planning process.

8. The major components of the strategic management process are defining the mission, vision, values, and major goals of the organization; analyzing the external and internal environments of the organization; choosing a business model and strategies that align an organization's strengths and weaknesses with external environmental opportunities and threats; and adopting organizational structures and control systems to implement the organization's chosen strategies.

9. Strategy can emerge from deep within an organization in the absence of formal plans as lower-level managers respond to unpredicted situations.

10. Strategic planning often fails because executives do not plan for uncertainty and ivory tower planners lose touch with operating realities.

11. In spite of systematic planning, companies may adopt poor strategies if their decision-making processes are vulnerable to groupthink and if individual cognitive biases are allowed to intrude into the decision-making process.

12. Devil's advocacy, dialectic inquiry, and the outside view are techniques for enhancing the effectiveness of strategic decision making.

13. Good leaders of the strategy-making process have a number of key attributes: vision, eloquence, and consistency; ability to craft the business model; commitment; being well informed; a willingness to delegate and empower; political astuteness; and emotional intelligence.

DISCUSSION QUESTIONS

1. Discuss the accuracy of the following statement: Formal strategic planning systems are irrelevant for firms competing in high-technology industries where the pace of change is so rapid that plans are routinely made obsolete by unforeseen events.

2. Between 1997 and 2004, Microsoft's ROIC fell from 32% to 17.5%. Over the same period, Microsoft's profits grew from $3.45 billion to $11.33 billion. How can a company have declining profitability (as measured by ROIC) but growing profits? What do you think explains this situation at Microsoft? For 2004, analysts predicted that Microsoft's ROIC would jump to 35%. Why do you think this was the case? Was it due to any change in the company's strategy?

3. What do we mean by strategy? How is a business model different from a strategy?

C L O S I N G   C A S E

Planning for the Chevy Volt

General Motors is a company in deep trouble. As car sales in North America collapsed in 2008, GM, which had already lost money in 2007, plunged deeply into the red. With losses estimated at $14 billion, the company was forced to go cap in hand to the government to beg for public finds to help it stave off bankruptcy. Fearing the economic consequences of a collapse of GM, the government agreed to loan funds to GM, but it insisted that the company have a clear plan charting its way back to profitability. Ironically, such a plan was already in place at GM. At the heart of it was a potentially huge gamble on a new type of car: the Chevy Volt.

The Chevy Volt, which is scheduled for market introduction in 2010, is a compact, four-door electric car with a reserve gasoline-powered engine. The primary power source is a large lithium ion battery (lithium ion batteries are typically found in small electric appliances such as cell phones). The battery can be charged by plugging it into a wall socket for six hours; when fully charged, it will fuel the car for 40 miles, which is less than most people's daily commute. After that, a gasoline engine kicks in, providing both drive power and recharging the lithium ion battery. GM estimates fuel economy will be over 100 miles per gallon, and charging the car overnight from a power outlet would cost about 80% less than filling it with gas at $3 per gallon. The car will cost somewhere between $30,000 and $40,000; however, because it uses a battery-powered technology, buyers will be able to take $7,500 tax credit.

The Volt was the brainchild of two men, Bob Lutz, GM's vice chairman, and Larry Burns, the head of R&D and strategic planning at GM. Although Lutz in particular had always championed large gas-hungry muscle cars, GM's planning told them that the market would probably move away from the SUVs that had been a profitable staple at GM for most of the 1990s. A number of trends were coming together to make this scenario likely.

First, oil prices, and by extension, gas prices, were increasing sharply. While driving an SUV that gets 12 miles to the gallon might make economic sense when gas was priced at $1 a gallon, it did not for most people when gas was $4 per gallon. GM's planning suggested that due to growing demand in developed nations, including China and India, and limited new supplies, the days of cheap oil were over. Second, global warming was becoming an increasing concern, and it seemed possible that tighter regulations designed to limit carbon emissions would be introduced in the future. As a major source of greenhouses gases, such as carbon dioxide, automobiles powered by internal combustion engines could hardly escape this trend. Third, the cost of manufacturing lithium ion batteries was falling, and new technology was promising to make them more powerful. Finally, GM's major competitor, Toyota, with its best selling hybrid, the Prius, had demonstrated that there was demand for fuel-efficient cars that utilized new battery technology (the Prius, however, uses a conventional fuel cell as opposed to a lithium ion battery).

Despite their analysis, when Lutz and Burns first proposed making the Volt in 2003, other managers at GM beat them down. For one thing, GM had already invested billions in developing fuel cells, and many in the company did not want to suddenly switch gears and focus on lithium ion batteries instead. Besides, said the critics, technologically it would be difficult to produce a large lithium ion battery. Others were skeptical given that GM had already had one failure with an electric car, the ill-fated EV1 introduced in the 1990s. Powered by a fuel cell, the EV1 had not sold well (according to many because the company had not put its weight behind it).

By 2006, however, the tide had started to turn. Not only were oil prices surging, as predicted by the strategic planning group, but also a small Silicon Valley start-up, Telsa Motors, had announced that it would be bringing a lithium ion sports car to market. Lutz' reaction was, "if a start-up can do it, GM can too!" So Lutz and Burns formed a skunk works within GM and quickly put together a Chevy Volt concept car, which they unveiled at the 2007 Detroit auto show. The concept car gained a lot of positive feedback, and Lutz used this to argue within the company that GM needed to commit to the project. Moreover, he argued, Toyota has gaining major benefits from its Prius, both in terms of sales, and the halo effect associated with making a green car. This time Lutz and Burns were able to persuade other senior managers to back the project, and it was officially launched in early 2007 with an aggressive goal of market introduction in 2010.

Case Discussion Questions

1. What does the Chevy Volt case tell you about the nature of strategic decision making at a large complex organization like GM?
2. What trends in the external environment favored the pursuit of the Chevy Volt project?
3. What impediments to pursuing this project do you think existed within GM?
4. The plan for the Chevy Volt seems to be based partly on the assumption that oil prices would remain high, and yet in late 2008, oil prices collapsed in the wake of a sharp global economic slowdown.
   a. What does this tell you about the nature of strategic plans?
   b. What do falling oil prices mean for the potential success of the Chevy Volt?
   c. Do you think oil prices will remain low?
5. What will it take for the Chevy Volt to be a successful car? In light of your analysis, how risky do you think this venture is for GM? What are the costs of failure? What are the costs of not pursuing the project?

OPPORTUNITIES AND THREATS—ANALYZING THE EXTERNAL ENVIRONMENT

LEARNING OBJECTIVES

After reading this chapter, you should be able to

- Review the main technique used to analyze competition in an industry environment—the five forces model
- Explore the concept of strategic groups and illustrate its implications for industry analysis

- Discuss how industries evolve over time, with reference to the industry life cycle model
- Show how trends in the macroenvironment can shape the nature of competition in an industry

The United States Steel Industry For decades, the United States steel industry was in deep economic malaise.

The problems of the industry were numerous. Since the 1970s, on, falling trade barriers have allowed cost-efficient foreign producers to sell steel in the United States, taking market share away from once-dominant integrated steel makers, such as U.S. Steel, Bethlehem Steel, and Wheeling Pittsburg. To make matters worse for incumbents, there was also new domestic competition in the form of minimills. Minimills were small steelmakers who used electric arc furnaces to smelt scrap steel and produce steel, often at a significantly lower cost than large established companies. The average minimill was about one-tenth of the size of a large integrated mill.

If the expansion in supply from foreign companies and minimills was not enough, demand for steel was also decreasing as customers switched to substitutes, including aluminum, plastics, and composites. The combination of growing supply and shrinking demand resulted in excess capacity. Indeed, at one time, as much as 45% of the steelmaking capacity in the United States was excess to requirements. As steelmakers struggled with excess capacity, they slashed their prices to try and capture more demand and cover their fixed costs, only to be matched by rivals. The result was intense price competition and low profits. More-over, customers for whom steel was mostly a commodity-type input could easily switch demand from company to company, and they used this leverage to further bargain down prices. To make matters worse, established steelmakers were typically unionized. A combination of high wage rates and inflexible work rules raised labor costs, making it even more difficult to make a profit in this brutally competitive industry. Strong unions, together with the costs of closing a plant, were also impediments to reducing excess capacity in the industry.

It is not surprising, then, that the steel industry as a whole rarely made money. Many of the old integrated steelmaking companies ultimately went bankrupt, including Bethlehem Steel and Wheeling Pittsburgh. Then, in the early 2000s, things started to change. There was a surge in demand for steel from the rapidly developing economies of China, India, Russia, and Brazil. By 2004, China alone was consuming almost one-third of all steel produced worldwide, and demand there was growing by more than 20% per year. Moreover, two decades of bankruptcies and consolidation had finally removed much of the excess capacity from the industry, not just in the United States but also worldwide. In the United States, the producers that survived the decades of restructuring were efficient enterprises with productive workforces and new technology. Finally competitive, for the first time they were able to hold their own against foreign imports. What helped was a decline in the value of the United States dollar after 2001 that made steel imports relatively more expensive and helped to create demand for steel exports *from* the United States.

As a result of this, competitive environment prices and profits surged. Hot rolled steel plate, for example, was priced at $260 per ton in June 2003. By June 2008, it had increased to $1,225 per ton. In 2003, U.S. Steel, the country's largest steel producer, lost $406 million. In 2008, it made $2 billion in net profit. Nucor Steel, long regarded as the most efficient steelmaker in the country, saw its profits increase from $63 million to $1.8 billion over the same period. How sustainable is this profit turnaround given the global economic slowdown that occurred in 2008? It is difficult to know for sure, but with governments around the world increasing state spending on infrastructure to try and jump-start their troubled economies, demand for steel may remain relatively strong, even in the face of a deep economic pullback.[1]

Overview

Strategy formulation begins with an analysis of the forces that shape competition in the industry in which a company is based. The goal is to understand the opportunities and threats confronting the firm and to use this understanding to identify strategies that will enable the company to outperform its rivals. **Opportunities** arise when a company can take advantage of conditions in its environment to formulate and implement strategies that enable it to become more profitable. For example, as discussed in the Opening Case, the growth in infrastructure spending in developing economies such as China and India represents an *opportunity* for steelmakers to expand their sales volume by creating products for the premium segment. **Threats** arise when conditions in the external environment endanger the integrity and profitability of the company's business. For two decades, the rise of foreign competitors and minimills was a threat to established producers in the United States steel industry.

This chapter begins with an analysis of the industry environment. First, it examines concepts and tools for analyzing the competitive structure of an industry and identifying industry opportunities and threats. Second, it analyzes the competitive implications that arise when groups of companies within an industry pursue similar and different kinds of competitive strategies. Third, it explores the way an industry evolves over time and the accompanying changes in competitive conditions. Fourth, it looks at the way in which forces in the macroenvironment affect industry structure and influence opportunities and threats. By the end of the chapter, you will understand that to succeed, a company must either fit its strategy to the external environment in which it operates or be able to reshape the environment to its advantage through its chosen strategy.

DEFINING AN INDUSTRY

An *industry* can be defined as a group of companies offering products or services that are close substitutes for each other, that is, products or services that satisfy the same basic customer needs. A company's closest competitors, its rivals, are those that serve the same basic customer needs. For example, carbonated drinks, fruit punches, and bottled water can be viewed as close substitutes for each other because they serve the same basic customer needs for refreshing and cold nonalcoholic beverages. Thus, we can talk about the soft drink industry, whose major players are Coca-Cola, PepsiCo, and Cadbury Schweppes. Similarly, desktop computers and notebook computers satisfy the same basic need that customers have for computer hardware on which to run personal productivity software; browse the Internet; send e-mail; play games; and store, display, and manipulate digital images. Thus, we can talk about the personal computer industry, whose major players are Dell, Hewlett-Packard, Lenovo (the Chinese company that purchased IBM's personal computer business), and Apple Computer.

The starting point of external analysis is to identify the industry that a company competes in. To do this, managers must begin by looking at the basic customer needs their company is serving, that is, they must take a customer-oriented view of their business as opposed to a product-oriented view (see Chapter 1). An industry is the supply side of a market, and companies in the industry are the suppliers. Customers are the demand side of a market and are the buyers of the industry's products. The basic customer needs that are served by a market define an industry's boundary. It is very important for managers to realize this, for if they define industry boundaries incorrectly, they may be caught flat-footed by the rise of competitors that serve the same basic customer needs with different product offerings. For example, Coca-Cola long saw itself as being in the soda industry—meaning carbonated soft drinks—whereas in fact it was in the soft drink industry, which includes noncarbonated soft drinks. In the mid-1990s, Coca-Cola was caught by surprise by the rise of customer demand for bottled water and fruit drinks, which began to cut into the demand for sodas. Coca-Cola moved quickly to respond to these threats, introducing its own brand of water, Dasani, and acquiring orange juice maker Minute Maid. By defining its industry boundaries too narrowly, Coca-Cola almost missed the rapid rise of the noncarbonated soft drinks segment of the soft drinks market.

Industry and Sector

An important distinction that needs to be made is between an industry and a sector. A sector is a group of closely related industries. For example, as illustrated in Figure 2.1, the computer sector comprises several related industries: the computer component industries (e.g., the disk drive industry, the semiconductor industry, and the modem industry), the computer hardware industries (e.g., the personal computer industry; the handheld computer industry, which includes smart phones such as the Apple iPhone; and the mainframe computer industry), and the computer software industry. Industries within a sector may be involved with each other in many different ways. Companies in the computer component industries are the suppliers of firms in the computer hardware industries. Companies in the computer software industry provide important complements to computer hardware: the software programs that customers purchase to run on their hardware. And companies in the personal, handheld, and mainframe industries are in indirect competition with each other because all provide products that are to a degree substitutes for each other.

Industry and Market Segments

It is also important to recognize the difference between an industry and the market segments within that industry. Market segments are distinct groups of customers within a market that can be differentiated from each other on the basis of their distinct attributes and specific demands. In the beer industry, for example, there are three main segments: consumers who drink long-established, mass-market brands (e.g., Budweiser); weight-conscious consumers who drink less-filling, low-calorie mass-market brands (e.g., Coors Light), and consumers who prefer premium-priced "craft beer" offered by microbreweries and many importers. Similarly, in the personal

Figure 2.1 The Computer Sector: Industries and Segments

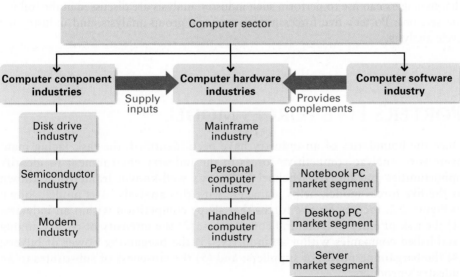

computer industry, there are different segments in which customers desire desktop machines, lightweight portable machines (laptops), and servers that sit at the center of a network of personal computers (see Figure 2.1). Personal computer manufacturers recognize the existence of these different segments by producing a range of product offerings that appeal to customers in different segments. Customers in all of these different segments, however, share a common need for PCs on which to run personal software applications.

Changing Industry Boundaries

Industry boundaries may change over time as customer needs evolve or new technologies emerge that enable companies in hitherto unrelated industries to satisfy established customer needs in new ways. We have noted that during the 1990s, as consumers of soft drinks began to develop a taste for bottled water and non-carbonated fruit-based drinks, Coca-Cola found itself in direct competition, and in the same industry, with the manufacturers of bottled water and fruit-based soft drinks.

For an example of how technological change can alter industry boundaries, consider the convergence that is currently taking place between the computer and telecommunications industries. Historically, the telecommunications equipment industry has been considered a distinct entity from the computer hardware industry. However, as telecommunications equipment has moved from traditional analog technology to digital technology, so telecommunications equipment has increasingly come to resemble computers. The result is that the boundaries between these different industries are blurring. A digital wireless phone, for example, is nothing more than a small handheld computer with a wireless connection, and small handheld computers often now come with wireless capabilities, transforming them into phones. Thus, Nokia and Motorola, who manufacture wireless phones, are now finding themselves competing directly with computer companies such as Apple and Microsoft.

Industry competitive analysis begins by focusing on the overall industry in which a firm competes before market segments or sector-level issues are considered. Tools that managers can use to perform such industry analysis are discussed in the following sections: Porter's five forces model, strategic group analysis, and industry life cycle analysis.

PORTER'S FIVE FORCES MODEL

Once the boundaries of an industry have been identified, the task facing managers is to analyze competitive forces in the industry environment to identify opportunities and threats. Michael E. Porter's well-known framework, known as the five forces model, helps managers with this analysis.[2] His model, shown in Figure 2.2, focuses on five forces that shape competition within an industry: (1) the risk of entry by potential competitors; (2) the intensity of rivalry among established companies within an industry; (3) the bargaining power of buyers; (4) the bargaining power of suppliers; and (5) the closeness of substitutes to an industry's products.

Figure 2.2   Porter's Five Forces Model

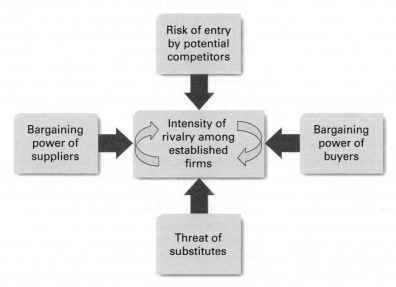

Porter argues that the stronger each of these forces is, the more limited is the ability of established companies to raise prices and earn greater profits. Within Porter's framework, a strong competitive force can be regarded as a threat because it depresses profits. A weak competitive force can be viewed as an opportunity because it allows a company to earn greater profits. The strength of the five forces may change over time as industry conditions change. The task facing managers is to recognize how changes in the five forces give rise to new opportunities and threats and to formulate appropriate strategic responses. In addition, it is possible for a company, through its choice of strategy, to alter the strength of one or more of the five forces to its advantage. This is discussed in the following chapters.

Risk of Entry by Potential Competitors

Potential competitors are companies that are not currently competing in an industry but have the capability to do so if they choose. For example, cable television companies have recently emerged as potential competitors to traditional phone companies. New digital technologies have allowed cable companies to offer telephone service over the same cables that transmit television shows.

Established companies already operating in an industry often attempt to discourage potential competitors from entering the industry because the more companies that enter, the more difficult it becomes for established companies to protect their share of the market and generate profits. A high risk of entry by potential competitors represents a threat to the profitability of established companies. But if the risk of new entry is low, established companies can take advantage of this opportunity to raise prices and earn greater returns.

The risk of entry by potential competitors is a function of the height of barriers to entry, that is, factors that make it costly for companies to enter an industry. The greater the costs that potential competitors must bear to enter an industry, the greater are the barriers to entry and the weaker this competitive force. High entry barriers may keep potential competitors out of an industry even when industry profits are high. Important barriers to entry include economies of scale, brand loyalty, absolute cost advantages, customer switching costs, and government regulation.[3] An important strategy is building barriers to entry (in the case of incumbent firms) or finding ways to circumvent those barriers (in the case of new entrants). We shall discuss this topic in more detail in subsequent chapters.

Economies of Scale   **Economies of scale** arise when unit costs fall as a firm expands its output. Sources of economies of scale include (1) cost reductions gained through mass-producing a standardized output; (2) discounts on bulk purchases of raw material inputs and component parts; (3) the advantages gained by spreading fixed production costs over a large production volume; and (4) the cost savings associated with spreading marketing and advertising costs over a large volume of output. If the cost advantages from economies of scale are significant, a new company that enters the industry and produces on a small scale suffers a significant cost disadvantage relative to established companies. If the new company decides to enter on a large scale in an attempt to obtain these economies of scale, it has to raise the capital required to build large-scale production facilities and bear the high risks associated with such an investment. A further risk of large-scale entry is that the increased supply of products will depress prices and result in vigorous retaliation by established companies. For these reasons, the threat of entry is reduced when established companies have economies of scale.

Brand Loyalty   **Brand loyalty** exists when consumers have a preference for the products of established companies. A company can create brand loyalty through continuous advertising of its brand-name products and company name, patent protection of products, product innovation achieved through company R&D programs, an emphasis on high product quality, and good after-sales service. Significant brand loyalty makes it difficult for new entrants to take market share away from established companies. Thus it reduces the threat of entry by potential competitors because they may see the task of breaking down well-established customer preferences as too costly. In the mass market segments of the beer industry, for example, the brand loyalty enjoyed by Anheuser Busch (Budweiser), Molson Coors (Coors), and SBA-Miller (Miller) is such that new entry into these segments of the industry is very difficult. Hence, most new entrants have focused on the premium segment of the industry, where established brands have less of a hold. (For an example of how a company circumvented brand-based barriers to entry in the market for carbonated soft drinks, see Strategy in Action 2.1.)

Absolute Cost Advantages   Sometimes established companies have an **absolute cost advantage** relative to potential entrants, meaning that entrants cannot expect to match the established companies' lower cost structure. Absolute cost advantages arise from three main sources: (1) superior production operations and processes due to accumulated experience, patents, or secret processes; (2) control of particular inputs required for production, such as labor, materials, equipment, or

2.1 STRATEGY IN ACTION

Circumventing Entry Barriers into the Soft Drink Industry

The soft drink industry has long been dominated by two companies—Coca-Cola and PepsiCo. By spending large sums of money on advertising and promotion, both companies have created significant brand loyalty and made it very difficult for new competitors to enter the industry and take market share away from these two giants. When new competitors do try to enter, both companies have responded by cutting prices, thus forcing the new entrant to curtail expansion plans.

However, in the late 1980s, the Cott Corporation, then a small Canadian bottling company, worked out a strategy for entering the soft drink market. Cott's strategy was deceptively simple. The company initially focused on the cola segment of the soft drink market. Cott signed a deal with Royal Crown Cola for exclusive global rights to its cola concentrate. RC Cola was a small player in the U.S. cola market. Its products were recognized as having a high quality, but RC Cola had never been able to effectively challenge Coke or Pepsi. Next, Cott signed a deal with a Canadian grocery retailer, Loblaw, to provide the retailer with its own private-label brand of cola. Priced low, the Loblaw private-label brand, known as President's Choice, was very successful and took share from both Coke and Pepsi.

Emboldened by this success, Cott decided to try to convince other retailers to carry private-label cola. To retailers, the value proposition was simple because, unlike its major rivals, Cott spent almost nothing on advertising and promotion. This constituted a major source of cost savings, which Cott passed on to retailers in the form of lower prices. For their part, the retailers found that they could significantly undercut the price of Coke and Pepsi and still make better profit margins on private-label brands than on branded colas.

Despite this compelling value proposition, few retailers were willing to sell private-label colas for fear of alienating Coca-Cola and PepsiCo., whose products were a major draw of grocery store traffic. Cott's breakthrough came in the early 1990s when it signed a deal with Walmart to supply the retailing giant with a private-label cola called "Sam's Choice" (named after Walmart founder Sam Walton). Walmart proved to be the perfect distribution channel for Cott. The retailer was just starting to get into the grocery business, and consumers went to Walmart not to buy branded merchandise but to get low prices. As Walmart's grocery business grew, so did Cott's sales. Cott soon added other flavors to its offerings, such as lemon-lime soda, which would compete with 7Up and Sprite. Moreover, pressured by Walmart, by the late 1990s, other U.S. grocers had also started to introduce private-label sodas, often turning to Cott to supply their needs.

By 2008, Cott had grown to become a $1.7 billion company. Cott captured more than 6% of the United States soda market, up from almost nothing a decade earlier, and held onto a 15% share of sodas in grocery stores, its core channel. The losers in this process have been Coca-Cola and PepsiCo, which are now facing the steady erosion of their brand loyalty and market share as consumers increasingly come to recognize the high quality and low price of private-label sodas.

Sources: A. Kaplan, "Cott Corporation," *Beverage World*, June 15, 2004, 32; J. Popp, "2004 Soft Drink Report," *Beverage Industry*, March 2004, 13–18; L Sparks, "From Coca-Colonization to Copy Catting: The Cott Corporation and Retailers Brand Soft Drinks in the UK and US," *Agribusiness*, March 1997, 153–127. Vol 13, Issue 2; E. Cherney, "After Flat Sales, Cott Challenges Pepsi, Coca-Cola," *Wall Street Journal*, January 8, 2003, B1, B8; Anonymous, "Cott Corporation: Company Profile," *Just-Drinks*, August 2006, 19–22; The Cott Corporation Web site, http://www.cott.com/about/history/en, accessed August 5, 2009.

management skills, that are limited in their supply; and (3) access to cheaper funds because existing companies represent lower risks than new entrants. If established companies have an absolute cost advantage, the threat of entry as a competitive force is weaker.

Customer Switching Costs Switching costs arise when it costs a customer time, energy, and money to switch from the products offered by one established company to the products offered by a new entrant. When switching costs are high, customers can be locked into the product offerings of established companies, even if new entrants offer better products.[4] A familiar example of switching costs concerns the costs associated with switching from one computer operating system to another. If a person currently uses Microsoft's Windows operating system and has a library of related software applications (for example, word processing software, spreadsheet, games) and document files, it is expensive for that person to switch to another computer operating system. To effect the change, this person would have to buy a new set of software applications and convert all existing document files to run with the new system. Faced with such an expense of money and time, most people are unwilling to make the switch unless the competing operating system offers a substantial leap forward in performance. Thus, the higher the switching costs are the higher the barrier to entry is for a company attempting to promote a new computer operating system.

Government Regulation   Historically, government regulation has constituted a major entry barrier into many industries. For example, until the mid-1990s, United States government regulation prohibited providers of long-distance telephone service from competing for local telephone service and vice versa. Other potential providers of telephone service, including cable television service companies such as Time Warner and Comcast (which could have used their cables to carry telephone traffic as well as TV signals), were prohibited from entering the market altogether. These regulatory barriers to entry significantly reduced the level of competition in both the local and long-distance telephone markets, enabling telephone companies to earn higher profits than might otherwise have been the case. All this changed in 1996 when the government deregulated the industry significantly. In the months that followed this announcement, local, long-distance, and cable TV companies all announced their intention to enter each other's markets, and a host of new players entered the market. The five forces model predicts that falling entry barriers due to government deregulation will result in significant new entry, an increase in the intensity of industry competition, and lower industry profit rates; indeed, that is what occurred.

In summary, if established companies have built brand loyalty for their products, have an absolute cost advantage with respect to potential competitors, have significant economies of scale, are the beneficiaries of high switching costs, or enjoy regulatory protection, the risk of entry by potential competitors is greatly diminished; it is a weak competitive force. Consequently, established companies can charge higher prices, and industry profits are higher. Evidence from academic research suggests that the height of barriers to entry is one of the most important determinants of profit rates in an industry.[5] Clearly, it is in the interest of established companies to pursue strategies consistent with raising entry barriers to secure these profits. By the same token, potential new entrants have to find strategies that allow them to circumvent barriers to entry.

Rivalry Among Established Companies

The second of Porter's five competitive forces is the intensity of rivalry among established companies within an industry. Rivalry refers to the competitive struggle between companies in an industry to gain market share from each other. The competitive struggle can be fought using price, product design, advertising and promotional spending, direct selling efforts, and after-sales service and support. More intense rivalry implies lower prices or more spending on non–price-competitive weapons, or both. Because intense rivalry lowers prices and raises costs, it squeezes profits out of an industry. Thus, intense rivalry among established companies constitutes a strong threat to profitability. Alternatively, if rivalry is less intense, companies may have the opportunity to raise prices or reduce spending on non–price-competitive weapons, which leads to a higher level of industry profits. The intensity of rivalry among established companies within an industry is largely a function of four factors: (1) industry competitive structure; (2) demand conditions; (3) cost conditions; and (4) the height of exit barriers in the industry.

Industry Competitive Structure   The competitive structure of an industry refers to the number and size distribution of companies in it, something that strategic managers determine at the beginning of an industry analysis. Industry structures vary, and different structures have different implications for the intensity of rivalry. A fragmented industry consists of a large number of small or medium-sized companies, none of which is in a position to determine industry price. A consolidated industry is dominated by a small number of large companies (an oligopoly) or, in extreme cases, by just one company (a monopoly), and companies often are in a position to determine industry prices. Examples of fragmented industries are agriculture, dry cleaning, video rental, health clubs, real estate brokerage, and tanning parlors. Consolidated industries include the aerospace, soft drink, automobile, pharmaceutical, stockbrokerage, and beer industries. In the beer industry, for example, the top three firms account for 80% of industry sales.

Many fragmented industries are characterized by low entry barriers and commodity-type products that are hard to differentiate. The combination of these traits tends to result in boom-and-bust cycles as industry profits rise and fall. Low entry barriers imply that whenever demand is strong and profits are high, new entrants will flood the market, hoping to profit from the boom. The explosion in the number of video stores, health clubs, and tanning salons in the 1980s and 1990s exemplifies this situation.

Often the flood of new entrants into a booming fragmented industry creates excess capacity, so companies start to cut prices to use their spare capacity. The difficulty companies face when trying to differentiate their products from those of competitors can exacerbate this tendency. The result is a price war, which depresses industry profits, forces some companies out of business, and deters potential new entrants. For example, after a decade of expansion and booming profits, many health clubs are now finding that they have to offer large discounts to hold on to their membership. In general, the more commodity-like an industry's product is, the more vicious will be the price war. This bust part of the cycle continues until overall industry capacity is brought into line with demand (through bankruptcies), at which point prices may stabilize again.

A fragmented industry structure, then, constitutes a threat rather than an opportunity. Most booms are relatively short-lived because of the ease of new entry and will be followed by price wars and bankruptcies. Because it is often difficult to differentiate products in these industries, the best strategy for a company is to try to minimize its costs so it will be profitable in a boom and survive any subsequent bust. Alternatively, companies might try to adopt strategies that change the underlying structure of fragmented industries and lead to a consolidated industry structure in which the level of industry profitability is increased. Exactly how companies can do this is something we shall consider in later chapters.

In consolidated industries, companies are interdependent because one company's competitive actions or moves (with regard to price, quality, and so on) directly affect the market share of its rivals and thus their profitability. When one company makes a move, this generally "forces" a response from its rivals, and the consequence of such competitive interdependence can be a dangerous competitive spiral. Rivalry increases as companies attempt to undercut each other's prices or offer customers more value in their products, pushing industry profits down in the process. The fare wars that have periodically created havoc in the airline industry provide a good illustration of this process. The steel industry also suffered from similar price-cutting until 2004 (see the Opening Case).

Companies in consolidated industries sometimes seek to reduce this threat by following the prices set by the dominant company in the industry.[6] However, companies must be careful, for explicit face-to-face price-fixing agreements are illegal. (Tacit, indirect agreements, arrived at without direct or intentional communication, are legal.) Instead, companies set prices by watching, interpreting, anticipating, and responding to each other's behavior. However, tacit price-leadership agreements often break down under adverse economic conditions, as has occurred in the breakfast cereal industry, profiled in Strategy in Action 2.2.

Industry Demand   The level of industry demand is a second determinant of the intensity of rivalry among established companies. Growing demand from new customers or additional purchases by existing customers tend to moderate competition by providing greater scope for companies to compete for customers. Growing demand tends to reduce rivalry because all companies can sell more without taking market share away from other companies. High industry profits are often the result. Conversely, declining demand results in more rivalry as companies fight to maintain market share and revenues (as in the breakfast cereal industry). Demand declines when customers leave the marketplace or each customer buys less. Now a company can grow only by taking market share away from other companies. Thus, declining demand constitutes a major threat, for it increases the extent of rivalry between established companies.

Cost Conditions   The cost structure of firms in an industry is a third determinant of rivalry. In industries where fixed costs are high, profitability tends to be highly leveraged to sales volume, and the desire to grow volume can spark intense rivalry. Fixed costs are the costs that must be borne before the firm makes a single sale. For example, before they can offer service, cable TV companies have to lay cable in the ground; the cost of doing so is a fixed cost. Similarly, to offer air express service, a company like FedEx must invest in planes, package-sorting facilities, and delivery trucks, all fixed costs that require significant capital investments. In industries where the fixed costs of production are high, if sales volume is low, firms cannot cover their fixed costs and will not be profitable. Thus, they have an incentive to cut their prices and/or increase promotion spending to drive up sales volume so that they can cover their fixed costs. In situations where demand is not growing fast enough and too many companies are engaged in the same actions (cutting prices and/or raising promotion spending in an attempt to cover fixed costs), the result can be intense rivalry and lower profits. Research suggests that often the weakest firms in an industry initiate such actions, precisely because they are the ones struggling to cover their fixed costs.[7]

2.2 STRATEGY IN ACTION

Price Wars in the Breakfast Cereal Industry

For decades, the breakfast cereal industry was one of the most profitable in the United States. The industry has a consolidated structure dominated by Kellogg's, General Mills, and Kraft Foods with its Post brand. Strong brand loyalty, coupled with control over the allocation of supermarket shelf space, helped to limit the potential for new entry. Meanwhile, steady demand growth of about 3% per annum kept industry revenues expanding. Kellogg's, which accounted for more than 40% of the market share, acted as the price leader in the industry. Every year Kellogg's increased cereal prices, its rivals followed, and industry profits remained high.

This favorable industry structure started to change in the early 1990s when growth in demand slowed and then stagnated as lattes and bagels or muffins replaced cereal as the morning fare for many American adults. Soon after, the rise of powerful discounters such as Walmart, which entered the grocery industry in the early 1990s, and began to aggressively promote their own brands of cereal, priced significantly below the brand-name cereals. As the decade progressed, other grocery chains such as Kroger's started to follow suit, and brand loyalty in the industry began to decline as customers realized that a $2.50 bag of wheat flakes from Walmart tasted about the same as a $3.50 box of Cornflakes from Kellogg's. As sales of cheaper, store-brand cereals began to take off, supermarkets, no longer as dependent on brand names to bring traffic into their stores, began to demand lower prices from the branded cereal manufacturers.

For several years, the manufacturers of brand cereals tried to hold out against these adverse trends, but in the mid-1990s, the dam broke. In 1996, Kraft (then owned by Philip Morris) aggressively cut prices by 20% for its Post brand in an attempt to gain market share. Kellogg's soon followed with a 19% price cut on two-thirds of its brands, and General Mills quickly did the same. The decades of tacit price collusion were officially over.

If the breakfast cereal companies were hoping that the price cuts would stimulate demand, they were wrong. Instead, demand remained flat while revenues and margins followed prices down, and Kellogg's operating margins dropped from 18% in 1995 to 10.2% in 1996, a trend experienced by the other brand cereal manufacturers.

By 2000, conditions had only worsened. Private-label sales continued to make inroads, gaining more than 10% of the market. Moreover, sales of breakfast cereals started to contract at 1% per annum. To cap it off, an aggressive General Mills continued to launch expensive price and promotion campaigns in an attempt to take share away from the market leader. Kellogg's saw its market share slip to just over 30% in 2001, behind the 31% now held by General Mills. For the first time since 1906, Kellogg's no longer led the market. Moreover, profits at all three major producers remained weak in the face of continued price discounting.

In mid-2001, General Mills finally blinked and raised prices a modest 2% in response to its own rising costs. Competitors followed, signaling perhaps that after a decade of costly price warfare, pricing discipline might once more emerge in the industry. Both Kellogg's and General Mills tried to move further away from price competition by focusing on brand extensions, such as Special K containing berries and new varieties of Cheerios. Kellogg's efforts with Special K helped the company recapture market leadership from General Mills. More importantly, the renewed emphasis on nonprice competition halted years of damaging price warfare, at least for the time being.

Sources: G. Morgenson, "Denial in Battle Creek," *Forbes,* October 7, 1996, 44; J. Muller, "Thinking out of the Cereal Box," *Business Week,* January 15, 2001, 54; A. Merrill, "General Mills Increases Prices," *Star Tribune,* June 5, 2001, 1D; S. Reyes, "Big G, Kellogg Attempt to Berry Each Other," *Brandweek,* October 7, 2002, 8.

Exit Barriers Exit barriers are economic, strategic, and emotional factors that prevent companies from leaving an industry.[8] If exit barriers are high, companies become locked into an unprofitable industry where overall demand is static or declining. The result is often excess productive capacity, which leads to even more intense rivalry and price competition as companies cut prices in the attempt to obtain the customer orders needed to use their idle capacity and cover their fixed costs.[9] Common exit barriers include the following:

- Investments in assets such as specific machines, equipment, and operating facilities that are of little or no value in alternative uses or cannot be sold off. If a company wishes to leave the industry, it has to write off the book value of these assets.
- High fixed costs of exit, such as the severance pay, health benefits, and pensions that have to be paid to workers who are being made redundant when a company ceases to operate.
- Emotional attachments to an industry, as when a company's owners or employees are unwilling to exit from an industry for sentimental reasons or because of pride.
- Economic dependence on an industry because a company relies on a single industry for its revenue and profit.
- The need to maintain an expensive collection of assets at or above some minimum level to participate effectively in the industry.
- Bankruptcy regulations, particularly in the United States, where Chapter 11 bankruptcy provisions allow insolvent enterprises to continue operating and reorganize themselves under bankruptcy protection. These regulations can keep unprofitable assets in the industry, result in persistent excess capacity, and lengthen the time required to bring industry supply in line with demand.

As an example of the effect of exit barriers in practice, consider the express mail and parcel delivery industry. The key players in this industry, such as FedEx and UPS, rely on the delivery business entirely for their revenues and profits. They have to be able to guarantee their customers that they will deliver packages to all major localities in the United States, and much of their investment is specific to this purpose. To meet this guarantee, they need a nationwide network of air routes and ground routes, an asset that is required to participate in the industry. If excess capacity develops in this industry, as it does from time to time, FedEx cannot incrementally reduce or minimize its excess capacity by deciding not to fly to and deliver packages in, say, Miami because that proportion of its network is underused. If it did that, it would no longer be able to guarantee that it would be able to deliver packages to all major locations in the United States, and its customers would switch to some other carrier. Thus, the need to maintain a nationwide network is an exit barrier that can result in persistent excess capacity in the air express industry during periods of weak demand. Finally, both UPS and FedEx managers and employees are emotionally tied to this industry: they were first movers, in the ground and air segments of the industry, respectively; their employees are also major owners of their companies' stock; and they are dependent financially on the fortunes of the delivery business.

The Bargaining Power of Buyers

The third of Porter's five competitive forces is the bargaining power of buyers. An industry's buyers may be the individual customers who ultimately consume its products (its end users) or the companies that distribute an industry's products to end users, such as retailers and wholesalers. For example, while soap powder made by Procter & Gamble and Unilever is consumed by end users, the principal buyers of soap powder are supermarket chains and discount stores, which resell the product to end users. The bargaining power of buyers refers to the ability of buyers to bargain down prices charged by companies in the industry or to raise the costs of companies in the industry by demanding better product quality and service. By lowering prices and raising costs, powerful buyers can squeeze profits out of an industry. Thus, powerful buyers should be viewed as a threat. Alternatively, when buyers are in a weak bargaining position, companies in an industry can raise prices and perhaps reduce their costs by lowering product quality and service, thus increasing the level of industry profits. Buyers are most powerful in the following circumstances:

- The industry that is supplying a particular product or service is composed of many small companies and the buyers are large and few in number. These circumstances allow buyers to dominate supplying companies.
- Buyers purchase in large quantities. In such circumstances, buyers can use their purchasing power as leverage to bargain for price reductions.
- The supply industry depends on the buyers for a large percentage of its total orders.
- When switching costs are low, buyers can play off the supplying companies against each other to force down prices.
- When it is economically feasible for buyers to purchase an input from several companies at once, buyers can play off one company in the industry against another.
- When buyers can threaten to enter the industry and produce the product themselves and thus supply their own needs, this tactic will force down industry prices.

The auto component supply industry, whose buyers are large automobile manufacturers such as GM, Ford, and Toyota, is a good example of an industry in which buyers have strong bargaining power and thus a strong competitive threat. Why? The suppliers of auto components are numerous and typically small in scale; their buyers, the auto manufacturers, are large in size and few in number. Additionally, to keep component prices down, both Ford and GM have used the threat of manufacturing a component themselves rather than buying it from auto component suppliers. The automakers have used their powerful position to play off suppliers against each other, forcing down the price they have to pay for component parts and demanding better quality. If a component supplier objects, the automaker uses the threat of switching to another supplier as a bargaining tool.

Another issue is that the relative power of buyers and suppliers tends to change in response to changing industry conditions. For example, because of changes now taking place in the pharmaceutical and health care industries, major buyers of pharmaceuticals (hospitals and health maintenance organizations) are gaining power over the suppliers of pharmaceuticals and have been able to demand lower prices. The Running Case discusses how Walmart's buying power has changed over the years as the company has become larger.

RUNNING CASE

Walmart's Bargaining Power over Suppliers

When Walmart and other discount retailers began in the 1960s, they were small operations with little purchasing power. To generate store traffic, they depended in large part on stocking nationally branded merchandise from well-known companies such as Procter & Gamble and Rubbermaid. Because the discounters did not have high sales volume, the nationally branded companies set the price. This meant that the discounters had to look for other ways to cut costs, which they typically did by emphasizing self-service in stripped-down stores located in the suburbs where land was cheaper. (In the 1960s, the main competitors for discounters were full-service department stores such as Sears, Roebuck that were often located in downtown shopping areas.)

Discounters such as Kmart purchased their merchandise through wholesalers, who in turned bought from manufacturers. The wholesaler would come into a store and write an order, and when the merchandise arrived, the wholesaler would come in and stock the shelves, saving the retailer labor costs. However, Walmart was located in Arkansas and placed its stores in small towns. Wholesalers were not particularly interested in serving a company that built its stores in such out-of-the-way places. They would do it only if Walmart paid higher prices.

Walmart's Sam Walton refused to pay higher prices. Instead, he took his fledgling company public and used the capital raised to build a distribution center to stock merchandise. The distribution center would serve all stores within a 300-mile radius, with trucks leaving the distribution center daily to restock the stores. Because the distribution center was serving a collection of stores and thus buying in larger volumes, Walton found that he was able to cut the wholesalers out of the equation and order directly from manufacturers. The cost savings generated by not having to pay profits to wholesalers were then passed on to consumers in the form of lower prices, which helped Walmart continue growing. This growth increased its buying power and thus its ability to demand deeper discounts from manufacturers.

Today Walmart has turned its buying process into an art form. Because 8% of all retail sales in the United States are made in a Walmart store, the company has enormous bargaining power over its suppliers. Suppliers of nationally branded products, such as Procter & Gamble, are no longer in a position to demand high prices. Instead, Walmart is now so important to Procter & Gamble that it is able to demand deep discounts from them. Moreover, Walmart has itself become a brand that is more powerful than the brands of manufacturers. People do not go to Walmart to buy branded goods; they go to Walmart for the low prices. This simple fact has enabled Walmart to bargain down the prices it pays, always passing on cost savings to consumers in the form of lower prices.

Since the early 1990s, Walmart has provided suppliers with real-time information on store sales through the use of individual stock keeping units (SKUs). These have allowed suppliers to optimize their own production processes, matching output to Walmart's demands and avoiding under- or overproduction and the need to store inventory. The efficiencies that manufacturers gain from such information are passed on to Walmart in the form of lower prices, which then passes on those cost savings to consumers.

Sources: "How Big Can It Grow? Wal-Mart," *Economist*, April 17, 2004, 74–76; H. Gilman, "The Most Underrated CEO Ever," Fortune, April 5, 2004, 242–247; K. Schaffner, "Psst! Want to Sell to Wal-Mart?" *Apparel Industry Magazine*, August 1996, 18–20.

The Bargaining Power of Suppliers

The fourth of Porter's five competitive forces is the bargaining power of suppliers: the organizations that provide inputs into the industry, such as materials, services, and labor (which may be individuals, organizations such as labor unions, or companies that supply contract labor). The bargaining power of suppliers refers to the ability of suppliers to raise input prices, or to raise the costs of the industry in other ways, for example, by providing poor-quality inputs or poor service. Powerful suppliers squeeze profits out of an industry by raising the costs of companies in the industry. Thus, powerful suppliers are a threat. Alternatively, if suppliers are weak, companies in the industry have the opportunity to force down input prices and demand higher-quality inputs (such as more productive labor). As with buyers, the ability of suppliers to make demands on a company depends on their power relative to that of the company. Suppliers are most powerful in the following situations:

- The product that suppliers sell has few substitutes and is vital to the companies in an industry.
- The profitability of suppliers is not significantly affected by the purchases of companies in a particular industry. In other words, the industry is not an important customer to the suppliers.
- Companies in an industry would experience significant switching costs if they moved to the product of a different supplier because a particular supplier's products are unique or different. In such cases, the company depends on a particular supplier and cannot play suppliers off against each other to reduce price.
- Suppliers can threaten to enter their customers' industry and use their inputs to produce products that would compete directly with those of companies already in the industry.
- Companies in the industry cannot threaten to enter their suppliers' industry and make their own inputs as a tactic for lowering the price of inputs.

An example of an industry in which companies are dependent on a powerful supplier is the personal computer industry. Personal computer firms are heavily dependent on Intel, the world's largest supplier of microprocessors for PCs. The industry standard for personal computers runs on Intel's microprocessor chips. Intel's competitors, such as Advanced Micro Devices (AMD), must develop and supply chips that are compatible with Intel's standard. Although AMD has developed competing chips, Intel still supplies about 85% of the chips used in PCs, primarily because only Intel has the manufacturing capacity required to serve a large share of the market. It is beyond the financial resources of Intel's competitors, such as AMD, to match the scale and efficiency of Intel's manufacturing systems. This means that while PC manufacturers can buy some microprocessors from Intel's rivals, most notably AMD, they still have to turn to Intel for the bulk of their supply. Because Intel is in a powerful bargaining position, it can charge higher prices for its microprocessors than would be the case if its competitors were more numerous and stronger (that is, if the microprocessor industry were fragmented).

Substitute Products

The final force in Porter's model is the threat of substitute products: the products of different businesses or industries that can satisfy similar customer needs. For example, companies in the coffee industry compete indirectly with those in the tea and soft drink industries because all three serve customer needs for nonalcoholic drinks. The existence of close substitutes is a strong competitive threat because this limits the price that companies in one industry can charge for their product, and thus industry profitability. If the price of coffee rises too much relative to that of tea or soft drinks, coffee drinkers may switch to those substitutes.

If an industry's products have few enough close substitutes that substitutes are a weak competitive force, then, other things being equal, companies in the industry have opportunities to raise prices and earn additional profits. For example, there is no close substitute for microprocessors, which gives companies like Intel and AMD the ability to charge higher prices.

A Sixth Force: Complementors

Andrew Grove, the former CEO of Intel, has argued that Porter's five forces model ignores a sixth force: the power, vigor, and competence of complementors.[10] Complementors are companies that sell products that add value to (complement) the products of companies in an industry because when used together, the products better satisfy customer demands. For example, the complementors to the personal computer industry are the companies that make software applications to run on those machines. The greater the supply of high-quality software applications to run on personal computers, the greater the value of personal computers to customers, creating greater demand for PCs and greater profitability for the personal computer industry.

Grove's argument has a strong foundation in economic theory, which has long argued that both substitutes and complements influence demand in an industry.[11] Moreover, recent research has emphasized the importance of complementary products in determining demand and profitability in many high-technology industries, such as the computer industry in which Grove made his mark.[12] The issue, therefore, is that when complements are an important determinant of demand for an industry's products, industry profits depend critically on there being an adequate supply of complementary products. When the number of complementors is increasing and they produce attractive complementary products, it boosts demand and profits in the industry and can open up many new opportunities for creating value. Conversely, if complementors are weak and are not producing attractive complementary products, it can be a threat that slows industry growth and limits profitability.

Porter's Model Summarized

The systematic analysis of forces in the industry environment using the Porter framework is a powerful tool that helps managers to think strategically. It is important to recognize that one competitive force often affects the others, thus all forces need to be considered and thought about when performing an industry analysis. Indeed, industry analysis leads managers to think systematically about how their strategic choices will be affected by the forces of industry competition and also about how their choices will affect the five forces and change conditions in the industry.

STRATEGIC GROUPS WITHIN INDUSTRIES

Companies in an industry often differ significantly from each other with respect to the way they strategically position their products in the market in terms of such factors as the distribution channels they use, the market segments they serve, the quality of their products, technological leadership, customer service, pricing policy, advertising policy, and promotions. As a result of these differences, within most industries,

Ethical Dilemma

You are a strategic analyst at a successful hotel enterprise that has been generating substantial excess cash flow. Your CEO instructed you to analyze the competitive structure of closely related industries to find one that the company could enter using your cash reserve to build a sustainable position. Your analysis, using Porter's five forces model, suggests that the highest profit opportunities are to be found in the gambling industry. You realize that it might be possible to add casinos to existing hotels, lowering entry costs into this industry. However, you personally have strong moral objections to gambling. Should your own personal beliefs influence your recommendations to the CEO?

it is possible to observe groups of companies in which each company follows a business model that is similar to that pursued by other companies in the group but different from the business model followed by companies in other groups. These different groups of companies are known as strategic groups.[13]

Normally, the basic differences between the business models that companies in different strategic groups use can be captured by a relatively small number of strategic factors. For example, in the pharmaceutical industry, two main strategic groups stand out (see Figure 2.3).[14] One group, which includes such companies as Merck, Eli Lilly, and Pfizer, is characterized by a business model based on heavy R&D spending and a focus on developing new, proprietary, blockbuster drugs. The companies in this proprietary strategic group are pursuing a high-risk, high-return strategy. It is a high-risk strategy because basic drug research is difficult and expensive. Bringing a new drug to market can cost up to $800 million in R&D money and a decade of research and clinical trials. The risks are high because the failure rate in new drug development is very high: only one out of every five drugs entering clinical trials is ultimately approved by the U.S. Food and Drug Administration. However, the strategy is also a high-return one because a single successful drug can be patented, giving the innovator a 20-year monopoly on its production and sale. This lets these proprietary companies charge a high price for the patented drug, allowing them to earn millions, if not billions, of dollars over the lifetime of the patent.

The second strategic group might be characterized as the generic drug strategic group. This group of companies, which includes Forest Labs, Mylan Labs, and Watson Pharmaceuticals, focuses on the manufacture of generic drugs: low-cost copies of drugs that were developed by companies in the proprietary group whose patents have now expired. Low R&D spending, production efficiency, and an emphasis on low prices characterize the business models of companies in this strategic group. They are pursuing low-risk, low-return strategies because they are not investing millions of dollars in R&D. The strategies are low return because the companies cannot charge high prices.

Figure 2.3　Strategic Groups in the Pharmaceutical Industry

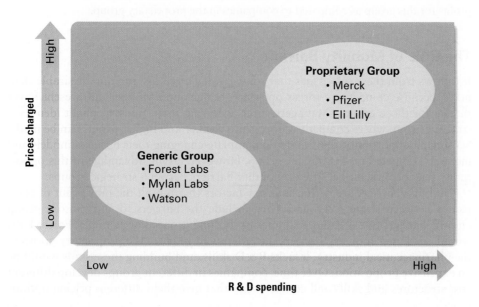

Implications of Strategic Groups

The concept of strategic groups has a number of implications for the identification of opportunities and threats within an industry. First, because all the companies in a strategic group are pursuing similar business models, customers tend to view the products of such enterprises as direct substitutes for each other. Thus, a company's closest competitors are those in its strategic group, not those in other strategic groups in the industry. The most immediate threat to a company's profitability comes from rivals within its own strategic group. For example, in the retail industry, there is a group of companies that might be characterized as discounters. Included in this group are Walmart, Kmart, Target, and Fred Meyer. These companies compete most vigorously with each other, rather than with other retailers in different groups, such as Nordstrom or Gap Inc. Kmart, for example, was driven into bankruptcy in the early 2000s not because Nordstrom or Gap Inc. took business from it but because Walmart and Target gained share in the discounting group by virtue of their superior strategic execution of the discounting business model.

A second competitive implication is that different strategic groups can have a different standing with respect to each of the competitive forces; thus, each strategic group may face a different set of opportunities and threats. The risk of new entry by potential competitors, the degree of rivalry among companies within a group, the bargaining power of buyers, the bargaining power of suppliers, and the competitive force of substitute and complementary products can each be a relatively strong or weak competitive force depending on the competitive positioning approach adopted by each strategic group in the industry. For example, in the pharmaceutical industry, companies in the proprietary group have historically been in a very powerful position in relation to buyers because their products are patented and there are no substitutes. Also, rivalry based on price competition within this group has been low because competition in the industry revolves around being the first to patent a new drug (so-called patent races), not around drug prices. Thus, companies in this group have been able to charge high prices and earn high profits. In contrast, companies in the generic group have been in much weaker positions because many companies are able to produce different versions of the same generic drug after patents expire. Thus, in the generic group, products are close substitutes, rivalry has been high, and price competition has led to lower profits for this group as compared to companies in the proprietary group.

The Role of Mobility Barriers

It follows from these two issues that some strategic groups are more desirable than other, because competitive forces open up greater opportunities and present fewer threats for those groups. Managers, after analyzing their industry, might identify a strategic group where competitive forces are weaker and higher profits can be made. Sensing an opportunity, they might contemplate changing their business models and move to compete in that strategic group. However, taking advantage of this opportunity may be difficult because of mobility barriers between strategic groups.

Mobility barriers are within-industry factors that inhibit the movement of companies between strategic groups. They include the barriers to entry into a group and the barriers to exit from a company's existing group. For example, Forest Labs would encounter mobility barriers if it attempted to enter the proprietary group in the pharmaceutical industry; it lacks R&D skills, and building these skills would be an expensive proposition. Over time, companies in different groups develop different cost structures and skills and competencies that give them different pricing options and choices. A company contemplating entry into another strategic group must evaluate whether it has the ability to imitate, and indeed outperform, its potential competitors in that strategic group. Managers must determine if it is cost-effective to overcome mobility barriers before deciding whether the move is worthwhile.

In summary, an important task of industry analysis is to determine the sources of the similarities and differences among companies in an industry and to work out the broad themes that underlie competition in an industry. This analysis often reveals new opportunities to compete in an industry by developing new kinds of products to meet the needs of customers better. It can also reveal emerging threats that can be countered effectively by changing competitive strategy. This issue is discussed in Chapters 5, 6, and 7, which examine crafting competitive strategy in different kinds of markets to build a competitive advantage over rivals and best satisfy customer needs.

INDUSTRY LIFE CYCLE ANALYSIS

An important determinant of the strength of the competitive forces in an industry (and thus of the nature of opportunities and threats) is the changes that take place in it over time. The similarities and differences between companies in an industry often become more pronounced over time, and its strategic group structure frequently changes. The strength and nature of each of the competitive forces also change as an industry evolves, particularly the two forces of risk of entry by potential competitors and rivalry among existing firms.[15]

A useful tool for analyzing the effects of industry evolution on competitive forces is the industry life cycle model, which identifies five sequential stages in the evolution of an industry that lead to five distinct kinds of industry environment: embryonic, growth, shakeout, mature, and decline (see Figure 2.4). The task facing managers is to anticipate how the strength of competitive forces will change as the industry environment evolves and formulate strategies that take advantage of opportunities as they arise and that counter emerging threats.

Figure 2.4   Stages in the Industry Life Cycle

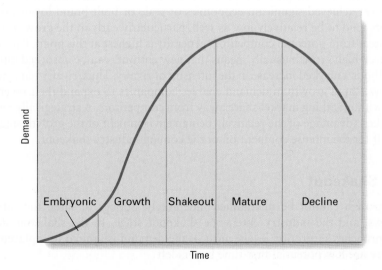

Embryonic Industries

An embryonic industry is just beginning to develop (e.g., personal computers and biotechnology in the 1970s, wireless communications in the 1980s, Internet retailing in the early 1990s, and nanotechnology today). Growth at this stage is slow because of such factors as buyers' unfamiliarity with the industry's product, high prices due to the inability of companies to reap any significant economies of scale, and poorly developed distribution channels. Barriers to entry tend to be based on access to key technological know-how rather than cost economies or brand loyalty. If the core know-how required to compete in the industry is complex and difficult to grasp, barriers to entry can be quite high, and established companies will be protected from potential competitors. Rivalry in embryonic industries is based not so much on price as on educating customers, opening up distribution channels, and perfecting the design of the product. Such rivalry can be intense; the company that is the first to solve design problems often has the opportunity to develop a significant market position. An embryonic industry may also be the creation of one company's innovative efforts, as happened with microprocessors (Intel), vacuum cleaners (Hoover), photocopiers (Xerox), small package express delivery (FedEx), and Internet search (Google). In such circumstances, the company has a major opportunity to capitalize on the lack of rivalry and build a strong hold on the market.

Growth Industries

Once demand for the industry's product begins to take off, the industry develops the characteristics of a growth industry. In a growth industry, first-time demand is expanding rapidly as many new customers enter the market. Typically, an industry grows when customers become familiar with the product; prices fall because experience and economies of scale have been attained, and distribution channels develop. The United States wireless telephone industry was in the growth stage for most of the 1990s. In 1990, there were only 5 million cellular subscribers in the nation. By 2008, this figure had increased to approximately 260 million with 84% of the population owning cell phones.

Normally, the importance of control over technological knowledge as a barrier to entry has diminished by the time an industry enters its growth stage. Because few companies have yet achieved significant economies of scale or built brand loyalty, other entry barriers tend to be relatively low as well, particularly early in the growth stage. Thus, the threat from potential competitors generally is highest at this point. Paradoxically, however, high growth usually means that new entrants can be absorbed into an industry without a marked increase in the intensity of rivalry. Thus, rivalry tends to be relatively low. Rapid growth in demand enables companies to expand their revenues and profits without taking market share away from competitors. A strategically aware company takes advantage of the relatively benign environment of the growth stage to prepare itself for the intense competition of the coming industry shakeout.

Industry Shakeout

Explosive growth cannot be maintained indefinitely. Sooner or later, the rate of growth slows, and the industry enters the shakeout stage. In the shakeout stage, demand approaches saturation levels; most of the demand is limited to replacement because there are few potential first-time buyers left.

As an industry enters the shakeout stage, rivalry between companies becomes intense. Typically, companies that have become accustomed to rapid growth continue to add capacity at rates consistent with past growth. However, demand is no longer growing at historic rates, and the consequence is the emergence of excess productive capacity. This condition is illustrated in Figure 2.5, where the solid curve indicates the growth in demand over time and the broken curve indicates the growth in productive capacity over time. As you can see, past point t_1, demand growth becomes slower as the industry becomes more mature. However, capacity continues to grow until time t_2. The gap between the solid and broken lines signifies excess capacity. In an attempt to use this capacity, companies often cut prices. The result can be a price war, which drives many of the most inefficient companies into bankruptcy, which is enough to deter any new entry.

Mature Industries

The shakeout stage ends when the industry enters its mature stage: the market is totally saturated, demand is limited to replacement demand, and growth is low or zero. What growth there is comes from population expansion that brings new customers into the market or an increase in replacement demand.

As an industry enters maturity, barriers to entry increase, and the threat of entry from potential competitors decreases. As growth slows during the shakeout, companies can no longer maintain historic growth rates merely by holding on to their market share. Competition for market share develops, driving down prices and often producing a price war, as happened in the airline and personal computer industry. To survive the shakeout, companies begin to focus on minimizing costs and building brand loyalty. The airlines, for example, tried to cut operating costs by hiring nonunion labor and build brand loyalty by introducing frequent-flyer programs. Personal computer companies have sought to build brand loyalty by providing excellent after-sales service and working to lower their cost structures. By the time an industry

Figure 2.5 Growth in Demand and Capacity

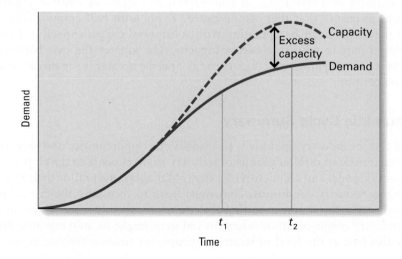

matures, the surviving companies are those that have brand loyalty and efficient low-cost operations. Because both these factors constitute a significant barrier to entry, the threat of entry by potential competitors is often greatly diminished. High entry barriers in mature industries can give companies the opportunity to increase prices and profits—although this does not always occur.

As a result of the shakeout, most industries in the maturity stage have consolidated and become oligopolies. Examples include the beer industry, the breakfast cereal industry, and the pharmaceutical industry. In mature industries, companies tend to recognize their interdependence and try to avoid price wars. Stable demand gives them the opportunity to enter into price-leadership agreements. The net effect is to reduce the threat of intense rivalry among established companies, thereby allowing greater profitability. Nevertheless, the stability of a mature industry is always threatened by further price wars. A general slump in economic activity can depress industry demand. As companies fight to maintain their revenues in the face of declining demand, price-leadership agreements break down, rivalry increases, and prices and profits fall. The periodic price wars that occur in the airline industry seem to follow this pattern.

Declining Industries

Eventually, most industries enter a decline stage: growth becomes negative for a variety of reasons, including technological substitution (e.g., air travel for rail travel); social changes (e.g., greater health consciousness hitting tobacco sales); demographics (e.g., the declining birthrate hurting the market for baby and child products); and international competition (e.g., low-cost foreign competition pushed the U.S. steel industry into decline for two decades until 2004—see Opening Case). Within a declining industry, the degree of rivalry among established companies usually increases. Depending on the speed of the decline and the height of exit barriers, competitive pressures can become as fierce as in the shakeout stage.[16] The main problem in a declining industry is that falling demand leads to the emergence of excess capacity. In trying to use this capacity, companies begin to cut prices, thus sparking a price war. The U.S. steel industry experienced these problems during the 1980s and 1990s because steel companies tried to use their excess capacity despite falling demand. The same problem occurred in the airline industry in 1990–1992, in 2001–2003, and again in 2008 as companies cut prices to ensure that they would not be flying with half-empty planes (that is, that they would not be operating with substantial excess capacity). Exit barriers play a part in adjusting excess capacity. The greater the exit barriers, the harder it is for companies to reduce capacity and the greater is the threat of severe price competition.

Industry Life Cycle Summary

A third task of industry analysis is to identify the opportunities and threats that are characteristic of different kinds of industry environments to develop an effective business model and competitive strategy. Managers must tailor their strategies to changing industry conditions. They must learn to recognize the crucial points in an industry's development so that they can forecast when the shakeout stage of an industry might begin or when an industry might be moving into decline. This is also true at the level of strategic groups, for new embryonic groups may emerge because of shifts in customer needs and tastes. Some groups may grow rapidly because of changes in technology, and others will decline as their customers defect.

LIMITATIONS OF MODELS FOR INDUSTRY ANALYSIS

The competitive forces, strategic groups, and life cycle models provide useful ways of thinking about and analyzing the nature of competition within an industry to identify opportunities and threats. However, each has its limitations, and managers need to be aware of their shortcomings.

Life Cycle Issues

It is important to remember that the industry life cycle model is a generalization. In practice, industry life cycles do not always follow the pattern illustrated in Figure 2.4. In some cases, growth is so rapid that the embryonic stage is skipped altogether. In others, industries fail to get past the embryonic stage. Industry growth can be revitalized after long periods of decline through innovation or social change. For example, the health boom brought the bicycle industry back to life after a long period of decline.

The time span of the stages can also vary significantly from industry to industry. Some industries can stay in maturity almost indefinitely if their products become basic necessities of life, as is the case for the car industry. Other industries skip the mature stage and go straight into decline, as in the case of the vacuum tube industry. Transistors replaced vacuum tubes as a major component in electronic products even though the vacuum tube industry was still in its growth stage. Still other industries may go through several shakeouts before they enter full maturity, as appears to be happening in the telecommunications industry.

Innovation and Change

Over any reasonable length of time, in many industries competition can be viewed as a process driven by innovation.[17] Indeed, innovation is frequently the major factor in industry evolution and causes movement through the industry life cycle. Innovation is attractive because companies that pioneer new products, processes, or strategies can often earn enormous profits. Consider the explosive growth of Toys"R"Us, Dell Computer, and Walmart. In a variety of different ways, all of these companies were innovators. Toys"R"Us pioneered a new way of selling toys (through large discount warehouse-type stores); Dell pioneered a whole new way of selling personal computers (directly via telephone and then the Web); Walmart pioneered the low-price discount superstore concept.

Successful innovation can transform the nature of industry competition. In recent decades, one frequent consequence of innovation has been to lower the fixed costs of production, thereby reducing barriers to entry and allowing new, and smaller, enterprises to compete with large established organizations. For example, two decades ago, large integrated steel companies such as U.S. Steel, LTV, and Bethlehem Steel dominated the steel industry. The industry was a typical oligopoly, dominated by a small number of large producers, in which tacit price collusion was practiced. Then along came a series of efficient minimill producers such as Nucor and Chaparral Steel, which used a new technology: electric arc furnaces. Over the past 20 years, they have revolutionized the structure of the industry. What was once a consolidated industry is now much more fragmented and price competitive. The successor company to U.S. Steel, USX, now has only a 12% market share, down from 55% in the mid-1960s. In contrast, the minimills now hold more than 40% of the market, up from 5% 20 years ago.[18] Thus, the minimill innovation has reshaped the nature of competition in the steel industry.[19] Porter's five forces model applied to the industry in 1970 would look very different from one applied in 2008 (see Opening Case for more details).

Michael Porter talks of innovations as "unfreezing" and "reshaping" industry structure. He argues that after a period of turbulence triggered by innovation, the structure of an industry once more settles down into a fairly stable pattern, and the five forces and strategic group concepts can once more be applied.[20] This view of the evolution of industry structure is often referred to as *punctuated equilibrium*.[21] The punctuated equilibrium view holds that long periods of equilibrium, when an industry's structure is stable, are punctuated by periods of rapid change when industry structure is revolutionized by innovation; there is an unfreezing and refreezing process.

Figure 2.6 shows what punctuated equilibrium might look like for one key dimension of industry structure: competitive structure. From time t_0 to t_1, the competitive structure of the industry is a stable oligopoly, with a few companies sharing the market. At time t_1, a major new innovation is pioneered by either an existing company or a new entrant. The result is a period of turbulence between t_1 and t_2. After a period of time, the industry settles down into a new state of equilibrium, but now the competitive structure is far more fragmented. Note that the opposite could have happened: the industry could have become more consolidated, although this seems

Figure 2.6   Punctuated Equilibrium and Competitive Structure

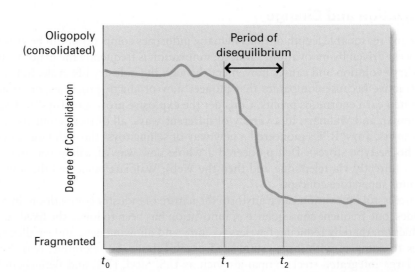

to be less common. In general, innovations seem to lower barriers to entry, allow more companies into the industry, and, as a result, lead to fragmentation rather than consolidation.

During a period of rapid change when industry structure is being revolutionized by innovation, value typically migrates to business models based on new positioning strategies.[22] In the stockbrokerage industry, value migrated away from the full-service broker model to the online trading model. In the steel industry, the introduction of electric arc technology led to a migration of value away from large, integrated enterprises and toward small minimills. In the book-selling industry, value has migrated away from small boutique "bricks and mortar" booksellers toward large bookstore chains such as Barnes & Noble and online bookstores such as amazon.com. Because the competitive forces and strategic group models are static, they cannot adequately capture what occurs during periods of rapid change in the industry environment when value is migrating.

Company Differences

Another criticism of industry models is that they overemphasize the importance of industry structure as a determinant of company performance and underemphasize the importance of variations or differences among companies within an industry or a strategic group.[23] As discussed in the next chapter, there can be enormous variance in the profit rates of individual companies within an industry. Research by Richard Rumelt and his associates suggests that industry structure explains only about 10% of the variance in profit rates across companies.[24] The implication is that individual company differences explain much of the remainder. Other studies have put the explained variance closer to 20%, which is still not a large figure.[25] Similarly, a growing number of studies have found only weak evidence of a link between strategic group membership and company profit rates, despite the fact that the strategic group model predicts a strong link.[26] Collectively, these studies suggest that the individual resources and capabilities of a company are far more important determinants of its profitability than is the industry or strategic group of which the company is a member. In other words, there are strong companies in tough industries where average profitability is low (e.g., Nucor in the steel industry), and weak companies in industries where average profitability is high.

Although these findings do not invalidate the five forces and strategic group models, they do imply that the models are only imperfect predictors of enterprise profitability. A company will not be profitable just because it is based in an attractive industry or strategic group. As we discuss in Chapters 3 and 4, more is required.

THE MACROENVIRONMENT

Just as the decisions and actions of strategic managers can often change an industry's competitive structure, so too can changing conditions or forces in the wider macroenvironment, that is, the broader economic, global, technological, demographic, social, and political context in which companies and industries are embedded (see Figure 2.7). Changes in the forces in the macroenvironment can have a direct impact on any or all of the forces in Porter's model, thereby altering the relative strength of these forces and, with it, the attractiveness of an industry.

Figure 2.7 The Role of the Macroenvironment

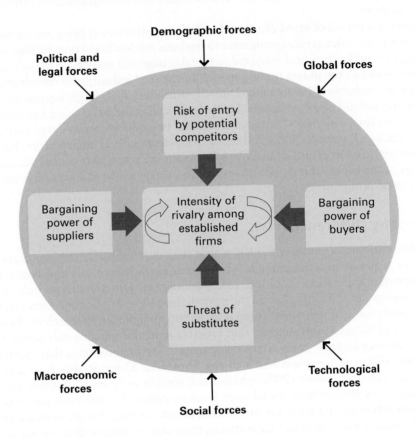

Macroeconomic Forces

Macroeconomic forces affect the general health and well-being of a nation or the regional economy of an organization, which in turn affect companies' and industries' abilities to earn an adequate rate of return. The four most important macroeconomic forces are the growth rate of the economy, interest rates, currency exchange rates, and inflation (or deflation) rates. Economic growth, because it leads to an expansion in customer expenditures, tends to produce a general easing of competitive pressures within an industry. This gives companies the opportunity to expand their operations and earn higher profits. Because economic decline (a recession) leads to a reduction in customer expenditures, it increases competitive pressures. Economic decline frequently causes price wars in mature industries.

Interest rates can determine the demand for a company's products. Interest rates are important whenever customers borrow money to finance their purchase of these products. The most obvious example is the housing market, in which mortgage rates directly affect demand. Interest rates also have an impact on the sale of autos, appliances, and capital equipment. For companies in such industries, rising interest rates are a threat and falling rates an opportunity. Interest rates are also important because they influence a company's cost of capital, and therefore its ability to raise funds and invest in new assets. The lower that interest rates are, the lower the cost of capital for companies will be, and the more investment there will be.

Currency exchange rates define the value of different national currencies against each other. Movement in currency exchange rates has a direct impact on the competitiveness of a company's products in the global marketplace. For example, when the value of the dollar is low compared with that of other currencies, products made in the United States are relatively inexpensive, and products made overseas are relatively expensive. A low or declining dollar reduces the threat from foreign competitors while creating opportunities for increased sales overseas. The fall in the value of the dollar against several major currencies during 2004–2008 helped to make the United States steel industry more competitive.

Price inflation can destabilize the economy, producing slower economic growth, higher interest rates, and volatile currency movements. If inflation keeps increasing, investment planning becomes hazardous. The key characteristic of inflation is that it makes the future less predictable. In an inflationary environment, it may be impossible to predict with any accuracy the real value of returns that can be earned from a project five years hence. Such uncertainty makes companies less willing to invest. Their holding back in turn depresses economic activity and ultimately pushes the economy into a recession. Thus, high inflation is a threat to companies.

Price deflation also has a destabilizing effect on economic activity. If prices are falling, the real price of fixed payments goes up. This is damaging for companies and individuals with a high level of debt who must make regular fixed payments on that debt. In a deflationary environment, the increase in the real value of debt consumes more of household and corporate cash flows, leaving less for other purchases and depressing the overall level of economic activity. Although significant deflation has not been seen since the 1930s, in the 1990s it started to take hold in Japan, and in 2008 there were concerns that it might reemerge in the United States as the country plunged into a deep recession.

Global Forces

Over the last half-century there have been enormous changes in the world economic system. We review these changes in some detail in Chapter 8 when we discuss global strategy. For now, the important points to note are that barriers to international trade and investment have tumbled, and more and more countries have enjoyed sustained economic growth. Economic growth in places like Brazil, China, and India has created large new markets for companies' goods and services and is giving companies an opportunity to grow their profits faster by entering these nations. Falling barriers to international trade and investment have made it much easier to enter foreign nations. For example, 20 years ago, it was almost impossible for a Western company to set up operations in China. Today, Western and Japanese companies are investing more than $50 billion a year in China. By the same token, however, falling barriers to international trade and investment have made it easier for foreign enterprises to enter the domestic markets of many companies (by lowering barriers to entry), thereby increasing the intensity of competition and lowering profitability. Because of these changes, many formally isolated domestic markets have now become part of a much larger, and more competitive, global marketplace, creating a myriad of threats and opportunities for companies.

Technological Forces

Over the last few decades, the pace of technological change has accelerated.[27] This has unleashed a process that has been called a "perennial gale of creative destruction."[28] Technological change can make established products obsolete overnight and simultaneously create a host of new product possibilities. Thus, technological change is both creative and destructive—both an opportunity and a threat.

One of the most important impacts of technological change is that it can impact the height of barriers to entry and therefore radically reshape industry structure. For example, the Internet lowered barriers to entry into the news industry. Providers of financial news now have to compete for advertising dollars and customer attention with new Internet-based media organizations that sprang up during the 1990s and 2000s, such as TheStreet.com, the Motley Fool, Yahoo!'s financial section, and, most recently, Google news. The resulting increase in rivalry has given advertisers more choices, enabling them to bargain down the prices that they must pay to media companies.

Demographic Forces

Demographic forces are outcomes of changes in the characteristics of a population, such as age, gender, ethnic origin, race, sexual orientation, and social class. Like the other forces in the general environment, demographic forces present managers with opportunities and threats and can have major implications for organizations. Changes in the age distribution of a population are an example of a demographic force that affects managers and organizations. Currently, most industrialized nations are experiencing the aging of their populations as a consequence of falling birth and death rates and the aging of the baby-boom generation. The aging of the population is increasing opportunities for organizations that cater to older people; the home healthcare and recreation industries, for example, are seeing an upswing in demand for their services. As the baby-boom generation from the late 1950s to the early 1960s has aged, it has created a host of opportunities and threats. During the 1980s, many baby boomers were getting married, creating an upsurge in demand for the customer appliances normally bought by newlyweds. Companies such as Whirlpool Corporation and GE capitalized on the resulting upsurge in demand for washing machines, dishwashers, dryers, and the like. In the 1990s, many of these same baby boomers were starting to save for retirement, creating an inflow of money into mutual funds and creating a boom in the mutual fund industry. In the next 20 years, many baby boomers will retire, creating a boom in retirement communities.

Social Forces

Social forces refer to the way in which changing social mores and values affect an industry. Like the other macroenvironmental forces discussed here, social change creates opportunities and threats. One of the major social movements of recent decades has been the trend toward greater health consciousness. Its impact has been immense, and companies that recognized the opportunities early have often reaped significant gains. Philip Morris, for example, capitalized on the growing health consciousness trend when it acquired Miller Brewing Company and then redefined competition in the beer industry with its introduction of low-calorie beer (Miller Lite). Similarly, PepsiCo was able to gain market share from its rival, Coca-Cola, by being the first to introduce diet colas and fruit-based soft drinks. At the same time, the health trend has created a threat for many industries. The tobacco industry, for example, is in decline as a direct result of greater customer awareness of the health implications of smoking.

Political and Legal Forces

Political and legal forces are outcomes of changes in laws and regulations. They result from political and legal developments within society and significantly affect managers and companies.

Political processes shape a society's laws, which constrain the operations of organizations and managers and thus create both opportunities and threats.[29] For example, throughout much of the industrialized world, there has been a strong trend toward deregulation of industries previously controlled by the state and privatization of organizations once owned by the state. In the United States, deregulation of the airline industry in 1979 allowed 29 new airlines to enter the industry between 1979 and 1993. The increase in passenger-carrying capacity after deregulation led to excess capacity on many routes, intense competition, and fare wars. To respond to this more competitive task environment, airlines have had to look for ways to reduce operating costs. The development of hub-and-spoke systems, the rise of non-union airlines, and the introduction of no-frills discount service are all responses to increased competition in the airlines' task environment. Despite these innovations, the airline industry still experiences intense fare wars, which have lowered profits and caused numerous airline company bankruptcies. The global telecommunications service industry is now experiencing the same kind of turmoil following the deregulation of that industry in the United States and elsewhere.

SUMMARY OF CHAPTER

1. An industry can be defined as a group of companies offering products or services that are close substitutes for each other. Close substitutes are products or services that satisfy the same basic customer needs.

2. The main technique used to analyze competition in the industry environment is the five forces model. The five forces are (a) the risk of new entry by potential competitors; (b) the extent of rivalry among established firms; (c) the bargaining power of buyers; (d) the bargaining power of suppliers; and (e) the threat of substitute products. The stronger each force is, the more competitive the industry and the lower the rate of return that can be earned.

3. The risk of entry by potential competitors is a function of the height of barriers to entry. The higher the barriers to entry are, the lower is the risk of entry and the greater the profits that can be earned in the industry.

4. The extent of rivalry among established companies is a function of an industry's competitive structure, demand conditions, cost conditions, and barriers to exit. Strong demand conditions moderate the competition among established companies and create opportunities for expansion. When demand is weak, intensive competition can develop, particularly in consolidated industries with high exit barriers.

5. Buyers are most powerful when a company depends on them for business but they themselves are not dependent on the company. In such circumstances, buyers are a threat.

6. Suppliers are most powerful when a company depends on them for business but they themselves are not dependent on the company. In such circumstances, suppliers are a threat.

7. Substitute products are the products of companies serving customer needs similar to the needs served by the industry being analyzed. The more similar the substitute products are to each other,

the lower is the price that companies can charge without losing customers to the substitutes.

8. Some argue for a sixth competitive force of some significance: the power, vigor, and competence of complementors. Powerful and vigorous complementors may have a strong positive impact on demand in an industry.

9. Most industries are composed of strategic groups: groups of companies pursuing the same or a similar strategy. Companies in different strategic groups pursue different strategies.

10. The members of a company's strategic group constitute its immediate competitors. Because different strategic groups are characterized by different opportunities and threats, it may pay a company to switch strategic groups. The feasibility of doing so is a function of the height of mobility barriers.

11. Industries go through a well-defined life cycle: from an embryonic stage, through growth, shakeout, and maturity, and eventually decline. Each stage has different implications for the competitive structure of the industry, and each gives rise to its own set of opportunities and threats.

12. The five forces, strategic group, and industry life cycles models all have limitations. The five forces and strategic group models present a static picture of competition that deemphasizes the role of innovation. Yet innovation can revolutionize industry structure and completely change the strength of different competitive forces. The five forces and strategic group models have been criticized for deemphasizing the importance of individual company differences. A company will not be profitable just because it is based in an attractive industry or strategic group; much more is required. The industry life cycle model is a generalization that is not always followed, particularly when innovations revolutionize an industry.

13. The macroenvironment affects the intensity of rivalry within an industry. Included in the macroenvironment are the macroeconomic environment, the global environment, the technological environment, the demographic and social environment, and the political and legal environment.

DISCUSSION QUESTIONS

1. Identify a growth industry, a mature industry, and a declining industry. For each industry, identify the following: (a) the number and size distribution of companies; (b) the nature of barriers to entry; (c) the height of barriers to entry; and (d) the extent of product differentiation. What do these factors tell you about the nature of competition in each industry? What are the implications for the company in terms of opportunities and threats?

2. Under what environmental conditions are price wars most likely to occur in an industry? What are the implications of price wars for a company? How should a company try to deal with the threat of a price war?

3. Discuss Porter's five forces model with reference to what you know about the United States steel industry (see the Opening Case). What does the model tell you about the level of competition in this industry?

C L O S I N G   C A S E

The United States Beer Industry

Over the last few decades, the United States beer industry has been characterized by a very clear trend toward an increase in the concentration of the market. Today, some 80% of all beer consumed in the United States is produced by just three companies—Anheuser-Busch (which is now owned by InBevof Belgium), SAB-Miller, and Molson Coors—up from 57% of the market in 1980. Anheuser-Busch had almost 50% of the market in 2008, up from just 28.2% in 1980. SAB-Miller (formed in 2002 when South African Breweries merged with Miller Beer) had around 19% of the market, and Molson Coors (formed in 2005 when Canada's Molson merged with Coors) had 11% of the market.

Anheuser Busch, SAB-Miller, and Molson Coors dominate the *mass market* segment of the industry, where competition revolves around aggressive pricing, brand loyalty, distribution channels, and national advertising spending. In contrast, there is another segment in the industry, the *premium beer* segment, which is served by a large number of microbrewers and importers, the majority of which have a market share of less than 1%. The premium segment focuses on discerning buyers. Producers are engaged in the art of craft brewing. They build their brands around taste and cover higher product costs by charging much higher prices—roughly twice as much for a six pack as the mass market brewers. The microbrewers and importers have been gaining share and currently account for about 11% of the total market.

Over the last two decades, the industry has changed in a number of ways. First, consumption of beer in the United States has been gradually declining (even though consumption of premium beer has been increasing). Per capita consumption of beer peaked at 30 gallons in 1980 and fell to a low of 21.8 gallons in 2007. The decline in consumption was partly due to the growing popularity of substitutes, particularly wine and spirits. In 1994, Americans consumed 1.75 gallons of wine per capita. By 2006, that at figure

had risen 2.16 gallons. Consumption of spirits increased from 1.27 gallons per capita in 1994 to 1.34 gallons per capita over the same period.

Second, advertising spending has steadily increased, putting smaller brewers at a disadvantage. In 1975, the industry was spending $0.18 per case on advertising; by 2002 it was spending $0.40 per case. (These figures are in inflation adjusted or constant dollars.) Smaller mass-market brewers could not afford the expensive national TV advertising campaigns required to match the spending of the largest firms in the industry, and they saw their market share shrink as a result.

Third, due to a combination of technological change in canning and distribution and increased advertising expenditures, the size that a mass-market brewer has to attain to reap all economies of scale—called the *minimum efficient scale* of production—has steadily increased. In 1970, the minimum efficient scale of production was estimated to be 8 million barrels of beer a year, suggesting that a market share of 6.4% was required to reap significant economies of scale. By the early 2000s, the minimum efficient scale had increased to 23 million barrels, implying that a market share of 13.06% was required to reap significant economies of scale.

By the early 2000s, only 24 mass-market brewers were left in the United States, down from 82 in 1970. Among the remaining mass-market brewers, Anheuser Busch is the most consistent performer due to its superior economies of scale. The company's ROIC has been high, fluctuating in the 17% to 23% range between 1996 and 2008, while net profits grew from $1.1 billion in 1996 to $2 billion in 2008. In contrast, both Coors and Miller, along with most other mass market brewers, have had mediocre financial performance at best. Coors and Miller merged with Molson and SAB, respectively, in an attempt to gain economies of scale.[30]

Case Discussion Questions

1. Why has the United States brewing industry become more concentrated over the last two decades?

2. Analyze the competitive structure of the industry using Porter's five forces model.

3. What are the implications of the evolving competitive structure in the brewing industry for the profitability and strategy of a smaller mass-market firm in the industry?

4. Are there different strategic groups in the industry? What are they? Do you think the nature of competition varies between groups?

3

COMPETENCIES AND PROFITABILITY ANALYZING INTERNAL RESOURCES

LEARNING OBJECTIVES

After reading this chapter, you should be able to

- Discuss the source of competitive advantage
- Identify and explore the role of efficiency, quality, innovation, and customer responsiveness in building and maintaining a competitive advantage
- Explain the concept of the value chain
- Understand the link between competitive advantage and profitability
- Explain what impacts the durability of a company's competitive advantage

Regaining McDonald's Competitive Advantage
McDonald's is an extraordinarily successful enterprise.

Started in 1955 when the legendary Ray Kroc decided to franchise the McDonald brothers' fast-food concept, McDonald's has grown into the largest restaurant chain in the world with almost 32,000 stores in 120 countries.

For decades, McDonald's success was grounded in a simple formula: give consumers value for money, good quick service, and consistent quality in a clean environment and they will come back time and time again. To deliver value for money and consistent quality, it standardized the process of order taking, making food, and service. Standardized processes raised the productivity of employees while ensuring that customers had the same experience in any restaurant. McDonald's also developed close ties with wholesalers and food producers, managing its supply chain to reduce costs. As it became larger, its buying power enabled it to realize economies of scale in purchasing and to pass on cost savings to customers in the form of low-priced meals, which drove forward demand. And then there was the ubiquity of McDonald's; wherever people went, they could find one of their restaurants. This, coupled with the consistent experience and low prices, drove brand loyalty.

T

The formula worked well until the late 1990s and early 2000s. By then, McDonald's was under attack for contributing to obesity. Its low-priced, high-fat foods were dangerous, claimed the critics. The company's image was tarnished by the best-selling book, *Fast Food Nation,* and by the documentary, *Super Size Me,* which featured a journalist who rapidly gained weight by eating only McDonald's "super size" meals for a month. By 2002, sales were stagnating, and profits were falling. It seemed that McDonald's had lost its edge.

What followed was a classic corporate makeover that has enabled the company to regain its competitive advantage. First, top management was changed. Then, the emphasis was shifted. McDonald's scrapped its super-size menu and added healthier options, such as salads and apple slices. Executives mined data to see what people were eating and found that people were eating more chicken and less beef. So they emphasized chicken, adding grilled chicken sandwiches, wraps with chicken, Southern-style chicken sandwiches, and, most recently, chicken for breakfast. To be sure, the company still sells many low-cost "dollar meals" consisting of cheeseburgers and fries. Indeed, in the recessionary environment of 2008–2009, sales of dollar meals surged. However, chicken sales doubled at McDonald's between 2002 and 2008, and the company now buys more chicken than beef. The company also decided to use white chicken only, ending the speculation about the "mystery meat" in chicken McNuggets.

The company also changed its emphasis on beverages. For decades, beverages were afterthoughts at McDonald's, but executives could not help but note the rapid growth of Starbucks. In 2006, McDonald's decided to offer better coffee, including lattes. McDonald's improved the quality of its coffee by buying high-quality beans, using better equipment, and filtering its water. The company did not lose sight of the need to keep costs low and service quick, however, and has been adding coffee-making machines that produce lattes and cappuccinos in 45 seconds at the push of a button. Starbucks it is not, but for many people, a latte from the McDonald's drive-through window is good enough. Today, the machines have been installed in almost half of the stores in the United States.

The next change is in the design of the restaurants. The aging design is being phased out, to be replaced with sleek new buildings with trendy furnishings and lights, wide screen TVs, and Wi-Fi connections. The idea is to raise the perception of quality and, thereby, capture more customers.

Thus far, the changes seem to be working. Both sales and profits have been growing at a healthy clip, despite a difficult economic environment. In 2008, net profits were $4 billion, up from $1.7 billion in 2002, while revenues expanded from $15.4 billion to $24 billion. Profitability has also improved, with McDonald's return on invested capital (ROIC) increasing from 9.4% in 2002 to 18% in 2008.[1]

Overview

Why, within a particular industry or market, do some companies outperform others? What is the basis of their (sustained) competitive advantage? The Opening Case provides some clues. The competitive advantage of McDonald's comes from efficiency, reliable quality, and customer responsiveness. McDonald's efficiency is due to its standardized processes, which boosts employee productivity, and its economies of scale in purchasing, both of which lower costs. Standardized processes also help to ensure reliable quality. While McDonald's does not sell high-quality food, the quality is reliably consistent—something that consumers value. In addition, recently, McDonald's has been taking steps to raise the perceived quality of its offerings, serving healthier meals, using only white chicken meat, serving higher-quality coffee, and changing the format of its restaurants to make them more appealing. McDonald's customer responsiveness is demonstrated by its shift toward healthier meals and its decision to offer higher quality drinks, such as lattes and cappuccinos. In this manner, McDonald's responds to changes in the tastes and preferences of its customer base. As described in this chapter, efficiency, customer responsiveness, and reliable quality are three of the four main building blocks of competitive advantage. The other building block is innovation.

This chapter focuses on internal analysis, which is concerned with identifying the strengths and weaknesses of a company. Together with an analysis of a company's external environment, internal analysis gives managers the information they need to choose the business model and strategies that will enable their company to attain a sustained competitive advantage. Internal analysis is a three-step process: (1) Managers must understand the process by which companies create value for customers and profit for themselves, and they need to understand the role of resources, capabilities, and distinctive competencies in this process; (2) they need to understand how important superior efficiency, innovation, quality, and customer responsiveness are in creating value and generating high profitability; and (3) they must be able to analyze the sources of their company's competitive advantage to identify what is driving the profitability of their enterprise and where opportunities for improvement might lie. In other words, managers must be able to identify how the strengths of the enterprise boost its profitability and how any weaknesses lead to lower profitability.

Three more critical issues in internal analysis are addressed in this chapter. First, what factors influence the durability of competitive advantage? Second, why do successful companies sometimes lose their competitive advantage? Third, how can companies avoid competitive failure and sustain their competitive advantage over time?

After reading this chapter, you will understand the nature of competitive advantage and why managers need to perform internal analysis, just as they must conduct industry analysis, to achieve superior performance and profitability.

THE ROOTS OF COMPETITIVE ADVANTAGE

A company has a *competitive advantage* over its rivals when its profitability is greater than the average profitability of all companies in its industry. It has a *sustained competitive advantage* when it is able to maintain above-average profitability over a number of years (as Walmart has done in the retail industry and McDonald's has done in the restaurant industry). The primary objective of strategy is to achieve a sustained competitive advantage, which in turn will result in superior profitability and profit growth. What are the sources of competitive advantage, and what is the link between strategy, competitive advantage, and profitability?

Distinctive Competencies

Competitive advantage is based on distinctive competencies. **Distinctive competencies** are firm-specific strengths that allow a company to differentiate its products from those offered by rivals and/or achieve substantially lower costs than its rivals.

McDonald's, for example, has a distinctive competence in managing fast-food franchises, which leads to higher employee productivity and lower costs (see the Opening Case). Similarly, it can be argued Toyota, which is the standard outperformer in the automobile industry, has distinctive competencies in the development and operation of manufacturing processes. Toyota pioneered a whole range of manufacturing techniques, such as just-in-time inventory systems, self-managing teams, and reduced setup times for complex equipment. These competencies, collectively known as the "Toyota lean production system," helped it attain superior efficiency and product quality, the basis of its competitive advantage in the global automobile industry.[2] Distinctive competencies arise from two complementary sources: resources and capabilities.[3]

Resources   **Resources** refer to the assets of a company. A company's resources can be divided into two types: tangible and intangible resources. **Tangible resources** are physical entities, such as land, buildings, plant, equipment, inventory, and money. **Intangible resources** are nonphysical entities that are created by managers and other employees, such as brand names, the reputation of the company, the knowledge that employees have gained through experience, and the intellectual property of the company, including that protected through patents, copyrights, and trademarks.

Resources are particularly *valuable* when they enable a company to create strong demand for its products, and/or to lower its costs. Toyota's valuable *tangible resources* include the equipment associated with its lean production system, much of which has been engineered specifically by Toyota for exclusive use in its factories. These valuable tangible resources allow Toyota to lower its costs, relative to its competitors. Similarly, Microsoft has a number of valuable *intangible resources*, including its brand name and the software code that underlies its Windows operating system. These valuable resources allow Microsoft to sell more of its products, relative to its competitors.

Valuable resources are more likely to lead to a sustainable competitive advantage if they are *rare*, in the sense that competitors do not possess them, and difficult for rivals to imitate; that is, if there are *barriers to imitation* (we will discuss the source of barriers to imitation in more detail later in this chapter). For example, the software code underlying Windows is rare because only Microsoft has full access to it. The code is also difficult to imitate. A rival cannot simply copy the software code underlying Windows and sell its own version of Windows because the code is protected by copyright law and copying it is illegal.

Capabilities   **Capabilities** refer to a company's skills at coordinating its resources and putting them to productive use. These skills reside in an organization's rules, routines, and procedures, that is, the style or manner through which it makes decisions and manages its internal processes to achieve organizational objectives.[4] More generally, a company's capabilities are the product of its organizational structure, processes, control systems, and hiring systems. They specify how and where decisions are made within a company, the kind of behaviors the company rewards, and the company's cultural norms and values. (We discuss how organizational structure and control systems help a company obtain capabilities in Chapters 12 and 13.) Capabilities are intangible. They reside not so much in individuals as in the way individuals interact, cooperate, and make decisions within the context of an organization.[5]

Like resources, capabilities are particularly valuable if they enable a company to create strong demand for its products and/or to lower its costs. The competitive advantage of Southwest Airlines is based in large part on its capability to select, motivate, and manage its workforce in such a way that leads to high employee productivity and lower costs (like McDonald's in the Opening Case). As with resources, valuable capabilities are also more likely to lead to a sustainable competitive advantage if they are both rare and protected from copying by barriers to imitation.

Resources, Capabilities, and Competencies   The distinction between resources and capabilities is critical to understanding what generates a distinctive competency. A company may have firm-specific and valuable resources, but unless it has the capability to use those resources effectively, it may not be able to create a distinctive competency. It is also important to recognize that a company may not need firm-specific and valuable resources to establish a distinctive competency so long as it has capabilities that no competitor possesses. For example, the steel mini-mill operator Nucor is widely acknowledged to be the most cost-efficient steelmaker in the United States. Its distinctive competency in low-cost steel-making does not come from any firm-specific and valuable resources. Nucor has the same resources (plant, equipment, skilled employees, know-how) as many other mini-mill operators. What distinguishes Nucor is its unique capability to manage its resources in a highly productive way. Specifically, Nucor's structure, control systems, and culture promote efficiency at all levels within the company.

In sum, for a company to have a distinctive competency, it must at a minimum have either (1) a firm-specific and valuable resource and the capabilities (skills) necessary to take advantage of that resource or (2) a firm-specific capability to manage resources (as exemplified by Nucor). A company's distinctive competency is strongest when it possesses both firm-specific and valuable resources and firm-specific capabilities to manage those resources.

The Role of Strategy   Figure 3.1 illustrates the relationship of a company's strategies, distinctive competencies, and competitive advantage. Distinctive competencies shape the strategies that a company pursues, which lead to competitive advantage and superior profitability. However, it is also very important to realize that the strategies a company adopts can build new resources and capabilities or strengthen the existing resources and capabilities of the company, thereby enhancing the distinctive competencies of the enterprise. Thus, the relationship between

Figure 3.1   Strategy, Resources, Capabilities, and Competencies

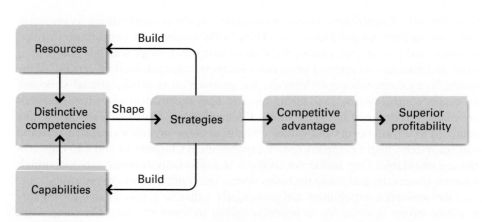

distinctive competencies and strategies is not a linear one; rather, it is a reciprocal one in which distinctive competencies shape strategies, and strategies help to build and create distinctive competencies.[6]

The history of the Walt Disney Company illustrates the way this process works. In the early 1980s, Disney suffered a string of poor financial years that culminated in a 1984 management shakeup when Michael Eisner was appointed CEO. Four years later, Disney's sales had increased from $1.66 billion to $3.75 billion, its net profits from $98 million to $570 million, and its stock market valuation from $1.8 billion to $10.3 billion. What brought about this transformation was the company's deliberate attempt to use its resources and capabilities more aggressively: Disney's enormous film library, its brand name, and its filmmaking skills, particularly in animation. Under Eisner, many old Disney classics were re-released, first in movie theaters and then on video, earning the company millions in the process. Then Eisner reintroduced the product that had originally made Disney famous: the full-length animated feature. Putting together its brand name and in-house animation capabilities, Disney produced a stream of major box office hits, including *The Little Mermaid*, *Beauty and the Beast*, *Aladdin*, *Pocahontas*, and *The Lion King*. Disney also started a cable television channel, the Disney Channel, to use this library and capitalize on the company's brand name. In other words, Disney's existing resources and capabilities shaped its strategies.

Through his choice of strategies, Eisner also developed new competencies in different parts of the business. In the filmmaking arm of Disney, for example, Eisner created a new low-cost film division under the Touchstone label, and the company had a string of low-budget box office hits. It entered into a long-term agreement with the computer animation company Pixar to develop a competency in computer-generated animated films. This strategic collaboration produced several hits, including *Toy Story* and *Monsters, Inc.* (In 2004, Disney acquired Pixar.) In sum, Disney's transformation was based not only on strategies that took advantage of the company's existing resources and capabilities but also on strategies that built new resources and capabilities such as those that underlie the company's competency in computer-generated animated films.

Competitive Advantage, Value Creation, and Profitability

Competitive advantage leads to superior profitability. At the most basic level, how profitable a company becomes depends on three factors: (1) the value customers place on the company's products; (2) the price that a company charges for its products; and (3) the costs of creating those products. The value customers place on a product reflects the *utility* they get from a product—the happiness or satisfaction gained from consuming or owning the product. Utility must be distinguished from price. Utility is something that customers get from a product. It is a function of the attributes of the product, such as its performance, design, quality, and point-of-sale and after-sale service. For example, most customers would place a much higher utility value on a top-end Lexus car from Toyota than on a low-end basic economy car from Kia (they would value it more), precisely because they perceive the Lexus to have better performance and superior design, quality, and service. A company that strengthens the utility (or value) of its products in the eyes of customers has more pricing options: it can raise prices to reflect that utility (value) or hold prices lower to induce more customers to purchase its products, thereby expanding unit sales volume.

Whatever pricing option a company chooses, however, the price a company charges for goods or service is typically less than the utility value placed on goods or service by the customer. This is because the customer captures some of that utility in the form of what economists call a *consumer surplus*.[7] The customer is able to do this because the company is competing with other companies for the customer's business, so the company must charge a lower price than it could were it a monopoly supplier. Moreover, it is normally impossible to segment the market to such a degree that the company can charge each customer a price that reflects that individual's unique assessment of the utility of a product—what economists refer to as a customer's reservation price. For these reasons, the price that gets charged tends to be less than the utility value placed on the product by many customers. Nevertheless, remember the basic principle here: the more utility that consumers get from a company's products or services, the more pricing options it has.

These concepts are illustrated in Figure 3.2: U is the *average* utility value per unit of a product to a customer; P is the average price per unit that the company decides to charge for that product; and C is the average unit cost of producing that product (including actual production costs and the cost of capital investments in production systems). The company's average profit per unit is equal to $P - C$, and the consumer surplus is equal to $U - P$. In other words, $U - P$ is a measure of the value the consumer captures, and $P - C$ is a measure of the value the company captures. The company makes a profit so long as P is more than C, and its profitability will be greater the lower C is relative to P. Bear in mind that the difference between U and P is in part determined by the intensity of competitive pressure in the marketplace; the lower the intensity of competitive pressure is, the higher the price that can be charged relative to U, but the difference between U and P is also determined by the company's pricing choice.[8] As we shall see, a company may choose to keep prices low relative to volume because lower prices enable the company to sell more products, attain economies of scale, and boost its profit margin by lowering C relative to P.

Note also that the value created by a company is measured by the difference between the utility a consumer gets from the product (U) and the costs of production (C), that is, $U - C$. A company creates value by converting factors of production that cost C into a product from which customers gets a utility of U. A company

Figure 3.2 Value Creation per Unit

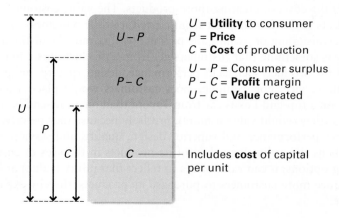

U = **Utility** to consumer
P = **Price**
C = **Cost** of production

$U - P$ = Consumer surplus
$P - C$ = **Profit** margin
$U - C$ = **Value** created

C ——— Includes **cost** of capital per unit

can create more value for its customers by lowering C or making the product more attractive through superior design, performance, quality, service, and the like. When customers assign a greater utility to the product (U increases), they are willing to pay a higher price (P increases). This discussion suggests that a company has a competitive advantage and high profitability when it creates more value for its customers than do rivals.[9]

The company's pricing options are captured in Figure 3.3. Suppose a company's current pricing option is the one pictured in the middle column of Figure 3.3. Imagine that the company decides to pursue strategies to increase the utility of its product offering from U to U^* to boost its profitability. Increasing utility initially raises production costs because the company has to spend money to increase product performance, quality, service, and other factors. Now there are two different pricing options that the company can pursue. Option 1 is to raise prices to reflect the higher utility: the company raises prices more than its costs increase, and profit per unit ($P - C$) increases. Option 2 involves a very different set of choices: the company lowers prices to expand unit volume. Basically, what is happening here is that customers recognize that they are getting a great bargain because price is now much lower than utility (the consumer surplus has increased), so they rush out to buy more (demand has increased). As unit volume expands due to increased demand, the company is able to realize economies of scale and reduce its average unit costs. Although creating the extra utility initially costs more and prices are now lowered, profit margins widen because the average unit costs of production fall as volume increases and economies of scale are attained.

Managers need to understand the dynamic relationships among utility, pricing, demand, and costs and make decisions on the basis of that understanding to maximize competitive advantage and profitability. Option 2 in Figure 3.3, for example, might not be a viable strategy if demand did not increase rapidly with lower prices or if there are few economies of scale to be had by increasing volume. Managers must

Figure 3.3 Value Creation and Pricing Options

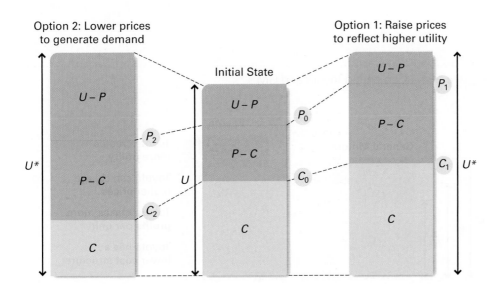

understand how value creation and pricing decisions affect demand and also how unit costs change with increases in volume. In other words, they must have a good grasp of the demand for the company's product and its cost structure at different levels of output if they are to make decisions that maximize profitability.

Consider the automobile industry. According to a 2008 study by Oliver Wyman, in 2007 Toyota made $922 in profit on every vehicle it manufactured in North America. GM, in contrast, lost $729 on every vehicle it made.[10] What accounts for the difference? First, Toyota has the best reputation for quality in the industry. According to annual surveys issued by J. D. Power and Associates, Toyota consistently tops the list in terms of quality, while GM cars are at best in the middle of the pack. The higher quality translates into a higher utility and allows Toyota to charge 5% to 10% higher prices than GM for equivalent cars. Second, Toyota has a lower cost per vehicle than GM, in part because of its superior labor productivity. For example, in Toyota's North American plants, it took an average of 30.37 employee hours to build a car, compared to 32.29 at GM plants in North America. That 1.94-hour productivity advantage translates into lower labor costs for Toyota; hence, a lower overall cost structure. Therefore, as summarized in Figure 3.4, Toyota's advantage over GM derives from greater utility (U), which has allowed the company to charge a higher price (P) for its cars, and from a lower cost structure (C), which taken together implies significantly greater profitability per vehicle ($P - C$).

Toyota's decisions with regard to pricing are guided by its managers' understanding of the relationship of utility, prices, demand, and costs. Given its ability to build more utility into its products, Toyota could have charged even higher prices than illustrated in Figure 3.4, but that might have led to lower sales volume, fewer economies of scale, higher unit costs, and lower profit margins. Toyota's managers have sought to find the pricing option that enables the company to maximize its profits given their assessment of demand for its products and its cost function. Thus, to create superior value, a company does not have to have the lowest cost structure in an industry or create the product with the highest utility in the eyes of customers. All that is necessary is that the gap between perceived utility (U) and costs of production (C) is greater than the gap attained by competitors.

Figure 3.4 Comparing Toyota and GM

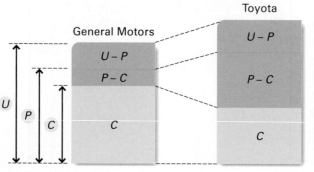

Note that Toyota has differentiated itself from General Motors by its superior quality, which allows it to charge higher prices; its superior productivity translates into a lower cost structure. Thus, its competitive advantage over General Motors is the result of strategies that have led to distinctive competencies, resulting in greater differentiation and a lower cost structure.

Indeed, at the heart of any company's business model is the combination of congruent strategies aimed at creating distinctive competencies that (1) differentiate its products in some way so that its consumers derive more utility from them, which gives the company more pricing options, and (2) result in a lower cost structure, which also gives it a broader range of pricing choices.[11] Achieving a sustained competitive advantage and superior profitability requires the right choices with regard to utility through differentiation and pricing given the demand conditions in the company's market and the company's cost structure at different levels of output. This issue is addressed in detail in the following chapters.

The Value Chain

All of the functions of a company—such as production, marketing, product development, service, information systems, materials management, and human resources—have a role in lowering the cost structure and increasing the perceived utility (value) of products through differentiation. As the first step in examining this concept, consider the value chain, which is illustrated in Figure 3.5.[12] The term **value chain** refers to the idea that a company is a chain of activities for transforming inputs into outputs that customers value. The transformation process involves a number of primary activities and support activities that add value to the product.

Primary Activities

Primary activities have to do with the design, creation, and delivery of the product, its marketing, and its support and after-sales service. In the value chain illustrated in Figure 3.5, the primary activities are broken down into four functions: research and development, production, marketing and sales, and customer service.

Research and Devlopment　Research and development is concerned with the design of products and production processes. Although we think of R&D as being associated with the design of physical products and production processes in manufacturing enterprises, many service companies also undertake R&D. For example, banks compete with each other by developing new financial products and new ways of delivering those products to customers. Online banking and smart debit cards are two recent examples of the fruits of new-product development in the banking industry. Earlier examples of innovation in the banking industry were ATM machines, credit cards, and debit cards.

By creating superior product design, R&D can increase the functionality of products, which makes them more attractive to customers, thereby adding value. Alternatively, the work of R&D may result in more efficient production processes, thereby lowering production costs. Either way, the R&D function can help to lower costs or raise the utility of a product and permit a company to charge higher prices. At Intel,

Ethical Dilemma

Your friend manages a highly profitable retailer. She attributes the principle source of competitive advantage to low labor costs, which are a result of her hiring minimum wage workers, denying worker benefits, and her consistent opposition to unionization at the company. Although she acknowledges that this approach leads to high employee turnover, she argues that the jobs are low skilled and easily refilled. Is your friend's approach to doing business ethical? Are there ways of achieving low labor costs without relying on placement of minimum wage workers? Would you council your friend to use an alternative approach?

Figure 3.5 The Value Chain

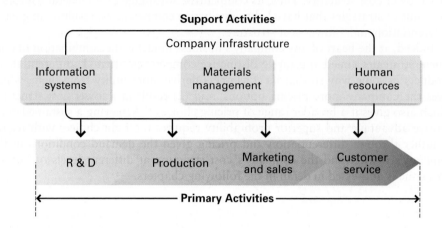

for example, R&D creates value by developing ever more powerful microprocessors and helping to pioneer ever more efficient manufacturing processes (in conjunction with equipment suppliers).

It is important to emphasize that R&D is not just about enhancing the features and functions of a product; it is also about the elegance of a product's design, which can create an impression of superior value in the minds of consumers. For example, part of the success of Apple Computer's iPod player has been based on the elegance and appeal of the iPod design, which has turned this piece of electronic equipment into a fashion accessory. For another example of how design elegance can create value, see Strategy in Action 3.1, which discusses value creation at the fashion house Burberry.

Production   Production is concerned with the creation of a good or service. For physical products, when we talk about production, we generally mean manufacturing. For services such as banking or retail operations, "production" typically takes place when the service is delivered to the customer, as when a bank makes a loan to a customer. By performing its activities efficiently, the production function of a company helps to lower its cost structure. For example, the efficient production operations of Honda and Toyota help those automobile companies achieve higher profitability relative to competitors such as General Motors. The production function can also perform its activities in a way that is consistent with high product quality, which leads to differentiation (and higher value) and lower costs.

Marketing and Sales   There are several ways in which the marketing and sales functions of a company can help to create value. Through brand positioning and advertising, the marketing function can increase the value that customers perceive to be contained in a company's product (and thus the utility they attribute to the product). Insofar as these help to create a favorable impression of the company's product in the minds of customers, they increase utility. For example, the French company Perrier persuaded U.S. customers that slightly carbonated bottled water was worth $1.50 per bottle rather than a price closer to the $0.50 that it cost to collect, bottle,

3.1 STRATEGY IN ACTION

Value Creation at Burberry

When Rose Marie Bravo, the highly regarded president of Saks Fifth Avenue, announced in 1997 that she was leaving to become CEO of the ailing British fashion house Burberry, people thought she was crazy. Burberry, best known as a designer of raincoats with the trademark tartan linings, had been described as an outdated, stuffy business with a fashion cachet of almost zero. When she stepped down from the Burberry position in 2006, Bravo was heralded in Britain and the United States as one of the world's best managers. During her tenure, she had engineered a remarkable turnaround, leading a transformation of Burberry into what one commentator called an "achingly hip" high-end fashion brand whose famous tartan bedecks everything from raincoats to bikinis and handbags to luggage in a riot of color from pink to blue to purple. In less than a decade, Burberry had become one of the most valuable luxury fashion brands in the world.

When asked how she achieved the transformation, Bravo explained that there was hidden brand value that was unleashed by constant creativity and innovation. Bravo hired world-class designers to redesign Burberry's tired fashion line and bought in Christopher Bailey, one of the very best, to lead the design team. The marketing department worked closely with advertisers to develop hip ads that would appeal to a younger, well-heeled audience. The ads featured supermodel Kate Moss promoting the line, using a top fashion photographer to shoot the model wearing Burberry. Burberry exercised tight control over distribution, pulling its products from stores whose image was not consistent with the brand, and expanding its own chain of Burberry stores.

Bravo also noted that "Creativity doesn't just come from designers … ideas can come from the sales floor, the marketing department, even from accountants, believe or not. People at whatever level they are working have a point of view and have something to say that is worth listening to." Bravo emphasized the importance of teamwork. "One of the things I think people overlook is the quality of the team. It isn't one person, and it isn't two people. It is a whole group of people—a team that works cohesively toward a goal—that makes something happen or not." She noted that her job is to build the team and then motivate them, "keeping them on track, making sure that they are following the vision."

Sources: Quotes from S. Beatty, "Bass Talk: Plotting Plaid's Future," *The Wall Street Journal*, September 9, 2004, B1. Also see C. M. Moore and G. Birtwistle, "The Burberry Business Model," *International Journal of Retail and Distribution Management* 32 (2004): 412–422; M. Dickson, "Bravo's Legacy in Transforming Burberry," *Financial Times*, October 6, 2005, 22.

and distribute the water. Perrier's marketing function essentially increased the perception of utility that customers ascribed to the product. Similarly, by helping to re-brand the company and its product offering, the marketing department at Burberry helped to create value (see Strategy in Action 3.1). Marketing and sales can also create value by discovering customer needs and communicating them back to the R&D function of the company, which can then design products that better match those needs.

Customer Service The role of the service function of an enterprise is to provide after-sales service and support. This function can create superior utility by solving customer problems and supporting customers after they have purchased the product. For example, Caterpillar, the U.S.-based manufacturer of heavy earth-moving equipment, can get spare parts to any point in the world within 24 hours, thereby minimizing the amount of downtime its customers have to face if their equipment malfunctions.

This is an extremely valuable support capability in an industry where downtime is expensive. It has helped to increase the utility that customers associate with Caterpillar products and, thus, the price that Caterpillar can charge for its products.

Support Activities

The **support activities** of the value chain provide inputs that allow the primary activities to take place. These activities are broken down into four functions: materials management (or logistics), human resources, information systems, and company infrastructure (see Figure 3.5).

Materials Management (Logistics)   The materials management (or logistics) function controls the transmission of physical materials through the value chain, from procurement through production and into distribution. The efficiency with which this is carried out can significantly lower costs, thereby creating more value. Dell has a very efficient materials management process. By tightly controlling the flow of component parts from its suppliers to its assembly plants and into the hands of consumers, Dell has dramatically reduced its inventory holding costs. Lower inventories mean lower costs and, hence, greater value creation. Another company that has benefited from very efficient materials management, the Spanish fashion company Zara, is discussed in Strategy in Action 3.2.

Human Resources   There are a number of ways in which the human resource function can help an enterprise create more value. This function ensures that the company has the right mix of skilled people to perform its value creation activities effectively. It is also the job of the human resource function to ensure that people are adequately trained, motivated, and compensated to perform their value creation tasks. If the human resources are functioning well, employee productivity rises (which lowers costs) and customer service improves (which raises utility), thereby enabling the company to create more value.

Information Systems   Information systems are largely electronic systems for managing inventory, tracking sales, pricing products, selling products, dealing with customer service inquiries, and so on. Information systems, when coupled with the communications features of the Internet, are holding out the promise of being able to improve the efficiency and effectiveness with which a company manages its other value creation activities. Again, Dell uses Web-based information systems to efficiently manage its global logistics network and increase inventory turnover. World-class information systems are also an aspect of Zara's competitive advantage (see Strategy in Action 3.2).

Company Infrastructure   Company infrastructure is the company-wide context within which all the other value creation activities take place: the organizational structure, control systems, and company culture. Because top management can exert considerable influence in shaping these aspects of a company, top management should also be viewed as part of the infrastructure of a company. Indeed, through strong leadership, top management can shape the infrastructure of a company and the performance of all other value-creation activities that take place within it. A good example of this process is given in Strategy in Action 3.1, which looks at how Rose Marie Bravo helped to engineer a turnaround at Burberry.

3.2 STRATEGY IN ACTION

Competitive Advantage at Zara

The fashion retailer Zara is one of Spain's fastest growing and most successful companies with sales of some $8.5 billion and a network of 2,800 stores in 64 countries. Zara's competitive advantage centers on one thing—speed. While it takes most fashion houses six to nine months to go from design to having merchandise delivered to a store, Zara can pull off the entire process in just five weeks. This rapid response time enables Zara to quickly respond to changing fashions.

Zara achieves this by breaking many of the rules of operation in the fashion business. While most fashion houses outsource production, Zara has its own factories and keeps about half of its production in-house. Zara also has its own designers and stores. Its designers are in constant contact with the stores, not only tracking what is selling on a real-time basis through information systems but also talking to store managers once a week to get their subjective impressions of what is hot. This information supplements data gathered from other sources, such as fashion shows.

Drawing on this information, Zara's designers create approximately 40,000 new designs per year from which 10,000 are selected for production. Zara then purchases basic textiles from global suppliers but performs capital intensive production activities in its own factories. These factories use computer-controlled machinery to cut pieces for garments. Zara does not produce in large volumes to attain economies of scale; instead it produces in small lots. Labor-intensive activities, such as sewing, are performed by subcontractors located close to Zara's factories. Zara makes a practice of having more production capacity than necessary, so that if an emerging fashion trend is spotted, the company can quickly respond by designing garments and ramping up production.

Once garments have been made, they are delivered to one of Zara's warehouses and then shipped to its stores weekly. Zara deliberately underproduces products, supplying small batches of products in hot demand before quickly shifting to the next fashion trend. Often the merchandise sells out quickly. The empty shelves in Zara stores create a scarcity value—which helps to generate demand. Customers quickly snap up products they like because they know they may soon be out of stock and not produced again.

As a result of this strategy, which is supported by competencies in design, information systems, and logistics management, Zara carries fewer inventories than competitors (Zara's inventory amounts to about 10% of sales, compared to 15% at rival stores like Gap Inc. and Benetton). This means fewer price reductions to move products that have not sold and higher profit margins.

Source: Staff Reporter, "Shining Examples," *The Economist: A Survey of Logistics*, June 17, 2006, 4–6; K. Capell, et al., "Fashion Conquistador," *Business Week*, September 4, 2006, 38–39; K. Ferdows, et al., "Rapid Fire Fulfillment," *Harvard Business Review* 82 (2004), 101–107.

THE BUILDING BLOCKS OF COMPETITIVE ADVANTAGE

Four factors help a company build and sustain competitive advantage: superior efficiency, quality, innovation, and customer responsiveness. Each of these factors is the product of a company's distinctive competencies. Indeed, in a very real sense they are "generic" distinctive competencies. These generic competencies allow a company to (1) differentiate its product offering and offer more utility to its customers and (2) lower its cost structure (see Figure 3.6). These factors can be considered generic distinctive competencies because any company, regardless of its industry or the products or services it produces, can pursue them. Although they are discussed sequentially,

Figure 3.6   Building Blocks of Competitive Advantage

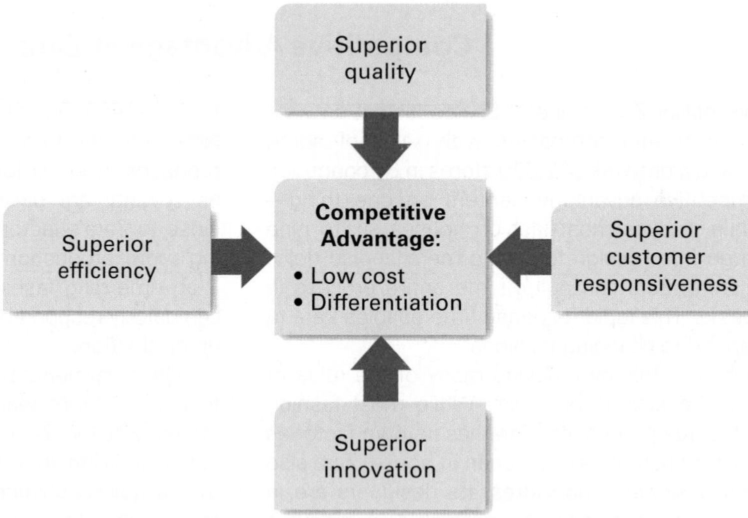

they are highly interrelated, and the important ways they affect each other here should be noted. For example, superior quality can lead to superior efficiency, and innovation can enhance efficiency, quality, and responsiveness to customers.

Efficiency

In one sense, a business is simply a device for transforming inputs into outputs. Inputs are basic factors of production, such as labor, land, capital, management, and technological know-how. Outputs are the goods and services that the business produces. The simplest measure of efficiency is the quantity of inputs that it takes to produce a given output, that is, efficiency = outputs/inputs. The more efficient a company is, the fewer the inputs required to produce a given output.

The most common measure of efficiency for many companies is employee productivity. **Employee productivity** refers to the output produced per employee. For example, if it takes GM 30 hours of employee time to assemble a car and it takes Ford 25 hours, we can say that Ford has higher employee productivity than GM and is, thus, more efficient. As long as other things are equal, such as wage rates, we can assume from this information that Ford will have a lower cost structure than GM. Thus, employee productivity helps a company attain a competitive advantage through a lower cost structure.

Quality as Excellence and Reliability

A product can be thought of as a bundle of attributes.[13] The attributes of many physical products include their form, features, performance, durability, reliability, style, and design.[14] A product is said to have *superior quality* when customers perceive that its attributes provide them with higher utility than the attributes of products sold by rivals. For example, a Rolex watch has attributes—such as design, styling, performance, and reliability—that customers perceive as being superior to the same attributes in many other watches. Thus, we can refer to a Rolex as a high-quality product: Rolex has differentiated its watches by these attributes.

When customers evaluate the quality of a product, they commonly measure it against two kinds of attributes: those related to *quality as excellence* and those related to *quality as reliability*. From a quality-as-excellence perspective, the important attributes are things such as a product's design and styling, its aesthetic appeal, its features and functions, the level of service associated with the delivery of the product, and so on. For example, customers can purchase a pair of imitation leather boots for $20 from Walmart, or they can buy a handmade pair of butter-soft leather boots from Nordstrom for $500. The boots from Nordstrom will have far superior styling, feel more comfortable, and look much better than those from Walmart. The utility consumers will get from the Nordstrom boots will in all probability be much greater than the utility derived from the Walmart boots, but of course, they will have to pay far more for them. That is the point: when excellence is built into a product offering, consumers have to pay more to own or consume it.

With regard to quality as reliability, a product can be said to be reliable when it consistently does the job it was designed for, does it well, and rarely, if ever, breaks down. As with excellence, reliability increases the utility a consumer gets from a product and, thus, the price the company can charge for that product. Toyota's cars, for example, have the highest reliability ratings in the automobile industry, and, therefore, consumers are prepared to pay more for them than for cars that are very similar in other attributes. As we shall see, increasing product reliability has been the central goal of an influential management philosophy that came out of Japan in the 1980s, which is commonly referred to as **total quality management (TQM)**.

The position of a product against two dimensions, reliability and other attributes, can be plotted on a figure similar to Figure 3.7. For example, a Lexus has attributes—such as design, styling, performance, and safety features—that customers perceive as demonstrating excellence in quality and that are viewed as being superior to those of most other cars. Lexus is also a very reliable car. Thus, the overall

Figure 3.7 A Quality Map for Automobiles

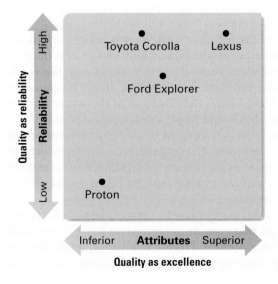

level of quality of the Lexus is very high, which means that the car offers consumers significant utility. This gives Toyota the option of charging a premium price for the Lexus. Toyota also produces another very reliable vehicle, the Toyota Corolla, but this product is positioned for less-wealthy customers and lacks many of the superior attributes of the Lexus. Thus, although the Corolla is also a high-quality car in the sense of being reliable, it is not as high-quality as a Lexus in the sense of being an excellent product. At the other end of the spectrum, we can find poor-quality products that have both low reliability and inferior attributes, such as poor design, performance, and styling. An example is the Proton, which is built by the Malaysian car firm of the same name. The design of the car is more than a decade old and has a dismal reputation for styling and safety. Moreover, Proton's reliability record is one of the worst of any car, according to J. D. Power.[15]

The concept of quality applies whether we are talking about Toyota automobiles, clothes designed and sold by Gap Inc. the customer service department of Citibank, or the ability of airlines to arrive on time. Quality is just as relevant to services as it is to goods.[16] The impact of high product quality on competitive advantage is twofold.[17] First, providing high-quality products increases the utility those products provide to customers, which gives the company the option of charging a higher price for them. In the automobile industry, for example, Toyota can charge a higher price for its cars because of the higher quality of its products.

The second impact of high quality on competitive advantage comes from the greater efficiency and the lower unit costs associated with reliable products. When products are reliable, less employee time is wasted making defective products or providing substandard services, and less time has to be spent fixing mistakes, which translates into higher employee productivity and lower unit costs. Thus, high product quality not only enables a company to differentiate its product from that of rivals, but if the product is reliable, it also lowers costs.

The importance of reliability in building competitive advantage has increased dramatically over the past decade. Indeed, so crucial is the emphasis placed on reliability by many companies that achieving high product reliability can no longer be viewed as just one way of gaining a competitive advantage. In many industries, it has become an absolute imperative for survival.

Innovation

Innovation refers to the act of creating new products or processes. There are two main types of innovation: **product innovation** and process innovation. Product innovation is the development of products that are new to the world or have superior attributes to existing products. Examples are Intel's invention of the microprocessor in the early 1970s, Cisco's development of the router for routing data over the Internet in the mid-1980s, and Apple's development of the iPod in the early 2000s. **Process innovation** is the development of a new process for producing products and delivering them to customers. Examples include Toyota, which developed a range of new techniques known as the Toyota lean production system for making automobiles: just-in-time inventory systems, self-managing teams, and reduced setup times for complex equipment.

Product innovation creates value by creating new products, or enhanced versions of existing products, that customers perceive as having more utility, thus increasing the company's pricing options. Process innovation often allows a company to create more value by lowering production costs. Toyota's lean production system, for example, helped to boost employee productivity, thus giving Toyota a cost-based competitive advantage.[18] Similarly, Staples' application of the supermarket business model to retail office supplies dramatically lowered the cost of selling office supplies. Staples passed on some of this cost saving to customers in the form of lower prices, which enabled the company to rapidly increase its market share.

In the long run, innovation of products and processes is perhaps the most important building block of competitive advantage.[19] Competition can be viewed as a process driven by innovations. Although not all innovations succeed, those that do can be a major source of competitive advantage because, by definition, they give a company something unique—something its competitors lack (at least until they imitate the innovation). Uniqueness can allow a company to differentiate itself from its rivals and charge a premium price for its product or, in the case of many process innovations, reduce its unit costs far below those of competitors.

Customer Responsiveness

To achieve superior responsiveness to customers, a company must be able to do a better job than its competitors of identifying and satisfying its customers' needs. Customers will then attribute more utility to its products, creating a differentiation based on competitive advantage. Improving the quality of a company's product offering is consistent with achieving responsiveness, as is developing new products with features that existing products lack. In other words, achieving superior quality and innovation is integral to achieving superior responsiveness to customers.

Another factor that stands out in any discussion of responsiveness to customers is the need to customize goods and services to the unique demands of individual customers or customer groups. For example, the proliferation of soft drinks and beers can be viewed partly as a response to this trend. Automobile companies have become more adept at customizing cars to the demands of individual customers. For instance, following the lead of Toyota, Saturn builds cars to order for individual customers, letting them choose from a wide range of colors and options.

An aspect of responsiveness to customers that has drawn increasing attention is **customer response time**: the time that it takes for a good to be delivered or a service to be performed.[20] For a manufacturer of machinery, response time is the time it takes to fill customer orders. For a bank, it is the time it takes to process a loan or the length of time that a customer must stand in line to wait for an available teller. For a supermarket, it is the time that customers must stand in checkout lines. For a fashion retailer, it is the time required to take a new product from design to a retail store (see Strategy in Action 3.2 for a discussion of how the Spanish fashion retailer Zara minimizes this). Survey after survey has shown that slow response time is a major source of customer dissatisfaction.[21]

Other sources of enhanced responsiveness to customers are superior design, service, and after-sales service and support. All of these factors enhance responsiveness to customers and allow a company to differentiate itself from its less-responsive competitors. In turn, differentiation enables a company to build brand loyalty and charge premium prices for its products. Consider how much more people are prepared to pay for next-day delivery of Express Mail, as opposed to standard delivery in three to four days. In 2009, a two-page letter sent overnight by Express Mail within the United States cost about $13, compared with 44 cents for regular mail. Thus, the price premium for express delivery (reduced response time) was $12.60, or a premium of about 2,757% over the regular price.

BUSINESS MODELS, THE VALUE CHAIN, AND GENERIC DISTINCTIVE COMPETENCIES

As noted in Chapter 1, a business model is a manager's conception, or gestalt, of how the various strategies that a firm pursues fit together into a congruent whole, enabling the firm to achieve a competitive advantage. More precisely, a business model represents the way in which managers configure the value chain of the firm through strategy, as well as the investments they make to support that configuration, so that they can build the distinctive competencies necessary to attain the efficiency, quality, innovation, and customer responsiveness required to support the firm's low-cost or differentiated position, thereby achieving a competitive advantage and generating superior profitability (see Figure 3.8).

For example, the main strategic goal of Walmart is to be the lowest-cost operator offering a wide range of general merchandise in the retail industry. Walmart's business model involves offering general merchandise in a self-service supermarket type of setting. Walmart's strategies flesh out this business model and help the company to attain its strategic goal. To reduce costs, Walmart limits investments in the fittings and fixtures of its stores. One of the keys to generating sales and lowering costs in this setting is rapid inventory turnover, which is achieved through strategic investments in logistics and information systems. Walmart makes major investments in process innovation to improve the effectiveness of its information and logistics systems, which enables the company to respond to customer demands for low-priced goods when they walk in the door and to do so in a very efficient manner.

Walmart's business model is much different from that found at a retailer such as Nordstrom. Nordstrom's business model is to offer high-quality, high-priced apparel in a full-service, sophisticated setting. This implies differences in the way

Figure 3.8 Competitive Advantage and the Value Creation Cycle

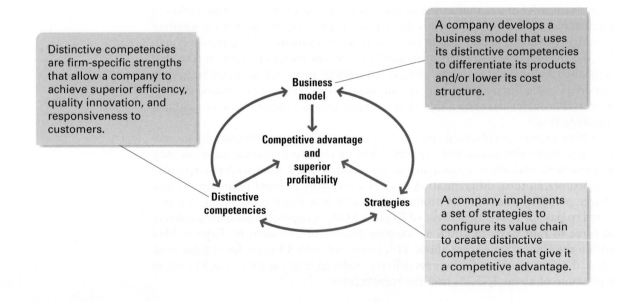

Distinctive competencies are firm-specific strengths that allow a company to achieve superior efficiency, quality innovation, and responsiveness to customers.

A company develops a business model that uses its distinctive competencies to differentiate its products and/or lower its cost structure.

Business model

Competitive advantage and superior profitability

Distinctive competencies

Strategies

A company implements a set of strategies to configure its value chain to create distinctive competencies that give it a competitive advantage.

the value chain is configured. Nordstrom devotes far more attention to in-store customer service than Walmart does, which implies significant investments in its salespeople. Moreover, Nordstrom invests far more in the furnishings and fittings for its stores, as opposed to Walmart, whose stores have a basic "warehouse feel" to them. Nordstrom recaptures the costs of its investment by charging higher prices for higher-quality merchandise. Thus, even though Walmart and Nordstrom both sell apparel (Walmart is the biggest seller of apparel in the United States), their business models imply very different positioning in the marketplace and a very different configuration of value chain activities and investments.

ANALYZING COMPETITIVE ADVANTAGE AND PROFITABILITY

If a company's managers are to perform a good internal analysis, they need to be able to analyze the financial performance of their company, identifying how its strategies contribute (or not) to profitability. To identify strengths and weaknesses effectively, they need to be able to compare, or benchmark, the performance of their company against that of competitors and the historic performance of the company itself. This will help them determine whether (1) they are more or less profitable than competitors and whether the performance of the company has been improving or deteriorating over time; (2) their company strategies are maximizing the value being created; (3) their cost structure is out of line with those of competitors; and (4) they are using the resources of the company to the greatest effect.

As we noted in Chapter 1, the key measure of a company's financial performance is its profitability, which captures the return that a company is generating on its investments. Although several different measures of profitability exist, such as return on assets and return on equity, many authorities on the measurement of profitability argue that ROIC is the best measure because "it focuses on the true operating performance of the company."[22] (However, return on assets is very similar in formulation to return on invested capital.)

ROIC is defined as net profit over invested capital, or ROIC = net profit/invested capital. Net profit is calculated by subtracting the total costs of operating the company from its total revenues (total revenues − total costs). *Net profit* is what is left over after the government takes its share in taxes. *Invested capital* is the amount that is invested in the operations of a company: property, plant, equipment, inventories, and other assets. Invested capital comes from two main sources: interest-bearing debt and shareholders' equity. Interest-bearing debt is money the company borrows from banks and those who purchase its bonds. Shareholders' equity is the money raised from selling shares to the public plus earnings that the company has retained in prior years that are available to fund current investments. ROIC measures the effectiveness by which a company is using the capital funds that it has available for investment. As such, it is recognized to be an excellent measure of the value a company is creating.[23]

A company's ROIC can be algebraically decomposed into two major components: return on sales and capital turnover.[24] Specifically:

ROIC = net profits/invested capital

      = (net profits/revenues) × (revenues/invested capital)

where net profits/revenues is the return on sales, and revenues/invested capital is capital turnover. Return on sales measures how effectively the company converts revenues into profits. Capital turnover measures how effectively the company employs its invested capital to generate revenues. These two ratios can be further decomposed into some basic accounting ratios, as shown in Figure 3.9 (these ratios are defined in Table 3.1).[25]

Figure 3.9   Drivers of Profitability (ROIC)

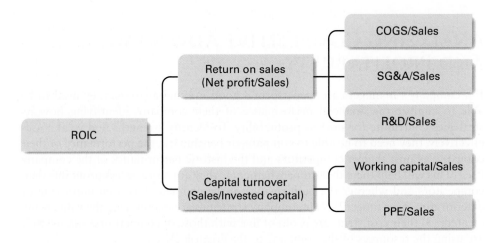

Table 3.1   Definitions of Basic Accounting Terms

Term	Definition	Source
Cost of Goods Sold (COGS)	Total costs of producing products	Income statement
Sales, General, and Administrative Expenses (SG&A)	Costs associated with selling products and administering the company	Income statement
R&D Expenses (R&D)	Research and development expenditure	Income statement
Working Capital	The amount of money the company has to "work" with in the short term: Current assets − current liabilities	Balance sheet
Property, Plant, and Equipment (PPE)	The value of investments in the property, plant, and equipment that the company uses to manufacture and sell its products; also known as *fixed capital*	Balance sheet
Return on Sales (ROS)	Net profit expressed as a percentage of sales; measures how effectively the company converts revenues into profits	Ratio
Capital Turnover	Revenues divided by invested capital; measures how effectively the company uses its capital to generate revenues	Ratio
Return on Invested Capital (ROIC)	Net profit divided by invested capital	Ratio
Net Profit	Total revenues minus total costs before tax	Income statement
Invested Capital	Interest-bearing debt plus shareholders' equity	Balance sheet

Figure 3.9 says that a company's managers can increase ROIC by pursuing strategies that increase the company's return on sales (ROS). To increase a company's ROS, they can: pursue strategies that reduce the cost of goods sold (COGS) for a given level of sales revenues (COGS/sales); reduce the level of spending on sales force, marketing, general, and administrative expenses (SG&A) for a given level of sales revenues (SG&A/sales); and reduce research and development (R&D) spending for a given level of sales revenues (R&D/sales). Alternatively, they can increase ROS by pursuing strategies that increase sales revenues more than they increase the costs of the business, as measured by COGS, SG&A, and R&D expenses. That is, they can increase the ROS by pursuing strategies that lower costs or increase value through differentiation, thus allowing the company to increase its prices more than its costs.

Figure 3.9 also states that a company's managers can boost the profitability of their company by getting greater sales revenues from the invested capital, thereby increasing capital turnover. They do this by pursuing strategies that reduce the amount of working capital, such as the amount of capital invested in inventories, needed to generate a given level of sales (working capital/sales), and then pursuing strategies that reduce the amount of fixed capital that they have to invest in plant, property, and equipment (PPE) to generate a given level of sales (PPE/sales). That is, they pursue strategies that reduce the amount of capital that they need to generate every dollar of sales and their cost of capital. The cost of capital is part of the cost structure of a company (see Figure 3.2). Hence, strategies designed to increase capital turnover also lower the cost structure.

To see how these basic drivers of profitability help to explain what is going on in a company and identify its strengths and weaknesses, compare the financial performance of Walmart against one of its closest and more efficient competitors—Target. This is done in the following Running Case.

On the other hand, you will notice that Walmart spends significantly less on SG&A expenses as a percentage of sales than Target (18.77% versus 22.95%). There are three reasons for this as outlined on the next page.

RUNNING CASE

Comparing Walmart and Target

For the financial year ending January 2008, Walmart earned a ROIC of 14.1%, while Target earned a respectable 10.6%. Walmart's superior profitability can be understood in terms of the impact of its strategies on the various ratios identified in Figure 3.9. These are summarized in Figure 3.10.

First, note that Walmart has a *lower* ROS than Target. This is because Walmart's COGS as a percentage of sales are higher than Target's (76.5% versus 66.1%). For a retailer, the COGS reflect the price that Walmart pays to its suppliers for merchandise. The lower COGS/Sales ratio implies that Walmart does not mark up prices as much as Target—its profit margin on each item sold is lower. Consistent with its long-time strategic goal, Walmart passes on the low prices it gets from suppliers to customers. Walmart's higher COGS/Sales ratio reflects its strategy of being the lowest-price retailer.

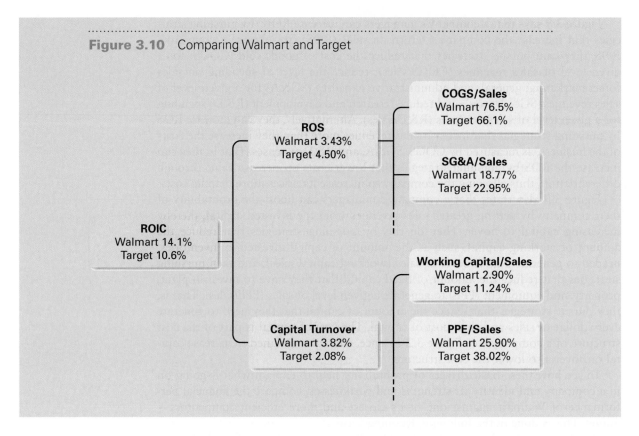

Figure 3.10 Comparing Walmart and Target

COGS/Sales
Walmart 76.5%
Target 66.1%

ROS
Walmart 3.43%
Target 4.50%

SG&A/Sales
Walmart 18.77%
Target 22.95%

ROIC
Walmart 14.1%
Target 10.6%

Working Capital/Sales
Walmart 2.90%
Target 11.24%

Capital Turnover
Walmart 3.82%
Target 2.08%

PPE/Sales
Walmart 25.90%
Target 38.02%

(1) Walmart's early strategy was to focus on small towns that could only support one discounter. In small towns, the company does not have to advertise heavily because it is not competing against other discounter.

(2) Walmart has become such a powerful brand that the company does not need to advertise as heavily as its competitors, even when its stores are located close to them in suburban areas.

(3) Because Walmart sticks to its low-price philosophy and manages its inventory so well, it does not usually have an overstock problem. Thus, the company does not have to hold periodic sales, nor does it have to bear the costs of promoting those sales (e.g., sending out advertisements and coupons in local newspapers). By reducing spending on sales promotions, these factors reduce Walmart's SG&A/sales ratio.

In addition, Walmart operates with a flat-organization structure that has very few layers of management between the head office and store managers (the company has no regional headquarters). This reduces administrative expenses (which are a component of SG&A), and hence, the SG&A/sales ratio. Walmart can operate with such flat structure because its information systems allow the company's top managers to monitor and control individual stores directly rather than relying on intervening layers of subordinates to do that for them.

It is when we consider the capital turnover side of the ROIC equation, however, that the financial impact of Walmart's competitive advantage in information systems and logistics becomes apparent. Walmart generates $3.82 for every dollar of capital invested in the business, whereas Target generates only $2.08 for every dollar of capital invested. Walmart is much more efficient in its use of capital than Target. Why?

A big reason is that Walmart has a much lower working capital/sales ratio than Target. In fact, Walmart has a *negative* ratio (−2.90%), while Target has a positive ratio (11.24%). The negative working capital ratio implies that Walmart does not need any capital to finance its day-to-day operations. In fact, Walmart is using its suppliers' capital to finance those operations. This is very unusual, but Walmart is able to do this for two reasons. First, Walmart is so powerful that it can demand and get very favorable payment terms from its suppliers. It does not have to pay for merchandise until 60 days after it is delivered. Second, Walmart turns over its inventory rapidly—7.72 times a year or every 47 days—that it typically sells merchandise *before* it has to pay its suppliers. Thus, suppliers finance Walmart's inventory and the company's short-term capital needs. Walmart's high inventory turnover is the result of strategic investments in information systems and logistics. It is these value chain activities, more than any other, that explain Walmart's competitive advantage.

Finally, note that Walmart has a significantly lower PPE/sales ratio than Target: 25.9% versus 35.02%. There are several explanations for this. First, many of Wamart's stores are still located in small towns where land is cheap, whereas most of Target's stores are located in more expensive suburban mall locations. Thus, on average, Walmart needs to spend less on a store than Target. Again, strategy has a clear impact on financial performance. Second, because Walmart turns its inventory over so rapidly, it does not need to devote as much space in stores to storing inventory. This means that more floor space can be devoted to selling merchandise. Other things being equal, this will result in a higher PPE/sales ratio. By the same token, efficient inventory management means that it needs less space at a distribution center to support a store, which again reduces total capital spending of PPE. Third, the higher PPE/sales ratio may also reflect the fact that Walmart's brand is so powerful and its commitment to low pricing so strong that store traffic is higher than at comparable discounters such as Target. The stores are simply busier. Hence, the PPE/sales ratio is higher.

In sum, Walmart's high profitability is a function of its strategy and the distinctive competencies that strategic investments have built over the years, particularly in the area of information systems and logistics. As in the Walmart example, the methodology described in this section can be a very useful tool for analyzing why and how well a company is achieving and sustaining a competitive advantage. It highlights a company's strengths and weaknesses, showing where there is room for improvement and where a company is excelling. As such, it can drive strategy formulation. Moreover, the same methodology can be used to analyze the performance of competitors, and gain a greater understanding of their strengths and weaknesses, which can in turn inform strategy.

THE DURABILITY OF COMPETITIVE ADVANTAGE

The next question we must address is how long a competitive advantage will last once it has been created. In other words, what is the durability of competitive advantage given that other companies are also seeking to develop distinctive competencies that will give them a competitive advantage? The answer depends on three factors: barriers to imitation, the capability of competitors, and the general dynamism of the industry environment.

Barriers to Imitation

A company with a competitive advantage will earn higher-than-average profits. These profits send a signal to rivals that the company has some valuable distinctive competency that allows it to create superior value. Naturally, its competitors will try to identify and imitate that competency, and insofar as they are successful, ultimately their increased success may whittle away the company's superior profits.[26]

How quickly rivals will imitate a company's distinctive competencies is an important issue because the speed of imitation has a bearing on the durability of a company's competitive advantage. Other things being equal, the more rapidly competitors imitate a company's distinctive competencies, the less durable its competitive advantage will be, and the more important it is that the company endeavor to improve its competencies to stay one step ahead of the imitators. It is important to stress that ultimately almost any distinctive competency can be imitated by a competitor. The critical issue is time: the longer it takes competitors to imitate a distinctive competency, the greater the opportunity the company has to build a strong market position and reputation with customers, which are then more difficult for competitors to attack. The longer it takes to achieve an imitation, the greater is the opportunity for the imitated company to improve on its competency or build other competencies, thereby staying one step ahead of the competition.

Barriers to imitation are a primary determinant of the speed of imitation. Barriers to imitation are factors that make it difficult for a competitor to copy a company's distinctive competencies; the greater the barriers to imitation, the more sustainable is a company's competitive advantage.[27] Barriers to imitation differ depending on whether a competitor is trying to imitate resources or capabilities.

Imitating Resources   In general, the easiest distinctive competencies for prospective rivals to imitate tend to be those based on the possession of firm-specific and valuable tangible resources, such as buildings, plant, and equipment. Such resources are visible to competitors and can often be purchased on the open market. For example, if a company's competitive advantage is based on sole possession of efficient-scale manufacturing facilities, competitors may move fairly quickly to establish similar facilities. Although Ford gained a competitive advantage over GM in the 1920s by being the first to adopt an assembly-line manufacturing technology to produce automobiles, GM quickly imitated that innovation, competing away Ford's distinctive competency in the process. A similar process is occurring in the auto industry now, as companies try to imitate Toyota's famous production system. However, Toyota has slowed down the rate of imitation by not allowing competitors access to its latest equipment.

Intangible resources can be more difficult to imitate. This is particularly true of brand names, which are important because they symbolize a company's reputation. In the heavy earth-moving equipment industry, for example, the Caterpillar brand name is synonymous with high quality and superior after-sales service and support. Similarly, the St. Michael's brand name used by Marks & Spencer, Britain's largest clothing retailer, symbolizes high-quality but reasonably priced clothing. Customers often display a preference for the products of such companies because the brand name is an important guarantee of high quality. Although competitors might like to imitate well-established brand names, the law prohibits them from doing so.

Marketing and technological know-how are also important intangible resources and can be relatively easy to imitate. The movement of skilled marketing personnel between companies may facilitate the general dissemination of marketing know-how. For example, in the 1970s, Ford was acknowledged as the best marketer among the big three U.S. auto companies. In 1979, it lost much of its marketing know-how to Chrysler when its most successful marketer, Lee Iacocca, joined Chrysler and subsequently hired many of Ford's top marketing people to work with him at Chrysler. More generally, successful marketing strategies are relatively easy to imitate because they are visible to competitors. Thus, Coca-Cola quickly imitated PepsiCo's Diet Pepsi brand with the introduction of its own brand, Diet Coke.

With regard to technological know-how, the patent system in theory should make technological know-how relatively immune to imitation. Patents give the inventor of a new product a 20-year exclusive production agreement; however, this is not always the case. In electrical and computer engineering, for example, it is often possible to invent "around" patents: that is, produce a product that is functionally equivalent but does not rely on the patented technology. One study found that 60% of patented innovations were successfully invented around in four years.[28] This suggests that, in general, distinctive competencies based on technological know-how can be relatively short-lived.

Imitating Capabilities Imitating a company's capabilities tends to be more difficult than imitating its tangible and intangible resources, chiefly because capabilities are based on the way in which decisions are made and processes are managed deep within a company. It is hard for outsiders to discern them.

On its own, the invisible nature of capabilities would not be enough to halt imitation; competitors could still gain insights into how a company operates by hiring people away from that company. However, a company's capabilities rarely reside in a single individual. Rather, they are the product of how numerous individuals interact within a unique organizational setting.[29] It is possible that no one individual within a company may be familiar with the totality of a company's internal operating routines and procedures. In such cases, hiring people away from a successful company as a way to imitate its key capabilities may not be helpful.

Capability of Competitors

According to Pankaj Ghemawat, a major determinant of the capability of competitors to imitate a company's competitive advantage rapidly is the nature of the competitors' prior strategic commitments.[30] By strategic commitment, Ghemawat means a company's commitment to a particular way of doing business, that is, to developing a particular set of resources and capabilities. Ghemawat's point is that once a company has made a strategic commitment, it will have difficulty responding to new competition if doing so requires a break with this commitment. Therefore, when competitors have long-established commitments to a particular way of doing business, they may be slow to imitate an innovating company's competitive advantage. Its competitive advantage will thus be relatively durable.

The U.S. automobile industry again offers an example. From 1945 to 1975, the industry was dominated by the stable oligopoly of GM, Ford, and Chrysler, all of which geared their operations to the production of large cars, which American customers demanded at the time. When the market shifted from large cars to small, fuel-efficient ones during the late 1970s, U.S. companies lacked the resources and capabilities required to produce these cars. Their prior commitments had built the wrong kind of products for this new environment. As a result, foreign producers, particularly the Japanese, stepped into the market breach by providing compact, fuel-efficient, high-quality, and low-cost cars. The failure of U.S. auto manufacturers to react quickly to the distinctive competency of Japanese auto companies gave the latter time to build a strong market position and brand loyalty, which subsequently have been difficult to attack.

Another determinant of the ability of competitors to respond to a company's competitive advantage is the absorptive capacity of competitors.[31] **Absorptive capacity** refers to the ability of an enterprise to identify, value, assimilate, and use new knowledge. For example, in the 1960s and 1970s, Toyota developed a competitive advantage based on its innovation of lean production systems. Competitors such as GM were slow to imitate this innovation, primarily because they lacked the necessary absorptive capacity. GM was a bureaucratic and inward-looking organization; thus, it was difficult for the company to identify, value, assimilate, and use the knowledge that underlies lean production systems. Indeed, long after GM had identified and understood the importance of lean production systems, it was still struggling to assimilate and use that new knowledge. Internal inertia forces can make it difficult for established competitors to respond to a rival whose competitive advantage is based on new products or internal processes, such as innovation.

Taken together, factors such as existing strategic commitments and low absorptive capacity limit the ability of established competitors to imitate the competitive advantage of a rival, particularly when that competitive advantage is based on innovative products or processes. This is why, when innovations reshape the rules of competition in an industry, value often migrates away from established competitors and toward new enterprises that are operating with new business models.

Industry Dynamism

A dynamic industry environment is one that is changing rapidly. We examined the factors that determine the dynamism and intensity of competition in an industry in Chapter 2 when we discussed the external environment. The most dynamic industries tend to be those with a high rate of product innovation, for example, the consumer electronics industry and the personal computer industry. In dynamic industries, the rapid rate of innovation means that product life cycles are shortening, and competitive advantage can be fleeting. A company that has a competitive advantage today may find its market position outflanked tomorrow by a rival's innovation.

In the personal computer industry, the rapid increase in computing power during the past two decades has contributed to a high degree of innovation and a turbulent environment. Reflecting the persistence of innovation, in the late 1970s and early 1980s, Apple had an industry-wide competitive advantage due to its innovation. In 1981, IBM seized the advantage by introducing its first personal computer. By the mid-1980s, IBM had lost its competitive advantage to high-power "clone" manufacturers such as Compaq that had beaten IBM in the race to introduce a computer based on Intel's 386 chip. In turn, in the 1990s, Compaq subsequently lost its competitive advantage to Dell, which pioneered new low-cost ways of delivering computers to customers using the Internet as a direct-selling device.

Summarizing Durability of Competitive Advantage

The durability of a company's competitive advantage depends on the height of barriers to imitation, the capability of competitors to imitate its innovation, and the general level of dynamism in the industry environment. When barriers to imitation are low, capable competitors abound, and the environment is dynamic, with innovations being developed all the time, then competitive advantage is likely to be transitory. But even within such industries, companies can build a more enduring competitive advantage if they are able to make investments that build barriers to imitation.

AVOIDING FAILURE AND SUSTAINING COMPETITIVE ADVANTAGE

How can a company avoid failure and escape the traps that have snared so many once-successful companies? How can managers build a sustainable competitive advantage? Much of the remainder of this book deals with these issues. Following, we identify several key points that set the scene for the coming discussion.

Why Companies Fail

When a company loses its competitive advantage, its profitability falls. The company does not necessarily fail; it may just have average or below-average profitability. It can remain in this mode for a considerable time, although its resource and capital base is shrinking. Failure implies something more drastic. A failing company is one whose profitability is now substantially lower than the average profitability of its competitors; it has lost the ability to attract and generate resources, so its profit margins and invested capital are shrinking rapidly.

Why does a company lose its competitive advantage and fail? The question is particularly pertinent because some of the most successful companies of the last half-century have seen their competitive position deteriorate at one time or another. IBM, GM, American Express, Digital Equipment Corporation (DEC), and Sears, among many others, which all at one time were held up as examples of managerial excellence, have gone through periods where their financial performance was poor and they clearly lacked any competitive advantage. We explore three related reasons for failure: inertia, prior strategic commitments, and the Icarus paradox.

Inertia   The inertia argument says that companies find it difficult to change their strategies and structures when adapting to changing competitive conditions.[32] IBM is a classic example of this problem. For 30 years, it was viewed as the world's most successful computer company. Then in the space of a few years, its success turned into a disaster: it lost $5 billion in 1992, leading to layoffs of more than 100,000 employees. IBM's troubles were caused by a dramatic decline in the cost of computing power as a result of innovations in microprocessors. With the advent of powerful low-cost microprocessors, the locus of the computer market shifted from mainframes to small, low-priced personal computers, leaving IBM's huge mainframe operations with a diminished market. Although IBM had a significant presence in the personal computer market, it had failed to shift the focus of its efforts away from mainframes and toward personal computers. This failure meant deep trouble for one of the most successful companies of the 20th century. (IBM has now executed a successful turnaround with a repositioning as a provider of e-commerce infrastructure and solutions.)

One reason that companies find it so difficult to adapt to new environmental conditions seems to be the role of capabilities in causing inertia. Organizational capabilities—the way a company makes decisions and manages its processes—can be a source of competitive advantage, but they are difficult to change. IBM always emphasized close coordination among operating units and favored decision processes that stressed consensus among interdependent operating units as a prerequisite for a decision to go forward.[33] This capability was a source of advantage for IBM during the 1970s, when coordination among its worldwide operating units was necessary to develop, manufacture, and sell complex mainframes. But the slow-moving bureaucracy that it had spawned was a source of failure in the 1990s, when organizations had to adapt readily to rapid environmental change.

Capabilities are difficult to change because a certain distribution of power and influence is embedded within the established decision-making and management processes of an organization. Those who play key roles in a decision-making process clearly have more power. It follows that changing the established capabilities of an organization means changing its existing distribution of power and influence; those whose power and influence would diminish then resist such change. Proposals for change trigger turf battles. This power struggle and the political resistance associated with trying to alter the way in which an organization makes decisions and manages its process—that is, trying to change its capabilities—bring on inertia. This is not to say that companies cannot change. However, because change is so often resisted by those who feel threatened by it, change in most cases has to be induced by a crisis. By then, the company may already be failing, as happened at IBM.

Prior Strategic Commitments   A company's prior strategic commitments not only limit its ability to imitate rivals but may also cause competitive disadvantage.[34] IBM, for instance, had major investments in the mainframe computer business, so when the market shifted, it was stuck with significant resources specialized to that particular business. IBM's manufacturing facilities were geared to the production of mainframes. Its research organization and sales force were similarly specialized. Because these resources were not well-suited to the newly emerging personal computer business, IBM's difficulties in the early 1990s were, in a sense, inevitable. Its prior strategic commitments locked it into a business that was shrinking. Shedding these resources was bound to cause hardship for all organization stakeholders.

The Icarus Paradox   Danny Miller has postulated that the roots of competitive failure can be found in what he termed the Icarus paradox.[35] Icarus is a figure in Greek mythology who used a pair of wings that his father made for him to escape from an island where he was being held prisoner. He flew so well that he went higher and higher, ever closer to the sun, until the heat of the sun melted the wax that held his wings together, and he plunged to his death in the Aegean Sea. The paradox is that his greatest asset, his ability to fly, caused his demise. Miller argues that the same paradox applies to many once successful companies. According to Miller, many companies become so dazzled by their early success that they believe more of the same type of effort is the way to future success. As a result, they can become so specialized and inner-directed that they lose sight of market realities and the fundamental requirements for achieving a competitive advantage. Sooner or later, this leads to failure. For example, Miller argues that Texas Instruments and Digital Equipment Corporation (DEC), achieved early success through engineering excellence. But then they became so obsessed with engineering details that they lost sight of market realities. (The story of DEC's demise is summarized in Strategy in Action 3.3.)

3.3 STRATEGY IN ACTION

The Road to Ruin at DEC

Digital Equipment Corporation (DEC) was one of the premier computer companies of the 1970s and 1980s. DEC's original success was founded on the minicomputer, a cheaper, more-flexible version of its mainframe cousins that Ken Olson and his brilliant team of engineers invented in the 1960s. DEC improved on its original minicomputers until they could not be beat for quality and reliability. In the 1970s, their VAX series of minicomputers was widely regarded as the most reliable series of computers ever produced, and DEC was rewarded by high profit rates and rapid growth. By 1990, it was number 27 on the Fortune 500 list of the largest corporations in America.

Buoyed by its success, DEC turned into an engineering monoculture—its engineers became idols; its marketing and accounting staff, however, were barely tolerated. Component specifications and design standards were all that senior managers understood. Technological fine-tuning became such an obsession that the needs of customers for smaller, more economical, user-friendly computers were ignored. DEC's personal computers, for example, bombed because they were out of touch with the needs of customers, and the company failed to respond to the threat to its core market presented by the rise of computer workstations and client-server architecture. Indeed, Ken Olson was known for dismissing such new products. He once said, "We always say that customers are right, but they are not always right." Perhaps. But DEC, blinded by its early success, failed to remain responsive to its customers and changing-market conditions. In another famous statement, when asked about personal computers in the early 1980s, Olson said, "I can see of no reason why anybody would ever want a computer on their desk."

By the early 1990s, DEC was in deep trouble. Olson was forced out in July 1992, and the company lost billions of dollars between 1992 and 1995. It returned to profitability in 1996, primarily because of the success of a turnaround strategy aimed at reorienting the company to serve precisely those areas that Olson had dismissed. In 1998, the company was acquired by Compaq Computer Corporation (which was subsequently purchased by Hewlett Packard) and disappeared from the business landscape as an independent entity.

Sources: D. Miller, *The Icarus Paradox* (New York: HarperBusiness, 1990); P. D. Llosa, "We Must Know What We Are Doing," *Fortune*, November 14, 1994, 68.

Steps to Avoid Failure

Given that so many traps wait for companies, the question arises as to how strategic managers can use internal analysis to find them and escape them. We now look at several tactics that managers can use.

Focus on the Building Blocks of Competitive Advantage   Maintaining a competitive advantage requires a company to continue focusing on all four generic building blocks of competitive advantage—efficiency, quality, innovation, and responsiveness to customers—and to develop distinctive competencies that contribute to superior performance in these areas. One of the messages of Miller's Icarus paradox is that many successful companies become unbalanced in their pursuit of distinctive competencies. DEC, for example, focused on engineering quality at the expense of almost everything else, including, most importantly, responsiveness to customers. Other companies forget to focus on any distinctive competency at all.

Institute Continuous Improvement and Learning   The only constant in the world is change. Today's source of competitive advantage may soon be rapidly imitated by capable competitors or made obsolete by the innovations of a rival. In such a dynamic and fast-paced environment, the only way that a company can maintain a competitive advantage over time is to continually improve its efficiency, quality, innovation, and responsiveness to customers. The way to do this is to recognize the importance of learning within the organization.[36] The most-successful companies are not those that stand still, resting on their laurels. They are those that are always seeking out ways of improving their operations and, in the process, are constantly upgrading the value of their distinctive competencies or creating new competencies. Companies such as GE and Toyota have a reputation for being learning organizations. This means that they are continually analyzing the processes that underlie their efficiency, quality, innovation, and responsiveness to customers. Their objective is to learn from prior mistakes and to seek out ways to improve their processes over time. This has enabled Toyota, for example, to continually upgrade its employee productivity and product quality, and thus stay ahead of imitators.

Track Best Industrial Practice and Use Benchmarking One of the best ways to develop distinctive competencies that contribute to superior efficiency, quality, innovation, and responsiveness to customers is to identify and adopt best industrial practice. Only in this way will a company be able to build and maintain the resources and capabilities that underpin excellence in efficiency, quality, innovation, and responsiveness to customers. (We discuss what constitutes best industrial practice in some depth in chapter 4.) It requires tracking the practice of other companies, and perhaps the best way to do so is through benchmarking: measuring the company against the products, practices, and services of some of its most efficient global competitors.

Overcome Inertia Overcoming the internal forces that are a barrier to change within an organization is one of the key requirements for maintaining a competitive advantage, and an entire chapter, Chapter 4, is spent discussing this issue. Suffice it to say that identifying barriers to change is an important first step. Once this step has been taken, implementing change requires good leadership, the judicious use of power, and appropriate changes in organizational structure and control systems.

The Role of Luck A number of scholars have argued that luck plays a critical role in determining competitive success and failure.[37] In its most extreme version, the luck argument devalues the importance of strategy altogether. Instead, it states that, in the face of uncertainty, some companies just happen to pick the correct strategy.

Although luck may be the reason for a company's success in particular cases, it is an unconvincing explanation for the persistent success of a company. Recall our argument that the generic building blocks of competitive advantage are superior efficiency, quality, innovation, and responsiveness to customers. Keep in mind also that competition is a process in which companies are continually trying to outdo each other in their ability to achieve high efficiency, superior quality, outstanding innovation, and quick responsiveness to customers. It is possible to imagine a company getting lucky and coming into possession of resources that allow it to achieve excellence on one or more of these dimensions. However, it is difficult to imagine how sustained excellence on any of these four dimensions could be produced by anything other than conscious effort, that is, by strategy. Luck may indeed play a role in success, and managers must always exploit a lucky break. However, to argue that success is entirely a matter of luck is to strain credibility. As the great banker of the early 20th century, J. P. Morgan, once said, "The harder I work, the luckier I seem to get." Managers who strive to formulate and implement strategies that lead to a competitive advantage are more likely to be lucky.

SUMMARY OF CHAPTER

1. Distinctive competencies are the firm-specific strengths of a company. Valuable distinctive competencies enable a company to earn a profit rate that is above the industry average.

2. The distinctive competencies of an organization arise from its resources (its financial, physical, human, technological, and organizational assets) and capabilities (its skills at coordinating resources and putting them to productive use).

3. In order to achieve a competitive advantage, a company needs to pursue strategies that build on its existing resources and capabilities and formulate strategies that build additional resources and capabilities (develop new competencies).

4. The source of a competitive advantage is superior value creation.

5. To create superior value, a company must lower its costs or differentiate its product so that it creates more value and can charge a higher price or do both simultaneously.

6. Managers must understand how value creation and pricing decisions affect demand and how costs change with increases in volume. They must have a good grasp of the demand conditions in the company's market and the cost structure of the company at different levels of output if they are to make decisions that maximize the profitability of their enterprise.

7. The four building blocks of competitive advantage are efficiency, quality, innovation, and responsiveness to customers. These are generic distinctive competencies. Superior efficiency enables a company to lower its costs; superior quality allows it to charge a higher price and lower its costs; and superior customer service lets it charge a higher price. Superior innovation can lead to higher prices, particularly in the case of product innovations, or lower unit costs, particularly in the case of process innovations.

8. If a company's managers are to perform a good internal analysis, they need to be able to analyze the financial performance of their company, identifying how the strategies of the company relate to its profitability, as measured by the ROIC.

9. The durability of a company's competitive advantage depends on the height of barriers to imitation, the capability of competitors, and environmental dynamism.

10. Failing companies typically earn low or negative profits. Three factors seem to contribute to failure: organizational inertia in the face of environmental change, the nature of a company's prior strategic commitments, and the Icarus paradox.

11. Avoiding failure requires a constant focus on the basic building blocks of competitive advantage, continuous improvement, identification and adoption of best industrial practice, and victory over inertia.

DISCUSSION QUESTIONS

1. It is possible for a company to be the lowest-cost producer in its industry and simultaneously have an output that is the most valued by customers. Discuss this statement.

2. Why is it important to understand the drivers of profitability, as measured by the ROIC?

3. What are the main implications of the material discussed in this chapter for strategy formulation?

C L O S I N G   C A S E

Southwest Airlines

Southwest Airlines has long been one of the stand-out performers in the U.S. airline industry. It is famous for its low fares, which are often some 30% lower than those of its major rivals. These are balanced by an even lower cost structure, enabling it to record superior profitability even in bad years such as 2002, when the industry faced slumping demand in the wake of the September 11 terrorist attacks. Indeed, from 2001 to 2005, quite possibly the worst four years in the history of the airline industry, while every other major airline lost money, Southwest made money every year and earned an ROIC of 5.8%. Even in 2008, an awful year for most airlines, Southwest made a profit and earned an ROIC of 4%.

Southwest operates somewhat differently from many of its competitors. While operators like American Airlines and United Airlines route passengers through hubs, Southwest Airlines flies point-to-point, often through smaller airports. By competing in a way that other airlines do not, Southwest has found that it can capture enough demand to keep its planes full. Moreover, because it avoids many hubs, Southwest has experienced fewer delays. In the first eight months of 2008, Southwest planes arrived on schedule 80% of the time, compared to 76% at United and 74% at Continental.

Southwest flies only one type of plane, the Boeing 737. This reduces training costs, maintenance costs, and inventory costs while increasing efficiency in crew and flight scheduling. The operation is nearly ticketless, with no seat assignments, which reduces cost and back-office accounting functions. There are no meals or movies in flight, and the airline will not transfer baggage to other airlines, reducing the need for baggage handlers.

Southwest also has high employee productivity. One-way airlines measure employee productivity is by the ratio of employees to passengers carried. According to figures from company 10-K statements, in 2008 Southwest had an employee-to-passenger ratio of 1 to 2,400, the best in the industry. By comparison, the ratio at United Airlines was 1 to 1,175 and, at Continental, it was 1 to 1,125.

Southwest devotes enormous attention to the people it hires. On average, the company hires only 3% of those interviewed in a year. When hiring, it emphasizes teamwork and a positive attitude. Southwest rationalizes that skills can be taught, but a positive attitude and a willingness to pitch in cannot. Southwest also creates incentives for its employees to work hard. All employees are covered by a profit-sharing plan, and at least 25% of an employee's share of the profit-sharing plan has to be invested in Southwest Airlines stock. This gives rise to a simple formula: the harder employees work, the more profitable Southwest becomes, and the richer the employees get. The results are clear. At other airlines, one would never see a pilot helping to check passengers onto the plane. At Southwest, pilots and flight attendants have been known to help clean the aircraft and check in passengers at the gate. They do this to turn around an aircraft as quickly as possible and get it into the air again because an aircraft does not make money while it is on the ground. This flexible and motivated workforce leads to higher productivity and reduces the company's need for more employees.

Because Southwest flies point-to-point rather than through congested airport hubs, there is no need for dozens of gates and thousands of employees to handle banks of flights that come in and then disperse within a two-hour window, leaving the hub empty until the next flights a few hours later. The result: Southwest can operate with far fewer employees than airlines that fly through hubs.[38]

Case Discussion Questions

1. How would you characterize the business model of Southwest Airlines? How does this differ from the business model used at many other airlines, such as United and American Airlines?
2. Identify the resources, capabilities, and distinctive competencies of Southwest Airlines.
3. How do Southwest's resources, capabilities, and distinctive competencies translate into superior financial performance?
4. How secure is Southwest's competitive advantage? What are the barriers to imitation here?

STRATEGY AT THE FUNCTIONAL LEVEL

LEARNING OBJECTIVES

After reading this chapter, you should be able to

- Explain how an enterprise can use functional-level strategies to increase its efficiency
- Explain how an enterprise can use functional-level strategies to increase its quality
- Explain how an enterprise can use functional-level strategies to increase its innovation
- Explain how an enterprise can use functional-level strategies to increase its customer responsiveness

Productivity Improvement at United Technologies

In 2007, George David, the long-time CEO of United Technologies, retired.

David could look back on a very impressive 15 years at the helm, during which time revenues tripled while net profits rose tenfold. Today, United Technologies is a $60 billion diversified manufacturing enterprise with businesses including jet-engine-maker Pratt & Whitney; Carrier, an air-conditioning business; and Otis Elevators.

A major source of the profit surge over the last 15 years has been productivity improvements. At the heart of these is a program known as Achieve Competitive Excellence (ACE). The program was a result of collaboration between David and a Japanese quality consultant, Yuzuru Ito, who at one time was a quality expert at Matsushita, the Japanese consumer electronics giant. David brought Ito in to figure

out why Otis Elevators performed so poorly compared to those from rival Mitsubishi. The number of times a building owner had to call a mechanic was 40 times per year for Otis products and just 0.5 times a year for those from Mitsubishi. What Ito uncovered was a range of problems ranging from bad design to poor manufacturing practices and a lack of quality control in Otis' factories. Ito explained to David how poor quality hurt employee productivity because time was wasted building defective products. Poor quality also hurt demand because customers were less likely to buy products from a company with a poor reputation for quality.

The solution to these problems at Otis included designing elevators so that they were easier to manufacture, which led to fewer errors in the assembly process, reconfiguring the manufacturing process, and empowering factory floor employees to identify and fix quality problems. For example, by changing the placement of elevator parts, allowing assembly line workers easier access, Otis took $300 off the cost of each elevator, which led to worldwide annual savings of $27 million. In addition, the production processes were streamlined, requiring fewer steps, less reaching and movement for workers, and easier access to parts, all of which boosted productivity.

ACE evolved out of the experience at Otis and was subsequently rolled out company wide. The main thrust of ACE is built around the belief that every person should be involved with continuous improvement, from top executives to the most junior workers. ACE "pilots" are production line workers who learn a quality improvement process in a matter of days and then are empowered to lead that process within their work groups. They learn to pinpoint potential problems, ranging from fundamental design flaws in a product, such as misplaced bolts, to a co-worker's fatigue from staying up with a newborn all night.

As the program was implemented across the company, the results were impressive. At Carrier, square footage assigned to manufacturing was reduced by 50%, while production rose 70%, all with 10% fewer employees. At Pratt & Whitney, dramatic improvements in the quality of jet engines were registered. The mean time between part failures in a jet engine went from 2,500 hours to 170,000 hours, a huge improvement resulting from better design and manufacturing processes. Customers noticed these quality improvements, and they increased their purchases of United Technology products, driving forward revenues and profits.[1]

Overview

In this chapter, we take a close look at **functional-level strategies**: those aimed at improving the effectiveness of a company's operations and, thus, its ability to attain superior efficiency, quality, innovation, and customer responsiveness.

It is important to keep in mind the relationships between functional strategies, distinctive competencies, differentiation, low cost, value creation, and profitability (see Figure 4.1). Distinctive competencies shape the functional-level strategies that a company can pursue. Managers, through their choices with regard to functional-level strategies, can build resources and capabilities that enhance a company's distinctive competencies. Note also that the ability of a company to attain superior efficiency, quality, innovation, and customer responsiveness will determine if its product offering is differentiated from that of its rivals and if it has a low cost structure. Recall that companies that increase the utility consumers get from their products through differentiation, while simultaneously lowering their cost structures, create more value than their rivals. This leads to a competitive advantage and superior profitability and profit growth.

The Opening Case illustrates some of these relationships. Managers at United Technologies pursued functional-level strategies that raised productivity, increasing the efficiency of their production processes, while also increasing the reliability of their final product offering. The superior efficiency enabled United Technologies to

Figure 4.1   The Roots of Competitive Advantage

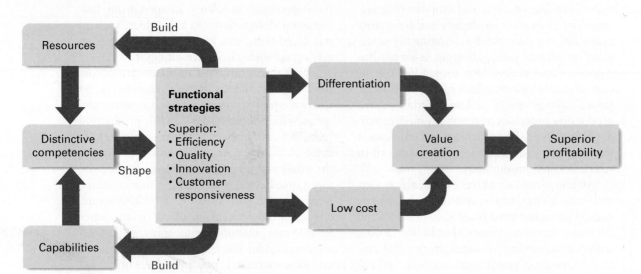

lower costs, while superior reliability enhanced product quality and helped to differentiate the product offerings of United Technologies, thereby boosting sales volume. The result: United Technologies created more value, and its profitability increased.

Consistent with the United Technologies example, much of this chapter is devoted to looking at the basic strategies that can be adopted at the functional level to improve competitive position. By the end of this chapter, you will understand how functional-level strategies can be used to build a sustainable competitive advantage.

ACHIEVING SUPERIOR EFFICIENCY

A company is a device for transforming inputs (labor, land, capital, management, and technological know-how) into outputs (the goods and services produced). The simplest measure of efficiency is the quantity of inputs that it takes to produce a given output; that is, efficiency = outputs/inputs. The more efficient a company is, the fewer the inputs required to produce a given output and the lower its cost structure will be. Put another way, an efficient company has higher productivity, and therefore lower costs, than its rivals. Following, we review the steps that companies can take at the functional level to increase their efficiency and thereby lower their cost structures.

Efficiency and Economies of Scale

Economies of scale are unit cost reductions associated with a large scale of output. You will recall from the previous chapter that it is very important for managers to understand how the cost structure of their enterprise varies with output because this understanding should help to drive strategy. For example, if unit costs fall significantly as output is expanded—that is, if there are significant economies of scale—a company may benefit by keeping prices down and increasing volume.

One source of economies of scale is the ability to spread fixed costs over a large production volume. **Fixed costs** are costs that must be incurred to produce a product whatever the level of output; examples are the costs of purchasing machinery, setting up machinery for individual production runs, building facilities, advertising, and R&D. For example, Microsoft spent approximately $5 billion to develop the latest version of its Windows operating system, Windows Vista. It can realize substantial scale economies by spreading the fixed costs associated with developing the new operating system over the enormous unit sales volume it expects for this system (95% of the world's 250 million personal computers use Microsoft operating systems). These scale economies are significant because of the trivial incremental (or marginal) cost of producing additional copies of Windows Vista. Once the master copy has been produced, additional CDs containing the operating system can be produced for a few cents. The key to Microsoft's efficiency and profitability (and that of other companies with high fixed costs and trivial incremental or marginal costs) is to increase sales rapidly enough that fixed costs can be spread out over a large unit volume so that substantial scale economies can be realized.

Another source of scale economies is the ability of companies producing in large volumes to achieve a greater division of labor and specialization. Specialization is said to have a favorable impact on productivity, mainly because it enables employees to become very skilled at performing particular tasks. The classic example of such economies is Ford's Model T car. The world's first mass-produced car, the Model T Ford, was introduced in 1923. Until then, Ford had made cars using an expensive hand-built craft production method. By introducing mass-production techniques, the company achieved greater division of labor (it split assembly into small, repeatable tasks) and specialization, which boosted employee productivity. Ford was also able to spread the fixed costs of developing a car and setting up production machinery over a large volume of output. As a result of these economies, the cost of manufacturing a car at Ford fell from $3,000 to less than $900 (in 1958 dollars).

These examples illustrate that economies of scale can boost profitability, as measured by ROIC, in a number of ways. Economies of scale exist in production, sales and marketing, and R&D, and the overall effect of realizing economies of scale is to reduce spending as a percentage of revenues on COGS, SG&A expenses, and R&D expenses, thereby boosting ROS and, by extension, ROIC (see Figure 3.9). Moreover, by making more intensive use of existing capacity, a company can increase the amount of sales generated from its PPE, thereby reducing the amount of capital it needs to generate a dollar of sales, thus increasing its capital turnover and its ROIC.

The concept of economies of scale is illustrated in Figure 4.2, which shows that as a company increases its output, unit costs fall. This process comes to an end at an output of Q1, where all scale economies are exhausted. Indeed, at outputs of greater than Q1, the company may encounter **diseconomies of scale**, which are the unit cost increases associated with a large scale of output. Diseconomies of scale occur primarily because of the increasing bureaucracy associated with large-scale enterprises and the managerial inefficiencies that can result.[2] Larger enterprises have a tendency to develop extensive managerial hierarchies in which dysfunctional political behavior is commonplace, information about operating matters is accidentally and deliberately distorted by the number of managerial layers through which it has to travel to reach top decision makers, and poor decisions are the result. As a result, past some point (such as Q1 in Figure 4.2), the inefficiencies that result from such

Figure 4.2 Economies and Diseconomies of Scale

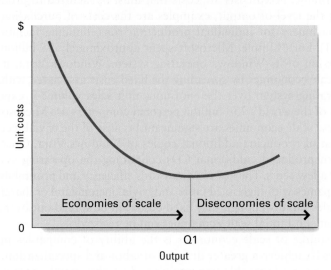

developments outweigh any additional gains from economies of scale, and unit costs start to rise as output expands.

Managers must know not only the extent of economies of scale but also where diseconomies of scale begin to occur. At Nucor for example, the realization that diseconomies of scale exist has led to a decision not to build plants that employ more than 300 individuals. The belief is that it is more efficient to build two plants, each employing 300 people, than one plant employing 600 people. Although the larger plant might theoretically be able to reap greater scale economies, Nucor's management believes that these would be swamped by the diseconomies of scale that come with larger organizational units.

Efficiency and Learning Effects

Learning effects are cost savings that come from learning by doing. Labor, for example, learns by repetition how best to carry out a task. Therefore, labor productivity increases over time, and unit costs fall as individuals learn the most efficient way to perform a particular task. Equally important, management in new manufacturing facilities typically learns over time how best to run the new operation. Hence, production costs decline because of increasing labor productivity and management efficiency. Japanese companies like Toyota are noted for making learning a central part of their operating philosophy.

Learning effects tend to be more significant when a technologically complex task is repeated because there is more to learn. Thus, learning effects will be more significant in an assembly process that has 1,000 complex steps than in one with 100 simple steps. Although learning effects are normally associated with the manufacturing process, there is every reason to believe that they are just as important in service industries. For example, one famous study of learning in the context of the health care industry found that more-experienced medical providers posted significantly lower mortality rates for a number of common surgical procedures, suggesting that learning effects are at work in surgery.[3] The authors of this study used the evidence to argue for establishing regional referral centers for the provision of highly specialized medical care. These centers would perform many specific surgical procedures (such as heart surgery), replacing local facilities with lower volumes and presumably higher mortality rates. Another recent study found strong evidence of learning effects in a financial institution. The study looked at a newly established document-processing unit with 100 staff members and found that, over time, documents were processed much more rapidly as the staff learned the process. Overall, the study concluded that unit costs fell every time the cumulative number of documents processed doubled.[4] Strategy in Action 4.1 looks at the determinants of differences in learning effects across a sample of hospitals performing cardiac surgery.

In terms of the unit cost curve of a company, although economies of scale imply a movement along the curve (say, from A to B in Figure 4.3), the realization of learning effects implies a downward shift of the entire curve (B to C in Figure 4.3) as both labor and management become more efficient over time at performing their tasks at every level of output. In accounting terms, learning effects in a production setting will reduce the COGS as a percentage of revenues, enabling the company to earn a higher ROS and ROIC.

No matter how complex the task is, however, learning effects typically die out after a limited period of time. Indeed, it has been suggested that they are really important only during the start-up period of a new process and cease after two or three years.[5] When changes occur to a company's production system—as a result of merger or the use of new information technology, for example—the learning process must begin again.

Efficiency and the Experience Curve

The **experience curve** refers to the systematic lowering of the cost structure, and consequent unit cost reductions, that have been observed to occur over the life of a product.[6] According to the experience-curve concept, unit manufacturing costs for a product typically decline by some characteristic amount each time accumulated output of the product is doubled (accumulated output is the total output of a product

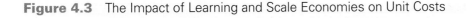

Figure 4.3   The Impact of Learning and Scale Economies on Unit Costs

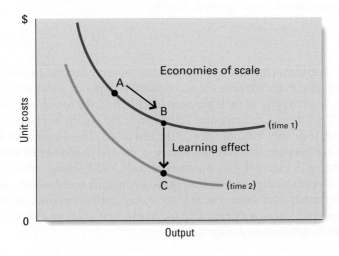

4.1 STRATEGY IN ACTION

Learning Effects in Cardiac Surgery

A study carried out by researchers at the Harvard Business School tried to estimate the importance of learning effects in the case of a specific new technology for minimally invasive heart surgery that was approved by federal regulators in 1996. The researchers looked at 16 hospitals and obtained data on the operations for 660 patients. They examined how the time required to undertake the procedure varied with cumulative experience. Across the 16 hospitals, they found that average time fell from 280 minutes for the first procedure with the new technology to 220 minutes by the time a hospital had performed 50 procedures. (Note that not all of the hospitals performed 50 procedures, and the estimates represent an extrapolation based on the data.)

Next they looked at differences across hospitals. They found evidence of very large differences in learning effects. One hospital, in particular, stood out. This hospital, which they called "Hospital M," reduced its net procedure time from 500 minutes on case 1 to 132 minutes by case 50. Hospital M's 88-minute procedure time advantage over the average hospital at case 50 translated into a cost saving of approximately $2,250 per case and allowed surgeons at the hospital to do one more revenue-generating procedure per day.

The researchers tried to find out why Hospital M was superior. They noted that all hospitals had similar state-of-the-art operating rooms and used the same set of FDA approved devices. All adopting surgeons went through the same training courses, and all surgeons came from highly respected training hospitals. Follow-up interviews, however, suggested that Hospital M differed in how it implemented the new procedure. The team was hand-picked by the adopting surgeon to perform the surgery. It had significant prior experience working together (That was apparently a key criterion for team members.) The team trained together to perform the new surgery. Before undertaking a single procedure, they met with the operating room nurses and anesthesiologists to discuss the procedure. Moreover, the adopting surgeon mandated that the surgical team and surgical procedure was stable in the early cases. The initial team went through 15 procedures, and new members were added or substituted 20 cases before the procedures were modified. The adopting surgeon also insisted that the team meet prior to each of the first 10 cases, and they also met after the first 20 cases to debrief.

The picture that emerges is one of a core team that was selected and managed to maximize the gains from learning. Unlike other hospitals in which there was less stability of team members and procedures, and less attention to briefing, debriefing, and learning, surgeons at Hospital M both learned much faster, and ultimately achieved higher productivity than their peers in other institutions. Clearly, differences in the implementation of the new procedure were very important.

Source: G. P. Pisano, R. M. J. Bohmer, and A. C. Edmondson, "Organizational Differences in Rates of Learning: Evidence from the Adoption of Minimally Invasive Cardiac Surgery," *Management Science* 47 (2001): 752–768.

since its introduction). This relationship was first observed in the aircraft industry, in which it was found that each time the accumulated output of airframes was doubled, unit costs declined to 80% of their previous level.[7] Thus, the fourth airframe typically cost only 80% of the second airframe to produce; the eighth airframe only 80% of the fourth; the 16th only 80% of the eighth; and so on. The outcome of this process is a relationship between unit manufacturing costs and accumulated output similar to that illustrated in Figure 4.4. Economies of scale and learning effects underlie the experience-curve phenomenon. Put simply, as a company increases the accumulated volume of its output over time, it is able to realize both economies of scale (as volume increases) and learning effects. Consequently, unit costs and cost structure fall with increases in accumulated output.

Figure 4.4 The Experience Curve

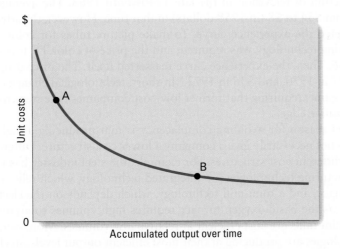

The strategic significance of the experience curve is clear: increasing a company's product volume and market share will lower its cost structure relative to its rivals. Thus, company B in Figure 4.4, because it is farther down the experience curve, has a cost advantage over company A because of its lower cost structure. The concept is very important in industries that mass-produce a standardized output (for example, the manufacture of semiconductor chips). A company that wishes to become more efficient and lower its cost structure must try to ride down the experience curve as quickly as possible. This means constructing efficient scale manufacturing facilities even before it has generated demand for the product and aggressively pursuing cost reductions from learning effects. It might also need to adopt an aggressive marketing strategy—cutting prices to the bone, stressing heavy sales promotions and extensive advertising to build up demand, hence, accumulating volume as quickly as possible. The need to be aware of the relationship of demand, price options, and costs noted in Chapter 3 is clear.

Once down the experience curve because of its superior efficiency, the company is likely to have a significant cost advantage over its competitors. For example, it has been argued that Intel uses such tactics to ride down the experience curve and gain a competitive advantage over its rivals in the market for microprocessors.[8]

However, there are three reasons why managers should not become complacent about efficiency-based cost advantages derived from experience effects. First, because neither learning effects nor economies of scale go on forever, the experience curve is likely to bottom out at some point; indeed, it must do so by definition. When this occurs, further unit cost reductions from learning effects and economies of scale will be hard to come by. Thus, in time, other companies can lower their cost structures and match the cost leader. Once this happens, a number of low-cost companies can have cost parity with each other. In such circumstances, a sustainable competitive advantage must rely on strategic factors besides the minimization of production costs by using existing technologies—factors such as better responsiveness to customers, product quality, or innovation.

Second, as noted in Chapter 2, changes that are always taking place in the external environment disrupt a company's business model, so cost advantages gained from experience effects can be made obsolete by the development of new technologies. The price of television picture tubes followed the experience-curve pattern from the introduction of television in the late 1940s until 1963. The average unit price dropped from $34 to $8 (in 1958 dollars) in that time. However, the advent of color TV interrupted the experience curve. To make picture tubes for color TVs, a new manufacturing technology was required, and the price of color TV tubes shot up to $51 by 1966. Then, the experience curve reasserted itself. The price dropped to $48 in 1968, $37 in 1970, and $36 in 1972.[9] In short, technological change can alter the rules of the game, requiring that former low-cost companies take steps to reestablish their competitive edge.

A further reason for avoiding complacency is that producing a high volume of output does not necessarily give a company a lower cost structure. Different technologies have different cost structures. For example, the steel industry has two alternative manufacturing technologies: an integrated technology, which relies on the basic oxygen furnace, and a mini-mill technology, which depends on the electric arc furnace. Whereas the basic oxygen furnace requires high volumes to attain maximum efficiency, mini-mills are cost efficient at relative low volumes. Moreover, even when both technologies are producing at their most efficient output levels, steel companies with basic oxygen furnaces do not have a cost advantage over mini-mills. Consequently, the pursuit of experience economies by an integrated company using basic oxygen technology may not bring the kind of cost advantages that a naive reading of the experience-curve phenomenon would lead the company to expect. Indeed, there have been significant periods of time when integrated companies have not been able to get enough orders to run at optimum capacity. Hence, their production costs have been considerably higher than those of mini-mills.[10] As we discuss next, new flexible manufacturing technologies in many industries hold out the promise of allowing small manufacturers to produce at unit costs comparable to those of large assembly-line operations.

Efficiency, Flexible Production Systems, and Mass Customization

Central to the concept of economies of scale is the idea that the best way to achieve high efficiency and a lower cost structure is through the mass production of a standardized output. The tradeoff implicit in this idea is between unit costs and product variety. Producing greater product variety from a factory implies shorter production runs, which implies an inability to realize economies of scale and higher costs. That is, a wide product variety makes it difficult for a company to increase its production efficiency and thus reduce its unit costs. According to this logic, the way to increase efficiency and achieve a lower cost structure is to limit product variety and produce a standardized product in large volumes (see Figure 4.5a).

This view of production efficiency has been challenged by the rise of flexible production technologies. The term **flexible production technology**—or lean production as it is sometimes called—covers a range of technologies designed to reduce setup times for complex equipment, increase the use of individual machines through better scheduling, and improve quality control at all stages of the manufacturing process.[11] Flexible production technologies allow the company to produce a wider variety of end products at a unit cost that at one time could be achieved only through the mass production of a standardized output (see Figure 4.5b). Indeed, research suggests that the adoption of flexible production technologies may increase efficiency

Figure 4.5 Tradeoff between Costs and Product Variety

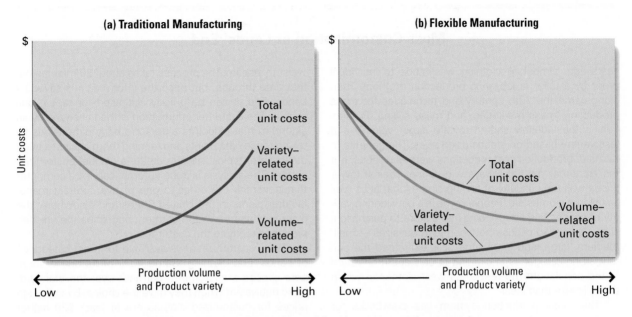

and lower unit costs relative to what can be achieved by the mass production of a standardized output, while at the same time enabling the company to customize its product offering to a much greater extent than was once thought possible. The term **mass customization** has been coined to describe the ability of companies to use flexible manufacturing technology to reconcile two goals that were once thought to be incompatible: low cost and differentiation through product customization.[12] For an extended example of the benefits of mass customization, see Strategy in Action 4.2, which looks at mass customization at Lands' End.

Flexible machine cells are a common flexible production technology. A flexible machine cell is a grouping of various types of machinery, a common materials handler, and a centralized cell controller (a computer). Each cell normally contains four to six machines capable of performing a variety of operations but dedicated to producing a family of parts or products. The settings on the machines are computer controlled, which allows each cell to switch quickly between the production of different parts or products.

Improved capacity utilization and reductions in work in progress (that is, stockpiles of partly finished products) and waste are major efficiency benefits of flexible machine cells. Improved capacity utilization arises from the reduction in setup times and the computer-controlled coordination of production flow between machines, which eliminates bottlenecks. The tight coordination between machines also reduces work in progress. Reductions in waste are due to the ability of computer-controlled machinery to identify ways to transform inputs into outputs while producing a minimum of unusable waste material. Freestanding machines might be in use 50% of the time; the same machines when grouped into a cell can be used more than 80% of the time and produce the same end product with half the waste, thereby increasing efficiency and resulting in lower costs.

The effects of installing flexible production technology on a company's cost structure can be dramatic. Ford is currently introducing flexible production

4.2 STRATEGY IN ACTION

Mass Customization at Lands' End

Years ago, almost all clothing was made to individual order by a tailor (a job shop production method). Then along came the 20th century and techniques for mass production, mass marketing, and mass selling. Production in the industry shifted toward larger volume and less variety based on standardized sizes. The benefits in terms of production cost reductions were enormous, but the customer did not always win. Offset against lower prices was the difficulty of finding clothes that fit as well as tailored clothes did. People come in a bewildering variety of shapes and sizes. Going into a store to purchase a shirt, you get to choose between just four-sizes—small, medium, large, and extra large. It is estimated the current sizing categories in clothing fit only about one-third of the population. The rest of us wear clothes in which the fit is less than ideal.

The mass production system has drawbacks for apparel manufacturers and retailers as well. Year after year, apparel firms find themselves saddled with billions of dollars in excess inventory that is either thrown away, or put on sale, because retailers had too many items of the wrong size and color. To try and solve this problem, Lands' End has been experimenting with mass customization techniques.

To purchase customized clothes from Lands' End, the customer provides information on Lands' End Web site by answering a series of 15 questions (for pants) or 25 questions (for shirts) covering nearly everything from waist to inseam. The process takes about 20 minutes the first time through, but once the information is saved by Lands' End, it can be quickly accessed for repeat purchases. The customer information is then analyzed by an algorithm that pinpoints a person's body dimensions by taking these data points and running them against a huge database of typical sizes to create a unique, customized pattern. The analysis is done automatically by a computer that transmits the order to one of five contract manufacturer plants in the United States and elsewhere; the plant cuts and sews the garment and ships the finished product directly to the customer.

Today customization is available for most categories of Lands' End clothing. Some 40% of its online shoppers choose a customized garment over the standard-sized equivalent when they have the choice. Even though prices for customized clothes are at least $20 higher and take about three to four weeks to arrive, customized clothing reportedly accounts for a rapidly growing percentage of Lands' End's $500 million online business. Lands' End states that its profit margins are roughly the same for customized clothes as regular clothes, but the reductions in inventories that come from matching demand to supply account for additional cost savings. Moreover, customers who customize appear to be more loyal, with reordering rates that are 34% higher than for buyers of standard-sized clothing.

Sources: J. Schlosser, "Cashing in on the New World of Me," *Fortune,* December 13, 2004, 244–249; V. S. Borland, "Global Technology in the Twenty-First Century," *Textile World,* January 2003, 42–56; http://www.landsend.com.

technologies into its automotive plants around the world. These new technologies should allow Ford to produce multiple models from the same line and to switch production from one model to another much more quickly than in the past. In total, Ford hopes to take $2 billion out of its cost structure between 2006 and 2010 through flexible manufacturing.[13]

More generally, in terms of the profitability framework developed in Chapter 3, flexible production technology should boost profitability (measured by ROIC) by reducing the COGS as a percentage of revenues, reducing the working capital needed to finance work-in-progress (because there is less of it), and reducing the amount of capital that needs to be invested in PPE to generate a dollar of sales (because less space is needed to store inventory).

Marketing and Efficiency

The marketing strategy that a company adopts can have a major impact on efficiency and cost structure. **Marketing strategy** refers to the position that a company takes with regard to pricing, promotion, advertising, product design, and distribution. Some of the steps leading to greater efficiency are fairly obvious. For example, riding down the experience curve to achieve a lower cost structure can be facilitated by aggressive pricing, promotions, and advertising, all of which are the task of the marketing function. Other aspects of marketing strategy have a less obvious but no less important impact on efficiency. One important aspect is the relationship of customer defection rates, cost structure, and unit costs.[14]

Customer defection rates (or "churn rates") are the percentage of a company's customers who defect every year to competitors. Defection rates are determined by customer loyalty, which in turn is a function of the ability of a company to satisfy its customers. Because acquiring a new customer entails certain one-time fixed costs for advertising, promotions, and the like, there is a direct relationship between defection rates and costs. The longer a company holds on to a customer, the greater is the volume of customer-generated unit sales that can be set against these fixed costs and the lower the average unit cost of each sale. Thus, lowering customer defection rates allows a company to achieve a lower cost structure.

One consequence of the defection-cost relationship is illustrated in Figure 4.6. Because of the relatively high fixed costs of acquiring new customers, serving customers who stay with a company only for a short time before switching to competitors often leads to a loss on the investment made to acquire those customers. The longer a customer stays with a company, the more the fixed costs of acquiring that customer can be spread out over repeat purchases, boosting the profit per customer. Thus, there is a positive relationship between the length of time that a customer stays with a company and profit per customer. If a company can reduce customer defection rates, it can make a much better return on its investment in acquiring customers and thereby boost its profitability. In terms of the profitability framework developed in Chapter 3,

Figure 4.6 The Relationship between Customer Loyalty and Profit per Customer

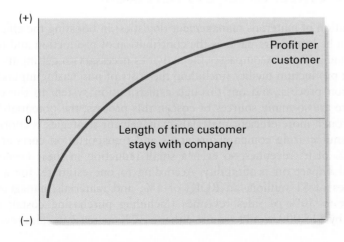

reduced customer defection rates mean that the company needs to spend less on SG&A expenses to generate a dollar of sales revenue, which increases both return on sales and ROIC.

For an example, consider the credit card business.[15] Most credit card companies spend an average of $50 to recruit a customer and set up a new account. These costs come from the advertising required to attract new customers, the credit checks required for each customer, and the mechanics of setting up an account and issuing a card. These one-time fixed costs can be recouped only if a customer stays with the company for at least two years. Moreover, when customers stay a second year, they tend to increase their use of the credit card, which raises the volume of revenues generated by each customer over time. As a result, although the credit card business loses $50 per customer in year 1, it makes a profit of $44 in year 3 and $55 in year 6.

Another economic benefit of long-time customer loyalty is the free advertising that customers provide for a company. Loyal customers can dramatically increase the volume of business through referrals. A striking example is Britain's largest retailer, the clothing and food company Marks & Spencer, whose success is built on a well-earned reputation for providing its customers with high-quality goods at reasonable prices. The company has generated such customer loyalty that it does not need to advertise in Britain, a major source of cost saving.

The key message, then, is that reducing customer defection rates and building customer loyalty can be major sources of a lower cost structure. One study has estimated that a 5% reduction in customer defection rates leads to the following increases in profits per customer over average customer life: 75% in the credit card business; 50% in the insurance brokerage industry; 45% in the industrial laundry business; and 35% in the computer software industry.[16]

A central component of developing a strategy to reduce defection rates is to identify customers who have defected, find out why they defected, and act on that information so that other customers do not defect for similar reasons in the future. To take these measures, the marketing function must have information systems capable of tracking customer defections.

MATERIALS MANAGEMENT, JUST-IN-TIME, AND EFFICIENCY

The contribution of materials management (logistics) in boosting the efficiency of a company can be just as dramatic as the contribution of production and marketing. Materials management encompasses the activities necessary to get inputs and components to a production facility (including the costs of purchasing inputs), through the production process, and out through a distribution system to the end user.[17] Because there are so many sources of cost in this process, the potential for reducing costs through more efficient materials-management strategies is enormous. For a typical manufacturing company, materials and transportation costs account for 50% to 70% of its revenues, so even a small reduction in these costs can have a substantial impact on profitability. According to one estimate, for a company with revenues of $1 million, an ROIC of 5%, and materials-management costs that amount to 50% of sales revenues (including purchasing costs), increasing total profits by $15,000 would require either a 30% increase in sales revenues or a

3% reduction in materials costs.[18] In a typical competitive market, reducing materials costs by 3% is usually much easier than increasing sales revenues by 30%.

Improving the efficiency of the materials-management function typically requires the adoption of a **just-in-time** (JIT) inventory system, which is designed to economize on inventory holding costs by having components arrive at a manufacturing plant just in time to enter the production process or to have goods arrive at a retail store only when stock is almost depleted. The major cost saving comes from increasing inventory turnover, which reduces inventory holding costs, such as warehousing and storage costs, and the company's need for working capital. For example, through efficient logistics Walmart can replenish the stock in its stores at least twice a week; many stores receive daily deliveries if they are needed. The typical competitor replenishes its stock every two weeks, so it has to carry a much higher inventory and needs more working capital per dollar of sales. Compared to its competitors, Walmart can maintain the same service levels with a lower investment in inventory, a major source of its lower cost structure. Thus, faster inventory turnover has helped Walmart achieve an efficiency-based competitive advantage in the retailing industry.[19]

More generally, in terms of the profitability model developed in Chapter 3, JIT inventory systems reduce the need for working capital (because there is less inventory to finance) and fixed capital to finance storage space (because there is less to store). This reduces capital needs, increases capital turnover, and, by extension, boosts the return on invested capital.

The drawback of JIT systems is that they deny companies buffer stocks of inventory. Although buffer stocks are expensive to store, they can help tide a company over shortages of inputs brought about by disruption among suppliers (for instance, a labor dispute at a key supplier) and can help a company respond quickly to increases in demand. However, there are ways around these limitations. For example, to reduce the risks linked to dependence on just one supplier for an important input, a company might decide to source inputs from multiple suppliers.

Recently, the efficient management of materials and inventory has been recast in terms of **supply-chain management**: the task of managing the flow of inputs and components from suppliers into the company's production processes to minimize inventory holding and maximize inventory turnover. One of the exemplary companies in terms of supply-chain management is Dell, whose goal is to streamline its supply chain to such an extent that it "replaces inventory with information."

R&D Strategy and Efficiency

The role of superior R&D in helping a company achieve a greater efficiency and a lower cost structure is twofold. First, the R&D function can boost efficiency by designing products that are easy to manufacture. By cutting down on the number of parts that make up a product, R&D can dramatically decrease the required assembly time, which translates into higher employee productivity, lower costs, and higher profitability. For example, after Texas Instruments redesigned an infrared sighting mechanism that it supplies to the Pentagon, it found that it had reduced, the number of parts from 47 to 12, the number of assembly steps from 56 to 13, the time spent fabricating metal from 757 minutes per unit to 219 minutes per unit, and unit assembly time from 129 minutes to 20 minutes. The result was a substantial decline in production costs. Design for manufacturing requires close coordination between the production and R&D functions of a company, of course. Cross-functional teams that contain production and R&D personnel who work jointly on the problem best achieve this.

The second way in which the R&D function can help a company achieve a lower cost structure is by pioneering process innovations. A process innovation is an innovation in the way production processes operate that improves their efficiency. Process innovations have often been a major source of competitive advantage. Toyota's competitive advantage is based partly on the company's invention of new flexible manufacturing processes that dramatically reduced setup times. This process innovation enabled it to obtain efficiency gains associated with flexible manufacturing systems years ahead of its competitors.

Human Resource Strategy and Efficiency

Employee productivity is one of the key determinants of an enterprise's efficiency, cost structure, and profitability.[20] Productive manufacturing employees can lower COGS as a percentage of revenues, a productive sales force can increase sales revenues for a given level of expenses, and productive employees in the company's R&D function can boost the percentage of revenues generated from new products for a given level of R&D expenses. Thus, productive employees lower the costs of generating revenues, increase ROS, and by extension boost the company's ROIC. The challenge for a company's human resource function is to devise ways to increase employee productivity. Among the choices it has are using certain hiring strategies, training employees, organizing the workforce into self-managing teams, and linking pay to performance. The running case in this chapter looks at the steps Walmart has taken to boost employee productivity.

Hiring Strategy   Many companies that are known for their productive employees devote considerable attention to hiring. Southwest Airlines hires people who have positive attitudes and work well in teams because it believes these people will work hard and interact well with customers, helping to create customer loyalty. Nucor hires people who are self-reliant and goal-oriented because its employees work in self-managing teams in which they need these qualities to perform well. As these examples suggest, it is important to make sure that the hiring strategy of the company is consistent with its own internal organization, culture, and strategic priorities. The people a company hires should have attributes that match the strategic objectives of the company.

Employee Training   Employees are a major input into the production process. Those who are highly skilled can perform tasks faster and more accurately and are more likely to learn the complex tasks associated with many modern production methods than individuals with lesser skills. Training upgrades employee skill levels, bringing the company productivity-related efficiency gains from learning and experimentation.[21]

Self-Managing Teams   The use of **self-managing teams**, whose members coordinate their own activities and make their own hiring, training, work, and reward decisions, has been spreading rapidly. The typical team comprises five to fifteen employees who produce an entire product or undertake an entire task. Team members learn all team tasks and rotate from job to job. Because a more flexible workforce is a result, team members can fill in for absent coworkers and take over managerial duties such

RUNNING CASE

Human Resource Strategy and Productivity at Walmart

Walmart has one of the most productive workforces of any retailer. The roots of Walmart's high productivity go back to the company's early days and the business philosophy of the company's founder, Sam Walton. Walton started off his career as a management trainee at JCPenney. There he noticed that all employees were called associates, and, moreover, that treating them with respect seemed to reap dividends in the form of high employee productivity.

When he founded Walmart, Walton decided to call all employees "associates" to symbolize their importance to the company. He reinforced this by emphasizing that at Walmart, "Our people make the difference." Unlike many managers who have stated this mantra, Walton believed it and put it into action. He believed that if he treated people well, they would return the favor by working hard, and that if he empowered them, ordinary people could work together to achieve extraordinary things. These beliefs formed the basis for a decentralized organization that operated with an open-door policy and open books. This allowed associates to see just how their store and the company were doing.

Consistent with the open-door policy, Walton continually emphasized that management needed to listen to associates and their ideas. As he noted:

> The folks on the front lines—the ones who actually talk to the customer—are the only ones who really know what's going on out there. You'd better find out what they know. This really is what total quality is all about. To push responsibility down in your organization, and to force good ideas to bubble up within it, you must listen to what your associates are trying to tell you.

For all of his belief in empowerment, however, Walton was notoriously tight on pay. Walton opposed unionization, fearing that it would lead to higher pay and restrictive work rules that would sap productivity. The culture of Walmart also encouraged people to work hard. One of Walton's favorite homilies was the "sun-down rule," which stated that one should never put off until tomorrow what can be done today. The sundown rule was enforced by senior managers, including Walton, who would drop in unannounced at a store, peppering store managers and employees with questions, but at the same time praising them for a job well done and celebrating the "heroes" who took the sundown rule to heart and did today what could have been put off for tomorrow.

The key to getting extraordinary effort out of employees, while paying them meager salaries, was to reward them with profit-sharing plans and stock-ownership schemes. Long before it became fashionable in American business, Walton was placing a chunk of Walmart's profits into a profit-sharing plan for associates, and the company put matching funds into employee stock-ownership programs. The idea was simple: reward associates by giving them a stake in the company, and they will work hard for low pay because they know they will make it up in profit sharing and stock price appreciation.

For years, this formula worked extraordinarily well, but there are now signs that Walmart's very success is creating problems. In 2008, the company had a staggering 2.1 million associates, making it the largest private employer in the world. As the company has grown, it has become increasingly difficult to hire people that Walmart has traditionally relied on—those willing to work long hours for low pay based on the promise of advancement and reward through profit sharing and stock ownership. The company has come under attack for paying its associates low wages and pressuring them to work long hours without overtime pay. Labor unions have made a concerted but so far unsuccessful attempt over time to unionize stores, and the company itself is the target of lawsuits from employees alleging sexual discrimination. Walmart claims that the negative publicity is based on faulty data, and perhaps that is right, but if the company has indeed become too big to put Walton's principles into practice, the glory days may be over.

Sources: S. Walton and J. Huey, *Sam Walton: Made in America* (New York: Bantam, 1993). S. Maich, "Walmart's Mid Life Crisis," *Maclean's,* August 23, 2004, 45; "The People Make It All Happen," *Discount Store News,* October 1999, 103–106. http://www.walmartstores.com.

as scheduling work and vacation, ordering materials, and hiring new members. The greater responsibility thrust on team members and the empowerment it implies are seen as motivators. (Empowerment is the process of giving lower-level employees decision-making power.) People often respond well to being given greater autonomy and responsibility. Performance bonuses linked to team production and quality targets work as an additional motivator.

The effect of introducing self-managing teams is reportedly an increase in productivity of 30% or more and a substantial increase in product quality. Further cost savings arise from eliminating supervisors and creating a flatter organizational hierarchy, which also lowers the cost structure of the company. In manufacturing companies, perhaps the most potent way to lower the cost structure is to combine self-managing teams with flexible manufacturing cells. For example, after the introduction of flexible manufacturing technology and work practices based on self-managing teams, a GE plant in Salisbury, North Carolina, increased productivity by 250% compared with GE plants that produced the same products four years earlier.[22]

Still, teams are no panacea; in manufacturing companies, self-managing teams may fail to live up to their potential unless they are integrated with flexible manufacturing technology. Also, teams put a lot of management responsibilities on team members, and helping team members to cope with these responsibilities often requires substantial training—a fact that many companies often forget in their rush to drive down costs, with the result that the teams do not work out as well as planned.[23]

Pay for Performance   It is hardly surprising that linking pay to performance can help increase employee productivity, but the issue is not quite so simple as just introducing incentive pay systems. It is also important to define what kind of job performance is to be rewarded and how. Some of the most efficient companies in the world, mindful that cooperation among employees is necessary to realize productivity gains, link pay to group or team (rather than individual) performance. Nucor divides its workforce into teams of 30 or so, with bonus pay, which can amount to 30% of base pay, linked to the ability of the team to meet productivity and quality goals. This link creates a strong incentive for individuals to cooperate with each other in pursuit of team goals; that is, it facilitates teamwork.

Information Systems and Efficiency

Ethical Dilemma

Reread the running case on Walmart then discuss the following question: Is it ethical for Walmart to pay its employees minimum wage and to oppose unionization, given that the organization also works its people very hard? Are Walmart's employment and compensation practices for lower-level employees (i.e., associates) ethical?

With the rapid spread of computers, the explosive growth of the Internet and corporate intranets (internal corporate computer networks based on Internet standards), and the spread of high-bandwidth fiber optics and digital wireless technology, the information systems function is moving to center stage in the quest for operating efficiencies and a lower cost structure.[24] The impact of information systems on productivity is wide ranging and potentially affects all other activities of a company. For example, Cisco Systems has been able to realize significant cost savings by moving its ordering and customer service functions online. The company has just 300 service agents handling all of its customer accounts, compared to the 900 it would need if sales were not handled online. The difference represents an annual saving of $20 million a year. Moreover, without automated customer service functions, Cisco calculates that it would need at least 1,000 additional service engineers, which would cost about $75 million.[25] Dell also makes extensive use of the Internet to lower its cost structure and differentiate itself from rivals.

Like Cisco and Dell, many companies are using Web-based information systems to reduce the costs of coordination between the company and its customers and the company and its suppliers. By using Web-based programs to automate customer and supplier interactions, companies can substantially reduce the number of people required to manage these interfaces, thereby reducing costs. This trend extends beyond high-tech companies. Banks and financial service companies are finding that they can substantially reduce costs by moving customer accounts and support functions online. Such a move reduces the need for customer service representatives, bank tellers, stockbrokers, insurance agents, and others. For example, it costs an average of about $1.07 to execute a transaction at a bank, such as shifting money from one account to another; executing the same transaction via the Internet costs $0.01.[26]

Similarly, the theory behind Internet-based retailers such as amazon.com is that by replacing physical stores and their supporting personnel with an online virtual store and automated ordering and checkout processes, a company can take significant costs out of the retailing system. Cost savings can also be realized by using Web-based information systems to automate many internal company activities, from managing expense reimbursements to benefits planning and hiring processes, thereby reducing the need for internal support personnel.

Infrastructure and Efficiency

A company's infrastructure—that is, its structure, culture, style of strategic leadership, and control system—determines the context within which all other value creation activities take place. It follows that improving infrastructure can help a company increase efficiency and lower its cost structure. Above all, an appropriate infrastructure can help foster a company-wide commitment to efficiency and promote cooperation among different functions in pursuit of efficiency goals. These issues are addressed at length in later chapters.

For now, it is important to note that strategic leadership is especially important in building a company-wide commitment to efficiency. The leadership task is to articulate a vision that recognizes the need for all functions of a company to focus on improving efficiency. It is not enough to improve the efficiency of production, or of marketing, or of R&D in a piecemeal fashion. Achieving superior efficiency requires a company-wide commitment to this goal that must be articulated by general and functional managers. A further leadership task is to facilitate the cross-functional cooperation needed to achieve superior efficiency. For example, designing products that are easy to manufacture requires that production and R&D personnel communicate; integrating JIT systems with production scheduling requires close communication between materials management and production; designing self-managing teams to perform production tasks requires close cooperation between human resources and production; and so on.

Summary: Achieving Efficiency

Table 4.1 summarizes the primary roles that various functions must take to achieve superior efficiency. Bear in mind that achieving superior efficiency is not something that can be tackled on a function-by-function basis. It requires an organization-wide commitment and an ability to ensure close cooperation among functions. Top management, by exercising leadership and influencing the infrastructure, plays a major role in this process.

Table 4.1   Primary Roles of Value Creation Functions in Achieving Superior Efficiency

Value Creation Function	Primary Roles
Infrastructure (leadership)	1. Provide company-wide commitment to efficiency
	2. Facilitate cooperation among functions
Production	1. Where appropriate, pursue economies of scale and learning economics
	2. Implement flexible manufacturing systems
Marketing	1. Where appropriate, adopt aggressive marketing to ride down the experience curve
	2. Limit customer defection rates by building brand loyalty
Materials management	1. Implement JIT systems
	2. Implement supply-chain coordination
R&D	1. Design products for ease of manufacture
	2. Seek process innovations
Information systems	1. Use information systems to automate processes
	2. Use information systems to reduce costs of coordination
Human resources	1. Institute training programs to build skills
	2. Implement self-managing teams
	3. Implement pay for performance

Achieving Superior Quality

In Chapter 3, we noted that quality can be thought of in terms of two dimensions: *quality as reliability* and *quality as excellence*. High-quality products are reliable, in the sense that they do the job they were designed for and do it well, and are also perceived by consumers to have superior attributes. We also noted that superior quality gives a company two advantages. First, a strong reputation for quality allows a company to differentiate its products from those offered by rivals, thereby creating more utility in the eyes of customers, which gives a company the option of charging a premium price for its products. Second, eliminating defects or errors from the production process reduces waste, increases efficiency, and lowers the cost structure of a company and increases its profitability. For example, reducing the number of defects in a company's manufacturing process will lower the COGS as a percentage of revenues, thereby raising the company's ROS and ROIC. In this section, we look in more depth at what managers can do to enhance the reliability and other attributes of a company's product offering.

Attaining Superior Reliability

The principal tool that most managers now use to increase the reliability of their product offering is the Six Sigma quality-improvement methodology. The Six Sigma methodology is a direct descendant of the TQM philosophy that was widely adopted, first by Japanese companies and then by American companies, during the 1980s and early 1990s.[27] The TQM concept was developed by a number of American management consultants, including W. Edwards Deming, Joseph Juran, and A. V. Feigenbaum.[28]

Originally, these consultants won few converts in the United States. However, managers in Japan embraced their ideas enthusiastically and even named their premier annual prize for manufacturing excellence after Deming. The philosophy underlying TQM, as articulated by Deming, is based on the following five-step chain reaction:

1. Improved quality means that costs decrease because of less rework, fewer mistakes, fewer delays, and better use of time and materials.
2. As a result, productivity improves.
3. Better quality leads to higher market share and allows the company to raise prices.
4. This increases the company's profitability and allows it to stay in business.
5. Thus the company creates more jobs.[29]

Deming identified a number of steps that should be part of any quality-improvement program: A company should have a clear business model to specify where it is going and how it is going to get there.

1. Management should embrace the philosophy that mistakes, defects, and poor-quality materials are not acceptable and should be eliminated.
2. Quality of supervision should be improved by allowing more time for supervisors to work with employees and giving them appropriate skills for the job.
3. Management should create an environment in which employees will not fear reporting problems or recommending improvements.
4. Work standards should not only be defined as numbers or quotas but also include some notion of quality to promote the production of defect-free output.
5. Management is responsible for training employees in new skills to keep pace with changes in the workplace.
6. Achieving better quality requires the commitment of everyone in the company.

It took the rise of Japan to the top rank of economic powers in the 1980s to alert western business to the importance of the TQM concept. Since then, quality-improvement programs have spread rapidly throughout western industry. Strategy in Action 4.3 describes one of the most successful implementations of a quality-improvement process, GE's Six Sigma program.

Despite such instances of spectacular success, quality-improvement practices are not universally accepted. A study by the American Quality Foundation found that only 20% of United States companies regularly review the consequences of quality performance, compared with 70% of Japanese companies.[30] Another study, this one by Arthur D. Little, of 500 American companies using TQM found that only 36% believed that TQM was increasing their competitiveness.[31] A prime reason for this, according to the study, was that many companies had not fully understood or

4.3 STRATEGY IN ACTION

GE's Six Sigma Quality Improvement Process

Six Sigma, a quality and efficiency program adopted by several major corporations, including Motorola, GE, and Allied Signal, aims to reduce defects, boost productivity, eliminate waste, and cut costs throughout a company. "Sigma" comes from the Greek letter that statisticians use to represent a standard deviation from a mean: the higher the number of sigma, the smaller the number of errors. At Six Sigma, a production process would be 99.99966% accurate, creating just 3.4 defects per million units. Although it is almost impossible for a company to achieve such perfection, several companies strive toward that goal.

GE is perhaps the most well-known adopter of Six Sigma programs. Under the direction of long-serving CEO Jack Welch, GE spent nearly $1 billion to convert all of its divisions to the Six Sigma faith.

One of the first products that was designed from start to finish using Six Sigma processes was a $1.25 million diagnostic computer tomography (CT) scanner, the Lightspeed, which produces rapid three-dimensional images of the human body. The new scanner captures multiple images simultaneously, requiring only 20 seconds to do full-body scans that once took three minutes—important because patients must remain perfectly still during the scan. GE spent $50 million to run 250 separate Six Sigma analyses designed to improve the reliability and lower the manufacturing cost of the new scanner. Its efforts were rewarded when the Lightspeed's first customers soon noticed that it ran without downtime from the start, a testament to the reliability of the product.

Achieving that reliability took a lot of work. GE's engineers deconstructed the scanner into its basic components and tried to improve the reliability of each component through a detailed step-by-step analysis. For example, the most important part of CT scanners is vacuum tubes that focus X-ray waves. The tubes that GE used in previous scanners, which cost $60,000 each, suffered from low reliability. Hospitals and clinics wanted the tubes to operate for 12 hours a day for at least six months, but typically they lasted only half that long. Moreover, GE was scrapping some $20 million in tubes each year because they failed preshipping performance tests, and a disturbing number of faulty tubes were slipping past inspection, only to be pronounced dead on arrival.

To try to solve the reliability problem, the Six Sigma team took the tubes apart. They knew that one problem was a petroleum-based oil used in the tube to prevent short circuits by isolating the anode, which has a positive charge, from the negatively charged cathode. The oil often deteriorated after a few months, leading to short circuits, but the team did not know why. By using statistical "what-if" scenarios on all parts of the tube, the researchers learned that the lead-based paint on the inside of the tube was adulterating the oil. Acting on this information, the team developed a paint that would preserve the tube and protect the oil. By pursuing this and other improvements, the Six Sigma team was able to extend the average life of a vacuum tube in the CT scanner from three months to over a year. Although the improvements increased the cost of the tube from $60,000 to $85,000, the increased cost was outweighed by the reduction in replacement costs, making it an attractive proposition for customers.

Sources: C. H. Deutsch, "Six-Sigma Enlightenment," *New York Times*, December 7, 1998, 1; J. J. Barshay, "The Six-Sigma Story," *Star Tribune*, June 14, 1999, 1; D. D. Bak, "Rethinking Industrial Drives," *Electrical/Electronics Technology*, November 30, 1998, 58.

embraced the TQM concept. They were looking for a quick fix, whereas implementing a quality-improvement program is a long-term commitment.

Implementing Reliability Improvement Methodologies

Among companies that have successfully adopted quality-improvement methodologies, certain imperatives stand out. These are discussed following in the order in which they are usually tackled in companies implementing quality-improvement programs. What needs to be stressed first, however, is that improvement in product reliability is a cross-functional process. Its implementation requires close cooperation among all functions in the pursuit of the common goal of improving quality; it is a process that cuts across functions. The roles played by the different functions in implementing reliability improvement methodologies are summarized in Table 4.2.

First, it is important that senior managers buy into a quality-improvement program and communicate its importance to the organization. Second, if a quality-improvement program is to be successful, individuals must be identified to lead the program. Under the Six Sigma methodology, exceptional employees are identified and put through a "black belt" training course on the Six Sigma methodology. The black belts are taken from their regular job roles and assigned to work solely on Six Sigma projects for the next two years. In effect, the black belts become internal consultants and project leaders. Because they are dedicated to Six Sigma programs, the black belts are not distracted from the task at hand by day-to-day operating responsibilities. To make a black belt assignment attractive, many companies now use it as a step in a career path. Successful black belts may not return to their prior jobs after two years but instead are promoted and given more responsibility.

Third, quality-improvement methodologies preach the need to identify defects that arise from processes, trace them to their source, find out what caused them, and make corrections so that they do not recur. Production and materials

Table 4.2 Roles Played by Different Functions in Implementing Reliability Improvement Methodologies

Infrastructure (leadership)	1. Provide leadership and commitment to quality
	2. Find ways to measure quality
	3. Set goals and create incentives
	4. Solicit input from employees
	5. Encourage cooperation among functions
Production	1. Shorten production runs
	2. Trace defects back to the source
Marketing	1. Focus on the customer
	2. Provide customers' feedback on quality
Materials management	1. Rationalize suppliers
	2. Help suppliers implement quality-improvement methodologies
	3. Trace defects back to suppliers
R&D	1. Design products that are easy to manufacture
Information systems	1. Use information systems to monitor defect rates
Human resources	1. Institute quality-improvement training programs
	2. Identify and train "black belts"
	3. Organize employees into quality teams

management typically have primary responsibility for this task. To uncover defects, quality-improvement methodologies rely upon the use of statistical procedures to pinpoint variations in the quality of goods or services. Once variations have been identified, they must be traced to their source and eliminated.

One technique that greatly helps in tracing defects to their source is reducing lot sizes for manufactured products. With short production runs, defects show up immediately. Consequently, they can be quickly traced to the source, and the problem can be addressed. Reducing lot sizes also means that when defective products are produced, their number will not be large, thus decreasing waste. Flexible manufacturing techniques can be used to reduce lot sizes without raising costs. JIT inventory systems also play a part. Under a JIT system, defective parts enter the manufacturing process immediately; they are not warehoused for several months before use. Hence, defective inputs can be quickly spotted. The problem can then be traced to the supply source and corrected before more defective parts are produced. Under a more traditional system, the practice of warehousing parts for months before they are used may mean that large numbers of defects are produced by a supplier before they enter the production process.

Fourth, another key to any quality-improvement program is to create a metric that can be used to measure quality. In manufacturing companies, quality can be measured by criteria such as defects per million parts. In service companies, with a little creativity, suitable metrics can be devised. For example, one of the metrics Florida Power & Light uses to measure quality is meter-reading errors per month.

Fifth, once a metric has been devised, the next step is to set a challenging quality goal and create incentives for reaching it. Under Six Sigma programs, the goal is 3.4 defects per million units. One way of creating incentives to attain such a goal is to link rewards, like bonus pay and promotional opportunities, to the goal.

Sixth, shop floor employees can be a major source of ideas for improving product quality, so their participation needs to be incorporated into a quality-improvement program.

Seventh, a major source of poor-quality finished goods is poor-quality component parts. To decrease product defects, a company must work with its suppliers to improve the quality of the parts they supply.

Eighth, the more assembly steps a product requires, the more opportunities there are for making mistakes. Thus, designing products with fewer parts is often a major component of any quality-improvement program.

Finally, implementing quality-improvement methodologies requires organization-wide commitment and substantial cooperation among functions. R&D must cooperate with production to design products that are easy to manufacture; marketing must cooperate with production and R&D so that customer problems identified by marketing can be acted on; human resource management has to cooperate with all the other functions of the company to devise suitable quality-training programs; and so on.

Improving Quality as Excellence

As we stated in Chapter 3, a product is a bundle of different attributes, and reliability is just one of them, albeit an important one. Products can also be *differentiated* by attributes that collectively define product excellence. These attributes include the form, features, performance, durability, and styling of a product. In addition, a company can create quality as excellence by emphasizing attributes of the service associated with the product, such as ordering ease, prompt delivery, easy installation, the availability of customer training and consulting, and maintenance services. Dell, for example, differentiates itself on ease of ordering (via the Web), prompt delivery, easy installation, and the ready availability of customer support and maintenance services. Differentiation can also be based on the attributes of the people in the company whom customers interact with when making a product purchase, such as their competence, courtesy, credibility, responsiveness, and communication. Singapore Airlines, for example, enjoys an excellent reputation for quality service, largely because passengers perceive their flight attendants as competent, courteous, and responsive to their needs. Thus, we can talk about the product attributes, the service attributes, and the personnel attributes associated with a company's product offering (see Table 4.3).

For a product to be regarded as high in the excellence dimension, a company's product offering must be seen as superior to that of its rivals. Achieving a perception of high quality on any of these attributes requires specific actions by managers. First, it is important for managers to collect marketing intelligence indicating which of these attributes are most important to customers. For example, consumers of personal computers may place a low weight on durability because they expect their PCs to be made obsolete by technological advances within three years, but they may place a high weight on features and performance. Similarly, ease of ordering and timely delivery may be very important attributes for customers of online booksellers (as they indeed are for customers of amazon.com), whereas customer training and consulting may be very important attributes for customers who purchase complex business-to-business software to manage their relationships with suppliers.

Second, once the company has identified the attributes that are important to customers, it needs to design its products, and the associated services, so that those attributes are embodied in the product, and it needs to make sure that personnel in the company are appropriately trained so that the correct attributes are emphasized. This requires close coordination between marketing and product development (the topic of the next section) and the involvement of the human resource management function in employee selection and training.

Third, the company must decide which of the significant attributes to promote and how best to position them in the minds of consumers, that is, how to tailor the marketing message so that it creates a consistent image in the minds of customers.[32]

Table 4.3 Attributes Associated with a Product Offering

Product Attributes	Service Attributes	Associated Personnel Attributes
Form	Ordering ease	Competence
Features	Delivery	Courtesy
Performance	Installation	Credibility
Durability	Customer training	Reliability
Reliability	Customer consulting	Responsiveness
Style	Maintenance and repair	Communication

At this point, it is important to recognize that although a product might be differentiated on the basis of six attributes, covering all of those attributes in the company's communication messages may lead to an unfocused message. Many marketing experts advocate promoting only one or two central attributes to customers. For example, Volvo consistently emphasizes the safety and durability of its vehicles in all marketing messages, creating the perception in the minds of consumers (backed by product design) that Volvo cars are safe and durable. Volvo cars are also very reliable and have high performance, but the company does not emphasize these attributes in its marketing messages. In contrast, Porsche emphasizes performance and styling in all of its marketing messages; thus, a Porsche is positioned differently in the minds of consumers than a Volvo is. Both are regarded as high-quality products because both have superior attributes, but the attributes that the two companies have chosen to emphasize are very different. They are differentiated from the average car in different ways.

Finally, it must be recognized that competition does not stand still, but instead produces continual improvement in product attributes and often the development of new-product attributes. This is obvious in fast-moving high-tech industries where product features that were considered leading edge just a few years ago are now obsolete, but the same process is also at work in more stable industries. For example, the rapid diffusion of microwave ovens during the 1980s required food companies to build new attributes into their frozen food products: they had to maintain their texture and consistency while cooked in microwaves. A product could not be considered high quality unless it could do that. This speaks to the importance of having a strong R&D function in the company that can work with marketing and manufacturing to continually upgrade the quality of the attributes that are designed into the company's product offerings. Exactly how to achieve this is covered in the next section.

ACHIEVING SUPERIOR INNOVATION

In many ways, innovation is the most important source of competitive advantage. This is because innovation can result in new products that better satisfy customer needs, can improve the quality (attributes) of existing products, or can reduce the costs of making products that customers want. The ability to develop innovative new products or processes gives a company a major competitive advantage that allows it to (1) *differentiate* its products and charge a premium price, and/or (2) *lower its cost structure* below that of its rivals. Competitors, however, attempt to imitate successful innovations and often succeed. Therefore, maintaining a competitive advantage requires a continuing commitment to innovation.

Successful new product launches are major drivers of superior profitability. Robert Cooper looked at more than 200 new product introductions and found that of those classified as successes, some 50% achieve a return on investment in excess of 33%; half have a payback period of two years or less; and half achieve a market share in excess of 35%.[33] Many companies have established a track record for successful innovation. Among them Sony, whose successes include the Walkman, the CD, and the PlayStation; Nokia, which has been a leader in the development of wireless phones; Pfizer, a drug company that during the 1990s and early 2000s produced eight blockbuster new drugs; 3M, which has applied its core competency in tapes and adhesives to developing a wide range of new products; Intel, which has consistently managed to lead in the development of innovative new microprocessors to run personal computers; and Cisco Systems, whose innovations helped to pave the way for the rapid growth of the Internet.

The High Failure Rate of Innovation

Although promoting innovation can be a source of competitive advantage, the failure rate of innovative new products is high. Research evidence suggests that only 10% to 20% of major R&D projects give rise to a commercial products.[34] Well-publicized product failures include Apple's Newton, a personal digital assistant, Sony's Betamax format in the video player and recorder market, and Sega's Dreamcast videogame console. Although many reasons have been advanced to explain why so many new products fail to generate an economic return, five explanations for failure appear on most lists.[35]

First, many new products fail because the demand for innovations is inherently uncertain. It impossible to know prior to market introduction whether the new product has tapped an unmet customer need, and if there is sufficient market demand to justify making the product. Although good market research can reduce the uncertainty about likely future demand for a new technology, it cannot be eradicated, so a certain failure rate is to be expected.

Second, new products often fail because the technology is poorly commercialized. This occurs when there is definite customer demand for a new product, but the product is not well adapted to customer needs because of factors such as poor design and poor quality. For instance, the failure of Apple to establish a market for the Newton, a handheld personal digital system that Apple introduced in the 1990s can be traced to poor commercialization of a potentially attractive technology. Apple predicted a $1 billion market for the Newton, but sales failed to materialize when it became clear that the Newton's handwriting software, an attribute that Apple chose to emphasize in its marketing promotions, could not adequately recognize messages written on the Newton's message pad.

Third, new products may fail because of poor positioning strategy. **Positioning strategy** is the specific set of options a company adopts for a product on four main dimensions of marketing: price, distribution, promotion and advertising, and product features. Apart from poor product quality, another reason for the failure of the Newton was poor positioning strategy. The Newton was introduced at such a high initial price (close to $1,000) that there would probably have been few buyers even if the technology had been adequately commercialized.

Fourth, many new product introductions fail because companies often make the mistake of marketing a technology for which there is not enough demand. A company can get blinded by the wizardry of a new technology and fail to examine whether there is customer demand for the product.

Finally, companies fail when they are slow to get their products to market. The more time that elapses between initial development and final marketing—the slower the "cycle time"—the more likely it is that someone else will beat the company to market and gain a first-mover advantage.[36] In the car industry, GM has suffered from being a slow innovator. Its product development cycle has been about five years, compared with two to three years at Honda, Toyota, and Mazda and three to four years at Ford. Because they are based on five-year-old technology and design concepts, GM cars are already out of date when they reach the market.

Reducing Innovation Failures

One of the most important things that managers can do to reduce the high failure rate associated with innovation is to make sure that there is tight integration between R&D, production, and marketing.[37] Tight cross-functional integration can help a company to ensure that:

1. Product development projects are driven by customer needs.
2. New products are designed for ease of manufacture.
3. Development costs are kept in check.
4. Time to market is minimized.
5. Close integration between R&D and marketing is achieved to ensure that product development projects are driven by the needs of customers.

A company's customers can be one of its primary sources of new product ideas. The identification of customer needs, and particularly unmet needs, can set the context within which successful product innovation takes place. As the point of contact with customers, the marketing function can provide valuable information. Moreover, integrating R&D and marketing is crucial if a new product is to be properly commercialized. Otherwise, a company runs the risk of developing products for which there is little or no demand.

Integration between R&D and production can help a company ensure that products are designed with manufacturing requirements in mind. Design for manufacturing lowers manufacturing costs and leaves less room for mistakes, which can lower costs and increase product quality. Integrating R&D and production can help lower development costs and speed products to market. If a new product is not designed with manufacturing capabilities in mind, it may prove too difficult to build, given existing manufacturing technology. In that case, the product will have to be redesigned, and both overall development costs and time to market may increase significantly. Making design changes during product planning can increase overall development costs by 50% and add 25% to the time it takes to bring the product to market.[38]

One of the best ways to achieve cross-functional integration is to establish cross-functional product development teams, composed of representatives from R&D, marketing, and production. The objective of a team should be to take a product development project from the initial concept development to market introduction. A number of attributes seem to be important for a product development team to function effectively and meet all its development milestones.[39]

First, a **heavyweight project manager**—one who has high status within the organization and the power and authority required to get the financial and human resources that the team needs to succeed—should lead the team and be dedicated primarily, if not entirely, to the project. The leader should believe in the project (a champion) and be skilled at integrating the perspectives of different functions and helping personnel from different functions work together for a common goal. The leader should also be able to act as an advocate of the team to senior management.

Second, the team should be composed of at least one member from each key function. The team members should have a number of attributes, including an ability to contribute functional expertise, high standing within their function, a willingness to share responsibility for team results, and an ability to put functional advocacy aside. It is generally preferable if core team members are 100% dedicated to the project for its duration. This makes sure that their focus is on the project, not on the ongoing work of their function.

Third, the team members should be physically co-located to create a sense of camaraderie and facilitate communication. Fourth, the team should have a clear plan and clear goals, particularly with regard to critical development milestones and development budgets. The team should have incentives to attain those goals; for example, pay bonuses when major development milestones are hit. Fifth, each team needs to develop its own processes for communication and conflict resolution. For example, one product development team at Quantum Corporation, a California-based manufacturer of disk drives for personal computers, instituted a rule that all major decisions would be made and conflicts resolved at meetings that were held every Monday afternoon. This simple rule helped the team to meet its development goals.[40]

Finally, there is good evidence that developing competencies in innovation requires managers to take proactive steps to learn from their experience with product development and incorporate the lessons from past successes and failures in future new product development processes.[41] This is easier said than done. To learn, managers need to undertake an objective postmortem of a product development project, identify key success factors and the root causes of failures, and allocate resources toward fixing failures. Leaders also need to admit their own failures if they are to encourage others to step up to the plate and identify what they did wrong. Strategy in Action 4.4 looks at how Corning learned from a prior mistake to develop a potentially promising new product.

The primary role that the various functions play in achieving superior innovation is summarized in Table 4.4. The table makes two matters clear. First, top management must bear primary responsibility for overseeing the whole development

Table 4.4 Functional Roles for Achieving Superior Innovation

Value Creation Function	Primary Roles
Infrastructure (leadership)	1. Manage overall project (i.e., manage the development function)
	2. Facilitate cross-functional cooperation
Production	1. Cooperate with R&D on designing products that are easy to manufacture
	2. Work with R&D to develop process innovations
Marketing	1. Provide market information to R&D
	2. Work with R&D to develop new products
Materials management	No primary responsibility
R&D	1. Develop new products and processes
	2. Cooperate with other functions, particularly marketing and manufacturing, in the development process
Information systems	1. Use information systems to coordinate cross-functional and cross-company product development work
Human resources	1. Hire talented scientists and engineers

4.4 *STRATEGY IN ACTION*

Corning: Learning from Innovation Failures

In 1998, Corning, then the world's largest supplier of fiber optic cable, decided to diversify into the development and manufacture of DNA microarrays (DNA chips). DNA chips are used to analyze the function of genes and are an important research tool in the drug development process. Corning tried to develop a DNA chip that could print all 28,000 human genes onto a set of slides. By 2000, Corning had invested more than $100 million in the project and its first chips were on the market, but the project was a failure; in 2001 it was pulled.

What went wrong? Corning was late to market—a critical mistake. The market was dominated by Affymetrix, which had been in the businesses since the early 1990s. By 2000, Affymetrix's DNA chips were the dominant design; researchers were familiar with them, they performed well, and few people were willing to switch to chips from unproven competitors. Corning was late because it adhered to its long-established innovation processes, which were not entirely appropriate in the biological sciences. In particular, Corning's own in-house experts in the physical sciences insisted on sticking to rigorous quality standards that customers and life scientists felt were higher than necessary. These quality standards proved to be very difficult to achieve. As a result, the product launch was delayed, giving Affymetrix time

to consolidate its hold on the market. Moreover, Corning failed to give prototypes of its chips to potential customers, and, consequently, it missed incorporating some crucial features that customers wanted.

After reviewing this failure, Corning decided that going forward, it needed to bring customers into the development process earlier; it needed to hire more outside experts if it was diversifying into an area where it lacked competencies to give those experts a larger say in the development process.

The project was not a total failure, however, for through it Corning discovered a vibrant and growing market: the market for drug discovery. By combining what it had learned about drug discovery with another failed businesses, photonics, which manipulates data using light waves, Corning created a new product called Epic. Epic is a revolutionary technology for drug testing that uses light waves instead of fluorescent dyes (the standard industry practice). Epic promises to accelerate the process of testing potential drugs and saving pharmaceutical companies valuable R&D money. Unlike its DNA microarray project, Corning had 18 pharmaceutical companies test Epic before development was finalized. Corning used this feedback to refine Epic. The company believes that ultimately Epic could generate $500 million annually.

Sources: V. Govindarajan and C. Trimble, "How Forgetting Leads to Innovation," *Chief Executive*, March 2006, 46–50. J. McGregor, "How Failure Breeds Success," *Business Week*, July 10, 2006, 42–52.

process. This entails both managing the development funnel and facilitating cooperation among the functions. Second, the effectiveness of R&D in developing new products and processes depends on its ability to cooperate with marketing and production.

ACHIEVING SUPERIOR RESPONSIVENESS TO CUSTOMERS

To achieve superior responsiveness to customers, a company must give customers what they want, when they want it, and at a price they are willing to pay—so long as the company's long-term profitability is not compromised in the process. Customer responsiveness is an important differentiating attribute that can help to build brand loyalty. Strong product differentiation and brand loyalty give a company more pricing options; the company can charge a premium price for its products or keep prices low to sell more goods and services to customers. Either way, the company that is more responsive to its customers' needs than its rivals will have a competitive advantage, all else being equal.

Achieving superior responsiveness to customers means giving customers value for money. Steps taken to improve the efficiency of a company's production process and the quality of its products should be consistent with this aim. In addition, giving customers what they want may require the development of new products with new features. In other words, achieving superior efficiency, quality, and innovation are all part of achieving superior responsiveness to customers. There are two other prerequisites for attaining this goal. First, a company has to develop competency in listening to and focusing on its customers and in investigating and identifying their needs. Second, it constantly needs to seek better ways to satisfy those needs.

Focusing on the Customer

A company cannot be responsive to its customers' needs unless it knows what those needs are. Thus, the first step to building superior responsiveness to customers is to motivate the whole company to focus on the customer. The means to this end are demonstrating leadership, shaping employee attitudes, and using mechanisms for bringing customers into the company.

Demonstrating Leadership   Customer focus must start at the top of the organization. A commitment to superior responsiveness to customers brings attitudinal changes throughout a company that ultimately can be built only through strong leadership. A mission statement that puts customers first is one way to send a clear message to employees about the desired focus. Another avenue is top management's own actions. For example, Tom Monaghan, the founder of Domino's Pizza, stayed close to the customers by visiting as many stores as possible every week, running some deliveries himself, insisting that other top managers do the same, and eating Domino's pizza regularly.[42]

Shaping Employee Attitudes   Leadership alone is not enough to attain a superior customer focus. All employees must see the customer as the focus of their activity and be trained to focus on the customer, whether their function is marketing, manufacturing, R&D, or accounting. The objective should be to make employees think of themselves as customers—to put themselves in customers' shoes. At that point, employees will be better able to identify ways to improve the quality of a customer's experience with the company.

To reinforce this mindset, incentive systems within the company should reward employees for satisfying customers. For example, senior managers at the Four Seasons hotel chain, who pride themselves on their customer focus, like to tell the story of Roy Dyment, a doorman in Toronto who neglected to load a departing guest's briefcase into his taxi. The doorman called the guest, a lawyer, in Washington DC, who desperately needed the briefcase for a morning meeting. Dyment hopped on a plane to Washington and returned it—without first securing approval from his boss. Far from punishing Dyment for making a mistake and not checking with management before going to Washington, the Four Seasons responded by naming Dyment

Employee of the Year.[43] This action sent a powerful message to Four Seasons employees about the importance of satisfying customer needs.

Bringing Customers into the Company "Know thy customer" is one of the keys to achieving superior responsiveness to customers. Knowing the customer not only requires that employees think like customers themselves; it also demands that they listen to what their customers have to say and, as much as possible, bring them into the company. Although this may not involve physically bringing customers into the company, it does mean bringing in customers' opinions by soliciting feedback on the company's goods and services and by building information systems that communicate the feedback to the relevant people.

For example, consider direct-selling clothing retailer Lands' End. Through its catalog, the Internet, and customer service telephone operators, Lands' End actively solicits comments from its customers about the quality of its clothing and the kind of merchandise they want it to supply. Indeed, it was customers' insistence that initially prompted the company to move into the clothing segment. Lands' End used to supply equipment for sailboats through mail-order catalogs. However, it received so many requests from customers to include outdoor clothing in its offerings that it responded by expanding the catalog to fill this need. Soon clothing became the main business, and Lands' End dropped the sailboat equipment. Today, the company still pays close attention to customer requests. Every month, a computer printout of customer requests and comments is given to managers. This feedback helps the company to fine-tune the merchandise it sells. Indeed, frequently new lines of merchandise are introduced in response to customer requests.[44]

Satisfying Customer Needs

Once a focus on the customer is an integral part of the company, the next requirement is to satisfy the customer needs that have been identified. As already noted, efficiency, quality, and innovation are crucial competencies that help a company satisfy customer needs. Beyond that, companies can provide a higher level of satisfaction if they differentiate their products by (1) customizing them, where possible, to the requirements of individual customers and (2) reducing the time it takes to respond to or satisfy customer needs.

Customization Customization is varying the features of a good or service to tailor it to the unique needs or tastes of groups of customers or, in the extreme case, individual customers. Although extensive customization can raise costs, the development of flexible manufacturing technologies has made it possible to customize products to a much greater extent than was feasible 10 to 15 years ago without experiencing a prohibitive rise in cost structure (particularly when flexible manufacturing technologies are linked with Web-based information systems). For example, online retailers such as amazon.com have used Web-based technologies to develop a homepage customized for each individual user. When a customer accesses amazon.com, he or she is offered a list of recommendations for books or music to purchase based on an analysis of prior buying history, a powerful competency that gives amazon.com a competitive advantage.

The trend toward customization has fragmented many markets, particularly customer markets, into ever smaller niches. An example of this fragmentation occurred in Japan in the early 1980s when Honda dominated the motorcycle market there. Second-place Yamaha decided to go after Honda's lead. It announced the opening of a new factory that, when operating at full capacity, would make Yamaha the world's largest manufacturer of motorcycles. Honda responded by proliferating its product line and stepping up its rate of new-product introduction. At the start of what became known as the "motorcycle wars," Honda had 60 motorcycles in its product line. Over the next 18 months, it rapidly increased its range to 113 models, customizing them to ever smaller niches. Honda was able to accomplish this without bearing a prohibitive cost penalty because it has a competency in flexible manufacturing. The flood of Honda's customized models pushed Yamaha out of much of the market, effectively stalling its bid to overtake Honda.[45]

Response Time Giving customers what they want when they want it requires speed of response to customer demands. To gain a competitive advantage, a company must often respond to customer demands very quickly, whether the transaction is a furniture manufacturer's delivery of a product once it has been ordered, a bank's processing of a loan application, an automobile manufacturer's delivery of a spare part for a car that broke down, or the wait in a supermarket checkout line. We live in a fast-paced society, where time is a valuable commodity. Companies that can satisfy customer demands for rapid response build brand loyalty, differentiate their products, and can charge higher prices for them.

Increased speed often lets a company choose a premium pricing option, as the mail delivery industry illustrates. The air express niche of the mail delivery industry is based on the notion that customers are often willing to pay considerably more for overnight Express Mail as opposed to regular mail. Another example of the value of rapid response is Caterpillar, the manufacturer of heavy earth-moving equipment, who can get a spare part to any point in the world within 24 hours. Downtime for heavy construction equipment is very costly, so Caterpillar's ability to respond quickly in the event of equipment malfunction is of prime importance to its customers. As a result, many of them have remained loyal to Caterpillar despite the aggressive low-price competition from Komatsu of Japan.

In general, reducing response time requires (1) a marketing function that can quickly communicate customer requests to production; (2) production and materials-management functions that can quickly adjust production schedules in response to unanticipated customer demands; and (3) information systems that can help production and marketing in this process.

Table 4.5 summarizes the steps different functions must take if a company is to achieve superior responsiveness to customers. Although marketing plays the critical role in helping a company attain this goal, primarily because it represents the point of contact with the customer, Table 4.5 shows that the other functions also have major roles. Moreover, like achieving superior efficiency, quality, and innovation, achieving superior responsiveness to customers requires top management to lead in building a customer orientation within the company.

Table 4.5 Primary Roles of Different Functions in Achieving Superior Responsiveness to Customers

Value Creation Function	Primary Roles
Infrastructure (leadership)	• Through leadership by example, build a company-wide commitment to responsiveness to customers
Production	• Achieve customization through implementation of flexible manufacturing • Achieve rapid response through flexible manufacturing
Marketing	• Know the customer • Communicate customer feedback to appropriate functions
Materials management	• Develop logistics systems capable of responding quickly to unanticipated customer demands (JIT)
R&D	• Bring customers into the product development process
Information systems	• Use Web-based information systems to increase responsiveness to customers
Human resources	• Develop training programs that get employees to think like customers themselves

SUMMARY OF CHAPTER

1. A company can increase efficiency through a number of steps: exploiting economies of scale and learning effects; adopting flexible manufacturing technologies; reducing customer defection rates; implementing JIT systems; getting the R&D function to design products that are easy to manufacture; upgrading the skills of employees through training; introducing self-managing teams; linking pay to performance; building a company-wide commitment to efficiency through strong leadership; and designing structures that facilitate cooperation among different functions in pursuit of efficiency goals.

2. Superior quality can help a company lower its costs, differentiate its product, and charge a premium price.

3. Achieving superior quality demands an organization-wide commitment to quality and a clear focus on the customer. It also requires metrics to measure quality goals and incentives that emphasize quality, input from employees regarding ways in which quality can be improved, a methodology for tracing defects to their source and correcting the problems that produce them, a rationalization of the company's supply base, cooperation with the suppliers that remain to implement TQM programs, products that are designed for ease of manufacturing, and substantial cooperation among functions.

4. The failure rate of new-product introductions is high because of factors such as uncertainty, poor commercialization, poor positioning strategy, slow cycle time, and technological myopia.

5. To achieve superior innovation, a company must build skills in basic and applied research; design good processes for managing development projects; and achieve close integration between the different functions of the company, primarily through the adoption of cross-functional product development teams and partly parallel development processes.

6. To achieve superior responsiveness to customers often requires that the company achieve superior efficiency, quality, and innovation.

7. To achieve superior responsiveness to customers, a company needs to give customers what they want when they want it. It must ensure a strong customer focus, which can be attained by emphasizing customer focus through leadership; training employees to think like customers; bringing customers into the company through superior market research; customizing products to the unique needs of individual customers or customer groups; and responding quickly to customer demands.

DISCUSSION QUESTIONS

1. In what sense might innovation be called the single most important building block of competitive advantage?

2. In the long run, will adoption of Six Sigma quality-improvement processes give a company a competitive advantage or will it be required just to achieve parity with competitors?

3. How are the four generic building blocks of competitive advantage related to each other?

CLOSING CASE

Boosting Efficiency at Matsushita

In 2000, when Kunio Nakamura became CEO of the venerable Japanese electronics giant, Matsushita, it was a company in deep trouble. Earnings had been going south for years, and the company's market capitalization had shrunk to less than half of that of long-time rival Sony. Employees were frustrated and moral was poor. By the time he retired in June 2006, Matsushita was delivering its best financial performance in more than a decade. After losing $3.7 billion in 2002, in 2006 the company registered profits of $1.37 billion. Moreover, earnings grew 20% to $1.7 billion in 2007.

For a long time, the policy at Matsushita had been to allow different divisions to develop identical products, although at the end of the day typically only one division was granted the right to market a product. Early in his tenure, Nakamura put an end to this internal competition, believing that it would produce efficiency gains. He also effectively ended the long-standing practice at Matsushita of lifetime employment. He slashed the domestic workforce by 19% and reduced the number of layers in the management hierarchy. He pushed factory managers to do everything possible to raise productivity, giving them challenging productivity goals, and tying bonuses to the attainment of those goals.

Matsushita's factory in Saga, Japan, exemplifies the obsession with productivity improvements. Employees at the factory, which makes cordless phones, faxes, and security cameras, doubled productivity between 2000 and 2004 by introducing robots into the assembly line, but factory managers were not happy. An analysis of flow in the production system showed that bottlenecks on the assembly line meant that robots sat idle for longer than they were working. So the plant's managers ripped out the assembly line conveyer belts and replaced them with clusters of robots grouped into cells. The cells allowed them to double up on slower robots to make the entire manufacturing process run more smoothly. Then they developed software to synchronize production so that each robot jumped into action as soon as the previous step was completed. If one robot broke down, the workflow could be shifted to another to do the same job.

The results were impressive. The time that it took to build products was drastically reduced. It formerly took two-and-one-half days into a production run before the first finished products came off the assembly line; now it takes as little as 40 minutes. Phones, for example, can now be assembled in one-third of the time, doubling weekly output from the same plant with the same number of employees. Shorter cycle times enabled the factory to slash inventories. Work in progress, such as partly finished products, along with components such as chipsets, keypads, and circuit boards now spent far less time in the factory.

The Saga factory is known as a "mother plant" within Matsushita. Once process improvements have been refined at a mother plant, they have to be transferred to other plants within the group as quickly as possible. There are six other plants in the Saga group in China, Malaysia, Mexico, and Britain. Most were able to quickly copy what was done at Saga and saw similar cuts in inventory and boosts in productivity.

Despite the faster pace of work, the factory employees paid close attention to product quality. The short cycle times helped employees to identify the source of defective products and quickly fix any errors that led to quality problems. Consequently, at less than 1% of output, by 2006 defect rates were at an all time low in every factory. The reduction in waste further boosted productivity and helped the company to strengthen its reputation for producing high-quality merchandise.[46]

Case Discussion Questions

1. What are the benefits of eliminating the long-standing policy at Matsushita that different divisions should be allowed to develop the same basic product? Are there any potential drawbacks of such a policy change?

2. What do you think were the benefits of lifetime employment at Matsushita? Why then did Nakamura effectively end this practice? What benefits did he realize for Matsushita by doing so?

3. What does the example of the Saga factory at Matsushita tell you about the benefits of optimizing workflow for (a) work in progress, (b) the productivity of both employees, and (c) the capital invested in plant and equipment?

4. What are the benefits to Matsushita of a reduction in defect rates?

5. What does the Matsushita example tell you about the importance of functional-level strategies for competitive advantage?

6. Matsushita is a manufacturing company. Do you think that the principles discussed in the case are as important for a service enterprise?

STRATEGY AT THE BUSINESS LEVEL

L E A R N I N G   O B J E C T I V E S

After reading this chapter, you should be able to

- Explain why a company must define its business and how managers do this through their choices about which customer groups, customer needs, and distinctive competencies to pursue
- Define competitive positioning and explain the tradeoffs between differentiation, cost, and pricing options
- Identify the choices managers make to pursue a business model based on some combination of

- the main generic business-level strategies: cost leadership, differentiation, and focus
- Explain why each business model allows a company to outperform its rivals, reach the value creation frontier, and obtain above average profitability
- Discuss why some companies can successfully make the competitive positioning decisions that allow them to sustain their competitive advantage over time while others cannot

---

Sony's Failure in Competitive Positioning

Just a few years ago, engineers at Sony turned out an average of four ideas for new products every day, and the company was the innovation leader in the consumer electronics industry.

Why? It had a policy of "self-promotion" that allowed Sony engineers to seek out projects anywhere in the company they thought they could contribute to new product innovation. Sony had hundreds of new product development teams in which its engineers churned out innovative electronics such as the Sony PlayStation, Trinitron TVs, and Walkman cassette players that allowed it to differentiate its products from competitors and charge customers premium prices.[1] By the early 2000s, Sony was the most profitable company in the electronics industry, but in 2009 it warned that instead of the $2.2 billion in profits, it expected to earn it now forecast a $2.9 billion operating loss—its first in 14 years.[2]

What went wrong? Sony's Welsh-born CEO Howard Stringer who had been hired in 2006 to develop a new business model that would allow it to maintain its leading industry position had no doubt that the company's problems were due to poor competitive positioning. On the one hand, Sony had failed to develop strategies to deal with competitors that were developing new and improved technologies and sustain its differentiated position. On the other hand, it had failed to develop strategies to deal with increasing low-cost competitors from Korea and Taiwan that were offering electronic products at rock-bottom prices. Stringer claimed that despite the fact that Sony had an "unbeatable" combination of top-notch consumer electronic products, and entertainment content such as blockbuster movies, TV programs, and music, it had not managed to fuse them together into a digital package that could be easily delivered to customers online.[3]

On the differentiation side, Sony's reputation as the most innovative company was challenged by the rapid advances of other electronics and computer companies. Companies like Samsung, Visio, and Sharp had been much faster than Sony in developing the flat screen LCD technology that had made its Trinitron TVs obsolete. Apple had revolutionized music hardware and software with its iPod and iTunes platform that had made Sony's Walkman obsolete.[4] And, because Sony made more than 55% of its profits from its PlayStation business group, the performance of this division had been badly affected by the increasing popularity of Nintendo's pioneering Wii, with its innovative "interactive" features, and from Microsoft's Xbox, with its sophisticated Internet-linked consol and services. Indeed, by 2009 Nintendo had sold 50 million Wiis worldwide and had become the most profitable consumer electronics company.

Why was Sony suffering from these failures in product positioning, despite the fact that it still had thousands of talented engineers continually working on developing its distinctive competence in innovation? Stringer said frankly that the problem was because of the intense competition between Sony's different product groups that had developed over time; groups were not sharing knowledge; they were hoarding it, and Sony's position as the industry leader suffered as a result. "Too often we have been late to market with new products and this practice cannot be tolerated going forward.[5]" Although he had made attempts to change the way Sony operated, in 2009, Stringer announced that he was changing Sony's traditional product-group decision-making to one based on speedier, top-down decision-making. He removed Ryoji Chubachi, Sony's powerful vice chairman and director of engineering, who he blamed for the slow pace of change. Stringer's goal was to force a change in Sony's competitive positioning by encouraging engineers to think about how consumers will use a new product before they focus on the product's technical capabilities when deciding which new products to invest in—to force a customer-oriented, not a product-oriented, business definition on the company.

On the cost side, however, Sony engineers' focus on technical innovation also had devastating effects on its product positioning. Stringer announced that Sony's practice of allowing its product divisions and individual engineers to champion whatever products they wished might increase innovation, but it had also resulted in a bloated cost structure that was draining the company's profits. Not only was the competition for resources between divisions for funds increasing costs, it had also led managers to ignore the need to manage the supply chain efficiently. For example, Sony was still making many components that other companies had outsourced to efficient suppliers long ago. Sony was now behind its competitors because of its higher cost structure, and Stringer changed the company's product positioning in major ways. To reduce costs, Stringer announced thousands of layoffs and p[...] to close 10 of its 57 factories w[...] and he ordered divisions to[...]

non-vital components. His top management team was instructed to conduct a top-to-bottom review of each of its business groups, from flat screen TVs to video games, to find ways to reduce operating costs and make Sony's value-creation chain run more efficiently. On the day he announced the new loss forecast, he also announced that he was doubling Sony's cost-cutting target to $2.8 billion by 2010.

Overview

As the Opening Case suggests, even an industry leader like Sony can experience major problems in managing its business model successfully over time to maintain its competitive advantage. This chapter examines how a company selects, pursues, and maintains a business model that will allow it to compete effectively in an industry and increase its profitability over time. A successful business model results from business-level strategies that create a competitive advantage over rivals and achieve superior performance in an industry.

In Chapter 2, we examined how the competitive forces at work inside an industry affect its profitability. As industry forces change, so they change the profitability of an industry and, thus, the profitability of any particular business model. Industry analysis is vital in formulating a successful business model because it determines (1) how existing companies will decide to change their business-level strategies to improve the performance of their business model over time; (2) whether established companies outside an industry may decide to create a business model to enter it; and (3) whether entrepreneurs can devise a business model that will allow them to compete successfully against existing companies in an industry.

In Chapter 3, we examined how competitive advantage depends on a company developing a business model that allows it to achieve superior efficiency, quality, innovation, and customer responsiveness—the building blocks of competitive advantage. In Chapter 4, we discussed how every function must develop the distinctive competencies that allow a company to implement a business model that will lead to superior performance and competitive advantage in an industry.

In this chapter, we examine the competitive decisions involved in creating a business model that will attract and retain customers and continue to do so over time so that a company enjoys growing profitability. To create a successful business model, strategic managers must (1) formulate business-level strategies that will allow a company to attract customers away from other companies in the industry (its competitors) and (2) implement those business-level strategies, which also involves the use of functional-level strategies to increase responsiveness to customers, efficiency, innovation, and quality. As the Opening Case suggests, Sony failed to do this, and, by 2009, it was unprofitable as a result.

By the end of this chapter, you will be able to distinguish between the principal generic business models and business-level strategies that a company uses to obtain a competitive advantage over its rivals. You will also understand why, and under what circumstances, strategic leaders of companies like Sony, Apple, Nintendo, and Microsoft change their company's strategies over time to pursue different kinds of business models to try to increase their competitive advantage over industry rivals.

COMPETITIVE POSITIONING AND THE BUSINESS MODEL

To create a successful business model, managers must choose a set of business-level strategies that work together to give a company a competitive advantage over its rivals; that is, they must optimize **competitive positioning**. As we noted in Chapter 1, to craft a successful business model, a company must first define its business, which entails decisions about (1) customer needs, or what is to be satisfied; (2) customer groups, or who is to be satisfied; and (3) distinctive competencies, or how customer needs are to be satisfied.[6] The decisions managers make about these three issues determine which set of strategies they formulate and implement to put a company's business model into action and create value for customers. Consequently, we need to examine the principal choices facing managers as they make these three decisions.

Formulating the Business Model: Customer Needs and Product Differentiation

Customer needs are desires, wants, or cravings that can be satisfied by means of the attributes or characteristics of a product (a good or service). For example, a person's craving for something sweet can be satisfied by a box of Godiva chocolates, a carton of Ben & Jerry's ice cream, a Snickers bar, or a spoonful of sugar. Two factors determine which product a customer chooses to satisfy these needs: (1) the way a product is differentiated from other products of its type so that it appeals to customers and (2) the price of the product. All companies must differentiate their products to a certain degree to attract customers. Some companies, however, decide to offer customers low-priced products and do not engage in much product differentiation. Companies that seek to create something *unique* about their product differentiate their products to a much greater degree than others so that they satisfy customers' needs in ways other products cannot.

   Product differentiation is the process of designing products to satisfy customers' needs. A company obtains a competitive advantage when it creates, makes, and sells a product in a way that better satisfies customer needs than its rivals do. Then the four building blocks of competitive advantage come into play, for a company's decision to pursue one or more of these building blocks determine its approach to product differentiation. If managers devise strategies to differentiate a product by innovation, excellent quality, or responsiveness to customers, they are choosing a business model based on offering customers *differentiated products*. On the other hand, if managers base their business model on finding ways to increase efficiency and reliability to reduce costs, they are choosing a business model based on offering customers *low-priced products*.

   Creating unique or distinctive products can be achieved in countless different ways, which explains why there are usually many different companies competing in an industry. Distinctiveness obtained from the physical characteristics of a product commonly results from pursuing innovation or quality, such as when a company focuses on developing state-of-the-art car safety systems or on engineering a sports utility vehicle (SUV) to give it sports car-like handling, something Porsche and BMW strive to achieve. Similarly, companies might try to design their cars with features such as butter-soft, hand-sewn leather interiors, fine wood fittings, and sleek, exciting body styling to appeal to customers' psychological needs, such as a personal need for prestige and status or to declare a particular "lifestyle," something Mercedes-Benz and Lexus strive for.[7]

Differentiation has another important aspect. Companies that invest their resources to create something distinct or different about their products can often charge a higher or *premium* price for their product. For example, superb design or technical sophistication allows companies to charge more for their products because customers are willing to pay these higher prices. Porsche and Mercedes-Benz buyers pay a high premium price to enjoy their sophisticated vehicles, as do customers of Godiva chocolates, which retail for about $26 a pound—much more than, say, a box of Whitman's candies or a Hershey bar.

Consider the high-price segment of the car market, in which customers are willing to pay more than $35,000 to satisfy their needs for a "personal luxury vehicle." In this segment, Cadillac, Mercedes-Benz, Infiniti, BMW, Jaguar, Lexus, Lincoln, Audi, Volvo, Acura, and others are engaged in a continuing battle to design the "perfect" luxury vehicle—the one that best meets the needs of those who want such a vehicle. Over time, the companies that attract the most luxury car buyers—because they have designed the cars that possess the innovative features or excellent quality and reliability these customers desire the most—are the ones that achieve a sustained competitive advantage over rivals. For example, some customers value a sporty ride and performance handling; Mercedes-Benz and BMW, because of their cutting-edge technical design, can offer this driving experience better than any other carmaker. Toyota's Lexus division is well known for the smoothness and quietness of its cars and their exceptional reliability. Lexus cars consistently outrank all other cars in published reliability rankings, and this excellence appeals to a large group of customers who appreciate these qualities. Infinity's reputation for both sportiness and reliability has increased steadily in the 2000s as has its market share, and both Bentley and Rolls-Royce that produce prestige cars can sell all they can make. Other luxury carmakers have not fared so well. Cadillac, Lincoln, Audi, Acura, Saab, and Volvo have found it more difficult to differentiate their cars, which sometimes compare unfavorably to their rivals in terms of ride, comfort, safety, or reliability. Although these less successful companies still sell many cars, customers often find their needs better satisfied by the attributes and qualities of their rivals' cars. It is the latter that can sustain their competitive advantage over time. Even in the luxury car segment, however, carmakers must be concerned with efficiency because price affects a buying decision, even for highly differentiated products. Luxury carmakers compete to offer customers the car with the ride, performance, and features that provide them with the most value (satisfies their needs best) given the price of the car. Thus, Lexus cars are always several thousand dollars less than comparable cars, and Toyota can price these cars lower because of its low cost structure. For example, the Lexus LS460 at about $64,000 costs at least $20,000 less than the BMW 7 Series and Mercedes S Class, its closest rivals. Most customers are discriminating and match price to differentiation, even in the luxury car segment of the market, so BMW and Mercedes have to offer customers something that justifies their vehicles' higher prices.

At every price range in the car market—under $15,000, from $15,000 to $25,000, from $25,000 to $35,000, and the luxury segment above $35,000—many models of cars compete to attract customers. For each price range, a carmaker has to decide how best to differentiate a particular car model to suit the needs of customers in that price range. Typically, the more differentiated a product is, the more it will cost to design and produce, and so differentiation leads to a higher cost structure. Thus, if a carmaker is to stay within the $15,000 to $25,000 price range and yet design and produce a differentiated car with a competitive advantage that allows it to outperform its rivals in the same price range, its managers have to make difficult choices.

They have to forecast what features customers will most value; for example, they may decide to trade-off sporty styling to increase safety features so that the car will not cost too much to produce, which allows them to make a profit and still sell the car for less than $25,000.

In sum, in devising a business model, strategic managers are always constrained by the need to differentiate their products against the need to keep their cost structure under control so that they can offer the product at a **competitive price**—a price that offers customers as much or more value than the products of its rivals. Companies that have built a competitive advantage through innovation, quality, and reliability can differentiate their products more successfully than their rivals. In turn, because customers perceive there is more value in their products, these companies can charge a premium price, as Sony used to be able to do.

Formulating the Business Model: Customer Groups and Market Segmentation

The second main choice involved in formulating a successful business model is to decide which kind of product(s) to offer to which customer group(s). Customer groups are the sets of people who share a similar need for a particular product. Because a particular product usually satisfies several different kinds of desires and needs, many different customer groups normally exist in a market. In the car market, for example, some customers need basic transportation, some desire top-of-the-line luxury, and others want the thrill of driving a sports car; these are three of the customer groups in the car market.

In the athletic shoe market, the two main customer groups are those people who use them for sporting purposes and those who like to wear them because they are casual and comfortable. Within each customer group, there are often subgroups composed of people who have an even more specific need for a product. Inside the group of people who buy athletic shoes for sporting purposes, for example, are subgroups of people who buy shoes suited to a specific kind of activity, such as running, aerobics, walking, and soccer (see Figure 5.1).

A company searching for a successful business model must group customers according to the similarities or differences in their needs to discover what kinds of products to develop for different kinds of customers. The marketing function performs research to discover a group of customers' primary need for a product, how they will use it, and their income or buying power (to determine the balance between differentiation and price). Other important attributes of a customer group are then identified that more narrowly target their specific needs. Once a group of customers who share a similar or specific need for a product has been identified, this group is treated as a market segment. Companies then decide whether to make and sell a product designed to satisfy the specific needs of this customer segment.

Three Approaches to Market Segmentation   **Market segmentation** is the way a company decides to group customers, based on important differences in their needs or preferences, to gain a competitive advantage.[8] First, the company must segment the market according to how much customers are able and willing to pay for a particular product, such as the different price ranges for cars mentioned above. Once price has been taken into consideration, customers can be segmented according to the specific needs that are being satisfied by a particular product, such as the economy, luxury, or speed of cars mentioned earlier.

....

Figure 5.1   Identifying Customer Groups and Market Segments

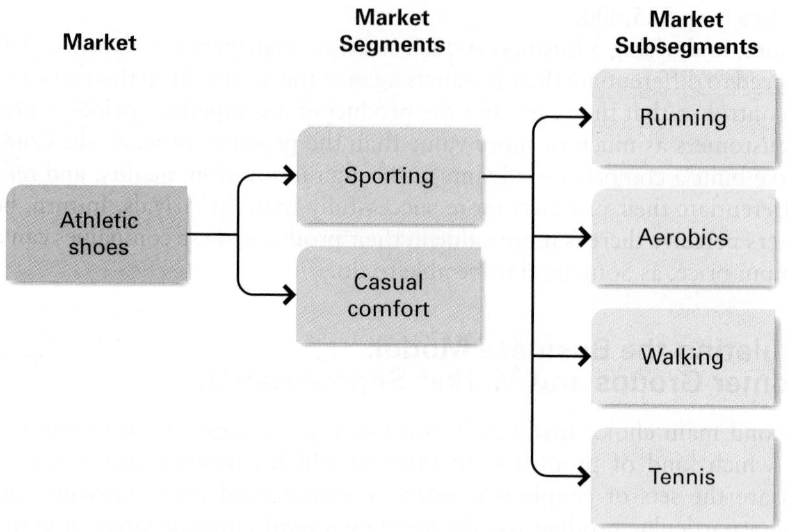

In crafting a business model, managers have to think strategically about which segments they are going to compete in and how they will differentiate their products for each segment. In other words, once market segments have been identified, a company has to decide how *responsive it should be to the needs of customers in the different segments* to obtain a competitive advantage. This decision determines a particular company's product range. There are three main approaches toward market segmentation in devising a business model (Figure 5.2):

1. First, a company might choose *not* to recognize that different market segments exist and make a product targeted at the average or typical customer. In this case, customer responsiveness is at a *minimum*, and competitive advantage is achieved through low price, not differentiation.
2. Second, a company can choose to recognize the differences between customer groups and make a product targeted toward most or all of the different market segments. In this case, customer responsiveness is *high* and products are being *customized* to meet the specific needs of customers in each group, so competitive advantage is obtained through differentiation, not low price.
3. Third, a company might choose to target just *one or two market segments* and devote its resources to developing products for customers in just these segments. In this case, it may be highly responsive to the needs of customers in only these segments, or it may offer a bare-bones product to undercut the prices charged by companies who do focus on differentiation. So, competitive advantage may be obtained through a focus on low price *or* differentiation.

Because a company's cost structure and operating costs increase when it makes a different product for each market segment rather than just one product for the whole market, why would a company devise a business model based on serving customers in multiple market segments? The answer is that although operating costs

....

Figure 5.2   Three Approaches to Market Segmentation

**No Market
Segmentation**
A product is targeted at
the "average customer."

**High Market
Segmentation**
A different product is offered
to each market segment.

**Focused Market
Segmentation**
A product is offered to one
or a few market segments.

increase, the decision to produce a range of products that are closely aligned with the needs of customers in different market segments attracts many more customers (because responsiveness to customers increases), and, therefore, sales revenues and profits increase. A car company that offers a wide range of cars customized to the needs of customers in different market segments increases the total number of cars it can sell. As long as a company's revenues increase faster than its operating costs as its product range expands, profitability increases.

This does *not* mean that all companies should decide to produce a wide range of products aimed at each market segment. Profitability increases to the degree that there are significant differences in customer needs for a product in a particular market or industry. In some industries, like cars, customer needs differ widely. There are considerable differences in buyers' primary needs for a car: income levels, lifestyles, ages, and so on. For this reason, major global carmakers broaden their product range and make vehicles to serve most market segments because this does increase profitability. A company that produces only a single model, compared to a company that produces 25 models, may therefore find itself at a serious competitive disadvantage.

On the other hand, in some markets customers have similar needs for a product, and so the relative price of competing products drives their buying choices. In this situation, a company that strives to gain a competitive advantage by using its resources to make and sell a single product as inexpensively as possible might be the most profitable. The average customer buys the product because it's "OK" and good "value for the money." This is the business model followed by companies that specialize in making a low-cost product, such as BIC, which makes low-cost razors and ballpoint pens, and Arm & Hammer, which makes baking soda. These are products that most people use in the same way. This is also the business model followed by companies like Walmart whose goal is to buy products from suppliers as cheaply as possible and then sell them to customers at the lowest possible prices. BIC and Walmart do not segment the market; they decide to serve the needs of customers who want to buy products as inexpensively as possible. Walmart promises everyday low prices and price rollbacks; BIC promises the lowest-priced razor blades that work acceptably.

The third approach to market segmentation is to target a product just at one or two market segments. To pursue this approach, a company must develop something very special or distinctive about its product to attract a large share of customers in those particular market segments. In the car market, for example, Rolls-Royce and Porsche target their products at specific market segments. Porsche, for example, targets its well-known sports cars at buyers in the high-priced sports car segment. In a similar way, specialty retailers compete for customers in a particular market segment, such as the segment composed of affluent people who can afford to buy expensive handmade clothing, or people who enjoy wearing "trendy" shoes or jeans. A retailer might also specialize in a particular style of clothing, such as western wear, beachwear, or accessories. In many markets, these are enormous opportunities for small companies to specialize in satisfying the needs of a specific market segment. Often, these companies can better satisfy their customers' needs because they are so close to them and understand how their needs are changing over time.

Market segmentation is an evolving, ongoing process that presents considerable opportunities for strategic managers to improve their company's business model. For example, in the car industry, savvy strategists often identify a "new" customer group whose specific needs have not been met and who have had to "satisfice" and buy a model that does not meet their needs exactly but is a reasonable compromise. Now a car company can decide to treat this group as a market segment and create a product designed to meet their specific needs, and, if it makes the right choice, it has a blockbuster product. This was the origin of the minivan; the SUV; crossover vehicles like the Honda Pilot, Toyota Scion, or Dodge Magnum; and hybrid vehicles such as Toyota's Prius and Honda's 2009 Insight. In the case of SUVs, many car buyers wanted a more rugged and powerful vehicle capable of carrying many passengers or towing heavy loads. They liked the comfort of a car but also the qualities of a pickup. By combining these two, carmakers created the SUV market segment. If managers make mistakes, however, and design a product for a market segment that is much smaller than they expected, the opposite can occur. After oil prices soared, United States carmakers ended production of many gas-guzzling vehicles, such as the luxury Lincoln truck and Excursion SUV, and massively reduced production of other models after customer demand collapsed; even Toyota had to temporarily suspend production of its blockbuster Tundra pickup.

Implementing the Business Model: Building Distinctive Competencies

To develop a successful business model, strategic managers have to devise a set of strategies that determine (1) how to differentiate and price their product and (2) how much to segment a market and how wide a range of products to develop. Whether these strategies will result in a profitable business model now depends on a strategic manager's ability to implement the business model, that is, to choose strategies that will create products that provide customers with the most value, while keeping the cost structure viable (because of the need to be price competitive).

In practice, this involves deciding how to invest a company's capital to build and shape distinctive competencies that result in a competitive advantage based on superior efficiency, quality, innovation, and/or responsiveness to customers. Hence, implementing a company's business model sets in motion *the specific set of functional-level strategies needed to create a successful differentiation and low-cost business strategy.* We discussed how functional strategies can build competitive advantage

RUNNING CASE

Walmart's Business Model and Competitive Positioning

As noted earlier, Walmart's business model is based on buying goods from suppliers as inexpensively as possible and then selling them to customers at the lowest possible prices. Figure 5.3 identifies strategies that Sam Walton, the company's founder, developed to allow the company to position itself to keep operating costs to a minimum so that he could offer customers everyday low prices and continuous price rollbacks. Walton chose strategies to increase efficiency, such as having low product differentiation (Walmart chooses minimal advertising and low responsiveness to customers) and targeting the mass market. His discount retail business model was based on the idea that lower costs mean lower prices.

Having devised a way to compete for customers, Walton's task was now to implement the business model in ways that would create a low-cost structure to allow him to charge lower prices. One business-level strategy he implemented was to locate his stores in small towns where there were no low-cost competitors; a second was to find ways to manage the value chain to reduce the costs of getting products from manufacturers to customers; and a third was to design and staff store operations to increase efficiency. The task of all functional managers in logistics, materials management, sales and customer service, store management, and so on, was to implement specific functional-level strategies that supported the low-cost/low-price business model. As Figure 5.3 suggests, Walmart has made thousands of specific strategic choices to allow it to implement its low-price business model successfully.

in Chapter 4. The better the fit between a company's business strategy and its functional-level strategies, the more value and profit a company creates, as the Running Case on Walmart suggests.

COMPETITIVE POSITIONING AND BUSINESS-LEVEL STRATEGY

Figure 5.4 presents a way of thinking about the competitive positioning decisions that strategic managers make to create a successful business model.[9] The decision to differentiate a product increases its perceived value to the customer so that market demand for the product increases. Differentiation is expensive, however; for example, strategies to improve product quality, support a higher level of service, or increase innovation increase operating costs. Therefore, the decision to increase product differentiation also raises a company's cost structure and results in a higher unit cost. (In some cases, if increased demand for the product allows a company to make large volumes of the product and achieve economies of scale, these economies can offset some of these extra costs; this effect is showed by the dashed line in Figure 5.4.)[10]

To maximize profitability, managers must choose a premium pricing option that compensates for the extra costs of product differentiation but is not so high that it chokes off the increase in expected demand (to prevent customers from deciding that the extra differentiation is not worth the higher price). Once again, to increase

Figure 5.3   Walmart's Business Model

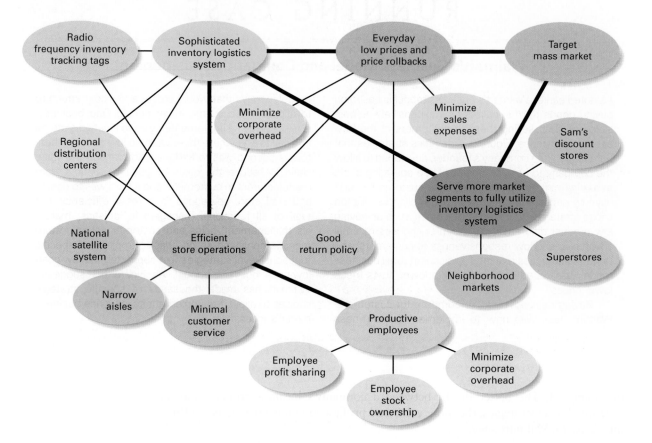

profitability, managers must also search for other ways to reduce the cost structure but not in ways that will harm the differentiated appeal of its products. There are many specific functional strategies a company can adopt to achieve this. For example, Nordstrom, the luxury department store retailer, differentiates itself in the retail clothing industry by providing a high-quality shopping experience with elegant store operations and a high level of customer service—all of which raise Nordstrom's cost structure. However, Nordstrom can still lower its cost structure by, for example, managing its inventories efficiently and increasing inventory turnover. Also, its strategy of being highly responsive to customers results in more customers and higher demand, which means that sales per square foot increase. This revenue enables it to make more intensive use of its facilities and salespeople, which leads to scale economies and lower costs. Thus, no matter what level of differentiation a company chooses to pursue in its business model, it always must recognize the way its cost structure will vary as a result of its choice of differentiation and the other specific strategies it adopts to lower its cost structure; in other words, *differentiation and cost structure decisions affect one another*.

The last main issue shown in Figure 5.4 concerns the impact of the industry's competitive structure on a company's differentiation, cost structure, and pricing choices. Recall that strategies are developed in an industry environment populated

Figure 5.4 Competitive Positioning at the Business Level

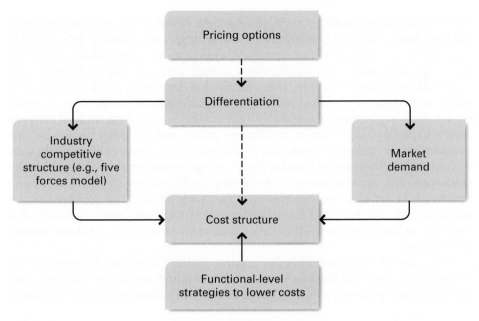

by watchful and agile competitors; therefore, one company's choice of competitive positioning is always made *with reference to those of its competitors*. If, for example, competitors start to offer products with new or improved features, a company may be forced to increase its level of differentiation to remain competitive, even if this reduces its profitability. Similarly, if competitors decide to develop products for new market segments, the company will have to follow suit or become uncompetitive. Thus, because differentiation increases costs, increasing industry competition can drive up a company's cost structure. When that happens, a company's ability to charge a premium price to cover these high costs may fall.

This is what happened to Sony when it lost its competitive advantage to competitors making flat screen LCD TVs and gaming consoles. Its cost structure rose, but it was unable to maintain its premium pricing, thus the result was lost profitability. Of course, its competitors, like Apple and Nintendo, experienced the opposite situation. Their innovative products, such as the iPhone and Wii, increased their cost structure, but the technological lead they obtained has allowed them to charge customers premium prices, which has made them the most profitable companies in these product markets. This is why competitive advantage can change so quickly in an industry and why it is vital to make the right product positioning choices. In sum, maximizing the profitability of a company's business model is about making the right choices with regard to value creation through differentiation, cost structure, and pricing, given the level of customer demand for its particular product and overall competitive conditions in the industry.

COMPETITIVE POSITIONING: GENERIC BUSINESS-LEVEL STRATEGIES

As we discussed previously, a successful business model is the result of the way a company formulates and implements a set of strategies to achieve a fit between its differentiation, cost, and pricing options. Although no diagram can ever model all the complexities involved in business-level strategy decisions, Figure 5.5 represents a way to bring together the three issues involved in developing a successful business model. In the figure, the vertical and horizontal axes represent the decisions of strategic managers to position a company's products with respect to the tradeoff between differentiating products (higher costs/higher prices) and achieving the lowest cost structure or cost leadership (lower costs/lower prices). The curve connecting the axes represents the **value creation frontier,** that is, the maximum amount of value that the products of different companies in an industry can provide to customers at any one time using the different business models. Companies on the value creation frontier are those that have built and maintained the most successful business models in a particular industry over time—they have a competitive advantage and above average profitability.

As Figure 5.5 illustrates, the value creation frontier is reached by pursuing one or more of the four building blocks of competitive advantage (quality has been split into its two components), which are listed from top to bottom in terms of how much

Figure 5.5   Competitive Positioning and the Value Creation Frontier

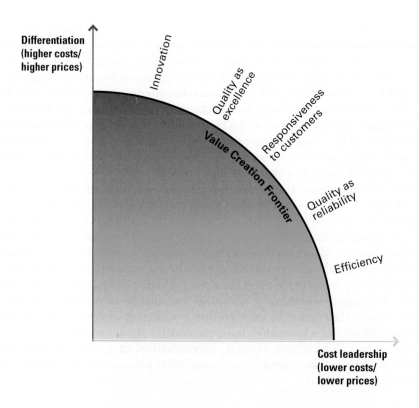

they can contribute to the creation of a differentiation or cost-leadership advantage. Thus innovation, a costly process that results in unique products, is nearest the differentiation axis, followed by quality as excellence, customer responsiveness, and quality as reliability; efficiency with its focus on lowering the cost structure is closest to the cost-leadership axis.

To reach the value creation frontier and so achieve above-average profitability, a company must formulate and implement a business model based on one or a combination of three generic business-level strategies: cost leadership, differentiation, and focused. A **generic business-level strategy** gives a company a specific form of competitive position and advantage vis-à-vis its rivals that results in above-average profitability.[11] *Generic* means that all companies can potentially pursue these strategies regardless of whether they are manufacturing, service, or nonprofit enterprises; they are also generic because they can be pursued across different kinds of industries.[12]

Cost Leadership

A company pursuing a **cost-leadership** business model chooses strategies that do everything possible to lower its cost structure so it can make and sell goods or services at a lower cost than its competitors. These strategies include both functional strategies designed to improve its operating performance and competitive strategies intended to influence industry competition in its favor. In essence, a company seeks to achieve a competitive advantage and above-average profitability by developing a cost-leadership business model that positions it on the value creation frontier as close as possible to the lower costs/lower prices axis.

Two advantages accrue to a company pursuing cost leadership. First, because the company has lower costs, it will be more profitable than its closest competitors, the companies that compete for the same set of customers and charge similar low prices for their products. Second, the cost leader gains a competitive advantage because it is able to charge a *lower price* than its competitors because of its lower cost structure. Offering customers the same kind of value from a product but at a lower price attracts many more customers, so that even though the company has chosen a lower price option, the increased volume of sales will cause profits to surge. If its competitors try to get lost customers back by reducing their prices and all companies start to compete on price, the cost leader will still be able to withstand competition better than the other companies because of its lower costs. It is likely to win any competitive struggle. For these reasons, cost leaders are likely to earn above-average profits. A company becomes a cost leader when its strategic managers make the following competitive positioning decisions.

Competitive Positioning Decisions   The cost leader chooses a low to moderate level of product differentiation relative to its competitors. Differentiation is expensive; the more a company spends resources to make its products distinctive, the more its costs rise.[13] The cost leader aims for a "sufficient" level of differentiation obtainable at low cost.[14] Walmart, for example, does not spend hundreds of millions of dollars on store design to create an attractive shopping experience as chains like Macy's, Dillard's, or Nordstrom's have done. As Walmart explains in its mission statement, "We think of ourselves as buyers for our customers, and we apply our considerable strengths to get the best value for you." Such value is not obtained by building lavish stores.[15] Cost leaders often wait until customers want a feature or service before providing it. For example, a cost leader like Vizio or Phillips is never the first to offer the state-of-the-art picture or sound quality; they increase their LCD TV capabilities only when it is obvious that customers demand it—or competitors start to do it first.

The cost leader also ignores the many different market segments in an industry. It positions its products to appeal to the "average" customer to avoid the high costs of developing and selling a wide range of products tailored to the needs of different market segments. In targeting the average customer, the goal is to provide the smallest number of products that will attract the largest number of customers—something at the heart of Dell's approach to building its PCs or Walmart's approach to stocking its stores. Thus, although customers may not get exactly the products they want, they are attracted by their lower prices.

To implement cost leadership, the overriding goal of the cost leader must be to choose strategies to increase its efficiency and lower its cost structure compared with its rivals. The development of distinctive competencies in manufacturing, materials management, and IT is central to achieving this goal. For example, manufacturing companies that pursue a cost-leadership strategy focus on doing everything they can to continually ride down the experience curve to continuously lower cost structure. Achieving a cost-leadership position requires a company to develop skills in flexible manufacturing, adopt efficient materials-management techniques, and do all it can to increase inventory turnover and reduce the cost of goods sold. (Table 4.1 outlined the ways in which a company's functions can be used to increase efficiency.)

Consequently, the main goal is to reduce the operating costs of the manufacturing and materials-management functions, and the other functions shape their distinctive competencies to help achieve this. The sales function, for example, may focus on capturing large, stable sets of customer orders so that manufacturing can make longer production runs and so obtain economies of scale that reduce costs. Similarly, Dell provides its online PC customers with a limited set of options to choose from so that it can provide customized PCs at a low cost.

By contrast, companies supplying services, such as retail stores like Walmart, must develop distinctive competencies in the specific functions that contribute most to their cost structure. For Walmart, this is the cost of purchasing products, so the logistics or materials-management function becomes of central importance for reducing product costs. Walmart continually takes advantage of advances in IT to lower the costs associated with transferring products from manufacturers to customers, just as Dell, the cost leader in the PC industry, uses the Internet to lower the cost of selling its computers. Another major source of cost savings in pursuing cost leadership is to choose an organizational structure and culture to implement this strategy in the most cost-efficient way. Thus, a low-cost strategy implies minimizing the number of managers in the hierarchy and the rigorous use of budgets to control production and selling costs. An interesting example of the way a company can craft a business model to become the cost leader in an industry is Ryanair, discussed in Strategy in Action 5.1.

Competitive Advantages and Disadvantages   Porter's five forces model, introduced in Chapter 2, explains why companies that employ each of the business models successfully reach the value creation frontier shown in Figure 5.5 and achieve a competitive advantage and above-average profitability. Recall that the five forces are threats from competitors, powerful suppliers, powerful buyers, substitute products, and new entrants. The cost leader has an advantage over industry competitors because

5.1 STRATEGY IN ACTION

Ryanair Takes Control over the Sky in Europe

Ryanair, based in Dublin, Ireland, imitated and improved on the cost-leadership business model pioneered by Southwest Airlines in the United States and used it to become a leading player in the European air travel market. Ryanair's CEO, the flamboyant Michael O'Leary, copied the specific strategies Southwest had developed to cut costs and position Ryanair as the lowest-cost, lowest-priced European airline. The average cost of a Ryanair ticket within Europe is $48, compared to $330 on British Airways and $277 on Lufthansa, which have long dominated the European air travel market. The result is that Ryanair now flies more passengers inside Britain than British Airways, and its share of the European market is growing as fast as it can gain access to new landing spots and buy the new planes needed to service its expanding route structure.

O'Leary also worked to improve Southwest's low-cost business model. Ryanair imitated the main elements of Southwest's model, such as using only one plane, the 737, to reduce maintenance costs, selling tickets directly to customers, and eliminating seat assignments and free in-flight meals. It also avoids high-cost airports like Heathrow and chooses smaller ones outside big cities, such as Luton, its London hub. However, to reduce airplane operating costs, O'Leary also eliminated free blankets, pillows, sodas or snacks, and even "sick" bags—perks a passenger expects to receive on a more

differentiated airline. "You get what you pay for" is Ryanair's philosophy. To implement his cost-leadership strategy, O'Leary and all employees are expected to find ways to continually shrink the operating costs that arise in performing the thousands of specific tasks needed to run an airline. Through these tactics, Ryanair has lowered its cost structure so far that no other European airline can come close to offering its low-cost fares and break even, let alone make a profit.

The other side of Ryanair's business model is to add to its revenues by getting its customers to spend as much as possible while they are on its flights. To this end, Ryanair offers snacks, meals, and a variety of drinks to encourage customers to open their wallets. In addition, to cut costs his planes have no back-seat LCD screens for viewing movies and playing games; passengers can rent a digital handheld device for $6 a flight to watch movies and sitcoms or play games or music. 14% of its revenues come from these sources; they are so important that the airline gives away millions of its unsold seats free to customers so that it can at least generate some revenue from passengers sitting in what otherwise would be empty seats. Ryanair and Southwest have together shown that the cost-leadership business model is the only one that will work in the future and globally; all large airlines are rushing to adopt the specific strategies that will allow them to pursue it.

Sources: D. McGinn, "Is This Any Way to Run an Airline?" *Newsweek*, October 4, 2004, E14–19; E. Torbenson, "Budget Carriers Rule the European Skies," *Dallas Morning News*, September 22, 2004, D1. http://www.ryanair.com.

it has a lower cost structure. Its lower costs also mean that it will be less affected than its competitors by increases in the price of inputs if there are powerful suppliers and less affected by the lower prices it can charge if powerful buyers exist. Moreover, because cost leadership usually requires a large market share, the cost leader purchases in relatively large quantities, increasing its bargaining power over suppliers, just as Walmart does. If substitute products begin to come onto the market, the cost leader can reduce its price to compete with them and retain its market share. Finally, the leader's cost advantage constitutes a barrier to entry because other companies are unable to enter the industry and match the leader's low costs or prices. The cost leader is therefore relatively safe as long as it can maintain its low-cost advantage.

The principal dangers of the cost-leadership approach arise when competitors are able to develop new strategies that lower their cost structure and beat the cost leader at its own game. For instance, if technological change makes experience-curve economies obsolete, new companies may apply lower-cost technologies that give them a cost advantage. The steel mini-mills discussed in Chapter 4 pursued this strategy to obtain a competitive advantage. Competitors may also obtain a cost advantage from labor-cost savings. Global competitors located in countries overseas often have very low labor costs; wage costs in the United States are roughly 600% more than they are in Malaysia, China, or Mexico. Most United States companies now assemble their products abroad as part of their low-cost strategy; many are forced to do so simply to compete and stay in business.

Competitors' ability to imitate the cost leader's methods easily is another threat to the cost-leadership strategy. For example, companies in China routinely take apart the electronic products of Japanese companies like Sony and Panasonic to see how they are designed and assembled. Then, using inexpensive Chinese-made components and domestic labor, they manufacture clones of these products and flood the United States market with lower-priced flat screen TVs, laptops, and mobile phones.

Finally, a danger arises if a strategic manager's single-minded desire to reduce costs to remain the cost leader results in decisions that might lower costs but also drastically reduce demand for the product. This happened to Gateway Computer when, to reduce the costs of customer service to better compete with Dell, customer support people were instructed not to help customers who were experiencing problems with their new Gateway PCs if they had installed their own new software on the machines. New buyers, most of whom install their own software, began to complain vociferously, and Gateway's sales plunged. Within six months, managers had reversed their decision, and once again began offering full customer support.

Focused Cost Leadership

A cost leader is not always a large, national company that targets the average customer. Sometimes a company can pursue a **focused cost leadership** business model based on combining the cost leadership and focused business-level strategies to compete for customers in just one or a few market segments. Focused cost leaders concentrate on a narrow market segment, which may be defined geographically, by type of customer, or by segment of the product line.[16] In Figure 5.6, focused cost leaders are represented by the smaller circles next to the cost leader's circle. For example, because a geographic niche can be defined by region or even by locality, a cement-making company, a carpet-cleaning business, or a pizza chain could pursue a cost-leadership strategy in one or more cities in a region. Figure 5.7 compares a focused cost-leadership business model with a pure cost-leadership model.

If a company uses a focused cost-leadership approach, it competes against the cost leader in the market segments where it can operate at no cost disadvantage. For example, in local lumber, cement, bookkeeping, or pizza delivery markets, the focuser may have lower materials or transportation costs than the national cost leader. The focuser may also have a cost advantage because it is producing complex or custom-built products that do not lend themselves easily to economies of scale in production and therefore offer few cost-saving possibilities. The focused cost leader concentrates on small-volume custom products, for which it has a cost advantage, and leaves the large-volume standardized market to the national cost leader—for example, low-priced Mexican food specials versus Big Macs.

Because it has no cost disadvantage in its market segments, a focused cost leader also operates on the value creation frontier and so earns above-average profits.

Figure 5.6   Generic Business Models and the Value Creation Frontier

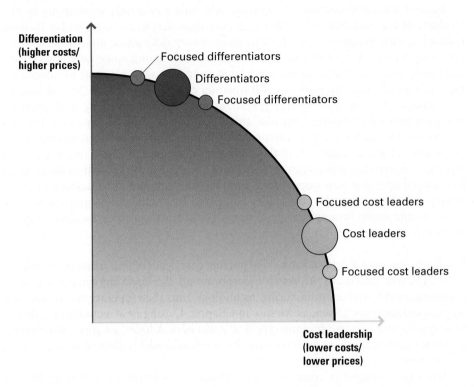

Such a company has great opportunity to enlarge its market segment and compete against companies pursuing cost-leadership or differentiated strategies. Ryanair, for example, began as a focus company because at first it operated flights only between Dublin and London. Because there was no cost leader in the European market, it was able to quickly expand its operations, and today it is the European cost leader. Similarly, Southwest began as a focused cost leader within the Texas market but is

Figure 5.7   Why Focus Strategies Are Different

now a national airline and competes against new companies that pursue focused cost leadership, such as JetBlue.

Because a focused company makes and sells only a relatively small quantity of a product, its cost structure will often be higher than that of the cost leader. In some industries, such as automotive, this can make it very difficult or impossible to compete with the cost leader. However, sometimes, by targeting some new market segment or by implementing a business model in a superior way—such as by adopting a more advanced technology—focused companies can be a threat to large cost leaders. For example, flexible manufacturing systems have opened up many new opportunities for focused companies because small production runs become possible at a lower cost. The steel mini-mills discussed in Chapter 4 provide another good example of how a focused company, in this case Nucor, by specializing in one market can grow so efficient that it becomes *the* cost leader. Similarly, the growth of the Internet has opened up many new opportunities for focused companies to develop business models based on being the cost leader compared to bricks-and-mortar companies. Amazon.com shows how effectively a company can craft a business model to become the cost leader.

Implications and Conclusions   To pursue cost leadership, strategic managers need to devote enormous efforts to incorporate all the latest information, materials management, and manufacturing technology into their operations to find new ways to reduce costs. Often, as we saw in Chapter 4, using new technology will also raise quality and increase responsiveness to customers. A low-cost approach requires ongoing strategic thinking to make sure the business model is aligned with changing environmental opportunities and threats.

Strategic managers in companies throughout the industry are watching the cost leader and will move quickly to imitate its innovations because they also want to reduce their costs. Today, a differentiator cannot let a cost leader get too great a cost advantage because the leader might then be able to use its high profits to invest more in product differentiation and beat the differentiator at its own competitive game. For example, Toyota and Honda began as focused cost leaders, manufacturing a reliable low-priced car. Their cars sold well, and they then invested their profits to design and make new models of cars that became increasingly differentiated in features and quality. Today, Toyota and Honda, with cars in every market segment, pursue a differentiation strategy, although Toyota also has the lowest cost structure of any global carmaker.

A cost leader must also imitate the strategic moves of its differentiated competitors, and increase the quality and features of its products when they do, to prosper in the long run. Even low-priced products, such as Timex watches and BIC razors, cannot be too inferior to the more expensive Seiko watches or Gillette razors if the lower costs/lower prices model is to succeed. Companies in an industry watch the strategies their rivals are pursuing, and the changes they make to those strategies. So, if Seiko or Swatch introduces a novel kind of LCD watch dial or Gillette a three- or four-bladed razor, managers at Timex and BIC will respond within months by incorporating these innovations in their low-priced products if required. This situation is also very common in the high-priced women's fashion industry. As soon as famous designers like Gucci and Dior have shown their spring and fall collections, their designs are copied and the plans are transmitted to factories in Malaysia, where workers are ready to manufacture low-priced imitations that within months will reach low-price clothing retail stores around the world.

Differentiation

A company pursuing a **differentiation** business model pursues business-level strategies that allow it to create a unique product, one that customers perceive as different or distinct in some important way. A differentiator (that is, a differentiated company) gains a competitive advantage because it has the ability to satisfy customers' needs in a way that its competitors cannot, which allows it to charge a premium price for its product. The ability to increase revenues by charging premium prices (rather than by reducing costs, as the cost leader does) allows the differentiator to reach the value frontier, outperform its competitors, and achieve superior profitability, as shown in Figure 5.6. Customers pay a premium price when they believe the product's differentiated qualities are worth the extra money, so differentiated products are priced as high as customers are willing to pay.

Mercedes-Benz cars are more expensive than the cars of its closest rivals because customers believe they offer more features and confer more status on their owners. Similarly, a BMW is not much more expensive to produce than a Honda, but its high price is determined by customers who want its distinctive sporty ride and the prestige of owning a BMW. (In fact, in Japan, BMW prices its entry cars quite modestly to attract young, well-heeled Japanese customers from Honda.) Similarly, Rolex watches do not cost much to produce—their design has not changed very much for years—and their gold content represents only a small fraction of their price. Customers, however, buy a Rolex because of the distinct qualities they perceive in it: its beautiful design and its ability to hold its value as well as to confer status on its wearer.

Competitive Positioning Decisions A differentiator invests its resources to gain a competitive advantage from superior innovation, excellent quality, and responsiveness to customer needs—the three principal routes to high product differentiation. For example, Procter & Gamble claims that its product quality is high and that Ivory soap is 99.44% pure. Toyota stresses reliability and the best repair record of any carmaker. IBM promotes the quality service provided by its well-trained sales force. Innovation is commonly the source of differentiation for technologically complex products, and many people pay a premium price for new and innovative products, such as a state-of-the-art gaming PC, gaming console, or car.

When differentiation is based on responsiveness to customers, a company offers comprehensive after-sales service and product repair. This is an especially important consideration for complex products such as cars and domestic appliances, which are likely to break down periodically. Whirlpool, Dell, and BMW all excel in responsiveness to customers. In service organizations, quality-of-service attributes are also very important. Neiman Marcus, Nordstrom, and FedEx can charge premium prices because they offer an exceptionally high level of service. Firms of lawyers, accountants, and consultants stress the service aspects of their operations to clients: their knowledge, professionalism, and reputation.

Finally, a product's appeal to customers' psychological desires is a source of differentiation. The appeal can be prestige or status, as it is with Rolls-Royce cars and Rolex watches; safety of home and family, as with Aetna or Prudential Insurance; or simply providing a superior shopping experience, as with Target and Macy's. Differentiation can also be tailored to age groups and socioeconomic groups. Indeed, the bases of differentiation are endless.

A company pursuing a business model based on differentiation pursues strategies to differentiate itself along as many competitive dimensions as possible. The less it resembles its rivals, the more it is protected from competition and the wider is its market appeal. Thus, BMWs offer more than prestige; they also offer technological sophistication, luxury, reliability, and good, although very expensive, repair service. All these bases of differentiation help increase sales.

Generally, a differentiator chooses to divide its market into many segments and offer different products in each segment, just as Sony, Toyota, and Dell do. Strategic managers recognize how much revenues can be increased when each of a company's products, targeted at different market segments, can attract more customers. A differentiator targets only the market segments in which customers are willing to pay a premium price, however. For example, Sony produces many flat screen TV models, but it targets only the niches from mid-priced to high-priced sets; its lowest-priced model is still a few hundred dollars above that of its low-cost competitors—despite its current problems.

Finally, in choosing how to implement its business model, a differentiated company concentrates on developing distinctive competencies in the functions that provide the source of its competitive advantage. Differentiation on the basis of innovation and technological competency depends on the R&D function, as discussed in Chapter 4. Efforts to improve service to customers depend on the quality of the sales and customer service function.

Pursuing a business model based on differentiation is expensive, so a differentiator has a cost structure that is higher than a cost leader's. Building new competencies in the functions necessary to sustain a company's differentiated appeal does not mean neglecting the cost structure, however. Even differentiators benchmark how cost leaders operate to find ways to imitate their cost-saving innovations while preserving their products' differentiated appeal. A differentiator must control its cost structure to ensure the price of its products does not exceed the price customers are willing to pay for them—something that Sony has failed to do. Also, superior profitability is a function of a company's cost structure, so it is important to keep costs under control but not to reduce them so far that a company loses the source of its differentiated appeal.[17] The owners of the famous Savoy Hotel in London, England, face just this problem. The Savoy's reputation has always been based on the incredibly high level of service it offers its customers. Three hotel employees serve the needs of each guest, and in every room, a guest can summon a waiter, maid, or valet by pressing a button at bedside. The cost of offering this level of service has been so high that the hotel makes less than 1% net profit every year, despite the fact that a room costs at least $500 a night![18] Its owners try to find ways to reduce costs to increase profits, but if they reduce the number of hotel staff (the main source of the Savoy's high costs), they will destroy the main source of its differentiated appeal.

Competitive Advantages and Disadvantages   The reason why the differentiation business model also allows a company to obtain a competitive advantage and reach the value creation frontier can also be explained by the five forces model. Differentiation protects a company from competitors when customers develop brand loyalty for its products, a valuable asset that allows it to charge a premium price. Because the differentiated company's strategy is geared more toward the premium price it can charge than toward costs, powerful suppliers become less of a problem, especially as differentiators can often pass on price increases to loyal customers. Thus, a differentiator can tolerate moderate increases in input prices better than the cost leader can. Differentiators are unlikely to experience problems with powerful buyers because they offer a distinctive product that commands brand loyalty and only they can supply it. Differentiation and brand loyalty also create a barrier to entry for other companies seeking to enter the industry. A new company must find a way to make its own product distinctive to be able to compete, which involves an expensive investment in building some kind of distinctive competence. Finally, substitute products are a threat only if a competitor can develop a product that satisfies a similar customer need as the differentiator's product, thus causing customers to switch to the new product. This can happen; wired phone companies have suffered as mobile phone companies offer an attractive wireless product, and lower-cost alternative ways of making phone calls through PCs and the Internet are becoming increasingly popular.

The main problems with a differentiation strategy center on how well strategic managers can maintain a product's perceived difference or distinctness to customers and hence maintain premium pricing. In the 2000s, it has become clear that it is easier than ever for agile competitors to imitate and copy successful differentiators. This has happened across many industries, such as retailing, computers, cars, home electronics, telecommunications, and pharmaceuticals. Patents and first-mover advantages (the advantages of being the first to market a product or service) last only so long, and as the overall quality of competing products increases, brand loyalty declines, as do prices. The problems L.L.Bean has had in maintaining its competitive advantage, described in Strategy in Action 5.2, highlight many of the threats that face a differentiator.

Implications and Conclusions   A business model based on differentiation requires a company to make strategic choices that reinforce each other and together increase the value of a good or service in the eyes of customers. When a product has distinctness, differentiators can charge a premium price. The disadvantages of pursuing differentiation are the ease with which competitors can imitate a differentiator's product and the difficulty of maintaining a premium price. When differentiation stems from the design or physical features of the product, differentiators are at great risk because imitation is easy; over time products such as LCD televisions and cell phones became commodity-like products, and customers became increasingly price sensitive. However, when differentiation stems from functional-level strategies that lead to superior service or reliability, or from any intangible source, such as FedEx's guarantee or the prestige of a Rolex, a company is much more secure. It is difficult to imitate intangible products, and a differentiator can often reap the benefits of premium prices for an indefinite time. Nevertheless, all differentiators must watch out for imitators and be careful that they do not charge a premium price that is higher than customers are willing to pay. These are issues that Sony neglected, contributing to its currently declining sales as it loses its competitive advantage.

Focused Differentiation

A company that pursues a business model based on **focused differentiation** chooses to combine the differentiation and focused generic business-level strategies and specializes in making distinctive products for one or two market segments. All the means of differentiation that are open to the differentiator are available to the focused differentiator. The point is that the focused company develops a business model that allows it to successfully position itself to compete with the differentiator

5.2 STRATEGY IN ACTION

L.L.Bean's New Business Model

In 1911, Leon Leonwood Bean, a hunter who grew weary of walking miles to hunt game as his feet became wetter and wetter, decided he would create waterproof boots. The ones he invented had leather uppers attached to large rounded rubber bases. Soon he began selling his boots through mail order. As word spread about their reliability, backed by his policy of being responsive to customers who complained (often replacing their boots years after a sale), his company's reputation spread. As the years went by, L.L.Bean expanded its now well-known product line to include products such as canvas tote bags and, of course, flannel dog beds. By 2000, the company's mail order revenues exceeded $1 billion a year, and L.L.Bean became known for offering one of the highest-quality product lines of sporting clothes and accessories.

To display its product line, the company built a 160,000-square-foot signature store in Freeport, Maine, that stocks hundreds of versions of its backpacks, fleece vests, shirts, moccasins, tents, and other items; more than 3 million visitors a year shop its store. L.L.Bean established this store partly to give customers hands-on access to its products so that they would have a better understanding of the high quality they were being offered. Of course, L.L.Bean expects to command a premium price for offering such a wide variety of high-quality products, and historically it has enjoyed high profit margins. Customers buy its products for their personal use but also as gifts for friends and relatives.

L.L. Bean's business model began to suffer when there was an explosion in the number of companies touting high-quality, high-priced products to customers; consequently, L.L. Bean's catalogue lost its unique appeal. Furthermore, the explosive growth of the Internet gave customers access to many more companies that offered quality products, often at much lower prices, such as Lands' End, which also began to feature fleece vests, dog baskets, and so on, in its product lineup. The problem facing any differentiator is how to protect the distinctiveness of its products from imitators who are always searching for ways to steal away its customers by offering them similar kinds of products at reduced prices.

Finding ways to protect L.L. Bean's business model has proved to be a major challenge. Its catalogue sales were stagnant for several years as buyers switched loyalty to lower-priced companies. To help the company rebuild its competitive advantage, it began to build a chain of L.L.Bean stores in major urban locations to encourage potential customers to examine the quality of its products and so attract them—either to buy them in the stores or to use its Web site.

This has not proved easy to date because physical retail stores have high cost structures; L.L. Bean has had to search for the right way to implement its strategy. It has also had to lower the price of its sporting clothes and accessories in these stores; the days of premium prices are gone. Another strategy has been to launch an aggressive advertising campaign aimed at younger customers who may not know the L.L. Bean story. Then, with physical stores, the Internet, and its catalogues, it may have a better chance of getting their business.

The jury is out, however. Not only are other differentiated sporting goods chains expanding, such as Dick's Sporting Goods and Gander Mountain, but sites like Amazon.com and Landsend.com, owned by Sears, are offering lower-priced products. Whether L.L.Bean's differentiation business model can be reworked to allow it to reach the value creation frontier remains to be seen, and because cost leadership is not an option, the company faces a rocky road ahead.

Sources: D. McGinn, "Swimming Upstream," *Newsweek*, October 1, 2004; E10–12 http://www.llbean.com.

in just one or a few segments. For example, Porsche, a focused differentiator, competes against Toyota and BMW only in the sports car and luxury SUV segments of the car market.

For the focused differentiator, selecting a market segment means the decision to focus on one type of customer, such as serving only the very rich, the very young, or the very adventurous; or to focus on only one kind of product in a particular market, such as organic or vegetarian foods, very fast cars, luxury designer clothes, or exclusive sunglasses. Focused differentiators reach the value frontier when they have developed a distinctive product that better meets the needs of customers in a particular segment than the differentiator (Figure 5.6). A competitive advantage may result, for example, because a focused differentiator possesses better knowledge (than the differentiator) about the needs of a small customer set (such as sports car buyers) or superior expertise in a particular field (such as corporate law, management consulting, or Web site management for retail customers or restaurants). Similarly, it might develop superior skills in responsiveness to customers because of its ability to serve the particular needs of regional or industry customers in ways that a national differentiator would find very expensive. Finally, concentration on a narrow range of products sometimes allows a focuser to develop innovations more quickly than a large differentiator can.

The focuser does not attempt to serve all market segments because that would bring it into direct competition with the differentiator. Instead, it concentrates on building market share in one or a few market segments; if it is successful, it may begin to serve more and more market segments and chip away at the differentiator's competitive advantage. However, if it is too successful at what it does, or if it does try to compete with the differentiator, it may run into trouble because the differentiator has the resources to imitate the focused company's business model. For example, when Ben & Jerry's innovated luxury ice cream, their huge success led other companies like Häagen-Dazs and Godiva to bring out their competing products. A good example of the way competition is changing, even among focused differentiators that make a similar luxury product, in this case designer clothing, is profiled in Strategy in Action 5.3.

In sum, a focused differentiator can protect its competitive advantage in a market segment to the extent that it can provide a good or service that its rivals cannot, for example, by being close to its customers and responding to their changing needs. However, a focused company cannot easily move to another market segment, so if its market segment disappears because of technological change or changes in customers' tastes this is a major danger. For example, few people today want a VCR even if it is state-of-the-art because of the shift to digital technology, and clothing store chain Brooks Brothers ran into great difficulty when business casual not formal suits, its main product, became the clothing norm at most companies. Similarly, corner diners have become almost a thing of the past because they are unable to compete with the low prices and speed of fast-food chains like McDonald's and the upscale atmosphere of Starbuck's.

THE DYNAMICS OF COMPETITIVE POSITIONING

Companies that successfully pursue one of the business models just discussed are able to outperform their rivals and reach the value creation frontier. They have developed the business-level strategies that result in competitive advantage and above-average profitability and are the most successful and well-known companies in their industry. Although some companies are able to develop the business model and strategies that allow them to reach the value creation frontier, many others cannot and so achieve only average or below-average profitability. For example, the most successful

Ethical Dilemma

You are a top manager of a small company that has pioneered the development of software that allows Web users to interface online in real time. A major rival recognized the value of your product and offered to buy your company at a price you think is inadequate. When you refused to sell your company, the rival began recruiting your top software engineers to obtain their specialized knowledge. One engineer left while others have banded together, threatening to leave if demands aren't met. Consequently, you stand to lose your competitive advantage. Is it ethical for you to apply for a court order preventing engineers from leaving to join your competitor? Is it ethical for your competitor to recruit your employees to obtain their knowledge? Given your answers to these questions, should you let the differentiator buy your company and take over your market niche?

5.3 *STRATEGY IN ACTION*

Zara Uses IT to Change the World of Fashion

Well-known fashion houses like Chanel, Dior, Gucci, and Armani charge thousands of dollars for the fashionable suits and dresses that they introduce twice yearly in the fall and spring. Because only the very rich can afford such differentiated and expensive clothing, to expand demand for its products, most luxury designers produce less expensive lines of clothing and accessories that are sold in upscale fashion retailers such as Neiman Marcus, Nordstrom, and Saks Fifth Avenue. In the 2000s, however, these luxury designers, which all pursue focused differentiation, have come under increasing pressure from small, agile fashion designers, such as England's Jaeger and Laura Ashley and Spain's Zara, that have developed capabilities in using IT that allow them to pursue a focused differentiation strategy but at a much lower cost than the luxury fashion houses. This has allowed them to circumvent barriers to entry into the high fashion segment and develop well-received brand names that still command a premium price.

Zara, in particular, has achieved significant success. Its sales have soared because it created innovative information and materials management systems that keep its cost structure low while reducing time to market. The result is that Zara can produce fashionable clothes at lower prices and turn them over quickly by selling them in its own chain of clothing stores. Major fashion houses like Dior and Gucci can take six or more months to design their collections and then three to six more before their moderately priced lines become available in upscale retailers. Zara's designers closely watch the trends in the high fashion industry and the kinds of innovations that the major houses are introducing. Then, using sophisticated IT that links Zara's designers to its suppliers and clothing manufacturers abroad, the company can create a new collection in only five weeks, and these clothes can then be made in a week and delivered to its stores soon after. This short time to market makes Zara very flexible and allows it to compete effectively in the rapidly changing fashion market, where customer tastes evolve quickly.

Because of the quick manufacturing-to-sales cycle and just-in-time fashion, Zara has been able to offer its collections at comparatively low prices and still make profits that are the envy of the fashion clothing industry.

Sources: C. Vitzthum, "Just-in-Time-Fashion," *Wall Street Journal*, May 18, 2001, B1, B4; http://www.zara.com.

companies in the retail industry, such as Neiman Marcus, Target, and Walmart, have reached the value frontier; but their competitors, such as Saks, JCPenney, and Sears/Kmart have not.

Moreover, few companies are able to continuously outperform their rivals and remain on the value frontier over time. For example, high-performing companies such as Sony and Dell that were on the frontier a few years ago have lost their competitive advantage to rivals such as Panasonic, Samsung, Apple, and Hewlett-Packard (HP). Companies such as Toyota, Walmart, and Zara that have maintained their position on the frontier are rare. Why is it so hard for companies to sustain their competitive advantage over time and remain on the frontier?

To understand why some companies perform better than others, and why the performance of one company can increase or decrease over time, it is necessary to understand the dynamics involved in positioning a company's business model so that it can compete successfully in an industry. In this section, we first explore another business model that helps explain why some companies are able to sustain and increase their competitive advantage over time. Second, we examine how the business model a company pursues places it in a strategic group composed of other companies that compete in a similar way and how this has a major affect on its profitability over time. Finally, we examine some competitive dynamics that explain why companies run into major problems that can affect their very survival.

Competitive Positioning for Superior Performance: Broad Differentiation

Companies that pursue cost leadership pursue a different business model and strategies than companies that choose differentiation, yet each business model is a path to superior performance and profitability. As we emphasize throughout this chapter, no matter what business model a company pursues, it must control its cost structure if it is to maintain and increase its profitability; at the same time, it also must find ways to differentiate its product in some way to attract customers. This is particularly important today because of intense global competition from companies abroad and rapid technological change that allows competitors to develop strategies that provide them with some kind of superior differentiation or cost advantage. In this dynamic situation, a company that can *combine* the strategies necessary to successfully pursue both cost leadership and differentiation will develop the most competitive and profitable business model in its industry.

Today, the most successful companies in an industry are often the ones that have developed strategies to achieve this; these companies are the most profitable because they can offer customers quality products at reasonable prices, that is, they offer customers a superior "value proposition" compared to their rivals. The middle of the value creation frontier is occupied by **broad differentiators**, companies that have developed business-level strategies to better differentiate their products and lower their cost structures *simultaneously*. Broad differentiators operate on the value frontier because they have chosen a level of differentiation that gives them a competitive advantage in the market segments they have targeted, and they have achieved this *in a way that has allowed them to lower their cost structure over time* (see Figure 5.8). Thus, although they may have higher costs than cost leaders, and offer a less differentiated product than differentiators, they have found a competitive position that offers their customers more value than industry rivals. Broad differentiators continually use their distinctive competencies to increase their product range, and they search for new market segments to enter to increase their market share and profits. At the same time, they work continuously to find ways to lower their cost structure and increase their profitability. For example, companies such as Dell, Amazon.com, Best Buy, and eBay have used the Internet as a way to become broad differentiators. These companies have been rapidly expanding the range of products they offer customers and taking advantage of their highly efficient information and/or materials-management systems to drive down costs compared to bricks-and-mortar retailers.

Importantly, broad differentiators that have developed the business-level strategies that enable them to reach this highly profitable position become an increasing threat to both differentiators and cost leaders over time. These companies make differentiated products so that they can charge higher prices than the cost leader, but they can also charge lower (but still premium) prices than differentiators because their cost structures are lower. The result is that many customers perceive the value of the products offered by the broad differentiator versus the cost leader is worth the higher price. At the same time, customers reluctant to pay the high premium prices of a differentiator's products decide that the lower price of the broad differentiator's product more than makes up for the loss of the "extra" differentiated features of the luxury premium-priced products. In essence, customers choose TVs from Panasonic

Figure 5.8   The Broad Differentiation Business Model

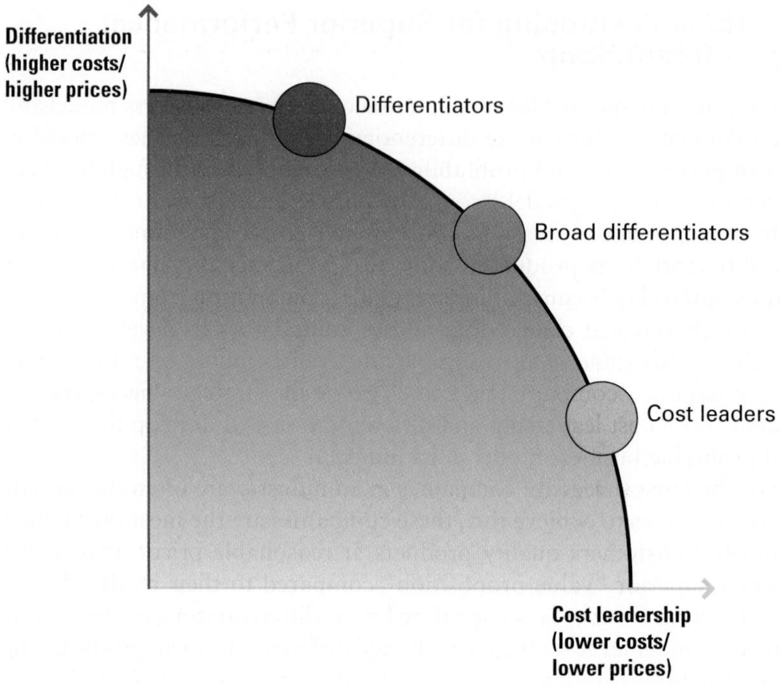

(a broad differentiator) over Vizio (a cost leader) or Sony (a differentiator), or a bottle of Pantene shampoo from Procter & Gamble (a broad differentiator) over a bottle from Estée Lauder (a differentiator) or Walmart (a cost leader).

As a result, if strategic managers have the skills to pursue this business model successfully, broad differentiators steadily increase their market share and profitability over time. This provides them with more capital to reinvest in their business, so they can continually improve their business model. For example, their growing profits allow broad differentiators to invest in new technology that both increases their differentiation advantage and lower their cost structure, which weakens the competitive position of their rivals. As they build their competitive advantage and become able to offer customers a better value proposition, they push the value creation frontier to the right and knock their competitors off the frontier, so they become less profitable. Toyota, profiled in Strategy in Action 5.4, provides a good example of a company that uses a broad differentiation business model that has increasingly put its rivals at a competitive disadvantage. The result today is that it has replaced GM as the largest and most profitable global carmaker.

Competitive Positioning and Strategic Groups

New developments such as (1) technological innovations that permit increased product differentiation, (2) the identification of new customer groups and market segments, and (3) the discovery of superior ways to lower cost structure continually change the competitive forces at work in an industry. In such a dynamic situation, the competitive position of companies can change rapidly. Higher performing

5.4 STRATEGY IN ACTION

Toyota's Goal? A High-Value Vehicle to Match Every Customer Need

The car industry has always been one of the most competitive in the world because of the huge revenues and profits that are at stake. Given the difficult economic conditions in the late 2000s, it is hardly surprising that rivalry has increased as global carmakers fight to develop new car models that better satisfy the needs of particular groups of buyers. One company at the competitive forefront is Toyota.

Toyota produced its first car 40 years ago, an ugly, boxy vehicle that was, however, cheap. As the quality of its car became apparent, sales increased. Toyota, which was then a focused cost leader, plowed back its profits into improving the styling of its vehicles and into efforts to continually reduce production costs. Over time, Toyota has taken advantage of its low cost structure to make an ever-increasing range of reasonably priced vehicles tailored to different segments of the car market. Its ability to go from the initial design stage to the production stage in two to three years allowed it to bring out new models faster than its competitors and capitalize on the development of new market segments. Toyota has been a leader in positioning its whole range of vehicles to take advantage of new, emerging market segments. In the SUV segment, for example, its first offering was the expensive Toyota Land Cruiser, then priced at over $35,000. Realizing the need for SUVs in lower price ranges, it next introduced the 4Runner, priced at $20,000 and designed for the average SUV customer; the RAV4, a small SUV in the low $20,000 range, followed; then came the Sequoia, a bigger, more powerful version of the 4Runner in the upper $20,000 range. Finally, taking the technology from its Lexus division, it introduced the luxury Highlander SUV in the low $30,000 range. Today it offers six SUVs, each offering a particular combination of price, size, performance, styling, and luxury to appeal to a particular customer group within the SUV segment of the car market. In a similar way, Toyota positions its sedans to appeal to the needs of different sets of customers. For example, the Camry is targeted at the middle of the market to customers who can afford to pay about $23,000 and want a balance of luxury, performance, safety, and reliability.

Toyota's broad differentiation business model is geared toward making a range of vehicles that optimizes the amount of value it can create for different groups of customers. At the same time, the number of models it makes is constrained by the need to maintain a low cost structure and car-pricing options that will generate maximum revenues and profits. Because competition in each car market segment is now intense, all global carmakers need to balance the advantages of having more cars to attract customers against the increasing costs that result when they expand the number of different models of car they make.

Source: http://www.toyota.com, 2009.

companies are able to gain if they can position themselves competitively to pursue broad differentiation. Poorer performing companies often do not realize how fast their competitive position is deteriorating because of their rivals' strategies and sometimes discover it is too late to rebuild their business models. Strategic group analysis, which we discussed in Chapter 2, is a tool that managers can use to better understand the dynamics of competitive positioning so that they can change their business models to maintain above-average profitability.

A company's business model determines how it will compete for customers in one or more market segments, and typically several companies compete for the same group of customers. This means that, over time, companies competing for the same customer group become rivals locked in a competitive struggle. The goal is to be the company that reaches or pushes out the value frontier by pursuing the business-level strategies that result in sustained competitive advantage and above average profitability.

Within most industries, **strategic groups**, that is, the set of companies that pursue a similar business model, emerge.[19] For example, those companies in an industry that compete to be the cost leader form one strategic group, those that seek some form of differentiation advantage form another, as do those companies that have developed a broad differentiation strategy. Companies pursuing focused differentiation or focused cost leadership form yet other strategic groups.

The concept of strategic groups has several implications for competitive positioning. First, strategic managers must map their competitors according to their choice of specific business model, for example, cost leadership and focused cost leadership. The managers must identify the differences among the specific set of strategies each company uses to pursue the same business model to explain their differences in profitability. For example, how has one company better identified which particular customer needs to satisfy or customer groups to serve, and how have they worked to developed a particular distinctive competence? Strategic managers can then use this knowledge to better position their business model so that they become closer to customers, differentiate themselves from their competitors, or learn how to reduce costs. Careful strategic-group analysis allows managers to uncover the most important ways to compete for customers in one or more market segments and helps reveal what strategies are needed in the future to maintain a competitive advantage.

Second, once a company has mapped its rivals, it can better understand how changes taking place in the industry are affecting its competitive advantage from a differentiation and cost structure perspective, as well as identify opportunities and threats. Often a company's nearest rivals are the competitors in its strategic group that are pursuing a similar business model. Customers tend to view the products of such companies as direct substitutes for each other. Thus, a major threat to a company's profitability can arise from within its own strategic group when its rivals find ways to either improve product differentiation and get closer to customers or lower their cost structure. This is why today companies benchmark their closest competitors on major performance dimensions to determine if they are falling behind in some important respect. For example, UPS and FedEx are constantly examining each other's performance.

In sum, strategic-group analysis involves identifying and charting the business models and business-level strategies that industry rivals are pursuing. Managers can then determine which strategies are successful and unsuccessful and why a certain business model is working or not. Importantly, they can also analyze how the relative competitive position of industry rivals, both those pursuing the same business model and those pursuing different business models, is changing over time. This knowledge allows them to either fine-tune or radically alter their business models and strategies to improve their competitive position and reach or remain on the value frontier.

Failures in Competitive Positioning

Successful competitive positioning requires that a company achieve a fit between its strategies and its business model. Thus, a cost leader cannot strive for a high level of market segmentation, and provide a wide range of products, as a differentiator does, because this strategy would raise its cost structure too much, causing the company to lose its low-cost advantage. Similarly, a differentiator with a competency in innovation that tries to reduce its R&D costs, or one with a competency in after-sales service that seeks to economize on its sales force to lower costs, is asking for trouble because it is using the wrong strategies to implement its business model.

To pursue a successful business model, managers must be careful to ensure that the set of business-level strategies they have formulated and implemented are working in harmony to support each other and do not result in conflicts that ruin the competitive position a company is aiming for through its choice of business model. Many companies, through neglect, ignorance, or error—perhaps because of the Icarus paradox discussed in Chapter 3—do not work to continuously improve their business model, do not perform strategic-group analysis, and often fail to identify and respond to changing opportunities and threats in the industry environment. As a result, a company's business model starts to fail because its business-level strategies do not work together and its profitability starts to decline, as happened to Sony. Sometimes a company's performance can decline so quickly, it cannot recover and is taken over by its competitors or goes bankrupt. For example, Circuit City could not find a buyer because of its poor competitive situation and declared bankruptcy in 2009.

These companies have lost their position on the value frontier, either because they have lost the source of their competitive advantage or because their rivals have found ways to push out the value creation frontier and leave them behind. Sometimes these companies initially pursued a successful cost-leadership or differentiation business model but then gradually began to pursue business-level strategies that worked against them. Unfortunately, it seems that most companies lose control of their business models over time, often because they become large, complex companies that are difficult to manage or because the environment is changing faster than they can change their business model—such as by adjusting product and market strategies to suit changing industry conditions. This is why it is so important that managers *think strategically*.

There are many factors that can cause a company to make competitive positioning errors. Although some focused companies may succeed spectacularly for a time, a focuser may make a major error if, in its rush to implement its business model, it overexpands and so loses control of its business model. For example, People Express, a United States airline, was the first cost leader to emerge after deregulation of the United States airline industry. It started out as a specialized air carrier serving a narrow market niche: low-priced travel on the eastern seaboard. In pursuing focused cost leadership, it was very successful, but in its rush to expand to other geographic regions, it decided to take over other airlines. These airlines were differentiators that had never pursued cost leadership. This strategy raised People Express' cost structure, and it lost its competitive advantage against other national carriers and was taken over. Herb Kelleher, the founder of Southwest Airlines, watching how People Express had failed, stuck to the cost-leadership business model. He took *20 years* to build his national airline, but he never deviated from the strategies necessary to turn his company from a focused cost leader into the cost leader in the United States airline industry.

Differentiators can also fail in the market and end up stuck in the middle if focused competitors attack their markets with more valuable or low-cost products that blunt their competitive edge. This happened to IBM in the mainframe computer market as PCs became more powerful and able to do the job of the much more expensive mainframes. It also happened to Sony when companies like Apple and Samsung introduced products that better met customer needs. No company is safe in the jungle of competition, and each must be constantly on the lookout to take advantage of new opportunities as they arise. The experience of Holiday Inn described in the closing case describes how a company can lose control of its business model but also how managers can devise strategies that match changing competitive conditions and return to the value frontier.

In sum, strategic managers must employ the tools discussed in this book to continually monitor how well the business-level strategies they use to implement their company's business model are working. There is no more important task than ensuring that their company is optimally positioned against its rivals to compete for customers. And, as we have discussed, the constant changes occurring in the external environment, as well as the actions of competitors who work to develop superior business-level strategies, make competitive positioning a complex, demanding task that requires the highest degree of strategic thinking. That is why companies pay tens of millions of dollars a year to CEOs and other top managers who have demonstrated their ability to create and sustain successful business models.

SUMMARY OF CHAPTER

1. To create a successful business model, managers must choose business-level strategies that give the company a competitive advantage over its rivals; that is, they must optimize competitive positioning. They must first decide on (a) customer needs, or what is to be satisfied; (b) customer groups, or who is to be satisfied; and (c) distinctive competencies, or how customer needs are to be satisfied. These decisions determine which strategies they formulate and implement to put a company's business model into action.

2. Customer needs are desires, wants, or cravings that can be satisfied through the attributes or characteristics of a product. Customers choose a product based on (a) the way a product is differentiated from other products of its type and (b) the price of the product. Product differentiation is the process of designing products to satisfy customers' needs in ways that competing products cannot. Companies that create something distinct or different can often charge a higher, or premium, price for their products.

3. If managers devise strategies to differentiate a product by innovation, excellent quality, or responsiveness to customers, they are choosing a business model based on offering customers differentiated products. If managers base their business model on finding ways to reduce costs, they are choosing a business model based on offering customers low-priced products.

4. The second main strategy in formulating a successful business model is to decide what kind of product(s) to offer to which customer group(s). Market segmentation is the way a company decides to group customers, based on important differences in their needs or preferences, to gain a competitive advantage.

5. There are three main approaches toward market segmentation. First, a company might choose to ignore differences and make a product targeted at the average or typical customer. Second, a company can choose to recognize the differences between customer groups and make a product targeted toward most or all of the different market segments. Third, a company might choose to target just one or two market segments.

6. To develop a successful business model, strategic managers have to devise a set of strategies that determine (a) how to differentiate and price their product and (b) how much to segment a market and how wide a range of products to develop. Whether these strategies will result in a profitable business model now depends on a strategic manager's ability to provide customers with the most value while keeping the cost structure viable.

7. The value creation frontier represents the maximum amount of value that the products of different companies inside an industry can give customers at any one time by using different business models. Companies on the value frontier are those that have the most successful business models in a particular industry.

8. The value creation frontier can be reached by choosing among four *generic competitive strategies*: cost leadership, focused cost leadership, differentiation, and focused differentiation.

9. A cost-leadership business model is based on lowering the company's cost structure so it can

make and sell goods or services at a lower cost than its rivals. A cost leader is often a large, national company that targets the average customer. Focused cost leadership is developing the right strategies to serve just one or two market segments.

10. A differentiation business model is based on creating a product that customers perceive as different or distinct in some important way. Focused differentiation is providing a differentiated product for just one or two market segments.

11. The middle of the value creation frontier is occupied by broad differentiators, which have pursued their differentiation strategy in a way that has also allowed them to lower their cost structure over time.

12. Strategic-group analysis helps companies in an industry better understand the dynamics of competitive positioning. In strategic-group analysis, managers identify and chart the business models and business-level strategies their industry rivals are pursuing. Then they can determine which strategies are successful and unsuccessful and why a certain business model is working or not. In turn, this allows them to either fine-tune or radically alter their business models and strategies to improve their competitive position.

13. Many companies, through neglect, ignorance, or error, do not work to continually improve their business model, do not perform strategic-group analysis, and often fail to identify and respond to changing opportunities and threats. As a result, their business-level strategies do not work together, their business model starts to fail, and their profitability starts to decline. There is no more important task than ensuring that one's company is optimally positioned against its rivals to compete for customers.

DISCUSSION QUESTIONS

1. What strategies does a company need to develop to become a broad differentiator? In what ways does this provide it with a competitive advantage over either cost leaders or differentiators?

2. What is the value creation frontier? How does each of the four generic business models allow a company to reach this frontier?

3. How do changes in the environment affect the success of a company's business model?

C L O S I N G   C A S E

Holiday Inns on Six Continents

The history of the Holiday Inn motel chain is one of the great success stories in United States business. Its founder, Kemmons Wilson, vacationing in the early 1950s, found motels to be small, expensive, and of unpredictable quality. This discovery, along with the prospect of unprecedented highway travel that would come with the new interstate highway program, triggered a realization: there was an unmet customer need—a gap in the market for quality accommodations.[20] Holiday Inn was founded to meet that need. From the beginning, Holiday Inn set the standard for offering motel features such as air-conditioning and icemakers while keeping room rates reasonable. These amenities enhanced the motels' popularity, and motel franchising, Wilson's invention, made rapid expansion possible. By 1960, Holiday Inns could be found in virtually every city and on every major highway. Before the 1960s ended, more than 1,000 were in full operation, and occupancy rates averaged 80%. The concept of mass accommodation had arrived.

The service Holiday Inn offered appealed to the average traveler, who wanted a standardized product (a room) at an average price—the middle of the hotel room market. But by the 1970s, travelers were beginning to make different demands on hotels and motels. Some wanted luxury and were willing to pay higher prices for better accommodations and service. Others sought low prices and accepted rock-bottom quality and service in exchange. As the market fragmented into different groups of customers with different needs, Holiday Inn was still offering an undifferentiated, average-cost, average-quality product.

Although Holiday Inn missed the change in the market and thus failed to respond appropriately to it, the competition did not. Companies such as Hyatt siphoned off the top end of the market, where quality and service sold rooms. Chains such as Motel 6 and Days Inn captured the basic-quality, low-price end of the market. In between were many specialty chains that appealed to business travelers, families, or self-caterers (people who want to be able to cook in their hotel rooms). Holiday Inn's position was attacked from all sides. As occupancy rates dropped drastically with increasing competition, profitability declined.

Wounded but not dead, Holiday Inn began a counterattack. The original chain was upgraded to suit quality-oriented travelers. Then, to meet the needs of different kinds of travelers, Holiday Inn created new hotel and motel chains: the luxury Crowne Plaza; Hampton Inn serving the low-priced end of the market; and the all-suite Embassy Suites. Thus, Holiday Inn attempted to meet the demands of the many niches, or segments, of the hotel market that have emerged as customers' needs have changed over time. These moves were successful in the early 1990s, and Holiday Inn grew to become one of the largest suppliers of hotel rooms in the industry. However, by the late 1990s, falling revenues made it clear that with intense competition in the industry from other chains such as Marriott, Holiday Inn was once again losing its differentiated appeal.[21]

In the fast-changing hotel and lodging market, positioning each hotel brand or chain to maximize customer demand is a continuing endeavor. In 2000, the pressure on all hotel chains to adapt to the challenges of global competition and become globally differentiated brands led to the takeover of Holiday Inn and its incorporation into the international Six Continents Hotels chain. Today, around the globe, more than 3,200 hotels flying the flags of Holiday Inn, Holiday Inn Express, Crowne Plaza, Staybridge Suites by Holiday Inn, and luxury Inter-Continental Hotels and Resorts are positioning themselves to offer the services, amenities, and lodging experiences that will cater to virtually every travel occasion and guest need.[22] In the 2000s, the company has undertaken a massive modernization campaign in the United States to take existing full-service Holiday Inns to their next evolution. Holiday Inn plans to have a room to meet the need of every segment of the lodging market anywhere in the world.

Case Discussion Questions

1. Why did Holiday Inn's business model and strategies change over time?

2. What are the strategies behind the Six Continents Hotels current business model? In what ways is it trying to improve its competitive advantage?

6

INDUSTRY ENVIRONMENT
AND BUSINESS—LEVEL STRATEGY

LEARNING OBJECTIVES

After reading this chapter, you should be able to

- Explain why strategic managers need to tailor their business models to the conditions that exist in different kinds of industry environments
- Identify the strategies managers can develop to increase profitability in fragmented industries
- Discuss the special problems that exist in embryonic and growth industries and how companies can develop successful business models to compete effectively

- Understand competitive dynamics in mature industries and discuss the strategies managers can develop to increase profitability even when competition is intense
- Outline the different strategies companies in declining industries can use to support their business models and profitability

OPENING CASE

Competition in the Microchip Business Speeds Up

Intel has always been the leader in the market for central processing units (CPUs) microchips; its Pentium, Atom, and new Nehalem chips provide the processing power for all kinds of PCs, including desktops, laptops, and smartbooks.

Its main competitor is AMD. The market for graphic processing units (GPUs) microchips that provide state-of-the-art animation, high-definition video, and the processing power needed to run high-powered computer games such as Crysis, World of Warcraft, and Grand Theft Auto and that allow for sophisticated 3D rendering of shapes and images has been dominated by Nvidia. Nvidia's GPU chips are a favorite among sophisticated gamers, animators, and visual designers. Nvidia's main competitor is ATI, which was bought by AMD (Intel's major CPU competitor) in 2006.

AMD's goal in buying ATI was to combine the different processing powers of the CPU and GPU chips to give PC users the best possible computer processing power and speed while providing stunning graphic capabilities. By combining both kinds of chips, AMD's goal was to obtain a competitive advantage over Intel. Intel's CPUs have only very basic graphic processing power—enough for ordinary PC tasks but not sufficient for powerful gaming applications, video processing, or sophisticated graphic interfaces such as those inside Apple's PCs. GPUs are the heart of all gaming consoles, and Nvidia provided the chip used in the first Xbox. Currently AMD's ATI division supplies the GPU that powers the Nintendo Wii, and Nvidia's GPU is inside the PlayStation3. Nvidia scored a major coup in 2009 when Apple announced that all its new PCs would contain Nvidia's advanced GPUs because of their state-of-the-art performance. Nevertheless, in 2009, ATI also introduced powerful new GPUs that compete with Nvidia's. Today, both Nvidia and ATI compete to provide the GPUs in the PCs offered by makers such as Dell, HP, and Lenovo; in addition, Intel and AMD compete to provide the CPU in these PCs.

The complex, competitive situation between these three companies has led to major changes in their business models, competitive positioning, and strategies in the maturing PC market. For example, fierce competition between AMD and Intel came to a head in 2005 when AMD introduced a new generation 64-bit CPU that performed better than Intel's, and its stock price shot up as Intel struggled to catch up. But Intel, a broad differentiator with massive resources invested heavily, innovated an even more powerful CPU, and by 2007, it had matched and outperformed AMD's. At the same time, Intel had the resources to make its next-generation CPUs smaller, something which is increasingly important today because of the need to cool the smaller-sized laptops. AMD's stock price plunged as Intel's soared because it had lost its lead in CPUs and because in 2007 it still had no viable GPU to compete with Nvidia's.

Then, as noted, in 2008 Nvidia received a major shock when AMD's ATI introduced its next-generation GPU chip that outperformed Nvidia's and offered these powerful GPUs at lower prices to regain market share. Then, Nvidia's stock price plunged; it was forced to reduce the price of its GPUs to compete. A price war began, and the profits of both companies fell. At the same time, ATI was still battling with Intel in the CPU market, in which Intel's new "dual core" processors had become the market leader. AMD introduced its next-generation chips that matched and even outperformed Intel's; the result again was a price war in which companies reduced the price of their CPUs to fight for market share. The result was that each of the three chipmakers' profits were falling because they locked in an intense competitive battle; at the same time, PC customers obtained more powerful PCs at lower and lower prices.

Then, in 2008, to worsen the competitive situation, Intel announced that it was developing its own state-of-the-art GPU code named Larrabee to compete directly against Nvidia and AMD. Intel had recognized how rapidly the GPU market was growing because of the increasing popularity of online video, animations, HD movies, and, of course, high-powered games played on PCs. With Intel, the giant in CPUs now competing in the GPU segment of the market, the stock price of Nvidia and AMD crumbled. Prices of all kinds of chips continued to plunge just as all three companies have had to spend billions on expensive new R&D to innovate improved chips, even as their profits plunge. The bottom line is that the intense competition in the computer chip market is leading to falling profitability of the three major companies, even though they are providing customers with much more value for their money. Clearly, the most innovative companies need to manage industry competition to ensure that they can provide their customers with superior products and, at the same time, obtain above-average profits so they can fund the innovation necessary to improve products and profitability over time.

Overview

As competition in the microchip industry suggests, even leading industry companies—those with the most successful business models—face major problems in maintaining their profitability over time. Even if strategic managers do create a successful business model, they still face another challenge: the need to continuously develop and improve their business-level strategies to sustain their competitive advantage over time as the industry environment changes. As the industry environment changes over the life cycle, the kinds of opportunities and threats that face a company change; its business model and strategies have to adapt and change to meet this changing environment.

This chapter first examines how companies in fragmented industries can develop new kinds of business-level strategies to strengthen their business models. It then considers the challenges of developing and sustaining a competitive advantage in embryonic, growth, mature, and declining industries. By the end of this chapter, you will understand how forces in the changing industry environment require managers to pursue new kinds of strategies to strengthen their company's business model and keep it at the value creation frontier where the most profit is earned.

STRATEGIES IN FRAGMENTED INDUSTRIES

A *fragmented industry* is one composed of a large number of small and medium-sized companies, for example, the dry cleaning, restaurant, health club, and legal services industries. There are several reasons that an industry may consist of many small companies rather than a few large ones.[1]

First, fragmented industries are characterized by low barriers to entry because they lack economies of scale. Many homebuyers, for example, prefer dealing with local real estate agents, whom they perceive as having better local knowledge than national chains. Second, in some industries, there may even be diseconomies of scale. In the restaurant business, for example, customers often prefer the unique food and style of a popular local restaurant rather than the standardized offerings of some national chain. Third, low entry barriers that permit constant entry by new companies also serve to keep an industry fragmented. The restaurant industry exemplifies this situation. The costs of opening a restaurant are moderate and can be borne by a single entrepreneur. High transportation costs, too, can keep an industry fragmented, and local or regional production may be the only efficient way to satisfy customers' needs, as in the dirt, cement, brick, or custom glass industries. Finally, an industry may be fragmented because customer needs are so specialized that only a small amount of a product is required, hence, there is no scope for a large mass-production operation to satisfy the market, for example, custom-made jewelry or catering.

If these conditions exist, in many fragmented industries the focus business model will be the most profitable to pursue. Companies may specialize by customer group, customer need, or geographic region so that many small specialty companies operate in local or regional markets. All kinds of specialized or custom-made products—furniture, clothing, hats, boots, houses, and so on—fall into this category, as do all small service operations that cater to personalized customer needs, such as laundries, restaurants, health clubs, and furniture rental stores.

However, strategic managers are eager to gain the cost advantages of pursuing cost leadership or the sales-revenue-enhancing advantages of differentiation by circumventing the competitive conditions that have allowed focus companies to dominate an industry. Essentially, companies search for a business model and strategies that will allow them to *consolidate* a fragmented industry to obtain the above average profitability possible in a consolidated industry. These companies include large retailers such as Walmart and Target and fast-food chains such as McDonald's and Subway; repair shops such as Midas, Inc.; and even lawyers, consultants, and tax preparers.

To grow, consolidate their industries, and become industry leaders, these companies have developed strategies—such as chaining, franchising, horizontal merger, and using the Internet and IT—to realize the advantages of a cost-leadership or differentiation business model. By doing so, many focus companies lost their competitive advantage and have disappeared (Figure 6.1).

Chaining

Companies such as Walmart and Midas pursue a **chaining** strategy to obtain the advantages of cost leadership. They establish networks of linked merchandising outlets that are interconnected by IT and function as one large company. The enormous buying power these companies possess through their chain of nationwide stores allows them to negotiate large price reductions with suppliers that promote their competitive advantage. They overcome the barrier of high transportation costs by establishing regional distribution centers that can economize on inventory costs and maximize responsiveness to the needs of regional stores and customers. They also realize economies of scale by sharing managerial skills across the chain, and they can use nationwide, rather than local, advertising.

Thus, by the use of chaining, companies achieve the cost and differentiation advantages enjoyed by industry leaders; indeed, they often become the new industry leaders. For example, the chaining strategy has been used in a wide range of retail industries, consolidating one after the other. Barnes & Noble and Borders used this strategy in book retailing; Staples applied it to office supplies; Best Buy to electronics retailing; Home Depot to building supplies; and so on. In each case, the companies that used chaining to pursue a business model based on cost leadership or differentiation changed the competitive structure of the industry to its advantage, consolidating the industry and weakening the five forces of competition in the process.

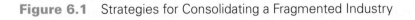

Figure 6.1 Strategies for Consolidating a Fragmented Industry

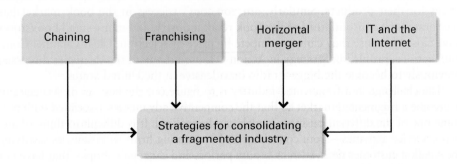

Franchising

Like chaining, franchising is a business-level strategy that allows companies, particularly service companies such as McDonald's or Century 21 Real Estate, to enjoy the competitive advantages that result from cost leadership or differentiation. In franchising, the franchisor (parent) grants to its franchisees the right to use the parent's name, reputation, and business model in a particular location or area in return for a sizable franchise fee and often a percentage of the profits.[2]

One particular advantage of this strategy is that because franchisees essentially own their businesses, they are strongly motivated to make the company-wide business model work effectively and make sure that quality and standards are consistently high so that customers' needs are always satisfied. Such motivation is particularly critical for a differentiator that must continually work to maintain its unique or distinctive appeal. In addition, franchising lessens the financial burden of swift expansion, which permits rapid growth of the company. Finally, a nationwide franchised company can reap the advantages of large-scale advertising, as well as economies in purchasing, management, and distribution, as McDonald's does very efficiently in pursuing its cost-leadership model.

Horizontal Merger

Companies such as Anheuser-Busch, Dillard's, and Blockbuster chose a strategy of *horizontal merger* to consolidate their respective industries. For example, Dillard's arranged the merger of regional store chains to form a national company. By pursuing horizontal merger, companies are able to obtain economies of scale and secure a national market for their product. As a result, they are able to pursue a cost-leadership or a differentiation business model (although, Dillard's has been struggling to pursue its differentiation model effectively). The many important strategic implications of horizontal merger are discussed in detail in Chapter 9.

Using Information Technology and the Internet

The development of new IT often gives a company the opportunity to develop new business strategies to consolidate a fragmented industry. eBay and amazon.com, for example, use the Internet and the associated strategies e-commerce makes possible to pursue a cost-leadership model and consolidate the fragmented auction and book-selling industries. Before eBay, the auction business was extremely fragmented, with local auctions in cities being the principal way in which people could dispose of their antiques and collectibles. By harnessing the Internet, eBay can now assure sellers that they are getting wide visibility for their collectibles and are likely to receive higher prices for their products. Similarly, amazon.com's success in the book market has accelerated the consolidation of the book retail industry, and many small bookstores have closed because they cannot compete by price or selection. Clear Channel Communications, profiled in Strategy in Action 6.1, used many of the strategies discussed previously to become the biggest radio broadcaster in the United States.

The challenge in a fragmented industry is to figure out the best set of strategies to overcome a fragmented market so that the competitive advantages associated with pursuing one of the different business models can be realized. It is difficult to think of any major service activities—from consulting and accounting firms to businesses satisfying the smallest customer need, such as beauty parlors and car repair shops—that have not been consolidated by companies seeking to pursue a more profitable business model.

6.1 STRATEGY IN ACTION

Clear Channel Creates a National Chain of Local Radio Stations

Clear Channel Communications started out with only one radio station in San Antonio in 1995. Historically, the radio broadcasting industry was fragmented because federal law did not allow one company to own more than 40 stations nationwide; as a result, most local radio stations were independently owned. Clear Channel took advantage of the repeal of this law in 1996 to purchase radio stations and, most importantly, develop a business model (which today is one of *broad differentiation*) that would allow it to obtain the gains from consolidating this fragmented industry; by the 2000s, it operated more than 1,200 United States radio stations.

Clear Channel's strategic managers recognized from the beginning that the major way to increase the profitability of local radio stations was to obtain economies of scale by operating and marketing them on a national level. The question was how to find ways to raise the quality of its programming to increase the number of listeners and thus increase advertising revenues (advertising rates are based on the number of listeners). At the same time, it needed to find ways to reduce each station's high operating costs, that is, lower its cost structure. How to do both simultaneously was the challenge. Clear Channel's managers took advantage of emerging digital technology that allowed for the easy and rapid manipulation and transfer of large volumes of data to accomplish both these goals.

By the late 1990s, music and programming could easily be recorded, stored in digital format, and edited. Its managers hit on a strategy called "voice tracking." To obtain economies of scale, Clear Channel employed popular regional or national DJs to record its daily programs, and these DJs customized their productions to suit the needs of local markets. For example, one technology allows DJs to isolate and listen to the end of one track and the beginning of the next; then they can insert whatever talk, news, or information is appropriate between tracks how and when they like. The local stations supply this local information; after they have customized their program, the DJs send it over the Internet, where the local operators handle it. This practice has enormous advantages. On the cost side, the programming costs of a limited number of popular DJs are much lower than the cost of employing an army of local DJs. On the differentiation side, the quality of programming is much higher because Clear Channel can invest more in its programming and because the appeal of some DJs is much higher than others. Over time, higher-quality programming increases the number of listeners, and this attracts more national advertisers, whose digital advertisements can be easily inserted in the programming by local operators.

In addition, Clear Channel developed its own proprietary brand name, KISS, across its radio stations so that when people travel, they will be attracted to its local stations wherever they are. It hoped that the resulting increased customer demand would drive up advertising revenues, thereby lowering its cost structure and increasing its future profitability. Clear Channel received a major shock in the 2000s when the growing popularity of MP3 players like the iPod and online videos began to sharply reduce the size of its listening audience, hurting its advertising revenues. It has been forced to experiment with new ways to tailor radio advertising to listeners, experimenting with short sound bites, and also partnered with Google to find ways to better tailor advertising to the particular needs of the local market. Once again, nothing stays the same for long in any competitive industry environment.

Sources: http://www.clearchannel.com, 2009; A. W. Mathews, "From a Distance: A Giant Chain Is Perfecting the Art of Seeming Local," *Wall Street Journal*, February 25, 2002, A1, A4.

STRATEGIES IN EMBRYONIC AND GROWTH INDUSTRIES

As Chapter 2 discusses, an embryonic industry is one that is just beginning to develop, and a growth industry is one in which first-time demand is expanding rapidly as many new customers enter the market. In choosing the strategies needed to pursue a business model, embryonic and growth industries pose special challenges because new groups of customers with different kinds of needs emerge. Strategic managers need to be aware of the way competitive forces in embryonic and growth industries change over time because they commonly have to build and develop new kinds of competencies and refine their business models to compete effectively in the long term.

Most embryonic industries emerge when a technological innovation creates a new product opportunity. For example, a century ago, the introduction of the internal combustion engine led to the development of "moving vehicles" and the rise of new industries making such products as motorcars, motorbuses, and motorbikes. In 1975, the PC industry was born after Intel developed new microprocessor (CPU) technology that allowed companies to build the world's first PCs; the PC software industry was born when Microsoft developed an operating system for IBM.[3] Customer demand for the products of an embryonic industry is limited at first for a variety of reasons. Reasons for slow growth in market demand include (1) the limited performance and poor quality of the first products; (2) customer unfamiliarity with what the new product can do for them; (3) poorly developed distribution channels to get the product to customers; (4) a lack of complementary products to increase the value of the product for customers; and (5) high production costs because of small volumes of production. Strategic managers who understand how markets develop are in a much better position to pursue a business model and strategies that will lead to a sustained competitive advantage.

Customer demand for the first cars, for example, was limited by their poor performance (they were no faster than a horse, far noisier, and frequently broke down), a lack of important complementary products such as a network of paved roads and gas stations, and high production costs that made them a luxury. Similarly, demand for the first PCs was limited because buyers had to be able to program computers to use them; there were no software programs to purchase that could run on the original PCs. Because of such problems, early demand for the products of embryonic industries came from a small set of technologically savvy customers willing and able to tolerate and even enjoy imperfections in their new purchase. Computer geeks who derive great joy out of tinkering with their (still) imperfect PCs and try to find ways to make them work better are the ones who buy the next-generation PCs—laptops, smartbooks, or smartphones.

An industry moves from the embryonic to the growth stage when a mass market, that is, one in which a large numbers of customers enter the market, starts to develop for its product. Mass markets start to develop when three things happen: (1) ongoing technological progress makes a product easier to use and increases its value for the average customer; (2) complementary products are developed that also increase its value; and (3) companies in the industry work to find ways to reduce the costs of making the new products so they can lower their prices and stimulate high demand.[4] For example, the mass market for cars emerged and the demand for cars surged when (1) technological progress increased the performance of cars; (2) a network of paved roads and gas stations was established; and (3) Henry Ford began to mass produce cars, something that dramatically reduced production costs, which allowed him to reduce car prices. Similarly, the mass market for PCs emerged when technological advances made them easier to use, a supply of complementary software such as spreadsheets and word processing programs was developed that increased the value of owning a PC, and companies in the industry such as Dell began to use mass production to build PCs at low cost.

The Changing Nature of Market Demand

Strategic managers who understand how the demand for a product is affected by the changing needs of customers can focus on developing new strategies that will protect and strengthen their business models, such as building competencies to lower manufacturing costs or speed product development. In most product markets, the changing needs of customers lead to the S-shaped growth curve illustrated in Figure 6.2, which illustrates how different groups of customers with different needs enter the market over time. The curve is S-shaped because as the stage of market development moves from embryonic to mature, customer demand first accelerates then decelerates as the market approaches the saturation point where most customers have already bought the product. This curve has major implications for a company's differentiation, cost, and pricing competitive positioning decisions.

The first group of customers to enter the market are referred to as the *innovators*. Innovators are "technocrats," people who are delighted by being the first to purchase and experiment with a product based on a new technology—even though it is imperfect and expensive. Frequently, they have an engineering mindset and want to "own" the technology because it is so new. In the PC market, the first customers were software engineers and computer hobbyists who wanted to write computer code at home.[5]

Early adopters are the second group of customers to enter the market; they understand that the technology may have important future applications and are willing to experiment with it to see if they can pioneer uses for it. Early adopters are often people who envision how the technology may be used in the future, and they try to be the first to profit from its use. Jeff Bezos, the founder of amazon.com, was an early adopter of Internet technology. He saw in 1994 before anyone else that the Internet could be used in innovative ways to sell books.

Both innovators and early adopters enter the market while the industry is in its embryonic stage. The next group of customers, the *early majority*, forms the leading wave or edge of the mass market, and their entry into the market signifies the beginning of the

Figure 6.2 Market Development and Customer Groups

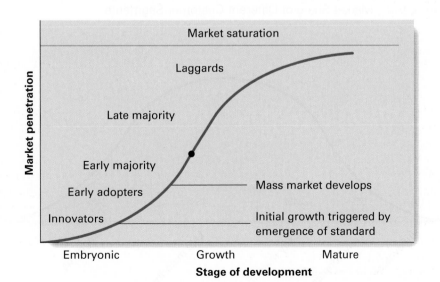

growth stage. Customers in the early majority are practical, understanding the new technology. They weigh the benefits of adopting its new products against their costs and wait to enter the market until they are confident they will benefit. When they decide to enter the market, a large number of new buyers may be expected. This is what happened in the PC market after IBM's introduction of the PC in 1981. For the early majority, IBM's entry into the market legitimized PC technology and signaled that the benefits of adopting it would be worth the cost to purchase and learn how to use a PC. The growth of the PC market was then further strengthened by the development of applications that added value to the PC, such as new spreadsheet and word processing programs. These applications transformed the PC from a hobbyist's toy into a business productivity tool.

When the mass market reaches a critical mass, with about 30% of the potential market penetrated, the next group of customers enters the market. This group is characterized as the *late majority*, the customers who purchase a new technology or product only when it is obvious it has great utility and is here to stay. A typical late majority customer group is the older set of customers, unfamiliar with the new technology that began to enter the PC market in the mid-1990s. However, by observing other people buying PCs to send e-mail and browse the Web, they overcame their hesitancy and started to purchase PCs. By 2002, some 65% of homes in the United States had at least one PC, suggesting that the product was well into the late majority group, and the market was approaching saturation. Indeed, the entry of the late majority signals the end of the growth stage.

Laggards, the last group of customers to enter the market, are people who are inherently conservative and distrustful of new technology. Laggards frequently refuse to adopt it even when its benefits are obvious or unless they are forced to do so by circumstances—for work reasons, for example. People who use typewriters rather than computers to write letters and books or insist on using fountain pens rather than "micro" ballpoints would be considered laggards.

In Figure 6.3, the bell-shaped curve represents the total market, and the divisions in the curve show the average percentage of customers who fall into each of these

Figure 6.3   Market Share of Different Customer Segments

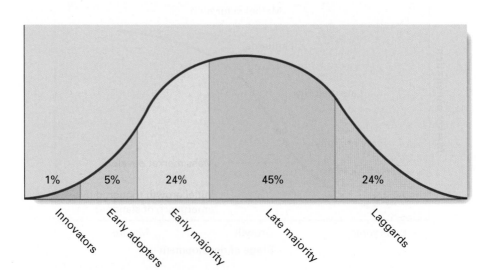

customer groups. Note that early adopters are a very small percentage of the market; hence, the figure illustrates a vital competitive dynamic—the highest market demand and industry profits arise when the early and late majority enters the market. And research has found that although early pioneering companies succeed in attracting innovators and early adopters, many of these companies often *fail* to attract a significant share of early and late majority customers and ultimately go out of business.

Strategic Implications: Crossing the Chasm

Why are pioneering companies often unable to create a business model that allows them to be successful over time and remain the market leaders? *Innovators and early adopters have very different customer needs from the early majority.* In an influential book, Geoffrey Moore argues that because of the differences in customer needs between these groups, the business-level strategies required for companies to succeed in the emerging mass market are quite different from those required to succeed in the embryonic market.[6] Pioneering companies that do not change the strategies they use to pursue their business model will therefore lose their competitive advantage to those companies that implement new strategies to remain on the value creation frontier. New strategies are often required to strengthen a company's business model as a market develops over time for the following reasons:

- Innovators and early adopters are technologically sophisticated customers willing to tolerate the limitations of the product; the early majority, however, value ease of use and reliability. Companies competing in an embryonic market typically pay more attention to increasing the performance of a product than to its ease of use and reliability. Those competing in a mass market need to make sure that the product is reliable and easy to use. Thus, the product development strategies required for success are different as a market develops over time.
- Innovators and early adopters are typically reached through specialized distribution channels, and products are often sold by word of mouth. Reaching the early majority requires mass-market distribution channels and mass media advertising campaigns that require a different set of marketing and sales strategies.
- Because innovators and the early majority are relatively few in number and are not particularly price sensitive, companies serving them typically pursue a focus model and produce small quantities of a product. To serve the rapidly growing mass market, a cost-leadership model based on large-scale mass production may be critical to ensure that a high-quality product can be produced reliably at a low price point.

In sum, the business model and strategies required to compete in an embryonic market populated by early adopters and innovators are very different from those required to compete in a high-growth mass market populated by the early majority. As a consequence, the transition between the embryonic market and the mass market is not a smooth, seamless one. Rather, it represents a *competitive chasm* or gulf that companies must cross. According to Moore, many companies do not or cannot develop the right business model; they fall into the chasm and go out of business. Thus, although embryonic markets are typically populated by a large number of small companies, once the mass market begins to develop, the number of companies falls sharply.[7]

Figure 6.4, which compares the strategies of AOL Time Warner and Prodigy Communications, illustrates Moore's thesis by showing that a chasm exists between innovators and the early majority, that is, between the embryonic market and the rapidly growing mass market. Note also that other chasms exist between other sets of

Figure 6.4   The Chasm: AOL and Prodigy

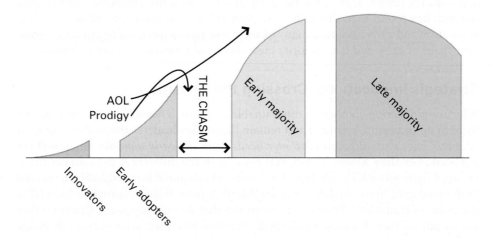

customers; these also represent important changes in customer demand that require changes in business-level strategy (for example, a different approach to market segmentation). To successfully cross a chasm, Moore implied a company must continually work to develop the right strategies and build new competencies to create a business model that will allow it to cross the chasm, survive, and prosper. Strategy in Action 6.2 describes how one company, AOL, successfully built a business model to cross a chasm, and how another company, Prodigy, failed.

The implication is clear: to cross this chasm successfully, managers must correctly identify the customer needs of the first wave of early majority users—the leading edge of the mass market. Then they must alter their business models by developing new strategies to redesign products and create distribution channels and marketing campaigns to satisfy the needs of the early majority. They must have available a suitable product at a reasonable price that they can sell to the early majority when they begin to enter the market in large numbers. At the same time, the industry pioneers must abandon their old focused business model that was directed solely at the needs of innovators and early adopters because this focus will lead them to ignore the needs of the early majority—and the need to develop the strategies needed to pursue a differentiation or cost-leadership business model and remain a dominant industry competitor.

Strategic Implications of Market Growth Rates

A final important issue that strategic managers must understand in embryonic and growth industries is that different markets develop at different rates. The speed at which a market develops can be measured by its growth rate, that is, the rate at which the industry's product is bought by customers in that market. A number of factors explain the variation in market growth rates for different products and thus the speed with which a particular industry develops. It is important for strategic managers to understand the source of these differences, for by their choice of business model and strategies, they can accelerate or retard the rate at which a particular market grows.[8] In other words, business-level strategy is a major determinant of industry profitability.

6.2 STRATEGY IN ACTION

AOL, Prodigy, and the Chasm between Innovators and the Early Majority

Before America Online (AOL) became a household name, Prodigy Communications was a market leader. When its online network was launched in 1990, Prodigy's business model was differentiation, and its goal was to build the largest proprietary online shopping network. It quickly attracted a half a million users. Competition was low at this time; the largest competitor, CompuServe, was conservatively managed, and it pursued a focused business model based on servicing the needs of technical and financial users. There was one smaller competitor, AOL, but as one Prodigy executive commented, "It was just a little thing off to the side." Ten years later, the little thing had become the largest online service in the world with 33 million members, and Prodigy had been forced to exit the online business altogether.

Why did Prodigy fail? The company appeared to be focusing on the mass market; its target customers were not computer-oriented early adopters but typical middle-class Americans. And its business model to sell products online seemed correct; surely this ultimately had to become a major Internet application. The problem was that Prodigy's managers did not choose the right set of strategies to formulate its business model to attract the early majority because they did not understand the full range of needs customers were trying to satisfy by using the Internet.

One of the surprise early drivers of customer demand for online services, and a major factor in creating the mass market, was e-mail. To attract the early majority, AOL's strategy was to offer its members unlimited e-mail, but Prodigy charged its members a fee for sending more than 30 e-mails per month—a big difference in business strategy. Another important application of online service that customers were increasingly embracing was chat rooms. AOL saw chat rooms as an important online application to satisfy customer needs; its strategy was to quickly develop the software that soon made chat rooms one of its most popular services. Prodigy's lawyers, however, feared it might be held legally liable for comments made in chat rooms or events that arose from them. They discouraged Prodigy from offering this service. This censorship, lack of chat rooms, and charges for e-mail rankled its members, and they began to switch to AOL.

By 1996, the battle was effectively over: AOL was growing by leaps and bounds, and Prodigy was losing customers at a rapid pace because it had not developed the right set of strategies to pursue a differentiation business model that allowed it remain on the value frontier. AOL, by correctly sensing the way customer needs were changing and then providing a differentiated product that met those needs, crossed the chasm with ease.

Sources: http://www.aol.com (2009); Kara Swisher, AOL.com (New York: Random House, 1998).

The first factor that accelerates customer demand is a new product's *relative advantage*, that is, the degree to which a new product is perceived as better at satisfying customer needs than the product it supersedes. For example, the early growth in demand for cell phones was partly driven by their economic benefits. Studies showed that because business customers could always be reached by cell phone, they made better use of their time—for example, by not showing up at a meeting that had been cancelled at the last minute—and saved two hours per week in time that would otherwise have been wasted. For busy executives, the early adopters, the productivity benefits of owning a cell phone outweighed the costs. Cell phones also diffused rapidly for social reasons, in particular, because they conferred glamour or prestige on their users (something that also drives demand for advanced kinds of handheld computers and smartphones).

Another factor driving growth in demand is *compatibility*, the degree to which a new product is perceived as being consistent with the current needs or existing values of potential adopters. Demand for cell phones grew rapidly because their operation was compatible with the prior experience of potential adopters who used traditional landline phones. *Complexity*, the degree to which a new product is perceived as difficult to understand and use, is a third factor. Early PCs with their clunky operating system interfaces were complex to use, and, hence, slow to be adopted. The first cell phones were simple to use and were adopted quickly. A fourth factor is *trialability*, the degree to which potential customers can experiment with a new product on a hands-on trial basis. Many people first used cell phones by borrowing them from colleagues to make calls, and the positive experiences helped accelerate growth rates. In contrast, early PCs were more difficult to experiment with because they were rare and expensive, and because some training was needed in how to use them. These complications led to slower growth rates. A final factor is *observability*, the degree to which the results of using and enjoying a new product can be seen and appreciated by other people. The Palm Pilot and later the Blackberry diffused rapidly because it was easy to see how quickly their users could schedule meetings, enter addresses, record expenses, and so on. When the convenience of the devices is clear, they are rapidly adopted.

Thus, strategic managers must be sure to devise strategies that help to educate customers about the value of their products if they are to grow their company's market share over time.

A related strategic issue when a market is growing rapidly is that the popularity of a new product often increases or spreads in a way that is analogous to a *viral model of infection*. Lead adopters (the first customers who buy a product) in a market become "infected" or enthused with the product, such as Blackberry or iPhone users. Subsequently, they infect other people by telling them about their advantages. After having observed the benefits of the product, these people also adopt it. Companies promoting new products can take advantage of viral diffusion by identifying and aggressively courting opinion leaders in a particular market—the customers whose views command respect. For example, when the manufacturers of new high-tech medical equipment, such as an MRI scanner, start to sell a new product, they first try to get well-known doctors at major research and teaching hospitals to use the product. They may give these opinion leaders free machines for their research purposes and work closely with them in developing the technology. Once these opinion leaders commit to the product and give it their stamp of approval, doctors at many other hospitals often follow.

In sum, understanding competitive dynamics in embryonic and growth industries is an important strategic issue. The ways in which different kinds of customer groups emerge and customer needs change are important determinants of the strategies that need to be pursued to make a business model successful over time. Similarly, understanding the factors that affect a market's growth rate allows managers to tailor their business model to a changing industry environment. (More is said about competition in high-tech industries in the next chapter.)

NAVIGATING THROUGH THE LIFE CYCLE TO MATURITY

Another crucial business decision that faces strategic managers at each stage of the industry life cycle is which investment strategy to pursue. An investment strategy determines the amount and type of resources and capital—human, functional, and financial—that must be spent to configure a company's value chain so that it can pursue a business model successfully over time.[9] In deciding on an investment strategy, managers must evaluate the potential return (on invested capital) from investing in a particular business model against the cost. In this way, they can determine whether pursuing a certain business model is likely to be profitable and how the profitability of a particular business model will change as competition within the industry changes.

Two factors are crucial in choosing an investment strategy: (1) the competitive advantage a company's business model gives it in an industry relative to its competitors and (2) the stage of the industry's life cycle in which the company is competing.[10] In determining the strength of a company's relative competitive position, market share and distinctive competencies become important. A large market share signals greater potential returns from future investment because it suggests a company has brand loyalty and is in a strong position to grow its profits in the future. Similarly, the more difficult it is to imitate a company's distinctive competencies, such as those in R&D or manufacturing and marketing, the more sustainable is the competitive advantage supplied by its business model and the greater the likelihood that investment in it will lead to higher profitability. These two attributes also reinforce one another; for example, a large market share may help a company create and develop distinctive competencies that strengthen its business model over time because high demand allows it to ride down the experience curve and lower its cost structure. Also, a large market share may create a large cash flow that allows a company to invest more to develop competencies in R&D or elsewhere. In general, companies with the largest market share and the strongest distinctive competencies are in the best position to build and sustain their competitive advantage. Companies with small market shares and little ability to develop distinctive competencies are in a much weaker competitive position.[15]

Because different kinds of opportunities and threats are found in each life cycle stage, the stage of the industry life cycle also influences a company's choice of how much to invest in its business model. Each stage, therefore, has different implications for the investment of resources needed to obtain a competitive advantage. Competition is strongest in the shakeout stage of the life cycle and least important in the embryonic stage, for example. The *risks* associated with pursuing a certain business model change over time. The difference in risk explains why the potential returns from investing in a particular business model depend on the life cycle stage.

Embryonic Strategies

In the embryonic stage, all companies, weak and strong, emphasize the development of a distinctive competency to build a successful business model. During this stage, investment needs are great because a company has to establish a competitive advantage. Many fledgling companies in the industry are seeking resources to develop a distinctive competency. Thus, the appropriate business-level investment strategy is a **share-building strategy**. The aim is to build market share by developing a stable and distinct competitive advantage to attract customers who have no knowledge of the company's products.

Companies require large amounts of capital to develop R&D or sales and service competencies. They cannot generate much of this capital internally. Thus, a company's success depends on its ability to demonstrate a distinctive competency to attract outside investors, or venture capitalists. If a company gains the resources to develop a distinctive competency, it will be in a relatively stronger competitive position. If it fails, its only option may be to exit the industry. In fact, companies in weak competitive positions at all stages in the life cycle may choose to exit the industry to cut their losses.

Growth Strategies

At the growth stage, the task facing a company is to strengthen its business model to provide the competitive foundation it needs to survive the coming shakeout. Thus, the appropriate investment strategy is the **growth strategy**. The goal is to maintain its relative competitive position in a rapidly expanding market and, if possible, to increase it—in other words, to grow with the expanding market. However, other companies are entering the market and catching up with the industry's innovators. As a result, the companies first into the market with a particular kind of product often require successive waves of capital infusion to maintain the momentum generated by their success in the embryonic stage. For example, differentiators need to engage in extensive R&D to maintain their technological lead, and cost leaders need to invest in state-of-the-art machinery and computers to obtain new experience-curve economies. All this investment to strengthen their business model is very expensive. And, as we discussed previously, many companies fail to recognize the changing needs of customers in the market and invest their capital in ways that do not lead to the distinctive competencies required for long-term success.

The growth stage is also the time when companies attempt to secure their grip over customers in existing market segments and enter new segments so that they can increase their market share. Increasing the level of market segmentation to become a broad differentiator is expensive as well. A company has to invest resources to develop a new sales and marketing competency, for example. Consequently, at the growth stage, companies must make investment decisions about the relative advantages of differentiation, cost-leadership, or focus business models given their financial needs and relative competitive position. If one or a few companies have emerged as the clear cost leaders, for example, other companies might realize that it is futile to compete head-to-head with these companies and instead decide to pursue a growth strategy using a differentiation or focus approach and invest resources in developing other competencies. As a result, strategic groups start to develop in an industry as each company seeks the best way to invest its scarce resources to maximize its competitive advantage.

Companies must spend a lot of money just to keep up with growth in the market, and finding additional resources to develop new competencies is a difficult task for strategic managers. Consequently, companies in a weak competitive position at this stage engage in a **market concentration** strategy to find a viable competitive position. They seek to specialize in some way and adopt a focus business model to reduce their investment needs. If they are very weak, they may also choose to exit the industry and sell out to a stronger competitor.

Shakeout Strategies

By the shakeout stage, customer demand is increasing, and competition by price or product characteristics becomes intense. Companies in strong competitive positions need resources to invest in a **share-increasing strategy** to attract customers from weak companies exiting the market. In other words, companies attempt to maintain and increase market share despite fierce competition. The way companies invest their resources depends on their business model.

For cost leaders, because of the price wars that can occur, investment in cost control is crucial if they are to survive the shakeout stage; they must do all they can to reduce their cost structure. Differentiators in a strong competitive position choose to forge ahead and increase their market share by investing in marketing, and they are likely to develop a sophisticated after-sales service network. Differentiators in a weak position reduce their investment burden by withdrawing to a focused model, the market concentration strategy, to specialize in serving the needs of customers in a particular market segment. A market concentration strategy indicates that a company is trying to turn around its business so that it can survive in the long run.

Weak companies exiting the industry engage in a harvest strategy. A company using a **harvest strategy** must limit or decrease its investment in a business and extract or milk its investment as much as it can. For example, a company reduces to a minimum the assets it employs in the business and forgoes investment to reduce its cost structure.[11] Then the company "harvests" all the sales revenues it can profitably obtain before it liquidates its assets and exits the industry. Companies that have lost their cost-leadership position to more efficient companies are more likely to pursue a harvest strategy because a smaller market share means higher costs and they are unable to move to a focus strategy. Differentiators, in contrast, have a competitive advantage in this stage if they can move to a focus model.

Maturity Strategies

By the maturity stage, companies want to reap the rewards of their previous investments in developing the business models that have made them dominant industry competitors. Until now, profits have been reinvested in the business, and dividends have been small. Investors in leading companies have obtained their rewards through the appreciation of the value of their stock, because the company has reinvested most of its capital to maintain and increase market share. As market growth slows in the maturity stage, a company's investment strategy depends on the level of competition in the industry and the source of the company's competitive advantage.

In industries in which competition is high because of technological change or low barriers to entry, companies need to defend their competitive position. Strategic managers need to continue to invest heavily in building the company's business model to maintain its competitive advantage. Both cost leaders and differentiators adopt a **hold-and-maintain strategy** to defend their business models and ward off threats from focused companies that might be attempting to grow and compete with the industry leaders. They expend resources to develop their distinctive competency so as to remain the market leaders. For example, differentiated companies may invest in improved after-sales service, and low-cost companies may invest in the latest production technologies.

It is at this point that many companies realize the benefits that can be obtained by investing resources to become broad differentiators to protect themselves from aggressive competitors (both at home and abroad) that are watching for any opportunity or perceived weakness to take the lead in the industry. Differentiators enter new market segments to increase their market share; they also take advantage of their growing profits to develop flexible manufacturing systems to reduce their production costs. Cost leaders also begin to enter more market segments and increase product differentiation to expand their market share. For example, Gallo moved from the bulk wine segment and began marketing premium wines and wine coolers to take advantage of its low production costs. Soon Gallo's new premium brands, such as Falling Leaf chardonnay, became best-selling wines in the United States. As time goes on, the competitive positions of the leading differentiators and cost leaders become closer, and the pattern of industry competition changes yet again, as we discuss in the next section.

STRATEGY IN MATURE INDUSTRIES

As a result of fierce competition in the shakeout stage, an industry becomes consolidated; hence, a mature industry is commonly dominated by a small number of large companies. Although they may also contain many medium-sized companies and a host of small, specialized ones, the large companies determine the nature of competition in the industry because they can influence the five competitive forces. Indeed, these large companies hold their leading positions because they have developed the most successful business models and strategies in the industry.

By the end of the shakeout stage, companies have learned how important it is to analyze each other's business model and strategies. They also know that if they change their strategies, their actions are likely to stimulate a competitive response from industry rivals. For example, a differentiator that starts to lower its prices because it has adopted a more cost-efficient technology not only threatens other differentiators but may also threaten cost leaders that see their competitive advantage being eroded. Hence, by the mature stage of the life cycle, companies have learned the meaning of competitive independence.

As a result, in mature industries, business-level strategy revolves around understanding how established companies *collectively* try to reduce the strength of industry competition to preserve both company and industry profitability. Interdependent companies can help protect their competitive advantage and profitability by adopting strategies and tactics, first, to deter entry into an industry, and second, to reduce the level of rivalry within an industry.

Strategies to Deter Entry: Product Proliferation, Price Cutting, and Maintaining Excess Capacity

Companies can use three main methods to deter entry by potential rivals and hence maintain and increase industry profitability: product proliferation, price cutting, and maintaining excess capacity (see Figure 6.5). Of course, *potential entrants* will try to circumvent such entry-deterring strategies by incumbent companies. Competition is rarely a one-way street.

Product Proliferation   As we noted earlier, in the maturity stage, most companies move to increase their market share by producing a wide range of products targeted at different market segments. Sometimes, however, to reduce the threat of entry, existing companies ensure that they are offering a product targeted at every segment in the market. This creates a barrier to entry because potential competitors find it hard to break into an industry and establish a "beachhead" when there is no obvious group of customers whose needs are not being met by existing companies.[12] This strategy of "filling the niches," or catering to the needs of customers in all market segments to deter entry, is known as **product proliferation**.

Figure 6.5   Strategies for Deterring Entry of Rivals

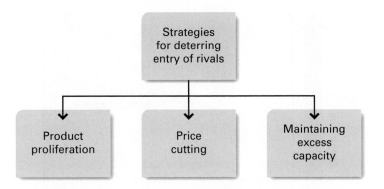

Because the large United States carmakers were so slow to fill the small-car niches (they did *not* pursue a product proliferation strategy), they were vulnerable to the entry of the Japanese into these market segments in the United States in the 1980s. Ford and GM had no excuse for this situation, for in their European operations, they had a long history of small-car manufacturing. Managers should have seen the opening and filled it 10 years earlier, but the (mistaken) view was that "small cars mean small profits." Better small profits than no profits! In the soap and detergent industry, on the other hand, competition is based on the production of new kinds of soaps and detergents to satisfy or create new desires by customers. Thus, the number of soaps and detergents, and especially the way they are packaged (powder, liquid, or tablets), proliferates, making it very difficult for prospective entrants to attack a new market segment. Figure 6.6 indicates how product proliferation can deter entry. It depicts product space in the restaurant industry along two dimensions: atmosphere, which ranges from fast food to candlelight dining, and quality of food, which ranges from average to gourmet. The circles represent product spaces filled by restaurants located along the two dimensions. Thus, McDonald's is situated in the average quality/fast food area. A gap in the product space gives a potential entrant or an existing rival an opportunity to enter the market and make inroads. The shaded unoccupied product space represents areas where new restaurants can enter the market. When all the product spaces are filled, this barrier to entry makes it much more difficult for a new company to gain a foothold in the market and differentiate itself.

Price Cutting   In some situations, pricing strategies can be used to deter entry by other companies, thus protecting the profit margins of companies already in an industry. One entry-deterring strategy is to cut prices every time a new company enters the industry or, even better, every time a potential entrant is *contemplating* entry, and then raise prices once the new or potential entrant has withdrawn. The goal is to send a signal to potential entrants that new entry will be met with price cuts. If incumbent companies in an industry consistently pursue such a strategy, potential entrants will come to understand that their entry will spark off a price war, the threat of new entry will be reduced, average prices will be higher, and industry profitability will increase. However, a price-cutting strategy will not keep out an entrant that plans to adopt a new technology that will give it a cost advantage over

Figure 6.6   Product Proliferation in the Restaurant Industry

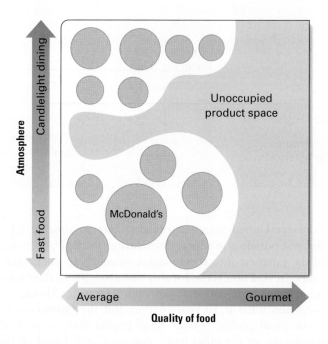

established companies or has pioneered a new business model that its managers expect will also give it a competitive advantage. In fact, many of the most successful entrants into mature industries are companies that have done just this. For example, the Japanese car companies were able to enter the United States market because they had pioneered new lean manufacturing technologies that gave them a cost and quality advantage over established United States companies.

A second price-cutting strategy is to charge a high price initially for a product and seize short-term profits but then to cut prices aggressively to build market share *and* deter potential entrants simultaneously.[13] The incumbent companies thus signal to potential entrants that if they enter the industry, the incumbents will use their competitive advantage to drive down prices to a level at which new companies will be unable to cover their costs. This pricing strategy also allows a company to ride down the experience curve and obtain substantial economies of scale. Because costs fall with prices, profit margins could still be maintained. However, this strategy is unlikely to deter a strong potential competitor—an established company that is trying to find profitable investment opportunities in other industries. It is difficult, for example, to imagine 3M being afraid to enter an industry because companies threaten to drive down prices. A company such as 3M has the resources to withstand any short-term losses. Hence, when faced with such a scenario, it may be in the interests of incumbent companies to accept new entry gracefully, giving up market share gradually to the new entrants to prevent price wars from developing and thus saving their profits, if this is feasible.

Maintaining Excess Capacity   A third competitive technique that allows companies to deter entry involves maintaining excess capacity, that is, maintaining the physical capability to produce more product than customers currently demand.

Existing industry companies may deliberately develop some limited amount of excess capacity to warn potential entrants that if they enter the industry, existing firms can retaliate by increasing output and forcing down prices until entry would become unprofitable. However, the threat to increase output has to be *credible*; that is, companies in an industry must collectively be able to raise the level of production quickly if entry appears likely.

Strategies to Manage Rivalry

Beyond seeking to deter entry, companies also wish to develop strategies to manage their competitive interdependence and decrease price rivalry. Unrestricted competition over prices reduces both company and industry profitability. Several strategies are available to companies to manage industry rivalry. The most important are price signaling, price leadership, non-price competition, and capacity control (Figure 6.7).

Price Signaling   A company's ability to choose the price option that leads to superior performance is a function of several factors, including the strength of demand for a product and the intensity of competition between rivals. Price signaling is a first means by which companies attempt to control rivalry among competitors so as to allow the *industry* to choose the most favorable pricing option.[14] **Price signaling** is the process by which companies increase or decrease product prices to convey their intentions to other companies and so influence the way they price their products.[15] Companies use price signaling to improve industry profitability.

Companies may use price signaling to announce that they will respond vigorously to hostile competitive moves that threaten them. For example, they may signal that if one company starts to cut prices aggressively, they will respond in kind. A **tit-for-tat strategy** is a well-known price signaling strategy in which a company does exactly what its rivals do: if its rivals cut prices, the company follows; if its rivals raise prices, the company follows. By pursuing this strategy consistently over time, a company sends a clear signal to its rivals that it will match any pricing moves they make, the idea being that, sooner or later, rivals will learn that the company will always pursue a tit-for-tat strategy. Because rivals now know that the company will match any price reductions and cutting prices will only reduce profits, price cutting

Figure 6.7   Strategies for Managing Industry Rivalry

becomes less common in the industry. Moreover, a tit-for-tat strategy also signals to rivals that price increases will be imitated, increasing the probability that rivals will initiate price increases to raise profits. Thus, a tit-for-tat strategy can be a useful way of shaping pricing behavior in an industry.[16]

The airline industry is a good example of the power of price signaling when prices typically rise and fall depending on the current state of customer demand. If one carrier signals the intention to lower prices, a price war frequently ensues as other carriers copy each other's signals. If one carrier feels demand is strong, it tests the waters by signaling an intention to increase prices, and price signaling becomes a strategy to obtain uniform price increases. Nonrefundable tickets, another strategy adopted to obtain a more favorable pricing option, originated as a market signal by one company that was quickly copied by all other companies in the industry. Carriers recognized that they could stabilize their revenues and earn interest on customers' money if they collectively acted to force customers to assume the risk of buying airline tickets in advance. In essence, price signaling allows companies to give one another information that enables them to understand each other's competitive product or market strategy and make coordinated, price-competitive moves.

Price Leadership   Price leadership—in which one company assumes the responsibility for setting the pricing option that maximizes industry profitability—is a second tactic used to reduce price rivalry between companies in a mature industry.[17] Formal price leadership, or price setting by companies jointly, is illegal under antitrust laws, so the process of price leadership is often very subtle. In the car industry, for example, prices are set by imitation. The price set by the weakest company—that is, the one with the highest cost structure—is often used as the basis for competitors' pricing. Thus, United States carmakers set their prices, and Japanese carmakers then set theirs with reference to the United States prices. The Japanese are happy to do this because they have lower costs than United States companies. They make higher profits than United States carmakers without competing with them on price. Pricing is done by market segment. The prices of different auto models in the model range indicate the customer segments that the companies are aiming for and the price range they believe the market segment can tolerate. Each manufacturer prices a model in the segment with reference to the prices charged by its competitors, not by reference to competitors' costs. Price leadership also allows differentiators to charge a premium price.

Although price leadership can stabilize industry relationships by preventing head-to-head competition and thus raise the level of profitability within an industry, it has its dangers. It helps companies with high cost structures, allowing them to survive without having to implement strategies to become more productive and efficient. In the long term, such behavior makes them vulnerable to new entrants that have lower costs because they have developed new low-cost production techniques. That is what happened in the United States car industry after the Japanese entered the market. After years of tacit price fixing, with GM as the price leader, the carmakers were subjected to growing low-cost Japanese competition, to which they were unable to respond. Indeed, most United States carmakers survived only because the Japanese carmakers were foreign firms. Had the foreign firms been new United States entrants, the government would probably not have taken steps to protect Chrysler, Ford, or GM, including bailing them out with billions of dollars in loans in 2009 to prevent them from going bankrupt.

Figure 6.8 Four Nonprice Competitive Strategies

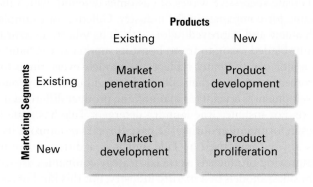

Nonprice Competition   A third very important aspect of product and market strategy in mature industries is the use of **nonprice competition** to manage rivalry within an industry. The use of strategies to try to prevent costly price cutting and price wars does not preclude competition by product differentiation. Indeed, in many industries, product-differentiation strategies are the principal tools companies use to deter potential entrants and manage rivalry within their industry.

Product differentiation allows industry rivals to compete for market share by offering products with different or superior features, such as more powerful, smaller, or sophisticated CPUs and GPUs as AMD, Intel, and Nvidia compete to do, or by applying different marketing techniques. In Figure 6.8, product and market segment dimensions are used to identify four nonprice competitive strategies based on product differentiation: market penetration, product development, market development, and product proliferation. (Notice that this model applies to new market segments, not new markets.)[18]

Market Penetration   When a company concentrates on expanding market share in its existing product markets, it is engaging in a strategy of **market penetration**.[19] Market penetration involves heavy advertising to promote and build product differentiation. For example, Intel has actively pursued penetration with its aggressive marketing campaign of "Intel Inside." In a mature industry, advertising aims to influence customers' brand choice and create a brand-name reputation for the company and its products. In this way, a company can increase its market share by attracting the customers of its rivals. Because brand-name products often command premium prices, building market share in this situation is very profitable.

In some mature industries—for example, soap and detergent, disposable diapers, and brewing—a market-penetration strategy becomes a way of life.[20] In these industries, all companies engage in intensive advertising and battle for market share. Each company fears that if it does not advertise, it will lose market share to rivals who do. Consequently, in the soap and detergent industry, Proctor & Gamble spends more than 20% of sales revenues on advertising, with the aim of maintaining and perhaps building market share. These huge advertising outlays constitute a barrier to entry for prospective entrants.

Product Development   **Product development** is the creation of new or improved products to replace existing ones.[21] The wet-shaving industry depends on product replacement to create successive waves of customer demand, which then create new sources of revenue for companies in the industry. Gillette, for example, periodically comes out with a new and improved razor, such as its vibrating razor that competes with Schick's four-bladed razor, to try to boost its market share. Similarly, in the car industry, each major car company replaces its models every three to five years to encourage customers to trade in their old models and buy the new one.

   Product development is crucial for maintaining product differentiation and building market share. For instance, the laundry detergent Tide has gone through more than 50 changes in formulation during the past 40 years to improve its performance. The product is always advertised as Tide, but it is a different product each year. Refining and improving products is a crucial strategy companies use to fine-tune and improve their business models in a mature industry, but this kind of competition can be as vicious as a price war because it is very expensive and can dramatically increase a company's cost structure. This happened in the chip industry where intense competition to make the fastest or most powerful CPU or GPU and become the market leader has dramatically increased the cost structure of Intel, AMD, and Nvidia and sharply reduced their profitability.

Market Development   **Market development** finds new market segments for a company's products. A company pursuing this strategy wants to capitalize on the brand name it has developed in one market segment by locating new market segments in which to compete—just as Mattel and Nike do by entering many different segments of the toy and shoe market, respectively. In this way, companies can leverage the product differentiation advantages of their brand name. The Japanese auto manufacturers provide an interesting example of the use of market development. When they entered the market, each Japanese manufacturer offered a car model aimed at the economy segment of the auto market, such as the Toyota Corolla and the Honda Accord. Then they upgraded each model over time, and now each is directed at a more expensive market segment. The Accord is a leading contender in the mid-sized car segment, and the Corolla fills the small-car segment. By redefining their product offerings, Japanese manufacturers have profitably developed their market segments and successfully attacked their United States rivals, wresting market share from these companies. Although the Japanese used to compete primarily as cost leaders, market development has allowed them to become differentiators as well. In fact, as we noted in the previous chapter, Toyota has used market development to become a broad differentiator. Figure 6.9 illustrates how, over time, Toyota has used market development to develop a vehicle for almost every main segment of the car market.[22]

Product Proliferation   **Product proliferation** can be used to manage rivalry within an industry and to deter entry. The strategy of product proliferation generally means that large companies in an industry all have a product in each market segment or niche and compete head-to-head for customers. If a new niche develops, such as SUVs, designer sunglasses, or Internet Web sites, then the leader gets a first-mover advantage, but soon all the other companies catch up. Once again, competition is stabilized, and rivalry within the industry is reduced. Product proliferation thus allows the development of stable industry competition based on product differentiation, not price—that is, nonprice competition based on the development of new products. The competitive battle is over a product's perceived uniqueness, quality, features, and performance, not over its price. The way in which Nike has used these

Figure 6.9 Toyota's Product Lineup

Price	Utility Vehicles (SUVs)	Passenger/ Sports Sedans	Passenger Vans	Personal Luxury Vehicles	Sporty Cars	Pickup Trucks
$11–$20K	Scion xB	Camry, Matrix, Corolla, Prism, Scion xA			Celica GT	Tacoma
$21–$30K	RAV4- 4Runner, Highlander	Venza, Avalon	Sienna	Avalon	MR2, Spyder	Tundra
$31–$45K	Sequoia, RX330	GS 300, IS 300		ES 330	Camry, Solara	Tundra Double Cab
$46–$75K	Land Cruiser GX, LX	GS 430		LS 430	SC 430	

Source: www.toyota.com, accessed August 2009.

nonprice competitive strategies to strengthen its differentiation business model is profiled in Strategy in Action 6.3.

Capacity Control Although nonprice competition helps mature industries avoid the cutthroat price cutting that reduces company and industry levels of profitability, price competition does periodically break out when excess capacity exists in an industry. Excess capacity arises when companies collectively produce too much output; to dispose of it, they cut prices. When one company cuts prices, the others quickly follow because they fear that the price cutter will be able to sell its entire inventory while they will be left with unwanted goods. The result is that a price war develops.

Excess capacity may be caused by a shortfall in demand, as when a recession lowers the demand for cars and causes car companies to give customers price incentives to purchase new cars. In this situation, companies can do nothing except wait for better times. By and large, however, excess capacity results from companies within an industry simultaneously responding to favorable conditions; they all invest in new plants to be able to take advantage of the predicted upsurge in demand. Paradoxically, each individual company's effort to outperform the others means that, collectively, the companies create industry overcapacity, which hurts them all. Although demand is rising, the consequence of each company's decision to increase capacity is a surge in industry capacity, which drives down prices. To prevent the accumulation of costly excess capacity, companies must devise strategies that let them control—or at least benefit from—capacity expansion programs. Before we examine these strategies, however, we need to consider in greater detail the factors that cause excess capacity.[23]

Factors Causing Excess Capacity The problem of excess capacity often derives from technological developments. Sometimes new low-cost technology is the culprit because all companies invest in it simultaneously to prevent being left behind. Excess capacity occurs because the new technology can produce more than the old. In addition, new technology is often introduced in large increments, which generate overcapacity. For instance, an airline that needs more seats on a route must add

6.3 STRATEGY IN ACTION

Nonprice Competitive Strategies at Nike

Nike, headquartered in Beaverton, Oregon, was founded by Bill Bowerman, a former University of Oregon track coach, and Phil Knight, an entrepreneur in search of a profitable business opportunity. Bowerman's goal was to dream up a new kind of sneaker tread that would enhance a runner's traction and speed, and he came up with the idea for Nike's "waffle tread" after studying the waffle iron in his home. Bowerman and Knight made their shoe and began by selling it out of the trunk of a car at track meets. From this small beginning, Nike has grown into a company that sold more than $18 billion worth of shoes in the $40 billion athletic footwear and apparel industries in 2008 and made more than $1.8 billion in profit.

Nike's amazing growth came from its business model, which from the beginning was based on differentiation; its strategy was to innovate state-of-the-art athletic shoes and then to publicize the qualities of its shoes through dramatic "guerrilla" marketing. Nike's marketing is designed to persuade customers that its shoes are not only superior but also a high fashion statement and a necessary part of a lifestyle based on sporting or athletic interests. Nike's strategy to emphasize the uniqueness of its product obviously paid off as its market share soared. However, the company received a shock in 1998, when its sales suddenly began to fall; it was becoming more and more difficult to design new shoes that its existing customers perceived to be significantly better and worth their premium price—in other words, its strategy of market penetration and product development was no longer paying off. Phil Knight recruited a team of talented top managers from leading consumer products companies to help him change Nike's business model in some fundamental ways.

In the past, Nike shunned sports like golf, soccer, rollerblading, and so on, and focused most of its efforts on making shoes for the track and basketball market segments. However, when its sales started to fall, it realized that using marketing to increase sales in a particular market segment (market penetration) can only grow sales and profits so far. So Nike took its existing design and marketing competencies and began to craft new lines of shoes for new market segments. In other words, it began to pursue market development and product proliferation as well as the other nonprice strategies. For example, it revamped its aerobics shoes and launched a line of soccer shoes and perfected their design over time; by the mid-2000s, it took over as the market leader from its archrival Adidas. In addition, it launched its Total 90 III shoes, which are aimed at the millions of casual soccer players throughout the world who want a shoe they can just "play" in.

To take advantage of its competencies in design and marketing, Nike decided to enter new market segments by purchasing other footwear companies that offered shoes that extended or complemented its product lines. Continuing its pursuit of product proliferation, it bought Converse, the maker of retro-style sneakers, and Official Starter, a licensor of athletic shoes and apparel whose brands include the low-priced Shaq brand. Allowing Converse to take advantage of Nike's in-house competencies has resulted in dramatic increases in the sales of its sneakers. Nike also entered another market segment when it bought Cole Haan, the dress shoemaker. Nike also entered the athletic apparel market to use its skills there, and by 2004, apparel sales were more than $1 billion. Nike's new strategies significantly strengthened its differentiation business model, which is why its market share and profitability have continued to increase and are the envy of its competitors.

Sources: http://www.nike.com, press release, 2004; "The New Nike," http://www.yahoo.com (2004), September 12; A. Wong, "Nike: Just Don't Do It," *Newsweek*, November 1, 2004, 84; http://www.nike, 2009.

another plane, thereby adding hundreds of seats even if only 50 are needed. To take another example, a new chemical process may operate efficiently at the rate of only 1,000 gallons a day, whereas the previous process was efficient at 500 gallons a day. If all companies within an industry change technologies, industry capacity may double, and enormous problems can result.

Overcapacity may also be caused by competitive factors within an industry. Entry into an industry is one such a factor. The entry of steel producers from the former Soviet Union countries into the global steel market produced excess capacity and plunging prices in the world steel market in the early 2000s. The recession of 2009 has once again caused global overcapacity, and the price of steel has plunged. Sometimes the age of a company's physical assets is the source of the problem. For example, in the hotel industry, given the rapidity with which the quality of hotel furnishings declines, customers are always attracted to new hotels. When new hotel chains are built alongside the old chains, excess capacity can result. Often, companies are simply making simultaneous competitive moves based on industry trends, but those moves eventually lead to head-to-head competition. Most fast-food chains, for instance, establish new outlets whenever demographic data show population increases. However, the companies seem to forget that all other chains use the same data (they are not anticipating their rivals' actions). Thus, a locality that has no fast-food outlets may suddenly see several being built at the same time. Whether they can all survive depends on the growth rate of demand relative to the growth rate of the chains.

Choosing a Capacity-Control Strategy   Given the various ways in which capacity can expand, companies clearly need to find some means of controlling it. If they are always plagued by price cutting and price wars, they will be unable to recoup the investments in their generic strategies. Low profitability within an industry caused by overcapacity forces not just the weakest companies but also sometimes the major players to exit the industry. In general, companies have two strategic choices: (1) each company individually must try to preempt its rivals and seize the initiative, or (2) the companies collectively must find indirect means of coordinating with each other so that they are all aware of the mutual effects of their actions.

To *preempt* rivals, a company must forecast a large increase in demand in the product market and then move rapidly to establish large-scale operations that will be able to satisfy the predicted demand. By achieving a first-mover advantage, the company may deter other firms from entering the market because the preemptor will usually be able to move down the experience curve, reduce its costs and therefore its prices as well, and threaten a price war if necessary.

This strategy, however, is extremely risky, for it involves investing resources before the extent and profitability of the future market are clear. Walmart, with its strategy of locating in small rural towns to tap an underexploited market for discount goods, preempted Sears and Kmart. Walmart has been able to engage in market penetration and market expansion because of the secure base it established in its rural strongholds. A preemptive strategy is also risky if it does not deter competitors and they decide to enter the market. If the competitors have a stronger generic strategy or more resources, such as Microsoft or Intel, they can make the preemptor suffer. Thus, for the strategy to succeed, the preemptor must generally be a credible company with enough resources to withstand a possible price war.

To *coordinate* with rivals as a capacity-control strategy, caution must be exercised because collusion on the timing of new investments is illegal under antitrust law. However, tacit coordination is practiced in many industries as companies attempt to understand and forecast one another's competitive moves. Generally, companies use market signaling to secure coordination. They make announcements about their future investment decisions in trade journals and newspapers. In addition, they share information about their production levels and their forecasts of demand within an industry to bring supply and demand into equilibrium. Thus, a coordination strategy reduces the risks associated with investment in the industry. This is very common in the chemical refining and oil businesses, where new capacity investments frequently cost hundreds of millions of dollars.

STRATEGIES IN DECLINING INDUSTRIES

Sooner or later, many industries enter into a decline stage, in which the size of the total market starts to shrink. Examples are the railroad industry, the tobacco industry, and the steel industry. Industries start declining for a number of reasons, including technological change, social trends, and demographic shifts. The railroad and steel industries began to decline when technological changes brought viable substitutes for their products. The advent of the internal combustion engine drove the railroad industry into decline, and the steel industry fell into decline with the rise of plastics and composite materials. As for the tobacco industry, changing social attitudes toward smoking, which are themselves a product of growing concerns about the health effects of smoking, have caused the decline.

The Severity of Decline

When the size of the total market is shrinking, competition tends to intensify in a declining industry, and profit rates tend to fall. The intensity of competition in a declining industry depends on four critical factors, which are indicated in Figure 6.10. First, the intensity of competition is greater in industries in which decline is rapid as opposed to industries such as tobacco in which decline is slow and gradual.

Second, the intensity of competition is greater in declining industries in which exit barriers are high. As you recall from Chapter 2, high exit barriers keep companies locked into an industry, even when demand is falling. The result is the emergence of excess productive capacity and, hence, an increased probability of fierce price competition.

Figure 6.10   Factors that Determine the Intensity of Competition
in Declining Industries

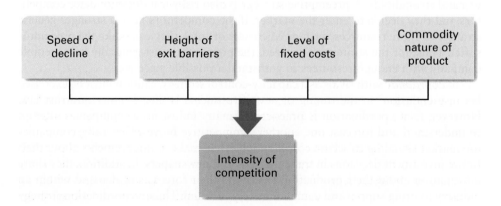

Third, and related to the previous point, the intensity of competition is greater in declining industries in which fixed costs are high (as in the steel industry). The reason is that the need to cover fixed costs, such as the costs of maintaining productive capacity, can make companies try to use any excess capacity they have by slashing prices, which can trigger a price war.

Finally, the intensity of competition is greater in declining industries in which the product is perceived as a commodity (as it is in the steel industry) in contrast to industries in which differentiation gives rise to significant brand loyalty, as was true until very recently of the declining tobacco industry.

Not all segments of an industry typically decline at the same rate. In some segments, demand may remain reasonably strong despite decline elsewhere. The steel industry illustrates this situation. Although bulk steel products, such as sheet steel, have suffered a general decline, demand has actually risen for specialty steels, such as those used in high-speed machine tools. Vacuum tubes provide another example. Although demand for them collapsed when transistors replaced them as a key component in many electronics products, vacuum tubes still had some limited applications in radar equipment for years afterward. Consequently, demand in this vacuum tube segment remained strong despite the general decline in the demand for vacuum tubes. The point, then, is that there may be pockets of demand in an industry in which demand is declining more slowly than in the industry as a whole or not declining at all. Price competition thus may be far less intense among the companies serving such pockets of demand than within the industry as a whole.

Choosing a Strategy

There are four main strategies that companies can adopt to deal with decline: (1) a **leadership strategy**, by which a company seeks to become the dominant player in a declining industry; (2) a **niche strategy**, which focuses on pockets of demand that are declining more slowly than the industry as a whole; (3) a **harvest strategy**, which optimizes cash flow; and (4) a **divestment strategy**, by which a company sells off the business to others. Figure 6.11 provides a simple framework for guiding strategic choice. Note that the intensity of competition in the declining industry is measured on the vertical axis and a company's strengths relative to remaining pockets of demand are measured on the horizontal axis.

Leadership Strategy   A leadership strategy aims at growing in a declining industry by picking up the market share of companies that are leaving the industry. A leadership strategy makes most sense when (1) the company has distinctive strengths that allow it to capture market share in a declining industry and (2) the speed of decline and the intensity of competition in the declining industry are moderate. Philip Morris has pursued such a strategy in the tobacco industry. Through aggressive marketing, Philip Morris has increased its market share in a declining industry and earned enormous profits in the process.

The tactical steps companies might use to achieve a leadership position include using aggressive pricing and marketing to build market share, acquiring established competitors to consolidate the industry, and raising the stakes for other competitors, for example, by making new investments in productive capacity. Such competitive tactics signal to other competitors that the company is willing and able to stay and compete in the declining industry. These signals may persuade other companies to exit the industry, which would further enhance the competitive position of the

....

Figure 6.11 Strategy Selection in a Declining Industry

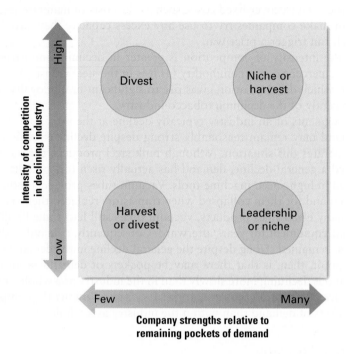

industry leader. Strategy in Action 6.4 offers an example of a company, Richardson Electronics, that has prospered by taking a leadership position in a declining industry. It is one of the last companies in the vacuum tube business.

Niche Strategy A niche strategy focuses on pockets of demand in the industry in which demand is stable or declining less rapidly than the industry as a whole. The strategy makes sense when the company has some unique strengths relative to those niches in which demand remains relatively strong. As an example, consider Naval, a company that manufactures whaling harpoons and small guns to fire them and makes money doing so. This might be considered rather odd because the world community has outlawed whaling. However, Naval survived the terminal decline of the harpoon industry by focusing on the one group of people who are still allowed to hunt whales, although only in very limited numbers: North American Eskimos. Eskimos are permitted to hunt bowhead whales, provided that they do so only for food and not for commercial purposes. Naval is the sole supplier of small harpoon whaling guns to Eskimo communities, and its monopoly position allows it to earn a healthy return in this small market.

Harvest Strategy As we noted earlier, a harvest strategy is the best choice when a company wishes to get out of a declining industry and optimize cash flow in the process. This strategy makes the most sense when the company foresees a steep decline and intense future competition or lacks strengths relative to remaining pockets of demand in the industry. A harvest strategy requires the company to cut all new investments in capital equipment, advertising, R&D, and the like. The inevitable result is

6.4 STRATEGY IN ACTION

How to Make Money in the Vacuum Tube Business

At its peak in the early 1950s, the vacuum tube business was a major industry in which companies such as Westinghouse, GE, RCA, and Western Electric had a large stake. Then along came the transistor, making most vacuum tubes obsolete, and one by one all the big companies exited the industry. One company, however, Richardson Electronics, not only stayed in the business but also demonstrated that high returns are possible in a declining industry. Primarily a distributor (although it does have some manufacturing capabilities), Richardson bought the remains of a dozen companies in the United States and Europe as they exited the vacuum tube industry. It now has a warehouse that stocks more than 10,000 different types of vacuum tubes. The company is the world's only supplier of many of them, which helps explain why its gross margin is in the 35% to 40% range.

Richardson survives and prospers because vacuum tubes are vital parts of some older electronic equipment that would be costly to replace with solid-state equipment. In addition, vacuum tubes still outperform semiconductors in some limited applications, including radar and welding machines. The United States government and GM are big customers of Richardson.

Speed is the essence of Richardson's business. The company's Illinois warehouse offers overnight delivery to some 40,000 customers, and it processes 650 orders a day at an average price of $550. Customers such as GM do not really care whether a vacuum tube costs $250 or $350; what they care about is the $40,000 to $50,000 downtime loss that they face when a key piece of welding equipment is not working. By responding quickly to the demands of such customers and being the only major supplier of many types of vacuum tubes, Richardson has placed itself in a position that many companies in growing industries would envy: a monopoly position. However, a new company, Westrex Corp., was formed to take advantage of the growing popularity of vacuum tubes in high-end stereo systems, and today it is competing head-to-head with Richardson in some market segments. Clearly, good profits can be made even in a declining industry.

Sources: P. Haynes, "Western Electric Redux," *Forbes*, January 26, 1998, 46–47; http://www.westrexcorp.com, 2009.

that it will lose market share, but because it is no longer investing in this business, initially its positive cash flow will increase. Essentially, the company is taking cash flow in exchange for market share. Ultimately, cash flow will start to decline, and at this stage it makes sense for the company to liquidate the business. Although this strategy is very appealing in theory, it can be somewhat difficult to put into practice. Employee morale in a business that is being run down may suffer. Furthermore, if customers catch on to what the company is doing, they may defect rapidly. Then market share may decline much faster than the company expected.

Divestment Strategy   A divestment strategy rests on the idea that a company can recover most of its investment in an underperforming business by selling it early, before the industry has entered into a steep decline. This strategy is appropriate when the company has few strengths relative to whatever pockets of demand are likely to remain in the industry and when the competition in the declining industry is likely to be intense. The best option may be to sell out to a company that is pursuing a leadership strategy in the industry. The drawback of the divestment strategy is that it depends for its success on the ability of the company to spot its industry's decline before it becomes serious and to sell out while the company's assets are still valued by others.

SUMMARY OF CHAPTER

1. In fragmented industries composed of a large number of small and medium-sized companies, the principal forms of competitive strategy are chaining, franchising, and horizontal merger, as well as using the Internet.

2. In embryonic and growth industries, strategy is determined partly by market demand. The innovators and early adopters have different needs from the early and the late majority, and a company must have the right strategies in place to cross the chasms and survive. Similarly, managers must understand the factors that affect a market's growth rate so that they can tailor their business model to a changing industry environment.

3. Companies need to navigate the difficult road from growth to maturity by choosing an investment strategy that supports their business models. In choosing this strategy, managers must consider the company's competitive position in the industry and the stage of the industry's life cycle. Some main types of investment strategy are share building, growth, market concentration, share increasing, harvest, and hold-and-maintain.

4. Mature industries are composed of a few large companies whose actions are so highly interdependent that the success of one company's strategy depends on the responses of its rivals.

5. The principal strategies used by companies in mature industries to deter entry are product proliferation, price cutting, and maintaining excess capacity.

6. The principal strategies used by companies in mature industries to manage rivalry are price signaling, price leadership, nonprice competition, and capacity control.

7. In declining industries, in which market demand has leveled off or is falling, companies must tailor their price and nonprice strategies to the new competitive environment. They also need to manage industry capacity to prevent the emergence of capacity expansion problems.

8. There are four main strategies a company can pursue when demand is falling: leadership, niche, harvest, and divestment. The choice is determined by the severity of industry decline and the company's strengths relative to the remaining pockets of demand.

DISCUSSION QUESTIONS

1. What are the key problems in maintaining a competitive advantage in embryonic and growth industry environments? What are the dangers associated with being the leader?

2. What kinds of strategies might a (a) small pizza place operating in a crowded college market and (b) detergent manufacturer seeking to bring out new products in an established market use to strengthen their business models?

3. Why are industries fragmented? What are the main ways in which companies can turn a fragmented industry into a consolidated one?

Warfare in Toyland

The rapid pace at which the world is changing is forcing strategic managers at all kinds of companies to speed up their decision making; otherwise they get left behind by agile competitors who respond faster to changing customer fads and fashions. Nowhere is this truer than in the global toy industry, in which the doll business, worth more than $10 billion a year in sales, vicious combat is raging. The largest global toy company, Mattel, has earned tens of billions of dollars from the world's best-selling doll, Barbie, since it introduced her almost 50 years ago.[24] Mothers who played with the original dolls bought them for their daughters and granddaughters and Barbie became an American icon. However, Barbie's advantage as best-selling global doll led Mattel's managers to make major strategic errors in the 2000s.

Barbie and all Barbie accessories accounted for almost 50% of Mattel's toy sales in the 1990s, so protecting its star product was crucial. The Barbie doll was created in the 1960s when most women were homemakers; her voluptuous shape was a response to a dated view of what the "ideal" woman should look like. Barbie's continuing success, however, led Bob Eckert, Mattel's CEO, and his top managers to underestimate how much the world had altered. Changing cultural views about the role of girls, women, sex, marriage, and women working in the last decades shifted the tastes of doll buyers. But Mattel's managers continued to bet on Barbie's eternal appeal and collectively bought into an "If it's not broken, don't fix it" approach. In fact, given that Barbie was the best-selling doll, they thought it might be very dangerous to make major changes to her appearance; customers might not like the product development changes and stop buying her. Mattel's top managers decided not to rock the boat; they left the brand and business model unchanged and focused their efforts on developing new digital kinds of toys.

As a result, Mattel was unprepared when a challenge came along in the form of a new kind of doll, the Bratz doll, introduced by MGA Entertainment. Many competitors to Barbie had emerged over the years, and the doll business is highly profitable, but no other doll had matched Barbie's appeal to young girls (or their mothers). The marketers and designers behind the Bratz line

of dolls had spent a lot of time to discover what the new generation of girls, especially those aged 7–11, wanted from a doll, however. It turned out that the Bratz dolls they designed met the desires of these girls. Bratz dolls have larger heads, oversized eyes, wear lots of makeup, short dresses, and are multicultural to give each doll "personality and attitude."[25] The dolls were designed to appeal to a new generation of girls brought up in a fast-changing fashion, music, and television market/age. The Bratz dolls met the untapped needs of "tween" girls, and the new line took off. MGA quickly licensed the rights to make and sell the doll to toy companies overseas, and Bratz quickly became a serious competitor to Barbie.

Mattel was in trouble. Its strategic managers had to change its business model and strategies and bring Barbie up to date; Mattel's designers must have been wishing they had been adventurous and made more radical changes earlier when they did not need to change. However, they decided to change Barbie's "extreme" vital statistics; they killed off her old-time boyfriend Ken and replaced him with Blaine, an Aussie surfer.[26] They also recognized they had waited much too long to introduce new lines of dolls to meet the changed needs of tweens and older girls in the 2000s. They rushed out the "My Scene" line of dolls in 2002, which were obvious imitations of Bratz dolls. This new line has not matched the popularity of Bratz dolls. Mattel also introduced a new line called Flava in 2003 to appeal to even younger girls, but this line flopped completely. At the same time, the decisions that they made to change Barbie and her figure, looks, clothing, and boyfriends came too late, and sales of Barbie dolls continued to fall.

By 2006, sales of the Barbie collection had dropped by 30%. This was serious because Mattel's profits and stock price hinged on Barbie's success and they both plunged. Analysts argue that Mattel had not paid enough attention to its customers' changing needs or moved quickly to introduce the new and improved products necessary to keep a company on top of its market. Mattel brought Ken back in 2006, but in recognition of its mounting problems in November 2006, Mattel's lawyers filed suit against

MGA Entertainment. They argued that the Bratz dolls' copyright rightfully belonged to them. Mattel complained that the head designer of Bratz was a Mattel employee when he made the initial drawings for the dolls and that they had applied for copyright protection on a number of early Bratz drawings. In addition, they claim that MGA hired key Mattel employees away from the firm, and these employees "stole" sensitive sales information and transferred it to MGA. In 2008, a judge ruled in Mattel's favor and ordered MGA to stop using the Bratz name; the case was still under appeal in 2009.

Case Discussion Questions

1. What business model and strategies made Mattel the industry leader?
2. What strategies have its rival, MGA, pursued that have threatened its competitive position?
3. What new strategies does Mattel need to pursue to regain its competitive advantage?

7

TECHNOLOGY

LEARNING OBJECTIVES

After reading this chapter, you should be able to

- Understand the tendency toward standardization in many high technology markets
- Describe the strategies that firms can use to establish their technology as the standard in a market
- Explain what the cost structure of many high technology firms looks like and articulate the strategic implications of this
- Explain the nature of technological paradigm shifts and their implications for enterprise strategy

The Format War in Smartphones

There is a format war unfolding in the smartphone business as a number of companies battle for dominance in what is fast evolving into the next large high-technology market.

Smartphones are wireless handsets with extended data capabilities that allow users to browse the Internet, send e-mails, and run a growing number of applications from spreadsheets and restaurant locators to games and music players. The development of smartphones is rapidly transforming wireless handsets into powerful general-purpose computing devices that can perform many of the functions we typically associate with desktop and laptop computers. A key feature of smartphones is the operating system that resides on the device and runs all of the onboard functions and applications.

The main competitors in this market include Research in Motion, with its Blackberry phones; Apple, with its iPhone; Nokia, which owns the Symbian operating system for smartphones; Microsoft, with its Windows mobile offering; and Google, with the Google phone. In 2008, some $45 billion worth of smartphones were sold worldwide. Despite a global economic slowdown, forecasts call for sales of close to $100 billion by 2013, when one-third of all phones sold will be smartphones. While Research in Motion, Apple, and Nokia make both the phone and the operating system and sell the integrated bundle to end users, Microsoft and Google make just the operating system and partner with various hardware manufacturers to sell the phone to end users. All companies sell their phones in conjunction with wireless service providers.

One of the key developments in the market was the introduction of the Apple iPhone. This revolutionary device, with its elegant touch screen interface, Apple operating system, and multimedia capabilities, helped to redefine the smartphone business and rapidly started to create a mass market for these devices. Prior to the iPhone, most adopters had been business users. Now, increasingly, they are consumers. By the end of 2008, Nokia's Symbian operating system had a 46% share of the market, followed by Apple with a 17% share, RIM with a 15% share, and Microsoft with a 13.6% share. Apple, however, is growing most rapidly and gaining ground on its rivals.

Observers wonder whether the same trends toward operating system standardization seen in the PC industry will also play out in the smartphone business, with the market ultimately settling on one or two dominant systems. Certainly, Apple's strategy with its iPhone is consistent with the attainment of such a goal. Apple has realized that applications add value to the iPhone. Toward this end, Apple has provided tools to developers to help them develop applications and a novel way of distributing those applications—Apple's online App store. Apple's hope is that more applications will drive adoption of more iPhones, and that adoption of more iPhones, because it increases the size of the addressable market, will result in more applications being written to run on the iPhone than competing devices. The result could be a positive feedback loop, similar to the one that led to the dominance of Microsoft in the PC operating system business. Apple is not having it all its own way, however. Other companies are pursuing a similar strategy. Google, for example, has opened its own online store for applications, and Microsoft has a large base of developers who are writing applications to run on Windows Mobile devices.[1]

Overview

The format war now unfolding in the smartphone business is typical of the nature of competition in high-technology industries (see the Opening Case). In this chapter, we will take a close look at the nature of competition and strategy in high-technology industries. **Technology** refers to the body of scientific knowledge used in the production of goods or services. **High-technology (high-tech) industries** are those in which the underlying scientific knowledge that companies in the industry use is advancing rapidly, and, by implication, so are the attributes of the products and services that result from its application. The computer industry is often thought of as the quintessential example of a high-tech industry. Other industries often considered high tech are telecommunications, in which new technologies based on wireless and the Internet have proliferated in recent years; consumer electronics, where the digital technology underlying products from high-definition DVD players to gaming terminals and digital cameras is advancing rapidly; pharmaceuticals, where new technologies based on cell biology, recombinant DNA, and genomics are revolutionizing the process of drug discovery; power generation, where new technologies based on fuel cells and cogeneration may change the economics of the industry; and aerospace, where the combination of new composite materials, electronics, and more efficient jet engines are giving birth to a new era of super efficient commercial jet aircraft, such as Boeing's 787.

This chapter focuses on high-technology industries for a number of reasons. First, technology is accounting for an ever-larger share of economic activity. Estimates suggest that 12% to 15% of total economic activity in the United States is in information technology industries.[2] This figure actually underestimates the true impact of technology on the economy because it ignores the other high-tech areas we just mentioned. Moreover, as technology advances, many low-technology industries are becoming more high tech. For example, the development of biotechnology and genetic engineering transformed the production of seed corn, long considered a low-technology business, into a high-tech business. Retailing used to be considered a low-technology business, but the shift to online retailing, led by companies such as Amazon, has changed this. Moreover, high-tech products are making their way into a wide range of businesses; today most automobiles contain more computing power than the multimillion-dollar mainframe computers used in the Apollo space program, and the competitive advantage of physical stores, such as Walmart, is based on their use of information technology. The circle of high-tech industries is both large and expanding, and even in industries not thought of as high tech, technology is revolutionizing aspects of the product or production system.

Although high-tech industries may produce very different products, when it comes to developing a business model and strategies that will lead to a competitive advantage, superior profitability, and profit growth, they often face a similar situation. For example, "winner-take-all" format wars are common in many high-tech industries, such as the consumer electronics and computer industries (see the Opening Case for an example of an ongoing format war). This chapter examines the competitive features found in many high-tech industries and the kinds of strategies that companies must adopt to build business models that will allow them to achieve superior profitability and profit growth.

After you have completed this chapter, you will have an understanding of the nature of competition in high-tech industries and the strategies that companies can pursue to succeed in those industries.

TECHNICAL STANDARDS AND FORMAT WARS

Especially in high-tech industries, the ownership of **technical standards**—a set of technical specifications that producers adhere to when making a product or a component of it—can be an important source of competitive advantage.[3] Indeed, in many cases the source of product differentiation is based on the technical standard. As in the high-definition DVD market, often only one standard will become the dominant standard, so many battles in high-tech industries revolve around companies competing to be the one that sets the standard.

Battles to set and control technical standards in a market are referred to as **format wars**; they are essentially battles to control the source of differentiation and thus the value that such differentiation can create for the customer. Because differentiated products often command premium prices and are often expensive to develop, the competitive stakes are enormous. The profitability and very survival of a company may depend on the outcome of the battle. For example, the outcome of the battle now being waged over the establishment and ownership of the standard for smartphone operating systems will help determine which companies will be leaders for the next decade in that marketplace (see the Opening Case).

Examples of Standards

A familiar example of a standard is the layout of a computer keyboard. No matter what keyboard you buy, the letters are all in the same pattern.[4] The reason is quite obvious. Imagine if each computer maker changed the ways the keys were laid out—if some started with QWERTY on the top row of letters (which is indeed the format used and is known as the QWERTY format), some with YUHGFD, and some with ACFRDS. If you learned to type on one layout, it would be irritating and time-consuming to have to relearn another layout. The standard format (QWERTY) makes it easy for people to move from computer to computer because the input medium, the keyboard, is set out in a standard way.

Another example of a technical standard concerns the dimensions of containers used to ship goods on trucks, railcars, and ships. All have the same basic dimensions—the same height, length, and width—and all make use of the same locking mechanisms to hold them onto a surface or to bolt against each other. Having a standard ensures that containers can easily be moved from one mode of transportation to another—from trucks, to railcars, to ships, and back to railcars. If containers lacked standard dimensions and locking mechanisms, it would suddenly become much more difficult to ship containers around the world. Shippers would have to make sure that they had the right kind of container to go on the ships and trucks and railcars scheduled to carry a particular container around the world—very complicated indeed.

Consider, finally, the PC. Most share a common set of features: an Intel or Intel-compatible microprocessor, random access memory (RAM), a Microsoft operating system, an internal hard drive, a CD or DVD drive, a keyboard, a monitor, a mouse, a modem, and so on. We call this set of features the dominant design for personal computers (a **dominant design** refers to a common set of features or design characteristics). Embedded in this design are several technical standards (see Figure 7.1). For example, there is the Wintel technical standard based on an Intel microprocessor and a Microsoft operating system. Microsoft and Intel "own" that standard, which is central to the PC. Developers of software applications, component parts, and peripherals such as printers adhere to this standard when developing their own products because this guarantees that their products will work well with a PC based on the Wintel standard. Another technical standard for connecting peripherals to the PC is the Universal Serial Bus (or USB), established by an industry standards-setting board. No one owns it; the standard is in the public domain. A third technical standard is for communication between a PC and the Internet via a modem. Known as TCP/IP, this standard was also set by an industry association and is in the public domain. Thus, as with many other products, the PC is actually based on several technical standards. It is also important to note that when a company owns a standard,

Figure 7.1 Technical Standards for Personal Computers

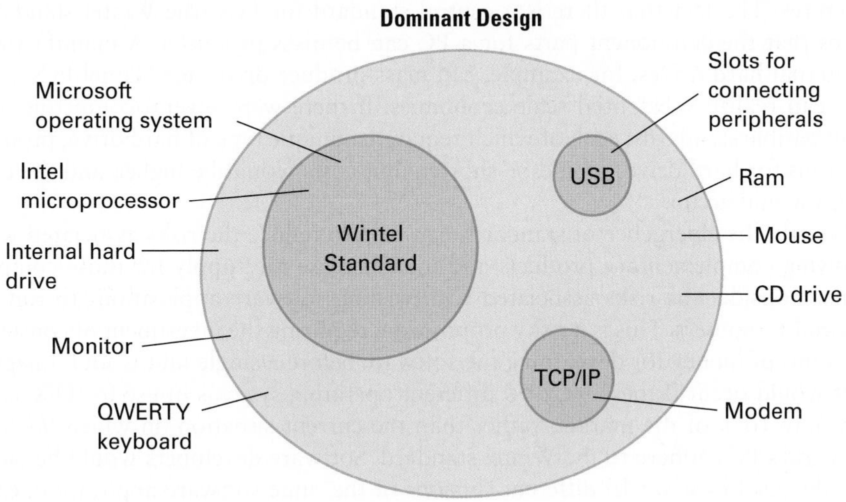

as Microsoft and Intel do with the Wintel standard, it may be a source of competitive advantage and high profitability.

Benefits of Standards

Standards emerge because there are economic benefits associated with them. First, having a technical standard helps to guarantee compatibility between products and their complements—other products used with them. For example, containers are used with railcars, trucks, and ships; PCs are used with software applications. Compatibility has the tangible economic benefit of reducing the costs associated with making sure that products work well with each other.

Second, having a standard can help to reduce confusion in the minds of consumers. Years ago, several consumer electronics companies were vying with each other to produce and market the first generation of DVD players and championing different variants of the basic DVD technology—different standards—that were incompatible with each other; a DVD disk designed to run on a DVD player made by Toshiba would not run on a player made by Sony, and vice versa. The companies feared that selling these incompatible versions of the same technology would produce confusion in the minds of consumers, who would not know which version to purchase and might decide to wait and see which technology ultimately dominated the marketplace. With lack of demand, the technology might fail to gain traction in the marketplace and would not be successful. To avoid this possibility, the developers of DVD equipment established a standard-setting body for the industry, the DVD Forum, which established a common technical standard for DVD players and disks that all companies adhered to. The result was that when DVDs were introduced, there was a common standard and no confusion in consumers' minds. This helped to boost demand for DVD players, making this one of the fastest-selling technologies of the late 1990s and early 2000s.

Third, the emergence of a standard can help to reduce production costs. Once a standard emerges, products based on that standard design can be mass-produced, enabling manufacturers to realize substantial economies of scale and lower their cost structures. The fact that there is a central standard for PCs (the Wintel standard) means that the component parts for a PC can be mass-produced. A manufacturer of internal hard drives, for example, can mass-produce drives for Wintel PCs, and, thus, can realize substantial scale economies. If there were several competing and incompatible standards, each of which required a unique type of hard drive, production runs for hard drives would be shorter, unit costs would be higher, and the cost of PCs would go up.

Fourth, the emergence of standards can help to reduce the risks associated with supplying complementary products and thus increase the supply for those complements. Consider the risks associated with writing software applications to run on personal computers. This is a risky proposition, requiring the investment of considerable sums of money for developing the software before a single unit is sold. Imagine what would occur if there were 10 different operating systems in use for PCs, each with only 10% of the market, rather than the current situation, in which 95% of the world's PCs adhere to the Wintel standard. Software developers would be faced with the need to write 10 different versions of the same software application, each for a much smaller market segment. This would change the economics of software development, increase its risks, and reduce potential profitability. Moreover, because of their higher cost structure and fewer economies of scale, the price of software programs would increase.

Thus, although many people complain about the consequences of Microsoft's near monopoly of PC operating systems, that monopoly does have at least one good effect: it substantially reduces the risks facing the makers of complementary products and the costs of those products. In fact, standards lead to both low-cost and differentiation advantages for individual companies and can help raise the level of industry profitability.

Establishment of Standards

Standards emerge in an industry in three main ways. First, recognizing the benefits of establishing a standard, companies in an industry might lobby the government to mandate an industry standard. In the United States, for example, the Federal Communications Commission (FCC), after detailed discussions with broadcasters and consumer electronics companies, has mandated a single technical standard for digital television (DTV) broadcasts and required broadcasters to have capabilities in place for broadcasting digital signals based on this standard by 2006. The FCC took this step because it believed that without government action to set the standard, the rollout of DTV would be very slow. With a standard set by the government, consumer electronics companies can have greater confidence that a market will emerge, and this should encourage them to develop DTV products.

Second, technical standards are often set by cooperation among businesses, without government help, often through the medium of an industry forum, such as the DVD Forum. Companies cooperate in this way when they decide that competition among them to create a standard might be harmful because of the uncertainty that it would create in the minds of consumers.

When standards are set by the government or an industry association, they fall into the **public domain**, meaning that any company can freely incorporate the knowledge and technology on which the standard is based into its products. For example, no one owns the QWERTY format, therefore, no one company can profit from it directly. Similarly, the language that underlies the presentation of text and graphics on the Web, hypertext markup language (HTML), is in the public domain; it is free for all to use. The same is true for TCP/IP, the communications standard used for transmitting data on the Internet.

Often, however, the industry standard is selected competitively by the purchasing patterns of customers in the marketplace—that is, by market demand. In this case, the strategy and business model a company has developed for promoting its technological standard are of critical importance because ownership of an industry standard that is protected from imitation by patents and copyrights is a valuable asset—a source of sustained competitive advantage and superior profitability. Microsoft and Intel, for example, both owe their competitive advantage to their ownership of format wars, which exist between two or more companies competing against each other to get their designs adopted as the industry standard. Format wars are common in high-tech industries because of the high stakes. The Wintel standard became the dominant standard for PCs only after Microsoft and Intel won format wars against Apple Computer's proprietary system and later against IBM's OS/2 operating system. Microsoft and Real Networks are currently competing head-to-head in a format war to establish rival technologies—Windows Media Player and RealPlayer—as the standard for streaming video and audio technology on the Web. The Opening Case tells how a number of firms are engaged in a format war in the smartphone business.

Network Effects, Positive Feedback, and Lockout

There has been a growing realization that when standards are set by competition between companies promoting different formats, network effects are a primary determinant of how standards are established.[5] **Network effects** arise in industries where the size of the "network" of complementary products is a primary determinant of demand for an industry's product. For example, the demand for automobiles early in the 20th century was an increasing function of the network of paved roads and gas stations. Similarly, the demand for telephones is an increasing function of the quantity of other numbers that can be called with that phone; that is, of the size of the telephone network (the telephone network is the complementary product). When the first telephone service was introduced in New York City, only 100 numbers could be called. The network was very small because of the limited number of wires and telephone switches, which made the telephone a relatively useless piece of equipment. As more and more people purchased telephones and as the network of wires and switches expanded, the value of a telephone connection increased. This led to an increase in the demand for telephone lines, which further increased the value of owning a telephone, setting up a positive feedback loop.

To understand why network effects are important in the establishment of standards, consider the classic example of a format war: the battle between Sony and Matsushita to establish their respective technology for videocassette recorders (VCRs) as the standard in the marketplace. Sony was first to market with its Betamax technology, followed by Matsushita with its VHS technology. Both companies sold VCR recorder-players, and movie studios issued films prerecorded on VCR tapes for rental to consumers. Initially, all tapes were issued in Betamax format to play on Sony's machine. Sony did not license its Betamax technology, preferring to make all of the player-recorders itself. When Matsushita entered the market, it realized that to make its VHS format players valuable to consumers, it would have to encourage movie studios to issue movies for rental on VHS tapes. The only way to do that, Matsushita's managers reasoned, was to increase the installed base of VHS players as rapidly as possible. They believed that the greater the installed base of VHS players, the greater the incentive would be for movie studios to issue movies for rental on VHS format tapes. The more prerecorded VHS tapes were available for rental, the greater the value of a VHS player became to consumers, and therefore, the greater the demand would be for VHS players (see Figure 7.2). Matsushita wanted to exploit a positive feedback loop.

To do this, Matsushita chose a licensing strategy under which any consumer electronics company was allowed to manufacture VHS format players under license. The strategy worked. A large number of companies signed on to manufacture VHS players. Soon, far more VHS players were available for purchase in stores than Betamax players. As sales of VHS players started to grow, movie studios issued more films for rental in VHS format, and this stoked demand. Before long, it was clear to anyone who walked into a video rental store that there were more and more VHS tapes available for rent and fewer and fewer Betamax tapes. This served to reinforce the positive feedback loop, and, ultimately, Sony's Betamax technology was shut out of the market. The pivotal difference between the two companies was strategy: Matsushita chose a licensing strategy, and Sony did not. As a result, Matsushita's VHS technology became the de facto standard for VCRs, while Sony's Betamax technology was locked out.

The general principle that emerges from this example is that when two or more companies are competing with each other to get their technology adopted as a standard in an industry, and when network effects and positive feedback loops are important, the company that wins the format war will be the one whose strategy best exploits positive feedback loops. It turns out that this is a very important strategic principle in many high-tech industries, particularly computer hardware, software, telecommunications, and consumer electronics. Microsoft is where it is today because it exploited a positive feedback loop. So did Dolby (see Strategy in Action 7.1).

Figure 7.2   Positive Feedback in the Market for VCRs

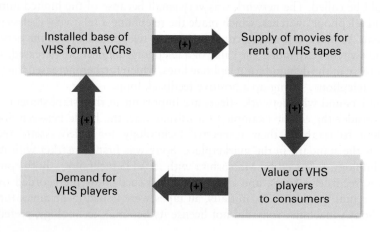

7.1 STRATEGY IN ACTION

How Dolby Became the Standard in Sound Technology

Inventor Ray Dolby's name has become synonymous with superior sound in homes, movie theaters, and recording studios. The technology produced by his company, Dolby Laboratories, is part of nearly every music cassette and cassette recorder, prerecorded videotape, and, most recently, DVD movie disc and player. Since 1976, close to 1.5 billion audio products that use Dolby's technology have been sold worldwide. More than 44,000 movie theaters now show films in Dolby Digital Surround Sound, and some 50 million Dolby Digital home theater receivers have been sold since 1999. Dolby technology has become the de facto industry standard for high-quality sound in the music and film industry. How did Dolby build this technology franchise?

The story goes back to 1965 when Dolby Laboratories was founded in London by Ray Dolby (the company's headquarters moved to San Francisco in 1976). Dolby, who had a PhD in physics from Cambridge University in England, had invented a technology for reducing the background hiss in professional tape recording without compromising the quality of the material being recorded. In 1968, Dolby reached an agreement to license his noise-reduction technology to KLH, a highly regarded American producer of audio equipment (record players and tape decks) for the consumer market. Soon other manufacturers of consumer equipment started to approach Dolby to license the technology. Dolby briefly considered manufacturing record players and tape decks for the consumer market, but as he later commented, "I knew that if we entered that market and tried to make something like a cassette deck, we would be in competition with any licensee that we took on.... So we had to stay out of manufacturing in that area in order to license in that area."

Dolby adopted a licensing business model and then had to determine what licensing fee to charge. He knew his technology was valuable, but he also understood that charging a high licensing fee would encourage manufacturers to invest in developing their own noise-reduction technology. He decided to charge a modest fee to reduce the incentive that manufacturers would have to develop their own technology. Then there was the question of which companies to license to. Dolby wanted the Dolby name associated with superior sound, so he needed to make sure that licensees adhered to quality standards. Therefore, the company set up a formal quality-control program for its licensees' products. Licensees have to agree to have their products tested by Dolby, and the licensing agreement states that they cannot sell products that do not pass Dolby's quality tests. By preventing products with substandard performance from reaching the market, Dolby has maintained the quality image of products featuring Dolby technology and trademarks. Today, Dolby Laboratories tests samples of hundreds of licensed products every year under this program. By making sure that the Dolby name is associated with superior sound quality, Dolby's quality assurance strategy has increased the power of the Dolby brand, making it very valuable to license.

Another key aspect of Dolby's strategy was born in 1970 when Dolby began to promote the idea of releasing prerecorded cassettes encoded with Dolby noise-reduction technology so that they would have low noise when played on players equipped with Dolby noise-reduction technology. Dolby decided to license the technology on prerecorded tapes for free, opting to collect licensing fees just from the sales of tape players that used Dolby technology. This strategy was hugely successful and set up a positive feedback loop that helped to make Dolby technology ubiquitous. Growing sales of prerecorded tapes encoded with Dolby technology created a demand for players that contained Dolby technology. As the installed base of players with Dolby technology grew, the proportion of prerecorded tapes that were encoded with Dolby technology surged, further boosting demand for players incorporating Dolby technology. By the mid-1970s, virtually all prerecorded tapes were encoded with Dolby noise-reduction technology. This strategy remains in effect today for all media recorded with Dolby technology and encompasses not only videocassettes but also video games and DVD releases encoded with Dolby Surround or Dolby Digital.

As a result of its licensing and quality assurance strategies, Dolby has become the standard for high-quality sound in the music and film industries. Although the company is not large—its revenues were $537 million in 2008—its influence is large. It continues to push the boundaries of sound-reduction technology (it has been

(continued)

a leader in digital sound since the mid-1980s) and has successfully extended its noise-reduction franchise, first into films, then into DVD and gaming technology, and finally onto the Web, where it has licensed its digital technology to a wide range of media companies for digital music delivery and digital audio players, such as those built into personal computers and handheld music players. Dolby has also licensed its technology for use in the newest generation of products: high-definition DVDs.

Sources: M. Snider, "Ray Dolby, Audio Inventor," *USA Today,* December 28, 2000, D3; D. Dritas, "Dealerscope Hall of Fame: Ray Dolby," *Dealerscope,* January 2002: 74–76; J. Pinkerton, "At Dolby Laboratories: A Clean Audio Pipe," *Dealerscope,* December 2000: 33–34; Company history archived at www.dolby.com; L. Himelstein, "Dolby Gets Ready to Make a Big Noise," *BusinessWeek,* February 9, 2004, 78; D. Pomerantz, "Seeing in Dolby," *Forbes,* January 30, 2006, 56.

An important implication of the positive feedback process is that as the market settles on a standard, companies promoting alternative standards can become locked out of the market when consumers are unwilling to bear the switching costs required for them to abandon the established standard and adopt the new standard. In this context, *switching costs* are the costs that consumers must bear to switch from a product based on one technological standard to a product based on another.

For illustration, imagine that a company developed an operating system for PCs that was both faster and more stable than the current standard in the marketplace, Microsoft Windows. Would this company be able to gain significant market share from Microsoft? They could do so only with great difficulty. Consumers buy PCs not for their operating systems but for the applications that run on that system. A new operating system would initially have a very small installed base, so few developers would be willing to take the risks in writing word processing programs, spreadsheets, games, and other applications for that operating system. Because there would be very few applications available, consumers who did make the switch would have to bear the switching costs associated with giving up some of their applications—something that they might be unwilling to do. Moreover, even if applications were available for the new operating system, consumers would have to bear the costs of purchasing those applications, another source of switching costs. In addition, they would have to bear the costs associated with learning to use the new operating system, yet another source of switching costs. Thus, many consumers would be unwilling to switch even if the new operating system performed better than Windows, and the company promoting the new operating system would be locked out of the market.

However, consumers will bear switching costs if the benefits of adopting the new technology outweigh the costs of switching. For example, in the late 1980s and early 1990s, millions of people switched from analog record players to digital CD players, even though the switching costs were significant: they had to purchase the new player technology, and many people purchased duplicate copies of their favorite music recordings. They nevertheless made the switch because for many people, the perceived benefit—the incredibly better sound quality associated with CDs—outweighed the costs of switching.

As this process started to get under way, a positive feedback started to develop, with the growing installed base of CD players leading to an increase in the number of music recordings issued on CDs, as opposed to or in addition to vinyl records. Past some point, the installed base of CD players got so big that music companies started to issue recordings on CDs only. Once this happened, even those who did not want to switch to the new technology were required to do so if they wished to purchase new music recordings. The industry standard had shifted: the new technology had locked in as the standard, and the old technology was locked out. It follows that despite its dominance, the Wintel standard for PCs could one day be superseded if a competitor finds a way of providing sufficient benefits that enough consumers are willing to bear the switching costs associated with moving to a new operating system. Indeed, there are signs that Apple is starting to chip away at the dominance of the Wintel standard, primarily by using elegant design and ease of use as tools to get people to bear the costs of switching from Wintel computers to Apple machines.

STRATEGIES FOR WINNING A FORMAT WAR

From the perspective of a company pioneering a new technological standard in a marketplace where network effects and positive feedback loops operate, the key question becomes, "What strategy should we pursue to establish our format as the dominant one?"

The various strategies that companies should adopt to win format wars revolve around *finding ways to make network effects work in their favor and against their competitors*. Winning a format war requires a company to build the installed base for its standard as rapidly as possible, thereby leveraging the positive feedback loop, inducing consumers to bear switching costs and ultimately locking the market into its technology. It requires the company to jump-start and then accelerate demand for its technological standard or format such that it becomes established as quickly as possible as the industry standard, thereby locking out competing formats. There are a number of key strategies and tactics that can be adopted to achieve this.[6]

Ensure a Supply of Complements

It is important for the company to make sure that, in addition to the product itself, there is an adequate supply of complements. For example, no one will buy the Sony PlayStation 3 unless there is an adequate supply of games to run on that machine. Companies normally take two steps to ensure an adequate supply of complements.

First, they may diversify into the production of complements and seed the market with sufficient supply to help jump-start demand for their format. Before Sony produced the original PlayStation in the early 1990s, it established its own in-house unit to produce video games for the PlayStation. When it launched the PlayStation, Sony also simultaneously issued 16 games to run on the machine, giving consumers a reason to purchase the format. Second, companies may create incentives or make it easy for independent companies to produce complements. Sony also licensed the right to produce games to a number of independent game developers, charged the developers a lower royalty rate than they had to pay to competitors such as Nintendo and Sega, and provided them with software tools that made it easier for them to develop the games (note that Apple is now doing the same thing with its smartphones— see the Opening Case). Thus, the launch of the Sony PlayStation was accompanied by the simultaneous launch of compatible games, which quickly helped to stimulate demand for the machine.

Leverage Killer Applications

Killer applications are applications or uses of a new technology or product that are so compelling that they persuade customers to adopt the new format or technology in droves, thereby "killing" demand for competing formats. Killer applications often help to jump-start demand for the new standard. For example, the killer applications that induced consumers to sign up to online services such as AOL in the 1990s were e-mail, chat rooms, and the ability to browse the Web.

Ideally, the company promoting a technological standard will want to develop the killer applications itself—that is, develop the appropriate complementary products. However, it may also be able to leverage the applications that others develop. For example, the early sales of the IBM PC following its 1981 introduction were driven primarily by IBM's decision to license two important software programs for the PC, VisiCalc (a spreadsheet program) and Easy Writer (a word processing program), both developed by independent companies. IBM saw that they were driving rapid adoption of rival PCs, such as the Apple II, so it quickly licensed them, produced versions that would run on the IBM PC, and sold them as complements to the IBM PC, a strategy that was to prove very successful.

Aggressively Pricing and Marketing

A common tactic to jump-start demand is to adopt a **razor and blade strategy**: pricing the product (razor) low to stimulate demand and increase the installed base and then trying to make high profits on the sale of complements (razor blades), which are priced relatively high. This strategy owes its name to the fact that it was pioneered by Gillette to sell its razors and razor blades. Many other companies have followed this strategy. For example, HP typically sells its printers at cost but makes significant profits on the subsequent sale of its replacement cartridges. In this case, the printer is the "razor," and it is priced low to stimulate demand and induce consumers to switch from their existing printer, while the cartridges are the "blades," which are priced high to make profits. The inkjet printer represents a proprietary technological format because only HP cartridges can be used with printers, not cartridges designed for competing inkjet printers, such as those sold by Canon. A similar strategy is used in the gaming industry: manufacturers price gaming consoles at cost to induce consumers to adopt their technology, while making profits on the royalties they receive from the sales of games that run on their system.

Aggressive marketing is also a key factor in jump-starting demand to get an early lead in an installed base. Substantial upfront marketing and point-of-sales promotion techniques are often used to get potential early adopters to bear the switching costs associated with adopting the format. If these efforts are successful, they can be the start of a positive feedback loop. Again, the Sony PlayStation provides a good example. Sony linked the introduction of the PlayStation with nationwide television advertising aimed at its primary demographic (18- to 34-year-olds) and in-store displays that allowed potential buyers to play games on the machine before making a purchase.

Cooperate with Competitors

Companies have been close to simultaneously introducing competing and incompatible technological standards a number of times. A good example is the compact disc. Initially four companies—Sony, Philips, JVC, and Telefunken—were developing CD players using different variations of the underlying laser technology. If this situation had persisted, they might have ultimately introduced incompatible technologies into the marketplace, so a CD made for a Philips CD player would not play on a Sony CD player. Understanding that the nearly simultaneous introduction of such incompatible technologies can create significant confusion among consumers and often leads them to delay their purchases, Sony and Philips decided to join forces with each other and cooperate on developing the technology. Sony contributed its error correction technology, and Philips contributed its laser technology. The result of this cooperation was that momentum among other players in the industry shifted toward the Sony-Philips alliances; JVC and Telefunken were left with little support. Most important, recording labels announced that they would support the Sony-Philips format but not the Telefunken or JVC format. Telefunken and JVC subsequently decided to abandon their efforts to develop CD technology. The cooperation between Sony and Philips was important because it reduced confusion in the industry and allowed a single format to rise to the fore, which speeded up adoption of the technology. The cooperation was a win-win situation for both Philips and Sony. It eliminated the competitors and enabled the companies to share in the success of the format.

License the Format

Another strategy often adopted is to license the format to other enterprises so that they can produce products based on it. The company that pioneered the format gains from the licensing fees that flow back to it and from the enlarged supply of the product, which can stimulate demand and help accelerate market adoption. This was the strategy that Matsushita adopted with its VHS format for the VCR. In addition to producing VCRs at its own factory in Osaka, Matsushita allowed a number of other companies to produce VHS format players under license (Sony decided not to license its competing Betamax format and produced all Betamax format players itself); hence, VHS players were more widely available. More people purchased VHS players, which created an incentive for film companies to issue more films on VHS tapes (as opposed to Betamax tapes), which further increased demand for VHS players and helped Matsushita to lock in VHS as the dominant format in the marketplace. Sony, ironically the first to market, saw its position marginalized by the reduced supply of the critical complement, prerecorded films, and ultimately withdrew Betamax players from the consumer marketplace.

Dolby, as we saw in Strategy in Action 7.1, adopted a similar licensing strategy to get its noise-reduction technology adopted as the technological standard in the music and film industries. By charging a modest licensing fee for use of the technology in recording equipment and forgoing licensing fees on media recorded using Dolby technology, Dolby deliberately sought to reduce the financial incentive that potential competitors might have to develop their own, possibly superior, technology. Dolby calculated that its long-run profitability would be maximized by adopting a licensing strategy that limited the incentive of competitors to enter the market.

The correct strategy to pursue in a particular scenario requires that a company consider all of these different strategies and tactics and pursue those that seem most appropriate given the competitive circumstances prevailing in the industry and the likely strategy of rivals. Although there is no one best mix of strategies and tactics, a company must keep the goal of rapidly increasing the installed base of products based on its standard at the front of its mind. By helping to jump-start demand for its format, a company can induce consumers to bear the switching costs associated with adopting its technology and leverage any positive feedback process that might exist. Also important is not pursuing strategies that have the opposite effect. For example, pricing high to capture profits from early adopters, who tend not to be as price sensitive as later adopters, can have the unfortunate effect of slowing demand growth and letting a more aggressive competitor pick up share and establish its format as the industry standard.

COSTS IN HIGH-TECHNOLOGY INDUSTRIES

In many high-tech industries, the fixed costs of developing the product are very high, but the costs of producing one extra unit of the product are very low. This is most obvious in the case of software. For example, it reportedly cost Microsoft $5 billion to develop Windows Vista, the latest version of its Windows operating system, but the cost of producing one more copy of Windows Vista is virtually zero. Once Windows Vista was completed, Microsoft produced master disks that it sent out to PC manufacturers, such as Dell Computer, who then loaded a copy of Windows Vista onto every PC it sold. The cost to Microsoft was effectively zero, yet it receives a significant licensing fee for each copy of Windows Vista installed on a PC.[7] For Microsoft, the marginal cost of making one more copy of Windows Vista is close to zero, although the fixed costs of developing the product are $5 billion.

Many other high-tech products have similar cost economics: very high fixed costs and very low marginal costs. Most software products share these features, although if the software is sold through stores, the costs of packaging and distribution will raise the marginal costs, and if it is sold by a sales force direct to end-users, this will also raise the marginal costs. Many consumer electronics products have the same basic economics. The fixed costs of developing a DVD player or a gaming console can be very expensive, but the costs of producing an incremental unit are very low. The costs of developing a new drug, such as Viagra, can run to more than $800 million, but the marginal cost of producing each additional pill is at most a few cents.

Comparative Cost Economics

To grasp why this cost structure is strategically important, a company must understand that, in many industries, marginal costs rise as a company tries to expand output (economists call this the *law of diminishing returns*). To produce more of a good, a company has to hire more labor and invest in more plant and machinery. At the margin, the additional resources used are not as productive, so this leads to increasing marginal costs. However, the law of diminishing returns often does not apply in many high-tech settings, such as the production of software or sending one more bit of data down a digital telecommunications network.

Consider two companies, α and β (see Figure 7.3). Company α is a conventional producer and faces diminishing returns, so as it tries to expand output, its marginal costs rise. Company β is a high-tech producer, and its marginal costs do not rise as output is increased. Note that in Figure 7.3, company β's marginal cost curve is drawn as a straight line near the horizontal axis, implying that marginal costs are close to zero and do not vary with output, whereas company α's marginal costs rise

Figure 7.3 Cost Structures in High-Technology Industries

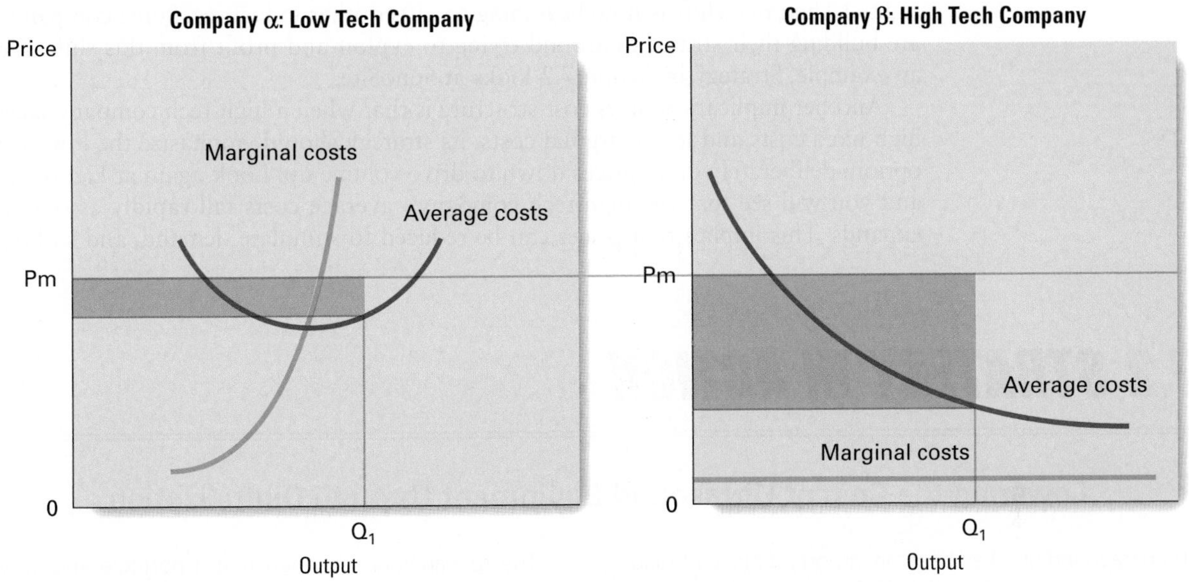

as output is expanded, illustrating diminishing returns. Company β's flat and low marginal cost curve means that its average cost curve will fall continuously over all ranges of output as it spreads its fixed costs out over greater volume. In contrast, the rising marginal costs encountered by company α mean that its average cost curve is the U-shaped curve familiar from basic economics texts. For simplicity, assume that both companies sell their product at the same price, Pm, and both sell exactly the same quantity of output, 0 − Q1. You will see from Figure 7.3 that at an output of Q1, company β has much lower average costs than company α and, as a consequence, is making far more profit (profit is the shaded area in Figure 7.3).

Strategic Significance

If a company can shift from a cost structure where it encounters increasing marginal costs to one where fixed costs may be high but marginal costs are much lower, its profitability may increase. In the consumer electronics industry, such a shift has been playing out for two decades. Music recordings previously were based on analog technology, where marginal costs rose as output expanded due to diminishing returns (as in the case of company α in Figure 7.3). Since the 1980s, digital systems such as CD players have replaced analog systems. Digital systems are software based, and this implies much lower marginal costs of producing one more copy of a recording. As a result, the music labels have been able to lower prices, expand demand, and see their profitability increase (their production system has more in common with company β in Figure 7.3).

This process is still unfolding. The latest technology for making copies of music recordings is based on distribution over the Internet (for example, by downloading onto an iPod). In this case, the marginal costs of making one more copy of a recording are lower still. In fact, they are close to zero and do not increase with output. The only problem is that the low costs of copying and distributing music recordings have created a major copyright problem that the major music labels have yet to solve. (We will discuss this in more detail shortly when we consider intellectual property rights.) The same shift is now beginning to affect other industries. Some companies are building their strategies around trying to exploit and profit from this shift. For an example, Strategy in Action 7.2 looks at SonoSite.

Another implication of its cost structure is that when a high-tech company faces high fixed costs and low marginal costs, its strategy should emphasize the low-cost option: deliberately drive prices down to drive volume up. Look again at Figure 7.3 and you will see that the high-tech company's average costs fall rapidly as output expands. This implies that prices can be reduced to stimulate demand, and so long

7.2 STRATEGY IN ACTION

Lowering the Cost of Ultrasound Equipment Through Digitalization

The ultrasound unit has been an important piece of diagnostic equipment in hospitals for some time. Ultrasound units use the physics of sound to produce images of soft tissues in the human body. They can produce detailed, three-dimensional color images of organs and, by using contrast agents, track the flow of fluids through an organ. A cardiologist, for example, can use an ultrasound in combination with contrast agents injected into the bloodstream to track the flow of blood through a beating heart. In additional to the visual diagnosis, ultrasound also produces an array of quantitative diagnostic information of great value to physicians.

Modern ultrasound units are sophisticated instruments that cost $250,000 to $300,000 each for a top-line model. They are fairly bulky instruments, weighing some 300 pounds, and are wheeled around hospitals on carts.

A few years back, a group of researchers at ATL, one of the leading ultrasound companies, came up with an idea for reducing the size and cost of a basic unit. They theorized that it might be possible to replace up to 80% of the solid circuits in an ultrasound unit with software, in the process significantly shrinking the size and reducing the weight of machines and thereby producing portable ultrasound units. Moreover, by digitalizing much of the ultrasound unit, replacing hardware with software, they could considerably drive down the marginal costs of making additional units and would thus be able to make a good profit at much lower price points.

The researchers reasoned that a portable and inexpensive ultrasound unit would find market opportunities in totally new niches. For example, a small, inexpensive ultrasound unit could be placed in an ambulance, carried into battle by an army medic, or purchased by family physicians for use in their offices. Although they realized that it would be some time, perhaps decades, before such small, inexpensive machines could attain the image quality and diagnostic sophistication of top-of-the-line machines, they saw the opportunity in terms of creating market niches that previously could not be served by ultrasound companies because of the high costs and bulk of the product.

The researchers ultimately became a project team within ATL and were then spun out of ATL as an entirely new company, SonoSite. In late 1999, they introduced their first portable product, weighing just six pounds and costing about $25,000. SonoSite targeted niches that full-sized ultrasound products could not reach: ambulatory care and foreign markets that could not afford the more expensive equipment. In 2008, the company sold more than $200 million worth of its product. In the long run, SonoSite plans to build more features and greater image quality into the small handheld machines, primarily by improving the software. This could allow the units to penetrate United States hospital markets that currently purchase the established technology, much as client-server systems based on PC technology came to replace mainframes for some functions in business corporations.

Source: Interviews by Charles W. L. Hill.

as prices fall less rapidly than average costs, per unit profit margins will expand as prices fall. This is a consequence of the fact that the firm's marginal costs are low and do not rise with output. This strategy of pricing low to drive volume and reap wider profit margins is central to the business model of some very successful high-tech companies, including Microsoft.

CAPTURING FIRST-MOVER ADVANTAGES

In high-tech industries, companies often compete by striving to be the first to develop revolutionary new products, that is, to be a **first mover**. By definition, the first mover with regard to a revolutionary product is in a monopoly position. If the new product satisfies unmet consumer needs and demand is high, the first mover can capture significant revenues and profits. Such revenues and profits signal to potential rivals that there is money to be made by imitating the first mover. As illustrated in Figure 7.4, in the absence of strong barriers to imitation, this implies that imitators will rush into the market created by the first mover, competing away the first mover's monopoly profits and leaving all participants in the market with a much lower level of returns.

Despite imitation, some first movers have the ability to capitalize on and reap substantial first-mover advantages—the advantages of pioneering new technologies and products that lead to an enduring competitive advantage. Intel introduced the world's first microprocessor in 1971 and today still dominates the microprocessor segment of the semiconductor industry. Xerox introduced the world's first photocopier and for a long time enjoyed a leading position in the industry. Cisco introduced the first Internet protocol network router in 1986 and still dominates the market for that equipment today. Some first movers can reap substantial advantages from their pioneering activities that lead to an enduring competitive advantage. They can, in other words, limit or slow the rate of imitation.

Figure 7.4   The Impact of Imitation on Profits of a First Mover

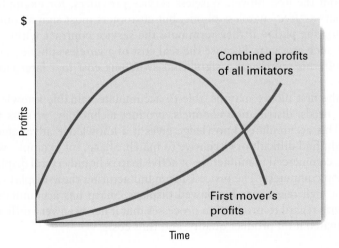

But there are plenty of counterexamples suggesting that first-mover advantages might not be easy to capture. In fact, that there might be **first-mover disadvantages**—the competitive disadvantages associated with being first. For example, Apple Computer was the first company to introduce a handheld computer, the Apple Newton, but the product failed; a second mover, Palm, succeeded where Apple had failed. In the market for commercial jet aircraft, DeHavilland was the first to market with the Comet, but it was the second mover, Boeing, with its 707 jetliner, that went on to dominate the market.

Clearly being a first mover does not by itself guarantee success. As we shall see, the difference between innovating companies that capture first-mover advantages and those that fall victim to first-mover disadvantages in part turns on the strategy that the first mover pursues. Before considering the strategy issue, however, we need to take a closer look at the nature of first-mover advantages and disadvantages.[8]

First-Mover Advantages

There are five main sources of first-mover advantages.[9] First, the first mover has an opportunity to exploit network effects and positive feedback loops, locking consumers into its technology. In the VCR industry, Sony could have exploited network effects by licensing its technology, but instead the company ceded its first-mover advantage to the second mover, Matsushita.

Second, the first mover may be able to establish significant brand loyalty, which is expensive for later entrants to break down. Indeed, if the company is successful in this endeavor, its name may become closely associated with the entire class of products, including those produced by rivals. People still talk of "Xeroxing" when they are going to make a photocopy or "FedExing" when they are going to send a package by overnight mail, and when we want to find something on the Web, we "Google" it.

Third, the first mover may be able to ramp up sales volume ahead of rivals and thus reap cost advantages associated with the realization of scale economies and learning effects (see Chapter 4). Once the first mover has these cost advantages, it can respond to new entrants by cutting prices to hold onto its market share and still earn significant profits.

Fourth, the first mover may be able to create switching costs for its customers that subsequently make it difficult for rivals to enter the market and take customers away from the first mover. Wireless service providers, for example, will give new customers a "free" wireless phone, but customers must sign a contract agreeing to pay for the phone if they terminate the service contract within a specified time period, such as a year. Because the real cost of a wireless phone may run from $100 to $200, this represents a significant switching cost that later entrants have to overcome.

Finally, the first mover may be able to accumulate valuable knowledge related to customer needs, distribution channels, product technology, process technology, and so on. This accumulated knowledge gives it a knowledge advantage that later entrants might find difficult or expensive to match. Sharp, for example, was the first mover in the commercial manufacture of active matrix liquid crystal displays (LCDs) used in laptop computers. The process for manufacturing these displays is very difficult, with a high reject rate for flawed displays. Sharp has accumulated such an advantage with regard to production processes that it has been very difficult for later entrants to match it on product quality, and thus costs.

First-Mover Disadvantages

Balanced against these first-mover advantages are a number of disadvantages.[10] First, the first mover has to bear significant pioneering costs that later entrants do not. The first mover has to pioneer the technology, develop distribution channels, and educate customers about the nature of the product. All of this can be expensive and time-consuming. Later entrants, by way of contrast, might be able to free-ride on the first mover's investments in pioneering the market and customer education.

Related to this, first movers are more prone to make mistakes because there are so many uncertainties in a new market. Later entrants may be able to learn from the mistakes made by first movers, improve on the product or the way in which it is sold, and come to market with a superior offering that captures significant market share from the first mover. For example, one of the reasons that the Apple Newton failed was that the handwriting software in the handheld computer failed to recognize human handwriting. The second mover in this market, Palm, learned from Apple's error. When it introduced the PalmPilot, it used software that recognized letters written in a particular way, Graffiti, and then persuaded customers to learn this method of inputting data into the handheld computer.

Third, first movers run the risk of building the wrong resources and capabilities because they are focusing on a customer set that is not going to be characteristic of the mass market. This is the *crossing the chasm* problem that we discussed in the previous chapter. You will recall that the customers in the early market—those we categorized as innovators and early adopters—have different characteristics from the first wave of the mass market, the early majority. The first mover runs the risk of gearing its resources and capabilities to the needs of innovators and early adopters and not being able to switch when the early majority enters the market. As a result, first movers run a greater risk of plunging into the chasm that separates the early market from the mass market.

Finally, the first mover may invest in inferior or obsolete technology. This can happen when its product innovation is based on underlying technology that is advancing rapidly. By basing its product on an early version of the technology, it may lock itself into something that rapidly becomes obsolete. In contrast, later entrants may be able to leapfrog the first mover and introduce products that are based on later versions of the underlying technology. This happened in France during the 1980s when, at the urging of the government, France Telecom introduced the world's first consumer online service, Minitel. France Telecom distributed crude terminals to consumers for free, which they could hook up to their phone line and use to browse phone directories. Other simple services were soon added, and before long the French could carry out online shopping, banking, travel, weather, and news—all years before the Web was invented. The problem was that by the standards of the Web, Minitel was very crude and inflexible, and France Telecom, as the first mover, suffered. The French were very slow to adopt PCs and the Internet, primarily because Minitel had such a presence. As late as 1998, only one-fifth of French households had computers, compared with two-fifths in the United States, and only 2% of households were connected to the Internet, compared to more than 30% in the United States. As the result of a government decision, France Telecom, and indeed an entire nation, was slow to adopt a revolutionary new online medium, the Web, because they were the first to invest in a more primitive version of the technology.[11]

Strategies for Exploiting First-Mover Advantages

The task facing a first mover is how to exploit its lead to capitalize on first-mover advantages and build a sustainable long-term competitive advantage while simultaneously reducing the risks associated with first-mover disadvantages. There are three basic strategies available: (1) develop and market the innovation itself, (2) develop and market the innovation jointly with other companies through a strategic alliance or joint venture, and (3) license the innovation to others and let them develop the market.

The optimal choice of strategy depends on the answers to three questions:

1. Does the innovating company have the complementary assets to exploit its innovation and capture first-mover advantages?
2. How difficult is it for imitators to copy the company's innovation? In other words, what is the height of barriers to imitation?
3. Are there capable competitors that could rapidly imitate the innovation?

Complementary Assets   Complementary assets are the assets required to exploit a new innovation and gain a competitive advantage.[12] Among the most important complementary assets are competitive manufacturing facilities capable of handling rapid growth in customer demand while maintaining high product quality. State-of-the-art manufacturing facilities enable the first mover to move quickly down the experience curve without encountering production bottlenecks or problems with the quality of the product. The inability to satisfy demand because of these problems, however, creates the opportunity for imitators to enter the marketplace. For example, in 1998, Immunex was the first company to introduce a revolutionary new biological treatment for rheumatoid arthritis. Sales for this product, Enbrel, ramped up very rapidly, hitting $750 million in 2001. However, Immunex had not invested in sufficient manufacturing capacity. In mid-2000, it announced that it lacked the capacity to satisfy demand and that bringing additional capacity online would take at least two years. This manufacturing bottleneck gave the second mover in the market, Johnson & Johnson, the opportunity to expand demand for its product rapidly, which by early 2002 was outselling Enbrel. Immunex's first-mover advantage had been partly eroded because it lacked an important complementary asset, the manufacturing capability required to satisfy demand.

Complementary assets also include marketing know-how, an adequate sales force, access to distribution systems, and an after-sales service and support network. All of these assets can help an innovator build brand loyalty and achieve market penetration more rapidly.[13] In turn, the resulting increases in volume facilitate more rapid movement down the experience curve and the attainment of a sustainable cost-based advantage due to scale economies and learning effects. One of the reasons that EMI, the first mover in the market for CT scanners, ultimately lost out to established medical equipment companies, such as GE Medical Systems, was that it lacked the marketing know-how, sales force, and distribution systems required to compete effectively in the world's largest market for medical equipment, the United States.

Developing complementary assets can be very expensive, and companies often need large infusions of capital for this purpose. That is why first movers often lose out to late movers that are large, successful companies in other industries with the resources to quickly develop a presence in the new industry. Microsoft and 3M exemplify companies that can move quickly to capitalize on the opportunities when other companies open up new product markets, such as CDs or floppy disks. For example, although Netscape pioneered the market for Internet browsers with the Netscape Navigator, Microsoft's Internet Explorer ultimately dominated the market for Internet browsers.

Height of Barriers to Imitation   Recall from Chapter 3 that barriers to imitation are factors that prevent rivals from imitating a company's distinctive competencies and innovations. Although ultimately any innovation can be copied, the higher the barriers are, the longer it takes for rivals to imitate, and the more time the first mover has to build an enduring competitive advantage.

Barriers to imitation give an innovator time to establish a competitive advantage and build more enduring barriers to entry in the newly created market. Patents, for example, are among the most widely used barriers to imitation. By protecting its photocopier technology with a thicket of patents, Xerox was able to delay any significant imitation of its product for 17 years. However, patents are often easy to "invent around." For example, one study found that this happened to 60% of patented innovations within four years.[14] If patent protection is weak, a company might try to slow imitation by developing new products and processes in secret. The most famous example of this approach is Coca-Cola, which has kept the formula for Coke a secret for generations. But Coca-Cola's success in this regard is an exception. A study of 100 companies has estimated that proprietary information about a company's decision to develop a major new product or process is known to its rivals within about 12 to 18 months of the original development decision.[15]

Capable Competitors   Capable competitors are companies that can move quickly to imitate the pioneering company. A competitor's capability to imitate a pioneer's innovation depends primarily on two factors: (1) R&D skills and (2) access to complementary assets. In general, the greater the number of capable competitors with access to the R&D skills and complementary assets needed to imitate an innovation, the more rapid imitation is likely to be.

In this context, R&D skills refer to the ability of rivals to reverse-engineer an innovation to find out how it works and quickly develop a comparable product. As an example, consider the CT scanner. GE bought one of the first CT scanners produced by EMI, and its technical experts reverse-engineered it. Despite the product's technological complexity, GE developed its own version, which allowed it to imitate EMI quickly and ultimately replace EMI as the major supplier of CT scanners.

With regard to complementary assets, the access that rivals have to marketing, sales know-how, or manufacturing capabilities is one of the key determinants of the rate of imitation. If would-be imitators lack critical complementary assets, not only do they have to imitate the innovation, but they may also have to imitate the innovator's complementary assets. This is expensive, as AT&T discovered when it tried to enter the PC business in 1984. AT&T lacked the marketing assets (sales force and distribution systems) necessary to support PC products. The lack of these assets and the time it takes to build them partly explain why, four years after it entered the market, AT&T had lost $2.5 billion and still had not emerged as a viable contender. It subsequently pulled out of this business.

Three Innovation Strategies   The way in which these three factors—complementary assets, height of barriers to imitation, and the capability of competitors—influence the choice of innovation strategy is summarized in Table 7.1. The competitive

Table 7.1   Strategies for Profiting from Innovation

Strategy	Does the Innovator Have the Required Complementary Assets?	Likely Height of Barriers to Imitation	Number of Capable Competitors
Going it alone	Yes	High	Very few
Entering into an alliance	No	High	Moderate number
Licensing the innovation	No	Low	Many

strategy of developing and marketing the innovation alone makes most sense when (1) the innovator has the complementary assets necessary to develop the innovation, (2) the barriers to imitating a new innovation are high, and (3) the number of capable competitors is limited. Complementary assets allow rapid development and promotion of the innovation. High barriers to imitation buy the innovator time to establish a competitive advantage and build enduring barriers to entry through brand loyalty or experience-based cost advantages. The fewer the capable competitors there are, the less likely it is that any one of them will succeed in circumventing barriers to imitation and quickly imitating the innovation.

The competitive strategy of developing and marketing the innovation jointly with other companies through a strategic alliance or joint venture makes most sense when (1) the innovator lacks complementary assets, (2) barriers to imitation are high, and (3) there are several capable competitors. In such circumstances, it makes sense to enter into an alliance with a company that already has the complementary assets—in other words, with a capable competitor. Theoretically, such an alliance should prove to be mutually beneficial, and each partner can share in high profits that neither could earn on its own. Moreover, such a strategy has the benefit of co-opting a potential rival. For example, had EMI teamed up with a capable competitor to develop the market for CT scanners, such as GE Medical Systems, instead of going it alone, the company might not only have been able to build a more enduring competitive advantage, but it would also have co-opted a potentially powerful rival into its camp.

The third strategy, licensing, makes most sense when (1) the innovating company lacks the complementary assets, (2) barriers to imitation are low, and (3) there are many capable competitors. The combination of low barriers to imitation and many capable competitors makes rapid imitation almost certain. The innovator's lack of complementary assets further suggests that an imitator will soon capture the innovator's competitive advantage. Given these factors, because rapid diffusion of the innovator's technology through imitation is inevitable, the innovator can at least share in some of the benefits of this diffusion by licensing out its technology.[16] Moreover, by setting a relatively modest licensing fee, the innovator may be able to reduce the incentive that potential rivals have to develop their own competing, and possibly superior, technology. This seems to have been the strategy Dolby adopted to get its technology established as the standard for noise reduction in the music and film businesses (see Strategy in Action 7.1).

TECHNOLOGICAL PARADIGM SHIFTS

Technological paradigm shifts occur when new technologies come along that revolutionize the structure of the industry, dramatically alter the nature of competition, and require companies to adopt new strategies to survive. A good example of a paradigm shift that is currently unfolding is the shift from chemical to digital photography (another example of digitalization). For more than half a century, the large incumbent enterprises in the photographic industry, such as Kodak and Fujifilm, have generated most of their revenues from selling and processing film using traditional silver halide technology. The rise of digital photography has been a huge disruptive threat to their business models. Digital cameras do not use film, the mainstay of Kodak's and Fuji's business. Moreover, these cameras are more like specialized computers than conventional cameras and are thus based on scientific knowledge that Kodak and Fuji have little expertise in. Although both Kodak and Fuji have invested heavily in the development of digital cameras, they are facing intense competition from companies such as Sony, Canon, and HP, which have developed their own digital cameras; from software developers such as Adobe and Microsoft, which make the software for manipulating digital images; and from printer companies such as HP and Canon, which are making the printers that consumers can use to print out their own high-quality pictures at home. As digital substitution gathers speed in the photography industry, it is not clear that the traditional incumbents will be able to survive this shift; the new competitors might well rise to dominance in the new market.

Kodak and Fuji are hardly the first large incumbents to be felled by a technological paradigm shift in their industry. In the early 1980s, the computer industry was revolutionized by the arrival of PC technology, which gave rise to client-server networks that replaced traditional mainframe and minicomputers for many business uses. Many incumbent companies in the mainframe era, such as Wang, Control Data, and DEC, ultimately did not survive, and even IBM went through a decade of wrenching changes and large losses before it reinvented itself as a provider of e-business solutions. In their place, new entrants such as Microsoft, Intel, Dell, and Compaq rose to dominance in this new computer industry.

Examples such as these raise four questions:

1. When do paradigm shifts occur, and how do they unfold?
2. Why do so many incumbents go into decline following a paradigm shift?
3. What strategies can incumbents adopt to increase the probability that they will survive a paradigm shift and emerge on the other side of the market abyss created by the arrival of new technology as a profitable enterprise?
4. What strategies can new entrants into a market adopt to profit from a paradigm shift?

We answer each of these questions in the remainder of this chapter.

Paradigm Shifts and the Decline of Established Companies

Paradigm shifts appear to be more likely to occur in an industry when one, or both, of the following conditions are in place.[17] First, the established technology in the industry is mature and approaching or at its "natural limit," and second, a new "disruptive technology" has entered the marketplace and is taking root in niches that are poorly served by incumbent companies using the established technology.

The Natural Limits to Technology   Richard Foster has formalized the relationship between the performance of a technology and time in terms of what he calls the technology S-curve (see Figure 7.5).[18] This curve shows the relationship over time of cumulative investments in R&D and the performance (or functionality) of a given technology. Early in its evolution, R&D investments in a new technology tend to yield rapid improvements in performance as basic engineering problems are solved. After a time, diminishing returns to cumulative R&D begin to set in, the rate of improvement in performance slows, and the technology starts to approach its natural limit, where further advances are not possible. For example, one can argue that there was more improvement in the first 50 years of the commercial aerospace business following the pioneering flight by the Wright Brothers than there has been in the second 50 years. Indeed, the venerable Boeing 747 is based on a 1960s design. In commercial aerospace, therefore, we are now in the region of diminishing returns and may be approaching the natural limit to improvements in the technology of commercial aerospace.

Similarly, it can be argued that we are approaching the natural limit to technology in the performance of silicon-based semiconductor chips. Over the past two decades, the performance of semiconductor chips has been increased dramatically by packing ever more transistors onto a single small silicon chip. This process has helped to increase the power of computers, lower their cost, and shrink their size. But we are starting to approach limits to the ability to shrink the width of lines on a chip and therefore pack ever more transistors onto a single chip. The limit is imposed by the natural laws of physics. Light waves are used to help etch lines onto a chip, and one cannot etch a line that is smaller than the wavelength of light being used. Semiconductor companies are already using light with very small wavelengths, such as extreme ultraviolet, to etch lines onto a chip, but there are limits to how far this technology can be pushed, and many believe that we will reach those limits within the decade. Does this mean that our ability to make smaller, faster, cheaper computers is coming to an end? Probably not. It is more likely that we will find another technology to replace silicon-based computing and enable us to continue building smaller, faster, cheaper computers. In fact, several exotic competing technologies are already being developed that may replace silicon-based computing. These include self-organizing molecular computers, three-dimensional microprocessor technology, quantum computing technology, and using DNA to perform computations.[19]

Figure 7.5   The Technology S-Curve

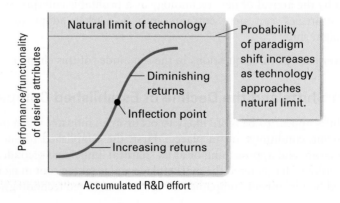

What does all of this have to do with paradigm shifts? According to Foster, when a technology approaches its natural limit, research attention turns to possible alternative technologies, and sooner or later one of those alternatives might be commercialized and replace the established technology. That is, the probability that a paradigm shift will occur increases. Thus, sometime in the next decade or two, another paradigm shift might shake the very foundations of the computer industry as exotic computing technology replaces silicon-based computing. If history is any guide, if and when this happens, many of the incumbents in today's computer industry will go into decline, and new enterprises will rise to dominance.

Foster pushes this point a little further, noting that, initially, the contenders for the replacement technology are not as effective as the established technology in producing the attributes and features that consumers demand in a product. For example, in the early years of the 20th century, automobiles were just starting to be produced. They were valued for their ability to move people from place to place, but so was the horse and cart (the established technology). When automobiles originally appeared, the horse and cart was still quite a bit better than the automobile at doing this (see Figure 7.6). After all, the first cars were slow, noisy, and prone to breakdown. Moreover, they needed a network of paved roads and gas stations to be really useful, and that network did not exist, so for most applications, the horse and cart was still the preferred mode of transportation—to say nothing of the fact that it was cheaper.

However, this comparison ignored the fact that in the early 20th century, automobile technology was at the very start of its S-curve and was about to experience dramatic improvements in performance as major engineering problems were solved (and those paved roads and gas stations were built). In contrast, after 3,000 years of continuous improvement and refinement, the horse and cart was almost definitely at the end of its technological S-curve. The result was that the rapidly improving automobile soon replaced the horse and cart as the preferred mode of transportation. At time T_1 in Figure 7.6, the horse and cart was still superior to the automobile. By time T_2, the automobile had surpassed the horse and cart.

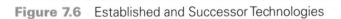

Figure 7.6   Established and Successor Technologies

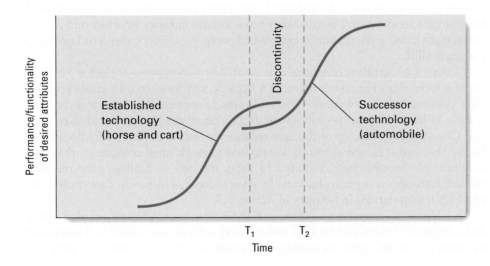

Figure 7.7   Swarm of Successor Technologies

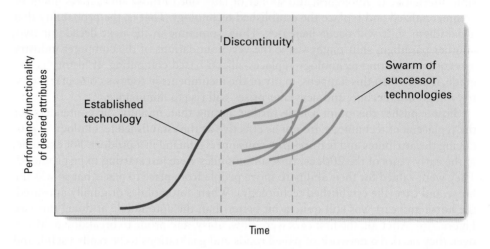

Foster notes that because the successor technology is initially less efficient than the established technology, established companies and their customers often make the mistake of dismissing it, only to be taken off-guard by its rapid performance improvement. A final point here is that often there is not one potential successor technology but a swarm of potential successor technologies, only one of which might ultimately rise to the fore (see Figure 7.7). When this is the case, established companies are put at a disadvantage. Even if they recognize that a paradigm shift is imminent, they may not have the resources to invest in all the potential replacement technologies. If they invest in the wrong one, something that is easy to do given the uncertainty that surrounds the entire process, they may be locked out of subsequent development.

Disruptive Technology   Clayton Christensen built on Foster's insights and his own research to develop a theory of disruptive technology that has become very influential in high-technology circles.[20] Christensen uses the term *disruptive technology* to refer to a new technology that gets its start away from the mainstream of a market and then, as its functionality improves over time, invades the main market. Such technologies are disruptive because they revolutionize industry structure and competition, often causing the decline of established companies. They cause a technological paradigm shift.

Christensen's greatest insight is that established companies are often aware of the new technology but do not invest in it because they listen to their customers, and their customers do not want it. Of course, this arises because the new technology is early in its development—only at the beginning of the S-curve for that technology. Once the performance of the new technology improves, customers do want it, but by this time it is new entrants, as opposed to established companies, that have accumulated the knowledge required to bring the new technology into the mass market. Christensen supports his view by several detailed historical case studies, one of which is summarized in Strategy in Action 7.3.

In addition to listening too closely to their customers, Christensen also identified a number of other factors that make it very difficult for established companies to adopt a new disruptive technology. He noted that many established companies

7.3 *STRATEGY IN ACTION*

Disruptive Technology in Mechanical Excavators

Excavators are used to dig out foundations for large buildings, trenches to lay large pipes for sewers and the like, and foundations and trenches for residential construction and farm work. Prior to the 1940s, the dominant technology used to manipulate the bucket on a mechanical excavator was based on a system of cables and pulleys. Although these mechanical systems could lift large buckets of earth, the excavators themselves were quite large, cumbersome, and expensive. Thus, they were rarely used to dig small trenches for house foundations, irrigation ditches for farmers, and the like. In most cases, these small trenches were dug by hand.

In the 1940s, a new technology made its appearance: hydraulics. In theory, hydraulic systems had certain advantages over the established cable and pulley systems. Most important, their energy efficiency was higher. For a given bucket size, a smaller engine would be required using a hydraulic system. However, the initial hydraulic systems also had drawbacks. The seals on hydraulic cylinders were prone to leak under high pressure, effectively limiting the size of bucket that could be lifted using hydraulics. Notwithstanding this drawback, when hydraulics first appeared, many of the incumbent firms in the mechanical excavation industry took the technology seriously enough to ask their primary customers whether they would be interested in products based on hydraulics. Because the primary customers of incumbents needed excavators with large buckets to dig out the foundations for buildings and large trenches, their reply was negative. For this customer set, the hydraulic systems of the 1940s were not reliable or powerful enough. Consequently, after consulting with their customers, these established companies in the industry made the strategic decision not to invest in hydraulics. Instead, they continued to produce excavation equipment based on the dominant cable and pulley technology.

It was left to a number of new entrants, which included J. I. Case, John Deere, J. C. Bamford, and Caterpillar, to pioneer hydraulic excavation equipment. Because of the limits on bucket size imposed by the seal problem, these companies initially focused on a poorly served niche in the market that could make use of small buckets: residential contractors and farmers. Over time, these new entrants were able to solve the engineering problems associated with weak hydraulic seals, and as they did so, they manufactured excavators with larger buckets. Ultimately, they invaded the market niches served by the old-line companies: general contractors that dug the foundations for large buildings, sewers, and so on. At this point, Case, Deere, Caterpillar, and their kin rose to dominance in the industry, while the majority of established companies from the prior era lost share. Of the 30 or so manufacturers of cable-actuated equipment in the United States in the late 1930s, only four survived to the 1950s.

Source: Christensen, *The Innovator's Dilemma.*

declined to invest in new disruptive technologies because initially they served such small market niches that it seemed unlikely that they would have an impact on the company's revenues and profits. As the new technology started to improve in functionality and invade the main market, their investment was often hindered by the fact that exploiting the new technology required a new business model totally different from the company's established model, and thus very difficult to implement.

Both of these points can be illustrated by reference to one more example: the rise of online discount stockbrokers during the 1990s such as Ameritrade and E*TRADE, which made use of a new technology, the Internet, to allow individual investors to trade stocks for a very low commission fee, whereas full-service stockbrokers such as Merrill Lynch, where orders had to be placed through a stockbroker who earned a commission for performing the transaction, did not.

Christensen also noted that a new network of suppliers and distributors typically grows up around the new entrants. Not only do established companies initially ignore disruptive technology but also their suppliers and distributors. This creates an opportunity for new suppliers and distributors to enter the market to serve the new entrants. As the new entrants grow, so does the associated network. Ultimately, Christensen suggests, the new entrants and their network may replace not only established enterprises but also the entire network of suppliers and distributors associated with established companies. Taken to its logical extreme, this view suggests that disruptive technologies may result in the demise of the entire network of enterprises associated with established companies in an industry.

The established companies in an industry that is being rocked by a technological paradigm shift often have to cope with internal inertia forces that limit their ability to adapt, but the new entrants do not and thereby have an advantage. They do not have to deal with an established and conservative customer set and an obsolete business model. Instead, they can focus on optimizing the new technology, improving its performance, and riding the wave of disruptive technology into new market segments until they invade the main market and challenge the established companies, by which time they may be well equipped to beat them.

Strategic Implications for Established Companies

Although Christensen uncovered an important tendency, it is by no means written in stone that all established companies are doomed to fail when faced with disruptive technologies, as we have seen with IBM and Merrill Lynch. Established companies must meet the challenges created by the emergence of disruptive technologies.[21]

First, having access to knowledge about how disruptive technologies can revolutionize markets is itself a valuable strategic asset. Many of the established companies that Christensen examined failed because they took a myopic view of the new technology and asked their customers the wrong question. Instead of asking, "Are you interested in this new technology?" they should have recognized that the new technology was likely to improve rapidly over time. Instead they should have asked, "Would you be interested in this new technology if it improves its functionality over time?" If they had done this, they may have made very different strategic decisions.

Second, it is clearly important for established enterprises to invest in newly emerging technologies that may ultimately become disruptive technologies. Companies have to hedge their bets about new technology. As we have noted, at any time, there may be a swarm of emerging technologies, any one of which might ultimately become a disruptive technology. Large, established companies that are generating significant cash flows can and often should establish and fund central R&D operations to invest in and develop such technologies. In addition, they may wish to acquire newly emerging companies that are pioneering potentially disruptive technologies or enter into alliances with them to develop the technology jointly. The strategy of acquiring companies that are developing potentially disruptive technology is one that Cisco Systems, a dominant provider of Internet network equipment, is famous for pursuing. At the heart of this strategy must be recognition on the part of the incumbent enterprise that it is better for the company to develop disruptive technology and then cannibalize its established sales base than to have that sales base taken away by new entrants.

However, Christensen makes the important point that even when established companies undertake R&D investments in potentially disruptive technologies, they often fail to commercialize those technologies because of internal forces that suppress change. For example, managers in the parts of the business that are currently generating the most cash may claim that they need the greatest R&D investment to maintain their market position and may lobby top management to delay investment in a new technology. Early on in the S-curve, when it is very unclear what the long-term prospects of a new technology may be, this can be a powerful argument. The consequence, however, may be that the company fails to build a competence in the new technology and will suffer accordingly.

In addition, Christensen argued that the commercialization of new disruptive technology often requires a radically different value chain with a completely different cost structure—a new business model. For example, it may require a different manufacturing system, a different distribution system, and different pricing options and involve very different gross margins and operating margins. Christensen argued that it is almost impossible for two distinct business models to coexist within the same organization. When companies try to do that, almost inevitably the established business model will suffocate the business model associated with the disruptive technology.

The solution to this problem is to separate out the disruptive technology and place it in its own autonomous operating division. For example, during the early 1980s HP built a very successful laser jet printer business. Then along came inkjet technology. Some in the company believed that ink jet printers would cannibalize sales of laser jets and consequently argued that HP should not produce inkjets. Fortunately for HP, senior management at the time saw inkjet technology for what it was: a potential disruptive technology. Far from not investing in it, they allocated significant R&D funds toward its commercialization. Furthermore, when the technology was ready for market introduction, they established an autonomous inkjet division at a different geographic location with its own manufacturing, marketing, and distribution activities. They accepted that the inkjet division might take sales away from the laser jet division and decided that it was better to have an HP division cannibalize the sales of another HP division than have those sales cannibalized by another company. Happily for HP, it turns out that inkjets cannibalize sales of laser jets only on the margin and that both have profitable market niches. This felicitous outcome, however, does not detract from the message of the story: if your company is developing a potentially disruptive technology, the chances of success will be enhanced if it is placed in a stand-alone product division and given its own mandate.

Strategic Implications for New Entrants

The work just discussed also holds implications for new entrants. The new entrants, or attackers, have several advantages over established enterprises. Pressures to continue the existing out-of-date business model do not hamstring new entrants, which do not have to worry about product cannibalization issues. They do not have to worry about their established customer base or relationships with established suppliers and distributors. Instead, they can focus all their energies on the opportunities offered by the new disruptive technology, ride the S-curve of technology improvement, and grow rapidly with the market for that technology. This does not mean that the new entrants have no problems to solve. They may be constrained by a lack of capital or have to manage the organizational problems associated with rapid growth; most important, they may need to find a way to take their technology from a small out-of-the-way niche into the mass market.

Perhaps one of the most important issues facing new entrants is the choice of whether to partner with an established company or go it alone in their attempt to develop and profit from a new disruptive technology. Although a new entrant may enjoy all of the advantages of the attacker, it may lack the resources required to exploit them fully. In such a case, it might want to consider forming a strategic alliance with a larger, established company to gain access to those resources. The main issues here are the same as those that we discussed earlier when examining the three strategies that companies can pursue to capture first-mover advantages: go it alone, enter into a strategic alliance, or license its technology.

SUMMARY OF CHAPTER

1. Technical standards are important in many high-tech industries: they guarantee compatibility, reduce confusion in the minds of customers, allow for mass production and lower costs, and reduce the risks associated with supplying complementary products.
2. Network effects and positive feedback loops often determine which standard comes to dominate a market.
3. Owning a standard can be a source of sustained competitive advantage.
4. Establishing a proprietary standard as the industry standard may require the company to win a format war against a competing and incompatible standard. Strategies for doing this include producing complementary products, leveraging killer applications, using aggressive pricing and marketing, licensing the technology, and cooperating with competitors.
5. Many high-tech products are characterized by high fixed costs of development but very low or zero marginal costs of producing one extra unit of output. These cost economics create a presumption in favor of strategies that emphasize aggressive pricing to increase volume and drive down average total costs.
6. It is very important for a first mover to develop a strategy to capitalize on first-mover advantages. A company can choose from three strategies: develop and market the technology itself, do so jointly with another company, or license the technology to existing companies. The choice depends on the complementary assets required to capture a first-mover advantage, the height of barriers to imitation, and the capability of competitors.
7. Technological paradigm shifts occur when new technologies come along that revolutionize the structure of the industry, dramatically alter the nature of competition, and require companies to adopt new strategies to survive.
8. Technological paradigm shifts are more likely to occur when progress in improving the established technology is slowing because it is giving diminishing returns and a new disruptive technology is taking root in a market niche.
9. Established companies can deal with paradigm shifts by hedging their bets with regard to technology or setting up a stand-alone division to exploit the technology.

DISCUSSION QUESTIONS

1. Why are standards so important in many high-tech industries? What are the competitive implications of this?
2. You work for a small company that has the leading position in an embryonic market. Your boss believes that the company's future is ensured because it has a 60% share of the market, the lowest cost structure in the industry, and the most reliable and highest-valued product. Write

a memo to him outlining why his assumptions might be incorrect.

3. Read the Closing Case on the emerging format war for high-definition DVD players. On the basis of the information contained in this case, who do you think is most likely to win this format war, Sony or Toshiba? Why?

C L O S I N G   C A S E

Blu-Ray versus HD DVD

Between 2004 and 2008, there was a format war in the consumer electronics industry between two different versions of next generation high-definition DVD players and discs. In one camp, there was Sony with its Blu-ray format; in the other was Toshiba, who was championing the rival HD DVD format. Both high-definition formats offer a dramatic improvement in picture and sound quality over established DVD technology and are designed to work with high-definition television sets. However, although each new format plays old DVDs, the two standards are incompatible with each other. Blu-ray players will not accept DVDs formatted for HD DVD, and vice versa.

Format wars like this have occurred many times in the past. VHS versus Betamax in the videocassette market and Windows versus Macintosh in PC operating systems are classic examples. If history is any guide, format wars tend to be "winner-take-all contests," with the loser being vanquished to a niche (as in the case of Apple's Macintosh operating system) or exiting the market altogether (as in the case of Sony's Betamax format). Format wars are high-stakes games.

Aware of this, both Sony and Toshiba worked hard to ensure that their format gained an early lead in sales. A key strategy of both companies was to line up film studios and get them to commit to issuing discs based on their format.

Initially, it looked as if Sony had the early advantage. Prior to the technology being launched in the market, Columbia Pictures and MGM (both owned by Sony), along with Disney and Fox Studios, all committed exclusively to Blu-ray. By late 2005, several other studios that had initially committed exclusively to HD DVD, including Warner Brothers and Paramount, also indicated that they would support Blu-ray as well. Warner and Paramount cited Blu-ray's

momentum among other studios and its strong copyright protection mechanisms. This left just Universal Studios committed exclusively to HD DVD.

To further strengthen its hand, Sony announced that it would incorporate Blu-ray technology in its next generation PS3 gaming console and its Vaio line of PCs. HP and Dell also indicated that they would support the Blu-ray format. Sony even licensed the Blu-ray format to several other consumer electronics firms, including Samsung, in a bid to increase the supply of Blu-ray players in stores.

Then things began to go wrong for Sony. The company had to delay delivery of its P3 gaming console by a year due to engineering problems, which sapped some of the momentum from Blu-ray. Microsoft took advantage of this misstep, announcing that it would market an HD DVD player that would work with its own gaming console, Xbox 360. In mid-2006, the first Blu-ray and HD DVD players hit the market: the Blu-ray players were more expensive, as much as twice the price of entry level HD DVD players. According to Toshiba, HD DVD players and discs are cheaper to manufacture, although Sony disputes this. To complicate matters, one of the first Blu-ray players, made by Sony licensee Samsung, was shipped with a bad chip that marred its image quality.

By late 2006, some firms were beginning to hedge their bets. HP reversed its earlier position and said that it would support both standards. Then in mid-2007, Toshiba persuaded Paramount to switch from Blu-ray and exclusively back the HD DVD format, paying it $150 million to do so. Paradoxically, Sony claimed that the Paramount defection was a sign that it was winning. The fact that Toshiba had to pay Paramount $150 million showed how desperate they were, claimed Sony.

As it turned out, Sony was right. By late 2007, sales of Blu-ray DVDs were outselling HD DVDs by a margin of two to one, primarily thanks to the P3, which after arriving late to the market, was selling reasonably well. To further accelerate its lead, Sony cut prices on stand-alone Blu-ray players. Then in early 2008, Warner announced that henceforth it would back Blu-ray exclusively, citing Blu-ray's market momentum. This proved to be the coup de grâce for HD DVD. Very quickly, the remaining fence sitters backed Blu-ray, and HD DVD was effectively dead. Some wonder, however, whether Sony's triumph might be something of a pyrrhic victory, for another technology was emerging that promised to make HD DVD players obsolete: video on demand and video downloads onto computer hard drives over the Internet.[22]

Case Discussion Questions

1. Why did both Sony and Toshiba perceive it to be so important to get an early lead in sales?
2. What strategies and assets enabled Sony to win this format war?
3. What might Toshiba have done that might have led to a different outcome?
4. The companies that developed first generation DVD technology decided not to compete on technology, instead harmonizing their technology under the auspices of the DVD Forum. Why do you think they chose a different approach this time around?
5. What are the risks associated with fighting a format war like this?

GLOBAL STRATEGY

After reading this chapter, you should be able to

- Understand the process of globalization and how it impacts a company's strategy
- Discuss the motives for expanding internationally

- Review the different strategies that companies use to compete in the global marketplace
- Explain the pros and cons of different modes for entering foreign markets

The Evolving Strategy of Coca-Cola

Coca-Cola, the iconic American soda maker, has long been among the most international of enterprises.

The company made its first move outside the United States in 1902, when it entered Cuba. By 1929, Coca-Cola was marketed in 76 countries. In World War II, Coca-Cola struck a deal to supply the United States military, wherever they might be, with its signature soda, Coca-Cola. During this era, the company built 63 bottling plants around the world. Its global push continued after the war, fueled in part by the belief that the United States market would eventually reach maturity and by the perception that huge growth opportunities lay overseas. By 2008, more than 59,000 of the company's 71,000 employees were located in 200 countries outside the United States, and 73% of

Coca-Cola's case volume was in international markets.

Until the 1980s, its strategy could best be characterized as one of considerable localization. Local operations were granted a high degree of independence to manage their own operations as they saw fit. This all changed in the 1980s and 1990s under the leadership of Roberto Goizueta, a talented Cuba immigrant who became the CEO of Coca-Cola in 1981. Goizueta placed renewed emphasis on Coca-Cola's flagship brands, which were extended with the introduction of Diet Coke, Cherry Coke, and the like. His prime belief was that the main difference between the United States and international markets was the lower level of penetration in the latter, where consumption per capita of colas was only 10–15% of the United States figure. Goizueta pushed Coca-Cola to become a global company, centralizing a great deal of management and marketing activities at the corporate headquarters in Atlanta, focusing on core brands, and taking equity stakes in foreign bottlers so that the company could exert more strategic control over them. This one-size-fits-all strategy was built around standardization and the realization of economies of scale by, for example, using the same advertising message worldwide.

Goizueta's global strategy was adopted by his successor, Douglas Ivester, but by the late 1990s, the drive toward a one-size-fits-all strategy was running out of steam, as smaller, more nimble local competitors marketing local beverages began to halt the Coke growth engine. With Coca-Cola failing to hit its financial targets for the first time in a generation, Ivester resigned in 2000 and was replaced by Douglas Daft. Daft instituted a 180-degree shift in strategy. Daft's belief was that Coca-Cola needed to put more power back in the hands of local country managers. He thought that strategy, product development, and marketing should be tailored to local needs. He laid off 6,000 employees, many of them in Atlanta, and granted country managers much greater autonomy. Moreover, in a striking move for a marketing company, he announced that the company would stop making global advertisements, and he placed advertising budgets and control over creative content back in the hands of country managers.

Ivester's move was in part influenced by the experience of Coca-Cola in Japan, the company's second-most profitable market, where the best selling Coke product is not a carbonated beverage but a canned cold coffee drink—Georgia Coffee—sold in vending machines. The Japanese experience seemed to signal that products should be customized to local tastes and preferences, and Coca-Cola would do well to decentralize more decision-making authority to local managers.

However, the shift toward localization did not produce the growth that had been expected; by 2002 the pendulum was swinging back toward more central coordination, with Atlanta exercising *oversight* over marketing and product development in different nations. But this time, it was not the one-size-fits-all ethos of the Goizueta era. Under the leadership of Neville Isdell, who became CEO in March 2004, Coca-Cola began reviewing and guiding local marketing and product development but adopted the belief that strategy, including pricing, product offerings, and marketing message, should be varied from market to market to match local conditions. Isdell's position, in other words, represents a midpoint between the strategy of Goizueta and Daft. Moreover, Isdell stressed the importance of leveraging good ideas across nations. A case in point is Georgia Coffee. Having seen the success of this beverage in Japan, in October 2007, Coca-Cola entered into a strategic alliance with Illycaffe, one of Italy's premier coffee makers, to build a global franchise for canned or bottled cold coffee beverages. Similarly, in 2003, the Coke subsidiary in China developed a low-cost, noncarbonated orange-based drink that has rapidly become one of the best-selling drinks in that nation. Seeing the potential of the drink, Coca-Cola is now rolling it out in other Asian countries. It has been a huge hit in Thailand, where it was launched in 2005, and seems to be gaining traction in India, where it was launched in 2007.[1]

Overview

This chapter begins with a discussion of ongoing changes in the global competitive environment and discusses models managers can use for analyzing competition in different national markets. Then the chapter discusses the various ways in which international expansion can increase a company's profitability and profit growth. It also looks at the advantages and disadvantages of different strategies companies can pursue to gain competitive advantages in the global marketplace. This is followed by a discussion of two related strategic issues: (1) how managers decide which foreign markets to enter, when to enter them, and on what scale; and (2) what kind of vehicle or means a company should use to expand globally and enter a foreign country. Once a company has entered a foreign market, it becomes a **multinational company**, that is, a company that does business in two or more national markets. The vehicles that companies can employ to enter foreign markets and become multinationals include exporting, licensing, setting up a joint venture with a foreign company, and setting up a wholly owned subsidiary. The chapter closes with a discussion of the benefits and costs of entering into strategic alliances with other global companies.

By the time you have completed this chapter, you will have a good understanding of the various strategic issues that companies face when they decide to expand their operations abroad to achieve competitive advantage and superior profitability.

Coca-Cola, profiled in the opening case, gives us a preview of some issues that we will explore in this chapter. Like many other companies, Coca-Cola moved into other countries because it saw huge growth opportunities there. It thought it could create value by transferring its iconic brand to local subsidiaries and letting them develop the market in conjunction with local bottlers. This worked for a long time, but by the 1980s, Coca-Cola felt the need for greater control over local strategy. It centralized power in Atlanta, while acquiring an equity stake in many local bottlers. For many companies, such a globally coordinated strategy seems to work, and for a time it did for Coca-Cola too. It rolled out centrally produced marketing messages and products worldwide. It realized economies of scale from standardization, and sales grew at a robust rate. But by the end of the 1990s, the strategy was running out of steam. New beverages were springing up in many countries, often marketed by local enterprises, and the growth of Coca-Cola's flagship brands was stalling. The company's response, as it has evolved in the 2000s, has been to allow country managers more strategic autonomy, while maintaining oversight and guidance from Atlanta. At the same time, Coca-Cola has placed more emphasis on trying to reignite growth by transferring good ideas across nations. As we shall see in this chapter, many other enterprises have followed a similar path, focusing first on localization then on global standardization. Like Coca-Cola, many of these companies have come to the conclusion that the best strategy is neither localization nor global standardization; the ideal strategy is one that combines elements of both and that leverages good ideas across nations. We call this orientation a *transnational strategy*, and we discuss it in depth later in the chapter. To begin with, however, we need to define exactly what we mean by strategy.

THE GLOBAL AND NATIONAL ENVIRONMENTS

In the 1950s, most national markets were isolated from each other by significant barriers to international trade and investment. In those days, managers could focus on analyzing just those national markets in which their company competed. They did not need to pay much attention to entry by global competitors, for there were few and entry was difficult. Nor did they need to pay much attention to entering foreign markets because that was often prohibitively expensive. All of this has now changed. Barriers to international trade and investment have tumbled, huge global markets for goods and services have been created, and companies from different nations are entering each other's home markets on a hitherto unprecedented scale, increasing the intensity of competition. Rivalry can no longer be understood merely in terms of what happens within the boundaries of a nation; managers now need to consider how globalization is impacting the environment in which their company competes and what strategies their company should adopt to exploit the unfolding opportunities and counter competitive threats. In this section, we look at the changes ushered in by falling barriers to international trade and investment, and we discuss a model for analyzing the competitive situation in different nations.

The Globalization of Production and Markets

The past half-century has seen a dramatic lowering of barriers to international trade and investment. For example, the average tariff rate on manufactured goods traded between advanced nations has fallen from around 40% to under 4%. Similarly, in nation after nation, regulations prohibiting foreign companies from entering domestic markets and establishing production facilities, or acquiring domestic companies, have been removed. As a result of these two developments, there has been a surge in both the volume of international trade and the value of foreign direct investment. The volume of world merchandise trade has grown faster than the world economy since 1950.[2] From 1970 to 2007, the volume of world merchandise trade expanded 28-fold, outstripping the expansion of world production, which grew about eight times in real terms. Moreover, between 1992 and 2007, the total flow of foreign direct investment from all countries increased by more than 500%, while world trade by value grew by some 145% and world output by about 40%.[3] These two trends have led to the globalization of production and the globalization of markets.[4]

The globalization of production has been increasing as companies take advantage of lower barriers to international trade and investment to disperse important parts of their production processes around the globe. Doing so enables them to take advantage of national differences in the cost and quality of factors of production such as labor, energy, land, and capital, which allow them to lower their cost structures and boost profits. For example, some 30% of the Boeing Company's commercial jet aircraft, the 777, is built by foreign companies. For its next jet airliner, the 787, Boeing is pushing this trend even further, with some 65% of the total value of the aircraft scheduled to be outsourced to foreign companies, 35% of which will go to three major Japanese companies, and another 20% going to companies located in Italy, Singapore, and the United Kingdom.[5] Part of Boeing's rationale for outsourcing so much production to foreign suppliers is that these suppliers are the best in the world at performing their particular activity. Therefore, the result of having foreign suppliers build specific parts is a better final product and higher profitability for Boeing.

As for the globalization of markets, it has been argued that the world's economic system is moving from one in which national markets are distinct entities, isolated from each other by trade barriers and barriers of distance, time, and culture, toward a system in which national markets are merging into one huge global marketplace. Increasingly, customers around the world demand and use the same basic product offerings. Consequently, in many industries, it is no longer meaningful to talk about the German market, the United States market, or the Japanese market; there is only the global market. The global acceptance of Coca-Cola, Citigroup credit cards, blue jeans, Starbucks, McDonald's hamburgers, the Nokia wireless phone, and Microsoft's Windows operating system are examples of this trend.[6]

The trend toward the globalization of production and markets has several important implications for competition within an industry. First, industry boundaries do not stop at national borders. Because many industries are becoming global in scope, actual and potential competitors exist not only in a company's home market but also in other national markets. Managers who analyze only their home market can be caught unprepared by the entry of efficient foreign competitors. The globalization of markets and production implies that companies around the globe are finding their home markets under attack from foreign competitors. For example, in Japan, American financial institutions such as JP Morgan have been making inroads against Japanese financial service institutions. In the United States, Finland's Nokia has taken market share from Motorola in the market for wireless phone handsets (see Strategy in Action 8.1). In the European Union, the once-dominant Dutch company Philips has seen its market share in the customer electronics industry taken by Japan's JVC, Matsushita, and Sony.

Second, the shift from national to global markets has intensified competitive rivalry in industry after industry. National markets that once were consolidated oligopolies, dominated by three or four companies and subjected to relatively little foreign competition, have been transformed into segments of fragmented global industries in which a large number of companies battle each other for market share in country after country. This rivalry has threatened to drive down profitability and made it all the more critical for companies to maximize their efficiency, quality, customer responsiveness, and innovative ability. The painful restructuring and downsizing that has been going on at companies such as Kodak is as much a response to the increased intensity of global competition as it is to anything else. However, not all global industries are fragmented. Many remain consolidated oligopolies, except that now they are consolidated global, rather than national, oligopolies. In the gaming industry, for example, three companies are battling for global dominance: Microsoft in the United States and Nintendo and Sony in Japan. In the market for wireless handsets, Nokia of Finland does global battle against: Motorola of the United States; Samsung and LG in South Korea; Sony-Ericsson, a joint venture between Sony of Japan and Ericsson of Sweden; and, most recently, Apple with its iPhone, and Research in Motion of Canada with its Blackberry.

Finally, although globalization has increased both the threat of entry and the intensity of rivalry within many formerly protected national markets, it has also created enormous opportunities for companies based in those markets. The steady decline in barriers to cross-border trade and investment has opened up many once protected markets to companies based outside them. Thus, for example, in recent years, western European, Japanese, and United States companies have accelerated their investments in the nations of Eastern Europe, Latin America, and Southeast Asia as they try to take advantage of growth opportunities in those areas.

National Competitive Advantage

Despite the globalization of production and markets, many of the most successful companies in certain industries are still clustered in a small number of countries. For example, many of the world's most successful biotechnology and computer companies are based in the United States, and many of the most successful consumer electronics companies are based in Japan and South Korea. Germany is the base for many successful chemical and engineering companies. These facts suggest that the nation-state within which a company is based may have an important bearing on the competitive position of that company in the global marketplace.

8.1 STRATEGY IN ACTION

Finland's Nokia

The wireless phone market is one of the great growth stories of the last decade. Starting from a very low base in 1990, annual global sales of wireless phones surged to reach 825 million units in 2005. By the end of 2008, there were more than 2 billion wireless subscribers worldwide, up from less than 10 million in 1990. Nokia is one of the dominant players in the world market for mobile phones. Nokia's roots are in Finland, not usually a country that comes to mind when one talks about leading-edge technology companies. In the 1980s, Nokia was a rambling Finnish conglomerate with activities that embraced tire manufacturing, paper production, consumer electronics, and telecommunications equipment. By 2008, it had transformed itself into a focused telecommunications equipment manufacturer with a global reach, sales of more than $75 billion, earnings of more than $10 billion, and a one-third share of the global market for wireless phones. How has this former conglomerate emerged to take a global leadership position in wireless telecommunications equipment? Much of the answer lies in the history, geography, and political economy of Finland and its Nordic neighbors.

In 1981, the Nordic nations cooperated to create the world's first international wireless telephone network. They had good reason to become pioneers: it cost far too much to lay down a traditional wire line telephone service in those sparsely populated and inhospitably cold countries. The same features made telecommunications all the more valuable: people driving through the Arctic winter and owners of remote northern houses needed a telephone to summon help if things went wrong. As a result, Sweden, Norway, and Finland became the first nations in the world to take wireless telecommunications seriously. They found, for example, that although it cost up to $800 per subscriber to bring a traditional wire line service to remote locations, the same locations could be linked by wireless cellular for only $500 per subscriber. As a consequence, 12% of people in Scandinavia owned cellular phones by 1994, compared with less than 6% in the

United States, the world's second-most developed market. This lead continued over the next decade. By the end of 2005, 90% of the population in Finland owned a wireless phone, compared with 70% in the United States.

Nokia, a long-time telecommunications equipment supplier, was well positioned to take advantage of this development from the start, but there were other forces at work that helped Nokia develop its competitive edge. Unlike virtually every other developed nation, Finland has never had a national telephone monopoly. Instead, the country's telephone services have long been provided by about 50 or so autonomous local telephone companies whose elected boards set prices by referendum (which naturally means low prices). This army of independent and cost-conscious telephone service providers prevented Nokia from taking anything for granted in its home country. With typical Finnish pragmatism, its customers were willing to buy from the lowest-cost supplier, whether that was Nokia, Ericsson, Motorola, or some other company. This situation contrasted sharply with that prevailing in most developed nations until the late 1980s and early 1990s, where domestic telephone monopolies typically purchased equipment from a dominant local supplier or made it themselves. Nokia responded to this competitive pressure by doing everything possible to drive down its manufacturing costs while staying at the leading edge of wireless technology.

The consequences of these forces are clear. Nokia is now a leader in digital wireless technology. Many now regard Finland as the lead market for wireless telephone services. If you want to see the future of wireless, you do not go to New York or San Francisco; you go to Helsinki, where Finns use their wireless handsets not just to talk to each other but also to browse the Web, execute e-commerce transactions, control household heating and lighting systems, or purchase Coke from a wireless-enabled vending machine. Nokia has gained this lead because Scandinavia started switching to digital technology five years before the rest of the world.

Sources: Lessons from the Frozen North," *Economist*, October 8, 1994, 76–77; "A Finnish Fable," *Economist*, October 14, 2000; D. O'Shea and K. Fitchard, "The First 3 Billion Is Always the Hardest," *Wireless Review*, Volume 22, September 2005, 25–31. P. Taylor, "Big Names Dominate in Mobile Phones," *Financial Times*, September 29, 2006, 26; http://www.nokia.com.

In a study of national competitive advantage, Michael Porter identified four attributes of a national or country-specific environment that have an important impact on the global competitiveness of companies located within that nation:[7]

1. *Factor endowments*: A nation's position in factors of production such as skilled labor or the infrastructure necessary to compete in a given industry
2. *Local demand conditions*: The nature of home demand for the industry's product or service
3. *Competitiveness of related and supporting industries*: The presence or absence in a nation of supplier industries and related industries that are internationally competitive
4. *Intensity of rivalry*: The conditions in the nation governing how companies are created, organized, and managed and the nature of domestic rivalry

Porter speaks of these four attributes as constituting the diamond, arguing that companies from a given nation are most likely to succeed in industries or strategic groups in which the four attributes are favorable (see Figure 8.1). He also argues that the diamond's attributes form a mutually reinforcing system in which the effect of one attribute is dependent on the state of others.

Factor Endowments   Factor endowments—the cost and quality of factors of production—are prime determinants of the competitive advantage that certain countries might have in certain industries. Factors of production include basic factors, such as land, labor, capital, and raw materials, and advanced factors, such as technological

Figure 8.1   National Competitive Advantage

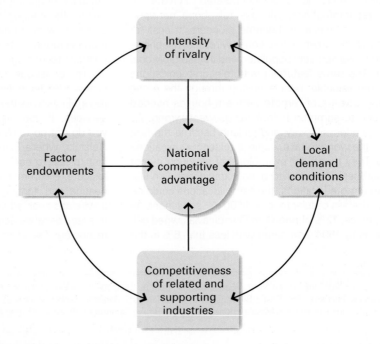

Source: Adapted from M. E. Porter, "The Competitive Advantage of Nations," *Harvard Business Review*, March–April 1990, 77.

know-how, managerial sophistication, and physical infrastructure (roads, railways, and ports). The competitive advantage that the United States enjoys in biotechnology might be explained by the presence of certain advanced factors of production—for example, technological know-how—in combination with some basic factors, which might be a pool of relatively low-cost venture capital that can be used to fund risky start-ups in industries such as biotechnology.

Local Demand Conditions   Home demand plays an important role in providing the impetus for "upgrading" competitive advantage. Companies are typically most sensitive to the needs of their closest customers. Thus, the characteristics of home demand are particularly important in shaping the attributes of domestically made products and creating pressures for innovation and quality. A nation's companies gain competitive advantage if their domestic customers are sophisticated and demanding and pressure local companies to meet high standards of product quality and produce innovative products. Japan's sophisticated and knowledgeable buyers of cameras helped stimulate the Japanese camera industry to improve product quality and introduce innovative models. A similar example can be found in the cellular phone equipment industry, where sophisticated and demanding local customers in Scandinavia helped push Nokia of Finland and Ericsson of Sweden to invest in cellular phone technology long before the demand for cellular phones took off in other developed nations. As a result, Nokia and Ericsson, together with Motorola, are significant players in the global cellular telephone equipment industry. The case of Nokia is reviewed in more depth in Strategy in Action 8.1.

Competitiveness of Related and Supporting Industries   The third broad attribute of national advantage in an industry is the presence of internationally competitive suppliers or related industries. The benefits of investments in advanced factors of production by related and supporting industries can spill over into an industry, thereby helping it achieve a strong competitive position internationally. Swedish strength in fabricated steel products (such as ball bearings and cutting tools) has drawn on strengths in Sweden's specialty steel industry. Switzerland's success in pharmaceuticals is closely related to its previous international success in the technologically related dye industry. One consequence of this process is that successful industries within a country tend to be grouped into clusters of related industries. Indeed, this was one of the most pervasive findings of Porter's study. One such cluster is the German textile and apparel sector, which includes high-quality cotton, wool, synthetic fibers, sewing machine needles, and a wide range of textile machinery.

Intensity of Rivalry   The fourth broad attribute of national competitive advantage in Porter's model is the intensity of rivalry of firms within a nation. Porter makes two important points here. First, different nations are characterized by different management ideologies, which either help them or do not help them build national competitive advantage. For example, Porter noted the predominance of engineers in top management at German and Japanese firms. He attributed this to these firms' emphasis on improving manufacturing processes and product design. In contrast, Porter noted a predominance of people with finance backgrounds leading many United States firms. He linked this to United States firms' lack of attention to improving manufacturing processes and product design. He argued that the dominance of finance led to an overemphasis on maximizing short-term financial returns. According to Porter, one consequence of these different management ideologies was a relative loss of United States competitiveness in those engineering-based industries where manufacturing processes and product design issues are all-important (such as the automobile industry).

Porter's second point is that there is a strong association between vigorous domestic rivalry and the creation and persistence of competitive advantage in an industry. Rivalry induces companies to look for ways to improve efficiency, which makes them better international competitors. Domestic rivalry creates pressures to innovate, improve quality, reduce costs, and invest in upgrading advanced factors. All this helps to create world-class competitors. The stimulating effects of strong domestic competition are clear in the story of the rise of Nokia of Finland in the market for wireless handsets and telephone equipment (see Strategy in Action 8.1).

Using the Framework   The framework just described can help managers identify from where their most significant global competitors are likely to come. For example, there is an emerging cluster of computer service and software companies in Bangalore, India, that includes two of the fastest-growing information technology companies in the world, Infosys and Wipro. These companies are emerging as aggressive competitors on the global stage. Indeed, there are signs that this is now happening, since both companies have recently opened up offices in the European Union and United States so they can better compete against the likes of IBM and EDS.

The framework can also be used to help managers decide where they might want to locate certain productive activities. Seeking to take advantage of United States expertise in biotechnology, many foreign companies have set up research facilities in San Diego, Boston, and Seattle, where United States biotechnology companies tend to be clustered. Similarly, in an attempt to take advantage of Japanese success in consumer electronics, many United States electronics companies have set up research and production facilities in Japan, often in conjunction with Japanese partners.

Finally, the framework can help a company assess how tough it might be to enter certain national markets. If a nation has a competitive advantage in certain industries, it might be challenging for foreigners to enter those industries. For example, the highly competitive retailing industry in the United States has proved to be a very difficult one for foreign companies to enter. Successful foreign retailers such as Britain's Marks & Spencer and IKEA from Sweden have found it tough going in the United States, precisely because the United States retailing industry is the most competitive in the world.

INCREASING PROFITABILITY AND PROFIT GROWTH THROUGH GLOBAL EXPANSION

In this section, we look at a number of ways in which expanding globally can enable companies to increase their profitability and grow their profits more rapidly. At the most basic level, global expansion increases the size of the market a company is addressing, thereby boosting profit growth. Moreover, as we shall see, global expansion offers opportunities for reducing the cost structure of the enterprise or adding value through differentiation, thereby potentially boosting profitability.

Expanding the Market: Leveraging Products

A company can increase its growth rate by taking goods or services developed at home and selling them internationally. Indeed, almost all multinationals started out doing just this. Procter & Gamble (P&G), for example, developed most of its best-selling products at home and then sold them around the world. Similarly, from its earliest days, Microsoft has always focused on selling its software around the world. Automobile companies like Ford, Volkswagen, and Toyota also grew by developing products at home and then selling them in international markets. The returns from such a strategy are likely to be greater if indigenous competitors in the nations a company enters lack comparable products. Thus, Toyota has grown its profits by entering the large automobile markets of North America and Europe and by offering products that are differentiated from those offered by local rivals (Ford and GM) by their superior quality and reliability.

It is important to note that the success of many multinational companies is based no only on the goods or services that they sell in foreign nations but also on the distinctive competencies (unique skills) that underlie the production and marketing of those goods or services. Toyota's success is based on its distinctive competency in manufacturing automobiles, and expanding internationally can be seen as a way of generating greater returns from this competency. Similarly, P&G's global success was based on more than its portfolio of consumer products; it was also based on the company's skills in mass-marketing consumer goods. P&G grew rapidly in international markets between 1950 and 1990 because it was one of the most skilled mass-marketing enterprises in the world and could "out-market" indigenous competitors in the nations it entered. Global expansion was thus a way of generating higher returns from its competency in marketing.

In other words, because distinctive competencies are in essence the most valuable aspects of a company's business model, the successful global expansion by manufacturing companies like Toyota and P&G was based on their ability to transfer aspects of their business models and apply them to foreign markets.

The same can be said of companies engaged in the service sectors of an economy, such as financial institutions, retailers, restaurant chains, and hotels. Expanding the market for their services often means replicating their business models in foreign nations (albeit with some changes to account for local differences, which we will discuss in more detail shortly). Starbucks, for example, is expanding rapidly outside the United States by taking the basic business model it developed at home and using that as a blueprint for establishing international operations. As detailed in the Running Case, Walmart has done the same thing, establishing stores in nine other nations since 1992, following the blueprint it developed in the United States.

Realizing Cost Economies from Global Volume

In addition to growing profits more rapidly, by expanding its sales volume through international expansion, a company can realize cost savings from economies of scale, thereby boosting profitability. Such scale economies come from several sources. First, by spreading the fixed costs associated with developing a product and setting up production facilities over its global sales volume, a company can lower its average unit cost. Thus, Microsoft can garner significant scale economies by spreading the $5 billion it cost to develop Windows Vista over global demand.

RUNNING CASE

Walmart's Global Expansion

In the early 1990s, managers at Walmart realized that the company's opportunities for growth in the United States were becoming more limited. By 1995, the company would be active in all 50 states. Management calculated that by the early 2000s, domestic growth opportunities would be constrained due to market saturation. So the company decided to expand globally. The critics scoffed. Walmart, they said, was too American a company. Although its business model was well suited to America, it would not work in other countries where infrastructure was different, consumer tastes and preferences varied, and where established retailers already dominated.

Unperturbed, in 1991, Walmart started to expand internationally with the opening of its first stores in Mexico. The Mexican operation was established as a joint venture with Cifera, the largest local retailer. Initially, Walmart made a number of missteps that seemed to prove the critics right. Walmart had problems replicating its efficient distribution system in Mexico. Poor infrastructure, crowded roads, and a lack of leverage with local suppliers, many of whom could not or would not deliver directly to Walmart's stores or distribution centers, resulted in stocking problems and raised costs and prices. Initially, prices at Walmart in Mexico were some 20% above prices for comparable products in the company's United States stores, which limited Walmart's ability to gain market share. There were also problems with merchandise selection. Many of the stores in Mexico carried items that were popular in the United States. These included ice skates, riding lawn mowers, leaf blowers, and fishing tackle. Not surprisingly, these items did not sell well in Mexico, so managers would slash prices to move inventory, only to find that the company's automated information systems would immediately order more inventory to replenish the depleted stock.

By the mid-1990s, however, Walmart had learned from its early mistakes and adapted its operations in Mexico to match the local environment. A partnership with a Mexican trucking company dramatically improved the distribution system, while more careful stocking practices meant that the Mexican stores sold merchandise that appealed more to local tastes and preferences. As Walmart's presence grew, many of Walmart's suppliers built factories close by its Mexican distribution centers so that they could better serve the company, which helped to drive down inventory and logistics costs. In 1998, Walmart acquired a controlling interest in Cifera. Today, Mexico is a leading light in Walmart's international operations, where the company is more than twice the size of its nearest rival.

The Mexican experience proved to Walmart that it could compete outside the United States. It subsequently expanded into 15 other countries. In Canada, Britain, Germany, Japan, and South Korea, Walmart entered by acquiring existing retailers and then transferring its information systems, logistics, and management expertise. In Puerto Rico, Brazil, Argentina, and China, Walmart established its own stores (although it added to its Chinese operations with a major acquisition in 2007). As a result of these moves, by 2008, the company had more than 3,000 stores outside the United States, 600,000 associates, and generated international revenues of more than $80 billion.

In addition to greater growth, expanding internationally has brought Walmart two other major benefits. First, Walmart has also been able to reap significant economies of scale from its global buying power. Many of Walmart's key suppliers have long been international companies; for example, GE (appliances), Unilever (food products), and P&G (personal care products) are all major Walmart suppliers that have long had their own global operations. By building international reach, Walmart has been able to use its enhanced size to demand deeper discounts from the local operations of its global suppliers, increasing the company's ability to lower prices to consumers, gain market share and ultimately earn greater profits. Second, Walmart has found that it is benefiting from the flow of ideas across the countries in which it now competes. For example, Walmart's Argentina team worked with Walmart's Mexican management to replicate a Walmart store format developed first in Mexico and to adopt the best practices in human resources and real estate that had been developed in Mexico. Other ideas, such as wine departments in its stores in Argentina, have now been integrated into layouts worldwide.

Moreover, Walmart realized that if it did not expand internationally, other global retailers would beat them to the punch. In fact, Walmart does face significant global competition from Carrefour of France, Ahold of Holland, and Tesco of the United Kingdom. Carrefour, the world's second-largest retailer, is perhaps the most global of the lot. The pioneer of the hypermarket concept now operates in 26 countries and generates more than 50% of its sales outside France. Compared to this, Walmart is a laggard with just 25% of its sales in 2008 generated from international operations. However, there is still room for significant global expansion. The global retailing market is still very fragmented. The top-25 retailers controlled only about a quarter of retail sales in 2008.

Still, for all of its success Walmart has hit some significant speed bumps in its drive for global expansion. In 2006, the company pulled out of two markets, South Korea—where it failed to decode the shopping habits of local customers—and Germany—where it could not beat incumbent discount stores on price. It is also struggling in Japan, where the company does not seem to have grasped the market's cultural nuances. One example was Walmart's decision to sell lower-priced gift fruits at Japanese holidays. It failed because customers felt spending less would insult the recipient. Interestingly, the markets where Walmart has struggled were all developed markets that it entered through acquisitions, where it faced long-established and efficient local competitors, and where shopping habits were very different than in the United States. In contrast, many of those markets where it has done better have been developing nations that lacked strong local competitors, and where Walmart has built operations from the ground up (e.g., Mexico, Brazil, and, increasingly, China).

Sources: A. Lillo, "Walmart Says Global Going Good," *Home Textiles Today*, Septmeber 15, 2003, 12–13. A. de Rocha and L. A. Dib, "The Entry of Walmart into Brazil," *International Journal of Retail and Distribution Management*, Vol 30, 2002, 61–73; Anonymous, "Walmart: Mexico's Biggest Retailer," *Chain Store Age*, June 2001, 52–54; M. Flagg, "In Asia, Going to the Grocery Increasingly Means Heading for a European Retail Chain," *Wall Street Journal*, April 24, 2001, A21; "A Long Way from Bentonville," *The Economist*, September 20, 2006, 38–39; "How Walmart Should Right Itself," *The Wall Street Journal*, April 20, 2007, C1, C5. http://www.walmart.com

Second, by serving a global market, a company can potentially utilize its production facilities more intensively, which leads to higher productivity, lower costs, and greater profitability. For example, if Intel sold microprocessors only in the United States, it might be able to keep its factories open only for one shift, five days a week. But by serving a global market from the same factories, it might be able to utilize those assets for two shifts, seven days a week. In other words, the capital invested in those factories is used more intensively if Intel sells to a global as opposed to a national market, which translates into higher capital productivity and a higher return on invested capital.

Third, as global sales increase the size of the enterprise, so its bargaining power with suppliers increases, which may allow it to bargain down the cost of key inputs and boost profitability that way. Walmart has been able to use its enormous sales volume as a lever to bargain down the price it pays suppliers for merchandise sold through its stores.

In addition to the cost savings that come from economies of scale, companies that sell to a global as opposed to local marketplace may be able to realize further cost savings from learning effects. We first discussed learning effects in Chapter 4, in which we noted that employee productivity increases with cumulative increases in output over time. (For example, it costs considerably less to build the 100th aircraft off a Boeing assembly line than the 10th because employees learn how to perform their tasks more efficiently over time.) By selling to a global market, a company may be able to increase its sales volume more rapidly and the cumulative output from its plants, which in turn should result in quicker learning, higher employee productivity, and a cost advantage over competitors that are growing more slowly because they lack international markets.

Realizing Location Economies

Earlier in this chapter we discussed how countries differ from each other along a number of dimensions, including differences in the cost and quality of factors of production. These differences imply that some locations are more suited than others for producing certain goods and services.[8] **Location economies** are the economic benefits that arise from performing a value creation activity in the optimal location for that activity, wherever in the world that might be (transportation costs and trade barriers permitting). Locating a value creation activity in the optimal location for that activity can have one of two effects: (1) it can lower the costs of value creation, helping the company achieve a low-cost position; or (2) it can enable a company to differentiate its product offering, which gives it the option of charging a premium price or keeping price low and using differentiation as a means of increasing sales volume. Thus, efforts to realize location economies are consistent with the business-level strategies of low cost and differentiation. In theory, a company that realizes location economies by dispersing each of its value creation activities to the optimal location for that activity should have a competitive advantage over a company that bases all of its value creation activities at a single location. It should be able to differentiate its product offering better and lower its cost structure more than its single-location competitor. In a world where competitive pressures are increasing, such a strategy may well become an imperative for survival.

For an example of how this works in an international business, consider Clear Vision, a manufacturer and distributor of eyewear. Started in the 1970s by David Glassman, the firm now generates annual gross revenues of more than $100 million. Not exactly small, but no corporate giant either, Clear Vision is a multinational firm with production facilities on three continents and customers around the world. Clear Vision began its move toward becoming a multinational in the early 1980s. The strong dollar at that time made United States-based manufacturing very expensive. Low-priced imports were taking an ever larger share of the United States eyewear market, and Clear Vision realized it could not survive unless it also began to import. Initially the firm bought from independent overseas manufacturers, primarily in Hong Kong. However, it became dissatisfied with these suppliers' product quality and delivery. As Clear Vision's volume of imports increased, Glassman decided that the best way to guarantee quality and delivery was to set up Clear Vision's own manufacturing operation overseas. Accordingly, Clear Vision found a Chinese partner, and together they opened a manufacturing facility in Hong Kong, with Clear Vision being the majority shareholder.

The choice of the Hong Kong location was influenced by its combination of low labor costs, a skilled workforce, and tax breaks given by the Hong Kong government. The firm's objective at this point was to lower production costs by locating value creation activities at an appropriate location. After a few years, however, the increasing industrialization of Hong Kong and a growing labor shortage had pushed up wage rates to the extent that it was no longer a low-cost location. In response, Glassman and his Chinese partner moved part of their manufacturing to a plant in mainland China to take advantage of the lower wage rates there. Again, the goal was to lower production costs. The parts for eyewear frames manufactured at this plant are shipped to the Hong Kong factory for final assembly and then distributed to markets in North and South America. The Hong Kong factory now employs 80 people and the China plant between 300 and 400.

At the same time, Clear Vision was looking for opportunities to invest in foreign eyewear firms with reputations for fashionable design and high quality. Its objective was not to reduce production costs but to launch a line of high-quality, differentiated, "designer" eyewear. Clear Vision did not have the design capability in-house to support such a line, but Glassman knew that certain foreign manufacturers did. As a result, Clear Vision invested in factories in Japan, France, and Italy, holding a minority shareholding in each case. These factories now supply eyewear for Clear Vision's Status Eye division, which markets high-priced designer eyewear.[9]

Some Caveats   Introducing transportation costs and trade barriers somewhat complicates this picture. New Zealand might have a comparative advantage for low-cost car assembly operations, but high transportation costs make it an uneconomical location from which to serve global markets. Factoring transportation costs and trade barriers into the cost equation helps explain why many United States companies have been shifting their production from Asia to Mexico. Mexico has three distinct advantages over many Asian countries as a location for value creation activities: low labor costs; Mexico's proximity to the large United States market, which reduces transportation costs; and the North American Free Trade Agreement (NAFTA), which has removed many trade barriers between Mexico, the United States, and Canada, increasing Mexico's attractiveness as a production site for the North American market. Thus, although the relative costs of value creation are important, transportation costs and trade barriers also must be considered in location decisions.

Another caveat concerns the importance of assessing political and economic risks when making location decisions. Even if a country looks very attractive as a production location when measured against cost or differentiation criteria, if its government is unstable or totalitarian, companies are usually well advised not to base production there. Similarly, if a particular national government appears to be pursuing inappropriate social or economic policies, this might be another reason for not basing production in that location, even if other factors look favorable.

Leveraging the Skills of Global Subsidiaries

Initially, many multinational companies develop the valuable competencies and skills that underpin their business model in their home nation and then expand internationally, primarily by selling products and services based on those competencies. However, for more mature multinational enterprises that have already established a network of subsidiary operations in foreign markets, the development of valuable skills can just as well occur in foreign subsidiaries.[10] Skills can be created anywhere within a multinational's global network of operations, wherever people have the opportunity and incentive to try new ways of doing things. The creation of skills that help to lower the costs of production, or enhance perceived value and support higher product pricing, is not the monopoly of the corporate center.

Leveraging the skills created within subsidiaries and applying them to other operations within the firm's global network may create value. For example, McDonald's increasingly is finding that its foreign franchisees are a source of valuable new ideas. Faced with slow growth in France, its local franchisees have begun to experiment not only with the menu but also with the layout and theme of restaurants. Gone are the ubiquitous Golden Arches; gone too are many of the utilitarian chairs and tables and other plastic features of the fast-food giant. Many McDonald's restaurants in France now have hardwood floors, exposed brick walls, and even armchairs. Half of the 930 or so outlets in France have been upgraded to a level that would make them unrecognizable to an American. The menu, too, has been changed to include premier sandwiches, such as chicken on focaccia bread, priced some 30% higher than the average hamburger. In France, at least, the strategy seems to be working. Following the change, increases in same-store sales rose from 1% annually to 3.4%. Impressed with the impact, McDonald's executives are now considering adopting similar changes at other McDonald's restaurants in markets where same-store sales growth is sluggish, including the United States.[11]

For the managers of a multinational enterprise, this phenomenon creates important new challenges. First, they must have the humility to recognize that valuable skills can arise anywhere within the firm's global network, not just at the corporate center. Second, they must establish an incentive system that encourages local employees to acquire new competencies. This is not as easy as it sounds. Creating new competencies involves a degree of risk. Not all new skills add value. For every valuable idea created by a McDonald's subsidiary in a foreign country, there may be several failures. The management of the multinational must install incentives that encourage employees to take the necessary risks, and the company must reward people for successes and not sanction them unnecessarily for taking risks that did not pan out. Third, managers must have a process for identifying when valuable new skills have been created in a subsidiary. Finally, they need to act as facilitators, helping to transfer valuable skills within the firm.

COST PRESSURES AND PRESSURES FOR LOCAL RESPONSIVENESS

Companies that compete in the global marketplace typically face two types of competitive pressures: *pressures for cost reductions* and *pressures to be locally responsive* (see Figure 8.2).[12] These competitive pressures place conflicting demands on a company. Responding to pressures for cost reductions requires that a company try to minimize its unit costs. To attain this goal, it may have to base its productive activities at the most favorable low-cost location, wherever in the world that might be. It may also have to offer a standardized product to the global marketplace to realize the cost savings that come from economies of scale and learning effects. On the other hand, responding to pressures to be locally responsive requires that a company differentiate its product offering and marketing strategy from country to country in an effort to accommodate the diverse demands arising from national differences in consumer tastes and preferences, business practices, distribution channels, competitive conditions, and government policies. Because differentiation across countries can involve significant duplication and a lack of product standardization, it may raise costs.

While some companies, such as Company A in Figure 8.2, face high pressures for cost reductions and low pressures for local responsiveness, and others, such as Company B, face low pressures for cost reductions and high pressures for local responsiveness, many

Figure 8.2   Pressures for Cost Reductions and Local Responsiveness

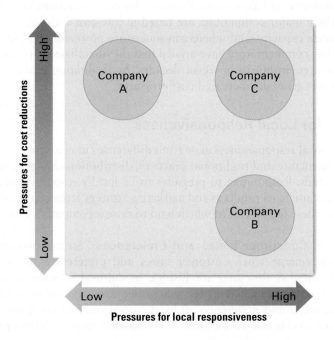

Pressures for local responsiveness

companies are in the position of Company C. They face high pressures for both cost reductions and local responsiveness. Dealing with these conflicting and contradictory pressures is a difficult strategic challenge, primarily because being locally responsive tends to raise costs.

Pressures for Cost Reductions

In competitive global markets, international businesses often face pressures for cost reductions. To respond to these pressures, a firm must try to lower the costs of value creation. A manufacturer, for example, might mass-produce a standardized product at the optimal location in the world, wherever that might be, to realize economies of scale and location economies. Alternatively, it might outsource certain functions to low-cost foreign suppliers in an attempt to reduce costs. Thus, many computer companies have outsourced their telephone-based customer service functions to India, where qualified technicians who speak English can be hired for a lower wage rate than in the United States. In the same vein, a retailer such as Walmart might push its suppliers (who are manufacturers) to also lower their prices. (In fact, the pressure that Walmart has placed on its suppliers to reduce prices has been cited as a major cause of the trend among North American manufacturers to shift production to China.)[13] A service business, such as a bank, might move some back-office functions, such as information processing, to developing nations where wage rates are lower.

Cost reduction pressures can be particularly intense in industries producing commodity-type products where meaningful differentiation on nonprice factors is difficult and price is the main competitive weapon. This tends to be the case for products that serve universal needs. Universal needs exist when the tastes and preferences of consumers in different nations are similar if not identical, such as for bulk chemicals, petroleum, steel, sugar, and the like. They also exist for many industrial and consumer products, such as handheld calculators, semiconductor chips, PCs, and liquid crystal display (LCD) screens. Pressures for cost reductions are also intense in industries where major competitors are based in low-cost locations, where there is persistent excess capacity, and where consumers are powerful and face low switching costs. Many commentators have argued that the liberalization of the world trade and investment environment in recent decades, by facilitating greater international competition, has generally increased cost pressures.[14]

Pressures for Local Responsiveness

Pressures for local responsiveness arise from differences in consumer tastes and preferences, infrastructure and traditional practices, distribution channels, and host government demands. Responding to pressures to be locally responsive requires that a company differentiate its products and marketing strategy from country to country to accommodate these factors, all of which tend to raise a company's cost structure.

Differences in Consumer Tastes and Preferences Strong pressures for local responsiveness emerge when customer tastes and preferences differ significantly between countries, as they may for historic or cultural reasons. In such cases, a multinational company's products and marketing message have to be customized to appeal to the tastes and preferences of local customers. The company is then typically pressured to delegate production and marketing responsibilities and functions to a company's overseas subsidiaries.

For example, the automobile industry in the 1980s and early 1990s moved toward the creation of "world cars." The idea was that global companies such as GM, Ford, and Toyota would be able to sell the same basic vehicle the world over, sourcing it from centralized production locations. If successful, the strategy would have enabled automobile companies to reap significant gains from global scale economies. However, this strategy frequently ran aground on the hard rocks of consumer reality. Consumers in different automobile markets seem to have different tastes and preferences, and these require different types of vehicles. North American consumers show a strong demand for pickup trucks. This is particularly true in the South and West where many families have pickup trucks as second or third vehicles. But in European countries, pickup trucks are seen purely as utility vehicles and are purchased primarily by firms rather than individuals. As a consequence, the product mix and marketing message need to be tailored to take into account the different nature of demand in North America and Europe.

Some commentators have argued that customer demands for local customization are on the decline worldwide.[15] According to this argument, modern communications and transport technologies have created the conditions for a convergence of the tastes and preferences of customers from different nations. The result is the emergence of enormous global markets for standardized consumer products. The worldwide acceptance of McDonald's hamburgers, Coca-Cola, Gap clothes, Nokia cell phones, and Sony television sets, all of which are sold globally as standardized products, are often cited as evidence of the increasing homogeneity of the global marketplace. Others, however, consider this argument to be extreme. For example, Christopher Bartlett and Sumantra Ghoshal have observed that in the consumer electronics industry, buyers reacted to an overdose of standardized global products by showing a renewed preference for products that are differentiated to local conditions.[16]

Differences in Infrastructure and Traditional Practices Pressures for local responsiveness also arise from differences in infrastructure or traditional practices among countries, creating a need to customize products accordingly. To meet this need, companies may have to delegate manufacturing and production functions to foreign subsidiaries. For example, in North America, consumer electrical systems are based on 110 volts, whereas in some European countries 240-volt systems are standard. Thus, domestic electrical appliances have to be customized to take this difference in infrastructure into account. Traditional practices also often vary across nations. For example, in Britain, people drive on the left-hand side of the road, creating a demand for right-hand-drive cars, whereas in France (and the rest of Europe), people drive on the right-hand side of the road and need left-hand-drive cars. Obviously, automobiles have to be customized to take this difference in traditional practices into account.

Although many of the country differences in infrastructure are rooted in history, some are quite recent. For example, in the wireless telecommunications industry, different technical standards are found in different parts of the world. A technical standard known as GSM is common in Europe, and an alternative standard, CDMA, is more common in the United States and parts of Asia. The significance of these different standards is that equipment designed for GSM will not work on a CDMA network, and vice versa. Thus, companies such as Nokia, Motorola, and Ericsson, which manufacture wireless handsets and infrastructure such as switches, need to customize their product offering according to the technical standard prevailing in a given country.

Differences in Distribution Channels A company's marketing strategies may have to be responsive to differences in distribution channels among countries, which may necessitate delegating marketing functions to national subsidiaries. In the pharmaceutical industry, for example, the British and Japanese distribution system is radically different from the United States system. British and Japanese doctors will not accept or respond favorably to a United States-style high-pressure sales force. Thus, pharmaceutical companies have to adopt different marketing practices in Britain and Japan compared with the United States—soft sell versus hard sell.

Similarly, Poland, Brazil, and Russia all have similar per capita income on a purchasing power parity basis, but there are big differences in distribution systems across the three countries. In Brazil, supermarkets account for 36% of food retailing, in Poland for 18%, and in Russia for less than 1%.[17] These differences in channels require that companies adapt their own distribution and sales strategy.

Differences in Host Government Demands Finally, economic and political demands imposed by host country governments may require local responsiveness. For example, pharmaceutical companies are subject to local clinical testing, registration procedures, and pricing restrictions—all of which make it necessary that the manufacturing and marketing of a drug should meet local requirements. Moreover, because governments and government agencies control a significant proportion of the health care budget in most countries, they are in a powerful position to demand a high level of local responsiveness.

More generally, threats of protectionism, economic nationalism, and local content rules (which require that a certain percentage of a product should be manufactured locally) dictate that international businesses manufacture locally. As an example, consider Bombardier, the Canadian-based manufacturer of railcars, aircraft, jet boats, and snowmobiles. Bombardier has 12 railcar factories across Europe. Critics

Ethical Dilemma

Because of low labor costs, your company has established a manufacturing subsidiary in Southern China. At the local minimum wage, employees work 10-hour days (sometimes 12-hour days due to mandatory overtime), six days a week. The factory does not adhere to the same standards for environmental protection and employee safety as those mandated in your home nation. You are concerned with the substandard working conditions and environmental protection and ask the expatriate manager heading operations if something should be done to improve conditions. He argues that he is complying with all local regulations and laws. Moreover, he notes that the company established this subsidiary to have a low-cost manufacturing base. Improving working conditions and environmental standards beyond those mandated by local laws would not be consistent with this goal. Is his position ethical? What are the potential negative consequences of continuing operations in this manner? What benefits might there be to improve conditions beyond local standards?

of the company argue that the resulting duplication of manufacturing facilities leads to high costs and helps explain why Bombardier makes lower profit margins on its railcar operations than on its other business lines. In reply, managers at Bombardier argue that in Europe, informal rules with regard to local content favor people who use local workers. To sell railcars in Germany, they claim, you must manufacture in Germany. The same goes for Belgium, Austria, and France. To try to address its cost structure in Europe, Bombardier has centralized its engineering and purchasing functions, but it has no plans to centralize manufacturing.[18]

Choosing a Global Strategy

Pressures for local responsiveness imply that it may not be possible for a firm to realize the full benefits from economies of scale and location economies. It may not be possible to serve the global marketplace from a single low-cost location, producing a globally standardized product, and marketing it worldwide to achieve economies of scale. In practice, the need to customize the product offering to local conditions may work against the implementation of such a strategy. For example, automobile firms have found that Japanese, American, and European consumers demand different kinds of cars, and this necessitates producing products that are customized for local markets. In response, firms like Honda, Ford, and Toyota are pursuing a strategy of establishing top-to-bottom design and production facilities in each of these regions so that they can better serve local demands. Although such customization brings benefits, it also limits the ability of a firm to realize significant scale economies and location economies.

In addition, pressures for local responsiveness imply that it may not be possible to leverage skills and products associated with a firm's distinctive competencies wholesale from one nation to another. Concessions often have to be made to local conditions. Despite being depicted as "poster boy" for the proliferation of standardized global products, even McDonald's has found that it has to customize its product offerings (its menu) to account for national differences in tastes and preferences.

Given the need to balance the cost and differentiation (value) sides of a company's business model, how do differences in the strength of pressures for cost reductions versus those for local responsiveness affect the choice of a company's strategy? Companies typically choose among four main strategic postures when competing internationally: a global standardization strategy, a localization strategy, a transnational strategy, and an international strategy.[19] The appropriateness of each strategy varies with the extent of pressures for cost reductions and local responsiveness. Figure 8.3 illustrates the conditions under which each of these strategies is most appropriate.

Global Standardization Strategy

Companies that pursue a **global standardization strategy** focus on increasing profitability by reaping the cost reductions that come from economies of scale and location economies; that is, their business model is based on pursuing a low-cost strategy on a global scale. The production, marketing, and R&D activities of companies pursuing a global strategy are concentrated in a few favorable locations. These companies try not to customize their product offering and marketing strategy to local conditions because customization, which involves shorter production runs and the duplication of functions, can raise costs. Instead, they prefer to market a standardized product

Figure 8.3 Four Basic Strategies

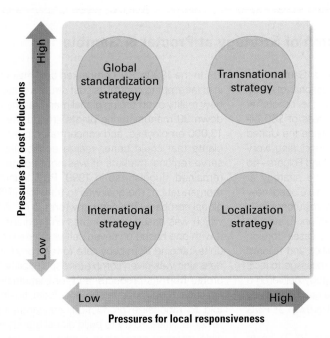

worldwide so that they can reap the maximum benefits from economies of scale. They also tend to use their cost advantage to support aggressive pricing in world markets.

This strategy makes most sense when there are strong pressures for cost reductions, and demand for local responsiveness is minimal. Increasingly, these conditions prevail in many industrial goods industries, whose products often serve universal needs. In the semiconductor industry, for example, global standards have emerged, creating enormous demands for standardized global products. Accordingly, companies such as Intel, Texas Instruments, and Motorola all pursue a global strategy.

These conditions are not always found in many consumer goods markets, where demands for local responsiveness remain high. However, even some consumer goods companies are moving toward a global standardization strategy in an attempt to drive down their costs. P&G, which is featured in Strategy in Action 8.2, is one example of such a company.

Localization Strategy

A **localization strategy** focuses on increasing profitability by customizing the company's goods or services so that they provide a good match to tastes and preferences in different national markets. Localization is most appropriate when there are substantial differences across nations with regard to consumer tastes and preferences and where cost pressures are not too intense. By customizing the product offering to local demands, the company increases the value of that product in the local market. On the downside, because it involves some duplication of functions and smaller production runs, customization limits the ability of the company to capture the cost reductions associated with mass-producing a standardized product for global consumption. The strategy may make sense, however, if the added value associated with local customization

8.2 STRATEGY IN ACTION

The Evolution of Strategy at Procter & Gamble

Founded in 1837, Cincinnati-based Procter & Gamble has long been one of the world's most international of companies. Today P&G is a global colossus in the consumer products business with annual sales in excess of $50 billion, some 54% of which are generated outside the United States. P&G sells more than 300 brands—including Ivory soap, Tide, Pampers, Iams pet food, Crisco, and Folgers—to consumers in 160 countries. Historically, the strategy at P&G was well established. The company developed new products in Cincinnati and then relied on semiautonomous foreign subsidiaries to manufacture, market, and distribute those products in different nations. In many cases, foreign subsidiaries had their own production facilities and tailored the packaging, brand name, and marketing message to local tastes and preferences. For years this strategy delivered a steady stream of new products and reliable growth in sales and profits. By the 1990s, however, profit growth at P&G was slowing.

The essence of the problem was simple; P&G's costs were too high because of extensive duplication of manufacturing, marketing, and administrative facilities in different national subsidiaries. The duplication of assets made sense in the world of the 1960s, when national markets were segmented from each other by barriers to cross-border trade. Products produced in Great Britain, for example, could not be sold economically in Germany due to high tariff duties levied on imports into Germany. By the 1980s, however, barriers to cross-border trade were falling rapidly worldwide, and fragmented national markets were merging into larger regional or global markets. Also, the retailers through which P&G distributed its products were growing larger and more global, such as Walmart, Tesco from the United Kingdom, and Carrefour from France. These emerging global retailers were demanding price discounts from P&G.

In the 1990s, P&G embarked on a major reorganization in an attempt to control its cost structure and recognize the new reality of emerging global markets. The company shut down 30 manufacturing plants around the globe, laid off 13,000 employees, and concentrated production in fewer plants that could better realize economies of scale and serve regional markets. It was not enough. Profit growth remained sluggish, so in 1999, P&G launched a second reorganization. The goal was to transform P&G into a truly global company. The company tore up its old organization, which was based on countries and regions, and replaced it with one based on seven self-contained global business units, ranging from baby care to food products. Each business unit was given complete responsibility for generating profits from its products, and for manufacturing, marketing, and product development. Each business unit was told to rationalize production, concentrating it in fewer larger facilities; to try to build global brands wherever possible, thereby eliminating marketing difference between countries; and to accelerate the development and launch of new products. P&G announced that as a result of this initiative, it would close another 10 factories and lay off 15,000 employees, mostly in Europe where there was still extensive duplication of assets. The annual cost savings were estimated to be about $800 million. P&G planned to use the savings to cut prices and increase marketing spending in an effort to gain market share, and thus further lower costs through the attainment of economies of scale. This time the strategy seemed to be working. Between 2003 and 2007, P&G reported strong growth in both sales and profits. Significantly, P&G's global competitors, such as Unilever, Kimberly-Clark, and Colgate-Palmolive, were struggling in 2003 to 2007.

Source: J. Neff, "P&G Outpacing Unilever in Five-Year Battle," *Advertising Age,* November 3, 2003, 1–3; G. Strauss, "Firm Restructuring into Truly Global Company," *USA Today,* September 10, 1999, B2; *Procter & Gamble 10K Report, 2005;* M. Kolbasuk McGee, "P&G Jump-Starts Corporate Change," *Information Week,* November 1, 1999, 30–34.

supports higher pricing, which would enable the company to recoup its higher costs, or if it leads to substantially greater local demand, enabling the company to reduce costs through the attainment of some scale economies in the local market.

MTV Networks is a good example of a company that has had to pursue a localization strategy. If MTV had not localized its programming to match the demands of viewers in different nations, it would have lost market share to local competitors, its advertising revenues would have fallen, and its profitability would have declined. Thus, even though it raised costs, localization became a strategic imperative at MTV.

At the same time, it is important to realize that companies like MTV still have to keep a close eye on costs. Companies pursuing localization strategies still need to be efficient and, whenever possible, capture some scale economies from their global reach. As noted earlier, many automobile companies have found that they have to customize some of their product offerings to local market demands—for example, by producing large pickup trucks for United States consumers and small, fuel-efficient cars for Europeans and Japanese. At the same time, these companies try to get some scale economies from their global volume by using common vehicle platforms and components across many different models and by manufacturing those platforms and components at efficiently scaled factories that are optimally located. By designing their products in this way, these companies have been able to localize their product offering, yet simultaneously capture some scale economies.

Transnational Strategy

We have argued that a global standardization strategy makes most sense when cost pressures are intense and demands for local responsiveness limited. Conversely, a localization strategy makes most sense when demands for local responsiveness are high but cost pressures are moderate or low. What happens, however, when the company simultaneously faces both strong cost pressures and strong pressures for local responsiveness? How can managers balance out such competing and inconsistent demands? According to some researchers, the answer is by pursuing what has been called a transnational strategy.

Two of these researchers, Christopher Bartlett and Sumantra Ghoshal, argue that in today's global environment, competitive conditions are so intense that, to survive, companies must do all they can to respond to pressures for both cost reductions and local responsiveness. They must try to realize location economies and economies of scale from global volume, transfer distinctive competencies and skills within the company, and simultaneously pay attention to pressures for local responsiveness.[20]

Moreover, Bartlett and Ghoshal note that, in the modern multinational enterprise, distinctive competencies and skills do not reside just in the home country but can develop in any of the company's worldwide operations. Thus, they maintain that the flow of skills and product offerings should not be all one way, from home company to foreign subsidiary. Rather, the flow should also be from foreign subsidiary to home country and from foreign subsidiary to foreign subsidiary. Transnational companies, in other words, must also focus on leveraging subsidiary skills.

In essence, companies that pursue **transnational strategies** are trying to develop business models that simultaneously achieve low costs, differentiate the product offerings across geographic markets, and foster a flow of skills between different subsidiaries in the companies' global networks of operations. As attractive as this may sound, the strategy is not an easy one to pursue because it places conflicting demands on a company. Differentiating the product to respond to local demands in different geographic markets raises costs, which runs counter to the goal of reducing costs. Companies such as Ford and ABB (one of the world's largest engineering conglomerates) have tried to embrace a transnational strategy and have found it difficult to implement in practice.

Indeed, how best to implement a transnational strategy is one of the most complex questions that large global companies are grappling with today. It may be that few if any companies have perfected this strategic posture. But some clues to the right approach can be derived from a number of companies. Consider, for example, the case of Caterpillar. The need to compete with low-cost competitors such as Komatsu of Japan forced Caterpillar to look for greater cost economies. However, variations in construction practices and government regulations across countries meant that Caterpillar also had to be responsive to local demands. Therefore, Caterpillar confronted significant pressures for both cost reductions and local responsiveness.

To deal with cost pressures, Caterpillar redesigned its products to use many identical components and invested in a few large-scale component-manufacturing facilities, sited at favorable locations, to fill global demand and realize scale economies. At the same time, the company augments the centralized manufacturing of components with assembly plants in each of its major global markets. At these plants, Caterpillar adds local product features, tailoring the finished product to local needs. Thus, Caterpillar is able to realize many of the benefits of global manufacturing while reacting to pressures for local responsiveness by differentiating its product among national markets.[21] Caterpillar started to pursue this strategy in 1979, and over the next 20 years it succeeded in doubling output per employee, significantly reducing its overall cost structure in the process. Meanwhile, Komatsu and Hitachi, which are still wedded to a Japan-centric global strategy, have seen their cost advantages evaporate and have been steadily losing market share to Caterpillar.

However, building an organization capable of supporting a transnational strategy is a complex and challenging task. Indeed, some would say it is too complex because the strategy implementation problems of creating a viable organizational structure and control systems to manage this strategy are immense. We will return to this issue in Chapter 13.

International Strategy

Sometimes it is possible to identify multinational companies that find themselves in the fortunate position of being confronted with low cost pressures and low pressures for local responsiveness. Typically these enterprises are selling a product that serves universal needs, but because they do not face significant competitors, they are not confronted with pressures to reduce their cost structure. Xerox found itself in this position in the 1960s after its invention and commercialization of the photocopier. The technology underlying the photocopier was protected by strong patents, so for several years Xerox did not face competitors: it had a monopoly. Because the product was highly valued in most developed nations, Xerox was able to sell the same basic product the world over and charge a relatively high price for it. At the same time, because it did not face direct competitors, the company did not have to deal with strong pressures to minimize its costs.

Historically, companies like Xerox have followed a similar developmental pattern as they build their international operations. They tend to centralize product development functions such as R&D at home. However, they also tend to establish manufacturing and marketing functions in each major country or geographic region in which they do business. Although they may undertake some local customization of product offering and marketing strategy, this tends to be rather limited in scope. Ultimately, in most international companies, the head office retains tight control over marketing and product strategy.

Other companies that have pursued this strategy include P&G, which historically always developed innovative new products in Cincinnati and then transferred them wholesale to local markets. Another company that has followed a similar strategy is Microsoft. The bulk of Microsoft's product development work takes place in Redmond, Washington, where the company is headquartered. Although some localization work is undertaken elsewhere, this is limited to producing foreign-language versions of popular Microsoft programs such as Office.

Changes in Strategy over Time

The Achilles heal of the international strategy is that, over time, competitors inevitably emerge, and if managers do not take proactive steps to reduce their cost structure, their company may be rapidly outflanked by efficient global competitors. That is exactly what happened to Xerox. Japanese companies such as Canon ultimately invented their way around Xerox's patents, produced their own photocopies in very efficient manufacturing plants, priced them below Xerox's products, and rapidly took global market share from Xerox. Xerox's demise was not due to the emergence of competitors, for ultimately that was bound to occur, but rather to its failure to proactively reduce its cost structure in advance of the emergence of efficient global competitors. The message in this story is that an international strategy may not be viable in the long term. To survive, companies that are able to pursue it need to shift toward a global standardization strategy or perhaps a transnational strategy in advance of competitors (see Figure 8.4).

Figure 8.4 Changes over Time

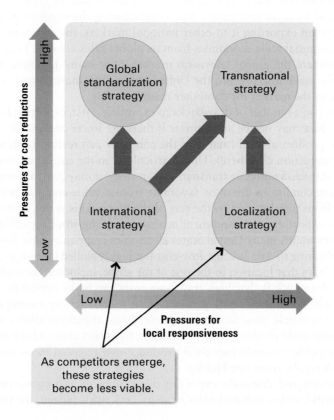

The same can be said about a localization strategy. Localization may give a company a competitive edge, but if it is simultaneously facing aggressive competitors, the company will also have to reduce its cost structure, and the only way to do that may be to adopt more of a transnational strategy. Thus, as competition intensifies, international and localization strategies tend to become less viable, and managers need to orientate their companies toward either a global standardization strategy or a transnational strategy.

THE CHOICE OF ENTRY MODE

Any firm contemplating entering a different national market has to determine the best mode or vehicle for such entry. There are five main choices of entry mode: exporting, licensing, franchising, entering into a joint venture with a host country company, and setting up a wholly owned subsidiary in the host country. Each mode has its advantages and disadvantages, and managers must weigh these carefully when deciding which mode to use.[22]

Exporting

Most manufacturing companies begin their global expansion as exporters and only later switch to one of the other modes for serving a foreign market. Exporting has two distinct advantages: it avoids the costs of establishing manufacturing operations in the host country, which are often substantial, and it may be consistent with scale economies and location economies. By manufacturing the product in a centralized location and then exporting it to other national markets, the company may be able to realize substantial scale economies from its global sales volume. That is how Sony came to dominate the global television market, how many Japanese auto companies originally made inroads into the United States auto market, and how Samsung gained share in the market for computer memory chips.

There are also a number of drawbacks to exporting. First, exporting from the company's home base may not be appropriate if there are lower-cost locations for manufacturing the product abroad (that is, if the company can realize location economies by moving production elsewhere). Thus, particularly in the case of a company pursuing a global standardization or transnational strategy, it may pay to manufacture in a location where conditions are most favorable from a value creation perspective and then export from that location to the rest of the globe. This is not so much an argument against exporting as an argument against exporting from the company's home country. For example, many United States electronics companies have moved some of their manufacturing to Asia because low-cost but highly skilled labor is available there. They export from that location to the rest of the globe, including the United States.

Another drawback is that high transport costs can make exporting uneconomical, particularly in the case of bulk products. One way of getting around this problem is to manufacture bulk products on a regional basis, thereby realizing some economies from large-scale production while limiting transport costs. Many multinational chemical companies manufacture their products on a regional basis, serving several countries in a region from one facility.

Tariff barriers, too, can make exporting uneconomical, and a government's threat to impose tariff barriers can make the strategy very risky. Indeed, the implicit threat from the United States Congress to impose tariffs on Japanese cars imported into the United States led directly to the decision by many Japanese auto companies to set up manufacturing plants in the United States.

Finally, a common practice among companies that are just beginning to export also poses risks. A company may delegate marketing activities in each country in which it does business to a local agent, but there is no guarantee that the agent will act in the company's best interest. Often foreign agents also carry the products of competing companies and thus have divided loyalties. Consequently, they may not do as good a job as the company would if it managed marketing itself. One way to solve this problem is to set up a wholly owned subsidiary in the host country to handle local marketing. In this way, the company can reap the cost advantages that arise from manufacturing the product in a single location and exercise tight control over marketing strategy in the host country.

Licensing

International licensing is an arrangement whereby a foreign licensee buys the rights to produce a company's product in the licensee's country for a negotiated fee (normally, royalty payments on the number of units sold). The licensee then puts up most of the capital necessary to get the overseas operation going.[23] The advantage of licensing is that the company does not have to bear the development costs and risks associated with opening up a foreign market. Licensing therefore can be a very attractive option for companies that lack the capital to develop operations overseas. It can also be an attractive option for companies that are unwilling to commit substantial financial resources to an unfamiliar or politically volatile foreign market where political risks are particularly high.

Licensing has three serious drawbacks, however. First, it does not give a company the tight control over manufacturing, marketing, and strategic functions in foreign countries that it needs to have to realize scale economies and location economies—as companies pursuing both global standardization and transnational strategies try to do. Typically, each licensee sets up its own manufacturing operations. Hence, the company stands little chance of realizing scale economies and location economies by manufacturing its product in a centralized location. When these economies are likely to be important, licensing may not be the best way of expanding overseas.

Second, competing in a global marketplace may make it necessary for a company to coordinate strategic moves across countries so that the profits earned in one country can be used to support competitive attacks in another. Licensing, by its very nature, severely limits a company's ability to coordinate strategy in this way. A licensee is unlikely to let a multinational company take its profits (beyond those due in the form of royalty payments) and use them to support an entirely different licensee operating in another country.

A third problem with licensing is the risk associated with licensing technological know-how to foreign companies. For many multinational companies, technological know-how forms the basis of their competitive advantage, and they would want to maintain control over the use to which it is put. By licensing its technology, a company can quickly lose control over it. RCA, for instance, once licensed its color television technology to a number of Japanese companies. The Japanese companies quickly assimilated RCA's technology and then used it to enter the United States market. Now the Japanese have a bigger share of the United States market than the RCA brand does.

There are ways of reducing this risk. One way is by entering into a cross-licensing agreement with a foreign firm. Under a cross-licensing agreement, a firm might license some valuable intangible property to a foreign partner and, in addition to a royalty payment, also request that the foreign partner license some of its valuable know-how to the firm. Such agreements are reckoned to reduce the risks associated with licensing technological know-how because the licensee realizes that if it violates the spirit of a licensing contract (by using the knowledge obtained to compete directly with the licensor), the licensor can do the same to it. Put differently, cross-licensing agreements enable firms to hold each other hostage, thereby reducing the probability that they will behave opportunistically toward each other.[24] Such cross-licensing agreements are increasingly common in high-technology industries. For example, the United States biotechnology firm Amgen has licensed one of its key drugs, Nuprogene, to Kirin, the Japanese pharmaceutical company. The license gives Kirin the right to sell Nuprogene in Japan. In return, Amgen receives a royalty payment, and through a licensing agreement it gains the right to sell certain of Kirin's products in the United States.

Franchising

In many respects, franchising is similar to licensing, although franchising tends to involve longer-term commitments than licensing. Franchising is basically a specialized form of licensing in which the franchiser not only sells intangible property to the franchisee (normally a trademark) but also insists that the franchisee agree to abide by strict rules as to how it does business. The franchiser will also often assist the franchisee to run the business on an ongoing basis. As with licensing, the franchiser typically receives a royalty payment, which amounts to some percentage of the franchisee revenues.

Whereas licensing is a strategy pursued primarily by manufacturing companies, franchising, which resembles it in some respects, is a strategy employed chiefly by service companies. McDonald's provides a good example of a firm that has grown by using a franchising strategy. McDonald's has established strict rules as to how franchisees should operate a restaurant. These rules extend to control over the menu, cooking methods, staffing policies, and restaurant design and location. McDonald's also organizes the supply chain for its franchisees and provides management training and financial assistance.[25]

The advantages of franchising are similar to those of licensing. Specifically, the franchiser does not have to bear the development costs and risks of opening up a foreign market on its own, for the franchisee typically assumes those costs and risks. Thus, using a franchising strategy, a service company can build up a global presence quickly and at a low cost.

The disadvantages are less pronounced than in the case of licensing. Because franchising is often used by service companies, there is no reason to consider the need for coordination of manufacturing to achieve experience curve and location economies. But franchising may inhibit the firm's ability to take profits out of one country to support competitive attacks in another. A more significant disadvantage of franchising is quality control. The foundation of franchising arrangements is that the firm's brand name conveys a message to consumers about the quality of the firm's product. Thus, a business traveler checking in at a Four Seasons hotel in Hong Kong can reasonably expect the same quality of room, food, and service that he or she would receive in New York. The Four Seasons name is supposed to guarantee consistent product quality. This presents a problem in that foreign franchisees may not be as concerned about quality as they are supposed to be, and the result of poor quality can extend beyond lost sales in a particular foreign market to a decline in the firm's worldwide reputation. For example, if a business traveler has a bad experience at the Four Seasons in Hong Kong, he or she may never go to another Four Seasons hotel and may urge his or her colleagues to do likewise. The geographical distance of the firm from its foreign franchisees can make poor quality difficult to detect. In addition, the sheer numbers of franchisees—in the case of McDonald's, tens of thousands—can make quality control difficult. Due to these factors, quality problems may persist.

To reduce this problem, a company can set up a subsidiary in each country or region in which it is expanding. The subsidiary, which might be wholly owned by the company or a joint venture with a foreign company, then assumes the rights and obligations to establish franchisees throughout that particular country or region. The combination of proximity and the limited number of independent franchisees that have to be monitored reduces the quality control problem. Besides, since the subsidiary is at least partly owned by the company, the company can place its own managers in the subsidiary to ensure the kind of quality monitoring it wants. This organizational arrangement has proved very popular in practice. It has been used by McDonald's, Kentucky Fried Chicken (KFC), and Hilton Hotels Corp. to expand their international operations, to name just three examples.

Joint Ventures

Establishing a joint venture with a foreign company has long been a favored mode for entering a new market. One of the most famous long-term joint ventures is the Fuji-Xerox joint venture to produce photocopiers for the Japanese market. The most typical form of joint venture is a 50/50 joint venture, in which each party takes a 50% ownership stake, and operating control is shared by a team of managers from both parent companies. Some companies have sought joint ventures in which they have a majority shareholding (for example, a 51% to 49% ownership split), which permits tighter control by the dominant partner.[26]

Joint ventures have a number of advantages. First, a company may feel that it can benefit from a local partner's knowledge of a host country's competitive conditions, culture, language, political systems, and business systems. Second, when the development costs and risks of opening up a foreign market are high, a company might gain by sharing these costs and risks with a local partner. Third, in some countries, political considerations make joint ventures the only feasible entry mode. For example, historically many United States companies found it much easier to get permission to set up operations in Japan if they went in with Japanese partners than if they tried to enter on their own. That is why Xerox originally teamed up with Fuji to sell photocopiers in Japan.

Despite these advantages, there are major disadvantages with joint ventures. First, as with licensing, a firm that enters into a joint venture risks giving control of its technology to its partner. Thus, a proposed joint venture in 2002 between Boeing and Mitsubishi Heavy Industries to build a new wide-body jet raised fears that Boeing might unwittingly give away its commercial airline technology to the Japanese. However, joint-venture agreements can be constructed to minimize this risk. One option is to hold majority ownership in the venture. This allows the dominant partner to exercise greater control over its technology. But it can be difficult to find a foreign partner who is willing to settle for minority ownership.

Another option is to "wall off" from a partner technology that is central to the core competence of the firm, while sharing other technology.

A second disadvantage is that a joint venture does not give a firm the tight control over subsidiaries that it might need to realize experience curve or location economies. Nor does it give a firm the tight control over a foreign subsidiary that it might need for engaging in coordinated global attacks against its rivals. Consider the entry of Texas Instruments (TI) into the Japanese semiconductor market. When TI established semiconductor facilities in Japan, it did so for the dual purpose of checking Japanese manufacturers' market share and limiting their cash available for invading TI's global market. In other words, TI was engaging in global strategic coordination. To implement this strategy, TI's subsidiary in Japan had to be prepared to take instructions from corporate headquarters regarding competitive strategy. The strategy also required the Japanese subsidiary to run at a loss if necessary. Few if any potential joint-venture partners would have been willing to accept such conditions because it would have necessitated a willingness to accept a negative return on investment. Indeed, many joint ventures establish a degree of autonomy that would make such direct control over strategic decisions all but impossible to establish.[27] Thus, to implement this strategy, TI set up a wholly owned subsidiary in Japan.

Wholly Owned Subsidiaries

A wholly owned subsidiary is one in which the parent company owns 100% of the subsidiary's stock. To establish a wholly owned subsidiary in a foreign market, a company can either set up a completely new operation in that country or acquire an established host-country company and use it to promote its products in the host market.

Setting up a wholly owned subsidiary offers three advantages. First, when a company's competitive advantage is based on its control of a technological competency, a wholly owned subsidiary will normally be the preferred entry mode because it reduces the company's risk of losing this control. Consequently, many high-tech companies prefer wholly owned subsidiaries to joint ventures or licensing arrangements. Wholly owned subsidiaries tend to be the favored entry mode in the semiconductor, computer, electronics, and pharmaceutical industries. Second, a wholly owned subsidiary gives a company the kind of tight control over operations in different countries that it needs if it is going to engage in global strategic coordination—taking profits from one country to support competitive attacks in another.

Third, a wholly owned subsidiary may be the best choice if a company wants to realize location economies and the scale economies that flow from producing a standardized output from a single or limited number of manufacturing plants. When pressures on costs are intense, it may pay a company to configure its value chain in such a way that value added at each stage is maximized. Thus, a national subsidiary may specialize in manufacturing only part of the product line or certain components of the end product, exchanging parts and products with other subsidiaries in the company's global system. Establishing such a global production system requires a high degree of control over the operations of national affiliates. Different national operations have to be prepared to accept centrally determined decisions as to how they should produce, how much they should produce, and how their output should be priced for transfer between operations. A wholly owned subsidiary would have to comply with these mandates, whereas licensees or joint venture partners would most likely shun such a subservient role.

On the other hand, establishing a wholly owned subsidiary is generally the most costly method of serving a foreign market. The parent company must bear all the costs and risks of setting up overseas operations—in contrast to joint ventures, where the costs and risks are shared, or licensing, where the licensee bears most of the costs and risks. But the risks of learning to do business in a new culture diminish if the company acquires an established host country enterprise. Acquisitions, though, raise a whole set of additional problems, such as trying to marry divergent corporate cultures, and these problems may more than offset the benefits. (The problems associated with acquisitions are discussed in Chapter 10.)

Choosing an Entry Strategy

The advantages and disadvantages of the various entry modes are summarized in Table 8.1. Inevitably, there are tradeoffs in choosing one entry mode over another. For example, when considering entry into an unfamiliar country with a track record of nationalizing foreign-owned enterprises, a company might favor a joint venture with a local enterprise. Its rationale might be that the local partner will help it establish operations in an unfamiliar environment and speak out against nationalization should the possibility arise. But if the company's distinctive competency is based on

Table 8.1 The Advantages and Disadvantages of Different Entry Modes

Entry Mode	Advantages	Disadvantages
Exporting	• Ability to realize location- and scale-based economies	• High transport costs • Trade barriers • Problems with local marketing agents
Licensing	• Low development costs and risks	• Inability to realize location- and scale-based economies • Inability to engage in global strategic coordination • Lack of control over technology
Franchising	• Low development costs and risks	• Inability to engage in global strategic coordination • Lack of control over quality
Joint ventures	• Access to local partner's knowledge • Shared development costs and risks • Political dependency	• Inability to engage in global strategic coordination • Inability to realize location- and scale-based economies • Lack of control over technology
Wholly owned subsidiaries	• Protection of technology • Ability to engage in global strategic coordination • Ability to realize location- and scale-based economies	• High costs and risks

proprietary technology, entering into a joint venture might mean risking loss of control over that technology to the joint venture partner, which would make this strategy unattractive. Despite such hazards, some generalizations can be offered about the optimal choice of entry mode.

Distinctive Competencies and Entry Mode When companies expand internationally to earn greater returns from their differentiated product offerings, entering markets where indigenous competitors lack comparable products, the companies are pursuing an international strategy. The optimal entry mode for such companies depends to some degree on the nature of their distinctive competency. In particular, we need to distinguish between companies with a distinctive competency in technological know-how and those with a distinctive competency in management know-how.

If a company's competitive advantage—its distinctive competency—derives from its control of proprietary technological know-how, licensing and joint venture arrangements should be avoided, if possible, to minimize the risk of losing control of that technology. Thus, if a high-tech company is considering setting up operations in a foreign country to profit from a distinctive competency in technological know-how, it should probably do so through a wholly owned subsidiary.

However, this rule should not be viewed as a hard and fast one. For instance, a licensing or joint venture arrangement might be structured in such a way as to reduce the risks that a company's technological know-how will be expropriated by licensees or joint venture partners. We consider this kind of arrangement in more detail later in the chapter when we discuss the issue of structuring strategic alliances. To take another exception to the rule, a company may perceive its technological advantage as being only transitory and expect rapid imitation of its core technology by competitors. In this situation, the company might want to license its technology as quickly as possible to foreign companies to gain global acceptance of its technology before imitation occurs.[28] Such a strategy has some advantages. By licensing its technology to competitors, the company may deter them from developing their own, possibly superior, technology. It also may be able to establish its technology as the dominant design in the industry (as Matsushita did with its VHS format for VCRs), ensuring a steady stream of royalty payments. Such situations apart, however, the attractions of licensing are probably outweighed by the risks of losing control of technology, and therefore licensing should be avoided.

The competitive advantage of many service companies, such as McDonald's or Hilton Hotels, is based on management know-how. For such companies, the risk of losing control of their management skills to franchisees or joint venture partners is not that great. The reason is that the valuable asset of such companies is their brand name, and brand names are generally well protected by international laws pertaining to trademarks. Given this fact, many of the issues that arise in the case of technological know-how do not arise in the case of management know-how. As a result, many service companies favor a combination of franchising and subsidiaries to control franchisees within a particular country or region. The subsidiary may be wholly owned or a joint venture. In most cases, however, service companies have found that entering into a joint venture with a local partner to set up a controlling subsidiary in a country or region works best because a joint venture is often politically more acceptable and brings a degree of local knowledge to the subsidiary.

Pressures for Cost Reduction and Entry Mode The greater the pressures for cost reductions are, the more likely it is that a company will want to pursue some combination of exporting and wholly owned subsidiaries. By manufacturing in the locations where factor conditions are optimal and then exporting to the rest of the world, a company may be able to realize substantial location economies and substantial scale economies. The company might then want to export the finished product to marketing subsidiaries based in various countries. Typically, these subsidiaries would be wholly owned and have the responsibility for overseeing distribution in a particular country. Setting up wholly owned marketing subsidiaries is preferable to a joint venture arrangement or using a foreign marketing agent because it gives the company the tight control over marketing that might be required to coordinate a globally dispersed value chain. In addition, tight control over a local operation enables the company to use the profits generated in one market to improve its competitive position in another market. Hence companies pursuing global or transnational strategies prefer to establish wholly owned subsidiaries.

GLOBAL STRATEGIC ALLIANCES

Global strategic alliances are cooperative agreements between companies from different countries that are actual or potential competitors. Strategic alliances run the range from formal joint ventures, in which two or more companies have an equity stake, to short-term contractual agreements, in which two companies may agree to cooperate on a particular problem (such as developing a new product).

Advantages of Strategic Alliances

Companies enter into strategic alliances with competitors to achieve a number of strategic objectives.[29] First, strategic alliances may facilitate entry into a foreign market. For example, many firms feel that if they are to successfully enter the Chinese market, they need local partners who understand business conditions and who have good connections. Thus, in 2004, Warner Brothers entered into a joint venture with two Chinese partners to produce and distribute films in China. As a foreign film company, Warner found that if it wanted to produce films on its own for the Chinese market, it had to go through a complex approval process for every film and farm out distribution to a local company, which made doing business in China difficult. Due to the participation of Chinese firms, however, the joint-venture films go through a streamlined approval process, and the venture may distribute any films it produces. Moreover, the joint venture may produce films for Chinese TV, something that foreign firms are not allowed to do.[30]

Second, strategic alliances allow firms to share the fixed costs (and associated risks) of developing new products or processes. An alliance between Boeing and a number of Japanese companies to build Boeing's latest commercial jetliner, the 787, was motivated by Boeing's desire to share the estimated $8 billion investment required to develop the aircraft. For another example of cost sharing, see Strategy in Action 8.3, which discusses the strategic alliances between Cisco and Fujitsu.

Third, an alliance is a way to bring together complementary skills and assets that neither company could easily develop on its own.[31] In 2003, for example, Microsoft and Toshiba established an alliance aimed at developing embedded microprocessors (essentially tiny computers) that can perform a variety of entertainment functions in an automobile (e.g., run a back-seat DVD player or a wireless Internet connection). The processors will run a version of Microsoft's Windows CE operating system. Microsoft brings its software engineering skills to the alliance, while Toshiba brings its skills in developing microprocessors.[32] The alliance between Cisco and Fujitsu was also formed to share know-how (see Strategy in Action 8.3).

Fourth, it can make sense to form an alliance that will help the firm establish technological standards for the industry that will benefit the firm. For example, in 1999 Palm Computer, the leading maker of personal digital assistants (PDAs), entered into an alliance with Sony under which Sony agreed to license and use Palm's operating system in Sony PDAs. The motivation for the alliance was in part to help establish Palm's operating system as the industry standard for PDAs, as opposed to a rival Windows-based operating system from Microsoft.[33]

8.3 STRATEGY IN ACTION

Cisco and Fujitsu

In late 2004, Cisco Systems, the world's largest manufacturer of Internet routers entered into an alliance with the Japanese computer, electronics, and telecommunications equipment firm, Fujitsu. The stated purpose of the alliance was to jointly develop next generation high-end routers for sales in Japan. Routers are the digital switches that sit at the heart of the Internet and direct traffic; they are, in effect, the traffic cops of the Internet. Although Cisco has long held the leading share in the market for routers—indeed, it pioneered the original router technology—it faces increasing competition from other firms, such as Juniper Technologies and China's fast growing Huawei Technologies. At the same time, demand in the market is shifting as more and more telecommunications companies adopt Internet-based telecommunications services. While Cisco has long had a strong global presence, management also felt that the company needed to have better presence in Japan, which is shifting rapidly to second generation high-speed Internet-based telecommunications networks.

By entering into an alliance with Fujitsu, Cisco feels it can achieve a number of goals. First, both firms can pool their R&D efforts, which will enable them to share complementary technology and develop products quicker, thereby gaining an advantage over competitors. Second, by combining Cisco's proprietary leading edge router technology with Fujitsu's production expertise,

the companies believe that they can produce products that are more reliable than those currently offered. Third, Fujitsu will give Cisco a stronger sales presence in Japan. Fujitsu has good links with Japan's telecommunications companies and a well-earned reputation for reliability. It will leverage these assets to sell the routers produced by the alliance, which will be co-branded as Fujitsu-Cisco products. Fourth, sales may be further enhanced by bundling the co-branded routers together with other telecommunications equipment that Fujitsu sells and marketing an entire solution to customers. Fujitsu sells many telecommunications products but lacks a strong presence in routers. Cisco is strong in routers but lacks strong offerings elsewhere. The combination of the two company's products will enable Fujitsu to offer Japan's telecommunications companies "end-to-end" communications solutions. Since many companies prefer to purchase their equipment from a single provider, this should drive sales.

The alliance introduced its first products in May 2006. If it is successful, both firms should benefit. Development costs will be lower than if they did not cooperate. Cisco will grow its sales in Japan, and Fujitsu can use the co-branded routers to fill out its product line and sell more bundles of products to Japan's telecommunications companies.

Sources: "Fujitsu, Cisco Systems to Develop High-End Routers for Web Traffic," *Knight Ridder-Tribune Business News,* December 6, 2004, 1; "Fujitsu and Cisco Introduce New High Performance Routers for IP Next Generation Networks," *JCN Newswire,* May 25, 2006.

Disadvantages of Strategic Alliances

The advantages we have discussed can be very significant. Despite this, some commentators have criticized strategic alliances on the grounds that they give competitors a low-cost route to new technology and markets.[34] For example, a few years ago some commentators argued that many strategic alliances between American and Japanese firms were part of an implicit Japanese strategy to keep high-paying, high-value-added jobs in Japan while gaining the project engineering and production process skills that underlie the competitive success of many United States companies.[35] They argued that Japanese success in the machine tool and semiconductor industries was built on United States technology acquired through strategic alliances. And they argued that American managers were aiding the Japanese by entering alliances that channel new inventions to Japan and provide an American sales and distribution network for the resulting products. Although such deals may generate short-term profits, so the argument goes, in the long run, the result is to "hollow out" United States firms, leaving them with no competitive advantage in the global marketplace.

These critics have a point; alliances have risks. Unless a firm is careful, it can give away more than it receives. But there are so many examples of apparently successful alliances between firms—including alliances between American and Japanese firms—that their position seems extreme. It is difficult to see how the Microsoft-Toshiba alliance, the Boeing-Mitsubishi alliance for the 787, or the Fujifilm-Xerox alliance fit the critics' thesis. In these cases, both partners seem to have gained from the alliance. Why do some alliances benefit both firms while others benefit one firm and hurt the other? The next section provides an answer to this question.

Making Strategic Alliances Work

The failure rate for international strategic alliances is quite high. For example, one study of 49 international strategic alliances found that two-thirds run into serious managerial and financial troubles within two years of their formation; although many of these problems are ultimately solved, 33% are ultimately rated as failures by the parties involved.[36] The success of an alliance seems to be a function of three main factors: partner selection, alliance structure, and the manner in which the alliance is managed.

Partner Selection One of the keys to making a strategic alliance work is to select the right kind of partner. A good partner has three principal characteristics. First, a good partner helps the company achieve strategic goals, such as achieving market access, sharing the costs and risks of new-product development, or gaining access to critical core competencies. In other words, the partner must have capabilities that the company lacks and that it values.

Second, a good partner shares the firm's vision for the purpose of the alliance. If two companies approach an alliance with radically different agendas, the chances are great that the relationship will not be harmonious and will end in divorce.

Third, a good partner is unlikely to try to exploit the alliance opportunistically for its own ends—that is, to expropriate the company's technological know-how while giving away little in return. In this respect, firms with reputations for fair play probably make the best partners. For example, IBM is involved in so many strategic alliances that it would not pay the company to trample over individual alliance partners (in the mid-2000s IBM reportedly had more than

150 major strategic alliances).[37] This would tarnish IBM's reputation of being a good ally and would make it more difficult for IBM to attract alliance partners. Because IBM attaches great importance to its alliances, it is unlikely to engage in the kind of opportunistic behavior that critics highlight. Similarly, their reputations make it less likely (but by no means impossible) that such Japanese firms as Sony, Toshiba, and Fuji, which have histories of alliances with non-Japanese firms, would opportunistically exploit an alliance partner.

To select a partner with these three characteristics, a company needs to conduct some comprehensive research on potential alliance candidates. To increase the probability of selecting a good partner, the company should collect as much pertinent, publicly available information about potential allies as possible; collect data from informed third parties, including companies that have had alliances with the potential partners, investment bankers who have had dealings with them, and some of their former employees; and get to know potential partners as well as possible before committing to an alliance. This last step should include face-to-face meetings between senior managers (and perhaps middle-level managers) to ensure that the chemistry is right.

Alliance Structure   Having selected a partner, the alliance should be structured so that the company's risk of giving too much away to the partner is reduced to an acceptable level. Figure 8.5 depicts the four safeguards against opportunism by alliance partners that we discuss. (**Opportunism**, which is often defined as self-interest seeking with guile, includes the "expropriation" of technology or markets.) First, alliances can be designed to make it difficult (if not impossible) to transfer technology not meant to be transferred. Specifically, the design, development, manufacture, and service of a product manufactured by an alliance can be structured so as to "wall off" sensitive technologies to prevent their leakage to the other participant. In the alliance between GE and Snecma to build commercial aircraft engines, for example, GE reduced the risk of "excess transfer" by walling off certain sections of the production process. The modularization effectively cut off the transfer of what GE regarded as key competitive technology while permitting Snecma access to final assembly. Similarly, in the alliance between Boeing and the Japanese to build the 767, Boeing walled off research, design, and marketing functions considered central to its competitive position, while allowing the Japanese to share in production technology. Boeing also walled off new technologies not required for 767 production.[38]

....

Figure 8.5   Structuring Alliances to Reduce Opportunism

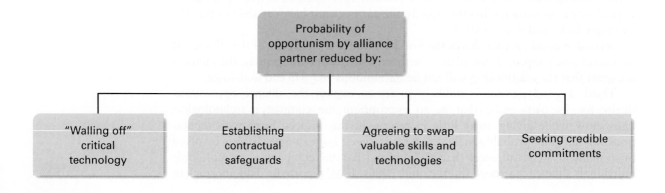

Second, contractual safeguards can be written into an alliance agreement to guard against the risk of opportunism by a partner. For example, TRW has three strategic alliances with large Japanese auto component suppliers to produce seat belts, engine valves, and steering gears for sale to Japanese-owned auto assembly plants in the United States. TRW has clauses in each of its alliance contracts that bar the Japanese firms from competing with TRW to supply American-owned auto companies with component parts. By doing this, TRW protects itself against the possibility that the Japanese companies are entering into the alliances merely as a means of gaining access to the North American market to compete with TRW in its home market.

Third, both parties to an alliance can agree in advance to swap skills and technologies that the other covets, thereby ensuring a chance for equitable gain. Cross-licensing agreements are one way to achieve this goal.

Fourth, the risk of opportunism by an alliance partner can be reduced if the firm extracts a significant credible commitment from its partner in advance. The long-term alliance between Xerox and Fuji to build photocopiers for the Asian market perhaps best illustrates this. Rather than enter into an informal agreement or a licensing arrangement (which Fuji Photo initially wanted), Xerox insisted that Fuji invest in a 50/50 joint venture to serve Japan and East Asia. This venture constituted such a significant investment in people, equipment, and facilities that Fuji Photo was committed from the outset to making the alliance work in order to earn a return on its investment. By agreeing to the joint venture, Fuji essentially made a credible commitment to the alliance. Given this, Xerox felt secure in transferring its photocopier technology to Fuji.

Managing the Alliance   Once a partner has been selected and an appropriate alliance structure agreed on, the task facing the company is to maximize the benefits from the alliance. One important ingredient of success appears to be sensitivity to cultural differences. Many differences in management style are attributable to cultural differences, and managers need to make allowances for these in dealing with their partner. Beyond this, maximizing the benefits from an alliance seems to involve building trust between partners and learning from partners.[39]

Managing an alliance successfully requires building interpersonal relationships between the firms' managers, or what is sometimes referred to as *relational capital*.[40] This is one lesson that can be drawn from a successful strategic alliance between Ford and Mazda. Ford and Mazda set up a framework of meetings within which their managers not only discuss matters pertaining to the alliance but also have time to get to know each other better. The belief is that the resulting friendships help build trust and facilitate harmonious relations between the two firms. Personal relationships also foster an informal management network between the firms. This network can then be used to help solve problems arising in more formal contexts (such as in joint committee meetings between personnel from the two firms).

Academics have argued that a major determinant of how much acquiring knowledge a company gains from an alliance is its ability to learn from its alliance partner.[41] For example, in a study of 15 strategic alliances between major multinationals, Gary Hamel, Yves Doz, and C. K. Prahalad focused on a number of alliances between Japanese companies and Western (European or American) partners.[42] In every case in which a Japanese company emerged from an alliance stronger than its Western partner, the Japanese company had made a greater effort to learn. Few Western companies studied seemed to want to learn from their Japanese partners. They tended to regard the alliance purely as a cost-sharing or risk-sharing device, rather than as an opportunity to learn how a potential competitor does business.

For an example of an alliance in which there was a clear learning asymmetry, consider the agreement between GM and Toyota to build the Chevrolet Nova. This alliance was structured as a formal joint venture, New United Motor Manufacturing, in which both parties had a 50% equity stake. The venture owned an auto plant in Fremont, California. According to one of the Japanese managers, Toyota achieved most of its objectives from the alliance: "We learned about United States supply and transportation. And we got the confidence to manage United States workers." All that knowledge was then quickly transferred to Georgetown, Kentucky, where Toyota opened a plant of its own in 1988. By contrast, although GM got a new product, the Chevrolet Nova, some GM managers complained that their new knowledge was never put to good use inside GM. They say that they should have been kept together as a team to educate GM's engineers and workers about the Japanese system. Instead, they were dispersed to different GM subsidiaries.[43]

When entering an alliance, a company must take some measures to ensure that it learns from its alliance partner and then puts that knowledge to good use within its own organization. One suggested approach is to educate all operating employees about the partner's strengths and weaknesses and make clear to them how acquiring particular skills will bolster their company's competitive position. For such learning to be of value, the knowledge acquired from an alliance has to be diffused throughout the organization—which did not happen at GM. To spread this knowledge, the managers involved in an alliance should be used as a resource in familiarizing others within the company about the skills of an alliance partner.

SUMMARY OF CHAPTER

1. For some companies, international expansion represents a way of earning greater returns by transferring the skills and product offerings derived from their distinctive competencies to markets where indigenous competitors lack those skills. As barriers to international trade have fallen, industries have expanded beyond national boundaries, and industry competition and opportunities have increased.

2. Because of national differences, it pays a company to base each value creation activity it performs at the location where factor conditions are most conducive to the performance of that activity. This strategy is known as focusing on the attainment of location economies.

3. By building sales volume more rapidly, international expansion can help a company gain a cost advantage through the realization of economies of scale and learning effects.

4. The best strategy for a company to pursue may depend on the kind of pressures it must cope with: pressures for cost reductions or for local responsiveness. Pressures for cost reductions are greatest in industries producing commodity-type products, where price is the main competitive weapon. Pressures for local responsiveness arise from differences in consumer tastes and preferences, as well as from national infrastructure and traditional practices, distribution channels, and host government demands.

5. Companies pursuing an international strategy transfer the skills and products derived from distinctive competencies to foreign markets while undertaking some limited local customization.

6. Companies pursuing a localization strategy customize their product offering, marketing strategy, and business strategy to national conditions.

7. Companies pursuing a global standardization strategy focus on reaping the cost reductions that come from scale economies and location economies.

8. Many industries are now so competitive that companies must adopt a transnational strategy. This involves a simultaneous focus on reducing costs, transferring skills and products, and being locally responsive. Implementing such a strategy may not be easy.

9. There are five different ways of entering a foreign market: exporting, licensing, franchising, entering into a joint venture, and setting up a wholly owned subsidiary. The optimal choice among entry modes depends on the company's strategy.

10. Strategic alliances are cooperative agreements between actual or potential competitors. The advantages of alliances are that they facilitate entry into foreign markets, enable partners to share the fixed costs and risks associated with new products and processes, facilitate the transfer of complementary skills between companies, and help companies establish technical standards.

11. The drawbacks of a strategic alliance are that the company risks giving away technological know-how and market access to its alliance partner while getting very little in return.

12. The disadvantages associated with alliances can be reduced if the company selects partners carefully, paying close attention to reputation, and structures the alliance so as to avoid unintended transfers of know-how.

DISCUSSION QUESTIONS

1. Licensing proprietary technology to foreign competitors is the best way to give up a company's competitive advantage. Discuss.

2. What kind of companies stand to gain the most from entering into strategic alliances with potential competitors? Why?

3. Plot the position of the following companies on Figure 8.3: Microsoft, Google, Coca-Cola, Dow Chemicals, Pfizer, and McDonald's. In each case, justify your answer.

CLOSING CASE

MTV Networks: A Global Brand Goes Local

MTV Networks has become a symbol of globalization. Established in 1981, the United States-based TV network has been expanding outside of its North American base since 1987 when it opened MTV Europe. Now owned by media conglomerate Viacom, MTV Networks, which includes Nickelodeon and VH1, the music station for the aging baby boomers, generates more than $2 billion in revenues outside the United States. Since 1987, MTV has become the most ubiquitous cable programmer in the world. By the late 2000s, the network reached some 450 million households, some 300 million of which were in 140 countries outside of the United States.

While the United States still leads in the number of households, the most rapid growth is elsewhere, particularly in Asia, where nearly two-thirds of the region's 3 billion people are younger than 35, the middle class is expanding quickly, and TV ownership is spreading rapidly. MTV Networks figures that every second of every day more than 2 million people are watching MTV around the world, the majority outside the United States.

Despite its international success, MTV's global expansion got off to a weak start. In 1987, when most of MTV's fare still consisted of music videos, it piped a single feed across Europe almost entirely composed of American programming with English-speaking hosts. Naively, the network's American managers thought Europeans would flock to the American programming. But while viewers in Europe shared a common interest in a handful of global superstars, who at the time included Madonna and Michael Jackson, their tastes turned out to be surprisingly local. What was popular in Germany might not be popular in Great Britain. Many staples of the American music scene left Europeans cold. MTV Networks suffered as a result. Soon local copycat stations were springing up in Europe that focused on the music scene in individual countries. They took viewers and advertisers away from MTV. As explained by Tom Freston, the former chairman of MTV Networks, "We were going for the most shallow layer of what united

viewers and brought them together. It didn't go over too well."

In 1995, MTV changed its strategy and broke Europe into regional feeds. There are approximately 25, including feeds for the United Kingdom and Ireland; another for Germany, Austria, and Switzerland; one for Italy; one for France; one for Spain; one for Holland; and one for Russia. The network adopted the same localization strategy elsewhere in the world. For example, in Asia it has 10 feeds: an English-Hindi channel for India; separate Mandrine feeds for China and Taiwan; a Korean feed for South Korea; a Bahasa-language feed for Indonesia; a Japanese feed for Japan; and so on. Digital and satellite technology have made the localization of programming cheaper and easier. MTV Networks can now beam a half-dozen feeds off one satellite transponder.

Although MTV Networks exercises creative control over these different feeds, and all the channels have the same familiar frenetic look and feel of MTV in the United States, a significant share of the programming and content is now local. When MTV opens a local station, it begins with expatriates from elsewhere in the world to do a "gene transfer" of company culture and operating principles. Once these are established, however, the network switches to local employees and the expatriates move on. The idea is to "get inside the heads" of the local population and produce programming that matches their tastes.

Although many of the programming ideas still originate in the United States, with staples such as *The Real World* having equivalents in different countries, an increasing share of programming is local in conception. In Italy, *MTV Kitchen* combines cooking with a music countdown. *Erotica* airs in Brazil and features a panel of youngsters discussing sex. The Indian channel produces 21 homegrown shows hosted by local veejays who speak "Hinglish," a city-bred breed of Hindi and English. Hit shows include *MTV Cricket in Control*, appropriate for a land where cricket is a national obsession; *MTV Housefull*, which hones in on Hindi film stars (India has the biggest film industry outside of Hollywood); and *MTV Bakra*, which is modeled after *Candid Camera*.

This localization push reaped big benefits for MTV, allowing the network to capture viewers back from local imitators. In India, for example, ratings increased by more than 700% between 1996, when the localization push began, and 2000. In turn, localization helps MTV to capture more of those all-important advertising revenues, even from other multinationals such as Coca-Cola, whose own advertising budgets are often locally determined.[44]

Case Discussion Questions

1. What strategy did MTV pursue when it initially started to expand internationally? What assumptions were managers at MTV making about foreign markets at the time?
2. Why strategy does MTV pursue today? What are the benefits of this strategy? What are the costs?
3. What must MTV do, in terms of its management and organization, to implement its current strategy?

STRATEGY AT THE CORPORATE LEVEL

LEARNING OBJECTIVES

After reading this chapter, you should be able to

- Discuss how corporate-level strategy can be used to strengthen a company's business model and business-level strategies
- Define horizontal integration and discuss the main advantages and disadvantages associated with this corporate-level strategy
- Explain the difference between a company's internal value chain and the industry value chain

- Define horizontal integration and describe the main advantages and disadvantages associated with this corporate-level strategy
- Describe why, and under what conditions, cooperative relationships such as strategic alliances and outsourcing may become a substitute for vertical integration

News Corp Forges Ahead

News Corp CEO Rupert Murdoch engineered acquisition or divestiture decisions for more than 50 years.

Murdoch has created one of the four largest and most powerful entertainment media companies in the world. What kinds of strategies did Murdoch use to create his media empire?[1] Murdoch was born into a newspaper family; his father owned and ran the *Adelaide News,* an Australian regional newspaper, and when his father died in 1952, Murdoch took control. He quickly enlarged the customer base by acquiring more Australian newspapers. One of these had connections to a major British "pulp" newspaper, and Murdoch used a sensational, *National Enquirer*-like, business model to establish his new newspaper, the *Sun,* as a leading British tabloid.

Murdoch's reputation as an entrepreneur grew because he showed that he could create a much higher return (ROIC) on the media assets he controlled than his competitors. This enabled him to borrow increasing amounts of money, which he used to buy well-known newspapers such as the *British Sunday Telegraph* and then his first United States newspaper, the *San Antonio Express*. Pursuing his sensational business model further, he launched the *National Star*. His growing profits and reputation allowed him to continue to borrow money, and in 1977, he bought the *New York Post*. Four years later, in 1981, he engineered a new coup when he bought the *Times* and *Sunday Times*, Britain's leading conservative publications—a far cry from the *Sun* tabloid.

Murdoch's strategy of horizontal integration through mergers allowed him to create one of the world's biggest newspaper empires. He realized, however, that industries in the entertainment and media sector can be divided into those that provide media content or "software" (newspapers, movies, and television programs) and those that provide the media channels or "hardware" necessary to bring software to customers (movie theaters, TV channels, TV cable, and satellite broadcasting). Murdoch decided that he could create the most profit by becoming involved in both the media software *and* hardware industries, that is, the entire value chain of the entertainment and media sector. This strategy of vertical integration gave him control over all the different industries, joined together like links in a chain that converted inputs such as stories into finished products like newspapers, books, TV shows, and movies.

In the 1980s, Murdoch began purchasing global media companies in both the software and hardware stages of the entertainment sector. He also launched new ventures of his own.

For example, sensing the potential of satellite broadcasting, in 1983 he launched Sky, the first satellite TV channel in the United Kingdom. He also began a new strategy of horizontal integration by purchasing companies that owned television stations; for Metromedia, which owned seven stations that reached more than 20% of United States households, he paid $1.5 billion. He scored another major coup in 1985 when he bought Twentieth Century Fox Movie Studios, a premium content provider. As a result, he had Fox's huge film library and its creative talents to make new films and TV programming.

In 1986, Murdoch decided to create the FOX Broadcasting Company and buy or create his own United States network of FOX affiliates that would show programming developed by his own FOX movie studios. After a slow start, the FOX network gained popularity with sensational shows like *The Simpsons*, which was FOX's first blockbuster program. Then, in 1994, FOX purchased the sole rights to broadcast all NFL games for more than $1 billion, thereby shutting out NBC. FOX became the "fourth network," which has forged and, with Murdoch's sensational business model, was one of the first to create the "reality" programming that has proved so popular in the 2000s.

By 2005, Murdoch's business model, based on strategies of horizontal and vertical integration, had created a global media empire. The company's profitability has ebbed and flowed because of the massive debt needed to fund Murdoch's acquisitions, debt that has frequently brought his company near to financial ruin. However, in 2009, his company is still a market leader because he engineered many new Internet acquisitions, such as MySpace, Rotten Tomatoes, and other popular Web sites that he has used to create even more value from his media assets.[2]

Overview

Over the last decades, Rupert Murdoch has acquired or started scores of companies to create a media empire, that is, a collection of businesses in different industries in the media sector. The overriding goal of managers is to maximize the value of the company for its shareholders; Murdoch embarked on his quest because he believed that by combining all these different businesses into one entity, he could increase their profitability. Clearly, the scale of Murdoch's mission and vision for News Corp takes the issue of strategy formulation to a new level of complexity.

The News Corp story illustrates the use of corporate-level strategy to identify (1) which businesses and industries a company should compete in; (2) which value creation activities it should perform in those businesses; and (3) how it should enter or leave businesses or industries to maximize its long-run profitability. In formulating corporate-level strategy, managers must adopt a long-term perspective and consider how changes taking place in an industry and in its products, technology, customers, and competitors will affect their company's current business model and its future strategies. They then decide how to implement specific corporate-level strategies to redefine their company's business model so that it can achieve a competitive position in the changing industry environment by taking advantage of the opportunities and countering the threats. Thus the principal goal of corporate-level strategy is to enable a company to sustain or promote its competitive advantage and profitability in its present business and in any new businesses or industries that it enters.

This chapter is the first of two that deals with the role of corporate-level strategy in repositioning and redefining a company's business model. We discuss three corporate-level strategies—horizontal integration, vertical integration, and strategic outsourcing—that are primarily directed toward improving a company's competitive advantage and profitability in its present business or product market. Diversification, which entails entry into new kinds of markets or industries, is examined in the next chapter, along with guidelines for choosing the most profitable way to enter new markets or industries or to exit others. By the end of this and the next chapter, you will understand how the different levels of strategy contribute to the creation of a successful and profitable business or multibusiness model. You will also be able to differentiate between the types of corporate strategies managers use to maximize long-term company profitability.

CORPORATE-LEVEL STRATEGY AND THE MULTIBUSINESS MODEL

The choice of corporate-level strategies is the final part of the strategy formulation process. Corporate-level strategies drive a company's business model over time and determine which types of business- and functional-level strategies managers will choose to maximize long-run profitability. The relationship between business-level strategy and functional-level strategy was discussed in Chapter 5. Strategic managers develop a business model and strategies that use their company's distinctive competencies to strive for a cost-leadership position and/or differentiate its products. Chapter 8 described how global strategy is also an extension of these basic principles. In this chapter and the next, we repeatedly emphasize that to increase profitability, a corporate-level strategy should enable a company or one or more of its business divisions or units *to perform value-chain functional activities (1) at a lower cost and/or (2) in a way that allows for differentiation.* Only when it selects the appropriate corporate-level strategies can a company choose the pricing option (lowest, average, or premium price) that will allow it to maximize profitability. In addition, corporate-level strategy will increase profitability if it helps a company reduce industry rivalry by reducing the threat of damaging price competition. In sum, a company's corporate-level strategies should be chosen to promote the success of its business-level strategies, which allows it to achieve a sustainable competitive advantage that leads to higher profitability.

Like News Corp, many companies choose to expand their business activities beyond one market or industry and enter others. When a company decides to expand into new industries, it must construct its business model at two levels. First, it must develop a business model and strategies for each business unit or division in every industry in which it competes. Second, it must also develop a higher-level *multibusiness model* that justifies its entry into different businesses and industries, something that Rupert Murdoch did for News Corp in the opening case. This multibusiness model should explain how and why entering a new industry will allow the company to use its existing functional competencies and business strategies to increase its overall profitability. This model should also explain any other ways in which a company's involvement in more than one business or industry can increase its profitability. Dell, for example, might argue that its entry into computer consulting and into the computer printer market will enable it to offer its customers a complete line of computer products and services, which allows it to better compete with HP or IBM. News Corp used its expertise in sensational marketing that it gained from its newspaper business and applied it to its FOX network to create reality TV programs, "racy" sitcoms, and a news service accused of political bias.

This chapter first focuses on the advantages of staying inside one industry by pursuing horizontal integration. It then looks at why companies use vertical integration and expand into new industries. In the next chapter, we examine two principal corporate strategies companies use to enter new industries to increase their profitability, related and unrelated diversification, and several other strategies companies may use to enter and compete in new industries.

HORIZONTAL INTEGRATION: SINGLE-INDUSTRY STRATEGY

Managers use corporate-level strategy to identify which industries their company should compete in to maximize its long-run profitability. For many companies, profitable growth and expansion often entail finding ways to compete successfully within a single market or industry over time. In other words, a company confines its value-creation activities to just one business or industry. Examples of such single-business companies include McDonald's, with its focus on the global fast-food business, and Walmart, with its focus on global discount retailing.

Staying inside an industry allows a company to focus its total managerial, financial, technological, and functional resources and capabilities on competing successfully in one area. This is important in fast-growing and changing industries in which demands on a company's resources and capabilities are likely to be substantial, but where the long-term profits from establishing a competitive advantage are also likely to be substantial.

A second advantage of staying inside a single industry is that a company "sticks to the knitting," meaning that it stays focused on what it knows and does best. A company does not make the mistake of entering new industries in which its existing resources and capabilities create little value and/or where a whole new set of competitive industry forces—new competitors, suppliers, and customers—present unanticipated threats. Coca-Cola, like many other companies, has committed this strategic error. Coca-Cola once decided to expand into the movie business and acquired Columbia Pictures; it also acquired a large California winemaker. It soon found it lacked the competencies to compete successfully in these new industries and had not foreseen the strong competitive forces that existed in these industries, from movie companies such as FOX and winemakers such as Gallo. Coca-Cola concluded that entry into these new industries had reduced rather than created value and lowered its profitability; it divested or sold off these new businesses at a significant loss.

Even when a company stays in one industry, sustaining a successful business model over time can be difficult because of changing conditions in the environment, such as advances in technology that allow new competitors into the market or because of changing customer needs. A decade ago, the strategic issue facing telecommunications companies was how to shape their line of "wired" phone service products to best meet customer needs in the local and long-distance phone service market. When a new kind of product, wireless phone service, emerged and quickly gained in popularity, wired phone companies like Verizon and AT&T had to quickly change their business models and lower the price of wired phone service and merge with wireless companies to ensure their very survival.

Even inside one industry, it is all too easy for strategic managers to fail to see the "forest" (changing nature of the industry that results in new product/market opportunities) for the "trees" (focusing only on how to position current products). A focus on corporate-level strategy can help managers anticipate future trends and change their business models so as to position their companies to compete successfully in a changing environment. Strategic managers must not become so committed to improving their company's *existing* product lines that they fail to recognize new product opportunities and threats. The task for corporate-level managers is to analyze how new emerging technologies will impact their business models, how and why these might change customer needs and customer groups in the future, and what kinds of new distinctive competencies will be needed to respond to these changes.

One corporate-level strategy that has been widely used to help managers strengthen their company's business model is horizontal integration. **Horizontal integration** is the process of acquiring or merging with industry competitors to achieve the competitive advantages that arise from a large size and scope of operations. An **acquisition** occurs when one company uses its capital resources, such as stock, debt, or cash, to purchase another company, and a **merger** is an agreement between equals to pool their operations and create a new entity. The Opening Case discusses how Rupert Murdoch made scores of acquisitions in the newspaper industry, and then in TV, so that all his companies could take advantage of the stories written by News Corp journalists anywhere in the world, which reduced costs.

Mergers and acquisitions have occurred in many industries. In the aerospace industry, Boeing merged with McDonald Douglas to create the world's largest aerospace company; in the pharmaceutical industry, Pfizer acquired Warner-Lambert to become the largest pharmaceutical firm; and in the computer hardware industry, Compaq acquired DEC and then itself was acquired by HP (see Closing Case). In the 2000s, the rate of mergers and acquisitions has increased as companies try to gain a global competitive advantage. Many of the largest mergers and acquisitions have been cross-border affairs as companies race to acquire overseas companies in the same industry. The result of this wave of global mergers and acquisitions has been to increase the level of concentration in a wide range of industries. The reason this has occurred is that horizontal integration can often significantly improve the competitive advantage and profitability of companies whose managers choose to stay inside one industry and focus on managing its competitive forces.

Benefits of Horizontal Integration

In pursuing horizontal integration, managers decide to invest their company's capital resources to purchase the assets of industry competitors to increase the profitability of its single-business model. Profitability increases when horizontal integration (1) lowers the cost structure, (2) increases product differentiation, (3) replicates the business model, (4) reduces rivalry within the industry, and (5) increases bargaining power over suppliers and buyers.

Lower Cost Structure   Horizontal integration can lower a company's cost structure because it creates increasing *economies of scale*. Suppose five major competitors exist, each of which operates a manufacturing plant in some region of the United States, but with none of the plants operating at full capacity. If one competitor buys up another and shuts down that plant, it can operate its own plant at full capacity and so reduce its manufacturing costs. Achieving economies of scale is very important in industries that have a high fixed-cost structure. In such industries, large-scale production allows companies to spread their fixed costs over a large volume and in this way drive down average unit costs. In the telecommunications industry, for example, the fixed costs of building an advanced Internet network are enormous, and to make such an investment pay off, a large volume of customers is required. Thus companies such as AT&T and Verizon bought other telecommunications companies to acquire their customers, build their customer base, and so increase utilization rates and reduce the cost of servicing each customer. Similar considerations were involved in News Corps' acquisitions and in the pharmaceutical industry in which mergers have resulted from the need to realize scale economies in sales and marketing. The fixed costs of building a nationwide pharmaceutical sales force are very high, and pharmaceutical companies need a good portfolio of products to effectively use that sales force. Pfizer acquired Warner-Lambert because its salespeople would have more products to sell when they visited physicians, thus increasing their productivity. In 2008, Pfizer acquired Wyeth pharmaceuticals to create a prescription drug company of unprecedented scale; the combined company had more than $70 billion in 2008.

A company can also lower its cost structure when horizontal integration allows it to *reduce the duplication of resources* between two companies, such as by eliminating the need for two sets of corporate head offices, two separate sales forces, and so on.

Increased Product Differentiation   Horizontal integration may also increase profitability when it increases product differentiation, for example, by increasing the flow of innovative new products that a company can sell to its customers at premium prices. Desperate for new drugs to fill its pipeline, for example, Eli Lily paid $6.5 billion to ImClone Systems to acquire its new cancer preventing drugs; it paid such a high price to outbid Bristol-Myers Squibb, another drug company seeking innovative new drugs.

Horizontal integration may also increase differentiation when it allows a company to combine the product lines of merged companies so that it can offer customers a wider range of products that can be bundled together. **Product bundling** involves offering customers the opportunity to buy a complete range of products at a single combined price. This increases the value of a company's product line because customers often obtain a price discount from buying a set of products and also become used to dealing with just one company and its representatives. A company may obtain a competitive advantage from increased product differentiation.

Another way to increase product differentiation is through **cross-selling**, which involves a company taking advantage of or "leveraging" its established relationship with customers by acquiring additional product lines or categories that it can sell to them. In this way, a company increases differentiation because it can provide a "total solution" and satisfy all of a customer's specific needs. Cross-selling and becoming a total solution provider is an important rationale for horizontal integration in the computer sector, where IT companies have tried to increase the value of their offerings by providing all of the hardware and service needs of corporate customers. Providing a total solution saves customers time and money because they do not have to deal with several suppliers, and a single sales team can ensure that all the different components of a customer's IT work seamlessly together. When horizontal integration increases the differentiated appeal and value of the company's products, the total solution provider gains market share. This was the business model Oracle pursued when it acquired many IT software companies and explains its current success, as discussed in Strategy in Action 9.1.

9.1 STRATEGY IN ACTION

Oracle Strives to Become the Biggest and the Best

Oracle Corporation, based in Redwood City, California, is the world's largest maker of database software and the third-largest global software company after Microsoft and IBM. This commanding position is not enough for Oracle, however, which has set its sights on becoming the global leader in the corporate applications software market. In this market, Germany's SAP, with 45% of the market, is the acknowledged leader, and Oracle, with only 19%, is a distant second. Corporate applications is a fast growing and highly profitable market, however, and Oracle has been snapping up leading companies in this segment. Its goal is to quickly build the distinctive competencies it needs to expand the range of products that it can offer to its existing customers and attract new customers to compete with SAP. Beginning in 2005, Oracle's CEO Larry Ellison spent $19 billion to acquire 14 leading suppliers of corporate software, including two of the top five companies: PeopleSoft, a leading human resource management (HRM) software supplier it bought for $10 billion, and Siebel Systems, a leader in customer relationship management (CRM) software, which cost Oracle $5.8 billion.

Oracle expects several competitive advantages to result from its use of acquisitions to pursue the corporate strategy of horizontal integration. First, it is now able to meld or bundle the best software applications of these acquired companies—with Oracle's own first-class set of corporate and database software programs—to create a new integrated software suite that will allow companies to manage all their functional activities, such as accounting, marketing, sales, HRM, CRM, and supply-chain management. Second, through these acquisitions, Oracle obtained access to thousands of new customers—the companies that use the software of the companies it acquired. All these companies now become potential customers for all of Oracle's other database and corporate software offerings. Third, beyond increasing the range of its products and number of its customers, Oracle's acquisitions have consolidated the corporate software industry. By taking over some of its largest rivals, Oracle has become the second-largest supplier of corporate software and is better positioned to compete with leader SAP.

Sources: www.sap.com, 2009
www.oracle.com, 2009

Replicating the Business Model   Given the many ways in which horizontal integration can be used to increase product differentiation and lower cost structure, a company that can replicate its successful business model in new *market segments* within its industry can also increase its profitability. In the retail industry, for example, Walmart took its low-cost/low-price discount retail business model to enter into the even lower-priced warehouse segment by opening its chain of Sam's Clubs. It also expanded the range of products it offers customers when it entered the supermarket business and established a nationwide chain of Walmart supercenters that sell groceries as well as all the clothing, toys, and electronics sold in regular Walmart stores. It has also replicated its business model globally by acquiring supermarket chains in several countries, such as Mexico, the United Kingdom, and Japan, where it used its efficient global materials-management practices to pursue its cost-leadership strategy. In the United States, Walmart has also been experimenting with new kinds of small-size supermarkets to expand its presence in this supermarket industry segment, as the Running Case discusses.

Reduced Industry Rivalry   Horizontal integration can help to reduce industry rivalry in two ways. First, acquiring or merging with a competitor helps to *eliminate excess capacity* in an industry, which, as we discuss in Chapter 6, often triggers price wars. By taking excess capacity out of an industry, horizontal integration creates a more benign environment in which prices might stabilize or even increase.

Second, by reducing the number of competitors in an industry, horizontal integration often makes it easier to implement *tacit price coordination* between rivals, that is, coordination reached without communication. (Explicit communication to fix prices is illegal.) In general, the larger the number of competitors in an industry, the more difficult it is to establish informal pricing agreements, such as price leadership by the dominant company, which reduces the possibility that a price war will erupt. By increasing industry concentration and creating an oligopoly, horizontal integration can make it easier to establish tacit coordination among rivals.

Both of these motives also seem to have been behind Oracle's many software acquisitions. There was significant excess capacity in the corporate software industry, and major competitors were offering customers discounted prices that had led to a price war and falling profit margins. Oracle hoped to be able to eliminate excess industry that would reduce price competition. By 2009, it was clear that the major corporate software competitors were focusing on finding ways to better differentiate their product suites to prevent a price war and continuing to make major acquisitions to help them build competitive advantage.

Increased Bargaining Power   Finally, some companies use horizontal integration because it allows them to obtain bargaining power over suppliers or buyers and so increase their profitability at the expense of suppliers or buyers. By consolidating the industry through horizontal integration, a company becomes a much larger buyer of suppliers' products and uses this as leverage to bargain down the price it pays for its inputs, thereby lowering its cost structure. Walmart is well-known for pursuing this strategy, for example. Similarly, by acquiring its competitors, a company gains control over a greater percentage of an industry's product or output. Other things being equal, it then has more power to raise prices and profits because customers have less choice of suppliers and are more dependent on the company for their products, which is something both Oracle and SAP are striving for to protect their customer base.

RUNNING CASE

Walmart's Growing Chain of "Neighborhood Markets"

After its entry into the supermarket industry, Walmart soon recognized that its huge supercenters and discount stores do not serve the needs of customers who want quick and convenient shopping experiences, for example, when they want to pick up food for evening meals. It also recognized that customers spend billions of dollars shopping in local stores such as neighborhood supermarkets, drugstores, and convenience stores, and that this was potentially a highly profitable segment of the retail market. Thus, in the 2000s, Walmart decided to enter this segment by opening a new chain of Walmart "Neighborhood Markets." Each of these supermarkets is approximately 40,000 square feet, about one-quarter the size of a Walmart supercenter, and stocks 20,000 to 30,000 items compared to more than 100,000 items available in supercenters. Walmart's strategy for the new chain stores was to position them to compete directly with local supermarkets, such as those run by Kroger and Safeway. They would be open 24 hours a day to maximize responsiveness to local customers, and they would also have high-profit-margin departments such as a pharmacy, drugs, health, and beauty products to draw off trade from drugstores such as CVS and Walgreens. As a result, customers could shop for food while they waited for their prescriptions to be filled or their film to be developed.

To test whether its cost-leadership model would work at this small scale of operations, Walmart opened stores slowly in good locations. Margins are small in the supermarket business, often between 1% and 2%, which is lower than Walmart was accustomed to. To keep costs low, it located its new stores in areas where it had efficient warehouse food preparation and delivery systems. Its strategy was to prepare high-margin items like bakery goods and meat and deli products in central locations and then ship them to supermarkets in prepackaged containers. Each neighborhood market store was also tied in by satellite to Walmart's retail link network so that food service managers would know what kind of food was selling and what was not. They could then customize the food each store sold to customer needs by changing the mix that was trucked fresh each day. Also, because the stores had no onsite butchers or bakers, costs were much lower.

As a result of these strategies, the 60-plus United States stores opened by 2004 were able to undercut the prices charged by supermarkets such as Publix, Winn-Dixie, Kroger, and Albertsons by 10%. A typical neighborhood market generates approximately $20 million per year in sales, has a staff of 90, and obtains a 2.3% profit margin, which is significantly higher than average in the supermarket industry. Encouraged by their success, Walmart continued to open more stores and had 145 neighborhood markets in operation by 2009, most of which are the southern United States.

Walmart is continuing to experiment with new kinds of small supermarkets to increase its share of this market segment. Its "Marketside" store concept is an even smaller "corner-store" format with store size in the 300–25,000 square feet range. It is also experimenting actively with a chain of stores geared to the needs of Hispanic consumers. One experimental "Hispanic Community" store in Texas is a large-format store at about 160,000 square feet, which in addition to its focus on Hispanic food and grocery also offers a large selection of non food products tailored toward Hispanic shoppers. Walmart is also looking into small "bodega" supermarkets tailored toward this customer group. Clearly, many profitable opportunities exist in this market segment. As at the global level, Walmart's managers are developing strategies to take advantage of them.

Sources: www.walmart.com, 2009; J. Birchall, "Walmart Looks to Hispanic Market," ft.com, March 12 2009; "Does 'Cool' Matter? A Blogger Compares Tesco and Walmart's 'Neighborhood Market' Offerings," www.bloggers-at-large.com, January 21, 2009.

When a company has greater ability to raise prices to buyers or bargain down the price paid for inputs, it has obtained increased market power.

Problems with Horizontal Integration

Although horizontal integration can strengthen a company's business model in several ways, there are problems, limitations, and dangers associated with pursuing this corporate-level strategy. We discuss many of these dangers in detail in Chapter 10; the important point to note is that a wealth of data suggests that the majority of mergers and acquisitions *do not* create value, and many actually *reduce* value.[3] For example, a well-known study by KPMG, a large accounting and management consulting company, looked at 700 large acquisitions and found that while 30% of these did increase the profitability of the acquiring company, 31% reduced profitability, and the remainder had little impact on it.[4] The implication is that *implementing* a horizontal integration strategy is not an easy task for managers.

As we discuss in Chapter 10, there are several reasons why mergers and acquisitions may fail to result in higher profitability: problems associated with merging very different company cultures; high management turnover in the acquired company when the acquisition is a hostile one; and a tendency of managers to overestimate the benefits to be had from a merger or acquisition and underestimate the problems involved in merging their operations.

Another problem with horizontal integration is that, when a company uses it to become a dominant industry competitor, an attempt to keep using the strategy to grow even larger brings a company into conflict with the Federal Trade Commission (FTC), the government agency responsible for enforcing antitrust law. Antitrust authorities are concerned about the potential for abuse of market power; more competition is generally better for consumers than less competition. So the FTC is concerned when a few industry companies try to make acquisitions that will allow them to raise prices to consumers above the level that would exist in a more competitive situation and thus abuse their market power. The FTC also wishes to prevent dominant companies from using their market power to crush potential competitors, for example, by cutting prices when a new competitor enters the industry and so force them out of business (then they raise prices after they have eliminated the threat). Because of these concerns, any merger or acquisition thought by the FTC to create too much consolidation and the *potential* for future abuse of market power may, for antitrust reasons, be blocked. The proposed merger between the two dominant satellite radio companies Sirius and XM was held up for many months, until July 2008, because of concerns this problem would arise in radio broadcasting. The merger was approved after it became clear that customers had many other ways to obtain high-quality radio programming, for example, through their computers and cell phones, so substantial competition would still exist in the industry.

VERTICAL INTEGRATION: ENTERING NEW INDUSTRIES TO STRENGTHEN THE "CORE" BUSINESS MODEL

Many companies that use horizontal integration to strengthen their business model and improve their competitive position also use the corporate-level strategy of vertical integration for the same purpose. In pursuing vertical integration, however, a company is entering new industries to support the business model of its "core" industry, the one that is the primary source of its competitive advantage and profitability. At this point, therefore, a company must formulate a multibusiness model that explains how entry into a new industry using vertical integration will enhance its long-term profitability. The model that justifies the pursuit of vertical integration is based on a company entering industries that *add value* to its core products because this increases product differentiation and/or lowers its cost structure, thus increasing its profitability.

A company pursuing a strategy of **vertical integration** expands its operations either backward into an industry that produces inputs for the company's products (*backward vertical integration*) or forward into an industry that uses, distributes, or sells the company's products (*forward vertical integration*). To enter an industry, it may establish its own operations and build the value chain needed to compete effectively in that industry; or it may acquire a company that is already in the industry. A steel company that supplies its iron ore needs from company-owned iron ore mines illustrates backward integration. A PC maker that sells its laptops through company-owned retail outlets illustrates forward integration. For example, Apple Computer entered the retail industry in 2001 when it decided to establish a chain of Apple stores to sell its PCs and iPods, something Sony and Dell have imitated. IBM is a highly vertically integrated company; it integrated backward into the chip and memory disk industry to produce the components that go into its mainframes and servers and integrated forward into the computer software and consulting services industries.

Figure 9.1 illustrates four *main* stages in a typical raw materials-to-customer value-added chain. For a company based in the final assembly stage, backward integration means moving into component parts manufacturing and raw materials production. Forward integration means moving into distribution and sales (retail). At each stage in the chain, *value is added* to the product, meaning that a company at that stage takes the product produced in the previous stage and transforms it in some way so that it is worth more to a company at the next stage in the chain and, ultimately, to the customer. It is important to note that each stage of the value-added chain is a separate industry or industries in which many different companies are competing. Moreover, within each industry, every company has a value chain composed of the value-creation activities we discussed in Chapter 3: R&D, production, marketing, customer service, and so on. In other words, we can think of a value chain that runs *across* industries, and embedded within that are the value chains of companies *within* each industry.

As an example of the value-added concept, consider how companies in each industry involved in the production of a PC contribute to the final product (Figure 9.2).

Figure 9.1 Stages in the Raw-Materials-to-Customer Value-Added Chain

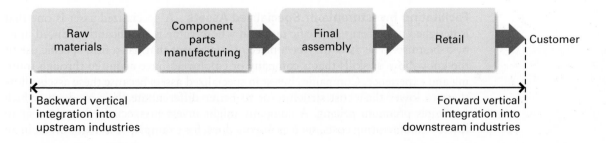

Figure 9.2   The Raw-Materials-to-Customer Value-Added Chain in the PC Industry

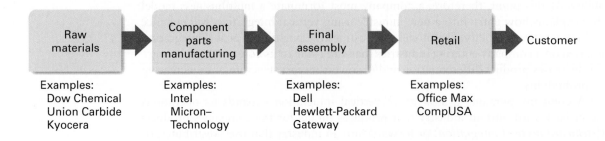

At the first stage in the chain are the raw materials companies that make specialty ceramics, chemicals, and metal, such as Kyocera of Japan, who manufactures the ceramic substrate for semiconductors. These companies sell their products to the makers of PC component products, such as Intel and AMD, who transform the ceramics, chemicals, and metals they purchase into PC components such as microprocessors, disk drives, and memory chips. In the process, they *add value* to the raw materials they purchase. At the third stage, these components are then sold to PC makers such as Apple, Dell, and HP, who decide which of these components to purchase and assemble to *add value* to their final PCs that they either make or outsource to a contract manufacturer. At stage four, the finished PCs are then either sold directly to the final customer over the Internet or sold to retailers such as Best Buy and Staples, which distribute and sell them to the final customer. Companies that distribute and sell PCs also *add value* to the product because they make it accessible to customers and provide customer service and support.

Thus companies in different industries add value at each stage in the raw-materials-to-customer chain. Viewed in this way, vertical integration presents companies with a choice about which industries in the raw-materials-to-customer chain to operate and compete in. This choice is determined by how much establishing operations at a stage in the value chain will increase product differentiation or lower costs—and therefore increase profitability—as we discuss in the following.

Increasing Profitability through Vertical Integration

As noted earlier, a company pursues vertical integration to strengthen the business model of its original or core business and to improve its competitive position.[5] Vertical integration increases product differentiation, lowers costs, or reduces industry competition when it (1) facilitates investments in efficiency-enhancing specialized assets, (2) protects product quality, and (3) results in improved scheduling.

Facilitating Investments in Specialized Assets   A specialized asset is one that is designed to perform a specific task and whose value is significantly reduced in its next-best use.[6] The asset may be a piece of equipment that has a firm-specific use or the know-how or skills that a company or employees have acquired through training and experience. Companies invest in specialized assets because these assets allow them to lower their cost structure or to better differentiate their products, which facilitates premium pricing. A company might invest in specialized equipment to lower manufacturing costs, such as Toyota does, for example, or it might invest in an advanced technology that allows it to develop better-quality products than its rivals, such as Apple does. Thus, specialized assets can help a company achieve a competitive advantage at the business level.

Just as a company invests in specialized assets in its own industry to build competitive advantage, it is often necessary that suppliers invest in specialized assets to produce the inputs that a specific company needs. By investing in these assets, a supplier can make higher-quality inputs that provide its customers with a differentiation advantage or inputs at a lower cost so it can charge its customers a lower price to keep their business. However, it is often difficult to persuade companies in adjacent stages of the raw materials-to-customer value-added chain to make investments in specialized assets. Often, to realize the benefits associated with such investments, a company has to vertically integrate and enter into adjacent industries and make the investments itself. Why does this happen?

Imagine that Ford has developed a unique energy-saving electrical engine system that will dramatically increase fuel efficiency and differentiate Ford's cars from those of its rivals, giving it a major competitive advantage. Ford has to decide whether to make the system in-house (vertical integration) or contract with a supplier such as a specialist outsourcing manufacturer to make the new engine system. Manufacturing these new systems requires a substantial investment in specialized equipment that can be used only for this purpose. In other words, because of its unique design, the equipment cannot be used to manufacture any other type of electrical engine for Ford or any other carmaker. Thus this is an investment in specialized assets.

Consider this situation from the perspective of the outside supplier deciding whether or not to make this investment. The supplier might reason that once it has made the investment, it will become dependent on Ford for business because *Ford is the only possible customer for the electrical engine made by this specialized equipment.* The supplier realizes that this puts Ford in a strong bargaining position and that Ford might use its power to demand lower prices for the engines. Given the risks involved, the supplier declines to make the investment in specialized equipment.

Now consider Ford's position. Ford might reason that if it outsources production of these systems to an outside supplier, it might become too dependent on that supplier for a vital input. Because specialized equipment is required to produce the engine systems, Ford cannot switch its order to other suppliers. Ford realizes that this increases the bargaining power of the supplier, which might use its bargaining power to demand higher prices.

The situation of *mutual dependence* that would be created by the investment in specialized assets makes Ford hesitant to allow outside suppliers to make the product, and makes suppliers hesitant to undertake such a risky investment. The problem is a lack of trust—neither Ford nor the supplier can trust the other to play fair in this situation. The lack of trust arises from the risk of **holdup**; that is, being taken advantage of by a trading partner *after* the investment in specialized assets has been made.[7] Because of this risk, Ford reasons that the only cost-effective way to get the new engine systems is for it to make the investment in specialized assets and manufacture them itself.

To generalize from this example, if achieving a competitive advantage requires one company to make investments in specialized assets so it can trade with another, **the risk of holdup** may serve as a deterrent, and the investment may not take place. Consequently, the potential for higher profitability from specialization will be lost. To prevent such loss, companies vertically integrate into adjacent stages in the value chain. Historically, the problems surrounding specific assets have driven automobile companies to vertically integrate backward into the production of component parts; steel companies to vertically integrate backward into the production of iron; computer companies to vertically integrate backward into chip production; and aluminum companies to vertically integrate backward into bauxite mining. The way specific asset issues have led to vertical integration in the aluminum industry is discussed in Strategy in Action 9.2.

Enhancing Product Quality   By entering industries at other stages of the value-added chain, a company can often enhance the quality of the products in its core business and so strengthen its differentiation advantage. For example, the ability to control the reliability and performance of complex components such as engine and transmission systems may increase a company's competitive advantage in the luxury sedan market and enable it to charge a premium price. Conditions in the banana industry also illustrate the importance of vertical integration in maintaining product quality. Historically, a problem facing food companies that import bananas has been the variable quality of delivered bananas, which often arrive on

9.2 STRATEGY IN ACTION

Specialized Assets and Vertical Integration in the Aluminum Industry

The metal content and chemical composition of bauxite ore, used to produce aluminum, vary from deposit to deposit, so each type of ore requires a specialized refinery—that is, the refinery must be designed for a particular type of ore. Running one type of bauxite through a refinery designed for another type reportedly increases production costs from 20% to 100%. Thus, the value of an investment in a specialized aluminum refinery and the cost of the output produced by that refinery depend on receiving the right kind of bauxite ore.

Imagine that an aluminum company has to decide whether to invest in an aluminum refinery designed to refine a certain type of ore. Also assume that this ore is extracted by a company that owns a single bauxite mine. Using a different type of ore would raise production costs by 50%. Therefore, the value of the aluminum company's investment is dependent on the price it must pay the bauxite company for this bauxite. Recognizing this, once the aluminum company has made the investment in a new refinery, what is to stop the bauxite company from raising bauxite prices? Nothing. Once it has made

the investment, the aluminum company is locked into its relationship with its bauxite supplier. The bauxite supplier can increase prices because it knows that as long as the increase in the total production costs of the aluminum company is less than 50%, the aluminum company will continue to buy its ore. Thus, once the aluminum company has made the investment, the bauxite supplier can *hold up* the aluminum company.

How can the aluminum company reduce the risk of holdup? The answer is by purchasing the bauxite supplier. If the aluminum company can purchase the bauxite supplier's mine, it need no longer fear that bauxite prices will be increased after the investment in an aluminum refinery has been made. In other words, vertical integration, by eliminating the risk of holdup, makes the specialized investment worthwhile. In practice, it has been argued that these kinds of considerations have driven aluminum companies to pursue vertical integration to such a degree that, according to one study, more than 90% of the total volume of bauxite is transferred within vertically integrated aluminum companies.

Source: J-F. Hennart, "Upstream Vertical Integration in the Aluminum and Tin Industries," *Journal of Economic Behavior and Organization* 9 (1988): 281–299.

the shelves of United States supermarkets too ripe or not ripe enough. To correct this problem, major United States food companies such as General Foods have integrated backward and now own banana plantations so they have control over the supply of bananas. As a result, they can distribute and sell bananas of a standard quality at the optimal time to better satisfy customers. Knowing they can rely on the quality of these brands, customers are also willing to pay more for them. Thus, by vertically integrating backward into plantation ownership, banana companies have built customer confidence, which in turn has enabled them to charge a premium price for their product.

The same considerations can promote forward vertical integration. Ownership of retail outlets may be necessary if the required standards of after-sales service for complex products are to be maintained. For example, in the 1920s, Kodak owned the retail outlets that distributed its photographic equipment because the company felt that few existing retail outlets had the skills necessary to sell and service its complex equipment. By the 1930s, new retailers had emerged that could provide satisfactory distribution and service for Kodak products, so it left the retail industry. McDonald's also has used vertical integration to protect product quality and increase efficiency, as Strategy in Action 9.3 relates.

9.3 STRATEGY IN ACTION

McDonald's: A Leader at Vertical Integration

By the 1990s, McDonald's faced a problem: after decades of rapid growth, the fast food market was beginning to show signs of market saturation. McDonald's response to the slowdown was to expand abroad rapidly. In 1980, 28% of the chain's new restaurant openings were abroad; in 1990 it was 60%, and by 2000, 70% and today it has more than 12,000 restaurants in 110 countries outside the United States. One of the keys to McDonald's successful global expansion is to replicate the value-creation skills that spurred its growth in the countries and world regions in which it operates. McDonald's United States success was built on a formula of close relations with suppliers, nationwide marketing might, and tight control over store-level operating procedures.

McDonald's biggest global problem has been to replicate its United States supply chain in other countries. United States suppliers are fiercely loyal to McDonald's; they must be because their fortunes are closely linked to those of McDonald's. McDonald's maintains very rigorous specifications for all the raw ingredients it uses— the key to its consistency and quality control. Outside of the United States, however, McDonald's has found suppliers far less willing to make the investments required to meet its specifications. In Great Britain, for example, McDonald's had problems getting local bakeries to produce the hamburger bun. After experiencing quality problems with two local bakeries, McDonald's had to vertically integrate backward and built its own bakeries to supply its British stores.

In a more extreme case, when McDonald's decided to operate in Russia, it found that local suppliers lacked the capability to produce ingredients of the quality it demanded. The firm was forced to vertically integrate through the local food industry on a heroic scale, importing potato seeds and bull semen and indirectly managing dairy farms, cattle ranches, and vegetable plots. It also had to construct the world's largest food-processing plant at a huge cost. In South America, McDonald's also bought huge ranches in Argentina to raise its own cattle. As a result, today, McDonald's is able to use vertical integration to protect product quality and reduce its global cost structure.

Source: www.mcdonalds.com, 2009.

Improved Scheduling   Sometimes important strategic advantages can be obtained when vertical integration makes it quicker, easier, and more cost-effective to plan, coordinate, and schedule the transfer of a product, such as raw materials or component parts, between adjacent stages of the value-added chain.[8] Such advantages can be crucial when a company wants to realize the benefits of JIT inventory systems. For example, in the 1920s, Ford profited from the tight coordination and scheduling made possible by backward vertical integration. Ford integrated backward into steel foundries, iron ore shipping, and iron ore mining. Deliveries at Ford were coordinated to such an extent that iron ore unloaded at Ford's steel foundries on the Great Lakes was turned into engine blocks within 24 hours, which lowered Ford's cost structure.

Very often, the improved scheduling that vertical integration makes possible also enables a company to respond better to sudden changes in the supply or demand for a particular product. For example, if demand drops, a company can quickly cut production of components; when demand increases, a company can quickly increase production capacity to get its products into the marketplace faster.[9]

Problems with Vertical Integration

Vertical integration can often be used to strengthen a company's business model and increase profitability. However, the opposite can occur when vertical integration results in (1) an increasing cost structure, (2) disadvantages that arise when technology is changing fast, and, (3) disadvantages that arise when demand is unpredictable. Sometimes these disadvantages are so great that vertical integration, rather than increasing profitability, may actually reduce it—in which case a company **vertically disintegrates** and exits industries adjacent to its core industry in the industry value chain. For example, Ford, which was highly vertically integrated, sold all its companies involved in mining iron ore and making steel when more efficient and specialized steel producers emerged that were able to supply lower-priced steel.

Increasing Cost Structure   Although vertical integration is often undertaken to lower a company's cost structure, it can raise costs if, over time, a company makes mistakes, such as continuing to purchase inputs from company-owned suppliers when low-cost independent suppliers that can supply the same inputs exist. For decades, for example, GM's company-owned suppliers made more than 60% of the component parts for its vehicles; this figure was far higher than any other major carmaker, which is why GM is a high-cost global carmaker. In the 2000s, it has vertically disintegrated by selling off many of its largest component operations, such as Delhi, its electrical components supplier. Thus, vertical integration can be a major disadvantage when company-owned suppliers develop a higher cost structure than those of independent suppliers. Why would a company-owned supplier develop such a high cost structure?

Company-owned or "in-house" suppliers know that they can always sell their components to the car-making divisions of their company—they have a "captive customer." Because company-owned suppliers do not have to compete with independent, outside suppliers for orders, they have much less *incentive* to look for new ways to reduce operating costs or increase component quality. Indeed, in-house suppliers simply pass on cost increases to the car-making divisions in the form of higher **transfer prices**, the prices one division of a company charges other divisions for its products. Unlike independent suppliers, which constantly have to increase their efficiency to protect their competitive advantage, in-house suppliers face no such competition, and the resulting rising cost structure reduces a company's profitability.

The term *bureaucratic costs* refers to the costs of solving the transaction difficulties that arise from managerial inefficiencies and the need to manage the handoffs or exchanges between business units to promote increased differentiation or to lower a company's cost structure. Bureaucratic costs become a significant component of a company's cost structure because considerable managerial time and effort must be spent to reduce or eliminate managerial inefficiencies, such as those that result when company-owned suppliers lose their incentive to increase efficiency or innovation.

Technological Change When technology is changing fast, vertical integration may lock a company into an old, inefficient technology and prevent it from changing to a new one that would strengthen its business model.[10] Consider a radio manufacturer that in the 1950s integrated backward and acquired a manufacturer of vacuum tubes to reduce costs. When transistors replaced vacuum tubes as a major component in radios in the 1960s, this company found itself locked into a technologically outdated business. However, if it had switched to transistors, the company would have had to write off its investment in vacuum tubes, and so managers were reluctant to adopt the new technology. Instead, they continued to use vacuum tubes in their radios while competitors that did not make vacuum tubes rapidly switched to the new transistor technology. As a result, the company lost its competitive advantage, and its failing business model led to a rapid loss in market share. Thus, vertical integration can pose a serious disadvantage when it prevents a company from adopting new technology or changing its suppliers or distribution systems to match the requirements of changing technology.

Demand Unpredictability Suppose the demand for a company's core product, such as cars or washing machines, is predictable, and a company knows how many units it needs to make each month or year. Under these conditions, vertical integration, by allowing a company to schedule and coordinate efficiently the flow of products along the industry value-added chain, may result in major cost savings. However, suppose the demand for cars or washing machines fluctuates wildly and is unpredictable. Now, if demand for cars suddenly plummets, the carmaker may find itself burdened with warehouses full of component parts it no longer needs, which is a major drain on profitability—something that has hurt major carmakers during the recent recession. Thus, vertical integration can be risky when demand is unpredictable because it is hard to manage the volume or flow of products along the value-added chain.

For example, a carmaker might vertically integrate backward to acquire a supplier of brake systems that can make exactly the number of systems the carmaker needs each month. However, if demand for cars falls because gas prices soar, the carmaker finds itself locked into a business that is now inefficient because it is not producing at full capacity. Its cost structure then starts to rise.

The Limits of Vertical Integration

Thus, although there are many ways that vertical integration can strengthen a company's business model, it may weaken when (1) bureaucratic costs increase because company-owned suppliers lack the incentive to reduce operating costs, and

(2) changing technology or uncertain demand reduces a company's ability to change its business model to protect its competitive advantage. It is clear that strategic managers must carefully assess the advantages and disadvantages of expanding the boundaries of their company by entering adjacent industries, either backward (upstream) or forward (downstream), in the industry value-added chain. Moreover, although the decision to enter a new industry to make crucial component parts may have been profitable in the past, it may make no economic sense today because so many low-cost global component parts suppliers exist that compete for the company's business. The risks and returns on investing in vertical integration have to be continually evaluated, and companies should be as willing to vertically disintegrate, as vertically integrate, to strengthen their core business model.

ALTERNATIVES TO VERTICAL INTEGRATION: COOPERATIVE RELATIONSHIPS

Is it possible to obtain the differentiation and cost-savings advantages associated with vertical integration without having to bear the problems and costs associated with this strategy? In other words, is there another corporate-level strategy that managers can use to obtain the advantages of vertical integration while allowing other companies to perform upstream and downstream activities? Today, companies have found that they can realize many of the benefits associated with vertical integration by entering into *long-term cooperative relationships* with companies in industries along the value-added chain. **Strategic alliances** are long-term agreements between two or more companies to jointly develop new products or processes that benefit all companies concerned. The advantages and disadvantages of strategic alliances are discussed in Chapter 8, in which we contrast the benefits of using strategic alliances against those obtained if a company decides to enter only into short-term contracts with other companies.

Short-Term Contracts and Competitive Bidding

Many companies use short-term contracts that last for a year or less to establish the price and conditions under which they will purchase raw materials or components from suppliers or sell their final products to distributors or retailers. A classic example is the carmaker that uses a *competitive bidding strategy*, in which independent component suppliers compete to be chosen to supply a particular component, made to agreed-upon specifications, at the lowest price. For example, GM typically solicits bids from global suppliers to produce a particular component and awards a one-year contract to the supplier that submits the lowest bid. At the end of the year, the contract is once again put out for competitive bid, and once again the lowest cost supplier is most likely to win the bid.

The advantage of this strategy for GM is that suppliers are forced to compete over price, which drives down the cost of its car components. However, GM has no long-term commitment to outside suppliers—and it drives a hard bargain. For this reason, suppliers are unwilling to make the expensive long-term investment in specialized assets that are required to produce higher-quality or better-designed component parts over time. In addition, suppliers will be reluctant to agree on the tight scheduling that makes it possible to use a JIT inventory system because this may help GM lower its costs but will increase a supplier's costs and reduce its profitability.

As a result, short-term contracting does not result in the specialized investments that are required to realize differentiation and cost advantages *because it signals a company's lack of long-term commitment to its suppliers*. Of course, this is not a problem when there is minimal need for cooperation, and specialized assets are not required to improve scheduling, product quality, or reduce costs. In this case, competitive bidding may be optimal. However, when there is a need for cooperation, something that is becoming increasingly significant today, the use of short-term contracts and competitive bidding can be a serious drawback.

Interestingly enough, in the past, GM did find itself at a competitive disadvantage when it used a competitive bidding approach to negotiate with suppliers. In 1992, the company instructed its parts suppliers to cut their prices by 10%—regardless of prior pricing agreements. In effect, GM tore up existing contracts and threatened to stop doing business with suppliers that did not agree to the price reduction. Although its action gave it a short-term benefit from lower costs, in the longer term the loss of trust and the hostility created between the company and its suppliers resulted in problems for GM from which it has never recovered. For example, several suppliers claimed that to reduce prices, they reduced the R&D spending necessary to design improved GM parts in the future, one kind of specialized investment. They also indicated that they would first share their new design knowledge with GM's competitors, such as Ford and Toyota, who both focus on forging cooperative long-term relationships with their suppliers.[11]

Strategic Alliances and Long-Term Contracting

Unlike short-term contracts, strategic alliances between buyers and suppliers are long-term, cooperative relationships; both companies agree to make specialized investments and work jointly to find ways to lower costs or increase product quality so that they both gain from their relationship. A strategic alliance becomes a *substitute* for vertical integration because it creates a relatively stable long-term partnership that allows both companies to obtain the same kinds of benefits that result from vertical integration. However, it also avoids the problems (bureaucratic costs) that arise from managerial inefficiencies that result when a company owns its own suppliers, such as those that arise because of a lack of incentives, or when a company becomes locked into an old technology even when technology is changing rapidly.

Consider the cooperative relationships that often go back decades, which many Japanese carmakers have with their component suppliers (the *keiretsu* system), which exemplifies the benefits of successful long-term contracting. Japanese carmakers and suppliers cooperate to find ways to maximize the "value added" they can obtain from being in adjacent stages of the value chain. For example, they do this by jointly implementing JIT inventory systems or sharing future component-parts designs to improve quality and lower assembly costs. As part of this process, suppliers make substantial investments in specialized assets to better serve the needs of a particular carmaker, and the cost savings that result are shared. Thus, Japanese carmakers have been able to capture many of the benefits of vertical integration without having to enter the component industry.

Similarly, component suppliers also benefit because their business and profitability grow as the companies they supply grow, and they can invest their profits in investing in ever more specialized assets.[12] An interesting example of this is the computer chip outsourcing giant Taiwan Semiconductor Manufacturing Company (TSMC) that makes the chips for many companies, such as Nvidia, Apple, and AMD. In 2009, the cost of investing in the machinery necessary to build a state-of-the-art chip factory can exceed $10 billion. TSMC is able to make this huge (risky) investment because it has developed cooperative long-term relationships with its computer chip partners. All parties recognize that they will benefit from this outsourcing arrangement, which does not preclude some hard bargaining between TSMC and the chip companies, because all parties want to maximize their profits and reduce their risks.

Building Long-Term Cooperative Relationships

How does a company create a long-term strategic alliance with another company given the fear of holdup and the possibility of being cheated that arises when one company makes a specialized investment with another company? How have companies such as Toyota managed to develop such profitable, enduring relationships with their suppliers?

There are several strategies companies can adopt to promote the success of a long-term cooperative relationship and lessen the chance one company will renege on its agreement and cheat the other. One strategy is for the company that makes the specialized investment to demand a *hostage* from its partner. Another is to establish a *credible commitment* from both companies that results in a trusting, long-term relationship.[13]

Hostage Taking   Hostage taking is essentially a means of guaranteeing that a partner will keep its side of the bargain. The cooperative relationship between Boeing and Northrop illustrates this type of situation. Northrop is a major subcontractor for Boeing's commercial airline division, providing many components for its aircraft. To serve Boeing's special needs, Northrop has to make substantial investments in specialized assets, and, in theory, having made this investment, Northrop becomes dependent on Boeing, which can threaten to switch orders to other suppliers as a way of driving down Northrop's prices. In practice, Boeing is highly unlikely to do this because it is a major supplier to Northrop's defense division and provides many parts for its Stealth aircraft; it also has made major investments in specialized assets to serve Northrop's needs. Thus, the companies are *mutually dependent*; each company holds a hostage—the specialized investment the other has made. Thus, Boeing is unlikely to renege on any pricing agreements with Northrop because it knows that Northrop would respond in kind.

Credible Commitments   A credible commitment is a believable promise or pledge to support the development of a long-term relationship between companies. Consider the way GE and IBM developed such a commitment. GE is one of the major suppliers of advanced semiconductor chips to IBM, and many of the chips are customized to IBM's requirements. To meet IBM's specific needs, GE has had to make substantial investments in specialized assets that have little other value. As a consequence, GE is dependent on IBM and faces a risk that IBM will take advantage of this dependence to demand lower prices. In theory, IBM could back up its demand by threatening to switch its business to another supplier. However, GE reduced this risk by having IBM enter into a contractual agreement that committed IBM to purchase chips from GE for a 10-year period. In addition, IBM agreed to share the costs of the specialized assets needed to develop the customized chips, thereby reducing the risks associated with GE's investment. Thus, by publicly committing itself to a long-term contract and putting some money into the chip development process, IBM made a *credible commitment* that it would continue to purchasing chips from GE.

Maintaining Market Discipline   Just as a company pursuing vertical integration faces the problem that its company-owned suppliers might become inefficient, so a company that forms a strategic alliance with an independent component supplier runs the risk that its alliance partner might become inefficient over time, resulting in higher component costs or lower quality. This also happens because the outside supplier knows it does not have to compete with other suppliers for the company's business. Consequently, a company seeking to form a mutually beneficial, long-term strategic alliance needs to possess some kind of power that it can use to discipline its partner—should the need arise.

A company holds two strong cards over its supplier partner. First, even long-term contracts are periodically renegotiated, usually every three to five years, so the supplier knows that if it fails to live up to its commitments, its partner may refuse to renew the contract. Second, many companies that form long-term relationships with suppliers use **parallel sourcing policies**—that is, they enter into long-term contracts with at least *two* suppliers for the *same* component (this is Toyota's policy, for example).[14] This arrangement protects a company against a supplier that adopts an uncooperative attitude because the supplier knows that if it fails to comply with the agreement, the company can switch *all* its business to its other supplier partner. When both the company and its suppliers recognize that the parallel sourcing policy allows a supplier to be replaced at short notice, most suppliers behave because the policy brings market discipline into their relationship.

The growing importance of JIT inventory systems as a way to reduce costs and enhance quality and differentiation is increasing the pressure on companies to form strategic alliances in a wide range of industries. The number of strategic alliances formed each year, especially global strategic alliances, is increasing, and the popularity of vertical integration is falling because so many low-cost global suppliers exist in countries like Malaysia, Korea, and China.

STRATEGIC OUTSOURCING

Vertical integration and strategic alliances are alternative ways of managing the value chain *across industries* to strengthen a company's core business model. However, just as low-cost suppliers of component parts exist, so today many *specialized companies* exist that can perform one of a company's *own value-chain activities* in a way that contributes to a company's differentiation advantage or that lowers its cost structure. For example, one specialist chip outsourcer, Taiwanese giant TSMC was discussed earlier; two other huge global contract manufacturers are Flextronics and Jabil Circuit.

Strategic outsourcing is the decision to allow one or more of a company's value-chain activities or functions to be performed by independent specialist companies that focus all their skills and knowledge on just one kind of activity. The activity to be outsourced may encompass an entire function, such as the manufacturing function, or it may be just one kind of activity that a function performs. For example, many companies outsource the management of their pension systems while keeping other HRM activities within the company. When a company chooses to outsource a value-chain activity, it is choosing to focus on a *fewer* number of value-creation activities to strengthen its business model.

There has been a clear move among many companies to outsource activities that managers regard as being "noncore" or "nonstrategic," meaning they are not a source of a company's distinctive competencies and competitive advantage.[15] One survey found that some 54% of the companies polled had outsourced manufacturing processes or services in the past three years.[16] Another survey estimates that some 56% of all global product manufacturing is outsourced to manufacturing specialists.[17] Some well-known companies that outsource include Nike, which does not make its athletic shoes; Gap Inc., which does not make its jeans and clothing; and Apple, which makes none of its own product. These products are made under contract at low-cost global locations by contract manufacturers that specialize in low-cost assembly.

Although manufacturing is the most popular form of strategic outsourcing, as we noted earlier, many other kinds of noncore activities are also outsourced. Microsoft has long outsourced its entire customer technical support operation to an independent company, as does Dell. Both companies have extensive customer support operations in India staffed by skilled operatives paid a fraction of what their United States counterparts earn. BP outsourced almost all of its human resource function to Exult, a San Antonio company, in a five-year deal worth $600 million; a few years later Exult won a 10-year $1.1 billion contract to handle HRM activities for all Bank of America's 150,000 employees. Similarly, American Express outsourced its entire IT function to IBM in a seven-year deal worth $4 billion, and the IT outsourcing market in North America was worth more than $250 billion by 2009.[18] In 2006, IBM announced it was outsourcing its purchasing function to an Indian company to save $2 billion a year, and it has steadily increased its use of outsourcing ever since. For example, in 2009 it announced it would lay off 5,000 IT employees in the United States and move their jobs to India.[19]

Companies engage in strategic outsourcing to strengthen their business models and increase their profitability. The process of strategic outsourcing typically begins with strategic managers identifying the value-chain activities that form the basis of a company's competitive advantage; these are obviously kept within the company to protect them from competitors. Managers then systematically review the noncore functions to assess whether independent companies that specialize in those activities can perform them more effectively and efficiently. Because these companies specialize in particular activities, they can perform them in ways that lower costs or improve differentiation. If managers decide there are differentiation or cost advantages, these activities are outsourced to those specialists.

This is illustrated in Figure 9.3, which shows the primary value-chain activities and boundaries of a company before and after it has pursued strategic outsourcing. In this example, the company decided to outsource its production and customer service functions to specialist companies, leaving just R&D and marketing and sales within the company. Once outsourcing has been executed, the relationships between the company and its specialists are then often structured as long-term contractual relationships, with rich information sharing between the company and the specialist organization to which it has contracted the activity. The term **virtual corporation** has been coined to describe companies that have pursued extensive strategic outsourcing.[20]

Benefits of Outsourcing

Strategic outsourcing has several advantages. It can help a company to (1) lower its cost structure, (2) increase product differentiation,[21] and (3) focus on the distinctive competencies that are vital to its long-term competitive advantage and profitability.

Figure 9.3 Strategic Outsourcing of Primary Value Creation Functions

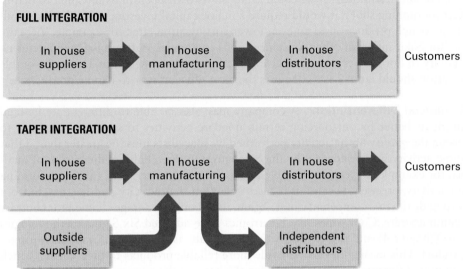

Lower Cost Structure   Outsourcing will reduce costs when the price that must be paid to a specialist company to perform a particular value-chain activity is less than what it would cost the company to internally perform that activity itself. Specialists are often able to perform an activity at a lower cost than the company, because they are able to realize scale economies or other efficiencies not available to the company. For example, performing HRM activities, such as managing pay and benefit systems, requires a significant investment in sophisticated HRM IT; purchasing these IT systems represents a considerable fixed cost for one company. But, by aggregating the HRM IT needs of many individual companies, a company that specializes in HRM, such as Exult and Paycheck, can obtain huge economies of scale in IT that any single company could not hope to achieve. Some of these cost savings are then passed to the client companies in the form of lower prices, which reduces their cost structure. A similar dynamic is at work in the contract manufacturing business. Once again, manufacturing specialists like Solectron, Flextronics, and Jabil Circuit make large capital investments to build efficient-scale manufacturing facilities, but then are able to spread those capital costs over a huge volume of output and drive down unit costs so that they can make a specific product—an Apple iPod or Motorola Krazr, for example—at a lower cost that the company.

Specialists are also likely to obtain the cost savings associated with learning effects much more rapidly than a company that performs an activity just for itself (see Chapter 4 for a review of learning effects). For example, because a company like Flextronics is manufacturing similar products for several different companies, it is able to build up *cumulative* volume more rapidly, and it learns how to manage and operate the manufacturing process more efficiently than any of its clients could. This drives down the specialists' cost structure and also allows them to charge client companies a lower price for a product than if they made it in-house.

Specialists are also often able to perform activities at lower costs than a specific company because they are based in low-cost global locations. Nike, for example, outsources the manufacture of its running shoes to companies based in China because of the much lower wage rates. The Chinese-based specialist can assemble shoes, which is a very labor-intensive activity, at a much lower cost than if assembled in the United States. Although Nike could establish its own operations in China to manufacture running shoes, it would require a major capital investment and limit its ability to switch production to an even lower-cost location later, for example, Vietnam. So, for Nike and most other consumer goods companies, outsourcing manufacturing activity to both lower costs and give it the flexibility to switch to a more favorable location should labor costs change is the most efficient way to handle production.

Enhanced Differentiation   A company may also be able to differentiate its final products better by outsourcing certain noncore activities to specialists. For this to occur, the *quality* of the activity performed by specialists must be greater than if that same activity was performed by the company. On the reliability dimension of quality, for example, a specialist may be able to achieve a lower error rate in performing an activity, precisely because it focuses solely on that activity and has developed a strong distinctive competency in it. Again, this is one advantage claimed for contract manufacturers. Companies like Flextronics have adopted Six Sigma methodologies (see Chapter 4) and driven down the defect rate associated with manufacturing a product. This means they can provide more reliable products to their clients, which can now differentiate their products on the basis of their superior quality.

A company can also improve product differentiation by outsourcing to specialists when they stand out on the excellence dimension of quality. For example, the excellence of Dell's United States customer service is a differentiating factor, and Dell outsources its PC repair and maintenance function to specialist companies. A customer who has a problem with a product purchased from Dell can get excellent help over the phone, and if it turns out that there is a defective part in the computer, a maintenance person will be dispatched to replace the part within a few days. The excellence of this service differentiates Dell and helps to guarantee repeat purchases, which is why HP has worked hard to match Dell's level of service quality. In a similar way, carmakers often outsource specific kinds of vehicle component design activities, such as microchips or headlights, to specialists that have earned a reputation for design excellence in this particular activity.

Focus on the Core Business   A final advantage of strategic outsourcing is that it allows managers to focus their energies and their company's resources on performing those core activities that have the most potential to create value and competitive advantage. In other words, companies can enhance their core competencies and so are able to push out the value frontier and create more value for their customers. For example, Cisco Systems remains the dominant competitor in the Internet router industry because it has focused on building its competencies in product design, marketing and sales, and supply-chain management. Companies that focus on the core activities essential for competitive advantage in their industry are better able to drive down the costs of performing those activities and better differentiate their final products.

Risks of Outsourcing

Although outsourcing noncore activities has many benefits, there are also risks associated with it, risks such as holdup and the possible loss of important information when an activity is outsourced. Managers must assess these risks before they decide to outsource a particular activity, although, as we discuss following, these risks can be reduced when the appropriate steps are taken.

Holdup   In the context of outsourcing, holdup refers to the risk that a company will become too dependent on the specialist provider of an outsourced activity and that the specialist will use this fact to raise prices beyond some previously agreed-on rate. As with strategic alliances, the risk of holdup can be reduced by outsourcing to several suppliers and pursuing a parallel sourcing policy, as Toyota and Cisco do. Moreover, when an activity can be performed well by any one of several different providers, the threat that a contract will not be renewed in the future is normally sufficient to keep the chosen provider from exercising bargaining power over the company. For example, although IBM enters into long-term contracts to provide IT services to a wide range of companies, it would be unadvisable to try to raise prices after the contract has been signed because it knows full well that such an action would reduce its chance of getting the contract renewed in the future. Moreover, the fact that IBM has many strong competitors in the IT services business, such as Accenture, Cap Gemini, and HP gives it a very strong incentive to deliver significant value to its client and not practice holdup.

Loss of Information   A company that is not careful can lose important competitive information when it outsources an activity. For example, many computer hardware and software companies have outsourced their customer technical support function to specialists. Although this makes good sense from a cost and differentiation perspective, it may also mean that a critical point of contact with the customer, and a source of important feedback, is lost. Customer complaints can be useful pieces of information and valuable inputs into future product design, but if those complaints are not clearly communicated to the company by the specialists performing the technical support activity, the company can lose the information. Again, this is not an argument against outsourcing. Rather, it is an argument for making sure that there is good communication flow between the outsourcing specialist and the company. At Dell, for example, a great deal of attention is paid to making sure that the specialist responsible for providing technical support and onsite maintenance collects and communicates all relevant data regarding product failures and other problems to Dell, so that Dell can design better products.

SUMMARY OF CHAPTER

1. A corporate strategy should enable a company, or one or more of its business units, to perform one or more of the value creation functions at a lower cost or in a way that allows for differentiation and a premium price.

2. The corporate-level strategy of horizontal integration is pursued to increase the profitability of a company's business model by (a) reducing costs, (b) increasing the value of the company's products through differentiation, (c) replicating the business model, (d) managing rivalry within the industry to reduce the risk of price warfare; and (e) increasing bargaining power over suppliers and buyers.

3. There are two drawbacks associated with horizontal integration: (a) the numerous pitfalls associated with making mergers and acquisitions, and (b) the fact that the strategy can bring a company into direct conflict with antitrust authorities.

4. The corporate-level strategy of vertical integration is pursued to increase the profitability of a company's "core" business model in its original

industry. Vertical integration can enable a company to achieve a competitive advantage by helping build barriers to entry, facilitating investments in specialized assets, protecting product quality, and helping to improve scheduling between adjacent stages in the value chain.

5. The disadvantages of vertical integration include increasing bureaucratic costs if a company-owned or in-house supplier becomes lazy or inefficient, and it reduces flexibility when technology is changing fast or demand is uncertain.

6. Entering into a long-term contract can enable a company to realize many of the benefits associated with vertical integration without having to bear the same level of bureaucratic costs. However, to avoid the risks associated with becoming too dependent on its partner, it needs to seek a credible commitment from its partner or establish a mutual hostage-taking situation.

7. The strategic outsourcing of noncore value creation activities may allow a company to lower its costs, better differentiate its products, and make better use of scarce resources, while also enabling it to respond rapidly to changing market conditions. However, strategic outsourcing may have a detrimental effect if the company outsources important value creation activities or becomes too dependent on the key suppliers of those activities.

DISCUSSION QUESTIONS

1. What value-creation activities should a company outsource to independent suppliers? What are the risks involved in outsourcing these activities?

2. Why was it profitable for GM and Ford to integrate backward into component-parts manufacturing in the past, and why are both companies now buying more of their parts from outside suppliers?

3. What is the difference between a company's internal value chain and the industry value chain? What is the relationship between vertical integration and the industry value chain?

CLOSING CASE

Beating Dell: Why HP Acquired Compaq

In 2001, Hewlett-Packard (now HP) shocked the business world when its former CEO, Carly Fiorina, announced that rival computer-maker Compaq had agreed to be acquired by HP. The announcement came at the end of a year in which slumping demand and strong competition from Dell had buffeted both companies. The merged company would have annual revenues of about $87.4 billion, putting it in the same league as IBM, and would be able to provide customers with a full range of computer products and services. With the exception of printers, in which HP is the market leader, there was significant product overlap between HP and Compaq.

To justify the acquisition, Fiorina claimed that it would yield a number of benefits. First, there would be significant cost savings. Some $2.5 billion per year would be taken out of annual expenses by eliminating redundant administrative functions and laying off 15,000 employees. In addition, combining the PC businesses of HP and Compaq would enable HP to capture significant scale economies and compete more efficiently with Dell. The same would be true in the computer server and storage businesses, areas in which Dell was gaining share. Critics, however, were quick to point out that Dell's competitive advantage was based on its cost-leadership business model that was based on the efficient management of its supply chain—an area in which both HP and Compaq lagged behind Dell. Although achieving economies of scale is desirable, would the merger allow HP to reduce its cost structure, such as by increasing its supply-chain efficiency? If HP could not change its PC business model to match Dell's low costs, then the merger would not provide any real benefit.

In addition to the cost advantages of the merger, Fiorina argued that the acquisition would give HP a critical mass in the computer service and consultancy business, in which it significantly lagged behind leader IBM. By being able to offer customers a total solution to their IT needs, both hardware *and* services, Fiorina argued that HP could gain new market share among corporate clients, who would now buy its PCs as part of the total "computer package"; moreover, HP would be entering the higher-margin service business. Here too, however, critics were quick to perceive flaws. They argued that HP would still be a minnow in the service and consultancy area, with less than 3% of market share.

In 2005, HP announced that it had achieved its cost savings target and that it was continuing to find ways to reduce the duplication of resources in the merged company. However, it also announced that Dell's entry into the printer business had hurt its profit margins, and the profit margins on the sales of its PCs were still well below those obtained by Dell. HP's stock price plunged, and its board of directors reacted by firing Fiorina and bringing in a new CEO, Mark Hurd, a person with proven skills in managing a company's cost structure. Hurd initiated another round of cost reductions by pruning HP's product line and workforce. In Spring 2006, the company astounded analysts when it announced much higher profit margins on its sales of PCs and higher profits across the company. Many of Fiorina's strategies had begun to pay off; HP's PCs were much more attractive to customers, and Dell's foray into printers had not proved highly successful against market leader HP. Neither had Dell's entry into other electronics industries such as MP3 players, televisions, and so on.

The result was that competitive advantage in the PC industry seemed to be moving away from Dell and toward HP. As a result, Dell has been forced to find ways to increase its level of differentiation to increase the attractiveness of its machines and so defend its position against HP and Apple. Dell and bought the upscale PC-maker Alienware in one move to increase differentiation; it also entered into physical retailing industry when it opened Dell PC stores in major shopping malls, imitating Apple's strategy. And, to find more cost savings, Dell also began to use AMD's cheaper chips and broke its long-term exclusive tie to Intel to find more cost savings. Analysts worry these moves will increase its cost structure, and the battle has heated up in the PC industry as Dell, HP, and Apple work to find new ways to lower costs and differentiate their products to increase their profitability and ROIC.

Case Discussion Questions

1. What kind of corporate-level strategies did HP and Dell pursue to strengthen their multibusiness models?

2. What are the advantages and disadvantages associated with these strategies?

10

CORPORATE DIVERSIFICATION STRATEGY

LEARNING OBJECTIVES

After reading this chapter, you should be able to

- Differentiate between multibusiness models based on related and unrelated diversification
- Explain the five main ways in which diversification can increase company profitability
- Discuss the conditions that lead managers to pursue related diversification versus unrelated

diversification and explain why some companies pursue both strategies
- Describe the three methods companies use to enter new industries: internal new venturing, acquisitions, and joint ventures
- Discuss the advantages and disadvantages associated with each of these methods

Samsung's Success Depends on Many Corporate Strategies

In the 2000s, Samsung Electronics (SE), based in Seoul, Korea, became the second-most profitable global technology company after Microsoft.

SE accomplished this when its pioneering CEO Lee Kun Hee decided to develop and build distinctive competences first in low-cost manufacturing, second in R&D, and then in new production in new industries.

SE's core industry is the consumer electronics industry. In the 1990s, its engineers studied how Japanese companies, Sony and Panasonic, innovated new products. Then, SE's engineers copied Japanese technology and used their low-cost skills to make low-priced versions of the products that they

could sell at lower prices than the Japanese companies. For example, SE decided to enter the cell phone industry and make lower-cost phones than companies such as Nokia and Motorola. SE also entered the semiconductor industry in which it worked to make the lowest-cost memory chips; soon it became the global cost leader. SE also entered other digital-product markets such as cameras, printers, and storage devices.

In essence, Samsung was pursuing the corporate-level strategy of related diversification.

Its goals were to increase its profitability by creating value by transferring and leveraging its distinctive competencies in product development and manufacturing by entering new industries and producing new products. SE's strategy was successful and profitable, but it was not playing in the same league as Sony, for example. Sony could charge premium prices for its leading electronics and continuously plow back profits into the R&D needed to make more advanced state-of-the-art electronics. CEO Hee decided to adopt new strategies that would allow his company to compete head-to-head with Japanese and European electronics companies and make it a global technology leader. SE's goal was not to copy technology innovated by Sony, Matsushita, Phillips, and Nokia but for SE's engineers to develop the research and engineering skills necessary to rapidly innovate leading-edge technologies, such as LCD displays, to create products more advanced than its competitors.

Within a decade, SE became the leading supplier of advanced flash memory chips and LCD screens, premium-priced products that it sold to other global electronics makers, including Japanese flat screen TV makers. Samsung also made the development of a new competence in global marketing an important part of its business model. For example, while Nokia was the leading cell phone innovator, Samsung was the first to realize customers wanted color screens for their phones to allow them to play games and built-in cameras to send photographs to their friends. Both of these incremental advances allowed Samsung to dramatically increase its share of the cell phone market. In 2009, it was the second-largest cell phone maker after Nokia.

By 2007, Samsung had become one of the most innovative global electronics makers with its four research divisions: semiconductors, telecommunications, digital media, and flat screen LCD displays. Because many of its products require components developed by all four divisions, to pursue its strategy of related diversification, SE teams up researchers, designers, engineers, and marketers from all its divisions at its research facility outside Seoul. In this way, they can spur the economies of scope and leveraging of competencies its strategy of related diversification permits. At the same time, it also can transfer its manufacturing competence between its divisions and make electronic products at lower cost than competitors.

In 2008, however, SE, like most other electronics companies, was forced to restructure its business divisions because of the global recession. The problem facing SE and other global electronics companies, such as Sony, was how to pursue related diversification while simultaneously reducing its cost structure and increasing its technological edge. In 2009, Samsung's new CEO Lee Yoon Woo announced a major restructuring that would consolidate its four divisions into two to reduce costs but still speed product development. SE's semiconductor and LCD display businesses were combined into a new Device Solutions Division, and its televisions, mobile phones and other consumer electronics, such as printers and computers were placed in the Digital Media and Communications Division. Because all of SE's products use in-house chips and LCD displays, this means that while SE is pursuing related diversification, it is also using its low-cost skills to benefit from vertical integration.

In addition, it is important to note that Samsung Electronics is only one division of the Samsung Corporation, which is a huge conglomerate that also pursues unrelated diversification. The parent Samsung Corporation has dozens of divisions that are involved in industries such as shipbuilding, construction, life insurance, leisure, and so on—in fact, the Samsung empire accounts for 20% of South Korea's total exports.

Overview

Samsung has developed a *multibusiness model* that allows each of the huge corporation's individual companies or divisions, such as Samsung Electronics, to pursue its own business model to achieve a competitive advantage in the industries in which it operates. The Opening Case discussed how Samsung's electronics division is pursuing the corporate-level strategies of related diversification and vertical integration to increase its profitability. The entire Samsung Corporation, however, is pursuing a strategy of unrelated diversification because it is involved in many industries that have no connection with each other.

In this chapter, we continue our discussion of how companies can strengthen their business models by pursuing the corporate-level strategies of related and unrelated diversification. A diversification strategy is based on a company's decision to enter one or more new industries to take advantage of its existing distinctive competencies and business model. We examine the different kinds of multibusiness models on which related and unrelated diversification are based. Then, we discuss three different ways companies can implement a diversification strategy: internal new ventures, acquisitions, and joint ventures. By the end of this chapter, you will understand the advantages and disadvantages associated with strategic managers' decisions to diversify and enter new markets and industries.

INCREASING PROFITABILITY THROUGH DIVERSIFICATION

Diversification is the process of entering new industries, distinct from a company's core or original industry, to make new kinds of products that can be sold profitably to customers in these new industries. A multibusiness model based on diversification aims to find ways to use a company's existing strategies and distinctive competencies to make products that are highly valued by customers in the new industries it enters. A **diversified company** is one that makes and sells products in two or more different or distinct industries (industries *not* in adjacent stages of an industry value chain as in vertical integration). In each industry a company enters, it establishes an operating division or business unit, which is essentially a self-contained company that makes and sells products to customers in one of more industry market segments. For example, Samsung created its consumer electronics division, and that division competes in many electronic market segments, including cell phones, flat screen TVs, and PCs. As in the case of the other corporate strategies, to increase profitability, a diversification strategy should enable a company or its individual business units to perform one or more of the value-chain functions (1) at a lower cost, (2) in a way that allows for differentiation and gives the company pricing options, or (3) in a way that helps the company to manage industry rivalry better.

The managers of most companies first consider diversification when they are generating **free cash flow**, that is, cash *in excess* of that required to fund investments in the company's existing industry and to meet any debt commitments.[1] In other words, free cash flow is cash in excess of that which can be profitably reinvested in an existing business (*cash* is simply *capital* by another name). When a company is generating free cash flow, managers must decide whether to return that cash to shareholders in the form of higher dividend payouts or invest it in diversification. Technically, any free cash flow belongs to the company's owners—its shareholders. So, for diversification to be a viable strategy, the return on investing free cash flow to pursue diversification opportunities, that is, the ROIC, *must* exceed the return that stockholders could get by investing that capital in a diversified portfolio of stocks and bonds. If this were not the case, it would be in the best interests of shareholders for the company to return any excess cash to them through higher dividends rather than pursue a diversification strategy. Thus, a diversification strategy is *not* consistent with maximizing returns to shareholders unless the multibusiness model managers use to justify entry into a new industry will significantly increase the value a company can create.

There are five main ways in which pursuing a multibusiness model based on diversification can increase company profitability. Diversification can increase profitability when strategic managers (1) transfer competencies between business units in different industries, (2) leverage competencies to create business units in new industries, (3) share resources between business units to realize economies of scope, (4) use product bundling, and (5) utilize *general* organizational competencies that increase the performance of *all* a company's business units.

Transferring Competencies

Transferring competencies involves taking a distinctive competency developed by a business unit in one industry and implanting it in a business unit operating in another industry. The second business unit is often one a company has acquired. Companies that base their diversification strategy on transferring competencies aim to use one or more of their existing distinctive competencies in a value-chain activity—for example, in manufacturing, marketing, materials management, or R&D—to significantly strengthen the business model of the acquired business unit or company. For example, over time, Philip Morris developed distinctive competencies in product development, consumer marketing, and brand positioning that had made it a leader in the tobacco industry. Sensing a profitable opportunity, it acquired Miller Brewing, which at the time was a relatively small player in the brewing industry. Then, to create valuable new products in the brewing industry, Philip Morris transferred some of its best marketing experts to Miller, where they applied the skills acquired at Philip Morris to turn around Miller's lackluster brewing business (see Figure 10.1). The result was the creation of Miller Light, the first light beer, and a marketing campaign that helped to push Miller from the number six to the number two company in the brewing industry in terms of market share.

Companies that base their diversification strategy on transferring competencies tend to acquire new businesses *related* to their existing business activities because of commonalities between one or more of their value-chain functions. A *commonality* is some kind of skill or attribute, which when it is shared or used by two or more business units, allows them to operate more effectively and efficiently and create more value for customers.

For example, Miller Brewing was related to Philip Morris's tobacco business because it was possible to create important marketing commonalities; both beer and tobacco are mass market consumer goods in which brand positioning, advertising, and product development skills are crucial to create successful new products. In general, such competency transfers increase profitability when they either (1) lower the cost structure of one or more of a diversified company's business units or (2) enable

Figure 10.1   Transfer of Competencies at Philip Morris

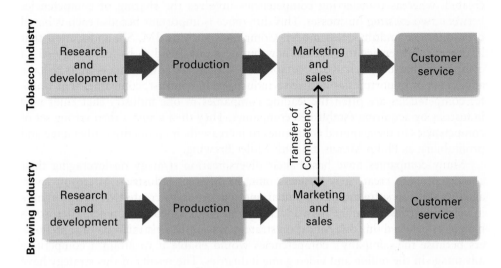

one or more of its business units to better differentiate their products, both of which give business unit pricing options to lower a product's price to increase market share or to charge a premium price.

For competency transfers to increase profitability, the competencies transferred must involve value-chain activities that become an important source of a specific business unit's competitive advantage in the future. In other words, the distinctive competency being transferred must have real strategic value. However, all too often companies assume that *any* commonality between their value chains is sufficient for creating value. When they attempt to transfer competencies, they find the anticipated benefits are not forthcoming because the different business units did not share some important attribute in common. For example, GM's acquisition of Hughes Aircraft, made simply because cars and car manufacturing were "going electronic" and Hughes was an electronics company, demonstrates the folly of overestimating the commonalities between different businesses. The acquisition failed to realize any of the anticipated gains for GM, whose competitive position did not improve, and GM subsequently sold off Hughes.

Leveraging Competencies

Leveraging competencies involves taking a distinctive competency developed by a business unit in one industry and using it to create a *new* business unit or division in a different industry, as SE did in the Opening Case when it used its low-cost manufacturing skills to enter the cell phone industry. Once again, the multi-business model is based on the premise that the set of distinctive competencies that are the source of a company's competitive advantage in one industry might be applied to create a differentiation- or cost-based competitive advantage for a new business unit in a different industry. For example, Canon used its distinctive competencies in precision mechanics, fine optics, and electronic imaging to produce laser jet printers, which, for Canon, was a new business in a new industry. Its competitive advantage in laser printers came from the fact that its competencies enabled it to produce high-quality (differentiated) printers that could be manufactured at a low cost.

The difference between leveraging competencies and transferring competencies is that in the case of leveraging competencies, an entirely *new* business unit is being created, whereas transferring competencies involves the sharing of competencies between two *existing* businesses. This difference is important because each is based on a different multibusiness model. Companies such as 3M, SE, and Canon that leverage competencies to establish new business units tend to be *technology-based* companies that use their R&D competencies to create new business units to take advantage of opportunities in diverse industries. In contrast, companies that transfer competencies are often the leading companies in one industry that enter new industries by acquiring established companies. They then transfer their strong set of competencies to the acquired companies to increase their competitive advantage and profitability, as Philip Morris did with Miller Brewing.

Many companies have based their diversification strategy on leveraging their competencies to create new business units in different industries. Microsoft leveraged its skills in software development and marketing to create two business units in new industries, its online network MSN and Xbox video game units. Microsoft's managers believed this diversification strategy was in the best interests of shareholders because the company's competencies would enable it to attain a competitive advantage in the online and video game industries. The results of this strategy have been mixed; in 2003 when Microsoft first broke its profits down by business unit, it turned out that the software business was generating almost all its profits, and most other business units were losing money. Its competitive situation has improved somewhat since its Xbox 360 has captured more market share from Sony, although the growing popularity of the Wii has not helped it. In its online business, it made a bid to buy Yahoo! in 2008 for $43 billion to strengthen MSN and especially to grow the popularity of its search engine because of increasing competition from Google, but it failed; the future profitability of its online businesses was in question in 2009.

Sharing Resources and Capabilities

A third way in which two or more business units that operate in different industries can increase a diversified company's profitability is when they way they share resources and capabilities results in economies of scope.[2] **Economies of scope** arise when one or more of a diversified company's business units are able to realize cost-saving or differentiation advantages because they can more effectively pool, share, and utilize expensive resources or capabilities, such as skilled people, equipment, manufacturing facilities, distribution channels, advertising campaigns, and R&D laboratories. If business units in different industries can share a common resource or function, they can collectively lower their cost structure.[3] For example, the costs of GE's consumer products advertising, sales, and service activities are spread over a wide range of products, such as light bulbs, appliances, air conditioning, furnaces, and so on, which reduces costs. There are two major sources of these cost reductions.

First, when companies can share resources or capabilities across business units, it lowers their cost structure compared to a company that operates in only one industry and has to bear the full costs of developing resources and capabilities. For example, P&G makes disposable diapers, toilet paper, and paper towels, which are all paper-based products that customers value for their ability to absorb fluids without disintegrating. Because these products need the same attribute—absorbency—P&G can share the R&D costs associated with developing and making even more

Figure 10.2 Sharing Resources at Proctor & Gamble

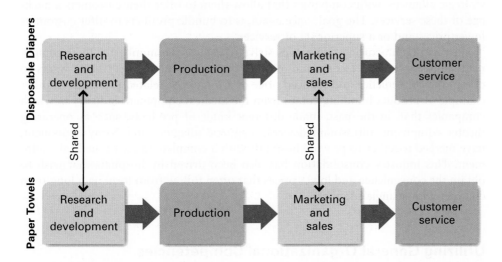

advanced absorbent paper-based products across the three distinct businesses (only two are shown in Figure 10.2). Similarly, because all these products are sold to retailers, P&G can use the same sales force to sell all their products (see Figure 10.2). In contrast, P&G competitors that make only one or two of these products cannot share these costs across industries, so their cost structure is higher. As a result, P&G has lower costs; it can use its marketing function to better differentiate its products, and it achieves a higher ROIC than companies that operate only in one or a few industries and are unable to obtain economies of scope from the ability to share resources across business units.

Once again, diversification to obtain economies of scope is possible only when there are *significant* commonalities between one or more of the value-chain functions in a company's different business units or divisions that result in increased profitability. In addition, managers need to be aware that the costs of coordination necessary to achieve economies of scope within a company sometimes may be *higher* that the value that can be created by such a strategy.[4] Consequently, diversification based on obtaining economies of scope should be pursued only when the sharing of competencies will result in a *significant* competitive advantage for one or more of a company's new or existing business units.

Using Product Bundling

In the search for new ways to differentiate their products, more and more companies are entering into industries that provide customers with new products that are connected or related to their existing products. This allows a company to expand and widen the range of products it produces so as to be able to satisfy customers' needs for a complete package of related products. This is currently happening in telecommunications in which customers are increasingly seeking package prices for wired phone service, wireless phone service, high-speed access to the Internet, VOIP phone service, television programming, online gaming, video on demand, or any combination of these services. To meet this need, large phone companies such as

AT&T and Verizon have been acquiring other companies that provide one or more of these services, while cable companies such as Comcast have acquired, or formed strategic alliances, with companies that allow them to offer their customers a package of these services. The goal, once again, is to bundle products to offer customers lower prices and/or a superior set of services.

Just as manufacturing companies strive to reduce the number of their component suppliers to reduce costs and increase quality, so the final customer wants to obtain the convenience and reduced price of a bundle of related products. Another example of product bundling comes from the medical equipment industry in which companies that, in the past, made different kinds of products, such as operating theater equipment, ultrasound devices, magnetic imaging, and X-ray equipment, have merged together to provide hospitals with a complete range of medical equipment. This industry consolidation has also been driven by hospitals that wish to obtain the convenience and lower prices that often follow from forming a long-term contract with a single supplier.

Utilizing General Organizational Competencies

General organizational competencies transcend individual functions or business units and are found at the top or corporate level of a multibusiness company. Typically, general competencies are the result of the skills of a company's top managers and functional experts. When these general competencies are present—and many times they are not—they help each business unit within a company perform at a higher level than it could if it operated as a separate or independent company—this increases the profitability of the *entire* corporation, such as with Samsung discussed in the opening case.[5] Three kinds of general organizational competencies help a company increase its performance and profitability: (1) entrepreneurial capabilities, (2) organizational design capabilities, and (3) strategic capabilities.

Entrepreneurial Capabilities   A company that generates significant excess cash flow can take advantage of it only if its managers are able to identify new opportunities and act on them to create a stream of new and improved products, both in its current industry and in new industries. Some companies seem to have a greater capability to stimulate their managers to act in entrepreneurial ways than others, for example, Apple, 3M, HP, and Samsung.[6]

These companies are able to promote entrepreneurship because they have an organizational culture that stimulates managers to act entrepreneurially. As a result, these companies are able to create profitable new business units more quickly than other companies; this allows them to take advantage of profitable opportunities for diversification. We discuss one of the strategies required to generate profitable new businesses later in this chapter: internal new venturing. For now, it is important to note that to promote entrepreneurship, a company must (1) encourage managers to take risks, (2) give them the time and resources to pursue novel ideas, (3) not punish managers when a new idea fails, and (4) make sure that its free cash flow is not wasted in pursuing too many risky new ventures that have a low probability of generating a profitable return on investment. Strategic managers face a significant challenge in achieving all four of these objectives. On the one hand, a company must encourage risk taking, and on the other hand, it must limit the number of risky ventures it engages in.

Companies that possess strong entrepreneurial capabilities achieve this balancing act. For example, 3M's goal of generating 40% of revenues from products introduced within the past four years focuses managers' attention on the need to develop new products and enter new businesses. 3M's long-standing commitment to help its customers solve problems also ensures that ideas for new businesses are customer focused. The company's celebration of employees who have created successful new businesses helps to reinforce the norm of entrepreneurship and risk taking. Similarly, there is a norm that failure should not be punished but viewed as a learning experience.

Capabilities in Organizational Design **Organizational design** is a company's ability to create a structure, culture, and control systems that motivate and coordinate employees to perform at a high level. Organizational design is a major factor that influences a company's entrepreneurial capabilities; it is also an important determinant of a company's ability to create the functional competencies that give it a competitive advantage. The way strategic managers make organizational design decisions such as how much autonomy to give to managers lower in the hierarchy, what kinds of norms and values should be developed to create an entrepreneurial culture, and even how to design its headquarters buildings to encourage the free flow of ideas, is an important determinant of a diversified company's ability to profit from its multibusiness model. Effective organizational structure and controls create incentives that encourage business unit (divisional) managers to maximize the efficiency and effectiveness of their units. Moreover, good organizational design helps prevent strategic managers from missing out on profitable new opportunities, as happens when employees become so concerned to protect their company's competitive position in *existing* industries that they lose sight of new or improved ways to do business and profitable opportunities to enter new industries.

The last two chapters of this book take an in-depth look at organizational design. To profit from pursuing the corporate-level strategy of diversification, a company must be able to continuously manage and change its structure and culture so as to motivate and coordinate its employees to work at a high level and develop the resources and capabilities on which its competitive advantage depends. The ever-present need to align a company's structure with its strategy is a complex, never-ending task, and only top managers with superior organizational design skills can do it.

Superior Strategic Management Capabilities For diversification to increase profitability, a company's top managers must have superior capabilities in strategic management. They must possess the intangible, hard-to-define governance skills that are required to manage different business units in a way that enables these units to perform better than they would if they were independent companies.[7] These governance skills are a rare and valuable capability. However, certain CEOs and top managers seem to have them; they have developed the aptitude of managing multiple businesses simultaneously and encourage the top managers of those business units to devise strategies to achieve superior performance. Examples of CEOs who possess superior strategic management capabilities include Jeffery Immelt at GE, Steve Ballmer at Microsoft, Steve Jobs at Apple, and Larry Ellison at Oracle—and, of course, the President of the United States, Barack Obama.

An especially important governance skill in a diversified company is the ability to diagnose the underlying source of the problems of a poorly performing business unit and then to understand how to proceed to solve those problems. This might involve recommending new strategies to the existing top managers of the unit or knowing when

Ethical Dilemma

Recently, many top managers have been convicted of illegally altering their company's financial statements or providing false information to hide the poor performance of their company from stockholders or simply for personal gain. You have been charged with the task of creating a control system for your company to ensure managers behave ethically and legally when reporting the performance of their business. To help develop the control system, you identify the five main ways managers use diversification to increase profitability—transferring and leveraging competences, sharing resources, product bundling, and the use of general managerial competencies. How might these five methods be associated with unethical behavior? Can you determine rules or procedures that could prevent managers from behaving in an unethical way?

to replace them with a new management team that is better able to fix the problems. Top managers who have such governance skills tend to be very good at probing business unit managers for information and helping them to think through strategic problems.

Related to this skill is the ability of the top managers of a diversified company to identify inefficient and poorly managed companies in other industries and then to acquire and restructure them to improve their performance—and thus the profitability of the total corporation. There are several ways to improve the performance of the acquired company. First, the top managers of the acquired company are replaced with a more aggressive top management team. Second, the new top management team sells off expensive assets, such as underperforming divisions, executive jets, and elaborate corporate headquarters; it also terminates managers and employees to reduce the cost structure. Third, the new management team works to devise new strategies to improve the performance of the operations of the acquired business and improve its efficiency, quality, innovativeness, and customer responsiveness.

Fourth, to motivate the new top management team and the other employees of the acquired company to work toward such goals, a company-wide pay-for-performance bonus system linked to profitability is introduced to reward employees at all levels for their hard work. Fifth, the acquiring company often establishes "stretch" goals for employees at all levels; these are challenging, hard-to-obtain goals that force employees at all levels to work to increase the company's efficiency and effectiveness. Finally, the new top management team clearly understands that if they fail to increase their division's performance and meet these stretch goals within some agreed-upon amount of time, they will be replaced. In sum, the system of rewards and sanctions corporate managers of the acquiring company establish provide the new top managers of the acquired unit with strong incentive to develop strategies to improve their unit's operating performance.

TWO TYPES OF DIVERSIFICATION

The last section discussed five principal ways in which companies can use diversification to transfer and implant their business models and strategies in other industries to increase their long-run profitability. The two corporate strategies of *related diversification* and *unrelated diversification* can be distinguished by how they attempt to realize these five profit-enhancing benefits of diversification.[8]

Related Diversification

Related diversification is a corporate-level strategy that is based on the goal of establishing a business unit (division) in a new industry that is *related* to a company's existing business units by some form of commonality or linkage between the value-chain functions of the existing and new business units. As you might expect, the goal of this strategy is to obtain the benefits from transferring competencies, leveraging competencies, sharing resources, and bundling products that are discussed above.

The multibusiness model of related diversification is based on taking advantage of strong technological, manufacturing, marketing, and sales commonalities between new and existing business units that can be successfully "tweaked" or modified to increase the competitive advantage of one or more business units. Figure 10.3 illustrates the commonalities or linkages possible among the different functions of three different business units or divisions. The greater the number of linkages that can be

....

Figure 10.3 Commonalities between the Value Chains of Three Business Units

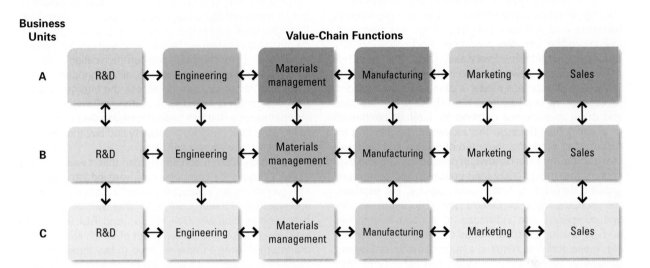

formed among business units, the greater the potential to realize the profit-enhancing benefits of the five reasons to diversify discussed previously.

One more advantage of related diversification is that it can also allow a company to use any general organizational competency it possesses to increase the overall performance of *all* its different industry divisions—such as the different divisions of the entire Samsung Corporation. For example, strategic managers may strive to create a structure and culture that encourages entrepreneurship across divisions as both Samsung and 3M have done; beyond these general competences, both companies have a set of distinctive competences that are shared among their different business units and which they continuously strive to improve. An example of a leading company that is increasingly pursuing related diversification is Cisco Systems, profiled in Strategy in Action 10.1.

10.1 STRATEGY IN ACTION

Cisco Systems Is Entering Many New Industries

Cisco Systems is famous for developing the Internet routers and switches on which the World Wide Web (WWW) is built. In 2009, Cisco still made most of its $10 billion yearly revenue from selling its Internet routers and switches to large companies, Internet service providers (ISPs), and the enormous data center storage companies that are emerging to satisfy the growing need for "cloud computing" or online data storage. However, the boom years of Internet building in the 1990s that allowed Cisco to make enormous profits are over; like all high-tech companies, Cisco was hit hard by the drop in demand for Internet hardware that followed the dot.com bust and by the recession that began in 2008. However, its CEO John Chambers, who has led the company from the beginning, has a reputation for acquiring high-tech companies when their stock price is low because of hard economic times and then using their competencies to spur its future growth. And, Cisco has billions in cash available to make whatever acquisitions Chambers decides will increase its future profitability.

(continued)

Realizing that the Internet router market by itself would not generate the huge profits necessary to drive up the company's ROIC, Chambers embarked on a major strategy of related diversification. From its core Internet hardware and software business, Cisco has been rapidly expanding into the consumer electronics industry to increase profitability. Every acquisition Chambers has made, however, is related to the Internet in some way. In fact, his multi-business model is based on acquiring companies that make products in the industries that facilitate and drive up customer demand for Internet bandwidth or usage. Why? Because this increases the demand for Cisco's core products: the Internet routers and switches that provide the extra bandwidth needed by ISPs and data centers that must satisfy their business' and customers' growing demand for fast Internet service. For example, the products made by Cisco's new acquisitions encourage companies and individuals to engage in activities such as sharing personal videos online or teleconferencing. These activities result in a huge demand for Internet bandwidth to increase the speed and capacity of their Internet service; online companies such as YouTube and Facebook, ISPs, major telecommunications companies such as AT&T and Sprint, and cable companies such as Comcast, are forced to spend billions of dollars to buy Cisco's routers to keep up with ever-increasing customer demand for fast Internet service.

While driving demand for the Internet is one part of its related diversification strategy, Cisco has been a pioneer in innovating new products from the beginning; it also seeks to transfer and leverage its R&D competencies across its new businesses and make them all work seamlessly together—resulting in economies of scope. For example, in 2003 to help customers get online more easily, Cisco bought home-networking equipment-maker Linksys for $500 million and implanted its technology in the company. Today, Linksys is the major supplier of home routers that customers use to create wireless home networks to give all family members instant access to the Web; this also drives up the need for bandwidth. The home routers share Cisco's Internet technology and work flawlessly with its routers and switches to make the Internet easier to access and use. In 2005, to increase TV viewers' ability to take advantage of the Internet to download TV shows and movies (and increase Internet usage), Chambers acquired Scientific Atlanta for $7 billion, which made the set-top boxes bought by subscription TV providers. Today, Cisco supplies all the set-top boxes to companies such as Comcast and Time Warner; of course, the boxes also work with its other Internet products. In addition, the boxes have the ability to provide both business and home users with video conferencing, which takes up enormous amounts of bandwidth.

In 2009, Cisco announced it would pay $590 million to purchase Pure Digital, the company that makes the colorful, pocket-sized flip video camcorders that allow people to quickly make and share their videos on the Web. Two million flips have been sold in the United States so far. Chambers claims this acquisition will help drive up demand for the next generation of entertainment and communication products, such as Wiis, iPhones, and laptops, all designed to make it easier and faster for users to access the Internet. Cisco's goal once again is to increase customer demand for fast Internet service that will force Internet-related companies to increase their bandwidth capacity and buy the networking giant's hardware and software.

In March 2009, Cisco announced that it was entering a new industry, the computer hardware industry, by internally venturing an advanced powerful computer server, code-named "Project California," that will bring it into direct competition with Dell, HP, Sun, and IBM. In 2009, to build any kind of data center, most of which are linked to the Internet, large companies have to buy three different kinds of products: computer servers linked into "racks" that combine their power, storage or memory banks, and the networking software and hardware that links them to the Internet. Different high-tech companies supply these three products; Cisco's goal is to provide all three as a unified package that can significantly reduce the server rack's complexity, power consumption, and cost. Each Cisco rack will contain seven servers powered by Intel's new powerful Nehalem chips, an integrated storage bank, and a new Cisco Internet networking switch, Nexus, which will allow the rack to deliver information that can be customized to the kind of communication technology and bandwidth requirements of any particular company. For example, many companies such as Google and IBM are competing to be the leader in online cloud computing, which allows customers to store their data in online datacenters. These datacenters require the use of thousands of racks of servers. In 2009, 50% of the eight million servers sold every year are based in Internet datacenters that use Cisco's routers. Cisco's new servers can therefore provide all the Internet hardware and software necessary to supply all the storage and bandwidth a company could ever need in a seamless way and, at a lower cost.

By 2009, Cisco's strategy of creating synergies and sharing and leveraging its competencies among all its Internet-related products has led it to enter 28 different industries, including smaller ventures into home digital music and public surveillance systems, all of which generate demand for bandwidth. Chambers announced that his goal was to come out of the 2009 recession with the products in place to make Cisco not just the global leader in communications technology but also in Internet-linked IT hardware for business and individual customers.

Source: http://www.cisco.com, 2009.

Unrelated Diversification

Unrelated diversification is a corporate-level strategy based on a multibusiness model whose goal is to increase profitability through the use of general organizational competencies to increase the performance of *all* the company's business units. Companies pursuing this strategy are often called *conglomerates*, business organizations that operate in many diverse industries. Companies pursuing a strategy of unrelated diversification have *no* intention of transferring or leveraging competencies between business units or sharing resources. The only goal of strategic managers is to use their company's general organizational competencies to strengthen the business models of each of its individual business units or divisions. If the strategic managers of conglomerates have the special skills needed to manage many companies in diverse industries, the strategy can result in superior performance and profitability often they do not have these skills, as is discussed later in the chapter. Some companies, such as United Technologies Corporation (UTC) discussed later in the chapter in Strategy in Action 10.2, have top managers who do seem to have these special skills.

THE LIMITS AND DISADVANTAGES OF DIVERSIFICATION

Many companies such as 3M, Samsung, UTC, and Cisco have achieved the benefits of pursuing either or both of the two diversification strategies just discussed, and they have managed to sustain their profitability over time. On the other hand, companies such as GM, Textron, and Phillips that pursued diversification failed miserably and became unprofitable. There are three principal reasons why a business model based on diversification may lead to a loss of competitive advantage: (1) changes in the industry or inside a company that occur over time, (2) diversification pursued for the wrong reasons, and (3) excessive diversification that results in increasing bureaucratic costs.

Changes in the Industry or Company

Diversification is a complex strategy. To pursue diversification, top managers must have the ability to recognize profitable opportunities to enter new industries and to implement the strategies necessary to make diversification profitable. Over time, a company's top management team often changes; sometimes its most able executives join other companies and become their CEOs, sometimes successful CEOs decide to retire or step down. When the managers who possess the hard-to-define skills leave, they often take their visions with them. A company's new leaders may lack the competency or commitment necessary to pursue diversification successfully over time; thus, the cost structure of the diversified company increases and eliminates any gains the strategy may have produced.

In addition, the environment often changes rapidly and unpredictably over time. When new technology blurs industry boundaries, it can destroy the source of a company's competitive advantage; for example, by 2009, it was clear that Apple's iPhone had become a direct competitor with Nintendo for playing games on small mobile devices. When such a major technological change occurs in a company's core business, the benefits it has previously achieved from transferring or leveraging distinctive competencies disappear. The company is now saddled with a collection of businesses that have all become poor performers in their respective industries because they are not based on the new technology—something that has happened to Sony. Thus, a major problem with diversification is that the future success of this strategy is hard to predict. For a company to profit from it over time, managers must be as willing to divest business units as they are to acquire them. Research suggests managers do not behave in this way, however.

Diversification for the Wrong Reasons

As we have discussed, when managers decide to pursue diversification, they must have a clear vision of how their entry into new industries will allow them to create new products that provide more value for customers and so increase their company's profitability. Over time, however, a diversification strategy may result in falling profitability for reasons noted earlier, but managers often refuse to recognize that their strategy is failing. Although they know they should divest unprofitable businesses, managers "make up" reasons why they should keep their collection of businesses together.

In the past, for example, one widely used (and false) justification for diversification was that the strategy would allow a company to obtain the benefits of risk pooling. The idea behind risk pooling is that a company can reduce the risk of its revenues and profits rising and falling sharply (something that sharply lowers its stock price) if it acquires and operates companies in several industries that have different business cycles. The business cycle is the tendency for the revenues and profits of companies in an industry to rise and fall over time because of "predictable" changes in customer demand. For example, even in a recession, people still need to eat; the profits earned by supermarket chains will be relatively stable, and sales at Walmart actually rise as shoppers attempt to get more value for their dollars. At the same time, a recession caused the demand for cars and luxury goods to plunge. Many CEOs argued by diversifying into industries that have different business cycles, the sales and revenues of some of their divisions would be rising while those in others would be falling, so the net result is a more stable stream of revenue and profits over time. An example of risk pooling occurred when U.S. Steel diversified into the oil and gas industry in an attempt to offset the adverse effects of cyclical downturns in the steel industry.

This argument ignores two important facts. First, stockholders can eliminate the risk inherent in holding an individual stock by diversifying their *own* portfolios, and they can do so at a much lower cost than a company can. Thus, attempts to pool risks through diversification represent an unproductive use of resources; instead, profits should be returned to shareholders in the form of increased dividends. Second, research suggests that corporate diversification is not an effective way to pool risks because the business cycles of different industries are *inherently difficult to predict*, so it is likely that a diversified company will find that an economic downturn affects *all* its industries simultaneously. If this happens, the company's profitability plunges.[9]

When a company's core business is in trouble, another mistaken justification for diversification is that entry into new industries will rescue it and lead to long-term growth and profitability. An example of a company that made this mistake is Kodak. In the 1980s, increased competition from low-cost Japanese competitors like Fuji, combined with the beginnings of the digital revolution, soon led its revenues and profits to plateau and then fall. Its managers should have done all they could to reduce its cost structure; instead they took its still huge free cash flow and spent tens of billions of dollars to enter new industries, such as health care, biotechnology, and computer hardware, in a desperate and mistaken attempt to find ways to increase profitability.

This was a disaster because every industry Kodak entered was populated by strong companies such as 3M, Canon, and Xerox. Also, Kodak's corporate managers lacked any general competencies to give their new business units a competitive advantage. Moreover, the more industries they entered, the greater the range of threats they encountered and the more time they had to spend dealing with these threats. As a result, they could spend much less time improving the performance of their core film business that continued to decline.

In reality, Kodak's diversification was just for growth itself, but *growth does not create value for stockholders*; growth is just the byproduct, not the objective, of a diversification strategy. However, in desperation, companies diversify for reasons of growth alone rather than to gain any well-thought-out strategic advantage.[10] In fact, a large number of academic studies suggest that *extensive* diversification tends to reduce rather than improve company profitability.[11] Many studies conclude that the corporate diversification strategies pursued by many companies can dissipate value instead of creating it.[12]

The Bureaucratic Costs of Diversification

A major reason why diversification often fails to boost profitability is that very often the *bureaucratic costs* of diversification exceed the benefits created by the strategy (that is, the increased profit that results when a company makes and sells a wider range of differentiated products and/or lower its cost structure). As we mention in the previous chapter, **bureaucratic costs** are the costs associated with solving the transaction difficulties that arise between a company's business units, and between business units and corporate headquarters, as the company attempts to obtain the benefits from transferring, sharing, and leveraging competencies. They also include the costs associated with using general organizational competencies to solve managerial and functional inefficiencies. The level of bureaucratic costs in a diversified organization is a function of two factors: (1) the number of business units in a company's portfolio and (2) the degree to which coordination is required between these different business units to realize the advantages of diversification.

Number of Businesses The greater the number of business units in a company's portfolio, the more difficult it is for corporate managers to remain informed about the complexities of each business. Managers simply do not have the time to assess the business model of each unit. This problem began to occur at GE in the 1970s when its growth-hungry CEO Reg Jones acquired many new businesses. As Jones commented,

> I tried to review each plan [of each business unit] in great detail. This effort took untold hours and placed a tremendous burden on the corporate executive office. After a while I began to realize that no matter how hard we would work, we could not achieve the necessary in-depth understanding of the 40-odd business unit plans.[13]

The inability of top managers in extensively diversified companies to maintain control over their multibusiness model over time often leads them to base important resource allocation decisions on only the most superficial analysis of each business unit's competitive position. For example, a promising business unit may be starved of investment funds, while other business units receive far more cash than they can profitably reinvest in their operations. Furthermore, because they are distant from the day-to-day operations of the business units, corporate managers may find that business unit managers try to hide information on poor performance to save their own jobs. For example, business unit managers might blame poor performance on difficult competitive conditions, even when it is the result of their inability to craft a successful business model. As such organizational problems increase, top managers have to spend an enormous amount of time and effort to solve them. This increases bureaucratic costs and cancels out the profit-enhancing advantages of pursuing diversification, such as those obtained from sharing or leveraging competencies.

Coordination among Businesses   The amount of coordination required to realize value from a diversification strategy based on transferring, sharing, or leveraging competencies is a major source of bureaucratic costs. The bureaucratic mechanisms needed to oversee and manage this coordination and handoffs between units, such as cross-business-unit teams and management committees, are a major source of these costs. A second source of bureaucratic costs arises because of the enormous amount of managerial time and effort required to accurately measure the performance and unique profit contribution of a business unit that is transferring or sharing resources with another. Consider a company that has two business units, one making household products (such as liquid soap and laundry detergent) and another making packaged food products. The products of both units are sold through supermarkets. To lower the cost structure, the parent company decides to pool the marketing and sales functions of each business unit, using an organizational structure similar to that illustrated in Figure 10.4. The company is organized into three divisions: a household products division, a food products division, and a marketing division.

Figure 10.4   Coordination among Related Business Units

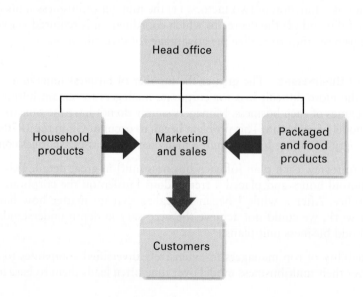

Although such an arrangement may significantly lower operating costs, it can also give rise to substantial control problems and hence bureaucratic costs. For example, if the performance of the household products business begins to slip, identifying who is to be held accountable—managers in the household products division or managers in the marketing division—may prove difficult. Indeed, each may blame the other for poor performance. Although these kinds of problems can be resolved if corporate management performs an in-depth audit of both divisions, the bureaucratic costs (managers' time and effort) involved in doing so may once again cancel out any value achieved from diversification.

In sum, while diversification can be a highly profitable strategy to pursue, it is also the most complex and difficult strategy to manage because it is based on a complex multibusiness model. Even when a company has pursued this strategy successfully in the past, changing conditions both in the industry environment and inside a company may quickly reduce the profit-creating advantages of pursuing this strategy. For example, such changes may result in one or more business units losing their competitive advantage, as happened to Sony. Or, changes may cause the bureaucratic costs associated with pursuing diversification to rise sharply and cancel out its advantages. Thus, the existence of bureaucratic costs places a limit on the amount of diversification that a company can profitably pursue. It makes sense for a company to diversify only when the profit-enhancing advantages of this strategy *exceed* the bureaucratic costs of managing the increasing number of business units required when a company expands and enters new industries.

CHOOSING A STRATEGY

Related versus Unrelated Diversification

Because related diversification involves more sharing of competencies, one might think it can boost profitability in more ways than unrelated diversification and so is the better diversification strategy. However, some companies, such as UTC, can create as much or more value from pursuing unrelated diversification, so that strategy must also have some substantial benefits. An unrelated company does *not* have to achieve coordination between business units; it has to cope only with the bureaucratic costs that arise from the number of businesses in its portfolio. In contrast, a related company has to achieve coordination *among* business units if it is to realize the gains that come from utilizing its distinctive competencies. Consequently, it has to cope with the bureaucratic costs that arise *both* from the number of business units in its portfolio *and* from coordination among business units. Thus, although it is true that related diversified companies can create value and profit in more ways than unrelated companies, they also have to bear higher bureaucratic costs to do so. These higher costs may cancel out the higher benefits, making the strategy no more profitable than one of unrelated diversification.

How then does a company choose between these strategies? The choice depends on a comparison of the benefits of each strategy against the bureaucratic costs of pursuing it. It pays a company to pursue related diversification when (1) the company's competencies can be applied across a greater number of industries, and (2) the company has superior strategic capabilities that allow it to keep bureaucratic costs under close control—perhaps by encouraging entrepreneurship or by developing a value-creating organizational culture.

Using the same logic, it pays a company to pursue unrelated diversification when (1) each business unit's functional competencies have few useful applications across industries, but the company's top managers are skilled at raising the profitability of poorly run businesses; and (2) the company's managers use their superior strategic management competencies to improve the competitive advantage of their business units and keep bureaucratic costs under control. Some well-managed companies, such as UTC, discussed in Strategy in Action 10.2, have managers who can successfully pursue unrelated diversification and reap its rewards.

10.2 STRATEGY IN ACTION

United Technologies Has an "ACE" in Its Pocket

United Technologies Corporation (UTC), based in Hartford, Connecticut, is a *conglomerate*, a company that owns a wide variety of other companies that operate separately in many different businesses and industries. Some of the companies in UTC's portfolio are better known than UTC itself, such as Sikorsky Aircraft Corporation; Pratt & Whitney, the aircraft engine and component maker; Otis Elevator Company; Carrier Air Conditioning; and Chubb, the security and lock maker that UTC acquired in 2003. Today, investors frown on companies like UTC that own and operate companies in widely different industries. There is a growing perception that managers can better manage a company's business model when the company operates as an independent or stand-alone entity. How can UTC justify holding all these companies together in a conglomerate? Why would this lead to a greater increase in total profitability than if they operated as independent companies? In the last decade, the boards of directors and CEOs of many conglomerates, such as Greyhound-Dial, ITT Industries, and Textron, have realized that by holding diverse companies together they were reducing, not increasing, the profitability of their companies. As a result, many conglomerates have been broken up, and their companies spun off to allow them to operate as separate, independent entities.

UTC's CEO George David claims that he has created a unique and sophisticated multibusiness model that adds value across UTC's diverse businesses. David joined Otis Elevator as an assistant to its CEO in 1975, but within one year, Otis was acquired by UTC. The 1970s was a decade when a "bigger is better" mindset ruled corporate America, and mergers and acquisitions of whatever kind were seen as the best way to grow profits. UTC sent David to manage its South American operations and later gave him responsibility for its Japanese operations.

Otis had formed an alliance with Matsushita to develop an elevator for the Japanese market, and the resulting "Elevonic 401," after being installed widely in Japanese buildings, proved to be a disaster. It broke down much more often than elevators made by other Japanese companies, and customers were concerned about its reliability and safety.

Matsushita was extremely embarrassed about the elevator's failure and assigned one of its leading total quality management (TQM) experts, Yuzuru Ito, to head a team of Otis engineers to find out why it performed so poorly. Under Ito's direction, all the employees—managers, designers, and production workers—who had produced the elevator analyzed why the elevators were malfunctioning. This intensive study led to a total redesign of the elevator, and when their new and improved elevator was launched worldwide, it met with great success. Otis's share of the global elevator market increased dramatically, and one result was that David was named president of UTC in 1992. He was given the responsibility to cut costs across the entire corporation, including its important Pratt & Whitney division, and his success in reducing UTC's cost structure and increasing its ROIC led to his appointment as CEO in 1994.

Now responsible for all of UTC's diverse companies, David decided that the best way to increase UTC's profitability, which had been declining, was to find ways to improve efficiency and quality in *all* its constituent companies. He convinced Ito to move to Hartford and take responsibility for championing the kinds of improvements that had by now transformed the Otis division, and Ito began to develop UTC's TQM system, which is known as "Achieving Competitive Excellence," or ACE.

ACE is a set of tasks and procedures that are used by employees from the shop floor to top managers to analyze all aspects of the way a product is made. The goal is to find ways to improve *quality and reliability*, to *lower the costs* of making a product, and especially to find ways to make the next generation of a particular product perform better—in other words, to encourage *technological innovation*. David makes every employee in every function and at every level personally responsible for achieving the incremental, step-by-step gains that result in state-of-the-art innovative and efficient products that allow a company to dominate its industry.

David calls these techniques "process disciplines," and he has used them to increase the performance of all UTC companies. Through these techniques, he has created the extra value for UTC that justifies it owning and operating such a diverse set of businesses. David's success can be seen in the performance that his company has achieved in the decade since he took control: he has quadrupled UTC's earnings per share, and its sales and profits have soared. UTC has been in the top three performers of the companies that make up the Dow Jones industrial average for most

the 2000s, and the company has consistently outperformed GE, another huge conglomerate, in its return to investors.

David and his managers believe that the gains that can be achieved from UTC's process disciplines are never-ending because its own R&D—in which it invests more than $2.5 billion a year—is constantly producing product innovations that can help all its businesses. Indeed, recognizing that its skills in creating process improvements are specific to manufacturing companies, UTC's strategy is to only acquire companies that make products that can benefit from the use of its ACE program—hence its Chubb acquisition. At the same time, David invests only in companies that have the potential to remain leading companies in their industries and so can charge above-average prices. His acquisitions strengthen the competencies of UTC's existing businesses. For example, he acquired a company called Sundstrand a leading aerospace and industrial systems company, and combined it with UTC's Hamilton aerospace division to create Hamilton Sundstrand which is now a major supplier to Boeing and makes products that command premium prices.

Source: http://www.utc.com, 2009.

The Web of Corporate-Level Strategy

Finally, it is important to note that while some companies may choose to pursue a strategy of related or unrelated diversification, there is nothing that stops them from pursuing both strategies at the same time—*as well as all the other corporate-level strategies we have discussed*. The purpose of corporate-level strategy is to increase long-term profitability. A company should pursue any and all strategies as long as strategic managers have weighed the advantages and disadvantages of those strategies and arrived at a multibusiness model that justifies them. The opening case discusses how Samsung pursues many different corporate-level strategies simultaneously; Figure 10.5 illustrates how Sony uses a web of corporate strategies to compete in many industries.

First, Sony's core business is its electronic consumer products business, which is well known for its innovative products that have made it one of the best-known brand names in the world. To protect the quality of its electronic products, Sony manufactures a high percentage of the component parts for its televisions, DVD players, and so on, and has pursued a strategy of backward vertical integration. Sony also engages in forward vertical integration: after acquiring Columbia Pictures and MGM in 2004, it now operates in the movie industry and has opened a chain of Sony stores in shopping malls. Sony also shared and leveraged its distinctive competencies by developing its own business units that operate in the computer and smartphone industries, a strategy of related diversification. Finally, when it decided to enter the home video game industry and develop its PlayStation to compete with Nintendo, it was pursuing a strategy of unrelated diversification. Today, this division contributes more to Sony's total profits than its core electronics business.

Figure 10.5   Sony's Web of Corporate-Level Strategy

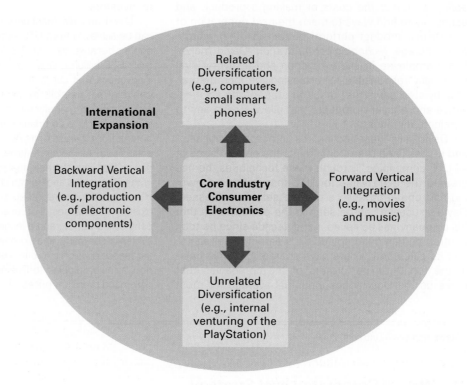

Although Sony has had enormous success pursuing these strategies in the past, in the 2000s its profitability has fallen dramatically. Analysts claim its multibusiness model led its managers to diversify into too many industries, in each of which the focus was on innovating high-quality product. This is very expensive, and, as a result, its cost structure increased so much that it swallowed up all the profits its businesses were generating. They also claim that its strategy of giving each business unit great autonomy has led each unit to pursue its own goals at the expense of the company's multibusiness model. Sony's escalating bureaucratic costs drained its profitability. Also, because its different divisions did not share their knowledge and expertise, it allowed competitors like Samsung to catch up and overtake it in areas such as cell phones and flat-screen LCDs. Sony has been responding to these problems. It has taken major steps to reduce bureaucratic costs, improve divisional cooperation to speed innovation, and lower its cost structure, including exiting industries such as PDAs. The next few years will show whether these changes will help the company better manage its web of corporate strategies to improve its profitability.

ENTERING NEW INDUSTRIES: INTERNAL NEW VENTURES

We have discussed all the corporate-level strategies managers use to formulate the multibusiness model. From this point, we can examine the three main methods managers employ to enter new industries: internal new ventures, acquisitions, and joint ventures. In this section, we consider the pros and cons of using internal new ventures. In the following sections, we look at acquisitions and joint ventures.

The Attractions of Internal New Venturing

Internal new venturing is typically used to implement corporate-level strategies when a company possesses one or more distinctive competencies in its core business model that can be leveraged or recombined to enter a new industry. **Internal new venturing** is the process of transferring resources to and creating a new business unit or division in a new industry. Internal venturing is used most by companies whose business model is based on using their technology to innovate new kinds of products and enter related markets or industries. Thus, technology-based companies that pursue related diversification, like DuPont, which has created new markets with products such as cellophane, nylon, Freon, and Teflon, are most likely to use internal new venturing. 3M has a near-legendary knack for creating new or improved products from internally generated ideas and then establishing new business units to create the business model that enables it to dominate a new market. Similarly, HP entered into the computer and printer industries by using internal new venturing.

A company may also use internal venturing to enter a newly emerging or embryonic industry—one in which no company has yet developed the competencies or business model that gives it a dominant position in that industry. This was Monsanto's situation in 1979 when it contemplated entering the biotechnology field to produce herbicides and pest-resistant crop seeds. The biotechnology field was young at that time, and there were no incumbent companies focused on applying biotechnology to agricultural products. Accordingly, Monsanto internally ventured a new division to develop the required competencies necessary to enter and establish a strong competitive position in this newly emerging industry.

Pitfalls of New Ventures

Despite the popularity of internal new venturing, there is a high risk of failure. Research suggests that somewhere between 33% and 60% of all new products that reach the marketplace do not generate an adequate economic return,[14] and most of these products were the result of internal new ventures. Three reasons are often put forward to explain the relatively high failure rate of internal new ventures: (1) market entry on too small a scale, (2) poor commercialization of the new-venture product, and (3) poor corporate management of the new venture division.[15]

Scale of Entry Research suggests that large-scale entry into a new industry is often a critical precondition for the success of a new venture. In the short run, this means that a substantial capital investment must be made to support large-scale entry; thus, there is a risk of major losses if the new venture fails. But, in the long run, which can be as long as five to twelve years depending on the industry, such a large investment results in far greater returns than if a company chooses to enter on a small scale to limit its investment to reduce potential losses.[16] Large-scale entrants can more rapidly realize scale economies, build brand loyalty, and gain access to distribution channels in the new industry, all of which increase the probability of a new venture's success. In contrast, small-scale entrants may find themselves handicapped by high costs due to a lack of scale economies and a lack of market presence limits their ability to build brand loyalty and gain access to distribution channels. These scale effects are particularly

Figure 10.6   Scale of Entry and Profitability

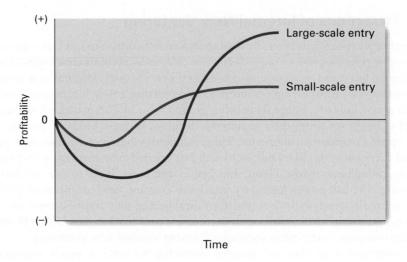

significant when a company is entering an *established* industry in which incumbent companies possess scale economies, brand loyalty, and access to distribution channels. In that case, the new entrant has to make a major investment to succeed.

Figure 10.6 plots the relationship between scale of entry and profitability over time for successful small-scale and large-scale ventures. The figure shows that successful small-scale entry is associated with lower initial losses, but in the long run, large-scale entry generates greater returns. However, because of the high costs and risks associated with large-scale entry, many companies make the mistake of choosing a small-scale entry strategy, which often means they fail to build the market share necessary for long-term success.

Commercialization   Many internal new ventures are driven by the opportunity to use a new or advanced technology to make better products for customers and outperform competitors. But, to be commercially successful, the products under development must be tailored to meet the needs of customers. Many internal new ventures fail when a company ignores the needs of customers in a market. Its managers become so focused on the technological possibilities of a new product that customer requirements are forgotten.[17] Thus, a new venture may fail because it is marketing a product based on a technology for which there is no demand, or the company fails to position or differentiate the product correctly in the market at attract customers.

For example, consider the desktop PC marketed by NeXT, the company started by the founder of Apple, Steve Jobs. The NeXT system failed to gain market share because the PC incorporated an array of expensive technologies that consumers simply did not want, such as optical disk drives and hi-fidelity sound. The optical disk drives, in particular, turned off customers because they made it tough to switch work from PC with floppy drives to NeXT machines with optical drives. In other words, NeXT failed because its founder was so dazzled by leading-edge technology that he ignored customer needs. However, Jobs redeemed himself when he successfully commercialized Apple's iPod, which dominates the MP3 player market, and iPhone, which has set the standard in the smartphone market.

Poor Implementation   Managing the new-venture process, and controlling the new venture division, creates many difficult managerial and organizational problems.[18] For example, one common mistake some companies make to try to increase their chances of making successful products is to establish *too many* different internal new-venture divisions at the same time. Managers attempt to spread the risks of failure by having many divisions, but this places enormous demands on a company's cash flow. Sometimes, companies are forced to reduce the funding each division receives to keep the whole company profitable, and this can result in the most promising ventures being starved of the cash they need to succeed.[19] Another common mistake is when corporate managers fail to do the extensive advanced planning necessary to ensure that the new venture's business model is sound and contains all the elements that will be needed later if it is to succeed. Sometimes corporate managers leave this process to the scientists and engineers championing the new technology. Focused on the new technology, they may innovate new products that have little strategic or commercial value. Corporate managers and scientists must work together to clarify how and why a new venture will lead to a product that has a competitive advantage, and jointly establish strategic objectives and a timetable to manage the venture until the product reaches the market.

The failure to anticipate the time and costs involved in the new-venture process constitutes a further mistake. Many companies have unrealistic expectations regarding the time frame and expect profits to flow in quickly. Research suggests that some companies operate with a philosophy of killing new businesses if they do not turn a profit by the end of the third year, which is clearly unrealistic given that it can take five years or more before a new venture generates substantial profits.

Guidelines for Successful Internal New Venturing

To avoid these pitfalls, a company should adopt a well-thought-out, structured approach to manage internal new venturing. New venturing is based on R&D. It begins with the *exploratory research* necessary to advance basic science and technology (the "R" in R&D), and *development research* to identify, develop, and perfect the commercial applications of a new technology (the "D" in R&D). Companies with strong track records of success at internal new venturing excel at both kinds of R&D: they help to advance basic science and discover important commercial applications for it.[20] To advance basic science, it is important for companies to have strong links with universities where much of the scientific knowledge that underlies new technologies is discovered. It is also important to make sure that research funds are being controlled by scientists who understand the importance of both "R" and "D" research. If the "D" is lacking, no matter how well a company does basic research, it will probably generate few successful commercial ventures. Companies can take a number of steps to ensure that good science ends up with good, commercially viable products.

First, many companies must place the funding for research in the hands of business unit managers who have the skill or know-how to narrow down and then select the best set of research projects—those that have the best chance of a significant commercial payoff. Second, to make effective use of its R&D competency, a company's top managers must work with its R&D scientists to continually develop and improve the business model and strategies that guide their efforts and make sure *all* its scientists and engineers understand what they have to do to make it succeed.[21]

Third, a company must also foster close links between R&D and marketing to increase the probability that a new product will be a commercial success in the future. When marketing works to identify the most important customer requirements for a new product and then communicates these requirements to scientists, it ensures that research projects meet the needs of their intended customers. Fourth, a company should also foster close links between R&D and manufacturing to ensure that it has the ability to make a proposed new product in a cost-effective way. Many companies successfully integrate the activities of the different functions by creating cross-functional project teams to oversee the development of new products from their inception to market introduction. This approach can significantly reduce the time it takes to bring a new product to market. For example, while R&D is working on design, manufacturing is setting up facilities, and marketing is developing a campaign to show customers how much the new product will benefit them.

Finally, because large-scale entry often leads to greater long-term profits, a company can promote the success of internal new venturing by "thinking big." Well in advance of a product's introduction, a company should construct efficient-scale manufacturing facilities and give marketing a large budget to develop a future campaign that will build market presence and brand loyalty quickly. And, corporate managers should not panic when customers are slow to adopt the new product. They need to accept the fact there will be initial losses and recognize that as long as market share is expanding, the product will eventually succeed.

ENTERING NEW INDUSTRIES: ACQUISITIONS

In Chapter 9, we explained that acquisitions are the main vehicle that companies use to implement a horizontal integration strategy. They are also a principal way companies enter new industries to pursue vertical integration and diversification, so it is necessary to understand both the benefits and risks associated with using acquisitions to implement a corporate-level strategy.

The Attraction of Acquisitions

In general, acquisitions are used to pursue vertical integration or diversification when a company lacks the distinctive competencies necessary to compete in a new industry, so it uses its financial resources to purchase an established company that has those competencies. A company is particularly likely to use acquisitions when it needs to move fast to establish a presence in an industry, commonly an embryonic or growth industry. Entering a new industry through internal venturing is a relatively slow process; acquisition is a much quicker way for a company to establish a significant market presence. A company can purchase a leading company with a strong competitive position in months, rather than waiting years to build a market leadership position by engaging in internal venturing. Thus, when speed is particularly, important, acquisition is the favored entry mode. Intel, for example, used acquisitions to build its communications chip business because it sensed that the market was developing very quickly, and it would take too long to develop the required competencies.

In addition, acquisitions are often perceived as being less risky than internal new ventures because they involve less commercial uncertainty. Because of the risks of failure associated with internal new venturing, it is difficult to predict its future success and profitability. By contrast, when a company makes an acquisition, it acquires a company with an already established reputation, and it knows exactly how big is that company's market share and profitability.

Finally, acquisitions are an attractive way to enter an industry that is protected by high barriers to entry. Recall from Chapter 2 that barriers to entry arise from factors such as product differentiation that leads to brand loyalty and high market share that leads to economies of scale. When entry barriers are high, it may be very difficult for a company to enter an industry through internal new venturing because it will have to construct large-scale manufacturing facilities and invest in a massive advertising campaign to establish brand loyalty—difficult goals that require huge capital expenditures. In contrast, if a company acquires a company already established in the industry, possibly the market leader, it can circumvent most entry barriers because that company has already achieved economies of scale and obtained brand loyalty. In general, the higher the barriers to entry, the more likely it is that acquisitions will be method used to enter the industry.

Acquisition Pitfalls

For these reasons, acquisitions have long been the most common method that companies use to pursue diversification. However, as we mentioned earlier, research suggests that many acquisitions fail to increase the profitability of the acquiring company and may result in losses. For example, a study of 700 large acquisitions found that although 30% of these resulted in higher profits, 31% led to losses, and the remainder had little impact.[22] Research suggests that many acquisitions fail to realize their anticipated benefits.[23] One study of the post-acquisition performance of acquired companies found that the profitability and market share of an acquired company often declines afterward, suggesting that many acquisitions destroy rather than create value.[24]

Acquisitions may fail to raise the performance of the acquiring companies for four reasons: (1) companies frequently experience management problems when they attempt to integrate a different company's organizational structure and culture into their own; (2) companies often overestimate the potential economic benefits from an acquisition; (3) acquisitions tend to be so expensive that they do not increase future profitability; and (4) companies are often negligent in screening their acquisition targets and fail to recognize important problems with their business models.

Integrating the Acquired Company Once an acquisition has been made, the acquiring company has to integrate the acquired company and combine it with its own organizational structure and culture. Integration involves the adoption of common management and financial control systems, the joining together of operations from the acquired and the acquiring company, the establishment of bureaucratic mechanisms to share information and personnel, and the need to create a common culture. Experience has shown that many problems can occur as companies attempt to integrate their activities.

After an acquisition, many acquired companies experience high management turnover because their employees do not like the acquiring company's way of operating—its structure and culture.[25] Research suggests that the loss of management talent and expertise, to say nothing of the damage from constant tension between the businesses, can materially harm the performance of the acquired unit.[26] Moreover, companies often have to take on an enormous amount of debt to fund acquisition and they frequently are unable to pay it once these management problems and sometimes the weaknesses of the acquired company's business model become clear.

Overestimating Economic Benefits Even when companies find it easy to integrate their activities, they often overestimate how much future profitability can be increased by combining the different businesses. Managers often overestimate the competitive advantages that will derive from the acquisition and so pay more for the acquired company than it is worth. One reason is that top managers typically overestimate their own personal general competencies to create valuable new products from an acquisition. Why? The very fact that they have risen to the top of a company gives them an exaggerated sense of their own capabilities and importance that distorts their strategic decision making.[27] Coca-Cola's acquisition of a number of medium-sized wine-making companies illustrates this. Reasoning that a beverage is a beverage, Coca-Cola's then-CEO decided he would be able to mobilize his company's talented marketing managers to develop the strategies needed to dominate the United States wine industry. After buying three wine companies and enduring seven years of marginal profits because of failed marketing campaigns, he subsequently decided that wine and soft drinks are very different products; in particular they have different kinds of appeal, pricing systems, and distribution networks. So, he eventually sold the wine operations to Joseph E. Seagram and took a substantial loss.[28]

The Expense of Acquisitions Perhaps the most important reason for the failure of acquisitions is that acquiring a company whose stock is publicly traded tends to be very expensive—and the expense of the acquisition can more than wipe out the value of the stream of future profits that are expected from the acquisition. One reason is that the top managers of a company that is "targeted" for acquisition are likely to resist any takeover attempt unless the acquiring company agrees to pay a substantial premium above its current market value. These premiums are often 100% above the usual value of a company's stock. Similarly, the stockholders of the target company are unlikely to sell their stocks unless they are paid major premiums over its market value prior to a takeover bid. To pay such high premiums, the acquiring company must be certain it can use its acquisition to generate the stream of future profits that justifies the high price of the target company. This is frequently a difficult thing to do, given how fast the industry environment can change and the other problems discussed earlier, such as integrating the acquired company. This is a major reason why acquisitions are frequently unprofitable for the acquiring company.

The reason why the acquiring company has to pay such a high premium is that the stock price of the acquisition target increases enormously during the acquisition process as investors speculate on the final price the acquiring company will pay to capture it. In the case of a contested bidding contest, where two or more companies simultaneously bid to acquire the target company, its stock price may rocket. Also, when many acquisitions are occurring in a particular industry, investors speculate that the value of the remaining industry companies that have *not* been acquired has increased and that a bid for these companies will be made at some future point. This also drives up their stock price and increases the cost of making acquisitions. This happened in the telecommunications sector when, to make sure they could meet the needs of customers who were demanding leading-edge equipment, many large companies went on acquisition "binges." Nortel, Corning, and Alcatel-Lucent engaged in a race to buy up smaller, innovative companies developing new telecommunications equipment. The result was that the stock prices for these companies were bid up by investors, and they were bought at a hugely inflated price. When the telecommunications boom turned to bust, the acquiring companies found that they had vastly overpaid for their acquisitions and had to take enormous accounting write-downs; the stock price of Nortel and Alcatel-Lucent plunged, and in 2009 they are fighting to survive.

Inadequate Preacquisition Screening As the problems of these companies suggest, top managers often do a poor job of preacquisition screening, that is, evaluating how much a potential acquisition may increase future profitability. Researchers have discovered that one important reason for the failure of an acquisition is that managers make the decision to acquire other companies without thoroughly analyzing potential benefits and costs.[29] In many cases, after an acquisition has been completed, many acquiring companies discover that instead of buying a well-managed business with a strong business model, they have bought a troubled organization. Obviously, the managers of the target company may manipulate company information or the balance sheet to make their financial condition look much better than it is. The acquiring company has to watch out and do extensive research. In 2009, IBM was in negotiations to purchase chip maker Sun Microsystems. After spending one week examining its books, IBM reduced its offer price by 10% after its negotiators had examined Sun's books and found its customer base was not as solid as they had expected.

Guidelines for Successful Acquisition

To avoid these pitfalls and make successful acquisitions, companies need to follow an approach to targeting and evaluating potential acquisitions that is based on four main steps: (1) target identification and preacquisition screening, (2) bidding strategy, (3) integration, and (4) learning from experience.[30]

Identification and Screening Thorough preacquisition screening increases a company's knowledge about a potential takeover target and lessens the risk of purchasing a problem company—one with a weak business model. It also leads to a more realistic assessment of the problems involved in executing a particular acquisition so that a company can plan how to integrate the new business and blend organizational structures and cultures. The screening process should begin with a detailed assessment of the strategic rationale for making the acquisition, an identification of the kind of company that would make an ideal acquisition candidate, and an extensive analysis of the strengths and weaknesses of its business model by comparing it to other possible acquisition targets.

Indeed, an acquiring company should select a set of top potential acquisition targets and evaluate each company using a set of criteria that focus on revealing (1) its financial position, (2) its distinctive competencies and competitive advantage, (3) changing industry boundaries, (4) its management capabilities, and (5) its corporate culture. Such an evaluation helps the acquiring company perform a detailed SWOT analysis that identifies the best target, for example, by measuring the potential economies of scale and scope that can be achieved between the acquiring company and each target company. This analysis also helps reveal the potential integration problems that might exist when it is necessary to integrate the corporate cultures of the acquiring and acquired companies. For example, Microsoft and SAP, the world's leading provider of enterprise resource planning software, sat down together to discuss a possible acquisition by Microsoft. Both companies decided that even though there was a strong strategic rationale for a merger—together they could dominate the software computing market that satisfies the need of large global companies—the problems of creating an organizational structure that could successfully integrate their hundreds of thousands of employees throughout the world, and blend two very different cultures, were insurmountable.

Once a company has reduced the list of potential acquisition candidates to the most favored one or two, it needs to contact expert third parties, such as investment bankers like Goldman Sachs and Merrill Lynch. These companies' business models are based on providing valuable insights about the attractiveness of a potential acquisition, current industry competitive conditions, and handling the many other issues surrounding an acquisition, such as how to select the optimal bidding strategy for acquiring the target company's stock to keep the purchase price as low as possible.

Bidding Strategy   The objective of the bidding strategy is to reduce the price that a company must pay for the target company. The most effective way a company can acquire another is to make a friendly takeover bid, which means the two companies work out an amicable way to merge the two companies that satisfies the needs of each company's stockholders and top managers. A friendly takeover prevents speculators from bidding up stock prices. By contrast, in a hostile bid, such as the ones between Oracle and PeopleSoft, and between Microsoft and Yahoo!, the price of the target company often gets bid up by speculators who expect that the offer price will be raised by the acquirer or by another company that might come in with a higher counteroffer.

Another essential element of a good bidding strategy is timing. For example, Hanson PLC, one of the most successful companies to pursue unrelated diversification, searched for essentially sound companies suffering from short-term problems because of the business cycle or because its performance was being seriously impacted by one underperforming division. Such companies are often undervalued by the stock market, so they can be acquired without paying a high stock premium. With good timing, a company can make a bargain purchase.

Integration   Despite good screening and bidding, an acquisition will fail unless the acquiring company possesses the essential organizational design skills needed to integrate the acquired company into its operations and quickly develop a viable multibusiness model. Integration should center on the source of the potential strategic advantages of the acquisition, for instance, opportunities to share marketing, manufacturing, R&D, financial, or management resources. Integration should also involve steps to eliminate any duplication of facilities or functions. In addition, any unwanted business units of the acquired company should be divested.

Learning from Experience   Research suggests companies that acquire many companies over time become expert in this process and so can generate significant value from their experience of the acquisition process.[31] Their past experience enables them to develop a "playbook," a clever plan that they can follow to execute an acquisition most efficiently and effectively. Tyco International, profiled in the Closing Case, did not make hostile acquisitions; it audited the accounts of the target company in detail, acquired companies to help it achieve a critical mass in an industry, moved quickly to realize cost savings after an acquisition, promoted managers one or two layers down to lead the newly acquired entity, and introducing profit-based incentive pay systems in the acquired unit.[32]

ENTERING NEW INDUSTRIES: JOINT VENTURES

Joint ventures are most commonly used to enter an embryonic or growth industry. Suppose a company is contemplating creating a new venture division in an embryonic industry, such a move involves substantial risks and costs because the company must make the huge investment necessary to develop the set of value-chain activities required to make and sell products in the new industry. On the other hand, an acquisition can be a dangerous proposition because there is rarely an established leading company in an emerging industry; even if there is it will be extremely expensive to purchase.

In this situation, a joint venture frequently becomes the most appropriate method to enter a new industry because it allows a company to share the risks and costs associated with establishing a business unit in the new industry with another company. This is especially true when the companies share *complementary* skills or distinctive competencies because this increases the probability of a joint venture's success. Consider the 50/50 equity joint venture formed between UTC and Dow Chemical to build plastic-based composite parts for the aerospace industry. UTC was already involved in the aerospace industry (it builds Sikorsky helicopters), and Dow Chemical had skills in the development and manufacture of plastic-based composites. The alliance called for UTC to contribute its advanced aerospace skills and Dow to contribute its skills in developing and manufacturing plastic-based composites. Through the joint venture, both companies became involved in new product markets. They were able to realize the benefits associated with related diversification without having to merge their activities into one company or bear the costs and risks of developing new products on their own. Thus, both companies enjoyed the profit-enhancing advantages of entering new markets without having to bear the increased bureaucratic costs.

Although joint ventures usually benefit both partner companies, under some conditions they may result in problems. First, while a joint venture allows companies to share the risks and costs of developing a new business, it also requires that they share in the profits if it succeeds. So, if it turns out later that one partner's skills are more important than the other partner's skills, that partner will have to "give away" profits to the other party because of the 50/50 agreement. This can create conflict and sour the working relationship as time goes on. Second, the joint venture partners may have different business models or time horizons, and problems can arise if they start to come into conflict about how to run the joint venture. The problems can tear it apart and result in business failure. Third, a company that enters into a joint venture runs the risk of giving away important company-specific knowledge to its partner, which might then use that knowledge to compete with its other partner in the future. For example, having gained access to Dow's expertise in plastic-based composites, UTC might have dissolved the alliance and produced these materials on its own. As the previous chapter discussed, this risk can be minimized if Dow gets a *credible commitment* from UTC, which is what it did. UTC had to make an expensive asset-specific investment to make the products the joint venture was formed to create.

RESTRUCTURING

Many companies expand into new industries to increase profitability. Sometimes, however, they need to exit industries to increase their profitability and spin-off and split apart their existing businesses into separate, independent companies. **Restructuring** is the process of reorganizing and divesting business units and exiting industries to refocus on a company's core business and rebuild its distinctive competencies.[33] Why are so many companies restructuring and how do they do it?

Why Restructure?

One main reason that diversified companies have restructured in recent years is that the stock market has valued their stock at a **diversification discount,** meaning that the stock of highly diversified companies is valued lower, relative to their earnings, than the stock of less-diversified companies.[34] Investors see highly diversified companies as less attractive investments for four reasons. First, as we discuss earlier, investors often feel these companies no longer have multibusiness models that justify their participation in many different industries. Second, the complexity of the financial statements of highly diversified enterprises disguises the performance of its individual business units; thus, investors cannot identify if their multibusiness models are succeeding. The result is that investors perceive the company as being riskier than companies that operate in one industry whose competitive advantage and financial statements are more easily understood. Given this situation, restructuring can be seen as an attempt to boost the returns to shareholders by splitting up a multibusiness company into separate and independent parts.

The third reason for the diversification discount is that many investors have learned from experience that managers often have a tendency to pursue too much diversification or do it for the wrong reasons: their attempts to diversify *reduce* profitability.[35] For example, some CEOs pursue growth for its own sake; they are empire builders who expand the scope of their companies to the point where fast-increasing bureaucratic costs become greater than the additional value their diversification strategy creates. Restructuring thus becomes a response to declining financial performance brought about by overdiversification.

A final factor leading to restructuring is that innovations in strategic management have diminished the advantages of vertical integration or diversification. For example, a few decades ago, there was little understanding of how long-term cooperative relationships or strategic alliances between a company and its suppliers could be a viable alternative to vertical integration. Most companies considered only two alternatives for managing the supply chain: vertical integration or competitive bidding. As we discuss in Chapter 9, in many situations, long-term cooperative relationships can create the most value, especially because they avoid the need to incur bureaucratic costs or dispense with market discipline. As this strategic innovation has spread throughout global business, the relative advantages of vertical integration have declined.

SUMMARY OF CHAPTER

1. Strategic managers often pursue diversification when their companies are generating free cash flow, that is, financial resources they do not need to maintain a competitive advantage in the company's core industry that can be used to fund profitable new business ventures.

2. A diversified company can create value by (a) transferring competencies among existing businesses, (b) leveraging competencies to create new businesses, (c) sharing resources to realize economies of scope, (d) using product bundling, and (e) taking advantage of general organizational competencies that enhance the performance of all business units within a diversified company. The bureaucratic costs of diversification rise as a function of the number of independent business units within a company and the extent to which managers have to coordinate the transfer of resources between those business units.

3. Diversification motivated by a desire to pool risks or achieve greater growth often results in falling profitability.

4. There are three methods companies use to enter new industries: internal new venturing, acquisition, and joint ventures.

5. Internal new venturing is used to enter a new industry when a company has a set of valuable competencies in its existing businesses that can be leveraged or recombined to enter a new business or industry.

6. Many internal ventures fail because of entry on too small a scale, poor commercialization, and poor corporate management of the internal venture process. Guarding against failure involves a carefully planned approach toward project selection and management, integration of R&D and marketing to improve the chance new products will be commercially successful, and entry on a scale large enough to result in competitive advantage.

7. Acquisitions are often the best way to enter a new industry when a company lacks the competencies required to compete in a new industry, and it can purchase a company that does have those competencies at a reasonable price. Acquisitions are also the method chosen to enter new industries when there are high barriers to entry and a company is unwilling to accept the time frame, development costs, and risks associated with pursuing internal new venturing.

8. Acquisitions are unprofitable when strategic managers (a) underestimate the problems associated with integrating an acquired company, (b) overestimate the profit that can be created from an acquisition, (c) pay too much for the acquired company, and (d) perform inadequate pre-acquisition screening to ensure the acquired company will increase the profitability of the whole company. Guarding against acquisition failure requires careful preacquisition screening, a carefully selected bidding strategy, effective organizational design to successfully integrate the operations of the acquired company into the whole company, and managers who develop a general managerial competency by learning from their experience of past acquisitions.

9. Joint ventures are used to enter a new industry when (a) the risks and costs associated with setting up a new business unit are more than a company is willing to assume on its own, and (b) a company can increase the probability that its entry into a new industry will result in a successful new business by teaming up with another company that has skills and assets that complement its own.

10. Restructuring is often required to correct the problems that result from (a) a business model that no longer creates competitive advantage, (b) the inability of investors to assess the competitive advantage of a highly diversified company from its financial statements, (c) excessive diversification because top managers who desire to pursue empire building that results in growth without profitability, and (d) innovations in strategic management such as strategic alliances and outsourcing that reduce the advantages of vertical integration and diversification.

DISCUSSION QUESTIONS

1. Imagine that IBM has decided to diversify into the telecommunications business to provide online "cloud computing" data services and broadband access for businesses and individuals. What method would you recommend that IBM pursue to enter this industry? Why?

2. Under which conditions are joint ventures a useful way to enter new industries?

3. What factors make it most likely that (a) acquisitions or (b) internal new venturing will be the preferred method to enter a new industry?

C L O S I N G   C A S E

Tyco's Changing Corporate-Level Strategies

Tyco has experienced success and failure as its multibusiness model has changed over time. In the 1990s, Tyco's success was attributed to the way its top managers used a multibusiness model to pursue unrelated diversification that was based on several consistent strategies. First, Tyco used acquisitions to become the dominant competitor in the industries it entered. For example, Tyco became one of the largest providers of security systems, basic medical supplies, and electronic components in the United States. In essence, through its acquisitions Tyco was able to consolidate fragmented industries and attain economies of scale that give it a cost-based advantage over smaller rivals.[36]

Second, Tyco sought out companies that made basic, low-tech products that commanded a large market share but had been underperforming their competitors, something that indicated there was a good opportunity to improve their performance. Once Tyco identified a potential target, it approached the company's top managers to see if they supported the idea of being acquired. If, after its auditors had carefully examined the target's books and decided the company had potential, Tyco made a formal bid. When the acquisition was completed, Tyco's top managers then worked to find ways to strengthen its business model and improve the performance of the acquired unit. Corporate overhead and the company's workforce were typically slashed, and the old top management team was retired and replaced by Tyco's managers. Also, unprofitable product lines were sold off or closed down, and manufacturing plants and sales forces were merged with Tyco's existing operations to reduce costs and obtain scale economies. For example, within months of acquiring AMP for $12 billion, the world's largest manufacturer of electronic components, Tyco had identified $1 billion in cost savings that could be obtained by closing unprofitable plants and reducing its workforce by 8,000. Once the new management team costs had reduced the cost structure, Tyco's corporate managers then established challenging performance goals to achieve, and strong financial incentives were used to motivate them to boost profitability.

Throughout the 1990s, this business model worked well, and Tyco's stock soared, but by 2000 the situation had changed. Tyco's most recent acquisitions had not contributed much to the company's total profitability; the company was growing, but its performance was deteriorating. Then industry analysts began to criticize the company's top managers for using inappropriate accounting methods to disguise the fact Tyco's business model was failing. Critics argued that Tyco's then CEO Dennis Kozlowski and its CFO Mark Swartz had illegally altered its financial reports to artificially increase the profitability of its business units and disguise its poor performance. They were forced to resign in 2003, and in 2005, these accusations were borne out when both men were sentenced to prison for grand larceny, securities fraud, falsifying business records, and conspiring to defraud Tyco of hundreds of millions of dollars to fund lavish lifestyles.

Tyco was a ship adrift in the mid-2000s. It seemed that there was no longer a rationale for keeping its empire together. Its business model was a failure, and its stock price plummeted. The company's stock traded with a "diversification discount" because investors found it impossible to evaluate the profitability of its individual business units. Thus, its new CEO, Edward Breen, decided that the best way to increase value to shareholders was to reverse the business model developed by Kozlowski.[37]

In 2006, Breen announced that he had decided to pursue a new "nondiversified" business model, and the different businesses Tyco owns will be able to create more value if they were split into three separate companies, each of which would be managed by its own top management team. Breen believed that each of the new companies would then be better positioned in their respective industries to maintain and grow market share and improve their profit margins. Essentially, Breen decided to abandon Tyco's strategy of unrelated diversification and "de-diversify" to increase the profitability of each company and thus returns to shareholders.

Tyco's electronics and health care units would be spun off in tax-free transactions, and Breen would continue to run its remaining operations, including its well-known ADT home-alarm systems and equipment security, fire-protection, and its pump and valve businesses. Breen believed that the managers of each independent company would be better positioned to develop the most successful business model for their industries. He also believed that the returns they will eventually generate will exceed those provided by Tyco's old multibusiness model that had resulted in growth without increased profitability.

The spinoff of these companies took place in 2007, and today Tyco International, Tyco Electronics, and Covidien, its old healthcare unit, operate as independent companies.[38] By 2009, it seemed that all three companies had developed the strong business models needed to boost their profitability in the way Breen had foreseen. However, the recession that began in 2008 is hurting the performance of all three companies, so the jury is still out.

Case Discussion Questions

1. In what ways has Tyco's multibusiness model changed over time? Why did its top managers make these changes?

2. Collect some recent information on the current performance of the three new companies that were created in 2007. What corporate strategies does each pursue? How well are they currently performing?

PERFORMANCE AND GOVERNANCE

The Fall of John Thain

When John Thain arrived as the new CEO at the beleaguered investment bank Merrill Lynch in November 2007, he was viewed as a potential savior.

Merrill Lynch was staggering under enormous losses related to America's mortgage crisis. The company had a large portfolio of collateralized debt obligations (CDOs), which are complex financial derivatives that were created to insure bonds backed by home mortgages against the possibility of default. The former CEO, Stan O'Neal, had taken Merrill Lynch into the CDOs when trading these instruments was very profitable. But as real estate prices collapsed in America and mortgage defaults soared, their value could not be accurately determined; they could not be resold, and companies like Merrill Lynch had to write billions off their balance sheets. O'Neal was fired by the board of directors and replaced by Thain.

Thain was recruited from the New York Stock Exchange, which he had led since 2004. At the NYSE, Thain followed hot on the heels of Richard Grasso, who had been dismissed from the NYSE in a scandal over excessive executive compensation (in one year Grasso had received more than $130 million in pay). Under Thain's leadership, the NYSE prospered, with its stock price rising 600% between 2004 and 2007, and Thain's reputation rose.

At Merrill Lynch, Thain found himself confronted by enormous challenges. Thain was able to raise additional capital for Merrill Lynch, helping to stave off bankruptcy. He also cut costs, laying off thousands of employees and exiting several businesses. To the employees that remained, he preached the virtues of tight cost control, telling them that miscellaneous personal expenses had to be reduced to a minimum. Ultimately, though, Thain recognized that Merrill Lynch could not survive as an independent entity. Although the federal government had already committed $10 billion in additional capital as part of its financial rescues package for the banking sector, Merrill Lynch needed more. In the fall of 2008, he engineered the sale of the company to Bank of America. The acquisition was to close in early 2009. For all of these actions, Thain received overwhelmingly positive press. Under the acquisition agreement, Thain was to continue working at Bank of America, reporting directly to CEO Ken Lewis. It was at this point that things started to go terribly wrong for him.

First, it was revealed that at the same time he was cutting jobs and preaching the virtues of cost controls, Thain also personally authorized spending of $1.2 million to redecorate his office at Merrill Lynch. He spent $800,000 to hire a well-known designer, $87,000 on an area rug, four pairs of curtains for $28,000, a pair of guest chairs for $87,000, and so on. If that was not bad enough, it was soon discovered that he had accelerated 2008 bonus payments at Merrill Lynch by several weeks, thereby allowing executives to collect bonuses *before* the acquisition by Bank of American closed. Many wondered why Merrill Lynch was granting any bonuses, given that the firm was booking large losses, the stock had lost over 80% of its value, and the government was lending $10 billion to the troubled company. Compensation and benefits at Merrill Lynch totaled $15 billion in 2008, including $2 billion in bonuses. The total compensation was down only 6% from the prior year. How, some asked, could this possibly be justified given the enormous destruction of stockholder wealth at Merrill Lynch? Moreover, newspapers were reporting that Thain had personally lobbied the compensation committee of the board of directors for a multimillion bonus for 2008, arguing that he had effectively saved the company by engineering a sale and should be rewarded for it. When this information became public, an embarrassed Thain quickly switched his position and stated that he would take no bonus for 2008.

Things came to a head in December 2008 when Thain revealed to Ken Lewis that Merrill Lynch's losses in the fourth quarter would be much bigger than previously thought, totaling some $15.3 billion. Lewis, who was reportedly furious at being misled, almost scuttled the buyout but was pressured to proceed by the federal government, which had already loaned money to Bank of America, and now committed another $20 billion in capital to help it with Merrill Lynch's losses. Three weeks after the deal closed, however, Bank of America announced that Thain would leave the company. Effectively, he had been fired.[1]

Overview

The story of John Thain detailed in the Opening Case illustrates some of the issues that we will deal with in this chapter. Thain arrived at Merrill Lynch as a highly regarded executive. He left with his reputation in tatters. Thain's decision to spend $1.2 million on his personal office at a time when Merrill Lynch was losing billions and laying off thousands of employees is, at best, an example of bad judgment and, at worst, an illustration of poor business ethics. His decision to accelerate bonuses, paying out some $4 billion at the loss-making enterprise, is also ethically suspect and suggests that Thain may not have been acting in shareholders' best interests, for few of them would have agreed to such extravagance amid mounting losses and a plunging stock price. His lobbying for a large bonus for himself indicates to the cynical that Thain was a man looking after his own best interests rather than those of the corporation and its shareholders. Finally, the failure to reveal, until very late in the acquisition process, that Merrill Lynch's losses were much bigger than previously thought suggests to some that Thain was trying to hide the true state of affairs from Ken Lewis for as long as possible for fear that it might derail the acquisition.

In this chapter, we take a close look at the governance mechanisms that shareholders put in place to make sure that managers are acting in their interests and pursuing strategies that maximize shareholder value. We also discuss how managers need to pay attention to other stakeholders as well, such as employees, suppliers, and customers. Balancing the needs of different stakeholder groups is in the long-run interests of the company's owners, its shareholders. Good governance mechanisms recognize this truth. In addition, we will spend some time reviewing the ethical implications of strategic decisions, and we will discuss how managers can make sure that their strategic decisions are founded on strong ethical principles, something that John Thain arguably did not do.

STAKEHOLDERS AND CORPORATE PERFORMANCE

A company's **stakeholders** are individuals or groups with interests, claims, or stakes in the company, in what it does, and in how well it performs.[2] They include stockholders, creditors, employees, customers, the communities in which the company does business, and the general public. Stakeholders can be divided into internal stakeholders and external stakeholders (see Figure 11.1). **Internal stakeholders** are stockholders and employees, including executive officers, other managers, and board members. **External stakeholders** are all other individuals and groups that have some

Figure 11.1 Stakeholders and the Enterprise

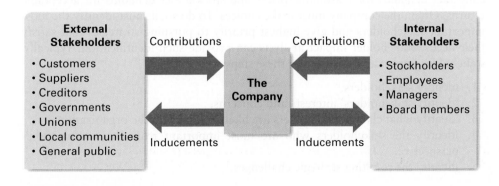

claim on the company. Typically, this group is comprised of customers, suppliers, creditors (including banks and bondholders), governments, unions, local communities, and the general public.

All stakeholders are in an exchange relationship with the company. Each of the stakeholder groups listed in Figure 11.1 supplies the organization with important resources (or contributions), and, in exchange, each expects its interests to be satisfied (by inducements).[3] Stockholders provide the enterprise with risk capital and, in exchange, expect management to try to maximize the return on their investment. Creditors, and particularly bondholders, also provide the company with capital in the form of debt, and they expect to be repaid on time with interest. Employees provide labor and skills and, in exchange, expect commensurate income, job satisfaction, job security, and good working conditions. Customers provide a company with its revenues and, in exchange, want high-quality, reliable products that represent value for money. Suppliers provide a company with inputs and, in exchange, seek revenues and dependable buyers. Governments provide a company with rules and regulations that govern business practice and maintain fair competition. In exchange, they want companies to adhere to these rules. Unions help to provide a company with productive employees, and, in exchange, they want benefits for their members in proportion to their contributions to the company. Local communities provide companies with local infrastructure and, in exchange, want companies that are responsible citizens. The general public provides companies with national infrastructure and, in exchange, seeks some assurance that the quality of life will be improved as a result of the company's existence.

A company must take these claims into account when formulating its strategies, or else stakeholders may withdraw their support. For example, stockholders may sell their shares, bondholders may demand higher interest payments on new bonds, employees may leave their jobs, and customers may buy elsewhere. Suppliers may seek more dependable buyers. Unions may engage in disruptive labor disputes. Government may take civil or criminal action against the company and its top officers, imposing fines and, in some cases, jail terms. Communities may oppose the company's attempts to locate its facilities in their area, and the general public may form pressure groups, demanding action against companies that impair the quality of life. Any of these reactions can have a damaging impact on an enterprise.

Stakeholder Impact Analysis

A company cannot always satisfy the claims of all stakeholders. The goals of different groups may conflict; in practice, few organizations have the resources to manage all stakeholders.[4] For example, union claims for higher wages can conflict with consumer demands for reasonable prices and stockholder demands for acceptable returns. Often, the company must make choices. To do so, it must identify the most important stakeholders and give highest priority to pursuing strategies that satisfy their needs. Stakeholder impact analysis can provide such identification. Typically, stakeholder impact analysis follows these steps:

1. Identify stakeholders.
2. Identify stakeholders' interests and concerns.
3. Identify what claims stakeholders are likely to make on the organization.
4. Identify the stakeholders who are most important from the organization's perspective.
5. Identify the resulting strategic challenges.[5]

Such an analysis enables a company to identify the stakeholders most critical to its survival and make sure that the satisfaction of their needs is paramount. Most companies that have gone through this process quickly come to the conclusion that three stakeholder groups must be satisfied above all others if a company is to survive and prosper: customers, employees, and stockholders.

The Unique Role of Stockholders

A company's stockholders are usually put in a different class from other stakeholder groups, and for good reason. Stockholders are legal owners and the providers of **risk capital**, a major source of the capital resources that allow a company to operate its business. The capital that stockholders provide to a company is seen as risk capital because there is no guarantee that stockholders will ever recoup their investment and or earn a decent return.

Recent history demonstrates all too clearly the nature of risk capital. For example, many investors who bought shares in Washington Mutual, the large Seattle-based bank and home loan lender, believed that they were making low risk investments. The company had been around for decades and paid a solid dividend, which it increased every year. It had a large branch network and billions in deposits. However, during the 2000s, Washington Mutual was also making increasingly risky mortgage loans, reportedly giving mortgages to people without ever properly verifying if they had the funds to pay back those loans on time. By 2008, many of the borrowers were starting to default on their loans, and Washington Mutual had to take multi-billion dollar write-downs on the value of its loan portfolio, effectively destroying its once-strong balance sheet. The losses were so large that people with deposits at the bank started to worry about its stability; those people withdrew some $16 billion in November 2008 from accounts at Washington Mutual. The stock price collapsed from approximately $40 at the start of 2008 to less than $2 a share. With the bank teetering on the brink of collapse, the federal government stepped in, seized the bank's assets, and engineered a sale to JP Morgan. What did Washington Mutual's shareholders get? Absolutely nothing; they were wiped out.

Over the past decade, maximizing returns to stockholders has taken on added importance as more and more employees have become stockholders in the company for which they work through employee stock ownership plans (ESOP). At Walmart, for example, all employees who have served for more than one year are eligible for the company's ESOP. Under an ESOP, employees are given the opportunity to purchase stock in their company, sometimes at a discount to the market value of the stock. The company may also contribute to a certain proportion of the purchase price. By making employees stockholders, ESOPs tend to increase the already strong emphasis on maximizing returns to stockholders, for they now help to satisfy two key stakeholder groups: stockholders and employees.

Profitability, Profit Growth, and Stakeholder Claims

Because of the unique position assigned to stockholders, managers normally seek to pursue strategies that maximize the returns that stockholders receive from holding shares in the company. As we noted in Chapter 1, stockholders receive a return on their investment in a company's stock in two ways: from dividend payments and from capital appreciation in the market value of a share (that is, by increases in stock market prices). The best way for managers to generate the funds for future dividend payments and keep the stock price appreciating is for them to pursue strategies that maximize the company's long-run profitability (as measured by the ROIC) and grow the profits of the company over time.[6]

As we saw in Chapter 3, ROIC is an excellent measure of the profitability of a company. It tells managers how efficiently they are using the capital resources of the company (including the risk capital provided by stockholders) to generate profits. A company that is generating a positive ROIC is covering all of its ongoing expenses and has money left over, which is then added to shareholders' equity, thereby increasing the value of a company and thus the value of a share of stock in the company. The value of each share will increase further if a company can grow its profits over time because then the profit that is attributable to every share (that is, the company's earning per share) will also grow. As we have described in this book, to grow their profits, companies must be doing one or more of the following: (1) participating in a market that is growing; (2) taking market share from competitors; (3) consolidating the industry through horizontal integration; and (4) developing new markets through international expansion, vertical integration, or diversification.

Although managers should strive for profit growth if they are trying to maximize shareholder value, the relationship between profitability and profit growth is a complex one because attaining future profit growth may require investments that reduce the current rate of profitability. The task of managers is to find the right balance between profitability and profit growth.[7] Too much emphasis on current profitability at the expense of future profitability and profit growth can make an enterprise less attractive to shareholders. Too much emphasis on profit growth can reduce the profitability of the enterprise and have the same effect. In an uncertain world, finding the right balance between profitability and profit growth is certainly as much art as it is science, but it is something that managers must try to do.

In addition to maximizing returns to stockholders, boosting a company's profitability and profit growth rate is also consistent with satisfying the claims of several other key stakeholder groups. When a company is profitable and its profits are growing, it can pay higher salaries to productive employees and also afford benefits such as health insurance coverage, all of which help to satisfy employees. In addition, companies with a high level of profitability and profit growth have no problem meeting their debt commitments, which provides creditors, including bondholders, with a measure of security. More profitable companies are also better able to undertake philanthropic investments, which can help to satisfy some of the claims that local communities and the general public place on a company. Pursuing strategies that maximize the long-run profitability and profit growth of the company is therefore generally consistent with satisfying the claims of various stakeholder groups.

There is an important cause-and-effect relationship here. Pursuing strategies to maximize profitability and profit growth helps a company to better satisfy the demands that several stakeholder groups place on it, not the other way around. The company that overpays its employees in the current period, for example, may have very happy employees for a short while, but such action will raise the company's cost structure and limit its ability to attain a competitive advantage in the marketplace, thereby depressing its long-run profitability and hurting its ability to award future pay increases. As far as employees are concerned, the way many companies deal with this situation is to make future pay increases contingent on improvements in labor productivity. If labor productivity goes up, labor costs as a percentage of revenues will fall, profitability will rise, and the company can afford to pay its employees more and offer greater benefits.

Of course, not all stakeholder groups want the company to maximize its long-run profitability and profit growth. Suppliers are more comfortable about selling goods and services to profitable companies because they can be assured that the company will have the funds to pay for those products. Similarly, customers may be more willing to purchase from profitable companies because they can be assured that those companies will be around in the long run to provide after-sales services and support. But neither suppliers nor customers want the company to maximize its profitability at their expense. Rather, they would like to capture some of these profits from the company in the form of higher prices for their goods and services (in the case of suppliers) or lower prices for the products they purchase from the company (in the case of customers). Thus, the company is in a bargaining relationship with some of its stakeholders, which was a phenomenon we discussed in Chapter 2.

Moreover, despite the argument that maximizing long-run profitability and profit growth is the best way to satisfy the claims of several key stakeholder groups, a company must do so within the limits set by the law and in a manner consistent with societal expectations. The unfettered pursuit of profit can lead to behaviors that are outlawed by government regulations, opposed by important public constituencies, or simply unethical. Governments have enacted a wide range of regulations to govern business behavior, including antitrust laws, environmental laws, and laws pertaining to health and safety in the workplace. It is incumbent on managers to make sure that the company is in compliance with these laws when pursuing strategies.

Unfortunately, there is plenty of evidence that managers can be tempted to cross the line between the legal and illegal in their pursuit of greater profitability and profit growth. For example, in mid-2003, the United States Air Force stripped Boeing of $1 billion in contracts to launch satellites when it was discovered that Boeing had obtained thousand of pages of proprietary information from rival Lockheed Martin. Boeing had used that information to prepare its winning bid for the satellite contract. This was followed by the revelation that Boeing's CFO, Mike Sears, had offered a government official, Darleen Druyun, a lucrative job at Boeing while Druyun was still involved in evaluating whether Boeing should be awarded a $17 billion contract to build tankers for the Air Force. Boeing won the contract against strong competition from Airbus, and Druyun was hired by Boeing. It was clear that the job offer may have had an impact on the Air Force decision. Boeing fired Sears and Druyun; shortly afterward, Boeing CEO Phil Condit resigned in a tacit acknowledgment that he bore responsibility for the ethics violations that had occurred at Boeing during his tenure as leader.[8] In another case, the CEO of Archer Daniels Midland, one of the world's largest producers of agricultural products, was sent to jail after an FBI investigation revealed that the company had systematically tried to fix the price for lysine by colluding with other manufacturers in the global marketplace. In another example of price fixing, the 76-year-old chairman of Sotheby's auction house was sentenced to a jail term and the former CEO to house arrest for fixing prices with rival auction house Christie's over a six-year period (see Strategy in Action 11.1).

Examples such as these beg the question of why managers would engage in such risky behavior. A body of academic work collectively known as *agency theory* provides an explanation for why managers might engage in behavior that is either illegal or, at the very least, not in the interest of the company's shareholders.

Ethical Dilemma

You work for a US-based textile company struggling with overseas competitors that have access to low-cost labor. While you pay your factory workers $14 an hour plus benefits, you know that a similar textile mill in Vietnam is paying its employees about $0.50 an hour, and the mill does not have to comply with the same safety and environmental regulations that your company does. Although your mill is marginally profitable, the Vietnamese factory clearly has a cost advantage. Your CEO wants to move production to Central America or Southeast Asia where labor and compliance costs are lower, resulting in mill closure and employee layoffs. Your mill is the only large employer in a small community. Many of the employees have worked there their entire working lives. What is the right action to take for stockholders? What is the most ethical course of action? Is there a conflict here?

11.1 *STRATEGY IN ACTION*

Price Fixing at Sotheby's and Christie's

Sotheby's and Christie's are the two largest fine art auction houses in the world. In the mid-1990s, the two companies controlled 90% of the fine art auction market, which at the time was worth some $4 billion a year. Traditionally, auction houses make their profit by the commission they charge on auction sales. In good times, these commissions can range as high as 10% on some items, but in the early 1990s, the auction business was in a slump, with the supply of art for auction drying up. With Sotheby's and Christie's desperate for works of art, sellers played the two houses off against each other, driving commissions down to 2% or even lower.

To try to control this situation, Sotheby's CEO, Dede Brooks, met with the CEO at Christie's, Christopher Davidge, in a series of clandestine meetings held in car parking lots that began in 1993. Brooks claims that she was acting on behalf of her boss, Alfred Taubman, the chairman and controlling shareholder of Sotheby's. According to Brooks, Taubman had agreed with the chairman of Christie's, Anthony Tennant, to work together in the weak auction market and limit price competition. In their meetings, Brooks and Davidge agreed to a fixed and nonnegotiable commission structure. Based on a sliding scale, the commission structure would range from 10% on a $100,000 item to 2% on a $5 million item. In effect, Brooks and Davidge were agreeing to

eliminate price competition between them, thereby guaranteeing both auction houses higher profits. The price-fixing agreement started in 1993 and continued unabated for six years until federal investigators uncovered the arrangement and brought charges against Sotheby's and Christie's.

With the deal out in the open, lawyers filed several class action lawsuits on behalf of sellers who had been defrauded by Sotheby's and Christie's. Ultimately, some 100,000 sellers signed on to the class action lawsuits, which the auction houses settled with a $512 million payment. The auction houses also pleaded guilty to price fixing and paid $45 million in fines to United States antitrust authorities. As for the key players, the chairman of Christie's, as a British subject, was able to avoid prosecution in the United States (price fixing is not an offense for which someone can be extradited). Christie's CEO, Davidge, struck a deal with prosecutors and in return for amnesty, handed over incriminating documents to the authorities. Brooks also cooperated with federal prosecutors and avoided jail (in April 2002, she was sentenced to three years' probation, six months' home detention, 1,000 hours of community service, and a $350,000 fine). Taubman, ultimately isolated by all his former co-conspirators, was sentenced to a year in jail and fined $7.5 million.

Sources: S. Tully, "A House Divided," *Fortune*, December 18, 2000, 264–275; J. Chaffin, "Sotheby's Ex CEO Spared Jail Sentence," *Financial Times*, April 30, 2002, 10; T. Thorncroft, "A Courtroom Battle of the Vanities," *Financial Times*, November 3, 2001, 3.

AGENCY THEORY

Agency theory looks at the problems that can arise in a business relationship when one person delegates decision-making authority to another. It offers a way of understanding why managers do not always act in the best interests of stakeholders and why they might sometimes behave unethically and perhaps also illegally.[9] Although agency theory was originally formulated to capture the relationship between management and stockholders, the basic principles have also been extended to cover the relationship with other key stakeholders, such as employees, as well as relationships between different layers of management within a corporation.[10] While the focus of attention in this section is on the relationship between senior management and stockholders, some of the same language can be applied to the relationship between other stakeholders and top managers and between top management and lower levels of management.

Principal-Agent Relationships

The basic propositions of agency theory are relatively straightforward. First, an agency relationship arises whenever one party delegates decision-making authority or control over resources to another. The principal is the person delegating authority, and the agent is the person to whom authority is delegated. The relationship between stockholders and senior managers is a classic example of an agency relationship. Stockholders, who are the principals, provide the company with risk capital, but they delegate control over that capital to senior managers, and particularly the CEO, who as their agent is expected to use that capital in a manner that is consistent with the best interests of stockholders. As we have seen, this means using that capital to maximize the company's long-run profitability and profit growth rate.

The agency relationship continues on down within the company. For example, in the large, complex, multibusiness company, top managers cannot possibly make all the important decisions, so they delegate some decision-making authority and control over capital resources to business unit (divisional) managers. Thus, just as senior managers such as the CEO are the agents of stockholders, business unit managers are the agents of the CEO (and in this context, the CEO is the principal). The CEO entrusts business unit managers to use the resources over which they have control in the most effective manner so that they maximize the performance of their units, which helps the CEO make sure that he or she maximizes the performance of the entire company, thereby discharging agency obligation to stockholders. More generally, whenever managers delegate authority to managers below them in the hierarchy and give them the right to control resources, an agency relation is established.

The Agency Problem

While agency relationships often work well, problems may arise if agents and principals have different goals and if agents take actions that are not in the best interests of their principals. Agents may be able to do this because there is an **information asymmetry** between the principal and the agent: agents almost always have more information about the resources they are managing than the principal does. Unscrupulous agents can take advantage of any information asymmetry to mislead principals and maximize their own interests at the expense of principals.

In the case of stockholders, information asymmetry arises because they delegate decision-making authority to the CEO, their agent, who by virtue of his or her position inside the company is likely to know far more than stockholders do about the company's operations. Indeed, there may be certain information about the company that the CEO is unwilling to share with stockholders because it would also help competitors. In such a case, withholding some information from stockholders may be in their best interests. More generally, the CEO, involved in the day-to-day running of the company, is bound to have an information advantage over stockholders, just as the CEO's subordinates may well have an information advantage over the CEO with regard to the resources under their control.

The information asymmetry between principals and agents is not necessarily a bad thing, but it can make it difficult for principals to measure how well an agent is performing, thus, holding the agent accountable for how well he or she is using the entrusted resources. There is a certain amount of performance ambiguity inherent in the relationship between a principal and agent. Principals cannot know for sure if the agents are acting in their best interests. They cannot know for sure if the agents are using the resources to which they have been entrusted as effectively and efficiently as possible. To an extent, principals have to trust the agents to do the right thing.

Of course, this trust is not blind. Principals put mechanisms in place whose purpose is to monitor agents, evaluate their performance, and, if necessary, take corrective action. As we shall see shortly, the board of directors is one such mechanism, for the board exists in part to monitor and evaluate senior managers on behalf of stockholders. Other mechanisms serve a similar purpose. In the United States, publicly owned companies must regularly file detailed financial statements with the Securities and Exchange Commission (SEC) that are in accordance with generally accepted accounting principles (GAAP). This requirement exists to give stockholders consistent and detailed information about how well management is using the capital with which it has been entrusted. Similarly, internal control systems within a company are there to help the CEO make sure that subordinates are using the resources with which they have been entrusted as efficiently and effectively as possible.

Despite the existence of governance mechanisms and comprehensive measurement and control systems, a degree of information asymmetry will always remain between principals and agents, and there is always an element of trust involved in the relationship. Unfortunately, not all agents are worthy of this trust. A minority will deliberately mislead principals for personal gain, sometimes behaving unethically or breaking laws in the process. The interests of principals and agents are not always the same; they diverge, and some agents may take advantage of information asymmetries to maximize their own interests at the expense of principals and engage in behaviors that the principals would never condone.

For example, some authors have argued that, like many other people, senior managers are motivated by desires for status, power, job security, and income.[11] By virtue of their position within the company, certain managers, such as the CEO, can use their authority and control over corporate funds to satisfy these desires at the cost of returns to stockholders. CEOs might use their position to invest corporate funds in various perks that enhance their status—executive jets, lavish offices, and expense-paid trips to exotic locations—rather than investing those funds in ways that increase stockholder returns. Economists have termed such behavior **on-the-job consumption**.[12] John Thain is an example of a CEO who appeared to engage in excessive on-the-job consumption (see the Opening Case)

Besides engaging in on-the-job consumption, CEOs, along with other senior managers, might satisfy their desires for greater income by using their influence or control over the board of directors to get the compensation committee of the board to grant pay increases. Critics of United States industry claim that extraordinary pay has now become an endemic problem and that senior managers are enriching themselves at the expense of stockholders and other employees. They point out that CEO pay has been increasing far more rapidly than the pay of average workers, primarily because of very liberal stock option grants that enable a CEO to earn huge pay bonuses in a rising stock market, even if the company underperforms the market and competitors.[13] In 1980, the average CEO in *Business Week*'s survey of CEO's of the largest 500 American companies earned 42 times what the average blue-collar worker earned. By 1990, this figure had increased to 85 times. Today, the average CEO in the survey earns more than 350 times the pay of the average blue-collar worker.[14]

What rankles critics is the size of some CEO pay packages and their apparent lack of relationship to company performance.[15] For example, in 2006 shareholders of Home Depot complained bitterly about the compensation package for CEO Bob Nardelli at the company's annual meeting. Nardelli, who was appointed in 2000, had received $124 million in compensation, despite mediocre financial performance at Home Depot and a 12% decline in the company's stock price since he joined. When unexercised stock options were included, his compensation exceeded $250 million.[16] Critics feel that the size of pay awards such as these is out of proportion to the achievement of the CEOs. If so, this represents a clear example of the agency problem.

A further concern is that in trying to satisfy a desire for status, security, power, and income, a CEO might engage in empire building, buying many new businesses in an attempt to increase the size of the company through diversification.[17] Although such growth may depress the company's long-run profitability and thus stockholder returns, it increases the size of the empire under the CEO's control and, by extension, the CEO's status, power, security, and income (there is a strong relationship between company size and CEO pay). Instead of trying to maximize stockholder returns by seeking the right balance between profitability and profit growth, some senior managers may trade long-run profitability for greater company growth by buying new businesses. Figure 11.2 graphs long-run profitability against the rate of growth in company revenues. A company that does not grow is probably missing out on some profitable opportunities.[18] A moderate revenue growth rate of G* allows a company to maximize long-run profitability, generating a return of Π^*. Thus, a growth rate of G1 in Figure 11.2 is not consistent with maximizing profitability ($\Pi 1 < \Pi^*$). By the same token, however, attaining growth in excess of G2 requires diversification into areas that the company knows little about. Consequently, it can be achieved only by sacrificing profitability; that is, past G*, the investment required to finance further growth does not produce an adequate return, and the company's profitability declines. Yet G2 may be the growth rate favored by an empire-building CEO, for it

Figure 11.2 The Tradeoff Between Profitability and Revenue Growth Rates

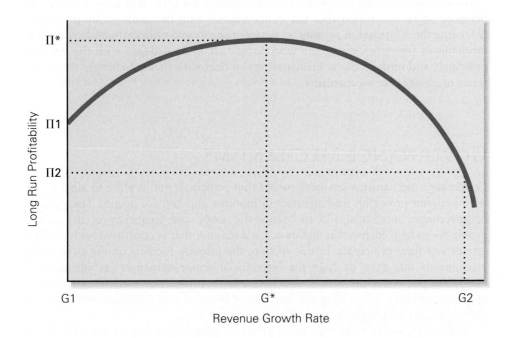

will increase his or her power, status, and income. At this growth rate, profitability is equal only to $\Pi2$. Because $\Pi^* > \Pi2$, a company growing at this rate is clearly not maximizing its long-run profitability or the wealth of its stockholders.

Just how serious agency problems could be was emphasized in the early 2000s when a series of scandals swept through the corporate world, many of which could be attributed to self-interest seeking by senior executives and a failure of corporate governance mechanisms to hold the largess of those executives in check. Between 2001 and 2004, accounting scandals unfolded at a number of major corporations, including Enron, WorldCom, Tyco, Computer Associates, HealthSouth, Adelphia Communications, Dynegy, Royal Dutch Shell, and the major Italian food company Parmalat. At Enron, some $27 billion in debt was hidden from shareholders, employees, and regulators in special partnerships that were kept off the balance sheet. At Parmalat, managers apparently "invented" some $8 to $12 billion in assets to shore up the company's balance sheet—assets that never existed. In the case of Royal Dutch Shell, senior managers knowingly inflated the value of the company's oil reserves by one-fifth, which amounted to 4 billion barrels of oil that never existed, making the company appear much more valuable than it actually was. At the other companies, earnings were systematically overstated, often by hundreds of millions of dollars, or even billions of dollars in the case of Tyco and WorldCom, which understated its expenses by $3 billion in 2001. Strategy in Action 11.2 discusses accounting fraud at Computer Associates. In all of these cases, the prime motivation seems to have been an effort to present a more favorable view of corporate affairs to shareholders than was actually the case, thereby securing senior executives significantly higher pay packets.[19]

It is important to remember that the agency problem is not confined to the relationship between senior managers and stockholders. It can also bedevil the relationship between the CEO and subordinates and between them and their subordinates. Subordinates might use control over information to distort the true performance of their unit to enhance their pay, increase their job security, or make sure their unit gets more than its fair share of company resources.

Confronted with agency problems, the challenge for principals is to (1) shape the behavior of agents so that they act in accordance with the goals set by principals, (2) reduce the information asymmetry between agents and principals, and (3) develop mechanisms for removing agents who do not act in accordance with the goals of principals and mislead them. Principals try to deal with these challenges through a series of governance mechanisms.

Governance Mechanisms

Governance mechanisms are mechanisms that principals put in place to align incentives between principals and agents and monitor and control agents. The purpose of governance mechanisms is to reduce the scope and frequency of the agency problem—to help ensure that agents act in a manner that is consistent with the best interests of their principals. In this section, the primary focus is on the governance mechanisms that exist to align the interests of senior managers (as agents) with their principals—stockholders. It should not be forgotten, however, that governance mechanisms also exist to align the interests of business unit managers with those of their superiors and so on down within the organization.

Following, we look at four main types of governance mechanisms for aligning stockholder and management interests: the board of directors, stock-based

11.2 STRATEGY IN ACTION

Self-Dealing at Computer Associates

Computer Associates is one of the world's largest software companies. During the 1990s, its stock price appreciated at a rapid rate, driven in large part by surging revenues and a commensurate rise in profits. Because its revenues were growing more rapidly than those of rivals during the late 1990s, investors assumed that the company was gaining market share and that high profitability would follow, so they bid up the price of the company's stock. The senior managers of Computer Associates were major beneficiaries of this process. Under a generous incentive program given to the company's three top managers by the board of directors—Charles Wang, then CEO and chairman of the board, Sanjay Kumar, the chief operating officer, and Russell Artzt, the chief technology officer—if the stock price stayed above $53.13 for 60 days, they would receive a special incentive stock award amounting to some 20 million shares. In May 1998, Kumar announced that Computer Associates had "record" revenues and earnings for the quarter. The stock price surged over the $53.13 trigger and stayed there long enough for all three to receive the special incentive stock award, then valued at $1.1 billion.

In late July 1998, after all three had received the award, Kumar announced that the effect of Asian economic turmoil and the year 2000 bug "leads us to believe that our revenue and earnings growth will slow over the next few quarters." The stock price promptly fell from the high 50s to less than $40 a share. What followed was a series of class action lawsuits, undertaken on behalf of stockholders, who claimed management had misled stockholders to enrich themselves. As a result of the lawsuits, the three were compelled to give back some of their gains, and the size of the award was reduced to 4.5 million shares. Wang stepped down as CEO, although he retained his position as chairman of the board, and Kumar became the CEO.

This was not the end of matters, however, for Computer Associates had attracted the attention of both the Justice Department and the SEC, which launched a joint investigation into the company's accounting practices. By 2002, they were reportedly focusing on a little-noticed action the company had taken in May 2000 to reduce its revenues by 10%, or $1.76 billion, below what it had previously reported for the three fiscal years that ended March 2000. The downward revisions, detailed in the company's 10-K filings with the SEC, retroactively took

hundreds of millions of dollars away from the top line in the 14 months preceding the May 1998 stock award to senior managers, including some $513 million for the year ending March 1998. According to the company, earnings were unaffected by the revision because the lost revenue was offset by a commensurate downward revision of expenses. The downward revision reportedly came at the urging of auditor KPMG, which replaced Ernst & Young as the company's accountant in June 1999.

The implication that some observers were drawing was that Computer Associates deliberately overstated its revenues in the period prior to May 1998 to enrich the three top managers. The losers in this process were stockholders who purchased shares at the inflated price and longer-term shareholders who saw the value of their holdings diluted by the stock awarded to Wang, Kumar, and Artzt. In a statement issued after a report of the ongoing investigation was published in the *Wall Street Journal*, Computer Associates stated that it changed how it classified revenue and expenses at the advice of its auditors. "We continue to believe CA has acted appropriately," the company spokesperson said. "This change in presentation had no impact on reported earnings, earnings per share, or cash flows."

By 2004, it was clear that Computer Associates had been acting anything but appropriately. According to the SEC investigation, between 1998 and 2000, the company adopted a policy of backdating contracts to boost revenues. For example, in January 2000, Computer Associates negotiated a $300 million contract with a customer but backdated the contract so that the revenues appeared in 1999. Although initially this may have been done to help secure the $1.1 billion special stock award, by 2000 the practice represented an increasingly desperate attempt to meet financial projects that the company was routinely missing. Under increasing pressure, in 2002 Charles Wang stepped down as chairman, and in 2004 Kumar was forced to resign as CEO by the board of Computer Associates, which had belatedly come to recognize that the company's financial statements were fraudulent. In late 2004, in a deal with federal regulators, the company admitted to $2.2 billion in fraud. As part of the deal, Kumar was indicted by federal prosecutors on charges of obstruction of justice and securities fraud. In November 2006, Kumar was sentenced to 12 years in jail for his part in the fraud.

Sources: J. Guidera, "Probe of Computer Associates Centers on Firm's Revenues," *Wall Street Journal*, May 20, 2002, A3, 15; Ronna Abramson, "Computer Associates Probe Focus on 1998, 1999 Revenue," *The Street.Com*, May 20, 2002; C. Forelle, M. Maremont, and G. Fields, "U.S. Indicts Sanjay Kumar for Fraud, Lies," *Wall Street Journal*, September 23, 2004, N. Varchaver, "Long Island Confidential," *Fortune*, November 27, 2006, 172–178.

compensation, financial statements, and the takeover constraint. The section closes with a discussion of governance mechanisms within a company to align the interest of senior and lower-level managers.

The Board of Directors

The board of directors is the centerpiece of the corporate governance system. Board members are directly elected by stockholders, and under corporate law they represent the stockholders' interests in the company. Hence, the board can be held legally accountable for the company's actions. Its position at the apex of decision making within the company allows it to monitor corporate strategy decisions and ensure that they are consistent with stockholder interests. If the board's sense is that corporate strategies are not in the best interest of stockholders, it can apply sanctions, such as voting against management nominations to the board of directors or submitting its own nominees. In addition, the board has the legal authority to hire, fire, and compensate corporate employees, including, most importantly, the CEO.[20] The board is also responsible for making sure that audited financial statements of the company present a true picture of its financial situation. Thus, the board exists to reduce the information asymmetry between stockholders and managers and monitor and control management actions on behalf of stockholders.

The typical board of directors is composed of a mix of inside and outside directors. **Inside directors** are senior employees of the company, such as the CEO. They are required on the board because they have valuable information about the company's activities. Without such information, the board cannot adequately perform its monitoring function. But because insiders are full-time employees of the company, their interests tend to be aligned with those of management. Hence, outside directors are needed to bring objectivity to the monitoring and evaluation processes. **Outside directors** are not full-time employees of the company. Many of them are full-time professional directors who hold positions on the boards of several companies. The need to maintain a reputation as competent outside directors gives them an incentive to perform their tasks as objectively and effectively as possible.[21]

There is little doubt that many boards perform their assigned functions admirably. For example, when the board of Sotheby's discovered that the company had been engaged in price fixing with Christie's, board members moved quickly to oust both the CEO and the chairman of the company (see Strategy in Action 11.1). But not all boards perform as well as they should. The board of now bankrupt, large energy company Enron signed off on that company's audited financial statements, which were later shown to be grossly misleading.

Critics of the existing governance system charge that inside directors often dominate the outsiders on the board. Insiders can use their position within the management hierarchy to exercise control over what kind of company-specific information the board receives. Consequently, they can present information in a way that puts them in a favorable light. In addition, because insiders have intimate knowledge of the company's operations and because superior knowledge and control over information are sources of power, they may be better positioned than outsiders to influence boardroom decision making. The board may become the captive of insiders and merely rubber-stamp management decisions instead of guarding stockholder interests.

Some observers contend that many boards are dominated by the company CEO, particularly when the CEO is also the chairman of the board.[22] To support this view, they point out that both inside and outside directors are often the personal nominees of the CEO. The typical inside director is subordinate to the CEO in the company's hierarchy and therefore unlikely to criticize the boss. Because outside directors are frequently the CEO's nominees as well, they can hardly be expected to evaluate the CEO objectively. Thus, the loyalty of the board may be biased toward the CEO, not the stockholders. Moreover, a CEO who is also chairman of the board may be able to control the agenda of board discussions in such a manner as to deflect any criticisms of his or her leadership.

In the aftermath of a wave of corporate scandals that hit the corporate world in the early 2000s, there are clear signs that many corporate boards are moving away from merely rubber-stamping top management decisions and are beginning to play a much more active role in corporate governance. In part, they have been prompted by new legislation, such as the 2002 Sarbanes-Oxley Act in the United States, which tightened rules governing corporate reporting and corporate governance. Also important has been a growing trend on the part of the courts to hold directors liable for corporate misstatements. Powerful institutional investors such as pension funds have also been more aggressive in exerting their power, often pushing for more outside representation on the board of directors and for a separation between the roles of chairman and CEO, with the chairman role going to an outsider. Partly as a result, more than 50% of big companies had outside directors in the chairman's role by the late 2000s, up from less than half of that number in 1990. Separating the role of chairman and CEO limits the ability of corporate insiders, and particularly that of the CEO, to exercise control over the board. Still, when all is said and done, it must be recognized that boards of directors do not work as well as they should in theory, and other mechanisms are need to align the interests of stockholders and managers.

Stock-Based Compensation

According to agency theory, one of the best ways to reduce the scope of the agency problem is for principals to establish incentives for agents to behave in their best interest through pay-for-performance systems. In the case of stockholders and top managers, stockholders can encourage top managers to pursue strategies that maximize a company's long-run profitability and profit growth, and thus the gains from holding its stock, by linking the pay of those managers to the performance of the stock price.

The most common pay-for-performance system has been to give managers **stock options**: the right to buy the company's shares at a predetermined (strike) price at some point in the future, usually within 10 years of the grant date. Typically, the strike price is the price that the stock was trading at when the option was originally granted. The idea behind stock options is to motivate managers to adopt strategies that increase the share price of the company, for in doing so they will also increase the value of their own stock options. Another stock-based pay for performance system is to grant managers stock if they attain predetermined performance targets.

Several academic studies suggest that stock-based compensation schemes for executives, such as stock options and stock grants, can align management and stockholder interests. For instance, one study found that managers were more likely to consider the effects of their acquisition decisions on stockholder returns if they themselves were significant shareholders.[23] According to another study, managers who were significant stockholders were less likely to pursue strategies that would maximize the size of the company rather than its profitability.[24] More generally, it is difficult to argue with the proposition that the chance to get rich from exercising stock options is the primary reason for the 14-hour days and six-day workweeks that many employees of fast-growing companies put in.

However, the practice of granting stock options has become increasingly controversial. Many top managers often earn huge bonuses from exercising stock options that were granted several years previously. While not denying that these options motivate managers to improve company performance, critics claim that they are often too generous. A particular cause for concern is that stock options are often granted at such low strike prices that the CEO can hardly fail to make a significant amount of money by exercising them, even if the company underperforms the stock market by a significant margin. Indeed, a serious example of the agency problem emerged in 2005 and 2006 when the SEC started to investigate a number of companies in which stock options granted to senior executives had apparently been "backdated" to a time when the stock price was lower, enabling the executives to earn more money than if those options had simply been dated on the day they were granted.[25] By late 2006, the SEC was investigating some 130 companies for possible fraud relating to stock option dating. Included in the list were major corporations, including Apple Computer, Jabil Circuit, United Health, and Home Depot.[26]

Other critics of stock options, including the famous investor Warren Buffett, complain that huge stock option grants increase the outstanding number of shares in a company and therefore dilute the equity of stockholders; accordingly, they should be shown in company accounts as an expense against profits. Under accounting regulations that were in force until 2005, stock options, unlike wages and salaries, were not expensed. However, this has now changed, and as a result, many companies are starting to reduce their use of options. At Microsoft, for example, which had long given generous stock option grants to high performing employees, stock options were replaced with stock grants in 2005.

Financial Statements and Auditors

Publicly trading companies in the United States are required to file quarterly and annual reports with the SEC that are prepared according to Generally Agreed Accounting Principals (GAAP). The purpose of this requirement is to give consistent, detailed, and accurate information about how efficiently and effectively the agents of stockholders—the managers—are running the company. To make sure that managers do not misrepresent this financial information, the SEC also requires that the accounts be audited by an independent and accredited accounting firm. Similar regulations exist in most other developed nations. If the system works as intended, stockholders can have a lot of faith that the information contained in financial statements accurately reflects the state of affairs at a company. Among other things, such information can enable a stockholder to calculate the profitability (ROIC) of a company in which he or she invests and compare its ROIC against that of competitors.

Unfortunately, in the United States at least, this system has not always worked as intended. Although the vast majority of companies do file accurate information in their financial statements and although most auditors do a good job of reviewing that information, there is substantial evidence that a minority of companies have abused the system, aided in part by the compliance of auditors. This was clearly an issue at Enron, where the CFO and others misrepresented the true financial state of the company to investors by creating off-balance-sheet partnerships that hid the true state of Enron's indebtedness from public view. Enron's auditor, Arthur Andersen, also apparently went along with this deception, in direct violation of its fiduciary duty. Arthur Anderson also had lucrative consulting contracts with Enron that it did not want to jeopardize by questioning the accuracy of the company's financial statements. The losers in this mutual deception were shareholders, who had to rely on inaccurate information to make their investment decisions.

There have been numerous examples in recent years of managers' gaming financial statements to present a distorted picture of their company's finances to investors. The typical motive has been to inflate the earnings or revenues of a company, thereby generating investor enthusiasm and propelling the stock price higher, which gives managers an opportunity to cash in stock option grants for huge personal gain, obviously at the expense of stockholders who have been mislead by the reports (see Strategy in Action 11.2 for an example).

The gaming of financial statements by companies such as Enron and Computer Associates raises serious questions about the accuracy of the information contained in audited financial statements. In response, in 2002, the United States passed the Sarbanes-Oxley bill into law, which represents the biggest overhaul of accounting rules and corporate governance procedures since the 1930s. Among other things, Sarbanes-Oxley set up a new oversight board for accounting firms, required CEOs and CFOs to endorse their company's financial statements, and barred companies from hiring the same accounting firm for auditing and consulting services.

The Takeover Constraint

Given the imperfections in corporate governance mechanisms, it is clear that the agency problem may still exist at some companies. However, stockholders still have some residual power, for they can always sell their shares. If they start doing so in large numbers, the price of the company's shares will decline. If the share price falls far enough, the company might be worth less on the stock market than the book value of its assets. At this point, it may become an attractive acquisition target and runs the risk of being purchased by another enterprise, against the wishes of the target company's management.

The risk of being acquired by another company is known as the **takeover constraint**. The takeover constraint limits the extent to which managers can pursue strategies and take actions that put their own interests above those of stockholders. If they ignore stockholder interests and the company is acquired, senior managers typically lose their independence and probably their jobs as well. So the threat of takeover can constrain management action and limit the worst excesses of the agency problem.

During the 1980s and early 1990s, the threat of takeover was often enforced by corporate raiders—individuals or corporations that buy up large blocks of shares in companies that they think are pursuing strategies inconsistent with maximizing stockholder wealth. Corporate raiders argue that if these underperforming companies pursued different strategies, they could create more wealth for stockholders. Raiders buy stock in a company either to take over the business and run it more efficiently or to precipitate a change in the top management, replacing the existing team with one more likely to maximize stockholder returns. Raiders are motivated not by altruism but by gain. If they succeed in their takeover bid, they can institute strategies that create value for stockholders, including themselves. Even if a takeover bid fails, raiders can still earn millions, for their stockholdings will typically be bought out by the defending company for a hefty premium. Called **greenmail**, this source of gain stirred much controversy and debate about its benefits. While some claim that the threat posed by raiders has had a salutary effect on enterprise performance by pushing corporate management to run their companies better, others claim there is little evidence of this.[27]

Although the incidence of hostile takeover bids has fallen off significantly since the early 1990s, this should not be taken to imply that the takeover constraint is no longer operating. Unique circumstances existed in the early 2000s that have made it more difficult to execute hostile takeovers. The boom years of the 1990s left many corporations with excessive debt (corporate America entered the new century with record levels of debt on its balance sheets), which limits the ability of companies to finance acquisitions, particularly hostile acquisitions, which are often particularly expensive. In addition, the market valuations of many companies got so out of line with underlying fundamentals during the stock market bubble of the 1990s that even after a substantial fall in certain segments of the stock market, such as the technology sector, valuations are still high relative to historic norms, making the hostile acquisition of even poorly run and unprofitable companies expensive. However, takeovers tend to go in cycles, and it seems likely that once excesses are worked out of the stock market and worked off corporate balance sheets, the takeover constraint will begin to reassert itself. It should be remembered that the takeover constraint is the governance mechanism of last resort and is often invoked only when other governance mechanisms have failed.

Governance Mechanisms inside a Company

Thus far, this section has focused on the governance mechanisms designed to reduce the agency problem that potentially exists between stockholders and managers. Agency relationships also exist within a company, and the agency problem can thus arise between levels of management. In this section, we explore how the agency problem can be reduced within a company by using two complementary governance mechanisms to align the incentives and behavior of employees with those of upper-level management: strategic control systems and incentive systems.

Strategic Control Systems Strategic control systems are the primary governance mechanisms established within a company to reduce the scope of the agency problem between levels of management. These systems are the formal target setting, measurement, and feedback systems that allow managers to evaluate whether a company is executing the strategies necessary to maximize its long-run profitability and, in particular, whether the company is achieving superior efficiency, quality, innovation, and customer responsiveness. These are discussed in more detail in other chapters.

The purpose of strategic control systems is to (1) establish standards and targets against which performance can be measured, (2) create systems for measuring and monitoring performance on a regular basis, (3) compare actual performance against the established targets, and (4) evaluate results and take corrective action if necessary. In governance terms, their purpose is to make sure that lower-level managers, as the agents of top managers, are acting in a way that is consistent with top managers' goals, which should be to maximize the wealth of stockholders, subject to legal and ethical constraints.

One increasingly influential model that guides managers through the process of creating the right kind of strategic control systems to enhance organizational performance is the balanced scorecard model.[28] According to the balanced scorecard model, traditionally managers have primarily used financial measures of performance such as ROIC to measure and evaluate organizational performance. Financial information is extremely important, but it is not enough by itself. If managers are to obtain a true picture of organizational performance, financial information must be supplemented with performance measures that indicate how well an organization has been achieving the four building blocks of competitive advantage: efficiency, quality, innovation, and responsiveness to customers. This is so because financial results simply inform strategic managers about the results of decisions they have already taken; the other measures balance this picture of performance by informing managers about how accurately the organization has in place the building blocks that drive future performance.[29]

One version of the way the balanced scorecard operates is presented in Figure 11.3. Based on an organization's mission and goals, strategic managers develop a set of strategies to build competitive advantage to achieve these goals. They then establish an organizational structure to use resources to obtain a competitive advantage.[30] To evaluate how well the strategy and structure are working, managers develop specific performance measures that assess how well the four building blocks of competitive advantage are being achieved:

1. *Efficiency* can be measured by the level of production costs, the productivity of labor (such as the employee hours needed to make a product), the productivity of capital (such as revenues per dollar invested in property, plant, and equipment), and the cost of raw materials.
2. *Quality* can be measured by the number of rejects, the number of defective products returned from customers, and the level of product reliability over time.
3. *Innovation* can be measured by the number of new products introduced, the percentage of revenues generated from new products in a defined period, the time taken to develop the next generation of new products versus the competition, and the productivity of R&D (how much R&D spending is required to produce a successful product).
4. *Responsiveness to customers* can be measured by the number of repeat customers, customer defection rates, level of on-time delivery to customers, and level of customer service.

Figure 11.3   A Balanced Scorecard Approach

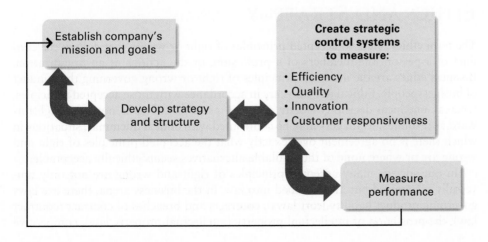

As Kaplan and Norton, the developers of this approach, suggest, "Think of the balanced scorecard as the dials and indicators in an airplane cockpit. For the complex task of navigating and flying an airplane, pilots need detailed information about many aspects of the flight. They need information on fuel, air speed, altitude, learning, destination, and other indicators that summarize the current and predicted environment. Reliance on one instrument can be fatal. Similarly, the complexity of managing an organization today requires that managers be able to view performance in several areas simultaneously."[31]

The way in which managers' ability to build a competitive advantage translates into organizational performance is then measured using financial measures, such as the ROIC, the return on sales, and the capital turnover ratio (see Chapter 3). Based on an evaluation of the complete set of measures in the balanced scorecard, strategic managers are in a good position to reevaluate the company's mission and goals and take corrective action to rectify problems, limit the agency problem, or exploit new opportunities by changing the organization's strategy and structure—which is the purpose of strategic control.

Employee Incentives Control systems alone may not be sufficient to align incentives between stockholders, senior management, and the rest of the organization. To help do this, positive incentive systems are often put into place to motivate employees to work toward goals that are central to maximizing long-run profitability. As already noted, employee stock ownership plans (ESOPs) are one form of positive incentive, as are stock option grants. In the 1990s, ESOPs and stock ownership grants were pushed down deep within many organizations. The logic behind such systems is straightforward: recognizing that the stock price, and therefore their own wealth, is dependent on the profitability of the company, employees will work toward maximizing profitability.

In addition to stock-based compensation systems, employee compensation can also be tied to goals that are linked to the attainment of superior efficiency, quality, innovation, and customer responsiveness. For example, the bonus pay of a manufacturing employee might depend on attaining quality and productivity targets, which if reached will lower the costs of the company, increase customer satisfaction, and boost profitability. Similarly, the bonus pay of a salesperson might be dependent on surpassing sales targets and that of an R&D employee on the success of new products he or she had a hand in developing.

ETHICS AND STRATEGY

The term **ethics** refers to accepted principles of right or wrong that govern the conduct of a person, the members of a profession, or the actions of an organization. **Business ethics** are the accepted principles of right or wrong governing the conduct of businesspeople. Ethical decisions are in accordance with those accepted principles, whereas unethical decisions violate accepted principles. This is not as straightforward as it sounds. Managers may be confronted with **ethical dilemmas**, situations in which there is no agreement over exactly what the accepted principles of right and wrong are or where none of the available alternatives seems ethically acceptable.

In our society, many accepted principles of right and wrong are not only universally recognized but also codified into law. In the business arena, there are laws governing product liability (tort laws), contracts and breaches of contract (contract law), the protection of intellectual property (intellectual property law), competitive behavior (antitrust law), and the selling of securities (securities law). Not only is it unethical to break these laws, it is illegal.

In this book, we argue that the preeminent goal of managers in a business should be to pursue strategies that maximize the long-run profitability and profit growth of the enterprise, thereby boosting returns to stockholders. Strategies, of course, must be consistent with the laws that govern business behavior: managers must act legally while seeking to maximize the long-run profitability of the enterprise. Unfortunately, as we have already seen in this chapter, there are examples of managers breaking the law. Moreover, managers may take advantage of ambiguities and gray areas in the law, of which there are many in our common law system, to pursue actions that are at best legally suspect and, in any event, clearly unethical. It is important to realize, however, that behaving ethically goes beyond staying within the bounds of the law. For example, see Strategy in Action 11.3, which discusses Nike's use of "sweatshop labor" in developing nations to make sneakers for consumers in the developed world. While Nike was not breaking any laws by using inexpensive laborers who worked long hours for poor pay in poor working conditions, and neither were its subcontractors, many considered it unethical to use subcontractors who by Western standards clearly exploited their workforce. In this section, we take a closer look at the ethical issues that managers may confront when developing strategy and at the steps managers can take to ensure that strategic decisions are not only legal but also ethical.

Ethical Issues in Strategy

The ethical issues that strategic managers confront cover a wide range of topics, but most are due to a potential conflict between the goals of the enterprise, or the goals of individual managers, and the fundamental rights of important stakeholders, including stockholders, customers, employees, suppliers, competitors, communities, and the general public. Stakeholders have basic rights that should be respected, and it is unethical to violate those rights.

Stockholders have the right to timely and accurate information about their investment (in accounting statements), and it is unethical to violate that right. Customers have the right to be fully informed about the products and services they purchase, including the right to information about how those products might cause harm to them or others, and it is unethical to restrict their access to such information. Employees have the right to safe working conditions, fair compensation for the work they perform, and just treatment by managers. Suppliers have the right to expect contracts to be respected, and the firm should not take advantage of a power disparity between itself and a supplier to opportunistically rewrite a contract. Competitors have the right to expect that the firm will abide by the rules of competition and not violate the basic principles of antitrust laws. Communities and the general public, including their political representatives in government, have the right to expect that a firm will not violate the basic expectations that society places on enterprises, for example, by dumping toxic pollutants into the environment or overcharging for work performed on government contracts.

Those who take the stakeholder view of business ethics often argue that it is in the enlightened self-interest of managers to behave in an ethical manner that recognizes and respects the fundamental rights of stakeholders because doing so will ensure the support of stakeholders and thus ultimately benefit the firm and its managers. Others go beyond this instrumental approach to ethics to argue that, in many cases, acting ethically is simply the right thing to do. They argue that businesses need

11.3 STRATEGY IN ACTION

Nike: The Sweatshop Debate

Nike is in many ways the quintessential global corporation. Established in 1972 by former University of Oregon track star Phil Knight, Nike is now one of the leading marketers of athletic shoes and apparel in the world. By 2004, the company had more than $12 billion in annual revenues, an ROIC of 17.5%, and sold its products in some 140 countries. Nike does not do any manufacturing. Rather, it designs and markets its products and contracts for their manufacture from a global network of 600 factories owned by subcontractors scattered around the globe that together employ some 550,000 people. This huge corporation has made founder Phil Knight into one of the richest people in America. Nike's marketing phrase, "Just Do It!" has become as recognizable in popular culture as its "swoosh" logo or the faces of its celebrity sponsors, such as Tiger Woods.

For all of its successes, however, the company has been dogged by repeated and persistent accusations that its products are made in "sweatshops," where workers, many of them children, slave away in hazardous conditions for wages that are below subsistence level. Nike's wealth, its detractors claim, has been built on the backs of the world's poor. Many see Nike as a symbol of the evils of globalization: a rich Western corporation exploiting the world's poor to provide expensive shoes and apparel to the pampered consumers of the developed world. Nike's "Niketown" stores have become standard targets for antiglobalization protestors. Several nongovernmental organizations, such as San Francisco-based Global Exchange, a human rights organization dedicated to promoting environmental, political, and social justice around the world, have targeted Nike for repeated criticism and protests. News programs such as CBS' *48 Hours*, hosted by Dan Rather, have run exposés on working conditions in foreign factories that supply Nike. And students on the campuses of several major United States universities with which Nike has lucrative sponsorship deals have protested against those deals, citing Nike's use of sweatshop labor.

Typical of the allegations were those detailed on *48 Hours* in 1996. The report painted a picture of young women at a Vietnamese subcontractor who worked six days a week, in poor working conditions with toxic materials, for only 20 cents an hour. The report also stated that a living wage in Vietnam was at least $3 a day, an income that could

not be achieved without working substantial overtime. Nike was not breaking any laws, and nor were its subcontractors, but this report and others like it raised questions about the ethics of using "sweatshop labor" to make what were essentially fashion accessories. It may have been legal; it may have helped the company to increase its profitability, but was it ethical to use subcontractors who by Western standards clearly exploited their workforce? Nike's critics thought not, and the company found itself the focus of a wave of demonstrations and consumer boycotts.

Adding fuel to the fire, in November 1997, Global Exchange obtained and leaked a confidential report by Ernst & Young of an audit that Nike had commissioned of a Vietnam factory owned by a Nike subcontractor. The factory had 9,200 workers and made 400,000 pairs of shoes a month. The Ernst & Young report painted a dismal picture of thousands of women, most younger than 25, laboring 10.5 hours a day, six days a week, in excessive heat and noise and foul air, for slightly more than $10 a week. The report also found that workers with skin or breathing problems had not been transferred to departments free of chemicals. More than half the workers who dealt with dangerous chemicals did not wear protective masks or gloves. The report stated that, in some parts of the plant, workers were exposed to carcinogens that exceeded local legal standards by 177 times, and 77% of the employees suffered from respiratory problems.

These exposés surrounding Nike's use of subcontractors forced the company to reexamine its policies. Realizing that its subcontracting policies were perceived as unethical, Nike's management took a number of steps. These included establishing a code of conduct for Nike subcontractors and setting up a scheme whereby all subcontractors would be monitored annually by independent auditors. Nike's code of conduct required that all employees at footwear factories be at least 18 years old and that exposure to potentially toxic materials would not exceed the permissible exposure limits established by the U.S. Occupational Safety and Health Administration (OSHA) for workers in the United States. In short, Nike concluded that behaving ethically required going beyond the requirements of the law. It required the establishment and enforcement of rules that adhere to accepted moral principles of right and wrong.

Sources: "Boycott Nike," CBS News *48 Hours,* October 17, 1996; D. Jones, "Critics Tie Sweatshop Sneakers to 'Air Jordan,'" *USA Today,* June 6, 1996, 1B; "Global Exchange Special Report: Nike Just Don't Do It," available at http://www.globalexchange.org/education/publications/newsltr6.97p2.html#nike; S. Greenhouse, "Nike Shoe Plant in Vietnam Is Called Unsafe for Workers," *New York Times,* November 8, 1997; V. Dobnik, "Chinese Workers Abused Making Nikes, Reeboks," *Seattle Times,* September 21, 1997, A4.

to recognize their noblesse oblige and give something back to the society that made their success possible. *Noblesse oblige* is a French term that refers to honorable and benevolent behavior that is considered the responsibility of people of high (noble) birth. In a business setting, it is taken to mean benevolent behavior that is the moral responsibility of successful enterprises.

Unethical behavior often arises in a corporate setting when managers decide to put the attainment of their own personal goals, or the goals of the enterprise, above the fundamental rights of one or more stakeholder groups (in other words, unethical behavior may arise from agency problems). The most common examples of such behavior involve self-dealing; information manipulation; anticompetitive behavior; opportunistic exploitation of other players in the value chain in which the firm is embedded (including suppliers, complement providers, and distributors); the maintenance of substandard working conditions; environmental degradation; and corruption.

Self-dealing occurs when managers find a way to feather their own nests with corporate monies, and we have already discussed several examples in this chapter (such as Computer Associates). **Information manipulation** occurs when managers use their control over corporate data to distort or hide information to enhance their own financial situation or the competitive position of the firm. As we have seen, many of the recent accounting scandals involved the deliberate manipulation of financial information. Information manipulation can also occur with regard to nonfinancial data. This occurred when managers at the tobacco companies suppressed internal research that linked smoking to health problems, violating the rights of consumers to accurate information about the dangers of smoking. When evidence of this came to light, lawyers brought class action suits against the tobacco companies, claiming that they had intentionally caused harm to smokers: they had broken tort law by promoting a product that they knew did serious harm to consumers. In 1999, the tobacco companies settled a lawsuit brought by the states who sought to recover health care costs associated with tobacco-related illnesses; the total payout to the states was $260 billion.

Anticompetitive behavior covers a range of actions aimed at harming actual or potential competitors, most often by using monopoly power, and thereby enhancing the long-run prospects of the firm. For example, in the 1990s, the Justice Department claimed that Microsoft used its monopoly in operating systems to force PC manufacturers to bundle Microsoft's Web browser, Internet Explorer, with Windows and to display Internet Explorer prominently on the computer desktop (the screen seen when starting PCs). Microsoft reportedly told PC makers that it would not supply them with Windows unless they did this. Since the PC makers had to have Windows to sell their machines, this was a powerful threat. The alleged aim of the action, an example of "tie-in-sales," which is illegal under antitrust laws, was to drive a competing browser maker, Netscape, out of business. The courts ruled that Microsoft was indeed abusing its monopoly power in this case, and under a 2001 consent decree, the company agreed to stop the practice.

Putting the legal issues aside, action such as that allegedly undertaken by managers at Microsoft is unethical on at least three counts. First, it violates the rights of end-users by unfairly limiting their choice; second, it violates the rights of downstream participants in the industry value chain, in this case PC makers, by forcing them to incorporate a particular product in their design; and third, it violates the rights of competitors to free and fair competition.

Opportunistic exploitation of other players in the value chain in which the firm is embedded is another example of unethical behavior. Exploitation of this kind typically occurs when the managers of a firm seek to unilaterally rewrite the terms of a contract with suppliers, buyers, or complement providers in a way that is more favorable to the firm, often using their power to force the revision through. For example, in the late 1990s, Boeing entered into a $2 billion contract with Titanium Metals Corporation to buy certain amounts of titanium annually for 10 years. In 2000, after Titanium Metals had already spent $100 million to expand its production capacity to fulfill the contract, Boeing demanded that the contract be renegotiated, asking for lower prices and an end to minimum purchase agreements. As a major purchaser of titanium, managers at Boeing probably thought they had the power to push this contract revision through, and the investment by Titanium Metals meant that they would be unlikely to walk away from the deal. Titanium Metals promptly sued Boeing for breach of contract. The dispute was settled out of court, and under a revised agreement Boeing agreed to pay monetary damages to Titanium Metals (reported to be in the $60 million range) and entered into an amended contract to purchase titanium.[32] Irrespective of the legality of this action, it was arguably unethical because it violated the rights of suppliers to have buyers who deal with them in a fair and open way.

Substandard working conditions arise when managers underinvest in working conditions, or pay employees below-market rates, to reduce their costs of production. The most extreme examples of such behavior occur when a firm establishes operations in countries that lack the workplace regulations found in developed nations such as the United States. The example of Nike (see Strategy in Action 11.3) falls into this category. In another recent example, The Ohio Art company ran into an ethical storm when newspaper reports alleged that it had moved production of its popular Etch A Sketch toy from Ohio to a supplier in Shenzhen province where employees, mostly teenagers, worked long hours for 24 cents per hour, below the legal minimum wage of 33 cents an hour in Shenzhen province. Moreover, production reportedly started at 7:30 a.m. and continued until 10 p.m., with breaks only for lunch and dinner. Saturdays and Sundays are treated as normal workdays. This translates into a workweek of seven 12-hour days, or 84 hours a week, well above the standard 40-hour week set by authorities in Shenzhen. Such working conditions clearly violate the rights of employees in China, as specified by local regulations (which are poorly enforced). Is it ethical for the Ohio Art company to use such a supplier? Many would say not.[33] As the next Running Case documents, Walmart has come under fire for having substandard working conditions, something that it is now trying hard to correct.

Environmental degradation occurs when a firm takes actions that directly or indirectly result in pollution or other forms of environmental harm. Environmental degradation can violate the rights of local communities and the general public for such things as clean air and water, land that is free from pollution by toxic chemicals, and properly managed forests (because forests absorb rainfall, improper deforestation results in land erosion and floods).

Finally, **corruption** can arise in a business context when managers pay bribes to gain access to lucrative business contracts. For example, it was alleged that Halliburton was part of a consortium that paid some $180 million in bribes to win a lucrative contract to build a natural gas plant in Nigeria.[34] Corruption is clearly unethical because it violates a bundle of rights, including the right of competitors to a level playing field when bidding for contracts, when government officials are involved, the right of citizens to expect that government officials act in the best interest of the local community or nation, and not in response to corrupt payments that feather their own nests.

RUNNING CASE

Working Conditions at Walmart

When Sam Walton founded Walmart, one of his core values was that if the company treated employees with respect, tied compensation to the performance of the enterprise, trusted them with important information and decisions, and provided ample opportunities for advancement, they would repay the company with dedication and hard work. For years the formula seemed to work. Employees were called "associates" to reflect their status within the company, even the lowest hourly employee was eligible to participate in profit-sharing plans and could use profit-sharing bonuses to purchase company stock at a discount to its market value. The company made a virtue of promoting from within (two-thirds of managers at Walmart started as hourly employees). At the same time, Walton and his successors always demanded loyalty and hard work from employees—managers for example, were expected to move to a new store on very short notice—and base pay for hourly workers was very low. Still, as long as the up side was there, little grumbling was heard from employees.

However, more recently the relationships between the company and its employees has been strained by a succession of lawsuits claiming that Walmart pressures hourly employees to work overtime without compensating them; systematically discriminates against women; and knowingly uses contractors who hire undocumented immigrant workers to clean its stores, paying them below minimum wage.

For example, a class-action lawsuit in Washington State claimed that Walmart routinely (1) pressured hourly employees not to report all their time worked; (2) failed to keep true time records, sometimes shaving hours from employee logs; (3) failed to give employees full rest or meal breaks; (4) threatened to fire or demote employees who would not work off the clock; and (5) required workers to attend unpaid meetings and computer training. Moreover, the suit claimed that Walmart has a strict "no overtime" policy, punishing employees who work more than 40 hours a week, yet the company also gives employees more work than can be completed in a 40-hour week. The Washington suit is one of more than 30 suits that have been filed around the nation in recent years.

With regard to discrimination against women, complaints date back to a 1996, when an assistant manager in a California store, Stephanie Odle, came across the W-2 of a male assistant manager who worked in the same store. The W-2 showed that he was paid $10,000 more than Odle. When she asked her boss to explain the disparity, she was told that her coworker had "a wife and kids to support." When Odle, a single mother, protested, she was asked to submit a personal household budget. She was then granted a $2,080 raise. Subsequently, Odle was fired, she claims for speaking up. In 1998, she filed a discrimination suit against the company. Others began to file suits around the same time, and by 2004 the legal action had evolved into a class action suit that covered 1.6 million current and former female employees at Walmart. The suit claims that Walmart did not pay female employees the same as their male counterparts and did not provide them with equal opportunities for promotion.

In the case of both undocumented overtime and discrimination, Walmart admits to no wrongdoing. The company does recognize that with more than 2 million employees, some problems are bound to arise, but it claims that there is no systematic company-wide effort to get hourly employees to work without pay or to discriminate against women. Indeed, the company claims that this could not be the case because hiring and promotion decisions are made at the store level.

For their part, critics charge that while the company may have no policies that promote undocumented overtime or discrimination, the hard driving cost containment culture of the company had created an environment in which abuses can thrive. Store managers, for example, are expected to meet challenging performance goals, and, in an effort to do so, they may be tempted to pressure subordinates to work additional hours without pay. Similarly, company policy requiring managers to move to different stores at short notice unfairly discriminates against women, who lack the flexibility to uproot their families and move them to another state at short notice.

While the lawsuits are ongoing and may take years to resolve, Walmart has taken steps to change

(continued)

its employment practices. For example, the company has created a director of diversity, a diversity compliance team, and restructured its pay scales to promote equal pay regardless of gender. Walmart has also taken action to stop employees working overtime without pay. For example, it programmed cash registers to shut down after an employee had exceeded a certain number of hours, and has told managers to make sure that employees take lunch and rest breaks.

Sources: S. Holt, "Walmart Workers Suit Wins Class Action Status," *Seattle Times,* October 9, 2004, E1, E4; C. Daniels, "Women versus Walmart," *Fortune,* July 21, 2003, 79–82; C. R. Gentry, "Off the Clock," *Chain Store Age,* February 2003, 33–36; M. Grimm, "Wal-Mart Uber Alles," *American Demographic,* October 2003, 38–42; S. Rosenbloom and M. Barbaro, "Green Light Specials, Now at Walmart," *New York Times,* January 25, 2009, B1, B4

The Roots of Unethical Behavior

Why do some managers behave unethically? What motivates them to engage in actions that violate accepted principles of right and wrong, trample on the rights of one or more stakeholder groups, or simply break the law? While there is no simple answer to this question, a few generalizations can be made.[35] First, it is important to recognize that business ethics are not divorced from **personal ethics**, which are the generally accepted principles of right and wrong governing the conduct of individuals. As individuals, we are taught that it is wrong to lie and cheat and right to behave with integrity and honor and stand up for what we believe to be right and true. The personal ethical code that guides our behavior comes from a number of sources, including our parents, our schools, our religion, and the media. Our personal ethical codes will exert a profound influence on the way we behave as businesspeople. An individual with a strong sense of personal ethics is less likely to behave in an unethical manner in a business setting; in particular, he or she is less likely to engage in self-dealing and more likely to behave with integrity.

Second, many studies of unethical behavior in a business setting have come to the conclusion that businesspeople sometimes do not realize that they are behaving unethically, primarily because they simply fail to ask the relevant question: Is this decision or action ethical? Instead, they apply a straightforward business calculation to what they perceive to be a business decision, forgetting that the decision may also have an important ethical dimension.[36] The fault here lies in processes that do not incorporate ethical considerations into business decision making. This may have been the case at Nike when managers originally made subcontracting decisions (see Strategy in Action 11.3). Those decisions were probably made on the basis of good economic logic. Subcontractors were probably chosen on the basis of business variables such as cost, delivery, and product quality, and key managers simply failed to ask, "How does this subcontractor treat its workforce?" If they thought about the question at all, they probably reasoned that it was the subcontractors' concern, not theirs.

Unfortunately, the climate in some businesses does not encourage people to think through the ethical consequences of business decisions. This brings us to the third cause of unethical behavior in businesses: an organizational culture that de-emphasizes business ethics and considers all decisions to be purely economic ones. A related fourth cause of unethical behavior may be pressure from top management to meet performance goals that are unrealistic, which can be attained only by cutting corners or acting in an unethical manner.

An organizational culture can "legitimize" behavior that society would judge as unethical, particularly when this is mixed with a focus on unrealistic performance goals, such as maximizing short-term economic performance regardless of the costs. In such circumstances, there is a greater-than-average probability that managers will violate their own personal ethics and engage in behavior that is unethical. By the same token, an organizational culture can do just the opposite and reinforce the need for ethical behavior. At HP, for example, Bill Hewlett and David Packard, the company's founders, propagated a set of values known as "The HP Way." These values, which shape the way business is conducted both within and by the corporation, have an important ethical component. Among other things, they stress the need for confidence in and respect for people, open communication, and concern for the individual employee.

This brings us to a fifth root cause of unethical behavior: *unethical leadership*. Leaders help to establish the culture of an organization, and they set the example that others follow. Other employees in a business often take their cues from business leaders, and if those leaders do not behave in an ethical manner, employees might not either. It is not what leaders say that matters, but what they do. A good example is Ken Lay, the former CEO of Enron. While constantly referring to Enron's code of ethics in public statements, Lay simultaneously engaged in behavior that was ethically suspect. Among other things, he failed to discipline subordinates who had inflated earnings by engaging in corrupt energy trading schemes. Such behavior sent a very clear message to Enron's employees: unethical behavior would be tolerated if it boosted earnings.

Behaving Ethically

What is the best way for managers to ensure that ethical considerations are taken into account? In many cases, there is no easy answer to this question, for many of the most vexing ethical problems involve very real dilemmas and suggest no obvious right course of action. Nevertheless, managers can and should do at least seven things to ensure that basic ethical principles are adhered to and that ethical issues are routinely considered when making business decisions. They can (1) favor hiring and promoting people with a well-grounded sense of personal ethics, (2) build an organizational culture that places a high value on ethical behavior, (3) make sure that leaders within the business not only articulate the rhetoric of ethical behavior but also act in a manner that is consistent with that rhetoric, (4) put decision-making processes in place that require people to consider the ethical dimension of business decisions, (5) use ethics officers, (6) put strong governance processes in place, and (7) act with moral courage.

Hiring and Promotion   It seems obvious that businesses should strive to hire people who have a strong sense of personal ethics and would not engage in unethical or illegal behavior. Similarly, one would rightly expect a business to not promote people, and perhaps fire people, whose behavior does not match generally accepted ethical standards. But doing so is actually very difficult. How do you know that someone has a poor sense of personal ethics? In our society, if someone lacks personal ethics, he or she may hide this fact to retain people's trust.

Is there anything that businesses can do to make sure that they do not hire people who turn out to have poor personal ethics, particularly given that people have an incentive to hide this from public view (indeed, unethical people may well lie about their nature)? Businesses can give potential employees psychological tests to try to discern their ethical predisposition, and they can check with prior employers regarding someone's reputation, such as by asking for letters of reference and talking to people who have worked with the prospective employee. The latter approach is certainly not uncommon and does indeed influence the hiring process. As for promoting people who have displayed poor ethics, it should not occur in a company in which the organizational culture values ethical behavior and where leaders act accordingly.

Organizational Culture and Leadership   To foster ethical behavior, businesses need to build an organizational culture that places a high value on ethical behavior. Three actions are particularly important. First, businesses must explicitly articulate values that place a strong emphasis on ethical behavior. Many companies now do this by drafting a **code of ethics**, a formal statement of the ethical priorities a business adheres to. Others have incorporated ethical statements into documents that articulate the values or mission of the business. For example, the food and consumer products giant Unilever has a code of ethics that includes the following points: "We will not use any form of forced, compulsory, or child labor" and "No employee may offer, give, or receive any gift or payment which is, or may be construed as being, a bribe. Any demand for, or offer of, a bribe must be rejected immediately and reported to management."[37] Unilever's principles send a very clear message to managers and employees within the organization.

Having articulated values in a code of ethics or some other document, it is important that leaders in the business give life and meaning to those words by repeatedly emphasizing their importance and then acting on them. This means using every relevant opportunity to stress the importance of business ethics and making sure that key business decisions not only make good economic sense but also are ethical. Many companies have gone a step further and hired independent firms to audit them and make sure that they are behaving in a manner consistent with their ethical code. Nike, for example, has in recent years hired independent auditors to make sure that its subcontractors are living up to Nike's code of conduct.

Finally, building an organizational culture that places a high value on ethical behavior requires incentive and reward systems, including promotion systems that reward people who engage in ethical behavior and sanction those who do not.

Decision-Making Processes   In addition to establishing the right kind of ethical culture in an organization, businesspeople must be able to think through the ethical implications of decisions in a systematic way. To do this, they need moral compasses, and both rights theories and Rawls's theory of justice help to provide such compasses. Beyond these theories, some experts on ethics have proposed a straightforward practical guide, or ethical algorithm, to determine whether a decision is ethical. A decision is acceptable on ethical grounds if a businessperson can answer "yes" to each of these questions:

1. Does my decision fall within the accepted values or standards that typically apply in the organizational environment (as articulated in a code of ethics or some other corporate statement)?
2. Am I willing to see the decision communicated to all stakeholders affected by it—for example, by having it reported in newspapers or on television?
3. Would the people with whom I have a significant personal relationship, such as family members, friends, or even managers in other businesses, approve of the decision?

Ethics Officers To make sure that businesses behave in an ethical manner, a number of firms now have ethics officers. These individuals are responsible for making sure that all employees are trained to be ethically aware, that ethical considerations enter the business decision-making process, and that the company's code of ethics is adhered to. Ethics officers may also be responsible for auditing decisions to make sure that they are consistent with this code. In many businesses, ethics officers act as internal ombudspersons with responsibility for handling confidential inquiries from employees, investigating complaints from employees or others, reporting findings, and making recommendations for change.

United Technologies (UTC), a large aerospace company with worldwide revenues of more than $28 billion, has had a formal code of ethics since 1990. There are now some 160 "business practice officers" within UTC this is the company's name for ethics officers) who are responsible for making sure that the code is adhered to. UTC also established an ombudsperson program in 1986 that allows employees to inquire anonymously about ethics issues. The program has received some 56,000 inquiries since 1986, and 8,000 cases have been handled by an ombudsperson.[38]

Strong Corporate Governance Strong corporate governance procedures are needed to make sure that managers adhere to ethical norms, in particular, that senior managers do not engage in self-dealing or information manipulation. The key to strong corporate governance procedures is an independent board of directors that is willing to hold top managers to account for self-dealing and is able to question the information provided to them by managers. If companies like Tyco, WorldCom, and Enron had had a strong board of directors, it is unlikely that they would have been racked by accounting scandals or that top managers would have been able to view the funds of these corporations as their own personal treasuries.

There are five cornerstones of strong governance. The first is a board of directors composed of a majority of outside directors who have no management responsibilities in the firm, are willing and able to hold top managers to account, and do not have business ties with important insiders. The outside directors should be individuals of high integrity whose reputation is based on their ability to act independently. The second cornerstone is a board in which the positions of CEO and chairman are held by separate individuals, with the chairman as an outside director. When the CEO is also chairman of the board of directors, he or she can control the agenda, thereby furthering his or her own personal agenda (which may include self-dealing) or limiting criticism against current corporate policies. The third cornerstone is a compensation committee formed by the board composed entirely of outside directors. It is the compensation committee that sets the level of pay for top managers, including stock option grants and the like. By making sure that the compensation committee is independent of managers, one reduces the scope of self-dealing. Fourth, the audit committee of the board, which reviews the financial statements of the firm, should also be composed of outsiders, thereby encouraging vigorous independent questioning of the firm's financial statements. Finally, the board should use outside auditors who are truly independent and do not have a conflict of interest. This was not the case in many recent accounting scandals, where the outside auditors were also consultants to the corporation and therefore less likely to ask hard questions of management for fear that doing so would jeopardize lucrative consulting contracts.

Moral Courage It is important to recognize that sometimes managers and others need significant moral courage. It is moral courage that enables managers to walk away from a decision that is profitable but unethical, that gives employees the strength to say no to superiors who instruct them to behave unethically, and that gives employees the integrity to go to the media and blow the whistle on persistent unethical behavior in a company. Moral courage does not come easily; there are well-known cases in which individuals have lost their jobs because they blew the whistle on corporate behaviors.

Companies can strengthen the moral courage of employees by committing themselves to not take retribution on employees that exercise moral courage, say no to superiors, or otherwise complain about unethical actions. For example, Unilever's code of ethics includes the following:

> Any breaches of the Code must be reported in accordance with the procedures specified by the Joint Secretaries. The Board of Unilever will not criticize management for any loss of business resulting from adherence to these principles and other mandatory policies and instructions. The Board of Unilever expects employees to bring to their attention, or to that of senior management, any breach or suspected breach of these principles. Provision has been made for employees to be able to report in confidence and no employee will suffer as a consequence of doing so.[39]

This statement gives "permission" to employees to exercise moral courage. Companies can also set up ethics hotlines that allow employees to anonymously register complaints with a corporate ethics officer.

Final Words The steps discussed in this chapter can help to ensure that, when managers make business decisions, they are fully cognizant of the ethical implications and do not violate basic ethical prescripts. At the same time, not all ethical dilemmas have clean and obvious solutions—that is why they are dilemmas. At the end of the day, there are clearly things that a business should not do, and there are things that they should do, but there are also actions that present managers with true dilemmas. In these cases, a premium is placed on the ability of managers to make sense out of complex, messy situations and to make balanced decisions that are as just as possible.

SUMMARY OF CHAPTER

1. Stakeholders are individuals or groups that have an interest, claim, or stake in the company, in what it does, and in how well it performs.

2. Stakeholders are in an exchange relationship with the company. They supply the organization with important resources (or contributions) and in exchange expect their interests to be satisfied (by inducements).

3. A company cannot always satisfy the claims of all stakeholders. The goals of different groups may conflict. The company must identify the most important stakeholders and give highest priority to pursuing strategies that satisfy their needs.

4. A company's stockholders are its legal owners and the providers of risk capital, a major source of the capital resources that allow a company to operate its business. As such, they have a unique role among stakeholder groups.

5. Maximizing long-run profitability and profit growth is the route to maximizing returns to stockholders, and it is also consistent with satisfying the claims of several other key stakeholder groups.

6. When pursuing strategies that maximize profitability, a company has an obligation to do so within the limits set by the law and in a manner consistent with societal expectations.

7. An agency relationship arises whenever one party delegates decision-making authority or control over resources to another.

8. The essence of the agency problem is that the interests of principals and agents are not always the same, and some agents may take advantage of information asymmetries to maximize their own interests at the expense of principals.

9. Several governance mechanisms serve to limit the agency problem between stockholders and managers, including the board of directors, stock-based compensation schemes, financial statements and auditors, and the threat of a takeover.

10. The term *ethics* refers to accepted principles of right or wrong that govern the conduct of a person, the members of a profession, or the actions of an organization. Business ethics are the accepted principles of right or wrong governing the conduct of businesspeople, and an ethical strategy is one that does not violate these accepted principles.

11. Unethical behavior is rooted in poor personal ethics—the inability to recognize that ethical issues are at stake, as when there are psychological and geographical distances between a foreign subsidiary and the home office: a failure to incorporate ethical issues into strategic and operational decision making; a dysfunctional culture; and failure of leaders to act in an ethical manner.

12. To make sure that ethical issues are considered in business decisions, managers should (a) favor hiring and promoting people with well-grounded senses of personal ethics; (b) build an organizational culture that places a high value on ethical behavior; (c) make sure that leaders within the business not only articulate the rhetoric of ethical behavior but also act in a manner that is consistent with that rhetoric; (d) put decision-making processes in place that require people to consider the ethical dimension of business decisions; (e) use ethics officers; (f) have strong corporate governance procedures; and (g) be morally courageous and encourage others to be the same.

DISCUSSION QUESTIONS

1. Under what conditions is it ethically defensible to outsource production to producers in the developing world who have much lower labor costs when such actions involve laying off long-term employees in the firm's home country?

2. How might a company configure its strategy-making processes to reduce the probability that managers will pursue their own self-interest at the expense of stockholders?

3. How prevalent has the agency problem been in corporate America during the last decade?

During the late 1990s, there was a boom in initial public offerings of Internet companies (dot-com companies). The boom was supported by sky-high valuations often assigned to Internet start-ups that had no revenues or earnings. The boom came to an abrupt end in 2001 when the NASDAQ stock market collapsed, losing almost 80% of its value. Who do you think benefited most from this boom: investors (stockholders) in those companies, managers, or investment bankers?

The Rise and Fall of Dennis Kozlowski

Under the leadership of Dennis Kozlowski, who became CEO of Tyco in 1990, the company's revenues expanded from $3.1 billion to almost $40 billion. Most of this growth was due to a series of acquisitions that took Tyco into a diverse range of unrelated businesses. Kozlowski was initially lauded in the business press as a great manager who bought undervalued assets and then enhanced their value by imposing tight financial controls at the acquired companies. Certainly both profits and the stock price advanced at a healthy clip during much of the 1990s.

Tyco financed the acquisitions by taking on significant debt commitments, which by 2002 exceeded $23 billion. As Tyco expanded, some questioned the company's ability to service its debt commitments. Others claimed that management was engaging in "accounting tricks" to pad its books and make the company appear significantly more profitable than it actually was. Tyco's defenders pointed out that its accounts were independently audited every year, and the outside accountants had detected no problems. These criticisms, which were ignored for some time, were finally shown to have some validity in 2002 when Kozlowski was forced out by the board and subsequently charged with tax evasion by federal authorities.

Among other charges, authorities claimed that Kozlowski treated Tyco as his personal treasury, drawing on company funds to purchase an expensive Manhattan apartment and a world-class art collection that he obviously thought were befitting of the CEO of a major corporation. Kozlowski even used company funds to help pay for an expensive birthday party for his wife—which included toga-clad ladies, gladiators, a naked-woman-with-exploding-breasts birthday cake and a version of Michelangelo's *David* that peed vodka! Kozlowski was replaced by a company outsider, Edward Breen. In 2003, after a special audit requested by Breen, Tyco took a $1.5 billion charge against earnings for accounting errors made during the Kozlowski era (i.e., Tyco's profits had been overstated by $1.5 billion during Kozlowski's tenure). Breen also set about dismantling parts of the empire that Kozlowski had built, divesting several businesses.

After a lengthy criminal trial in June 2005, Dennis Kozlowski and Mark Swartz, the former chief financial officer of Tyco, were convicted of 23 counts of grand larceny, conspiracy, securities fraud, and falsifying business records in connection with what prosecutors described as the systematic looting of millions of dollars from the conglomerate (Kozlowski was found guilty of looting $90 million from Tyco). Both were sentenced to jail for a minimum of eight years. As for Tyco, in 2006, CEO Ed Breen announced that the company would be broken up into three parts, a testament to the strategic incoherence of the conglomerate that Kozlowski built.[40]

Case Discussion Questions

1. Under the leadership of Dennis Kozlowski, Tyco grew rapidly for a decade. Why do you think Kozlowski pursued his growth through acquisition strategy? How did it benefit Tyco? How did it benefit Kozlowski?

2. What do you think leads top managers to engage in accounting manipulations to pad earnings, as apparently happened at Tyco?

3. During the period when Tyco's profits were apparently overstated to the tune of $1.5 billion, its accounts were audited every year by a major independent accounting firm that signed off on them. Why do you think that the accounting firm did not catch the manipulations at Tyco?

4. Why do you think Kozlowski and Swartz, both bright successful businessmen, engaged in the behavior that they did? What motivated them to take such risks? How risky do you think they thought their behavior was?

CORPORATE SINGLE INDUSTRY STRATEGY

After reading this chapter, you should be able to

- Understand how organizational design requires strategic managers to select the right combination of organizational structure, control, and culture
- Discuss how effective organizational design enables a company to increase product differentiation, reduce its cost structure, and build competitive advantage
- Explain why it is so important that strategic managers keep the organizational hierarchy as flat as possible and what factors determine the

way they to decide to centralize or decentralize authority
- Explain the many advantages of a functional structure and why and when it becomes necessary to move to a more complex form of organizational structure
- Differentiate between the more complex forms of organizational structure managers adopt to implement specific kinds of business-level strategies

A New Look for Liz Claiborne

Liz Claiborne, like other well-known apparel makers, embarked on a major product expansion strategy in the 1990s when it acquired many smaller-branded clothing and accessory companies and internally ventured new brands of its own.

The company's goal was to achieve greater operating efficiencies so that rising sales would also result in rising profits. By 2005, it had grown to 36 different brands, but while revenues had soared from $2 billion to more than $5 billion, its profits had not kept pace. In fact, profits were falling because costs were rising due to the enormous complexity and expense involved in managing so many brands. Also, in the 2000s, clothing

retailers like Walmart, Macy's, and Target were increasingly offering their own private-label brands; this put pressure on apparel makers to reduce their prices if they wished to keep selling their brands in these store chains.[1]

Liz Claiborne recruited a new CEO, William McComb, to turn around the troubled company. Within months, he decided to reverse course, shrink the company, and move to a new

OPENING CASE

form of organizational structure that would reduce the problems associated with managing its 36 different brands and once again allow it to grow, but this time with increasing profitability. McComb believed the company had developed a "culture of complexity" that had gotten out of control. Liz Claiborne's core merchandising culture that had made it so successful had been lost because of its rapid growth and overly complex organizational structure.

Liz Claiborne's former top managers had created five different apparel divisions to manage its 36 brands; brands were grouped into different divisions according to nature of the clothing or accessories they made. For example, luxury designer lines such as Ellen Tracy were grouped into one division; clothes for working women such as its signature Liz Claiborne and Dana Buchman brands were in a second division; trendy, hip clothing directed at young customers such as its Juicy Couture line were in a third division, and so on. Each division was controlled by a separate management team, and each division performed all the functional activities that marketing and design needed to support its brands. The problem was that over time it had become increasingly difficult both to differentiate between apparel brands in *each* division, as well as between the brands of *different* divisions, because fashion styles change quickly in response to changing customer tastes. Also, costs were rising because of the duplication of activities between divisions, and, as noted earlier, increasing industry competition was pressuring the company to lower prices to retail stores to protect its sales.

McComb decided to streamline and change Liz Claiborne's organizational structure to meet the changing needs of customers and increasing competition in the retailing industry. First, he decided the company would either sell, license, or close down 16 of its 36 brands and focus on the remaining 20 brands that had the most chance of generating good future profits.[2] To better manage these 20 brands, he reorganized the company's structure and reduced its five divisions to just two. This eliminated an entire level of top management. It also eliminated the duplication in marketing, distribution, and retail functions across the original five divisions. The result was a huge drop in operating costs and a simpler organization to manage.

The two remaining divisions were now its retail division called "direct brands" and its wholesale division called "partnered brands." Its new structure was intended to bring focus, energy, and clarity to the way each division operated. The retail division, for example, was responsible for the brands that were sold primarily through Liz Claiborne's retail store chains, such as its Kate Spade, Lucky Brand Jeans, and Juicy Couture chains. The goal of grouping together its fastest growing brands was to allow divisional managers to make better marketing and distribution decisions to differentiate its products and attract more customers.[3] On the other hand, the problem in the wholesale division, which sells branded apparel lines such as Liz Claiborne and Dana Buchman directly to department stores and other retailers, is to reduce costs to slow down the growing threat from private labels. For example, sales of Macy's private labels increased from 15% in 2005 to 18% in 2007. If managers of the wholesale division could find ways to reduce costs by turning inventory over more quickly, sharing marketing costs, and so forth, it could offer stores such as Macy's lower prices for its clothing, encouraging them to stick with its brands and still make higher profits.

McComb realized that to reduce complexity and allow each division to build the right merchandising culture, it was necessary to change Liz Claiborne's organizational structure. From grouping clothing brands into divisions according to their quality or price, he changed to two divisions in which clothing brands were grouped according to the needs of each division's customers—either the people in its stores or the retail chains that buy its clothes to resell to individual customers. The real problem is that each division faces a quite different set of strategic and operational problems; with its new structure, managers in each division can focus on solving a specific set of problems to achieve the best performance from their particular brands. McComb's hope is that the company's sales will grow rapidly, but this time its new structure will lead to rising profitability.

Overview

As the story of Liz Claiborne suggests, organizational structure and culture can have a direct bearing on a company's profits. This chapter examines how managers can best implement their strategies through their organization's structure and culture to achieve a competitive advantage and superior performance. A well-thought-out business model becomes profitable only if it can be implemented successfully. In practice, however, implementing strategy through structure and culture is a difficult, challenging, and never-ending task. Managers cannot just create an organizing framework for a company's value-chain activities and then assume it will keep working efficiently and effectively over time—just as they cannot select strategies and assume that these strategies will still work in a future in a changing competitive environment.

We begin by discussing the main elements of organizational design and the way they work together to create an organizing framework that allows a company to implement its strategy. We also discuss how strategic managers can use structure, control, and culture to pursue functional-level strategies that create and build distinctive competencies. The discussion then moves to the industry level and the implementation issues facing managers in a single industry. The next chapter takes up where this one leaves off and examines strategy implementation across industries and countries, that is, corporate and global strategy. By the end of this chapter and the next, you will understand why the fortunes of a company often rest on its managers' ability to design and manage its structure, control systems, and culture to best implement its business model.

IMPLEMENTING STRATEGY THROUGH ORGANIZATIONAL DESIGN

Strategy implementation involves the use of **organizational design**, the process of deciding how a company should create, use, and combine organizational structure, control systems, and culture to pursue a business model successfully. **Organizational structure** assigns employees to specific value creation tasks and roles and specifies how these tasks and roles are to be linked together in a way that increases efficiency, quality, innovation, and responsiveness to customers—the distinctive competencies that build competitive advantage. The purpose of organizational structure is to *coordinate and integrate* the efforts of employees at all levels—corporate, business, and functional—and across a company's functions and business units so that they work together in a way that will allow it to achieve the specific set of strategies in its business model.

Organizational structure does not, by itself, provide the set of incentives through which people can be *motivated* to make it work. Hence, there is a need for control systems. The purpose of a **control system** is to provide managers with (1) a set of incentives to motivate employees to work toward increasing efficiency, quality, innovation, and responsiveness to customers and (2) specific feedback on how well an organization and its members are performing and building competitive advantage so that managers can continuously take action to strengthen a company's business model. Structure provides an organization with a skeleton; control gives it the muscles, sinews, nerves, and sensations that allow managers to regulate and govern its activities.

Figure 12.1   Implementing Strategy Through Organizational Design

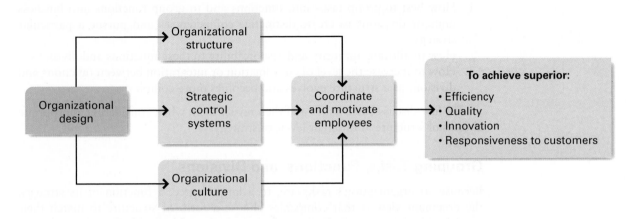

Organizational culture, the third element of organizational design, is the specific collection of values, norms, beliefs, and attitudes that are shared by people and groups in an organization and that control the way they interact with each other and with stakeholders outside the organization.[4] Organizational culture is a company's way of doing something: it describes the characteristic ways—"this is the way we do it around here"—in which members of an organization get the job done. Top managers, because they can influence which kinds of beliefs and values develop in an organization, are an important determinant of how organizational members will work toward achieving organizational goals, as we discuss later.[5]

Figure 12.1 sums up the discussion so far. Organizational structure, control, and culture are the means by which an organization motivates and coordinates its members to work toward achieving the building blocks of competitive advantage.

Top managers who wish to find out why it takes a long time for people to make decisions in a company, why there is a lack of cooperation between sales and manufacturing, or why product innovations are few and far between need to understand how the design of a company's structure and control system, and the values and norms in its culture, affect employee motivation and behavior. *Organizational structure, control, and culture shape people's behaviors, values, and attitudes and determine how they will implement an organization's business model and strategies.*[6] On the basis of such an analysis, top managers can devise a plan to reorganize or change their company's structure, control systems, and culture to improve coordination and motivation. Effective organizational design allows a company to obtain a competitive advantage and achieve above-average profitability.

BUILDING BLOCKS OF ORGANIZATIONAL STRUCTURE

After formulating a company's business model and strategies, managers must make designing an organizational structure their next priority. The value creation activities of organizational members are meaningless unless some type of structure is used to assign people to tasks and connect the activities of different people and functions.[7] Managers must make three basic choices:

1. How best to group tasks into functions and to group functions into business units or divisions to create distinctive competencies and pursue a particular strategy
2. How to allocate authority and responsibility to these functions and divisions
3. How to increase the level of coordination or integration between functions and divisions as a structure evolves and becomes more complex

We first discuss basic issues and then revisit them when considering appropriate choices of structure at different levels of strategy.

Grouping Tasks, Functions, and Divisions

Because an organization's tasks are, to a large degree, a function of its strategy, the dominant view is that companies choose a form of structure to match their organizational strategy. Perhaps the first person to address this issue formally was the Harvard business historian Alfred D. Chandler.[8] After studying the organizational problems experienced in large United States corporations such as DuPont and GM as they grew in the early decades of the 20th century, Chandler reached two conclusions: (1) in principle, organizational structure follows the range and variety of tasks that the organization chooses to pursue; and (2) structures of United States companies' structures change as their strategy changes in a predictable way over time.[9] In general, this means that most companies first group people and tasks into functions and then functions into divisions.[10]

As we discussed earlier, a *function* is a collection of people who work together and perform the same types of tasks or hold similar positions in an organization.[11] For example, the salespeople in a car dealership belong to the sales function. Together, car sales, car repair, car parts, and accounting are the set of functions that allow a car dealership to sell and maintain cars.

As organizations grow and produce a wider range of products, the amount and complexity of the *handoffs*, that is, the work exchanges or transfers among people, functions, and subunits, increase. The communications and measurement problems and the managerial inefficiencies surrounding these transfers or handoffs are a major source of *bureaucratic costs*, which we discussed in Chapter 10. Recall that these are the costs associated with monitoring and managing the functional exchanges necessary to add value to a product as it flows along a company's value chain to the final customer.[12] We discuss why bureaucratic costs increase as companies pursue more complex strategies later in the chapter.

For now, it is important to note that managers group tasks into functions and then group functions into a business unit or division to reduce bureaucratic costs. For example, as Liz Claiborne started to produce an increasing number of clothing brands, it created five separate divisions, each with its own marketing, sales, and accounting functions. A *division* is a way of grouping functions to allow an organization to better produce and transfer its goods and services to customers. In developing an organizational structure, managers must decide how to group an organization's activities by function and division in a way that achieves organizational goals effectively.[13]

Top managers can choose from among many kinds of structures to group their activities. The choice is made on the basis of the structure's ability to implement the company's business models and strategies successfully.

Allocating Authority and Responsibility

As organizations grow and produce a wider range of goods and services, the size and number of their functions and divisions increase. The number of handoffs or transfers between employees also increases. To economize on bureaucratic costs and effectively coordinate the activities of people, functions, and divisions, managers must develop a clear and unambiguous **hierarchy of authority**, or chain of command, that defines each manager's relative authority, from the CEO down through the middle managers and first-line managers, to the nonmanagerial employees who actually make goods or provide services.[14] Every manager, at every level of the hierarchy, supervises one or more subordinates. The term **span of control** refers to the number of subordinates who report directly to a manager. When managers know exactly what their authority and responsibilities are, information distortion problems that promote managerial inefficiencies are kept to a minimum, and handoffs or transfers can be negotiated and monitored to economize on bureaucratic costs. For example, managers are less likely to risk invading another manager's turf and thus can avoid the costly fights and conflicts that inevitably result from such encroachments.

Tall and Flat Organizations Companies choose the number of hierarchical levels they need on the basis of their strategy and the functional tasks necessary to create distinctive competencies.[15] As an organization grows in size or complexity (measured by the number of its employees, functions, and divisions), its hierarchy of authority normally lengthens, making the organizational structure taller. A **tall structure** has many levels of authority relative to company size; a **flat structure** has fewer levels relative to company size (see Figure 12.2). As the hierarchy becomes taller, problems that make the organization's structure less flexible and slow managers' response to

Figure 12.2 Tall and Flat Structures

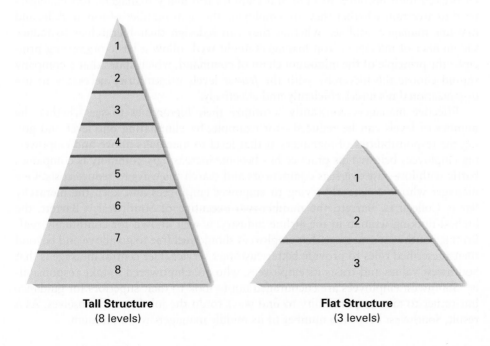

Tall Structure
(8 levels)

Flat Structure
(3 levels)

changes in the competitive environment may result. It is vital that managers understand how these problems arise so they know how to change a company's structure to respond to them.

First, communication problems may arise. When an organization has many levels in the hierarchy, it can take a long time for the decisions and orders of top managers to reach managers farther down in the hierarchy, and it can take a long time for top managers to learn how well their decisions worked out. Feeling out of touch, top managers may want to verify that lower-level managers are following orders and may require written confirmation from them. Lower-level managers, who know they will be held strictly accountable for their actions, start devoting more time to the process of making decisions to improve their chances of being right. They might even try to avoid responsibility by making top managers decide what actions to take.

A second communication problem that can result is the distortion of commands and orders as they are transmitted up and down the hierarchy, which causes managers at different levels to interpret what is happening differently. Accidental distortion of orders and messages occurs when different managers interpret messages from their own narrow functional perspectives. Intentional distortion can occur because managers lower in the hierarchy decide to interpret information to increase their own personal advantage.

A third problem with tall hierarchies is that they usually indicate that an organization is employing too many managers, and managers are expensive. Managerial salaries, benefits, offices, and secretaries are a huge expense for organizations. Large companies such as IBM, GM, and Dell pay their managers billions of dollars a year. In the recent recession, millions of middle and lower managers were laid off as companies strived to survive by reorganizing and simplifying their structures and downsizing their workforce to reduce their cost structure.

The Minimum Chain of Command   To ward off the problems that result when an organization becomes too tall and employs too many managers, top managers need to ascertain whether they are employing the right number of top, middle, and first-line managers and see whether they can redesign their hierarchies to reduce the number of managers. Top managers might well follow a basic organizing principle: the **principle of the minimum chain of command**, which states that a company should choose the hierarchy with the *fewest* levels of authority necessary to use organizational resources efficiently and effectively.

Effective managers constantly scrutinize their hierarchies to see whether the number of levels can be reduced—for example, by eliminating one level and giving the responsibilities of managers at that level to managers above and empowering employees below. This practice has become increasingly common as companies battle with low-cost overseas competitors and search for ways to reduce costs. One manager who is constantly trying to empower employees and keep the hierarchy flat is Colleen C. Barrett, the number-two executive of Southwest.[16] Barrett, the highest-ranking woman in the airline industry, is well known for continually reaffirming Southwest's message that employees should feel free to go above and beyond their prescribed roles to provide better customer service. Her central message is that Southwest values and trusts its employees, who are empowered to take responsibility. Southwest employees are encouraged not to look to their superiors for guidance but rather to take responsibility to find ways to do the job better themselves. As a result, Southwest keeps the number of its middle managers to a minimum.

When companies become too tall and the chain of command too long, strategic managers tend to lose control over the hierarchy, which means they lose control over their strategies. Disaster often follows because a tall organizational structure decreases, rather than promotes, motivation and coordination between employees and functions, and bureaucratic costs escalate as a result. Strategy in Action 12.1 discusses how this happened at Walt Disney.

Centralization or Decentralization?   One important way to reduce the problems associated with too-tall hierarchies and reduce bureaucratic costs is to *decentralize authority*—that is, vest authority in managers at lower levels in the hierarchy as well as at the top. Authority is *centralized* when managers at the upper levels of a company's hierarchy retain the authority to make the most important decisions. When authority is decentralized, it is delegated to divisions, functions, and employees at lower levels in the company. Delegating authority in this fashion reduces bureaucratic costs because it avoids the communication and coordination problems that arise when information has to be constantly sent up the hierarchy, sometimes to the top of the organization, for decisions to be made and then back down again. There are three advantages to decentralization.

First, when top managers delegate operational decision-making responsibility to middle- and first-level managers, they reduce information overload and so are able to spend more time on positioning the company competitively and strengthening

12.1 *STRATEGY IN ACTION*

Bob Iger Flattens Disney

In 2006, Bob Iger, who had been COO of Disney under its then-CEO Michael Eisner, took control of the troubled company. For several years, Disney had been plagued by slow decision making, and analysts claimed it had made many mistakes in putting its new strategies into action. Its Disney stores were losing money; its Internet properties were not getting many "hits," and even its theme parks seemed to have lost their luster as few new rides or attractions had been introduced.

Iger believed that one of the main reasons for Disney's declining performance was that it had become too tall and bureaucratic and its top managers were following financial rules that did not lead to innovative strategies. So, one of Iger's first moves to turn around the performance of the poorly performing company was to dismantle Disney's central strategic planning office. In this office, several levels of managers were responsible for sifting through all the new ideas and innovations sent up by Disney's different business divisions, such as theme parks, movies, gaming, and then deciding which ones to present to the CEO. Iger saw the strategic planning office as a bureaucratic bottleneck that actually reduced the number of ideas coming from below. So he dissolved the office and reassigned its managers back to the different business units.

The result of cutting out an unnecessary layer in Disney's hierarchy has been that more new ideas are being generated by its different business units. The level of innovation has increased because managers are more willing to speak out and champion their ideas when they know they are dealing directly with the CEO and a top management team searching for innovative new ways to improve performance rather than a layer of strategic planning "bureaucrats" only concerned for the bottom line.

Sources: J. McGregor, "The World's Most Innovative Companies," http://www.businessweek.com/innovate/content/May2007/id20070504_051674.htm, May 4, 2007; R. Nakashima, "Iger: Disney to Reap $1 Billion Online," http://www.sfgate.com/cgi-bin/article.cgi?f=/n/a/2008/03/10/financial/f165821D16.DTL$type=tech, March 11, 2008.

its business model. Second, when managers in the bottom layers of the company become responsible for implementing strategies to suit local conditions, their motivation and accountability increase. The result is that decentralization promotes flexibility and reduces bureaucratic costs because lower-level managers are authorized to make on-the-spot decisions; handoffs are not needed. The third advantage is that when lower-level employees are given the right to make important decisions, fewer managers are needed to oversee their activities and tell them what to do—a company can flatten its hierarchy.

If decentralization is so effective, why don't all companies decentralize decision making and avoid the problems of tall hierarchies? The answer is that centralization has its advantages, too. Centralized decision making allows for easier coordination of the organizational activities needed to pursue a company's strategy. If managers at all levels can make their own decisions, overall planning becomes extremely difficult, and the company may lose control of its decision making.

Centralization also means that decisions fit broad organization objectives. When its branch operations were getting out of hand, for example, Merrill Lynch increased centralization by installing more information systems to give corporate managers greater control over branch activities. Similarly, HP centralized R&D responsibility at the corporate level to provide a more directed corporate strategy. Furthermore, in times of crisis, centralization of authority permits strong leadership because authority is focused on one person or group. This focus allows for speedy decision making and a concerted response by the whole organization. How to choose the right level of centralization for a particular strategy is discussed later. Strategy in Action 12.2, however, discusses one company that benefits from centralizing authority and one company that benefits from decentralizing authority.

Integration and Integrating Mechanisms

Much coordination takes place among people, functions, and divisions through the hierarchy of authority. Often, however, as a structure becomes complex, this is not enough, and top managers need to use various **integrating mechanisms** to increase communication and coordination among functions and divisions. The greater the complexity of an organization's structure, the greater is the need for coordination among people, functions, and divisions to make the organizational structure work efficiently.[17] We discuss three kinds of integrating mechanisms that illustrate the kinds of issues involved.[18] Once again, these mechanisms are employed to economize on the information distortion problems that commonly arise when managing the handoffs or transfers among the ideas and activities of different people, functions, and divisions.

Direct Contact   Direct contact among managers creates a context within which managers from different functions or divisions can work together to solve mutual problems. However, several problems are associated with establishing this contact. Managers from different functions may have different views about what must be done to achieve organizational goals. But if the managers have equal authority (as functional managers typically do), the only manager who can tell them what to do is the CEO. If functional managers cannot reach agreement, no mechanism exists to resolve the conflict apart from the authority of the boss. In fact, one sign of a poorly performing organizational structure is the number of problems sent up the hierarchy for top managers to solve. The need to solve everyday conflicts and handoff or transfer problems raises bureaucratic costs. To reduce such conflicts and solve transfer

12.2 *STRATEGY IN ACTION*

To Centralize or Decentralize? That Is the Question

Union Pacific (UP), one of the biggest rail freight carriers in the United States, was experiencing a crisis in the 1990s. An economic boom had led to a record increase in the amount of freight the railroad had to transport—but, at the same time, the railroad was experiencing record delays in moving the freight. UP's customers were irate and complaining bitterly about the problem, and the delays were costing the company millions of dollars in penalty payments. The problem stemmed from UP's decision to centralize authority high in the organization to cut costs. All scheduling and route planning were handled centrally at its headquarters to promote operating efficiency. The job of regional managers was largely to ensure the smooth flow of freight through their regions. Now, recognizing that efficiency had to be balanced by the need to be responsive to customers, UP's CEO Dick Davidson announced a sweeping reorganization. In the future, regional, not top managers, would have the authority to make operational decisions; they could alter scheduling and routing to accommodate customer requests even if it raised costs. The goal of the organization was to "return to excellent performance by simplifying our processes and becoming easier to deal with." In deciding to decentralize authority, UP was following the lead of its competitors who had already decentralized their operations; its managers, would continue to "decentralize decision making into the field, while fostering improved customer responsiveness, operational excellence, and personal accountability."

Yahoo!, on the other hand, has been forced by circumstances to pursue a different approach to decentralization. In 2009, after the failed merger between Yahoo! and Microsoft, the company's stock price plunged.

Jerry Wang, one of the company' founders, who had come under intense criticism for preventing the merger, resigned as CEO and was replaced by Carol Bartz. Bartz, with a long history of success in managing online companies, had to move quickly to find ways to reduce Yahoo!'s cost structure and simplify its operations to maintain its strong online brand identity. Intense competition from the growing popularity of new online companies such as Facebook, Twitter, and established companies such as Google and Microsoft were threatening its popularity.

Bartz decided the best way to rebuild Yahoo!'s business model was to recentralize authority. To both gain more control over its different business units and reduce operating costs, she decided to centralize functions that had been previously performed by Yahoo!'s different business units, such as product development and marketing activities. For example, all the company's publishing and advertising functions were centralized and put under the control of Hilary Schneider. The control over Yahoo!'s European, Asian, and emerging markets divisions was centralized and another top Yahoo! executive took control. Her goal was to find out how she could make the company work better. While she was centralizing authority, she was also holding many "town hall" meetings. Bartz was asking Yahoo!'s employees, across all departments, "What would you do if you were me?" Even as she centralized authority to help Yahoo! recover its dominant industry position, she was looking for the input of employees at any level in the hierarchy. Once Yahoo! has regained its competitive advantage, she will likely decentralize authority to increase Yahoo!'s profitability, given her general managerial competences.

Source: http://www.unionpacific.com, 2009.

problems, top managers use more complex integrating mechanisms to increase coordination among functions and divisions.

Liaison Roles   Managers can increase coordination among functions and divisions by establishing liaison roles. When the volume of contacts between two functions increases, one way to improve coordination is to give one manager in each function or division the responsibility for coordinating with the other. These managers may meet daily, weekly, monthly, or as needed to solve handoff issues and transfer problems. The responsibility for coordination is part of the liaison's full-time job, and usually an informal relationship forms between the people involved, greatly easing strains between functions. Furthermore, liaison roles provide a way of transmitting information across an organization, which is important in large organizations where employees may know no one outside their immediate function or division.

Teams   When more than two functions or divisions share many common problems, direct contact and liaison roles may not provide sufficient coordination. In these cases, a more complex integrating mechanism, the **team**, may be appropriate. One manager from each relevant function or division is assigned to a team that meets to solve a specific mutual problem; team members are responsible for reporting back to their subunits on the issues addressed and the solutions recommended. Teams are increasingly being used at all organizational levels.

STRATEGIC CONTROL SYSTEMS

Strategic managers choose the organizational strategies and structure they hope will allow the organization to use its resources most effectively to pursue its business model and create value and profit. Then they create **strategic control systems**, tools that allow them to monitor and evaluate whether, in fact, their strategy and structure are working as intended, how they could be improved, and how they should be changed if they are not working.

Strategic control is not just about monitoring how well an organization and its members are performing currently or about how well the firm is using its existing resources. It is also about how to create the incentives to keep employees motivated and focused on the important problems that may confront an organization in the future so that they work together to find solutions that can help an organization perform better over time.[19] To understand the vital importance of strategic control, consider how it helps managers obtain superior efficiency, quality, innovation, and responsiveness to customers—the four basic building blocks of competitive advantage:

1. *Control and efficiency.* To determine how *efficiently* they are using organizational resources, managers must be able to measure accurately how many units of inputs (raw materials, human resources, and so on) are being used to produce a unit of output. They must also be able to measure the number of units of outputs (goods and services) they produce. A control system contains the measures or yardsticks that allow managers to assess how efficiently they are producing goods and services. Moreover, if managers experiment to find a more efficient way to produce goods and services, these measures tell managers how successful they have been. Without a control system in place, managers have no idea how well their organizations are performing and how they can make it perform better, something that is becoming increasingly important in today's highly competitive environment.[20]

2. *Control and quality.* Today, competition often revolves around increasing the *quality* of goods and services. In the car industry, for example, within each price range, cars compete against one another in terms of their features, design, and reliability. So whether a customer buys a Ford 500, a GM Impala, a Chrysler 300, a Toyota Camry, or a Honda Accord depends significantly on the quality of each company's product. Strategic control is important in determining the quality of goods and services because it gives managers feedback on product quality. If managers consistently measure the number of customers' complaints

and the number of new cars returned for repairs, they have a good indication of how much quality they have built into their product.

3. *Control and innovation.* Strategic control can help to raise the level of *innovation* in an organization. Successful innovation takes place when managers create an organizational setting in which employees feel empowered to be creative and in which authority is decentralized to employees so that they feel free to experiment and take risks, such as at Apple, 3M, and Nvidia. Deciding on the appropriate control systems to encourage risk taking is an important management challenge. As discussed later in the chapter, an organization's culture becomes important in this regard.

4. *Control and responsiveness to customers.* Finally, strategic managers can help make their organizations more *responsive to customers* if they develop a control system that allows them to evaluate how well employees with customer contact are performing their jobs. Monitoring employees' behavior can help managers find ways to help increase employees' performance level, perhaps by revealing areas in which skills training can help employees or by finding new procedures that allow employees to perform their jobs better. When employees know their behaviors are being monitored, they may have more incentive to be helpful and consistent in the way they act toward customers.

Strategic control systems are the formal target-setting, measurement, and feedback systems that allow strategic managers to evaluate whether a company is achieving superior efficiency, quality, innovation, and customer responsiveness and implementing its strategy successfully. An effective control system should have three characteristics. It should be *flexible* enough to allow managers to respond as necessary to unexpected events; it should provide *accurate information*, thus giving a true picture of organizational performance; and it should supply managers with the information in a *timely manner* because making decisions on the basis of outdated information is a recipe for failure.[21] As Figure 12.3 shows, designing an effective strategic control system requires four steps: establishing standards and targets, creating measuring and monitoring systems, comparing performance against targets, and evaluating the result.

Figure 12.3 Steps in Designing an Effective Strategic Control System

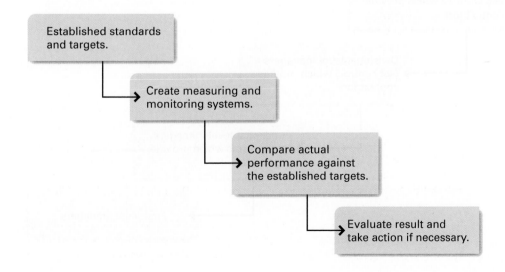

Established standards and targets.

Create measuring and monitoring systems.

Compare actual performance against the established targets.

Evaluate result and take action if necessary.

Levels of Strategic Control

Strategic control systems are developed to measure performance at four levels in a company: corporate, divisional, functional, and individual. Managers at all levels must develop the most appropriate set of measures to evaluate corporate-, business-, and functional-level performance. As the balanced scorecard approach discussed in Chapter 11 suggests, these measures should be tied as closely as possibly to the goals of developing distinctive competencies in efficiency, quality, innovativeness, and responsiveness to customers. Care must be taken, however, to ensure that the standards used at each level do not cause problems at the other levels—for example, that a division's attempts to improve its performance do not conflict with corporate performance. Furthermore, controls at each level should provide the basis on which managers at lower levels design their control systems. Figure 12.4 illustrates these links.

Types of Strategic Control Systems

In Chapter 11, the balanced scorecard approach was discussed as a way to ensure that managers complement the use of ROIC with other kinds of strategic controls to ensure they are pursuing strategies that maximize long-run profitability. In this chapter, we consider three more types of control systems: *personal control, output control,* and *behavior control.*

Figure 12.4 Levels of Organizational Control

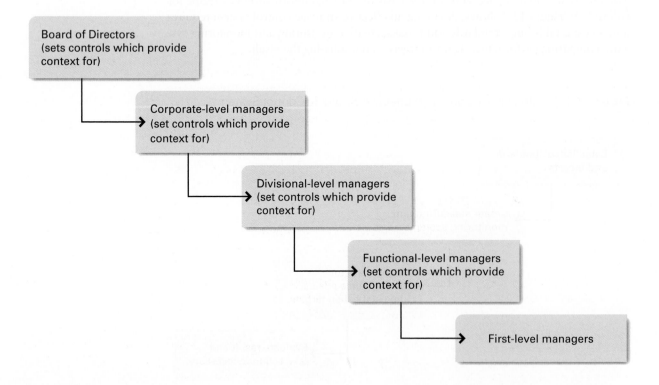

Personal Control   **Personal control** is the desire to shape and influence the behavior of a person in a *face-to-face interaction* in the pursuit of a company's goals. The most obvious kind of personal control is direct supervision from a manager farther up in the hierarchy. The personal approach is useful because managers can question and probe subordinates about problems or new issues they are facing to get a better understanding of the situation, as well as to ensure that subordinates are performing their work effectively and not hiding any information that could cause problems down the line. Personal control also can come from a group of peers, such as when people work in teams. Once again, personal control at the group level means that there is more possibility for learning to occur and competencies to develop, as well as greater opportunities to prevent free-riding or shirking.

Output Control   **Output control** is a system in which strategic managers estimate or forecast appropriate performance goals for each division, department, and employee and then measure actual performance relative to these goals. Often a company's reward system is linked to performance on these goals, so output control also provides an incentive structure for motivating employees at all levels in the organization. Goals keep managers informed about how well their strategies are creating a competitive advantage and building the distinctive competencies that lead to future success. Goals exist at all levels in an organization.

Divisional goals state corporate managers' expectations for each division concerning performance on dimensions such as efficiency, quality, innovation, and responsiveness to customers. Generally, corporate managers set challenging divisional goals to encourage divisional managers to create more effective strategies and structures in the future. At Liz Claiborne, for example, each division is given clear performance goals to achieve, and divisional managers are given considerable autonomy to formulate a strategy to meet these goals.

Output control at the functional and individual levels is a continuation of control at the divisional level. Divisional managers set goals for functional managers that will allow the division to achieve its goals. As at the divisional level, functional goals are established to encourage the development of generic competencies that provide the company with a competitive advantage, and functional performance is evaluated by how well a function develops a competency. In the sales function, for example, goals related to efficiency (such as cost of sales), quality (such as number of returns), and customer responsiveness (such as the time needed to respond to customer needs) can be established for the whole function.

Finally, functional managers establish goals that individual employees are expected to achieve to allow the function to achieve its goals. Sales personnel, for example, can be given specific goals (related to functional goals) that they are required to achieve. Functions and individuals are then evaluated on the basis of achieving or not achieving their goals; in sales, compensation is commonly pegged to achievement. The achievement of these goals is a sign that the company's strategy is working and meeting organizational objectives.

The inappropriate use of output control can promote conflict among divisions. In general, setting across-the-board output targets, such as ROIC targets for divisions, can lead to destructive results if divisions single-mindedly try to maximize divisional ROIC at the expense of corporate ROIC. Moreover, to reach output targets, divisions may start to distort the numbers and engage in strategic manipulation of the figures to make their divisions look good—which increases bureaucratic costs.[22]

Behavior Control **Behavior control** is control through the establishment of a comprehensive system of rules and procedures to direct the actions or behavior of divisions, functions, and individuals.[23] The intent of behavior controls is not to specify the goals but to standardize the *way or means* of reaching them. Rules standardize behavior and make outcomes predictable. If employees follow the rules, then actions are performed and decisions are handled the same way time and time again. The result is predictability and accuracy, the aim of all control systems. The main kinds of behavior controls are operating budgets, standardization, and rules and procedures.

Once managers at each level have been given a goal to achieve, they establish operating budgets that regulate how managers and workers are to attain those goals. An **operating budget** is a blueprint that states how managers intend to use organizational resources to most efficiently achieve organizational goals. Most commonly, managers at one level allocate to managers at a lower level a specific amount of resources to use in the production of goods and services. Once they have been given a budget, lower-level managers must decide how they will allocate certain amounts of money for different organizational activities. They are then evaluated on the basis of their ability to stay inside the budget and make the best use of it. For example, managers at GE's washing machine division might have a budget of $50 million to develop and sell a new line of washing machines; they have to decide how much money to allocate to R&D, engineering, sales, and so on, so that the division generates the most revenue and hence makes the biggest profit. Most commonly, large companies treat each division as a stand-alone profit center, and corporate managers evaluate each division's performance by its relative contribution to corporate profitability, something discussed in detail in the next chapter.

Standardization refers to the degree to which a company specifies how decisions are to be made so that employees' behavior becomes predictable.[24] In practice, there are three things an organization can standardize: *inputs, conversion activities,* and *outputs.*

When managers standardize, they screen *inputs* according to preestablished criteria, or standards that determine which inputs to allow into the organization. If employees are the input in question, for example, then one way of standardizing them is to specify which qualities and skills they must possess and then select only applicants who possess them. If the inputs in question are raw materials or component parts, the same considerations apply. The Japanese are renowned for the high quality and precise tolerances they demand from component parts to minimize problems with the product at the manufacturing stage. JIT inventory systems also help standardize the flow of inputs.

The aim of standardizing *conversion activities* is to program work activities so that they are done the same way time and time again. The goal is predictability. Behavior controls, such as rules and procedures, are among the chief means by which companies can standardize throughputs. Fast-food restaurants such as McDonald's and Burger King standardize all aspects of their restaurant operations; the result is consistent fast food.

The goal of standardizing *outputs* is to specify what the performance characteristics of the final product or service should be—the dimensions or tolerances the product should conform to, for example. To ensure that their products are standardized, companies apply quality control and use various criteria to measure this standardization. One criterion might be the number of goods returned from customers or the number of customers' complaints. On production lines, periodic sampling of products can indicate whether they are meeting performance characteristics.

As with other kinds of controls, the use of behavior control is accompanied by potential pitfalls that must be managed if the organization is to avoid strategic problems. Top management must be careful to monitor and evaluate the usefulness of behavior controls over time. Rules constrain people and lead to standardized, predictable behavior. However, rules are always easier to establish than to get rid of, and over time the number of rules an organization uses tends to increase. As new developments lead to additional rules, often the old rules are not discarded, and the company becomes overly bureaucratized. Consequently, the organization and the people in it become inflexible and are slow to react to changing or unusual circumstances. Such inflexibility can reduce a company's competitive advantage by lowering the pace of innovation and reducing its responsiveness to customers.

Using Information Technology

Information technology is playing an increasing role in strategy implementation at all organizational levels. In fact, it is making it much easier for organizations to cost-effectively develop output and behavior controls that give strategic managers much more and much better information to monitor the many aspects of their strategies and respond appropriately. IT, which provides a way of standardizing behavior through the use of a consistent, often cross-functional software platform, is a form of behavior control. IT is also a form of output control; when all employees or functions use the same software platform to provide up-to-date information on their activities, it codifies and standardizes organizational knowledge and makes it easier to monitor progress toward strategic objectives. IT is also a kind of integrating mechanism; it provides people at all levels in the hierarchy and across all functions with more of the information and knowledge they need to perform their roles effectively. For example, today functional-level employees are able to access information easily from other functions using cross-functional software systems that keep them all informed about changes in product design, engineering, manufacturing schedules, and marketing plans having an impact on their activities. In this sense, IT overlays the structure of tasks and roles that is normally regarded as the "real" organizational structure.

As an example of how IT can help a company change quickly to respond to changing industry conditions, consider the fast-moving semiconductor business organizational in which Cypress Semiconductor CEO T. J. Rodgers was facing a problem. How could he exert effective control over his 2,000 employees without developing a bureaucratic management hierarchy? Rodgers believes that a tall hierarchy hinders the ability of an organization to adapt to changing conditions. He is committed to maintaining a flat and decentralized organizational structure with a minimum of management layers. At the same time, he wants to control his employees to ensure that they performed in a manner consistent with company goals. The solution Rodgers adopted was to implement an IT information system that allows him to monitor what every employee and team is doing in his decentralized organization. Each employee maintains a list of 10 to 15 goals, such as "Meet with marketing for new product launch" or "Make sure to check with customer X." Also noted is when each goal is agreed on, its progress, and when it is completed. Rodgers can use IT to review the goals of all employees in hours, and he does so each week. He can achieve this because he "manages by exception." He looks only for employees who seem to be falling behind and then he contacts them, not to scold, but to ask if there is anything he can do to help them get their jobs done. His control system allows Rodgers to exercise control over his organization without resorting to the expensive layers of a management hierarchy.[25]

Strategic Reward Systems

Organizations strive to control employees' behavior by linking reward systems to their control systems.[26] Based on a company's strategy (cost leadership or differentiation, for example), strategic managers must decide which behaviors to reward. They then create a control system to measure these behaviors and link the reward structure to them. Determining how to relate rewards to performance is a crucial strategic decision because it determines the incentive structure that affects the way managers and employees behave at all levels in the organization. As Chapter 11 pointed out, top managers can be encouraged to work in shareholders' interests by being rewarded with stock options linked to a company's long-term performance. Companies such as Kodak and GM require managers to buy company stock. When managers become shareholders, they are more motivated to pursue long-term rather than short-term goals. Similarly, in designing a pay system for salespeople, the choice is whether to motivate them through straight salary or salary plus a bonus based on how much they sell. Neiman Marcus, the luxury retailer, pays employees a straight salary because it wants to encourage high-quality service and discourage a hard-sell approach. Thus, there are no incentives based on quantity sold. On the other hand, the pay system for rewarding car salespeople encourages high-pressure selling; it typically contains a large bonus based on the number and price of cars sold.

ORGANIZATIONAL CULTURE

The third element that goes into successful strategy implementation is managing *organizational culture*, the specific collection of values and norms shared by people and groups in an organization.[27] Organizational values are beliefs and ideas about what kinds of goals the members of an organization should pursue and about the appropriate kinds or standards of behavior organizational members should use to achieve these goals. Bill Gates is famous for the set of organizational values that he created for Microsoft: entrepreneurship, ownership, creativity, honesty, frankness, and open communication. By stressing entrepreneurship and ownership, he strives to get his employees to feel that Microsoft is not one big bureaucracy but a collection of smaller and very adaptive companies run by the members. Gates emphasizes that lower-level managers should be given autonomy and encouraged to take risks—to act like entrepreneurs, not corporate bureaucrats.[28]

From organizational values develop organizational norms, guidelines, or expectations that prescribe appropriate kinds of behavior by employees in particular situations and control the behavior of organizational members toward one another. The norms of behavior for software programmers at Microsoft include working long hours and weekends, wearing whatever clothing is comfortable (but never a suit and tie), consuming junk food, and communicating with other employees by e-mail and the company's state-of-the-art intranet.

Organizational culture functions as a kind of control because strategic managers can influence the kind of values and norms that develop in an organization—values and norms that specify appropriate and inappropriate behaviors and that shape and influence the way its members behave.[29] Strategic managers such as Gates deliberately cultivate values that tell their subordinates how they should perform their roles; at Microsoft and Nokia, innovation and creativity are stressed. These companies establish and support norms that tell employees they should be innovative and entrepreneurial and should experiment even if there is a significant chance of failure.

Other managers might cultivate values that tell employees they should always be conservative and cautious in their dealings with others, consult with their superiors before they make important decisions, and record their actions in writing so they can be held accountable for what happens. Managers of organizations such as chemical and oil companies, financial institutions, and insurance companies—any organization in which great caution is needed—may encourage a conservative, vigilant approach to making decisions.[30] In a bank or mutual fund, for example, the risk of losing investors' money makes a cautious approach to investing highly appropriate. Thus, we might expect that managers of different kinds of organizations will deliberately try to cultivate and develop the organizational values and norms that are best suited to their strategy and structure.

Organizational socialization is the term used to describe how people learn organizational culture. Through socialization, people internalize and learn the norms and values of the culture so that they become organizational members.[31] Control through culture is so powerful that once these values have been internalized, they become part of the individual's values, and the individual follows organizational values without thinking about them.[32] Often the values and norms of an organization's culture are transmitted to its members through the stories, myths, and language that people in the organization use, as well as by other means.

Culture and Strategic Leadership

Organizational culture is created by the strategic leadership provided by an organization's founder and top managers. The organization's founder is particularly important in determining culture because the founder imprints his or her values and management style on the organization. Walt Disney's conservative influence on the company he established continued well after his death. Managers were afraid to experiment with new forms of entertainment because they were afraid "Walt Disney wouldn't like it." It took the installation of a new management team under Michael Eisner to turn around the company's fortunes and allow it to deal with the realities of the new entertainment industry.

The leadership style established by the founder is transmitted to the company's managers; as the company grows, it typically attracts new managers and employees who share the same values. Moreover, members of the organization typically recruit and select only those who share their values. Thus, a company's culture becomes more and more distinct as its members become more similar. The virtue of these shared values and common culture is that they *increase integration and improve coordination among organizational members*. For example, the common language that typically emerges in an organization because people share the same beliefs and values facilitates cooperation among managers. Similarly, rules and procedures and direct supervision are less important when shared norms and values control behavior and motivate employees. When organizational members buy into cultural norms and values, they feel a bond with the organization and are more committed to finding new ways to help it succeed. The Running Case on Walmart profiles how its founder Sam Walton built a strong culture.

RUNNING CASE

Sam Walton Created Walmart's Culture

Walmart, headquartered in Bentonville, Arkansas, is the largest retailer in the world. In 2009, it sold more than $700 billion worth of products. A large part of Walmart's success is due to the nature of the culture that its founder, the late Sam Walton, established for the company. Walton wanted all his managers and workers to take a hands-on approach to their jobs and be totally committed to Walmart's main goal, which he defined as total customer satisfaction. To motivate his employees, Walton created a culture that gave all employees, called "associates," continuous feedback about their performance and the company's performance.

To involve his associates in the business and encourage them to develop work behaviors focused on providing quality customer service, Walton established strong cultural values and norms for his company. One of the norms associates are expected to follow is the "10-foot attitude." This norm encourages associates, in Walton's words, to "promise that whenever you come within 10 feet of a customer, you will look him in the eye, greet him, and ask him if you can help him." The "sundown rule" states that employees should strive to answer customer requests by sundown of the day they are made. The Walmart cheer ("Give me a W, give me an A," and so on) is used in all its stores.

The strong customer-oriented values that Walton created are exemplified in the stories Walmart members tell one another about associates' concern for customers. They include stories like the one about Sheila, who risked her own safety when she jumped in front of a car to prevent a little boy from being struck; about Phyllis, who administered CPR to a customer who had suffered a heart attack in her store; and about Annette, who gave up the Power Ranger she had on layaway for her own son to fulfill the birthday wish of a customer's son. The strong Walmart culture helps to control and motivate employees to achieve the stringent output and financial targets the company sets for itself.

A notable way Walmart builds its culture is through its annual stockholders' meeting, its extravagant ceremony celebrating the company's success. Every year, Walmart flies thousands of its highest performers to its annual meeting its corporate headquarters in Arkansas for a show featuring famous singers, rock bands, and comedians. Walmart feels that expensive entertainment is a reward its employees deserve and that the event reinforces the company's high-performance values and culture. The proceedings are even broadcast live to all of Walmart's stores so that employees can celebrate the company's achievements together.

Since Sam Walton's death, public attention to Walmart, which has more than 1 million employees, has revealed the "hidden side" of its culture. Critics claim that few Walmart employees receive reasonably priced health care or other benefits, and the company pays employees at little above the minimum wage. They also contend that employees do not question these policies because managers have convinced them into believing that this has to be the case—that the only way Walmart can keep its prices low is by keeping their pay and benefits low. In 2009, Walmart was threatened by proposed changes to health care laws that would force it to pay a much higher percentage of employee benefits. Will its loyal employees decide to follow Sam Walton's 10-foot-attitude rule in the future?

Sources: http:// www.walmart.com, 2009; "Associates Keystone to Structure," *Chain Store Age,* December, 1999, 17; M. Troy, "The Culture Remains the Constant," *Discount Store News,* June 8, 1998, 95–98; S. Voros, "3D Management," *Management Review,* January 2000, 45–47; "Neurosis, Arkansas-Style," *Fortune,* April 17, 2000, 36.

Strategic leadership also affects organizational culture through the way managers design organizational structure, that is, the way they delegate authority and divide task relationships. Thus, the way an organization designs its structure affects the cultural norms and values that develop within the organization. Managers need to be aware of this fact when implementing their strategies. Michael Dell, the founder of Dell Computer, for example, has always kept his company as flat as possible. He has decentralized authority to lower-level managers and employees and made them responsible for getting as close to the customer as possible. As a result, he has created a cost-conscious customer service culture at Dell, and employees strive to provide high-quality customer service.

Traits of Strong and Adaptive Corporate Cultures

Few environments are stable for a prolonged period of time. If an organization is to survive, managers must take actions that enable it to adapt to environmental changes. If they do not take such action, they may find themselves faced with declining demand for their products.

Managers can try to create an **adaptive culture**, one that is innovative and that encourages and rewards middle- and lower-level managers for taking the initiative.[33] Managers in organizations with adaptive cultures are able to introduce changes in the way the organization operates, including changes in its strategy and structure that allow it to adapt to changes in the external environment. Organizations with adaptive cultures are more likely to survive in a changing environment and indeed should have higher performance than organizations with inert cultures.

Several scholars in the field have tried to uncover the common traits that strong and adaptive corporate cultures share and find out whether there is a particular set of values that dominates adaptive cultures that is missing from weak or inert ones. An early but still influential attempt is T. J. Peters and R. H. Waterman's account of the values and norms characteristic of successful organizations and their cultures.[34] They argue that adaptive organizations show three common value sets. First, successful companies have values promoting a *bias for action*. The emphasis is on autonomy and entrepreneurship, and employees are encouraged to take risks—for example, to create new products—even though there is no assurance that these products will be winners. Managers are closely involved in the day-to-day operations of the company and do not simply make strategic decisions isolated in some ivory tower. Employees have a hands-on, value-driven approach.

The second set of values stems from the *nature of the organization's mission*. The company must stick with what it does best and develop a business model focused on its mission. A company can easily get sidetracked into pursuing activities outside its area of expertise just because they seem to promise a quick return. Management should cultivate values so that a company "sticks to its knitting," which means strengthening its business model. A company must also establish close relationships with customers as a way of improving its competitive position. After all, who knows more about a company's performance than those who use its products or services? By emphasizing customer-oriented values, organizations are able to identify customer needs and improve their ability to develop products and services that customers desire. All of these management values are strongly represented in companies such as McDonald's, Walmart, and Toyota, which are sure of their mission and continually take steps to maintain it.

The third set of values bears on *how to operate the organization*. A company should try to establish an organizational design that will motivate employees to do their best. Inherent in this set of values is the belief that productivity is obtained through people and that respect for the individual is the primary means by which a company can create the right atmosphere for productive behavior. An emphasis on entrepreneurship and respect for the employee leads to the establishment of a structure that gives employees the latitude to make decisions and motivates them to succeed. Because a simple structure and a lean staff best fit this situation, the organization should be designed with only the number of managers and hierarchical levels that are necessary to get the job done. The organization should also be sufficiently decentralized to permit employees' participation but centralized enough for management to make sure that the company pursues its strategic mission and that cultural values are followed.

In summary, these three main sets of values are at the heart of an organization's culture, and management transmits and maintains them through strategic leadership. Strategy implementation continues as managers build strategic control systems that help perpetuate a strong adaptive culture, further the development of distinctive competencies, and provide employees with the incentive to build a company's competitive advantage. Finally, organizational structure contributes to the implementation process by providing the framework of tasks and roles that reduces transaction difficulties and allows employees to think and behave in ways that enable a company to achieve superior performance.

BUILDING DISTINCTIVE COMPETENCIES AT THE FUNCTIONAL LEVEL

In this section, we turn to the issue of creating specific kinds of structures, control systems, and cultures to implement a company's business model. The first level of strategy to examine is the functional level because, as Chapters 3 and 4 discussed, a company's business model is implemented through the functional strategies managers adopt to develop the distinctive competencies that allow a company to pursue a particular business model.[35] What is the best kind of structure to use to group people and tasks to build competencies? The answer for most companies is to group them by function and create a functional structure.

Functional Structure: Grouping by Function

In the quest to deliver a final product to the customer, two related value chain management problems increase. First, the range of value chain activities that must be performed expands, and it quickly becomes clear that a company lacks the expertise needed to perform them effectively. For example, in a new company, it quickly becomes apparent that the expertise necessary to perform them effectively is lacking. It becomes apparent, perhaps, that the services of a professional accountant, a production manager, or a marketing expert are needed to take control of specialized tasks as sales increase. Second, it also becomes clear that a single person cannot successfully perform more than one value chain activity without becoming overloaded. The new company's founder, for instance, who may have been performing many value chain activities, realizes that he or she can no longer simultaneously make and sell the product. As most entrepreneurs discover, they have to decide how to group new employees to perform the various value chain activities most efficiently. Most choose the functional structure.

Functional structures group people on the basis of their common expertise and experience or because they use the same resources.[36] For example, engineers are

Figure 12.5 Functional Structure

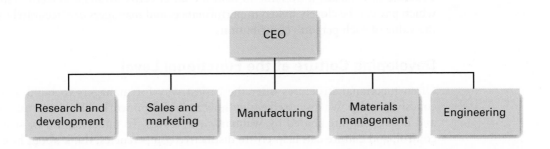

grouped in a function because they perform the same tasks and use the same skills or equipment. Figure 12.5 shows a typical functional structure. Each of the rectangles represents a different functional specialization—R&D, sales and marketing, manufacturing, and so on—and each function concentrates on its own specialized task.[37]

Functional structures have several advantages. First, if people who perform similar tasks are grouped together, they can learn from one another and become more specialized and productive at what they do. This can create capabilities and competencies in each function. Second, they can monitor each other to make sure that all are performing their tasks effectively and not shirking their responsibilities. As a result, the work process becomes more efficient, reducing manufacturing costs and increasing operational flexibility. A third important advantage of functional structures is that they give managers greater control of organizational activities. As already noted, many difficulties arise when the number of levels in the hierarchy increases. If people are grouped into different functions, each with their own managers, then *several different hierarchies are created*, and the company can avoid becoming too tall. There will be one hierarchy in manufacturing, for example, and another in accounting and finance. Managing the business is much easier when different groups specialize in different organizational tasks and are managed separately.

The Role of Strategic Control

An important element of strategic control is to design a system that sets ambitious goals and targets for all managers and employees and then develops performance measures that *stretch and encourage managers and employees* to excel in their quest to raise performance. A functional structure promotes this goal because it increases the ability of managers and employees to monitor and make constant improvements to operating procedures. The structure also encourages organizational learning because managers, working closely with subordinates, can mentor them and help develop their technical skills.

Grouping by function also makes it easier to apply output control. Measurement criteria can be developed to suit the needs of each function to encourage members to stretch themselves. Each function knows how well it is contributing to overall performance and, indeed, the part it plays in reducing the cost of goods sold or the gross margin. Managers can look closely to see if they are following the principle of the minimum chain of command and whether they need several levels of middle managers. Perhaps, instead of using middle managers, they could practice **management by objectives**, a system in which employees are encouraged to help set their own goals so that managers, like Cypress's Rodgers, *manage by exception*, intervening only when they sense something is not going right. Given this increase in control, a functional structure also makes it possible to institute an effective strategic reward system in which pay can be closely linked to performance, and managers can accurately assess the value of each person's contributions.

Developing Culture at the Functional Level

Often functional structures offer the easiest way for managers to build a strong, cohesive culture. We discussed earlier how Sam Walton worked hard to create values and norms that are shared by Walmart's employees. To understand how structure, control, and culture can help create distinctive competencies, think about how they affect the way these three functions operate: manufacturing, R&D, and sales.

Manufacturing   In manufacturing, functional strategy usually centers on improving efficiency and quality. A company must create an organizational setting in which managers can learn how to economize on costs and lower the cost structure. Many companies today follow the lead of Japanese companies like Toyota and Honda that have strong capabilities in manufacturing because they pursue TQM and flexible manufacturing systems (see Chapter 4).

Pursuing TQM, the inputs and involvement of all employees in the decision-making process are necessary to improve production efficiency and quality. Thus, it becomes necessary to decentralize authority to motivate employees to improve the production process. In TQM, work teams are created, and workers are given the responsibility and authority to discover and implement improved work procedures. Managers assume the role of coach and facilitator, and team members jointly take on the supervisory burdens. Work teams are often given the responsibility to control and discipline their own members and even decide who should work in their team. Frequently, work teams develop strong norms and values, and work-group culture becomes an important means of control; this type of control matches the new decentralized team approach. Quality control circles are created to exchange information and suggestions about problems and work procedures. A bonus system or employee stock ownership plan (ESOP) is frequently established to motivate workers and to allow them to share in the increased value that TQM often produces.

Nevertheless, to move down the experience curve quickly, most companies still exercise tight control over work activities and create behavior and output controls that standardize the manufacturing process. For example, human inputs are standardized through the recruitment and training of skilled personnel; the work process is programmed, often by computers; and quality control is used to make sure that outputs are being produced correctly. In addition, managers use output controls such as operating budgets to continuously monitor costs and quality. The extensive use of output controls and the continuous measurement of efficiency and quality ensure that the work team's activities meet the goals set for the function by management. Efficiency and quality increase as new and improved work rules and procedures are developed to raise the level of standardization. The aim is to find the match between structure and control and a TQM approach so that manufacturing develops the distinctive competency that leads to superior efficiency and quality.

R&D   The functional strategy for an R&D department is to develop distinctive competencies in innovation and quality as excellence that result in products that fit customers' needs. Consequently, the R&D department's structure, control, and culture should provide the coordination necessary for scientists and engineers to bring high-quality products quickly to market. Moreover, these systems should motivate R&D scientists to develop innovative products.

In practice, R&D departments typically have a flat, decentralized structure that gives their members the freedom and autonomy to experiment and be innovative. Scientists and engineers are also grouped into teams because their performance can typically be judged only over the long term (it may take several years for a project to be completed). Consequently, extensive supervision by managers and the use of behavior control are a waste of managerial time and effort.[38] By letting teams manage their own transfer and handoff issues rather than using managers and the hierarchy of authority to coordinate work activities, managers avoid the information distortion problems that cause bureaucratic costs. Strategic managers take advantage of scientists' ability to work jointly to solve problems and enhance each other's performance. In small teams, too, the professional values and norms that highly trained employees bring to the situation promote coordination. A culture for innovation frequently emerges to control employees' behavior, as it did at Nokia, Intel, and Microsoft, where the race to be first energizes the R&D teams. To create an innovative culture and speed product development, Intel uses a team structure in its R&D function. Intel has many work teams that operate side by side to develop the next generation of chips. So, when it makes mistakes, as it has recently, it can act quickly to join each team's innovations together to make a state-of-the-art chip that does meet customer needs, such as for multimedia chips. At the same time, to sustain its leading-edge technology, the company creates healthy competition between teams to encourage its scientists and engineers to champion new product innovations that will allow Intel to control the technology of tomorrow.[39]

To spur teams to work effectively, the reward system should be linked to the performance of the team and company. If scientists, individually or in a team, do not share in the profits a company obtains from its new products, they may have little motivation to contribute wholeheartedly to the team. To prevent the departure of their key employees and encourage high motivation, companies such as Merck, Intel, and Microsoft give their researchers stock options, stock, and other rewards that are tied to their individual performance, their team's performance, and the company's performance.

Sales   Salespeople work directly with customers, and when they are dispersed in the field, these employees are especially difficult to monitor. The cost-effective way to monitor their behavior and encourage high responsiveness to customers is usually to develop sophisticated output and behavior controls. Output controls, such as specific sales goals or goals for increasing responsiveness to customers, can be easily established and monitored by sales managers. These controls can then be linked to a bonus reward system to motivate salespeople. Behavior controls, such as detailed reports that salespeople file describing their interactions with customers, can also be used to standardize behavior and make it easier for supervisors to review performance.[40]

Usually, few managers are needed to monitor salespeople's activities, and a sales director and regional sales managers can oversee large sales forces because outputs and behavior controls are employed. Frequently, however, and especially when salespeople deal with complex products such as pharmaceutical drugs or even luxury clothing, it becomes important to develop shared employee values and norms about the importance of patient safety or high-quality customer service; managers spend considerable time training and educating employees to create such norms.

Similar considerations apply to the other functions, such as accounting, finance, engineering, and human resource management. Managers must implement functional strategy through the combination of structure, control, and culture to allow each function to create the competencies that lead to superior efficiency, quality, innovation, and responsiveness to customers. Strategic managers must also develop the incentive systems that motivate and align employees' interests with those of their companies.

Functional Structure and Bureaucratic Costs

No matter how complex their strategies become, most companies always retain a functional orientation because of its many advantages. Whenever different functions work together, however, bureaucratic costs inevitably arise because of information distortions that lead to the communications and measurement problems discussed in Chapter 10. These problems often arise from the transfers or handoffs across different functions that are necessary to deliver the final product to the customer.[41] Indeed, the need to economize on the bureaucratic costs of solving such problems leads managers to adopt new organizational arrangements that reduce the scope of information distortions. Usually, companies divide their activities according to more complex plans to match their business models and strategies in discriminating ways. These more complex structures are discussed later in the chapter. First, we review five areas in which information distortions can arise: communications, measurement, customers, location, and strategy.

Communication Problems   As separate functional hierarchies evolve, functions can grow more remote from one another, and it becomes increasingly difficult to communicate across functions and coordinate their activities. This communication problem stems from *differences in goal orientations*—the various functions develop distinct outlooks or understandings of the strategic issues facing a company.[42] For example, the pursuit of different competencies can often lead to different time or goal orientations. Some functions, such as manufacturing, have a short time frame and concentrate on achieving short-run goals, such as reducing manufacturing costs. Others, such as R&D, have a long-term point of view; their product development goals may have a time horizon of several years. These factors may cause each function to develop a different view of the strategic issues facing the company. Manufacturing, for example, may see the strategic issue as the need to reduce costs, sales may see it as the need to increase customer responsiveness, and R&D may see it as the need to create new products. These communication and coordination problems among functions increase bureaucratic costs.

Measurement Problems   Often a company's product range widens as it develops new competencies and enters new market segments. When this happens, a company may find it difficult to gauge or measure the contribution of a product or a group of products to its overall profitability. Consequently, the company may turn out some unprofitable products without realizing it and may also make poor decisions about resource allocation. This means that the company's measurement systems are not complex enough to serve its needs.

Customer Problems   As the range and quality of an organization's goods and services increase, often more and different kinds of customers are attracted to its products. Servicing the needs of more customer groups and tailoring products to suit new kinds of customers result in increasing handoff problems among functions. It becomes increasingly difficult to coordinate the activities of value chain functions across the growing product range. Also, functions such as production, marketing, and sales have little opportunity to differentiate products and increase value for customers by specializing in the needs of particular customer groups. Instead, they are responsible for servicing the complete product range. Thus, the ability to identify and satisfy customer needs may fall short in a functional structure.

Location Problems   Being in a particular location or geographical region may also hamper coordination and control. Suppose a growing company in the Northeast begins to expand and sell its products in many different regional areas. A functional structure will not be able to provide the flexibility needed for managers to respond to the different customer needs or preferences in the various regions.

Strategic Problems   The combined effect of all these factors is that long-term strategic considerations are frequently ignored because managers are preoccupied with solving communication and coordination problems. The result is that a company may lose direction and fail to take advantage of new strategic opportunities–thus bureaucratic costs escalate.

Experiencing one or more of these problems is a sign that bureaucratic costs are increasing. In that case, managers must change and adapt their organization's structure, control systems, and culture to economize on bureaucratic costs, build new distinctive competencies, and strengthen the company's business model. These problems indicate that the company has outgrown its structure and that managers need to develop a more complex structure that can meet the needs of their competitive strategy. An alternative, however, is to reduce these problems by adopting the outsourcing option.

The Outsourcing Option

Rather than move to a more complex, expensive structure, companies are increasingly turning to the outsourcing option (discussed in Chapter 9) and solving the organizational design problem by contracting with other companies to perform specific functional tasks. Obviously, it does not make sense to outsource activities in which a company has a distinctive competency, because this would lessen its competitive advantage. But it does make sense to outsource and contract with companies to perform particular value chain activities in which they specialize and therefore have a competitive advantage.

Thus, one way of avoiding the kinds of communication and measurement problems that arise when a company's product line becomes complex is to reduce the number of functional value chain activities it performs. This allows a company to focus on those competencies that are at the heart of its competitive advantage and to economize on bureaucratic costs. Today, responsibility for activities such as a company's marketing, pension and health benefits, materials management, and information systems is being increasingly outsourced to companies that specialize in the needs of a company in a particular industry. More outsourcing options, such as using a global network structure, are considered in Chapter 13.

IMPLEMENTING STRATEGY IN A SINGLE INDUSTRY

Building capabilities in organizational design that allow a company to develop a competitive advantage starts at the functional level. However, to pursue its business model successfully, managers must find the right combination of structure, control, and culture that *links and combines* the competencies in a company's value chain functions so that it enhances its ability to differentiate products or lower the cost structure. Therefore, it is important to coordinate and integrate across functions and business units or divisions. In organizational design, managers must consider two important issues: one concerns the revenue side of the profit equation and the other concerns the cost side, as Figure 12.6 illustrates.

First, effective organizational design improves the way in which people and groups choose the business-level strategies that lead to increasing differentiation, more value for customers, and the opportunity to charge a premium price. For example, capabilities in managing its structure and culture allow a company to more rapidly and effectively combine its distinctive competencies or transfer or leverage competencies across business units to create new and improved, differentiated products.

Second, effective organizational design reduces the bureaucratic costs associated with solving the measurement and communications problems that derive from factors such as transferring a product in progress between functions or a lack of cooperation between marketing and manufacturing or between business units. A poorly designed or inappropriate choice of structure or control system or a slow-moving bureaucratic culture (for example, a structure that is too centralized, an incentive system that causes functions to compete instead of cooperate, or a culture in which value and norms have little impact on employees) can cause the motivation, communication, measurement, and coordination problems that lead to high bureaucratic costs.

Effective organizational design often means moving to a more complex structure that economizes on bureaucratic costs. A more-complex structure will cost more to

---

Figure 12.6   How Organizational Design Increases Profitability

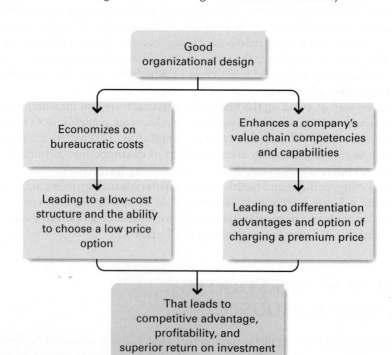

operate because additional, experienced, and more highly paid managers will be needed; a more expensive IT system will be required; there may be a need for extra offices and buildings; and so on. However, these are simply costs of doing business, and a company will happily bear this extra expense provided its new structure leads to increased revenues from product differentiation and/or new ways to lower its *overall* cost structure by obtaining economies of scale or scope from its expanded operations.

In the following sections, we first examine the implementation and organizational design issues involved in pursuing a cost-leadership or differentiation business model. Then we describe different kinds of organizational structures that allow companies to pursue business models oriented at (1) managing a wide range of products; (2) being responsive to customers; (3) expanding nationally; (4) competing in a fast-changing, high-tech environment; and (5) focusing on a narrow product line.

Implementing Cost Leadership

The aim of a company pursuing cost leadership is to become the lowest-cost producer in the industry, and this involves reducing costs across *all* functions in the organization, including R&D and sales and marketing.[43] If a company is pursuing a cost-leadership strategy, its R&D efforts probably focus on product and process development rather than on the more expensive product innovation, which carries no guarantee of success. In other words, the company stresses competencies that improve product characteristics or lower the cost of making existing products. Similarly, a company tries to decrease the cost of sales and marketing by offering a standard product to a mass market rather than different products aimed at different market segments, which is also more expensive.[44]

To implement cost leadership, a company chooses a combination of structure, control, and culture compatible with lowering its cost structure while preserving its ability to attract customers. In practice, the functional structure is the most suitable provided that care is taken to select integrating mechanisms that will reduce communication and measurement problems. For example, a TQM program can be effectively implemented when a functional structure is overlaid with cross-functional teams because team members can now search for ways to improve operating rules and procedures that lower the cost structure or standardize and raise product quality.[45]

Cost leadership also requires that managers continuously monitor their structures and control systems to find ways to restructure or streamline them so that they operate more effectively. For example, managers need to be alert to ways of using IT to standardize operations and lower costs. To reduce costs further, cost leaders use the cheapest and easiest forms of control available: output controls. For each function, a cost leader adopts output controls that allow it to closely monitor and evaluate functional performance. In the manufacturing function, for example, the company imposes tight controls and stresses meeting budgets based on production, cost, or quality targets.[46] In R&D, the emphasis also falls on the bottom line; to demonstrate their contribution to cost savings, R&D teams focus on improving process technology. Cost leaders are likely to reward employees through generous incentive and bonus plans to encourage high performance. Their culture is often based on values that emphasize the bottom line, such as those of Dell, Walmart, and McDonald's.

Implementing Differentiation

Effective strategy implementation can improve a company's ability to add value and to differentiate its products. To make its product unique in the eyes of the customer, for example, a differentiated company must design its structure, control, and culture around the *particular source* of its competitive advantage.[47] Specifically, differentiators need to design their structures around the source of their distinctive competencies, the differentiated qualities of their product, and the customer groups they serve. Commonly, in pursuing differentiation, a company starts to produce a wider range of products to serve more market segments, which means it has to customize its products for different groups of customers. These factors make it more difficult to standardize activities and usually increase the bureaucratic costs associated with managing the handoffs or transfers between functions. Integration becomes much more of a problem; communications, measurement, location, and strategic problems increasingly arise; and the demands on functional managers increase.

To respond to these problems, strategic managers develop more sophisticated control systems, increasingly make use of IT, focus on developing cultural norms and values that overcome problems associated with differences in functional orientations and focus on cross-functional objectives. The control systems used to match the structure should be geared to a company's distinctive competencies. For successful differentiation, it is important that the various functions do not pull in different directions; indeed, cooperation among the functions is vital for cross-functional integration. However, when functions work together, output controls become much harder to use. In general, it is much more difficult to measure the performance of people in different functions when they are engaged in cooperative efforts. Consequently, a differentiator must rely more on behavior controls and shared norms and values.

This explains why companies pursuing differentiation often have a markedly different kind of culture from those pursuing cost leadership. Because human resources—scientists, designers, or marketing employees—are often the source of differentiation, these organizations have a culture based on professionalism or collegiality that emphasizes the distinctiveness of the human resources rather than the high pressure of the bottom line.[48] HP, Motorola, and Coca-Cola, all of which emphasize some kind of distinctive competency, exemplify companies with professional cultures.

In practice, the implementation decisions that confront managers who must simultaneously strive for differentiation and a low cost structure are dealt with together as strategic managers move to implement new, more complex kinds of organizational structure. As a company's business model and strategies evolve, strategic managers usually start to *superimpose* a more complex divisional grouping of activities on its functional structure to better coordinate value chain activities. This is especially true of companies seeking to become *broad differentiators*—companies that have the ability to both increase differentiation and lower their cost structures. These companies are the most profitable in their industry, and they have to be especially adept at organizational design. This is a major source of a differentiation and cost advantage (see Figure 12.6). No matter what their business model, however, more complex structures cost more to operate than a simple functional structure. Managers are willing to bear this extra cost, however, as long as the new structure makes better use of functional competencies, increases revenues, and lowers the overall cost structure.

Product Structure: Implementing a Wide Product Line

The structure that organizations most commonly adopt to solve the control problems that result from producing many different kinds of products for many different market segments is the *product structure*. The intent is to break up a company's growing product line into a number of smaller, more manageable subunits to reduce bureaucratic costs due to communication, measurement, and other problems. Nokia moved to a product structure as it grew in size; its structure is shown in Figure 12.7.

An organization that chooses a product structure first divides its overall product line into product groups or categories (see Figure 12.7). Each product group focuses on satisfying the needs of a particular customer group and is managed by its own team of managers. Second, to keep costs as low as possible, value chain support functions such as basic R&D, marketing, materials, and finance are centralized at the top of the organization, and the different product groups share their services. Each support function, in turn, is divided into product-oriented teams of functional specialists who focus on the needs of one particular product group. This arrangement allows each team to specialize and become expert in managing the needs of its product group. Because all of the R&D teams belong to the same centralized function, however, they can share knowledge and information with each other and build their competence over time.

Strategic control systems can now be developed to measure the performance of each product group separately from the others. Thus, the performance of each product group is easy to monitor and evaluate, and corporate managers at the center can move more quickly to intervene if necessary. Also, the strategic reward system can be linked more closely to the performance of each product group, although top managers can still decide to make rewards based on corporate performance an important part of the incentive system. Doing so will encourage the different product groups to share ideas and knowledge and promote the development of a corporate culture, as well as the product group culture that naturally develops inside each product group. A product structure is commonly used by food processors, furniture makers, personal and health products companies, and large electronics companies like Nokia.

Figure 12.7 Nokia's Product Structure

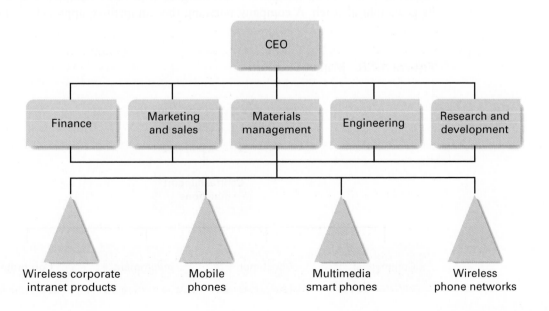

Market Structure: Increasing Responsiveness to Customer Groups

Suppose the source of competitive advantage in an industry depends on the ability to meet the needs of distinct and important sets of customers or different customer groups. What is the best way of implementing strategy now? Many companies develop a **market structure** that is conceptually quite similar to the product structure except that the focus is on customer groups instead of product groups.

For a company pursuing a strategy based on increasing responsiveness to customers, it is vital that the nature and needs of each different customer group be identified. Then, employees and functions are grouped by customer or market segment. A different set of managers becomes responsible for developing the products that each group of customers wants and tailoring or customizing products to the needs of each particular customer group. In other words, to promote superior responsiveness to customers, a company will design a structure around its customers, and a market structure is adopted. A typical market structure is shown in Figure 12.8.

A market structure brings customer group managers and employees closer to specific groups of customers. These people can then take their detailed knowledge and feed it back to the support functions, which are kept centralized to reduce costs. For example, information about changes in customer preferences can be quickly fed back to R&D and product design so that a company can protect its competitive advantage by supplying a constant stream of improved products for its installed customer base. This is especially important when a company serves well-identified customer groups such as Fortune 500 companies or small businesses. The Opening Case describes how Liz Claiborne uses a market structure to maximize its responsiveness to important customer groups while at the same time keeping its overall cost structure as low as possible.

Geographic Structure: Expanding Nationally

Suppose a company starts to expand nationally through internal expansion or by engaging in horizontal integration and merging with other companies to expand its geographical reach. A company pursuing this competitive approach frequently

Figure 12.8 Market Structure

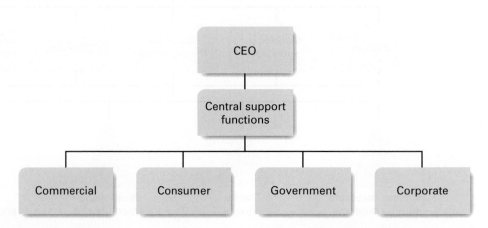

moves to a **geographic structure** in which geographic regions become the basis for the grouping of organizational activities (see Figure 12.9). A company may divide its manufacturing operations and establish manufacturing plants in different regions of the country, for example. This allows it to be responsive to the needs of regional customers and reduces transportation costs. Similarly, as a service organization such as a store chain or bank expands beyond one geographic area, it may begin to organize sales and marketing activities on a regional level to better serve the needs of customers in different regions.

A geographic structure provides more coordination and control than a functional structure does because several regional hierarchies are created to take over the work, just as in a product structure, where several product group hierarchies are created. A company such as FedEx clearly needs to operate a geographic structure to fulfill its corporate goal: next-day delivery. Large merchandising organizations, such as Neiman Marcus, Dillard's Department Stores, and Walmart, also moved to a geographic structure as they started building stores across the country. With this type of structure, different regional clothing needs (for example, sun wear in the South, down coats in the Midwest) can be handled as required. At the same time, because the information systems, purchasing, distribution, and marketing functions remain centralized, they can leverage their skills across all the regions. Thus, in using a geographic structure, a company can achieve economies of scale in buying, distributing, and selling and lower its cost structure while at the same time being more responsive (differentiated) to customer needs.

Figure 12.9 Geographic Structure

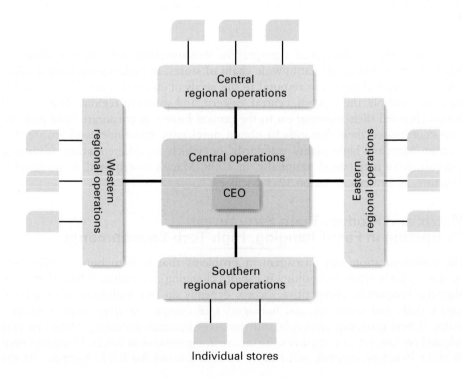

Individual stores

12.3 *STRATEGY IN ACTION*

Macy's Changes Its Geographic Structure

Since the recession started in 2008, all companies have been searching for ways to reduce their cost structure to remain profitable or reduce their losses. Macy's, the national department store chain, is one company that has been forced to take major steps to reduce its cost structure. To become a national retail chain, Macy's acquired many regional department store chains, but during this process its managers paid attention only to the differentiation side of the equation. They focused their efforts on making their clothes appealing to customers and had thought through the issue of how to combine and streamline the functional operations of the acquired companies, for example, how to merge all the regional purchasing and shipping operations of the acquired store chains to increase efficiency and reduce its cost structure. As a result, when the recession struck in 2008, Macy's sales plunged due to its high cost structure, and it was soon losing billions of dollars.

To survive, Macy's CEO decided that a major change in organizational structure was needed to cut operating costs. The operations of all four of Macy's regional head-quarters offices were centralized at its New York headquarters. This level in the hierarchy was eliminated, as were the jobs of 7,000 (40%) executives, mainly at the regional level. However, once it had eliminated these four large regional offices, realizing that it had to maintain effective control over its hundreds of stores and be responsive to the needs of customers in different geographic reasons, Macy's established eight new, much smaller regional offices in Chicago, Houston, Miami, Los Angeles, New York, Pittsburgh, San Francisco, and Washington, DC, to manage these activities.

All its major functions such as purchasing and shipping will still be centralized in New York. The new regional executives communicate customer needs to New York and work to increase the efficiency of its regional and district store operations. This change in operating structure is expected to save Macy's $400 million a year. It will also allow it to find ways to improve its functional competences so, for example, it can cut back on the level of store inventory, a major cost for a retailer, and move clothing and other products faster to stores.

Neiman Marcus developed a geographic structure similar to the one shown in Figure 12.9 to manage its nationwide chain of stores. In each region, it established a team of regional buyers to respond to the needs of customers in each geographic area, for example, the western, central, eastern, and southern regions. The regional buyers then fed their information to the central buyers at corporate headquarters, who coordinated their demands to obtain purchasing economies and ensure that Neiman Marcus's high-quality standards, on which its differentiation advantage depends, were maintained nationally. In 2009, Macy's reorganized its geographic structure, as Strategy in Action 12.3 discusses.

Matrix and Product-Team Structures: Competing in Fast-Changing, High-Tech Environments

The communication and measurement problems that lead to bureaucratic costs escalate quickly when technology is rapidly changing and industry boundaries are blurring. Frequently, competitive success depends on fast mobilization of a company's skills and resources, and managers face complex strategy implementation issues. A new grouping of people and resources becomes necessary, often one that is based on fostering a company's distinctive competencies in R&D. Managers need to make structure, control, and culture choices around the R&D function. At the same time, they need to ensure that implementation will result in new products that cost-effectively meet customer needs and will not result in products so expensive that customers will not wish to buy them.

Matrix Structure   To address these problems, many companies choose a matrix structure.[49] In a **matrix structure**, value chain activities are grouped in two ways (see Figure 12.10). First, activities are grouped vertically by *function* so that there is a familiar differentiation of tasks into functions such as engineering, sales and marketing, and R&D. In addition, superimposed on this vertical pattern is a horizontal pattern based on grouping by *product or project* in which people and resources are grouped to meet ongoing product development needs. The resulting network of reporting relationships among projects and functions is designed to make R&D the focus of attention.

Figure 12.10   Matrix Structure

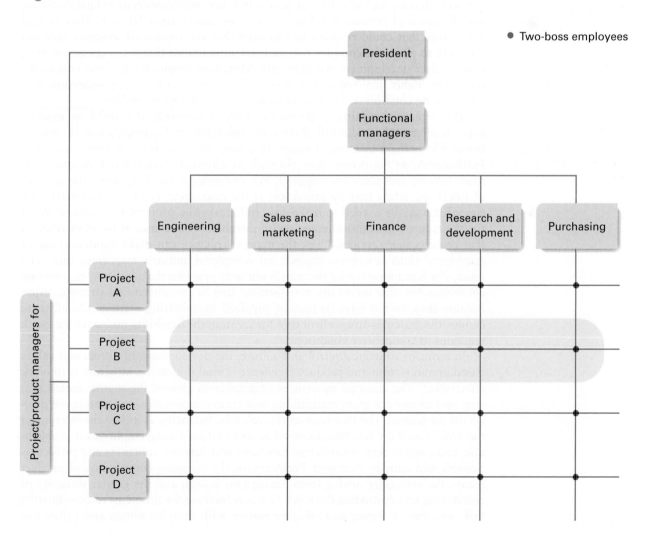

Matrix structures are flat and decentralized, and employees inside a matrix have two bosses: a *functional boss,* who is the head of a function, and a *product or project boss,* who is responsible for managing the individual projects. Employees work on a project team with specialists from other functions and report to the project boss on project matters and the functional boss on matters relating to functional issues. All employees who work on a project team are called **two-boss employees** and are responsible for managing coordination and communication among the functions and projects.

Implementing a matrix structure promotes innovation and speeds product development because this type of structure permits intensive cross-functional integration. Integrating mechanisms such as teams help transfer knowledge among functions and are designed around the R&D function. Sales, marketing, and production targets are geared to R&D goals, marketing devises advertising programs that focus on technological possibilities, and salespeople are evaluated on their understanding of new-product characteristics and their ability to inform potential customers about them.

Matrix structures were first developed by companies in high-technology industries such as aerospace and electronics, for example, TRW and Hughes. These companies were developing radically new products in uncertain, competitive environments, and the speed of product development was the crucial consideration. They needed a structure that could respond to this need, but the functional structure was too inflexible to allow the complex role and task interactions that are necessary to meet new-product development requirements. Moreover, employees in these companies tend to be highly qualified and professional and perform best in autonomous, flexible working conditions. The matrix structure provides such conditions.

This structure requires a minimum of direct hierarchical control by supervisors. Team members control their own behavior, and participation in project teams allows them to monitor other team members and to learn from each other. Furthermore, as the project goes through its different phases, different specialists from various functions are required. For example, at the first stage, the services of R&D specialists may be called for; at the next stage, engineers and marketing specialists may be needed to make cost and marketing projections. As the demand for the type of specialist changes, team members can be moved to other projects that require their services. Thus, the matrix structure can make maximum use of employees' skills as existing projects are completed and new ones come into existence. The freedom given by the matrix not only provides the autonomy to motivate employees but also leaves top management free to concentrate on strategic issues because they do not have to become involved in operating matters. On all these counts, the matrix is an excellent tool for creating the flexibility necessary for quick reactions to competitive conditions.

In terms of strategic control and culture, the development of norms and values based on innovation and product excellence is vital if a matrix structure is to work effectively.[50] The constant movement of employees around the matrix means that time and money are spent establishing new team relationships and getting the project off the ground. The two-boss employee's role, balancing as it does the interests of the project with the function, means that cooperation among employees is problematic, and conflict between different functions and between functions and projects is possible and must be managed. Furthermore, the changing composition of product teams, the ambiguity arising from having two bosses, and the greater difficulty of monitoring and evaluating the work of teams increase the problems of coordinating task activities. A strong and cohesive culture with unifying norms and values can mitigate these problems, as can a strategic reward system based on a group- and organizational-level reward system.

Product-Team Structure   A major structural innovation in recent years has been the **product-team structure**. Its advantages are similar to those of a matrix structure, but it is much easier and far less costly to operate because of the way people are organized into permanent cross-functional teams, as Figure 12.11 illustrates. In the product-team structure, as in the matrix structure, tasks are divided along product or project lines. However, instead of being assigned only *temporarily* to different projects, as in the matrix structure, functional specialists become part of a *permanent* cross-functional team that focuses on the development of one particular range of products, such as luxury cars or computer workstations. As a result, the problems associated with coordinating cross-functional transfers or handoffs are much lower than in a matrix structure, in which tasks and reporting relationships change rapidly. Moreover, cross-functional teams are formed at the beginning of the product development process so that any difficulties that arise can be ironed out early, before they lead to major redesign problems. When all functions have direct input from the beginning, design costs and subsequent manufacturing costs can be kept low. Moreover, the use of cross-functional teams speeds innovation and customer responsiveness because, when authority is decentralized, team decisions can be made more quickly.

A product-team structure groups tasks by product, and each product group is managed by a cross-functional product team that has all the support services necessary to bring the product to market. This is why it is different from the product structure, in which support functions remain centralized. The role of the product team is to protect and enhance a company's differentiation advantage and at the same time coordinate with manufacturing to lower costs.

Figure 12.11   Product-Team Structure

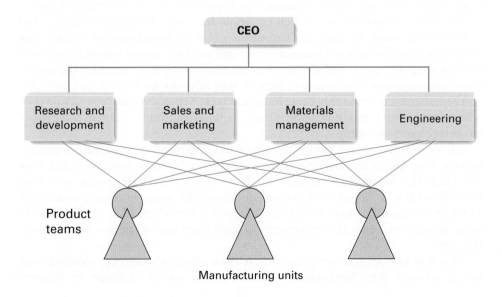

Focusing on a Narrow Product Line

As Chapter 5 discussed, a focused company concentrates on developing a narrow range of products aimed at one or two market segments, which may be defined by type of customer or location. As a result, a focuser tends to have a higher cost structure than a cost leader or differentiator, because output levels are lower, making it harder to obtain substantial scale economies. For this reason, a focused company must exercise cost control. On the other hand, some attribute of its product gives the focuser its distinctive competency—possibly its ability to provide customers with high-quality, personalized service. For both reasons, the structure and control system adopted by a focused company has to be inexpensive to operate but flexible enough to allow a distinctive competency to emerge.

A company using a focus strategy normally adopts a functional structure to meet these needs. This structure is appropriate because it is complex enough to manage the activities necessary to make and sell a narrow range of products for one or a few market segments. At the same time, the handoff problems are likely to be relatively easy to solve because a focuser remains small and specialized. Thus, a functional structure can provide all the integration necessary, provided that the focused firm has a strong, adaptive culture, which is vital to the development of some kind of distinctive competency.[51] Additionally, because such a company's competitive advantage is often based on personalized service, the flexibility of this kind of structure allows the company to respond quickly to customers' needs and change its products in response to customers' requests.

RESTRUCTURING AND REENGINEERING

To improve performance, a single business company often employs restructuring and reengineering. **Restructuring** a company involves two steps: (1) streamlining the hierarchy of authority and reducing the number of levels in the hierarchy to a minimum and (2) reducing the number of employees to lower operating costs. Restructuring and downsizing become necessary for many reasons.[52] Sometimes a change in the business environment occurs that could not have been foreseen; perhaps a shift in technology made the company's products obsolete. Sometimes an organization has excess capacity because customers no longer want the goods and services it provides; perhaps the goods and services are outdated or offer poor value for the money. Sometimes organizations downsize because they have grown too tall and inflexible and bureaucratic costs have become much too high. Sometimes they restructure even when they are in a strong position simply to build and improve their competitive advantage and stay on top.

All too often, however, companies are forced to downsize and lay off employees because they fail to monitor and control their basic business operations and have not made the incremental changes to their strategies and structures over time that allow them to adjust to changing conditions. Advances in management, such as the development of new models for organizing work activities, or IT advances offer strategic managers the opportunity to implement their strategies in more effective ways.

One way of helping a company operate more effectively is to use **reengineering**, which involves the "fundamental rethinking and radical redesign of business processes to achieve dramatic improvements in critical, contemporary measures of performance, such as cost, quality, service, and speed."[53] As this definition suggests, strategic managers who use reengineering must completely rethink how they organize their value chain activities. Instead of focusing on how a company's *functions* operate, strategic managers make business *processes* the focus of attention.

A **business process** is any activity that is vital to delivering goods and services to customers quickly or that promotes high quality or low costs (such as IT, materials management, or product development). It is not the responsibility of any one function but *cuts across functions*. Because reengineering focuses on business processes, not on functions, a company that reengineers always has to adopt a different approach to organizing its activities. Companies that take up reengineering deliberately ignore the existing arrangement of tasks, roles, and work activities. They start the reengineering process with the customer (not the product or service) and ask, "How can we reorganize the way we do our work—our business processes—to provide the best quality and the lowest-cost goods and services to the customer?"

Frequently, when companies ask this question, they realize that there are more effective ways to organize their value chain activities. For example, a business process that encompasses members of 10 different functions working sequentially to provide goods and services might be performed by one person or a few people at a fraction of the cost. Often individual jobs become increasingly complex, and people are grouped into cross-functional teams as business processes are reengineered to reduce costs and increase quality.

Hallmark Cards, for example, reengineered its card design process with great success. Before the reengineering effort, artists, writers, and editors worked separately in different functions to produce all kinds of cards. After reengineering, these same artists, writers, and editors were put on cross-functional teams, each of which now works on a specific type of card, such as birthday, Christmas, or Mother's Day. The result is that the time it takes to bring a new card to market dropped from years to months, and Hallmark's performance increased dramatically.

Reengineering and TQM, discussed in Chapter 4, are highly interrelated and complementary. After reengineering has taken place and value chain activities have been altered to speed the product to the final customer, TQM takes over, with its focus on how to continue to improve and refine the new process and find better ways of managing task and role relationships. Successful organizations examine both issues simultaneously and continuously attempt to identify new and better processes for meeting the goals of increased efficiency, quality, and customer responsiveness. Thus, they are always seeking to improve their visions of their desired future.

Another example of reengineering is the change program that took place at IBM Credit, a wholly owned division of IBM that manages the financing and leasing of IBM computers, particularly mainframes, to IBM's customers. Before reengineering took place, a financing request arrived at the division's headquarters in Old Greenwich, Connecticut, and went through a five-step approval process that involved the activities of five different functions. First, the IBM salesperson called the credit department, which logged the request and recorded details about the potential customer. Second, this information was taken to the credit-checking department, where a credit check on the potential customer was done. Third, when the credit check was complete, the request was taken to the contracts department, which wrote the contract. Fourth, from the contracts department, it went to the pricing department, which determined the actual financial details of the loan, such as the interest rate and the term of the loan. Finally, the whole package of information was assembled by the dispatching department and delivered to the sales representative, who gave it to the customer.

This series of cross-functional activities took an average of seven days to complete, and sales representatives constantly complained that this delay resulted in a low level of customer responsiveness that reduced customer satisfaction. Also, potential customers were tempted to shop around for financing and even to look at competitors' machines. The delay in closing the deal caused uncertainty for all concerned.

The change process began when two senior IBM credit managers reviewed the finance approval process. They found that the time spent by different specialists in the different functions actually processing a loan application was only ninety minutes. The seven-day approval process was caused by the delay in transmitting information and requests between departments. Managers also learned that the activities taking place in each department were not complex; each department had its own computer system containing its own work procedures, but the work done in each department was routine.

Armed with this information, IBM managers realized that the approval process could be reengineered into one overarching process handled by one person with a computer system containing all the necessary information and work procedures to perform the five loan-processing activities. If the application were complex, a team of experts stood ready to help process it, but IBM found that, after the reengineering effort, a typical application could be done in four hours rather than the previous seven days. A sales representative could go back to the customer the same day to close the deal, and all the uncertainty surrounding the transaction was removed.

As reengineering consultants Hammer and Champy note, this dramatic performance increase was brought about by a radical change to the process as a whole. Change through reengineering requires managers to go back to the basics and pull apart each step in the work process to identify a better way to coordinate and integrate the activities necessary to provide customers with goods and services. As this example makes clear, the introduction of new IT is an integral aspect of reengineering. IT also allows a company to restructure its hierarchy because it provides more and better-quality information. IT today is an integral part of the strategy implementation process.

SUMMARY OF CHAPTER

1. Implementing a company's business model and strategies successfully depends on organizational design, the process of selecting the right combination of organizational structure, control systems, and culture. Companies need to monitor and oversee the organizational design process to achieve superior profitability.

2. Effective organizational design can increase profitability in two ways. First, it economizes on bureaucratic costs and helps a company lower its cost structure. Second, it enhances the ability of a company's value creation functions to achieve superior efficiency, quality, innovativeness, and customer responsiveness and obtain the advantages of differentiation.

3. The main issues in designing organizational structure are how to group tasks, functions, and divisions; how to allocate authority and responsibility (whether to have a tall or flat organization or to have a centralized or decentralized structure); and how to use integrating mechanisms to improve coordination between functions (such as direct contacts, liaison roles, and teams).

4. Strategic control provides the monitoring and incentive systems necessary to make an organizational structure work as intended and extends corporate governance down to all levels inside the company. The main kinds of strategic control systems are personal control, output control, and behavior control. IT is an aid to output and behavior control, and reward systems are linked to every control system.

5. Organizational culture is the set of values, norms, beliefs, and attitudes that help to energize and motivate employees and control their behavior. Culture is a way of doing something, and a company's founder and top managers help determine which kinds of values emerge in an organization.

6. At the functional level, each function requires a different combination of structure and control system to achieve its functional objectives.

7. To successfully implement a company's business model, structure, control, and culture must be combined in ways that increase the relationships among all functions to build distinctive competencies.

8. Cost leadership and differentiation each require a structure and control system that strengthens the business model that is the source of their competitive advantage. Managers have to use organizational design in a way that balances pressures to increase differentiation against pressures to lower the cost structure.

9. Other specialized kinds of structures include the product, market, geographic, matrix, and product-team structures. Each has a specialized use and is implemented as a company's strategy warrants.

10. Restructuring and reengineering are two ways of implementing a company's business model more effectively.

DISCUSSION QUESTIONS

1. What kind of structure best describes the way your (a) business school and (b) university operate? Why is the structure appropriate? Would another structure fit better?

2. For each of the structures discussed in the chapter, outline the most suitable control systems.

3. What is the relationship among organizational structure, control, and culture? Give some examples of when and under what conditions a mismatch among these components might arise.

CLOSING CASE

Strategy Implementation at Dell Computer

Dell Computer was one of the fastest-growing companies of the 1990s, and its stock price increased at the rate of 100% per year, delighting its stockholders. Achieving this high return has been a constant challenge for Michael Dell. One of his biggest battles has been to manage and change Dell's organizational structure, control systems, and culture as his company grows.

Michael Dell was 19 in 1984, when he took $1,000 and spent it on the computer parts he assembled into PCs that he sold over the phone. Increasing demand for his PCs meant that within a few weeks, he needed to hire people to help him. Soon he found himself supervising three employees who worked together around a six-foot table to assemble computers while two more employees took orders over the phone.[54]

By 1993, Dell employed 4,500 workers and was hiring more than 100 new workers each week just to keep pace with the demand for the computers. When he found himself working 18-hour days managing the company, he realized that he could not lead the company single-handedly. The company's growth had to be managed, and he knew that he had to recruit and hire strategic managers who had experience in managing different functional areas, such as marketing, finance, and manufacturing. He recruited executives from IBM and Compaq. With their help, he created a functional structure, one in which employees were grouped by their common skills or tasks they performed, such as sales or manufacturing, to organize the value chain activities necessary to deliver his PCs to customers. As a part of this organizing process, Dell's structure also became taller, with more levels in the management hierarchy, to ensure that he and his managers had sufficient control over the different activities of his growing business. Michael Dell delegated authority to control Dell's functional value chain activities to his managers, which gave him the time he needed to perform his entrepreneurial task of finding new opportunities for the company.

Dell's functional structure worked well and, under its new management team, the company's growth continued to soar. Moreover, Dell's new structure had given functional managers the control they needed to squeeze out costs, and Dell had become the lowest-cost PC maker. Analysts also reported that Dell had developed a lean organizational culture, meaning that employees had developed norms and values that emphasized the importance of working hard to help each other find innovative new ways of making products to keep costs low and increase their reliability. Indeed, Dell rose to the top of the customer satisfaction rankings for PC makers because few customers complained about its products. Its employees became known for the excellent customer service they gave to PC buyers who were experiencing problems with setting up their computers.

However, Michael Dell realized that new and different kinds of problems were arising. Dell was now selling huge numbers of computers to different kinds of customers, for example, home, business, and educational customers and different branches of government. Because customers were demanding computers with different features or more computing power, the company's product line broadened rapidly. It became more difficult for employees to meet the needs of these customers efficiently because each employee needed information about all product features or all of Dell's thousands of different sales offers across its product range.

By the late 1990s, Michael Dell moved to change his company to a market structure and created separate divisions, each geared to the needs of a different group of customers: a consumer division, a business division, and so on. In each division, teams of employees specialized in servicing the needs of one of these customer groups. This move to a more complex structure also allowed each division to develop a unique subculture that suited its tasks, and employees were able to obtain in-depth knowledge about the needs of their market that helped them to respond better to their customers' needs. So successful was this change in structure and culture that by 2000, Dell's revenues were more than $35 billion and its profits in excess of $3 billion, a staggering increase from 1984.[55]

Michael Dell has continued to change his company's structure in the 2000s to respond to changing customer needs and increasing competitive challenges from Apple and HP. For example, Michael Dell realized that he could leverage his company's strengths in materials management, manufacturing, and Internet sales over a wider range of computer hardware products. He decided to begin assembling servers, workstations, and storage devices to compete with IBM, Sun, and HP. The increasing importance of the Internet also led him to pay more attention to more specialized groups of customers and find the best way to customize its approach to best meet each group's specific needs over the Internet. Today, for example, Dell can offer large and small companies and private buyers a complete range of computers, workstations, and storage devices that can be customized to their needs.

To help coordinate its growing activities, Dell is increasingly making use of its corporate Intranet to standardize activities across divisions and integrate its activities across functions to reduce costs. Dell's hierarchy is shrinking as managers increasingly delegate decision making to employees who use its

advanced IT to access the information they need to provide excellent customer service. To reduce costs, Dell has also outsourced most of its customer service function to India.[56] As a result of these moves, Dell's smaller United States workforce has become even more committed to maintain a low-cost advantage. Its cost-conscious culture is more than ever an important factor affecting its competitive advantage that has been threatened by the many cost-saving moves made by competitors such as Apple and HP that have imitated and even improved on its cost-saving strategies.[57]

Case Discussion Questions

1. Why has Dell moved to different kinds of organizational structures over time?
2. Has Dell's performance been improved?
3. Search the Internet to find out how Dell has been trying to increase its performance and how its competitors such as Apple and HP have also been working to improve theirs.

13

CORPORATE STRATEGIES ACROSS COUNTRIES AND INDUSTRIES

LEARNING OBJECTIVES

After reading this chapter, you should be able to

- Discuss the reasons why companies pursuing different corporate strategies need to implement these strategies using different combinations of organizational structure, control, and culture
- Describe the advantages and disadvantages of a multidivisional structure
- Explain why companies that pursue different kinds of global expansion strategies choose different kinds of global structures and control systems to implement them
- Discuss the strategy implementation problems associated with the three main methods used to enter new industries: internal new venturing, joint ventures, and mergers
- Identify the ways in which advanced IT may reduce bureaucratic costs and allow a company to more effectively implement its business model

Avon Is Calling for a New Global Structure

After a decade of profitable growth under its CEO Andrea Jung, Avon's global sales suddenly began to fall in the mid-2000s in developing markets in Central Europe, Russia, and China, which had been major contributors to its rising sales, as well as in the United States and Mexico.

Avon's stock price plunged in 2006, and Jung was shocked by the turn of events. For the first time as CEO, she was in the position of having to find ways to solve Avon's problems—rather than ways to add to its success.[1]

After several months jetting around the globe to visit the managers of Avon's divisions, she came to a surprising conclusion. Avon's rapid global expansion had given these global managers *too* much autonomy and authority to control operations in their respective countries and world regions. As a result, they made decisions that benefitted their own global divisions, but these decisions had hurt the performance of the whole company. Avon's country-level managers from Poland to Mexico ran their own factories, made their own product development decisions, and developed their own advertising campaigns. Many of these decisions had been based on poor marketing knowledge, with little concern for operating costs, because their goal was to increase their division's sales as fast as possible. When too much authority is decentralized to managers lower in an organization's hierarchy, the managers often recruit more managers to help them build their country "empires." The result was that Avon's global organizational hierarchy had exploded: it had risen from 7 to 15 levels of managers in a decade as tens of thousands of extra managers were hired around the globe![2] Because Avon's profits were rising fast, Jung and her top management team had not paid enough attention to the way Avon's organizational structure was becoming taller—just as it was getting wider as it entered more countries to expand cosmetics sales.

This was a nightmare scenario. Jung had to confront the need to lay off thousands of global managers and restructure the organizational hierarchy to reduce costs and boost profitability. She embarked on a program to take away the authority of Avon's country-level managers and transfer authority to regional and corporate headquarters managers to streamline decision making and reduce costs. She cut out seven levels of management and eliminated 25% of its global managers in its 114 worldwide markets. Then, using teams of expert managers from corporate headquarters, she embarked on a detailed examination of all of Avon's functional activities, country by country, to find out why costs had risen so quickly and what could be done to bring them under control. The duplication of marketing efforts in countries around the world was one source of these high costs. In Mexico, one team found that country managers' desire to expand their empires had led to the development of a staggering 13,000 different products. Not only

had this caused product development costs to soar, it had led to major marketing problems. How could Avon's Mexican sales reps learn all about the 13,000 products—and then find an easy way to tell customers about them?

In Avon's new structure, all new major product development is now centralized in the United States. While the input from global managers is used to customize products to the likes of each country, for example, fragrance, packaging and so on, the more than 1,000 new products a year Avon introduces are developed in its United States R&D laboratories. Similarly, to reduce costs, all marketing campaigns targeted toward the average "global" customer are developed by Avon's United States marketing function. Then they can be easily customized to a particular country or world region by, for example, using the appropriate language or the nationality of the models to market the product. Other initiatives have been to increase the money spent on global marketing, which had not kept pace with its rapid global expansion, and a major push to increase the number of Avon salespeople in developing nations, who number in the millions, to attract more customers.[3]

Country-level managers now are responsible for managing this army of Avon reps and for making sure that marketing dollars are being directed toward the right channels for maximum impact. However, they no longer have the authority to engage in major product development or build new manufacturing capacity—or hire new managers without the permission of regional or corporate level managers who are now focused on reducing Avon's cost structure. The major changes Jung made to Avon's organizational structure and culture has totally changed the balance of power and changed the way the company implements its web of global strategies. Today, Jung and all her managers are focusing on developing strategies that strengthen the business model of the entire company, not just its individual global divisions.

Overview

The story of Andrea Jung's efforts to develop a new organizational structure and culture to compete effectively in countries around the world suggests how complex strategic thinking becomes at the corporate level. Companies have to continuously examine and improve the way they implement their business and multibusiness models to increase their long-run profitability. If they fail to, like Avon, the result can be a nightmare. This chapter begins where the last one ends; it examines how to implement strategy when a company decides to enter and compete in new industries or in new countries when it expands globally. The strategy implementation issue remains the same: how to use organizational design and combine organizational structure, control, and culture to strengthen a company's multibusiness model and increase its profitability.

Once a company decides to compete across industries and countries, it confronts a new set of problems; however, some of them continuations of the organizational problems we discussed in Chapter 12, and some of them are a direct consequence of the decision to enter and compete in overseas markets and new industries. As a result, strategic managers have to make a new series of organizational design decisions to successfully implement their company's new global multibusiness model. By the end of the chapter, you will appreciate the many complex issues that confront global multibusiness companies and understand why effective strategy implementation is an integral part of achieving competitive advantage and superior performance.

Managing Corporate Strategy Through the Multidivisional Structure

As Chapter 10 discusses, corporate-level strategies such as vertical integration or diversification can be used in many ways to strengthen a company's business model and improve its competitive position. However, important implementation problems also arise when a company enters new industries, often due to the increasing bureaucratic costs associated with managing a collection of business units that operate in different industries. Bureaucratic costs are especially high when a company seeks to gain the differentiation and low-cost advantages of transferring, sharing, or leveraging its distinctive competencies across its business units in different industries. For companies pursuing a multibusiness model based on related diversification, for example, the problems and costs of managing the handoffs or transfers between the value chain functions of its different business units to boost profitability rise sharply. The need to economize on these costs propels strategic managers to search for improved ways to implement the corporate-level strategies necessary to pursue a multibusiness model.

As a company begins to enter new industries and produce different kinds of products, such as cars, fast food, and computers, the structures described in Chapter 12, such as the functional and product structures, are not up to the task. These structures cannot provide the level of coordination between managers and functions necessary to implement a multibusiness model effectively. As a result, the control problems that give rise to bureaucratic costs, such as those related to measurement, customers, location, or strategy, escalate. Experiencing these problems is a sign that a company has outgrown its structure. Strategic managers need to invest more resources to develop a more complex structure—one that allows it to implement its multibusiness model and strategies successfully. The answer for most large, complex companies is to move to a multidivisional structure, design a cross-industry control system, and fashion a corporate culture to reduce these problems and economize on bureaucratic costs.

A multidivisional structure has two organizational design advantages over a functional or product structure that allow a company to grow and diversify in a way that reduces the coordination and control problems that are inevitable when it enters and competes in new industries. First, in each industry in which a company operates, strategic managers group all its different business operations in that industry into one division or subunit. Normally, each division contains a full set of the value chain functions it needs to pursue its industry business model and is called a *self-contained division*. For example, GE competes in more than 150 different industries, and in each industry, all of its divisions are self-contained, performing all the value creation functions necessary to give the division a competitive advantage.

Second, the office of *corporate headquarters staff* is created to monitor divisional activities and exercise financial control over each division.[4] This staff contains the corporate-level managers who oversee the activities of divisional managers. Hence, the organizational hierarchy is taller in a multidivisional structure than in a product or functional structure. The role of the new level of corporate management is to develop strategic control systems that lower a company's overall cost structure, including finding ways to economize on the costs of controlling the handoffs and transfers between divisions. The extra cost of these corporate managers is more than justified if their actions can lower the cost structure of the operating divisions or increase the divisions' ability to differentiate their product—both of which boost a company's ROIC.

In the multidivisional structure, the day-to-day operations of each division are the responsibility of divisional management; that is, divisional management has *operating responsibility*. The corporate headquarters, which includes top executives as well as their support staff, is responsible for overseeing the company's long-term multibusiness model and providing guidance for interdivisional projects. These executives have *strategic responsibility*. Such a combination of self-contained divisions with a centralized corporate management provides the extra coordination and control necessary to enter new industries successfully.

Figure 13.1 illustrates a typical multidivisional structure found in a large chemical company such as DuPont. Although this company might easily have 20 different divisions, only three—the oil, pharmaceuticals, and plastics divisions—are represented in this figure. Each division possesses the value chain functions it needs to pursue its own industry business model. Each division is treated by corporate managers as an independent profit center, and measures of profitability such as ROIC are used to monitor and evaluate each division's individual performance.[5] The use of this kind of output control makes it easier for corporate managers to identify high-performing and underperforming divisions and to take corrective action as necessary.

Because the division operates independently, the strategic or divisional managers in charge of each individual division can choose which organizational structure (for example, a product, matrix, or market structure), control systems, and culture to adopt to implement its business model and strategies most effectively. Figure 13.1 illustrates how this process works. It shows that managers of the oil division have chosen a functional structure to pursue its cost leadership strategy. The pharmaceuticals division has adopted a product-team structure to encourage the speedy

Figure 13.1 Multidivisional Structure

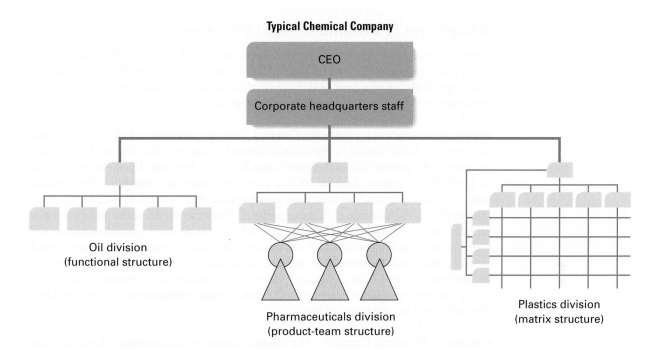

Typical Chemical Company

Oil division
(functional structure)

Pharmaceuticals division
(product-team structure)

Plastics division
(matrix structure)

development of new drugs. And managers of the plastics division implement a matrix structure that promotes cooperation between functions and speeds the innovation of improved plastic products that suit the changing needs of customers. These two divisions are pursuing differentiation based on a distinctive competence in innovation.

The CEO famous for employing the multidivisional structure to great advantage was Alfred Sloan, GM's first CEO, who implemented a multidivisional structure in 1921, noting that GM "needs to find a principle for coordination without losing the advantages of decentralization." Sloan placed each of GM's different car brands in a self-contained division so it possessed its own functions—sales, production, engineering, and finance. Each division was treated as a profit center and evaluated on its return on investment. Sloan was clear about the main advantage of decentralization: it made it much easier to evaluate the performance of each division. And, Sloan observed, it (1) "increases the morale of the organization by placing each operation on its own foundation…assuming its own responsibility and contributing its share to the final result"; (2) "develops statistics correctly reflecting…the true measure of efficiency"; and (3) "enables the corporation to direct the placing of additional capital where it will result in the greatest benefit to the corporation as a whole."[6]

Sloan recommended that exchanges or handoffs between divisions be set by a *transfer-pricing system* based on the cost of making a product plus some agreed-on rate of return. He recognized the risks that internal suppliers might become inefficient and raise the cost structure, and he recommended that GM should benchmark competitors to determine the fair price for a component. He established a centralized headquarters management staff to perform these calculations. Corporate management's primary role was to audit divisional performance and plan strategy for the total organization. Divisional managers were to be responsible for all competitive product-related decisions.

Advantages of a Multidivisional Structure

When managed effectively at both the corporate and the divisional levels, a multidivisional structure offers several strategic advantages. Together, they can raise corporate profitability to a new peak because they allow a company to more effectively implement its multibusiness model and strategies.

Enhanced Corporate Financial Control   The profitability of different business divisions is clearly visible in the multidivisional structure.[7] Because each division is its own profit center, financial controls can be applied to each business on the basis of profitability criteria such as ROIC. Corporate managers establish performance goals for each division, monitor their performance on a regular basis, and intervene selectively if a division starts to underperform. They can then use this information to identify the divisions in which investment of the company's financial resources will yield the greatest long-term ROIC. As a result, they can allocate the company's funds among competing divisions in an optimal way, that is, a way that will maximize the profitability of the *whole* company. Essentially, managers at corporate headquarters act as "internal investors" who channel funds to high-performing divisions in which they will produce the most profits.

Enhanced Strategic Control   The multidivisional structure makes divisional managers responsible for developing each division's business model and strategies; this allows corporate managers to focus on developing the multibusiness model, which is their main responsibility. The structure gives corporate managers the time they need to contemplate wider long-term strategic issues and develop a coordinated response to competitive changes, such as quickly changing industry boundaries. Teams of managers at corporate headquarters can also be created to collect and process crucial information that leads to improved functional performance at the divisional level. These managers also perform long-run strategic and scenario planning to find new ways to increase the performance of the entire company, such as evaluating which of the industries they compete in will likely be the most profitable in the future and vice versa. Then they can decide which industries they should expand into and which they should exit.

Profitable Long-Run Growth   The division of responsibilities between corporate and divisional managers in the multidivisional structure allows a company to overcome organizational problems, such as communication problems and information overload. Divisional managers work to enhance their divisions' profitability; teams of managers at corporate headquarters devote their time to finding opportunities to expand or diversify its existing businesses so that the entire company enjoys profitable growth. Communication problems are also reduced because corporate managers use the same set of standardized accounting and financial output controls to evaluate all divisions. Also, from a behavior control perspective, corporate managers can implement a policy of management by exception, which means that they intervene only when problems arise.

Stronger Pursuit of Internal Efficiency   As a single-business company grows, it often becomes difficult for top managers to accurately assess the profit contribution of each functional activity because their activities are so interdependent. This means that it is often difficult for top managers to evaluate how well their company is performing relative to others in its industry—and to identify or pinpoint the specific source of the problem. As a result, inside one company, considerable degrees of organizational slack—that is, the unproductive use of functional resources—can go undetected. For example, the head of the finance function might employ a larger staff than is required for efficiency to reduce work pressures inside the department and to bring the manager higher status. In a multidivisional structure, however, corporate managers can compare the performance of one division against another in terms of its cost structure, sales, and the profit it generates. The corporate office is thus in a better position to identify the managerial inefficiencies that result in bureaucratic costs; divisional managers have no excuses for poor performance.

Problems in Implementing a Multidivisional Structure

Although research suggests large companies that adopt multidivisional structures outperform those that retain functional structures, multidivisional structures have their disadvantages as well.[8] Good management can eliminate some of them, but others are inherent in the way the structure operates. Corporate managers have to continually pay attention to the way they operate to detect problems, such as the one Andrea Jung experienced at Avon described in the Opening Case.

Establishing the Divisional-Corporate Authority Relationship The authority relationship between corporate headquarters and the divisions must be correctly established. The multidivisional structure introduces a new level in the management hierarchy: the corporate level. The problem for corporate managers is to decide how much authority and control to delegate to divisional managers and how much authority to retain at corporate headquarters to give them the power to increase long-run profitability. Sloan encountered this problem when he implemented GM's multidivisional structure.[9] He found that when corporate managers retained too much power and authority, the managers of its business divisions lacked the autonomy required to change its business model to meet rapidly changing competitive conditions; the need to gain approval from corporate managers slowed down decision making. On the other hand, when too much authority is delegated to divisions, managers may start to pursue strategies that benefit their own divisions but add little to the whole company's profitability. The Opening Case describes how Avon recentralized control over its functional operations to United States corporate managers to prevent this problem.

The most important issue in managing a multidivisional structure is how much authority should be *centralized* at corporate headquarters and how much should be *decentralized* to the divisions. Corporate managers must consider how their company's multibusiness model and strategies will be affected by the way they make this decision now and in the future. There is no easy answer because every company is different. Also, as the environment changes or a company alters its multibusiness model, the optimal balance between centralization and decentralization of authority will change over time.

Restrictive Financial Controls Lead to Short-Run Focus Suppose corporate managers place too much emphasis on each division's *individual* profitability, for example, by establishing very high and stringent ROIC targets for each division.

Divisional managers may begin to distort the information they supply to corporate managers to hide declining divisional performance or start to pursue strategies that increase short-run profitability but reduce future profitability. For example, divisional managers may attempt to make the ROIC of their division look better by cutting investments in R&D, product development, or marketing—all of which increase ROIC in the short run. In the long run, however, cutting back on the investments and expenditures necessary to maintain the division's performance, particularly the crucial R&D investments that lead a stream of innovative products, will reduce its long-term profitability. Hence, corporate managers must carefully control their interactions with divisional managers to ensure that both the short- and long-term goals of the business are being met. In sum, the problem stems from the use of too restrictive financial controls; Chapter 11 discusses the "balanced scorecard" approach that helps solve it.

Competition for Resources   The third problem of managing a multidivisional structure is that when the divisions compete among themselves for scarce resources, this rivalry can make it difficult or impossible to obtain the gains from transferring, sharing, or leveraging distinctive competencies across business units. For example, every year the funds available to corporate managers to allocate or distribute to the divisions is fixed, and, usually, the divisions that have obtained the highest ROIC receive proportionally more of these funds. In turn, because they have more money to invest in their business, this usually will raise their performance the next year so strong divisions grow ever stronger. This is what leads to competition for resources and reduces interdivisional coordination; there are many recorded instances in which one division manager tells another, "You want our new technology? Well you have to pay us $2 billion to get it." When divisions battle over transfer prices, the potential gains from pursuing a multibusiness model are lost.

Transfer Pricing   As just noted, competition among divisions may lead to battles over **transfer pricing**, that is, conflicts over establishing the fair or "competitive" price of a resource or skill developed in one division that is to be transferred and sold to other divisions that require it. As Chapter 9 discusses, a major source of bureaucratic costs are the problems that arise from handoffs or transfers between divisions to obtain the benefits of the multibusiness models when pursuing a vertical integration or related diversification strategy. The problem of setting prices for resource transfers between divisions is a major source of these problems, because every supplying division has the incentive to set the highest possible transfer price for its products or resources to maximize its *own* profitability. The "purchasing" divisions realize the supplying divisions' attempts to charge high prices will reduce their profitability; the result is competition between divisions that undermines cooperation and coordination. Such competition can completely destroy the corporate culture and turn a company into a battleground. If such battles go unresolved, the benefits of the multibusiness model will not be achieved. Hence, corporate managers must be sensitive to this problem and work hard with the divisions to design incentive and control systems to make the multidivisional structure work. Indeed, managing transfer pricing is one of corporate managers' most important tasks.

Duplication of Functional Resources   Because each division has its own set of value chain functions, functional resources are duplicated across divisions; thus, multidivisional structures are expensive to operate. R&D and marketing are especially costly functional activities; to reduce their cost structure, some companies centralize most of the activities of these two functions at the corporate level in which they service the needs of all divisions. The expense involved in duplicating functional resources does not result in major problems if the differentiation advantages that result from the use of separate sets of specialist functions are substantial. Corporate managers must decide whether the duplication of functions is financially justified. And, they should always be on the lookout for ways to centralize or even outsource functional activities when this will reduce a company's cost structure and increase long-run profitability.

In sum, the advantages of divisional structures must be balanced against the problems of implementing them, but an observant, professional set of corporate (and divisional) managers who are sensitive to the issues involved can respond to and manage these problems. Indeed, advances in IT have made strategy implementation easier, as we discuss later in the chapter.

Structure, Control, Culture, and Corporate-Level Strategy

Once corporate managers select a multidivisional structure, they must then make choices about what kind of integrating mechanisms and control systems to use to make the structure work efficiently. Such choices depend on whether a company chooses to pursue a multibusiness model based on a strategy of unrelated diversification, vertical integration, or related diversification.

As Chapter 9 discusses, many possible differentiation and cost advantages derive from vertical integration. A company can coordinate resource transfers between divisions operating in adjacent industries to reduce manufacturing costs and improve quality, for example.[10] This might mean locating a rolling mill next to a steel furnace to save the costs of reheating steel ingots, making it easier to control the quality of the final product.

The principal benefits from related diversification also derive from transferring, sharing, or leveraging functional competencies across divisions, such as sharing distribution and sales networks to increase differentiation or lower the overall cost structure. With both strategies, the benefits to the company result from some *exchange* of distinctive competencies among divisions. To secure these benefits, managers must coordinate the activities of the various divisions, so an organization's structure and control systems must be designed to manage the handoffs or transfers among divisions.

In the case of unrelated diversification, the multibusiness model is based on using general strategic management capabilities, for example, in corporate finance or organizational design. Corporate managers' ability to create a culture that supports entrepreneurial behavior that leads to rapid product development, or restructure an underperforming company and establish an effective set of financial controls, can result in major increases in profitability. With this strategy, however, there are *no* exchanges among divisions; each division operates separately and independently. The only exchanges that need to be coordinated are those between the divisions and corporate headquarters. Structure and control must therefore be designed to allow each division to operate independently, while at the same time making it easy for corporate managers to monitor divisional performance and intervene if necessary.

The choice of structure and control mechanisms depends on the degree to which a company using a multidivisional structure needs to control the handoffs and interactions among divisions. The more interdependent the divisions—that is, the more they

Table 13.1   Corporate Strategy, Structure, and Control

Corporate Strategy	Appropriate Structure	Need for Integration	Type of Control		
			Financial Control	Behavior Control	Organizational Culture
Unrelated Diversification	Multidivisional	Low (no exchanges between divisions)	Great use (e.g., ROIC)	Some use (e.g., budgets)	Little use
Vertical Integration	Multidivisional	Medium (scheduling resource transfers)	Great use (e.g., ROIC, transfer pricing)	Great use (e.g., standardization, budgets)	Some use (e.g., shared norms and values)
Related Diversification	Multidivisional	High (achieving synergies between divisions by integrating roles)	Little use	Great use (e.g., rules, budgets)	Great use (e.g., norms, values, common language)

depend on each other for skills, resources, and competencies—the greater are the bureaucratic costs associated with obtaining the potential benefits from a particular corporate-level strategy.[11] Table 13.1 illustrates what forms of structure and control companies should adopt to economize on the bureaucratic costs associated with the three corporate strategies of unrelated diversification, vertical integration, and related diversification.[12] We examine these strategies in detail in the next sections.

Unrelated Diversification   Because there are *no exchanges or linkages* among divisions, unrelated diversification is the easiest and cheapest strategy to manage; it is associated with the lowest level of bureaucratic costs. The main advantage of the structure and control system is that it allows corporate managers to evaluate divisional performance accurately. Thus, companies use multidivisional structures, and each division is evaluated by output controls such as ROIC. A company also uses an IT-based system of financial controls to allow corporate managers to obtain information quickly from the divisions and compare their performance on many dimensions. UTC, Tyco, Textron, and Dover are good examples of companies that use sophisticated financial controls to manage their structures and track divisional performance on a daily basis.

Divisions usually have considerable autonomy *unless* they fail to reach their ROIC goals, in which case corporate managers will intervene in the operations of a division to help solve problems. As problems arise, corporate managers step in and take corrective action, such as replacing managers or providing additional funding, depending on the reason for the problem. If they see no possibility of a turnaround, they may decide to divest the division. The multidivisional structure allows the unrelated company to operate its businesses as a portfolio of investments that can be bought and sold as business conditions change. Typically, managers in the various divisions do not know one another; they may not even know what other companies are in the corporate portfolio. Hence, the idea of a corporate-wide culture is meaningless.

The use of financial controls to manage a company means that no integration among divisions is necessary. This is why the bureaucratic costs of managing an unrelated company are low. The biggest problem facing corporate managers is to make capital allocations decisions between divisions to maximize the overall profitability of the portfolio and monitor divisional performance to ensure they are meeting ROIC targets.

Alco Standard, based in Valley Forge, Pennsylvania, demonstrates how to operate a successful strategy of unrelated diversification. Alco is one of the largest office supply companies in the United States, distributing office and paper supplies and materials through a nationwide network of wholly owned distribution companies. The policy of Alco's top management is that authority and control should be completely decentralized to the managers in each of the company's 50 divisions. Each division is left alone to make its own manufacturing or purchasing decisions, even though some potential benefits that could be obtained from corporate-wide purchasing or marketing are lost. Corporate managers pursue this nonintervention policy because they believe that the gains from allowing its managers to act as independent entrepreneurs exceed the potential cost savings that would result from coordinating divisional activities. It believes that a decentralized operating system allows a big company to act similar to a small company and avoids the problems that arise when companies become bureaucratic and hard to change.

Vertical Integration   Vertical integration is a more expensive strategy to manage than unrelated diversification because *sequential resource flows* from one division to the next must be coordinated. Once again, the multidivisional structure economizes on the bureaucratic costs associated with achieving such coordination because it provides the centralized control necessary for a vertically integrated company to benefit from resource transfers. Corporate managers are responsible for devising financial output and behavior controls that solve the problems of transferring resources from one division to the next; for example, they solve transfer pricing problems. Also, rules and procedures are created that specify how resource exchanges are made to solve potential handoff problems; complex resource exchanges may lead to conflict among divisions; and corporate managers must try to prevent this.

The way to distribute authority between corporate and divisional managers must be considered carefully in vertically integrated companies. The involvement of corporate managers in operating issues at the divisional level runs the risk that divisional managers feel they have no autonomy, so their performance suffers. These companies must strike the right balance of centralized control at corporate headquarters and decentralized control at the divisional level if they are to implement this strategy successfully.

Because the interests of their divisions are at stake, divisional managers need to be involved in decisions concerning scheduling and resource transfers. For example, the plastics division in a chemical company has a vital interest in the activities of the oil division because the quality of the products it gets from the oil division determines the quality of its own products. Integrating mechanisms must be created between divisions that encourage their managers to freely exchange or transfer information and skills.[13] To facilitate communication among divisions, corporate managers create teams composed of both corporate and divisional managers, **integrating roles** whereby an experienced corporate manager assumes the responsibility for managing complex transfers between two or more divisions. The use of integrating roles to coordinate divisions is common in high-tech and chemical companies, for example.

Thus, a strategy of vertical integration is managed through a combination of corporate and divisional controls. As a result, the organizational structure and control systems used to economize on the bureaucratic costs of managing this strategy are more complex and difficult to implement than those used for unrelated diversification. However, as long as the benefits that derive from vertical integration are realized, the extra expense in implementing this strategy can be justified.

Related Diversification   In the case of related diversification, the gains from pursuing this multibusiness model derive from the transfer, sharing, and leveraging of R&D knowledge, industry information, customer bases, and so on, across divisions. Also, with this structure, the high level of divisional resource sharing and the exchange of functional competencies makes it difficult for corporate managers to evaluate the performance of each individual division.[14] Thus, bureaucratic costs are substantial. The multidivisional structure helps to economize on these costs because it provides some of the extra coordination and control that is required. However, if a related company is to obtain the potential benefits from using its competencies efficiently and effectively, it has to adopt more complicated forms of integration and control at the divisional level to make the structure work.

First, output control is difficult to use because divisions share resources, so it is not easy to measure the performance of an individual division. Therefore, a company needs to develop a corporate culture that stresses cooperation among divisions and corporate rather than purely divisional goals. Second, corporate managers must establish sophisticated integrating devices to ensure coordination among divisions. Integrating roles and even integrating teams of corporate and divisional managers are essential because they provide the forum in which managers can meet, exchange information, and develop a common vision of corporate goals. An organization with a multidivisional structure must have the right mix of incentives and rewards for cooperation if it is to achieve gains from sharing skills and resources among divisions.[15] With unrelated diversification, divisions operate autonomously, and the company can quite easily reward managers on their division's individual performance. With related diversification, however, rewarding divisions is more difficult because they are engaged in so many shared activities, and corporate managers must be alert to the need to achieve equity in the rewards the different divisions receive. The goal is always to design a company's structure and control systems to maximize the benefits from pursuing a particular strategy while economizing on the bureaucratic costs of implementing it.

The Role of Information Technology

The expanding use of IT is increasing the advantages and reducing the problems associated with implementing a multibusiness model effectively because it facilitates output control, behavior control, and integration between divisions and among divisions and corporate headquarters.

On the advantage side, IT provides a common software platform that can make it much less problematic for divisions to share information and knowledge and obtain the benefits from leveraging their competencies. IT facilitates output and financial control, making it easier for corporate headquarters to monitor divisional performance and decide when to intervene selectively. It also helps corporate managers better use their strategic and implementation skills because they can react more quickly given that they possess higher-quality, more timely information from the use of a sophisticated, cross-organizational IT infrastructure.

In a similar fashion, IT makes it easier to manage the problems that occur when implementing a multidivisional structure. Because it provides both corporate and divisional managers with more and better information, it makes it easier for corporate managers to decentralize control to divisional managers and yet react quickly, if the need arises. IT can also make it more difficult to distort information and hide bad news because divisional managers must provide standardized information that can be compared across divisions. Finally, IT eases the transfer pricing problem because divisional managers have access to detailed, up-to-date information about how much certain resources or skills would cost to buy in the external marketplace. Thus, a fair transfer price is easier to determine. The way in which SAP's enterprise resource planning (ERP) software helps to integrate the activities of divisions in a multidivisional structure is discussed in Strategy in Action 13.1.

13.1 STRATEGY IN ACTION

SAP's ERP System

SAP is the world's leading supplier of enterprise resources planning (ERP) software; it introduced the world's first ERP system in 1973. So great was the demand for its software that it had to train thousands of IT consultants from companies such as IBM, HP, Accenture, and Cap Gemini to install and customize it to meet the needs of companies around the globe. SAP's ERP system is popular because it manages functional activities at all stages of a company's value chain, as well as resource transfers among a company's different divisions.

First, SAP's software has modules specifically designed to manage each core functional activity. Each module contains the set of best practices that SAP's IT engineers have found works in building competencies in efficiency, quality, innovation, and responsiveness to customers. Each function inputs its data into its functional module in the way specified by SAP. For example, sales inputs all the information about customer needs required by SAP's sales module, and materials management inputs information about the product specifications it requires from suppliers into SAP's materials-management module. Each SAP module functions as an *expert system* that can reason through the information that functional managers put into it. It then provides managers with real-time feedback about the current state of vital functional operations and gives recommendations that allow managers to improve them. However, the magic of ERP does not stop there. SAP's ERP software connects across functions inside each division. This means that managers in all functions of a division have access to other functions' expert systems; SAP's software is designed to alert managers when their functional operations are affected by changes taking place in another function. *Thus, SAP's ERP software allows managers throughout a division to better coordinate their activities*, which is a major source of competitive advantage.

Moreover, SAP software, running on corporate mainframe computers, takes the information from all the different expert systems in the divisions and creates a company-wide ERP system that provides corporate managers with an overview of the operations of all a company's divisions. In essence, SAP's ERP system creates a sophisticated corporate-level expert system that can reason through the huge volume of information being provided by all its divisions and functions. The ERP system can then recognize and diagnose common issues and problems and recommend organization-wide solutions, such as suggesting new ways to leverage, transfer, and share competencies and resources. Top managers, armed with the knowledge that their ERP software provides, can also use it to adjust their business model with the changing environment. The result, SAP claims, is that when a multidivisional company implements its corporate-wide ERP software, it can achieve productivity gains of 30% to 50%, which amounts to billions of dollars of savings for large multinational companies like Nestlé and Exxon.

Source: http://www.sap.com, 2008 and 2009.

IMPLEMENTING STRATEGY ACROSS COUNTRIES

Global strategy can play a crucial role in strengthening the business model of both single-business and multibusiness companies. Indeed, few large companies that have expanded into new industries have not already expanded globally and replicated their business model in new countries to grow their profits. Companies can use four basic strategies as they begin to market their products and establish production facilities abroad:

1. A *localization strategy* is oriented toward local responsiveness, and a company decentralizes control to subsidiaries and divisions in each country in which it operates to produce and customize products to local markets.
2. An *international strategy* is based on R&D and marketing being centralized at home and all the other value creation functions being decentralized to national units.
3. A *global standardization strategy* is oriented toward cost reduction, with all the principal value creation functions centralized at the optimal global location.
4. A *transnational strategy* is focused so that it can achieve local responsiveness and cost reduction. Some functions are centralized; others are decentralized at the global location best suited to achieving these objectives.

The need to coordinate and integrate global value chain activities increases as a company moves from a localization to an international, to a global standardization, and then to a transnational strategy. To obtain the benefits of pursuing a transnational strategy, a company must transfer its distinctive competencies to the global location where it can create the most value and establish a global network to coordinate its divisions at home and abroad. The objective of such coordination is to obtain the benefits from transferring or leveraging competencies across a company's global business units. Thus, the bureaucratic costs associated with solving the communication and measurement problems that arise in managing handoffs or transfers across countries are much higher for companies pursuing a transnational strategy than it is for those pursuing the other strategies. The localization strategy does not require coordinating activities on a global level because value creation activities are handled locally, by country or world region. The international and global standardization strategies fit between the other two strategies although products have to be sold and marketed globally; hence, global product transfers must be managed, and there is less need to coordinate skill and resource transfers when using an international strategy than when using a transnational strategy.

The implication is that, as companies change from localization to international, global standardization, or transnational strategies, they require more complex structures, control systems, and cultures to coordinate the value creation activities associated with implementing those strategies. More complex structures economize on bureaucratic costs. In general, the choice of structure and control systems for managing a global business is a function of three factors:

1. The decision about how to distribute and allocate responsibility and authority between managers at home and abroad so that effective control over a company's global operations is maintained
2. The selection of the organizational structure that groups divisions both at home and abroad in a way that allows the best use of resources and serves the needs of foreign customers most effectively
3. The selection of the right kinds of integration and control mechanisms and organizational culture to make the overall global structure function effectively

Table 13.2 Global Strategy/Structure Relationships

	Localization Strategy	International Strategy	Global Standardization Strategy	Transnational Strategy
		Need for Coordination		
	Low	**Bureaucratic Costs**		**High**
Centralization of Authority	Decentralized to national unit	Core competencies centralized; others decentralized to national units	Centralized at optimal global location	Simultaneously centralized and decentralized
Horizontal Differentiation	Global-area structure	Global-division structure	Global product-group structure	Global-matrix structure, matrix-in-the-mind
Need for Complex Integrating Mechanisms	Low	Medium	High	Very high
Organizational Culture	Not important	Quite important	Important	Very important

Table 13.2 summarizes the appropriate design choices for companies pursuing each of these strategies.

Implementing a Localization Strategy

When a company pursues a localization strategy, it generally operates with a global-area structure (see Figure 13.2). When using this structure, a company duplicates all value creation activities and establishes overseas divisions in every country or world area in which it operates. Authority is decentralized to managers in each overseas division, and these managers devise the appropriate strategy for responding to the needs of the local environment. Managers at global headquarters use market and output controls such as ROIC, growth in market share, and operating costs to evaluate the performance of overseas divisions. On the basis of such global comparisons, they can make decisions about capital allocation and orchestrate the transfer of new knowledge among divisions.

A company that makes and sells the same products in many different countries often groups its overseas divisions into world regions to simplify the coordination of products across countries. Europe might be one region, the Pacific Rim another, and the Middle East a third. Grouping allows the same set of output and behavior controls to be applied across all divisions inside a region. Thus, global companies can reduce communications and transfer problems because information can be transmitted more easily across countries with broadly similar cultures. For example, consumers' preferences regarding product design and marketing are likely to be more similar among countries in one world region than among countries in different world regions.

Figure 13.2   Global-Area Structure

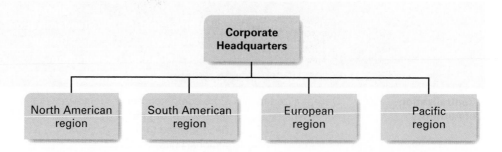

Because the overseas divisions themselves have little or no contact with others in different regions, no integrating mechanisms are needed. Nor does a global organizational culture develop because there are no transfers of skills or resources or transfer of managerial personnel among the various world regions. Historically, car companies such as GM and Ford used global-area structures to manage their overseas operations. Ford of Europe, for example, had little or no contact with its United States parent; capital was the principal resource exchanged.

One problem with a global-area structure and a localization strategy is that the duplication of specialist activities across countries raises a company's overall cost structure. Moreover, the company is not taking advantage of opportunities to transfer, share, or leverage its competencies and capabilities on a global basis; for example, it cannot apply the low-cost manufacturing expertise that it has developed in one world region to another. Thus, localization companies lose the many benefits of operating globally. As Chapter 8 discussed, the popularity of this strategic orientation has decreased.

Implementing an International Strategy

A company pursuing an international strategy adopts a different route to global expansion. Normally, a company shifts to this strategy when it decides to sell domestically made products in markets abroad. Until the 1990s, for example, companies such as Mercedes-Benz and Jaguar made no attempt to produce in foreign markets; instead, they distributed and sold their domestically produced cars internationally. Such companies usually just add a *foreign sales organization* to their existing structure and continue to use the same control system. If a company is using a functional structure, this department has to coordinate manufacturing, sales, and R&D activities with the needs of the foreign market. Efforts at customization are minimal. In overseas countries, a company usually establishes a subsidiary to handle local sales and distribution. For example, the Mercedes-Benz overseas subsidiaries allocate dealerships; organize supplies of spare parts; and, of course, sell cars. A system of behavior controls is then established to keep the home office informed of changes in sales, spare parts requirements, and so on.

A company with many different products or businesses operating from a multidivisional structure has the challenging problem of coordinating the flow of different products across different countries. To manage these transfers, many companies create *global divisions*, which they add to their existing divisional structures (see Figure 13.3).[16] Global operations are managed as a separate divisional business,

Figure 13.3 Global Division Structure

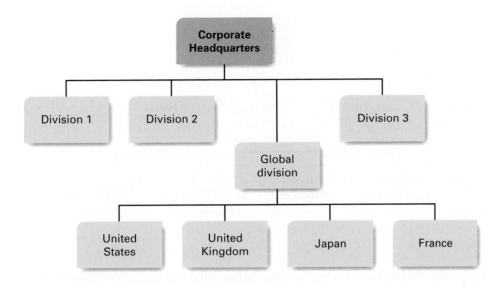

with managers given the authority and responsibility for coordinating domestic product divisions with overseas markets. The global division also monitors and controls the overseas subsidiaries that market the products and decides how much authority to delegate to managers in these countries.

This arrangement of tasks and roles reduces the transaction of managing hand-offs across countries and world regions. However, managers abroad are essentially under the control of managers in the global division, and if domestic and overseas managers compete for control of strategy making, conflict and lack of cooperation may result. Companies such as IBM, Citibank, and DaimlerChrysler have experienced this problem. Very often, significant strategic control has been decentralized to overseas divisions. When cost pressures force corporate managers to reassess their strategy and they decide to intervene, such intervention frequently provokes resistance, much of it due to differences in culture—not just corporate but also country differences.

Implementing a Global Standardization Strategy

When a company embarks on a global standardization strategy today, it locates its manufacturing and other value chain activities at the global location that will allow it to increase efficiency, quality, and innovation. In doing so, it has to solve the problems of coordinating and integrating its global value chain activities. It has to find a structure that lowers the bureaucratic costs associated with resource transfers between corporate headquarters and its overseas divisions and provides the centralized control that a global standardization strategy requires. The answer for many companies is a *global product-group structure* (see Figure 13.4).

In this structure, a product-group headquarters is created to coordinate the activities of a company's home and overseas operations. The managers at each product group's headquarters decide where to locate the different functions at the

Figure 13.4   Global Product-Group Structure

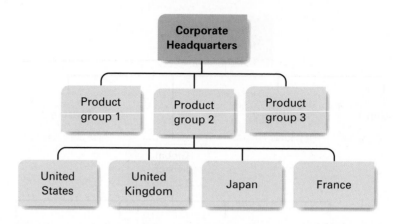

optimal global location for performing that activity. For example, Phillips has one product group responsible for global R&D, manufacturing, marketing, and sales of its light bulbs; another for medical equipment; and so on. The headquarters of the medical division and its R&D is located in Bothell, Washington; manufacturing is done in Taiwan; and the products are sold by sales subsidiaries in each local market.

The product-group structure allows managers to decide how best to pursue a global standardization strategy, for example, to decide which value chain activities, such as manufacturing or product design, should be performed in which country to increase efficiency. Increasingly, American and Japanese companies are moving manufacturing to low-cost countries such as China but establishing product design centers in Europe or the United States to take advantage of foreign skills and capabilities and thus obtain the benefits from this strategy. The Running Case describes how Walmart has used its sophisticated global supply chain to allow it to establish product groups to pursue a global standardization strategy.

Implementing a Transnational Strategy

The main failing of the global product-group structure is that, although it allows a company to achieve superior efficiency and quality, it is weak when it comes to responsiveness to customers because the focus is still on centralized control to reduce costs. Moreover, this structure makes it difficult for the different product divisions to trade information and knowledge and obtain the benefits from transferring, sharing, and leveraging their competencies. Sometimes the potential gains from sharing product, marketing, or R&D knowledge among product groups are high, but so too are the bureaucratic costs associated with achieving these gains. Is there a structure that can simultaneously economize on these costs and provide the coordination necessary to obtain these benefits?

In the 1990s, many companies implemented a *global-matrix structure* to simultaneously lower their global cost structures *and* differentiate their activities through superior innovation and responsiveness to customers globally.

RUNNING CASE

How Walmart Implements Global Expansion

Retailing giant Walmart has been aggressively expanding globally in recent years to boost its profitability. After moving into Mexico and Europe and establishing two global product groups in these regions, its managers turned their focus to Japan, where the supermarket business is extremely lucrative. They envisaged creating a highly profitable Japanese global product group that would benefit from the fact that, although Japanese customers pay some of the highest prices for food in the world, its supermarket chains are highly inefficient. Why?

Unlike efficient Japanese carmakers, which employ state-of-the-art IT materials-management systems to collect the detailed information needed to increase the quality and efficiency of their operations, Japan's retailers had lagged behind in adopting these systems. A major reason was that until the 1990s, Japan's Large Scale Retail Store Law allowed small Japanese retailers to block large supermarket chains from opening large, efficient new stores in their neighborhoods for 10 years or more. Although the Japanese government weakened the law so that local storeowners could delay a store opening for only 18 months, there was no history of low-cost competition in the Japanese retail market.

A second factor that led to low supermarket efficiency related to the way products such as groceries were distributed and sold in Japan. Traditionally, Japanese manufacturers sold their products only to wholesalers, with which they had developed long-term business relationships, not directly to retailers. Wholesalers add their own price markup and control distribution, making it much more difficult for supermarkets to compete on price and lowered competition. As a result, there were few incentives for Japanese retailers to invest in expensive materials-management systems to increase their efficiency.

In contrast, Walmart's focus on developing a sophisticated global supply chain to lower the costs of its purchasing, shipping, and sales activities has made it the most efficient global discount retailer and grocer. In addition, Walmart's supply chain management eliminates the need for wholesalers because the company is such a huge, powerful buyer. So, Walmart managers thought that entering the Japanese supermarket industry might be very profitable indeed. They bought a significant stake in Seiyu Ltd., Japan's fourth-largest supermarket, to gain a foothold in the Japanese market. An opportunity to expand and strengthen its base arose when Japan's third-largest supermarket chain, Daiei, which had been losing money for years, was put up for sale.

Walmart's Japanese strategy was to acquire Daiei and then combine it with its Seiyu operations to create a strong Japanese global product group. Its product group managers believed that if Walmart could leverage its IT-based global supply chain across an expanded chain of Japanese supermarkets, it would significantly increase Seiyu's and Daiei's efficiency and make the product group highly profitable. Also, as in the United States, they hoped that over time, the Japanese group's growing competitive advantage would either force other Japanese supermarket chains either to go out of business or sell out to Walmart so that it would eventually dominate the Japanese supermarket industry. To accomplish this, product group managers put into motion major plans to identify lower-priced groceries from abroad that would be attractive to Japanese customers and then use its IT system to purchase these groceries efficiently from producers around the world.

To Walmart's annoyance, Japan's Industrial Revitalization Corp., which had the power to decide which company could buy Daiei, decided it did not want Walmart to establish a powerful product group and become one of the largest retailers in Japan. It rejected Walmart's bid for Daiei; however, the world's largest retailer is still watching for other opportunities to expand its presence in the lucrative Japanese market.

Figure 13.5 shows such a structure that might be used by a company such as Ford, HP, SAP, or Nestlé. On the vertical axis, instead of functions, are the company's product *groups*. These groups provide specialist services such as R&D, product design, and marketing information to its overseas divisions, which are often grouped by world region. They might be the petroleum, plastics, pharmaceuticals, or fertilizer product groups. On the horizontal axis are the company's *overseas divisions* in the various countries or world regions in which it operates. Managers at the regional or country level control local operations. Through a system of output and behavior controls, they then report to managers in product-group headquarters in the United States and ultimately to the CEO. Managers for world regions or countries are also responsible for working with U.S. product-group managers to develop the control and reward systems that will promote transfer, sharing, or leveraging of competencies.

Implementing a matrix structure thus decentralizes control to overseas managers and provides them with considerable flexibility for managing local issues, but it can still give product-group and top corporate executives in the United States the centralized control they need to coordinate company activities on a global level. The matrix structure can allow knowledge and experience to be transferred among divisions in both product groups and geographic regions because it offers many opportunities for face-to-face contact between managers at home and abroad. The matrix also facilitates the transmission of a company's norms and values and, hence, the development of a global corporate culture. This is especially important for a company with far-flung global operations for which lines of communication are longer. Club Med, for instance, uses a matrix to standardize high-quality customer service across its global vacation villages. Nestlé's experience with the global-matrix structure is profiled in Strategy in Action 13.2.

Figure 13.5   Global-Matrix Structure

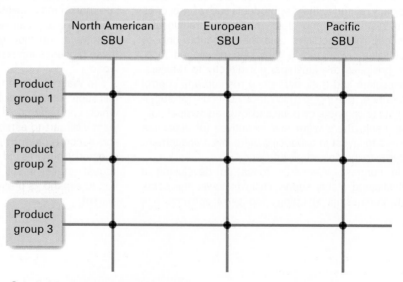

● Individual operating companies

13.2 STRATEGY IN ACTION

Nestlé's Global Matrix Structure

Nestlé, based in Vevey, Switzerland, is the world's largest food company, with global sales in excess of $70 billion in 2009. The company has been pursuing an ambitious program of global expansion by acquiring many famous companies, for example, Perrier, the French mineral water producer, and Rowntree, the British candy maker. In the United States, Nestlé bought Carnation, Stouffer Foods, Contadina, Ralston Purina, and Dreyer's Grand Ice Cream.

In the past, Nestlé pursued a localization strategy and managed its operating companies through a global-area structure. In each country, its individual divisions (such as its Carnation division) were responsible for managing business-level strategy. For example, they had the authority to make all product development, marketing, and manufacturing decisions. Nestlé's corporate managers at its Vevey headquarters made the vital acquisition, expansion, and corporate resource decisions, such as how best to invest its capital, and the size of the corporate staff had increased dramatically to manage its rapid global expansion.

In the 1990s, Nestlé realized it had major problems. Corporate managers had become remote from the divisional managers in its thousands of operating divisions. They did not understand the problems divisions faced, and because authority was centralized, Nestlé was often slow to respond to the fast-changing food products industry. Moreover, the way the company operated made it impossible to obtain the potential benefits from sharing and leveraging its distinctive competencies in food product development and marketing, both among divisions in a product group and among product groups and world regions. Because each product group operated separately, corporate executives could not integrate product-group activities around the world. To raise corporate performance, Nestlé's managers had to find a new way to organize its activities.

Its CEO at the time, Helmut Maucher, started restructuring Nestlé from the top down. He stripped away the power of corporate managers by decentralizing authority to the managers of seven global product groups that he created to oversee the company's major product lines (for example, coffee, milk, and candy). Each global product group was to integrate the activities of all the operating divisions in its group to transfer and leverage distinctive competencies to increase profitability. After the change, managers in the candy product group, for instance, began orchestrating the marketing and sale of Rowntree candy products, such as After Eight Mints and Smarties throughout Europe and the United States, and sales climbed by 60%.

Maucher then grouped all divisions within a country or world region into one national or regional strategic business unit (SBU) and created a team of SBU managers to link, coordinate, and oversee their activities. When the different divisions started to share joint purchasing, marketing, and sales activities, major cost savings resulted. In the United States, the SBU management team reduced the number of sales offices nationwide from 115 to 22 and the number of suppliers of packaging materials from 43 to 3.

Finally, Maucher decided to use a matrix structure to integrate the activities of the seven global-product groups with the operations of Nestlé's country-based SBUs. The goal of this matrix structure is to allow the company to pursue a transnational strategy and obtain the benefits of differentiation from global learning and from cost reductions from higher cooperation among divisions inside each product group. For example, regional SBU managers spend considerable time in Vevey with product-group executives discussing ways to take advantage of transferring and sharing the resources of the company on a global basis and inside each product group.

To further increase integration, Nestlé signed a $300 million contract with SAP to install and maintain a company-wide ERP system to integrate across *all* its global operations. Nestlé's top managers use their ERP system to provide them with the information they need to centralize control over its far-flung operations that they found the matrix structure did not provide by itself. Using the ERP system, for example, provides them with real-time information about the way Nestlé's global divisions are performing. They no longer need to rely solely on divisional managers for this information, so they can intervene on a global level as necessary.

Source: http://www.nestle.com, 2009.

Nestlé is not the only company to find the task of integrating and controlling a global-matrix structure a difficult task. Some, such as ABB, Motorola, and Ford have dismantled their matrix structures and moved to a simplified global product-group approach using IT to integrate across countries. If a matrix is chosen, however, other possible ways of making it work effectively include developing a strong global organizational culture to facilitate communication and coordination among country-based managers. For example, many companies transfer managers between their domestic and overseas operations, so they can implant their domestic culture in their new global division.

Toyota has made great efforts to understand how to manage car plants in overseas locations and how to transplant its culture into those plants. When it decided to manufacture cars in the United States, it first formed a joint venture with GM, and the companies combined their expertise in this venture, which was known as NUMMI. Toyota was responsible for implanting its knowledge of lean production in this plant; all the workers were cross-trained and taught how to monitor and benchmark their own performance and how to work on quality teams to improve it. Toyota then took all the learning from this venture and transferred it to its wholly owned car plants in Georgetown, Kentucky, where it manufactures cars with as good a reliability record as those made in its Japanese plants. Every Toyota plant is under the control of Japanese managers, however, and managers from Toyota's Japanese headquarters monitor their performance and work to transfer and implant Toyota's latest R&D innovations into its next car models.

ENTRY MODE AND IMPLEMENTATION

As we discuss in Chapter 10, many organizations today are altering their business models and strategies and entering or leaving industries to find better ways to use their resources and capabilities to create value. This section focuses on the implementation issues that arise when companies use internal new venturing, joint ventures, and/or acquisitions to enter new industries.

Internal New Venturing

Chapter 10 discusses how companies enter new industries by using internal new venturing to transfer and leverage their existing competencies to create the set of value chain activities necessary to compete effectively in a new industry. How can managers create a setting in which employees are encouraged to think about how to apply their functional competencies in new industries? In particular, how can structure, control, and culture be used to increase the success of the new-venturing process?

At the heart of this issue is that corporate managers must treat the internal new-venturing process as a form of entrepreneurship and the managers who are to pioneer and lead new ventures as **intrapreneurs**, that is, as inside or internal entrepreneurs. This means that organizational structure, control, and culture must be designed to encourage creativity and give new-venture managers real autonomy to develop and champion new products. At the same time, corporate managers want to make sure that their investment in a new market or industry will be profitable because commonalities exist between the new industry and its core industry so that the potential benefits of transferring or leveraging competencies will be obtained.[17] Apple, 3M, and Google are examples of companies that carefully select the right mix of structure, control, and culture to create a work context that facilitates the new-venturing process and promotes product innovation. For example, 3M's goal is that at least 30% of its growth in sales each year should come from new products developed within the past five years. To meet this challenging goal, 3M designed a sophisticated control and incentive system that provides its employees with the freedom and motivation to experiment and take risks.

Another approach to internal new venturing is championed by managers who believe that the best way to encourage new-product development is to separate the new venture unit from the rest of the organization. To provide the new-venture's managers with the autonomy to experiment and take risks, a company establishes a **new-venture division**, that is, a separate and independent division to develop a new product. The reason for creating an autonomous unit is that if a new venture's managers work within a company's existing structure under the scrutiny of its corporate managers, they will not have the autonomy they need to pursue exciting new product ideas. In a separate unit in a new location, however, new venture managers will be able to act as if they were external entrepreneurs as they work to create a new product and develop a business model to bring it to market successfully.

The new-venture unit or division uses controls that reinforce its entrepreneurial spirit. Strict output controls are inappropriate because they may promote short-term thinking and inhibit risk taking. Instead, stock options are often used to create a culture for entrepreneurship. Another issue is how to deal with corporate managers. The upfront R&D costs of new venturing are high, and its success is uncertain. After spending millions of dollars, corporate managers often become concerned about how successful the new-venture division will be. As a result, they might attempt to introduce strict output controls, including restrictive budgets to make the managers of the new venture more accountable—but which at the same time harm its entrepreneurial culture.[18] Corporate managers may believe it is important to use output and behavior controls to limit the new venture manager's autonomy; otherwise, they might make costly mistakes and waste resources on frivolous ideas.

Recently, there have been some indications that 3M's internal approach may be superior to the use of external new-venture divisions. It appears that many new-venture divisions have failed to get successful new products to market. And even if they do, the new-venture division eventually begins to operate like any other divisions and the whole company's cost structure rises because of the duplication of value chain activities. Another issue is that scientists are often not the best people to develop successful business models because they lack formal training. Just as many medical doctors are earning MBAs today to understand the many strategic issues they must confront when they decide to become the managers of hospitals, so scientists need to be able to think strategically. If this skill is lacking in a new-venture division, the result is failure.

Joint Ventures

Joint ventures are a second method used by large, established companies to maintain their momentum and grow their profits by entering new markets and industries.[19] A joint venture occurs when two companies agree to pool some combination of their resources and capabilities and establish a new business unit to develop a new product and a business model that will allow it bring the new product to market successfully. These companies believe that through collaboration, by sharing their technology or marketing skills to develop an improved product for example, they will be able to create more value and profit in the new industry than if they decide to "go it alone." Both companies transfer competent managers, who have a proven track record of success, to manage the new subunit that they both own. Sometimes they take an equal "50/50" ownership stake, but sometimes one company insists on having a 51% share or more, giving it the ability to buy out the other party at some point in the future should problems emerge. The way a joint venture is organized and controlled becomes an important issue in this context.

Allocating authority and responsibility is the first major implementation issue on which companies have to decide. Both companies need to be able to monitor the progress of the joint venture so that they can learn from its activities and benefit from their investment in it. Some companies insist on 51% ownership stakes because only then do they have the authority and control over the new ventures. Future problems could arise such as what to do if the new venture performs poorly or how to proceed if conflict develops between the parent companies over time—because one partner feels "cheated." For example, what will happen in the future is unknown, and frequently one parent company benefits much more from the product innovations the new company develops; if the other company demands "compensation," they come into conflict.[20] Also, as discussed in Chapter 8, a company also risks losing control of its core technology or competence when it enters into a strategic alliance. One parent company might come to believe this is taking place and so feels threatened by the other. A joint venture can also be dangerous not only because one parent might decide to take the new technology and then "go it alone" in the development process but also because its partner might be acquired by a competitor. For example, Compaq shared its proprietary server technology with a company in the computer storage industry to promote joint product development. Then, it watched helplessly as that company was acquired by Sun Microsystems, which consequently obtained Compaq's technology.

The implementation issues are strongly dependent on whether the purpose of the joint venture is to share and develop technology, jointly distribute and market products and brands, or share access to customers. Sometimes companies can simply realize the joint benefits from collaboration without having to form a new company. For example, Nestlé and Coca-Cola announced a 10-year joint venture, to be called Beverage Partners Worldwide, through which Coca-Cola will distribute and sell Nestlé's Nestea iced tea, Nescafé, and other brands throughout the globe.[21] Similarly, Starbuck's Frappuccino is distributed by Pepsi. In this kind of joint venture, both companies can gain from sharing and pooling different competencies so that both realize value that would not otherwise be possible. In these cases, issues of ownership and control are less important.

Once the ownership issue has been settled, one company appoints the CEO who becomes responsible for creating a cohesive top management team out of the managers transferred from the parent companies. The job of the top management team is to develop a successful business model. These managers then need to choose an organizational structure, such as the functional or product team, that will make the best use of the resources and skills they receive from the parent companies. The need to create an effective organizational design that integrates people and functions is of paramount importance to ensure that the best use is made of limited resources. So is the need to build a new culture for their new company that unites managers who used to work in companies with different cultures.

Managing these implementation issues is difficult, expensive, and time-consuming, so it is not surprising that when a lot is at stake and the future uncertain, many companies decide they would be better off acquiring another company and integrating it into their operations. This is Microsoft's favored strategy when it decides to enter new industries in the computer sector. Usually, it takes a 51% stake in an emerging company, which gives it the right to buy out the company and integrate its technology into its existing software divisions should it prove to have some competency vital to Microsoft's future interests. First, however, Microsoft shares its resources and expertise with the new company to spur the development of its R&D competence. If the risks are lower, however, and it is easier to forecast the future, as in the venture between Coca-Cola and Nestlé, then to reduce bureaucratic costs, a strategic alliance, which does not require the creation of a new subunit, may be quite capable of managing the transfers of complementary resources and skills between companies.

Mergers and Acquisitions

Mergers and acquisitions are the third method companies use to enter new industries or countries.[22] How to implement structure, control systems, and culture to manage a new acquisition is important because many acquisitions are unsuccessful. And, one of the main reasons acquisitions perform poorly is that many companies do not anticipate the difficulties associated with merging or integrating new companies into their existing operations.[23]

At the level of organizational structure, managers of both the acquiring and acquired companies have to confront the problem of how to establish new lines of authority and responsibility that will allow them to make the best use of both companies' competencies. The massive merger between HP and Compaq illustrates the issues. Before the merger, the top management teams of both companies spent thousands of hours analyzing the range of both companies' activities and performing a value chain analysis to determine how cost and differentiation advantages might be achieved. Based on this analysis, they merged all of both company's divisions into four main product groups.

Imagine the problems deciding who would control which group and which operating division and to whom these managers would report. To counter fears that infighting would prevent the benefits of the merger from being realized, the companies' CEOs were careful to announce in press releases that the process of merging divisions was going smoothly and that battles over responsibilities and control of resources were being resolved. One problem with a mishandled merger is that skilled managers who feel they have been demoted will leave the company, and if many leave, the loss of their skills may prevent the benefits of the merger from being realized. In 2009, after Cisco acquired the maker of the popular Flip camcorder, it announced that it was establishing a $15 million fund to reward Flip executives who decide to stay with the company.

Once managers have established clear lines of authority, they must decide how to coordinate and streamline the operations of both merged companies to reduce costs and leverage and share competencies. For large companies like HP, the answer is to choose the multidivisional structure, but important control issues still have to be resolved. In general, the more similar or related are the acquired companies' products and markets, the easier it is to integrate their operations. If the acquiring company has an efficient control system, it can be adapted to the new company to standardize the way its activities are monitored and measured. Or managers can work hard to combine the best elements of each company's control systems and cultures or introduce a new IT system to integrate their operations.

If managers make unrelated acquisitions, however, and then try to interfere with a company's strategy in an industry they know little about or apply inappropriate structure and controls to manage the new business, then major strategy implementation problems can arise. For example, if managers try to integrate unrelated companies with related ones in the search for some elusive benefits, apply the wrong kinds of controls at the divisional level, or interfere in business-level strategy, corporate performance can suffer as bureaucratic costs skyrocket. These mistakes explain why related acquisitions are sometimes more successful than unrelated ones.[24]

Even in the case of related diversification, the business processes of each company frequently are different, and their computer systems may be incompatible. The issue facing the merged company is how to use output and behavior controls to standardize business processes and reduce the cost of handing off and transferring resources. After Nestlé installed SAP's ERP software, for example, managers discovered that each of Nestlé's 150 different United States divisions was buying its own supply of vanilla from the same set of suppliers. However, the divisions were not sharing information about these purchases, and vanilla suppliers, dealing with each Nestlé division separately, tried to charge each division as much as they could, with the result that each division paid a different price for the same input![25] Each division at Nestlé used a different code for its independent purchase, and managers at United States headquarters did not have the information to discover this until SAP's software provided it.

Finally, even when acquiring a company in a closely related industry, managers must realize that each company has a unique culture, norms, values, and a way of doing things. Such idiosyncrasies must be understood to integrate the operations of the merged company effectively. Indeed, such idiosyncrasies are likely to be especially important when companies from different countries merge. Over time, top managers can change the culture and alter the internal workings of the company, but this is a difficult implementation task.

In sum, corporate managers' capabilities in organizational design are vital in ensuring the success of a merger or acquisition. Their ability to integrate and connect divisions to leverage competencies ultimately determines how well the new merged company will perform.[26] The path to merger and acquisition is fraught with danger, which is why some companies claim that internal new venturing is the safest path and that it is best to grow organically from within. Yet with industry boundaries blurring and new global competitors emerging, companies often do not have the time or resources to go it alone. How to enter a new industry or country is a complex implementation issue that requires thorough strategic analysis.

INFORMATION TECHNOLOGY, THE INTERNET, AND OUTSOURCING

The many ways in which advances in IT affect strategy implementation is an important issue today. Evidence that managerial capabilities in managing IT can be a source of competitive advantage is growing; companies that do not adopt leading-edge information systems are likely to be at a competitive disadvantage. IT includes the many different varieties of computer software platforms and databases and the computer hardware on which they run, such as mainframes and servers. IT also encompasses a broad array of communication media and devices that link people, including voice mail, e-mail, voice conferencing, videoconferencing, the Internet, groupware and corporate intranets, cell phones, fax machines, personal digital assistants (PDAs), smartphones, and so on.[27]

Information Technology and Strategy Implementation

At the level of organizational structure, control, and culture, advanced IT drastically increases the number of ways in which strategic managers can implement their strategies effectively. First, IT is an important factor that promotes the development of functional competencies and capabilities. Indeed, a company's IT capabilities are often a major source of competitive advantage because they are embedded in a company and are difficult to imitate. Walmart, for example, takes steps to legally protect its core competency in IT by blocking the movement of some of its key programmers to dot-coms like Amazon or Target. A company's ability to pursue a cost-leadership or differentiation business model depends on its possession of distinctive competencies in efficiency, quality, innovation, and customer responsiveness—and IT is a major facilitator of these sources of competitive advantage.[28]

Second, IT enables a company to transfer its knowledge and expertise across functional groups and integrate that knowledge into a function's operations, so it can deliver new and improved products to customers. The way in which Citibank implemented an organization-wide IT system to increase responsiveness to customers is instructive. After studying its business model, Citibank's managers found that the main customer complaint was the amount of time they had to wait for a response to some banking question, so they set out to solve this problem. Teams of managers examined the way Citibank's current IT system worked and then redesigned it to reduce the handoffs between people and functions necessary to provide customers with answers more quickly. Employees were then given extensive training in operating the new IT system. These changes resulted in significant time and cost savings, as well as an increase in the level of personalized service it is able to offer its clients, and these have changes have increased customer satisfaction and the number of customers.[29]

IT also has important effects on a company's ability to innovate and perform R&D. It improves the knowledge base that employees draw on when they engage in problem solving and decision making. IT also provides a mechanism to promote collaboration and information sharing both inside and across a company's functions and business units that speeds up product development. However, the availability of knowledge alone is not enough to promote innovation; organizational members' ability to use knowledge creatively is the key to promoting innovation and creating competitive advantage.[30] IT allows new ideas to be transmitted easily and quickly to the product team, function, or divisions that can use it to add value to products and boost profitability. The project-based work that is characteristic of matrix structures provides a vivid example of this process.

As a project progresses, the need for particular team members waxes and wanes. Some employees will be part of a project from beginning to end, but others only participate at key times when their expertise is required. IT provides managers with the real-time capability to monitor project progress and needs, to allocate each expert's time accordingly, and so increase the value each employee can add to a product.

Traditionally, product design has involved sequential processing across functions, with handoffs as each stage of the process is completed (see Chapter 4). Using advanced IT, this linear process has been replaced by parallel engineering that allows employees in different functions to work simultaneously and interact in real time to share information about design improvements, opportunities to reduce costs, and so on. This also promotes innovation.

IT has major effects on other aspects of a company's structure and control systems. The increasing use of IT has allowed managers to flatten the organizational hierarchy and reduce the number management levels to coordinate the work process. Because it provides managers with so much more useful, quality, and timely information, IT also permits greater decentralization of authority while simultaneously increasing integration within organizations. E-mail systems, the development of organization-wide corporate intranets, and, of course, ERP systems, have broken down the communication between functions and divisions. The result has been improved performance.[31] To facilitate the use of IT and make organizational structure work, however, a company must create a control and incentive structure to motivate people and subunits, as Strategy in Action 13.3 suggests.

Some companies are taking full advantage of IT's ability to help them integrate their activities to respond better to customer needs. These companies make the most cost-effective use of their employees' skills by using a virtual organizational structure. The **virtual organization** is composed of people who are linked by laptops, smartphones, computer-aided design (CAD) systems, and global video teleconferencing and who may rarely, if ever, see one another face-to-face. People join and leave a project team as their services are needed, much as in a matrix structure.

Accenture, the global management consulting company, is such a virtual organization. Its consultants connect through their laptops to its centralized **knowledge management system**, a company-specific information system that systematizes the knowledge of its employees and provides them with access to other employees who have the expertise to solve the problems that they encounter as they perform their jobs. The consultants pool their knowledge in a massive internal database that they can easily access externally through the Internet. The company's 40,000 consultants often work from their homes, traveling to meet the company's clients throughout the world and only rarely stopping at Accenture's branch offices to meet their superiors and colleagues. CEO George Shaheen says that the company's headquarters are wherever he happens to be at the time. (He spends 80% of his time traveling.)[32]

Strategic Outsourcing and Network Structure

IT has also affected a company's ability to pursue strategic outsourcing to strengthen its business model. As Chapter 9 discusses, strategic outsourcing is increasing rapidly because companies recognize the many opportunities it offers to promote differentiation, reduce costs, and increase flexibility. Recall that outsourcing occurs as companies use short- and long-term contracts and strategic alliances to form relationships with other companies. IT increases the efficiency of these relationships. For example, it allows for the more efficient movement of raw materials and component parts between a company and its suppliers and distributors. It also promotes the transfer, sharing, and leveraging of competencies between companies that have formed a strategic alliance that can lead to design and engineering improvements that increase differentiation and lower costs.

13.3 STRATEGY IN ACTION

Oracle's New Approach to Control

Oracle is the second-largest software provider after Microsoft. In the early 2000s, its cofounder and CEO Larry Ellison recognized that his company had developed a major problem. Its performance was slipping because it had not implemented the Internet-based software it had developed to allow companies to better control and make use of functional resources even though its customers were using its software to increase the performance of their functions. Ellison moved quickly to change Oracle's functional control systems so that they were Internet-based.

One of the main advantages of Internet-based control software is that it gives corporate managers the ability to monitor and evaluate a company's complex and widespread global operations. Corporate managers can easily compare the performance of different divisions spread around the world in real time and quickly identify problems and take corrective action. However, Ellison discovered that Oracle's financial and human resource information control systems were located in more than 70 independent data centers operating around the world. Consequently, it took days or weeks to track basic details, such as the size of the company's global workforce and changes in the global sales of its leading products, so that corrective action often came too late and many opportunities were being lost.

Recognizing the irony of the situation, Ellison ordered his managers to implement its Internet-based control systems as quickly as possible. His goal was to have all of Oracle's global sales, cost, profit, and human resource information and control systems consolidated in two locations and to make their services available to all its managers with one click of a mouse. In addition, he instructed managers to study which kinds of functional activities were still being handled by "real" people and wherever possible to develop Internet-based software that could substitute or improve on their efforts. For example, Oracle had 300 people responsible for monitoring and managing its paper-based travel planning and expense-reporting systems. These tasks were automated into a software system and put online. Each employee is now responsible for filing his or her own reports that are processed by the software to ensure compliance with company procedures. The 300 people were then transferred into sales and consulting positions, and more than $1 billion in cost savings a year resulted.

The use of Internet-based software control systems also allowed Oracle's functional managers to get closer to their customers and understand their changing needs, so they could sell them more of its products. Oracle's salespeople were taught how to use its new customer relationship management software, which requires they enter detailed information about customers' purchases, future plans, Web orders, and service requests into the system. As a result, corporate managers could track sales orders easily. If the system revealed problems such as lost sales or multiple service requests, they could move quickly to contact customers and find new ways to solve those problems.

So amazed was Ellison at the results of implementing Internet software systems that he radically rethought Oracle's control systems. Because of the advances in modern IT, especially ERP systems, he decided that Oracle's employees should perform only one of three tasks: building its products, servicing its products, or selling its products. All other activities should be automated by developing new information control systems, and it should be the manager's job to use control only to facilitate one of these three front-line activities. In addition, as we discussed in Chapter 8, Oracle has moved quickly in the 2000s to become a major player in the ERP market competing directly against SAP. A focus on effective strategy implementation can lead to major changes in a company's business model and strategies that boost its profitability.

Sources: M. Moeller, "Oracle: Practicing What It Preaches," *Business Week* (August 16, 1999): 1–5; http://www.oracle.com. 2009.

As a consequence, there has been growing interest in electronic **business-to-business (B2B)** networks in which companies in adjacent industries, for example, carmakers and car component makers, use the same software platform to link to each other and negotiate over prices, quality specifications, and delivery terms. The purchasing companies list the quantity and specifications of the inputs they require and invite bids from the thousands of component suppliers around the world. Because suppliers use the same software platform, electronic bidding, auctions, and transactions are conducted more efficiently between buyers and sellers around the world. The goal is to achieve joint gains for buyers and suppliers to help drive down costs and raise quality at the industry level. Strategy in Action 13.4, which describes the role of Li & Fung in managing the global supply chain for companies in Southeast Asia, illustrates how this process works.

To implement outsourcing effectively, strategic managers must decide what organizational arrangements to adopt. Increasingly, a **network structure**—the set of virtual strategic alliances an organization forms with suppliers, manufacturers, and distributors to produce and market a product—is becoming the structure of choice to implement outsourcing. An example of a network structure is the series of strategic alliances that Japanese carmakers such as Toyota and Honda have formed with their parts suppliers. All members of the network work together on a long-term basis

13.4 STRATEGY IN ACTION

Li & Fung's Global Supply-Chain Management

Identifying the overseas suppliers that offer the lowest-priced and highest-quality products is an important but difficult task for strategic managers because the suppliers are located in thousands of cities in many countries around the world. To help them, global companies use the services of foreign intermediaries or brokers, located near these suppliers, to find the ones that best suit their purchasing needs. Li & Fung, run by brothers Victor and William Fung, is one of the brokers that have helped hundreds of global companies identify suitable foreign suppliers, especially suppliers in mainland China.

In the 2000s, managing global companies' supply chains became an even more complicated task because overseas suppliers were increasingly specializing in just one part of the task of producing a product in their search for ways to reduce costs. In the past, a company such as Target might have negotiated with a supplier to manufacture 1 million units of a shirt at a certain cost per unit. But with specialization, Target might find it can reduce the costs of making shirts even more by splitting the operations involved in producing the shirt and negotiating with different suppliers, often in different countries, to perform each separate operation. For example, to reduce the unit cost of a shirt, Target might first negotiate with a yarn manufacturer in Vietnam to make the yarn, ship the

yarn to a Chinese supplier to weave it into cloth, and ship the cloth to several different factories in Malaysia and the Philippines to cut the cloth and sew the pieces into shirts. Another company might take responsibility for packaging and shipping the shirts to wherever in the world they are required. Because a company like Target has thousands of different clothing products under production and these products change all the time, there are clearly enormous problems associated with managing a global supply chain to obtain the most potential cost savings.

This is the opportunity that Li & Fung capitalized on. Realizing that many global companies do not have the time or expertise to find such specialized low-price suppliers, they moved quickly to provide this service. Li & Fung employs 3,600 agents who travel across 37 countries to find new suppliers and inspect existing suppliers to find new ways to help their clients, global companies, get lower prices or higher-quality products. Global companies are happy to outsource their supply-chain management to Li & Fung because they realize significant cost savings. And although they pay a hefty fee to Li & Fung, they avoid the costs of employing their own agents. As the complexity of supply-chain management continues to increase, more and more companies like Li & Fung will be appearing.

Sources: "Business Link in the Global Chain," *Economist* (June 2, 2001): 62–63; http://www.li&fung.com. 2006.

to find new ways to reduce costs and increase car component quality. Moreover, developing a network structure allows an organization to avoid the high bureaucratic costs of operating a complex organizational structure. Finally, a network structure allows a company to form strategic alliances with foreign suppliers, which gives managers access to low-cost foreign sources of inputs. The way Nike uses a global network structure to produce and market its sports, casual, and dress shoes is instructive.

Nike, located in Beaverton, Oregon, is the largest and most profitable sports shoemaker in the world. The key to Nike's success is the network structure that Philip Knight, its founder and CEO, created to allow his company to design and market its shoes. Today, the most successful companies simultaneously pursue a low-cost and a differentiation strategy. Knight realized this early and created the network structure to allow his company to achieve this goal.

By far, the largest function at Nike's headquarters in Beaverton is the design function, which is staffed by talented designers who pioneer the innovations in sports shoe design that have made Nike so successful. Designers use computer-aided design (CAD) to innovate new shoe models, and all new-product information, including manufacturing instructions, is stored electronically. When the designers have done their work, they relay the blueprints for the new products via the Internet to its network of suppliers and manufacturers throughout Southeast Asia with which Nike has formed contracts and alliances. Instructions for the design of a new sole, for example, may be sent to a supplier in Taiwan, and instructions for the leather uppers may be sent to a supplier in Malaysia. These suppliers produce the shoe parts that are then sent for final assembly to a contract manufacturer in China. From China, a shipping company that has also partnered with Nike, will ship its shoes to wholesalers and distributors throughout the world. Of the 100 million pairs of shoes Nike makes each year, 99% are made in Southeast Asia.

There are three main advantages to this network structure for Nike (and other companies). First, Nike can lower its cost structure because wages in Southeast Asia are a fraction of what they are in the United States. Second, Nike can respond to changes in sports shoe fashion very quickly. Using its global IT system, it can, literally overnight, change the instructions it gives to each of its suppliers so that within a few weeks contract manufacturers abroad can produce the new models of shoes. Any alliance partners that fail to meet Nike's standards are replaced with new partners, so Nike has great control over its network structure. In fact, the company works closely with its suppliers to take advantage of any new developments in technology that can help it reduce costs and increase quality. Third, the ability to outsource all its manufacturing abroad allows Nike to keep its United States structure fluid and flexible. Nike uses a functional structure to organize its activities and decentralizes control of the design process to teams that are assigned to develop each of the new kinds of sports shoes for which Nike is known.

In conclusion, the implications of IT for strategy implementation are still evolving and will continue to do so as new software and hardware reshape a company's business model and its strategies. IT is changing the nature of value chain activities both inside and among organizations, affecting all four building blocks of competitive advantage. For the multibusiness company, as for the single-business company, the need to be alert to such changes to strengthen its position in its core business has become vital, and the success of companies like Nike, Toyota, and Walmart compared to the failure of others like GM and Kmart can be traced, in part, to their success in developing the IT capabilities that lead to sustained competitive advantage.

SUMMARY OF CHAPTER

1. A company uses organizational design to combine structure, control systems, and culture in ways that allow it to implement its multibusiness model successfully.

2. As a company grows and diversifies, it adopts a multidivisional structure. Although this structure costs more to operate than a functional or product structure, it economizes on the bureaucratic costs associated with operating through a functional structure and enables a company to handle its value creation activities more effectively.

3. As companies change their corporate strategies over time, they must change their structures because different strategies are managed in different ways. In particular, the move from unrelated diversification to vertical integration to related diversification increases the bureaucratic costs associated with managing a multibusiness model. Each requires a different combination of structure, control, and culture to economize on those costs.

4. As a company moves from a localization to an international, global standardization, and transnational strategy, it also needs to switch to a more complex structure that allows it to coordinate increasingly complex resource transfers. Similarly, it needs to adopt a more complex integration and control system that facilitates resource sharing and the leveraging of competencies around the globe. When the gains are substantial, companies frequently adopt a global-matrix structure to share knowledge and expertise or implement their control systems and culture.

5. To encourage internal new venturing, companies must design internal venturing processes that give new-venture managers the autonomy they need to develop new products. Similarly, when establishing a joint venture with another company, managers need to carefully design the new unit's structure and control systems to maximize its chance of success.

6. The profitability of mergers and acquisitions depends on the structure and control systems that companies adopt to manage them and the way a company integrates them into its existing operating structure.

7. IT is having increasingly important effects on the way multibusiness companies implement their strategies. Not only does IT help improve the efficiency with which the multidivisional structure operates, it also allows for the better control of complex value chain activities. The growth of outsourcing has also been promoted by IT, and some companies have developed network structures to coordinate their global value chain activities.

DISCUSSION QUESTIONS

1. If a related company begins to buy unrelated businesses, in what ways should it change its structure or control mechanisms to manage the acquisitions?

2. What are the problems associated with implementing a strategy of related diversification through acquisitions?

3. When would a company decide to change from a functional to a multidivisional structure?

Ford's CEO Designs a New Global Structure

Designing a global organization structure to operate efficiently across many countries is a critical issue for multinational companies, as Ford has discovered over time. Ford realized early in its history that a major opportunity to increase its profitability was to take its American car-manufacturing skills and apply them in countries abroad. Over time, it established car-manufacturing divisions in different countries in Europe, Asia, and Australia. Ford decentralized decision-making authority to each global division, which controlled its own activities and developed cars suited to the local market. The result was that each division came to operate independently from its United States parent company. Ford of Europe, for example, became the largest and most profitable carmaker in Europe.

Ford remained a highly profitable company until Japanese carmakers began to flood the world with their small, reliable, low-priced cars in the 1980s. As car buyers began to buy the Japanese imports in large numbers, Ford tried to draw on the skills of its European unit to help build smaller, more fuel-efficient cars for the United States market. But it had never before tried to get its United States and European design and manufacturing units to cooperate; this proved difficult to achieve because its decentralized global organizational structure did not encourage them to cooperate. In the 1990s, Ford embarked on a massive project to create a new global-matrix structure that would solve the decentralized task and authority problems that were preventing it from utilizing its resources effectively.

In the 2000 plan, Ford laid out a timetable of how all its global carmaking units would learn to cooperate using one set of global support functions, such as design, purchasing, and so on. Country managers continued to resist the changes, however, to preserve their country empires and forced Ford to redesign its proposed global structure again and again. By the mid-2000s, Ford's United States, European, and Asia/Pacific divisions were still operating as a collection of different autonomous "empires." Ford had failed to lower its cost structure or design and make a profitable "world car" that could be sold to customers around the globe.

Once again, Ford decided to restructure itself. It moved to a "world structure," in which one set of managers was given authority over the whole of a specific global operation such as manufacturing or car design. Then Ford began to design cars for the global market. Its new structure never worked to speed car design and production, even as it constantly changed global lines of authority and the locations in which it operated to increase profitability. Ford went through multiple reorganizations to try to meet the Japanese challenge, but nothing worked. Losing billions of dollars, Ford announced in 2006 a revamped "Way Forward" plan to turn around its United States and global operations, a plan that called for cutting 44,000 jobs; closing 16 plants; and freshening 70% of the company's Ford, Mercury, and Lincoln car lineup.

In October 2006, Ford also appointed a new president and CEO, Alan Mulally, an expert in organizational design, to help turn around its operations. Mulally, a former Boeing executive, had led that company's global reorganization effort. He began to work out how to change Ford's global structure to reduce costs and speed product development. In the structure Mulally inherited, Ford's American unit reported to the CEO, but its other global and functional operations reported to the next two most senior executives, Mark Fields, president of Ford's Americas operation, and Mark Schulz, president of international operations. Mulally decided that Ford's downsizing should be accompanied by a major reorganization of its hierarchy, and he decided to flatten Ford's structure and recentralize control. At the same time, however, he put the focus on teamwork and adopted a cross-functional approach to handling the enormous value chain challenges that still confronted the organization.

The position of president of international operations was eliminated, and Mark Fields continues to report to Mulally but so also do the heads of the other two world regions: Lewis Booth, head of Ford of Europe, and John Parker, head of Ford of Asia Pacific and Africa and Mazda. Two levels in the hierarchy are gone, and Mulally's new organizational design clearly defines each global executive's role in the company's hierarchy. Ford can begin acting like one company instead of separate global units, each with their own interests.[33] In addition, the heads of its global value chain functions also now report directly to Mulally, not to Fields. These heads include Tony Brown, global head of purchasing; Nick Smither, head of IT; Richard Parry-Jones, chief technical officer; and Bennie Fowler, head of quality and advanced manufacturing engineering. Mulally's goal is to provide a centralized focus on using the company's global functional assets to better support its carmaking business units.

At the same time, Mulally also took a major restructuring step, announcing the creation of a new position, global product development chief, who is responsible for overseeing the development of Ford's entire global lines of vehicles. He appointed Derrick Kuzak, head of product development in the Americas, to head Ford's new global engineering design effort, and he also reports directly to Mulally. Kuzak oversees efforts to streamline product development and engineering systems around the world. As Mulally commented, "An integrated, global product development team supporting our automotive business units will enable us to make the best use of our global assets and capabilities and accelerate development of the new vehicles our customers prefer, and do so more efficiently."[34]

Mulally's goal was to force a cross-functional approach on all his top managers—one that he will personally oversee—to standardize its global carmaking and allow functional units to continuously improve quality, productivity, and the speed at which new products can be introduced. But beyond streamlining and standardizing its approach, its new-product development group must also ensure that its new vehicles are customized to better meet the needs of regional customers. All Ford's executives now understand the company's very survival was at stake; they had to work together to accelerate efforts to reduce costs and catch up to more efficient competitors such as Toyota.

Despite the fact that in 2009 Ford was still losing billions of dollars as the 2008 recession continued, its new global organizational structure did seem to be working. Ford was in the best competitive position of any United States carmaker, and it had not needed to borrow billions of dollars from the United States government so that it could continue to operate. Only time will tell, but Mulally remains confident.[35]

Case Discussion Questions

1. What kind of global strategy did Ford pursue at the beginning? What kind of global strategy does it pursue now?

2. In what main ways has Ford changed its global structure to allow it to coordinate the production and sale of its products more effectively around the world? In particular, what different forms of organizational structure has it adopted?

CASES

Analyzing a Case Study and Writing a Case Study Analysis

What Is Case Study Analysis?

Case study analysis is an integral part of a course in strategic management. The purpose of a case study is to provide students with experience of the strategic management problems that actual organizations face. A case study presents an account of what happened to a business or industry over a number of years. It chronicles the events that managers had to deal with, such as changes in the competitive environment, and charts the managers' response, which usually involved changing the business- or corporate-level strategy. The cases in this book cover a wide range of issues and problems that managers have had to confront. Some cases are about finding the right business-level strategy to compete in changing conditions. Some are about companies that grew by acquisition, with little concern for the rationale behind their growth, and how growth by acquisition affected their future profitability. Each case is different because each organization is different. The underlying thread in all cases, however, is the use of strategic management techniques to solve business problems.

Cases prove valuable in a strategic management course for several reasons. First, cases provide you, the student, with experience of organizational problems that you probably have not had the opportunity to experience firsthand. In a relatively short period of time, you will have the chance to appreciate and analyze the problems faced by many different companies and to understand how managers tried to deal with them.

Second, cases illustrate the theory and content of strategic management. The meaning and implications of this information are made clearer when they are applied to case studies. The theory and concepts help reveal what is going on in the companies studied and allow you to evaluate the solutions that specific companies adopted to deal with their problems. Consequently, when you analyze cases, you will be like a detective who, with a set of conceptual tools, probes what happened and what or who was responsible and then marshals the evidence that provides the solution. Top managers enjoy the thrill of testing their problem-solving abilities in the real world. It is important to remember that no one knows what the right answer is. All that managers can do is to make the best guess. In fact, managers say repeatedly that they are happy if they are right only half the time in solving strategic problems. Strategic management is an uncertain game, and using cases to see how theory can be put into practice is one way of improving your skills of diagnostic investigation.

Third, case studies provide you with the opportunity to participate in class and to gain experience in presenting your ideas to others. Instructors may sometimes call on students as a group to identify what is going on in a case, and through classroom discussion the issues in and solutions to the case problem will reveal themselves. In such a situation, you will have to organize your views and conclusions so that you can present them to the class. Your classmates may have analyzed the issues differently from you, and they will want you to argue your points before they will accept your conclusions, so be prepared for debate. This mode of discussion is an example of the dialectical approach to decision making. This is how decisions are made in the actual business world.

Instructors also may assign an individual, but more commonly a group, to analyze the case before the whole class. The individual or group probably will be responsible for a thirty- to forty-minute presentation of the case to the class. That presentation must cover the issues posed, the problems facing the company, and a series of recommendations for resolving the problems. The discussion then will be thrown open to the class, and you will have to defend your ideas. Through such discussions and presentations, you will experience how to convey your ideas effectively to others. Remember that a great deal of managers' time is spent in these kinds of situations: presenting their ideas and engaging in discussion with other managers who have their own views about what is going on. Thus, you will experience in the classroom the actual process of strategic management, and this will serve you well in your future career.

If you work in groups to analyze case studies, you also will learn about the group process involved in working as a team. When people work in groups, it is often difficult to schedule time and allocate responsibility for the case analysis. There are always group members who shirk their responsibilities and group members who are so sure of their own ideas that they try to dominate the group's analysis. Most of the strategic management takes place in groups, however, and it is best if you learn about these problems now.

ANALYZING A CASE STUDY

The purpose of the case study is to let you apply the concepts of strategic management when you analyze the issues facing a specific company. To analyze a case study, therefore, you must examine closely the issues confronting the company. Most often you will need to read the case several times—once to grasp the overall picture of what is happening to the company and then several times more to discover and grasp the specific problems.

Generally, detailed analysis of a case study should include eight areas:

1. The history, development, and growth of the company over time
2. The identification of the company's internal strengths and weaknesses
3. The nature of the external environment surrounding the company
4. A SWOT analysis
5. The kind of corporate-level strategy that the company is pursuing
6. The nature of the company's business-level strategy
7. The company's structure and control systems and how they match its strategy
8. Recommendations

To analyze a case, you need to apply the concepts taught in this course to each of these areas. To help you further, we next offer a summary of the steps you can take to analyze the case material for each of the eight points we just noted:

1. *Analyze the company's history, development, and growth.* A convenient way to investigate how a company's past strategy and structure affect it in the present is to chart the critical incidents in its history—that is, the events that were

the most unusual or the most essential for its development into the company it is today. Some of the events have to do with its founding, its initial products, how it makes new-product market decisions, and how it developed and chose functional competencies to pursue. Its entry into new businesses and shifts in its main lines of business are also important milestones to consider.

2. *Identify the company's internal strengths and weaknesses.* Once the historical profile is completed, you can begin the SWOT analysis. Use all the incidents you have charted to develop an account of the company's strengths and weaknesses as they have emerged historically. Examine each of the value creation functions of the company, and identify the functions in which the company is currently strong and currently weak. Some companies might be weak in marketing; some might be strong in research and development. Make lists of these strengths and weaknesses. The SWOT Checklist (Table 1) gives examples of what might go in these lists.

3. *Analyze the external environment.* To identify environmental opportunities and threats, apply all the concepts on industry and macroenvironments to analyze the environment the company is confronting. Of particular importance at the industry level are Porter's five forces model and the stage of the life cycle model. Which factors in the macroenvironment will appear salient depends on the specific company being analyzed. Use each factor in turn (for instance, demographic factors) to see whether it is relevant for the company in question.

   Having done this analysis, you will have generated both an analysis of the company's environment and a list of opportunities and threats. The SWOT Checklist table also lists some common environmental opportunities and threats that you may look for, but the list you generate will be specific to your company.

4. *Evaluate the SWOT analysis.* Having identified the company's external opportunities and threats as well as its internal strengths and weaknesses, consider what your findings mean. You need to balance strengths and weaknesses against opportunities and threats. Is the company in an overall strong competitive position? Can it continue to pursue its current business- or corporate-level strategy profitably? What can the company do to turn weaknesses into strengths and threats into opportunities? Can it develop new functional, business, or corporate strategies to accomplish this change? *Never merely generate the SWOT analysis and then put it aside.* Because it provides a succinct summary of the company's condition, a good SWOT analysis is the key to all the analyses that follow.

5. *Analyze corporate-level strategy.* To analyze corporate-level strategy, you first need to define the company's mission and goals. Sometimes the mission and goals are stated explicitly in the case; at other times, you will have to infer them from available information. The information you need to collect to find out the company's corporate strategy includes such factors as its lines of business and the nature of its subsidiaries and acquisitions. It is important to analyze the relationship among the company's businesses. Do they trade or exchange resources? Are there gains to be achieved from synergy? Alternatively, is the company just running a portfolio of investments? This analysis should enable you to define the corporate strategy that the company is pursuing (for example, related or unrelated diversification, or a combination of both) and to conclude whether the company operates in just one core business. Then, using your SWOT analysis, debate the merits of this strategy. Is it appropriate given the environment the company is in? Could a change in corporate strategy provide the company with new opportunities or transform a weakness into a strength? For example, should the company diversify from its core business into new businesses?

Table 1 A SWOT Checklist

Potential Internal Strengths	Potential Internal Weaknesses
Many product lines?	Obsolete, narrow product lines?
Broad market coverage?	Rising manufacturing costs?
Manufacturing competence?	Decline in R&D innovations?
Good marketing skills?	Poor marketing plan?
Good materials management systems?	Poor material management systems?
R&D skills and leadership?	Loss of customer good will?
Information system competencies?	Inadequate human resources?
Human resource competencies?	Inadequate information systems?
Brand name reputation?	Loss of brand name capital?
Portfolio management skills?	Growth without direction?
Cost of differentiation advantage?	Bad portfolio management?
New-venture management expertise?	Loss of corporate direction?
Appropriate management style?	Infighting among divisions?
Appropriate organizational structure?	Loss of corporate control?
Appropriate control systems?	Inappropriate organizational
Ability to manage strategic change?	structure and control systems?
Well-developed corporate strategy?	High conflict and politics?
Good financial management?	Poor financial management?
Others?	Others?

Potential Environmental Opportunities	Potential Environmental Threats
Expand core business(es)?	Attacks on core business(es)?
Exploit new market segments?	Increases in domestic competition?
Widen product range?	Increase in foreign competition?
Extend cost or differentiation advantage?	Change in consumer tastes?
Diversify into new growth businesses?	Fall in barriers to entry?
Expand into foreign markets?	Rise in new or substitute products?
Apply R&D skills in new areas?	Increase in industry rivalry?
Enter new related businesses?	New forms of industry competition?
Vertically integrate forward?	Potential for takeover?
Vertically integrate backward?	Existence of corporate raiders?
Enlarge corporate portfolio?	Increase in regional competition?
Overcome barriers to entry?	Changes in demographic factors?
Reduce rivalry among competitors?	Changes in economic factors?
Make profitable new acquisitions?	Downturn in economy?
Apply brand name capital in new areas?	Rising labor costs?
Seek fast market growth?	Slower market growth?
Others?	Others?

Other issues should be considered as well. How and why has the company's strategy changed over time? What is the claimed rationale for any changes? Often, it is a good idea to analyze the company's businesses or products to assess its situation and identify which divisions contribute the most to or detract from its competitive advantage. It is also useful to explore how the company has built its portfolio over time. Did it acquire new businesses, or did it internally venture its own? All of these factors provide clues about the company and indicate ways of improving its future performance.

6. *Analyze business-level strategy.* Once you know the company's corporate-level strategy and have done the SWOT analysis, the next step is to identify the company's business-level strategy. If the company is a single-business company, its business-level strategy is identical to its corporate-level strategy. If the company is in many businesses, each business will have its own business-level strategy. You will need to identify the company's generic competitive strategy—differentiation, low-cost, or focus—and its investment strategy, given its relative competitive position and the stage of the life cycle. The company also may market different products using different business-level strategies. For example, it may offer a low-cost product range and a line of differentiated products. Be sure to give a full account of a company's business-level strategy to show how it competes.

Identifying the functional strategies that a company pursues to build competitive advantage through superior efficiency, quality, innovation, and customer responsiveness and to achieve its business-level strategy is very important. The SWOT analysis will have provided you with information on the company's functional competencies. You should investigate its production, marketing, or research and development strategy further to gain a picture of where the company is going. For example, pursuing a low-cost or a differentiation strategy successfully requires very different sets of competencies. Has the company developed the right ones? If it has, how can it exploit them further? Can it pursue both a low-cost and a differentiation strategy simultaneously?

The SWOT analysis is especially important at this point if the industry analysis, particularly Porter's model, has revealed threats to the company from the environment. Can the company deal with these threats? How should it change its business-level strategy to counter them? To evaluate the potential of a company's business-level strategy, you must first perform a thorough SWOT analysis that captures the essence of its problems.

Once you complete this analysis, you will have a full picture of the way the company is operating and be in a position to evaluate the potential of its strategy. Thus, you will be able to make recommendations concerning the pattern of its future actions. However, first you need to consider strategy implementation, or the way the company tries to achieve its strategy.

7. *Analyze structure and control systems.* The aim of this analysis is to identify what structure and control systems the company is using to implement its strategy and to evaluate whether that structure is the appropriate one for the company. Different corporate and business strategies require different structures. You need to determine the *degree of fit between the company's strategy and structure.* For example, does the company have the right level of vertical differentiation (e.g., does it have the appropriate number of levels in the hierarchy or decentralized control?) or horizontal differentiation (does it use a functional structure when it should be using a product structure?)? Similarly, is the company using the right integration or control systems to

manage its operations? Are managers being appropriately rewarded? Are the right rewards in place for encouraging cooperation among divisions? These are all issues to consider.

In some cases, there will be little information on these issues, whereas in others there will be a lot. In analyzing each case, you should gear the analysis toward its most salient issues. For example, organizational conflict, power, and politics will be important issues for some companies. Try to analyze why problems in these areas are occurring. Do they occur because of bad strategy formulation or because of bad strategy implementation?

Organizational change is an issue in many cases because the companies are attempting to alter their strategies or structures to solve strategic problems. Thus, as part of the analysis, you might suggest an action plan that the company in question could use to achieve its goals. For example, you might list in a logical sequence the steps the company would need to follow to alter its business-level strategy from differentiation to focus.

8. *Make recommendations.* The quality of your recommendations is a direct result of the thoroughness with which you prepared the case analysis. Recommendations are directed at solving whatever strategic problem the company is facing and increasing its future profitability. Your recommendations should be in line with your analysis; that is, they should follow logically from the previous discussion. For example, your recommendation generally will center on the specific ways of changing functional, business, and corporate strategies and organizational structure and control to improve business performance. The set of recommendations will be specific to each case, and so it is difficult to discuss these recommendations here. Such recommendations might include an increase in spending on specific research and development projects, the divesting of certain businesses, a change from a strategy of unrelated to related diversification, an increase in the level of integration among divisions by using task forces and teams, or a move to a different kind of structure to implement a new business-level strategy. Make sure your recommendations are mutually consistent and written in the form of an action plan. The plan might contain a timetable that sequences the actions for changing the company's strategy and a description of how changes at the corporate level will necessitate changes at the business level and subsequently at the functional level.

After following all these stages, you will have performed a thorough analysis of the case and will be in a position to join in class discussion or present your ideas to the class, depending on the format used by your professor. Remember that you must tailor your analysis to suit the specific issue discussed in your case. In some cases, you might completely omit one of the steps in the analysis because it is not relevant to the situation you are considering. You must be sensitive to the needs of the case and not apply the framework we have discussed in this section blindly. The framework is meant only as a guide, not as an outline.

WRITING A CASE STUDY ANALYSIS

Often, as part of your course requirements, you will need to present a written case analysis. This may be an individual or a group report. Whatever the situation, there are certain guidelines to follow in writing a case analysis that will improve the evaluation your work will receive from your instructor. Before we discuss these guidelines and before you use them, make sure that they do not conflict with any directions your instructor has given you.

The structure of your written report is critical. Generally, if you follow the steps for analysis discussed in the previous section, *you already will have a good structure for your written discussion.* All reports begin with an *introduction* to the case. In it, outline briefly what the company does, how it developed historically, what problems it is experiencing, and how you are going to approach the issues in the case write-up. Do this sequentially by writing, for example, "First, we discuss the environment of Company X. . . . Third, we discuss Company X's business-level strategy. . . . Last, we provide recommendations for turning around Company X's business."

In the second part of the case write-up, the *strategic analysis* section, do the SWOT analysis, analyze and discuss the nature and problems of the company's business-level and corporate strategies, and then analyze its structure and control systems. Make sure you use plenty of headings and subheadings to structure your analysis. For example, have separate sections on any important conceptual tool you use. Thus, you might have a section on Porter's five forces model as part of your analysis of the environment. You might offer a separate section on portfolio techniques when analyzing a company's corporate strategy. Tailor the sections and subsections to the specific issues of importance in the case.

In the third part of the case write-up, present your *solutions and recommendations.* Be comprehensive, and make sure they are in line with the previous analysis so that the recommendations fit together and move logically from one to the next. The recommendations section is very revealing because your instructor will have a good idea of how much work you put into the case from the quality of your recommendations.

Following this framework will provide a good structure for most written reports, though it must be shaped to fit the individual case being considered. Some cases are about excellent companies experiencing no problems. In such instances, it is hard to write recommendations. Instead, you can focus on analyzing why the company is doing so well, using that analysis to structure the discussion. Following are some minor suggestions that can help make a good analysis even better:

1. Do not repeat in summary form large pieces of factual information from the case. The instructor has read the case and knows what is going on. Rather, use the in formation in the case to illustrate your statements, defend your arguments, or make salient points. Beyond the brief introduction to the company, you must avoid being *descriptive;* instead, you must be *analytical.*

2. Make sure the sections and subsections of your discussion flow logically and smoothly from one to the next. That is, try to build on what has gone before so that the analysis of the case study moves toward a climax. This is particularly important for group analysis, because there is a tendency for people in a group to split up the work and say, "I'll do the beginning, you take the middle, and I'll do the end." The result is a choppy, stilted analysis; the parts do not flow from one to the next, and it is obvious to the instructor that no real group work has been done.

3. Avoid grammatical and spelling errors. They make your work look sloppy.

4. In some instances, cases dealing with well-known companies end in 1998 or 1999 because no later information was available when the case was written. If possible, do a search for more information on what has happened to the company in subsequent years.

Many libraries now have comprehensive web-based electronic data search facilities that offer such sources as *ABI/Inform, The Wall Street Journal Index,* the *F&S Index,* and the *Nexis-Lexis* databases. These enable you to identify any article that has been written in the business press on the company of your choice within the past few years. A number of nonelectronic data sources are also useful. For example, *F&S Predicasts* publishes an annual list of articles relating to major companies that appeared in the national and international business press. *S&P Industry Surveys* is a great source for basic industry data, and *Value Line Ratings and Reports* can contain good summaries of a firm's financial position and future prospects. You will also want to collect full financial information on the company. Again, this can be accessed from web-based electronic databases such as the *Edgar* database, which archives all forms that publicly quoted companies have to file with the Securities and Exchange Commission (SEC; e.g., 10-K filings can be accessed from the SEC's *Edgar* database). Most SEC forms for public companies can now be accessed from Internet-based financial sites, such as Yahoo's finance site (http://finance.yahoo.com/).

5. Sometimes instructors hand out questions for each case to help you in your analysis. Use these as a guide for writing the case analysis. They often illuminate the important issues that have to be covered in the discussion.

If you follow the guidelines in this section, you should be able to write a thorough and effective evaluation.

THE ROLE OF FINANCIAL ANALYSIS IN CASE STUDY ANALYSIS

An important aspect of analyzing a case study and writing a case study analysis is the role and use of financial information. A careful analysis of the company's financial condition immensely improves a case write-up. After all, financial data represent the concrete results of the company's strategy and structure. Although analyzing financial statements can be quite complex, a general idea of a company's financial position can be determined through the use of ratio analysis. Financial performance ratios can be calculated from the balance sheet and income statement. These ratios can be classified into five subgroups: profit ratios, liquidity ratios, activity ratios, leverage ratios, and shareholder-return ratios. These ratios should be compared with the industry average or the company's prior years of performance. It should be noted, however, that deviation from the average is not necessarily bad; it simply warrants further investigation. For example, young companies will have purchased assets at a different price and will likely have a different capital structure than older companies do. In addition to ratio analysis, a company's cash flow position is of critical importance and should be assessed. Cash flow shows how much actual cash a company possesses.

Profit Ratios

Profit ratios measure the efficiency with which the company uses its resources. The more efficient the company, the greater is its profitability. It is useful to compare a company's profitability against that of its major competitors in its industry to determine whether the company is operating more or less efficiently than its rivals. In addition, the change in a company's profit ratios over time tells whether its performance is improving or declining.

A number of different profit ratios can be used, and each of them measures a different aspect of a company's performance. Here, we look at the most commonly used profit ratios.

Return on Invested Capital   This ratio measures the profit earned on the capital invested in the company. It is defined as follows:

$$\text{Return on invested capital (ROIC)} = \frac{\text{Net profit}}{\text{Invested capital}}$$

Net profit is calculated by subtracting the total costs of operating the company away from its total revenues (total revenues − total costs). Total costs are the (1) costs of goods sold, (2) sales, general, and administrative expenses, (3) R&D expenses, and (4) other expenses. Net profit can be calculated before or after taxes, although many financial analysts prefer the before-tax figure. Invested capital is the amount that is invested in the operations of a company—that is, in property, plant, equipment, inventories, and other assets. Invested capital comes from two main sources: interest-bearing debt and shareholders' equity. Interest-bearing debt is money the company borrows from banks and from those who purchase its bonds. Shareholders' equity is the money raised from selling shares to the public, *plus* earnings that have been retained by the company in prior years and are available to fund current investments. ROIC measures the effectiveness with which a company is using the capital funds that it has available for investment. As such, it is recognized to be an excellent measure of the value a company is creating.[1] Remember that a company's ROIC can be decomposed into its constituent parts.

Return on Total Assets (ROA)   This ratio measures the profit earned on the employment of assets. It is defined as follows:

$$\text{Return on total assests} = \frac{\text{Net profit}}{\text{Total assets}}$$

Return on Stockholders' Equity (ROE)   This ratio measures the percentage of profit earned on common stockholders' investment in the company. It is defined as follows:

$$\text{Return on stockholders equity} = \frac{\text{Net profit}}{\text{Stockholders equity}}$$

If a company has no debt, this will be the same as ROIC.

Liquidity Ratios

A company's liquidity is a measure of its ability to meet short-term obligations. An asset is deemed liquid if it can be readily converted into cash. Liquid assets are current assets such as cash, marketable securities, accounts receivable, and so on. Two liquidity ratios are commonly used.

[1]Tom Copeland, Tim Koller, and Jack Murrin, *Valuation: Measuring and Managing the Value of Companies* (New York: Wiley, 1996).

Current Ratio　The current ratio measures the extent to which the claims of short-term creditors are covered by assets that can be quickly converted into cash. Most companies should have a ratio of at least 1, because failure to meet these commitments can lead to bankruptcy. The ratio is defined as follows:

$$\text{Current ratio} = \frac{\text{Current assets}}{\text{Current liabilities}}$$

Quick Ratio　The quick ratio measures a company's ability to pay off the claims of short-term creditors without relying on selling its inventories. This is a valuable measure since in practice the sale of inventories is often difficult. It is defined as follows:

$$\text{Quick ratio} = \frac{\text{Current assets} - \text{inventory}}{\text{Current liabilities}}$$

Activity Ratios

Activity ratios indicate how effectively a company is managing its assets. Two ratios are particularly useful.

Inventory Turnover　This measures the number of times inventory is turned over. It is useful in determining whether a firm is carrying excess stock in inventory. It is defined as follows:

$$\text{Inventory turnover} = \frac{\text{Cost of goods sold}}{\text{Inventory}}$$

　　Cost of goods sold is a better measure of turnover than sales because it is the cost of the inventory items. Inventory is taken at the balance sheet date. Some companies choose to compute an average inventory, beginning inventory, and ending inventory, but for simplicity, use the inventory at the balance sheet date.

Days Sales Outstanding (DSO) or Average Collection Period　This ratio is the average time a company has to wait to receive its cash after making a sale. It measures how effective the company's credit, billing, and collection procedures are. It is defined as follows:

$$\text{DSO} = \frac{\text{Accounts receivable}}{\text{Total sales}/360}$$

　　Accounts receivable is divided by average daily sales. The use of 360 is the standard number of days for most financial analysis.

Leverage Ratios

A company is said to be highly leveraged if it uses more debt than equity, including stock and retained earnings. The balance between debt and equity is called the *capital structure*. The optimal capital structure is determined by the individual company. Debt has a lower cost because creditors take less risk; they know they will get their interest and principal. However, debt can be risky to the firm because if enough profit is not made to cover the interest and principal payments, bankruptcy can result. Three leverage ratios are commonly used.

Debt-to-Assets Ratio　The debt-to-assets ratio is the most direct measure of the extent to which borrowed funds have been used to finance a company's investments. It is defined as follows:

$$\text{Debt-to-assets ratio} = \frac{\text{Total debt}}{\text{Total assets}}$$

Total debt is the sum of a company's current liabilities and its long-term debt, and total assets are the sum of fixed assets and current assets.

Debt-to-Equity Ratio   The debt-to-equity ratio indicates the balance between debt and equity in a company's capital structure. This is perhaps the most widely used measure of a company's leverage. It is defined as follows:

$$\text{Debt-to-equity ratio} = \frac{\text{Total debt}}{\text{Total equity}}$$

Times-Covered Ratio   The times-covered ratio measures the extent to which a company's gross profit covers its annual interest payments. If this ratio declines to less than 1, the company is unable to meet its interest costs and is technically insolvent. The ratio is defined as follows:

$$\text{Times-covered ratio} = \frac{\text{Profit before interest and tax}}{\text{Total interest charges}}$$

Shareholder-Return Ratios

Shareholder-return ratios measure the return that shareholders earn from holding stock in the company. Given the goal of maximizing stockholders' wealth, providing shareholders with an adequate rate of return is a primary objective of most companies. As with profit ratios, it can be helpful to compare a company's shareholder returns against those of similar companies as a yardstick for determining how well the company is satisfying the demands of this particularly important group of organizational constituents. Four ratios are commonly used.

Total Shareholder Returns   Total shareholder returns measure the returns earned by time $t + 1$ on an investment in a company's stock made at time t. (Time t is the time at which the initial investment is made.) Total shareholder returns include both dividend payments and appreciation in the value of the stock (adjusted for stock splits) and are defined as follows:

$$\text{Total shareholder returns} = \frac{\text{Stock price } (t + 1) - \text{stock price } (t)}{+ \text{ sum of annual dividends per share}}{\text{Stock price } (t)}$$

If a shareholder invests $2 at time t and at time $t + 1$ the share is worth $3, while the sum of annual dividends for the period t to $t + 1$ has amounted to $0.20, total shareholder returns are equal to $(3 - 2 + 0.2)/2 = 0.6$, which is a 60 percent return on an initial investment of $2 made at time t.

Price-Earnings Ratio   The price-earnings ratio measures the amount investors are willing to pay per dollar of profit. It is defined as follows:

$$\text{Price-earnings ratio} = \frac{\text{Market price per share}}{\text{Earnings per share}}$$

Market-to-Book Value   Market-to-book value measures a company's expected future growth prospects. It is defined as follows:

$$\text{Market-to-book value} = \frac{\text{Market price per share}}{\text{Earnings per share}}$$

Dividend Yield   The dividend yield measures the return to shareholders received in the form of dividends. It is defined as follows:

$$\text{Dividend yield} = \frac{\text{Dividend per share}}{\text{Market price per share}}$$

Market price per share can be calculated for the first of the year, in which case the dividend yield refers to the return on an investment made at the beginning of the year. Alternatively, the average share price over the year may be used. A company must decide how much of its profits to pay to stockholders and how much to reinvest in the company. Companies with strong growth prospects should have a lower dividend payout ratio than mature companies. The rationale is that shareholders can invest the money elsewhere if the company is not growing. The optimal ratio depends on the individual firm, but the key decider is whether the company can produce better returns than the investor can earn elsewhere.

Cash Flow

Cash flow position is cash received minus cash distributed. The net cash flow can be taken from a company's statement of cash flows. Cash flow is important for what it reveals about a company's financing needs. A strong positive cash flow enables a company to fund future investments without having to borrow money from bankers or investors. This is desirable because the company avoids paying out interest or dividends. A weak or negative cash flow means that a company has to turn to external sources to fund future investments. Generally, companies in strong-growth industries often find themselves in a poor cash flow position (because their investment needs are substantial), whereas successful companies based in mature industries generally find themselves in a strong cash flow position.

A company's internally generated cash flow is calculated by adding back its depreciation provision to profits after interest, taxes, and dividend payments. If this figure is insufficient to cover proposed new investments, the company has little choice but to borrow funds to make up the shortfall or to curtail investments. If this figure exceeds proposed new investments, the company can use the excess to build up its liquidity (that is, through investments in financial assets) or repay existing loans ahead of schedule.

CONCLUSION

When evaluating a case, it is important to be *systematic*. Analyze the case in a logical fashion, beginning with the identification of operating and financial strengths and weaknesses and environmental opportunities and threats. Move on to assess the value of a company's current strategies only when you are fully conversant with the SWOT analysis of the company. Ask yourself whether the company's current strategies make sense given its SWOT analysis. If they do not, what changes need to be made? What are your recommendations? Above all, link any strategic recommendations you may make to the SWOT analysis. State explicitly how the strategies you identify take advantage of the company's strengths to exploit environmental opportunities, how they rectify the company's weaknesses, and how they counter environmental threats. Also, do not forget to outline what needs to be done to implement your recommendations.

WYNN RESORT

ROAD TO GOLD TIMELINE

October 25, 2002
- IPO NASDAQ WYNN

October 31, 2002
- Groundbreaking of Wynn Las Vegas

April 28, 2005
- Doors open at the Wynn Las Vegas

September 6, 2006
- Doors open at the Wynn Macau

December 15, 2007
- 2nd phase of Wynn Macau is complete

2009
- Expected completion of the Encore Las Vegas Diamond Suites

Future
- Wynn Resorts on the Cotai Strip

"KNOW WHEN TO HOLD 'EM; KNOW WHEN TO FOLD 'EM"

Millions of people travel to Las Vegas each year with big dreams of hitting the jackpot; most of them leave Las Vegas empty handed, heartbroken, and even further in debt. Very few people win big, and even fewer make their lives' fortune in "Sin City"; Steve Wynn is one of the lucky few who has. He went from humble beginnings in a family-run bingo parlor in Maryland to Chief Executive Officer (CEO) and Chairman of Wynn Resorts, Ltd. premium-destination world-class casinos and resorts. Seen by many in the entertainment industry as a visionary, Steve Wynn has revolutionized the city of Las Vegas one casino at a time.[1]

He started with small stakes in the Frontier Hotel in 1967 as a newcomer to Vegas to upping the ante with a complete renovation of the Golden Nugget from a dingy downtown Vegas casino to a four-star resort and gaming facility. Mr. Wynn was not satisfied with his accomplishment of attracting high networth clientele to downtown Vegas; he had dreams of expanding his casino empire, starting with a twin Golden Nugget resort in Atlantic City, a rival gambling destination. Also on his repertoire of great successes are the magnificent Mirage (1989), Treasure Island (1993), and the breathtaking Bellagio (1998). After what was considered the largest merger in the gaming industry's history, the Mirage became a part of MGM, Inc. for $6.4 million. Steve Wynn stepped down as Chairman and CEO of the Mirage and set his sights on developing his largest casino resort yet, the Five Diamond Wynn Las Vegas.

Wynn Resorts, Ltd. owns and operates the Wynn Las Vegas and the Wynn Macau, a casino resort located in the Macau Special Administrative Region of the People's Republic of China (PRC). The company is in the process of developing an expansion

---

This case was prepared by Victoria Page, Bentley College and Alan N. Hoffman, Bentley University.

The authors would like to thank Khalifa Al Jalahma, Erin Cavanaugh, Sevgi Eason, Gary Held, Kelley Henry, John Kinnecome, Deb Lahteine, Antoinette Paone, Farah Syed, and Will Hoffman for their research. Please address all correspondence to Dr. Alan N. Hoffman, MBA Program Director, LaCava 295, Bentley University, 175 Forest Street, Waltham, MA 02452; ahoffman@bentley.edu. Printed by permission of Dr. Alan N. Hoffman.

to the Wynn Las Vegas, called the Encore Diamond Suites. In addition, the company continues to explore opportunities to develop additional gaming or related businesses in other markets, both domestic and international.

The officers of the company include the following:

- *Stephen A. Wynn,* Chairman of the Board and Chief Executive Officer
- *Marc D. Schorr,* Chief Operating Officer
- *John Strzemp,* Executive Vice President and Chief Administrative Officer
- *Matt Maddox,* Chief Financial Officer and Treasurer

As mentioned, Mr. Wynn was previously the Chairman of the Board, President, and CEO of Mirage Resorts. In 1997, under his leadership, Mirage Resorts was ranked by *Fortune* magazine as the second-most admired company among American companies. It was also rated in the top three for innovativeness and quality for product and services. Steve Wynn is a man who is obsessed with details and continually strives for perfection.

The Wynn Las Vegas Resort and Casino opened on April 28, 2005. The property, which encompasses 217 acres of land, is located at the intersection of the Las Vegas Strip and Sands Avenue. The resort not only features an 111,000 square-foot casino with 137 table games, but also luxury hotel accommodations of 2,674 hotel rooms and suites, 36 fairway villas, and 6 private entry villas. The property offers its guests 18 restaurants; a Ferrari and Maserati car dealership; 76,000 square feet of high-end retail shops; recreational facilities, including an 18-hole golf course; five swimming pools; full cabanas; a full service spa and salon; and lavish nightlife (nightclubs and lounge entertainment). The Wynn Las Vegas has been described on the strip as "intimate" because it is significantly smaller than some of its competitors' structures. Because of the demand for the services provided by Wynn Las Vegas, the Encore Diamond Suites are currently in development. Encore will be located on the Strip, adjacent to Wynn Las Vegas and is expected to be completed in 2009.

Wynn Resorts is constantly looking for additional locations and opportunities to expand both domestically and internationally. In addition, Wynn is currently looking at opportunities for possible resorts in the Philippines as well as expanding into new markets, such as horseracing.

WHO IS THE PIT BOSS?

The greatest operational strength Wynn Resorts, Ltd. has is the founder himself, Steve Wynn. With more than 30 years experience in Las Vegas, this man has contacts, alliances, and knowledge that could not be easily replaced. As told by a bartender at Wynn Las Vegas, Mr. Wynn continues to be a very hands-on CEO. He can be seen regularly on the casino floor, talking with customers and employees. His passion for perfection can be seen throughout Las Vegas, from the Golden Nugget to the Bellagio. When talking about the Wynn Macau and its scale in comparison to some other casinos, Mr. Wynn stated, "Bigger ain't better. Better is better." This is the idea that lays the foundation in which Wynn Resorts relies to differentiate their resorts from those in direct competition.

Many of the other senior executives joined Mr. Wynn when he left the Mirage. The management team at Wynn Resorts has a tremendous amount of experience with building quality resort casinos. As Wynn Resorts continues its growth, the combined experience of these individuals will ensure the resort continues to build world-class operations. However, that Wynn Resorts is able to maintain competitive advantages is due in large part to the executive involvement of Steve Wynn.[2] If Steve Wynn left the company for any reason other than death or a severe disability, the resort would lose all lines of credit. Although Mr. Wynn is an operational strength, the company's complete dependence on him is a significant weakness.

ACES WILD

According to the Travel Industry Association of America (TIA), the U.S. tourism industry is the third largest retail industry after automotive and food stores and provides the nation with one of its largest service export industries.[3] The hotel/tourism industry has changed in recent years due to possible threats of terrorism and cutbacks in consumer spending on travel. In the years that followed the September 11, 2001, terrorist attacks, the United States has introduced stricter visa and passport requirements. Recent escalating airline fuel costs have also brought airfare increases. These changes impact the number of people who choose to travel and vacation farther away from home, thus affecting the overall industry.

There are many opportunities in the gaming industry from a social and demographic vantage point. As the legalization of gambling is spreading in the United States, the social acceptance of the pastime is beginning to spread as rapidly. In the past, gambling was negatively tied to addiction and corruption, but today gambling is being seen more and more as a socially acceptable and fun recreational activity, especially among the elderly.

In 2006, the Las Vegas strip had 38.9 million visitors, and Wynn Las Vegas enjoyed 94.4% occupancy at its 2,716-room hotel, far exceeding the area's average.[4] Wynn Resort's brand is synonymous with luxury in the casino market, and it capitalizes on this reputation, appealing to the high-end market.

Based on demographic trends in the United States, Wynn Las Vegas is in the right industry at the right time. In a 2006 report provided by Mintel Research on casino and casino-style gambling, they note that the population is aging, which is good news for the industry. The assumption is that, as people get older, they are more likely to gamble. As the report indicates, "Overall, the U.S. population is growing older . . . Casino gambling is very much a sport of a graying generation. Retirees and empty nesters typically enter casinos with a disposable income, financial security, and free time."[5]

Currently in the United States, the baby boomers are in the process of retiring; they are healthier and wealthier than earlier generations and have greater spending power. As the boomers retire, they are spending more money on leisure and recreation, and they are piling into the casinos. This growing market segment represents an opportunity for the gaming industry and for Wynn Resorts specifically.

There are a few social and demographic threats that Wynn Resorts must take into account. First is that social norms in the United States differ from those practiced in Macau and should not be universally applied. The occupancy rate at the Wynn Macau resorts is 80%, which is significantly less than that of the Las Vegas resort.[6]

Of those who visit Macau, only 25% actually stay overnight. Those that did stay overnight tended to stay for a short period of time (one to two nights). This is significantly different than the average visitor in Las Vegas. Although Wynn is investing in expansion of the Macau facility, it is important to bear in mind this distinction. Macau visitor behavior may change, but analysts agree that it will not happen overnight. Investing in the hotel arena may not be a safe bet for Wynn and other casinos.[7] Wynn's ideal client is what is referred to as a "whale" aka the risk-friendly, deep-pocketed, high-roller gambler. With increased global competition, it will be imperative for Wynn Resorts to maintain its social status and high brand image to attract and retain the "whale," customers. If they go elsewhere, it will be a substantial loss for the company.

PUT ON YOUR POKER FACE

Within the gaming and resort entertainment industry, there are many competing properties, including the Mirage, Las Vegas Sands, the Venetian, Paris, and the Bellagio, to name a few. Each casino has their own theme, attracting a significant number of visitors and directly competing with the Wynn Las Vegas.

- *Ameristar Casino* has casinos in Black Hawk, Colorado; North Chicago, Indiana; Council Bluffs, Iowa; Vicksburg, Mississippi; Kansas City and St. Charles, Missouri; and Jackpot, Nevada. They are established as the premier gaming and entertainment facility in these areas.
- *MGM Mirage* owns featured resorts such as the Mirage, Bellagio, Mandalay Bay, and Luxor, just to name a few.
- *Las Vegas Sands Corporation* is one of the leading international developers of multiuse integrated resorts. The company owns the Venetian Resort Hotel Casino, the Sands Expo and Convention Center in Las Vegas, the Sands Macau in the PRC Special Administrative Region of Macau. the company has recently opened 2 new resorts in 2007: the Palazzo Resort Hotel Casino in Las Vegas and the Venetian Macau Resort Hotel Casino in Macau. They are also developing the Cotai Strip, a development of resort casino properties in Macau, and were selected by the Singapore government to build the Marina Bay Sands, an integrated resort scheduled to open in Singapore by the end of 2009.
- *Boyd Gaming Corporation* is one of the premier casino entertainment companies in the United States. They have operations in Illinois, Indiana, Louisiana, Mississippi, New Jersey, and Nevada.
- *Harrah's* owns, operates, and/or manages about 50 casinos: Bally's, Caesars, Harrah's, and

Horseshu just to name a few. The majority of the casinos are based primarily in the United States and the United Kingdom. Operations include casino hotels, dockside and riverboat casinos, and Native American gaming establishments.

Steve Wynn feels unaffected by competition, as he believes his casinos cater to travelers who have higher demands. Wynn's main focus is to target high-end players with fancy new suites and baccarat tables. Wynn focuses on differentiating the company by concentrating on the atmosphere and design of the resorts and by enhancing customer service and luxury as a full-service provider.

The timing could not be better for Steve Wynn to start something new. The $9.4 billion merger between Harrah's and Caesar's Entertainment, along with MGM and Mandalay Bay coming together, give Wynn several top managers to choose from when developing his casinos. In addition, due to such mergers, it could be expected that casinos like Harrah's, which traditionally target middle-market gamblers, will reduce their focus away from the Caesar's Palace high-end customer to target the middle-class gambler. Such a move could result in additional revenues for Wynn, as such gamblers will look to Wynn Resort for higher-class amenities.

In general, rival casino operators say that new properties are good for Vegas because they create more reasons for people to come to town. Behind the scenes, however, they compete for the kind of gamblers who feel comfortable betting $10,000 or more per hand. MGM may already have launched its counteroffensive. "They're throwing tons of events, shopping sprees, baccarat tournaments, fishing trips," said Steve Conigliaro, an independent businessman who hosts high-rollers at various casinos. "Steve Wynn is going to take some business away. He knows what people like."[8]

LUCK OF THE DRAW

In the resort casino industry, the ability to find land and licenses in legal areas is very difficult because many countries have strict regulations about gaming resorts. Gaming licenses are difficult to obtain due to government regulations and limited availability. It is arguably more difficult to find a location that not only can support the size but also meets the legal requirements of that location. Today, Wynn Resorts, Ltd. has a premier

spot on the Las Vegas strip that is also home to the strip's only golf course. Wynn is also the holder of one of only four licenses in Macau. Having such scarce resources provides the company with a remarkable advantage.

Regulations regarding expansion in China remain questionable and could potentially be a barrier to entry. In Wynn Reports 10-K, they note certain risk factors for the company, including the fact that their concession in Macau effectively expires in June 2017, at which time the government in Macau has the right to take over the operation. The company also notes that there are currently only three gaming concessions granted until 2009. If the government in Macau were to revise this situation by granting more concessions, they would, in essence, alleviate this particular barrier to entry for other casinos and Wynn could potentially see more competition in the area.

Macau, an island located 37 miles southwest of Hong Kong and an hour ferry ride away, has become a popular gaming destination. At this time, there are 24 operating casinos in Macau with several others in the construction and development phase. Sociedade de Jogos de Macau (SJM) owns and operates 17 of these 24 casinos. Most are relatively small facilities that are not on the high-end like the Wynn. However, SJM controls three of the largest casinos in Macau: the Hotel Lisboa, the Greek Mythology Casino, and the Jai Alai.[9]

Currently, Wynn Macau is charged a 35% tax on gross gaming revenue and expected to contribute up to 4% of gross gaming revenue for the promotion of public interests, social security, infrastructure, and tourism in Macau.[10] If regulations were to change and taxes lowered, Wynn Resorts would be able to retain more of its earnings.

Currently, the Chinese government does not allow casinos on its mainland, only Macau,[11] so the breaking of the casino monopoly in Macau has provided an enormous growth opportunity for Wynn Resorts.[12] The government of Macau is trying to turn Macau into the "tourist destination of choice" in Asia.[13] In 2002, the government-sanctioned casino monopoly in Macau ended when the government granted concessions to three outside companies to operate casinos in Macau. Each of the three was allowed, with the approval of the government, to grant one sub-concession to another gaming operator.[14] If this legal situation were to occur in other areas of the globe, it could provide additional global growth opportunity for Wynn Resorts. Under the concession granted to Wynn Resorts, Wynn is able to develop an unlimited number of casino resorts in Macau with the government of Macau's approval.[15] This legal opportunity provides significant value for Wynn Resorts because they are one of a select few with such a right. In addition, because a limited number of companies have casino operating rights in Macau, Wynn is operating in a somewhat restricted competitive environment because they hold one of those six gaming licenses.[16]

Recently, Wynn Resorts was granted concession for its land application for 52 acres in Macau's Coati Strip. This legal right is essential for Wynn Resorts' future expansion plans. Steve Wynn stated during Wynn Resorts' third quarter 2007 conference call that he plans to build "the most beautiful hotel on Earth" in Coati. Currently, the designs include a 1,500- to 2,000-suites hotel to occupy all 52 acres. Wynn stated this hotel will have things that have never been seen before; it will be expensive but "it will be an experience."

The Chinese government has and is expected to continue to relax restrictions on travel and currency movements between China and Macau. Thus far, by relaxing its currency and travel restrictions, Chinese citizens from certain urban and economically developed areas are able to visit Macau without tour groups and are now allowed to bring more money into Macau.[17] If the Chinese government continues to loosen its restriction on travel and currency, tourism to Macau will grow, and the profit potential for Wynn Resorts will increase.

In 1999, Portugal returned Macau to Chinese control after 450 years of Portuguese control. Macau's legislative, regulatory, and legal institutions are still in a phase of transition because this change in control occurred less than eight years ago.[18] The long-term success of Wynn Macau will depend on the successful development of the political, economic, and regulatory framework in Macau. Wynn Resorts could be affected if an unfavorable environment develops in Macau.

By doing business in an emerging market, there are significant political, economic, and social risks for Wynn Macau.[19] For example, domestic or international unrest, health epidemics such as the bird flu, terrorism, or military conflicts in China or Macau will drastically affect Wynn Macau by not only reducing the inflow of customers from a decrease in tourism, but also by decreasing discretionary consumer spending and increasing the risk of higher taxes and government controls over gaming operations.

Furthermore, under Wynn Resorts' agreement with the government of Macau, the government has the right at any time to "assume temporary custody and control over the operation of a casino in certain circumstances."[20] The ability of the government to take control of the casino at any time it deems appropriate is a significant threat to the success of Wynn Resorts because it could lose control of its operations in Macau.

Additionally, Wynn Macau is subject to strict regulatory controls by the government, which limits its freedom of operations and creativity. For example, one of the regulations requires Wynn Macau to have an executive director who is a permanent resident of Macau and holds at least 10% of the company's capital stock.[21] The Macau government must approve this executive director and any successor, and they have to approve all contracts for the management of the casino's operation in Macau. This is just one example of the type of restrictions and the level of control the government holds over Wynn Macau.

The Macau land concession poses additional threats to Wynn Resorts. Under the agreement, Wynn Macau is leasing the 16 acres from the government of Macau for 25 years. The government of Macau may redeem the concession beginning June 24, 2017, and Wynn Macau will be entitled to fair compensation based on the amount of revenue generated during the previous tax year.[22] If the government takes back the land, the long-term plans of Wynn Resorts would be derailed, possibly leaving them with high debt and no means to repay. However, if the government does not take back the land, the concession may be renewed but the semiannual payments to use the land could substantially increase, taking away from Wynn's bottom line.

After April 1, 2009, the government of Macau obtained the right to offer additional concessions for the operation of casinos in Macau.[23] If additional concessions are granted, Wynn Macau will face further competition because these competitors already own land in Macau but do not have concessions to build yet. In addition, if the efforts to legalize gaming in Thailand or Taiwan are successful, Wynn will face competition from the surrounding area.[24] This competition will draw away customers, reducing the level of potential profits, and Wynn Macau could lose key employees to more attractive employment opportunities elsewhere in Asia.

Another threat exists in the possibility of Wynn Resorts, Ltd. being unable to collect on its gaming debts. This could have a significant negative impact on Wynn Macau's operating results if the company cannot collect its earnings. In Macau, taxes are due on gross gaming revenue regardless of whether revenue was actually collected. In essence, Wynn Macau would have to pay taxes on money it never received if it was unable to collect on the debt.[25]

As the competitive environment in Macau increases, the available employee talent pool will decrease, which could hamper future expansion plans in Macau. Wynn Resorts will need to petition the government to allow visas for more immigrant workers. If they are unable to do so, they run the risk of having employees who cannot run the facilities. If Wynn is successful, the strict immigration laws will take time to change that could threaten Wynn's future in Macau.

Wynn Resorts has positioned itself well in the growing gaming markets, particularly in Macau. The development of a casino in this area is a strategic opportunity. From an economic standpoint, Macau's GDP has grown nearly 30% in the first two quarters of 2007. The growth in gambling has also resulted in increased foreign investment in the area. United States exports to Macau have seen a tremendous increase as well.[26]

Macau's gross domestic product (GDP) growth is not likely to be sustainable. With increased competition in the region, Wynn's first-mover advantage will be diminished. Also, the company only has two casinos producing revenue, and with development efforts underway on their next projects, cash flow is undoubtedly going to be an issue.

PUT YOUR MONEY WHERE YOUR MOUTH IS

One of Wynn Resorts' greatest marketing strengths is strategic development of its product. The product that Wynn sells is a luxury destination experience that makes customers feel pampered and valued through high-quality amenities and customer service. This lavish experience allows consumers to justify spending significant amounts of money gambling, dining, drinking, shopping, and at the spas. The company strategically developed the Wynn brand name to be synonymous with high-quality goods and services. Continuous promotion of the brand is part of Wynn's overall company strategy.[27]

Steve Wynn is known for raising the luxury bar in Las Vegas. The packaging of Wynn's product is the glitz and glamour of its hotels, casinos, restaurants, and shops (such as a Ferrari and Maserati dealership). As customers enter the lobby of a Wynn hotel, they are instantly struck with grandiose decor. This feel extends throughout the hotel in the hallways, hotel rooms, suites, villas, and private-entry villas. The casino takes flash and glitz to another level. A mere glimpse of the lights and sounds would make any customer excited to gamble. The casino floor is designed specifically for the high-end customer and contains many private VIP areas and high-roller tables. These special areas and tables further contribute to the high-end customer experience.

The resort is able to charge a premium price due to the clout of the Wynn name, the high-income base of its customers, and the high quality of its products and services. In 2006, Wynn generated the highest room rate on the Las Vegas Strip. The average room rate for the quarter ending December 31, 2006, was $291, with the next highest being the Bellagio at $260 and then the Venetian at $243.[28]

Wynn is further segmenting the high-income customer market with the introduction of the Encore at Wynn Las Vegas, an all-suite hotel with its own casino, restaurants, nightclub, pool, and spa. This product layering allows Wynn to capitalize on the "celebrity" obsession with Las Vegas. The Encore at Wynn Las Vegas will be superior to Wynn Las Vegas in luxury, amenities, and, of course, price. This will serve to keep out people who cannot afford the price and will be attractive to elite customers who seek privacy as well as luxury.

Steve Wynn is by no means a newcomer to Las Vegas, and he knows the importance of strategic placement on the Vegas Strip. Wynn owns 235 acres on the strip, which houses hotels, casinos, and a golf course, the only golf course on the strip. Wynn was also strategic in the purchase of land in Macau and Coati, obtaining significant portions of land in the middle of all the excitement.

Wynn has been successful in the past with direct marketing to its high-end target customer. This past year, it expanded its promotion to include various media channels, such as print media, radio, and television.[29] Wynn Macau provides the opportunity for cross marketing with Wynn Las Vegas. Because the target market segment in both Wynn Las Vegas and Wynn Macau is high income, customers have the resources to travel and vacation in other parts of the world, which can make cross-marketing very effective. Wynn is the only gaming operator to target high-end customers in both Las Vegas and Macau.[30] Wynn Las Vegas already has a strong client base of Asian customers, and Macau provides the opportunity to increase this customer segment. Wynn recognizes that the Chinese economy is on the rise and that the population is becoming increasingly educated and wealthy. The "premium customer" in China, those in the top income brackets, will increase to approximately 180–200 million over the next 10 years.[31]

Because Wynn has the highest rates on the strip, it would be tough to extend its customer base beyond high-end clients. In addition, the already high prices may cause Wynn to increase rates at a slower percentage per year than other hotels on the strip. For the quarter ending December 31, 2006, Wynn's average room rate increased 4.4% from 2005 to 2006, while competitors' rates increased from 5.0% to 9.5%.[32]

Wynn faces the challenge of understanding the customer in Macau and other global markets. To accomplish this, Wynn has marketing executives located in offices around the world. However, a sole marketing executive in strategic global locations may not be sufficient to conduct thorough market research and adjust the product as necessary. Finally, focusing solely on the high-end market could be a marketing weakness in that Wynn is missing a large customer base of middle-income clients. This segment includes vacationers and younger people looking for a relatively inexpensive place to stay with the understanding that most of their budget will go to dining and entertainment.

When a customer pulls into the Wynn entrance off the Las Vegas or Macau strip, the feel is that of just being removed from a busy crowded city street and dropped into a tropical paradise. Entering the casino, one is surrounded by beautiful flower gardens and soothing sounds of water. Though close in the distance are the sounds of the casino floor, a gaming atmosphere is not the first to strike a person. Wynn Resort makes customers feel at ease by inviting them to relax and enjoy the serene surroundings. In the restaurants, specifically the Mediterranean-themed Bartolotta's, the renowned chef comes out and interacts with the diners. Every moment in the casino and each interaction with staff are designed to be the ultimate customer experience. The staff is focused on giving the customer a luxury experience and quality customer service.

Wynn Resorts' goal is to attract high-end gaming customers. In August 2006, Wynn Resorts, Ltd.

changed its tip-pooling policy to include pit bosses and table supervisors. Operationally, this move made it feasible for experienced dealers to take positions as supervisors, who, up until that point, generally earned less than the dealers. The company expects that the new tip-pooling policy will ensure that pit bosses and table supervisors will have more invested in keeping high-rolling gamblers happy. They will give more comps, and in return, customers will stay longer and return more often. This tip-pooling policy is an example of the kind of moves Wynn has made to further the luxury experience the customer receives.

SMALL BLIND, BIG BLIND

It is clear that Steve Wynn has been successful at building and operating a casino resort empire that turned his personal worth into $1.6 billion. This feat was accomplished with his personal ambition, business savvy, and vision for what entertainment really means to the world. Although Steve Wynn appears to be the epitome of casino resort gurus, this label does not hold the key for guaranteed future success of Wynn Resorts, Ltd. There are many challenges that Wynn will have to face, and the future may throw some curveballs along the way. Currently, there are three major challenges the firm will need to address in the future. The first is the need to secure a way to maintain the competitive advantage as increased competition is introduced both domestically and abroad into the gaming industry. Second, the Macau government reserves the right to take control of the Wynn Casino in 2017, as mentioned earlier; this would be detrimental to the profits for the company, and some solutions will need to be devised to ensure that the survival of the company is not majorly dependent on the revenues generated by the Wynn Macau resort and casino. A third concern about future success, but certainly not the final concern, is the loss of Steve Wynn himself. Losing Steve Winn would mean losing his expertise, passion, and governmental ties (concessions and licenses). In the most likely scenario, a loss of Steve Wynn may result in the sale of the firm to a competing company, such as MGM Inc. Although, the Wynn Resorts is not guaranteed future success, it is certainly on the right track and quite the remarkable company.

Financial Statements (February 22, 2008 10-K Edgar Online)
WYNN RESORTS, LIMITED AND SUBSIDIARIES
CONSOLIDATED STATEMENTS OF OPERATIONS
(amounts in thousands, except per share data)

	Year Ended December 31		
	2007	2006	2005
Operating revenues:			
Casino	$1,949,870	$ 800,591	$ 353,663
Rooms	339,391	283,084	170,315
Food and beverage	353,983	309,771	173,700
Entertainment, retail and other	245,201	205,213	125,230
Gross revenues	2,888,445	1,598,659	822,908
Less: promotional allowances	(200,926)	(166,402)	(100,927)
Net revenues	2,687,519	1,432,257	721,981
Operating costs and expenses:			
Casino	1,168,119	439,902	155,075
Rooms	83,237	73,878	44,171
Food and beverage	212,622	194,403	118,670
Entertainment, retail and other	161,087	134,530	80,185
General and administrative	310,820	231,515	118,980
Provision for doubtful accounts	36,109	21,163	16,206
Pre-opening costs	7,063	62,726	96,940
Depreciation and amortization	219,923	175,464	103,344
Contract termination fee	—	5,000	—
Property charges and other	60,857	25,060	14,297
Total operating costs and expenses	2,259,837	1,363,641	747,868
Equity in income from unconsolidated affiliates	1,721	2,283	1,331
Operating income (loss)	429,403	70,899	(24,556)
Other income (expense):			
Interest and other income	47,765	46,752	28,267
Interest expense, net of capitalized interest	(143,777)	(148,017)	(102,699)
Distribution to convertible debenture holders	—	(58,477)	—
Increase (decrease) in swap fair value	(6,001)	1,196	8,152
Gain on sale of subconcession right, net	—	899,409	—

(continued)

Financial Statements (February 22, 2008 10-K Edgar Online)
WYNN RESORTS, LIMITED AND SUBSIDIARIES
CONSOLIDATED STATEMENTS OF OPERATIONS
(amounts in thousands, except per share data) (*continued*)

	Year Ended December 31		
	2007	**2006**	**2005**
Loss from extinguishment of debt	(157)	(12,533)	—
Other income (expense), net	(102,170)	728,330	(66,280)
Income (loss) before income taxes	327,233	799,229	(90,836)
Provision for income taxes	(69,085)	(170,501)	—
Net Income (loss)	$ 258,148	$ 628,728	$ (90,836)
Basic and diluted income (loss) per common share:			
Net income (loss):			
Basic	$ 2.43	$ 6.29	$ (0.92)
Diluted	$ 2.34	$ 6.24	$ (0.92)
Weighted average common shares outstanding:			
Basic	106,030	99,998	98,308
Diluted	112,685	111,627	98,308

WYNN RESORTS, LIMITED AND SUBSIDIARIES
CONSOLIDATED BALANCE SHEETS
(amounts in thousands, except share data)

	December 31	
	2007	**2006**
ASSETS		
Current assets:		
Cash and cash equivalents	$ 1,275,120	$ 789,407
Restricted cash and investments	—	58,598
Receivables, net	179,059	140,232
Inventories	73,291	64,368
Deferred income taxes	24,746	13,727
Prepaid expenses and other	29,775	30,659
Total current assets	1,581,991	1,096,991
Restricted cash and investments	531,120	178,788

(*continued*)

WYNN RESORTS, LIMITED AND SUBSIDIARIES
CONSOLIDATED BALANCE SHEETS
(amounts in thousands, except share data) (*continued*)

	December 31	
	2007	2006
Property and equipment, net	3,939,979	3,157,622
Intangibles, net	60,074	65,135
Deferred financing costs	83,087	74,871
Deposits and other assets	97,531	80,792
Investment in unconsolidated affiliates	5,500	5,981
Total assets	$ 6,299,282	$4,660,180
LIABILITIES AND STOCKHOLDERS' EQUITY		
Current liabilities:		
Accounts and construction payable	$ 182,718	$ 123,061
Current portion of long-term debt	3,273	6,115
Current portion of land concession obligation	5,738	7,433
Income taxes payable	138	87,164
Accrued interest	12,478	15,495
Accrued compensation and benefits	93,097	71,223
Gaming taxes payable	75,014	46,403
Other accrued expenses	18,367	10,742
Customer deposits and other related liabilities	177,605	127,751
Construction retention	16,755	15,700
Total current liabilities	585,183	511,087
Long-term debt	3,533,339	2,380,537
Other long-term liabilities	39,335	5,214
Long-term land concession obligation	6,029	11,809
Deferred income taxes	152,953	97,064
Construction retention	34,284	8,884
Total liabilities	4,351,123	3,014,595
Commitments and contingencies (Note 18)		
Stockholders' equity:		
Preferred stock, par value $0.01; 40,000,000 shares authorized; zero shares issued and outstanding	—	—

(continued)

WYNN RESORTS, LIMITED AND SUBSIDIARIES
CONSOLIDATED BALANCE SHEETS
(amounts in thousands, except share data) (*continued*)

	December 31	
	2007	2006
Common stock, par value $0.01; 400,000,000 shares authorized; 116,259,411 and 101,887,031 shares issued; 114,370,090 and 101,887,031 shares outstanding	1,162	1,018
Treasury stock, at cost; 1,889,321 shares	(179,277)	—
Additional paid-in capital	2,273,078	2,022,408
Accumulated other comprehensive loss	(2,905)	(94)
Accumulated deficit	(143,899)	(377,747)
Total stockholders' equity	1,948,159	1,645,585
Total liabilities and stockholders' equity	$6,299,282	$4,660,180

WYNN RESORTS, LIMITED AND SUBSIDIARIES
CONSOLIDATED STATEMENTS OF CASH FLOWS
(amounts in thousands)

	Year Ended December 31		
	2007	2006	2005
Cash flows from operating activities:			
Net income (loss)	$258,148	$628,728	$(90,836)
Adjustments to reconcile net income (loss) to net cash provided by operating activities:			
Depreciation and amortization	219,923	175,464	103,344
Deferred income taxes	68,152	170,321	—
Stock-based compensation	18,527	16,712	4,676
Amortization and writeoffs of deferred financing costs, and other	19,318	23,419	14,045
Loss on extinguishment of debt	157	11,316	—
Provision for doubtful accounts	36,109	21,163	16,206
Property charges and other	60,857	25,060	14,297
Equity in income of unconsolidated affiliates, net of distributions	481	(911)	(1,331)
Decrease (increase) in swap fair value	6,001	(1,196)	(8,152)
Gain on sale of subconcession right	—	(899,409)	—

(continued)

WYNN RESORTS, LIMITED AND SUBSIDIARIES
CONSOLIDATED STATEMENTS OF CASH FLOWS
(amounts in thousands) (*continued*)

	Year Ended December 31		
	2007	2006	2005
Increase (decrease) in cash from changes in:			
Receivables net	(75,029)	(72,927)	(104,418)
Inventories and prepaid expenses and other	(7,565)	(21,261)	(58,934)
Accounts payable and accrued expenses	54,093	164,287	159,578
Net cash provided by operating activities	659,172	240,766	48,475
Cash flow from investing activities:			
Capital expenditures, net of construction payables and retention	(1,007,370)	(643,360)	(877,074)
Restricted cash and investments	(293,734)	205,216	499,765
Investment in unconsolidated affiliates	—	—	(3,739)
Purchase of intangibles and other assets	(43,216)	(59,456)	(40,181)
Proceeds from sale of subconcession right, net	—	899,409	—
Proceeds from sale of equipment	21,581	—	109
Net cash provided by (used in) investing activities	(1,322,739)	401,809	(421,120)
Cash flows from financing activities:			
Proceeds from exercise of stock options	9,180	21,790	1,404
Proceeds from issuance of common stock	664,125	—	—
Cash distributions	(683,299)	(608,299)	—
Proceeds from issuance of long-term debt	1,672,987	746,948	627,131
Principal payments on long-term debt	(297,321)	(440,929)	(121,933)
Proceeds from termination of interest rate swap	—	6,605	—
Purchase of treasury stock	(179,277)	—	—
Payments on long-term land concession obligation	(7,411)	(9,000)	(8,921)
Payment of deferred financing costs and other	(27,045)	(4,572)	(21,008)
Net cash provided by (used in) financing activities	1,151,939	(287,457)	476,673
Effect of exchange rate on cash	(2,659)	—	—
Cash and cash equivalents:			

(*continued*)

WYNN RESORTS, LIMITED AND SUBSIDIARIES
CONSOLIDATED STATEMETS OF CASH FLOWS
(amounts in thousands) (*continued*)

	Year Ended December 31		
	2007	**2006**	**2005**
Increase in cash and cash equivalents	485,713	355,118	104,028
Balance, beginning of period	789,407	434,289	330,261
Balance, end of period	$ 1,275,120	$ 789,407	$ 434,289
Supplemental cash flow disclosures:			
Cash paid for interest, net of amounts capitalized	$ 178,072	$ 133,850	$ 95,839
Cash distributions to convertible debenture holders	—	58,477	—
Cash paid for income taxes	79,168	180	—
Equipment purchases financed by debt and accrued assets	—	—	860
Stock-based compensation capitalized into construction	809	1,353	2,651

BOARD OF DIRECTORS

(http://phx.corporate-ir.net/phoenix.zhtml?c=132059&p= irol-govboard)

Stephen A. Wynn Chairman of the Board and Chief Executive Officer
Kazuo Okada Vice Chairman of the Board

Linda Chen Director
Dr. Ray R. Irani Director
Robert J. Miller Director
John A. Moran Director
Alvin V. Shoemaker Director
D. Boone Wayson Director
Elaine P. Wynn Director
Allan Zeman Director

Endnotes

1. http://www.investingvalue.com/investment-leaders/steve-wynn/index.htm.
2. Michael Schuman, "Egos Bigger than China," *Time*, Vol. 168, Issue 7, October 23, 2006.
3. "The North America Hospitality and Tourism Sectors," *Mergent Industry Report*. October, 2006.
4. "Wynn Resorts, Limited: Form 10-K," *United States Securities and Exchange Commission*. Filed 31 December 2006. Available Online. Thompson Research.
5. "Casino and Casino-style Gambling- US-November 2006,," http://academic.mintel.com.ezp.bentley.edu/sinatra/oxygen_academic/search_results/show&/display/id=177167/display/id=247080.
6. "Wynn Resorts, Limited: Form 10-K," *United States Securities and Exchange Commission*. Filed 31 December 2006. Available Online. Thompson Research.
7. Muhammad Cohen, "No Sure Thing," *Macau Business*. December 2006. Available Online. http://www.macaubusiness.com/index.php?id=634.
8. Steve Freiss, "In Las Vegas, a $2.7b Haven for High Rollers," *Boston Globe*. April 29,2005.
9. "Wynn Resorts, Limited: Form 10-K," *United States Securities and Exchange Commission*. Filed 31 December 2006. Available Online. Thompson Research.
10. "Wynn Resorts, Limited: Form 10-K," *United States Securities and Exchange Commission*. Filed 31 December 2006. Available Online. Thompson Research.
11. Kopin Tan, "Gambling on LVS, Wynn in Macau," 25 November 2007. Available Online. http://online.wsj.com/article/SB119594535268803103.html?mod=googlenews_wsj.

12. "Macau Wow," *Economist*. 1 September 2007. Vol. 384, Issue 8544, Pg 62. Available Online. Business Sources Premier.
13. "Wynn Resorts, Limited: Form 10-K," *United States Securities and Exchange Commission*. Filed 31 December 2006. Available Online. Thompson Research.
14. "Wynn Resorts, Limited: Form 10-K," *United States Securities and Exchange Commission*. Filed 31 December 2006. Available Online. Thompson Research.
15. "Wynn Resorts, Limited: Form 10-K," *United States Securities and Exchange Commission*. Filed 31 December 2006. Available Online. Thompson Research.
16. "Wynn Resorts Ltd: Stock Report," *Standard & Poor's*. 22 September 2007. Available Online. www.etrade.com.
17. "Wynn Resorts, Limited: Form 10-K," *United States Securities and Exchange Commission*. Filed 31 December 2006. Available Online. Thompson Research.
18. "Wynn Resorts, Limited: Form 10-K," *United States Securities and Exchange Commission*. Filed 31 December 2006. Available Online. Thompson Research.
19. "Wynn Resorts, Limited: Form 10-K," *United States Securities and Exchange Commission*. Filed 31 December 2006. Available Online. Thompson Research.
20. "Wynn Resorts, Limited: Form 10-K," *United States Securities and Exchange Commission*. Filed 31 December 2006. Available Online. Thompson Research.
21. "Wynn Resorts, Limited: Form 10-K," *United States Securities and Exchange Commission*. Filed 31 December 2006. Available Online. Thompson Research.
22. "Wynn Resorts, Limited: Form 10-K," *United States Securities and Exchange Commission*. Filed 31 December 2006. Available Online. Thompson Research.
23. "Wynn Resorts, Limited: Form 10-K," *United States Securities and Exchange Commission*. Filed 31 December 2006. Available Online. Thompson Research.
24. "Wynn Resorts, Limited: Form 10-K," *United States Securities and Exchange Commission*. Filed 31 December 2006. Available Online. Thompson Research.
25. "Wynn Resorts, Limited: Form 10-K," *United States Securities and Exchange Commission*. Filed 31 December 2006. Available Online. Thompson Research.
26. "Macau," *BuyUsa.Gov*. 18 September 2007. Available Online. www.buyusa.gov/hongkong/en/macau.html.
27. Wynn 10k
28. Ron Kramer, *Wynn Resorts*, Bear Stearns Retail, Restaurants and Consumer Conference, March 1, 2007.
29. Wynn 10k
30. Ron Kramer, *Wynn Resorts*, Bear Stearns Retail, Restaurants and Consumer Conference, March 1, 2007.
31. Ibid.
32. Ron Kramer, *Wynn Resorts*, Bear Stearns Retail, Restaurants and Consumer Conference, March 1, 2007.

APPLE IN 2008

INTRODUCTION

In 1997, Apple Computer was in deep trouble. The company that had pioneered the personal computer (PC) market with its easy-to-use Apple II in 1978 and introduced the first graphical user interface (GUI) with the Macintosh in 1984 was bleeding red ink. Apple's worldwide market share, which had been fluctuating between 7% and 9% since 1984, had sunk to 4%. Sales were declining. Apple was on track to lose $378 million on revenues of $7 billion, on top of a $740 million loss in 1996. In July 1997, the cofounder of the company, Steve Jobs, who had been fired from Apple in 1985, returned as CEO. At an investor conference, Michael Dell, CEO of Dell Computer, was asked what Jobs should do as head of Apple. Dell quipped "I'd shut it down and give the money back to shareholders."[1]

By 2008, the situation looked very different. Apple was on track to book record sales of more than $32 billion and net profits of close to $4.7 billion. The stock price, which had traded as low as $6 a share in 2003 was about $170, with the market capitalization at $140 billion, which far surpassed that of Dell Computer which was about $41 billion. Driving the transformation were strong sales of Apple's iPod music player, music downloads from the iTunes store, and Apple's iPhone. In addition, strong sales of Apple's iMac laptop and desktop computers had lifted Apple's market share in the United States PC business to 8.5%, up from a low of under 3% in 2004.[2] Apple now ranked third in the United States PC market behind Dell with 32% and HP 25%. Moreover, analysts were predicting that the halo effect of the iPod and iPhone, together with Apple's adoption of Intel's microprocessor architecture, would drive strong sales going forward. To emphasize the broadening product portfolio of the company, Apple had dropped "computer" from its name.

For the first time in 20 years, it looked as if Apple, the perennial also-ran, might be seizing the initiative. But questions remained. Could the company continue to build on its momentum? Could the company break out of its niche and become a mainstream player in the computer industry? How sustainable was the iPod driven sales boom? Would the iPhone continue to gain market traction? And with new competitors coming along, could Apple hold onto its market leading position in the market for digital music players?

APPLE 1976–1997

The Early Years

Apple's genesis is the stuff of computer industry ledged.[3] On April Fools Day 1976, two young electronics enthusiasts, Steve Jobs and Steve Wozniak, started a company to sell a primitive personal computer that Wozniak's had designed. Steve Jobs was just 20 years old; Wozniak, or Woz as he was commonly called, was five years older. They had known each other for several years, having been introduced by a mutual friend who realized that they shared an interest in consumer electronics. Woz had designed the computer just for the fun of it. That is what people did in 1976. The idea that somebody would actually want to purchase his machine had not occurred

This case was prepared by Charles W. L. Hill, the University of Washington. Copyright Charles W. L. Hill © 2008. Reprinted by permission.

to Woz, but it did to Jobs. Jobs persuaded a reluctant Woz to form a company and sell the machine. The location of the company was Steve Jobs' garage. Jobs suggested they call the company Apple and their first machine, Apple I. They sold about 200 computers at $666 each. The price point was picked as something of a prank.

The Apple I had several limitations: no case, keyboard, or power supply being obvious ones. It also required several hours of laborious assembly by hand. By late 1976, Woz was working on a replacement to the Apple I, the Apple II.[4] In October 1976, with the Apple II under development, Jobs and Woz were introduced to Mike Markkula. Only 34, Markkula was already a retired millionaire, having made a small fortune at Fairchild and Intel. Markkula had no plans to get back into business anytime soon, but a visit to Jobs' garage changed all that. He committed to investing $92,000 for one-third of the company and promised that his ultimate investment would be $250,000. Stunned, Jobs and Woz agreed to let him join as a partner. It was a fateful decision. The combination of Woz's technical skills, Jobs' entrepreneurial zeal and vision, and Markkula's business savvy and connections, was a powerful one. Markkula told Jobs and Woz that neither of them had the experience to run a company and persuaded them to hire a President, Michael Scott, who had worked for Markkula at Fairchild.

The Apple II was introduced in 1977 at a price of $1,200. The first version was an integrated computer with a Motorola microprocessor and included a keyboard, a power supply, a monitor, and the BASIC programming software. It was Steve Jobs who pushed Woz to design an integrated machine: he wanted something that was easy to use, not just a toy for geeks. Jobs also insisted that the Apple II looked good. It had an attractive case and no visible screws or bolts. This differentiated it from most personal computers at the time that looked as if they had been assembled by hobbyists at home (as many had).

In 1978, Apple started to sell a version of the Apple II that incorporated something new: a disk drive. The disk drive turned out to be a critical innovation, for it enabled third-party developers to write software programs for the Apple II that could be loaded via floppy disks. Soon programs started to appear, among them EasyWriter, a basic word-processing program, and VisiCalc, a spreadsheet program. VisiCalc was an instant hit, and pulled in a new customer set, business types who could use VisiCalc for financial planning and accounting. Because VisiCalc was only available for the Apple II, it helped to drive demand for the machine.

By the end of 1980, Apple had sold more than 100,000 Apple IIs, making the company the leader in the embryonic personal computer industry. The company had successfully executed an IPO, was generating over $200 million in annual sales, and was profitable. With the Apple II series selling well, particularly in the education market, Apple introduced its next product, the Apple III, in the fall of 1980. It was a failure. The computer was filled with bugs and crashed constantly. The Apple III had been rushed to market too quickly. Apple reintroduced a reengineered Apple III in 1981, but it continued to be outsold by Apple II. Indeed, successive versions of the Apple II family, each an improvement on the proceeding version, continued to be produced by the company until 1993. In total, more than two million Apple II computers were sold. The series became a standard in American classrooms, where it was valued for its intuitive ease of use. Moreover, the Apple II was the mainstay of the company until the late 1980s, when an improved version of the Macintosh started to garner significant sales.

The IBM PC and Its Aftermath

Apple's success galvanized the world's largest computer company, IBM, to speed up development of its entry into the personal computer market. IBM had a huge and very profitable mainframe computer business, but it had so far failed to develop a personal computer, despite two attempts. To get to market quickly with this, its third PC project, IBM broke with its established practice of using its own proprietary technology to build the PC. Instead, IBM adopted "open architecture," purchasing the components required to make the IBM PC from other manufacturers. These components included a 16-bit microprocessor from Intel and an operating system, MS-DOS, which was licensed from a small Washington state company, Microsoft.

Microsoft had been in the industry from its inception, writing a version of the BASIC software programming language for the MITS Atari in 1977, the first PC ever produced. IBM's desire to license BASIC brought them to Redmond to talk with the company's CEO, Bill Gates. Gates, still in his early 20s, persuaded IBM to adopt a 16-bit processor (originally IBM had been considering a less-powerful 8-bit processor). He was also instrumental in pushing IBM to adopt an open architecture, arguing that IBM would benefit from the software and peripherals that other companies could then make.

Initially IBM was intent on licensing the CP/M operating system, produced by Digital Research, for the IBM PC. However, the current version of CP/M was designed to work on an 8-bit processor, and Gates had persuaded IBM that it needed a 16-bit processor. In a series of quick moves, Gates purchased a 16-bit operating system from a local company, Seattle Computer, for $50,000. Gates then hired the designer of the operating system, Tim Paterson, renamed the system MS-DOS and offered to license it to IBM. In what turned out to be a masterstroke, Gates persuaded IBM to accept a non-exclusive license for MS-DOS (which IBM called PC-DOS).

To stoke sales, IBM offered a number of applications for the IBM PC that were sold separately, including a version of VisiCalc, a word processor called EasyWriter, and well-known series of business programs from Peachtree Software.

Introduced in 1981, the IBM PC was an instant success. Over the next two years, IBM would sell more than 500,000 PCs, seizing market leadership from Apple. IBM had what Apple lacked, an ability to sell into corporate America. As sales of the IBM PC mounted, two things happened. First, independent software developers started to write programs to run on the IBM PC. These included two applications that drove adoptions of the IBM PC; word-processing programs (Word Perfect) and spreadsheet programs (Lotus 1-2-3). Second, the success of IBM gave birth to clone manufacturers who made "IBM-compatible" PCs that also utilized an Intel microprocessor and Microsoft's MS-DOS operating system. The first and most successful of the clone makers was Compaq, which in 1983 introduced its first personal computer, a 28-pound "portable" PC. In its first year, Compaq booked $111 million in sales, which at the time was a record for first year sales of a company. Before long, a profusion of IBM clone makers entered the market, including Tandy, Zenith, Leading Edge, and Dell. The last was established in 1984 by Michael Dell, then a student at the University of Texas, who initially ran the company out of his dorm room.

The Birth of the Macintosh

By 1980, two other important projects were underway at Apple; Lisa and the Macintosh. Lisa was originally conceived as a high-end business machine and the Macintosh as a low-end portable machine.

The development of both the Lisa, and ultimately the Macintosh, were influenced by two visits Steve Jobs paid to Xerox's fabled Palo Alto Research Center (PARC) in November and December 1979. Funded out of Xerox's successful copier business, PARC had been set up to do advanced research on office technology. Engineers at PARC had developed a number of technologies that were later to become central to personal computers, including a GUI, software programs that were made tangible through on screen icons, a computer mouse that let a user click on and drag on screen objects, and a laser printer. Jobs was astounded by what he saw at PARC and decided on the spot that these innovations had to be incorporated into Apple's machines.

Jobs initially pushed the Lisa team to implement PARC's innovations, but he was reportedly driving people on the project nuts with his demands, so President Mike Scott pulled him of the project. Jobs reacted by essentially hijacking the Macintosh project, and transforming it into a skunk works that would put his vision into effect. By one account:

> He hounded the people on the Macintosh project to do their best work. He sang their praises, bullied them unmercifully, and told them they weren't making a computer, they were making history. He promoted the Mac passionately, making people believe that he was talking about much more than a piece of office equipment.[5]

It was during this period that Bud Tribble, a software engineer on the Mac project, quipped that Steve Jobs could create a "reality distortion field." Jobs insisted that the Mac would ship by early 1982. Tribble knew that the schedule was unattainable, and when asked why he did not point this out to Jobs, he replied: "Steve insists that we're shipping in early 1982, and won't accept answers to the contrary. The best way to describe the situation is a term from Star Trek. Steve has a reality distortion field.... In his presence, reality is malleable. He can convince anyone of practically anything. It wears off when he's not around, but it makes it hard to have realistic schedules."[6]

Andy Hertzfeld, another engineer on the Macintosh project, thought Tribble was exaggerating, "until I observed Steve in action over the next few weeks. The reality distortion field was a confounding mélange of a charismatic rhetorical style, an indomitable will, and an eagerness to bend any fact to fit the purpose at hand. If one line of argument failed to persuade, he would deftly switch to another. Sometimes, he would throw you off balance by suddenly adopting your position as his own, without acknowledging that he ever thought differently.[7]

Back at Apple, things were changing too. Mike Scott had left the company after clashes with other executives, including Markkula, who had become chairman. Steve Jobs persuaded John Sculley to join Apple as CEO. Sculley was the former vice president of marketing at Pepsi, where he had become famous for launching the Pepsi Challenge. Jobs had reportedly asked Sculley, "Do you want to sell sugar water for the rest of your life, or do you want to change the world?" Sculley opted for changing the world. A Wharton MBA, Sculley had been hired for his marketing savvy, not his technical skills.

While the Lisa project suffered several delays, Jobs pushed the Macintosh team to finish the project and beat the Lisa team to market with a better product. Introduced in 1984, the Macintosh certainly captured attention for its stylish design and utilization of a graphical user interface, icons, and a mouse, all of which made the machine easy to use and were not found on any other personal computer at the time. Jobs, ever the perfectionist, again insisted that not a single screw should be visible on the case. He reportedly fired a designer who presented a mockup with a screw that could be seen by lifting a handle.

Early sales were strong; then they faltered. For all of its appeal, the Macintosh lacked some important features: it had no hard disk drive, only one floppy drive, and insufficient computer memory. Moreover, there were few applications available to run on the machine, and the Mac proved to be a more difficult machine to develop applications for than the IBM PC and its clones. Jobs, however, seemed oblivious to the problems, and continued to talk about outsized sales projections, even when it was obvious to all around him that they were unattainable.

In early 1985, Apple posted its first loss. Aware that drastic action was necessary, but could not be taken while Jobs was running the Macintosh division, Sculley got backing from the board of directors to strip Jobs of his management role and oversight of the Macintosh division. In late 1985, an embittered Jobs resigned from Apple, sold all of his stock, and left to start another computer company, aptly named NeXT.

....

Exhibit 1   The Macintosh

Source: Courtesy of Apple Inc.

The Golden Years

With Jobs gone, Sculley shut down the Lisa line, which had done poorly in the market due to a very high price point of $10,000. He pushed developers to fix the problems with the Macintosh. In January 1986, a new version of the Macintosh, the Mac Plus, was introduced. This machine fixed the shortcomings of the original Mac, and sales started to grow again.

What also drove sales higher was Apple's domination of the desktop publishing market. Several events came together to make this happen. Researchers from Xerox PARC formed a company, Adobe, to develop and commercialize the PostScript page description language. PostScript enabled the visual display and printing of high quality page layouts loaded with graphics (e.g., colored charts, line drawings, and photos). Apple licensed PostScript and used it as the output for its Apple LaserWriter, which was introduced in 1985. Shortly afterward, a Seattle company, Aldus, introduced a program called PageMaker for the Mac. PageMaker used Adobe's PostScript page description language for output. Although Aldus introduced a version of PageMaker for MS-DOS in 1986, Apple already had a lead, and with the Mac's GUI interface appealing to graphic artists, Apple's tightened its hold on the desktop publishing segment. Apple's position in desktop publishing was further strengthened by the release of Adobe Illustrator in 1987 (a freehand drawing program) and Adobe Photoshop in 1990.

The period between 1986 and 1991 were in many ways the golden years for Apple. Because it made both hardware and software, Apple was able to control all aspects of its computers, offering a complete desktop solution that allowed customers to "plug and play." With the Apple II series still selling well in the education market, and the Mac dominating desktop publishing, Apple was able to charge a premium price for its products. Gross margins on the Mac line got as high as 55%. In 1990, Apple sales reached $5.6 billion; its global market share, which had fallen rapidly as the IBM-compatible PC market had grown, stabilized at 8%. The company had a strong balance sheet and was the most profitable personal computer manufacturer in the world.

During this period executives at Apple actively debated the merits of licensing the Mac operating system to other computer manufacturers, allowing them to make Mac clones. Sculley was in favor of this move. So was Microsoft's Bill Gates, who wrote two memos to Sculley laying out an argument for licensing the Mac OS. Gates argued that the closed architecture of the Macintosh prevented independent investment in the standard by third parties, and put Apple at a disadvantage against the IBM PC standard. However, some senior executives at Apple were against the licensing strategy, arguing that once Apple licensed its intellectual property, it would be difficult to protect it. In one version of events, senior executives debated the decision at a meeting, and took a vote on whether to license. Given the controversial nature of the decision, it was decided that the vote in favor had to be unanimous. It was not: a single executive voted against the licensing decision, and it was never pursued.[8] In another version of events, Jean-Louis Gassee, head of R&D at Apple, vigorously opposed Sculley's plans to clone, and Sculley backed down.[9] Gassee was deeply distrustful of Microsoft and Bill Gates and believed that Gates' probably had an ulterior motive, given how the company benefited from the IBM standard.

Ironically, in 1985 Apple had licensed its "visual displays" to Microsoft. Reportedly Gates had strong-armed Sculley, threatening that Microsoft would stop developing crucial applications for the Mac unless Apple granted Microsoft the license. At the time, Microsoft had launched development of its own GUI. Called Windows, it mimicked the look and feel of the Mac operating system, and Microsoft did not want to be stopped by a lawsuit from Apple. Several years later, when Apple filed a lawsuit against Microsoft, arguing that Windows 3.1 imitated the "look and feel" of the Mac, Microsoft was able to point to the 1985 license agreement to defend its right to develop Windows: a position that the judge in the case agreed with.

1990–1997

By the early 1990s, the prices of IBM-compatible PCs were declining rapidly. As long as Apple was the only company to sell machines that utilized GUIs, its differential appeal gave it an advantage over MS-DOS-based PCs with their clunky text-based interfaces, and the premium price could be justified. However, in 1990, Microsoft introduced Windows 3.1, its own GUI that sat on top of MS-DOS, and Apple's differential appeal began to erode. Moreover, the dramatic growth of the PC market had turned Apple into a niche player. Faced with the choice of writing software to work with MS-DOS/Windows operating systems and Intel microprocessors (now the dominant standard found on 90% of all personal computers), or the Mac OS and Motorola processors, developers logically opted for the dominant standard (desktop publishing remained an exception to this rule). Reflecting on this logic, Dan Eilers, then vice president of strategic planning at Apple, reportedly stated that "The company was on a glide path to history."[10]

Sculley too, thought that the company was in trouble. Apple seemed boxed into its niche. Apple had a high cost structure. It spent significantly more on R&D as a percentage of sales than its rivals. (In 1990, Apple spent 8% of sales on R&D, Compaq about 4%.) Its microprocessor supplier, Motorola, lacked the scale of Intel, which translated into higher costs for Apple. Moreover, Apple's small market share made it difficult to recoup the spiraling cost of developing a new operating system, which by 1990 amounted to at least $500 million.

Sculley's game plan to deal with these problems involved a number of steps.[11] First, he appointed himself chief technology officer in addition to CEO—a move that raised some eyebrows given Sculley's marketing background. Second, he committed the company to bring out a low-cost version of the Macintosh to compete with IBM clones. The result was the Mac Classic, introduced in October 1990 and priced at $999. He also cut prices for the Macs and Apple IIs by 30%. The reward was a 60% increase in sales volume, but lower gross margins. So, third, he cut costs. The workforce at Apple was reduced by 10%, the salaries of top managers (including Sculley's) were cut by as much as 15%, and Apple shifted much of its manufacturing to subcontractors (for example, the PowerBook was built in Japan—a first for Apple). Fourth, he called for the company to maintain its technological lead by bringing out hit products every 6 to 12 months. The results include the first Apple portable, the PowerBook notebook, which was shipped in late 1991 and garnered very favorable reviews, and the Apple Newton handheld computer, which bombed. Fifth, Apple entered into an alliance with IBM, whose managers realized that it had lost its hold on the PC market to companies such as Intel, Microsoft, and Compaq.

The IBM alliance had several elements. One was the decision to adopt IBM's Power PC microprocessor architecture, which IBM would also use in its own offerings. A second was the establishment of two joint ventures: Taligent to create a new operating system, and Kaleida to develop multimedia applications. A third was a project to help IBM and Apple machines work better together.

Although Sculley's game plan helped to boost the top line, the bottom line shrunk in 1993 due to a combination of low gross margins and continuing high costs. In 1994, Sculley left Apple. He was replaced by Michael Spindler, a German engineer who had gained prominence as head of Apple Europe.

In 1994, Spindler finally took the step that had been long debated in the company: he decided to license the Mac-OS to a handful of companies, allowing them to make Mac clones. The Mac-OS would be licensed for $40 a copy. It was too little too late—the industry was already waiting for the introduction of Microsoft's Windows 95. When it came, it became clear that Apple was in serious trouble. Windows 95 was a big improvement over Windows 3.1, and it closed the gap between Windows and the Mac. While many commentators criticized Apple for not licensing the Mac-OS in the 1980s, when it still had a big lead over Microsoft, ironically Bill Gates disagreed. In a 1996 interview with *Fortune*, Gates noted:

> As Apple has declined, the basic criticism seems to be that Apple's strategy of doing a unique hardware/software combination was doomed to fail. I disagree. Like all strategies, this one fails if you execute poorly. But the strategy can work, if Apple picks its markets and renews the innovation in the Macintosh.[12]

Spindler responded to Windows 95 by committing Apple to develop a next-generation operating system for the Macintosh—something that raised questions about the Taligent alliance with IBM. At the end of 1995, IBM and Apple parted ways, ending Taligent, which after $500 million in investments, had produced little.

By then, Spindler had other issues on his mind. The latter half of 1995 proved to be a disaster for Apple. The company seemed unable to predict demand for its products. It overestimated demand for its low-end Macintosh Performa computers and was left with excess inventory, while underestimating demand for its high end machines. To compound matters, its new PowerBooks had to be recalled after batteries started to catch fire, and a price war in Japan cut margins in one of its best markets. As a consequence, in the last quarter of 1995, gross margins slumped to 15%, down from 29% in 1994, and Apple lost $68 million. Spindler responded in January 1996 by announcing 1,300 layoffs. He suggested that up to 4,000 might ultimately go—some 23% of the workforce.[13] That was his last significant act. He was replaced in February by Gilbert Amelio.

Amelio, who joined Apple from National Semiconductor where he had gained a reputation for his turnaround skills, lasted just 17 months. He followed through on Spindler's plans to cut personnel and stated that Apple would return to its differentiation strategy. His hope was that the new Mac operating system would help, but work on that was in total disarray. He took the decision to scrap the project after an investment of more than $500 million. Instead, Apple purchased NeXT, the computer company founded by none other than Steve Jobs, for $425 million. The NeXT machines had received strong reviews but had gained no market traction due to a lack of supporting applications. Amelio felt that the NeXT OS could be adapted to run on the Mac. He also hired Steve Jobs as a consultant, but Jobs was rarely seen at Apple; he was too busy running Pixar, his computer animation company that was riding a wave of success after a huge hit with the animated movie, *Toy Story*.[14]

Amelio's moves did nothing to stop the slide in Apple's fortunes. By mid-1997, market share had slumped to 3%, from 9% when Amelio took the helm. The company booked a loss of $742 million in 1996 and was on track to lose another $400 million in 1997. It was too much for the board. In July 1997, Amelio was fired. With market share falling, third-party developers and distributors were rethinking their commitments to Apple. Without them, the company would be dead.

THE RETURN OF STEVE JOBS

Following Amelio's departure, Steve Jobs was appointed interim CEO. In April 1998, he took the position on a permanent basis, while staying on at Pixar as CEO. Jobs moved quickly to fix the bleeding. His first act was to visit Bill Gates and strike a deal with Microsoft. Microsoft agreed to invest $150 million in Apple and to continue producing Office for the Mac through until at least 2002. Then he ended the licensing deals with the clone makers, spending more than $100 million to acquire the assets of the leading Mac clone maker, Power Computing, including its license. Jobs killed slow-selling products, most notably the Apple Newton handheld computer, and reduced the number of product lines from 60 to just four. He also pushed the company into online distribution, imitating Dell Computer's direct-selling model. While these fixes brought the company time and a favorable reaction from the stock market, they were not a recipe for growth.

New Computer Offerings

Almost immediately, Jobs started to think about a new product that would embody the spirit of Apple. What emerged in May 1998 was the iMac. The differentiator for the iMac was not its software, its power, or its monitor: it was the design of the machine itself. A self-contained unit that combined the monitor and central processing unit in translucent teal and with curved lines, the iMac was a bold departure in a world dominated by putty-colored PC boxes.

To develop the iMac, Jobs elevated a team of designers headed by Jonathan Ive, giving them an unprecedented say in the development project. Ive's team worked closely with engineers, manufacturers, marketers and Jobs himself. To understand how to make a plastic shell look exciting rather than cheap, the designers visited a candy factory to study the finer points of making jelly beans. They spent months working with Asian partners designing a sophisticated process capable of producing millions of iMacs a year. The designers also pushed for the internal electronics to be redesigned, to make sure that they looked good through the thick shell. Apple may have spent as much as $65 a machine on the casing, compared with perhaps $20 for the average PC.[15]

Priced at $1,299, iMac sales were strong, with orders placed for 100,000 units even before the machine was available. Moreover, according to Apple's research, one-third of iMac purchases were by first-time buyers according to Apple's research.[16] The iMac line was continually updated, with faster

Exhibit 2 The iMac and iBook

Source: Courtesy of Apple, Inc.

processors, more memory, and bigger hard drives being added. The product was also soon available in many different colors. In 1999, Apple followed up the iMac with introduction of the iBook portable. Aimed at consumers and students, the iBook had the same design theme as the iMac and was priced aggressively at $1,599.

Sales of the iMac and iBook helped push Apple back into profitability. In 1999, the company earned $420 million on sales of $6.1 billion. In 2000, it made $611 million on sales of almost $8 billion.

To keep sales growing, Apple continued to invest in the development of a new operating system, based on the technology acquired from NeXT. After three years work by nearly 1,000 software engineers and a cost of approximately $1 billion, the first version of Apple's new operating systems was introduced in 2001. Known as OS X, it garnered rave reviews from analysts who saw the UNIX-based program as offering superior stability and faster speed than the old Mac OS. OS X also had an enhanced ability to run multiple programs at once, to support multiple users, connected easily to other devices such as digital camcorders, and was easier for developers to write applications for. In typical Apple fashion, OS X also sported a well-designed and intuitively appealing interface. Since 2001, new versions of OS X have been introduced almost once a year. The most recent version, OS X Leopard, was introduced in 2008 and retailed for $129.

To get the installed base of Mac users to upgrade to OS X, who at the time numbered 25 million, Apple had to offer applications. The deal with Microsoft ensured that its popular Office program would be available for the OS X. Steve Jobs had assumed that the vote of confidence by Microsoft would encourage other third-party developers to write programs for OS X, but it did not always happen. Most significantly, in 1998, Adobe Systems refused to develop a Mac version of their consumer video-editing program, which was already available for Windows PCs.

Shocked, Jobs directed Apple to start working on its own applications. The first fruits of this effort were two video-editing programs: Final Cut Pro for professionals and iMovie for consumers. Next was iLife, a bundle of multimedia programs preinstalled on every Mac, which included iMovie, iDVD, iPhoto, Gargage Band, and the iTunes digital jukebox. Apple also developed its own Web browser, Safari.

Meanwhile, Apple continued to update its computer lines with eye-catching offerings. In 2001, Apple introduced its Titanium PowerBook G4 notebooks. Cased in Titanium, these ultralight and fast notebooks featured a clean post-industrial look that marked a distinct shift from the whimsical look of the iMac and iBook. As with the iMac, Jonathan Ive's design team played a central part in the products development. A core team of designers set up a design studio in a San Francisco warehouse, far

Exhibit 3 iMac-5 introduced in 2004

Source: Courtesy of Apple, Inc.

away from Apple's main campus. They worked for six weeks on the basic design, and then headed to Asia to negotiate for widescreen flat panel displays and to work with tool makers.[17]

The Titanium notebooks were followed by a redesigned desktop line that appealed to the company's graphic design customers, including the offering of elegantly designed very wide screen cinema displays. In 2004, Ive's design team came out with yet another elegant offering, the iMac G5 computer, which *PC Magazine* described as a "simple stunning all in one design."[18] This was followed in 2008 with the release of yet another strong design, the ultra-thin MacBook Air that weighed just 3 pounds and was only 0.76 of an inch thick at its widest point.

For all of Apple's undisputed design excellence and the loyalty of its core user base, graphic artists and students, during the early 2000s Apple's global market share remained anemic, trailing far behind industry leaders Dell, Hewlett Packard, and IBM/Lenovo. Weak demand, combined with its low market share, translated into another loss for Apple in 2001, leading some to question the permanence of Steve Job's turnaround. However, while Apple's share in its core U.S. market fell to

less than 3% in 2004, it started to pick up again in 2005, and the company made strong share gains in 2006–2008 (see Exhibit 4). Momentum was particularly strong in the United States, where

Exhibit 4 Worldwide Market Share and United States Market Share, Second Quarter 2008

Company	Global Market Share (%)	U.S. Market Share (%)
HP	18.1%	25.3%
Dell	15.6%	31.9%
Acer	9.4%	8.1%
Lenova	7.8%	4.0%
Toshiba	4.4%	5.5%
Apple	1.9%	8.5%
Other	42.9%	16.8%
Total	100%	100%

Source: Gartner Press release: "Worldwide PC Market Grew 16% in Second Quarter of 2008," July 16, 2008.

Apple shipments surged. During the second quarter of 2008, for example, Apple's shipments were up over 40% compared to the prior year, and its growth rate was three times that of the industry. Driving growth during the 2005–2008 period, according to many analysts, was the surging popularity of Apple's iPod music player and, in 2007, the iPhone. These two products had raised Apple's profile among younger consumers and was having a spill-over effect on Mac sales.[19]

Intel Inside, Windows on the Desktop

Since the company's inception, Apple had not used Intel microprocessors, which had become the industry standard for microprocessors since the introduction of the IBM PC in 1981. In June 2005, Apple announced that it would start to do so. Driving the transition was growing frustration with the performance of the PowerPC chip line made by IBM that Apple had been using for over a decade. The PowerPC had failed to keep up with the Intel chips, which were both faster and had lower power consumption—something that was very important in the portable computer market, in which Apple had a respectable market share.

The transition created significant risks for Apple. Old applications and OS X had to be rewritten to run on Intel processors. By the spring of 2006, Apple had produced Intel compatible versions of OS X and its own applications, but many other applications had not been rewritten for Intel chips. To make the transition easier, Apple provided a free software program, known as Rosetta, which enabled users to run older applications on Intel-based Macs. Moreover, Apple went a step farther by issuing a utility program, known as Boot Camp, which enabled Mac owners to run Windows XP on their machines. Boot Camp was included was part of OS X Leopard, and allows Mac owners to run Windows XP or Vista if they should so chose.

Reviews of Apple's Intel-based machines were generally favorable, with many reviewers noting the speed improvement over the older PowerPC Macs.[20] In the fall of 2006, Apple reported that its transition to an Intel-based architecture was complete, some six months ahead of schedule. The move to Intel architecture may have helped Apple to close the price differential that had long existed between Windows-based PCs and Apple's offerings. According to one

analysis, by September 2006, Apple's products were selling at a *discount* to comparable product offerings from Dell and Hewlett Packard.[21]

Moving into Retail

In 2001, Apple made another important strategic shift: the company opened its first retail store. In an industry that had long relied on third-party retailers or direct sales, as in the case of Dell, this shift seemed risky. One concern was that Apple might encounter a backlash from Apple's long-standing retail partners. Another was that Apple would never be able to generate the sales volume required to justify expensive retail space; the product line seemed too thin. However, Apple clearly felt that it was hurt by a lack of retail presence. Many computer retailers did not carry Apple machines, and some of those that did often buried Mac displays deep in the store.

From the start, Apple's stores exhibited the same stylish design that characterized its products: clean lines, attractive displays, and postindustrial feel (see Exhibit 6). Steve Jobs himself was intimately involved in the design process. Indeed, he is one of the named inventors on a patent Apple secured for the design of the signature glass staircase found in many stores, and he was apparently personally involved in the design of a glass cube atop a store on New York's Fifth Avenue that opened in 2006. In an interview, Jobs noted that "We spent a lotof time designing the store, and it deserves to be built perfectly."[22]

Customers and analysts were immediately impressed by the product fluency that employees in Apple stores exhibited. Indeed, one hallmark of Apple stores seems to be the personal attention paid to customers by smiling sales staff, an approach that is remonstrant of upscale retailers like Nordstrom. They also liked the highlight of many stores, a "genius bar" where technical experts helped customers fix problems with their Apple products. The wide-open interior space, however, did nothing to allay the fears of critics that Apple's product portfolio was just too narrow to generate the traffic required to support premium space.

The critics could not have been more wrong. Spurred on by booming sales of the iPod, Apple's stores did exceptionally well. By early 2008, Apple had some 200 stores in upscale locations that generated some 20% of the company's total revenues, and the company was planning to open another

Exhibit 5 Inside an Apple Store

Source: Courtesy of Apple, Inc.

40 stores. Sales per square foot are apparently now significantly in excess of $4,000, making Apple the envy of other retailers.[23]

The iPod Revolution

In the late 1990s and early 2000s, the music industry was grappling with the implications of two new technologies. The first was the development of inexpensive portable MP3 players that could store and play digital music files, such as Diamond Media's

Rio, which was introduced in 1997 and could hold two hours of music. The second was the rise of peer-to-peer computer networks, such as Napster, Kazaa, Grokster, and Morpheus, that enabled individuals to efficiently swap digital files over the Internet. By the early 2000s, millions of individuals were downloading music files over the Internet without the permission of the copyright holders, the music publishing companies. For the music industry, this development had been devastating. After years of steady growth, global sales of music peaked in 1999 at $38.5 billion, falling to $32 billion in 2003. Despite the fall in

Exhibit 6 Sales of Apple's Main Product Lines 2003–2007 (millions)

	2003	2004	2005	2006	2007
Computers	$4,491	$4,923	$6,275	$ 7,375	$10,314
iPod	$ 345	$1,306	$4,540	$ 7,676	$ 8,305
iTunes	$ 36	$ 278	$ 899	$ 1,885	$ 2,496
Software	$ 644	$ 821	$1,091	$ 1,279	$ 1,508
Peripherals	$ 691	$ 951	$1,126	$ 1,100	$ 1,260
iPhone					$ 123

sales, the International Federation of the Phonographic Industry (IFPI) claimed that the demand for music was higher than ever, but the decline in sales reflected the fact that "the commercial value of music is being widely devalued by mass copying and piracy."[24]

The music industry had tried to counter piracy over the Internet by taking legal action to shut down the peer-to-peer networks, such as Napster, and filing lawsuits against individuals who made large numbers of music files available over the Internet. Its success had been limited, in part because peer-to-peer networks offered tremendous utility to consumers. They were fast, immediate, and enabled consumers to unbundled albums, downloading just the tracks they wanted while ignoring junk filler tracks. And, of course, they were free.

The music industry was desperate for a legal alternative to illegal downloading. Its own initiatives, introduced in 2002, had gained little traction. MusicNet, which offered songs from Warner Music, BMG, and EMI, had a single subscription plan: $9.85 a month for 100 streams and 100 downloads. After 30 days downloads expired and could not be played. Pressplay, which offered music from Sony, Universal, and EMI, had four subscription plans, from $9.95 to $24.95 a month, for up to 1,000 streams and 100 downloads. The higher subscription fee service from Pressplay allowed users to burn up to 20 songs a month onto CDs that would not expire, but no more than two songs could be burned from any one artist.[25]

Then along came the iPod and iTunes. These products were born out of an oversight: in the late 1990s, when consumers were starting to burn their favorite CDs, Macs did not have CD burners, or software to manage their digital music collections. Realizing the mistake, CEO Steve Jobs ordered Apple's software developers to create the iTunes program to help Mac users manage their growing digital music collections. The first iTunes program led to the concept of the iPod. If people were going to maintain the bulk of their music collection on a computer, they needed portable MP3 players to take music with them—a Sony Walkman for the digital age. While there were such devices on the market already, they could only hold a few dozen songs each.

To run the iPod, Apple licensed software from PortalPlayer. Apple also learned that Toshiba was building a tiny 1.8-inch hard drive that could hold more than 1,000 songs. Apple quickly cut a deal with Toshiba, giving it exclusive rights to the drive for 18 months. Meanwhile, Apple focused on designing the user interface, the exterior styling, and the synchronization software to make it work with the Mac. As with so many product offerings unveiled since Jobs had returned to the helm, the design team led by Jonathan Ive played a pivotal role in giving birth to the iPod. Ive's team worked in secrecy in San Francisco. The members, all paid extremely well by industry standards, worked together in a large open studio with little personal space. The team was able to figure out how to put a layer of clear plastic over the white and black core of an iPod, giving it tremendous depth of texture. The finish was superior to other MP3 players, with no visible screws or obvious joins between parts. The serial number of the iPod was not on a sticker, as with most products, it was elegantly etched onto the back of the device. This attention to detail and design elegance, although not with cost implications, was to turn the iPod into a fashion accessory.[26]

The iPod was unveiled in October 2001 to mixed reviews. The price of $399 was significantly above that of competing devices, and because the iPod only worked with Apple computers, it seemed destined to be a niche product. However, initial sales were strong. It turned out that consumers were willing to pay a premium price for the iPod's huge storage capacity. Moreover, Jobs made the call to develop a version of the iPod that would be compatible with Windows. After it was introduced in mid-2002, sales took off.

By this time, Jobs was dealing with a bigger strategic issue—how to persuade the music companies to make their music available for legal downloads. Jobs met with executives from the major labels. He persuaded them that it was in their best interest to support a legal music download business as an alternative to widespread illegal downloading of music over peer-to-peer networks that the music industry had not been able to shut down. People would pay to download music over the Internet, he argued. Although all of the labels were setting up their own online businesses, Jobs felt that because they were limited to selling music owned by the parent companies, demand would also be limited. What was needed was a reputable independent online music retailer, and Apple fit the bill. If it was going to work, however, all of the labels needed to get on board. Under Jobs' scheme, iTunes files would be downloaded for $0.99 each. The only portable digital player that the files could be stored and played on was an iPod. Job's argument was that this closed world made it easier to protect copyrighted material from unauthorized distribution.

Jobs also meet with 20 of the world's top recording artists, including U2's Bono, Sheryl Crow, and Mick Jagger. His pitch to them was that digital distribution is going to happen, and the best way to protect your interests is to support a legal online music distribution business. Wooed by Jobs, these powerful stakeholders encouraged the music recording companies to take Apple's proposal seriously.[27]

By early 2003, Jobs had all of the major labels onboard. Launched in April 2003, within days it was clear that Apple had a major hit on its hands. A million songs were sold in the first week. In mid-2004, iTunes passed the 100 million-download mark, and sales kept accelerating, hitting the 150 million-download mark in October 2004. At that point, customers were downloading more than 4 million songs per week, which represented a run rate of more than 200 million a year. While Steve Jobs admitted that Apple did not make much money from iTunes downloads, probably only $0.10 a song, it did make good margins on sales of the iPod—and sales of the iPod ballooned (see Exhibit 6).

As the installed base of iPods expanded, an ecosystem of companies selling iPod accessories emerged. The accessories include speakers, headphones, and add-on peripherals that allowed iPods to record voice, charge on the go, play tunes over the radio, or use the iPod wirelessly with a remote. There are also cases, neck straps, belt clips, and so on. By 2006, it was estimated that there were more than 100 companies in this system. Apple collects an unspecified royalty from companies whose products access the iPod's ports and benefits indirectly from the preference of buyers for the iPod over competing products that lack the same accessories.[28]

Success such as this attracts competitors. RealNetworks, Walmart, Yahoo!, Napster, and Amazon all set up legal downloading services to compete with iTunes. However, iTunes continued to outsell its rivals by a wide margin. In mid-2008, iTunes was accounting for about 90% of all legal music downloads.[29] iTunes was also the largest music retailer in the United States—the other three all had physical stores.

The iPod also had plenty of competition including offerings from SanDisk and Microsoft (Zune). Many of these were priced aggressively, well designed, and had as much storage capacity as the iPod. Few, however, manage to gain share against the iPod, which accounted for 73.5% of all unit sales in the United States in July 2008 and 88% of total dollar sales. SanDisk was second with an 8% share of unit sales, and Microsoft was third with a 2.6% share of unit sales. Moreover, Apple's seems to have yet again stolen a march on its competitors in late 2007 when it introduced the iPod touch, which had Web-browsing capability and quickly generated strong sales volume. However, the overall market for digital music players was maturing by 2007, with growth rates dropping into the low single digits. Apple needed another new product driver to keep sales expanding.

The iPhone

In June 2007, Apple introduced the iPhone. First announced in January 2007, the iPhone was essentially a smartphone that was also able to browse the Web, take pictures, and function as a digital music player. The iPhone was differentiated from established smartphone offerings by revolutionary touch screen design that replaced the traditional mechanical keypad and allowed users to quickly and easily switch between functions. The phone used a version of Apple's OS X operating system and the company's Safari Web browser. Apple struck a deal with AT&T, under which it was to be the exclusive provider of wireless service for the iPhone. Under the deal, AT&T would share a percentage of its service fees from iPhone users with Apple (the percentage was rumored to be 30%, but neither company would confirm this).

Priced between $499 and $599 depending on the model, the iPhone was positioned at the high end of the smartphone market. Some were skeptical that the device would be able to gain share from established smartphones such as Research in Motion with its Blackberry and offerings from Palm, Motorola, and Nokia, all of which had gained a following among business users.

Steve Jobs announced that the goal was to try and grab 1% of the total global market for cell phones in the first full year that the iPhone was on the market. With a total market in excess of 1 billion units, most of which were not smartphones, this suggested a goal of selling 10 million iPhones in fiscal 2008 (which ended September 2008).

There was some disappointment that the iPhone would use AT&T's slower data network, rather than the faster 3G network that was more suited to Web browsing. There was also disappointment that the iPhone did not contain a GPS location-finding function.

Despite the high price and perceived limitations, early demand for the iPhone was strong, with long lines forming outside Apple stores on the day the device was released. Although some consumers experienced activation problems, most were happy with their purchase. The device got rave reviews for its design elegance, ease of use, and compelling touch screen interface. Apple sold more than 250,000 iPhones in the first two days the device was on the market; it soon became clear that the company had another hit on its hands.

In June 2008, Apple introduced a second version of its iPhone, the iPhone 3G. Designed to run on a faster 3G networks, the new phone also incorporated GPS functionality. AT&T was again picked as the exclusive service provider in the United States. However, Apple shifted the business model. Instead of giving a share of service fees to Apple, AT&T agreed to pay a subsidy to Apple for each iPhone sold. The subsidy allowed Apple to drop the price for the iPhone to as low as $199 for an entry-level model. Yet again, long lines formed outside Apple stores, and in the first three days, the iPhone 3G was on the market, more than 1 million units were sold. By August, analysts were issuing forecasts calling for Apple to sell 11 million iPhones in fiscal 2008, and 25 million in 2009, with much of the growth coming from rapidly expanding sales in 40 other countries. While the 25 million still only represented only a small slice of the 1.2 billion wireless handsets forecast to be sold globally in 2009, it would make Apple one of the top-three makers of smartphones in the world and the only one with a strong position among consumers as opposed to business users.[30]

One feature of the iPhone 3G that started to garner a lot of attention was the rapid growth in third-party applications for the phone. In July 2008, Apple opened an online store for applications that were written to run on the iPhone. In the first month, the phone was on the market, more than 60 million programs were downloaded. While many applications were free, Apple was selling $1 million worth of applications a day and suggested that sales could reach a $500 million annual run rate fairly quickly. Apple kept 30% of the proceeds from application sales, just about enough to cover the costs of the store, letting program creators keep the other 70%. Among the big sellers were some games applications, such as Super Monkeyball from Sega, which sold 300,000 copies in 20 days at $9.99 a copy.[31]

THE PERSONAL COMPUTER INDUSTRY IN THE 2000S

For all of its product success, Apple remained a niche player in the computer industry, albeit one that was gaining share among consumers. After years of growth, sales of PCs had fallen for the first time ever in 2001, but the growth path had soon resumed. In 2004, 179 million PCs were sold worldwide, and by 2008 this figure had increased to 293 million.[32] Sales to consumers accounted for about 1/3 of this figure, and some 60% of the year on year growth in PC sales was now coming from emerging markets.

The industry is characterized by a handful of players who collectively account for about half the market, and a long tail of small enterprises that produce unbranded or locally branded "white box" computers, often selling their machines at a significant discount to globally branded products.

Among the larger players, consolidation has been a theme for several years. In 2002, Hewlett Packard acquired Compaq, Gateway and eMachines merged in 2004, and the Chinese firm Lenovo acquired the personal computer business of IBM in 2005. The large PC firms compete aggressively by offering ever-more powerful machines, producing them as efficiently as possible and lowering prices to sell more volume. The average selling price of a PC has fallen from approximately $1,700 in 1999 to less than $1,000 in 2006, and projections are that it may continued to fall, fueled in part by aggressive competition between Dell Computer and Hewlett Packard.[33]

All of these players focus on the design, assembly, and sales of personal computers, while purchasing the vast majority of component parts from independent companies. In recent years, the top personal computer companies have reduced their R&D

spending as a percentage of sales, as the industry has transitioned toward a commodity business.

The existence of the long tail of white box makers is made possible by the open architecture of the dominant PC standard based on Intel-compatible microprocessors, and a Microsoft operating system, and the low-tech nature of the assembly process. The components for these boxes, which are themselves commodities, can be purchased cheaply off the shelf. White box makers have a strong position in many developing nations. In Mexico, for example, domestic brands accounted for 60% of all sales in 2005, up from 44% in 2000. In Latin America as a whole, 70% of personal computers are produced locally. White box makers have a much weaker position in the United States, Western Europe, and Japan, where consumers display a stronger preference for branded products that incorporate leading-edge technology. In contrast, in the developing world, consumers are willing to accept older components if it saves a few hundred dollars.[34]

During the 1990s and early 2000s, Dell grew rapidly to capture the market lead. Dell's success was based on the inventory management efficiencies associated with its direct selling model (Dell could build machines to order, which reduced its need to hold inventory). Dell was also helped by the problems Hewlett Packard faced when it merged with Compaq. By 2005, however, a resurgent Hewlett Packard had lowered its costs, could price more aggressively, and was starting to gain ground against Dell. Apple continued to be the odd man out in this industry, and was the only major manufacturer that did not adhere to the Windows architecture.

STRATEGIC ISSUES

As 2008 drew to a close, Apple was in an enviable position. Revenue and profits growth was strong, driven by new product introductions, such as the iPhone, and strong sales of Apple's line of personal computers. While the iPod boom was starting to run its course as the market reached saturation, the company might have found a new growth driver in its iPhone business. In the PC market, Apple was still a niche player, albeit one with renewed growth prospects and an increasingly strong brand among consumers. In the business market, by contrast, Apple had very limited presence. Going forward, observers wondered whether Apple could continue to maintain its growth rate, particularly given concerns that CEO Steve Jobs, considered the architect of Apple's revival, was ill and might not be at the helm for much longer.

Endnotes

1. Quoted in Pete Burrows, "Steve Jobs" Magic Kingdom, *BusinessWeek,* February 6, 2006, 62–68.
2. N. Wingfield, "Apple Unveils New Computers," *Wall Street Journal,* August 8, 2006, B3. "Apple Increases PC Market Share, Ranks Third Behind Dell and HP," ChattahBox.com.
3. Much of this section is drawn from P. Freiberger and M. Swaine, *Fire in the Valley* (New York: McGraw-Hill, 2000).
4. For a detailed history of the development of the Apple II, see Steve Weyhrich, *Apple II History,* http://apple2history .org/history/ah01.html.
5. P. Freiberger and M. Swaine, *Fire in the Valley,* 357.
6. Andy Hertzfeld, "Reality Distortion Field," http://www .folklore.org/ProjectView.py?project=Macintosh.
7. Ibid.
8. This version of events was told to the author by a senior executive who was present in the room at the time.
9. Jim Carlton, "Playing Catch Up—Apple Finally Gives in an Attempts Cloning," *Wall Street Journal,* October 17, 1994, A1.
10. D. B. Yoffie, "Apple Computer 1992," Harvard Business School Case no. 792–081.
11. Andrew Kupfer, "Apple's Plan to Survive and Grow," *Fortune,* May 4, 1992, 68–71. B. R. Schlender, "Yet Another Strategy for Apple," *Fortune,* October 22, 1990. 81–85.
12. B. Schlender, "Paradise Lost: Apple's Quest for Life after Death," *Fortune,* February 1996, 64–72.
13. Jim Carlton, "Apple's Losses to Stretch into 2nd Period," *Wall Street Journal,* January 18, 1996, B7.
14. Peter Burrows, "Dangerous Limbo," *BusinessWeek,* July 21, 1997, 32.
15. Peter Burrows, The Man Behind Apple's Design Magic," *BusinessWeek,* September 2005, 27–34.
16. A. Reinhardt, "Can Steve Jobs Keep His Mojo Working?" *BusinessWeek,* August 2, 1999, 32.

17. Peter Burrows, The Man Behind Apple's Design Magic," 27–34.
18. Apple iMac G5 Review, *PC Magazine,* http://www .pcmag.com/article2/0,1759,1648796,00.asp.
19. *Standard & Poor's Industry Surveys,* Computers: Hardware, "Global Demand for PCs Accelerates," December 8, 2005. Mark Veverka, *Wall Street Journal,* "Barron's Insight: Apple's Horizon Brightens," July 23, 2006, A4.
20. Peter Lewis, "Apple's New Core," *Fortune,* March 29, 2006, 182–184.
21. Citigroup Global Markets, "Apple Computer: New Products Position Apple Well for Holidays," September 13, 2006.
22. N. Wingfield, "How Apple's Store Strategy Beat the Odds," *Wall Street Journal,* May 17, 2006, B1.
23. M. Frazier, "The Bigger Apple," *Advertising Age,* February 13, 2006, pp, 4–6. K. Hafner, "Inside Apple Stores," *New York Times,* December 27, 2007, C1.
24. *IFPI News* release. Global Music Sales Down 5% in 2001. www.ifpi.org.
25. W. S. Mossberg, "Record Labels Launch Two Feeble Services to Replace Napster," *Wall Street Journal,* February 7, 2002, B1.
26. Peter Burrows, "The Man Behind Apple's Design Magic," 27–34.
27. N. Wingfield and E. Smith, "U2's Gig: Help Apple Sell iPods," *Wall Street Journal,* October 20, 2004, D5. Apple Computer Press Release, "iTunes Music Store Downloads Top 150 Million Songs," October 14, 2004.
28. Paul Taylor, "iPod Ecosystem Offers Rich Pickings," *FT.com,* January 24, 2006, 1.
29. T. Braithwaite and K. Allison, "Crunch Time for Apple's Music Icon," *Financial Times,* June 14, 2006, 27.
30. P. Borrows, "Apple's Ambitious iPhone 3G Plans," *BusinessWeek,* August 25, 2008, 28.
31. N. Wingfield, "iPhone Software Sales Take Off," *Wall Street Journal,* August 11, 2008, B1.
32. "Gartner Says Worldwide PC Shipments to Grow 11% in 2008," Gartner Press release, March 25, 2008.
33. *Standard & Poor's Industry Surveys,* Computers: Hardware, "Global Demand for PCs Accelerates", December 8, 2005.
34. M. Dickerson, "Plain PCs Sitting Pretty," *Los Angeles Times,* December 11, 2005, C1.

INTRODUCTION

IKEA is one of the world's most successful global retailers. In 2007, IKEA had 300 home furnishing superstores in 35 countries and was visited by some 583 million shoppers. IKEA's low-priced, elegantly designed merchandise, displayed in large warehouse stores, generated sales of €21.2 billion in 2008, up from €4.4 billion in 1994. Although the privately held company refuses to publish figures on profitability, its net profit margins were rumored to be approximately 10%, high for a retailer. The founder, Ingvar Kamprad, now in his 80s but still an active "advisor" to the company, is rumored to be one of the world's richest men.

COMPANY BACKGROUND

IKEA was established by Ingvar Kamprad in Sweden in 1943 when he was just 17 years old. The fledgling company sold fish, Christmas magazines, and seeds from his family farm. His first business had been selling matches; the enterprising Kamprad purchased them wholesale in 100-box lots (with help from his grandmother who financed the enterprise) and then resold individually at a higher markup. The name IKEA was an acronym: I and K his initials; E stood for Elmtaryd, the name of the family farm; and A stood for Agunnaryd, the name of the village in southern Sweden where the farm was located. Before long, Kamprad had added ballpoint pens to his list and was selling his products via mail order. His warehouse was a shed on the family farm. The customer fulfillment system used the local milk truck, which picked up goods daily and took them to the train station.

In 1948, Kamprad added furniture to his product line; in 1949, he published his first catalog, distributed then as now, for free. In 1953, Kamprad was struggling with a problem: the milk truck had changed its route, and he could no longer use it to take goods to the train station. His solution was to buy an idle factory in nearby Almhult and convert it into a warehouse. With business now growing rapidly, Kamprad hired a 22-year-old designer, Gillis Lundgren. Lundgren originally helped Kamprad do photo shoots for the early IKEA catalogs, but he started to design more and more furniture for IKEA, eventually designing as many as 400 pieces, including many best sellers.

IKEA's goal over time was to provide stylish functional designs with minimalist lines that could be cost-efficiently manufactured under contract by suppliers and priced low enough to allow most people to afford them. Kamprad's theory was that "good furniture could be priced so that the man with a flat wallet would make a place for it in his spending and could afford it."[1] Kamprad was struck by the fact that furniture in Sweden was expensive at the time, something that he attributed to a fragmented industry dominated by small retailers. Furniture was also often considered family heirlooms, passed down across the generations. He wanted to change this: to make it possible for people of modest means to buy their own furniture. Ultimately, this led to the concept of what IKEA calls "democratic design"—a design

This case was prepared by Charles W. L. Hill, School of Business, University of Washington. Reprinted by permission.

that, according to Kamprad, "was not just good, but also from the start adapted to machine production and thus cheap to assemble."[2] Gillis Lundgren was instrumental in the implementation of this concept. Time and time again, he would find ways to alter the design of furniture to save on manufacturing costs.

Gillis Lundgren also stumbled on what was to become a key feature of IKEA furniture: self-assembly. Trying to efficiently pack and ship a long-legged table, he hit upon the idea of taking the legs off and mailing them packed flat under the tabletop. Kamprad quickly realized that flat-packed furniture reduced transport and warehouse costs, and damage (IKEA had been having a lot of problems with furniture damaged during the shipping process). Moreover, customers seemed willing to take on the task of assembly in return for lower prices. By 1956, self-assembly was integral to the IKEA concept.

In 1957, IKEA started to exhibit and sell its products at home furnishing fairs in Sweden. By cutting retailers out of the equation and using the self-assembly concept, Kamprad could undercut the prices of established retail outlets, much to their chagrin. Established retailers responded by prohibiting IKEA from taking orders at the annual furniture trade in Stockholm. Established outlets claimed that IKEA was imitating their designs. This was to no avail, however, so the retailers went further, pressuring furniture manufacturers not to sell to IKEA. This had two unintended consequences. First, without access to the designs of many manufacturers, IKEA was forced to design more of its products in-house. Second, Kamprad looked for a manufacturer who would produce IKEA-designed furniture. Ultimately, he found one in Poland.

To his delight, Kamprad discovered that furniture manufactured in Poland was as much as 50% cheaper than furniture made in Sweden, allowing him to cut prices even more. Kamprad also found that doing business with the Poles required the consumption of considerable amounts of vodka to celebrate business transactions, and for the next 40 years his drinking was legendary. Alcohol consumption apart, the relationship that IKEA established with the Poles was to become the archetype for future relationships with suppliers. According to one of the Polish managers, there were three advantages of doing business with IKEA: "One concerned the decision making; it was always one man's decision, and you could rely upon what had been decided. We were given long-term

contracts, and were able to plan in peace and quiet.... A third advantage was that IKEA introduced new technology. One revolutionary idea, for instance, was a way of treating the surface of wood. They also mastered the ability to recognize cost savings that could trim the price."[3] By the early 1960s, Polish-made goods were to be found on more than half of the pages of the IKEA catalog.

By 1958, an expanded facility at the Almhult location became the first IKEA store. The original idea behind the store was to have a location where customers could come and see IKEA furniture set up. It was a supplement to IKEA's main mail-order business; but it very quickly became an important sales point in its own right. The store soon started to sell car roof racks so customers could leave with flat-packed furniture loaded on top. Noticing that a trip to an IKEA store was something of an outing for many shoppers (Almhult was not a major population center, and people often drove in from long distances), Kamprad experimented with adding a restaurant to the store so that customers could relax and refresh themselves while shopping. The restaurant was a hit, and it became an integral feature of all IKEA stores.

The response of IKEA's competitors to its success was to argue that IKEA products were of low quality. In 1964, just after 800,000 IKEA catalogs had been mailed to Swedish homes, the widely read Swedish magazine *Allt i Hemmet* (Everything for the Home) published a comparison of IKEA furniture to that sold in traditional Swedish retailers. The furniture was tested for quality in a Swedish design laboratory. The magazine's analysis, detailed in a 16-page spread, was that not only was IKEA's quality as good if not better than that from other Swedish furniture manufacturers, the prices were much lower. For example, the magazine concluded that a chair bought at IKEA for 33 kronor ($4) was better than a virtually identical one bought in a more expensive store for 168 kronor ($21). The magazine also showed how a living room furnished with IKEA products was as much as 65% less expensive than one furnished with equivalent products from four other stores. This publicity made IKEA acceptable in middle-class households, and sales began to take off.

In 1965, IKEA opened its first store in Stockholm, Sweden's capital. By now, IKEA was generating the equivalent of €25 million and had already opened a store in neighboring Norway. The Stockholm store, its third, was the largest furniture store in Europe and had an innovative circular design that was modeled on the famous Guggenheim Art Museum in New York. The location of the store was to set the pattern at IKEA for decades. The store was situated on the outskirts of the city, rather than downtown, with ample space for parking and good access roads. The new store generated a large amount of traffic, so much so that employees could not keep up with customer orders, and long lines formed at the checkouts and merchandise pick-up areas. To try and reduce the lines, IKEA experimented with a self-service pick-up solution, allowing shoppers to enter the warehouse, load flat-packed furniture onto trolleys, and then take them through the checkout. It was so successful that this soon became the company norm in all stores.

International Expansion

By 1973, IKEA was the largest furniture retailer in Scandinavia with nine stores. The company enjoyed a market share of 15% in Sweden. Kamprad, however, felt that growth opportunities were limited. Starting with a single store in Switzerland over the next 15 years, the company expanded rapidly in Western Europe. IKEA met with considerable success, particularly in West Germany, where it had 15 stores by the late 1980s. As in Scandinavia, Western European furniture markets were largely fragmented and served by high-cost retailers located in expensive downtown stores, selling relatively expensive furniture that was not always immediately available, for delivery. IKEA's elegant functional designs with their clean lines, low prices, and immediate availability, were a breath of fresh air, as was the self-service store format. The company was met with almost universal success even though, as one former manager put it: "We made every mistake in the book, but money nevertheless poured in. We lived frugally, drinking now and again, yes perhaps too much, but we were on our feet bright and cheery when the doors were open for the first customers, competing in good Ikean spirit for the cheapest solutions."[4]

The man in charge of the European expansion was Jan Aulino, Kamprad's former assistant, who was just 34 years old when the expansion started. Aulino surrounded himself with a young team. Aulino recalled that the expansion was so fast paced that the stores were rarely ready when IKEA moved in. Moreover, it was hard to get capital out of Sweden due to capital controls; the trick was to make a quick profit and get a positive cash flow going as soon as possible. In the haste to expand, Aulino and his team did not always pay attention to detail. He reportedly clashed with Kamprad on several occasions and considered himself fired at least four times, although he never was. Eventually the European business was reorganized, and tighter controls were introduced.

IKEA was slow to expand in the UK, however, where the locally grown company Habitat had built a business that was similar in many respects to IKEA, offering stylish furniture at a relatively low price. IKEA also entered North America, opening 7 stores in Canada between 1976 and 1982. Emboldened by this success, in 1985, the company entered the United States. It proved to be a challenge of an entirely different nature.

On the face of it, America looked to be fertile territory for IKEA. As in Western Europe, furniture retailing was a very fragmented business in the United States. At the low end of the market were the general discount retailers, such as Walmart, Costco, and Office Depot, who sold a limited product line of basic furniture, often at very low prices. This furniture was very functional, lacked the design elegance associated with IKEA, and was generally of a fairly low quality. Then there were higher-end retailers, such as Ethan Allen, that offered high-quality, well-designed, high-priced furniture. They sold this furniture in full-service stores staffed by knowledgeable salespeople. High-end retailers would often sell ancillary services as well, such as interior design. Typically these retailers would offer home delivery service, including set up in the home, either for free or a small additional charge. Because it was expensive to keep large inventories of high-end furniture, much of what was on display in stores was not readily available, and the client would often have to wait a few weeks before it was delivered.

IKEA opened its first United States store in 1985 in Philadelphia. The company had decided to locate on the coasts. Surveys of American consumers suggested that IKEA buyers were more likely to be people who had travelled abroad, considered themselves risk takers, and liked fine food and wine. These people were concentrated on the coasts. As one manager put it, "There are more Buicks driven in the middle than on the coasts."[5]

Although IKEA initially garnered favorable reviews, and enough sales to persuade it to start opening additional stores, by the early 1990s, it was clear that things were not going well in America. The company found that its European-style offerings did not always resonate with American consumers. Beds were measured in centimeters, not the king, queen, and twin sizes with which Americans are familiar. American sheets did not fit on IKEA beds. Sofas were not big enough, wardrobe drawers not deep enough, glasses too small, curtains too short, and kitchens did not fit American-size appliances. In a story often repeated at IKEA, managers noted that customers were buying glass vases and using them to drink out of, rather than the small glasses for sale at IKEA. The glasses were apparently too small for Americans who like to add liberal quantities of ice to their drinks. To make matters worse, IKEA was sourcing many of the goods from overseas, priced in the Swedish kronor, which was strengthening against the American dollar. This drove up the price of goods in IKEA's American stores. Moreover, some of the stores were poorly located, and not large enough to offer the full IKEA experience familiar to Europeans.

Turning around its American operations required IKEA to take some decisive actions. Many products had to be redesigned to fit with American needs. Newer and larger store locations were chosen. To bring prices down, goods were sourced from lower-cost locations and priced in dollars. IKEA also started to source some products from factories in the United States to reduce both transport costs and dependency on the value of the dollar. At the same time, IKEA noticed a change in American culture. Americans were becoming more concerned with design, and more open to the idea of disposable furniture. It used to be said that Americans changed their spouses about as often as they changed their dining room tables, about 1.5 times in a lifetime, but something was shifting in American culture. Younger people were more open to risks and more willing to experiment. There was a thirst for design elegance and quality. Starbucks was tapping into this, as was Apple Computer, and so did IKEA. According to one manager at IKEA, "Ten or 15 years ago, travelling in the United States, you couldn't eat well. You couldn't get good coffee. Now you can get good bread in the supermarket, and people think that is normal. I like that very much. That is more important to good life

than the availability of expensive wines. That is what IKEA is about." [6]

To tap into America's shifting culture, IKEA reemphasized design and started promoting the brand with a series of quirky hip advertisements aimed at a younger demographic: young married couples, college students, and 20- to 30-something singles. One IKEA commercial, called "Unboring," made fun of the reluctance of Americans to part with their furniture. One famous ad featured a discarded lamp, forlorn and forsaken in some rainy American city. A man turned to the camera sympathetically. "Many of you feel bad for this lamp," he said in thick Swedish accent. "That is because you are crazy." Hip people, the commercial implied, bought furniture at IKEA. Hip people did not hang onto their furniture either; after a while they discarded it and replaced it with something else from IKEA.

The shift in tactics worked. IKEA's revenues doubled in a four-year period to $1.27 billion in 2001, up from $600 million in 1997. By 2008, the United States was IKEA's second-largest market after Germany, with 35 stores accounting for 10% of its total revenues, or around $2.4 billion, and expansion plans called for 50-plus stores in the United States by 2012.

Having learned vital lessons about competing in foreign countries outside continental Western Europe, IKEA continued to expand internationally in the 1990s and 2000s. It first entered the UK in 1987, and by 2008, it had 17 stores in the country. IKEA also acquired Britain's Habitat in the early 1990s and continued to run it under the Habitat brand name. In 1998, IKEA entered China, where it had 4 stores by 2008, followed by Russia in 2000 (11 stores by 2008), and Japan in 2006, a country where it had failed miserably 30 years earlier (by 2008 IKEA had four stores in Japan). In total, by 2008, there were 285 IKEA stores in 36 countries and territories. The company had plans to continue opening between 20 and 25 stores a year for the foreseeable future. According to one manager, an important limiting factor on the pace of expansion was building the supply network.

As with the United States, some local customization has been the order of the day. In China, for example, the store layout reflected the layout of many Chinese apartments, and because many Chinese apartments have balconies, IKEA's Chinese stores included a balcony section. IKEA also has had

e car ownership
IKEA stores are
and have lots
re located near
rs delivery ser-
get their pur-
d a deep price
some items as
EA stores out-
has sourced a
in China from

ess Model

wardly mobile
or low-priced
nd household
ewhat wacky,
ve traffic into
large ware-
colors of the
items, from
is plenty of
_____, and the stores are located with good access to major roads.

The interior of the stores is configured almost like a maze that requires customers to pass through each department to get to the checkout. The goal is simple; to get customers to make more impulse purchases as they wander through the IKEA wonderland. Customers who enter the store planning to buy a $40 coffee table can end up spending $500 on everything from storage units to kitchenware. The flow of departments is constructed with an eye to boosting sales. For example, when IKEA managers noticed that men would get bored while their wives stopped in the home textile department, they added a tool section just outside the textile department, and sales of tools skyrocketed. At the end of the maze, just before the checkout, is the warehouse where customers can pick up their flat-packed furniture. IKEA stores also have restaurants (located in the middle of the store) and child-care facilities (located at the entrance for easy drop off) so that shoppers stay as long as possible.

Products are designed to reflect the clean Swedish lines that have become IKEA's trademark. IKEA has a product strategy council, which is a group of senior managers who establish priorities for IKEA's product lineup. Once a priority is established, product developers survey the competition and then set a price point that is 30% to 50% below that of rivals. As IKEA's Web site states, "We design the price tag first, then the product." Once the price tag is set, designers work with a network of suppliers to drive down the cost of producing the unit. The goal is to identify the appropriate suppliers and the least-costly materials, a trial and error process that can take as long as three years. By 2008, IKEA had 1,380 suppliers in 54 countries. The top sourcing countries were China (21% of supplies), Poland (17%), Italy (8%), Sweden (6%), and Germany (6%).

IKEA devotes considerable attention to finding the right supplier for each item. Consider the company's best-selling Klippan love seat. Designed in 1980, the Klippan, with its clean lines, bright colors, simple legs, and compact size, has sold some 1.5 million units since its introduction. IKEA originally manufactured the product in Sweden but soon transferred production to lower-cost suppliers in Poland. As demand for the Klippan grew, IKEA then decided that it made more sense to work with suppliers in each of the company's big markets to avoid the costs associated with shipping the product all over the world. Today there are five suppliers of the frames in Europe, plus three in the United States and two in China. To reduce the cost of the cotton slipcovers, IKEA has concentrated production in four core suppliers in China and Europe. The resulting efficiencies from these global sourcing decisions enabled IKEA to reduce the price of the Klippan by some 40% between 1999 and 2005.

Although IKEA contracts out manufacturing for most of its products, since the early 1990s, a certain proportion of goods have been made internally (in 2008, about 90% of all products were sources from independent suppliers, with 10% being produced internally). The integration into manufacturing was born out of the collapse of communist governments in Eastern Europe after the fall of the Berlin Wall in 1989. By 1991, IKEA was sourcing some 25% of its goods from Eastern European manufacturers. It had invested considerable energy in building long-term relationships with these suppliers, and had often helped them to develop and purchase new technology so that they could make IKEA products at a lower cost. As communism collapsed and new bosses came in to the factories, many did not feel bound by the relationships with IKEA. They effectively tore up contracts, tried to raise prices, and underinvested in new technology.

With its supply base at risk, IKEA purchased a Swedish manufacturer, Swedwood. IKEA then used Swedwood as the vehicle to buy and run furniture manufacturers across Eastern Europe, with the largest investments being made in Poland. IKEA invested heavily in its Swedwood plants, equipping them with the most modern technology. Beyond the obvious benefits of giving IKEA a low-cost source of supply, Swedwood has also enabled IKEA to acquire knowledge about manufacturing processes that are useful both in product design and in relationships with other suppliers, giving IKEA the ability to help suppliers adopt new technology and drive down their costs.

For illustration, consider IKEA's relationship with suppliers in Vietnam. IKEA has expanded its supply base in Vietnam to help support its growing Asian presence. IKEA was attracted to Vietnam by the combination of low-cost labor and inexpensive raw materials. IKEA drives a tough bargain with its suppliers, many of whom say that they make thinner margins on their sales to IKEA than they do to other foreign buyers. IKEA demands high quality at a low price. But there is an upside; IKEA offers the prospect of forging a long-term, high-volume business relationship. Moreover, IKEA regularly advises its Vietnamese suppliers on how to seek out the best and cheapest raw materials, how to set up and expand factories, what equipment to purchase, and how to boost productivity through technology investments and management process.

Organization and Management

In many ways, IKEA's organization and management practices reflect the personal philosophy of its founder. A 2004 article in *Fortune* describes Kamprad, then one of the world's richest men, as an informal and frugal man who "insists on flying coach, takes the subway to work, drives a 10-year-old Volvo, and avoids suits of any kind. It has long been rumored in Sweden that when his self-discipline fails and he drinks an overpriced Coke out of a hotel mini bar, he will go down to a grocery store to buy a replacement."[7] Kamprad's thriftiness is attributed to his upbringing in Smaland, a traditionally poor region of Sweden. Kamprad's frugality is now part of IKEA's DNA.

Managers are forbidden to fly first class and are expected to share hotel rooms.

Under Kamprad, IKEA became mission driven. He had a cause, and those who worked with him adopted it too. It was to make life better for the masses, to democratize furniture. Kamprad's management style was informal, nonhierarchical, and team based. Titles and privileges are taboo at IKEA. There are no special perks for senior managers. Pay is not particularly high, and people generally work there because they like the atmosphere. Suits and ties have always been absent, from the head office to the loading docks. The culture is egalitarian. Offices have an open plan and are furnished with IKEA furniture; private offices are rare. Everyone is called a "co-worker," and first names are used throughout. IKEA regularly stages antibureaucracy weeks during which executives work on the store floor or tend to registers. In a 2005 *Business Week* article Andres Dahlvig, the CEO, described how he spent time earlier in the year unloading trucks and selling beds and mattresses.[8] Creativity is highly valued, and the company is replete with stories of individuals taking the initiative; from Gillis Lundgren's pioneering of the self-assemble concept to the store manager in the Stockholm store who let customers go into the warehouse to pick up their own furniture. To solidify this culture, IKEA had a preference for hiring younger people who had not worked for other enterprises and then promoting from within. IKEA has historically tended to shy away from hiring the highly educated, status-oriented elite, because they often adapted poorly to the company.

Kamprad seems to have viewed his team as extended family. Back in 1957, he bankrolled a weeklong trip to Spain for all 80 employees and their families as reward for hard work. The early team of employees all lived near each other. They worked together, played together, drank together, and talked about IKEA around the clock. When asked by an academic researcher what the fundamental key was to good leadership, Kamprad replied "Love." Recollecting the early days, he noted that "When we were working as a small family in Aluhult, we were as if in love. Nothing whatsoever to do with eroticism. We just liked each other so damn much."[9] Another manager noted that "We who wanted to join IKEA did so because the company suits our way of life. To escape thinking about status, grandeur and smart clothes."[10]

As IKEA grew, the question of taking the company public arose. While there were obvious advantages associated with doing so, including access to capital, Kamprad decided against it. His belief was that the stock market would impose short-term pressures on IKEA that would not be good for the company. The constant demands to produce profits, regardless of the business cycle, would, in Kamprad's view, make it more difficult for IKEA to take bold decisions. At the same time, as early as 1970, Kamprad started to worry about what would happen if he died. He decided that he did not want his sons to inherit the business. His worry was that they would either sell the company, or they might squabble over control of the company, and thus destroy it. All three of his sons, it should be noted, went to work at IKEA as managers.

The solution to this dilemma created one of the most unusual corporate structures in the world. In 1982, Kamprad transferred his interest in IKEA to a Dutch-based charitable foundation, Stichting Ingka Foundation. This is a tax-exempt, nonprofit legal entity that in turn owns Ingka Holding, a private Dutch firm that is the legal owner of IKEA. A five-person committee, chaired by Kamprad and including his wife, runs the foundation. In addition, the IKEA trademark and concept was transferred to IKEA Systems, another private Dutch company, whose parent company, Inter-IKEA, is based in Luxembourg. The Luxembourg company is, in turn, owned by an identically named company in the Netherlands Antilles, whose beneficial owners remain hidden from public view, but they are almost certainly the Kamprad family. Inter-IKEA earns its money from a franchise agreement it has with each IKEA store. The largest franchisee is none other than Ingka Holdings. IKEA states that franchisees pay 3% of sales to Inter-IKEA. Thus, Kamprad has effectively moved ownership of IKEA out of Sweden, although the company's identity and headquarters remain there, and established a mechanism for transferring funds to himself and his family from the franchising of the IKEA concept. Kamprad himself moved to Switzerland in the 1980s to escape Sweden's high taxes, and he has lived there ever since.

In 1986, Kamprad gave up day-to-day control of IKEA to Andres Moberg, a 36-year-old Swede who had dropped out of college to join IKEA's mail-order department. Despite relinquishing management control, Kamprad continued to exert influence over the company as an advisor to senior management and as an ambassador for IKEA, a role he was still pursuing with vigor in 2008, despite being in his 80s.

Looking Forward

In its half century, IKEA had established an enviable position for itself. It had become one of the most successful retail establishments in the world. It had expanded into numerous foreign markets (Exhibit 2), learning from its failures and building on its successes. It had bought affordable, well-designed, functional furniture to the masses, helping them to, in Kamprad's words, achieve a better everyday life. IKEA's goal was to continue to grow by opening 20 to 25 stores a year for the foreseeable future. Achieving that growth would mean expansion into non-Western markets, including most notably China where it had recently established a beachhead. Could the company continue to do so? Was its competitive advantage secure?

Exhibit 1   IKEA by the Numbers in 2008

IKEA Stores	285 in 35 countries
IKEA Sales	€21.2 billion
IKEA Suppliers	1,380 in 54 countries
The IKEA Range	9,500 products
IKEA Coworkers	127,800 in 39 countries

Source: http://franchisor.ikea.com/showContent .asp?swfId=facts9.

Exhibit 2   Sales and Suppliers

Top Five Sales Countries		Top Five Supplying Countries	
Germany	15%	China	21%
United States	10%	Poland	17%
France	10%	Italy	8%
UK	7%	Sweden	6%
Sweden	6%	Germany	6%

Source: http://www.ikea.com/ms/en_GB/about_ikea/facts_ and_figures/index.html.

References & Reading

1. Anonymous, "Furnishing the World," *The Economist*, November 19, 1995, 79–80.
2. Anonymous. "Flat pack accounting," *The Economist*, May 13, 2006, 69–70.
3. K. Capell, A. Sains, C. Lindblad, and A. T. Palmer, "IKEA," *BusinessWeek*, November 14, 2005, 96–101.
4. K. Capell et al., "What a Sweetheart of a Love Seat," *BusinessWeek*, November 14, 2005, 101.
5. C. Daniels, "Create IKEA, Make Billions, Take Bus," *Fortune*, May 3, 2004, 44.
6. J. Flynn and L. Bongiorno, "IKEA's New Game Plan," *BusinessWeek*, October 6, 1997, 99–102.
7. R. Heller, "Folk Fortune," *Forbes*, September 4, 2000, 67.
8. IKEA Documents at www.ikea.com.
9. J. Leland, "How the Disposable Sofa Conquered America," *New York Times Magazine*, October 5, 2005, 40–50.
10. P. M. Miller, "IKEA with Chinese Characteristics," *Chinese Business Review*, July–August 2004, 36–69.
11. B. Torekull, *Leading by Design: The IKEA Story* (New York: Harper Collins, 1998).

Endnotes

1. Quoted in R. Heller, "Folk Fortune," *Forbes*, September 4, 2000, 67.
2. B. Torekull, *Leading by Design: The IKEA Story* (New York: Harper Collins, 1998), 53.
3. Ibid.
4. Ibid.
5. J. Leland, "How the Disposable Sofa Conquered America," *New York Times Magazine*, October 5, 2005, 45.
6. Ibid.
7. C. Daniels and A. Edstrom, "Create IKEA, Make Billions, Take a Bus," *Fortune*, May 3, 2006, 44.
8. K. Capell et al., "Ikea," *Business Week*, November 14, 2005, 96–106.
9. B. Torekull, *Leading by Design: The IKEA Story*, 82.
10. B. Torekull, *Leading by Design: The IKEA Story*, 83.

INTRODUCTION: THE GOOGLE JUGGERNAUT

In the early 2000s, many Internet users started to gravitate toward a new search engine. It was called Google, and it delivered remarkable results. Put in a keyword, and in a blink of an eye the search engine would return a list of links, with the most relevant links appearing at the top of the page. People soon realized that Google was an amazing tool, enabling users to quickly find almost anything they wanted on the Web—to effortlessly sort through the vast sea of information contained in billions of Web pages and retrieve the precise information they desired. It seemed like magic. Before long, "to Google" became a verb (in June 2006, the verb *Google* was added to the *Oxford English Dictionary*). To find out more about a person, you would "Google them." To find out more about a subject, you would "Google it." If you wanted to find a good or service, enter a key word in Google, and a list of relevant links would be returned in an instant. For many users, Google became the "go to" page every time they wanted information about anything. As a result, by mid-2008, some 62% of all United States Internet searches were conducted through Google, far ahead of Yahoo!'s search engine, with a 20.5% share, and Microsoft's, which accounted for 9% of searches.[1] Moreover, Google had been gaining share; only two years earlier, its share had stood at 45%.[2]

What captured the attention of the business community, however, was the ability of Google to monetize its search engine. Google's core business model was the essence of simplicity. The company auctioned off the keywords used in searches to advertisers. The highest bidders would have links to their sites placed on the right-hand side of a page returning search results. The advertisers would then pay Google every time someone clicked on a link and was directed to their site. Thus, when bidding for a keyword, advertisers would bid for the price per click. Interestingly, Google did not necessarily place the advertiser who bid the highest amount per click at the top of the page. Rather, the top spot was determined by the amount per click multiplied by Google's statistical estimate of the likelihood that someone would actually click on the advertisement. This refinement maximized the revenue that Google got from its valuable real estate.

As more users gravitated to Google's site, more advertisers were attracted to it, and Google's revenues and profits took off. From a standing start in 2001, revenues had grown to $16.6 billion and net income to $4.2 billion by 2007. Google had become the gorilla in the online advertising space. In 2001, Google garnered 18.4% of total United States search ad spending. By 2005, its share had increased to 48.5%, and according to the research firm eMarketer, 75% of all United States search-advertising dollars went to Google in 2007.[3] Moreover, the future looked bright. Estimates suggested that Internet advertising spending could become a $51 billion market in the United States in 2012, up from $16.9 billion in 2006.[4] Forecasts called for Google's revenues to exceed $42 billion by 2012 as more and more advertisers move from traditional media to the Web.[5]

Flushed by this success, Google introduced a wave of new products, including mapping services

---

This case was prepared by Charles W. L. Hill, University of Washington Reprinted by permission.

(Google Maps and Google Earth); a free e-mail service (gmail); Google Desktop (which enables users to search files on their own computers); free online word-processing and spreadsheet programs that had much of the look, feel, and functionality of Microsoft's Word and Excel offerings; and in September 2008, its own Web browser. These products fueled speculation that Google's ambitions extended beyond search, and the company was trying to position itself as a platform company supporting an ecosystem that would rival that fostered by Microsoft, long the dominant player in the software industry. Google's competitors, however, had no intention of being steamrollered. Both Yahoo! and Microsoft were investing significant amounts in search in an attempt to grow their share. A number of smaller search companies, including Ask.com and snap.com, were looking to increase their share, too. Moreover, few of Google's new products had gained share against entrenched competitors, suggesting to some that the company might be overreaching itself.

SEARCH ENGINES[6]

A *search engine* connects the keywords that users enter (queries) to a database it has created of Web pages (an index). It then produces a list of links to pages (and summaries of content) that it believes are most relevant to a query.

Search engines consist of four main components: a Web crawler, an index, a runtime index, and a query processor (the interface that connects users to the index). The Web crawler is a piece of software that goes from link to link on the Web, collecting the pages it finds and sending them back to the index. Once in the index, Web pages are analyzed by sophisticated algorithms that look for statistical patterns. Google's page rank algorithm, for example, looks at the links on a page, the text around those links, and the popularity of the pages that link to that page, to determine how relevant a page is to a particular query (in fact, Google's algorithm looks at more than 100 factors to determine a page's relevance to a query term).

Once analyzed, pages are tagged. The tag contains information about the pages, for example, whether it is porn or spam, written in a certain language, or updated infrequently. Tagged pages are then dumped into a runtime index, which is a database that is ready to serve users. The runtime index forms a bridge between the back end of an engine, the Web crawler and index, and the front end, the query processor and user interface. The query processor takes a keyword input by a user, transports it to the runtime index, where an algorithm matches the keyword to pages, ranking them by relevance, and then transports the results back to the user, where they are displayed on the user interface.

The computing and data storage infrastructure required to support a search engine is significant. It must scale with the continued growth of the Web and with demands on the search engine. In 2007, Google had $2.7 billion in information technology assets on its balance sheet, close to 400,000 computers configured in large-scale clusters dedicated to the job of running its search engine, and spent around $600 million on maintaining its system.[7]

THE EARLY DAYS OF SEARCH

Search did not begin with Google. The first Internet search engine was Archie. Created in 1990, before the World Wide Web had burst onto the scene, Archie connected users through queries to the machines on which documents they wanted were stored. The users than had to dig through the public files on those machines to find what they wanted. The next search engine, Veronica, improved on Archie insofar as it allowed searchers to connect directly to the document they had queried.

The Web started to take off after 1993, with the number of Web sites expanding from 130 to more than 600,000 by 1996. As this expansion occurred, the problem of finding the information wanted on the Web became more difficult. The first Web-based search engine was the WWW Wanderer, developed by Matthew Gray at MIT. This was soon surpassed, however, by Web Crawler, a search engine developed by Brian Pinkerton of the University of Washington. Web Crawler was the first search engine to index the full text of Web pages, as opposed to just the title. Web Crawler was sold to AOL for $1 million in 1995. This marked the first time anyone had ascribed an economic value to a search engine.

In December 1995, the next search engine appeared on the scene, Alta Vista. Developed by an employee at Digital Equipment (DEC), Louis Monier, Alta Vista, like Web Crawler, indexed the entire text of a Web page. Unlike Web Crawler, however, Alta Vista sent out thousands of Web crawlers, which enabled it to build the most complete index of the Web to date. Avid Web users soon came to value the service, but the search engine was handicapped by two things. First, it was very much a stepchild within DEC, which saw itself as a hardware-driven business and did not really know what to do with Alta Vista. Second, there was no obvious way for Alta Vista to make much money, which meant that it was difficult for Monier to get the resources required for Alta Vista to keep up with the rapid growth of the Web. Ultimately DEC was acquired by Compaq Computer. Compaq then sold Alta Vista and related Internet properties to a high-flying Internet firm, CMGI, at the height of the Internet boom in 1999 for $2.3 billion in CMGI stock. CMGI had plans to spin off Alta Vista in an initial public offering (IPO), but it never happened. The NASDAQ stock market collapsed in 2000, taking CMGI's stock down with it, and the market had no appetite for another dot-com IPO.

Around the same time that Alta Vista was gaining traffic, two other companies introduced search engines, Lycos and Excite. Both search engines represented further incremental improvement. Lycos was the first search engine to use algorithms to try and determine the relevance of a Web page for a search query. Excite utilized similar algorithms. However, neither company developed a way of making money directly from search. Instead they saw themselves as portal companies, like Yahoo!, AOL, and MSN. Search was just a tool to increase the value of their portal as a destination site, enabling them to capture revenues from banner ads, e-commerce transactions, and the like. Both Lycos and Excite went public and then squandered much of the capital raised on acquiring other Internet properties, before seeing their value implode as the Internet bubble burst in 2000–2001.

Another company that tried to make sense out of the Web for users was Yahoo!, but Yahoo! did not use a search engine. Instead it created a hierarchical directory of Web pages. This helped drive traffic to its site. Other content kept users coming back, enabling Yahoo! to emerge as one of the most popular portals on the Web. In contrast to many of its smaller competitors, Yahoo!'s industry leading scale allowed it to make good money from advertising on its site.

The company added a search engine to its offering, but until 2003 it always did so through a partner. At one time, Alta Vista powered Yahoo!'s search function, then Inktomi, and ultimately Google. Yahoo!'s managers considered developing their own search engine, but they saw it as too capital intensive—search required a lot of computing power, storage, and bandwidth. Besides, there was no business model for monetizing search. That, however, was all about to change, and it was not Google that pioneered the way; it was a serial entrepreneur Bill Gross.

GoTo.com: A Business Model Emerges[8]

Bill Gross made his first million with Knowledge Adventure, which developed software to help kids learn. After he sold Knowledge Adventure to Cendant for $100 million, Gross created IdeaLab, a business incubator that subsequently generated a number of Internet start-ups including GoTo.com.

GoTo.com was born of Gross' concern that a growing wave of spam was detracting from the value of search engines such as Alta Vista. Spam arose because publishers of Web sites realized that they could drive traffic to their sites by including commonly used search key words such as "used cars" or "airfares" on their sites. Often the words were in the same color as the background of the Web site (e.g., black words on a black background) so that they could not be seen by Web users, who would suddenly wonder why their search for used cars had directed them to a porn site.

Gross also wanted a tool that would help drive good traffic to the Web sites of a number of Internet businesses being developed by IdeaLab. In Gross' view, much of the traffic arriving at Web sites was undifferentiated—people who had come to a site because of spam, bad portal real estate deals, or poor search engine results. Gross established GoTo.com to build a better search engine, one that would defeat spam, produce highly relevant results, and eliminate bad traffic.

Gross concluded that a way to limit spam was to charge for search. He realized that it was unworkable to charge the Internet user, so why not charge the advertiser? This led to his key insight—the keywords that Internet users typed into a search engine were inherently valuable to the owners of Web sites. They drove traffic to their sites, and many sites made money from that traffic, so why not charge for the keywords? Moreover, Gross realized that if a search engine directed higher quality traffic to a site, it would be possible to charge more for relevant keywords.

By this time, GoTo.com had decided to license search engine technology from Inktomi and focus its efforts on developing the paid search model. However, GoTo.com faced a classic chicken and egg problem: to launch a service, the company needed both audience and advertisers, but it had neither.

To attract advertisers, GoTo.com adopted two strategies.[9] First, GoTo.com would charge advertisers only when somebody clicked on a link and was directed to their Web site. To Gross' way thinking, for merchants this pay-per-click model would be more efficient than advertising through traditional media, or through banner ads on Web pages. Second, GoTo.com initially priced keywords low—as low as $0.01 a click (although they could, of course, be bid above that).

To capture an audience, a Web site alone would not be enough. GoTo.com needed to tap into the traffic already visiting established Web sites. One approach was to pay the owners of high traffic Web sites to place banner ads that would direct traffic to GoTo.com's Web site. A second approach, which ultimately became the core of GoTo.com's business, was to syndicate its service, allowing affiliates to place a co-branded GoTo.com search box on their site or to use GoTo.com's search engine and identify the results as "partner results." GoTo.com would then split the revenues from search with them. GoTo.com had to pay an upfront fee to significant affiliates, who viewed their Web sites as valuable real estate. For example, in late 2000, GoTo.com paid AOL $50 million to syndicate GoTo.com's listings on its sites, which included AOL, CompuServe, and Netscape.

To finance its expansion, GoTo.com raised some $53 million in venture capital funding—a relatively easy proposition in the heady days of the dot-com boom. In June 1999, GoTo.com raised another $90 million through an IPO.[10]

GoTo.com launched its service in June 1998 with just 15 advertisers. Initially, GoTo.com was paying more to acquire traffic than it was earning from click-through ad revenue. According to its IPO filing, in its first year of operation, GoTo.com was paying 5.5 cents a click to acquire traffic from Microsoft's MSN sites, and about 4 cents a click to acquire traffic from Netscape. The average yield from this traffic, however, was still less than the cost of acquisition, resulting in red ink, not an unusual situation for a dot-com in the 1990s.

However, the momentum was beginning to shift toward the company. As traffic volumes grew, and as advertisers began to understand the value of keywords, yields improved. By early 1999, the price of popular keywords was starting to rise. The highest bidder for the keyword "software" was $0.59 a click, "books" was $0.38 a click, "vacations" was $0.36 a click, and "porn" (the source of so much spam) was $0.28 a click.[11]

The turning point was the AOL syndication deal signed in September 2000. Prior to signing with AOL, GoTo.com was reaching 24 million users through its affiliates. After the deal, it was reaching 60 million unique users, or some 75% of the United States Internet audience. (AOL itself had 23 million subscribers, CompuServe 3 million, and Netscape—which was owned by AOL—another 31 million registered users).[12] With more than 50,000 advertisers now in its network and a large audience pool, both keyword prices and click through rates increased. GoTo.com turned profitable shortly after the AOL deal was put into effect. In 2001, the company earned net profits of $20.2 million on revenues of $288 million. In 2002, it earned $73.1 million on revenues of $667.7 million, making it one of the few dot-com companies to break into profitability.

In 2001, GoTo.com changed its name to Overture Services. The name change reflected the results of a strategic shift. By 2001, the bulk of revenues were coming from affiliate sites, with the GoTo.com Web site only garnering 5% of the company's total traffic.[13] Still, the fact that GoTo.com had its own Web site that was in effect competing with traffic going to affiliates created potential channel conflict. Many in the company feared that channel conflict might induce key affiliates, such as AOL, to switch their allegiance. After much internal debate, the company decided to phase out the GoTo.com Web site, focusing all of its attention on the syndication network.

Around the same time, Bill Gross apparently talked to the founders of another fast-growing search engine, Google, about whether they would be interested in merging the two companies. At the time, Google had no business model. Gross was paying attention to the fast growth of traffic going to Google's Web site. He saw a merger as an opportunity to join a superior search engine with Overture's advertising and syndication network (the company was still using Inktomi's search engine). The talks stalled, however, reportedly because Google's founders stated that they would never be associated with a company that mixed paid advertising with organic results.[14]

Within months, however, Google had introduced its own advertising service using a pay-for-click model that looked very similar in conception to Overture's. Overture promptly sued Google for patent infringement. To make matters worse, in 2002, AOL declined to renew its deal with Overture and switched to Google for search services.

By 2003, it was clear that although still growing and profitable, Overture was losing traction to Google (Overture's revenues were on track to hit $1 billion in 2003 with 80,000 advertisers in its network).[15] Moreover, Overture was invisible to many of its users, who saw the service as a part of the offering of affiliates, many of whom were powerful brands in their own right, including Yahoo! and with MSN. Yahoo! and Microsoft were also waking up to the threat posed by Google. Realizing that paid search was becoming a highly profitable market, both began to look at Overture to jump-start their own paid search services. While Microsoft apparently decided to build its own search engine and ad service from scratch, Yahoo! decided to bid for Overture. In June 2003, a deal was announced, with Overture being sold to Yahoo! for $1.63 billion in cash. The payday was a bittersweet one for Bill Gross. IdeaLab had done very well out of Overture, but Gross could not help but feel that a bigger opportunity had slipped through his fingers and into the palms of Google's founders.

As for the patent case, this settled in 2004 when Google agreed to hand over 2.7 million shares to Yahoo!. This represented about 1% of the outstanding stock, which at the time was valued at $330. Today the value of those shares is closer to $1 billion.[16]

GOOGLE RISING

Google started as a research project undertaken by Larry Page while he was a computer science PhD student at Stanford in 1996. Called BackRub, the goal of the project was to document the link structure of the Web. Page had observed that while it was easy to follow links from one page to another, it was much more difficult to discover links *back*. Put differently, just by looking at a page, it was impossible to know who was linking to that page. Page reasoned that this might be very important information. Specifically, one might be able to rank the value of a Web page by discovering which pages were linking to it, and if those pages were themselves linked to by many other pages.

To rank pages, Page knew that he would have to send out a Web crawler to index pages and archive links. At this point, another PhD student, Sergey Brin, became involved in the project. Brin, a gifted mathematician, was able to develop an algorithm that ranked Web pages according to not only the number of links into that site but also the number of links into each of the linking sites. This methodology had the virtue of discounting links from pages that themselves had few if any links into them.

Brin and Page noticed that the search results generated by this algorithm were superior to those returned by Alta Vista and Excite, both of which often returned irrelevant results, including a fair share of spam. They had stumbled onto the key ingredient for a better search engine: rank search results according to their relevance using a back link methodology. Moreover, they realized that the bigger the Web got, the better the results would be.

With the basic details of what was now a search engine worked out, Brin and Page released it on the Stanford Web site in August 1996. They christened their new search engine Google after googol, the term for the number 1 followed by 100 zeros. Early on, Brin and Page talked to several companies about the possibility of licensing Google. Executives at Excite took a look but passed, as did executives at Infoseek and Yahoo!. Many of these companies were embroiled in the portal wars—and portals were all about acquiring traffic, not about sending it away via search. Search just did not seem central to their mission.

By late 1998, Google was serving some 10,000 queries a day and rapidly outgrowing the computing resources available at Stanford. Brin and Page realized that to get the resources required to keep scaling Google, they needed capital, and that meant starting a company. Here Stanford's deep links into Silicon Valley became useful. Before long, they found themselves sitting together with Andy Bechtolsheim, one of the founders of another Stanford start-up, Sun Microsystems. Bechtolsheim watched a demo of Google and wrote a check on the spot for $100,000.

Google was formally incorporated on September 7, 1998, with Page as CEO and Brin as president. From that point on, things began to accelerate rapidly. Traffic was growing by nearly 50% a month, enough to attract the attention of several investors (including Amazon founder Jeff Bezos), who collectively put in another million. That was not enough; search engines have a veracious appetite for computing resources. To run its search engine, Brin and Page had custom designed a low-cost, Linux-based server architecture that was modular and could be scaled rapidly. But to keep up with the growth of the Web and return answers to search queries in a fraction of a second, they needed even more machines (by late 2005, the company was reportedly using more than 250,000 Linux servers to handle more than 3,000 searches a second).[17]

To finance the growth of their search engine in early 1999, Brin and Page started to look for venture capital funding. It was the height of the dot-com boom, and money was easy to find. Never mind that there was no business model, Google's growth was enough to attract considerable interest. By June 1999, the company had closed its first round of venture capital financing, raising $25 million from two of the premier firms in Silicon Valley, Sequoia Capital and Kleiner Perkins Caufield & Byers. Just as importantly perhaps, the legendary John Doerr, one of Silicon Valley's most successful investors and a Kleiner Perkins partner, took a seat on Google's board.

By late 1999, Google had grown to about 40 employees, and it was serving some 3.5 million searches a day. However, the company was burning through $500,000 a month, and there was still no business model. They had some licensing deals with companies that used Google as their search technology, but they were not bringing in enough money to stem the flow of red ink. At this point, Google started to experiment with ads, but they were not yet pay-per-click ads. Rather, Google began selling text-based ads to clients who were interested in certain keywords. The ads would then appear on the page returning search results, but not in the list of relevant sites. For example, if someone typed in "Toyota Corolla," an ad would appear at the top of the page, above the list of links for Toyota Corolla cars. These ads were sold on a "cost per thousand impressions"

basis, or CPM (the M being the Roman numeral for thousand). In other words, the cost of an ad was determined by how many people were estimated to have viewed it—not how many clicked on it. It did not work very well.

The management team also started to ponder placing banner ads on Google's Web site as a way of generating additional revenue, but before they made that decision, the dot-com boom imploded, the NASDAQ crashed, and the volume of online advertising dropped precipitously. Google clearly needed to figure out a different way to make money.

GOOGLE GETS A BUSINESS MODEL

Brin and Page now looked closely at the one search company that seemed to be making good money, GoTo.com. They could see the value of the pay-per-click model and auctioning off keywords, but there were things about GoTo.com that they did not like. GoTo.com would give guarantees that Web sites would be included more frequently in Web crawls, making sure they were updated, provided that the owners were prepared to pay more. Moreover, the purity of GoTo.com's search results was biased by the desire to make money from advertisers, with those who paid the most being ranked highest. Brin and Page were ideologically attached to the idea of serving up the best possible search results to users, uncorrupted by commercial considerations. At the same time, they needed to make money.

Although Bill Gross pitched the idea of GoTo.com teaming up with Google, Brin and Page decided to go it alone. They believed they could do as good a job as GoTo.com, so why share revenues with the company?[18]

The approach that Google ultimately settled on combined the innovations of GotTo.com with Google's superior relevance-based search engine. Brin and Page had always believed that Google's Web page should be kept as clean and elegant as possible—something that seemed to appeal to users. Moreover, they knew that users valued the fact that Google served up relevant search results that were unbiased by commercial considerations. The last thing they wanted to do was alienate their rapidly growing user base. So they decided to place text-based ads on the right-hand side of a page, clearly separated from search results by a thin line.

Like GoTo.com, they decided to adopt a pay-per-click model. Unlike GoTo.com, Brin and Page decided that in addition to the price an advertiser had paid for a keyword, ads should also be ranked according to relevance. Relevance was measured by how frequently users clicked on ads. More popular ads rose to the top of the list, less popular ones fell. In other words, Google allowed their users to rank ads. This had a nice economic advantage for Google; an ad that was generating $1.00 a click but is being clicked on three times as much as an ad generating $1.50 a click would make significantly more money for Google. It also motivated advertisers to make sure that their ads were appealing.

The system that Google used to auction off keywords was also different in detail from that used by GoTo.com. Google used a *Vickery second price auction* methodology. Under this system, the winner pays only one cent more than the bidder directly below them. Thus, if there are bids of $1, $0.50 and $0.25 for a keyword, the winner of the top place pays just $0.51 cents, not $1, the winner of the second place $0.26, and so on. The auction is nonstop, with the price for a keyword rising or falling depending on bids at each moment in time. Although the minimum bid for a keyword was set at $0.05, most were above that, and the range was wide. One of the most expensive search terms was reputed to be "mesothelioma," a type of cancer caused by exposure to asbestos. Bids were around $30 per click! They came from lawyers vying for a chance to earn lucrative fees by representing clients in lawsuits against asbestos producers.[19]

While developing this service, Google continued to grow like wildfire. In mid-2000, the service was dealing with 18 million search queries a day, and the index surpassed one billion documents, making it by far the largest search engine on the Web. By late 2000, when Google introduced the first version of its new service, which it called AdWords, the company was serving up 60 million search queries a day—giving it a scale that GoTo.com never came close to achieving. In February 2002, Google introduced a new version of AdWords that included for the first time the full set of pay-per-click advertising, keyword auctions, and advertising links ranked by relevance. Sales immediately started to accelerate. Google had hit on the business model that would propel the company into the big league.

In 2003, Google introduced a second product, AdSense. AdSense allowed third-party publishers large and small to access Google's massive network of advertisers on a self-service basis. Publishers could sign up for AdSense in a matter of minutes. AdSense would then scan the publisher's site for content and place contextually relevant ads next to that content. As with AdWords, this is a pay-per-click service, but with AdSense Google splits the revenues with the publishers. In addition to large publishers, such as online news sites, AdSense has been particularly appealing to many small publishers, such as Web bloggers. Small publishers found that by adding a few lines of code to their site, they could suddenly monetize their content. However, many advertisers feel that AdSense is not as effective as AdWords in driving traffic to their sites. Google allowed advertisers to opt out of AdSense in 2004. Despite this, AdSense has also grown into a respectable business, accounting for 15% of Google's revenues in 2005—or close to $1 billion.

GOOGLE GROWS UP

Between 2001 and 2008, Google changed in a number of ways. First, in mid-2001, the company hired a new CEO to replace Larry Page, Eric Schmidt. Schmidt had been the chief technology officer of Sun Microsystems, and then CEO of Novell. Schmidt was brought on to help manage the company's growth with the explicit blessing of Brin and Page. Both Brin and Page were still in their twenties, and the board felt they needed a "grown-up" who had run a large company to help Google transition to the next stage (Google turned a profit the month after Schmidt joined). Brin and Page became the president of technology and president of products, respectively. When Schmidt was hired, Google had more than 200 employees and was handling more than 100 million searches a day.

According to knowledgeable observers, Schmidt, Brin, and Page acted as a triumvirate, with Brin and Page continuing to exercise a very strong influence over strategies and policies at Google. Schmidt may be CEO, but Google was still very much Brin and Page's company.[20] Working closely together, the three drove the development of a set of values and an organization that would come to define the uniquely Google way of doing things.

Vision and Values

As Google's growth started to accelerate, there was concern that rapid hiring would quickly dilute the vision, values, and principles of the founders. In mid-2001, Brin and Page gathered a core group of early employees and asked them to come up with a policy for ensuring that the company's culture did not fracture as the company added employees. From this group, and subsequent discussions, emerged a vision and list of values that have continued to shape the evolution of the company. These were not new; rather, they represented the formalization of principles that Brin and Page felt they had always adhered to.

The central vision of Google is to "organize the world's information, and make it universally acceptable and useful."[21] The team also articulated a set of 10 core philosophies (values) that are now listed on its Web site.[22] Perhaps the most significant and certainly the most discussed of these values is captured by the phrase *Don't be evil*. The central message underlying this phrase was that Google should never compromise the integrity of its search results. Google would never let commercial considerations bias its rankings. Don't be evil, however, has become more than that at Google; it has become a central organizing principle of the company, albeit one that is far from easy to implement. Google got positive press from libertarians when it refused to share its search data with the United States government, who wanted the data to help fight child porn. However, the same constituency reacted with dismay when the company caved into the Chinese government, and removed from its Chinese service offending results for search terms such as "human rights" and "democracy." Brin justified the Chinese decision by saying that "it will be better for Chinese Web users, because ultimately they will get more information, though not quite all of it."[23]

Another core value at Google is "focus on the user, and all else will follow." In many ways, this value captures what Brin and Page initially did. They focused on giving the user the best possible search experience—highly relevant results, delivered with lightening speed to an uncluttered and elegant interface. The value also reflects a belief at Google that it is okay to deliver value to users first, and then figure out the business model for monetizing that value. This belief seems to reflect Google's own early experience.

Yet another key principle, although it is not one that is written down anywhere, is captured by the phrase *launch early and often*. This seems to underpin Google's approach to product development. Google has introduced a rash of new products over the last few years, not all of which are initially that compelling, but through rapid upgrades, it has subsequently improved the efficacy of those products.

Google also prides itself on being a company where decisions are *data driven*. Opinions are said to count for nothing unless they are backed up by hard data. It is not the loudest voice that wins the day in arguments over strategy, it is the data. In some meetings, people are not allowed to say "I think . . ." but instead "The data suggests. . . ."[24]

Finally, Google devotes considerable resources to making sure that its employees are working in a supportive and stimulating environment. To quote from the company's Web site:

Google Inc. puts employees first when it comes to daily life in our Googleplex headquarters. There is an emphasis on team achievements and pride in individual accomplishments that contribute to the company's overall success. Ideas are traded, tested and put into practice with an alacrity that can be dizzying. Meetings that would take hours elsewhere are frequently little more than a conversation in line for lunch and few walls separate those who write the code from those who write the checks. This highly communicative environment fosters a productivity and camaraderie fueled by the realization that millions of people rely on Google results. Give the proper tools to a group of people who like to make a difference, and they will.[25]

Organization

By all accounts, Google has a flat organization. In November 2005, Google had one manager for every 20 line employees. At times, the ratio has been as high as 1:40. For a while, one manager had 180 direct reports.[26] The structure is reportedly based on teams. Big projects are broken down and allocated to small, tightly focused teams. Hundreds of projects may be going on at the same time. Teams often throw out new software in six weeks or less and look at how users respond hours later. Google can try a new user interface, or some other tweak, with just 0.1% of its users and get massive feedback very quickly, letting it decide a project's fate in weeks.[27]

One aspect of Google's organization that has garnered considerable attention is the company's approach toward product development. Employees are expected to spend 20% of their time on something that interests them, away from their main jobs. Seemingly based on 3M's famous 15% rule, Google's 20% rule is designed to encourage creativity. The company has set up forums on its internal network where anyone can post ideas, discuss them, and solicit help from other employees. As a natural part of this process, talent tends to gravitate to those projects that seem most promising, giving those who post the most interesting ideas the ability to select a talented team to take them to the next level.

Like 3M, Google has established a process by which projects coming out of 20% time can be evaluated, receive feedback from peers, and ultimately garner funding. Marissa Myer, one of Google's early employees, acts as a gatekeeper, helping to decide when projects are ready to be pitched to senior management (and that typically means Brin and Page). Once in front of the founders, advocates have 20 minutes, and no more, to make their pitch.[28] Myer has also articulated a number of other principles that guide product development at Google.[29] These include:

1. Ideas come from everywhere: Set up a system where good ideas rise to the top.
2. Focus on users, not money: Money follows consumers. Advertisers follow consumers. If you amass a lot of consumers you will find ways to monetize your ideas.
3. Innovation, not instant perfection: Put products on the market, learn and iterate.
4. Don't kill projects, morph them: If an idea has managed to make its way out of the door, there is usually some kernel of truth to it. Don't walk away from ideas; think of ways to replace or rejuvenate them.

One of the early products to come out of 20% time was Google News, which returns news articles ranked by relevance in response to a keyword query. Put the term "oil prices" into Google News, for example, and the search will return news dealing with changes in oil prices, with the most relevant at the top of the list. A sophisticated algorithm determines relevance on a real-time basis by looking at the quality of the news source (e.g., *The New York Times* rates higher than local newspapers), publishing date, the number of other people who click on that source, and numerous other factors. The project was initiated by Krishna Bharat, a software engineer from India, who in response to the events of September 11, 2001, had a desire to learn what was being written and said around the world. Two other employees worked with Bharat to construct a demo that was released within Google. Positive reaction soon got Bharat in front of Brin and Page, who were impressed and gave the project a green light; Bharat started to work full-time on the project.[30]

Another feature of Google's organization is its hiring strategy. Like Microsoft, Google has made a virtue out of hiring people with high IQs. The hiring process is very rigorous. Each prospect has to take an "exam" to test his/her conceptual abilities. This is followed by interviews with eight or more people, each of whom rate the applicant on a 1 to 4 scale (4 being "I would hire this person"). Applicants also undergo detailed background checks to find out what they are like to work with. Reportedly, some brilliant prospects do not get hired when background checks find out that they are difficult to work with. In essence, all hiring at Google is by committee, and while this can take considerable time, the company insists that the effort yields dividends.

While accounts of Google's organization and culture tend to emphasize their positive aspects, not everyone has such a sanguine view. Brian Reid, who was recruited into senior management at Google in 2002 and fired two years later, told author John Battelle that "Google is a monarchy with two kings, Larry and Sergey. Eric is a puppet. Larry and Sergey are arbitrary, whimsical people . . . they run the company with an iron hand. . . . Nobody at Google from what I could tell had any authority to do anything of consequence except Larry and Sergey."[31] According to Battelle, several other former employees made similar statements to him.

Other former employees have noted that in practice 20% time turns out to be 120% time, since people still have their regular workload. There are also complaints that the culture is one of long workdays and seven-day work weeks, with little consideration for family issues. And several employees have complained that Google's organization is not scaling that well; with nearly 14,000 employees on the books, the firm's personnel department is "collapsing" and "absolute chaos reigns." One former employee noted that when she was hired, nobody knew when or where she was supposed to work.[32]

Many of the early employees, who are now financially wealthy, are starting to leave. As a result, employee turnover is increasing. At the same time, there are reports that the company's free-wheeling culture has led to a rather anarchic resource allocation process, and extensive duplication, with multiple teams working on the same project.[33]

The IPO

As Google's growth started to accelerate, the question of if and when to undertake an IPO became more pressing. There were two obvious reasons for doing an IPO: gaining access to capital and providing liquidity for early backers and the large number of employees who had equity positions. On the other hand, from 2001 onward, the company was profitable, generating significant cash flows, and could fund its expansion internally. Moreover, management felt that the longer they could keep the details of what was turning out to be an extraordinarily successful business model private, the better. In the end, the company's hand was forced by an obscure Securities and Exchange Commission (SEC) regulation that required companies that give stock options to employees to report as if they were a public company by as early as April 2004. Realizing that the cat would be out of the bag anyway, Google told its employees in early 2004 that it would go public.

True to form, Google flouted Wall Street tradition in the way it structured its IPO. The company decided to auction off shares directly to the public, using an untested and modified version of a Dutch auction, which starts by asking for a high price and then lowers it until someone accepts. Two classes of shares were created, Class A and B, with Class B shares having 10 times the votes of Class A shares. Only Class A shares were auctioned off. Brin, Page, and Schmidt were holders of Class B shares. Consequently, although they would own one-third of the company after the IPO, they would control 80% of the votes. Google also announced that it would not provide regular financial guidance to Wall Street financial analysts. In effect, Google had thumbed its nose at Wall Street.

The controversial nature of the IPO, however, was overshadowed by the first public glimpse of Google's financials, which were contained in the offering document. They were jaw dropping. The company had generated revenues of $1.47 billion in 2003, an increase of 230% over 2002. Google earned

net profits of $106 million in 2003, but accountants soon figured out that the number was depressed by certain one-time accounting items, and cash flow in 2003 had been more than $500 million!

Google went public on August 19, 2004, at $85 a share. The company's first quarterly report showed sales doubling over the prior year, and by November, the price was $200.

In September 2005, with the stock close to $300 a share, Google undertook a secondary offering, selling 14 million shares to raise $4.18 billion. With positive cash flow adding to this, by June 2008, Google was sitting on $12.8 billion in cash and short-term investments, prompting speculation as to the company's strategic intentions.

Strategy

Since 2001, Google has endeavored to keep enhancing the efficacy of its search engine, continually improving the search algorithms and investing heavily in computing resources. The company has branched out from being a text-based search engine. One strategic thrust has been to extend search to as many digital devices as possible. Google started out on PCs but can now be accessed through PDAs and cell phones. A second strategy has been to widen the scope of search to include different sorts of information. Google has pushed beyond text into indexing and offering up searches of images, news reports, books, maps, scholarly papers, a blog search, a shopping network (Froogle), and videos. Google Desktop, which searches files on a user's personal computer, also fits in with this schema. However, not all of these new search formats have advertising attached to them (for example, images and scholarly papers do not include sponsored links, while maps and book search does).

Not all of this has gone smoothly. Book publishers have been angered by Google's book project, which seeks to create the world's largest searchable digital library of books by systematically scanning books from the libraries of major universities (e.g., Stanford). The publishers have argued that Google has no right to do this without first getting permission from the publishers and is violating copyright by doing so. Several publishers have filed a complaint with the U.S. District Court in New York. Google has responded that users will not be able to download entire books, and that in any event creating an easy-to-use index of books is fair use under copyright law and will increase the awareness and sales of books, directly benefiting copyright holders. On another front, the World Association of Newspapers has formed a task force to examine the exploitation of content by search engines.[34]

Over the last six years, Google has introduced a rash of product offerings that do not have a strong affinity with the company's search mission. Many of these products grew out of the company's new product development process. They include free e-mail (gmail) and online chat programs; a calendar; a blog site (Blogger); a social networking site (Orkut), finance site (Google Money); a service for finding, editing and sharing photos (Picasa); and plans to offer citywide free Wi-Fi networks.

Google has also introduced several Web-based applications that seem aimed squarely at Microsoft's Office franchise; they are collectively known as Google Apps. In March of 2006, the company acquired a word-processing program, Writely. This was quickly followed by the introduction of a spreadsheet program, Google Spreadsheets. These products have the look and feel of Microsoft Word and Excel, respectively. Both products are designed for online collaboration. They can save files in formats used by Microsoft products, although they lack the full feature set of Microsoft's offerings. Google states that the company is not trying to match the features of Office, and "90% of users don't necessarily need 90% of the functions that are in there."[35]

In July 2006, Google introduced a product to compete with PayPal, a Web-based payment system owned by the online auction giant, eBay. Google's product, known as Checkout, offers secure online payment functionality for both merchants and consumers. For merchants, the fee for using Checkout is priced below that of PayPal's. Moreover, Checkout is being integrated into Google's AdWords product, so merchants who participate will be highlighted in Google's search results. In addition, merchants who purchase Google's search advertising will get a discount on processing fees. According to one analysis, a merchant with monthly sales of $100,000 who uses Checkout and AdWords stands to reduce its transaction costs by 28%, or $8,400 a year. If the merchant uses only Checkout, the merchant will reduce its transaction costs by 4%, or $1,200 a year.[36] However, with 105 million accounts in mid-2006, PayPal will be difficult to challenge.

In late 2007, Google announced another new product, this time a suite of mobile software, including an operating system and applications that work with it, for smart handsets. Android, as the suite is called, seems to be aimed squarely at Apple's iPhone and Research in Motion's Blackberry, which are the two runaway successes in the smartphones space.

The attraction for Google is that advertising is increasingly being inserted into content viewed on mobile handsets. By one estimate, worldwide spending on mobile advertising will rise to $19 billion in 2012, up from $2.7 billion in 2007.[37] Although Google announced that it had lined up more than 30 partners, including T-Mobile, Sprint, and China Mobile, no phones had reached the market by September 2008.

Google's track record with new product offerings has been mixed. In mid-2006, two years after its introduction, gmail generated 25% of the traffic of e-mail on Yahoo! and MSN. Also in mid-2006, Froogle was ranked number 8 among shopping networks; Google Talk was ranked 10 in the world, with 2% of the users of market leader MSN. After two years, Orkut had just 1% of the visitors of market leader MySpace. Google Maps and Google News, both seen as successful, were the number two offerings in their competitive space behind Map-Quest and Yahoo! News, respectively. Google Finance had a tiny market share, way behind market leader Yahoo!, although it was only three months old in mid-2006.[38] By late 2008, Google Apps was also gaining modest market traction with some one million registered users and expected bookings of "several hundred million dollars" in 2008, leaving it far behind the $19 billion that Microsoft generated from its Office franchise.[39]

Some analysts have questioned the logic behind Google's new product efforts. One noted that "Google has product ADD. They don't know why they are getting into all of these products. They have fantastic cash flow, but terrible discipline on products."[40] Another has accused Google of having an insular culture and argued that "Neither Froogle or Google's travel efforts has gained any traction, at least partly because of Google's tendency to provide insufficient support to its ecosystem partners and its habit of acting in an independent, secretive manner."[41] However, others argue that Google has been successful in upgrading the quality of its new offerings, and several products that were once laggards, such as Google News, are now the best in breed.[42]

Google has also entered into several partnership agreements. In late 2005, Google renewed its three-year-old pact to provide search engine services to AOL. In addition, however, AOL agreed to make more AOL content available to Google users. To support the partnership, Google invested $1 billion in AOL for a 5% stake in the company. At the time, it was reported that Microsoft was also negotiating with AOL on a similar deal, but Google's offer was apparently more compelling to Time Warner management.

In mid-2006, Google inked a deal with Fox Interactive under which Google provides advertising across Fox's online network, including Fox's market leading social networking service, MySpace. (Social networking sites let users post diaries, pictures, videos, and music to share with friends online.) MySpace is one of the two dominant enterprises in the social networking field (the other is Facebook.) with some 250 million registered users in 2008. Google is the exclusive provider of search service to Fox Interactive, and has the right of first refusal on display advertising. To get access to MySpace, Google committed itself to making minimum payments of $900 million by 2010.[43]

In another mid-2006 partnership agreement, Google announced that it had reached a deal with Dell Computer under which Dell would preload Google software onto all of its systems, including Google's desktop search product and toolbar, along with a co-branded Internet homepage. Google's search would also be set as the default on Dell machines.

On the acquisition front, until 2006, Google stuck to purchasing small technology firms. This changed in October 2006 when Google announced that it would purchase YouTube for $1.64 billion in stock. YouTube is a simple, fun Web site to which anybody can upload and share video clips. By October 2006, some 65,000 video clips were being uploaded every day, and 100 million were being watched. Like Google in its early days, YouTube had no business model. The thinking was that Google would find ways to sell advertising that is linked to video clips on YouTube.[44]

Over the next two years YouTube continued to grow at a rapid pace, accounting for 35% of all videos viewed online in May 2008, double its share in 2006. Some 4.2 billion videos were watched on YouTube in mid 2008. Yet Google has been relatively ineffective at selling ads on YouTube, collecting about $100 million in 2007 and a projected $200 million in 2008. One often-heard complaint from advertisers is that YouTube lacks enough content alongside which they want to run their ads.

In addition, Google is mired in legal disputes with copyright holders over video clips uploaded to YouTube. Viacom, for example, has filed a lawsuit against Google, claiming some $1 billion in copyright infringement from YouTube videos.

Another notable Google acquisition was its $3.1 billion purchase of DoubleClick in 2007. DoubleClick is a specialist in online display advertising, such as banner ads that are targeted at building brand awareness. Internet publishers pay DoubleClick to insert display ads on their Web sites as users visit their sites. While display advertising has not grown as rapidly as search-based advertising, it is a big business accounting for some 21% of all Internet advertising revenue, with significant potential upside potential as companies begin to apply demographic technology to increase the effectiveness of Internet display ads.[45] The DoubleClick deal was criticized by Google's rivals, including Microsoft, on antitrust grounds, but regulators in the United States and the European Union approved the deal, which closed in 2008.

Critics argue that as Google moves into these additional areas its profit margins will be compressed. Henry Blodget of Cherry Hill Research notes that in its core business, Google makes profit margins of about 60%. In its more recent business of placing advertisements on Web pages belonging to other people, such as bloggers, its profit margins are 10%–20%, because it is harder to make the advertisements as relevant to the audience and it must share the resulting revenues. Display advertising also offers lower returns. Google, not surprisingly, does not see things this way. The company argues that since its costs are mostly fixed, and incremental revenues are profit, it makes good sense to push into other markets, even if its average revenue per viewer is only 1 cent (compared with 50 cents for each click on the Web).[46]

THE ONLINE ADVERTISING MARKET IN 2008

There is an old adage in advertising that half of all the money spent on advertising is wasted—advertisers just don't know which half. Estimates suggest that out of $511 billion in worldwide advertising in 2008, a staggering $250 billion will be wasted because the wrong message is sent to the wrong audience.[47] The problem is that traditional media advertising is indiscriminate. Consider a 30-second ad spot on broadcast TV. Advertisers pay a rate (CPM) for such a spot. The CPM is based on estimates of how many people are watching a show. There are numerous problems with this system. The estimates of audience numbers are only approximations at best. The owners of the TV may leave the room while commercials are airing. They may channel surf during a commercial break, be napping, or talking on the telephone. The viewer may not be among the intended audience—a Viagra commercial might be wasted on a teenage girl, for example. Or the household might be using a TiVo or a similar digital video recorder that skips commercials.

By contrast, new advertising models based on pay-for-click are more discriminating. Rather than sending out ads to a large audience, only a few of whom will be interested in the products being advertised, consumers select in search-based ads. They do this twice, first, by entering a keyword in a search engine and, second, by scanning the search results as well as the sponsored links and clicking on a link. In effect, potential purchasers pull the ads toward them through the search process. Advertisers pay only when someone clicks on their ad. Consequently, the conversion rate for search-based ads is far higher than the conversion rate for traditional media advertising.

Moreover, traditional advertising is so wasteful that most firms advertise only 5% to 10% of their products in the mass media, hoping that other products will benefit from a halo effect. In contrast, the targeted nature of search-based advertising makes it cost effective to advertise products that only sell in small quantities. In effect, search-based Internet advertising allows producers to exploit the economics of the long tail. Pay-for-click models also make it economical for small merchants to advertise their wares on the Web.

The Growth Story

Powered by the rapid growth of search-based pay-for-click advertising, total global advertising spending on the World Wide Web exceeded $50 billion in 2008, and was predicted to hit $78 billion in 2010, around 50% of which will be in the United States (Exhibit 1).[48] Some view the growth figures as conservative, given that Web advertising is still underrepresented. Estimates suggest that all Web advertising accounted for about 10.2% of total advertising spending worldwide in 2008, even though consumers in many developed nations are now spending over 25% of their media time online (see Exhibit 2).[49]

In terms of the mix of advertising online, search-based advertising now dominates, followed by display advertising and classifieds (see Exhibit 3). However, the growth rate in search-based advertising in the United States has slowed from 31% in 2006 to 22% in 2008 and is forecasted to grow 14% in 2010.[50]

Exhibit 1   Internet Ad Revenues ($ billion)

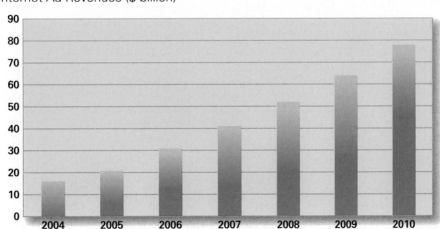

Exhibit 2 % Share of Global Ad Spending by Medium 2008

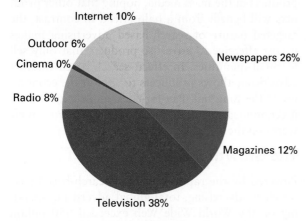

Exhibit 3 The Source of United States Internet Advertising Revenues (% of total) 2008

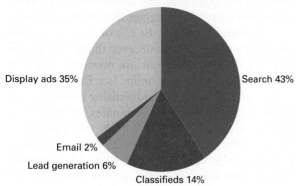

Google has been the main beneficiary of this trend. In July 2008, Google was the dominant search engine in America, with a 61.9% share of all searches, up from 45% two years earlier. Yahoo! was second with a 20.5% share, and Microsoft was third with 8.9% share (see Exhibit 4).[51] Google's share of total United States paid search advertising was even larger and stood at 75% in 2007. Yahoo!, at number two collected a mere 9%.[52]

Google's rise is reflected in its significant share of all Internet traffic. In mid-2006, Google's Web sites had the fourth largest unique audience on the Web, close behind the longer established portal sites maintained by Microsoft (MSN), Yahoo!, and Time Warner (AOL), respectively (see Exhibit 5). By mid-2006, Google's Web sites ranked number 1, in no small part due to the addition of YouTube.[53]

One blemish in the growth story has been concern over click fraud. Click fraud occurs whenever a person or computer program clicks on an ad to generate a fake or improper charge per click. Perpetrators of click fraud set up bogus Web sites and contract with a search company like Google to place search ads on them. Then they use computer programs and anonymous proxy servers to create the illusion that visitors are clicking on the ads, resulting in charges to the advertiser, which as an affiliate site they then split with Google. The fraud perpetrators and search engine gain from this action—the advertisers lose. Early estimates suggest that click fraud was running as high as 20% of all clicks, but more recent estimates suggest

Exhibit 4 Share of United States Search Queries 2006 and 2008

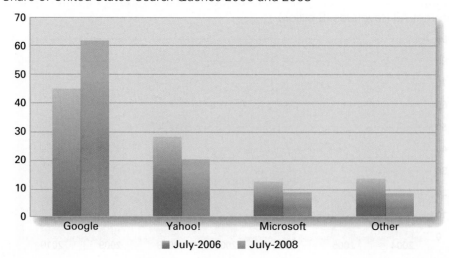

·····

Exhibit 5 Unique Visitors May 2006 and June 2008

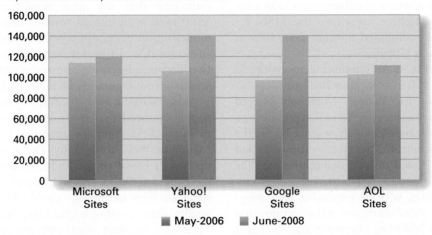

that the figures are much lower, perhaps only 5%. Nevertheless, click fraud remains a problem. To deal with this, some search engines are mulling over a "cost-per-action" business model, in which an advertiser pays only when a potential customer does something that signals genuine interest, such as placing an item into an online shopping cart, filling out a form, or making a purchase.[54]

Google's Competitors

Google's most significant competitors are Yahoo! and MSN, respectively. As paid search has grown, all three have increased their investment in search.[55] Both Yahoo! and Microsoft have been playing catch-up, trying to improve their search engine technology and gain market share at the expense of Google. Both have so far failed to gain share from Google; indeed the opposite has happened.

Until 2004, when Yahoo! purchased Overture, the company used Google's search technology. In 2005, Yahoo! announced that it was making a major investment in its search engine technology to increase its monetization of search. Driving this investment were estimates that Google generated between 30% and 50% more revenue per search than Yahoo!. About one-third of the higher search revenue was due to a higher price per click on Google, and two-thirds was due to higher click-through rates, a consequence of Google's superior search engine ranking model.[56] The goal of Yahoo!'s search engine upgrade was to shift from advertising results based on maximum bid price (the old Overture model), to results based on a series of factors, including relevancy. The new search engine

was scheduled to be introduced in the third quarter of 2006, but the introduction was delayed until 2007, and it has failed to stem Yahoo!'s market share erosion. Yahoo! was expected to benefit from a rise in online brand advertising. Yahoo! has been the leader in providing brand building graphical video and display ads, an area in which Google has been historically weak. However, Google's purchase of DoubleClick may nullify Yahoo!'s advantage in display ads.

Microsoft too, has been investing heavily in its online search capabilities. In May 2006, after two years in development, Microsoft introduced AdCenter, a platform that will ultimately enable advertisers to place ads everywhere, from search results and Web pages to videos games, cell phones, and Internet-connected TV. Prior to AdCenter, Microsoft had been buying ad services from Yahoo!. With AdCenter, Microsoft will attempt to leverage its array of platform assets, including Xbox Live, MSN, Windows Mobile, Microsoft TV, MediaCenter, Windows Live, and Microsoft Office Live. Microsoft's goal is to link users and advertisers together across all these platforms. In the middle will sit AdCenter, which is intended to work as the advertising engine. The first version of AdCenter, however, is limited to placing text ads on search result pages. Microsoft is attempting to differentiate AdCenter by providing advertisers with demographic and behavioral data that should help them to place their ads and result in a higher click-through rate.[57]

However, for all of its capabilities and investments Microsoft has significant ground to make up in the search economy. Not only is it trailing Google and Yahoo! by a wide margin, but data suggest that

Microsoft's MSN has the lowest conversion rate of homepage use to primary searching—less than one-third of MSN homepage users also use MSN for their search needs, compared to more than 40% at Yahoo! and 60% at Google.[58]

With its market share continuing to erode, in February 2008, Microsoft launched an unsolicited takeover bid for Yahoo!. Microsoft offered $44.6 billion, or $31 a share, for Yahoo!, representing a 62% premium over the closing share price before the takeover announcement. Microsoft's rationalization for the takeover rested on the assumption that the combined entity would be able to realize substantial scale economies, with its expanded Web properties offering a more attractive value proposition to advertisers. In addition, Microsoft argued that it would be able to reduce costs by $1 billion a year by combining some assets, such as data centers.

Critics immediately pointed to several potential problems with the proposed takeover, including the problems associated with combining the different cultures of the two companies, the possibility that talented Yahoo! employees might jump ship, and the difficulties posed in merging Web properties that had such different brand identities. Yahoo!'s top management too, was not impressed by the bid, arguing that it undervalued the company, and they rejected it.

After several months of difficult negotiations, during which Microsoft raised its bid to $33 a share and also threatened to fight a proxy battle to replace Yahoo!'s board with one favorable to the bid, Microsoft eventually withdrew its offer to acquire Yahoo!. In rationalizing its decision, Microsoft argued that Yahoo!'s continuing market share erosion during the months of negotiations had made the acquisition far less compelling. Yahoo's managers, for their part, continued to argue that Microsoft was not offering enough.

In June 2008, an embattled Yahoo! announced that it had reached a pact with Google under which it would display some ads sold by its rival. Yahoo! estimated that the deal would generate some $800 million in annual revenue through improved monetization of certain types of searches. Observers suspected that any deal between the number one and two Internet advertising companies would face intense scrutiny from regulators on antitrust grounds.

After walking away from the Yahoo! bid, Microsoft announced that it would acquire Powerset, a privately held company that has been developing "semantic Web" technology. This technology serves up results based on an understanding of a word's meaning and the context of its use. In theory at least, semantic Web technology could offer better search results than existing technology, and might allow Microsoft to start regaining ground on Google. Around the same time, Microsoft announced that it would extend an existing deal with Facebook, the number two social networking site, to link its search technology with Facebook, enabling people on Facebook sites to use Microsoft's Live Search technology. Microsoft is already the exclusive provider of traditional banner advertising on Facebook.

LOOKING FORWARD

With online advertising predicted to grow strongly, Google seems to be in the driver's seat. It has the largest market share in search, the greatest name recognition, and is capturing a proportionately greater share of search-based advertising than its rivals.

However, despite market share losses, Microsoft and Yahoo! cannot be dismissed. Will they be able to leverage their substantial assets and capabilities to gain ground on Google? As for Google, what is its long-term game plan? Recent strategic moves suggest that it is attempting to expand beyond search, but where will this take the company, and what does that mean for other Internet companies?

Endnotes

1. comScore releases July 2008 U.S. Search Engine Rankings," comScore Press release, August 21, 2008.
2. Nielsen/Net Ratings. "Google Accounts for Half of all U.S. Searches," May 25, 2006.
3. David Hallerman, "Search Marketing: Players and Problems," eMarketer, April 2006. "Search Marketing Still Dominates Online Advertising," eMarketer Press release, January 29, 2008.
4. Citigroup Global Markets, Internet Industry Note, "Key Takeaways from Conference Call on MSFT/GOOG Search Competition," June 4, 2006. "eMarketer Revises US Online Ad Spend Numbers," eMarketer, March 19, 2008.
5. "Google Inc.," Value Line Analysts Report, *Value Line*, August 22, 2008.

6. This section draws heavily on the excellent description of search given by John Battelle. See John Battelle, *The Search*, (Penguin Portfolio, New York, 2005).

7. Google 10-K for 2007.

8. The basic story of GoTo.com is related in John Battelle, *The Search*, (Penguin Portfolio, New York, 2005).

9. Karl Greenberg, "Pay-for-Placement Search Services Offer Ad Alternatives," *Adweek*, September 25, 2000, 60.

10. M. Gannon, "GoTo.com Inc.," *Venture Capital Journal*, August 1, 1999, 1.

11. Tim Jackson, "Cash is the Key to a True Portal," *Financial Times*, February 2, 1999, 16.

12. Karl Greenberg, "Pay-for-Placement Search Services Offer Ad Alternatives," 60.

13. Sarah Heim, "GoTo.com Changes to Overture Services, Launches Campaign," *Adweek*, September 10, 2001, 7.

14. This little gem comes from John Battelle, *The Search*, (Penguin Portfolio, New York, 2005). There is no independent confirmation of the story.

15. Anonymous, "Yahoo! to Acquire Overture Services for 2.44 Times Revenues," *Weekly Corporate Growth Service*, July 21, 2003, 8.

16. Richard Waters, "Google Settles Yahoo! Case with Shares," *Financial Times*, August 19, 2004, 29.

17. Fred Vogelstein, "Gates vs. Google: Search and Destroy," *Fortune*, May 2, 2005, 72–82.

18. This is according to David A. Vise, *The Google Story* (Random House, New York, 2004).

19. Ibid.

20. John Battelle, *The Search*. There is no independent confirmation of the story.

21. http://www.google.com/corporate/index.html

22. http://www.google.com/corporate/tenthings.html

23. Andy Kessler, "Sellout.com," *Wall Street Journal*, January 31, 2006, A14.

24. Quentin Hardy, "Google Thinks Small," *Fortune*, November 14, 2005, 198–199.

25. http://www.google.com/corporate/tenthings.html.

26. Quentin Hardy, "Google Thinks Small," 198–199.

27. Ibid.

28. Ben Elgin, "Managing Google's Idea Factory," *Business Week*, October 3, 2005, 88–90.

29. Michael Krauss, "Google's Mayer Tells How Innovation Gets Done," *Marketing News*, April 1, 2007, 7–8.

30. David A. Vise, *The Google Story*.

31. John Battelle, *The Search*, 233.

32. "Inside the Googleplex," The Economist, September 1, 2007, 53–56.

33. B. Lashinsky and Y. W. Yen, "Where Does Google Go Next?" *Fortune*, May 26, 2008, 104–110.

34. Jacqueline Doherty "In the Drink," *Barrons*, February 13, 2006, 31–36.

35. K. J. Delaney and R. A. Guth, "Google's Free Web Services Will Vie with Microsoft Office," *Wall Street Journal*, October 11, 2006, B1.

36. Mark Mahany, "Building out the Option Value of Google," *Citigroup Portfolio Strategist*, July 13, 2006.

37. "Mobile Ad Spending t Soar," eMarketer Press Release, August 20, 2008.

38. Ben Elgin, "So Much Fanfare, So Few Hits," *Business Week*, July 10, 2006, 26–30.

39. B. Lashinsky, and Y. W. Yen, "Where Does Google Go Next?" 104–110.

40. Ben Elgin, "So Much Fanfare, So Few Hits," 27.

41. David Card, "Understanding Google," *Jupiter Research*, March 10, 2006.

42. Mark Mahany, "Building out the Option Value of Google," *Citigroup Portfolio Strategist*, July 13, 2006.

43. Aline Duyn and Richard Waters, "MySpace Teams up with Google," *Financial Times*, August 8, 2006, 15.

44. "Two Kings Get Together; Google and YouTube," The Economist, October 14, 2006, 82–83.

45. R. Hof, "Ad Wars: Google's Green Light," *BusinessWeek*, March 3, 2008, 22.

46. "Inside the Googleplex," 53–56.

47. "The Ultimate Marketing Machine," The Economist, July 8, 2006, 61–64. K. J. Delaney, "Google Push to Sell Ads on YouTube Hits Snag," *Wall Street Journal*, July 9, 2008, A1.

48. ZanithOptimedia Press release, "Western Ad Markets Continue to Slow," June 30, 2008.

49. "The Ultimate Marketing Machine," 61–64.

50. Citi Investment Research, Google Inc., June 19, 2008.

51. comScore Press release, "comScore releases July 2008 search engine rankings," August 21, 2008.

52. eMarketer press release, "Search marketing still dominates online advertising," January 29, 2008.

53. Nielsen/Net Ratings Press Release, "U.S. Broadband Composition Reaches 72 percent at Home," June 21, 2006. comScore press release, comScore Media Matrix Ranks top 50 U.S. Web Properties for June 2008. July 21, 2008.

54. Chris Nuttall, "Google Moves to Tackle Click Fraud," *Financial Times*, July 27, 2006, 22.

55. David Hallerman "Search Marketing, Players and Problems," *eMarketer*, April 2006.

56. Mark Mahaney, "Yahoo!: Revisiting the Long Thesis," *Citigroup Global Market*, August 17, 2006.

57. Brian Morrissey, "Microsoft Takes Giant Steps in Advertising," *Adweek*, May 8, 2006, 6–8.

58. Brian Haven, "Search Loyalty Is Hard to Find," *Forrester Research*, December 19, 2005.

INTEL IN 2008

INTRODUCTION

In 2008, Intel was the leading manufacturer of micro-processors for personal computers (PCs) in the world, a position that it had held for two decades. Some 77% of all personal computers in 2008 used Intel micro-processors. The company was on track to record revenues in excess of $40 billion and net profits of over $7 billion. Meanwhile Intel's only viable competitor, AMD, which in the early 2000s had been gaining market share from Intel, was expected to lose $1 billion on sales of $6 billion. However, with growth rates in personal computer sales slowing down, Intel was looking for new growth opportunities outside its core business. In recent years, it had turned its attention to mobile wireless Internet devices, where Intel hoped to establish a strong position that would compliment its dominance in the PC market.

THE FOUNDATION OF INTEL

Two executives from Fairchild Semiconductor, Robert Noyce and Gordon Moore, founded Intel in 1968. Fairchild Semiconductor was one of the leading semi-conductor companies in the world and a key enter-prise in an area south of San Francisco that would come to be known as Silicon Valley. Noyce and Moore were no ordinary executives. They had been among the eight founders of Fairchild Semiconductor. Noyce was general manager at the company, while Moore was head of research and development (R&D). Three years earlier, Moore had articulated what came to be known as *Moore's Law*. He had observed that since 1958, due to process improvements, the industry had doubled the number of transistors that could be put on a chip every year (in 1975, he altered this to doubling every two years).

Fairchild Semiconductor had been established in 1957 with funding from Sherman Fairchild, who had backed the founders on the understanding that Fairchild Semiconductor would be a subsidiary of his Fairchild Camera and Instrument Corporation in New York. By 1968, Noyce and Moore were chafing at the bit under management practices imposed from New York, and both decided it was time to strike out on their own. Such were the reputations of Noyce and Moore that they were able to raise $2.3 million to fund the new venture "in an afternoon on the basis of a couple of sheets of paper containing one of the sketchiest business plans ever financed."[1]

When business reporters got wind of the new venture, they asked Noyce and Moore what they were intending to do, only to be greeted by vague replies. The two executives, however, knew exactly what they were going to do. They were going to manufacture silicon memory chips—they just didn't want potential competitors to know that. At the time, sales of mainframe computers were expanding. While these machines used integrated circuits to perform logic calculations, programs and data were stored on magnetic devices. Although inexpensive to produce, accessing information on a magnetic device was relatively slow. Noyce and Moore knew that if they could build a silicon-based integrated circuit that could function as a memory device, they could speed up computers, making them more powerful.

This, in turn, would expand their applications and allow them to shrink in size.

These memory chips were known as dynamic random access memories (DRAMs). While much of the theoretical work required to design an integrated circuit that could function as a memory device had already been done, manufacturing DRAMs cost effectively had so far proved impossible. At the same time, some key research on manufacturing was being done at Fairchild. This research included a technique known as metal oxide on silicon (MOS). Noyce and Moore wanted to mass produce DRAMs. After looking at other possible alternatives, they concluded that commercializing the MOS research was the way to do it. This prompted some cynics to note that Intel was established to steal the MOS process from Fairchild.

ANDY GROVE

Noyce and Moore hired a number of researchers away from Fairchild to help them, including, most notably, a young Hungarian Jewish émigré named Andy Grove. At Fairchild, Grove had reported directly to Moore. At Intel, he became the director of operations, with responsibility for getting products designed on time and built on cost. Through the force of his own personality, Grove would transmute this position into control over just about everything Intel did. This made him effectively the equal of Noyce and Moore, long before he was elevated to the CEO position in 1987.

Grove was an interesting character. Born in 1936, he went into hiding when the Germans invaded Hungary during World War II and managed to escape the Holocaust. After WWII, the tyranny of the Germans was replaced by the tyranny of the Soviets, as Hungary became a satellite state of the Soviet Union. In 1956, after the failure of an uprising against the Soviet puppet government, Grove escaped across the border to Austria and made his way to the United States. He put himself through college in New York by waiting on tables. He then went to UC Berkley for graduate work, where he received a PhD in chemical engineering in 1963. His next stop was Fairchild, where he worked until Moore recruited him away in 1968.

Over the next three decades, Grove would stamp his personality and management style on Intel. Regarded by many as one of the most effective managers of the late twentieth century, Grove was a very demanding and, according to some, autocratic leader who set high expectations for everyone, including himself. He was detail oriented, pushed hard to measure everything, and was constantly looking for ways to drive down costs and speed up development processes. He was known for a confrontational, "in your face" management style, and would frequently intimidate employees, shouting at those who failed to meet his expectations. Grove himself, who seemed to enjoy a good fight, characterized this behavior as "constructive confrontation." He would push people to their limits to get things done. As he once noted, "there is a growth rate at which everybody fails, and the whole situation results in chaos. I feel it is my most important function . . . to identify the maximum growth rate at which this wholesale failure begins."[2]

Grove demanded discipline. For example, he insisted that everybody be at their desks at 8 A.M., even if they had worked long into the night. He instituted a "late list," requiring people who arrived after 8 a.m. to sign in. If people arrived late for meetings, he would not let them attend. Every year, he circulated a memo to employees reminding them that Christmas Eve was not a holiday, and that they were expected to work a full day. Known as the "Scrooge memo," many would be returned with nasty comments scrawled over them. "May you eat yellow snow," said one. A very neat man, Grove would publically criticize employees if their desks were messy. According to one observer, "Andy Grove had an approach to discipline and control that made you wonder how much he had been unwittingly influenced by the totalitarian regime he had been so keen to escape."[3]

Grove controlled managers through a regular budgeting process that required them to make detailed revenue and cost projections. He also insisted that all managers establish medium-term objectives, and a set of key results by which success or failure would be measured. He instituted regular one-on-one meetings, during which performance was reviewed against objectives, holding managers accountable for shortfalls. He also required monthly management reviews, where managers from different parts of the company would meet to hear a presentation of its current strengths, weaknesses, opportunities, and threats. The goal was to get managers to step back and look at the bigger picture, and to encourage them to help each other solve problems.

Grove would also practice management by inspecting facilities and offices, demanding that they be clean, something that earned him the nickname "Mr. Clean." He pushed the human resource department to institute a standard system of ranking and rating that had four performance categories: "superior," "exceeds expectations," "meets expectations," or "does not meet expectations." People were compared against others of their rank. Pay raises and later, stock option awards, were based on these rankings.

Despite his autocratic style, Grove was grudgingly admired within the company. He was a brilliant problem solver, a man with tremendous control of facts and details, and someone who was determined to master the challenging technical projects that Intel was working on. Moreover, while he drove everyone hard, he drove himself harder still, thereby earning the respect of many employees.

THE MEMORY CHIP COMPANY

Making a DRAM using MOS methods proved to be extremely challenging. One major problem encountered was that small amounts of dust would contaminate the circuits during manufacturing, making them useless. So Intel had to develop "clean rooms" for keeping dust out of the process. Another challenge was how to etch circuit lines on silicon wafers, without having the etched lines fracture and break as the wafer was heated and cooled repeatedly during the manufacturing process. The solution to this problem, identified by Moore, was to "dope" the metal oxide with impurities, making it less brittle. Intel subsequently went to some lengths to keep this aspect of the manufacturing process secret from competitors for as long as possible.

Intel, of course, was not alone in the race to develop a commercial process for manufacturing DRAMs. Among the potential competitors was another semiconductor company started in 1969 by Jerry Sanders, a former marketing director at Fairchild. Sanders started his company (AMD) with the help of several other Fairchild employees who had not been recruited by Intel. AMD found it tough to raise capital until it received an investment from none other than Robert Noyce, who saw something he liked in the flamboyant Sanders.

Driven by constant pressure from Andy Grove, whose "in your face" management style was bearing fruit albeit at some human cost, by October 1970 Intel succeeded in producing a DRAM chip, named the 1103, in relatively high yields (which implied that relatively few chips had to be discarded). The 1103 could store 1,024 bits of information (zeros or ones), which was four times as much as the highest capacity semiconductor memory device currently available. Since the fixed costs required to establish a manufacturing facility were very high, the key to making money on the 1103 was high yields and high volume. If Intel could achieve both, unit costs would fall, thereby enabling Intel to make a lot of profit at low price points. In turn, low prices implied that DRAMs would start to gain wide adoption among computer manufacturers.

The 1103 put Intel firmly on the map. The chip soon became the memory technology of choice for computer makers. By the end of 1971, 14 out of the world's 18 leading mainframe computer makers were using the 1103. However, Intel did not have the market entirely to itself. Computer makers did not want to become dependent on a single source of supply for critical components. To avoid this, most computer makers mandated that components had to be at least duel sourced. For Intel, this meant that if it wanted business, it had to license its technology to other companies. Intel first licensed the rights to produce the 1103 to a Canadian firm named MIL in exchange for an upfront payment and per unit royalty fee. Before long, MIL was competing against Intel in the market for the 1103. However, MIL made a critical mistake in its manufacturing processes and it wasn't long before a stream of former MIL customers were knocking on Intel's door.

Along the way, Intel received an inquiry from two disgruntled engineers at Honeywell, asking if Intel was interested in building memory systems. The idea was to mount thousands of 1103 chips on a circuit board that could then be plugged into a mainframe computer to increase its memory capability. Impressed by the idea, Intel promptly hired the two engineers and set up a division to do this. Before long, the new division was selling circuit boards to customers running IBM mainframes. This was something of a coup: IBM would not even consider buying the 1103 and had started making its own memory chips. Now Intel had access to a formerly closed market that accounted for 70% of all memory sales.

Around the same time, an accidental discovery at Intel led to a second product line: erasable programmable read only memory (EPROM). Read only memory chips (ROM) were finding wide applications in computing. ROM had desired data, a program for example, permanently burnt into its circuits. ROM was used to store programs, such as a machine operating system, or a part of that system. The troubling thing about ROM is that if an engineer made a mistake in programming the chip, he or she would have to burn another chip, which was a painstaking and time-consuming process. Dov Froham, another ex-Fairchild researcher at Intel, explored the reason for the failure of 1103 chips in the manufacturing process. He found that the cause was that some of the "gates" inside the chips had become disconnected; they were floating. Froham realized that this flaw in the 1103 had a potential use. It might enable an engineer to design a ROM chip that could be programmed with ease in a few minutes. Moreover, he found that the data on such chips could be erased and rewritten by shinning an ultra violet light on them. Thus, the EPROM was born.

Engineers loved the EPROM chip. Once Intel solved the manufacturing problem and started to produce EPROM chips in large quantities, demand surged. Better still, for two years Intel had a virtual monopoly on the product. While other companies tried to produce similar chips, they were unable to solve the manufacturing problems involved. This enabled Intel to charge a relatively high price for a product whose cost was falling every day with advances in cumulative volume.

THE BIRTH OF THE MICROPROCESSOR

By 1971, Intel had already created two revolutionary innovations in the semiconductor industry: DRAM and the EPROM chips. A third, the microprocessor, was also created that year. The microprocessor was born out of an inquiry from a Japanese company. The company asked Intel if it could build a set of eight logic chips to perform arithmetic functions in a calculator it was planning to produce. Intel took on the project. Ted Hoff, one of the inventors of the DRAM, wondered if it might not make more sense to build a miniaturized general purpose computer, which could then be programmed to do the arithmetic for the company's calculator.

The project was assigned to Federico Faggin, an Italian engineer who made some of the basic breakthroughs on MOS technology while working at Fairchild. Although the Japanese company subsequently decided not to build the calculator, Intel pushed ahead with the project. Faggin, who worked 12- to 14-hour days for weeks on end, produced several prototypes in short order. (A source of irritation for Faggin was that despite the long hours, his boss, following Grove's lead, constantly complained that Faggin was late for work!)

Due to Faggin's efforts, by November 1971, Intel had its third product, the 4004 microprocessor. In an article in *Electronic News* that accompanied its introduction and which described the 4004 as a computer on a chip, Gordon Moore heralded the 4004 as "one of the most revolutionary products in the history of mankind." No one paid much attention. People in the computer industry viewed the 4004 as a fascinating novelty. Although small and cheap, it could process only 4 bits of information at a time, which made it slow and thus unsuitable for use in the computers of the time. The 4004 was followed by the 8008 microprocessor, which could process eight bits of information at a time. Although faster, it too was a product in search of a market. In an attempt to speed adoption, Intel started to sell development tools that made it easier and faster for outside engineers to develop and test programs for new microprocessors. Slowly the microprocessor began to make inroads into the computer industry, primarily in peripherals such as printers and tape drives.

THE PERSONAL COMPUTER REVOLUTION

By the mid-1970s, an embryonic new industry was appearing—the personal computer industry. A company named MITS based in Albuquerque, New Mexico, produced the first true personal computer. The MITS Altair used an Intel 8080 microprocessor, which was priced at $360. The first program offered for sale with the Altair was a version of BASIC programming language, written by Bill Gates and Paul Allen, and designed to run on the 8080. The two had moved to Albuquerque to be near to MITS, and had established a company of their own, Microsoft. The Altair was sold primarily to hobbyists who wanted to write computer code at home (for which Microsoft Basic came in handy).

In short order, a number of companies sprung up making personal computers. The most successful of the early companies was Apple Computer, which introduced its revolutionary Apple II in 1977. By this time, a number of other companies were also producing microprocessors, including Motorola, whose processor Apple used in the Apple II. The Apple II was a large commercial success in no small part because it was easy to use. Additionally, one of the most successful early programs, a spreadsheet called VisiCalc, was written to run on the Apple II.

The commercial success of the Apple II got the world's largest computer company, IBM, to take the nascent personal computer seriously. IBM started to develop its own personal computer in 1979 as a top secret project. To speed the product to market, IBM made a monumental strategic decision. It decided to use "off-the-shelf components" to build the PC rather than develop everything itself, which had been the norm at IBM. Originally, the company planned to use a microprocessor from Motorola and an operating system called CP/M from a company called Digital Research. However, Motorola was late developing its product, and Digital Research's CEO, Gary Kildall, proved to be difficult to work with. Casting around for alternatives, IBM contacted Intel and offered to purchase its latest microprocessor, the 8088, which was a derivative of Intel's 8086 chip. However, IBM did not tell Intel what the microprocessor was to be used for (originally Intel was told that it was to go in a printer). As part of the deal, IBM insisted on alternative sources for the 8088. Reluctantly Intel allowed AMD and a number of other companies to produce the 8088 under license. A 1982 cross-licensing agreement with AMD, which gave AMD the right to produce the 8088 chip, would come to haunt Intel for years to come.

For the operating system of its first PC, IBM decided to use MS-DOS, a Microsoft operating system. Originally developed by Seattle Computer, and called Q-DOS (which stood for quick and dirty

operating system), it was purchased by Microsoft for $50,000 when Bill Gates heard that IBM was looking for an operating system. Gates renamed the product, quickly turning around and licensing MS-DOS to IBM. In what was to be a stroke of genius that had enormous implications for the future of all parties involved, Gates, sensing that IBM executives were desperate to get their hands on an operating system to get the IBM PC to market on time, negotiated a *non-exclusive* license with IBM.

Executives at Intel, who by now had realized that IBM was developing a personal computer, were profoundly unimpressed with the choice of MS-DOS and Microsoft. After a visit to Microsoft, one Intel executive noted: "These people are flakes. They're not original, they don't really understand what they are doing, their ambitions are very low, and it's not really clear that they have succeeded even at that."[4] For its part, Microsoft had to produce a version of MS-DOS that would run on the Intel microprocessor. From that point on, like it or not, Microsoft and Intel would be joined at the hip.

Introduced in 1981, the IBM PC was an instant success. To stoke sales, IBM offered a number of applications for it that were sold separately, including a version of VisiCalc, a word processor called EasyWriter, and a well-known series of business programs from Peachtree Software. Over the next two years, IBM would sell more than 500,000 PCs, seizing market leadership from Apple. IBM had what Apple lacked—an ability to sell into corporate America.

As sales of the IBM PC mounted, two things occurred. First, independent software developers started to write programs to run on the IBM PC. These included two applications that drove adoptions of the IBM PC: word processing programs (WordPerfect) and a spreadsheet (Lotus 1-2-3). Second, the success of IBM gave birth to clone manufacturers who made "IBM-compatible" PCs that also utilized an Intel microprocessor and Microsoft's MS-DOS operating system. The first and most successful of the clone makers was Compaq, which in 1983 introduced its first personal computer, a 28-pound "portable" PC. In its first year, Compaq booked $111 million in sales, at the time a record for first year sales of a company. Before long, a profusion of IBM clone makers entered the market, including Tandy, Zenith, Leading Edge, and Dell Computer. This influx led to market share fragmentation in the PC industry.

By 1982 Intel had a replacement chip ready for the IBM PC, the 80286 microprocessor. The 80286 was desperately needed because the 8088 was painfully slow running some of the newer applications. IBM introduced a new PC named the AT to use the 80286 chip, and priced it at a premium. Demand was so strong that IBM put the AT on allocation, which opened the door to clone makers, particularly Compaq. By this time, 70% of the microprocessors sold to PC manufacturers were made by Intel, with AMD accounting for a significant portion of the remainder. For the 80286, Intel had cut the number of licenses down to four. It also ran an intensive marketing and sales campaign called Checkmate, which was successful in getting many original equipment manufacturers (OEMs) to use Intel's version of the 80286 in their machines.

THE DRAM DEBACLE

In 1984, Intel booked revenues of $1.6 million and made almost $200 million net profit, up from $134 million in revenues and $20 million in net profit a decade earlier. The growth had been dramatic. However, Intel's share of the DRAM market had been sliding for years. New entrants, particularly from Japan, had been grabbing DRAM sales. They had done this by undertaking large-scale investment to build efficient fabrication facilities (fabs) and paying meticulous attention to quality and costs, doing everything possible to drive up yields. One source suggested that, while peak yields in United States DRAM plants such as Intel's were around 50%, in Japan they were closer to 80%. This translated into a huge cost advantage for Japanese producers.

American manufacturers, Intel included, had made the crucial mistake of underestimating the Japanese threat. Demands from computer companies for second sources had helped to facilitate diffusion of the underlying product technology and commoditized DRAMs. In such a market, the advantage went to the most efficient manufacturer, and this was the Japanese. Moreover, Japanese companies seized the lead in developing more powerful DRAM chips. While Intel had created the market for DRAMs, and dominated the market for 1K chips, in each subsequent generation it fell further and

further behind. By 1983 when fifth generation 256K DRAMs started to appear, Intel was a year behind in the development cycle. Consequently, it was at a distinct cost disadvantage when it introduced its product. Somehow, despite Grove's aggressive leadership, Intel's share had fallen to only 1% of the total DRAM market. To regain market share, management understood that Intel would have to build a new fabrication facility at a cost of $600 million and throw company R&D resources behind an effort to bring a next generation 1 megabyte DRAM chip to the market. To make matters worse, the DRAM market was in a large slump brought on by overcapacity as a result of aggressive investments by Asian producers, and Intel was losing money in the DRAM business.

Faced with this bleak prospect, Intel's senior management had to decide whether to continue to compete in the DRAM business—the market they had created—or to focus resources on the more profitable microprocessor market. It was not an easy decision. Irrespective of the economics, there was enormous emotional attachment within the company to the DRAM business. Many at Intel wanted to build a 1MB DRAM. There were also valid arguments for staying in the DRAM business. Some thought that DRAMs were the technology driver in semiconductor manufacturing, and without the knowledge gained from making DRAMs, Intel's microprocessor business would suffer. In addition, there was the argument that customers would prefer to buy from a company that offered a full product range. If it exited the DRAM business, Intel would not be able to do that.

As Andy Grove describes it, a crucial point arrived when he and Gordon Moore were discussing what Intel's strategy should be. Grove asked Moore, "If we got kicked out, and the board brought in a new CEO, what would he do?" Moore replied, "He would get us out of memories." Grove then said, "Why don't we just walk out of the door, and come back and do it ourselves." It was one thing to make the decision another to implement it. Grove removed the head of the DRAM division, recognizing that he was not the man to wield the ax, and replaced him. The new manager promptly "went native" and started to argue for going ahead with the 1MB DRAM chip. He too was replaced, and a year after the decision was made, Intel finally exited the DRAM business.

THE MICROPROCESSOR BUSINESS

In 1987, Gordon Moore stepped down as CEO of Intel, passing the torch on to Andy Grove, although Moore remained as Chairman. Grove, who held the CEO position until 1998, and was then chairman until 2005, had no intention of letting Intel's dominance in microprocessors go the same way as its DRAM business.

Chip Design

By this point it was well understood at Intel that the market had an unquenchable thirst for more powerful microprocessors. Software was advancing rapidly, with new applications becoming available all the time. Running these applications quickly required more computing power, and users were willing to pay a premium for this. Intel knew that consumers would be only too happy to replace their old PCs with better, faster machines. It thus became critical to develop and introduce newer microprocessors. At the same time, the market demanded backward compatibility. The new machines had to run older software, and this meant that each new generation of chip should be able to run older programs. This requirement also implied that to a degree, Intel was locked into the microprocessor architecture that had started with the 8086 (from which the 8088 was derived), and continued with the 80286. The next microprocessor in what was now known as the x86 architecture was the 80386, or i386 for short.

First introduced in October 1985, the i386 was a 32-bit microprocessor that was much faster than the i286. Intel had been trying for over a year to get IBM to introduce a machine based on the i386, but IBM seemed to be dragging its feet. The problem for IBM was that an i386 PC would be very close in power to minicomputers that IBM was making a lot of money on. Fearing that i386 machines would cannibalize its product line, IBM seemed to want to keep the i386 off the market as long as possible. At the same time, Apple had introduced a new machine, the first Macintosh, which used a Motorola microprocessor. The Apple Mac was the first computer with a graphical user interface (GUI) and a mouse. As it started to gain market share, Grove feared that the market might switch to the Apple standard. This

made it more critical than ever to get i386-based machines on the market.

Intel had an ally in Compaq. In 1986, Compaq took advantage of IBM's sloth to be the first to introduce a PC built around the i386. Compaq seized the lead from IBM, other computer makers quickly followed, and from that point on IBM began to lose influence and share in the PC business. As the high margin i386 chip gained traction, Intel's sales exploded, hitting $2.9 billion in 1988, while profits surged to $450 million.

Over the next two decades Intel continued to drive the industry forward with regular advances in its x86 architecture. These included the i486 (introduced in 1989), the first Pentium chip (1993), the Pentium Pro (1995), various derivatives of the Pentium Pro architecture, and, more recently, its 64-bit Core 2 Duo and Quad processor line, first introduced in 2006 (see Exhibit 1). The latest Intel processors have pushed the limits of performance by building two or four processors into a chip. Intel prices new chips at a premium and then drops prices as manufacturing yields improve. It is not unusual to see prices drop by 30%–50% in one year.

By continually increasing the performance of its chips, Intel was able to vanquish several potential competitors. This included a series of fast chips from AMD in the early 2000s and several chips based on an architecture known as reduced instruction set computing (RISC) that during the 1990s seemed to threaten Intel's market dominance. One notable RISC chip arose out of an attempt by Apple, Motorola, and IBM to seize momentum away from Intel with a RISC processor called the PowerPC. However, few companies outside Apple adopted the processor. The limited volume meant high costs, which were further compounded by manufacturing problems at Motorola, and the PowerPC never gained wide acceptance. In 2006, Apple effectively killed the PowerPC when it announced that it would henceforth use Intel microprocessors in its machines.

Following Moore's law, successive generations of Intel chips have used ever smaller micron geometries to cram ever more transistors on a chip (see Exhibit 1). The size of features on the Core 2 Quad chip for example, is 0.065 micron (a micron is one millionth of a meter), and fast versions can run at 3.33 GHz (3.33 billion cycles per second). By comparison, the Intel 80286 used a feature size of 1.5 microns, and the fastest model ran at

Exhibit 1 Intel's Chips

Intel Chip	Number of Transistors	Year of Introduction
Intel 4004	2,300	1971
Intel 8088	29,000	1979
Intel 80286	134,000	1982
Intel 80386	275,000	1985
Intel 80486	1,200,000	1989
Pentium	3,100,000	1993
Pentium II	7,500,000	1997
Pentium III	9,500,000	1999
Pentium 4	42,000,000	2000
Core 2 Duo	291,000,000	2006
Core 2 Quad	582,000,000	2006

Source: Intel Corporation.

25 MHz (million cycles per second). By 2007 Intel was working with chips that had a feature size of just 0.045 microns. Driving chip design forward requires very heavy R&D spending. By the mid-2000s, Intel was spending over $5.5 billion a year on R&D, or 15% of sales. This spending was divided between chip design and improving manufacturing processes.

Manufacturing Processes

Designing and manufacturing these devices requires constantly pushing against the limits of physics and technology. Microprocessors are built in layers on a silicon wafer through various processes using chemicals, gas, and light. It is an extremely demanding process involving more than 300 steps. On modern chips, 20 layers are connected with microcircuitry to form a complex three-dimensional structure.

The high-tech fabrication plants required to manufacture microprocessors cost up to $3 billion each (by 2008 Intel had 15 of these plants around the world). To equip its plants, Intel works very closely with equipment vendors. Due to its scale, Intel enjoys considerable leverage over equipment suppliers. In some cases, Intel will design a new machine itself

and then have equipment vendors manufacture it. In others, Intel works closely with vendors on the design of a piece of equipment. As a result, Intel itself holds hundreds of patents relating to the process for manufacturing semiconductors. Whenever equipment is developed specifically for Intel's requirements, vendors are generally prohibited from selling that equipment to other companies, such as AMD, for a given period.

When installing new equipment, the goal is to gain manufacturing efficiencies through increased yields, or other process improvements. For example, in the 2000s Intel switched from using 200 mm to 300 mm wafers in its manufacturing processes, which enabled it to put more microprocessors on a wafer, increasing throughput and lowering costs. Next generation equipment, which is scheduled for introduction in 2012, will use 400 mm wafers.

To boost yields, raising the percentage of processors that come off the line functioning perfectly, Intel uses sophisticated statistical process control procedures. Over time, Intel has turned this into a precise science; with each succeeding generation of microprocessor geometry, the company seems able to achieve a steeper learning curve (see Exhibit 2). By constantly pushing the envelope with regard to manufacturing technology, product design, and yields, Intel has reportedly been able to reduce its unit manufacturing costs for a processor by as much as 25%–30% per year.

Intellectual Property

From the i386 chip onward, Grove was determined to ensure that Intel was the only supplier in the world of its architecture. AMD, however, believed that under the terms of the 1982 technology-sharing agreement between the two companies, it had rights to Intel's designs. Intel simply refused to hand over technical specifications for the i386 to AMD, sparking a lengthy court battle between the two that persisted until 1995. In the end, the two chipmakers agreed to drop all pending lawsuits against each other, settled existing lawsuits, and signed a cross-licensing agreement. Irrespective of the final settlement, AMD had spent $40 million a year on legal fees alone, and senior management attention had been diverted by the ongoing legal battle. AMD had been slow to develop its own version of the i386, waiting instead to get specifications from Intel, which only shared them after ordered to in a 1990 ruling.

Exhibit 2   Yields in Microprocessor Manufacturing at Intel

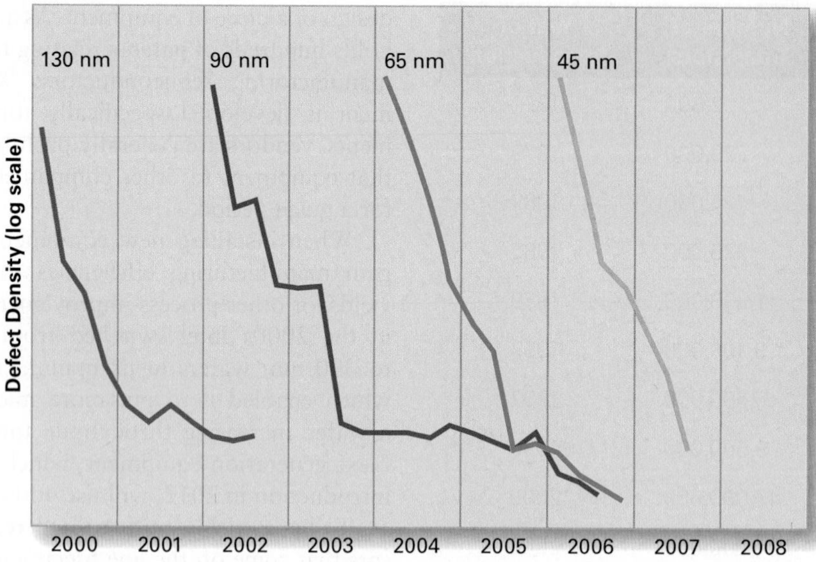

Source: Intel Corporation, http://www.intel.com/technology/itj/2008/v12i2/5-design/8-manufacturability.htm.

Intel Inside

For years, Intel had viewed its customers as OEMs, focusing its marketing efforts on engineers within those companies. But the nature of the end market was changing. By the early 1990s, increasingly sophisticated customers were making their own purchasing decisions, often in computer super-stores or buying direct from companies like Dell and Gateway. Consumers now had influence on the process and could exercise choice over not only the machine but also the components that went into it, including the microprocessor.

In 1991, Intel started to market directly to consumers with its *Intel Inside* campaign, effectively telling them that a computer with an Intel chip inside would guar-antee advanced technology and compatibility with prior software. Supported by slick advertisements, the campaign was a stunning success. Within a year, Intel was listed as the third most valuable brand name on the planet. In 1993, Grove was able to claim that the number of consumers who preferred a PC with an Intel microprocessor had risen from 60% to 80%. By 1994, some 1,200 computer companies had signed on to the campaign, adhering "Intel Inside" logos on their machines, or including the logo on their product ads.

Complicating matters, one aspect of the long-running legal battle between Intel and AMD was a trademark dispute. Intel had claimed that "386" referred to its trademark, and competitors like AMD could not use it. However, in 1991 a court had ruled that the name "386" was so widely used that it had become generic. The ruling infuriated Grove, who believed that clone makers would now be able to piggyback on Intel's marketing campaigns for the 386 and 486. He suggested that the next chip, which was to have been known as the i586, be given another name that could be trademarked, and the Pentium was born.

Forward Vertical Integration and Customers

Intel vertically integrated forward into the produc-tion of PCs in the mid-1980s, selling "boxes" without a screen, keyboard, or brand logo to well-known computer companies who put their own brand on them and resold them. The move led to complaints from several of Intel's customers, who felt that Intel was indirectly competing against them in the end market and lowering barriers to entry into the PC industry. After push back, in the early 1990s, Intel exited this business. However, the company continued to make motherboards (large, printed circuit boards that hold the microprocessors), other critical chips, slots for connecting memory and graphics cards, and so on.

Intel's move into motherboards assured more rapid diffusion of each new generation of chips, by making it much easier for PC companies to incorporate them into their machines. The move infuriated PC manufacturers such as Compaq and IBM who generally made their own motherboards. Compaq had been able to gain a competitive advantage by bringing PCs containing the latest generation Intel chips to market early. Compaq responded by trying to reduce their dependence on Intel. They used chips from AMD and initially refused to participate in the Intel inside branding scheme. However, by the mid-1990s, Intel's position was so strong that this had only marginal impact on the company.

Intel continued to make motherboards through the 2000s, even though profit margins were lower than on sales of stand-alone microprocessors. By 2007, some 24% of Intel's revenues came from the sale of motherboards. At this point, large branded OEMs with a global reach (HP, Dell, Lenovo, Acer, Toshiba, and Apple), accounted for approximately 50%–53% of global PC sales, with the remainder being captured by a long tail of smaller local brands. As of 2007, 18% of Intel's total sales (stand-alone chips and motherboards) went to Dell. Hewlett-Packard (HP) accounted for another 17%, with no other company accounting for more than 10%.

The Microsoft Connection

Throughout the 1980s and much of the 1990s, the relationship between Intel and Microsoft was an uneasy one. When Microsoft introduced Windows 3.0 in 1990, its first operating system with a GUI, it boosted demand for new PCs to run graphics heavy programs. The same happened when Windows 95 was introduced five years later. In both cases, Intel was a beneficiary of the resulting upgrade cycle. Intel clearly needed Microsoft, but that did not mean that Intel respected them. Intel was frustrated that Microsoft did not seem particularly interested in optimizing its software to run on Intel's chips. Microsoft's engineers seemed more concerned with adding features to their products than in streamlining code so that it took advantage of the full capabilities of Intel's microprocessors.

Microsoft, on the other hand, was interested in making its Windows operating system as ubiquitous as possible. This logically implied making a version of Windows that would run on other microprocessors, such as the new generation of RISC chips. During the 1990s, Microsoft was eyeing users of powerful computer workstations, many of which used RISC chips. This potential nightmare for Intel became all too real when Microsoft announced the development of Windows NT, a high end version of Windows that would run on both Intel and RISC microprocessors, including the PowerPC. What stopped the nightmare from occurring was the development of the Pentium Pro, which was so fast and efficient that it effectively eclipsed rivals who used RISC architecture.

Reflecting these underlying tensions, the relationships between Andy Grove and Microsoft's Bill Gates were often rocky, and there were reports of meetings dissolving into shouting matches. This started to change in the mid-1990s. It may have been that after the failure of the RISC challenge to Intel, the two companies and their respective leaders recognized their interdependence and decided cooperation was better than conflict. Beginning in 1996, quarterly meetings were held between Grove and Gates, aimed at coordinating strategy and resolving differences.

THE BARRETT ERA

In 1998, Craig Barrett succeeded Andy Grove as CEO. A former Stanford engineering professor who had become chief operating officer of Intel in 1993, Barrett's tenure as CEO was marked by an aggressive push into new markets. By the 1990s, the Internet was starting to take center place in computing, and Barrett saw opportunities in extending Intel's reach into chips to drive computer networking gear and wireless handsets. Moreover, Barrett was concerned that without product diversification, Intel would not be able to maintain its growth rate given the maturation of the PC market in many developed nations. In his first three years as CEO, Intel spent $12 billion on acquisitions and new internal ventures designed to strengthen the company's position in these emerging areas.

Barrett's push into these areas failed to yield any quick returns. By 2004, Intel only had 6% of the market for chips used in networking gear and 7% of the market for processing chips within wireless phones. Part of the problem was that Intel ran into stiff competition from embedded competitors. In the market for wireless phone chips, for example, Intel was competing against the likes of Texas Instruments and Qualcomm, both of whom had a strong market and technological position.

Moreover, Barrett's tenure was marred by some embarrassing product delays, capacity constraints that drove some customers to AMD, and product recalls. To make matters worse, in the early 2000s, AMD seized the lead in chip design for the first time. For two years AMD could boast that it was technological leader in the industry until Intel recaptured the lead with newer chips. Complicating matters, the PC industry went through a sharp contraction in 2001 that led to slumping sales and profits for Intel. While the industry recovered in 2002, growth rates since 2002 have been lower than in the 1990s.

Some observers have blamed the problems of the Barrett era on management issues at Intel. The company, they say, had become too large, too bureaucratic, and was no longer the egalitarian entity of its early years. The "constructive confrontation" of the Grove years, which had kept managers on their toes, had been replaced by an autocratic culture dominated by people who got promoted for managing upward. A management vacuum following Grove's departure led to a lack of accountability and control. To quote one critic: "In the Grove era, each leader who spearheaded an unsuccessful attempt left the company after the project failed. However, throughout the Barrett era each figurehead has remained at Intel after the project failed."[5]

PAUL OTELLINI'S PLATFORM STRATEGY

In 2005, Barrett became chairman and was replaced as CEO by Paul Otellini. Another long time Intel employee, Otellini was the first Intel CEO to not have an engineering background (Otellini was an MBA with a career in finance and marketing). As head of company-wide sales and marketing, Otellini gained prominence at Intel during the late 1990s by pushing the company to adopt a more aggressive approach to market segmentation. By the late 1990s, prices for low-end PCs were falling to under $1,000, and in this commodity market OEMs were casting around for cheaper microprocessor and motherboard options. Otellini came up with the idea of reserving the Pentium brand for higher end chips and creating a new brand, Celeron, for lower performance chips aimed at low-cost PCs.

During the early 2000s, Otellini pushed for the creation of the Centrino chip platform for laptop computers. While Intel engineers were focused on designing faster, more powerful processors, Otellini argued that laptop users cared more about heat generation, battery life, and wireless capabilities. The Centrino platform was designed for them. It combined an Intel microprocessor with a Wi-Fi chip (for wireless networking) and associated software. Personal computer manufacturers were initially skeptical about the value of the Centrino platform. For a while, they continued to buy Intel microprocessors while purchasing Wi-Fi chips from other companies. But when performance tests showed that the Centrino platform worked well, most manufacturers shifted to purchasing this platform for their laptops, and Centrino quickly became a recognizable brand.

Introduced in 2003, the Centrino was a huge hit and helped to pull Intel out of its sales slump. Indeed, by 2008 Intel was dominating the market for laptop chips with its chipset offerings. After succeeding Barrett, Otellini called for the Centrino strategy to be applied to other areas of the computer industry. He wanted Intel to design separate "platforms" for corporate computers, home computers, and laptop computers. Each platform was to combine several chips and focus on providing utility to a specific customer set. The platforms for corporate computers was to package a microprocessor with chips and software that enhanced the security of computers, keeping them virus free, and allowed for the remote management and servicing of computers (which could bring large cost savings to corporations). The platform for home computers was to combine a microprocessor with chips and software for a wireless base station (for home networking), chips for showing digital movies, and chips for three dimensional graphics processing (for computer games).

The goal was to enable Intel to capture more of the value going into every computer sold, thus increasing the company's profitability and profit growth. To implement this plan, Otellini announced a sweeping reorganization of Intel, creating separate market-focused divisions for mobile computing (laptops), corporate computing, home computing, and health care computing (which Intel regards as a promising growth market with its own unique set of customer requirements). Each division has its own engineering, software, and marketing personnel, and is charged with developing a platform for its target market.

INTEL IN 2008

Intel entered 2008 gaining market share from AMD, which, after seizing the technological lead from Intel in the early 2000s, was stumbling again. Intel's worldwide share of microprocessors for PCs hit 77.46% in 2007, up from 75.12% a year earlier, while AMD's share slipped to 22.26% from 23.06%. In the server market, where chips typically carry higher margins, Intel was even more dominant, capturing an 84.73% market share, up from 75.60% in 2006. AMD's share fell sharply to 14.27% from 24.17% in 2006. A big part of Intel's success could be attributed to its pioneering introduction of very powerful microprocessors with four computing cores. After a rough start, Otellini's strategy seemed to be bearing fruit.

In 2006, Intel exited its struggling communications chip business. Between 2006 and 2008 the workforce was cut by 20,000, while costs were reduced by $3 billion. However, the company did not lose sight of the need to produce processors for mobile devices. In mid-2008, Intel introduced a new line of low-power consumption chips called Atom that were aimed at mobile Internet devices (MIDs). These are devices that fall somewhere between a smartphone and a conventional laptop and include netbooks (very small laptops meant primarily for web surfing). Forecasts suggest that $3.5 billion worth of MIDs may be sold in 2008, with the figure rising to over $25 billion by 2013. Early reports suggested that the demand for Atom was very strong, with Intel selling $200 million worth in its first quarter in the market.

Intel has also been making moves into the graphics chip business, integrating graphics capabilities into its chipsets. Although Intel has gained some share at the low end, ATI and Nvidia currently dominate the high-end graphics chip business. The most important and demanding applications for graphics chips are computer games. In 2006, AMD purchased ATI for $5.4 billion, signaling its intention to bundle microprocessors and graphics chips together. As of late 2008, there were rumors that Intel might acquire Nvidia.

For its part, AMD reopened its legal battle with Intel, launching an antitrust suit against them. AMD claims that, as it started to gain share on Intel in the early 2000s, Intel responded by offering deep discounts and rebates to certain customers (mostly in Japan), which enticed them to significantly reduce their demand for AMD microprocessors over two years. AMD's share of Sony's business, for example, dropped from 23% in 2002 to almost zero in 2004. AMD's claim is that Intel was essentially using its monopoly power to engage in predatory pricing. They claimed that the goal was to keep AMD from gaining 30%–35% of the microprocessor market because at that point, Intel's stranglehold on the market would probably break. No ruling on the case is expected before the end of the decade.

Meanwhile, by late 2008, the market for PCs seems to be facing a global slowdown, brought on by the crisis that rocked world financial markets in late 2008, and seems likely to reduce consumer spending worldwide for anything from a few months to several years.

Exhibit 3 Intel's Recent Financial Performance

$ Billions	2005	2006	2007
Revenues ($ Billions)	$38.8	$35.4	$38.3
Cost of Good Sold	$18.4	$ 17.2	$15.2
R&D Spending	$ 5.1	$ 5.9	$ 5.8
Selling, General, and Administrative Expenses	$ 5.7	$ 6.1	$ 5.4
Net Profit ($ Billions)	$ 8.7	$ 5.0	$ 7.0
Return on Invested Capital	22.7%	13.1%	15.6%

Endnotes

1. Tim Jackson, *Inside Intel* (New York, Penguin Books, 1997), 18.
2. R. S. Redlow, "The Education of Andy Grove," *Fortune* (December 12, 2005), 116.
3. Tim Jackson, *Inside Intel* (New York, Penguin Books, 1997), 33.
4. Ibid., 206.
5. B. Coleman and L. Shrine, "Losing Faith: How the Grove Survivors Led the Decline of Intel's Corporate Culture," (Logan and Shrine, 2006), 117.

References & Readings

1. Anonymous, "Intel's Right Hand Turn," *The Economist*, May 14 2005, 67.
2. Anonymous, "The Empire Strikes Back," *The Economist*, December 2 2006, 69.
3. Anonymous, "Battlechips," *The Economist*, June 7 2008, 75–76.
4. B. Colman and L. Shrine, *Losing Faith*, Colman and Shrine, 2006.
5. R. P. Colwell, *The Pentium Chronicles*, John Wiley, New Jersey, 2006.
6. C. Edwards, "Getting Intel Back on the Inside Track," *Business Week*, November 29 2004, 39.
7. C. Edwards, "Shaking up Intel's Insides," *Business Week*, January 31 2005, 35.
8. P. Frieberger and M. Swaine, *Fire in the Valley*, McGraw Hill, New York, 2000.
9. A. Hesseldahl, "AMD vs Intel: The Challengers New Plan," *Business Week Online*, July 11 2008, 1.
10. A. Hesseldahl, "AMD Wins Another Round Against Intel," *Business Week Online*, June 9 2008, 12.
11. Intel Corporation, Form 10K, 2007.
12. T. Jackson, *Inside Intel*, Penguin Books, New York, 1997.
13. A. Lashinsky, "Is This the Right Man for Intel?," *Fortune*, April 18 2005, 110–120.
14. R. Parloff, "Intel's Worst nightmare," *Fortune*, August 21, 2006, 60–70.
15. B. Snyder Bulik, "Intel's New Strategy Demands a New Partner," *Advertising Age*, March 14 2005, 4–5.

The Global Auto Industry

INTRODUCTION

As the first decade of the 21st century drew to a close, the global automobile industry was facing unprecedented economic challenges. A deep recession had driven automobile sales down to levels not seen since the 1960s. Many long-established companies, including General Motors (GM), Chrysler, and Toyota, sought government aid to help them survive the downturn. Ultimately, Chrysler had to seek Chapter 11 bankruptcy protection. General Motors, also went down that road. In contrast, Toyota, with $19 billion in cash on its balance sheet, looked well positioned to survive the downturn in good shape.

At the same time, two seismic shifts were taking place in the structure of global demand. First, while demand imploded in many developed nations during 2008, growth continued in some developed nations, particularly China, which experts predicted could become the world's biggest automobile market sometime between 2016 and 2020. Reflecting this, several automobile companies from developing nations were using their strong home markets as springboards to expand their global reach. These included Tata Motors of India, which purchased Jaguar and Land Rover from Ford in 2008, and China's Geely, which, in mid-2009, was reportedly bidding for General Motor's Saab unit and Ford's Volvo subsidiary, both of which were based in Sweden.[1] In addition, high fuel costs were driving a migration in demand away from large vehicles, such as the sports utility (SUVs) vehicles so beloved by Americans, toward smaller more fuel-efficient cars, including hybrids such as the Ford Focus and Toyota Prius.

BACKGROUND

Some 50 years ago, renowned management author Peter Drucker called the automobile industry the "industry of industries." In many respects, his characterization is still true today. The industry makes over 50 million cars and trucks a year, employs millions of people in factories scattered around the globe, and accounts for about 10% of the gross domestic product in many developed countries. The industry consumes nearly half the world's output of rubber, 25% of its glass, and 15% of its steel.[2] Its products are responsible for almost half of the world's oil consumption and are a major source of rising carbon dioxide levels in the atmosphere, the greenhouse gas implicated in global warming. Modern cities, with their attendant suburban sprawl, have been designed around the automobile. The automobile has shaped our landscape, changed our atmosphere, and exerted a profound influence on the global economy. It is indeed still the industry of industries—and today the industry of industries is going through wrenching changes.

The emergence of the modern industry dates back to 1913 and Henry Ford's first implementation of the production technology—the continuously moving assembly line—that would revolutionize so much of industrial capitalism over the next few decades. Ford quickly became the master of mass production, churning out thousands of black Model T Fords from his Highland Park plant in Michigan. Mass production dramatically lowered the costs of building cars and paved the way for the emergence of a mass consumer market. It was not Ford, however, but Alfred Sloan, the CEO of General Motors, who in the mid-1920s realized that the key to success in the industry was serving customers by offering them "a car for every purse and purpose."[3] Under Sloan, GM segmented the market, producing a differentiated range of models to consumers. In doing so, the company seized market leadership from Ford and has not relinquished it since.

By the 1960s, General Motors, Ford, and Chrysler dominated the United States market; then by far the world's largest. GM at one point made more than 60% of all automobile sales in the United States, and collectively the three companies accounted for more than 90% of sales. Moreover, the companies were now multinationals, with significant operations outside of North America, particularly in Europe, the world's second-largest car market. This, however, was all about to change. Riding the wave of economic disruption caused by the OPEC oil price hikes of the 1970s, foreign manufacturers of fuel-efficient cars began to invade the United States market. First there was Volkswagen, with its revolutionary VW Beetle, followed by a slew of Japanese manufacturers, including, most notably, Honda, Nissan, and Toyota.

It was the invading Toyota that was to usher in the next revolution in car making. Faced with a small and intensely competitive home market and constrained by a lack of capital, Toyota started to tweak the mass production system first developed by Ford. Engineers tried to find ways to build cars efficiently in smaller volumes and with less capital. After years of experimentation, by the 1970s, a new production system emerged at Toyota. Later dubbed "lean production," it was based on innovations that reduced setup times for machinery and made shorter production runs economical. When coupled with the introduction of just-in-time (JIT) inventory systems, flexible work practices, an organization-wide focus on quality, and the practice of stopping the assembly line to fix defects (which was the antithesis of Ford's continually moving assembly line), the lean production system yielded significant gains in productivity and product quality. In turn, it lowered costs, improved brand equity, and gave Toyota a competitive advantage. Toyota capitalized on its lean production system to grow faster than its rivals; by 2008, the company had replaced General Motors as the world's largest automobile manufacturer.

As was the case with mass production, Toyota's innovation of lean production was imitated, with varying degrees of success, by other volume carmakers. Japanese competitors were the first to try to adopt Toyota's innovation. During the 1990s, the American volume carmakers jumped on the bandwagon. Despite this, Toyota still enjoys an advantage in the automobile industry, based on production excellence, although the gap has closed significantly. Just as importantly, the sluggish American response to Japanese and European invasions of their home market allowed the foreigners to capture even more market share.

By the end of the first decade of the new century, America's big three (now often referred to as the Detroit Three) were rapidly losing their grip on the domestic market. Collectively, GM, Ford, and Chrysler accounted for 47.9% of car and light truck sales in the United States in 2008, down from 61.8% in 2003 and 74% in 1997 (light trucks include pickup trucks and SUVs, both segments in which the big three have traditionally been very strong).[4] The other 52.1% of sales were attributed to foreign producers, up from 26% percent in 1997. Moreover, in stark contrast to the situation in the 1980s when most foreign cars were imported into the United States, by 2008, most foreign nameplates were built in "transplant" factories located in North America.

What saved the Detroit Three during the 1990s and early 2000s were robust sales of light trucks, particularly SUVs. Foreign manufacturers had been caught off-guard by the American appetite for SUVs, which surged as oil prices remained low and the economy boomed. In 2003, GM, Ford, and Chrysler still accounted for 74% of light truck sales. But there, too, market share was eroding due to gains made by Japanese and European SUV models.[5] The rapid rise in oil prices between 2004 and 2008, when oil peaked at nearly $150 a barrel, up from $20 a barrel in 2001, brought an end to the two-decade boom in SUV sales, removing the main source of strength for American manufacturers. With competition in the passenger car segment intensifying, the outlook for the Detroit Three looked increasingly grim. Then the economic recession of 2008 hit the industry.

THE 2008 GLOBAL FINANCIAL CRISIS AND AUTOMOBILE SALES

The recession started in the United States housing market. Over the prior decade, mortgage lenders had been making increasingly risky loans to American homebuyers, some of whom clearly could not afford the loans that they were taking on. However, low "teaser rates" that expired after one to five years, to be replaced by much higher interest rates, persuaded many borrowers to take on mortgage debt obligations. Moreover, many believed, incorrectly as it turned out, that if they could not meet their mortgage payments, they could always sell their home and pay off the loan.

For their part, mortgage lenders were encouraged to make risky loans by the development of a market for mortgage-backed securities. This enabled them to bundle mortgages into bonds and sell them off to other financial institutions, thereby shifting the risk. The institutions that purchased these mortgage-backed securities were themselves able to buy insurance that protected them against the risk of default by mortgage payees, which would have significantly reduced the value of the bonds they held. This insurance took the form of complex derivatives, known as collateralized debt obligations, or CDOs, that were then traded between institutions. CDOs were viewed as relatively safe investments because default rates on mortgages were low.

The entire system seemed to work as long as housing prices continued to rise and defaults stayed low. But in 2007, a two-decade rise in United States housing prices came to an abrupt end. Furthermore, the interest rates were starting to rise on many adjustable rate mortgages that had been sold with low teaser rates. As rates started to rise, defaults surged, homes were foreclosed at record rates, and an increase in the supply of homes for sale drove prices down even further. At this point, the United States financial system went into a tailspin. The value of mortgage-backed securities and derivatives such as CDOs plunged, damaging the balance sheets of many financial institutions. Because financial institutions from all over the world had been purchasing American mortgage-backed securities and derivatives, the crisis immediately became global. With assets on their balance sheets, financial institutions

had no choice but to dramatically reduce the new loans that they made, and after decades of easy credit, suddenly it became very difficult to borrow money.

The credit squeeze hit the automobile industry particularly hard because cars are, for many people, their second-biggest purchases after homes and are often financed with loans. Moreover, even for those people who used cash to buy cars, the financial crisis suddenly made them very nervous; they responded by putting off any purchases of big-ticket items such as automobiles as they waited for the crisis to resolve. As a consequence, demand for automobiles plunged. For 2008, United States automobile sales were down 18% from 16.1 million units in 2007 to 13.2 million units in 2008. Most of the sales fall occurred in the second half of the year, with monthly sales figures recording some of the lowest levels since the 1960s. Moreover, little relief was seen for 2009. Standard and Poor's, for example, was forecasting United States sales of 11.5 million units in 2009, a 39% drop from 2007.[6]

What complicated the situation was that at the same time the financial crisis was unfolding, oil prices surged to record highs, hitting $150 a barrel in mid-2008. As prices at the gas pump rose, people who were buying cars switched to more fuel-efficient vehicles, many of which were made not by American producers, but by smaller foreign firms such as Hyundai and Kia of Korea and Subaru of Japan. Even though oil prices subsequently fell as the recession took hold, the perception had taken hold that once the economy recovered, oil prices would again increase, and demand for pickup trucks and SUVs remained weak.

While the slump in demand was most dramatic in America, other markets also saw sharp declines, and for many of the same reasons: the global financial crisis caused credit contraction and increased uncertainty about the future, which hit automobile sales particularly hard. In France, for example, sales fell 15.8% in December 2008 compared with a year earlier. In Japan, the figure was 22%; in Italy, 13.3%; and Spain, 49.9%.[7] Looking forward, forecasts called for global automobile sales of approximately 46.6 million units in 2009, down from a peak of 54.92 million units in 2007.[8]

However, while demand declines have been the norm in developed nations, there is a different story in developing nations (see Exhibit 1). In China, India, and Brazil, for example, the sales declines were much

Exhibit 1 Global Automobile Sales: 2000, 2007, 2008, and 2009 Forecast (millions of units)

	2000	2007	2008	2009 Forecast
Total Global Sales	46.64	54.92	52.17	46.66
North America	19.77	18.83	15.85	12.80
Canada	*1.55*	*1.65*	*1.64*	*1.38*
United States	*17.35*	*16.09*	*13.19*	*10.50*
Western Europe	14.75	14.75	13.54	12.46
Eastern Europe	2.38	3.58	4.01	3.41
Asia	7.85	14.42	15.07	14.44
China	*0.61*	*5.15*	*5.04*	*5.29*
India	*0.60*	*1.18*	*1.20*	*1.23*
South America	1.89	3.34	3.70	3.55
Brazil	*1.17*	*1.98*	*2.19*	*2.24*

Source: "Auto Production Swings from Reverse into Drive," Global Auto Report, *Global Economic Research,* April 29, 2009.

smaller, and growth had already resumed by early 2009. In all of these countries, relatively low levels of automobile ownership, coupled with fast underlying economic growth rates, suggest that sales will continue to grow at a robust rate in coming years.

Two factors made the sharp sales declines particularly painful for automobile manufacturers. One was their high level of fixed costs. As sales fall below breakeven run rates, high fixed costs imply rapidly rising losses. Exacerbating the situation was the fact that between 2004 and 2008, some 19 million units of new productive capacity had been added to the global industry.

The combination of expanding global capacity, followed by a sharp drop in demand, when coupled with a demand shift to smaller cars, proved toxic for several companies. Hardest hit were General Motors and Chrysler. Both companies were forced to seek government aid in an attempt to stave off bankruptcy. In total, the United States government had committed $17.4 billion in aid to GM and Chrysler by early 2009. In contrast, Ford, who had raised significant capital from private investors in 2007, declined government aid and signaled that, despite operating losses, it would be able to survive the recession. Despite the aid both Chrysler and GM were forced into bankruptcy. Under an agreement negotiated after Chrysler's bankruptcy, the Italian company Fiat will take over management of the company's assets. Fiat itself had undergone a dramatic turnaround between 2004 and 2008 under the leadership of Sergio Marchionne, primarily through a combination of production efficiencies and new product launches, including small cars that have sold well in an environment of high fuel prices. As of May 2009, Fiat was also reported to be bidding for Opel, the European arm of General Motors.

Toyota, too, reported a loss of $3.6 billion for the financial year that ended in March 2009, its first-ever as a public company, primarily due to the sharp sales declines in the United States and Japan. However, with $19 billion in cash on its balance sheet, the result of years of high profits, Toyota was financially secure. Despite this, Toyota's finance arm had apparently sought some $2 billion in government aid from the Bank of Japan to help its finance arms survive the global credit crunch.

Other governments, eager to protect jobs, were also putting up cash to support their local producers. French government officials said that automakers could expect approximately $7.8 billion in loans and loan guarantees. Germany unveiled a similar plan. In Britain, automobile producers (which are almost entirely in foreign hands) sought about $3.3 billion in government loans. Similarly, the Swedish government provided around $3.4 billion in loan guarantees to Volvo and Saab (which at the time were owned by Ford and GM, respectively). In Brazil, where the market continued to grow, the government instructed Banco de Brasil to make $1.7 billion available to the financing units of local automakers so that they could cope with the global credit crisis.[9]

The flurry of government aid for ailing automakers prompted a caution from Pascal Lamy, the Director General of the World Trade Organization. Although he chose his words carefully, Lamy seemed to suggest that loans and loan guarantees were, in effect, subsidies to inefficient producers, and going forward they could distort world trade and discriminate against efficient producers who did not receive similar subsidies.

Most forecasts called for 2009 to be another rough year for the global automobile industry, although many believed that demand would start to recover toward the end of the year and the recovery would be sustained through 2011. During that time period, growth was predicted to be strongest in the emerging markets of China, India, and Brazil. The structure of the global industry, however, may be irreversibly altered.

INDUSTRY TRENDS

Several important trends characterized the competitive landscape of the global automobile industry in the first decade of the 21st century. Most important among these were the decline of America's big three, the shifting patterns of global demand (and particularly the growth of China as a major market and producer), and the increasing attention paid to non-traditional engines, including hybrids and fuel cells.

The Decline of America's Big Three

The decline of America's big three auto producers has been ongoing for decades. Once accounting for as much as 90% of all cars and trucks sold in the United States, by the mid-1990s the figure had fallen to 75%, and today it is about 44% (see Exhibit 2). Taking up market share have been the Japanese trio of Honda, Nissan, and Toyota and, to a lesser extent, Volkswagen, Hyundai, and Subaru. The decline has been notably steeper in the passenger car segment of the industry in which the big three saw their share decline to under 42% by 2008. In contrast, the light truck segment has long been a source of strength for the American producers, and collectively they still account for around 70% of the share in this segment. However, sales declines have been sharp in this segment due to the relatively poor fuel economy of most light trucks.

Many foreign companies now build a significant proportion of their output in North America. Japanese investments began in the early 1980s as a response to the threat of import controls on exports from Japan. By the early 2000s, foreign-owned producers had the capacity to build some 3 million automobiles in the United States, up from zero in 1981.[10] The foreign investment shows no sign of slowing down. Hyundai opened its first United States factory in Montgomery, Alabama, in 2005, making it the first Korean car company to build in North America. Meanwhile, Toyota opened its sixth North American factory in San Antonio, Texas, in 2006. Collectively, foreign-owned auto factories accounted for close to 30% United States automobile production by 2008.

Exhibit 2 U.S. Market Share, Passenger Cars and Light Trucks, February 2009

Producer	Share %
General Motors	18.9%
Toyota	16.9%
Ford	14.3%
Chrysler	10.9%
Honda	10.6%
Nissan	8%
Other Asian makers	12.8%
European makers	7.6%

Source: *Ward's Auto World*, March 2009.

Many states offered financial incentives such as tax breaks in an effort to attract inward investment by foreign producers and the associated jobs. Estimates suggest that by mid-decade the cumulative value of incentives given to attract new factories amounted to between $1.2 billion and $2 billion, which translates into an investment incentive of $1,000 for every car built by a foreign-owned factory.[11]

The addition of foreign capacity created an excess capacity situation in the American market, which became particularly evident during 2008–2009 when excess productive capacity exceeded 40%. Predictably, the result was significant price competition. This included zero rate financing, cash back on purchases, and large reductions from sticker prices, none of which was enough to prevent bankruptcy for Chrysler and General Motors.

The rise of foreign competitors in the United States market has been attributed to a number of factors, including better designs and more fuel-efficient offerings (particularly in the passenger car segment) superior product quality, higher employee and capital productivity, and lower costs due to smaller pension and health care commitments.

Quality seems to be an important factor explaining market share changes in the industry. J. D. Power and Associates produces quality rankings for automobiles sold in the United States market. Over the years, Toyota and Honda brands have consistently had among the best quality rankings in the industry. However, it is notable that American producers have made great strides, and by the mid-2000s, they were closing the gap. Nevertheless, as of 2008, foreign producers still dominated J. D. Power's vehicle dependability rankings, which measure problems per 100 vehicles within their first three years on the market. As can be seen from Exhibit 3, in March 2009, the industry average was 170 problems per 100 vehicles over three years. Although Buick and Jaguar, brands then owned by GM and Tata Motors of India topped the list, Toyota and Honda brands both scored consistently better than most major brands of Ford, Chrysler, and GM (Tata Motors purchased Jaguar from Ford in June 2008.) This being said, Ford has shown particularly strong improvement in recent years. It is clear that by 2009, the quality deficit that had longed plagued American made cars had been eliminated for some brands.[12]

With regard to productivity differences, the story is similar. American-owned plants have long had a productivity disadvantage compared to their foreign competitors. However, the gap has narrowed substantially in recent years as American-owned producers have worked to improve their productivity by implementing improved manufacturing techniques based on Toyota's model. According to the *Harbour Report,* an annual survey of manufacturing productivity in American assembly plants, although a substantial gap remained in 2003, by 2007 it had been reduced significantly (see Exhibit 4).[13] Indeed, Chrysler's plants matched those of Toyota, and General Motors outperformed Nissan.

Exhibit 3   J. D. Power Vehicle Dependability Study, 2009: Problems per 100 Vehicles over 3 Years

Brand	Rating
Buick	122
Jaguar	122
Lexus	126
Toyota	129
Acura	146
Cadillac	148
Honda	148
Ford	159
Chrysler	165
Industry Average	*170*
GM	174
Chevrolet	185
Volvo	186
Nissan	199
Dodge	202
Jeep	220
Pontiac	220
Volkswagen	260
Suzuki	263

Source: "Buick and Jaguar Tie to Rank Highest for Vehicle Dependability," J. D. Power press release, March 19, 2009.

Exhibit 4 Productivity Differences Measured by Total Labor Hours per Unit and Profit per Vehicle among U.S. Plants

Manufacturer	2003	2007	2007 Profit per Vehicle($)
Ford	38.60	33.88	−1,467
Chrysler	37.42	30.37	−412
General Motors	35.20	32.29	−729
Nissan	32.94	32.96	1,641
Honda	32.36	31.33	1,641
Toyota	30.01	30.37	922

Note: Productivity measures are for assembly, stamping, engine, and transmission combined.
Source: Oliver Wyman, *The Harbour Report, 2008,* Media Release, June 5, 2008.

Despite the closing of the productivity gap, American vehicle makers still lost money on every car they made in 2007, while their Japanese competitors made money (see Exhibit 4). The main reason was higher labor costs at the big three. This was due not just to higher wage rates but also to the pension and health care obligations that American manufacturers have long borne not just for their current employees but also for their retirees. General Motors, for example, has 2.4 pensioners for every current employee. In the early 2000s, both Ford and GM had to issue bonds worth billions of dollars to plug the holes in their pension funds. GM now has to pay out $1 billion a year in interest payments just to service these bonds. Moreover, the company has to pay out some $3 billion a year to cover health care costs for retirees. Just as troubling, GM may have to increase funds going into its pension plan if the fund does not earn a long-term return of 9% per annum.[14]

As a consequence of such factors, in 2007, the average labor cost at the American big three was $75 an hour, compared to $45 an hour at Toyota's American assembly plants. However, all three American companies have been renegotiating their contracts with the Union of Auto Workers (UAW), and trying to shift the obligations for retirees onto the union. Indeed, bankruptcy protection has enabled Chrysler and GM to accelerate this process. According to the *Harbour Report,* the implication is that by 2011, hourly labor rates for the big three may be down to $54.

Labor costs may fall still further for American manufacturers under an agreement negotiated with the UAW in early 2009. The agreement was required by the federal government as a condition for its loans to GM and Chrysler, which totaled $17.4 billion. The agreement was to cut pay for laid off workers, ease work rules to allow for greater job flexibility, and eliminate wage increases tied to the cost of living. Although Ford took no government aid, the UAW has the same agreement with all American manufacturers, so Ford also benefits from the government requirement.[15]

Among the American manufacturers, Ford seems best positioned to come out of the 2008–2009 recession in the industry. Ford raised some $23.5 billion in cash in 2006, before the recession hit, by mortgaging almost all of its plants and assets while interest rates were low. At the start of 2009, it still had $13.4 billion in cash on its balance sheet, which will be enough to see it through the recession without additional capital injections unless the recession continues well into 2010. As noted earlier, despite receiving $4 billion in government assistance, Chrysler entered bankruptcy protection in May 2009 and Fiat has taken over management of the company. GM, despite receiving $13.4 billion in federal assistance, also entered bankruptcy. The problems at GM and Chrysler seem to have been benefitting Ford, which started to pick up market share from its rivals in early 2009.

Shifting Patterns of Global Demand

While America's automobile market was in a deep recession in 2008–2009, as was most of Europe and Japan, some developing markets continued to expand. As recently as 2000, the United States market accounted for 37% of global demand. By 2008, this figure was 25%, and it was forecasted to fall to 22% in 2009 (see Exhibit 1). Leading the growth in developed nations was China. In 2002, there were just 16 vehicles per 1,000 people in this fast-growing country of 1.3 billion. This was compared to more than 800 vehicles per 1,000 people in the United States and 585 per 1,000 in Germany. By 2008, the figure for China had increased to 30 per 1,000 people, which is still very low. India, too, has a large population, fast economic growth, and a low level of car ownership (17 per 1,000 in 2008), so there, too, rapid growth in demand has been occurring.[16]

J. D. Power estimates that demand in China will climb to 14.6 million units per annum in 2013, up from a little over 5 million in 2008. By 2018, J. D. Power foresees demand for 19.9 million units per annum in China, compared with demand for 17.6 million units in the United States, which would make China the world's largest market. In fact, sales in China surged in early 2009 as their government offered subsidies on purchases of small fuel-efficient cars. For the first four months of 2009, sales in China outstripped those in the United States. J. D. Power also sees rapid growth in demand for automobiles in Brazil, India, and Russia, and by 2018 believes that demand in developing nations will outstrip demand in developed nations.

To serve the growing demand, foreign automobile makers have been investing heavily in these markets. Automobile production in China, which stood at 2 million units in 2001, was approaching 10 million units by 2009. Ironically, one of the most successful foreign companies in China has been GM, which produces cars in China through two joint ventures; a 50–50 partnership with Shanghai Automotive Industry, which makes and sells Chevrolets, Buicks, and Cadillacs in China, and a one-third stake in SAIC-GM-Wuling. China requires foreign auto manufacturers to enter into joint ventures with local producers. GM plans to double its Chinese capacity to 2 million vehicles a year and launch 30 new models tailored to the Chinese market by 2014. However, it is of note that most of GM's sales gain has come at its SAIC joint venture, in which SAIC has a controlling 51% ownership stake.[17] In May 2009, GM announced that it would start exporting cars to America from its SAIC joint venture.

China also has its own home grown industry. In addition to companies like SAIC and Shanghai Automotive, automakers include Brilliance, Geely, and Chery Automobile. While these companies are starting to export production to other developing nations, they have not yet broken into developed markets such as the United States and Western Europe. Among other constraints, their cars would not currently pass stringent United States emission requirements. In 2009, rumors swirled that these companies were considering purchasing parts of GM and Ford, including Saab, Volvo, and Hummer. Such a purchase would give them access not only to well-known global brands but also to technological know-how, which currently is the weak spot of Chinese manufacturers.[18] It would also follow the lead set by India's Tata Motors, another emerging automobile company, which, in 2008, purchased the Jaguar and Land Rover brands from Ford.

Changes in Operations

In an effort to cope with the tough competitive conditions in the North American market and elsewhere, automobile companies are looking hard at additional ways to take costs out of their system or capture more of the available demand. Among the most notable initiatives underway have been an industry-wide attempt to streamline product development, offer a wider range of niche cars, work more closely with suppliers, develop systems for building cars to order, and introduce a new breed of hybrid cars.

Historically, it took four years and cost as much as $1 billion to develop a new car model and prepare a factory for its production. To recoup those fixed costs, automobile companies needed high-volume sales, which required selling cars without a major update for four years and sometimes as long as seven years. To attain maximum economies of scale, automobile manufacturers tried to run their plants at full capacity, producing 240,000 units a year. The ideal was to have each plant produce just one model.

In recent years, the automobile market has become increasingly fragmented. Models are now updated more frequently to keep pace with changing consumer tastes and competitive pressures, shortening product life cycles. Customers have demanded more variety, and automobile companies have been willing to give it to them, bringing a wider variety of niche cars to the market. The Ford Taurus, for example, was once the best-selling passenger car in America with annual sales of approximately 500,000 (equivalent to two plants running at full capacity). As sales slipped, Ford decided to kill the Taurus and replace it with two models, one smaller than the Taurus and one bigger.

To recoup the costs of such offerings, development and manufacturing costs have to be reduced. Automobile companies are trying to do this by using a common platform and parts in a wider range of cars. An example depicting the industry's evolving philosophy is GM's 2005 roadster, the Pontiac Solstice. Under the old economics, the Solstice would never have made it off the drawing board. The car was forecasted to sell only 25,000 units a year. With a projected sticker price of $20,000, the volume was insufficient under the old paradigm to recoup costs. To make the car economically, GM revolutionized its product design philosophy. By digitalizing much of the design of the car and tools, GM was able to cut $50 million out of the design costs. It used to take 12 design engineers three months to produce a clay model, an essential step in the design process. Now a single designer can take an idea on a computer screen to an animated video of a vehicle in three weeks. GM saved another $80 million by designing the car so that it could use existing tools at its factory. More money was saved by a decision to base the car on a common platform architecture called Kappa, which would be used for other small rear-drive cars. According to GM, the company could make an almost unlimited number of bodies on the Kappa architecture, and each vehicle would be profitable with a volume of 20,000 to 25,000 a year.[19]

Using the same platform across a wide model range is fast becoming industry standard practice. As with so many other industry trends, the Japanese pioneered the practice. Honda, for example, builds its Odyssey minivan, the Pilot SUV, and the Acura MDX SUV on the same platform. In 2004, Chrysler based its vehicle fleet on 13 distinct platforms, but by 2008, the company had decreased this to just four platforms, in the process reducing the product development budget from $42 billion to $30 billion. Ford and General Motors have similar aims. The Kappa platform for GM's Pontiac Solstice will also be used for its new Saturn coupe and at least one more GM car. As GM develops its next generation Chevy Silverado and GMC Sierra pickups, it plans to reuse much of the existing platform, cutting development costs in half to nearly $3 billion. Over the next eight years, Ford plans to use its Mazda 6 sedan platform (Ford owns Mazda) as the basis for 10 new vehicles. The idea, according to Ford's head of operations, is to engineer it once and use it often.[20]

Another design goal is to try and use the same parts in a wider variety of car models and, where appropriate, use parts from old models in new cars. Detroit auto designers formerly boasted that new models were completely redesigned from the floor up with all new parts. Now that is seen as costly and time-consuming. At General Motors the current goal is to reuse 40%–60% of parts from one car generation to the next, thereby reducing design time and tooling costs. At Ford, the number of parts has been slashed. For example, Ford engineers now choose from just four steering wheels, instead of contemplating 14 different designs.

As a result of all these changes, the costs and time for bringing new cars to market is shrinking. Most of GM's new development projects are now on 24-month schedules—a far cry from the late 1980s when GM engineers celebrated because they were able to bring out the Chevrolet Corsica in *just* 45 months![21] Ford has reduced its product development time by 25% since the late 1990s and is still getting better by 10% per year.

Hand in hand with changes in design philosophy, automobile companies are retooling their factories to reduce costs and make them capable of producing several car models from the same line. By doing so, they hope to be able to reduce the break-even point for a new car model. With the Solstice, for example, GM cut design costs by using a common platform and parts. It has cut tooling and production costs by investing in flexible manufacturing technologies that can be used to produce multiple designs based on the Kappa platform from the same basic line. GM has also worked hard to get unions to agree to changes in inflexible work rules. Assembly line workers now perform several different jobs, which reduces waste and boosts productivity.

Ford hopes to have 75% of its production built on flexible assembly lines by 2010. If successful, its investments in flexible factories could reduce annual costs by some $2 billion a year.[22] Ford spent $400 million modernizing an 80-year old assembly plant in Chicago. This plant is now capable of making eight models from two different chassis.

Reengineering their plants to accommodate a wider range of models is not cheap. In 2003, GM spent some $7.3 billion on capital improvements at its automobile plants, up from an average of $5.4 billion in the early 1990s. In the early 1990s, Ford spent some $3.5 billion annually on capital improvements. More recently, its capital spending has been running at a $7.5–$8 billion annual rate. Chrysler, too, has increased its spending, while Toyota spent some $9 billion upgrading its factories in the mid-2000s.[23]

Companies are also changing the way they manage their suppliers. At one time, the American automobile companies were highly vertically integrated, producing as much as 70% of their component parts in-house. Those parts that were not made in-house were often purchased using an annual competitive bidding process. The last decade has seen enormous changes here. Both Ford and GM have sold off major chunks of their in-house suppliers. GM spun off its in-house suppliers in 1999 as Delphi Automotive. Delphi took some 200,000 former GM employees with it, about one-third of the total, many of whom were union members. Ford spun off its in-house suppliers the following year as Visteon Corporation. Delphi and Visteon are now the number one and two auto parts suppliers in the United States. In an effort to assert their independence, both companies are moving rapidly to build a more diverse set of customers.

The Detroit Three have also been reconfiguring their relationships with independent suppliers. The automobile companies are now expecting their Tier 1 or major suppliers to produce modules—larger vehicle parts that comprise several components such as fully assembled chassis, finished interiors, and "ready for the road" exterior trim. These modules are then bolted and welded together to make finished vehicles, rather like toy models being snapped together. For such an approach to work, the suppliers have to get involved earlier in the process of designing and developing new models and engineering assembly tools. To create an incentive for them to do so, the automobile manufacturers have been entering into longer-term contracts with their Tier 1 suppliers. At the same time, Tier 1 suppliers face intense price pressures and requirements for quality

improvements. If they do not meet these, the automobile companies have shown a willingness to walk away from long-term deals. In 2003, for example, Chrysler pulled a $90 million contract from a supplier of interior products, Collins & Aikman, because of poor product quality.[24]

Another trend has been to encourage major suppliers to locate new facilities next to assembly plants. Ford's refurbished plant in Chicago has a supplier park located next door. The idea is to get suppliers to deliver inventory to the assembly line on a JIT basis. At the Chicago plant, the average component now needs to travel only half a mile, as compared to 450 miles in the past. The proximity has saved suppliers transportation costs, which are passed onto Ford in the form of lower prices. In addition, Ford has reduced inventory on hand at its Chicago plant from two to three days' worth to just eight hours' worth.[25]

Once a car is built, it spends between 40 and 80 days sitting in factory lots, distribution centers, and dealers' forecourts before it is actually sold. This represents a huge amount of working capital that is tied up in inventory. To make matters worse, one of the biggest problems in the automobile industry is predicting what demand will be. To a large extent, repeated rounds of price cutting (disguised as incentives) in the American automobile industry have been initiated in an attempt to move slow-selling inventory sitting on dealers' lots. If automobile companies could predict demand more accurately, they might be able to reduce the mismatch between inventories and demand—and hence the need to resort to incentives.

In an effort to improve this end of the value chain, the automobile companies have been trying to reduce the time between ordering and delivery. The ultimate goal is to have cars built to order, with cars being assembled and shipped to a dealer within days of a customer placing an order. This is similar in conception to the way that Dell sells computers, with customers ordering a computer and paying for it, online, while the machine is shipped out within days. Nissan has calculated that if it could move to a build-to-order system with a short cycle time, it could reduce costs by as much as $3,600 a vehicle.[26]

Achieving this goal, however, is easier in theory than in practice. One obvious problem is that if the flow of orders is lumpy or seasonal, so will be the output of a factory, which might result in periods where capacity is not being fully utilized. Another problem involves changing buyer behavior. In America, at least many consumers look for instant gratification and expect to be able to purchase a car when they walk onto a dealer's lot, which is the antithesis of a build-to-order system. Still, there are some signs of a shift away from this mentality. Honda, for example, has been building its best-selling MDX SUV to order—although the delivery time is more like two months than two days. In Germany, BMW now builds some 60% of its cars to order, but once again the delivery time can be as long as two months. Toyota, too, is trying to build more cars to order. By the mid-2000s Toyota was building about 12% of the cars it sold in the United States to order, with a build time of just 14 days.[27]

New Technologies

For years, automobile companies have experimented with alternative power sources, most notably fuel cells. These investments have been driven by national and local government demands for lower emissions of carbon dioxide, carbon monoxide, and nitrogen oxides. Of particular concern has been the global buildup of carbon dioxide, the greenhouse gas implicated in global warming. In Europe, the European Commission has persuaded carmakers to agree to a voluntary deal to cut overall emissions across their car fleet by 25% by 2008 or face the imposition of strict emission rules on specific models. In California, draft regulations may require car manufacturers to reduce emissions of carbon dioxide by 30%, starting in 2009. In addition, California already has regulations in place that require 2% of car makers' fleets to be zero emission vehicles (ZEV), although this requirement is proving to be a "soft" one. In May 2009, the United States government raised the stakes by introducing tough new standards for fuel efficiency, which called for automobile manufacturers to make fleets that, on average, achieved 35.5 miles per gallon, up from 25.3 miles per gallon.

The only conceivable ZEV at this juncture is a car powered by an electric motor that runs on a fuel cell. A fuel cell combines hydrogen with oxygen from the air to produce water. The process generates an electric current strong enough to power a car. For all of their promise, however, fuel cells have drawbacks. It costs about 10 times more to produce a fuel cell than an internal combustion engine, the range of cars using fuel cells is still too limited for most customers, and replenishing hydrogen will require a network of hydrogen filling stations, which currently are not available.

Automakers have also been experimenting with modified internal combustion engines that use hydrogen rather than gasoline as a fuel. Here too, however, progress has been held back by the total absence of a network of hydrogen filling stations and serious technical problems associated with storing liquid hydrogen (which requires very cold temperatures).

More promising in the short to medium term are hybrid cars. In hybrid cars, at low speed the power comes from an electric motor that gets electricity from an onboard battery. At higher speed, the internal combustion engine kicks in and provides power, while simultaneously recharging the battery through a generator. When braking, energy from the slowing wheels is sent back through the electric motor to charge the batteries. The result can be substantial savings in fuel consumption, with little in the way of a performance penalty. Toyota's Prius hybrid can go from a standstill to 60 mph in 10 seconds and averages 60 mpg in the city and 51 mpg highway driving. This makes the Prius an ideal commuting car. The big drawback is that the hybrid propulsion system adds about $3,000 to $5,000 to a vehicle's sticker price, and the battery has to be replaced about every 100,000 miles at a cost of about $2,000. At a gas price of $2 a gallon, it takes some five years for a hybrid to repay the additional investment.

Introduced in 1997, Toyota had sold some 200,000 Prius cars by mid-2004. Sales started to increase rapidly in 2003 and 2004 as higher fuel prices made consumers more concerned about fuel economy. In 2004, sales in the United States were limited only by supply constraints to 47,000 units. By 2008, with fuel prices hitting $4 a gallon in the United States, Toyota was selling 250,000 Priuses a year. In May 2009, the company introduced its third-generation Prius in Japan, with plans to roll the car out globally over the next few months. Pre-orders in Japan were for 80,000 units, far surpassing the automaker's goal of selling 10,000 a month in its home market. In total, Toyota hopes to sell some 300,000–400,000 of the new Priuses a year.[28] In addition to the Prius, Toyota also sells hybrid versions of some of its other models, including the Lexus SUV, the Highlander SUV, and the Camry sedan. The company aims to increase its overall hybrid sales to $1 million by 2010–2012 and offer hybrid versions of all of its vehicles by 2020.

Toyota is not alone in developing hybrid technology. Most notably, both Honda and Ford have introduced hybrid models, and both are reportedly selling well. Bob Lutz, the vice chairman of GM, who was at one time well known for his resistance to alternative technologies, said that GM will aim to build about one-third of its vehicles as hybrids by 2015 and 80% by 2020.

In addition to hybrids, GM is also placing a bet on another technology, lithium ion batteries, with its Chevy Volt. Scheduled for market introduction in 2010, the Chevy Volt is a compact four-door electric car with a reserve gasoline-powered engine. The primary power source is a large lithium ion battery (lithium ion batteries are typically found in small electric appliances such as cell phones). The battery can be charged by plugging it into a wall socket for six hours, and fully charged, it will fuel the car for 40 miles, which is less than most people's daily commute. After that, a gasoline engine kicks in, providing both drive power and recharging the lithium ion battery. GM estimates fuel economy will be over 100 miles a gallon, and charging the car overnight from a power outlet would cost about 80% less than filling it with gas at $3 per gallon. The car will cost somewhere between $30,000 and $40,000; because it uses battery-powered technology, buyers will be able to take a $7,500 tax credit.

Endnotes

1. F. Balfour, "China's Geely Eyes GM's Saab, Ford's Volvo," *Business Week*, May 8, 2009, 18.
2. "A Survey of the Car Industry; Perpetual Motion," *The Economist*, September 4, 2004, 3–4.
3. The phrase first appeared in GM's 1924 Annual Report to Shareholders, and more than anything else, it captured the essence of Sloan's revolutionary marketing philosophy. For details, visit GM's Web site at http://www.gm.com/company/corp_info/history/index.html.
4. Standard & Poor's, *Industry Survey: Autos & Auto Parts*, December 25, 2008.
5. Figures from Standard & Poor's, *Industry Survey: Autos & Auto Parts*, June 24, 2004.
6. Standard & Poor's, *Industry Survey: Autos & Auto Parts*, December 25, 2008.
7. "Global Car Sales Fall by Double Digits," *CNNMoney.com*, January 5, 2009.
8. "Auto Production Swings from Reverse into Drive," Global Auto Report, *Global Economic Research*, April 29, 2009.
9. "Too Many Moving Parts," *The Economist*, February 7, 2009, 71.
10. A Survey of the Car Industry, "Detroit's Nine Lives," *The Economist*, September 4, 2004, 6–9.
11. Ibid.
12. "Buick and Jaguar Tie to Rank Highest for Vehicle Dependability," J. D. Power press release, March 19, 2009.
13. Oliver Wyman, *The Harbour Report, 2008*, Media Release, June 5, 2008.
14. D. Welch, "Has GM Outrun Its Pension Problems?" *Business Week*, January 19, 2004, 70.
15. M. Dolan, "Ford Benefits as GM and Chrysler Stumble," *Wall Street Journal*, Feburary 20, 2009, B1.
16. Standard & Poor's, *Industry Survey: Autos & Auto Parts*, December 25, 2008.
17. I. Rowley, "Would Bankruptcy Stall GM's China Growth?" *Business Week Online*, April 28, 2009, 14.
18. K. Marr, "As Detroit Crumbles, China Emerges as Auto Epicenter," *Washington Post*, May 18, 2009, A1.
19. M. Phelan, "GM Predicts Sporty Profits Even from Fewer Sales," *Knight Rider Tribune Business News*, March 13, 2004, 1.
20. D. Welch and K. Kerwin, "Detroit Tries It the Japanese Way," *Business Week*, January 26, 2004, 76; A. Taylor, "Detroit Buffs Up," *Fortune*, February 9, 2004, 90–94.
21. D. Winter, "Shrinking Product Development Time," *Ward's Auto World*, June 2003, 36–40.
22. J. Muller, "The Little Car That Could," *Forbes*, December 8, 2003, 82; "The Year of the Car," *The Economist*, January 3, 2004, 47.
23. Standard & Poor's, *Industry Survey: Autos & Auto Parts*, June 24, 2004.
24. Ibid.
25. K. Kerwin, "Ford to Suppliers: Let's Get Cozier," *Business Week*, September 20, 2004, 8.
26. A Survey of the Car Industry, "Fighting Back," *The Economist*, September 4, 2004, 14–16.
27. R. Rosmarin, "Your Custom Car Is Ready at Toyota," *Business* vol. 2 (October 2004): 150–151.
28. Y. Takahashi, "New Prius Is Set to Race Insight," *Wall Street Journal*, 2009, May 19, B2.

TOYOTA IN 2009

INTRODUCTION

The growth of Toyota has been one of the great success stories of Japanese industry during the last half century. In 1947, the company was a little-known domestic manufacturer producing about 100,000 vehicles a year. As 2008 drew to a close, Toyota stated that the company and its affiliates produced 9.3 million vehicles in 2008, enabling the company to surpass General Motors (GM) and become the largest producer in the global industry.

However, in a remarkably rapid turn of events, Toyota's success was tempered by the arrival of the worst economic recession in a generation. In 2008, a crisis in the American financial services industry reverberated around the world. American financial institutions had been too eager to make risky loans throughout the 2000s, particularly mortgage loans. In 2008, housing prices collapsed after a long period of price increases. Mortgage default rates started to soar. This ravaged the balance sheets of banks, which responded by dramatically tightening credit, making it more difficult for consumers to borrow funds for big-ticket items such as automobile purchases. The impact on the automobile industry was nothing short of catastrophic. Throughout 2008 and into 2009, sales plunged. People could either no longer afford to buy cars, or were too worried about the future to risk making a purchase. To complicate matters, gasoline prices had surged to record levels, hitting demand for large cars, such as SUVs.

In the United States, the world's largest market, sales fell by more than 40%, to levels not seen since the 1960s. Chrysler and General Motors sought government assistance, but that did not save either of them from bankruptcy. Many thought that Toyota would weather the storm better than others, but in the first quarter of 2009, the company reported a $7.8 billion loss, its first quarterly loss in 70 years, on the back of a 41% plunge in sales. With more than $19 billion in cash on its balance sheet, however, Toyota's financial position remained strong; for the first time in decades, the company clearly faced significant challenges.

THE ORIGIN OF TOYOTA

The original idea behind the founding of the Toyota Motor Company came from the fertile mind of Toyoda Sakichi.[1] The son of a carpenter, Sakichi was an entrepreneur and inventor whose primary interest lay in the textile industry, but he had been intrigued by automobiles since a visit to the United States in 1910. Sakichi's principal achievement was the invention of an automatic loom that held out the promise of being able to lower the costs of weaving high-quality cloth. In 1926, Sakichi established Toyoda Automatic Loom to manufacture this product. In 1930, Sakichi sold the patent rights to a British textile concern, Platt Brothers, for about 1 million yen, a considerable sum in those days. Sakichi urged his son, Toyoda Kiichiro, to use this money to study the possibility of manufacturing automobiles in Japan. A mechanical engineer with a degree from the University of Tokyo,

---

This case was prepared by Charles W. L. Hill, Foster School of Business, University of Washington.

Kiichiro became managing director of loom production at Toyoda Automatic Loom in 1930.

Kiichiro was at first reluctant to invest in automobile production. The Japanese market was at that time dominated by Ford and General Motors, both of which imported knockdown car kits from the United States and assembled them in Japan. Given this, the board of Toyoda Automatic Loom, including Kiichiro's brother-in-law and the company's president, Kodama Risaburo, opposed the investment on the grounds that it was too risky. Kiichiro probably would not have pursued the issue further, but his father made a deathbed request in 1930 that Kiichiro explore the possibilities of automobile production. Kiichiro had to push, but in 1933, he was able to get permission to set up an automobile department within Toyoda Automatic Loom.

Kiichiro's belief was that he would be able to figure out how to manufacture automobiles by taking apart American-made vehicles and examining them piece by piece. He also felt that it should be possible to adapt United States mass-production technology to manufacture cost efficiently at lower volumes. His confidence was based in large part on the already considerable engineering skills and capabilities at his disposal through Toyoda Automatic Loom. Many of the precision engineering and manufacturing skills needed in automobile production were similar to the skills required to manufacture looms.

Kiichiro produced his first 20 vehicles in 1935, and in 1936 produced 1,142 vehicles: 910 trucks, 100 cars, and 132 buses. At this time, however, the production system was essentially craft-based rather than a modern assembly line. Despite some progress, the struggle might still have been uphill had not fate intervened in the form of the Japanese military. Japan had invaded Manchuria in 1931 and quickly found American-made trucks useful for moving men and equipment. As a result, the military felt that it was strategically important for Japan to have its own automobile industry. The result was the passage of an automobile manufacturing law in 1936 that required companies producing more than 3,000 vehicles per year in Japan to get a license from the government. Moreover, to get a license, over 50% of the stock had to be owned by Japanese investors. The law also placed a duty on imported cars, including the knock-down kits that Ford and GM brought into Japan. As a direct result of this legislation, both GM and Ford exited from the Japanese market in 1939.

Once the Japanese government passed this law, Risaburo decided that the automobile venture could be profitable and switched from opposing to proactively supporting Kiichiro (in fact, Risaburo's wife, who was Kiichiro's elder sister, had been urging him to take this step for some time). The first priority was to attract the funds necessary to build a mass-production facility. In 1937, Risaburo and Kiichiro decided to incorporate the automobile department as a separate company to attract outside investors—which they were successful in doing. Kiichiro was appointed president of the new company. The company was named the Toyota Motor Company. (The founding family's name, Toyoda, means "abundant rice field" in Japanese. The new name had no meaning in Japanese.)

Upon incorporation, Risaburo and Kiichiro's vision was that Toyota should expand its passenger car production as quickly as possible. However, once again fate intervened in the form of the Japanese military. Toyota had barely begun passenger car production when war broke out; in 1939, the Japanese government, on advice from the military, prohibited passenger car production and demanded that the company specialize in the production of military trucks.

THE EVOLUTION OF TOYOTA

After the end of World War II, Kiichiro was determined that Toyota should reestablish itself as a manufacturer of automobiles.[2] Toyota, however, faced a number of problems in doing this:

1. The Japanese domestic market was too small to support efficient-scale, mass-production facilities such as those common in America by that time.
2. The Japanese economy was starved of capital, which made it difficult to raise funds to finance new investments.
3. New labor laws introduced by the American occupiers increased the bargaining power of labor and made it difficult for companies to lay off workers.
4. North America and Western Europe were full of large auto manufacturers eager to establish operations in Japan.

In response to the last point, in 1950, the new Japanese government prohibited direct foreign investment in the automobile industry and imposed high tariffs on the importation of foreign cars. This protection, however, did little to solve the other problems facing the company at this time.

Limitations of Mass Production

At this juncture, a remarkable mechanical engineer entered the scene: Ohno Taiichi. More than anyone else, it was Ohno who was to work out a response to the above problems. Ohno had joined Toyoda Automatic Loom in 1932 as a production engineer in cotton thread manufacture and entered Toyota when the former company was absorbed into the latter in 1943. He worked in auto production for two years, was promoted, and managed auto assembly and machine shops between 1945 and 1953; in 1954, he was appointed company director.

When Ohno Taiichi joined Toyota, the mass-production methods pioneered by Ford had become the accepted method of manufacturing automobiles. The basic philosophy behind mass production was to produce a limited product line in massive quantities to gain maximum economies of scale. The economies came from spreading the fixed costs involved in setting up the specialized equipment required to stamp body parts and manufacture components over as large a production run as possible. Since setting up much of the equipment could take a full day or more, the economies involved in long production runs were reckoned to be considerable. Thus, for example, Ford would stamp 500,000 right-hand door panels in a single production run and then store the parts in warehouses until they were needed in the assembly plant, rather than stamp just those door panels that were needed immediately and then change the settings and stamp out left-hand door panels, or other body parts.

A second feature of mass production was that each assembly worker should perform a single task only, rather than a variety of tasks. The idea was that as the worker became completely familiar with a single task, he or she could perform it much faster, thereby increasing labor productivity. Assembly line workers were overseen by a foreman who did not perform any assembly tasks; the foreman ensured that the workers followed orders. In addition, a number of specialists were employed to perform non-assembly operations, such as tool repair, die changes, quality inspection, and general "housecleaning."

After working in Toyota for five years and visiting Ford's United States plants, Ohno became convinced that the basic mass-production philosophy was flawed. He saw five problems with the mass-production system:

1. Long production runs created massive inventories that had to be stored in large warehouses. This was expensive both because of the cost of warehousing and because inventories tied up capital in unproductive uses.
2. If the initial machine settings were wrong, long production runs resulted in the production of a large number of defects.
3. The sheer monotony of assigning assembly line workers to a single task generated defects, because workers became lax about quality control. In addition, because assembly line workers were not responsible for quality control, they had little incentive to minimize defects.
4. The extreme division of labor resulted in the employment of specialists such as foremen, quality inspectors, and tooling specialists, whose jobs logically could be performed by assembly line workers.
5. The mass-production system was unable to accommodate consumer preferences for product diversity.

In addition to these flaws, Ohno knew that the small domestic market in Japan and the lack of capital for investing in mass-production facilities made the American model unsuitable for Toyota.

Reducing Setup Times

Given these flaws and the constraints that Toyota faced, Ohno decided to take a fresh look at the techniques used for automobile production. His first goal was to try to economically manufacture auto-body parts in small batches. To do this, he needed to reduce the time it took to set up the machines for stamping out body parts. Ohno and his engineers began to experiment with a number of techniques to speed up the time it took to change the dies in stamping equipment. This included using rollers to move dies in and out of position, along with a number of simple and mechanized adjustment mechanisms to fine-tune the settings. These techniques were relatively simple to master, so Ohno directed production workers to perform the die changes themselves. This reduced the need for specialists and eliminated the idle time that workers previously enjoyed while waiting for the dies to be changed.

Through a process of trial and error, Ohno succeeded in reducing the time required to change dies on stamping equipment from a full day to 15 minutes by 1962, and to as little as 3 minutes by 1971. By comparison, even in the early 1980s, many American and European plants required between 2 and 6 hours to change dies on stamping equipment. As a consequence, American and European plants found it economical to manufacture in lots equivalent to 10 to 30 days' supply and to reset equipment only every other day. In contrast, because Toyota could change the dies on stamping equipment in a matter of minutes, it manufactured in lots equivalent to just one day's supply, while resetting equipment three times per day.

Not only did these innovations make small production runs economical, but they also had the added benefit of reducing inventories and improving product quality. Making small batches eliminated the need to hold large inventories, thereby reducing warehousing costs and freeing up scarce capital for investment elsewhere. Small production runs and the lack of inventory also meant that defective parts were produced in small numbers and entered the assembly process almost immediately. This had the added effect of making those in the stamping shops far more concerned about quality. In addition, once it became economical to manufacture small batches of components, much greater variety could be included into the final product at little or no cost penalty.

Organization of the Workplace

One of Ohno's first innovations was to group the workforce into teams. Each team was given a set of assembly tasks to perform, and team members were trained to perform each task that the team was responsible for. Each team had a leader who was also an assembly line worker. In addition to coordinating the team, the team leader was expected to perform basic assembly line tasks and fill in for any absent worker. The teams were given the job of housecleaning, minor tool repair, and quality inspection (along with the training required to perform these tasks). Time was also set aside for team members to discuss ways to improve the production process (the practice now referred to as "quality circles").

The immediate effect of this approach was to reduce the need for specialists in the workplace and create a more flexible workforce in which individual assembly-line workers were not treated simply as human machines. All of this resulted in increased worker productivity.

None of this would have been possible, however, had it not been for an agreement reached between management and labor after a 1950 strike. The strike was brought on by management's attempt to cut the workforce by 25% (in response to a recession in Japan). After lengthy negotiations, Toyota and the union worked out a compromise. The workforce was cut by 25% as originally proposed, but the remaining employees were given two guarantees—one for lifetime employment and the other for pay graded by seniority and tied to company profitability through bonus payments. In exchange for these guarantees, the employees agreed to be flexible in work assignments. In turn, this allowed for the introduction of the team concept.

Improving Quality

One of the standard practices in mass-production automobile assembly plants was to fix any errors that occurred during assembly in a rework area at the end of the assembly line. Errors routinely occurred in most assembly plants because either bad parts were installed or good parts were installed incorrectly. The belief was that stopping an assembly line to fix such errors would cause enormous bottlenecks in the production system. Thus it was thought to be more efficient to correct errors at the end of the line.

Ohno viewed this system as wasteful for three reasons: (1) because workers understood that any errors would be fixed at the end of the line, they had little incentive to correct errors themselves; (2) once a defective part had been embedded in a complex vehicle, an enormous amount of rework might be required to fix it; and (3) because defective parts were often not discovered until the end of the line when the finished cars were tested, a large number of cars containing the same defect may have been built before the problem was found.

In an attempt to get away from this practice, Ohno decided to look for ways to reduce the amount of rework at the end of the line. His approach involved two elements. First, he placed a cord above every workstation and instructed workers to stop the assembly line if a problem emerged that could not be fixed. It then became the responsibility of the whole team to come over and work on the problem. Second, team members were taught to trace every defect back to its ultimate cause and then to ensure that the problem was fixed so that it would not reoccur.

Initially, this system produced enormous disruption. The production line was stopping all the time, and workers became discouraged. However, as team members began to gain experience in identifying problems and tracing them back to their root causes, the number of errors began to drop dramatically, so stops in the line became much rarer. Today, in most Toyota plants, the line virtually never stops.

Developing the Kanban System

Once reduced setup times had made small production runs economical, Ohno began to look for ways to coordinate the flow of production within the Toyota manufacturing system so that the amount of inventory in the system could be reduced to a minimum. Toyota produced about 25% of its major components in-house; the rest were contracted out to independent suppliers. Ohno's initial goal was to arrange for components and/or subassemblies manufactured in-house to be delivered to the assembly floor only when they were needed, not before. (This goal was later extended to include independent suppliers.)

To achieve this, in 1953, Ohno began experimenting with what came to be known as the kanban system. Under the kanban system, component parts are delivered to the assembly line in containers. As each container is emptied, it is sent back to the previous step in the manufacturing process. This then becomes the signal to make more parts. The system minimizes work in progress by increasing inventory turnover. The elimination of buffer inventories also means that defective components show up immediately in the next process. This speeds up the processes of tracing defects back to their source and facilitates correction of the problem before too many defects are made. Moreover, the elimination of buffer stocks, by removing all safety nets, makes it imperative that problems be solved before they become serious enough to jam up the production process, thereby creating a strong incentive for workers to ensure that errors are corrected as quickly as possible. In addition, by decentralizing responsibility for coordinating the manufacturing process to lower-level employees, the kanban system does away with the need for extensive centralized management to coordinate the flow of parts between the various stages of production.

After perfecting the kanban system in one of Toyota's machine shops, Ohno had a chance to apply the system broadly in 1960 when he was made general manager of the Motomachi assembly plant. Ohno already had converted the machining, body stamping, and body shops to the kanban system, but because many parts came from shops that had yet to adopt the system, or from outside suppliers, the impact on inventories was initially minimal. However, by 1962, Ohno had extended the kanban system to forging and casting; between 1962 and 1965, he began to bring independent suppliers into the system.

Organizing Suppliers

Assembly of components into a final vehicle accounts for only about 15% of the total manufacturing process in automobile manufacturing. The remaining 85% of the process involves manufacturing more than 10,000 individual parts and assembling them into about 100 major components, such as engines, suspension systems, transaxles, and so on. Coordinating this process so that everything comes together at the right time had always been a problem for auto manufacturers. Historically, the response at Ford and GM to this problem was massive vertical integration. The belief was that control over the supply chain would allow management to coordinate the flow of component parts into the final assembly plant. In addition, American firms held the view that vertical integration made them more efficient by reducing their dependence on other firms for materials and components and limiting their vulnerability to opportunistic overcharging.

As a consequence of this philosophy, even as late as the mid-1990s, General Motors made 68% of its own components in-house, while Ford made 50%. (In the late 1990s, both GM and Ford de-integrated, spinning off much of their in-house supply operations as independent enterprises.) When they did not, vertically integrated United States auto companies tried to reduce the procurement costs that remained through competitive bidding—asking a number of companies to submit contracts and giving orders to suppliers offering the lowest price.

Under the leadership of Kiichiro Toyoda during the 1930s and 1940s, Toyota followed the American model and pursued extensive vertical integration into the manufacture of component parts. In fact, Toyota had little choice in this matter, because only a handful of Japanese companies were able to make the necessary components. However, the low volume of production during this period meant that the scale of integration was relatively small. In the 1950s, however, the volume of auto production began to increase dramatically. This presented Toyota with a dilemma: should the company increase its capacity to manufacture components in-house in line with the growth in the production of autos, or should the company contract out?

In contrast to American practice, the company decided that while it should increase in-house capacity for essential subassemblies and bodies, it would do better to contract out for most components. Four reasons seem to bolster this decision:

1. Toyota wanted to avoid the capital expenditures required to expand capacity to manufacture a wide variety of components.
2. Toyota wanted to reduce risk by maintaining a low factory capacity in case factory sales slumped.
3. Toyota wanted to take advantage of the lower wage scales in smaller firms.
4. Toyota managers realized that in-house manufacturing offered few benefits if it was possible to find stable, high-quality, and low-cost external sources of component supply.

At the same time, Toyota managers felt that the American practice of inviting competitive bids from suppliers was self-defeating. While competitive bidding might achieve the lowest short-run costs, the practice of playing suppliers off against each other did not guarantee stable supplies, high quality, or cooperation beyond existing contracts to solve design or engineering problems. Ohno and other Toyota managers believed that real efficiencies could be achieved if the company entered into long-term relationships with major suppliers. This would allow them to introduce the kanban system, thereby further reducing inventory holding costs and realizing the same kind

of quality benefits that Toyota was already beginning to encounter with its in-house supply operations. In addition, Ohno wanted to bring suppliers into the design process since he believed that suppliers might be able to suggest ways of improving the design of component parts based on their own manufacturing experience.

As it evolved during the 1950s and 1960s, Toyota's strategy toward its suppliers had several elements. The company spun off some of its in-house supply operations into quasi-independent entities in which it took a minority stake, typically holding between 20% and 40% of the stock. It then recruited a number of independent companies, hoping to establish long-term relationships with them for the supply of critical components. Sometimes, but not always, Toyota took a minority stake in the companies as well. All of these companies were designated as "first-tier suppliers." First-tier suppliers were responsible for working with Toyota as an integral part of the new product development team. Each first tier was responsible for the formation of a "second tier" of suppliers under its direction. Companies in the second tier were given the job of fabricating individual parts. Both first- and second-tier suppliers were formed into supplier associations.

By 1986, Toyota had three regional supply organizations in Japan with 62, 135, and 25 first-tier suppliers. A major function of the supplier associations was to share information regarding new manufacturing, design, or materials management techniques among themselves. By this process, concepts such as statistical process control, total quality control, and computer-aided design were rapidly diffused among suppliers.

Toyota also worked closely with its suppliers, providing them with management expertise, engineering expertise, and sometimes capital to finance new investments. A critical feature of this relationship was the incentives that Toyota established to encourage its suppliers to focus on realizing continuous process improvements. The basic contract for a component was for four to five years, with the price agreed on in advance. If by joint efforts the supplier and Toyota succeeded in reducing the costs of manufacturing the components, then the additional profit would be shared between the two. If the supplier by its own efforts came up with an innovation that reduced costs, the supplier would keep the additional profit that the innovation generated for the lifetime of the contract.

As a consequence of this strategy, Toyota outsourced more production than almost any other major auto manufacturer. By the late 1980s, Toyota was responsible for only about 27% of the value going into a finished automobile, with the remainder coming from outside suppliers. In contrast, General Motors was responsible for about 70% of the value going into a finished automobile. Other consequences included long-term improvements in productivity and quality among Toyota's suppliers that were comparable to the improvements achieved by Toyota itself. In particular, the extension of the kanban system to include suppliers, by eliminating buffer inventory stocks, in essence forced suppliers to focus more explicitly on the quality of their product.

Consequences

The consequences of Toyota's production system included a surge in labor productivity and a decline in the number of defects per car. Exhibit 1 compares the number of vehicles produced per worker at General Motors, Ford, Nissan, and Toyota between 1965 and 1983. These figures are adjusted for the degree of vertical integration pursued by each company. As can be seen, in 1960, productivity at Toyota already outstripped that of Ford, General Motors, and its main Japanese

competitor, Nissan. As Toyota refined its production system over the next 18 years, productivity doubled. In comparison, productivity essentially stood still at General Motors and Ford during the same period.

Exhibit 2 provides another way to assess the superiority of Toyota's production system. Here, the performance of Toyota's Takaoka plant is compared with that of General Motors's Framingham plant in 1987. As can be seen, the Toyota plant was more productive, produced far fewer defects per 100 cars, and kept far less inventory on hand.

A further aspect of Toyota's production system was that the short setup times made it economical to manufacture a much wider range of models than was feasible at a traditional mass-production assembly plant. In essence, Toyota soon found that it could supply much greater product variety than its competitors with little in the way of a cost penalty. In 1990, Toyota was offering consumers around the world roughly as many products as General Motors (about 150), even though Toyota was still only half GM's size. Moreover, it could do this at a lower cost than GM.

Distribution and Customer Relations

Toyota's approach to its distributors and customers as it evolved during the 1950s and 1960s was in many ways just as radical as its approach toward suppliers. In 1950, Toyota formed a subsidiary, Toyota Motor Sales, to handle distribution and sales. The new subsidiary was headed by Kaymiya Shotaro from its inception until 1975. Kaymiya's philosophy

Exhibit 1 Vehicles Produced per Worker (adjusted for vertical integration), 1965–1983

Year	General Motors	Ford	Nissan	Toyota
1965	5.0	4.4	4.3	8.0
1970	3.7	4.3	8.8	13.4
1975	4.4	4.0	9.0	15.1
1979	4.5	4.2	11.1	18.4
1980	4.1	3.7	12.2	17.8
1983	4.8	4.7	11.0	15.0

Source: M. A. Cusumano, *The Japanese Automotive Industry* (Cambridge, Mass.: Harvard University Press, 1989), Table 48, 197.

Exhibit 2 General Motors's Framingham Plant versus Toyota's Takaoka Plant, 1987

	GM Framingham	Toyota Takaoka
Assembly hours per car	31	16
Assembly defects per 100 cars	135	45
Inventory of parts	2 weeks	2 hours

Source: J. P. Womack, D. T. Jones, and D. Roos, *The Machines That Changed the World* (New York: Macmillan, 1990), Figure 4.2, 83.

was that dealers should be treated as "equal partners" in the Toyota family. To back this up, he had Toyota Motor Sales provide a wide range of sales and service training for dealership personnel. Kaymiya then used the dealers to build long-term ties with Toyota's customers. The ultimate aim was to bring customers into the Toyota design and production process. To this end, through its dealers, Toyota Motor Sales assembled a huge database of customer preferences. Much of these data came from monthly or semiannual surveys conducted by dealers. They asked Toyota customers their preferences for styling, model types, colors, prices, and other features. Toyota also used these surveys to estimate the potential demand for new models. This information was then fed directly into the design process.

Kaymiya began this process in 1952 when the company was redesigning its Toyopet model. The Toyopet was primarily used by urban taxi drivers. Toyota Motor Sales surveyed taxi drivers to try to find out what type of vehicles they preferred. They wanted something reliable, inexpensive, and with good city fuel mileage—which Toyota engineers then set about designing. In 1956, Kaymiya formalized this process when he created a unified department for planning and market research, whose function was to coordinate the marketing strategies developed by researchers at Toyota Motor Sales with product planning by Toyota's design engineers. From this time on, marketing information played a critical role in the design of Toyota's cars and in the company's strategy. In particular, the research department at Toyota Motor Sales provided the initial stimulus for Toyota to start exporting during the late 1960s after predicting, correctly, that growth in domestic sales would slow down considerably during the 1970s.

Expanding Internationally

Large-scale overseas expansion did not become feasible at Toyota until the late 1960s for one principal reason: despite the rapid improvement in productivity, Japanese cars were still not competitive.[3] In 1957, for example, the Toyota Corona sold in Japan for the equivalent of $1,694. At the same time the Volkswagen Beetle sold for $1,111 in West Germany, while Britain's Austin Company was selling its basic model for the equivalent of $1,389 in Britain. Foreign companies were effectively kept out of the Japanese market, however, by a 40% value-added tax and shipping costs.

Despite these disadvantages, Toyota tried to enter the United States market in the late 1950s. The company set up a United States subsidiary in California in October 1957 and began to sell cars in early 1958, hoping to capture the American small car market (which at that time was poorly served by the United States automobile manufacturers companies). The result was a disaster. Toyota's cars performed poorly in road tests on United States highways. The basic problem was that the engines of Toyota's cars were too small for prolonged high-speed driving and tended to overheat and burn oil, while poorly designed chassis resulted in excessive vibration. Sales were slow, and in 1964, Toyota closed down its United States subsidiary and withdrew from the market.

The company was determined to learn from its United States experience and quickly redesigned several of its models based on feedback from American consumer surveys and road tests. As a result, by 1967, the picture had changed considerably. The quality of Toyota's cars was now sufficient to make an impact in the United States market, while production costs and retail prices had continued to fall and were now comparable with international competitors in the small car market.

In the late 1960s, Toyota reentered the United States market. Although sales were initially slow, they increased steadily. Then the OPEC-engineered fourfold increase in oil prices that followed the 1973 Israeli/Arab conflict gave Toyota an unexpected boost. United States consumers began to turn to small fuel-efficient cars in droves, and Toyota was one of the main beneficiaries. Driven primarily by a surge in American demand, worldwide exports of Toyota cars increased from 157,882 units in 1967 to 856,352 units by 1974 and 1,800,923 units by 1984. Put another way, in 1967, exports accounted for 19% of Toyota's total output. By 1984, they accounted for 52.5%.

Success brought its own problems. By the early 1980s, political pressures and talk of local content regulations in the United States and Europe were forcing an initially reluctant Toyota to rethink its exporting strategy. Toyota already had agreed to "voluntary" import quotas with the United States in 1981. The consequence for Toyota was stagnant export growth between 1981 and 1984. Against this background, in the early 1980s, Toyota began to seriously think about setting up manufacturing operations overseas.

Transplant Operations

Toyota's first overseas operation was a 50/50 joint venture with General Motors established in February 1983 under the name New United Motor Manufacturing, Inc. (NUMMI). NUMMI, based in Fremont, California, began producing Chevrolet Nova cars for GM in December 1984.[4] The maximum capacity of the Fremont plant was about 250,000 cars per year.

For Toyota, the joint venture provided a chance to find out whether it could build quality cars in the United States using American workers and suppliers. It also provided Toyota with experience dealing with an American union (the United Auto Workers Union) and a means of circumventing "voluntary" import restrictions. For General Motors, the venture provided an opportunity to observe in full detail the Japanese approach to manufacturing. While General Motors' role was marketing and distributing the plant's output, Toyota designed the product and designed, equipped, and operated the plant. At the venture's start, 34 executives were loaned to NUMMI by Toyota and 16 by General Motors. The chief executive officer (CEO) and chief operating officer were both Toyota personnel.

By the fall of 1986, the NUMMI plant was running at full capacity. The early indications were that the NUMMI plant was achieving productivity and quality levels close to those achieved at Toyota's major Takaoka plant in Japan. For example, in 1987, it took the NUMMI plant 19 assembly hours to build a car, compared to 16 hours at Takaoka, while the number of defects per 100 cars was the same at NUMMI as at Takaoka—45.[5]

Encouraged by its success at NUMMI, in December 1985, Toyota announced that it would build an automobile manufacturing plant in Georgetown, Kentucky. The plant, which came on-stream in May 1988, officially had the capacity to produce 200,000 Toyota Camrys a year. Such was the success of this plant, however, that by early 1990, it was producing the equivalent of 220,000 cars per year. This success was followed by an announcement in December 1990 that Toyota would build a second plant in Georgetown with a capacity to produce an additional 200,000 vehicles per year.[6]

By 2008, Toyota had 10 vehicle assembly plants in the United States that were producing 1.3 million vehicles per year. An 11th plant, slated to produce Toyota's best-selling hybrid car, the Prius, is expected to open in 2010. In addition, the company had six other plants producing a range of components, including engines and transmissions. The company also has two R&D and design centers in the United States, its only such facilities outside Japan. By 2008, Toyota's cumulative investment in the United States exceeded $17 billion. In total, Toyota's United States facilities employed more than 36,000 people directly and supported another 200,000 in suppliers and distributors. More than 50% of all Toyota vehicles sold in the United States were now locally produced.

In addition to its North American transplant operations, Toyota moved to set up production in Europe in anticipation of the 1992 lowering of trade barriers among the 12 members of the European Economic Community. In 1989, the company announced that it would build a plant in England, with a capacity to manufacture 200,000 cars per year by 1997. It opened a second plant in France in 2001, and by 2008, Toyota had four assembly plants in Europe, with a total production capacity of 800,000 vehicles.

The company also expanded to China during the first decade of the 21st century. In China, it had 3 assembly plants by 2008 that were capable of producing more than 440,000 vehicles a year. In the rest of Southeast Asia, Toyota had another 10 plants that could produce almost one million vehicles. There were also significant assembly plants in South Africa, Australia, and South America.

Despite Toyota's apparent commitment to expand global assembly operations, it was not all smooth sailing. One problem was building an overseas supplier network comparable to Toyota's Japanese network. For example, in a 1990 meeting of Toyota's North American supplier's association, Toyota executives informed their North American suppliers that the defect ratio for parts produced by 75 North American and European suppliers was 100 times greater than the defect ratio for parts supplied by 147 Japanese suppliers—1,000 defects per million parts versus 10 defects per million among Toyota's Japanese suppliers. Moreover, Toyota executives pointed out that parts manufactured by North American and European suppliers tended to be significantly more expensive than comparable parts manufactured in Japan.

Because of these problems, Toyota had to import many parts from Japan for its United States assembly operations. For political reasons, however, Toyota was being pushed to increase the local content of cars assembled in North America. By the mid-2000s, the local content of cars produced in North America was more than 70%. To improve the efficiency of its American-based suppliers, Toyota embarked upon an aggressive supplier education process. In 1992, it established the Toyota Supplier Support Center to teach its suppliers the basics of the Toyota production system. By the mid-2000s, more than 100 supplier companies had been through the center. Many had reportedly seen double- and triple-digit productivity growth as a result, as well as dramatic reductions in inventory levels.[7]

Product Strategy

Toyota's initial production was aimed at the small car/basic transportation end of the automobile market. This was true both in Japan and of its export sales to North America and Europe. During the 1980s, however, Toyota progressively moved up market and abandoned much of the lower end of the market to new entrants such as South Korea. Thus, the company's Camry and Corolla models, which initially were positioned toward the bottom of the market, had been constantly upgraded and were then aimed at the middle-income segments of the market. This upgrading reflects two factors: (1) the rising level of incomes in Japan and the commensurate increase in the ability of Japanese consumers to purchase mid-range and luxury cars; and (2) a desire to hold onto its American consumers, many of whom initially purchased inexpensive Toyotas in their early 20s and had since traded up to more expensive models.

The upgrading of Toyota's models reached a logical conclusion in September 1989 when the company's Lexus division began marketing luxury cars to compete with Jaguars, BMWs, and the like. Although the Lexus brand initially got off to a slow start—in large part due to an economic recession—by 2001, Toyota was selling more than 200,000 Lexus models a year in the United States, making it the best-selling luxury brand in the country.

In the mid-1990s, Toyota's United States research suggested that the company was losing younger buyers to hipper brands like Volkswagen. The result was a brand designed specially for the United States market, the Scion. Established with its own dealer network, the Scion was a hit for Toyota.

TOYOTA IN 2000–2008

The first eight years of the 21st century were ones of solid growth for Toyota. In 2004, it overtook Ford to become the second largest car company in the world. The company surpassed General Motors in 2008, and seemed on track to meet its goal of capturing 15% of the global automobile market by 2010. Toyota was a truly international company. Its overseas operations had grown from 11 production facilities in 9 countries in 1980 to 48 production facilities in 26 countries around the world.[8] In the important United States market, the world's largest, Toyota held an 18.4% share of passenger car sales in mid-2008, up from 11% in 2000. Ford's share was 15.4%, while GM held onto a 19.3% share.[9]

The company was very profitable. In the financial year ending March 2008, it earned $17.5 billion net profits on sales of $183 billion. Both General Motors and Ford lost money that year.

According to data from J.D. Power, Toyota was the quality leader in the United States market in 2008. For cars that had been on the market for more than three years, Toyota's Lexus brand led the pack for the 14th consecutive year with 120 problems per 100 vehicles, compared to an industry average of 206 problems per 100 vehicles. The Toyota brand had 159 problems per 100 vehicles, compared to 177 for Honda, 204 for Ford, 226 for GM, 229 for Chrysler, and 253 for Volkswagen. Toyota also had a strong record in the industry when measured by problems reported in the first 90 days after a sale: 99 problems per 100 cars for the Lexus brand and 104 for the Toyota brand versus an industry average of 118 problems per 100 cars.[10]

J. D. Power also found that Toyota led the market in Japan. A survey found that for vehicles purchased in 2002, Toyota had 89 problems per 100 vehicles compared to an industry average of 104. Honda was next with 91 problems per 100 vehicles, followed by Nissan with 108 problems per 100 vehicles.[11]

On the productivity front, Toyota's lead seemed to have narrowed (refer to Exhibit 3). While it was clearly the productivity leader in the United States in 2003, where it took an average of 30.1 hours to make a car, compared to 35.2 hours at General Motors and 38.6 hours at Ford, by 2007 Toyota was taking 30.37 to build a car, compared to 32.29 at GM and 33.88 at Ford.[12] On the other hand, accord-

Exhibit 3 Total Manufacturing Productivity in the U.S. Automobile Industry (total labor hours per unit)

Company	2003	2007
Ford	38.6	33.88
Chrysler	37.42	30.37
General Motors	35.2	32.39
Nissan	32.94	32.96
Honda	32.36	31.33
Toyota	30.01	30.37

Note: Includes assembly, stamping, engine, and transmission plants.

Source: *Oliver Wyman's Harbour Report,* Oliver Wyman, June 2008.

ing to J. D. Power, Toyota had the three most efficient assembly plants in the world, all of which are located in Japan.[13]

Higher quality and greater productivity helped Toyota to make far more money per car than its large rivals. In 2007, Toyota made a pretax profit of $922 per vehicle in the United States, compared with losses of $729 and $1,467 at GM and Ford, respectively. These losses also reflect the fact that Ford and GM still pay more for health care, pensions, and sales incentives than Toyota. Also, Ford and GM support more dealers relative to their market share than Toyota.[14]

Toyota's ability to stay on top of productivity and quality rankings can be attributed to a companywide obsession with continuing to improve the efficiency and effectiveness of its manufacturing operations. The latest round of these was initiated in 2000 by Fujio Cho, Toyota's president. Cho, who worked for a while under Toyota's legendary engineer, Ohno Taiichi, introduced an initiative known as "Construction of Cost Competitiveness for the 21st Century" or CCC21. The initiative had as a goal slashing component part costs by 30% on all new models. Attaining this goal necessitated Toyota working closely with suppliers—something it had long done.

By the mid-2000s, Toyota was close to attaining its CCC21 goal. In implementing CCC21, no detail has been too small. For example, Toyota took a close look at the grip handles mounted above the doors

inside most cars. By working closely with suppliers, they managed to reduce the number of parts in these handles from 34 to 5, which cut procurement costs by 40% and reduced the time needed for installation from 12 seconds to 3 seconds.[15]

More generally, Toyota continues to refine its lean production system. For example, in die-making, by 2004, Toyota had reduced the lead time to engineered and manufactured die sets for large body panels to 1.7 months, down from 3 months in 2002. By reducing lead time, Toyota reduced the startup costs associated with producing a new model and the development time.[16]

In welding, Toyota has developed and installed a simplified assembly process known as the "Global Body Line" or GBL. First developed in a low-volume Vietnamese assembly plant in 1996 and introduced into its first Japanese plant in 1998, the GBL was operating in some 20 of the company's 50 assembly plants by 2004; it was found in all plants by 2007. The GBL system replaced Toyota's Flexible Body Line (FBL) assembly philosophy that had been in place since 1985. The GBL system is based upon a series of programmable robotic welding tools. Under the old FBL system, each car required three pallets to hold body parts in place during the welding process: each gripping either a major body side assembly or the roof assembly. The GBL system replaces these three pallets with a single pallet that holds all three major body panels in place from the inside as welding proceeds.[17]

According to Toyota, the GBL system has the following consequences:

- 30% reduction in the time a vehicle spends in the body shop
- 70% reduction in the time required to complete a major body change
- 50% cut in the cost to add or switch models
- 50% reduction in the investment to set up a line for a new model
- 50% reduction in assembly-line footprint

The floor space freed up by the GBL allowed two assembly lines to be placed in the space traditionally required for one, effectively doubling plant capacity. Moreover, using GBL technology, as many as eight different models could be produced on a single assembly line. To achieve this, Toyota pushed for consistency in design across model ranges, particularly in regard to the "hard points" that are grasped by the single master pallet.

Meanwhile, Toyota was also accelerating the process of moving toward fewer vehicle platforms, the goal being to build a wide range of models on a limited range of platforms that use many of the same component parts or modules. The company is reportedly working toward a goal of having just 10 platforms, down from more than 20 in 2000.[18]

Toyota is undoubtedly making progress refining its manufacturing efficiency, the fact remains that the productivity and quality gap between Toyota and its global competitors has narrowed. General Motors and Ford have both made significant strides in improving their quality and productivity in recent years. Moreover, in the American market at least, Toyota has suffered from the perception that its product offerings lack design flair and are not always as well attuned to consumer tastes as they might be. In this example too, however, there are signs that Toyota is improving matters interestingly enough, by listening more to its American designers and engineers.

A pivotal event in the changing relationship between Toyota and its American designers occurred in the late 1990s. Japanese managers had resisted their United States colleagues' idea that the company should produce a V8 pickup truck for the American market. To change their minds, the United States executives flew their Japanese counterparts over from Japan and took them to a Dallas Cowboys football game—with a pit stop in the Texas Stadium parking lot. There the Japanese saw row upon row of full-size pickups. Finally, it dawned on them that Americans see the pickup as more than a commercial vehicle, considering it primary transportation. The result of this was Toyota's best-selling V8 pickup truck, the Toyota Tundra.[19]

American designers also pushed Toyota to redesign the Prius, the hybrid car first introduced in Japan in 1997. The Americans wanted a futuristic design change so that people would notice the technology. The result, the new Prius, has become a surprise hit, with Toyota hitting cumulative global sales of more than one million vehicles in mid-2008. Toyota now plans to make more than one million hybrids a year by 2010.[20]

Toyota's Americanization runs deeper than just product design issues. On the sales front, the company now sells more cars and trucks in North America than it does in Japan, and 70% to 80% of Toyota's global profits come from North America. On the personnel front, President Cho made his reputation

by opening Toyota's first United States production plant in Georgetown, Kentucky, in 1988. Another senior executive, Yoshi Inaba, spent eight years in the United States and has an MBA from Northwestern University. Americans are also starting to make their way into Toyota's top ranks. Two Americans from Toyota's United States subsidiary now rank among Toyota's top 42 executives, and each spends one to two weeks a month in Japan.[21]

Another concern of Toyota has been the aging of its customer base. According to J.D. Power, the average Toyota customer is 44 years old, compared with 38 for Volkswagen and 41 for Honda. Concerned that it was losing its hold with the younger generation, some 60 million of whom will reach driving age over the next few years, Toyota introduced the Scion, in America in June 2004. Currently the brand has three models, all priced in the $13,000 to $17,000 range. The cars are targeted at young, entry-level buyers and can be purchased on the Web, in addition to traditional Toyota dealers. Toyota's initial sales goals for the brand were 100,000 cars in 2005, but in October 2004, it raised that target to 170,000. The average buyer in the months following launch was 31 years old.[22]

THE 2008–2009 CRISIS

Starting in mid-2008, sales in the global automobile industry collapsed at unprecedented rates, falling by about 40%. The sales collapse was a direct consequence of the global financial crisis that started in the American mortgage market and then spilled over into other sectors. A combination of tight credit and uncertainty about the future caused consumers to buy far fewer new cars. For an industry with high fixed costs, a sales decline of this level was catastrophic.

Toyota was caught flat-footed by the decline. Toyota had been adding to its production capacity in the United States, its largest market, and was pushing into the full-sized pickup truck segment, when the storm hit. It had also been adding significant capacity elsewhere, a move that seemed sensible only 12 months earlier given that the company had been struggling to keep up with demand for its vehicles. Indeed, between 2001 and 2007, Toyota added about 500,000 cars worth of production capacity per year, a pace that now seems to be aggressive.[23]

By April 2009, Toyota's sales in the United States were down 42% compared to the same month a year earlier. Moreover, there were sales declines in all other major national markets as well, including China, where Toyota sales fell by 17% in the first quarter of 2009, even though that market was one of the few that continued to grow. Toyota's problems in China reflected a slow response to increasing demand outside of China's big cities for small affordable cars. Toyota exports from Japan were also hit hard by a rise in the value of the Japanese yen against the dollar and euro during 2008 and early 2009.

In the United States, Toyota responded to the recession by placing the planned addition of a new production plant in Mississippi on hold and idling a production line in Texas. In Japan, production was cut by as much as 40% in some factories. These actions created a huge problem for Toyota, which adheres to a policy of lifetime employment, and has not made any significant workforce reductions since the 1950s. Toyota's initial response was to send under-utilized employees to training sessions and have them work on identifying ideas for cost savings. However, the company did start to lay off temporary workers, and many questioned whether Toyota would be able to stick to its commitment of lifetime employment, particularly if the recession dragged on.

Toyota also launched an "Emergency Profit Improvement Committee," whose job was to find $1.4 billion in savings in 2009. These cost savings came upon some $3.3 billion in cost reductions attained during the preceding few years. In typical Toyota style, no action seems too small. Employees have been encouraged to take the stairs rather than use elevators to save electricity. The heat in factories has been turned down. Teams of workers are looking for ways to shave costs out of a production system that is already the world's most efficient.[24]

To try and boost sales in the United States, Toyota introduced 0% financing in late 2008, but sales continued to falter. Ironically, one of Toyota's best-selling cars in the United States during much of 2007 and 2008, the fuel-efficient Prius, which carries a relative high price sticker, also saw steep sales declines in early 2009 as gasoline prices fell, and consumers who purchased cars switched to low priced small cars from Kia and even Ford.

Meanwhile, Toyota is also going through a changing of senior management ranks. In June 2009, Akio Toyoda, grandson of the company's founder, will succeed outgoing CEO Katsuaki Watanabe. With an MBS from Babson College in the United States, and time working in both New York and London, Toyoda is without question the most cosmopolitan CEO to take the helm at Toyota. He does so at a particularly challenging time for the company. His major challenge is to weather the storm and return the company to its growth path.

Endnotes

1. This section is based primarily on the account given in M. A. Cusumano, *The Japanese Automobile Industry* (Cambridge, Mass: Harvard University Press, 1989), XX.
2. The material in this section is drawn from three main sources: M. A. Cusumano, *The Japanese Automobile Industry;* Ohno Taiichi, *Toyota Production System* (Cambridge, Mass: Productivity Press, 1990; Japanese Edition, 1997); J. P. Womack, D. T. Jones, and D. Roos, *The Machine That Changed the World* (New York: Macmillan, 1999).
3. The material in this section is based on M. A. Cusumano, *The Japanese Automobile Industry.*
4. Niland Powell, "U.S.-Japanese Joint Venture: New United Motor Manufacturing, Inc.," *Planning Review,* January–February 1989, 40–45.
5. From J. P. Womack, D. T. Jones, and D. Roos, *The Machine That Changed the World.*
6. J. B. Treece, "Just What Detroit Needs: 200,000 More Toyotas a Year," *BusinessWeek,* December 10, 1990, 29.
7. P. Strozniak, "Toyota Alters the Face of Production," *Industry Week,* August 13, 2001, 46–48.
8. Anonymous, "The Car Company out in Front," *The Economist,* January 29, 2005, 65–67.
9. R. Newman, "How Toyota Could Become the U.S. Sales Champ," *US News and World Reports,* June 9, 2008.
10. J. D. Power press release, "Lexus Ranks Highest in Vehicle Dependability for 14th Consecutive Year," August 7, 2008; J. D. Power press release, "Overall Initial Quality Improves Considerably with Gains Shared Across Most Manufacturers," June 4, 2008.
11. J. D. Power press release, "Toyota Ranks Highest in Japan's First Long-Term Vehicle Dependability Study," September 2, 2004.
12. *Oliver Wyman's Harbour Report,* Oliver Wyman, June 2008.
13. Ibid.
14. Ibid.

15. B. Bremner and C. Dawson, "Can Anything Stop Toyota?" *Business Week*, November 17, 2003, 114–117.

16. M. Hara, "Moving Target," *Automotive Industries*, June 2004, 26–29.

17. B. Visnic, "Toyota Adopts New Flexible Assembly Process," *Wards Auto World*, November 2002, 30–31; M. Bursa, "A Review of Flexible Automotive Manufacturing," *Just Auto*, May 2004, 15.

18. M. Hara, "Moving Target," 26–29.

19. C. Dawson and L. Armstrong, "The Americanization of Toyota," *Business Week*, April 15, 2002, 52–54.

20. Chuck Squatriglia, "Prius Sales Top 1 Million," *Autopia*, May 15, 2008.

21. A. Taylor, "The Americanization of Toyota," *Fortune*, December 8, 2004, 165.

22. N. Shirouzu, "Scion Plays Hip-Hop Impresario to Impress Young Drivers," *Wall Street Journal*, October 5, 2004, B1.

23. Y. Takahashi, "Toyota Record $7.74 Billion Quarterly Loss," *Wall Street Journal*, May 11, 2009, 3.

24. I. Rowly, "Toyota's Cost Cutting Drive," *Business Week*, January 1, 2009, 15.

GM IN 2009

General Motors (GM) was once the largest and most profitable industrial company in the world. But during the last decades, it became one of the least profitable; in 2008, after the economic recession caused a 40% plunge in United States car sales, it was losing so much money that it was forced to ask the government for a loan of billions of dollars to keep it afloat. As an indication of how much the company has shrunk, in 1995, GM employed more than 700,000 people globally; by 2005, this had dropped to 325,000, and by the end of 2009, less than 200,000 as GM continued to lay off or offer buyouts to tens of thousands of its managers and employees.

GM has reported losses of more than $90 billion since 2005, and its share of the United States vehicle market has dropped to 19% from more than 40% in 1980. To understand why GM has performed so poorly over the last decades to become one of the least-profitable global carmakers—and why it was forced to enter bankruptcy in 2009—it is necessary to examine the history of the company.

GM's ORIGINS

The company was founded in 1908 when William C. Durant formed the General Motors Corporation by bringing together 25 independent car companies, including Buick and Cadillac. At the beginning, each company retained its own identity, and GM was simply a holding company—a central administrative office surrounded by its 25 car divisions that produced hundreds of models of cars targeted at wealthy customers, the only people who could afford them at the time, because the cost of manufacturing cars was so high.

GM's main competitor was the Ford Motor Car Company, and in 1908, Henry Ford announced the development of the Model T car that was to be produced by the revolutionary method of mass production. Ford's new mass production technology was based on continuously moving conveyor belts that brought the car being assembled to unskilled workers who performed each of the individual operations necessary to complete the final vehicle. Before mass production, small teams of skilled workers assembled cars. Ford also pioneered the use of standardized car parts that could be easily fitted together to make the assembly process easier and faster. As a result, the costs of manufacturing cars plummeted, and Ford created a mass market for the Model T; it became the industry leader. GM found itself in the losing situation of making a wide variety of expensive cars bought by a small number of wealthy customers as compared to Ford's single, inexpensive product targeted at the middle of the United States market. Ford grew rich during the period from 1910 to 1920, while GM struggled to keep its head above water.

In 1920, Alfred P. Sloan became GM's CEO. He decided major strategic changes were necessary to compete effectively with Ford. It was clear to Sloan that operating 25 different car companies that produced hundreds of different models was very

For the most recent financial results of the company discussed in this case, go to http://finance.yahoo.com, click on symbol lookup at top of page, input the company's symbol into the search box, and then follow the appropriate links on the yahoo page for the information you require (e.g., click profile to find link to company's Web site for its annual financial reports, or click on Yahoo! links to the company's SEC filings or Financials).

inefficient compared to Ford's strategy of producing one model of car in large quantities. Moreover, GM's high-priced cars were competing against one another for the same set of wealthy customers.

GM'S NEW STRUCTURE

Sloan searched for a way to reorganize GM's car companies to increase their competitive advantage. He needed to reduce costs and increase efficiency, but he also saw that Ford's strategy to produce only one model of car for the whole market meant that it was ignoring the needs of other market segments—such as the luxury segment GM served. He realized that customers in the middle of the market might want a superior product to the standard Ford Model T, and there was a lot of opportunity to produce cars for market segments between those served by the inexpensive Model T and expensive GM models.

To achieve both superior efficiency and customer responsiveness, Sloan chose to group the 25 companies into five major self-contained operating divisions: Chevrolet, Pontiac, Oldsmobile, Buick, and Cadillac. Each of the different divisions was given its own set of support functions, such as sales, manufacturing, engineering, and finance. Each division was given the responsibility to produce a range of cars targeted at a specific socioeconomic customer segment. Sloan's plan was that GM's five divisions would make and market five brands of cars to customers in five different socioeconomic segments. Also, each division was instructed to imitate the mass production method that had been developed by Ford.

Chevrolet, for example, would make inexpensive cars for customers at the entry level of the market; Pontiac, Oldsmobile, and Buick would produce cars for progressively more prosperous customer segments, while Cadillac would specialize in making high-price, luxury cars directed at wealthy customers. Sloan's goal was to be responsive to customers in each segment of the car market by producing cars to meet their specific needs. He hoped that customers would move up to the next most expensive line of GM car as they prospered. GM carefully priced the cars of the different divisions to entice customers to move up: from a Chevrolet to a Buick or a Buick to a Cadillac. So customers would not be confused about the number of GM models they would be choosing

from, Sloan insisted that each division should develop a range of cars that had a unique image, thus the cars of the different divisions could be clearly differentiated by customers. Thus, Cadillac customers should believe that the Cadillacs they were buying were clearly superior to Buicks—not just more expensive cars with a different name.

Sloan also reorganized GM into five different car divisions to allow each division to operate as an independent profit center that could be evaluated on its profitability; ROI decision-making would be decentralized to the managers of each division, who would be in control of its business model and responsible for bottom-line results. Sloan's goal was that this would create competition between the managers of the five divisions, who would be motivated to improve their division's efficiency and receive a greater share of GM's capital to grow their division in the future— and boost their chances of becoming top corporate executives. The results of this change in GM's business model and strategies were dramatic. By 1925, demand for the Model T plummeted, because customers could buy better equipped, more prestigious, or more luxurious GM cars at comparable prices to Ford's. GM became the dominant United States car company as Sloan's new business model took away market share from Ford—demand for its Model T plummeted as customers switched to GM's upscale and affordable cars. Ford was forced to close down his factory for several months to retool the production line to imitate GM and produce new models of cars targeted at different kinds of customers. He never made up lost ground.

With its new strategy and structure in place, GM became the United States car market leader and obtained the largest market share of any global car manufacturer ever since—more than 70% at the highest point. From 1925 to 1975, GM embarked on a continuous program to expand its product range to include all kinds of models of vehicles, from cars to full-size trucks, lightweight trucks, and various forms of specialized vehicles such as vans and ambulances. As it grew bigger, GM also decided to take over more and more of its suppliers. It became highly vertically integrated; at the highest point, it made more than 65% of the components that went into its vehicles. For example, it took over Fisher Body Company, which had made the car bodies for GM cars. GM also internally developed many of its own car parts manufacturing operations, such as its

Delco division, which supplied GM with most of its electrical/electronic components. From 1925 to 1975, GM dominated the United States car market, controlling, on average, more than 65% of domestic sales. Together, GM, Ford, and Chrysler, the big three carmakers, controlled more than 90% of the United States vehicle market.

1970s: Big Changes in the Global Car Industry

GM's preeminent position in the United States car market was broken in the 1970s by a combination of two factors that altered competition in the car industry forever: (1) the global oil crisis and (2) the emergence of low-cost/high-quality Japanese competitors. The oil embargo of 1973 revealed the inefficiency of American "gas guzzler" cars that frequently obtained only six to nine miles per gallon. United States customers began to demand smaller, fuel-efficient vehicles that the big three did not have the technology to build—; but the Japanese had developed the competence to make these small, fuel-efficient cars. American customers began to switch to the Japanese vehicles; when they did, they also discovered that cars such as the Honda Accord and the Toyota Celica were not only inexpensive but also were reliable and much less prone to breaking down.

The switch in customer demand to small, reliable cars and the ability of the Japanese to serve the small-car niche precipitated a crisis for GM in the 1970s and 1980s. Demand for its large sedans plummeted, and divisions such as Buick and Cadillac began to lay off thousands of employees. GM's operating philosophy had been that large cars mean large profits; this was now revealed as false by Japanese carmakers that had been developing efficient, quality-enhancing "lean production" techniques to reduce manufacturing costs. Japanese companies began to make enormous profits selling their economy cars to United States customers who flocked to the rapidly expanding network of Japanese car dealerships that were spreading across the United States during the 1970s. By the end of the 1970s, the big three were revealed as high-cost, low-quality carmakers; their large, luxurious, boxy cars were now compared unfavorably either to inexpensive (ugly) Japanese

cars or to the sleek European luxury cars made by Mercedes and BMW that also began to make inroads into the United States luxury car market during the 1970s and 1980s. As GM lost market share both in the inexpensive and luxury segments of the car market, its profits plummeted as the sales of its large cars slowed to a trickle. It has never recovered; this explains why GM finally went bankrupt in 2009.

GM "Fights Back"

In 1980, GM still earned $3.3 billion on more than $60 billion in sales. Its huge cash flow and cash reserves still allowed it to act like a dominant competitor—despite the fact that its business model was clearly inferior to the new model Japanese carmakers had developed. A new CEO, Roger Smith, took control of GM in 1980 to rebuild its competitive advantage. Under his control, GM began several major programs to reduce costs and improve quality that by 1990 had cost the company more than $100 billion—enough money, analysts pointed out, to have purchased Toyota and Honda given their market value at that time! Did Smith's new strategies work? No, but they allowed GM's top managers to avoid confronting the harsh competitive realities it was facing. Also, GM's managers did not need to confront its central problems—solving the internal issues that stemmed from its high-cost internal suppliers and its high-cost labor agreements with the United Auto Workers (UAW) union that had led to its high (unprofitable) cost structure.

Focusing only on the differentiation side of the equation, to enhance its competitive position in cars and trucks, GM invested more than $50 billion to improve and update its technology to gain expertise from Japanese lean manufacturing techniques. Beginning in the early 1980s, Roger Smith started to champion the development of automated factories and robots as a way of raising quality and productivity. As in Japanese factories, GM used automated equipment and robots to mold parts, assemble car components, and pick up and distribute parts along the assembly line. These automated factories proved very expensive to operate; however, vehicle axles made in its new factories cost twice as much as ones produced conventionally. GM seemed to lack the Japanese know-how to efficiently operate automated factories.

A major experiment that GM began in 1982 to develop low-cost manufacturing skills and produce quality cars was to create a new division it called Saturn. The Saturn division was charged to imitate Japanese manufacturing techniques and produce small cars at the same low cost as Japanese makers. The division was deliberately kept separate from GM's other divisions so its managers and employees could learn new production skills from scratch. Saturn's new $2 billion car plant was the biggest construction undertaking in GM's history. It went into full production in 1990. Saturn cars were priced to compete with the Honda Civic and Toyota Corolla. By 1991, Saturn had built just 50,000 cars, far short of its 240,000 yearly capacity and lost $800 million in 1991. By 1992, Saturn car sales had picked up; its cars were ranked in the top 10 of customer satisfaction, but it still lost $700 million. Eventually, GM realized Saturn would never be able to match the low costs of Japanese manufacturers—one major reason because Saturn did not have Toyota's or Honda's efficient low-cost supply chain, something essential to the success of "lean" manufacturing. And, it was burdened with high labor costs due to its previous agreements with the UAW.

Another way GM attempted to learn Japanese techniques in lean manufacturing was by creating a joint venture with Toyota in 1983 called New United Motor Manufacturing, Inc. (NUMMI) to produce Chevrolet Novas in GM's Freemont, California, plant. This plant had closed in 1982 because of poor quality and bad labor-management relations. In 1984, NUMMI reopened under the control of Japanese management. By 1986, its productivity was higher than that of any other GM factory, and it was operating at twice the old level under GM management. One of the primary reasons for its success was the use of flexible work teams. At the NUMMI factory, Toyota divided the workforce into 350 flexible work teams consisting of 5–7 people plus a team leader. Each worker was trained to perform the jobs of other workers and regularly rotated jobs. In addition, all workers were taught the procedures for analyzing jobs to improve work procedures. Team members designed all the team's jobs, timing each other using stopwatches and continually attempting to find better ways to perform tasks. Before GM had employed 80 managers to perform this analysis; now not only did flexible work teams do it, but they were also responsible for monitoring product quality. The role of managers in the new factory was to provide shop-floor workers with support, not to monitor or supervise their activities. From this venture, GM finally learned how Toyota's lean production system worked and that work relationships are at least as important as automated factories in increasing productivity and reducing costs. From this point on, GM began to implement the new system across all its hundreds of manufacturing plants. Although this was a slow process, by 2005, GM could claim it was the most efficient United States carmaker, although it still trailed the Japanese, because the Japanese never ceased to work to continuously lower costs and increase quality.

In sum, although by the 2000s, GM reduced operating costs and increased vehicle quality, its Japanese and European competitors were always one step ahead. Moreover, during the 1990s, the United States had become an inexpensive country in which to make cars compared to Japan and Europe. Global carmakers were anxious to avoid the United States government imposing tariffs on their growing imports of cars or limiting the number of cars that could be imported, something that had occurred during the 1970s and 1980s. So, Toyota, Honda, Nissan, BMW, and Mercedes began to open their own plants in the United States. When it became clear that car plants operated by Japanese managers could attain quality levels close to those achieved in Japan, they began to rapidly expand the number of these plants. Toyota and Honda led the quality ranking of American-made cars, and, by 1995, they made more than 1.5 million cars a year in the United States. Their market share was rapidly growing.

A New Management Team Takes Over

Even though GM's market share had declined rapidly from 50% in 1978 to 35% by 1992, it had not reduced the number of its manufacturing plants or downsized its workforce in any significant way—its managers still chose to believe it was experiencing only a temporary setback and that its sales and revenues would soon turn around. Smith had even said that GM would reach a 50% market share again! Everyone except GM's top executives recognized that the company had at least 100,000 excess white-collar employees and an even greater number of production employees who were draining the company's resources and profitability.

In 1990, Roger Smith's hand-picked successor, Robert Stempel, became CEO. Like Smith, Stempel did not want to downsize the corporation and make the huge cuts in its workforce that analysts thought imperative to turn the company around. Luckily for GM in 1991, an activist GM director, John Smale, insisted that to stop GM's losses, a new CEO must be found. In 1992, he convinced the board to appoint Jack Smith, the former head of GM's European operations, as president, and Smale became CEO. Together, they forced through a new policy of downsizing: GM announced it would lay off 80,000 workers and close 10 United States assembly plants, 4 engine factories, and 11 parts plants by 2005. Also, GM's corporate staff was to be reduced from 13,500 to approximately 2,300 managers. Eventually, Jack Smith replaced Smale as CEO.

Smith soon defined GM's future strategies: to become profitable, an aggressive focus on reducing costs and improving quality, an aggressive marketing of redesigned vehicles that better satisfy customers needs, and a new more-flexible decentralized organizational structure had to be implemented. All these strategies seemed appropriate, yet Smith could not find the right way to implement them. Why didn't Jack Smith's business model and strategies improve GM's performance? Indeed, why did its performance continue to decline?

New Production Manufacturing Initiatives

Smith had been in charge of GM's European operations and successfully implemented new lean production techniques to raise quality; he had a clear vision of what GM needed to do to reduce its cost structure. First, he understood the importance of dropping unsuccessful products and reducing the number of models to reduce costs. By 1993, GM had reduced the number of models in production from 85 to 65—but it had introduced more than 20 new cars and trucks. GM had also imitated other carmakers in lowering costs by reducing the number of its vehicle-making platforms from 14 to 8; by 2000, it was focusing on small, medium, and large cars and trucks. But its Japanese competitors only made 8 to 12 different models, using only 4 to 5 different vehicle platforms. This difference lowered Japan's cost structures, giving them a major competitive advantage over GM.

One continuing part of GM's new efficiency program was to build new state-of-the-art assembly plants and close down old inefficient ones. In 2000, GM started to build a $1 billion manufacturing plant in Lansing, Michigan, to advanced flexible manufacturing technologies and help raise quality nearer to its Japanese competitors. The new plant began operations in 2005 and did achieve significant quality improvements, but still its high cost structure, due to labor and component costs, meant it could never become profitable.

In another attempt to reduce value-chain costs, GM finally closed down its Oldsmobile division in 2004. Doing so allowed it to reduce the number of its car models. In developing its unsuccessful line of new models in the 1980s, GM learned the need to standardize components across models and reduce the number of parts needed to produce a car to reduce value-chain costs and speed product development. Smith directed GM's engineers to work to reduce the number of parts used to make a car's basic metal frame by one-third.

GM also changed the way it managed relationships with suppliers, to find more cost-effective ways to manage its supply chain. In 1992, GM obtained 57% of its parts from its own component divisions, compared to Chrysler's 30% and Toyota's 5%. GM's car assembly divisions were locked into their own "allied plant" suppliers such as Central Foundry for casting, Delco for brakes, and so on. In 1993, GM introduced a new strategy that its in-house high-cost components divisions would no longer be protected from efficient outside suppliers.

To help suppliers reduce costs, GM imitated Toyota and implemented a Purchased Input Concept Optimization with Suppliers (PICOS) strategy, in which teams of GM engineers visit supplier plants and work with suppliers to reduce costs. However, with the program up and running, GM, unlike Toyota, began to bargain hard with its suppliers to get lower component prices. It started to give one supplier's plans to other suppliers to get lower prices from them, essentially trading off one against the other, and made suppliers rebid contracts year by year to try to get them to lower their bids. This angered outside suppliers, who told GM that if it bought mainly on price, they would not invest money to improve the components that GM wanted them to make and would move their business to Ford, Chrysler, and Japanese companies operating in the United States. As a result, GM had to rethink its aggressive strategy.

GM also extended its supply chain management program globally and began to develop hundreds of alliances with overseas parts manufacturers to produce components that could be used in its cars assembled around the world. For example, GM formed a joint venture with a Hungarian company to build axles and diesel engines for assembly in cars sold under the Opel name throughout Western Europe. The next major development in the supply chain management process took place in 2000 when GM, Ford, and Chrysler announced they would form an organization called Covisint to coordinate their purchase of standardized car components through the Internet. Billed as the world's largest virtual marketplace, Covisint gives large carmakers considerable power over global suppliers, who are essentially forced to compete to obtain the Big Three's business. However, at the same time, there is the opportunity to create economies of scale in producing many kinds of components. During this same period, Japanese carmakers established many factories inside the United States and also created networks of efficient, high-quality component suppliers, allowing them to maintain their lead in productivity and quality. Toyota, for example, was the first to launch a joint program with its suppliers to radically reduce the number of steps needed to make components and car parts; it saw costs fall by $2.6 billion.

Structural Changes

Side-by-side with changes to its production and supply chain operations, GM also radically altered its corporate structure. Starting in 1990, GM realized the need to streamline its operations, decentralize decision making, and integrate its design and manufacturing operations. In 1992, it consolidated its nine engine groups into five and combined all its car divisions' engineering and manufacturing units to eliminate redundancy. Also, five design and technical departments at GM's Technical Center were combined into three to speed product development. GM created a new product design system to provide strong, single point management of a vehicle program and accelerate the vehicle development process. GM's goal was to achieve economies of scale through integrating and coordinating its functional activities in product development, engineering, manufacturing, and marketing around the world. In this way, it could avoid unnecessary duplication of activities between divisions and facilitate the sharing and learning about cost-saving processes and quality innovations across divisions and countries.

Given its inability to lower its cost structure significantly, promoting innovation became a key element of GM's strategy. Its strategy was to improve vehicle design and engineering to develop new vehicle models that targeted customer needs in profitable market segments such as SUVs and trucks and provide high-margin, add-on vehicle accessories, such as its OnStar service, to increase the profit made on each car sale. Global cooperation became vital to achieve these goals in the 1990s because GM's engineers needed to share resources and best practices to develop a wide range of vehicles for different customer needs from GM's remaining six vehicle platforms.

To promote such cooperation, GM changed its global organizational structure and adopted the global matrix structure shown in Exhibit 1. The vertical axis consists of GM's five main business units, the four world regions in which GM operates: North America; Europe; Asia-Pacific; and Latin America, Africa, and the Middle East. The fifth business unit is GM's financial services division that is responsible for financing the sale of GM's cars throughout the world. On the horizontal axis are the main value chain activities required to efficiently orchestrate the global production of its cars: supply chain management, product development, production, marketing, and business services. Where the axes intersect are found the hundreds of assembly plants and engineering facilities that belong to a specific GM car division, such as Cadillac, Buick, and so on. While each car division operates as an independent entity, it is also embedded in the global value-chain organization GM needed to compete against its highly efficient global rivals.

GM also invested heavily in IT to help implement its new global structure to provide the integration necessary to manage the enormously complex transactions required to operate global assembly and value chain activities using a matrix structure. Using software and consultancy services from IBM, GM harmonized all its IT systems across the company in an attempt to speed information transfer between its divisions all around the world. GM's new IT system

Exhibit 1 GM's Global Matrix Structure

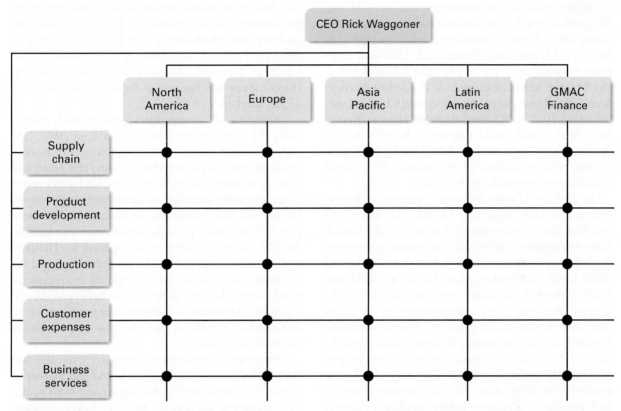

● GM assembly, design, and operating units located in countries around the world.

helped to better implement GM's business model; it permitted faster global coordination in design and engineering development and reduced the duplication of work by engineers in different research areas. It also increased the efficiency of GM's supply chain operations, for example, in 2004, it cut its component costs by 3% in North America and by 3.5% in Europe.

The problem for GM was that its Japanese competitors continued to obtain more than double the cost savings it achieved each year, so that despite GM's improving performance, it was still falling behind. To lower its cost structure quickly, GM decided to spin off several of its component parts divisions and vertically disintegrate. For example, in 1999, GM spun off its huge Delphi electronics components division into a separate company, in the hope that Delco could lower its cost structure and supply GM, which remained its biggest customer, with lower cost components.

Global Expansion under New Leadership

In the 1990s, GM watched Japanese carmakers rapidly expand their manufacturing operations in Europe and Asia, and GM's managers decided that to compete effectively on a global level, they needed to bolster its global presence. To further its efforts to learn lean manufacturing techniques, in 1996, GM formed joint ventures with Japanese companies Isuzu Motors and Suzuki to establish facilities and make specialized engines and transmissions for GM cars in specific market segments, such as the European diesel engine market. GM took a minority equity stake in these ventures. Also, in its European Opel and Vauxhall divisions, GM invested heavily to update its factories and improve its skills in lean production to compete against the Japanese. In 2000, GM also acquired a 20% equity stake in Fuji, the manufacturer of Subaru brand vehicles. Finally, it established a strategic alliance with Honda.

While Japan was an important market, GM also decide to strengthen its presence in the rapidly developing Chinese and Eastern European markets. In 2002, GM formed an alliance with a Russian company to produce a line of low-cost Chevrolets tailored to the needs of customers in Eastern Europe. After several years of cooperation with Chinese companies, in 2001, GM's new assembly plant in Shanghai, China, began production of the Regal economy car for the Chinese market. All global makers were rushing to seize a share of this market they hoped would prove profitable in the future.

In 2000, GM went through a change in leadership when Rick Waggoner became the new CEO and Jack Smith stayed on as chairman of the board. Both of these executives had extensive experience in global operations, which led them to champion GM's rapid global expansion. In Europe, GM and Ford competed viciously against each other to acquire premium European carmakers in the belief that they needed to offer United States customers a broad line of premium, differentiated cars. To achieve this, both companies were willing to pay enormously inflated prices. Ford won the battle against GM to acquire the UK carmaker Jaguar and Sweden's Volvo, two highly inefficient companies with high cost structures. To fight back, GM acquired Saab in 2000 and also bought a 20% stake in Fiat with an option to buy the whole company later.

The problem, of course, was that they were buying premium car brand names—but they were not buying state-of-the-art technology to build quality, low-cost vehicles. Japanese companies never made a move to acquire highly inefficient European carmakers, and why would they? They soon developed their own premium brands such as Toyota's Lexus and Nissan's Infinity. The mistake in United States carmakers' strategies became increasingly obvious over time. In 2005, GM had to pay $2 billion to terminate its ill-fated Fiat alliance. Its Saab operation also proved to be a disaster, losing GM hundreds of millions of dollars. In the meantime, GM's established European Brands such as Opel, its German subsidiary, and Vauxhall, its British unit, were struggling to compete against Japanese companies that had established efficient operations inside the European Union. French carmaker Renault adopted

a different strategy. In 2000, it bought a controlling interest in Nissan at a time when, because of poor car design and management, Nissan was struggling to compete against Toyota and Honda in Japan and globally. After installing a star Renault manager to head its Japanese subsidiary, Carlos Goshen (now CEO of Renault), Nissan's performance soared; the company has become a major competitor in all global markets.

Watching its competitors enter China, potentially the largest market in the world, in 2000, GM also decided to acquire the car operations of Korean conglomerate Daewoo to help it enter the Asian and Chinese markets. In South America, GM also opened a car assembly complex in Brazil utilizing state-of-the-art modular assembly techniques to produce cars for the rapidly growing South American market. Similar assembly plants were opened in Thailand and Germany as part of GM's program to extend the learning it was gaining from its global matrix operations. Meanwhile, the joint venture between GM and Shanghai Automotive Industry Corporation led to its launch of the Buick Sail, the first modern family car built in China.

As global competition increased over the last decade, finding the right way to brand and market its cars in the United States (the biggest and most profitable market in the world) has been GM's principal problem. For example, although it achieved some success with its Cadillac brand, its Oldsmobile division had lost its customer base and closed down. Also its Pontiac and Saturn divisions were losing customer support because their models were aging. GM's Chevrolet division eventually became the keystone of its plan to increase its SUV and truck sales around the world. GM invested hundreds of millions to develop and market the trucks and SUVs Chevrolet is known for around the world. To promote its SUV sales, GM acquired the Hummer brand from AM General Corp. in 2000. GM's small and mid-sized car business was still suffering, however. In 2002, GM announced it would end production of its Chevrolet Camaro and Pontiac Firebird because it had lost this market niche for sporty cars to Ford, Nissan, and Toyota. Then, in 2003, GM announced that it would revamp its entire range of midsize American car models and focus on a few strong brands. GM's strategy was to introduce 10 new or restyled mid-size vehicles between 2003 and 2006 to strengthen its product line and regain market share—despite its high cost structure.

The Legacy of the Past: A High Cost Structure

GM has spent hundreds of billions of dollars since 1980 to update and revamp its factories and improve its car-assembly skills, redesign its vehicles to appeal to modern customer needs, and improve customer service. In some areas, it had some success, such as increasing sales of its SUVs, trucks, and luxury vehicles. But GM profitability did not increase in the 2000s, and its problems increased. Why? The main reason is that none of its CEOs has been able or willing to confront and solve the huge problems that have resulted from the legacies of its prosperous past: from its union contracts, huge car dealer network, and high-cost internal suppliers.

GM's CEOs only dealt with its problems in a "piecemeal" fashion. Little by little they worked to spin off internal high-cost component suppliers and reduce value-chain costs as discussed previously, but they never caught up with their competitors. One reason it took GM so long to take major corrective actions is because of its complex long-term agreements with the UAW. Until the 1980s, GM's high profitability and dominance of the United States vehicle market meant that it was hard to resist the UAW's demands for higher pay and benefits, especially pensions and healthcare benefits. Shareholders, managers, and workers were all enjoying GM's prosperity. When Japanese carmakers ended this fortunate situation, GM, like Ford and Chrysler, found itself saddled with strict union rules that prevented it from retraining and moving its workers from job to job or from laying off employees or closing down facilities except at a high cost. If employees were laid off, GM had agreed to pay 60% of their salaries. Also, rising healthcare costs, which had not been considered an important factor, became hugely significant in the 1990s, as did GM's pension liabilities to former and current employees. In 2002, it was estimated that GM had more than $45 billion in *unfunded* liabilities. And, GM still paid its workforce much more than its competitors in benefits; for example, GM paid an average of $35 for each employee's pension and medical costs compared to the $11 Toyota pays for the same benefits.

It has been estimated that the costs of paying these high pensions and benefits gives Toyota and Honda a cost advantage of about $1,500 a car—which is a major reason for their higher profitability. Moreover, GM cannot charge a $1,500 premium for its cars—it has to charge less than its stronger competitors because its quality is lower—which is why its profit margins have been low or nonexistent and why it sells many of its vehicles at a loss. In 2004, although Toyota's revenues were 33% lower than GM's, its net earnings were 60% higher; Toyota's ROIC was almost 6% in 2004, while GM's was 1% and Ford's 0.6%.

Of course, GM's managers and white-collar employees also enjoyed better-than-average pay and benefits; even though GM had made major reductions to its corporate, divisional, and functional staff, it still employed tens of thousands of managers it could not afford given its weak competitive condition. So, at the input (component) and throughput (design and production) stages of the value chain, GM's cost structure was strangling its profitability; at the distribution stage, its contracts with its 5,600 dealerships also were draining its profitability. Each of GM's brands was distributed by different car dealerships, and all these dealerships had contracts that guaranteed them a supply of cars and favorable financing from GM's financial division, GMAC. When GM's vehicles were market leaders, its many thousands of dealerships were a competitive advantage. But once it was forced to reduce the number of models of cars it produced and shut down divisions such as Oldsmobile, these dealerships became a major liability—and it was locked into contracts with them. The greater the number of dealerships, the higher GM's distribution, financing, and operating costs. When GM's sales plunged in the 2000s, its excessive number of dealerships cost GM billions of dollars a year.

Indeed, in the 2000s, the main reason that GM remained profitable at all was because of the profits made by its financing division, GMAC. This division earned the company the billions of dollars it needed to offset the losses made by its vehicle production operations. The bottom line was that GM made most of its profit by *financing* the sale of its vehicles to customers, rather than *actually making the vehicle itself*.

Growing Problems in 2008

By 2008, GM was in a desperate situation: as prices had risen to more than $4 a gallon, and GM was struggling with a vehicle line-up composed of gas-guzzling SUVs and trucks that no longer matched customer demand for smaller, more fuel-efficient cars. Bravely, GM decided to devote a substantial amount of its dwindling capital to develop an all-electric vehicle, the Chevrolet Volt. Powered by lithium ion batteries, the car can propel for about 40 miles on a single charge before a gasoline engine kicks in to power the vehicle and recharge the battery. Only 4-cylinder engines are needed for this purpose. But will Americans really give up their love affairs with V6 and V8 engines coupled with the large SUVs and pickups trucks, especially if gas prices remain under $3 as they were by 2009? Prior to the financial meltdown in 2008, the United States congress had approved a $25 billion loan to American carmakers, to rebuild decades-old car plants and help fund the development of advanced batteries and gas-electric hybrids. In January 2009, GM established the first lithium-ion battery-pack factory in the United States to produce batteries for its Volt, with output starting in 2010. This money funded GM's new battery plant, but producing lithium-ion batteries on the scale needed to power cars is still not a well-developed technology; it was not clear in 2009 if this would be cost-effective.

Despite GM's claims that it intended to reduce the range of its different models to lower its cost structure, its managers still continued its old strategy of diluting brands and brand cannibalism. For example, in 2008, Chevrolet introduced the Traverse, a crossover vehicle that was based on a "lambda platform." But Buick and GMC had already released crossover vehicles under their brand names based on exactly the same platform—and Saturn's crossover looked exactly the same. Why would GM produce four different versions of the same car if its goal is to reduce its cost structure? Finally, GM decided its Pontiac brand should be downsized and decided to eliminate all but two of its models by 2010, but why the wait? Clearly, the overhead fixed costs of maintaining the Pontiac brand are enormous, and one reason was its contracts with Pontiac car dealerships and the UAW. Once again, a major change in strategy to eliminate a major drain on its profitability could not be pursued; exit costs were just too high. (In fact, after the government bailout, it announced it would end the Pontiac brand in 2009.)

Similarly, its large, gas-guzzling Hummer brand has become a major liability since 2008. The Hummer brand used to have status as a "macho" exclusive SUV, but, by 2008, it too was seen as a gas-guzzling dinosaur out of synch with customer tastes for new,

greener vehicles. GM put its Hummer brand up for sale in late 2008. GM also shut down three plants in the fall of 2008 that produced its Cadillacs, Hummers, and GMC cars and trucks, because their sales plummeted.

In an unusual move to strengthen its business model, in October 2008, GM and Chrysler managers met to consider a merger to unite their vehicles lines, a move that would once again raise GM's United States market share to more than 33%. But, would this merger also increase profitability? Chrysler's vehicle brands were in worse shape than GM's; they were aging and unreliable, with no competitive advantage that would stop overseas carmakers from continuing to take away United States carmakers' market share. Talks ended after growing public criticism of a merger that was seen as designed mainly to help GM's managers avoid bankruptcy.

In 2009, Fiat emerged as a prospective buyer for Chrysler; after Chrysler declared Chapter 11 bankruptcy, Fiat bought its assets to enter the United States market with at least five new European-designed vehicles that will be built in Chrysler's United States plants. Ford was luckier than GM or Chrysler, because, foreseeing the global recession and plunging car sales, it borrowed several billion dollars at low interest rates before the credit markets collapsed. Ford claimed that it did not need government bailout money and has new fuel-efficient car models lined up to come out when the recession ends that will bring it back to profitability quickly.

In fact, after the recession and meltdown of vehicles sales that started in 2008, GM's top managers had to confront the fact that their strategy of offering global customers a broad line of premium to low-cost branded vehicles had been a total disaster. Not only had this prevented them from bringing their supply chain management costs under control, it had diluted the company's resources by forcing it to make too many investments in too many companies in too many countries around the world. So, GM decided to spin off, sell, or divest many of its global assets. In November 2008, GM sold its entire holding of 16,000,000 shares in Suzuki Motors back to Suzuki and used the proceeds to bolster its cash flow. Then, in February 2009, after it failed to find a buyer for Saab, GM announced that it was essentially abandoning or "cutting loose" this division after the Swedish government refused to give GM any loans to help keep the division out of bankruptcy. Saab entered bankruptcy proceedings in Sweden and laid off 750 of its 4,100 employees, while it tried to reorganize to find a buyer that could provide the capital needed to rejuvenate its brand image. Similarly, in March 2009, GM announced that it wanted to sell its German Opel and UK Vauxhall divisions and was looking for buyers. Given the credit crunch, a potential buyer would need loans from the German and UK governments, which had resisted helping to pay for what they regarded as GM's mistakes. However, the jobs of 50,000 European workers were at stake, and, in May 2009, the Italian company, Fiat, emerged as a potential buyer. Both governments were negotiating over loan guarantees with the eventual buyer to protect the future of Opel and Vauxhall workers. At the end of May, however, Canadian component parts maker, Magna, beat Fiat to acquire GM's Opel and Vauxhall divisions to provide a market for its components and use GM's Opel technology as a platform to enter the Russian car market. Half, or 25,000, of GM's European workforce were expected to lose their jobs, however, and plant closings were also expected. GM sold its global car assets off at rock-bottom prices and, in the process, lost tens of billions of shareholder wealth.

THE INCREDIBLE SHRINKING COMPANY

While it was selling off or closing down its United States and European divisions, GM still had to deal with the problems of lowering its cost structure by reducing its United States workforce. Every GM CEO resisted making the massive cuts necessary to create a profitable business model, in part because each believed that GM could regain market share from the Japanese, and because contracts with the UAW made laying off workers an expensive undertaking. By the end of 2008, however, even though GM's total workforce was less than half what it was in 1988, there was no choice. After a 40% fall in sales in December 2008, GM announced it would temporarily idle 30% of its assembly plants during the first quarter of 2009 and reduce vehicle production by 250,000 units. In February 2009, GM announced it would cut its global salaried workforce by 10,000 to 63,000 and cut the pay of the remaining salaried workforce. Higher-level employees would have their base pay cut by 10%, lower-level employees by 3%–7%. GM also aimed to cut an additional 37,000 hourly jobs worldwide by the end of 2009 by offering workers generous severance packages.

One executive employee terminated by the United States government was CEO Rick Waggoner. He was replaced as CEO by Fritz Henderson, a highly respected GM executive, and an activist board member, Kent Kresa, a former CEO of Northrop Grumman, became chairman. Under increasing pressure from the United States government to reduce its cost structure to avoid a bankruptcy that was becoming more likely every day, in March 2009, GM's new CEO announced further business and job reductions. After cutting production in the spring by 250,000 units, GM announced that it was scheduling multiple down weeks at 13 assembly plants to remove another 200,000 vehicles from its 2009 production schedule, and more would come in the fall of 2009 unless the economy turned around. As a result, GM is scheduled to produce 1 million fewer cars in 2009 than in 2008. In April 2009, GM said it would close at least 6 additional production plants and phase out its Pontiac brand, and that the number of its North American production facilities would fall to 27 by 2012 from the 47 operating in 2008. This was truly the end of the old GM; this would effectively eliminate its ability to make the excess one million vehicles that it was no longer able to sell. Also in May 2009, GM announced that a number of potential buyers had expressed interest in buying the Saturn brand and dealer network, and there was a prospective buyer for the Hummer brand.

GM's top managers had been forced to pursue these drastic strategies because of the need to secure government financing to avoid bankruptcy. By April 2009, GM had received more than $19 billion to keep it going. Still trying to avoid bankruptcy, in May 2009, GM and the UAW began negotiating a major new labor agreement to reduce labor costs and pensions by billions of dollars a year—something also demanded by the United States government in return for billions in future loans. Only at the last minute, on May 29, 2009, did GM and the UAW reach an agreement on a major cost-saving deal. Three-quarters of UAW members voted to accept a freeze on pay and an end to bonuses that will cut labor costs by $2 billion a year. The UAW also agreed to cut health benefits to retired employees, and instead of the company funding healthcare costs for former workers, a UAW health trust will receive 17.5% of shares in the "new GM" to fund this. The UAW also agreed not to strike until 2015. Beyond its new agreement with the UAW, GM also announced plans to eliminate more than 2,600 of its 6,000 United States dealerships and close 250 Canadian dealerships to reduce its cost structure.

GM's Bankruptcy in June 2009

Over time, GM's CEOs have responded to the pressures of global competition, have adopted strategies to reduce its cost structure, and championed the introduction of innovative vehicle models. So why was GM forced to enter bankruptcy on June 1, 2009? Primarily because GM's legacy problems with its high cost structure coincided with a plunge in vehicle sales due to the recession that started in 2008. The credit crunch that resulted from this recession prevented its GMAC financing division from making the loans to customers that generated the profits it needed to fund its ongoing operations; indeed, its GMAC division incurred a loss, which was why the company had to ask the United States government for billions of dollars in loans to allow it to keep operating in 2009. Beginning in the third quarter of 2008, GM reported lower global vehicle sales of 11.4% to 2.1 million vehicles, while sales in the United States fell 19% because of credit tightening, along with high gas prices. This plunge in vehicle sales became steadily worse, and by the spring of 2009, United States vehicle sales had dropped by over 40%. GM's cash flow also plunged, but it still needed billions of dollars a month to pay its suppliers, workforce, and fixed costs. By April 2009, GM had received more than $19 billion in loans that allowed it to avoid declaring Chapter 11 bankruptcy, but this still was not enough. By this time a team of United States government financial experts had more or less taken control of GM's financial decision making and future strategy because they had control over loans. As a sign of their power over GM, they ousted CEO Rick Waggoner in May 2009 after deciding that a fresh leadership approach was needed to help turn around the company—even if GM was forced to enter bankruptcy to accomplish this.

By the end of May 2009, it was clear that GM would soon declare bankruptcy. In return for the $19 billion in loans it had already received, plus additional United States government aid of $30 billion and Canadian government aid of $9 billion, the United States will own 60% of the shares in the new GM, and the Canadian government will own 12.5% once restructuring is complete. The UAW health trust will own 17.5%, and GM's bondholders finally agreed to swap their ownership of $27 billion of GM's debt for the remaining 10% of shares, although they have warrants to buy an additional 15% stake under certain conditions. The government plan envisions the slimmed-down new GM with $17 billion in long-term debt and $9 billion in debt-like preferred shares. Only $8 billion of United States government loans would remain on GM's books; the rest of the $50 billion in loans has been converted into stock in the new GM.

To push through the restructuring, GM was allowed to enter Chapter 11 bankruptcy on June 1, 2009, in order to legally erase most of its debt, ratify its new agreements with the UAW, and allow it to sever its contracts with its dealerships. Hopefully, a leaner, stronger, and better-managed company will emerge that can develop a competitive advantage, retain its market share, and make cars profitably. If GM returns to profitability and its stock rises, it would allow the government to sell its GM stock and regain some percentage of the money loaned to GM. GM's vice chairman and car design champion, Bob Lutz commented that, "We will come out of this rid of some of the historic legacy costs that have been dragging us down for the last 20 years or so; we will come out of it with an all new focus on product development."

For the most up-to-date financial results and analysis of the company in this case go to http://finance.yahoo.com, *click on symbol lookup at top of page, input the company's symbol into the search box, and then follow the appropriate links on the yahoo page for the information you require (e.g., click profile to find link to company's website for its annual financial reports, or click on Yahoo! links to the company's SEC filings or Financials).*

TATA MOTORS' ACQUISITION OF LAND ROVER

"Acquisition of JLR provides the company with a strategic opportunity to acquire iconic brands with a great heritage and global presence, and increase the company's business diversity across markets and product segments."[1]

—Tata Motors, in April 2008

"If they run the brands as a British company and invest properly in new product, it will be successful because they are still attractive brands."[2]

—Charles Hughes,[3] Founder, Brand Rules LLC,[4] in 2008

"Market conditions are now extremely tough, especially in the key US market, and the Tatas will need to invest in a lot of brand building to make and keep JLR profitable."[5]

—Ian Gomes, Global Head, Emerging Markets, KPMG, in 2008

ACQUISITION OF BRITISH ICONS

On June 02, 2008, India-based Tata Motors[6] completed the acquisition of the Jaguar and Land Rover (JLR) units from the US-based auto manufacturer Ford Motor Company (Ford) for US$ 2.3 billion,[7] on a cash free-debt free[8] basis. JLR was a part of Ford's Premier Automotive Group[9] (PAG) and were considered to be British icons. Jaguar was involved in the manufacture of high-end luxury cars, while Land Rover manufactured high-end SUVs. Forming a part of the purchase consideration were JLR's manufacturing plants, two advanced design centers in the UK,[10] national sales companies spanning across the world, and also licenses of all necessary intellectual property rights.

Tata Motors had several major international acquisitions to its credit. It had acquired Tetley, South Korea-based Daewoo's commercial vehicle unit, and Anglo-Dutch Steel maker Corus (Refer to Exhibit 1 for the details of the group's international acquisitions). Tata Motors' long-term strategy included consolidating its position in the domestic Indian market and expanding its international footprint by leveraging on in-house capabilities and products and also through acquisitions and strategic collaborations.

This case was written by **Indu P.**, under the direction of **Vivek Gupta**, ICFAI Center for Management Research (ICMR). It was compiled from published sources, and is intended to be used as a basis for class discussion rather than to illustrate either effective or ineffective handling of a management situation.

Exhibit 1 International Acquisitions by Tata Group

Year	Company	Country	Acquired for (US$)	Acquired by
2000	Tetley	UK	432 million	Tata Tea
2004	Daewoo Motors (Commercial Vehicles)	South Korea	102 million	Tata Motors
2005	Nat Steel Ltd.	Singapore	286 million	Tata Steel
	Eight O'Clock Coffee	USA	220 million	Tata Coffee
2006	Teleglobe Intl. Holdings Ltd.	USA	239 million	VSNL
	Tyco Intl.*	USA	130 million	VSNL
	Energy Brands Inc. (30%)**	USA	677 million	Tata Tea
2007	Corus	Anglo-Dutch	12 billion	Tata Steel
2008	PT Bumi Resources (30% in coal mines)	Indonesia	1.3 billion	Tata Power
	General Chemical Industrial Products Inc.	USA	1.01 billion	Tata Chemicals

*Global undersea fiber optic cable network unit

**Sold the stake for US$ 1.2 billion in January 2007 to Coca-Cola.

Compiled from various sources.

Analysts were of the view that the acquisition of JLR, which had a global presence and a repertoire of well established brands, would help Tata Motors become one of the major players in the global automobile industry. On acquiring JLR, Ratan Tata, Chairman, Tata Group, said, "We are very pleased at the prospect of Jaguar and Land Rover being a significant part of our automotive business. We have enormous respect for the two brands and will endeavor to preserve and build on their heritage and competitiveness, keeping their identities intact. We aim to support their growth, while holding true to our principles of allowing the management and employees to bring their experience and expertise to bear on the growth of the business."[11]

Ford had bought Jaguar for US$ 2.5 billion in 1989 and Land Rover for US$ 2.7 billion in 2000. However, over the years, the company found that it was failing to derive the desired benefits from these acquisitions. In 2006, Ford announced a major restructuring program 'The Way Forward,'[12] which involved plans to shut down unprofitable operations.

As a part of the program, Ford decided to dismantle PAG and in June 2007, announced that it was considering selling JLR. There were several bidders for JLR but Ford was more concerned about handing over the management of JLR to a company that would take into consideration the interests of the workers. The labor unions of JLR were not in favor of moving the existing manufacturing facilities and factories out of Britain as it would lead to elimination of jobs. These factors, among others, made Tata Motors the preferred bidder. Ford and Tata Motors announced a definitive agreement in March 2008, under which Tata Motors was to purchase JLR for US$ 2.3 billion.

News of the proposed acquisition by Tata Motors was greeted with much hope and enthusiasm. One of the suppliers to JLR, Grant Adams, Managing Director of Sertec Group Holdings, a UK body panel and stampings supplier for JLR, said, "We are very positive, especially when you look at the other companies that Tata Group has bought such as Corus and Tetley. Both have gone from strength to strength."[13] However, Moody's downgraded Tata Motors' credit ratings from Ba1 to Ba2, citing concerns about operations integration and the impact of the acquisition on the company's finances. According to Moody's, "This acquisition also comes at a time when there is intense competition and rising cost pressure in Tata Motors' domestic market. Furthermore, there are inherent challenges with any major M&A transactions. This deal therefore raises the immediate business risk profile of Tata Motors."[14]

BRITISH MARQUES UNDER FORD

Ford Motors Company (Ford) is a leading automaker and the third largest multinational corporation in the automobile industry. The company acquired Jaguar from British Leyland Limited[15] in 1989 for US$ 2.5 billion.

After Ford acquired Jaguar, adverse economic conditions worldwide in the 1990s led to tough market conditions and a decrease in the demand for luxury cars. The sales of Jaguar in many markets declined, but in some markets like Japan, Germany, and Italy, it still recorded high sales. In March 1999, Ford established the PAG with Aston Martin, Jaguar, and Lincoln. During the year, Volvo was acquired for US$ 6.45 billion, and it also became a part of the PAG.

Ford bought Land Rover[16] in 2000 for US$ 2.7 billion from BMW, and it became a part of the PAG. Since 2002, the activities of both Jaguar and Land Rover were fully integrated. They had a single engineering team, shared technologies and powertrains, and functioned through co-managed engineering facilities. Most of the back office functions like Purchasing, HR, IT, quality and finance were also integrated. Under Ford, the Range Rover MK III was launched in 2002, and the Discovery 3 in 2004. The Freelander 2 was introduced in 2006.

When it acquired Jaguar, Ford had plans to produce around 400,000 units a year to compete with the likes of Mercedes Benz, Audi, and BMW. However, its objective did not materialize as its plans to revive Jaguar's E-type sports car and F-type car failed. Some of the Jaguar models released in 2001 which targeted young customers failed to impress. In 2002, the sales of Jaguar reached 130,000. Analysts were of the view that under Ford, the engineering standards of Jaguar had improved but its image had taken a downturn. According to Paul Horrell, who writes for BBC's *Top Gear* magazine, "The trouble with Ford was, around the Millennium, it became very fashionable to build retro looking cars. A policy of building modern cars that looked like old cars developed. The Jaguar gradually became known as basically an old man's car."[17]

The customers of Jaguar and Land Rover were seen as being highly nationalistic and brand loyal. Jaguar customers were considered to be traditionalists. Analysts cited the case of the X-Type launched by Ford, which consumers did not accept as they did not like the design. They felt that it was more like a Ford Mondeo than a Jaguar. In order to control costs, Ford built Jaguar on the Mondeo platform, but this only served to dilute Jaguar's premium image. Jaguar recorded losses of US$ 426 million in 2004. By 2006, it was believed that Ford had spent over US$ 10 billion on Jaguar since acquiring it. However, it had little to show in terms of profit. In the fiscal 2006, Jaguar reported a loss of US$ 327 million.

Ford reported losses of US$ 12.7 billion in the year 2006, the worst loss in the history of the company. It lost around US$ 6 billion in the American operations, and a further investment of US$ 12 billion was required to make these operations profitable by the year 2009.

By the time the results for the year 2006 were out, analysts believed that in order to salvage the North American business, Ford needed to sell JLR. Strategic reviews conducted by Ford on the two brands ended with recommendations of sale. However, some analysts voiced the view that both brands were on the path to revival. Jaguar had several new models lined up and had introduced the XK in 2006. Land Rover was on its way to profits and recorded sales of 192,000 units in 2006.

JLR had three manufacturing sites spanning an area of around 800 acres. These were located at Hale Wood, Solihull, and Castle Bromwich. Two advanced design centers were located at Gaydon and Whitley. The design centers employed around 5,000 of the total 16,000 workforce in JLR. The facilities available at the advanced design centers included testing facilities, workshops, prototype building facilities, design studio, vehicle development, power train engineering, power train development, and power train integration. (Refer to Exhibit 2 for Assets and Liabilities of JLR).

Exhibit 2   Assets and Liabilities—Jaguar Land Rover (Held-for-Sale Operations)

	December 31, 2007 (US$ millions)	December 31, 2006 (US$ millions)
ASSETS		
Receivables	758	590
Inventories	1,530	1,404
Net Property	2,246	2,119
Goodwill and other net intangibles	2,010	3,210
Pension assets	696	3
Other assets	297	122
Total Assets of the held-for-sale Operations	**7,537**	**7,448**
LIABILITIES		
Payables	2,395	2,202
Pension liabilities	19	380
Warranty liabilities	645	759
Other liabilities	2,022	2,050
Total Liabilities of the held-for-sale Operations	**5,081**	**5,391**

Source: Annual Report, Ford, 2007.

By the end of 2007, Jaguar had 859 dealers and a presence in 93 markets across the world. The vehicle sales were at 60,485 units, with Europe accounting for 57% of the sales and North America for 26%. Land Rover had a presence in 175 markets through 1397 dealers. Europe accounted for 60% of the sales and North America for 23%. (Refer to Exhibit 3 for JLR's worldwide sales and to Exhibit 4 for the financial performance of Jaguar and Land Rover).

FORD SELLS JLR

In September 2006, after Allan Mulally (Mulally) assumed charge as the President and CEO of Ford, he decided to dismantle the PAG. In March 2007, Ford sold the Aston Martin sports car unit for

Exhibit 3   Jaguar and Land Rover—Worldwide Sales

No (in units)	2007	2006	2005
Jaguar	57,578	72,680	86,651
Western Europe	33,024	41,367	46,789
America	16,836	22,136	32,131
Rest of the World	7,718	9,177	7,731
Land Rover	202,609	174,940	170,156
Western Europe	109,785	95,399	97,303
America	57,092	53,638	51,634
Rest of the World	35,732	25,903	21,219

Source: Annual Report, Ford, 2007.

Exhibit 4   Jaguar Land Rover—Financial Performance *(in US$ millions)*

	2005	2006	2007	Q1 2007	Q1 2008
Revenue	12,462	12,969	14,942	3,548	4,145
Cost of Sales	(10,955)	(11,292)	(12,258)	(2,747)	(3,161)
Gross Profit	1,507	1,677	2,684	801	984
Marketing & Selling	(1,112)	(1,057)	(1,069)	(265)	(275)
R&D	(821)	(683)	(829)	(183)	(226)
Admin	(408)	(360)	(352)	(88)	(82)
Other	336	66	215	24	16
EBIT (excl. special items*)	(498)	(357)	649	289	417
Special Items	(1,434)	(1,751)	(30)	(15)	(417)
EBIT (Incl. special items)	1,933	2,108	620	274	0

Special Items:

- Impairments of the asset base (2005: $(1,300)m, 2006: $(1,600)m, 2008 Q1: $(421)m)
- Restructuring costs, primarily personnel separation costs (2005: $(134)m, 2006: $(151)m, 2007: $(52)m, 2007 Q1 $(15)m)
- Variable marketing accrual methodology (2007: $(53)m)
- Mark to market of forward year hedging contracts (2007: $143m, 2008 Q1: $(18)m)
- Other incl. transaction fees relating to the sale of JLR and D&A "held for sale" treatment (2007: $(68), 2008 Q1: $22m)

Source: Presentation by Tata Motors.

US$ 931 million. In June 2007, Ford announced that it was considering selling JLR. Commenting on the sale of JLR, Lord Bhattacharya, Head, Warwick Manufacturing Group, said, "How often do two such icons come up for sale at the same time? Land Rover is now sustainably profitable and you are about to see a renaissance of Jaguar. But what you really have to look at is the timing."[18]

The bids for JLR came to close in the third week of July 2007. Several private equity firms and automobile manufacturers from across the world expressed an interest in acquiring JLR. These included Cerberus Capital Management LLC,[19] Ripplewood Holdings,[20] One Equity Partners LLC,[21] TPG Capital,[22] Tata Motors, and Mahindra & Mahindra (M&M).[23]

In November 2007, Ford announced the three preferred bidders: Tata Motors, M&M, and One

Equity Partners. Analysts were of the view that Ford was concerned more about the interests of the workers employed with JLR than the price, as it was of the view that any misstep in this direction could adversely affect its image in the UK, which was its second largest market.

JLR's labor unions were looking at a company that would guarantee job security and were against selling it to private equity firms. According to one of the union members, "That's because of the way it operates, loading debt on to companies that they take over, which has the effect of squeezing pay and pensions—and in many cases putting pressure on jobs as well."[24]

In November 2007, Tata Motors secured the support of Unite, the union that represented Ford.[25] All the three shortlisted bidders gave a presentation to representatives of the union. During the presentation, the Managing Director of Tata Motors, Ravi Kant, assured the union representatives that the company did not intend to close any of the plants and would continue to manufacture JLR in the UK. He even came out with plans to employ more people in the next two to three years. He said the executives from JLR were welcome to stay with the company. Most of the union representatives opted for Tata Motors over M&M and One Equity.

On January 03, 2008, Ford announced that it had decided on Tata Motors as the preferred bidder and had entered into focused negotiations with the company. According to an industry expert, "The manner in which the Tata group handled the Corus Steel deal in late 2006 created a major positive impression among the unions and the employees at large. Finally, it was one of the key factors that led to a successful completion of the Jaguar and Land Rover deal."[26]

However, there was widespread skepticism about an Indian company acquiring such iconic brands. According to Ken Gorin, Head of Jaguar's American dealers, "I don't believe the US public is ready for ownership out of India for a luxury-car brand such as Jaguar...."[27]

THE DEAL

On March 26, 2008, Tata Motors entered into an agreement with Ford for the purchase of JLR. Tata Motors agreed to pay US$ 2.3 billion in cash for a 100% acquisition of the businesses of JLR. As part of the acquisition, Tata Motors did not inherit any of the debt liabilities of JLR—the acquisition was totally debt free. On the reasons why Ford sold off the brands, John Wolkonowicz, Analyst, Global Insight, said, "They had almost 20 years of playing with Jaguar without success. Ford realized they don't want to put good money after bad any more and it is in a position where they need the money to shore up their core business."[28]

As a part of the acquisition, Tata Motors acquired the manufacturing plants, two advanced design and engineering centers, and a worldwide network of 26 national sales companies.[29] The IPRs on key technologies were to be transferred from Ford to JLR. In case the technology was shared from Ford, a royalty

free license for using these technologies was part of the purchase consideration. Ford also provided minimum guaranteed capital allowances of US$ 1.1 billion for taxation.

Ford was to continue supplying JLR with vehicle components like powertrains, stampings, environment and platform technologies, and services like engineering support, R&D, IT, and accounting. Ford also agreed to provide critical supplies including engines, access to test facilities, and key services in the areas of IT, accounting, etc. The supply of engines included new engines being developed by JLR, produced at the Ford manufacturing plant. The engine supplies were to continue for a period ranging between 7 and 9 years. The design development cooperation included sharing certain platforms, technical support, joint development, and advanced research projects. Ford did not disclose the time period for which it would provide this support. Ford Motor Credit Company, the captive credit division of Ford, agreed to continue providing financing to dealers and customers of JLR during the transition period.[30]

Tata committed itself to following Ford's business plan for JLR till 2011. The plan included new product launches; reducing the dependence on the matured markets, which accounted for 80% of JLR's sales, through strategies to increase sales from the emerging markets; complying with the EU norms pertaining to emissions, etc.

These arrangements would help JLR to continue with their plans and to develop own capabilities. After the deal, not many changes were expected in the employment terms of the around 16,000 employees of JLR.

Tata Motors said it did not have any plans to bring in any major changes in either the brands or the way the companies were run. At the Geneva Motor Show, in March 2008, Ratan Tata said, "We plan to retain the image, touch, and feel of these brands and not tinker with them in any way.

These brands belong to Britain and they will continue to belong to Britain. Who owns them is not as material as the brands belonging to Britain and the West Midlands."[31]

On the completion of sale, Ford was to contribute US$ 600 million out of the purchase consideration toward the pension fund of JLR in the UK. Tata Motors was also required to contribute to the fund. Ford had funded a substantial part of the deficit as on October 31, 2007. The next evaluation was planned for April 2009.

Tata Motors signed an agreement with the employees of JLR, and those belonging to Unite, safeguarding the jobs till 2011. According to an officer at Unite, "Unite has secured written guarantees for all the plants on staffing levels, employee terms and conditions, including pensions, and sourcing agreements. The sale ensures the future of our members."[32]

The trade unions in the UK announced that the deal was good news for the automotive industry in the UK. The unions were happy about the fact that, "Tata recognize the Britishness of the two brands and have no intention of closing any plants in the UK."[33] Analysts were of the view that the support that Tata Motors received from Unite was due to Tata's track record of managing its employees well and keeping its promises to them. Tata Steel's acquisition of Corus, where it had kept its promise to the employees, convinced unions about the management's sincerity. The unions were reportedly in touch with the employees of Tetley and Corus to understand how Tata operated. They found that Tata had not outsourced any jobs and had not even moved the jobs offshore.

However, investors of Tata Motors did not appear too pleased with the deal. When Ford announced that Tata Motors would be the preferred bidder, the share price of the company on the National Stock Exchange (NSE) was at Rs.794.25. It had fallen to Rs.679.40 by the time the deal was announced. Investors expressed concern over how Tata Motors would finance the acquisition (Refer to Exhibit 5 for stock price chart of Tata Motors).

Initially, Tata Motors obtained a bridge loan of US$ 3 billion underwritten by a consortium of banks. The additional funding was meant for engine and component supply, for which Tata Motors had entered into a separate agreement with Ford, for any contingencies and requirements that may arise in the future, and for the working capital requirements of JLR. The amount required was to be obtained through a bridge loan raised by Tata Motors UK, a special purpose vehicle, 100% subsidiary of Tata Motors (Refer to Exhibit 6 for the acquisition structure).

To refinance the bridge loan, the company planned to raise amount of around US$ 2.3 billion equity and equity linked instruments. Of this, it planned to obtain US$ 1.7 billion through three simultaneous but unlinked rights issues and overseas flotation. This rights issues consisted of normal shares and also shares with differential voting rights.[34] The rights issue was priced at Rs.340 for the normal shares and Rs.305 for the shares with differential voting rights.

Exhibit 5 Tata Motors—Stock Price Chart

Source: www.investing.businessweek.com.

Exhibit 6   Tata Motors— JLR Acquisition Structure

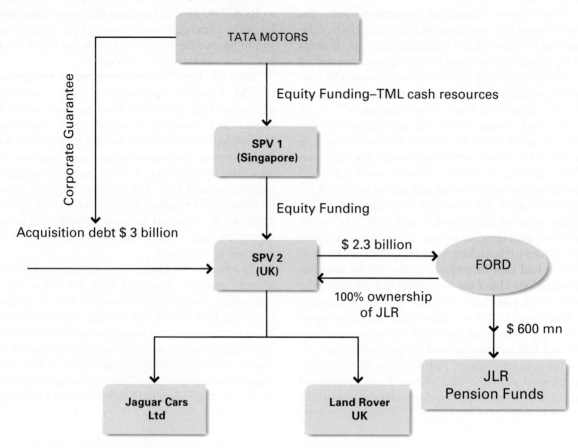

SPV 1: TML Holdings Pte. Ltd
SPV 2: Jaguar Land Rover Ltd
Source: Investor Presentation, Tata Motors, June 06, 2008.

THE BENEFITS

Tata Motors was interested in acquiring JLR as it would reduce the company's dependence on the Indian market, which accounted for 90% of i ts sales. The company was of the view that the acquisition would provide it with the opportunity to spread its business across different geographies and across different customer segments.

The acquisition provided Tata Motors an opportunity to establish its presence in the high-end premier segment of the global automobile market. According to Peter Cooke, Professor, Automotive Industries Management, University of Buckingham, "For any

company with aspiration to become a global player, there's a good opportunity there."[35]

Analysts were of the opinion that Land Rover fitted into the position above the utility vehicles Tata Motors already had. Tata Motors said it was looking forward to synergies in the areas of component sourcing, engineering, and design. The vehicles from the Tata would have better technology in the future, due to its association with JLR. Tata Motors would also benefit from JLR's service and distribution networks.

Unlike in the case of Ford, there would not be any overlap with Tata Motors' existing models. The acquisition would mean that the company would be able to compete both at the low-end of the market, with Nano priced at US$ 2500 and at the top-end with the Jaguar XF priced at US$ 64,000.

Another brand that Tata Motors had obtained through the deal was Lanchester, which Jaguar had acquired from Daimler in 1960. The deal also included the right to use the Daimler brand. According to Ratan Tata, "We are looking at whether we can resurrect the Daimler brand, which is sort of moribund."[36] Tata Motors planned to place in it in the super luxury segment, competing with Bentley and Rolls-Royce.

Both Jaguar and Land Rover had many new models lined up for the next few years. These launches were expected to take Jaguar's sales volumes beyond the 100,000 vehicle mark for 2008. The XF in particular had received rave reviews and *Auto Car UK* had rated it ahead of the BMW 5 while *What Car*

magazine had awarded it the Car of the Year award for the year 2008.

The new products in the offing from the Jaguar stable included the much awaited X351, which would replace the popular XJ Sedan. Another product was a two-seat sports car, based on the XK Coupe. Land Rover had plans of launching a small crossover vehicle by 2010. This would be one of the several small vehicles, including two door and four door vehicles that Land Rover planned to bring out from a common platform (Refer to Exhibit 7 for the list of Jaguar and Land Rover products to be unveiled in the next few years).

The success Tata Group had had with other international acquisitions, especially Corus, was often cited as an example of Tata's ability to succeed in its international ventures. According to an analyst from

....

Exhibit 7   Jaguar and Land Rover New Products Pipeline

Year (Expected)	Models	Description
2009	Jaguar XFR	High performance version of XF Sedan
	Jaguar XKR	High performance version of XK coupe
	Range Rover	Facelift version, with 5.0-liter V8, redesigned interiors
	Range Rover Sport	Facelift version, with 5.0-liter V8, redesigned interiors
2010	Jaguar XJ	Flagship sedan with XF styling, more leg and shoulder room
	Land Rover LR3	Facelift version, with new interiors
2011	Land Rover LRX	Urban chic car also includes hybrid model
2012	Jaguar F Type	Two seat sports car priced around US$ 50,000
	Land Rover LRX	Spin off of LRX with seven seats
2013	Jaguar Coupe	Range extension with low-roofline style
	All new Range Rover	Replacement of the flagship product
2014	All New Jaguar XF	Aluminum body construction
	All New Range Rover Sport	Variant of the new range rover, with aluminum body.
	All New Land Rover Defender	Similar to Toyota land cruiser targeted at the developing countries.

Adapted from Julian Rendell, "New Lease on Life," *Autoweek,* April 07, 2008.

Lehman Brothers in Mumbai, "When they bought Corus, a lot of people said they were stupid. Maybe it's the same with Jaguar. If anyone has a chance to emerge as a big auto player from India, it's Tata."[37]

THE CHALLENGES

Morgan Stanley reported that JLR's acquisition appeared negative for Tata Motors, as it had increased the earnings volatility, given the difficult economic conditions in the key markets of JLR including the US and Europe. Moreover, Tata Motors had to incur a huge capital expenditure as it planned to invest another US$ 1 billion in JLR. This was in addition to the US$ 2.3 billion it had spent on the acquisition. Tata Motors had also incurred huge capital expenditure on the development and launch of the small car Nano and on a joint venture with Fiat to manufacture some of the company's vehicles in India and Thailand. This, coupled with the downturn in the global automobile industry, was expected to impact the profitability of the company in the near future.

Many analysts were skeptical about the synergies Tata expected to achieve out of the deal. They pointed out that even after spending over US$ 10 billion over a span of 18 years, Ford had not been able do revive the fortunes of Jaguar. Prof. Garel Rhys, Director, Center for Automotive Industry Research, Cardiff Business School, said, "With Jaguar, Tata has to prove it can succeed where Ford failed. Ford couldn't turn the company around despite its knowledge of the European market."[38]

Analysts were of the view that Tata Motors would not get much of a value through the deal. They reiterated that as Tata Motors was a major truck manufacturer and was dealing in the low end of the passenger car market, JLR, which catered to the needs of the premium segment, did not go well with its existing line-up. According to an analyst from Morgan Stanley, "Buying Jaguar, Land Rover was value-destructive given the lack of synergies and the high-cost operations involved."[39]

Analysts were also skeptical about Tata Motors' ability to market such high end products, as it had neither manufactured nor marketed high-end luxury vehicles earlier. The luxury car market was highly competitive, with several prestigious brands vying for the space. These were backed by huge conglomerates like Porsche-Volkswagen, Daimler, BMW, and Toyota. These companies boasted significant financial resources, technology, and vast experience in dealing with the luxury brands that Tata Motors did not possess, they pointed out.

One of the major challenges that Tata Motors could face was the cost of key components. While Ford had agreed to provide access to engine and engine technology for some time, if the prices of these components go up after the deal, Tata Motors might have to incur extra costs on producing the vehicles. Experts were of the view that Ford was highly unlikely to supply the components as per the fixed price contracts as these prices were highly volatile.

The European Commission had decided to adopt a proposal for legislation in December 2007. The proposal aimed at reducing the CO_2 emissions from passenger cars from 160 grams per kilometer to 130 grams per kilometer by 2012. The permitted CO_2 emissions for new vehicles were stipulated depending on the mass of the vehicle. This meant that cars which were heavier needed to bring in more improvements than the lighter ones. Manufacturers could make cars with higher emissions provided they also made smaller cars with lower emissions that would offset the higher emissions.

And this was another problem area for Tata Motors. Jaguar and Land Rover had comparatively high emissions. For example, Jaguar's most fuel efficient model, the X-type, emitted around 194 grams of CO_2 per kilometer. If Jaguar and Land Rover were with Ford, the higher emissions of the two could have been balanced by the lower emissions from Ford's others brands. But Tata Motors did not sell its cars in the UK, nor did it sell any other car in Europe. The company could thus end up facing a proposed penalty in the form of 'excess emissions premium'. For the first year, ie, 2012, the penalty was proposed at € 20 per gram/kilometer, which would increase to € 35 per gram/kilometer by 2013 and to € 95 by 2015. According to Wright, "Neither Jaguar or Land Rover is very well placed in the race to significantly lower the average emissions of their respective ranges."[40] However, Tata Motors on its part was planning to launch Nano in Europe by 2012, after meeting the crash standards and Euro 5 emission standards.

THE ROAD AHEAD

Tata Motors had formed an integration committee with senior executives from the JLR and Tata Motors, to set milestones and long-term goals for the acquired entities. One of the major problems for Tata Motors could be the slowing down of the European and US automobile markets. It was expected that the company would address this issue by concentrating on countries like Russia, China, India, and the Middle East. As of 2008, China was the fastest growing auto market in the world and was estimated to be Land Rover's fifth largest market and Jaguar's seventh largest market. Russia was expected to be Land Rover's third largest market and Jaguar's eighth in 2008.

Though several analysts were skeptical about Tata Motors being able to turn Jaguar profitable, Tata Motors itself was confident about it. According to C Ramakrishnan, CFO, Tata Motors, "I think Ford has put in several building blocks in terms of turning Jaguar around very successfully. You are looking at the business at a point of time when they are still making losses, but well on their way to a full recovery and we believe some of the work that has already been happened in this company, will take it forward successfully."[41]

Analysts were of the view that Tata Motors needed to understand how to market to the premium segment to take advantage of the opportunities provided by the acquisition of JLR. Going forward, the way Tata Motors managed these brands and derived synergies from them would hold the key to the success of JLR's acquisition. Harbir Singh, Management Professor at Wharton commented, "My sense is that the Tatas are trying to expand their portfolio in general and they are trying to offer [various brands]. I don't think it's a question of the customer viewing Nano, and Jaguar and Land Rover as all offerings of the same company. It's much more a question of like Louis Moet Hennessy having a set of brands and really doing the best you can for Land Rover and the best you can for Jaguar. In terms of the economic sense of the transaction, I think another way of looking at it is: What's the replacement value of those brands, right? And clearly whatever price they pay is much lower than the replacement value. So the real challenge here for them is to make sure that they can enhance Jaguar in its own terms and enhance Land Rover in its own terms."[42]

References & Readings

1. Buyers Line up for Jaguar and Land Rover, Professional Engineering, July 25, 2007.
2. Fighting over Ford, Business India Intelligence, The Economist Intelligence Unit, September 05, 2007.
3. Gail Edmondson, Is Jaguar an Endangered Species?, BusinessWeek Online, September 20, 2007
4. James Franey, New day Nears for Jaguar-Land Rover, Automotive News Europe, October 01, 2007.
5. Bidders Drop out of Race for Land Rover and Jaguar as Deal Stalls, Professional Engineering, October 03, 2007.
6. Amy Wilson, Mark Rechtin, Some Jaguar Dealers Uneasy about Indian Owner, Automotive News, December 10, 2007.
7. Jorn Madslien, What Price for Jaguar and Land Rover? news.bbc.co.uk, December 21, 2007.
8. Stephen Power, Eric Bellman, Jaguar Dealers Head Favors Sale to U.S Group, www.online.wsj.com, December 07, 2007.
9. Ford to Lose Jaguar, Land Rover Design Staff, Ward's Autoworld, January 2008.
10. Ford in Advanced Talks with Tata over Jaguar, www.msnbc.msn.com, January 03, 2008.
11. India's Jewel Crown could put the Glint Back into UK Marques, Marketing Week, January 03, 2008.
12. Manu P. Toms, Uptrend in Land Rover, Jaguar Sales, The Hindu Business Line, January 04, 2008.
13. Tata Squeezes Ahead of Equity Firms in Fight for Jaguar and Land Rover, Professional Engineering, January 16, 2008.
14. ANALYSIS—Tata Seen Under-Powered for Jaguar, Land Rover, www.in.news.yahoo.com, March 04, 2008.
15. Tata Motors Appoints SBI as Lead Manager to Raise $3 Billion Acquisition Corpus, www.in.ibtimes.com, March 18, 2008.
16. SBI Initiates Fund-Raising for Tata JLR Deal, Financial Express, March 18, 2008.
17. Tata Buys Jaguar in £1.15 bn Deal, www.news.bbc.co.uk, March 26, 2008.
18. Tata Motors Enters into Definitive Agreement with Ford for Purchase of Jaguar Land Rover, www.tatamotors.com, March 26, 2008.
19. From Cars for Rs One Lakh to Rs One Crore, Tata Makes Them All, www.economictimes.com, March 26, 2008.
20. A Used Car Bargain, The Economist, March 26, 2008.
21. Sudeshna Sen, Close Take on Tatas' $2.30 bn Jaguar Land Rover Deal, The Economic Times, March 26, 2008.
22. Jorn Madslien, Who Gains Most as Tata Buys UK Legends? www.news.bbc.co.uk, March 27, 2008.
23. Ian Rowley, Nandini Lakshman, Can Tata Rev up Jaguar, BusinessWeek Online, March 27, 2008.
24. Ford Clears New Path with Sale of Jaguar, Land Rover, www.economictimes.com, March 27, 2008.
25. David Kiley, Jaguar: Finally Ready to Roar? BusinessWeek Online, March 27, 2008.
26. International Media Divided over Tata-JLR Deal, Financial Express, March 27, 2008.
27. Andrew English, Tata must keep up to the Marque, www.telegraph.co.uk, March 27, 2008.

28. Sudeshna Sen, Lijee Philip, Kausik Datta, Jaguar, Land Rover Find a New Driver in Tatas, The Economic Times, March 27, 2008.

29. S. Muralidhar, Jaguar, Land Rover: From Utilitarian to Premium, The Hindu Business Line, March 27, 2008.

30. Bryce G Hoffman, Ford Unloads Jaguar, Land Rover to Tata, The Detroit News, March 27, 2008.

31. JLR Deal is a Heavy Burden, Feel Rating Agencies, The Economic Times, March 27, 2008.

32. Not Thought of Bringing JLR Tech to India Yet: Ravi Kant, www.moneycontrol.com, March 27, 2008.

33. Rashmee Roshan Lall, UK's Unions Support Tata-JLR Deal, www.economictimes.com, March 28, 2008.

34. Amy Blackburn, A Very British Luxury Brand, www.bbc.co.uk, March 28, 2008.

35. Jaguar-Land Rover Buy is a Long-term Strategic Decision, The Hindu Business Line, March 28, 2008.

36. Lijee Philip, George Smith Alexander On-Road Price Tag for Jaguar & Land Rover Runs to $3 bn, The Economic Times, March 29, 2008.

37. Now What? Economist, March 29, 2008.

38. John Revill, Tony Lewin, A Brighter Future for Jaguar, Land Rover, Automotive News Europe, March 31, 2008.

39. Ford Sale Opens Door to Strong New Competitor, Automotive News Europe, March 31, 2008.

40. Mark Rechtin, Expect Most Ford-Bred Executives to Stay Put, Automotive News, March, 31, 2008.

41. Edward Lapham, Tip for Tata: Let British Brands be British Brands, Automotive News, March 31, 2008.

42. Richard Truett, Concern . . . Confidence . . . Curiosity—Welcome to America, Tata, Automotive News, March 31, 2008.

43. Lawrence White, Tata Says Hello to Land Rover and Jaguar, Euromoney, April 2008.

44. Jaguar Land Rover Confident as Tata Agrees Business Plan, Automotive Engineer, April 2008.

45. Ford Pulls Trigger on Jag, Land Rover Sale, Ward's Autoworld, April 2008.

46. Antoinette Odoi, Tata Takes Turn with British Icons, Marketing, April 02, 2008.

47. Classic Names are Part of Tata Deal, Automotive News, April 07, 2008.

48. Julian Rendell, New Lease on Life, AutoWeek, April 07, 2008.

49. Tata Luxury Takeover Welcomed, Professional Engineering, April 09, 2008.

50. Tata Name Helped Clinch Jaguar-Rover Deal, www.economictimes.com, April 06, 2008.

51. Tata Luxury Takeover Welcomed, Professional Engineering, April 09, 2008.

52. The Tata Bid Really Blew us out of the Water, www.outlokbusiness.com, April 19, 2008.

53. Krishna Gopalan, In the Driver's Seat, Business Today, April 20, 2008.

54. No Lenders Yet for Tata Motors $3bn Bridge. Euroweek, April 25, 2008.

55. Jaguar and Land Rover: Tata Motors Acquires a Rich Legacy, Domain-b.com, March 26, 2008.

56. Tata Motors Plans to Raise $1.7 bln for Jag Deal, www.reuters.com, May 28, 2008.

57. Tough Road Ahead for Tata's Jaguar-Land Rover Ride in Europe, The Economic Times, May 28, 2008.

58. UPDATE 1-India Tata Motors Shares Trip on Rights Issues Plan, www.in.reuters.com, May 29, 2008.

59. Vipin V. Nair, Tata Motors Plunges in Mumbai on Fund-Raising Plan, www.bloomberg.com, May 29, 2008.

60. Tata Plans $1.7 Billion Rights Issue for Jaguar, www.uk.reuters.com, May 29, 2008.

61. Tata Motors Sinks on Fundraising Plan, CNNMoney.com, May 29, 2008

62. Tata Motors to Take Rights Road for JLR, Business Standard, May 29, 2008.

63. David Isaiah, India: Tata Motors to Raise Rs72bn Through Triple Rights Issue, www.automotiveworld.com, May 29, 2008.

64. Satish John, Tata Motors' Differential Rights Likely to Set Trend, www.dnaindia.com, May 30, 2008

65. Ford Completes £1.7bn Jaguar Deal, news.bbc.co.uk, June 02, 2008.

66. Tata Motors Completes Acquisition of Jaguar & Land Rover, The Economic Times, June 02, 2008.

67. EXT-Moody's release on Tata Motors Ltd, in.reuters.com, June 03, 2008.

68. Downgraded by Moody's after JLR Acquisition, The Times of India, June 04, 2008.

69. Tata Motors plans 40% Discount on Rights Issue, The Times of India, June 04, 2008.

70. Jaguar, Land Rover See Opportunities in New Markets, The Economic Times, June 06, 2008.

71. Tata's Takeover of Jaguar, Land Rover Hailed by Local Leaders, The Hindu, June 06, 2008.

72. JLR Buy: Tata Motors to Revive Daimler Brand, The Times of India, July 25, 2008.

73. Peter Hutchison, Tata Shelves Cash Call for Jaguar Bill after Shares Fall by a Third, Telegraph.co.uk, August 21, 2008.

74. Rhys Blakley, Tata Turns to Asset Sales to Pay for Jaguar and Land Rover, Times Online, August 21, 2008.

75. Production Cut at Tata Jaguar in UK, Hindustan Times, August 24, 2008

76. Tata Motors Revises Terms for Mega Rights Issue, The Hindu, September 02, 2008.

77. Baiju Kalesh, JM to Underwrite Tata Motors Issue, www.livemint.com, September 06, 2008.

78. BSE Announcement on Tata Motors Rights Issue, www.tradingmarkts.com, September 08, 2008.

79. Investor Presentations, Tata Motors

80. Annual Reports, Ford

81. Annual Reports, Tata Motors

82. www.tata.com

83. www.tatamotors.com

84. www.ford.com

85. www.jaguar.com

86. www.landrover.com

Endnotes

1. Tata Motors, Annual Report, 2007–08.
2. David Kiley, "Jaguar: Finally Ready to Roar?" Business-Week Online, March 27, 2008.
3. Charles Hughes was involved in the launch of Land Rover North America in the US in the 1980s.
4. Brand Rules LLC is a marketing consulting consortium that provides advice about shaping and sustaining brands.
5. Sudeshna Sen, Lijee Philip, Kausik Datta, "Jaguar, Land Rover Find a New Driver in Tatas," www.economictimes.com, March 27, 2008.
6. Tata Motors, part of the Tata Group, one of the largest business conglomerates in India with a presence in over 80 countries and a work force of around 290,000 people. Tata Motors is the largest automobile company in India with gross revenue of Rs.330.93 billion in 2007–08. Tata Motors is also the second largest bus manufacturer and the fourth largest truck manufacturer in the world. Tata Motors unveiled the cheapest car in the world, the Tata Nano, priced at around US$ 2,500, in early 2008.
7. As of September 19, 2008 1 US$ = Rs.46.36 (Indian Rupee).
8. Cash-free, debt-free transaction refers to the amount the buyer would pay if the seller had no debt and no cash on the balance sheet of the company.
9. Premier Automotive Group of Ford consisted of Jaguar, Land Rover, Aston Martin, Volvo and Lincoln.
10. The plants were located at Solihull, Castle Bromwich, and Halewood while the design centers were located at Gaydon and Whitley.
11. "Tata Buys Jaguar in £1.15 bn Deal," www.news.bbc.co.uk, March 26, 2008.
12. 'The Way Forward' was Ford's restructuring plan. The plan included resizing the company, selling off some of the unprofitable models, and closing down some of the vehicle plants and component factories. This was estimated to lead to a 28% reduction in the company's workforce in a span of five years from 2006.
13. John Revill, Tony Lewin, "A Brighter Future for Jaguar, Land Rover," Automotive News Europe, March 31, 2008.
14. "Downgraded by Moody's after JLR Acquisition," The Times of India, June 04, 2008.
15. Jaguar was founded in 1922 by William Lyons and William Walmsley. In 1966, Jaguar merged with the British Motor Corporation to form British Motor Holdings. In 1968, it merged with Leyland Motors Ltd. to form British Leyland Motor Corporation (BLMC). After BLMC faced financial crisis in the early 1970s, it was given government support, resulting in its nationalization and formation of British Leyland Limited. In 1984, Jaguar was floated as a separate company.
16. Land Rover was founded in the 1860s and the name Rover was introduced in 1884. It became one of the top car manufacturers in Britain by 1920s. It became a part of Leyland Motors in 1967 and was acquired by British Aerospace in 1988. It was sold to BMW in 1994. BMW split the company into two and Rover was sold to Ford.
17. Amy Blackburn, "A Very British Luxury Brand," www.bbc.co.uk, March 28, 2008.
18. "A Used Car Bargain," The Economist, March 26, 2008.
19. Cerberus acquired 80.1% equity stake in Chrysler from DaimlerChrysler for US$ 7.4 billion.
20. Ripplewood Holdings is a US-based private equity firm. Nick Scheele, President of Ford, served as an advisor with Ripplewood Holdings between 2001 and 2005.
21. Jacques Nasser was the CEO of Ford between 1999 and 2001. After leaving Ford, he became a senior partner of One Equity Partners.
22. TPG Capital played a major role in turning around Italian Motorcycle brand Ducati.
23. Mahindra & Mahindra is an India-based auto manufacturer. It is the flagship company of the Mahindra Group. The company's revenues in 2008 were at US$ 6.7 billion.
24. "Tata Squeezes Ahead of Equity Firms in Fight for Jaguar and Land Rover," Professional Engineering, January 16, 2008.
25. Unite is a British Irish Trade union.
26. "Tata Name Helped Clinch Jaguar-Rover Deal," www.economictimes.com, April 06, 2008.
27. "From Cars for Rs One Lakh to Rs One Crore, Tata Makes Them All," www.economictimes.com, March 26, 2008.
28. "Ford Clears New Path with Sale of Jaguar, Land Rover," www.economictimes.com, March 27, 2008.
29. Existing national sales companies of JLR and the national sales companies to be created by carving out the Ford operations in some countries.
30. The transition period was expected to be around 12 months.
31. "Tata Motors Appoints SBI as Lead Manager to Raise $3 Billion Acquisition Corpus," www.in.ibtimes.com, March 18, 2008.
32. Krishna Gopalan, "In the Driver's Seat," Business Today, April 20, 2008.
33. Rashmee Roshan Lall, "UK's Unions Support Tata-JLR Deal," www.economictimes.com, March 28, 2008.
34. The shares with differential voting rights had one vote for every ten shares and were offered at a discount of 12.8% over the regular rights shares and were given 5% extra dividend.
35. "Bidders Drop out of Race for Land Rover and Jaguar as Deal Stalls," Professional Engineering, October 03, 2007.
36. "JLR Buy: Tata Motors to Revive Daimler Brand," The Times of India, July 25, 2008.
37. Ian Rowley, Nandini Lakshman, "Can Tata Rev up Jaguar," BusinessWeek Online, March 27, 2008.
38. "Tata Luxury Takeover Welcomed," Professional Engineering, April 09, 2008.
39. "A Used Car Bargain," The Economist, March 26, 2008.
40. Jorn Madslien, "Who Gains Most as Tata Buys UK Legends?" news.bbc.co.uk, March 27, 2008.
41. Tata Motors Conference Call, Acquisition of Jaguar and Land Rover, April 02, 2008.
42. "Tata's Takeover of Jaguar and Land Rover: Bumpy Road or Smooth Ride?" India Knowledge@Wharton, April 03, 2008.

THE HOME VIDEO GAME INDUSTRY

AN INDUSTRY IS BORN

In 1968, Nolan Bushell, the 24-year-old son of a Utah cement contractor, graduated from the University of Utah with a degree in engineering.[1] Bushnell then moved to California, where he worked briefly in the computer graphics division of Ampex. At home, Bushnell turned his daughter's bedroom into a laboratory. There, he created a simpler version of Space War, a computer game that had been invented in 1962 by an MIT graduate student, Steve Russell. Bushnell's version of Russell's game, which he called Computer Space, was made of integrated circuits connected to a 19-inch black-and-white television screen. Unlike a computer, Bushnell's invention could do nothing but play the game, which meant that, unlike a computer, it could be produced cheaply.

Bushnell envisioned video games like his standing next to pinball machines in arcades. With hopes of having his invention put into production, Bushnell left Ampex to work for a small pinball company that manufactured 1,500 copies of his video game. The game never sold, primarily because the player had to read a full page of directions before he or she could play the game—way too complex for an arcade game. Bushnell left the pinball company and with a friend, Ted Dabney, put up $500 to start a company that would develop a simpler video game. They wanted to call the company Syzygy, but the name was already taken, so they settled on Atari, a Japanese word that was the equivalent of "check in the go."

In his home laboratory, Bushnell built the simplest game he could think of. People knew the rules immediately, and it could be played with one hand. The game was modeled on table tennis, and players batted a ball back and forth with paddles that could be moved up and down sides of a court by twisting knobs. He named the game "Pong" after the sonar-like sound that was emitted every time the ball connected with a paddle.

In the fall of 1972, Bushnell installed his prototype for Pong in Andy Capp's tavern in Sunnyvale, California. The only instructions were "avoid missing the ball for a high score." In the first week, 1,200 quarters were deposited in the casserole dish that served as a coin box in Bushnell's prototype. Bushnell was ecstatic; his simple game had brought in $300 in a week. The pinball machine that stood next to it averaged $35 a week.

Lacking the capital to mass-produce the game, Bushnell approached established amusement game companies, only to be repeatedly shown the door. Down but hardly out, Bushnell cut his hair, put on a suit, and talked his way into a $50,000 line of credit from a local bank. He set up a production line in an abandoned roller skating rink and hired people to assemble machines while Led Zeppelin and the Rolling Stones played at full volume over the speaker system of the rink. Among his first batch of employees was a skinny 17-year-old named Steve Jobs, who would later found a few companies of his own, including Apple Computer, NeXT, and Pixar. Like others, Jobs had been attracted by a classified ad that read "Have Fun and Make Money."

In no time at all, Bushnell was selling all the machines that his small staff could make—about

---

This case was prepared by Charles W. L. Hill, the University of Washington. This case is intended to be used as a basis for class discussion rather than as an illustration of either effective or ineffective handling of the situation. Reprinted by permission of Charles W. L. Hill.

10 per day; to grow, however, he needed additional capital. The ambience at the rink, with its mix of rock music and marijuana fumes, put off most potential investors, but Don Valentine, one of the country's most astute and credible venture capitalists, was impressed with the growth story. Armed with Valentine's money, Atari began to increase production and expand its range of games. New games included Tank and Breakout; the latter was designed by Jobs and a friend of his, Steve Wozniak, who had left Hewlett-Packard to work at Atari.

By 1974, 100,000 Pong-like games were sold worldwide. Although Atari manufactured only 10% of the games, the company still made $3.2 million that year. With the Pong clones coming on strong, Bushnell decided to make a Pong system for the home. In fact, Magnavox had been marketing a similar game for the home since 1972, although sales had been modest.[2] Bushnell's team managed to compress Atari's coin-operated Pong game down to a few inexpensive circuits that were contained in the game console. Atari's Pong had a sharper picture and more sensitive controllers than Magnavox's machine. It also cost less. Bushnell then went on a road show, demonstrating Pong to toy buyers, but he received an indifferent response and no sales. A dejected Bushnell returned to Atari with no idea of what to do next. Then the buyer for the sporting goods department at Sears came to see Bushnell, reviewed the machine, and offered to buy every home Pong game Atari could make. With Sears's backing, Bushnell boosted production. Sears ran a major television ad campaign to sell home Pong, and Atari's sales soared, hitting $450 million in 1975. The home video game had arrived.

Boom and Bust

Nothing attracts competitors like success, and by 1976 about 20 different companies were crowding into the home video game market, including National Semiconductor, RCA, Coleco, and Fairchild. Recognizing the limitations of existing home video game designs, in 1976, Fairchild came out with a home video game system capable of playing multiple games. The Fairchild system consisted of three components—a console, controllers, and cartridges. The console was a small computer optimized for

graphics processing capabilities. It was designed to receive information from the controllers, process it, and send signals to a television monitor. The controllers were handheld devices used to direct on-screen action. The cartridges contained chips encoding the instructions for a game. The cartridges were designed to be inserted into the console.

In 1976, Bushnell sold Atari to Warner Communications for $28 million. Bushnell stayed on to run Atari. Backed by Warner's capital, in 1977, Atari developed and brought out its own cartridge-based system, the Atari 2600. The 2600 system was sold for $200, and associated cartridges retailed for $25 to $35. Sales surged during the 1977 Christmas season. However, a lack of manufacturing capacity on the part of market-leader Atari and a very cautious approach to inventory by Fairchild led to shortages and kept sales significantly below what they could have been. Fairchild's cautious approach was the result of prior experience in consumer electronics. A year earlier, it had increased demand for its digital watches, only to accumulate a buildup of excess inventory that had caused the company to take a $24.5 million write-off.[3]

After the 1977 Christmas season, Atari claimed to have sold about 400,000 units of the 2600 VCA, about 50% of all cartridge-based systems in American homes. Atari had also earned more than $100 million in sales of game cartridges. By this point, second-place Fairchild sold about 250,000 units of its system. Cartridge sales for the year totaled about 1.2 million units, with an average selling price of about $20. Fresh from this success and fortified by market forecasts predicting sales of 33 million cartridges and an installed base of 16 million machines by 1980, Bushnell committed Atari to manufacturing 1 million units of the 2600 for the 1978 Christmas season. Atari estimated that total demand would reach 2 million units. Bushnell was also encouraged by signals from Fairchild that it would again be limiting production to approximately 200,000 units. At this point, Atari had a library of nine games, while Fairchild had 17 games.[4]

Atari was not the only company to be excited by the growth forecasts. In 1978, a host of other companies, including Coleco, National Semiconductor, Magnavox, General Instrument, and a dozen other companies, entered the market with incompatible cartridge-based home systems. The multitude of choices did not seem to entice consumers, however, and the 1978 Christmas season brought unexpectedly low sales. Only Atari and Coleco survived an industry shakeout. Atari lost Bushnell, who was ousted by Warner executives. (Bushnell went on to start Chuck E. Cheese Pizza Time Theater, a restaurant chain that had 278 outlets by 1981.) Bushnell later stated that part of the problem was a disagreement over strategy. Bushnell wanted Atari to price the 2600 at cost and make money on sales of software; Warner wanted to continue making profits on hardware sales.[5]

Several important developments occurred in 1979. First, several game producers and programmers defected from Atari to set up their own firm, Activision, and to make games compatible with the Atari 2600. Their success encouraged others to follow suit. Second, Coleco developed an expansion module that allowed its machine to play Atari games. Atari and Mattel (who entered the market in 1979) did likewise. Third, the year 1979 saw the introduction of three new games to the home market—Space Invaders, Asteroids, and Pac Man. All three were adapted from popular arcade games and all three helped drive demand for players.

Demand recovered strongly in late 1979 and kept growing for the next three years. In 1981, United States sales of home video games and cartridges hit $1 billion. In 1982, they surged to $3 billion, with Atari accounting for half of this amount. It seemed as if Atari could do no wrong; the 2600 was everywhere. About 20 million units were sold, and by late 1982, a large number of independent companies, including Activision, Imagic, and Epyx, were now producing hundreds of games for the 2600. Second-place Coleco was also doing well, partly because of a popular arcade game, Donkey Kong, which it had licensed from a Japanese company called Nintendo.

Atari was also in contact with Nintendo. In 1982, the company very nearly licensed the rights to Nintendo's Famicom, a cartridge-based video game system machine that was a big hit in Japan. Atari's successor to the 2600, the 5200, was not selling well, and the Famicom seemed like a good substitute. The negotiations broke down, however, when Atari discovered that Nintendo had extended its Donkey Kong license to Coleco. This allowed Coleco to port a version of the game to its home computer, which was a direct competitor to Atari's 800 home computer.[6]

After a strong 1982 season, the industry hoped for continued growth in 1983. Then the bottom dropped out of the market. Sales of home video games plunged to $100 million. Atari lost $500 million in the first nine months of the year, causing the stock of parent company Warner Communications to drop by half. Part of the blame for the collapse was laid at the feet of an enormous inventory overhang of unsold games. About 15 to 20 million surplus game cartridges were left over from the 1982 Christmas season (in 1981, there were none). On top of this, approximately 500 new games hit the market in 1993. The average price of a cartridge plunged from $30 in 1979 to $16 in 1982 and then to $4 in 1983. As sales slowed, retailers cut back on the shelf space allocated to video games. It proved difficult for new games to make a splash in a crowded market. Atari had to dispose of 6 million ET: The Extraterrestrial games. Meanwhile, big hits from previous years, such as Pac Man, were bundled with game players and given away free to try to encourage system sales.[7]

Surveying the rubble, commentators claimed that the video game industry was dead. The era of dedicated game machines was over, they claimed. Personal computers were taking their place.[8] It seemed to be true. Mattel sold off its game business, Fairchild moved on to other things, Coleco folded, and Warner decided to break up Atari and sell its constituent pieces—at least, those pieces for which it could find a buyer. No one in America seemed to want to have anything to do with the home video game business; no one, that is, except for Minoru Arakawa, the head of Nintendo's United States subsidiary, Nintendo of America (NOA). Picking through the rubble of the industry, Arakawa noticed that there were people who still packed video arcades, bringing in $7 billion a year, more money than the entire movie industry. Perhaps it was not a lack of interest in home video games that had killed the industry. Perhaps it was bad business practice.

THE NINTENDO MONOPOLY

Nintendo was a century-old Japanese company that had built up a profitable business making playing cards before diversifying into the video game business. Based in Kyoto and still run by the founding Yamauchi family, the company started to diversify into the video game business in the late 1970s. The first step was to license video game technology from Magnavox. In 1977, Nintendo introduced a home video game system in Japan based on this technology that played a variation of Pong. In 1978, the company began to sell coin-operated video games. It had its first hit with Donkey Kong, designed by Sigeru Miyamoto.

The Famicom

In the early 1980s, the company's boss, Hiroshi Yamauchi, decided that Nintendo had to develop its own video game machine. He pushed the company's engineers to develop a machine that combined superior graphics-processing capabilities and low cost. Yamauchi wanted a machine that could sell for $75, less than half the price of competing machines at the time. He dubbed the machine the Family Computer, or Famicom. The machine that his engineers designed was based on the controller, console, and plug-in cartridge format pioneered by Fairchild. It contained two custom chips—an 8-bit central processing unit and a graphics-processing unit. Both chips had been scaled down to perform only essential functions. A 16-bit processor was available at the time, but to keep costs down, Yamauchi refused to use it.

Nintendo approached Ricoh, the electronics giant, which had spare semiconductor capacity. Employees at Ricoh said that the chips had to cost no more that 2,000 yen. Ricoh thought that the 2,000-yen price point was absurd. Yamauchi's response was to guarantee Ricoh a 3-million-chip order within two years. Since the leading companies in Japan were selling, at most, 30,000 video games per year at the time, many within the company viewed this as an outrageous commitment, but Ricoh went for it.[9]

Another feature of the machine was its memory—2,000 bytes of random access memory (RAM), compared to the 256 bytes of RAM in the Atari machine. The result was a machine with superior graphics-processing capabilities and faster action that could handle far more complex games than Atari games. Nintendo's engineers also built a new set of chips into the game cartridges. In addition to chips that held the game program, Nintendo developed memory map controller (MMC) chips that took over some of the graphics-processing work from the chips in the console and enabled the system to handle more complex games. With the addition of the MMC chips, the potential for more-

sophisticated and complex games had arrived. Over time, Nintendo's engineers developed more powerful MMC chips, enabling the basic 8-bit system to do things that originally seemed out of reach. The engineers also figured out a way to include a battery backup system in cartridges that allowed some games to store information independently—to keep track of where a player had left off or track high scores.

The Games

Yamauchi recognized that great hardware would not sell itself. The key to the market, he reasoned, was great games. Yamauchi had instructed the engineers, as they were developing the hardware, to make sure that "it was appreciated by software engineers." Nintendo decided that it would become a haven for game designers. "An ordinary man," Yamauchi said, "cannot develop good games no matter how hard he tries. A handful of people in this world can develop games that everyone wants. Those are the people we want at Nintendo."[10]

Yamauchi had an advantage in the person of Sigeru Miyamoto. Miyamoto had joined Nintendo at the age of 24. Yamauchi had hired Miyamoto, a graduate of Kanazawa Munici College of Industrial Arts, as a favor to his father and an old friend, although he had little idea what he would do with an artist. For three years, Miyamoto worked as Nintendo's staff artist. Then in 1980, Yamauchi called Miyamoto into his office. Nintendo had started selling coin-operated video games, but one of the new games, Radarscope, was a disaster. Could Miyamoto come up with a new game? Miyamoto was delighted. He had always spent a lot of time drawing cartoons, and as a student, he had played video games constantly. Miyamoto believed that video games could be used to bring cartoons to life.[11]

The game Miyamoto developed was nothing short of a revelation. At a time when most coin-operated video games lacked characters or depth, Miyamoto created a game around a story that had both. Most games involved battles with space invaders or heroes shooting lasers at aliens; Miyamoto's game did neither. Based loosely on *Beauty and the Beast* and *King Kong*, Miyamoto's game involved a pet ape who runs off with his master's beautiful girlfriend. His master is an ordinary carpenter called Mario, who has a bulbous nose, a bushy mustache, a pair of large pathetic eyes, and a red cap (which Miyamoto added because he was not good at hairstyles). He does not carry a laser gun. The ape runs off with the girlfriend to get back at his master, who was not especially nice to the beast. The man, of course, has to get his girlfriend back by running up ramps, climbing ladders, jumping off elevators, and the like, while the ape throws objects at the hapless carpenter. Since the main character is an ape, Miyamoto called him Kong; because the main character is as stubborn as a donkey, he called the game Donkey Kong.

Released in 1981, Donkey Kong was a sensation in the world of coin-operated video arcades and a smash hit for Nintendo. In 1984, Yamauchi again summoned Miyamoto to his office. He needed more games, this time for Famicom. Miyamoto was made the head of a new research and development (R&D) group and told to come up with the most imaginative video games ever.

Miyamoto began with Mario from Donkey Kong. A colleague had told him that Mario looked more like a plumber than a carpenter, so a plumber he became. Miyamoto gave Mario a brother, Luigi, who was as tall and thin as Mario was short and fat. They became the Super Mario Brothers. Since plumbers spend their time working on pipes, large green sewer pipes became obstacles and doorways into secret worlds. Mario and Luigi's task was to search for the captive Princess Toadstool. Mario and Luigi are endearing bumblers, unequal to their tasks yet surviving. They shoot, squash, or evade their enemies—a potpourri of inventions that include flying turtles and stinging fish, man-eating flowers and fire-breathing dragons—while they collect gold coins, blow air bubbles, and climb vines into smiling clouds.[12]

Super Mario Brothers was introduced in 1985. For Miyamoto, this was just the beginning. Between 1985 and 1991, Miyamoto produced eight Mario games. About 60 to 70 million were sold worldwide, making Miyamoto the most successful game designer in the world. After adapting Donkey Kong for Famicom, he also went on to create other top-selling games, including another classic, The Legend of Zelda. While Miyamoto drew freely from folklore, literature, and pop culture, the main source for his ideas was his own experience. The memory of being lost among a maze of sliding doors in his family's home was re-created in the labyrinths of the Zelda games. The dog that attacked him when he was a child attacks Mario in Super Mario. As a child,

Miyamoto had once climbed a tree to catch a view of far-off mountains and had become stuck. Mario gets himself in a similar fix. Once Miyamoto went hiking without a map and was surprised to stumble across a lake. In the Legend of Zelda, part of the adventure is in walking into new places without a map and being confronted by surprises.

Nintendo in Japan

Nintendo introduced Famicom into the Japanese market in May 1983. Famicom was priced at $100, more than Yamauchi wanted, but significantly less than the products of competitors. When he introduced the machine, Yamauchi urged retailers to forgo profits on the hardware because it was just a tool to sell software, and that is where they would make their money. Backed by an extensive advertising campaign, 500,000 units of Famicom were sold in the first two months. Within a year, the figure stood at 1 million, and sales were still expanding rapidly. With the hardware quickly finding its way into Japanese homes, Nintendo was besieged with calls from desperate retailers frantically demanding more games.

At this point, Yamauchi told Miyamoto to come up with the most imaginative games ever. However, Yamauchi also realized that Nintendo alone could not satisfy the growing thirst for new games, so he initiated a licensing program. To become a Nintendo licensee, companies had to agree to an unprecedented series of restrictions. Licensees could issue only five Nintendo games per year, and they could not write those titles for other platforms. The licensing fee was set at 20% of the wholesale price of each cartridge sold (game cartridges wholesaled for around $30). It typically cost $500,000 to develop a game and took around six months. Nintendo insisted that games not contain any excessively violent or sexually suggestive material and that they review every game before allowing it to be produced.[13]

Despite these restrictions, six companies (Bandai, Capcom, Konami, Namco, Taito, and Hudson) agreed to become Nintendo licensees, not least because millions of customers were now clamoring for games. Bandai was Japan's largest toy company. The others already made either coin-operated video games or computer software games. Because of these licensing agreements, they saw their sales and earnings surge. For example, Konami's earnings went from $10 million in 1987 to $300 million in 1991.

After the six licensees began selling games, reports of defective games began to reach Yamauchi. The original six licensees were allowed to manufacture their own game cartridges. Realizing that he had given away the ability to control the quality of the cartridges, Yamauchi decided to change the contract for future licensees. Future licensees were required to submit all manufacturing orders for cartridges to Nintendo. Nintendo charged licensees $14 per cartridge, required that they place a minimum order for 10,000 units (later the minimum order was raised to 30,000), and insisted on cash payment in full when the order was placed. Nintendo outsourced all manufacturing to other companies, using the volume of its orders to get rock bottom prices. The cartridges were estimated to cost Nintendo between $6 and $8 each. The licensees then picked up the cartridges from Nintendo's loading dock and were responsible for distribution. In 1985, there were 17 licensees. By 1987, there were 50. By this point, 90% of the home video game systems sold in Japan were Nintendo systems.

Nintendo in America

In 1980, Nintendo established a subsidiary in America to sell its coin-operated video games. Yamauchi's American-educated son-in-law, Minoru Arakawa, headed the subsidiary. All of the other essential employees were Americans, including Ron Judy and Al Stone. For its first two years, Nintendo of America (NOA), based originally in Seattle, struggled to sell second-rate games such as Radarscope. The subsidiary seemed on the brink of closing. NOA could not even make the rent payment on the warehouse. Then they received a large shipment from Japan: 2,000 units of a new coin-operated video game. Opening the box, they discovered Donkey Kong. After playing the game briefly, Judy proclaimed it a disaster. Stone walked out of the building, declaring that "It's over."[14] The managers were appalled. They could not imagine a game less likely to sell in video arcades. The only promising sign was that a 20-year employee, Howard Philips, rapidly became enthralled with the machine.

Arakawa, however, knew he had little choice but to try to sell the machine. Judy persuaded the owner of the Spot Tavern near Nintendo's office to take one of the machines on a trial basis. After one night, Judy discovered $30 in the coin box, a phenomenal amount. The next night there was $35, and $36 the night after that. NOA had a hit on its hands.

By the end of 1982, NOA had sold more than 60,000 copies of Donkey Kong and had booked sales in excess of $100 million. The subsidiary had outgrown its Seattle location. They moved to a new site in Redmond, a Seattle suburb, where they located next to a small but fast-growing software company run by an old school acquaintance of Howard Philips, Bill Gates.

By 1984, NOA was riding a wave of success in the coin-operated video game market. Arakawa, however, was interested in the possibilities of selling Nintendo's new Famicom system in the United States. Throughout 1984, Arakawa, Judy, and Stone met with numerous toy and department store representatives to discuss the possibilities, only to be repeatedly rebuffed. Still smarting from the 1983 debacle, the representatives wanted nothing to do with the home video game business. They also met with former managers from Atari and Coleco to gain their insights. The most common response they received was that the market collapsed because the last generation of games were awful.

Arakawa and his team decided that if they were going to sell Famicom in the United States, they would have to find a new distribution channel. The obvious choice was consumer electronics stores. Thus, Arakawa asked the R&D team in Kyoto to redesign Famicom for the United States market so that it looked less like a toy (Famicom was encased in red and white plastic), and more like a consumer electronics device. The redesigned machine was renamed the Nintendo Entertainment System (NES).

Arakawa's big fear was that illegal, low-quality Taiwanese games would flood the United States market if NES was successful. To stop counterfeit games from being played on NES, Arakawa asked Nintendo's Japanese engineers to design a security system into the U.S. version of Famicom so that only Nintendo-approved games could be played on NES. The Japanese engineers responded by designing a security chip that was embedded in the game cartridges. NES would not work unless the security chips in the cartridges unlocked, or shook hands with, a chip in NES. Since the code embedded in the security chip was proprietary, the implication of this system was that no one could manufacture games for NES without Nintendo's specific approval.

To overcome the skepticism and reluctance of retailers to stock a home video game system, Arakawa decided in late 1985 to make an extraordinary commitment. Nintendo would stock stores and set up displays and windows. Retailers would not have to pay for anything they stocked for 90 days. After that, retailers could pay Nintendo for what they sold and return the rest. NES was bundled with Nintendo's best-selling game in Japan, Super Mario Brothers. It was essentially a risk-free proposition for retailers, but even with this, most were skeptical. Ultimately, thirty Nintendo personnel descended on the New York area. Referred to as the Nintendo SWAT team, they persuaded some stores to stock NES after an extraordinary blitz that involved 18-hour days. To support the New York product launch, Nintendo also committed itself to a $5 million advertising campaign aimed at the 7- to 14-year-old boys who seemed to be Nintendo's likely core audience.

By December 1985, between 500 and 600 stores in the New York area were stocking Nintendo systems. Sales were moderate, about half of the 100,000 NES machines shipped from Japan were sold, but it was enough to justify going forward. The SWAT team moved first to Los Angeles, then to Chicago, then to Dallas. As in New York, sales started at a moderate pace, but by late 1986 they started to accelerate rapidly, and Nintendo went national with NES.

In 1986, around 1 million NES units were sold in the United States. In 1987, the figure increased to 3 million. In 1988, it jumped to over 7 million. In the same year, 33 million game cartridges were sold. Nintendo mania had arrived in the United States. To expand the supply of games, Nintendo licensed the rights to produce up to five games per year to 31 American software companies. Nintendo continued to use a restrictive licensing agreement that gave it exclusive rights to any games, required licensees to place their orders through Nintendo, and insisted on a 30,000-unit minimum order.[15]

By 1990, the home video game market was worth $5 billion worldwide. Nintendo dominated the industry, with a 90% share of the market for game equipment. The parent company was, by some measures, now the most profitable company in Japan. By 1992, it was netting over $1 billion in gross profit annually, or more than $1.5 million for each employee in Japan. The company's stock market value exceeded that of Sony, Japan's premier consumer electronics firm. Indeed, the company's net profit exceeded that of all the American movie studios combined. Nintendo games, it seemed, were bigger than the movies.

As of 1991, there were more than 100 licensees for Nintendo, and more than 450 titles were available for NES. In the United States, Nintendo products were distributed through toy stores (30% of volume), mass merchandisers (40% of volume), and department stores (10% of volume). Nintendo tightly controlled the number of game titles and games that could be sold, quickly withdrawing titles as soon as interest appeared to decline. In 1988, retailers requested 110 million cartridges from Nintendo. Market surveys suggested that perhaps 45 million could have been sold, but Nintendo allowed only 33 million to be shipped.[16] Nintendo claimed that the shortage of games was in part due to a worldwide shortage of semiconductor chips.

Several companies had tried to reverse-engineer the code embedded in Nintendo's security chip, which competitors characterized as a lockout chip. Nintendo successfully sued them. The most notable was Atari Games, one of the successors of the original Atari, which in 1987 sued Nintendo of America for anticompetitive behavior. Atari claimed that the purpose of the security chip was to monopolize the market. At the same time, Atari announced that it had found a way around Nintendo's security chip and would begin to sell unlicensed games.[17] NOA responded with a countersuit. In a March 1991 ruling, Atari was found to have obtained Nintendo's security code illegally and was ordered to stop selling NES-compatible games. However, Nintendo did not always have it all its own way. In 1990, under pressure from Congress, the Department of Justice, and several lawsuits, Nintendo rescinded its exclusivity requirements, freeing up developers to write games for other platforms. However, developers faced a real problem: what platform could they write for?

SEGA'S SONIC BOOM

Back in 1954, David Rosen, a 20-year-old American, left the U.S. Air Force after a tour of duty in Tokyo.[18] Rosen had noticed that Japanese people needed lots of photographs for ID cards, but local photo studios were slow and expensive. He formed a company, Rosen Enterprises, and went into the photo-booth business, which was a big success. By 1957, Rosen had established a successful nationwide chain. At this point, the Japanese economy was booming, so Rosen decided it was time to get into another business—entertainment. As his vehicle, he chose arcade games, which were unknown in Japan at the time. He picked up used games on the cheap from America and set up arcades in the same Japanese department stores and theaters that typically housed his photo booths. Within a few years, Rosen had 200 arcades nationwide. His only competition came from another American-owned firm, Service Games (SeGa), whose original business was jukeboxes and fruit machines.

By the early 1960s, the Japanese arcade market had caught up with the United States market. The problem was that game makers had run out of exciting new games to offer. Rosen decided that he would have to get into the business of designing and manufacturing games, but to do that he needed manufacturing facilities. SeGa manufactured its own games, so in 1965 Rosen approached the company and suggested a merger. The result was Sega Enterprise, a Japanese company with Rosen as its CEO.

Rosen designed Sega's first game, Periscope, in which the objective was to sink chain-mounted cardboard ships by firing torpedoes, represented by lines of colored lights. Periscope was a big success not only in Japan but also in the United States and Europe. It allowed Sega to build up a respectable export business. Over the years, the company continued to invest heavily in game development, always using the latest electronic technology.

Gulf and Western (G&W), a United States conglomerate, acquired Sega in 1969, with Rosen running the subsidiary. In 1975, Gulf and Western (G&W) took Sega public in the United States but kept Sega Japan as a G&W subsidiary. Hayao Nakayama, a former Sega distributor, was drafted as president. In the early 1980s, Nakayama pushed G&W to invest more in Sega Japan so that the company could enter the then-booming home video game market. When G&W refused, Nakayama suggested a management buyout. G&W agreed, and in 1984, for the price of just $38 million, Sega became a Japanese company once more. (Sega's Japanese revenues were about $700 million, but by now the company was barely profitable.)

Sega was caught off guard by the huge success of Nintendo's Famicom. Although it released its own 8-bit system in 1986, the machine never commanded more than 5% of the Japanese market. Nakayama, however, was not about to give up. From years in the arcade business, he understood that great games drove sales. Nevertheless, he also understood that more powerful technology gave game developers the tools to develop more appealing games. This philosophy underlay Nakayama's decision to develop a 16-bit game system, Genesis.

Sega took the design of its 16-bit arcade machine and adapted it for Genesis. Compared to Nintendo's 8-bit machine, the 16-bit machine featured an array of superior technological features, including high-definition graphics and animation, a full spectrum of colors, two independent scrolling backgrounds that created an impressive depth of field, and near CD quality sound. The design strategy also made it easy to port Sega's catalog of arcade hits to Genesis.

Genesis was launched in Japan in 1989 and in the United States in 1990. In the United States, the machine was priced at $199. The company hoped that sales would be boosted by the popularity of its arcade games, such as the graphically violent Altered Beast. Sega also licensed other companies to develop games for the Genesis platform. In an effort to recruit licensees, Sega asked for lower royalty rates than Nintendo, and it gave licensees the right to manufacture their own cartridges. Independent game developers were slow to climb on board, however, and the $200 price tag for the player held back sales.

One of the first independent game developers to sign up with Sega was Electronic Arts (EA). Established by Trip Hawkins, EA had focused on designing games for personal computers and consequently had missed the Nintendo 8-bit era. Now Hawkins was determined to get a presence in the home video game market, and aligning his company's wagon with Sega seemed to be the best option. The Nintendo playing field was already crowded, and Sega offered a far less restrictive licensing deal than Nintendo. EA subsequently wrote several popular games for Genesis, including John Madden football and several gory combat games.[19]

Nintendo had not been ignoring the potential of the 16-bit system. Nintendo's own 16-bit system, Super NES, was ready for market introduction in 1989—at the same time as Sega's Genesis. Nintendo introduced Super NES in Japan in 1990, where it quickly established a strong market presence and beat Sega's Genesis. In the United States, however, the company decided to hold back longer to reap the full benefits of the dominance it enjoyed with the 8-bit NES system. Yamauchi was also worried about the lack of backward compatibility between Nintendo's 8-bit and 16-bit systems. (The company had tried to make the 16-bit system so that it could play 8-bit games but concluded that the cost of doing so was prohibitive.) These concerns may have led the company to delay market introduction until the 8-bit market was saturated.

Meanwhile, in the United States, the Sega bandwagon was beginning to gain momentum. One development that gave Genesis a push was the introduction of a new Sega game, Sonic the Hedgehog. Developed by an independent team that was contracted to Sega, the game featured a cute hedgehog that impatiently tapped his paw when the player took too long to act. Impatience was Sonic's central feature—he had places to go—and quickly. He zipped along, collecting brass rings when he could find them, before rolling into a ball and flying down slides with loops and underground tunnels. Sonic was Sega's Mario.

In mid-1991, in an attempt to jump-start slow sales, Tom Kalinske, head of Sega's American subsidiary, decided to bundle Sonic the Hedgehog with the game player. He also reduced the price for the bundled unit to $150, and he relaunched the system with an aggressive advertising campaign aimed at teenagers. The campaign was built around the slogan "Genesis does what Nintendon't." The shift in strategy worked, and sales accelerated sharply.

Sega's success prompted Nintendo to launch its own 16-bit system. Nintendo's Super NES was introduced at $200. However, Sega now had a two-year head start in games. By the end of 1991, about 125 game titles were available for Genesis, compared to 25 for Super NES. In May 1992, Nintendo reduced the price of Super NES to $150. At this time Sega was claiming a 63% share of the 16-bit market in the United States, and Nintendo claimed a 60% share. By now, Sega was cool. It began to take more chances with mass media-defined morality. When Acclaim Entertainment released its bloody *Mortal Kombat* game in September 1992, the Sega version let players rip off heads and tear out hearts. Reflecting Nintendo's image of their core market, its version was sanitized. The Sega version outsold Nintendo's two to one.[20] Therefore, the momentum continued to run in Sega's favor. By January 1993, there were 320 titles available for Sega Genesis and 130 for Super NES. In early 1994, independent estimates suggested that Sega had 60% of the United States market and Nintendo had 40%, figures that Nintendo disputed.

3DO

Trip Hawkins, whose first big success was EA, founded 3DO in 1991.[21] Hawkins's vision for 3DO was to shift the home video game business away from the existing cartridge-based format and toward a CD-ROM-based platform. The original partners in 3DO were EA, Matsushita, Time Warner, AT&T, and the venture capital firm Kleiner Perkins. Collectively, they invested more than $17 million in 3DO, making it the richest start-up in the history of the home video game industry. 3DO went public in May 1993 at $15 per share. By October of that year, the stock had risen to $48 per share, making 3DO worth $1 billion—not bad for a company that had yet to generate a single dollar in revenues.

The basis for 3DO's $1 billion market cap was a patented computer system architecture and a copyrighted operating system that allowed for much richer graphics and audio capabilities. The system was built around a 32-bit reduced instruction set computing (RISC) microprocessor and proprietary graphics processor chips. Instead of a cartridge, the 3DO system stored games on a CD-ROM that was capable of holding up to 600 megabytes of content, sharply up from the 10 megabytes of content found in the typical game cartridge of the time. The slower access time of a CD-ROM compared to a cartridge was alleviated somewhat by the use of a double-speed CD-ROM drive.[22]

The belief at 3DO—a belief apparently shared by many investors—was that the superior storage and graphics-processing capabilities of the 3DO system would prove very attractive to game developers, allowing them to be far more creative. In turn, better games would attract customers away from Nintendo and Sega. Developing games that used the capabilities of a CD-ROM system altered the economics of game development. Estimates suggested that it would cost approximately $2 million to produce a game for the 3DO system and could take as long as 24 months to develop. However, at $2 per disc, a CD-ROM cost substantially less to produce than a cartridge.

The centerpiece of 3DO's strategy was to license its hardware technology for free. Game developers paid a royalty of $3 per disc for access to the 3DO operating code. Discs typically retailed for $40 each.

Matsushita introduced the first 3DO machine into the United States market in October 1993. Priced at $700, the machine was sold through electronic retailers that carried Panasonic high-end electronics products. Sega's Tom Kalinsky noted, "It's a noble effort. Some people will buy 3DO, and they'll have a wonderful experience. It's impressive, but it's a niche. We've done the research. It does not become a large market until you go below $500. At $300, it starts to get interesting. We make no money on hardware. It's a cutthroat business. I hope Matsushita understands that."[23] CD-ROM discs for the 3DO machine retailed for about $75. The machine came bundled with Crash 'n' Burn, a high-speed combat racing game. However, only 18 3DO titles were available by the crucial Christmas period, although reports suggested that 150 titles were under development.[24]

Sales of the hardware were slow, reaching only 30,000 by January 1994.[25] In the same month, AT&T and Sanyo both announced that they would begin to manufacture the 3DO machine. In March, faced with continuing sluggish sales, 3DO announced that it would give hardware manufacturers two shares of 3DO stock for every unit sold at or below a certain retail price. Matsushita dropped the price of its machine to $500. About the same time, Toshiba, LG, and Samsung all announced that they would start to produce 3DO machines.

By June 1994, cumulative sales of 3DO machines in the United States stood at 40,000 units. Matsushita announced plans to expand distribution beyond the current 3,500 outlets to include the toy and mass merchandise channels. Hawkins and his partners announced that they would invest another $37 million in 3DO. By July, there were 750 3DO software licensees, but only 40 titles were available for the format. Despite these moves, sales continued at a very sluggish pace, and the supply of new software titles started to dry up.[26]

In September 1996, 3DO announced that it would either sell its hardware system business or move it into a joint venture.[27] The company announced that about 150 people, one-third of the workforce, would probably lose their jobs in the restructuring. According to Trip Hawkins, 3DO would now focus on developing software for online gaming. Hawkins stated that the Internet and Internet entertainment constituted a huge opportunity for 3DO. The stock dropped $1.375 to $6.75.

SEGA'S SATURN

3DO was not alone in moving to a CD-ROM-based format. Both Sega and Sony also introduced CD-ROM-based systems in the mid-1990s. Sega

had, in fact, beaten 3DO to the market with its November 1992 introduction of the Sega CD, a $300 CD-ROM add-on for the 16-bit Genesis. Sega sold 100,000 units in its first month alone. Sales then slowed down, however, and by December 1993 were standing at just 250,000 units. One reason for the slowdown, according to critics, was a lack of strong games. Sega was also working on a 32-bit CD-ROM system, Saturn, which was targeted for a mid-1995 introduction in the United States. In January 1994, Sega announced that Microsoft would supply the operating system for Saturn.[28]

In March 1994, Sega announced the Genesis Super 32X, a $150 add-on cartridge designed to increase the performance of Genesis cartridge and CD-ROM games. The 32X contained the 32-bit Hitachi microprocessor that was to be used in Saturn. Sega called the 32X "the poor man's 32-bit machine" because it sold for a mere $149. Introduced in the fall of 1994, the 32X never lived up to its expectations. Most users appeared willing to wait for the real thing, Sega Saturn, promised for release the following year.

In early 1995, Sega informed the press and retailers that it would release Saturn on "Sega Saturn Saturday, Sept 2nd," but Sega released the 32-bit Saturn in May 1995. It was priced at $400 per unit and accompanied by the introduction of just 10 games. Sega apparently believed that the world would be delighted by the May release of the Saturn. However, Saturn was released without the industry fanfare that normally greets a new game machine. Only four retail chains received the Saturn in May, while the rest were told they would have to wait until September. This move alienated retailers, who responded by dropping Sega products from their stores.[29] Sega appeared to have made a marketing blunder.[30]

SONY'S PLAYSTATION

In the fall of 1995, Sony entered the fray with the introduction of the Sony PlayStation.[31] PlayStation used a 32-bit RISC microprocessor running at 33 MHz and using a double-speed CD-ROM drive. PlayStation cost an estimated $500 million to develop. The machine had actually been under development since 1991, when Sony decided that the home video game industry was getting too big to ignore. Initially, Sony was in an alliance with Nintendo to develop the machine. Nintendo walked away from the alliance in 1992, however, after a disagreement over who owned the rights to any future CD-ROM games. Sony went alone.[32]

From the start, Sony felt that it could leverage its presence in the film and music business to build a strong position in the home video game industry. A consumer electronics giant with a position in the Hollywood movie business and the music industry (Sony owned Columbia Pictures and the Columbia record label), Sony believed that it had access to significant intellectual property that could form the basis of many popular games.

In 1991, Sony established a division in New York: Sony Electronic Publishing. The division was to serve as an umbrella organization for Sony's multimedia offerings. Headed by Iceland native Olaf Olafsson, then just 28 years old, this organization ultimately took the lead role in both the market launch of Play-Station and in developing game titles.[33] In 1993, as part of this effort, Sony purchased a well-respected British game developer, Psygnosis. By the fall of 1995, this unit had 20 games ready to complement PlayStation: the Haldeman Diaries, Mickey Mania (developed in collaboration with Disney), and Johnny Mnemonic, based on the William Gibson short story. To entice independent game developers such as EA, Namco, and Acclaim Entertainment, Olafsson used the promise of low royalty rates. The standard royalty rate was set at $9 per disc, although developers that signed on early enough were given a lower royalty rate. Sony also provided approximately 4,000 game development tools to licensees in an effort to help them speed games to market.[34]

To distribute PlayStation, Sony set up a retail channel separate from Sony's consumer electronics sales force. It marketed the PlayStation as a hip and powerful alternative to the outdated Nintendo and Sega cartridge-based systems. Sony worked closely with retailers before the launch to find out how it could help them sell the PlayStation. To jump-start demand, Sony set up in-store displays to allow potential consumers to try the equipment. Just before the launch, Sony had lined up an impressive 12,000 retail outlets in the United States.[35]

Sony targeted its advertising for PlayStation at males in the 18- to 35-year age range. The targeting was evident in the content of many of the games. One of the big hits for PlayStation was Tomb Raider, whose central character, Lara Croft, combined sex appeal with savvy and helped to recruit an older generation to PlayStation.[36] PlayStation was initially priced at $299, and games retailed for as much as $60. Sony's Tokyo-based executives had reportedly been insisting on a $350 to $400 price for PlaySta-tion, but Olafsson pushed hard for the lower price. Because of the fallout from this internal battle, in January 1996, Olafsson resigned from Sony. By then, however, Sony was following Olafsson's script.[37]

Sony's prelaunch work was rewarded with strong early sales. More than 800,000 PlayStations and 4 million games had been sold in the United States by January 1996. In May 1996, with 1.2 million PlayStations shipped, Sony reduced the price of PlayStation to $199. Sega responded with a similar price cut for its Saturn. The prices on some of Sony's initial games were also reduced to $29.99. The weekend after the price cuts, retailers reported that PlayStation sales were up by between 350% and 1,000% over the prior week.[38] The sales surge continued through 1996. By the end of the year, sales of PlayStation and associated software amounted to $1.3 billion, out of a total for United States sales at $2.2 billion for all video game hardware and software. In March 1997, Sony cut the price of Play-Station again, this time to $149. It also reduced its suggested retail price for games by $10 to $49.99. By this point, Sony had sold 3.4 million units of PlayStation in the United States, compared to Saturn's 1.6 million units.[39] Worldwide, PlayStation had outsold Saturn by 13 million to 7.8 million units, and Saturn sales were slowing.[40] The momentum was clearly running in Sony's favor, but the company now had a new challenge to deal with: Nintendo's latest generation game machine, the N64.

NINTENDO STRIKES BACK

In July 1996, Nintendo launched Nintendo 64 (N64) in the Japanese market. This release was followed by a late fall introduction in the United States. N64 is a 64-bit machine developed in conjunction with Silicon Graphics. Originally targeted for introduction a year earlier, N64 had been under development since 1993. The machine used a plug-in cartridge format rather than a CD-ROM drive. According to Nintendo, cartridges allow for faster access time and are far more durable than CD-ROMs (an important consideration with children).[41]

The most-striking feature of the N64 machine, however, was its 3D graphics capability. N64 provides fully rounded figures that can turn on their heels and rotate through 180 degrees. Advanced ray-tracing techniques borrowed from military simulators and engineering workstations added to the sense of realism by providing proper highlighting, reflections, and shadows.

N64 was targeted at children and young teenagers. It was priced at $200 and launched with just four games. Despite the lack of games, initial sales were very strong. Indeed, 1997 turned out to be a banner year for both Sony and Nintendo. The overall United States market was strong, with sales of hardware and software combined reaching a record $5.5 billion. Estimates suggest that PlayStation accounted for 49% of machines and games by value. N64 captured a 41% share, leaving Sega trailing badly with less than 10% of the market. During the year, the average price for game machines had fallen to $150. By year-end there were 300 titles available for PlayStation, compared to 40 for N64. Games for PlayStation retailed for $40, on average, compared to more than $60 for N64.[42]

By late 1998, PlayStation was widening its lead over N64. In the crucial North American market, PlayStation was reported to be outselling N64 by a two-to-one margin, although Nintendo retained a lead in the under-12 category. At this point, there were 115 games available for N64 versus 431 for PlayStation.[43] Worldwide, Sony had now sold close to 55 million PlayStations. The success of PlayStation had a major impact on Sony's bottom line. In fiscal 1998, PlayStation business generated revenues of $5.5 billion for Sony, 10% of its worldwide revenues, but accounted for $886 million, or 22.5%, of the company's operating income.[44]

THE 128-BIT ERA

When Nintendo launched its 64-bit machine in 1996, Sony and Sega did not follow, preferring instead to focus on the development of even more powerful 128-bit machines.

Sega was the first to market a 128-bit video game console, which it launched in Japan in late 1998 and

in the United States in late 1999. The Dreamcast came equipped with a 56-kilobit modem to allow for online gaming over the Internet. By late 2000, Sega had sold approximately 6 million Dreamcasts worldwide, accounting for about 15% of console sales since its launch. Sega nurtured Dreamcast sales by courting outside software developers who helped develop new games, including Crazy Taxi, Resident Evil, and Quake III Arena. The company had a goal of shipping 10 million units by March 2001, a goal it never reached.[45]

Despite its position as first mover with a 128-bit machine, and despite solid technical reviews, by late 2000 the company was struggling. Sega was handicapped first by product shortages due to constraints on the supply of component parts and then by a lack of demand as consumers waited to see whether Sony's 128 bit offering, the much anticipated PlayStation 2 (PS2), would be a more attractive machine. In September 2000, Sega responded to the impending United States launch of Sony's PS2 by cutting the price for its console from $199 to $149. Then in late October, Sega announced that, due to this price cut, it would probably lose more than $200 million for the fiscal year ending March 2001.[46]

Sony's PlayStation 2

PS2 was launched in Japan in mid-2000 and in the United States at the end of October 2000. Initially priced at $299, PS2 is a powerful machine. At its core was a 300-megahertz graphics processing chip that was jointly developed with Toshiba and consumed about $1.3 billion in R&D. Referred to as the Emotion Engine processor, the chip allows the machine to display stunning graphic images previously found only on supercomputers. The chip made the PS2 the most powerful video game machine yet.

The machine was set up to play different CD and DVD formats, as well as proprietary game titles. As is true with the original PlayStation, PS2 could play audio CDs. The system was also compatible with the original PlayStation: any PlayStation title could be played on the PS2. To help justify the initial price tag, the unit doubled as a DVD player with picture quality as good as current players. The PS2 did not come equipped with a modem, but it did have networking capabilities, and a modem could be attached using one of two USB ports.[47]

Nintendo GameCube

Nintendo had garnered a solid position in the industry with its N64 machine by focusing on its core demographic, 7- to 12-year-olds. In 1999, Nintendo took 33% of the hardware market and 28% of the game market. Nintendo's next generation video game machine, GameCube, packed a modem and a powerful 400-megahertz, 128-bit processor made by IBM into a compact cube. GameCube marked a shift away from Nintendo's traditional approach of using proprietary cartridges to hold game software. Instead, software for the new player came on 8-centimeter CDs, which are smaller than music CDs. The disks held 1.5 gigabytes of data each, far greater storage capacity than the old game cartridges. Players could control GameCube by using wireless controllers.[48]

Nintendo tried to make the GameCube easy for developers to work with rather than focusing on raw peak performance. While developers no doubt appreciated this, by the time GameCube hits store shelves in late 2001, PS2 had been on the market for 18 months and boasted a solid library of games. Despite its strong brand and instantly recognized intellectual property, which included Donkey Kong, Super Mario Brothers, and the Pokémon characters, Nintendo was playing catch-up to Sony. Moreover, another new entrant into the industry launched its 128 bit offering at about the same time: Microsoft.

Microsoft's Xbox

Microsoft was first rumored to be developing a video game console in late 1999. In March 2000, Bill Gates made it official when he announced that Microsoft would enter the home video game market in fall 2001 with a console code named Xbox. In terms of sheer computing power, the 128-bit Xbox had the edge over competitors. Xbox had a 733-megahertz Pentium III processor, a high-powered graphics chip from Nvidia Corp, a built-in broadband cable modem to allow for online game playing and high-speed Internet browsing, 64 megabytes of memory, CD and DVD drives, and an internal hard disk drive. The operating system was a stripped-down version of its popular Windows system optimized for graphics-processing capabilities. Microsoft claimed that because the Xbox was based on familiar PC technology, it would be much easier for software developers to write games for, and it would be relatively easy to convert games from the PC to run on the Xbox.[49]

Although Microsoft was a new entrant to the video game industry, it was no stranger to games. Microsoft had long participated in the PC gaming industry and was one of the largest publishers of PC games, with hits such as Microsoft Flight Simulator and Age of Empires I and II to its credit. Sales of Microsoft's PC games increased 50% annually between 1998 and 2001, and the company controlled about 10% of the PC game market in 2001. Microsoft also offered online gaming for some time, including its popular MSN Gaming Zone site. Started in 1996, by 2001 the Web site had become the largest online PC gaming hub on the Internet, with nearly 12 million subscribers paying $9.95 a month to play premium games, such as Asheron's Call or Fighter Ace. Nor was Microsoft new to hardware; its joysticks and game pads outsell all other brands, and it had an important mouse business.

To build the Xbox, Microsoft chose Flextronics, a contract manufacturer that already made computer mice for Microsoft. Realizing that it would probably have to cut Xbox prices over time, Microsoft guaranteed Flextronics a profit margin, effectively agreeing to subsidize Flextronics if selling prices fell below a specified amount. By 2003, Microsoft was thought to be losing $100 on every Xbox sold. To make that back and turn a profit, Microsoft reportedly had to sell between six and nine video games per Xbox.[50]

Analysts speculated that Microsoft's entry into the home video game market was a response to a potential threat from Sony. Microsoft was worried that Internet-ready consoles like PS2 might take over many Web-browsing functions from the personal computer. Some in the company described Internet-enabled video game terminals as Trojan horses in the living room. In Microsoft's calculation, it made sense to get in the market to try and keep Sony and others in check. With annual revenues in excess of $20 billion worldwide, the home video game market is huge and an important source of potential growth for Microsoft. Still, by moving away from its core market, Microsoft was taking a big risk, particularly given the scale of investments required to develop the Xbox, reported to run as high as $1.5 billion.

Mortal Combat:
Microsoft versus Sony

The launch of Xbox and GameCube helped propel sales of video game hardware and software to a record $9.4 billion in 2001, up from $6.58 billion in 2000. Although both Xbox and Nintendo initially racked up strong sales, the momentum started to slow significantly in 2002. Microsoft, in particular, found it very difficult to penetrate the Japanese market. By September 2002, Sony had sold 11.2 million units of PS2 in the United States versus 2.2 million units of Xbox and 2.7 million units of Nintendo's GameCube. Unable to hold onto market share in the wake of the new competition, Sega withdrew from the console market, announcing that, henceforth, it would focus just on developing games for other platforms.

In June 2002, Sony responded to the new entry by cutting the price for PS2 from $299 to $199. Microsoft quickly followed, cutting the price for Xbox from $299 to $199, while Nintendo cut its price from $299 to $149.[51] A year later, Sony cut prices again, this time to $179 a console. Again, Microsoft followed with a similar price cut, and in March 2004 it took the lead, cutting Xbox prices to $149. Sony followed suit two months later.[52]

Microsoft's strategy, however, involved far more than just cutting prices. In November 2002 Microsoft announced that it would introduce a new service for gamers, Xbox Live. For $50 a year, Xbox Live subscribers with broadband connections would be able to play online-enabled versions of Xbox games with other online subscribers. To support Xbox Live, Microsoft invested some $500 million in its own data centers to host online game playing.

Online game playing was clearly a strategic priority from the outset. Unlike the PS2 and GameCube, Xbox came with a built in broadband capability. The decision to make the Xbox broadband capable was made back in 1999 when less than 5% of United States homes were linked to the Internet with a broadband connection. Explaining the decision to build broadband capabilities into the Xbox at a time when rivals lacked them, the head of Xbox, Jay Allard, noted that "My attitude has always been to bet on the future, not against it."[53] While Sony's PS2 can be hooked up to the Internet via a broadband connection, doing so requires the purchase of a special network adapter for $40.

By mid-2003, Xbox Live had some 500,000 subscribers, versus 80,000 who had registered to play PS2 games online. By this time there were 28 online games for Xbox and 18 for PS2. By January 2004, the comparative figures stood at 50 for Microsoft and 32 for Sony. By mid-2004, Xbox Live reportedly had over one million subscribers, with Sony claiming a similar number of online players.[54] In May 2004, Microsoft struck a deal with EA, the world's largest video game publisher, to bring EA games, including its best selling Madden Football, to the Xbox Live platform. Until this point, EA had only produced live games for Sony's platform.

In spite of all these strategic moves, by late 2004, Xbox was still a distant second to PS2 in the video game market, having sold 14 million consoles against Sony's 70 million (Nintendo had sold 13 million GameCube consoles). While Sony was making good money from the business, Microsoft was registering significant losses. In fiscal 2004, Microsoft's home and entertainment division, of which Xbox is the major component, registered $2.45 billion in revenues, but lost $1.135 billion. By way of contrast, Sony's game division had $7.5 billion of sales in fiscal 2004 and generated operating profits of $640 million.

Microsoft, however, indicated that it was in the business for the long term. In late 2004, the company got a boost from the release of Halo 2, the sequel to Halo, one of its best-selling games. As first-day sales for Halo 2 were totaled, executives at Sony had to be worried. Microsoft announced that Halo 2 had sales of $125 million in its first 24 hours on the market in the United States and Canada, an industry record. These figures represented sales of 2.38 million units and put Halo 2 firmly on track to be one of the biggest video games ever with a shot at surpassing Nintendo's Super Mario 64, which had sold $308 million in the United States since its September 1996 debut. Moreover, the company was rumored to be ahead of Sony by as much as a year to bring the next generation video game console to market. In late 2004, reports suggested that Xbox 2 would be on the market in time for the 2005 Christmas season, probably a full year ahead of Sony's PlayStation 3 (PS3). Sony was rumored to be running into technical problems while developing the PS3.[55]

THE NEXT GENERATION

As the battle between PS2 and Xbox drew to a close, it was clear that Sony was the big winner. From 2001 through the fall of 2006, when PS3 hit the market, Sony had sold about 110 million PS2 consoles, versus 25 million for Microsoft's Xbox and 21 million for Nintendo's GameCube.[56] Sony's advantage in its installed base translated into a huge lead in number of games sold: approximately 1.08 billion for PS2 by mid-2006 versus 200 million for the Xbox.[57] With the console companies reportedly making an average royalty on third-party software of $8 per game sold, the financial implications of Sony's lead with PS2 are obvious.[58] Indeed, in 2005 Sony's games division contributed to 6.24% of the company's total revenue but 38% of operating profit. In contrast, Microsoft's home and entertainment division lost $4 billion between the launch of Xbox and mid-2006.

However, by 2006, this was all history. In November 2005, Microsoft introduced its next generation machine, Xbox 360, beating Sony and Nintendo to the market by a solid year. The Xbox 360 represented a big technological advance over the original Xbox. To deliver improved picture quality, the Xbox 360 could execute 500 million polygons per second: a four-fold increase over the Xbox. The main microprocessor was 13 times faster than the chip in the Xbox. Xbox 360 had 512 megabytes of memory, an 8-fold increase, and a 20-gigabyte hard drive, 2.5 times bigger than that found on the Xbox. Xbox 360 is, of course, enabled for a broadband connection to the Internet.

The machine was made by Flextronics and Wistron, two contract manufacturers (a third started production after launch). Priced at $299, Xbox 360 was sold at a loss. The cost for making Xbox 360 was estimated to be as high as $500 at launch, falling to $350 by late 2006. Microsoft's goal was to ultimately break even on sales of the hardware as manufacturing efficiencies drove down unit costs.

To seed the market with games, Microsoft took a number of steps. Taking a page out of its Windows business, Microsoft provided game developers with tools designed to automate many of the key software programming tasks and reduce development time and costs. The company had also expanded its own in-house game studios, in part by purchasing several independent game developers, including Bungie Studios, makers of Halo. This strategy enabled Microsoft to offer exclusive content for the Xbox 360, something that third parties were reluctant to do.

With the costs of game development increasing to between $10 and $15 million for more complex games, and development time stretching out to between 24 and 36 months, Microsoft also had to provide an inducement to get third-party developers onboard. Although details of royalty terms are kept private, it is believed that Microsoft offered very low royalty rates, and perhaps even zero royalties, for a specified period of time to game developers who committed early to Xbox 360. One of those to commit early was EA, the leading independent game development company, which reportedly budgeted as much as $200 million to develop some 25 versions of its best-selling games, such as its sports games, for Xbox 360. Microsoft budgeted a similar amount to develop its own games.[59]

In the event, some 18 games were available for the November 2005 launch of Xbox 360, and by the end of 2006, this figure had increased to about 160. Halo 3, which was expected to be one of the biggest games for Xbox 360, was released in September 2007. Exclusive to the Xbox 360, Halo 3 racked in first-day sales of $170 million, which was an industry record. Grand Theft Auto 4, the most popular franchise on PS2, was also launched simultaneously for both Xbox 360 and PS3 in 2007: a major coup for Microsoft.

The initial launch of Xbox 360 was marred by shortages of key components, which limited the number of machines that Microsoft could bring to market. Had Sony been on time with its launch of PS3, this could have been a serious error, but Sony delayed its launch of PS3, first until spring of 2006 and then November 2006. By the time Sony launched PS3 in November 2006, some 6 million Xbox 360 consoles had been sold, and Microsoft was predicting sales of 10 million by the end of 2006.

As with Xbox, Microsoft pushed Xbox Live with Xbox 360. The company invested as much as $1 billion in Live from its inception. By late 2006 Microsoft was claiming that some 60% of Xbox 360 customers had also signed on for Xbox Live and that the service had 4 million subscribers. By early 2008, there were more than 10 million subscribers. Xbox Live allowed users to play against each other online and to download digital content from Xbox Live

Marketplace. Looking forward, there is little doubt that Microsoft sees Xbox Live as a critical element of its strategy, enabling Xbox owners to download any digital content—games, film, music—onto their consoles, which could become the hub of a home digital entertainment system.

The business model for Xbox 360 depends on the number of games sold per console, the percentage of console owners who sign up for Xbox Live, sales of hardware accessories (e.g., controllers, an HD-DVD drive, wireless networking adapter), and the console itself achieving break-even production costs. Reports suggest that Microsoft will break even if each console owner buys six to seven games, two to three accessories, and some 10 million sign on to Xbox Live (Microsoft splits Xbox Live revenues with game developers). By the end of 2006, it was estimated that some 33 million games had been sold for Xbox 360.[60]

Sony finally introduced PS3 on November 11, 2006 in Japan and November 17, 2006 in the United States. The delay in the launch of PS3 was due to Sony's decision to bundle a Blu-ray drive with PS3, along with problems developing the "cell" processor that sits at the core of the PS3. Blu-ray is Sony's proprietary HD-DVD format. The company is currently locked in a format war with Toshiba, which is pushing its rival HD-DVD format (which can be purchased as an accessory for the Xbox 360). Sony has argued that the combination of its cell processor and Blu-ray DVD drive will give PS3 a substantial performance edge over Xbox 360. While this is true in a technical sense (the Blu-ray discs have five times the storage capacity of the DVD discs for Xbox 360), few reviewers have noticed much in the way of difference from a game playing perspective—perhaps because few games were initially available that showed the true power of the PS3.

What is certain is that incorporating Blu-ray drives in the PS3 has significantly raised the costs of the PS3. Sony is selling its standalone Blu-ray drives for $999, which suggests that the PS3, initially priced at between $500 and $600 depending on configuration, is in a sense a subsidized Blu-ray player. Shortages of blue diodes, a critical component in HD-DVD drives, also limited supply of the PS3 after its launch. Only 93,000 PS3 players were available for the Japanese launch. At launch, there were some 20 games available for the PS3. Sony also announced its own live offering to compete with Xbox Live and stated that it would be free to PS3 users.

Nintendo is also back in the fray. In November 2006, it launched its own next generation offering, Wii. When developing the Wii, Nintendo made a number of interesting strategic decisions. First, it decided not to compete with Microsoft and Sony on graphics processing power. Instead of developing a high-powered machine crammed full of expensive custom-built components, they used off-the-shelf components to assemble a much cheaper machine that could be sold at a much lower price point (the initial price was $250). Although this machine did not offer the graphics processing capabilities of Xbox 360 or PS3, the games were cheaper to develop, about $5 million each as opposed to as much as $20 million for the PS3. Second, Nintendo decided to target a new demographic, indifferent people who had no interest in video games, as opposed to the stereotypical game player. Nintendo already had some evidence that this market could be tapped and would be extremely lucrative. In 2004, Nintendo had introduced a game for its handheld player, the DS, that was aimed not at its core 7- to 12-year-old demographic but at much wider market. The game, Brain Age, based on a brain training regime developed by a Japanese neuroscientist, was a huge hit in Japan, with sales of more than 12 million units. It made the DS a hit in such unlikely places as nursing homes. Third, rather than processing power, Nintendo decided to focus on developing a motion sensitive, wireless controller that could detect arm and hand motions and transfer them to the screen. This enabled the development of interactive games, with players physically controlling the action on screen by moving their arms, whether by swinging an imaginary bat, driving a go-kart, or slashing a sword through the air.[61]

By early 2007, it was clear that the Wii was turning into a surprise hit. The combination of low price, innovative design, and a portfolio of recognizable games based on Nintendo's long-established franchises, such as Mario Brothers and Pokémon, helped to drive sales forward. Moreover, as planned, the Wii seemed to have appeal to a broad range of age groups and both genders. Soon articles started to appear explaining how retirement homes were buying the Wii so that residents could play virtual baseball with their visiting grandchildren, and sales started to accelerate.

Exhibit 1   Cumulative Sales of Platform Through September 2008 (millions of units)

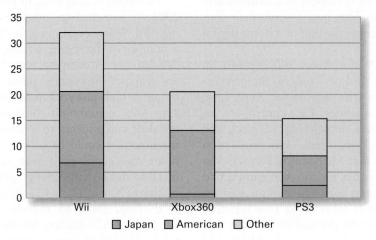

Source: Raw data from VG Chartz at http://www.vgchartz.com/.

By 2008, Nintendo had seized the leadership position in the industry (see Exhibit 1). Cumulatively, the Wii had sold some 32 million units worldwide by September 2008, compared to 20.6 million units for Xbox 360 and 15.3 million units for the PS3. Moreover, Nintendo had established a strong position in all major markets, unlike Microsoft for example, which had been unable to garner significant Xbox 360 sales in Japan. The popularity of the Wii helped to drive Nintendo's sales and earnings to record levels, with net profits forecasted to reach a record $3.78 billion for the year ending March 2009. Nintendo's market capitalization on the Japanese stock market surpassed Sony's, and in September 2008 it was second only to Toyota. It would appear that Nintendo was back.

Endnotes

1. A good account of the early history of Bushnell and Atari can be found in S. Cohen, *Zap! The Rise and Fall of Atari*, New York: McGraw-Hill, 1984.
2. R. Isaacs, "Video Games Race to Catch a Changing Market," *Business Week*, December 26, 1977, 44B.
3. P. Pagnano, "Atari's Game Plan to Overwhelm Its Competitors," *Business Week*, May 8, 1978, 50F.
4. R. Isaacs, "Video Games Race to Catch a Changing Market," *Business Week*, December 26, 1977, 44B.
5. P. Pagnano, "Atari's Game Plan to Overwhelm Its Competitors," *Business Week*, May 8, 1978, 50F; and D. Sheff, *Game Over*, New York: Random House, 1993.
6. S. Cohen, *Zap! The Rise and Fall of Atari*, New York: McGraw-Hill, 1984.
7. L. Kehoe, "Atari Seeks Way out of Video Game Woes," *Financial Times*, December 14, 1983, 23.
8. M. Schrage, "The High Tech Dinosaurs: Video Games, Once Ascendant, Are Making Way," *Washington Post*, July 31, 1983, F1.
9. D. Sheff, *Game Over*, New York: Random House, 1993.
10. Quoted in D. Sheff, *Game Over*, New York: Random House, 1993, 38.
11. D. Sheff, *Game Over*, New York: Random House, 1993.
12. D. Golden, "In Search of Princess Toadstool," *Boston Globe*, November 20, 1988, 18.
13. N. Gross, and G. Lewis, "Here Come the Super Mario Bros.," *Business Week*, November 9, 1987, 138.
14. D. Sheff, *Game Over*, New York: Random House, 1993.
15. D. Golden, "In search of Princess Toadstool," *Boston Globe*, November 20, 1988, 18.

16. Staff Reporter, "Marketer of the Year," *Adweek*, November 27, 1989, 15.

17. C. Lazzareschi, "No Mere Child's Play," *Los Angeles Times*, December 16, 1988, 1.

18. For a good summary of the early history of Sega, see J. Battle, and B. Johnstone, "The Next Level: Sega's Plans for World Domination," *Wired*, release 1.06, December 1993.

19. D. Sheff, *Game Over*, New York: Random House, 1993.

20. J. Battle, and B. Johnstone, "The Next Level: Sega's Plans for World Domination," *Wired*, release 1.06, December 1993.

21. For background details, see J. Flower, "3DO: Hip or Hype?" *Wired*, release 1.02, May/June 1993.

22. R. Brandt, "3DO's New Game Player: Awesome or another Betamax?" *Business Week*, January 11, 1993, 38.

23. J. Flower, "3DO: Hip or Hype?" *Wired*, release 1.02, May/June 1993.

24. S. Jacobs, "Third Time's a Charm (They Hope)," *Wired*, release 2.01, January 1994.

25. A. Dunkin, "Video Games: The Next Generation," *Business Week*, January 31, 1994, 80.

26. J. Greenstein, "No Clear Winners, Though Some Losers: The Video Game Industry in 1995," *Business Week*, December 22, 1995, 42.

27. Staff Reporter, "3DO Says 'I Do' on Major Shift of Its Game Strategy," *Los Angeles Times*, September 17, 1996, 2.

28. J. Battle, and B. Johnstone, "The Next Level: Sega's Plans for World Domination," *Wired*, release 1.06, December 1993.

29. J. Greenstein, "No Clear Winners, Though Some Losers: The Video Game Industry in 1995," *Business Week*, December 22, 1995, 42.

30. D. P. Hamilton, "Sega Suddenly Finds Itself Embattled," *Wall Street Journal*, March 31, 1997, A10.

31. S. Taves, "Meet Your New Playmate," *Wired*, release 3.09, September 1995.

32. Kunni, I., "The Games Sony Plays," *Business Week*, June 15, 1998, 128.

33. C. Platt, "WordNerd," *Wired*, release 3.10, October 1995.

34. I. Kunni, "The Games Sony Plays," *Business Week*, June 15, 1998, 128.

35. J. A. Trachtenberg, "Race Quits Sony Just Before U.S. Rollout of Its PlayStation Video-Game System," *Wall Street Journal*, August 8, 1995, B3.

36. S. Beenstock, "Market Raider: How Sony Won the Console Game," *Marketing*, September 10, 1998, 26.

37. J. A. Trachtenberg, "Olafsson Calls It Quits as Chairman of Sony's Technology Strategy Group," *Wall Street Journal*, January 23, 1996, B6.

38. J. Greenstein "Price Cuts Boost Saturn, PlayStation Hardware Sales," *Video Business*, May 31, 1996, 1.

39. Greenstein, J., "Sony Cuts Prices of PlayStation Hardware," *Video Business*, March 10, 1997, 1.

40. D. Hamilton, "Sega Suddenly Finds Itself Embattled," *Wall Street Journal*, March 31, 1997, A10.

41. Staff Reporter, "Nintendo Wakes Up," *The Economist*, August 3, 1996, 55–56.

42. D. Takahashi, "Game Plan: Video Game Makers See Soaring Sales Now—And Lots of Trouble Ahead," *Wall Street Journal*, June 15, 1998, R10.

43. D. Takahashi, "Sony and Nintendo Battle for Kids under 13," *Wall Street Journal*, September 24, 1998, B4.

44. I. Kunni, "The Games Sony Plays," *Business Week*, June 15, 1998, 128.

45. R. A. Guth, "Sega Cites Dreamcast Price Cuts for Loss Amid Crucial Time for Survival of Firm," *Wall Street Journal*, October 30, 2000, A22.

46. R. Guth, "Sega Cites Dreamcast Price Cuts for Loss Amid Crucial Time for Survival of Firm," *Wall Street Journal*, October 30, 2000, A22.

47. T. Oxford, and S. Steinberg, "Ultimate Game Machine Sony's PlayStation 2 Is Due on Shelves Oct. 26. It Brims with Potential—But at This Point Sega's Dreamcast Appears a Tough Competitor," *Atlanta Journal/Atlanta Constitution*, October 1, 2000, P1.

48. R. A. Guth, "New Players from Nintendo Will Link to Web," *Wall Street Journal*, August 25, 2000, B1.

49. D. Takahashi, "Microsoft's X-Box Impresses Game Developers," *Wall Street Journal*, March 13, 2000, B12.

50. K. Powers, "Showdown," *Forbes*, August 11, 2003, 86–87.

51. *The Economist*, "Console Wars," June 22, 2002, 71.

52. R. A. Guth, "Game Gambit: Microsoft to Cut Xbox Price," *Wall Street Journal*, March 19, 2004, B1.

53. K. Powers, "Showdown," *Forbes*, August 11, 2003, 86–87.

54. E. Taub, "No Longer a Solitary Pursuit: Video Games Move Online," *New York Times*, July 5, 2004, C4.

55. J. Greene and C. Edwards, "Microsoft Plays Video Leapfrog," *Business Week*, May 10, 2004, 44–45.

56. "Playing a Long Game," *The Economist*, November 18, 2006, 63–65.

57. B. Thill, "Microsoft: Gat Game? Update on Vista, Xbox and the Tender," *Citigroup Capital Markets*, August 30, 2006.

58. Ibid.

59. D. Takahashi, *The Xbox 360 Uncloaked*, Spider Works, 2006.

60. B. Thill, "Microsoft: Gat Game? Update on Vista, Xbox and the Tender," *Citigroup Capital Markets*, August 30, 2006.

61. J. M. O'Brian and C. Tkaczyk, "Wii Will Rock You," *Fortune*, June 11, 2007, 82–92.

NUCOR IN 2009

Nucor Corporation was the classic American success story, arising anew on the world stage while "old steel" gave up. But in January 2009, Daniel DiMicco, CEO of Nucor, faced challenges as great as any in Nucor's 54-year history. In December 2008, he announced earnings for the fourth quarter of 2008 would plunge and told Jim Cramer on CNBC how sales for the steel industry "went off the edge of a cliff." After three record quarters, capacity utilization fell "immediately" to 50%. The United States mortgage crisis led to a global financial meltdown that effected the growth and economic health of developed and developing economies alike. Iron ore and scrap metal prices that had soared only months before, due to the voracious hunger for infrastructure in China and India, plummeted to bargain basement prices, along with demand for steel and steel products. With the financial markets in disarray and governments globally working to bail out financial institutions and others, consumers who had spent freely on big-ticket items suddenly became risk adverse. Nucor, which had risen to be the world's 10th largest steelmaker by 2005, had dropped to the 12th largest by 2007, as it and its competitors carried out acquisitions around the world. DiMicco, who had led the company during the downs and ups of 2001 and 2005, respectively, had a big job ahead: to assess the threats and opportunities facing Nucor and select the best strategies and structure for the company as it moved further into the 21st century.

BACKGROUND

Nucor can be traced back to the company that manufactured the first Oldsmobile in 1897, known as the Reo Truck Company. As that company declined into bankruptcy in the postwar years, a 1955 merger created Nuclear Corporation of America. Following the "conglomerate" trend of the period, Nuclear acquired various high-tech businesses, such as radiation sensors, semi-conductors, rare earths, and air-conditioning equipment. However, the company lost money continually, and a fourth reorganization in 1966 put 44-year-old Ken Iverson in charge. The building of Nucor had begun.

Ken Iverson had joined the Navy after high school in 1943 and had been transferred from officer training school to Cornell's Aeronautical Engineering Program. On graduation, he selected mechanical engineering/metallurgy for a Master's degree to avoid the long drafting apprenticeship in aeronautical engineering. His college work with an electron microscope earned him a job with International Harvester. After five years in their lab, his boss and mentor prodded him to expand his vision by going with a smaller company.

Over the next 10 years, Iverson worked for four small metals companies, gaining technical knowledge and increasing his exposure to other business functions. He enjoyed working with the presidents of these small companies and admired their ability to achieve outstanding results. Nuclear Corp., after failing to buy the company Iverson worked for, hired him as a consultant to find another metals business to buy. In 1962, the firm bought a small joist plant in South Carolina that Iverson found, on the condition that he would run it.

Over the next four years, Iverson built up the Vulcraft division as Nuclear Corporation struggled. The president, David Thomas, was described as a great promoter and salesman but a weak manager. A partner with Bear Stearns actually made a personal

---

This case was prepared by Frank C. Barnes, Belk College of Business University of North Carolina–Charlotte, and Beverly B. Tyler, College of Management, North Carolina State University. Reprinted by permission of the authors.

loan to the company to keep it going. In 1966, when the company was on the edge of bankruptcy, Iverson, who headed the only successful division, was named president and moved the company's headquarters to Charlotte, North Carolina. He immediately began getting rid of the esoteric, but unprofitable, high-tech divisions and concentrated on the steel joist business he found successful. Nucor built more joist plants and, in 1968, began building its first steel mill in South Carolina to make steel cheaper than that steel purchased from importers. By 1984, Nucor had six joist plants and four steel mills, using the new "mini-mill" technology.

The original owner of Vulcraft, Sanborn Chase, was known at Vulcraft as "a scientific genius." He had been a man of great compassion who understood the atmosphere necessary for people to self-motivate. Chase, an engineer by training, invented a number of things in diverse fields. He also established the incentive programs for which Nucor later became known. With only one plant, he was able to operate in a decentralized manner. Before his death in 1960, while still in his 40s, the company was studying the building of a steel mill using newly developed mini-mill technology. His widow ran the company until it was sold to Nucor in 1962.

Dave Aycock met Ken Iverson when Nuclear purchased Vulcraft, and they worked together closely for the next year and a half. Located in Phoenix at the corporate headquarters, Aycock reported to Iverson on all the joist operations and was given the task of planning and building a new joist plant in Texas. In late 1963, he was transferred to Norfolk, where he lived for the next 13 years and managed a number of Nucor's joist plants. Then in 1977, he was named the manager of the Darlington, South Carolina, steel plant. In 1984, Aycock became Nucor's president and chief operating officer (COO), while Iverson became chairman and CEO.

Aycock had this to say about Iverson: "Ken was a very good leader, with an entrepreneurial spirit. He is easy to work with and has the courage to do things, to take lots of risks. Many things didn't work, but some worked very well." There is the old saying, "Failure to take risk is failure." This saying epitomizes a cultural value personified by the company's founder and reinforced by Iverson during his time at the helm. Nucor was very innovative in steel and joists. The plant was years ahead in wire rod welding at Norfolk. In the late 1960s, Nucor had one of the first computer inventory management systems and design/engineering programs. Nucor was sophisticated in purchasing, sales, and managing, beating out competition often by speedy design efforts.

By 1984, the bankrupt conglomerate became a leading United States steel company. It was a fairy-tale story. Tom Peters used Nucor's management style as an example of "excellence," while the barons of old steel ruled over creeping ghettos. NBC featured Nucor on television, and the *New Yorker* magazine serialized a book about how a relatively small American steel company built a team, which led the whole world into a new era of steelmaking. As the NBC program asked: "If Japan can, why can't we?" Nucor had. Iverson was rich, owning $10 million in stock but with a salary that rarely reached $1 million, compared to some United States executives whose salaries were in the range of $50 to $100 million. The 40-year-old manager of the South Carolina Vulcraft plant had become a millionaire. Stockholders chuckled, and non-unionized hourly workers, who had never seen a layoff in 20 years, earned more than the unionized workers of old steel and more than 85% of the people in the states where they worked. Many employees were financially quite secure.

Nucor owed much of its success to its benchmark organizational style and the empowered division managers. There were two basic lines of business: (1) the six steel joist plants that made the steel frames seen in many buildings and (2) the four steel mills that utilized the innovative mini-mill technology to supply the joist plants at first and, later, outside customers. In 1984, Nucor was only the seventh-largest steel company in America, but it had established the organization design, management philosophy, and incentive system, which lead to its continued success.

NUCOR'S FORMULA FOR SUCCESS, 1964–1999

In the early 1990s, Nucor's 22 divisions, one for every plant, had a general manager, who was also a vice president of the corporation. The divisions were of three basic types: joist plants, steel mills, and miscellaneous plants. The corporate staff consisted of less than 25 people. In the beginning, Iverson had chosen Charlotte "as the new home base for what he had envisioned as a small cadre of executives who would guide a decentralized operation with liberal authority delegated to managers in the field," according to *South Magazine*. The divisions did their own manufacturing, selling, accounting, engineering, and personnel management and there were only four levels from top to bottom (see Exhibit 1 for Nucor's structure in 1991).

Iverson gave his views on keeping a lean organization:

> Each division is a profit center, and the division manager has control over the day-to-day decisions that make that particular division profitable or not profitable. We expect the division to provide contribution, which is,

earnings before corporate expenses. And we expect a division to earn 25% return on total assets employed, before corporate expenses, taxes, interest, or profit sharing. And we have a saying in the company: if a manager doesn't provide that for a number of years, we are either going to get rid of the division or get rid of the general manager, and it's generally the division manager.

Nucor strengthened its position by developing strong alliances with outside parties. It did no internal research and development. Instead, Nucor monitored others' work worldwide and attracted investors who brought the company new technical applications at the earliest possible dates. Though Nucor was known for constructing new facilities at the lowest possible costs, the company's engineering

Exhibit 1   Nucor Organization Chart: Executive Management, 1991

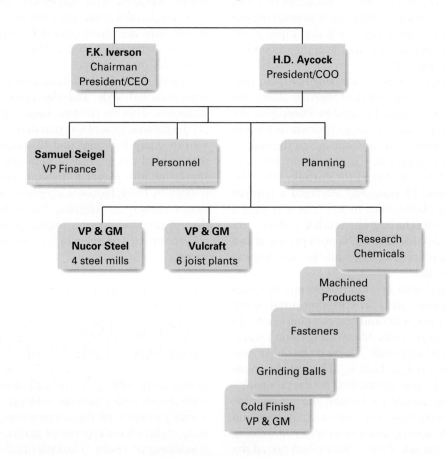

and construction team consisted of only three individuals. Nucor did not attempt to specify exact equipment parameters but asked the equipment supplier to provide this information and then held the manufacturer accountable. Nucor had alliances with selected construction companies around the country who knew the kind of work Nucor wanted. Nucor bought 95% of its scrap steel from an independent broker who followed the market and made recommendations regarding scrap purchases. Nucor did not have a corporate advertising department, a corporate public relations department, or a corporate legal or environmental department; resources outside Nucor had long-term contracts to provide these services.

The steel industry had established a pattern of absorbing the cost of shipments so, regardless of the distance from the mill, all users paid the same delivered price. Nucor broke with this tradition and stopped equalizing freight. It offered all customers the same sales terms. Nucor also gave no volume discounts, feeling that with modern computer systems there was no justification. Customers located next to the plant guaranteed themselves the lowest possible costs for steel purchases. Two tube manufacturers, two steel service centers, and a cold rolling facility had located adjacent to the Arkansas plant. These facilities accounted for 60% of the shipments from the mill. The plants were linked electronically to each other's production schedules, allowing them to function in a just-in-time inventory mode. All new mills were built on large enough tracks of land to accommodate collaborating businesses.

Iverson didn't feel greater centralization would be good for Nucor. Hamilton Lott, a Vulcraft plant manager, commented in 1997, "We're truly autonomous; we can duplicate efforts made in other parts of Nucor. We might develop the same computer program six times. But the advantages of local autonomy make it worth it." Joe Rutkowski, manager at Darlington steel, agreed. "We're not constrained; headquarters doesn't restrict what I spend. I just have to make my profit contribution at the end of year."

South Magazine observed that Iverson had established a characteristic organizational style described as "stripped down" and "no nonsense." "Jack Benny would like this company," observed Roland Underhill, an analyst with Crowell, Weedon and Co. of Los Angeles, "so would Peter Drucker." Underhill pointed out that Nucor's thriftiness does not end with its spartan office staff or modest offices. "There are no corporate perquisites," he recited. "No company planes. No country club memberships. No company cars."

Fortune noted, "Iverson takes the subway when he is in New York, a Wall Street analyst reports in a voice that suggests both admiration and amazement." The general managers reflected this style in the operation of their individual divisions. Their offices were more like plant offices or the offices of private companies built around manufacturing rather than for public appeal. They were simple, routine, and businesslike.

Division Managers

The corporate personnel manager described management relations as informal, trusting, and not bureaucratic. He felt there was a minimum of paperwork, that a phone call was more common than memos and no confirming memo was thought to be necessary.

A Vulcraft manager commented: "We have what I would call a very friendly spirit of competition from one plant to the next. And, of course, all of the vice presidents and general managers share the same bonus systems so we are in this together as a team even though we operate our divisions individually."

The divisions managed their activities with a minimum of contact with the corporate staff. Each day, disbursements were reported to corporate office. Payments flowed into regional lockboxes. On a weekly basis, joist divisions reported total quotes, sales cancellations, backlog, and production. Steel mills reported tons rolled, outside shipments, orders, cancellations, and backlog.

Each month the divisions completed a two-page (11" × 17") operations analysis that was sent to all managers. Its three main purposes were (1) financial consolidation, (2) sharing information among the divisions, and (3) corporate management examination. The summarized information and the performance statistics for all the divisions were then returned to the managers.

The general managers met three times a year. In late October, they presented preliminary budgets and capital requests. In late February, they met to finalize budgets and address miscellaneous matters. Then, at a meeting in May, they handled personnel matters, such as wage increases and changes of policies or benefits. The general managers as a group considered the raises for the department heads, the next lower level of management for all the plants.

Vulcraft: The Joist Divisions

One of Nucor's major businesses was the manufacture and sale of open web steel joists and joist girders at Vulcraft divisions located in Florence, South Carolina; Norfolk, Nebraska; Ft. Payne, Alabama; Grapeland, Texas; St. Joe, Indiana; Brigham City, Utah; and Chemung, New York. Open web joists, in contrast to solid joists, were made of steel angle iron separated by round bars or smaller angle iron (Exhibit 2). These joists cost less, were of greater strength for many applications, and were used primarily as the roof support systems in larger buildings, such as warehouses and shopping malls.

The joist industry was characterized by high competition among many manufacturers for many small customers. With an estimated 40% of the market, Nucor was the largest supplier in the United States. It utilized national advertising campaigns and prepared competitive bids on 80% to 90% of the buildings using joists. Competition was based on price and delivery performance. Nucor had developed computer programs to prepare designs for customers and compute bids based on current prices and labor standards. In addition, each Vulcraft plant maintained its own engineering department to help customers with design problems or specifications. The Florence manager commented, "Here on the East Coast, we have six or seven major competitors; of course, none of them are as large as we are." He added, "It has been said to us by some of our competitors that in this particular industry we have the finest selling organization in the country."

Nucor aggressively sought to be the lowest-cost producer in the industry. Materials and freight were two important elements of cost. Nucor maintained its own fleet of almost 150 trucks to ensure on-time delivery to all of the states, although most business was regional due to transportation costs. Plants were located in rural areas near the markets being served. Nucor's move into steel production was a move to lower the cost of steel used by the joist business.

On the basic assembly line used at the joist divisions, three or four of which might make up any one plant, about six tons of joists per hour would be assembled. In the first stage, eight people cut the angles to the right lengths or bend the round bars to the desired form. These were moved on a roller conveyer to six-man assembly stations, where the component parts would be tacked together for the next stage, welding. Drilling and miscellaneous work were done by three people between the lines. The nine-man welding station completed the welds before passing the joists on roller conveyers to two-man inspection teams. The last step before shipment was painting.

The workers had control over and responsibility for quality. There was an independent quality control inspector who had the authority to reject the run of joists and cause them to be reworked. The quality control people were not under the incentive system and reported to the engineering department.

Exhibit 2   Illustration of Joists

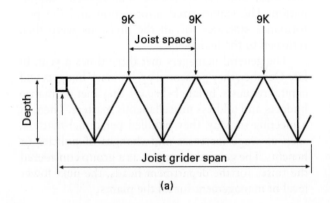

(a)

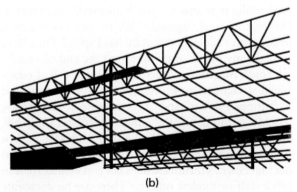

(b)

Daily production might vary widely, because each joist was made for a specific job. The wide range of joists made control of the workload at each station difficult; bottlenecks might arise anywhere along the line. Each workstation was responsible for identifying such bottlenecks so that the foreman could reassign people promptly to maintain productivity. Since workers knew most of the jobs on the line, including the more skilled welding job, they could be shifted as needed. Work on the line was described by one general manager as "not machine type but mostly physical labor." He said the important thing was to avoid bottlenecks.

There were four lines of about 28 people each on two shifts at the Florence division. The jobs on the line were rated on responsibility and assigned a base wage, from $11 to $13 per hour. In addition, a weekly bonus was paid on the total output of each line. Each worker received the same percent bonus on his base wage. The Texas plant was typical with the bonus running 225%, giving a wage of $27.00 an hour in 1999.

The amount of time required to make a joist had been established as a result of experience. As a job was bid, the cost of each joist was determined through a computer program. The time required depended on the length, number of panels, and depth of the joist. At the time of production, the labor value of production, the standard, was determined in a similar manner. The South Carolina general manager stated, "In the last nine or ten years, we have not changed a standard." The Grapeland plant maintained a time chart, which was used to estimate the labor required on a job. The plant teams were measured against this time for bonus. The chart was based on the historical time required on the jobs. The production manager at Grapeland considered himself an example for the Nucor policy—"The sky is the limit." He had started in an entry position and risen to the head of this plant of 200 people.

Steel Divisions

Nucor moved into the steel business in 1968 to provide raw material for the Vulcraft plants. Iverson said, "We got into the steel business because we wanted to build a mill that could make steel as cheaply as we were buying it from foreign importers or from offshore mills." Thus, they entered the industry using the new mini-mill technology after taking a task force of four people around the world to investigate new technological advancements. A case writer from Harvard recounted the development of the steel divisions:

> By 1967, about 60% of each Vulcraft sales dollar was spent on materials, primarily steel. Thus, the goal of keeping costs low made it imperative to obtain steel economically. In addition, in 1967, Vulcraft bought about 60% of its steel from foreign sources. As the Vulcraft Division grew, Nucor became concerned about its ability to obtain an adequate economical supply of steel and in 1968 began construction of its first steel mill in Darlington, South Carolina. By 1972, the Florence, South Carolina, joist plant was purchasing over 90% of its steel from this mill. The Fort Payne, Alabama, plant bought about 50% of its steel from Florence. Since the mill had excess capacity, Nucor began to market its steel products to outside customers. In 1972, 75% of the shipments of Nucor steel was to Vulcraft and 25% was to other customers.

Between 1973 and 1981, Nucor constructed three more bar mills and their accompanying rolling mills to convert the billets into bars, flats, rounds, channels, and other products. Iverson explained in 1984:

> In constructing these mills, we experimented with new processes and new manufacturing techniques. We serve as our own general contractor and design and build much of our own equipment. In one or more of our mills, we have built our own continuous casting unit, reheat furnaces, cooling beds, and, in Utah, even our own mill stands. All of these to date have cost under $125 per ton of annual capacity—compared with projected costs for large integrated mills of $1,200–1,500 per ton of annual capacity, ten times our cost. Our mills have high productivity. We currently use less than four man hours to produce a ton of steel. Our total employment costs are less than $60 per ton compared with the average employment costs of the seven largest U.S. steel companies of close to $130 per ton. Our total labor costs are less than 20% of our sales price.

In 1987, Nucor was the first steel company in the world to begin to build a mini-mill to manufacture steel sheets, the raw material for the auto industry and other major manufacturers. This project opened up another 50% of the total steel market. The first plant in Crawfordsville, Indiana, was successful, and three additional sheet mills were constructed between 1989 and 1990. Through the years, these steel plants were significantly modernized and expanded until the total capacity was three million tons per year at a capital cost of less than $170 per ton by 1999. Nucor's total steel production capacity was 5.9 million tons per year at a cost of $300 per ton of annual capacity. The eight mills sold 80% of their output to outside customers and the balance to other Nucor divisions.

The Steel Making Process

A steel mill's work is divided into two phases: preparation of steel of the proper "chemistry" and the forming of steel into the desired products. The typical mini mill utilized scrap steel, such as junk auto parts, instead of the iron ore, which would be used in larger, integrated steel mills. The typical bar mini-mill had an annual capacity of 200,000 to 600,000 tons, compared with the 7 million tons of Bethlehem Steel's Sparrow's Point, Maryland, integrated plant.

In bar mills, a charging bucket fed loads of scrap steel into electric arc furnaces. The melted load, called a heat, was poured into a ladle to be carried by an overhead crane to the casting machine. In the casting machine, the liquid steel was extruded as a continuous red-hot solid bar of steel and cut into lengths weighing some 900 pounds called "billets." In the typical plant the billet, about four inches in cross-section and about 20 feet long, was held temporarily in a pit, where it cooled to normal temperatures. Periodically, billets were carried to the rolling mill and placed in a reheat oven to bring them up to 2,000°F; at this temperature they would be malleable. In the rolling mill, presses and dies progressively converted the billet into the desired round bars, angles, channels, flats, and other products. After cutting to standard lengths, they were moved to the warehouse.

Nucor's first steel mill, which employed more than 500 people, was located in Darlington, South Carolina. The mill, with its three electric arc furnaces, operated 24 hours per day, 5.5 days per week. Nucor had made a number of improvements in the melting and casting operations. Thus, less time and lower capital investment were required at Darlington than other mini-mills at the time of its construction. The casting machines were "continuous casters," as opposed to the old batch method. All research projects had not been successful. The company spent approximately $2,000,000 in an unsuccessful effort to utilize resistance-heating. They lost even more on an effort at induction melting. As Iverson told *Metal Producing*, "That costs us a lot of money. Time wise it was very expensive. But you have got to make mistakes and we've had lots of failures." The Darlington design became the basis for plants in Nebraska, Texas, and Utah. The Texas plant had costs under $80 per ton of annual capacity. Whereas the typical mini-mill at the time cost approximately $250 per ton, the average cost of Nucor's four mills was under $135. An integrated mill was expected to cost between $1,200 and $1,500 per ton.

The Darlington plant was organized into 12 natural groups for the purpose of incentive pay. Two mills each had two shifts with three groups: melting and casting, rolling mill, and finishing. In melting and casting, there were three or four different standards, depending on the material, established by the department manager years ago based on historical performance. The general manager stated, "We don't change the standards." The caster, key to the operation, was used at a 92% level—one greater than the claims of the manufacturer. For every good ton of billet above the standard hourly rate for the week, workers in the group received 4% bonuses. Workers received 4% to 6% bonuses for every good ton sheared per hour for the week over the computed standard. A manager stated "Melt shop employees don't ask me how much it costs Chaparral or LTV to make a billet. They want to know what it costs Darlington, Norfolk, Jewitt to put a billet on the ground—scrap costs, alloy costs, electrical costs, refractory, gas, etc. Everybody from Charlotte to Plymouth watches the nickels and dimes."

Management Philosophy

Aycock, while still the Darlington manager, stated:

> The key to making a profit when selling a product with no aesthetic value, or a product that you really can't differentiate from your competitors, is cost. I don't look at us as a fantastic marketing organization, even though I think we are pretty good; but we don't try to overcome unreasonable costs by mass marketing. We maintain low costs by keeping the employee

force at the level it should be, not doing things that aren't necessary to achieve our goals, and allowing people to function on their own and by judging them on their results.

To keep a cooperative and productive workforce you need, number one, to be completely honest about everything; number two, to allow each employee as much as possible to make decisions about that employee's work, to find easier and more productive ways to perform duties; and number three, to be as fair as possible to all employees. Most of the changes we make in work procedures and in equipment come from the employees. They really know the problems of their jobs better than anyone else.

To communicate with my employees, I try to spend time in the plant and at intervals have meetings with the employees. Usually if they have a question, they just visit me. Recently a small group visited me in my office to discuss our vacation policy. They had some suggestions and, after listening to them, I had to agree that the ideas were good.

In discussing his philosophy for dealing with the workforce, the Florence manager stated:

I believe very strongly in the incentive system we have. We are a non-union shop, and we all feel that the way to stay so is to take care of our people and show them we care. I think that's easily done because of our fewer layers of management. . . . I spend a good part of my time in the plant, maybe an hour or so a day. If a man wants to know anything, for example an insurance question, I'm there, and they walk right up to me and ask me questions, which I'll answer the best I know how.

We don't lay our people off and we make a point of telling our people this. In the slowdown of 1994, we scheduled our line for four days, but the men were allowed to come in the fifth day for maintenance work at base pay. The men in the plant on an average running bonus might make $17 to $19 an hour. If their base pay is half that, on Friday they would only get $8–$9 an hour. Surprisingly, many of the men did not want to come in on Friday. They felt comfortable with just working four days a week. They are happy to have that extra day off." About 20% of the people took the 5th day

at base rate, but still no one had been laid off, in an industry with a strong business cycle.

In an earlier business cycle, the executive committee decided in view of economic conditions that a pay freeze was necessary. The employees normally received an increase in their base pay the first of June. The decision was made at that time to freeze wages. The officers of the company, as a show of good faith, accepted a 5% pay cut. In addition to announcing this to the workers with a stuffer in their pay envelopes, meetings were held. Each production line, or incentive group of workers, met in the plant conference room with all supervision: foremen, plant production managers, and division managers. The economic crisis that the company was facing was explained to the employees by the production managers, and all of their questions were answered.

The Personnel Policies

The foremost characteristic of Nucor's personnel system was its incentive plan. Another major personnel policy was providing job security. Also, all employees at Nucor received the same fringe benefits. There was only one group insurance plan. Holidays and vacations did not differ by job. Every child of every Nucor employee received up to $1,200 a year for four years if they chose to go on to higher education, including technical schools. The company had no executive dining rooms or restrooms, no fishing lodges, company cars, or reserved parking places.

Jim Coblin, Nucor's vice president of Human Resources, described Nucor's systems for *HRMagazine* in a 1994 article, "No-frills HR at Nucor: a lean, bottom-line approach at this steel company empowers employees." Coblin, as benefits administrator, received part-time help from one of the corporate secretaries in the corporate office. The plants typically used someone from their finance department to handle compensation issues, although two plants had personnel generalists. Nucor plants did not have job descriptions, finding they caused more problems than they solved, given the flexible workforce and non-union status of Nucor employees. Surprisingly, Coblin found performance appraisal a waste of time. If an employee was not performing well, the problem was dealt with directly. The key, he believed, was not to put a maximum on what an employee could earn and pay them directly for productivity. Iverson firmly believed that the bonus should be direct and involve no discretion on part of a manager.

Employees were kept informed about the company. Charts showing the division's results in return-on-assets and bonus payoff were posted in prominent places in the plant. The personnel manager commented that as he traveled around to all the plants, he found everyone in the company could tell him the level of profits in their division. The general managers held dinners at least once but usually twice a year with each of their employees. The dinners were held with 50 or 60 employees at a time, resulting in as many as 20 dinners per year. After introductory remarks, the floor was open for discussion of any work-related problems. There was a new employee orientation program and an employee handbook that contained personnel policies and rules. The corporate office sends all news releases to each division, where they were posted on bulletin boards. Each employee in the company also received a copy of the annual report. For the last several years, the cover of the annual report contained the names of all Nucor employees.

Absenteeism and tardiness was not a problem at Nucor. Each employee had four days of absences before pay was reduced. In addition to these, missing work was allowed for jury duty, military leave, or the death of close relatives. After this, a day's absence cost them bonus pay for that week and lateness of more than a half-hour meant the loss of bonus for that day.

Safety was a concern of Nucor's critics. With 10 fatalities in the 1980s, Nucor was committed to doing better. Safety administrators had been appointed in each plant, and safety had improved in the 1990s. The company also had a formal grievance procedure, although the Darlington manager could not recall the last grievance he had processed.

The average hourly worker's pay was more than twice the average earnings paid by other manufacturing companies in the states where Nucor's plants were located. In many rural communities where Nucor was located, the company provided better wages than most other manufacturers. The new plant in Hertford County (North Carolina) illustrated this point as reported in a June 21, 1998, article in the *Charlotte Observer*, entitled "Hope on the Horizon: In Hertford County, Poverty Reigns and Jobs Are Scarce." In this article, the author wrote, "In North Carolina's forgotten northeastern corner, where poverty rates run more than twice the state average, Nucor's $300 million steel mill is a dream realized." The plant on the banks of the Chowan River in North Carolina's banks coastal district would have their employees earning a rumored $60,000 a year, three times the local average manufacturing wage upon completion. Nucor had recently begun developing its plant sites with the expectation of other companies co-locating to save shipping costs. Four companies announced plans to locate close to Nucor's property, adding another 100 to 200 jobs. People could not believe such wages, but calls to the plant's chief financial officer (CFO) were confirmed. "We don't like to promise too much, but $60,000 might be a little low." The average wage for the jobs at Darlington was $70,000. The plant's CFO added that Nucor did not try to set pay "a buck over Walmart" but went for the best workers. The article noted that steel work is hot and often dangerous, and turnover at the plant may be high as people adjust to this and Nucor's hard-driving team system. He added, "Slackers don't last." The state of North Carolina had given $155 million in tax credits over 25 years. The local preacher said "In 15 years, Baron (a local child) will be making $75,000 a year at Nucor, not in jail. I have a place now I can hold in front of him and say 'Look, right here. This is for you.'"

The Incentive System

There were four incentive programs at Nucor, one each for production workers; department heads; staff people, such as accountants, secretaries, or engineers; and senior management, which included the division managers (Managers of each division). All of these programs were based on group performance.

Within the production program, groups ranged in size from 25 to 30 people and had definable and measurable operations. The company believed that a program should be simple, and that bonuses should be paid promptly. "We don't have any discretionary bonuses—zero. It is all based on performance. Now we don't want anyone to sit in judgment, because it never is fair," said Iverson. The personnel manager stated: "Their bonus is based on roughly 90% of historical time it takes to make a particular joist. If during a week they make joists at 60% less than the standard time, they receive a 60% bonus." This was paid with the regular pay the following week. The complete paycheck amount, including overtime, was multiplied by the bonus factor. A bonus was not paid when equipment was not operating: "We have the philosophy that when equipment is not operating, everybody suffers, and the bonus for downtime is zero." The foremen were also part of the group and received the same bonus as the employees they supervised.

The second incentive program was for department heads in the various divisions. The incentive pay for them was based on division contribution, defined as the division earnings before corporate expenses and profit sharing are determined. Bonuses were reported to run between 0 and 90% (average 35%–50%) of a person's base salary. The base salaries at this level were set at 75% of industry norms.

There was a third plan for people who were not production workers, department managers, or senior managers. Their bonus was based on either the division return-on-assets or the corporate return-on-assets depending on the unit they were a part of. Bonuses were typically 30% or more of a person's base salary for corporate positions.

The fourth program was for the senior officers. The senior officers had no employment contracts, pension or retirement plans, or other perquisites. Their base salaries were set at about 75% of what an individual doing similar work in other companies would receive. Once return-on-equity reached 9%, slightly below the average for manufacturing firms, 5% of net earnings before taxes went into a pool, which was divided among the officers based on their salaries. "Now if return-on-equity for the company reaches, say 20%, which it has, then we can wind up with as much as 190% of our base salaries and 115% on top of that in stock. We get both." Half the bonus was paid in cash and half was deferred. Individual bonuses ranged from zero to several hundred percent, averaging 75% to 150%.

However, the opposite was true as well. In 1982, the return was 8%, and the executives received no bonus. Iverson's pay in 1981 was approximately $300,000 but dropped the next year to $110,000. "I think that ranked by total compensation I was the lowest paid CEO in the Fortune 500. I was kind of proud of that, too." In his 1997 book, *Plain Talk: Lessons from a Business Maverick*, Iverson said, "Can management expect employees to be loyal if we lay them all off at every dip of the economy, while we go on padding our own pockets?" Even so by 1986, Iverson's stock was worth over $10 million dollars, and the once Vulcraft manager was a millionaire.

In lieu of a retirement plan, the company had a profit-sharing plan with a deferred trust. Each year 10% of pretax earnings was put into profit sharing for all people below officer level. Twenty percent of this was set aside to be paid to employees in the following March as a cash bonus, and the remainder was put into trust for each employee on the basis of the percent of their earnings as a percent of total wages paid within the corporation. The employee was vested after the first year. Employees received a quarterly statement of their balance in profit sharing.

The company had an Employer Monthly Stock Investment Plan to which Nucor added 10% to the amount the employee contributed on the purchase of any Nucor stock and paid the commission. After each five years of service with the company, the employee received a service award consisting of five shares of Nucor stock. Moreover, if profits were good, extraordinary bonus payments would be made to the employees. For example, in December 1998, each employee received an $800 payment. According to Iverson:

> I think the first obligation of the company is to the stockholder and its employees. I find in this country too many cases where employees are underpaid, and corporate management is making huge social donations for self-fulfillment. We regularly give donations, but we have a very interesting corporate policy. First, we give donations where our employees are. Second, we give donations that will benefit our employees, such as to the YMCA. It is a difficult area, and it requires a lot of thought. There is certainly a strong social responsibility for a company, but it cannot be at the expense of the employees or the stockholders.

Having welcomed a parade of visitors over the years, Iverson had become concerned with the pattern apparent at other companies' steel plants: "They only do one or two of the things we do. It's not just incentives or the scholarship program; its all those things put together that results in a unified philosophy for the company."

Building on Their Success

Throughout the 1980s and 1990s, Nucor continued to take the initiative and be the prime mover in steel and the industries vertically related to steel. For example, in 1984, Nucor broke with the industry pattern of basing the price of an order of steel on the quantity ordered. Iverson noted, "Some time ago we began to realize that with computer order entry and billing, the extra charge for smaller orders was not cost justified." In a seemingly risky move in 1986, Nucor began construction of a $25 million plant in Indiana to manufacture steel fasteners. Imports had grown to 90% of this market as United States companies failed to compete. Iverson said, "We're going to bring that business back; we can make bolts as cheaply as foreign producers." A second plant, in 1995, gave Nucor 20% of the United States market for steel fasteners. Nucor also acquired a steel bearings manufacturer in 1986, which Iverson called "a good fit with our business, our policies, and our people."

In early 1986, Iverson announced plans for a revolutionary plant at Crawfordsville, Indiana, which would be the first mini-mill in the world to manufacture flat-rolled or sheet steel, the last bastion of the integrated manufacturers. This market alone was twice the size of the existing market for mini-mill products. It would be a quarter-of-a-billion dollar gamble on a new technology. The plant was expected to halve the integrated manufacturer's $3 of labor per ton and save $50–$75 on a $400-per-ton selling price. If it worked, the profit from this plant alone would come close to the profit of the whole corporation. *Forbes* commented, "If any mini-mill can meet the challenge, it's Nucor. But expect the going to be tougher this time around." If successful, Nucor had the licensing rights to the next two plants built in the world with this technology. Nucor had spent millions trying to develop the process when it heard of some promising developments at a German company. In the spring of 1986, Aycock flew to Germany to see the pilot machine at SMS Schloemann-Siemag AG. In December, the Germans came to Charlotte for the first of what they thought would be many meetings to hammer out a deal with Nucor. Iverson shocked them when he announced Nucor was ready to proceed to build the first plant of its kind.

Keith Busse was given the job of building the Crawfordsville, Indiana, steel sheet plant. The process of bringing this plant online was so exciting it became the basis for a best-selling book by Robert Preston, which was serialized in the *New Yorker* magazine. Preston reported on a conversation at dinner during construction between Iverson and Busse. Thinking about the future, Busse worried that Nucor might someday become like Big Steel. He asked, "How do we allow Nucor to grow without expanding the bureaucracy?" He commented on the vice presidents stacked on vice presidents, research departments, assistants to assistants, and so on. Iverson agreed. Busse seriously suggested, "Maybe we're going to need group vice presidents." Iverson's heated response was, "Do you want to ruin the company? That's the old Harvard Business School thinking. They would only get in the way, slow us down." He said the company could at least double, to $2 billion, before it added a new level of management. "I hope that by the time we have group vice presidents, I'll be collecting Social Security."

The gamble on the new plant paid off, and Busse, the general manager of the plant, became a key man within Nucor. The new mill began operations in August 1989 and reached 15% of capacity by the end of the year. In June 1990, it had its first profitable month, and Nucor announced the construction of a second plant in Arkansas.

The supply and cost of scrap steel to feed the mini-mills was an important future concern to Iverson. So at the beginning of 1993, Nucor announced the construction of plant in Trinidad to supply its mills with iron carbide pellets. The innovative plant would cost $60 million and take a year and a half to complete. In 1994, the two existing sheet mills were expanded, and a new $500 million, 1.8 million ton sheet mill in South Carolina was announced, to begin operation in early 1997.

In what the *New York Times* called Nucor's "most ambitious project yet," in 1987, Nucor began a joint venture with Yamato Kogyo, Ltd., to make structural steel products in a mill on the Mississippi River in direct challenge to the Big Three integrated steel companies. He put John Correnti in charge of the operation. Correnti built and then became the general manager of Nucor-Yamato when it started up in 1988. In 1991, he surprised many people by deciding to double Nucor-Yamato's capacity by 1994. It became Nucor's largest division and the largest wide flange producer in the United States. By 1995, Bethlehem Steel was the only other wide flange producer of structural steel products left and had plans to leave the business.

Nucor started up its first facility to produce metal buildings in 1987. A second metal buildings facility began operations in late 1996 in South Carolina, and a new steel deck facility, in Alabama, was announced for 1997. At the end of 1997, the Arkansas sheet mill was undergoing a $120 million expansion to include a galvanizing facility.

In 1995, Nucor became involved in its first international venture, an ambitious project with

Brazil's Companhia Siderurgica National to build a $700 million steel mill in the state of Ceara. While other mini-mills were cutting deals to buy and sell abroad, Nucor was planning to ship iron from Brazil and process it in Trinidad.

Nucor set records for sales and net earnings in 1997. In the spring of 1998, as Iverson approached his 73rd birthday, he commented, "People ask me when I'm going to retire. I tell them our mandatory retirement age is 95, but I may change that when I get there." It surprised the world when, in October 1998, Ken Iverson left the board. He retired as chairman at the end the year. Although sales for 1998 decreased 1% and net earnings were down 10%, management made a number of long-term investments and closed draining investments. Start-up began at the new South Carolina steam mill and at the Arkansas sheet mill expansion. The plans for a North Carolina steel plate mill in Hertford were announced. This would bring Nucor's total steel production capacity to 12 million tons per year. Moreover, the plant in Trinidad, which had proven much more expensive than was originally expected, was deemed unsuccessful and closed. Finally, directors approved the repurchase of up to 5 million shares of Nucor stock.

Still, the downward trends at Nucor continued. Sales and earnings were down 3% and 7%, respectively, for 1999. However, these trends did not seem to affect the company's investments. Expansion was underway in the steel mills, and a third building systems facility was under construction in Texas. Nucor was actively searching for a site for a joist plant in the Northeast. A letter of intent was signed with Australian and Japanese companies to form a joint venture to commercialize the strip casting technology. To understand the challenges facing Nucor, industry, technology, and environmental trends in the 1980s and 1990s need to be considered.

EVOLUTION OF THE U.S. STEEL INDUSTRY

The early 1980s had been the worst years in decades for the steel industry (AISI). Data from the American Iron and Steel Institute showed shipments falling from 100 million tons in 1979 to the mid-80 levels in 1980 and 1981. A slackening in the economy, particularly in auto sales, led to the decline. In 1986, when industry capacity was at 130 million tons, the outlook was for a continued decline in per-capita consumption and movement toward capacity in the range of 90–100 million tons. The chairman of Armco saw "millions of tons chasing a market that's not there; excess capacity that must be eliminated."

The large, integrated steel firms, such as U.S. Steel and Armco, which made up the major part of the industry, were the hardest hit. The *Wall Street Journal* stated, "The decline has resulted from such problems as high labor and energy costs in mining and processing iron ore, a lack of profits and capital to modernize plants, and conservative management that has hesitated to take risks." These companies produced a wide range of steels, primarily from ore processed in blast furnaces and found it difficult to compete with imports, usually from Japan, giving up market share to imports. Thus, these companies sought the protection of import quotas.

Imported steel accounted for 20% of the United States steel consumption, up from 12% in the early 1970s. The United States share of world production of raw steel declined from 19% to 14% over the period. *Iron Age* stated that exports, as a percentage of shipments in 1985, were 34% for Nippon, 26% for British Steel, 30% for Krupp, 49% for Usinor SA of France, and less than 1% for every American producer on the list. The consensus of steel experts was that imports would average 23% of the market in the last half of the 1980s.

By the mid-1980s, the integrated mills were moving fast to get back into the game: they were restructuring, cutting capacity, dropping unprofitable lines, focusing products, and trying to become responsive to the market. The industry made a pronounced move toward segmentation. Integrated producers focused on mostly flat-rolled and structural grades, reorganized steel companies focused on a limited range of products, mini-mills dominated the bar and light structural product areas, and specialty steel firms sought niches. There was an accelerated shutdown of older plants, an elimination of products by some firms, and the installation of new product lines with new technologies by others.

The road for the integrated mills was not easy. As *Purchasing* pointed out, tax laws and accounting rules slowed the closing of inefficient plants. Shutting down a 10,000-person plant could require a firm to hold a cash reserve of $100 million to fund health, pension, and insurance liabilities. The chairman of

Armco commented: "Liabilities associated with a planned shutdown are so large that they can quickly devastate a company's balance sheet."

Joint ventures had arisen to produce steel for a specific market or region. The chairman of USX called them "an important new wrinkle in steel's fight for survival" and stated, "If there had been more joint ventures like these two decades ago, the U.S. steel industry might have built only half of the dozen or so hot-strip mills it put up in that time and avoided today's overcapacity."

The AISI reported steel production in 1988 of 99.3 million tons, up from 89.2 million tons in 1987, and the highest in seven years. As a result of modernization programs, 60.9% of production was from continuous casters. Exports for steel increased and imports fell. Some steel experts believed that the United States was now cost competitive with Japan. However, 1989 proved to be a year of "waiting for the other shoe to drop," according to *Metal Center News*. United States steel production was hampered by a new recession, the expiration of the voluntary import restraints, and labor negotiations in several companies. Declines in car production and consumer goods hit flat-rolled companies hard. AUJ Consultants told MCN, "The U.S. steel market has peaked. Steel consumption is tending down. By 1990, we expect total domestic demand to dip under 90 million tons."

The economic slowdown of the early 1990s led to a decline in the demand for steel through early 1993, but by 1995 America was in its best steel market in 20 years, and many companies were building new flat-roll mini-mills. A *Business Week* article at the time described it as "the race of the Nucor look-alikes." Six years after Nucor pioneered the low-cost German technology in Crawfordsville, Indiana, the competition was finally gearing up to compete. Ten new projects were expected to add 20 million tons per year of flat-rolled steel, raising United States capacity by as much as 40% by 1998. These mills opened in 1997 just as the industry was expected to move into a cyclical slump. It was no surprise that worldwide competition increased and companies that had previously focused on their home markets began a race to become global powerhouses. The foreign push was new for United States firms that had focused on defending their home markets. United States mini-mills focused their international expansion primarily in Asia and South America.

Meanwhile in 1994, U.S. Steel, North America's largest integrated steel producer, began a major business process re-engineering project to improve order fulfillment performance and customer satisfaction on the heels of a decade of restructuring. According to *Steel Times International*:

> U.S. Steel had to completely change the way it did business. Cutting labor costs and increasing reliability and productivity took the company a long way toward improving profitability and competitiveness. However, it became clear that this leaner organization still had to implement new technologies and business processes if it was to maintain a competitive advantage.

The goals of the business process reengineering project included a sharp reduction in cycle time, greatly decreased levels of inventory, shorter order lead times, and the ability to offer real-time promise dates to customers. In 1995, they successfully installed integrated planning/production/order fulfillment software, and the results were very positive. U.S. Steel believed that the reengineering project had positioned it for a future of increased competition, tighter markets, and raised customer expectations.

In late 1997 and again in 1998, the decline in demand prompted Nucor and other United States companies to slash prices to compete with the unprecedented surge of imports. By the last quarter of 1998, these imports had led to the filing of unfair trade complaints with United States trade regulators, causing steel prices in the spot market to drop sharply in August and September before they stabilized. A press release by the U.S. Secretary of Commerce, William Daley, stated, "I will not stand by and allow U.S. workers, communities, and companies to bear the brunt of other nations' problematic policies and practices. We are the most open economy of the world. But we are not the world's dumpster."

The Commerce Department concluded in March 1999 that six countries had illegally dumped stainless steel in the United States at prices below production costs or home market prices. The Commerce Department found that Canada, South Korea, and Taiwan were guilty of dumping only, while Belgium, Italy, and South Africa also gave producers unfair subsidies that effectively lowered prices. However, on June 23, 1999, the *Wall Street Journal* reported that the Senate decisively shut off an attempt to restrict United States imports of steel despite industry complaints that a flood of cheap imports were driving them out of business. Advisors of President Clinton were reported to have said the President would likely veto the bill if it passed. Administrative officials opposed the bill because it would violate international trade law and leave the United States open to retaliation.

The AISI reported that in May 1999, United States steel mills shipped 8,330,000 net tons, a decrease of 6.7% from the 8,927,000 net tons shipped in May 1998. They also stated that for the first five months of 1999, shipments were 41,205,000 net tons, down 10% from the same period in 1998. AISI President and CEO, Andrew Sharkey, III, said, "Once again, the May data show clearly that America's steel trade crisis continues. U.S. steel companies and employees continue to be injured by high levels of dumping and subsidized imports. . . . In addition, steel inventory levels remain excessive, and steel operating rates continue to be very low."

As the 1990s ended, Nucor was the second-largest steel producer in the United States, behind USX. The company's market capitalization was about two times that of the next smaller competitor. Even in a tight industry, someone can win. Nucor was in the best position because the industry was very fragmented, and there were many marginal competitors.

Steel Technology and the Mini-Mill

A new type of mill, the mini-mill, had emerged in the United States during the 1970s to compete with the integrated mill. The mini-mill initally used electric arc furnaces to manufacture a narrow product line from scrap steel. The leading United States mini-mills in the 1980s were Nucor, Florida Steel, Georgetown Steel, North Star Steel, and Chaparral. Between the late 1970s and 1980s, the integrated mills' market share fell from about 90% to about 60%, with the integrated steel companies averaging a 7% return on equity, the mini mills averaging 14%, with some—such as Nucor—achieving about 25%. In the 1990s, the integrated mills, market share fell to about 40%, while mini-mills, share rose to 23%; reconstructed mills increased their share from 11% to 28%, and specialized mills increased their share from 1% to 6%.

Some experts believed that a relatively new technology, the twin shell electric arc furnace, would help mini-mills increase production and lower costs

and take market share. According to the *Pittsburgh Business Times*, "With a twin shell furnace, one shell—the chamber holding the scrap to be melted—is filled and heated. During the heating of the first shell, the second shell is filled. When the heating is finished on the first shell, the electrodes move to the second. The first shell is emptied and refilled before the second gets hot." This increased production by 60%. Twin shell production had been widely adopted in the last few years. For example, Nucor began running a twin shell furnace in November 1996 in Berkeley, South Carolina, and installed another in Norfolk, Nebraska, which began operations in 1997. "Everyone accepts twin shells as a good concept because there's a lot of flexibility of operation," said Rodney Mott, vice president and general manager of Nucor-Berkeley. However, this move toward twin shell furnaces could mean trouble in the area of scrap availability. According to an October 1997 quote in *Pittsburgh Business Times* by Ralph Smaller, vice president of process technology at Kvaerner, "Innovations that feed the electric furnaces' production of flat-rolled (steel) will increase the demand on high quality scrap and alternatives. The technological changes are just beginning and will accelerate over the next few years."

According to a September 1997 *Industry Week* article, steelmakers around the world were now closely monitoring the development of continuous "strip casting" technology, which may prove to be the next leap forward for the industry. "The objective of strip casting is to produce thin strips of steel (in the 1 millimeter to 4 millimeter range) as liquid steel flows from a tundish: the stationary vessel that received molten steel from the ladle. It would eliminate the slab-casting stage and all of the rolling that now takes place in a hot mill." Strip casting was reported to have some difficult technological challenges, but companies in Germany, France, Japan, Australia, Italy, and Canada had strip-casting projects underway. In fact, all of the significant development work in strip casting was taking place outside the United States.

Larry Kavanaph, AISI vice president for manufacturing and technology, said, "Steel is a very high-tech industry, but nobody knows it." Today's most-productive steelmaking facilities incorporate advanced metallurgical practices, sophisticated process-control sensors, state-of-the-art computer controls, and the latest refinements in continuous casting and rolling mill technology. Michael Shot, vice president of manufacturing at Carpenter Technology Corp., Reading, Pennsylvania, a specialty steels and premium-grade alloys company, said, "You don't survive in this industry unless you have the technology to make the best products in the world in the most efficient manner."

Environmental and Political Issues

Not all stakeholders were happy with the way Nucor did business. In June, 1998 *Waste News* reported that Nucor's mill in Crawfordsville, Indiana, was cited by the United State Environmental Protection Agency for alleged violations of federal and state clean-air rules. The Pamlico-Tar River Foundation, the North Carolina Coastal Federation, and the Environmental Defense Fund had concerns about the state's decision to allow the company to start building the plant before the environmental review were completed. According to the *News & Observer* Web site, "The environmental groups charge that the mill will discharge 6,720 tons of pollutants into the air each year."

Moreover, there were other concerns about the fast-track approval of the facility being built in Hertford County. First, this plant was located on the banks of one of the most important and sensitive stretches of the Chowan, a principal tributary to the national treasure Albemarle Sound and the last bastion of the state's once-vibrant river-herring fishery. North Carolina passed a law in 1997 that required the restoration of this fishery through a combination of measures designed to prevent over-fishing, restore spawning and nursery habitats, and improve water quality in the Chowan. "New federal law requires extra care in protecting essential habitat for the herring, which spawn upstream," according to an article in the *Business Journal*. Also, there were concerns regarding the excessive incentives the state gave to convince Nucor to build a $300 million steel mill in North Carolina. Some questioned whether the promise of 300 well-paying jobs in Hertford County was worth the $155 million in tax breaks the state was giving Nucor to locate here.

Management Evolution

Only five, not six, members of the board were in attendance during the board of directors meeting in the fall of 1998, due to the death of Jim Cunningham.

Near its end, Aycock read a motion, drafted by Siegel, that Ken Iverson be removed as chairman. It was seconded by Hlavacek and passed. It was announced in October that Iverson would be a chairman emeritus and a director, but after disagreements, Iverson left the company completely. It was agreed Iverson would receive $500,000 a year for five years. Aycock left retirement to become chairman.

The details of Iverson's leaving did not become known until June 1999 when John Correnti resigned after disagreements with the Board; Aycock took his place. All of this was a complete surprise to investors and decreased the stock price by 10%. Siegel commented, "The board felt Correnti was not the right person to lead Nucor into the 21st century." Aycock assured everyone he would be happy to move back into retirement as soon as replacements could be found.

Aycock moved to increase the corporate office staff by adding a level of executive vice presidents over four areas of business and adding two specialist jobs in strategic planning and steel technology. When Siegel retired, Aycock promoted Terry Lisenby to CFO and treasurer and hired a Director of IT to report to Lisenby (see Exhibit 3 for the organization chart in 2000).

Jim Coblin, vice president of human resources, believed the additions to management were necessary, "It's not bad to get a little more like other companies." He noted that the various divisions did their business cards and plant signs differently; some did not even want a Nucor sign. Sometimes six different Nucor salesmen would call on the same customer. "There is no manager of human resources in the plants, so at least we needed to give additional training to the person who does most of that work at the plant," he stated. With these new additions, there would be a director of information technology and two important committees: one for environmental issues and the second for audit.

He believed the old span of control of 20 might have worked well when there was less competition. Aycock considered it "ridiculous." "It was not possible to properly manage, to know what was going on. The top managers have totally lost contact with the company." Coblin was optimistic that having executive vice presidents would improve management. The three meetings of the general managers had slowly increased from about one-and-a-half days to about two-and-a-half days and became more

Exhibit 3 Nucor Organization Chart, 2000

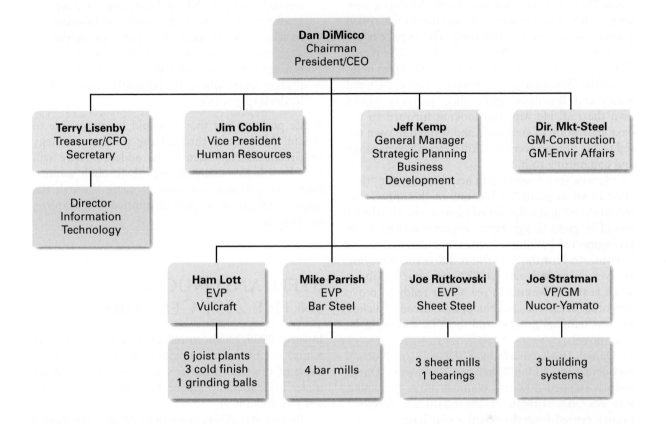

focused. The new executive vice president positions would bring a perspective above the level of the individual plants. Instead of 15 individual, detailed presentations, each general manager would give a short, five-minute briefing, and then there would be an in-depth presentation on the group, with team participation. After some training by Lisenby, the divisions had recently done a pretty good job with a SWOT analysis. Coblin thought these changes would make Nucor a stronger global player.

According to Jeff Kemp, the new general manager of strategic planning and business development, the big issue was how to sustain earnings growth. In the United States steel industry, there were too many marginal competitors. The United States government had recently added to the problem by giving almost a billion dollars to nine mills, which simply allowed them to limp along and weaken the industry as a whole. He was looking for Nucor's opportunities within the steel industry. He asked why Nucor had bought

a bearing company. His experience in the chemical industry suggested a need for Nucor to establish a position of superiority and grow globally, driving industry competition rather than reacting. He argued that a company should protect its overall market position, which could mean sacrifices for individual plants. Aycock liked Kemp's background in law and accounting and had specifically sought someone from outside the steel industry to head up Nucor's strategic planning. By June 2000, Kemp had conducted studies of other industries in the United States market and developed a working document that identified opportunities worthy of further analysis.

"Every company hits a plateau," Aycock observed. "You can't just go out and build plants to grow. How do you step up to the next level? I wouldn't say it's a turning point, but we have to get our strategic vision and strategic plans." He stated, "We are beginning Nucor's first ever strategic planning sessions; it was not necessary before."

Aycock believed Nucor needed to be quick to recognize developing technology in all production areas. He noted the joint venture to develop a new strip caster, which would cast the current flat-rolled material in a more finished form. The impact could be explosive, allowing Nucor to build smaller plants closer to markets. This would be particularly helpful on the West Coast. Nucor would own the United States and Brazilian rights; their partners would own the rest. He was also looking forward to the next generation of steel mills and wanted to own the rights. He praised Iverson's skill at seeing technology and committing to it.

He was very interested in acquisitions, but "they must fit strategically." A bar mill in the upper central Midwest and a flat-rolled plant in the Northeast would be good. A significant opportunity existed in preengineered buildings. Aycock intended to concentrate on steel for the next five to six years, achieving an average growth rate of 15% per year. In about seven years, he wanted to see Nucor ready to move into other areas. He said Nucor had already "picked the low hanging grapes" and must be careful in its next moves.

Daniel DiMicco assumed the role of Nucor's president and CEO in September 2000, when David Aycock stepped down as planned. Peter Browning was elected chairman of the board of directors. Aycock retired from the board a year later.

Sales for 2000 increased 14% over 1999, reaching a record level. Earnings were also at record levels, 27% over 1999. The year had begun on strong footing but had turned weak by year-end. While Nucor remained profitable, other steel companies faced bankruptcy. A Vulcraft plant was under construction in New York. It was Vulcraft's first northeastern operation and expanded the geographical coverage into a new region. Nucor was also attempting a breakthrough technological step in strip casting at Crawfordsville, known as the Castrip process. They sold its Grinding Ball process and the Bearing Products operation because they were not a part of its core business.

In the company's annual report, DiMicco laid out Nucor's plans for 2000 and beyond:

Our targets are to deliver an average annual earnings growth of 10%–15% over the next 10 years, deliver a return well in excess of our cost of capital, maintain a minimum average return on equity of 14% and deliver to return on sales a 8%–10%. Our strategy will focus on Nucor becoming a market leader in every product group and business in which we compete. This calls for significant increases in market share for many of our core products and the maintenance of market share where we currently enjoyed a leadership position.

While pointing out that it would be impossible to obtain this success through the previous strategy of Greenfield construction, he added, "There will now be a heavy focus on growth through acquisitions. We will also continue growing through the commercialization of new disruptive and leapfrog technologies."

STEEL AND NUCOR IN THE 21ST CENTURY

In early 2009, DiMicco reflected over his nine-year tenure as CEO of Nucor with pride. These had been some of the steel industry's rockiest times, and yet under his leadership Nucor had almost doubled its size (see Exhibit 4).

By October 2001, more than 20 steel companies in the United States, including Bethlehem Steel Corp. and LTV Corp., the nations' third and fourth largest steel producers, respectively, had filed for bankruptcy protection. More than a dozen producers were operating under Chapter 11 bankruptcy protection, which allows them to maintain market share by selling steel cheaper than non-Chapter 11 steelmakers. On October 20, *The Economist* noted that of the 14 steel companies followed by Standard & Poor's, only Nucor was indisputably healthy. In the fall of 2001, 25% of domestic steel companies were in bankruptcy proceedings, although the United States was the largest importer of steel in the world. Experts believed that close to half of the United States steel industry might be forced to close before conditions improved.

In 2001, the world steel industry found itself in the middle of one of its most unprofitable and volatile periods ever, in part due to a glut of steel that had sent prices to 20-year lows. While domestic steel producers were mired in red ink, many foreign

Exhibit 4   Nucor Organization Chart: Executive Management, 2009

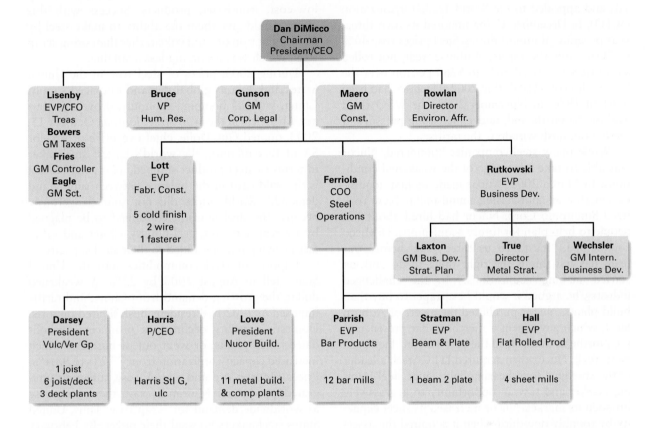

steel-makers desperately needed to continue to sell in the relatively open U.S. market to stay profitable. The industry was hovering around 75% capacity utilization, a level too low to be profitable for many companies. Three European companies—France's Usinor SA, Luxembourg's Arbed SA, and Spain's Aceralia Corp.—merged to form the world's largest steel company. Two Japanese companies—NKK Corp. and Kawasaki Steel Corp.—merged to form the world's second-biggest steelmaker. These new mega steel-makers could out-muscle United States competitors, which were less efficient, smaller, and financially weaker than Asian and European competitors. At this time the largest United States steel maker, USX-U.S. Steel Group, was only the 11th largest producer in the world. Furthermore, while in 1990, mini-mills accounted for 36% of the domestic steel market, by 2000, the more efficient mini-mill had seized 50% of the market, and the resulting competition had driven prices lower for integrated steel as well as mini-mills.

The year 2001 turned out to be one of the worst years ever for steel. There were the 9/11 terrorist attacks, a recession, and a surge of imports. DiMicco broke with Nucor's traditional opposition to government intervention to make a major push for protective tariffs. He stated, "The need to enforce trade rules is similar to the need to enforce any other law. If two merchants have stores side by side, but one sells stolen merchandise at a vast discount, we know that it's time for the police to step in." In March 2002, President George W. Bush, after an investigation and recommendation by the International Trade Commission, imposed anti-dumping tariffs under section 201 of the Trade Act of 1974. This restricted some imports of steel and placed quotas of up to 30% on others. The move was opposed by many, including steel users. Columnist George Will, in his editorial on March 10, 2002, criticized President Bush for abandoning free trade and pointed out that protection would hamper the necessary actions to restructure the steel industry in America by reducing excess capacity. The European Union immediately threatened reprisals and appealed to the World Trade Organization (WTO). In December, China imposed its own three-year program of import duties. Steel prices rose 40% in 2002 after the tariffs. Within a year, hot-rolled steel prices increased 50% to $260 per ton over the 20-year low of $210 during 2002. The price had been $361 in 1980. In November 2003, the WTO ruled against the tariffs and, under increasing pressure of retaliation, Bush withdrew the tariffs.

While many steel companies floundered, Nucor was able to take advantage of the weakened conditions. In March 2001, Nucor made its first acquisition in 10 years, purchasing a mini-mill in New York from Sumitomo Corp. Nucor had hired about five people to help plan for future acquisitions. DiMicco commented, "It's taken us three years before our team has felt this is the right thing to do and get started making acquisitions." In the challenged industry, he argued it would be cheaper to buy than build plants. Nucor purchased the assets of Auburn Steel, which gave them a merchant bar presence in the Northeast and helped the new Vulcraft facility in New York. Nucor then acquired ITEC Steel, a leader in the emerging load-bearing light gauge steel framing market and saw an opportunity to aggressively broaden its market. Nucor increased its sheet capacity by roughly one-third when it acquired the assets of Trico Steel Co. in Alabama for $120 million. In early 2002, Nucor acquired the assets of Birmingham Steel Corp. The $650 million purchase of four mini-mills was the largest acquisition in Nucor's history. However, 2002 also proved to be a difficult year for Nucor. Although Nucor increased its steelmaking capacity by more than 25%, revenue increased 11%, and earnings improved 43% over a weak 2001, Nucor's other financial goals were not met.

This did not stop Nucor from continuing its expansion through acquisitions to increase market share and capacity in steel and by actively working on new production processes that would provide them with technological advantages. Nucor acquired the United States and Brazilian rights to the promising Castrip process for strip casting, the process of directly casting thin sheet steel. After development work on the process in Indiana, full-time production began in May 2002 and produced 7,000 tons in the last 10 months of 2002. Moreover, in April 2002, Nucor entered into a joint venture with a Brazilian mining company, CVRD, the world's largest producer of iron-ore pellets, to jointly develop low-cost, iron-based products. Success with this effort would give them the ability to make steel by combining iron ore and coke rather than using scrap steel, which was becoming less available.

During 2003, prices of steel rose in the United States and Asia as global demand outpaced supply. China, with its booming economy, drove the market. An article in the *Wall Street Journal*, October 15, 2003, quoted Guy Dolle, chief executive of Arcelor SA of Luxembourg, the world's largest steelmaker in terms of steel product shipped, as saying, "China is the wild card in the balance between supply and demand." World prices did not soar dangerously because the steel industry continued to be plagued by overcapacity. Yet steel-hungry China and other fast-growing nations added to their steel capacity.

Imports of steel commodities into the United States fell in August 2003 by 22%. A weakened dollar, the growing demand from China, and tariffs imposed in 2002 by President Bush limited imports. Domestic capacity declined as producers consolidated, idled plants, or went out of business, which increased capacity utilization from 77.2% to 93.4%. Prices for iron ore and energy rose, affecting integrated producers. Mini-mills saw their costs rise as worldwide demand for scrap rose. Thus, United States steelmakers boosted their prices. By February 2004, a growing coalition of United States steel producers and consumers were considering whether to petition to limit soaring exports of scrap steel from the United States, the world's largest producer of steel scrap. The United States had exported an estimated 12 million metric tons of scrap steel in 2003, a 21% increase from 2002. Moreover, the price of scrap steel was up 83% from a year earlier, at $255 a ton. At the same time, the price of hot-rolled sheet steel rose 30% to $360 a ton. One result was that the International Steel Group (ISG) replaced Nucor as the most profitable US steel producer. ISG was created when investor Wilbur Ross acquired the failing traditional steel producers in America, including LTV, Bethlehem, and Weirton. These mills used iron ore rather than scrap steel.

When 2003 ended, Nucor struck a positive note by reminding its investors that the company had been profitable every single quarter since beginning operations in 1966. But while Nucor set records for both steel production and steel shipments, net earnings declined 61%. Although the steel industry as a whole struggled, Nucor increased its market share and held on to profitability. Nucor worked on expanding its business with the automotive industry, continued its joint venture in Brazil to produce pig iron, and pursued a joint venture with Japan and China to make iron without the usual raw materials. In February 2004, Nucor was "optimistic about the prospects for obtaining commercialization" of its promising Castrip process for strip casting in the United States and Brazil. The mini-mills could not produce sheet steel, a large share of the market. Moreover, Nucor was optimistic because the administration was using its trade laws to curtail import dumping, and Nucor expected higher margins.

Global competition continued. According to the *Wall Street Journal*, Posco steelworks in Pohang, South Korea, enjoyed the highest profits in the global steel industry as of 2004. Moreover, *Business Week* reported that the company had developed a new technology called Finex, which turned coal and iron ore into iron without coking and sintering and was expected to cut production costs by nearly a fifth and harmful emissions by 90%. The company had also expanded their 80 Korean plants by investing in 14 Chinese joint ventures. By December 2004, demand in China had slowed, and it had become a net steel exporter, sparking concerns of global oversupply.

Global consolidation also continued. In October 2004, London's Mittal family announced that they would merge their Ispat International NV with LNM Group and ISG, to create the world's largest steelmaker, with an estimated annual revenue of $31.5 billion and an output of 57 million tons. This would open a new chapter for the industry's consolidation, which had been mostly regional. Although the world's steel industry remains largely fragmented with the world's top 10 steelmakers supplying less than 30% of global production, Mittal Steel would have about 40% of the United States market in flat-rolled steel. Moreover Mittal, which had a history of using its scale to buy lower-cost raw materials and import modern management techniques into previously inefficient state-run mills, was buying ISG, a United States company that already owned the lowest-cost, highest profit mills in the United States. In January 2005, Mittal announced plans to buy 37% of China's Hunan Valin Iron & Steel Group Co.

In 2004 and 2005, Nucor continued its aggressive geographic expansion and introduction of new products. For example, Nuconsteel ("Nucon"), a wholly owned subsidiary of Nucor that specialized in load-bearing light gauge steel framing systems for commercial and residential construction markets, introduced two new low-cost automated fabrication systems for residential construction. And in March 2005, Nucor formed a joint venture with Lennar Corporation, named Nextframe LP, to provide comprehensive light gauge steel framing for residential construction. Nucor's 25% joint venture with the Rio Tinto Group, Mitsubishi Corporation, and Chinese steelmaker Shougang Corporation for a Hlsmelt commercial plant in Kwinana, Australia, started up in 2005. In 2004, Nucor acquired assets of an idled direct-reduced iron (DRI) plant in Louisiana and moved them to Trinidad. By December 2006, construction was completed and by 2008, Nu-Iron Unlimited produced 1,400,000 metric tons of DRI from Brazilian iron ore for the United States.

By 2005, Nucor had 16 steel facilities producing three times as much as in 1999. The number of bar mills had grown to nine mills, with capacity of 6,000,000 tons by the addition of Birmingham's four mills with 2,000,000 tons and Auburn's 400,000 tons. The sheet mills grew to four and increased capacity by one-third with the acquisition of Trico. Nucor-Yamato's structural steel capacity was increased by half a million tons from the South Carolina plant. A new million ton plate mill, Nucor's second, had opened in North Carolina in 2000. Ninety-three percent of production was sold to outside customers.

By 2006, DiMicco had made many acquisitions while still managing to instill Nucor's unique culture in the new facilities. A *Business Week* article in May 2006 stated Nucor's culture and compensation system had changed very little since the 1990s. Michael Arndt reported that "Nucor gave out more than $220 million in profit sharing and bonuses to the rank and file in 2005. The average Nucor steelworker took home nearly $79,000 last year. Add to that a $2,000 one-time bonus to mark the company's record earnings and almost $18,000, on average, in profit sharing." He also noted that executive pay was still geared toward team building as "the bonus of a plant manager, a department manager's boss, depends on the entire corporation's return on equity. So there's no glory in winning at your plant if the others are failing."

Globally, steel mergers and acquisitions boomed during 2006–2008. For example, Arcelor SA took over

Canadian steelmaker Dofasco Inc. for $4.85 billion in March 2006, followed by a merger in June with Mittal Steel Co. NV to create the world's largest steel company. In January 2007, Russian steelmaker Evraz SA acquired Oregon Steel Mills, a Portland-based producer of specialty steel, for $2.3 billion, and in March, Indian-based Tata Steel Ltd. completed its acquisition of UK-based Corus Group Plc for $12.4 billion. SSAB (Svenskt Stal AB of Sweden) completed its acquisition of IPSCO Inc. of Lisle, Illinois, for $7.7 billion in July 2007, and in October, Steel Dynamics completed the acquisition of privately held OmniSource Corp., a scrap processor and trading company. In May 2008, OAO Severstal, a Russian-based steel company acquired ArcelorMittal's Sparrow Point steel plant in Maryland, and in June, outbid Essar Steel Holdings Ltd., an India-based steel company for Esmark Inc. Also in June 2008, Tangsham Iron & Steel Group merged with Handan Iron & Steel Group; the new company, called Hebei Iron & Steel Group Co., surpassed Baosteel Group Co. as China's largest steel producer. This merger activity was due to a combination of low borrowing costs, high stock prices, and large amounts of cash. Another factor prompting mergers was a rise in raw materials costs. Despite all the transactions in 2006, 2007, and 2008, the industry remained fragmented, both domestically and internationally, and more mergers were expected.

Future merger activity was expected to differ slightly as steel companies attempted to become more vertically integrated. Examples were integration forward with Esmark's service center's combination with Wheeling-Pittsburgh's steel production and integration backward into scrap with the takeover of OmniSource by Steel Dynamics in 2007 and Nucor's acquisition of David J. Joseph Co. in 2008. These represented a trend toward becoming less dependent on outside vendors. This was due to the rising cost of scrap, which jumped from $185/ton in January 2006 to $635/ton in June 2008, and the highly concentrated nature of iron ore sources. BHP Billiton Ltd. based in Australia, Rio Tinto plc headquartered in London, UK, and Brazil-based Vale accounted for 75% of iron ore shipments worldwide.

Nucor was also active in mergers. In March 2007, Nucor acquired Harris Steel Group Inc. of Canada for $1.06 billion in cash, adding 770,000 tons of rebar fabrication capacity and over 350,000 tons of capacity in other downstream steel products. This acquisition showed that Nucor saw growth opportunities in finishing steel products for its customers and in distribution rather than additional steelmaking capacity. While many large steel companies were buying other primary steelmakers around the world, Nucor was focusing its investments largely in North America's manufacturing infrastructure, such as reinforced steel bars, platform grating, and wire mesh for construction products ranging from bridges to airports and stadiums, which according to DiMicco "significantly advances Nucor's downstream growth initiatives." Through the acquisition of Harris, Nucor also acquired a 75% interest in Novosteel SA, a Swiss-based steel trading company that matched buyers and sellers of steel products on a global basis and offered its customers logistics support, material handling, quality certifications, and schedule management.

Nucor had a joint venture with Harris for the previous three years and already owned a 50% stake in the company. Harris kept its name as a Nucor subsidiary and was led by the previous chairman and CEO John Harris. However, the Harris board consisted of Harris and three Nucor representatives. This was the first time Nucor had broken from its non-union tradition, as about half of Harris's 3,000 employees belonged to a mix of iron workers', autoworkers', and steelworkers' unions. As Timna Tanners, a steel analyst in New York said, "It's definitely a stretch for Nucor, culturally, since they have managed to keep its other operations non-union by offering higher salaries and production incentives. But there are not many non-union options left in North America when it comes to acquisitions and expansion."

The Harris team was operating as a growth platform within Nucor and had completed several acquisitions, including rebar fabricator South Pacific Steel Corporation in June 2007, Consolidated Rebar Inc. in August 2007, a 90% equity interest in rebar fabricator Barker Steel Company Inc. in December 2007, as well as smaller transactions. Nucor made several other acquisitions, which combined with the Laurel Steel, Fisher & Ludlow, and LEC businesses that came with the Harris acquisition and some internal organic growth, increased Nucor's cold finish and drawn products' capacity by over 75% from 490,000 tons in 2006 to 860,000 tons at the end of 2007. In addition it resulted in 90,000 tons of steel grating capacity, and steel mesh capacity almost tripled to 233,000 tons per year.

Nucor continued to invest in other downstream and upstream businesses. In the third quarter of 2007, Nucor completed the acquisition of Magnatrax Corporation, a leading provider of custom-engineering metal buildings, for $275.2 million in cash. The Magnatrax acquisition, when combined with its existing building systems divisions and a newly constructed buildings systems division in Brigham City, Utah, made Nucor the second largest metal building producer in the United States, more than doubling its annual capacity to 480,000 tons of pre-engineered metal buildings.

In 2007, Nucor's seven Vulcraft facilities supplied more than 40% of the total domestic buildings using steel joists and joist girders. In both 2006 and 2007, 99% of its steel requirements were obtained from Nucor bar mills. Nucor's nine steel deck plants supplied almost 30% of total domestic sales in decking; six of these plants were constructed by Nucor adjacent to Vulcraft joist facilities, and three were acquired in November 2006 as a wholly owned subsidiary called Verco Decking. These decking plants obtained 99% of their steel requirements from Nucor sheet plants in 2006 but only 76% in 2007.

In March 2008, Nucor completed the acquisition of the David J. Joseph Company, the largest broker of ferrous and nonferrous scrap in the United States and one of the nation's largest processors of ferrous scrap, for $1.44 billion. The company had been a supplier of scrap to Nucor since 1969. DJJ operated more than 30 scrap processing facilities. This acquisition expanded Nucor's scrap-processing capabilities to 4 million short tons from 500,000 short tons, providing them additional steelmaking raw materials through their brokerage operations, and provided rail services and logistics through its private fleet of some 2,000 scrap-related railcars. This allowed Nucor to capture further margins in the steelmaking supply chain and to more closely control its raw materials inputs. In May, Nucor announced a plan to raise $3 billion for expansions and acquisitions, two-thirds to come from selling 25 million new shares.

United States steelmakers saw a major transition in 2008. In the first quarter, the combination of higher volume and increased prices led to a sizable gain in profits. Furthermore, data showed that the four leading domestic steel companies, AK Steel Holding Corp., Nucor Corp., Steel Dynamics Inc., and United States Steel Corp., which Standard & Poor's followed as a proxy for industry performance, collectively accounted for 45.5% of industry shipments in 2007. The rise in revenues for this proxy group reflected a 9.3% increase in revenue per ton, volume gained at the expense of imports and the impact of acquisitions. At the end of July, major United States steelmakers' results were still supported by months of steel-price increases, which eased the burden of rising raw materials prices, as demand from emerging markets kept global steel supplies tight.

However, in September 2008, steelmakers in the United States experienced a sharp pullback from buyers who were concerned with the credit crisis and a slowdown in the automobile and construction markets. This caused inventories to rise and prices on some key products to drop 10%. The *Wall Street Journal* reported on November 17, 2008, that "Metals prices fell 35% in just four weeks last month—the steepest decline ever recorded, according to Barclays Capital." They also reported that big steelmakers worldwide were cutting production as much as 35% and that U.S. Steel Corp. planned to lay off 2% of its workforce. Chinese demand also slowed. This was a swift reversal in an industry that saw its profits increase 20-fold in five years. The pricing volatility was intensified by the global financial crisis, as many hedge funds, pension funds, and other investors desperate to raise cash rapidly sold their commodities holdings. Still, the article said that ultimately the industry's problems were rooted in weakened demand, particularly in China, rather than the financial crisis.

So as 2009 began, with prices for steel, iron ore, and scrap metal plummeting, competition in the global steel industry was expected to increase. And further consolidation was expected as the major players sought to maintain their dominant positions (see Exhibit 5). In a December 2008 interview on CNBC, Cramer said to DiMicco, "Nucor's great CEO," it was "amazing you can be profitable" with an overnight 40% drop in sales. DiMicco said it showed the success of Nucor's business model. He believed Nucor's acquisitions over the past 10 years, with its integration into steel products markets and into raw materials, would position Nucor to survive and even prosper—where there were threats, there were also opportunities.

Exhibit 5 Top 12 Global Steel Producers as of the End of 2007 According to the International Iron and Steel Institute, September 21, 2008

Company Name	2007 Rank	Million Metric Tons	2006 Rank	Million Metric Tons
ArcelorMittal	1	116.4	1	117.2
Nippon Steel	2	35.7	2	34.7
JFE	3	34.0	3	32.0
POSCO	4	31.1	4	30.1
Baosteel	5	28.6	6	22.5
Tata Steel*	6	26.5	45	6.4
Anshan-Benxi	7	23.6	5	22.6
Jiangsu Shagang	8	22.9	17	14.6
Tangshan	9	22.8	9	19.1
U.S. Steel	10	21.5	7	21.2
Wuhan	11	20.4	16	15.1
Nucor	12	20.0	8	20.3

*2007 figure includes Corus

SATELLITE RADIO (A)

THE BIRTH OF A MARKET

More than anyone else, Canadian-born David Margolese was the key player in the creation of the satellite radio business. In 1978, at the age of 20, Margolese dropped out of college to create a Vancouver-based paging company. He soon turned his attention to the nascent cellular telephone business. When he tried to obtain funding to establish a cellular telephone business in Canada, he was initially rebuffed by venture capitalists who told him that the industry would never amount to much. At best, they said, cellular phones would be used only by a few CEOs and diplomats. Undeterred, Margolese persisted in his fund-raising efforts. In 1980, when cellular was still little more than a dream, he convinced Ameritech to invest in his company, Cantel.

Using these funds, he acquired licenses to cellular phone rights in Canada. Along the way, he joined forces with others, including Ted Rodgers of Rodgers Communications, to create what became Rogers Wireless, which by 2001 was Canada's largest cellular telephone company. In the late 1980s, when he was just 31, Margolese sold his stake for $2 billion in cash and set himself up as a venture capitalist.

It was in that capacity that Margolese met Robert Briskman, a former NASA engineer and the operations chief at Geostar, a satellite messaging company that went bankrupt in 1991. Briskman had designed the core technology for satellite radio, called the unified S-band. He and other former Geostar employees had established a company named Satellite Radio CD to commercialize the technology, but they were without funding and needed to overcome numerous regulatory hurdles.

Initially Margolese invested just $1 million in the business, whose name was changed to CD Radio, but he soon decided that this was the best business he had ever seen. What attracted Margolese was that radio programs beamed from satellite using the unified S-band technology and digital signals could deliver nationwide coverage and CD quality sound. Established radio was local, the quality of the analog signal was often poor, and it faded quickly outside the local area. Moreover, the local markets served by established radio businesses were too small to support niche programming, such as stations devoted to jazz, classical music, or Reggae, but this might not be the case for a radio company that could serve a nationwide market. However, numerous hurdles stood in the way of established a viable satellite radio business. It would be very expensive to put satellites into space, easily several hundred million dollars. The Federal Communications Commission (FCC) had to be persuaded to allocate radio spectrum to satellite radio. Receiving the radio signal from space would require special receivers, and how could potential customers be persuaded to purchase these when they already had radios in their cars and at home? Moreover, it would be difficult to get advertisers to support a service that initially had no listeners—a classic chicken and egg problem—and without the advertisers, how would the service generate revenues?

By 1994, Margolese was estimating that satellite radio would be operational by 1997 and cost some $500 million, but CD Radio faced substantial roadblocks. Despite lobbying from Margolese, the FCC had not yet decided if it would license radio spectrum for satellite radio. Fierce opposition from the

---

This case was prepared by Charles W. L. Hill, School of Business University of Washington. Reprinted by permission.

National Association of Broadcasters (NAB), which represented existing radio stations, was slowing things down. Among other things, NAB filings with the FCC argued that satellite radio would lead to the demise of local radio service, hundreds of which would close, to the detriment of local communities that relied on AM (amplitude modulated) and FM (frequency modulated) radio for important local news.

It was not until 1997 that the FCC finally auctioned off the spectrum for satellite radio. There were four bidders for the spectrum. The FCC decided to license two providers, creating a duopoly. CD Radio and XM Radio won the auction, paying $83.3 million and $89.8 million, respectively. Established in 1992, XM Radio was a development stage company backed by American Mobile Satellite Corp., which was itself owned by Hughes Electronics (then a subsidiary of General Motors) and McCaw Cellular. With spectrum in hand, CD Radio, which in 1999 changed its name to Sirius, and XM Radio now had to deliver on their promise to establish a nationwide satellite radio service. If they did not, the FCC would not renew the licenses when they came up for review in 2007. If not renewed, the licenses would expire on February 14, 2010.

THE RADIO INDUSTRY

The radio industry dates back to 1921 when the first radio station was licensed. Radio involves the transmission of sound waves, which are sent from AM or FM stations. AM radio operates on relatively low frequencies and was the earliest broadcast service. FM radio, which was first patented in 1933, operates at much higher frequencies but was very slow to catch on because of heavy investment by stations and listeners in AM equipment.

Radios are ubiquitous and can be found in 99 out of 100 American households. The average number of radios per household is 5.6, including radios in cars (there are approximately 150 million radios in vehicles). Some 95.4% of radio owners listen to the radio during any given week. The typical adult listener tunes in for 3 hours and 12 minutes every weekday, and 5 hours 30 minutes on weekends. On a typical weekday, the average person 12 years or older spends 41.7% of radio listening time in a car or truck, 37.3% while at home, and 21% at work or other places. On weekends, car listening jumps

to 47.3%, home listening to 40.5%, and listening elsewhere falls to 12.1%. On average, some 13% to 17% of airtime every hour is devoted to advertising on FM/AM radio stations.[1]

Encouraged by broadcast deregulation, the number of radio stations in the United States increased from 10,500 in 1985 to roughly 13,000 by the end of 2001.[2] In 1996, the Telecommunications Act removed limits on the number of radio stations that a company could own in a given market (a "market" is generally defined as discrete geographical area, such as a city or county). Prior to 1996, a company could only own two FM and two AM stations in any one market, no matter how populated that market. Under the new regulations, a company could own or operate up to eight stations in any one market, with up to five in one service (AM or FM). These new rules facilitated consolidation in the industry and led to the growth of large radio broadcasting companies that own many stations. The leader among these, Clear Channel Communications, owned 1,182 United States radio stations at the end of 2003, reached an audience of 180 million, and generated $3.70 billion in revenues from radio advertising.[3] The next largest radio broadcasting company in terms of revenues, Infinity Broadcasting, owned 180 radio stations, which were concentrated in the most populated markets in the United States. By 2002, the 10 largest broadcasters owned about 17% of all United States stations and accounted for more than 40% of radio industry advertising revenues (the largest broadcasters are focused on the largest markets where advertising revenues are greater). Most analysts believe that the industry will continue to consolidate over the next few years.

Due to the limited range of their signal, radio stations focus on the market in which they are located. Radio stations earn their revenues from advertising. Advertising rates are a function of a station's ability to attract an audience that has certain demographic characteristics. Stations offer programs of a specific format to attract the demographic that advertisers are interested in. Popular formats include news/talk radio, rock, oldies, sports, country, or jazz. The ability of radio to offer different programs that target different demographics is a big selling point, attracting advertisers pursuing narrowly defined audiences. Also important are the number of other stations and advertising media competing in that market. Advertising rates are normally highest during the morning and evening drive time hours.

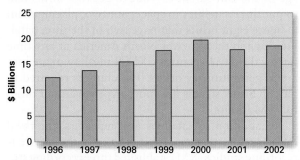

Exhibit 1   Radio Advertising Spending ($ billions)

Source: Standard & Poor's Industry Survey, Broadcasting and Cable Industry, July 2002.

In 2002, advertising revenues for radio stations was $18.6 billion, an increase from $12.41 billion in 1996 (see Exhibit 1). Advertising revenues dropped by almost $2 billion in 2001 compared to 2000 due to a week national economy and the impact of September 11, 2001. The cost structure of radio broadcasters is largely fixed, making the profitability of radio stations sensitive to the overall level of advertising revenues.

THE BUSINESS PLAN FOR SATELLITE RADIO

The Business Case

The business case for Sirius and XM was based on the argument that the number of radio stations in local markets is limited, most of these stations focus on the same five formats, and the geographic range of service is also limited with the signal fading outside the market area. According to market data, more than 48% of all commercial radio stations use one of only three general programming formats—country, news/talk/sports, and adult contemporary, and more than 71% of all commercial radio stations use one of only five general formats—the same three plus oldies and religion.[4] The small number of available programming choices means that artists representing other niche music formats are likely to receive little or no airtime in many markets. Radio stations prefer featuring artists they believe appeal to the broadest market. Meanwhile, according to the Recording Industry Association of America, recorded music sales of niche

music formats, such as classical, jazz, movie and Broadway soundtracks, religious programming, new age, children's programming, and others, comprised up to 27% of total recorded music sales in 2001.

Both Sirius and XM planned to offer approximately 100 channels. Sirius planned to keep 50 channels of music commercial free, while selling advertising spots on the remaining news, sports, and information channels. XM planned to have 15–20 channels commercial free, while limiting advertising spots to just seven minutes an hour on other channels. The channels would focus on a wide range of different music formats and news/information/talk formats. For example, XM planned to offer music channels focusing on each decade from the 1940s to the 1990s, plus contemporary music channels, several different country formats (e.g., bluegrass, Nashville), Christian rock channels, numerous news formats, information formats, and so on. Both Sirius and XM also planned to enter into agreements with established broadcasters to offer satellite radio formats of their services. These formats included MTV, VH1, CNN, the BCC, ESPN, Court TV, C-Span, and Playboy. XM also partnered with Clear Channel Communications to offer Clear Channel program formats, such as the KISS pop music station, over XM Satellite radio.

To generate revenues, in addition to advertising fees, both Sirius and XM decided to charge a subscription-based fee for their services that would run approximatley $10–$12 per month. When it was pointed out that existing radio is offered for free to consumers, executives at Sirius and XM noted that the same is true for traditional broadcast TV, but, nevertheless, consumers have been more than willing to pay a monthly subscription fee for cable TV service and satellite TV service. Penetration data relating to cable television, satellite television, and premium movie channels suggest that consumers are willing to pay for services that expand programming choice or enhance quality. There were more than 22.9 million digital cable subscribers and 22.3 million satellite subscribers in early 2004. As of 2004, some 69% of TV households subscribed to basic cable television and 20% of TV households subscribed to satellite television.[5]

Infrastructure

Although the technology used by Sirius and XM Radio differs in important ways, both companies followed the same basic business plan. Sirius and XM decided to place satellites in orbit to serve the United States. Sirius planned to put three satellites in elliptical orbits 23,000 miles above the earth, while XM planned to put a pair of more powerful satellites in geostationary orbits at 22,300 miles. The satellites were expected to have a useful life of up to 15 years. Both Sirius and XM planned to keep a spare satellite in storage that could be launched quickly in the event of failure of one of their satellites. If an orbiting satellite were to fail, it would take approximately six months to get a replacement satellite into space. Service would be partially interrupted during this time. Initial plans called for Sirius to launch its satellites in 1999 and XM in 2000, with service starting soon thereafter.

The satellites broadcast a digital signal that can be converted into CD quality sound by radios fitted with the appropriate chip-set and receivers that decode, decompress, and output digital signals from a satellite. The S-band signal used by both companies can be picked up by moving vehicles and will not be "weathered out" by dense cloud cover. The radios were expected to cost between $200 and $400. Since the digital signal cannot be picked up by a standard radio, this required customers to invest in new radio equipment.

At least initially, a radio with a Sirius receiver would not pick up XM Radio, and vice versa. On February 16, 2000, XM and Sirius signed an agreement to develop a unified standard for satellite radios, enabling consumers to purchase one radio capable of receiving both Sirius and XM services. The technology relating to this unified standard was jointly developed and funded by the two companies, who share ownership of it. The unified standard was mandated by the FCC, which required interoperability with both licensed satellite radio systems. Radios based on the unified standard started to become available at the end of 2004.

To offer truly seamless nationwide coverage, satellites alone would not be enough. To receive a satellite signal, a clear line of sight is needed. In tunnels, buildings, and the urban canyons of American cities, a clear line of sight is not available. To solve this problem, both companies had plans to build a nationwide network of terrestrial repeaters. Sirius initially planned to put up 105 repeaters in 42 cities, and XM some 1,700 repeaters in about 70 cities. Sirius could get away with fewer repeaters because

the orbits of its satellites allowed for a better coverage of the United States—but to get that Sirius had to put three satellites in space, not two, placing them in figure eight orbits that have two of the three satellites high in the sky over North America at any time during the day. In contrast, XM Radio's two satellites are in geostationary orbits. The chipsets required to pickup Sirius signals are more expensive than those for XM Radio.

In addition to satellites and repeaters, the third infrastructure element required to offer the service is recording studios. XM established three recording studios, one in Washington, D.C. one in New York City, and one in Nashville. Taken together, the three studios comprise an all digital radio complex that is one of the largest in the world, with more than 80 soundproof studios of different configurations. Sirius built a single studio complex in New York City.

By mid-2000, Sirius was expecting to spend $1.2 billion and XM Radio $1.1 billion to develop this infrastructure. These estimates had increased considerably from the initial estimates made in the mid-1990s, which were approximately $500 million. Given the infrastructure and operational and advertising costs, the companies estimated that they needed to have 2–3 million subscribers each to make a profit. In 2000, forecasts by market research agencies and securities analysts suggest that in total, satellite radio could have as many as 15 million subscribers by 2006, 36 million by 2010 and about 50 million by 2014.[6]

Distribution

Both Sirius and XM believe that installation in cars and trucks was likely to drive early growth for satellite radio. In the early 2000s, 17 to 18 million new cars and light trucks were sold in the United States each year. Some 30 million car radios were sold, either embedded in new cars or in the aftermarket. In total there were more than 210 million vehicles on American roads. Both companies made deals with major automobile manufacturers to have satellite radios installed in new cars as optional—and ultimately standard—equipment. The price of the radio is embedded in the price of the car, with the customer signing up for service at the time of purchase. XM has an exclusive deal with GM and Honda, and Sirius with Ford and DaimlerChrysler. Both companies have now entered into an agreement with the FCC under which they have agreed to refrain from making any more exclusive deals. Plans called for satellite radio to be offered as an option on certain models, with the offering to be increased to more models over time.

The exclusive deals with automobile companies do not come cheap. As part of its deal with DaimlerChrysler, Sirius reimbursed DaimlerChrysler for some advertising expenses and hardware costs, and issued to DaimlerChrysler a warrant to purchase 4,000,000 shares of Sirius common stock at an exercise price of $3.00 per share. The deal with Ford was very similar. The deal between Sirius and DaimlerChrysler expires in October 2007, while the Ford deal expires May 2007.

The agreement between XM and GM required XM to guarantee annual, fixed payment obligations to GM. However, the agreement was subject to renegotiation if GM did not achieve and maintain specified installation levels, starting with 1,240,000 by November 2005 and installations of 600,000 per year thereafter. The GM agreement expires September 2013. For its part, Honda has committed to shipping 400,000 cars with XM Radios in 2005.

The companies also lined up manufacturers of aftermarket car receivers and signed retail arrangements with the Best Buy and Circuit City chains to distribute them.

Capital Requirements and Investors

Financing these two ventures was not trivial. XM Radio raised some $2.6 billion in equity and debt proceeds through January 2004 from investors and strategic partners to fund its infrastructure build out and operations. The strategic investors in XM Radio included GM, Hughes Electronics/DIRECTV, Clear Channel Communications, American Honda, and Hearst Communications. Financial investors in XM included Columbia Capital, Madison Dearborn Partners, AEA Investors, BayStar Capital, and Eastbourne Capital. XM Radio went public in late 1999. Honda and GM are major investors in XM Radio, with stakes of 13% and 8.6%, respectively, in late 2004.[7] Similarly, Sirius, which went public in 1995, had raised around $2.5 billion by 2004.

Much of the funds raised went into building out the infrastructure. At the end of 2003, XM Radio reported that it had spent $470 million to put its two satellites in orbit and purchase a spare satellite, $267 million to set up a system of ground repeaters

covering 60 cities, and $130 million on satellite control facilities and studios. Sirius is believed to have spent similar amounts.

Competition

Satellite radio faces competition from three main sources. Traditional AM/FM radio stations are obvious competitors. The big advantage of AM/FM radio is its local content, such as local news, sports, and weather, which listeners want. Although AM/FM radio is predominantly local, the emergence of consolidators such as Clear Channel Communications is beginning to change this. Clear Channel has made an effort to realize scale economies by developing a nationwide branded format for radio shows, most notably its pop format that goes under the KISS brand. KISS offers standard programming developed in a national studio. Local content such as news, weather, sports, and some dialog is spliced into KISS programming to make it seem as if the broadcast is local.[8] There are also signs that traditional AM/FM radio will ultimately move toward digital broadcasting, although doing so will require that consumers purchase radios capable of receiving a digital signal.

Internet radio is a second potential competitor. A number of FM and AM radio stations are now broadcasting digital signals over the Internet that can be accessed anywhere in the world by users with the appropriate equipment (computers, Internet connections, and media players).

A third competitor comes in the form of satellite TV and cable TV systems. Both satellite and cable providers are offering digital radio services as part of a package of digital services, with the radio being bundled with TV service, typically at no additional cost to the consumer.

LAUNCHING THE SERVICES

Initially, Sirius was thought to have the lead over XM Radio, but this changed when technical problems with the chip-sets to go in the radio receivers delayed the launch of Sirius' service for two years (the receivers, which were built by Lucent, did a poor job of picking up the digital signal and had to be redesigned).

XM Radio also had some delays due to problems with the Boeing rockets that were to launch its satellites but was able to launch its two satellites—named "Rock" and "Roll"—in early 2001, more than a year behind its initial schedule. XM started offering national service in November 2001 for a monthly fee of $9.95. XM Radio's launch was supported by an advertising campaign in excess of $100 million.

Beset by technical problems, Sirius did not launch its final satellite until early 2002 and did not start offering service until July 2002. Sirius charged $12.95 a month, justifying its price premium over XM because all of Sirius' 60 music channels ran without commercials. XM has limited commercials of about two minutes per hour on 35 of its 70 music channels (see Exhibit 2 for a comparison between XM and Sirius). Sirius stated that it will depend on subscriptions for about 85% of it revenue. XM initially expected to rely somewhat more on advertising revenues.

By the end of 2003, Sirius had 133 terrestrial repeaters in 92 urban markets where high buildings interfere with line of sight. XM had some 800 repeaters in 60 markets.

The nine-month lead that XM gained as a result of Sirius' technical problems proved to be invaluable. By the end of 2002, XM had 347,000 subscribers, while Sirius had just 30,000. XM passed the 500,000 subscriber milestone in April 2003 and was projecting that it would end 2003 with more than 1 million subscribers. This rapid subscriber accrual helped XM Radio sell faster than CD and DVD players did in their first year on the market.[9] Sirius, meanwhile, was aiming to end 2003 with some 300,000 subscribers and had just over 100,000 by mid year. Both companies were now estimating that

Exhibit 2   XM versus Sirius in 2003

	XM	Sirius
Monthly Cost	$9.99	$12.95
Radio Cost	$325 factory installed radio, $400–$500 for dealer-installed $200–$299 for home radio	$400–$500 for dealer-installed no home radio
Programming	101 channels 70 music 30 talk, sports, news 1 premium channel (Playboy)	100 channels 60 music 40 sports, talk, news
Commercials	None of 35 music channels Limited commercials on rest (about 2 minutes per hour)	None on music channels
Key Formats	Classic (3 channels) Pop (10 channels) Jazz/Blues (7 channels) Country (6 channels) Rock (12 channels) Latin (5 channels) Franks' Place The Joint (Reggae) Broadway Old Time Radio Classics	Classic (3 channels) Pop (9 channels) Jazz/standards (5 channels) Hip Hop (5 channels) Country (5 channels) Dance (6 channels) R&B (4 channels) Rock (13 channels) Broadway Radio Classics
News	Fox, CNN, CNBC, ESPN, Others	Fox, CNN, CNBC, ESPN, Others
Automotive Partners	GM, Honda	Ford, DaimlerChrysler, BMW
Subscribers as of Mid-2003	692,253	105,186

they needed 2 to 3 million subscribers to break even, with XM predicting that it would be cash-flow positive by late 2004.

In addition to XM's nine-month lead in the market, analysts attribute much of the company's early gains to an aggressive push by GM. GM rolled out XM's satellite radio as optional factory installed equipment in 25 of its 57 car, light truck, and sport utility models, including the entire Cadillac line. GM planned to increase that figure to 44 models for the 2004 model year, and the company expected to sell some 800,000 cars autos with XM's radio installed during 2004 and 1.1 million during 2005. The GM-installed radio, which is built by GM-supplier Delphi, costs $325 and is bundled into the price of the vehicle. In addition to being a shareholder of XM, GM is believed to get about $100 from XM for every radio it installs.

In early 2003, Honda stated that it planned to include XM radios as standard equipment in the 2004 Acura RL and as factory installed options in the 2004 Accord. In September 2003, Honda announced that XM radios would be installed as standard equipment in certain Honda Accord models. An XM Satellite Radio spokesman said that between the Accord, the Pilot and S2000 models, Honda will release about 200,000 automobiles that have an XM radio receiver as a factory-installed feature during the 2004 model year and 400,000 during the 2005 model year.[10] In addition to GM and Honda, XM radios are now available as dealer-installed options on certain offerings from Toyota, Volkswagen, and Audi, among others.

In contrast, Sirius' main partners are not as far along putting Sirius radios into their vehicles. DaimlerChrysler and BMW offer Sirius radios as a dealer-installed option, as opposed to factory installed, meaning that a buyer has to request that the dealer install the equipment. In 2004, DaimlerChrsyler committed to factory install 550,000 radios by mid-2007. Ford reportedly planned to offer factory-installed radios in select models for the 2004 model year, but that did not transpire. Now Ford has announced that it will begin factory installing Sirius Radios in the 2006 model year and will be factory installing Sirius radios in 20 of its 21 car lines by 2007.[11]

The wild card in the industry may be Toyota, which had not aligned itself with either XM or Sirius by late 2004, although Toyota did offer XM Radio as a dealer-installed option on some models. Nissan, too, has not aligned itself with either company, but the company again offers either XM or Sirius radios as a dealer-installed option.

Both XM and Sirius are also starting to offer an array of satellite radios for home use. The best selling of these in 2002 and 2003 was the Delphi XM SkyFi radio, which is made by Delphi for XM and sold through major consumer electronics chains for between $199 and $230 a unit. By mid-2003 some 80,000 Delphi XM SkyFi units had been sold, and Walmart, the nation's largest retailer, now stocked the item. The SkyFi radio could be used both at home, where it slots into an audio player, and adapted to fit into a car. In late 2004, XM Radio and Delphi announced that they would start selling a handheld portable radio, the Delphi MyFi, in December 2004.

Early surveys suggest high customer satisfaction with satellite radio. Surveys carried out by GM reportedly give a 90% satisfaction rate among customers who chose satellite radio as an option, with 70%–75% saying that they are likely to order satellite radio for their next vehicle.[12] Several consumer products reporters have also given satellite strong reviews, although some have complained that the sound quality is not quite CD quality.[13]

Sirius' late entry into the market and relatively low traction has left it in a very shaky financial condition. In October 2001, CEO David Margolese abruptly resigned, presumably a casualty of the company's failure to launch its service on time. Margolese continues as non-executive chairman of Sirius. The delay in the launch of its service resulted in Sirius running down its cash reserves, and mid-2002, it looked almost certain that the company would default on debt payments and have to file for Chapter 11 bankruptcy protection. However, at the last minute in October 2002, Sirius was able to pull off something of a coup, converting $700 million in debt and $525 million in preferred stock into common equity. In addition, three of the original investors in Sirius agreed to supply the company with another $200 million in cash. As a result of the recapitalization plan, the existing holders of the company's common stock ended up owning just 8% of the recapitalized company. It remains to be seen whether these funds will be sufficient to see the company through to profitability.

XM Radio also returned to the capital markets in early 2003, lining up an additional $475 million in funding. Of the $475 million, $225 million came from new investors, and the remainder from GM in the form of deferred payments and credit facilities. Critical to the deal's success was the agreement by more than 90% of the holders of $325 million in XM bonds to swap them for newly issued debt that pays no interest until 2006.

Although XM did launch on schedule, it too has experienced some technological problems that represent a potential cloud on the horizon. XM's two satellites, "Rock" and "Roll," are experiencing unexpected degradation of their solar power panels. The degradation has prompted XM to cut their useful life to 2008 from 2015. However, XM believes that it will be able to launch additional satellites by the time the degradation impacts signal strength. XM believes that its current insurance policies cover this problem and will be able to claim sufficient funds from insurance to be able to launch additional satellites.

By mid-2003, some analysts remained very bullish about the potential of XM Radio, although the future of Sirius was somewhat hazy. A May 2002 study by the Yankee Group projected satellite radio would achieve 15 million subscribers by 2006. Other market studies conducted for XM Radio project that as many as 50 million people may subscribe to satellite radio by 2012. More conservative investment analysts were suggesting that satellite radio might garner 4 to 5 million subscribers by mid-decade, and the ultimate total may be closer to 40 to 50 million. According to some projections made in early 2003, if XM hits 10 million subscribers in 2007, it could earn $500 million, or $1.50 a share. If XM Radio were ultimately to garner 30 million subscribers, it could earn $7 or more a share.[14]

SIGNIFICANT DEVELOPMENTS IN 2004

As 2004 drew to a close, subscription data suggested that XM Radio was continuing to capitalize on its early lead over Sirius in the industry. Analysts were now expecting XM to end 2004 with 3.11 million subscribers versus about 1 million for Sirius (see Exhibit 3). During 2004, XM Radio's net subscriber additions (gross additions less cancellations) were 1.75 million, versus 0.76 million for Sirius. XM was

Exhibit 3   Forecasted Subscriber Growth

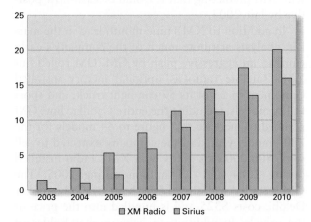

Source: Salomon Smith Barney Estimates. 2003 figures are actual figures.

forecasted to have 5.31 million subscribers in 2005, versus 2.14 million for Sirius.

Sirius had tried to differentiate itself by aggressively signing valuable branded content. In December 2003, Sirius signed a seven-year exclusive deal with the National Football League to broadcast football games, beginning with the 2005–2006 season. The deal cost Sirius $188 million in cash over the course of the contract, plus 32 million in warrants. In early October 2004, Sirius signed up "shock jock" Howard Stern to an exclusive five-year deal for $500 million, which would start to air on January 1, 2006. The branded content was used by Sirius to justify the premium subscription price of its service.

XM Radio has responded to these moves with deals of its own. In October 2004, XM signed an 11-year, $650 million deal with Major League Baseball, giving XM exclusive rights to the satellite broadcast of games beginning 2005, including the World Series. Also in October 2004, XM launched a premium channel dedicated to shock jocks Opie and Anthony, who had previously been removed from the air due to profanity. The Opie and Anthony channel will cost subscribers an additional $1.99 a month.

By late 2004, the business models at XM Radio and Sirius were starting to crystallize. It was now clear that earlier statements regarding break-even subscription levels were too low. A detailed research report on XM Radio by Salomon Smith Barney suggested that the company would not start to generate positive earnings before interest, taxes, depreciation, and amortization

(EBITDA) until 2007, when the subscriber base was forecasted to be about 11 million (see Exhibit 4).[15] On the same basis, Sirius was not expected to start generating a positive EBITDA until 2008.

The key variables in analysts' estimation of break-even volume were subscription revenues, fixed costs, variable costs, customer acquisition costs, and customer churn rates. For 2004, Salomon Smith Barney estimated that XM Radio would have revenues of $243 million, with only $6 million of those being attributed to advertising revenues. Fixed costs—which included costs related to equipment, broadcasting, programming and content, and customer support—were estimated to be around $175 million. Variable costs—including revenue sharing with partners such as GM, royalties paid for the right to broadcast songs, and customer care costs—amounted to $96.5 million. The average cost of acquiring a customer—including advertising, marketing, and subsidies given to equipment suppliers—was pegged at $130/customer and forecasted to hit $279.9 million in 2004. In its 2003 10-K, XM Radio estimated that 1.3% of its paying

customers left the service every month. However, if nonpaying customers who received the service on a trial basis through automobile companies were counted in, the churn rate rises to 3.5% a month.

Sirius had a similar revenue and cost structure to XM Radio, although accounting differences make a direct comparison difficult (see Exhibit 5). The largest difference was that Sirius still charged a premium price for subscriptions but was also committed to paying higher fees for content on an annualized basis. In 2006, for example, forecasts suggested that programming costs per subscriber will be $3.88 at Sirius and $1.31 at XM Radio.[16] Sirius also had a larger customer churn rate than XM Radio in 2004, around 1.7% a month, and a larger customer acquisitions cost, which was forecasted to be about $247 per customer in 2005. The higher customer acquisition costs, relative to XM Radio, were because Sirius paid a larger subsidy to equipment manufacturers, and it had a small base over which to spread its marketing costs. In Exhibit 5, customer acquisition costs are bundled in with marketing expenses.

Exhibit 4   Financial Performance and Forecasts for XM Radio (in $ millions)

	2003	2004E	2005E	2006E	2007E
Revenue	$91.8	$243.5	$469.7	$790	$1,183.2
Variable Costs	($52.4)	($96.5)	($150.9)	($231.5)	($324.3)
Fixed Costs	($143.1)	($175.9)	($248.7)	($281.1)	($299.6)
Customer Acquisition Costs	($192.4)	($279.9)	($347.4)	($412.5)	($508.1)
EBITDA	($296.1)	($308.8)	($277.2)	($135.7)	$51.1

Source: Company Reports and Salomon Smith Barney.

Exhibit 5   Financial Performance and Forecasts for Sirius (in $ millions)

	2003	2004	2005	2006	2007
Revenue	$12.9	$68.2	$186.7	$520.7	$1383.4
Non-Marketing Operating expense	($160.9)	($224.7)	($258.3)	($469.6)	($614.4)
Marketing Expenses	($194.1)	($294.4)	($339.8)	($542.5)	($489.5)
EBITDA	($342.2)	($450.9)	($411.3)	($513.7)	($154.2)

Source: Company Reports and Salomon Smith Barney.

References & Readings

1. K. Bachman. "The Next Wave," *Mediaweek*, April 12, 1999, 26–31.
2. K. Bachman. "Reaching for the Stars," *Mediaweek*, March 25, 2002, 22–27.
3. A. Barry. "A Sound Idea," *Barrons*, February 17, 2003, 17–19.
4. A. Barry. "Interference," *Barrons*, April 21, 2003, 13–14.
5. A. Cosper. "Sirius Competition," *Satellite Broadband*, March 2002, 24–29.
6. K. Batchman, "Reaching for the Stars," 22–30.
7. P. Lewis. "Satellite Radio," *Fortune*, October 15, 2001, 253–256.
8. P. Lewis. "Sirius Competition," *Fortune*, June 23, 2003, 130–132.
9. A.W. Mathews, "From a Distance," *Wall Street Journal*, February 25, 2002, A1.
10. B. McLean. "Satellite Killed the Radio Star," *Fortune*, January 22, 2001, 94–99.
11. E. Rathbun. "Radio Flyer," *Broadcasting & Cable*, June 5, 2000, 18–23.
12. A. Rodgers. "A Little Space Music," *Newsweek*, November 12, 2001, 67–69.
13. Sirius Radio 2002 and 2003 10-K Form.
14. Standard & Poor's *Industry Survey*, Broadcasting and Cable, July 25, 2002.
15. XM Radio 2002 and 2003 10-K Form.
16. Salomon Smith Barney, XM Satellite Radio Holdings, October 26, 2004.

Endnotes

1. Statistics from Standard & Poor's Industry Survey, Broadcasting and Cable, July 25, 2002.
2. Standard & Poor's *Industry Survey*.
3. Clear Channel Communications 2002 10-K Form.
4. XM Radio 2003 10K form.
5. National Cable Television Association Web site and skyreport.com Web site.
6. XM Radio 2002 10K Form. Smith Barney, *XM Satellite Radio Holdings*, October 26, 2004.
7. Smith Barney, *XM Satellite Radio Holdings*.
8. A.W. Mathews, "From a Distance," *Wall Street Journal*, February 25, 2002, A1.
9. Anonymous, "Outstanding Subscriber Growth for XM," *Dealerscope*, June 2003, 5.
10. Anonymous, "XM Satellite Radio to Be Standard Equipment on Honda Accord Models," *Dow Jones News Wire*, September 9, 2003.
11. Smith Barney, *XM Satellite Radio Holdings*.
12. A. Barry. "A Sound Idea," *Barron's*, February 17, 2003, 17–19.
13. K. Batchman, "Reaching for the Stars," *Mediaweek*, March 25, 2003, 22–30.
14. A. Barry. "A Sound Idea," 17–19.
15. Smith Barney, *XM Satellite Radio Holdings*.
16. Smith Barney, *Sirius Satellite Radio*, October 26, 2004.

SATELLITE RADIO (B)

INTRODUCTION

As 2005 unfolded, the good times seemed to be just around the corner for the satellite radio business. XM Radio ended 2005 with almost 6 million subscribers, and Sirius with a shade over 3.3 million, both surpassing forecasts made a year earlier. Moreover, with churn rates only 1.5% a month, the lowest for any major subscription business, both companies could argue that their users clearly placed a high value on the product offering. Mel Karmazin, the CEO of Sirius, argued this was because, "Our programming is so compelling, so strong, and so sticky."[1] Forecasts called for the two companies to have a combined subscriber base of 44 million by 2010, divided more or less evenly between the two companies. For 2006, the subscriber base was expected to reach 15 million.

GROWTH RATES SLOW

Late 2005 proved to be the high point of expectations for satellite radio. As 2006 progressed, the growth rate started to decelerate. The two companies ended the year with 14 million subscribers, one million less than forecasted (Sirius had 6 million and XM Radio 8 million subscribers). Moreover both companies continued to lose money; Sirius lost $513 million in 2006 and XM Radio lost $719 million. As investors fretted about whether the companies would ever gain enough subscribers to cover their fixed costs, the stock prices of both fell sharply. Despite subscriber growth throughout 2007—XM ended the year with 9 million subscribers and Sirius with 8.3 million—losses continued to mount. Sirius lost $327 million in 2007 and XM $682 million. The 44 million subscribers forecasted for 2010 now seemed out of reach. One analyst forecasted 32 million subscribers for the two companies by 2011.

Various reasons were offered to explain the slowing growth rate. One was competition from other formats for listening to music. By 2007, some 57 million Americans were listening to some form of Web radio every week and analysts worried that in the near future, Web radio might be streamed to cars using WiMax technology. Of more immediate concern, increasingly people were listening to music using iPods, more than 200 million of which had been sold by 2007. Many cars were now fitted with racks for iPods (about 40% of cars sold in 2007 came with sound systems that were compatible with iPods).

Another problem was the core demographic for satellite radio seemed to be middle aged people. Many younger people would rather listen to their own playlists downloaded from iTunes and played on iPods. While satellite radio offered music programming, people with iPods preferred to program their own music. A study by Forrester Research

---

This case was prepared by Charles W. L. Hill, School of Business, University of Washington. Reprinted by permission.

estimated that only about 13% of the population actually wanted satellite radio and that the percentage would shrink significantly if the satellite radio companies started to run advertising.

Compounding matters was the auto business facing a sharp downturn. Because auto dealers were the major distribution channel for satellite radio, as car sales shrank so did the number of new subscriber additions. What was a slowdown in sales became a major crisis in 2008, as tight credit in the United States led to a sharp contraction in auto sales. Auto sales for 2008 were expected to total only 13.5 million, down from 16.1 million in 2007. Forecasts for 2009 suggested sales of 13.1 million.

MERGER PROPOSAL

In February 2007, the Sirius and XM Radio announced plans to merge. Under the merger agreement, Sirius offered 4.6 of its shares for each XM share, leaving each side with 50% of the new venture. Sirius closed on the day before the announcement at $3.70 a share while XM was at $13.98. The merger valued the combined companies at $13 billion. The stock price of both companies dropped following the merger announcement, knocking $2 billion off the market capitalization of the combined entity.

The main benefit claimed for the merger was cost reduction, particularly marketing and programming costs. About 34% of XM's revenue in 2006 went to programming and marketing expenses, while 47% of Sirius' revenue was eaten up by these costs, many of which were fixed. The costly war for content between the two companies, exemplified by Sirius $50 million deal with Howard Stern, would also come to an end. One analyst estimated that the combined company could save up to $4 billion through cost reductions over six years.

The merger would also enable the new company to offer a wider range of channels. Although duplicate channels would be eliminated, no longer, for example, would the National Football League be exclusive to one provider and Major League Baseball to another. This could help with subscriber retention and growth.

Implementation problems included making radio receivers that were compatible with both satellite systems (something that the companies had already been working on under a Federal Communications Commission mandate) and in the long run, rationalizing the satellite system. From a practical point of view, many subscribers might balk at having to replace their radios with ones that can receive signals from both satellites, which could stretch out the implementation over years.

The proposed merger faced two regulatory hurdles. The Department of Justice had to agree to the merger, which created a monopoly in satellite radio, and the Federal Communications Commission (FCC) also had to sign off. The FCC would have to reverse its mandate in 1995, when it allocated satellite radio spectrum, that "one (satellite radio) licensee will not be permitted to acquire control of the other remaining" one.

Opposition to the merger quickly emerged from the National Association of Broadcasters (NAB), which represented conventional radio broadcaster. The NAB argued that a national satellite radio monopoly could overwhelm local broadcasters. They claimed that the new company might win additional business in the biggest markets by offering them channels with local news, weather and information.

In the end, the key issues centered on the definition of the "relevant market" for Sirius and XM Radio. If the relevant market was defined narrowly as the market for satellite radio, then the merger seemed doomed on antitrust grounds. Alternatively, the satellite radio companies argued that the relevant market was all broadcast radio, of which satellite radio was just a small segment. The satellite companies pointed out that 240 million people listened to conventional radio, and that satellite radio in total comprised less than 5% of the combined satellite and terrestrial broadcast market. They also argued that their service was competing with Internet radio and other ways of consuming music, such as the iPod.

In March 2008, the Justice Department gave the go-ahead to the merger, and the FCC followed with a green light in July 2008. Both government bodies agreed on a broad definition of the relevant market. However, as part of the price for allowing the merger to proceed, the FCC required that new company to offer more content *a la carte* pricing schemes, with lower priced subscriptions schemes being offered for access to limited content, and higher priced schemes offered for access to *premium* content. This raised the possibility that many subscribers might opt for a less expensive monthly subscription rate, which could materially impact the revenues of the new company.

The FCC also mandated that there would be no increase in the price of the base subscription plan, which stood at $12.95 a month, for three years.

IMMEDIATE AFTERMATH

The merger was consummated on July 29, 2008. The new company was called Sirius XM. Mel Karmazin, the CEO of Sirius, became the CEO of the combined entity. For the time being, XM would function as a wholly owned subsidiary of Sirius. In early September, Sirius XM estimated that the net synergies from the merger would total $425 million, $25 million more than originally thought, and that the company would generate positive cash flow in 2009. Sirius forecasted that it would end 2008 with 19.5 million subscribers and 2009 with 21.5 million. However, the continuing contraction in the United States automobile industry, a result of the 2008 financial crisis, raised questions about how attainable this actually was. Some 80% of all new subscriptions came though sales at auto dealers in 2007.

Having lost some $4 billion between 2005 and 2007, and with no prospect of becoming profitable soon, Sirius XM now faces substantial funding issues. The company has $1.05 billion of debt that will become due in 2009. Its cash on hand, which stood at $442 million in September 2008, could fall substantially in 2009 as it pays down debt and spends $100 million on a new satellite that is planned. Mel Karmazin has pledged to not issue any new equity to pay down debt, so a significant portion of the debt coming due in 2009 will have to be refinanced—not an easy prospect given the credit crunch in United States financial markets.

By October 2008, the stock of the new company was trading at under $0.40 a share, down from a high $3.40. The market capitalization of the new company was down to $1.2 billion. If the stock trades at under $1 for 30 consecutive days, it faces possible delisting from the NASDAQ stock exchange, which would have adverse consequences on its ability to raise capital. To avoid this possibility, Sirius XM was looking at the potential for a reverse 10 for 1 stock split.

References & Readings

1. Anonymous, "Howard's Way," *The Economist*, January 14, 2006, 65.
2. Anonymous, "They Cannot Be Sirius," *The Economist*, February 24, 2007, 77.
3. J. C. Anselmo and M. A. Taverna, "Urge to Merge," *Aviation Week and Space Technology*, February 26, 2007, 92.
4. Argus Research, *Sirius XM Radio Inc*, September 15, 2008.
5. C. Holahan and A. Hesseldahl, "Sirius and XM Get the Justice Go-Ahead," *Business Week Online*, March 26, 2008.
6. Olga Kharif, "The FCC Approves the XM-Sirius Merger," *Business Week Online*, July 28, 2008.
7. Olga Kharif, "Sirius XM Is in a Serious Bind," *Business Week Online*, September 18, 2008.
8. T. Lowry and P. Lehman, "XM and Sirius: What a Merger Won't Fix," *Business Week*, March 5, 2007, 31.

THE RISE OF IBM

From its beginnings as a company that developed instruments to measure time, IBM grew to become the world's largest computer company. At its height in 1966, its stock was valued at $140; in 1993, its stock was trading at $42 a share, and shareholders had lost hundreds of billions of dollars of their investments. How could a giant company like IBM have fallen so low? How could the company strengths that contributed to its success have led to its fall? Why did IBM lose control of its customers and markets? To understand the problems that IBM currently faces, we need to look at IBM's past and at the way its strategy and structure developed over time.

BEFORE THE COMPUTER

In 1900, Charles Flint, a financier and arms merchant, owned, among other businesses, the International Time Recording Company (ITR), a clock manufacturer, and Computing Scale Company of America, a weighing scale and food slicing machine manufacturer.[1] These two business machine manufacturers formed the seeds of what was to become IBM. In the search for new markets for its products, ITR began to produce new kinds of time measuring machines that, among other things, permitted the rapidly expanding Bell telephone company to time its customers' long-distance calls. By 1910, ITR had become the leader in the time recording industry and had sales over $1 million. Computing Scale's main product was a scale that weighed items and calculated the cost per unit; the company also sold meat and cheese slicers to retail stores.[2]

Toward the end of the 19th century, an engineer named Herman Hollerith invented a calculating machine that sorted cards by punched holes. Any kind of data could be recorded by punching holes according to a standard procedure; and then the data could be analyzed statistically to provide a picture of the overall results. Potential customers for this device were organizations, such as government agencies, railroads, and retail establishments, that needed a way of managing and manipulating large amounts of information. The U.S. Census Bureau, for example, saw the potential of this device for handling its national data collection efforts, and Hollerith was awarded a contract for managing the data processing of the 1890 census. Holes were punched in cards to represent different census attributes, such as age, sex, and national origin. The cards were then sorted by the punched holes, and Hollerith's calculating machine supplied the requested data, such as the statistics for the percentage of people in a certain age group in a certain state.

The punch card machine required a huge number of punched cards—in the census, one for every family unit—that could be used only once, so each machine sale provided card revenue. Thus, although the machines performed quickly and accurately, they were expensive to operate. Nevertheless, the potential uses of the machine were limitless because any kind of data could be recorded on these cards. James Powers, an employee of the U.S. Census Bureau, immediately saw the potential of the calculating machine; from his experience with Hollerith's machines at the Census Bureau, he understood its strengths and weaknesses. Using this information,

For the most recent financial results of the company discussed in this case, go to http://finance.yahoo.com, input the company's stock symbol, and download the latest company report from its homepage.

Powers stole a march on Hollerith by inventing an improved calculating machine; using his contacts at the Census Bureau, he managed to get the contract for the 1910 census.[3]

Hollerith was now in a difficult position; he had lost his principal customer and lacked the resources to improve his machine and find new customers. He approached Flint to get him to invest in the business, but Flint, seeing the opportunity to broaden his company's line of business machines, decided to acquire Hollerith's Tabulating Machine Company. In 1911, Flint merged it with ITR and Computing Scale to form the Computing Tabulating & Recording Company (CTR).[4]

Although Power's machine was technologically better, Hollerith had developed the practice of only leasing his machines to customers. Customers liked this arrangement because it lowered their costs. Also, Hollerith provided a repair service for the machines, which were prone to breakdown. Using CTR's resources, the calculating machines were continually improved over time, and the new and improved machines were leased to customers. These leases provided CTR with a continuing source of revenues, but, more importantly, each of CTR's customers were required to buy their punch cards from CTR; 75% of the tabulating revenues came from the sale of the punched cards, while only 25% came from the lease of the actual machines. In 1912, CTR's profits were $541,000, with two-thirds coming from ITR. Its time machine division, however, saw profits rise to $613,000 in 1913 with most of the increase coming from the calculators. This proved very important to CTR because the next year, 1914, profits plunged to $490,000 due to a decline in the time clock sector, and the calculating business kept the company afloat.[5]

Thomas Watson Arrives at CTR

In 1914, to build CTR's business, Flint agreed to hire Thomas Watson as the general manager of CTR.[6] Watson was a former employee of National Cash Register (NCR), another major business machine company, which Watson had joined in 1895 when he was 21 years old. Watson had a passion for selling and began selling pianos, sewing machines, and organs when he was 18. However, the opportunity to earn large commissions eventually led him to NCR, where a mentor took an interest in his career and helped him develop selling skills until he became the star salesman at NCR within three years. Watson became an NCR branch manager in 1899.[7]

To exploit Watson's talents, NCR assigned him to create an independent company, called Watson's Cash Register and Secondhand Exchange, using NCR funds to beat NCR's competitors in the used cash register market. Just as NCR had a virtual monopoly over the sale of new cash registers, Watson set out to monopolize the used cash register market by deliberately undercutting competitors' prices. With their businesses failing, NCR then acquired its competitors. In 1912, Watson and 29 other NCR managers were indicted for a violation of antitrust laws. Watson was fined and sentenced to one year in jail; however, although he won an appeal, he decided to leave NCR. Watson had other offers in the boat, auto, and retail industries, but because he wanted to use his knowledge of business machines, he accepted the offer at CTR.[8]

Watson's career at NCR was significant because he implemented many of NCR's sales practices at CTR. Although NCR's competitors had higher quality cash registers than NCR, NCR consistently beat the competition because of the way it organized and rewarded its sales force. NCR had a strong sales force in which salespeople were granted exclusive territories and paid on commission. This made them aggressively pursue all sales opportunities in their territories. They continually called on customers and built strong, personal relationships with them. This sales strategy had been developed by the leader of NCR, John Patterson, who believed that a product was worthless until it was sold. Patterson insisted that NCR salespeople answer repair calls immediately and instilled in them that they were selling a *service* not just a *product*. NCR created a training school in 1894 for its salespeople; it also established the NCR "Hundred Point Club," which recognized and rewarded salespeople who had exceeded their quotas. Members of the club received bonuses and trips to conventions in big cities, coverage in the company newspaper, and congratulations from Patterson.[9] As described following, Watson took full advantage of his knowledge of NCR's sales practices at CTR. However, he also took full advantage of his entrepreneurial ability to sense unmet customer needs. He was fascinated with the potential of the punch-card calculating machine.

In 1904, Watson had seen a friend at Eastman Kodak using a Hollerith punch card calculating machine to monitor salespeople. Each time a sale was completed, all the data was entered onto a card, which was sorted and tabulated monthly to generate reports indicating what each person sold, which products were selling best in which regions, etc. The cards were permanent records that could be filed, accumulated, and printed automatically.[10] The punch card system eliminated boring jobs such as copying ledger entries and writing bills. Furthermore, the machines were relatively inexpensive compared to employing clerks to keep records, dependable, and fast. Thus as head of CTR, Watson was most interested in the calculating machine side of the business, even though the time measurement business generated the highest sales and profits.

When Watson became president of CTR in 1915 after NCR, he convinced Flint that CTR should devote most of its resources to developing the tabulator side of the business. Watson implemented a plan to develop new tabulators, recorders, and printers to print the output of the tabulating machine. To achieve this new plan, the company funded the development of a research laboratory to improve the tabulating machines and established a facility to train salespeople. His goal was to create a sales force like NCR's sales force and make better tabulating machines than CTR's competitors. To help provide the revenue to achieve this, Watson licensed foreign companies to produce and sell the tabulators in foreign markets. The licensees paid a royalty to CTR based on sales. This was the beginning of CTR's international strategy. Within two years, CTR's research laboratory created a new line of tabulators that were easier to use than competitors' models and priced below their prices, offered for lease on favorable terms. Powers was CTR's major competitor at this time.

To compete with Powers, who had tabulators as good as CTR, Watson used the strategy that NCR had developed in the cash register business: Watson, like Patterson, emphasized that the salesperson's role was to provide good quality customer service, not merely to lease and install a machine. He established the "100 Percent Club" to reward salespeople, and those who met quotas were honored at conventions. Employees were also paid on commission, and quotas were increased each year.[11] In addition, employees received a premium salary and good benefits, and the company's policy of internal promotion made it possible for hard-working employees to advance quickly in the organization.[12] These employment practices made it easy for CTR to attract and retain good employees and gain the commitment of its workforce.[13]

By 1917, CTR's sales had increased to $8.3 million from $4.2 million in 1914. All three of its divisions were doing well. Computing Scale's products were now used in shipyards and factories throughout the United States to measure the quantity of products, such as nuts and bolts. ITR had record sales due to World War I. CTR had leased 1,400 tabulators by the end of the war. Virtually all big insurance companies, railroads, and government agencies used CTR's tabulators. In addition to leasing the machines, sales of punch cards were also increasing and contributing to company revenues. In 1919, CTR launched a new printer that displayed the data collected and analyzed in the Hollerith tabulators and card sorters. The printer was also priced less than the machine made by Powers and was so successful that CTR had a backorder for the printers. Watson planned to build a new production plant to meet the high demand.[14]

The large expenditures on research and development (R&D) and developing a skilled national sales force put a severe strain on the company's resources. It was so severe that when sales revenues dropped from a record $16 million in 1920 to $10.6 million in 1921 due to slump in the economy, CTR was in trouble and needed external funds to survive. Fortunately for the company, Guaranty Trust Bank loaned CTR the money it needed to meet current liabilities. In 1922, sales revenues rebounded, and the company made a profit. However, the company had to cut costs in every area, including sales and R&D. CTR learned not to let cash balances go too low and implemented policies of low dividends, high revenues, and careful cost controls. In addition, the company intentionally refrained from introducing new products until a mass market had developed for its new range of tabulating machines.[15]

Watson became chairman of CTR in 1924 and renamed the company International Business Machines (IBM). This new name not only presented an integrated image of the company's three main product lines but also indicated the direction Watson planned for the company: providing advanced business machines for both domestic and foreign markets.

IBM's strategy from the 1920s on was to produce and lease business machines that collected, processed, and presented large amounts of data. From 1924 to 1941, IBM's primary business was the production and lease of punch card tabulating machines, and punch cards contributed most to the revenues of the company. As the technology of punch card machines became more advanced, they could sort 400 cards a minute and print paychecks and address labels. Tabulating machines were increasingly used by large companies to keep records on their employees, suppliers, and customer accounts.[16] Companies usually leased IBM's machines; IBM developed a specific punch card system to meet the needs of each individual customer.[17] For example, IBM developed a coding system appropriate to each client's information processing needs.

The potential of punch card tabulating machines had been recognized by other companies as well. Although the Powers Accounting Machine Corporation had long been IBM's competitor, new competitors included Burroughs, NCR, Remington Rand, and Underwood Elliot Fisher. Underwood, created in 1927, ruled the typewriter industry with its Model 5 and had a sales force as good as IBM's, while Burroughs was the leader in adding machines. At this time, IBM was not interested in mass producing machines like typewriters and adding machines unless such machines could be made part of the tabulating system. Its strategy was to lease its machines and then support the machines with trained service representatives who were available to handle customers' problems and make suggestions for improving customers' information processing as their individual businesses changed. Leasing gave IBM several competitive advantages over Burroughs, NCR, and Remington Rand who all sold machines. First, it allowed the company to retain control over outdated technology that could not be resold in the used market (a problem NCR had encountered). Second, leasing made it easier for the customers because they were not committed to a large capital outlay or purchasing outmoded machines. Third, leasing provided IBM with a steady cash flow. Moreover, by leasing machines, IBM was also able to force customers to purchase the thousands of cards they used each month from

IBM. The practice of making customers buy its cards led to an antitrust law suit in 1936. The Supreme Court ruled that IBM should discontinue requiring customers to buy cards from IBM alone. However, this ruling had no impact because IBM was the only effective supplier of cards, and its sales force made sure that customers were kept happy.

During the 1920s and 1930s, IBM also began to develop specialized tabulators to handle specific types of information processing needs for customers. For example, IBM developed a proofing machine for banks that could sort and add checks, a very labor-intensive process. This proof machine, which was called the IBM 405 and launched in 1932, became IBM's most profitable product at the time. The 405 consisted of a punch, a sorter, and an accounting machine. Operators punched holes in cards to represent data. The sorter put the cards in the appropriate bins. The cards were then taken out of the bin and run through the accounting machines, which generated printouts of the data and could also print checks. Some customers rented verifiers that attached to the punch to ensure the cards were properly prepared. IBM trained its customers' employees on how to use the 405 at no cost to ensure a demand for their products.

By 1939, IBM was the biggest and most powerful business machine company in the United States. IBM owned about 80% of the keypunches, sorters, and accounting machines used for tabulating purposes. By this time, Remington Rand and Burroughs were minor competitors, and the Powers company had disappeared, unable to match IBM's strengths in sales and R&D.[18]

By 1939, Watson had also reorganized the company's business divisions. The punch card tabulating division was now the center of the company's business, and he was building the company's other divisions around this division. For example, Watson decided to keep ITR, which sold time clocks among other things, because customers bought many time cards, which were similar to punched cards. However, he sold off the largest part of the scale division because it no longer fit the company's new direction. On the other hand, Watson bought Electromatic Typewriter Company because it was working on keypunch consoles. By 1945, IBM developed this company to become the United States leader in electric typewriters, which were sold by IBM's large and well-trained sales force.[19]

In 1939, total revenues were $34.8 million, and profits were $9.1 million. Sales of punch cards were about $5 million of this total and had higher profit margins than any other product.[20] However, the start of World War II accelerated the demand for IBM's tabulating machines, and sales rose to $143.3 million by 1943. However, profits were only $9.7 million compared to $9.1 million due to the wartime excess profits tax. Higher sales were achieved because IBM created mobile punch card units that followed supply controllers across war zones, and bookkeeping was done on the battle-field.[21] For example, a mobile unit would go to a Pacific island and compute the soldiers' payrolls. The tabulators also recorded bombing results, casu-alties, prisoners, displaced persons, and supplies. A punch card record was maintained on every man drafted and followed him until he was discharged from the military.[22]

THE COMPUTER AGE

Toward the end of World War II, a research team at the University of Pennsylvania constructed a computer to solve math problems for the army; the machine, called the ENIAC, could compute ballistic tables for the big guns of World War II. In 1946, the ENIAC was the only working computer in the world. This computer was the size of a small house and had 18,000 vacuum tubes, which tended to burn out. The machine cost $3 million to build, took a long time to set up, and was very difficult to use. The inventors of the computer, J. Presper Eckert and John Mauchley, realized that computers could take the place of punch card tabulating machines and that they would eventually be used in business. They created a company to develop and manufac-ture a computer for commercial use, the Univac (standing for UNIVersal Automatic Computer). In 1948, they received an order from the U.S. Census Bureau for their computer (just as Hollerith had 60 years before), and in the same year, Prudential Insurance also ordered a Univac.[23] These organiza-tions were two of IBM's largest customers, and so IBM became interested in the new computer tech-nology.[24] However, in 1950, Remington Rand, which also sold typewriters, tabulators, filing cabinets, and electric shavers, forestalled IBM and bought Eckert

and Mauchley's company to gain entry into the new computer market. Just as Watson had realized the potential of the punch card machine, so Remington realized the potential of the computer. The race was on to become the company that would dominate the next generation of business machines—computers.

IBM had not ignored technical developments in the tabulating industry. By 1948, it had developed an electromechanical machine called the MARK I that was 51 feet long by 8 feet high and cost $1 million. This machine was more advanced than a punch card machine, but it was still not a true computer. It was slower than the Univac.[25]

Tom Watson's two sons, Tom Jr. and Arthur ("Dick"), joined IBM at the end of the war.[26] Tom Jr. convinced his father that IBM would lose everything if it did not embrace the new technology and enter the computer market.[27] Large insurance companies such as Prudential and Metropolitan Life were IBM companies that had been complaining for a long time that the punch card system required too much storage space and was becoming too slow and cumbersome to handle the volume of information these companies were generating. IBM began investigating new kinds of storage systems, such as magnetic tapes, and look-ing at computers that used new electronic circuits to sort data and handle calculations. After looking at the ENIAC computer, which used the new elec-tronic circuits, Watson Jr. encouraged IBM's research laboratory managers to recruit more electronic spe-cialists.[28] He prodded IBM to incorporate electronic circuits in punch card machines because a primitive electronic circuit could perform 5,000 additions per second compared to 4 per second for the fastest mechanism in a punch card machine.

Working quickly, and with access to the com-pany's large resource base, IBM developed a new machine in 1946 that could compute payroll in one-tenth the time a punch card machine could do it. The 603 Electronic Multiplier was not a true com-puter; numbers were processed from punch cards rather than from signals recorded in the machine's memory circuits. The machine was upgraded to the 604, which had electronic circuits that could divide. When it was introduced in mid-1948, it sold by the thousands. Both machines matched IBM's exist-ing punch card equipment, which made it easy for IBM's customers to upgrade to the new machines. The machine's success convinced Tom Watson Jr. and Senior that electronics would grow even faster. From this time on, the company committed its resources to developing an advanced new computer system, just as 30 years before Tom Sr. had bet CTR's future on advanced punch card machines.[29]

IBM began working on its first family of electronic computers, called the 701 in 1949. Tom Jr. became president of the domestic division of IBM in 1952, the same year in which the 701 was launched.[30] The 701 was a scientific computer for use in laboratories, but it was not as advanced as the Univac. However, although Remington Rand was ahead in technology, the company lacked IBM's vision, and Rand would not permit punch card salespeople to sell Univacs. Tom Jr., however, placed IBM's sales force behind its computer and required both senior executives and engineers to help train its sales force in operating the new machine. By 1953, IBM installed 32 of its 701 computer machines and had 164 on order compared to Remington Rand's 33 installations and 24 orders.

The 702, a commercial computer for general accounting applications, was launched in 1954. This machine was faster than the Univac, and with this machine, IBM took the technological lead. By 1956, IBM had 87 computers installed at various businesses and 190 on order, compared to all other competitors combined installations of 41 and combined orders of 40 computers.[31] Because all its machines were leased, it was easy for IBM to upgrade its customers to its new advanced machines. When the 705 was developed to replace the 702, and the 704 to replace the 701, IBM retained and increased its market share.[32] Between 1950 and 1956, IBM's revenues tripled from $214.9 million to $743.3 million.[33] The average growth rate of the company from 1946 to 1955 was 22%. Watson Jr. decided to expand IBM's product line as fast as the market would allow.

IBM's technological success was due to the way Watson Jr. had totally changed the company's R&D thrust. IBM's research lab had been dominated by engineers because its punch card machines operated on mechanical principles. None of its engineers understood electronics, however, so Watson Jr. hired a new lab chief and increased the staff from 500 mechanical engineers and technicians in 1950 to more than 4,000 electrical engineers by 1956. Watson Jr. also created a smaller lab in California to specialize in storage devices. In less than three years, this lab invented the computer disk that stores data

on magnetic tape that became the backbone of IBM's future computer systems.

Watson Jr. also led the development of the IBM 650 in 1956 that provided enough data processing power for most general commercial applications. The 650 was less powerful than the 700 series, but it was much cheaper. The 650 introduced thousands of punch card customers to computers. It was designed to work with ordinary punch card equipment but made the punch card system much more powerful and versatile. For example, life insurance companies compute insurance premiums from actuarial tables based upon the age, sex, and other customer factors. Using a 650, these actuarial tables could be loaded into the computer memory, and when the punch card containing information on a customer was loaded into the machine, the computer did the calculations and furnished the total.[34] Previously, a clerk had to figure the totals and record the information on a punch card for recording purposes; the 650 did everything.

IBM put its huge sales force behind the 650 machine, and as a result of its efforts, within a year almost 1,000 machines were sold. Most computers were used in administrative offices and in factories for controlling the manufacturing process.[35] By the end of the 1950s, IBM had a 75% market share. The remaining market was divided among Remington Rand, Honeywell Electronics, NCR, and a few others. Although Underwood Typewriter and NCR attempted to launch small computers, the 650 was a better performer.

The Transistor

In 1956, the transistor, developed by William Shockley at Bell Labs, weighed 100 times less than the vacuum tube. Compared to a vacuum tube, the transistor required a lot less electrical power, could perform calculations at a much faster rate, and had the potential to miniaturize computing systems. The transistor made it feasible both to design a more complex and powerful computer and sell it at a price that most companies could afford.[36]

IBM researchers had been successfully using the vacuum tube, and like the mechanical engineers before them, they were reluctant to change to a transistor-based computer technology. Watson Jr. sent a memo to development personnel stating that no more IBM machines would be designed using vacuum tubes.[37] This memo started a whole new thrust in IBM's research efforts that ultimately led to the 7000 computer series, IBM's first computers based on transistors instead of vacuum tubes.[38] However, scientists had a hard time wiring transistors together until the integrated circuit was invented in 1959 by a Fairchild Semiconductor engineer. The whole circuit board was the size of a fingernail. By the early 1960s, IBM computers guided Polaris missiles and air force jets. When integrated circuits were mass produced, their cost fell from $1,000 per circuit in 1960 to a few cents per circuit by 1970. IBM developed successive generations of more powerful machines to exploit the new technology.[39]

Redefining the Industry

By 1960, IBM's computer division was disorganized and had a product line consisting of eight newer transistor-based computers and several older vacuum tube machines. This caused several problems for IBM's customers because the computers were not compatible. For example, if a customer expanded and wanted to upgrade to a larger or newer computer, the customer had to lease a whole new range of equipment and rewrite all the programs to make the computer work in the company. The disjointed product line was also causing problems for IBM's personnel. Because IBM's product line had grown so large, Watson Jr. decided to split the data processing division into two units: one for machines that rented for over $10,000 a month and one for machines that rented for less than $10,000 a month. However, this product division caused competition between managers of the different product lines, each of whom fought to obtain resources to develop and improve their particular product line. This also led to a duplication of R&D efforts. The diverse range of computers made it more difficult for IBM's sales force to learn the different systems associated with each computer and to efficiently inform customers about their suitability for their particular business.

IBM's technological thrust had outpaced the ability of the company to adequately service its products. Its attempt to become the leader in the industry resulted in the development of a fragmented product line that was confusing its customers and employees. The company needed a new strategy to grow. Watson Jr.'s answer was that IBM needed to build a line of computers that would cover the needs of the whole computer market. The project was called the System/360, representing 360 degrees in a circle, because IBM wanted to meet the needs of every user in both the scientific and business community. The 360 was intended to make all other computers, both IBM's and its competitor's, obsolete. All of the 360 computers would be compatible with one another. Moreover, they would all use the same operating language, software, disk drives, printers, etc. The goal of this design was to lock in customers to IBM's computer systems and make it difficult for customers to change to competing products. Their incentive would be keep buying new IBM products when they wanted to upgrade their systems. The other goal of the system was to make better use of IBM's R&D resources and make it easier for its sales force to sell an integrated package of products to customers. The project was challenging because hardware and software had to be coordinated, and IBM began producing its own electronic parts for the first time.[40] IBM opened six new plants around the world to manufacture the System/360 computers. Over a four-year period, $5 billion was invested, and 50,000 new employees were hired.[41]

The System/360 mainframe computer was launched in 1964 and captured 70% of the market.[42] The project was an immense success and put IBM way ahead of its competitors. Although before the 360, competitors such as RCA, Burroughs, Honeywell, Univac, and General Electric sold machines that performed much better than IBM computers for the same price, the compatible design and the power of the System/360 beat all competitors.[43] Moreover, marketing played as large a role in the success of the project as did technology. Although all its competitors had access to integrated circuits and could produce an advanced computer, only IBM had the capacity to sell a machine, install it correctly, and provide the quality service that allowed it to retain and lock in its customers.

Due to the success of the System/360 mainframes and the IBM sales force, IBM dominated the computer industry.[44] The 360 spurred growth in the whole industry. In 1963, there were only 11,700 computers in the United States, however; this figure doubled in 1965 and redoubled in 1969. By 1969, IBM had revenues of $7.196 billion and earnings of $934 million. Although, the situation was masked by increasing revenues from world trade and interest earned from investments, by 1970, IBM was starting to slow down. Its stock price actually declined in 1970. The company had grown at an annual rate of 22% from 1946 to 1955, but its growth was only 16% per year from 1955 to 1970 and slowed further after 1970. The reason was that IBM was beginning to face competition from other companies who had begun to produce computers for other segments of the computer market. Before we examine the new competition in the computer industry, it is useful to discuss the scope of IBM's domestic and foreign operations to understand how large and complex the company had become.

GLOBAL DEVELOPMENT

IBM's movement into global markets began in 1908 when Herman Hollerith made a licensing agreement with the British Tabulating Company (BTC) to produce and sell Hollerith tabulators throughout the British Empire. Tom Watson Sr. continued with Hollerith's vision of IBM as an international company and established IBM's foreign department. After WWI, he began to build small manufacturing plants in Germany, France, and Great Britain to evade the tariffs these countries levied on foreign imports. Sales and marketing agencies were also created throughout Europe, Latin America, and parts of Asia. The branches were called Watson Business Machines and their function, as in the United States, was to provide the high level of customer service that supported IBM's business machines. In 1935, foreign revenue was $1.6 million, with punch cards once again being the biggest contributor. By 1939, more than 12% of IBM's revenues came from foreign operations.

During WWII, IBM's plants in Europe and Japan were seized. However, even though IBM's German plant, which contributed 50% of the foreign department's revenue, was in ruins, by 1945, foreign revenues were almost $2 million. After the war, IBM's British plant became the largest facility outside North America. In 1949, IBM renegotiated the 1908 agreement with BTC whereby BTC, would receive a free, nonexclusive license on all current IBM products in exchange for letting IBM sell its new products through its own sales organization. This agreement resulted in the creation of a new subsidiary called

IBM UK, which, selling IBM's new advanced computers, soon came to dominate the British and European markets.

In 1949, Dick Watson, who spoke German, French, Italian, and Spanish, was put in charge of IBM's international operations. In 1950, the foreign department was renamed the IBM World Trade Division and became an independent subsidiary that would receive product and financial support from the IBM domestic Division but would operate on its own. By 1950, the World Trade Division had 10 factories producing machines and more than 20 facilities making cards throughout the world. The World Trade Division operated in 58 countries through subsidiaries such as IBM Deutschland, IBM France, and many smaller units in Latin America and Africa.[45]

Of World Trade's 16,000 employees in 1954, only 200 were Americans because Dick Watson believed that most success would be achieved if each subsidiary was responsive to the needs of its own region or country. Dick Watson set high standards for the World Trade Division, hired good people as country managers, and was responsive to local customs. So, for example, the German subsidiary would be staffed by German nationals who could be responsive to the needs of its German customers and understand their specific problems.[46] By 1967, foreign revenues were $1.6 billion and net earnings were $209 million. World Trade sales were equal to IBM's domestic sales. Although IBM operated in 130 countries, Europe accounted for two-thirds of foreign revenue.[47] In 1970, Dick Watson resigned from IBM to become the United States ambassador to France. With his departure, the World Trade Division was further divided into world regions: Europe, the Middle East, Africa, the Americas, and the Far East. By 1970, foreign revenues had increased to $3.5 billion.[48]

DOMESTIC OPERATIONS

IBM Domestic, which was led by Tom Watson Jr., was limited to operations in the continental United States, but as the parent company, it was also responsible for R&D and financing operations for the entire company.[49] The rapid growth of the company began to produce enormous problems for the company. By 1950, not only was IBM designing and manufacturing many different models of computers, it was also designing and manufacturing many of the component parts used in the computers, such as disk drives and transistors peripheral equipment such as printers file storage, and servers. The range of the company's activities had increased enormously, and IBM's operating structure had lagged behind the growth in the company, which began to cause many problems.

Despite IBM's growth (in 1955, the company reached $500 million in revenues), it was run by Tom Watson Sr. until he retired in 1955. Watson Sr. oversaw all of IBM's operations, and a line of top managers was always waiting to see him. No formal organizational chart existed because Watson believed that people should be interested in all aspects of IBM's activities rather than focusing on specific jobs. The company had no clear chain of command, no policy of decentralization that gave lower level managers the right to make independent decisions, and no formal planning process or business policies. Knowledge was simply in employees' heads, and strategy emerged gradually over time from discussions and negotiations between Watson Sr. and his top management team.

After Watson Sr.'s retirement, Tom Watson Jr. and Al Williams, IBM's president at the time, decided to construct an organizational chart to see who reported to Watson. They found that 38 to 40 top managers had been reporting directly to him. It was obvious to them that this highly centralized management style could not continue if the rapidly growing company was going to stay on top of the computer industry. Unmade decisions were accumulating because managers lacked the authority to make decisions.

Watson Jr. wanted to break with his father's centralized, autocratic style of decision making and speed up the process, so he and Williams reorganized IBM's operating structure to decentralize control to managers who were given the responsibility of managing the different functional areas of the company. The organization chart they devised put Red Lamotte in charge of sales and R&D and Al Williams in charge of finance, while Watson Jr. would take control of the company's strategy. However, this reorganization simply divided the chaos among three people instead of one; there were still far too many managers reporting to the three top managers, and they were unable to control IBM's operations. So, in 1956, IBM was reorganized along divisional

lines. IBM Domestic was broken up into five individual divisions: the field engineering division, which primarily served commercial customers; the federal systems division, which primarily served government agencies; the systems manufacturing division, which manufactured the computers; the component manufacturing division, which manufactured the components; and the research division, which performed the basic research and design activities. In each division, a general manager would make decisions for the division. The World Trade Division would continue to operate separately from the now subdivided Domestic Division.[50]

This divisional structure ensured that each executive had clearly defined tasks. Watson Jr. created a top management team of six people, consisting of himself and the heads of the five divisions to oversee the company. Each of the five general managers was responsible for a major part of IBM, and Watson Jr. oversaw the entire company. Watson Jr. claimed that his ability to choose and retain an intelligent top management team was his greatest contribution to IBM.[51] He created a corporate staff of experts in sales and marketing, finance, manufacturing, personnel, and communications to advise him and oversee the activities of the divisions. The corporate staff was seen as staff or advisory managers, while divisional managers were seen as line managers, with responsibility for the bottom line operating results. The line managers were responsible for meeting production targets, beat sales quotas, and increase market share. The staff managers gave advice to line managers; the heads of the divisions, who were their superiors, conveyed policy from corporate headquarters to the operating divisions and ensured that the proper objectives were in place and being met. Each line manager would be evaluated solely on his or her unit's results, and each staff manager would be rated on his or her effort in making IBM a world leader.

IBM's divisional structure produced many tensions between corporate (staff) and divisional (line) personnel. For example, as a part of their roles, staff managers would often identify problems that needed to be addressed and would write memos to line managers suggesting how to solve it. Line managers, however, viewed these moves as interference and intrusions into their areas of operations. They began to guard their territories from corporate personnel who had no direct authority over divisional managers. To resolve these tensions, Williams created a check and balance system in IBM called "contention management." This system forced both staff and line managers to meet and encouraged them to debate the merits of an idea; no operating plan became final without staff approval. When line and staff managers could not agree, the problem was sent to the corporate management committee—the top six executives. Over time, however, an increasing number of issues were sent to the top of the organization to resolve, and it became accepted that top management would resolve important strategic issues. Thus, despite Watson's claimed policy of decentralizing authority to divisional managers and their subordinates, much of IBM's decision making remained centralized at the top of the organization. Managers from IBM's mainframe division, its chief revenue earner, had the most power in shaping corporate decision making.

IBM's policy of long-term employment, commitment, and loyalty to the company's objectives became entrenched during this period, and the company became known throughout the industry for its job security and good pay.[52] With its high rate of growth, internal promotions were easy to come by, and employees rose rapidly throughout the corporate ranks. In 1955, employee stock options were offered for the first time. In 1966, managers were required to attend an in-house IBM management school, where they were trained on IBM's philosophy on communications, sales and service efforts, meetings, and employee treatment (such as visiting workers with sick spouses).[53] This policy taught employees the IBM way and helped to cement IBM's corporate culture and its style of doing business.

NEW MANAGEMENT AND NEW CHALLENGES

In 1970, Dick Watson resigned to become the United States ambassador to France, and Tom Watson Jr. suffered a heart attack that resulted in his retirement in 1971. When Tom Watson Jr. appointed T. V. Learson as CEO in 1971, the period of the Watson family's control over IBM came to an end. IBM was the largest, most successful computer company in the world and had achieved complete domination over the global computer industry. The question for Learson was, what new challenges could IBM confront? How should it use its vast resources to exploit a computer market that was growing by leaps and bounds? How could the company exploit its privileged position to dominate the computer market of the future? The answers were not long in coming.

Endnotes

1. David Mercer, *The Global IBM* (New York: Dodd, Mead & Co., 1988), 27–31.
2. Robert Sober, *IBM: Colossus In Transition*, (New York: Times Books, 1981), 11.
3. Ibid. 15–19, 21.
4. David Mercer, *The Global IBM*, 27–31.
5. Robert Sober, *IBM: Colossus in Transition*, 49–59.
6. David Mercer, *The Global IBM*, 31–42.
7. Robert Sobel, *IBM: Colossus in Transition*, 32–38.
8. Ibid. 49–59, 61.
9. Ibid. 24, 27–30.
10. Thomas Watson Jr. and Peter Petre, *Father Son & Co.: My Life At IBM And Beyond*. (New York: Bantam Books, 1990), 70.
11. Robert Sober, *IBM: Colossus in Transition*, 49–59, 61.
12. David Mercer, *The Global IBM*, 31–42.
13. Robert Sober, *IBM: Colossus in Transition*, 62.
14. Ibid. 63.
15. David Mercer, *The Global IBM*, 31–42.
16. Thomas Watson Jr. & Peter Petre, Father Son & Co., 70.
17. David Mercer, *The Global IBM* 31–42.
18. Robert Sobel, *IBM: Colossus in Transition*, 72, 75–82, 86–87, 92.
19. Ibid. 83.
20. Ibid. 84.
21. David Mercer, *The Global IBM*, 31–42.
22. Thomas Watson Jr. & Peter Petre, Father Son & Co., 112.
23. "The Machine That Changed the World."
24. Thomas Watson Jr. & Peter Petre, Father Son & Co., 192.
25. Ibid. 190.
26. David Mercer, *The Global IBM*, 41–43.
27. "The Machine That Changed the World."
28. Thomas Watson Jr. & Peter Petre, Father Son & Co., 24–35.
29. Ibid. 136–137, 189, 192.
30. Ibid. 24–35.
31. Ibid. 243.
32. Robert Sober, *IBM: Colossus in Transition*, 127–128.

33. David Mercer, *The Global IBM*, 46.
34. Thomas Watson Jr. & Peter Petre, Father Son & Co., 244.
35. "The Machine That Changed the World."
36. "The Machine That Changed the World."
37. Thomas Watson Jr. & Peter Petre, Father Son & Co., 24–35.
38. Lewis, 92-98. BW 14 Feb. 1988, 92–98.
39. "The Machine That Changed the World."
40. Thomas Watson Jr. & Peter Petre, Father Son & Co., 292, 346–350.
41. David Mercer, *The Global IBM*, 51.
42. Lewis, 92-98. BW 14 Feb. 1988, 92–98.
43. Thomas Watson Jr. & Peter Petre, Father Son & Co., 346–350.
44. Robert Sober, IBM: *Colossus in Transition*, 169.
45. Ibid. 131–137, 197–199, 202, 204.
46. David Mercer, *The Global IBM*, 251–254.
47. Robert Sober, IBM: *Colossus in Transition*, 131–137, 197–199, 202, 204.
48. Ibid. 203–204, 207.
49. "The Intimate Tale of IBM's First Family." *Fortune*, 14 June 1990, 92–132. Book Excerpt from *Father, Son & Co.: My Life at IBM and Beyond*, By Thomas Watson Jr. and Peter Petre, Bantam Books (1990).
50. David Mercer, *The Global IBM*, 52–53.
51. Thomas Watson Jr. & Peter Petre, Father Son & Co., 24–35.
52. Ibid. 288–289.
53. Ibid. 24–35.

The Fall of IBM

T. V. Learson took over as CEO of IBM after Tom Watson Jr. in 1971 and became the head of a company that had a 75% share of the world market for mainframe computers—computers powerful enough to manage the information processing needs of an entire company. Learson had made a major personal contribution to IBM's emergence as the dominant global mainframe manufacturer when he led the development of IBM's highly successful System/360 mainframe series that led to the rapid rise in the company's fortunes. IBM's 360 mainframes fully automated a company's manual information processing systems, such as payroll, accounting, and customer record keeping, making the punch card obsolete. As the former head of the 360 program, Learson understood the critical importance of research and development (R&D) in maintaining and defending IBM's preeminent position in the mainframe market. Because of this, he initiated and oversaw the development of IBM's new, more powerful System/370 computer series.

Technical advances lowered the System/370's price per calculation to 60% less than that of the System/360s, plus the 370 had a larger information storage system. The 370s still used the software of the 360s however, making them primarily an upgrade rather than a replacement. Nevertheless, the 370 machines became the backbone of IBM's mainframe product line from the early 1970s on. Most of the advances that IBM traded to its mainframe computers from this time on were designed primarily to either improve the 370 machines' processing power or the performance of its various components, such as its software, its printers, and, especially, its storage capacity. The 370 series became the industry standard that IBM's competitors tried to match and outperform.

Under Learson's control, and then under the control of Frank Cary who became CEO when Learson retired in 1973, IBM continued to enjoy its domination of the mainframe market. By 1980, IBM had a market value of $26 billion, four times its size in 1971.

Increasing Competition

Although IBM's continued domination of the mainframe market produced record increases in revenues and profits every year, its performance masked some major problems that were developing during the 1970s and 1980s. The first major problem, which Cary had recognized as early as 1970, was that the mainframe computer market was starting to mature. Almost every large United States business possessed a mainframe computer, as did most scientific and higher education institutions. Furthermore, IBM also had saturated the international market. As a result, IBM's rate of growth was falling; even though its revenues were increasing, they were increasing at a decreasing rate. Competition was increasing from companies that were trying to find ways to attract IBM's customers and share in the huge revenues in the mainframe computer market. Its major competitors at the time were Amdahl, Honeywell, Burroughs, Univac, NCR, and Control Data.

Many of these companies began offering IBM's customers mainframe systems at a lower cost than the expensive IBM systems. Initially, IBM faced competition only from companies selling IBM-compatible peripheral equipment such as disk drives, storage devices, and printers at lower prices than IBM's products. Its sales force had been able to ward off such threats. Now, however, the nature of competition was changing. IBM's competitors began selling cheaper, higher performing, IBM-compatible central processing units (CPUs)—the brain of the computer and the source of its processing power. For the first time, competitors were offering a low-price alternative to the IBM mainframe. At the same time, IBM was still pursuing its high-priced lease strategy, which was backed by excellent customer service. Another emerging low-price threat came from leasing companies. These leasing companies would buy old 360s from IBM and lease them on better terms than IBM offered, attracting price-conscious IBM customers. While these competitive threats were small, they nevertheless gave IBM cause for concern.

From 1970 on IBM became concerned about the threat of low-cost, foreign competition in the mainframe computer market after witnessing the decline of several United States industries, including automobiles, due to the entry of low-cost Japanese competitors. The price of integrated circuits, the heart of a mainframe computer, was plummeting at this time, and Japanese companies had the technical capability to build a powerful computer that could match or exceed the IBM 370. The existence of a low-cost global competitor was a major threat to IBM's domination of both the United States market and the global market.

In response to the threat of low-cost competition, Cary announced that IBM would spend $10 billion to build new automated plants to produce low-cost computers over a six-year period. In this way, IBM would be able to meet the challenge of low-priced computers should the threat materialize and its customers start to switch to low-cost competitors. John Opel, who became IBM's CEO in 1981, was also concerned about competition from Japan and carried on with Cary's low-cost producer strategy. Under his control IBM spent $32 billion

from 1980 to 1985 to determine ways to reduce manufacturing costs.

IBM's push to reduce manufacturing costs did not fit well with its strategy of offering excellent customer service and using its very expensive sales force to sell and service its machines. It was unlikely that IBM would ever be able to compete on price with its competitors because its customer service and support activities raised its costs so much. Moreover, competing on price had never been a part of its strategy; IBM always had competed on its unique ability to provide customers with an integrated, full-line computer service. Analysts wondered whether Opel was spending too much to lower manufacturing costs and whether the $32 billion could not be better spent in some other way.

CHANGES IN TECHNOLOGY

Changes in mainframe technology also caused a change in IBM's strategy during the 1970s. As a result of technological innovations, particularly the plunging costs of integrated circuits, the life span of a mainframe computer—the time it could be used until it was technologically outdated—was shortening rapidly, and development costs were increasing. Formerly, customers would use the same IBM mainframe for several years. Now, however, IBM was forced to replace its leased computers every two or three years. This made it difficult to recoup development costs and obtain the premium price on its machines that it was accustomed to.

Because the computer life span was getting shorter and because of the growth low-cost competition, IBM under Cary, and then Opel, decided to phase out IBM's system of leasing machines to customers. Instead they decided to begin selling machines—a major change in IBM's strategy. Although this move increased revenue in the short term, it had major repercussions for the company in the long term. First, the leasing system had tied IBM to its customers and ensured that when customers upgraded and expanded their computer systems, they would look first at IBM machines. Moreover, leasing facilitated IBM's strategy of providing customers with excellent customer service and guaranteed the company a steady cash flow and control of the used machine market. With the end of leasing, IBM would be more susceptible to fluctuations in the demand for its products because its customers would be able to shop around.

From 1980 on, IBM began to face major competition from 370 clone manufacturers, large companies like Amdahl (which had a faster 370 processor than IBM), and Hitachi Data Systems (whose low-price machine generated record sales throughout the 1980s). IBM's customers began to feel more comfortable about buying 370 clones from companies that also promised quality support and service at low cost. IBM's sales growth for its biggest mainframe dropped from 12% annually in 1984 to 5% annually in 1990 as a result of the increased competition. Increased mainframe competition with Amdahl and Hitachi Data Systems also led to price discounting, despite the fact that IBM attempted to offer its customers a unique package that included software and services via addition to hardware. The days when IBM could demand whatever price it wanted for its machines were over.

The end of its leasing program also led to increased competition from independent computer leasing companies that would buy older mainframes and then sell the older processors at a price that was frequently only 10% of the cost of IBM's newest machine. These companies also disassembled mainframes to make smaller computers; for example, they could make two smaller machines out of one larger machine. In response to this price competition, IBM was forced to reduce the price of its machines.

The end of leasing, combined with a growth in low-cost competition, changed the nature of industry competition in ways that the company did not expect. IBM's strategy was now to protect its mainframe market from competitors and hang on to its customers at all costs. IBM devoted most of its immense resources to developing technically superior mainframe products, lowering the cost of production, and supporting its very expensive but very successful sales force.

IBM's focus on protecting its mainframe market blinded it to threats from the emergence of new kinds of computers. Even when it did recognize the competitive threat, IBM's operating structure and culture, shaped by its preeminent position as the world's leading mainframe computer company, made it difficult for IBM's managers to see emerging problems in its environment and react quickly to the changes that technology was bringing about

in the computer industry. The way IBM handled the emerging threat from new kinds of computers, such as minicomputers, personal computers (PCs), and workstations, illustrates many of the problems it experienced as a result of a corporate mindset that "mainframes were king."

THE MINICOMPUTER MARKET

One of the new computer markets that emerged in the 1970s was the minicomputer. Minicomputers were smaller and priced anywhere from $12,000 to $700,000, which was significantly cheaper than mainframe computers. The steadily falling price of integrated circuits during the 1960s and 1970s made it feasible to build a minicomputer that was affordable to small businesses or could be used in specialized technical or scientific applications. IBM had ignored this new market segment, preferring to focus its resources on developing and improving its profitable 360 and 370 series computers.

Two researchers from the Massachusetts Institute of Technology pioneered the development of a smaller, more powerful computer. They founded the Digital Equipment Corporation (DEC), which, in 1965, launched the PDP-8, a computer that could handle the smaller information processing needs and tasks of companies such as small businesses, offices, factories, and laboratories. The venture was very successful, and by 1968, DEC's sales reached $57 million, and its earnings were $6.8 million. DEC's computer competed with the lower end of the 360 range. The computer sold well in research facilities, but it did not do as well in business, because IBM dominated this market with its powerful sales force. However, DEC had plans to develop a more powerful machine. As it grew, it was quickly expanding its own national service network, imitating IBM's.

To meet DEC's challenge, which was still seen as a minor issue, Cary formed the General Systems Division in 1969. Its goal was to produce the System/3 which was to be IBM's small, powerful minicomputer. IBM did not, however, rethink its technology or invest resources to develop new minicomputer technology to make a product to suit this new market segment. Rather, IBM tried to adapt its existing mainframe technology to the minicomputer market.

IBM's top managers had risen up the ranks of IBM from the mainframe division and were conditioned by the idea that the level of computing power was everything. "The bigger the better" was the philosophy of these managers. Moreover, big machines meant big revenues. IBM's mainframe managers saw the potential earning power of the minicomputer as insignificant when compared to the huge revenues generated by its mainframes. More fundamentally, however, IBM's top managers did not want competition from a new computer division inside the company that would absorb large amounts of the company's resources and might change the company's future direction and strategy.

The result was that when the System/3s were developed, they were too big and too expensive to compete with DEC's machine and too small to compete with IBM's own mainframes. This caused them to fail to make much inroad into what was becoming a very big market segment. As the minicomputer segment of the market continued to grow rapidly in the 1970s, Cary tried to increase the importance of the minicomputer group inside IBM's corporate hierarchy by reorganizing IBM's Data Processing Division and splitting it into two units: General Systems to make minicomputers and Data Systems to make the mainframes. He hoped that this change would force IBM managers to change their mindset and support the company's move into the new markets.

So strong was the entrenched position of mainframe managers that Cary's change of structure created huge divisional rivalry between mainframe and minicomputer managers. The mainframe division saw itself as being in direct competition for resources with the minicomputer division. Managers in both units failed to cooperate and share technological resources to develop the new range of machines. When the General Systems Division finally produced a minicomputer called the 8100, it did not have a technological edge over the DEC machine. Nevertheless, it was successful, as many IBM customers had large sums of money invested in IBM mainframes and were reluctant to switch suppliers. Moreover, IBM's powerful sales force (although at first reluctant to push minicomputers for fear of reducing their commissions) could service the needs of the minicomputer

users. By the end of 1980, more than 100,000 minicomputers had been sold. IBM and DEC were the industry leaders, while the new companies that had sprung up, such as Hewlett-Packard (HP) and Wang, were also increasing their market share.

In 1986, DEC introduced its new VAX 9000 minicomputer. This new minicomputer shocked IBM's mainframe managers because it had the same speed and capacity as IBM's largest 370 mainframe, the 3090, but cost only 25% as much. For the first time, mainframe managers were forced to accept the fact that minicomputers might be feasible substitutes for mainframes in many applications. Although DEC gained business with its new machine in market segments previously dominated solely by IBM, such as large financial service companies and corporate data processing centers, it still could not seize many of IBM's loyal customers who were locked into IBM systems. Nevertheless, DEC's share of the minicomputer market grew from 19% in 1984 to 25% in 1988, while IBM's share dropped from 24% to 16% in the same period.

Finally, in 1988, IBM brought out the AS/400 series, a minicomputer that was superior to DEC's VAX. The AS/400 series was based on RISC (reduced instruction set computing) technology. Fast RISC chips could equal and exceed the speed of large mainframes, including IBM's own mainframes. Many large companies that had a great deal of money invested in IBM mainframes moved to adopt the IBM minicomputer system because it was compatible with their IBM mainframe systems. As a result of the success of its new minicomputers, IBM increased its market share from about 16% in 1988 to 28% in 1992, while DEC's market share fell. DEC then planned to produce its own machines based on RISC, but in the interim, it introduced new machines to compete with IBM's AS/400s on price. IBM now had a $14 billion business in minicomputers, which have gross margins of 56%.

THE PERSONAL COMPUTER

Another technological breakthrough, the microprocessor or "computer on a chip," sparked the development of the personal computer (PC), which was developed in 1977 by Steven Jobs and Stephen Wozniak, the cofounders of Apple

Computer. By 1980, Apple's sales had grown to $117 million. Once again, IBM stood by and watched as a new market segment was created. This time, recognizing the mistakes it had made in the minicomputer market by not moving quickly enough to develop a machine to compete with the industry leader, it decided to move quickly to create its own machine to compete with Apple's.

In the mainframe market, IBM made its own chips, circuit boards, disk drives, terminals, tape drives, and printers; wrote its own proprietary software for its machines; and helped to develop software to meet the needs of its customers. As a result, its machines were not compatible with those of its rivals that used their own proprietary hardware and software. The machines of different manufacturers would not work together. In 1981, however, in an effort to enter the PC market quickly, IBM outsourced and bought the inputs it needed from other companies make its PC. For example, Intel supplied the 8088 microchip that was the heart and Microsoft delivered MS-DOS, the programming language and software applications for the new IBM machine. Finally, computer stores, not the IBM sales force, were used to sell the new IBM PCs to get the machines to individual customers quickly.

IBM's first PC, more powerful than the first Apple computer, was introduced at a price of $1,565 in 1981. Intel's 8088 chip had more main memory and was more powerful than the chip used in the Apple II computer, and Microsoft's operating system, MS-DOS, was better than the current industry standard. These features, combined with the power of the IBM brand name, made the IBM PC an immediate success; it quickly became the industry standard for all other PCs. Backed by IBM's legendary service, business users turned to the machines in the thousands. By 1984, IBM had seized 40% of the personal computer market, but the IBM PC still could not be produced or distributed fast enough to meet the enormous customer demand.

Even the runaway success of the IBM PC became a threat to the company because its competitors rapidly imitated it; soon clone manufacturers were selling IBM-compatible personal computers as powerful or more powerful than IBM's own machines. For example, Compaq, founded in 1981, began to clone IBM PCs and produced a high-powered machine that seized a large share of the high-price business market. In 1986, Compaq beat IBM to the market with a machine using Intel's powerful new 386 chip. At the same time, other clone makers, such as Zenith and Packard Bell, attacked the low-price segment of the computer market and began producing PCs that undercut IBM's.

IBM, threatened both in the high-price and low-price end of the PC markets fought back with the PS/2. It had a proprietary hardware channel that IBM made sure could not be imitated, as its first personal computer had been. However, customers resisted buying the new PS/2. They did not want to become locked into a new IBM system that was not compatible with IBM's old system and their other software or hardware investments. In the face of hostility from its customers, and losing market share, IBM was forced to back down. In 1988 IBM began producing PS/2s that were compatible with the existing industry standard—ironically, its own older standard.

It was suddenly clear to IBM that it no longer controlled the rules of the competitive game in the personal computer industry. Nonetheless, it was still slow to change its strategy. Despite the fact that its cheaper rivals had machines that were as powerful as its own, IBM still attempted to charge a premium price for its product. In response, its customers went elsewhere. IBM's share of PC sales in the United States dropped from about 37% in 1985 to 24% in 1988. Clone makers continued to improve IBM's older standard, and IBM's market share declined to 16.5% in 1990.

In 1991, a major price war broke out in the PC market, brought on in large part by the steadily dropping price of computer hardware, such as Intel's microprocessors. IBM reduced prices three times to compete, and prices of the PS/2 were cut by as much as 25%. Partly due to price competition, a typical 386 PC, which had cost $3,500 in early 1991, cost $1,600 in late 1991 and only $1,200 in early 1992. In 1992, IBM also introduced new low-priced lines of computers such as the PS/Value Point. This computer was targeted at the fastest growing segment of the computer market, the home market, and business customers who did not need all the features of the high-end PS/2. These new models were very successful and in great demand. Nonetheless, IBM did not hold a dominant position in the PC market; in 1992, its market share was 12%, the same as its rival Apple and about twice that of rivals like Dell, Compaq, and NEC.

The PC price wars continued into 1993. In February 1993, Dell Computer, a rapidly growing clone maker, introduced price cuts of 5% to 22% across its entire product line. In response, IBM cut prices by as much as 16% on some models, including the PS/Value Point. Apple cut prices five times in 1993, for a reduction of up to 33%, on its three highest-priced computers in an effort to increase United States sales. PC makers also battled over distribution and the offering of extras, such as warranties. PCs ranged from $500 clones to $2,000 laptops to $25,000 network hubs. PCs dominated the computer industry, with world sales of $93 billion in 1993 compared to mainframe sales of $50 billion. The laptop segment of the PC market alone reached $5.67 billion in 1990. IBM, however, did not have a product for this market segment until 1991. It also faced tough competition from market leader Toshiba as well as from Apple.

By 1992, it was clear to IBM and industry analysts that IBM was just one more competitor in a very competitive market. Since 1990, IBM's PC division had yet to show a profit. This was due to intense price competition and because IBM's costs were above competitors such as Compaq, which moved quickly to slash costs in 1990 when the price of PCs began tumbling.

IBM's response to competition in the personal computer industry throughout the 1980s clearly was affected by its "mainframe mindset." Even though it was clear that new segments of the computer market were developing and that new uses for computers were being found, IBM managers still discounted the potential threat to mainframes from either the minicomputer or the personal computer. IBM was not alone in being unable to sense the significance of changes in the environment. Kenneth Olsen, one of the founders of the minicomputer maker DEC, went on record saying, "Personal computers are just toys" in discounting the challenge of PCs to minicomputers, just as IBM had discounted the threat of minicomputers to mainframes 10 years earlier. The Olsen philosophy blinded IBM's top management to the prospect that powerful PCs could become a threat to IBM's main line of business mainframes. This predicament was somewhat surprising given that the computer industry always had been dominated by technological change. IBM's success was itself the result of moving quickly and decisively to exploit the opportunities of new technology: the punch card machine, the transistor, and the integrated circuit.

Throughout the 1980s, IBM's personal computer division (which is the biggest personal computer operation in the world) could not respond quickly to the price cutting moves of its rivals and introduce new kinds of personal computers because of its centralized decision making style. Whenever a competitor reduced prices, managers of the personal computer division had to get approval from the corporate management committee to cut prices, a process that sometimes took months. As a result, the PC division was never able to forestall its rivals. Moreover, just as in the case of minicomputers, rivalry between PC and mainframe managers hampered efforts to quickly exploit the potential of the powerful new microprocessors.

IBM's competitors moved quickly to increase the power of their PCs by exploiting the power of the new generation of microprocessors. They also encouraged the development of powerful new netware software. This software could link PCs together and to a more powerful computer, such as a minicomputer or a workstation, so that a network of PCs could work as effectively as a mainframe—but more conveniently and at only a fraction of the cost.

WORKSTATIONS

Workstations are the fourth wave of computers following mainframes, minicomputers, and PCs. While PCs are designed for individual jobs such as word processing and financial analysis, workstations essentially are very powerful PCs designed to be connected to each other and to a mainframe through software. Workstations can analyze financial results and track inventories much faster than PCs and much more cheaply than minicomputers or mainframes. A network of workstations can also be linked to an even more powerful workstation (or minicomputer) called a file server, which contains a company's files and databases or which can retrieve them from a company's mainframe computer. Workstations, usually priced from $5,000 to $100,000, were first developed for scientists and engineers but increasingly were utilized by business professionals. New network software links workstations so that many people can work together simultaneously on the same project. These desktop machines have "user friendly" graphic displays and allow people at different machines to share data and software. By 1988, the workstation market was $4.7 billion. Workstations have a 45% profit margin compared to 58% for minicomputers.

Prior to 1989, IBM was a small player in this segment. Underestimating the potential power of personal computers and slow to develop powerful minicomputers (its AS/400 series was not introduced until 1988), IBM managers once again failed to see the potential of an emerging market. IBM had only a 3.9% market share in 1987, compared to Sun Microsystems's 29% and Apollo's 21%, the two upstart companies that were the innovators of the workstation. Once they realized the importance of this market segment, both IBM and DEC introduced workstations based on RISC processors, which make machines two to three times faster by eliminating all insignificant instructions. IBM introduced the IBM RT PC workstation in 1986, but the machine failed due to an underpowered microprocessor. Notwithstanding its problems, IBM launched the RS/6000 workstation in 1989 and captured 18% of the market by the end of 1991.

Competition in the workstation market was increasing as a result of market growth. This segment was growing 27% annually by 1992, compared to 5% for the computer industry as a whole. As the price of workstations fell, more and more small businesses, which could not afford to use mainframe or minicomputers, could afford workstations. The workstation market also was very important to large computer makers because workstations could be used in networks with larger mainframe computers. Thus, controlling the workstation market protected a company's mainframe market. By the end of 1991, the workstation market was $11.3 billion, and IBM was facing severe competition from DEC, Sun, Apollo, and HP, all of which sold RISC workstations.

Software and Services

Designing software (the instructions that allow computers to perform tasks) and providing customer service, particularly assistance in the design of programs to manage company-specific databases and systems, have been rapidly expanding segments of the computer industry for the past 20 years. IBM has always realized the importance of developing proprietary software that can link and join its mainframes,

minicomputers, workstations, and personal computers to provide customers with a completely integrated computer package. It failed, however, to recognize the developing market for more general operating language and software applications.

By 1981, 33% of the total computer industry revenue came from software and services, a figure that rose to an estimated 50% in 1993. Although software and services accounted for 33% of IBM's total revenues by 1990, 68% of this revenue came from supporting customers' IBM mainframe computer systems, which represented a declining share of the computer market. Thus IBM, tied to software that supports mainframes, was not in a strong position to compete in the new software and services market.

IBM's failure to realize the potential for software seems surprising given that it had outsourced the operating language for its personal computer to Microsoft and saw the success of the MS-DOS operating system. IBM's focus was mainframes and its continuing belief that its own proprietary hardware and software would become the industry standard seems to have been the source of its reluctance to enlarge and expand its software operations. In 1980, when IBM had the opportunity to indirectly control the software market by purchasing a large chunk of Microsoft stock at a low price, it declined to do so.

IBM soon found that developing new applications software was a difficult business to be in. First, IBM had a hard time recruiting talented programmers. They were not attracted to IBM's bureaucratic and conservative corporate culture, in which centralized decision making limited their opportunities to be creative and take risks. Second, talented software programmers found they could make more money in business for themselves; any programmer who could develop a new system generally started his or her own company. Microsoft recognized this problem early on; consequently, Bill Gates, Microsoft's chairman, gives his top programmers large stock options to encourage their best performance. Many of them have become millionaires as a result.

In today's computer market, developing better and more advanced software is crucial to selling more hardware or computers of all kinds. So, late as usual, IBM embarked on a program to forge alliances with many small, independent software companies to develop software for IBM machines quickly: mainframes, minicomputers, workstations, and PCs. One of IBM's goals was to rejuvenate sales of its mainframe by encouraging software companies to write programs that make mainframes the key part of a computer network that links personal computers and workstations. IBM spent $100 million in 1989 to acquire equity stakes in 12 software developers, including Interactive Images for Graphics, Inc.; Polygen Corporation for scientific software; and American Management Systems, Inc., for mainframe software. Marketing agreements were also made with several other firms. IBM loaned software developers up to $50,000 for startup costs and took a seat on the developer's board. For example, IBM was working on a project called Systems Application Architecture (SAA), which is a set of rules for links between programs and computers. SAA would facilitate the creation of networks with all types of machines, including mainframes and PCs.

In 1988, IBM created a new unit to launch applications software and established a position called "complementary resource marketing manager," responsible for connecting software "business partners" with IBM customers. Salespeople were expected to sell the products of these software partners as well as IBM products. Although most of the programs were for mainframes, many could be adapted to work with networks based on PCs. Software and services accounted for 40% of IBM's revenue in 1992. IBM wanted to achieve 50% of revenues from software and services by the year 2000.

SYSTEMS INTEGRATION AND OUTSOURCING

Traditionally, IBM limited its service activities to providing support for its own proprietary software and hardware. It did not use its skills to analyze various aspects of a customer's business, such as its inventory control or warehousing operations, and then custom design and install an appropriate mix of hardware and software to meet the customer's needs, a service known as systems integration. Moreover, it had not recognized the developing market for outsourcing data processing, whereby one company agrees to take over and manage all aspects of the data processing function for another company in return for a fee. By 1992, however, the systems integration and outsourcing market generated more revenues than the mainframe market.

IBM's failure to see the developing market segment for systems integration and outsourcing had not been lost on one of IBM's star salesmen, Ross Perot. When IBM capped the amount of money that Perot could earn from commissions in selling computers and ignored his plan to start an IBM division whose function would be to provide data management services to customers to advise them on ways to manage their data files and systems, Perot left IBM and started Electronic Data Services (EDS).

The systems integration market and outsourcing market were now growing at 19% annually. IBM's failure to enter this market early allowed its competitors—principally EDS and Andersen Consulting, the accounting firm that early on established a computer consulting division—to gain a first-mover advantage and dominate the market. At the time, EDS had 50% of the outsourcing business of managing a company's data storage and management needs, compared to IBM's 6%. Andersen dominated the market for advising companies on their software and hardware needs. IBM led primarily in the market for government contracts.

To quickly develop a presence in this lucrative market, IBM began developing alliances with various organizations. It formed a joint venture with Coopers & Lybrand to provide management consulting in selected industries. IBM also teamed with AT&T to make IBM's mainframes work better with AT&T's network management systems. IBM established the Integrated Systems Solutions Corporation subsidiary in 1991 to provide a platform for IBM to enter the data processing outsourcing market. Its business was increasing; for example, in 1992, it received a 10-year, $3 billion agreement to run the computer systems for McDonnell Douglas Corporation. The subsidiary did outsourcing for 30 companies, including Continental Bank. IBM would run all of a client company's systems, from mainframes and workstations to voice and data telecommunication. It was aggressively advertising its strengths and services in this area.

THE NEW COMPUTER INDUSTRY

By 1990, IBM received about 50% of its gross profit from mainframe hardware, software, peripherals, and maintenance; 6% from minicomputers; 18.5%

from PCs and workstations; and 12.4% from non-maintenance software and services. However, the future revenue-generating potential of each of these market segments was uncertain as the boundaries between the segments grew less clear. Would workstations replace minicomputers? Would workstations and minicomputers replace mainframes? Would a network of PCs linked by advanced software to a mainframe eliminate the need for minicomputers or workstations? Obviously, IBM had the most to gain from making mainframes the center of a computer network, while its competitors had as much to gain from making minicomputers and powerful workstations the wave of the future.

By 1990, IBM was facing stiff competition in all the developing segments of the computer market, from companies that were mainly specialized in one market niche, for example, Microsoft in the software segment or Sun Computer in the workstation niche. IBM was fighting to increase its market share in each market segment but was suffering because of tough competition from strong competitors that had developed their own loyal customer following.

Moreover, the market for mainframe computers, IBM's principal source of revenue, was declining as machines such as PCs and workstations were able to perform mainframe tasks at lower cost. It had been estimated that, while 80% of 1986 computer industry profits were attributable to mainframe computer sales, by 1991, sales of mainframe computer systems accounted for only 20%. The PC revolution had reduced costs and allowed customers to buy much cheaper computer systems to do work previously performed by expensive mainframes and minicomputers.

As a result of this shift, suppliers of computer components such as chips and software were the winners, as their share of industry profits rose from 20% in 1986 to 31% in 1991. Thus, for example, the share prices of Microsoft and Intel, which control the software and microprocessor markets, respectively, soared. Similar growth occurred in the share prices of Conner, Quantum, and Seagate, which dominated disk drives, as well as Andersen Consulting and EDS, which were the leaders in system integration. IBM's share price, however, fell dramatically from a high of $160 in 1987 to less than $50 in 1992.

To fight the trend toward PCs and workstations, IBM attempted to make its 370 computer the central component of a network of computers that link individual users to the mainframe. It did not succeed, however, as sales growth for its biggest mainframe, the 370, dropped from 4% per year in 1990 to less than 2% per year in 1992. Even many of IBM's 370 users began switching to IBM AS/400 minicomputers because they could perform the same task more easily and cheaply. The mainframe market was now the third-largest market behind PCs and minicomputers.

IBM FIGHTS BACK

In 1985, John Akers became CEO and was charged with the task of using IBM's vast resources to make it the market leader in the new lucrative market segments of the computer industry and reduce IBM's dependence on mainframes. He took over a company in which managers were still arrogant and complacent and believed completely in IBM's preeminence despite all the warning signs that it had lost its competitive edge. Its top management committee, staffed primarily by managers from its mainframe division, seemed unable to make the type of innovative decisions that would allow IBM to respond quickly to the rapidly changing computer environment. The result was a failure to develop products fast enough and a mistaken commitment to the mainframe computer. Even its renowned salespeople had become a problem for the company. Committed to the IBM product, they had become oriented to selling and servicing the mainframe; they were not oriented toward satisfying customer needs, which might be for a minicomputer or a workstation.

Akers launched a "year of the customer" in 1987 to refocus the sales force on meeting the needs of the customer rather than the needs of the mainframe. Most importantly, Akers realized the need to restructure the company and change IBM's highly centralized style of decision making if it was to innovate the next generation of products and emerge as a market leader in the new market segments. Akers recognized that the biggest problem for IBM was its highly bureaucratic organizational structure that slowed decision making and continually frustrated attempts to be innovative and entrepreneurial.

The 1998 Restructuring

To speed decision making, in January 1998, Akers reorganized IBM into seven divisions based on the main product market segments in which the company was competing: personal computer systems, mid-range systems, mainframes, information systems and communications, technology development (such as microchips), programming, and software. The idea behind the reorganization was to demolish the mainframe mindset by giving the managers of each division the autonomy and responsibility for developing new products for their respective markets. No longer would mainframe managers be able to stifle the pace of change and discourage the development of products that threatened the dominance of the mainframe. The sales force, however, was to remain a separate entity whose job would still be to sell the whole line of IBM products. The logic for this was that the sales force could sell customers integrated IBM computer systems: networks of PCs, file servers, and mainframes and provide the computer software, service, and systems consulting to tailor the system to customers' individual needs.

The disadvantage of the single sales force was that each division would not be able to devise a sales strategy specific to its own competitive environment, and salespeople would not be able to focus on a single product line. IBM felt that the economies of scale and scope provided by a unified sales force outweighed these disadvantages. Twenty-thousand employees were transferred from staff and lab positions to the sales force, and the commission system was revamped so that salespeople were evaluated on total revenue, not on the number of units rented or sold.

IBM's Contention System

If the first purpose of the reorganization was to focus IBM's activities more closely on the main segments of the computer market, the second purpose was to shorten the product development cycle and speed products to market. Since the early 1970s, IBM had taken advantage of its dominance in the market to use a "contention" system to control new product development. In this system, two or more project teams designed competing product prototypes, and a series of committees at both the divisional level and the corporate level met over a period of months to debate the merits of each project. A project would be approved after six committee members rated the two processes, which could take months or years; then the committee met to finalize the product plan. During this process, if any committee member said,

"I non-concur," meaning that he or she disagreed with the project, it would be sent back for further review or scrapped.

The result of the contention system was that the projects that were approved were generally successful. However, the time frame associated with making the decision was generally so long that products were late to market, putting IBM at a competitive disadvantage. For example, the small, independent team charged with the development of the first IBM PC launched the product in one year. However, once the PC group was put into the Information Systems and Communication Division and decision making became constrained by IBM's contention system, the speed of the development process slowed significantly. For example, the PS/2 was not introduced until 1987, missing the 1985 target. This delay allowed clone makers of the older PCs to gain 33% of the market share in PCs. Other symptoms of IBM's overly bureaucratic approach to decision making included its failure to enter new market segments quickly. For example, IBM entered the PC market four years late; it was also a laggard in workstations. Similarly, IBM's top managers refused to recognize the importance of the growth of minicomputers and were hesitant to launch products that would compete with the mainframes.

The reorganization was designed to shorten the time it took to get a product to market and overcome the hurdles to product development. In the 1980s, IBM no longer had the luxury of taking a long time to make competitive decisions, as smaller and more agile competitors were forging ahead and the product life cycle of computers was shortening.

In an attempt to cut costs, increase profitability, get close to the customers, and reduce bureaucracy, Akers embarked on a major campaign to downsize the organization. The 1985 workforce of 405,000 was reduced to 389,300 in 1988 through early retirement and attrition. In addition, overtime and temporary employees, equivalent to 12,500 full-time employees, were cut. Despite the fact that IBM closed plants, cut spending, and reduced capital outlays, costs grew faster than revenues during most of the reorganization. Moreover, analysts could not discern any noticeable change in IBM's strategy or the way it made decisions. Products were still late to market.

The 1988 reorganization was a failure. Although each division was supposed to become more autonomous, in reality, most decisions still required approval by IBM's corporate headquarters managers—managers who had risen through the ranks from the powerful mainframe computer division. Products that might have cannibalized the sale of mainframes were still discouraged by corporate managers, who, having achieved their success during the mainframe era, were hesitant to introduce products to compete with mainframes. One example of the mainframe mindset involved the PC unit's push to get into the laptop market in 1989 by competitively pricing their laptop at $4,995. Corporate headquarters insisted on a price of $5,995 to meet corporate profit in margin targets. As a result, many competitors were able to price their products lower than IBM's machines. Even though IBM later priced the machine lower, it never regained lost market share.

To allow the personal computer division to respond faster to the quickly changing PC market, Akers decided to place the PC business in a separate operating unit. In 1991, Akers formed the IBM Personal Computer Company and gave it control over the design, production, distribution, and marketing of IBM PCs. Prior to this change, distribution was performed by IBM's large sales and marketing division. After the change, 1,200 former marketing and sales employees were transferred to the new PC unit, which also was to handle telephone sales. The corporate sales force was to continue to sell to big corporate customers. In decentralizing authority to managers in the PC division, Akers was showing managers his plans for the IBM of the future.

The 1991 Restructuring

IBM announced another restructuring at the end of 1991, which was aimed at decentralizing decision making authority to the divisions and reducing the role of IBM corporate headquarters in setting divisional strategy. Akers divided IBM into 13 separate divisions: nine divisions were based on the company's main product lines, and four divisions were to be marketing and service operations organized geographically. The nine manufacturing divisions were to supply the four marketing divisions. The goal of the restructuring effort was to make the divisions independent units operating under a broad IBM umbrella, thus freeing them from corporate control.

Aker's plan was that each division would be an autonomous operating unit that could freely negotiate transfer prices of inputs with other divisions and, if a division wanted to, buy from and sell to outside companies. The divisions were to treat each other as they would outside companies; no favorable prices were to be granted to IBM divisions. Moreover, the performance of each division would be reported separately, and each division would be accountable for its individual profits and losses. The heads of the divisions were responsible for developing annual business plans and were to guarantee IBM a certain return on money invested in their division. In the past, most managers did not know the details, such as profit and loss statements, of an individual division's financial performance. Each divisional manager signed a contract to meet objectives in revenue growth, profit, ROA (return on assets), cash flow, customer satisfaction, quality, and morale. If the divisional heads were successful, they would get a share of the profits. If they failed, their jobs were on the line. Financial results for all 13 units were to be made public by 1994.

The goal of this restructuring was to free up IBM's powerful resources and make it more competitive. Division heads would have control over long-term development and business level strategy. For example, the Personal Systems Division's manager could decide how PCs and workstations were produced and designed, and the PC division's R&D function would not compete directly with the mainframe division for resources. The hope was that the divisions would be able to compete with their smaller, more entrepreneurial rivals once they were freed from corporate bureaucracy.

The sales divisions would still be responsible for selling the whole range of IBM products, however, and control over sales would be centralized at corporate headquarters. The logic, once again, was that customers wanted a sales force that could handle their entire computer needs, and there were synergies from having one sales force provide a full set of products and services. IBM's traditional focus on service was still a strong competitive advantage. Analysts were skeptical however, of having only one sales force, especially one in which representatives were still biased toward mainframes. Many analysts felt that one sales force was a mistake; giving each division its own sales force would be a better source of competitive advantage. Moreover, the huge costs of operating the sales force could be hard to allocate between divisions, causing rivalry among them.

To demonstrate the commitment of IBM's thirteen operating divisions top management to IBM's more autonomous and entrepreneurial approach to doing business, IBM's PC division was given total control over its own sales and named an independent unit in 1992. James Cannavino, the head of the PC unit, took total control over the PC division's strategy and organized the PC division around products instead of functions. The five product groups of the PC division were the low cost Value Points; PS/2; PS/1, aimed at home and small business users; portable products; and Ambra, a line of PCs built by an Asian contractor and sold in Europe. Each product group was in charge of its own brand development, manufacturing, pricing, and marketing. This change was designed to allow the product groups to respond much more quickly to changes in the PC market, where products may have a life span of only six months to a year. In addition, Cannavino met with 32 CEOs of Silicon Valley startups and told them that he wanted to form alliances with them to speed the development of new hardware and software products, such as multimedia and CD-ROM products. The IBM PC division was the world's largest company.

NEW MANAGEMENT AND NEW PLANS

Despite the 1991 organization, IBM's profits and revenues continued to decline; 1991 revenues fell 5% from 1990, the first decline since 1946. The company's 1991 loss of $2.8 billion was the first loss in IBM's history. In 1992, IBM's losses increased to $5 billion on $65 billion in revenues. In January 1993, the stock fell below $46, the lowest price in 17 years. Pressure for change at the top was increasing.

Under pressure from investors and the public, John Akers resigned in January 1993. Although Akers reorganized and restructured, critics claimed that he never went far enough in implementing the reforms that would really turn around IBM. For example, despite the fact that between 1985 to 1992 a total of 100,000 IBM workers were cut mainly through early retirement and that Akers had removed the whole of IBM's former top management team to try to rid IBM of the "mainframe mindset," critics

claimed that Akers had avoided initiating the major layoffs that were needed to restore profitability.

In 1993, the board of directors searched for a replacement for Akers. Shunning an insider for fear that he could not bring a fresh perspective to IBM's problems, they chose an outsider to be the CEO of IBM, marking the first time an outsider had occupied the top job. Louis Gerstner, former CEO of RJR Nabisco, was recruited in March 1993. Gerstner had no experience in the computer industry, and IBM's stock price dropped $3 to a new low when he took over.

Gerstner immediately hired outsiders to form a new top management team to run the company. Jerry York, former chief financial officer (CFO) at Chrysler was recruited as IBM's CFO. Gerry Czarnecki, who was in charge of cutbacks at Honolulu's Honfed Bank, became a vice president. These outsiders were tough cost cutters, experienced at restructuring large companies. Gerstner hired another outsider, Abby Kohnstamm, a former senior vice president of card-member marketing at American Express, to be vice president of corporate marketing.

Gerstner and his top management team spent all of 1993 analyzing how IBM worked as a prelude to "reengineering the corporation." Reengineering refers to a two-step process whereby an organization first identifies and analyzes each of the core business processes—manufacturing, marketing, R&D, and so on—that make a business work and then changes or reengineers them from the bottom up to improve the way they function. Gerstner formed an 11-person "corporate executive committee" of IBM's top managers to spearhead the reengineering effort. Gerstner then gave each manager responsibility for heading a task force. Eleven task forces were formed to analyze IBM's main processes, which were modeled on the reengineering effort that Cannavino had performed in the PC division. As discussed previously, the result of that effort led to the move to a product group structure, in which each group took control over its own manufacturing and marketing—a change that had been very successful. Gerstner hoped that a corporate-wide effort would also prove successful.

Despite the fact that most analysts felt Gerstner would continue with Akers' approach of decentralizing decision making to the divisions, and even spinning off IBM's businesses into independent companies, Gerstner showed no sign of following this strategy. Gerstner preferred to restructure the relationship between the corporate center and the divisions. Moreover, Gerstner announced his belief that IBM should continue to follow its traditional strategy of providing customers with a full line of hardware and software products and services and announced his support for the mainframe division.

As a part of this full-line strategy, and despite expectations that he would decentralize IBM's sales force and give each division responsibility for its own sales, Gerstner announced in 1993 that he would not change the current companywide sales force structure. The current sales force of 40,000 salespeople would still pursue the strategy of one face to a customer because customers "do not want to be bothered by several salespeople." Apparently, Gerstner and his top management team believed that IBM's core strategy of being a full service company was appropriate. They believed the company's main problem was that it was too big. To reduce size in 1992, Gerstner announced plans to shed 115,000 more jobs in 1993 and 1994, reducing the workforce to 250,000 from a peak of 405,000 in 1985. Announcing in 1993 that "the last thing that IBM needs now is a corporate vision," Gerstner nevertheless identified four goals he had for IBM: (1) to get the company to the right size; (2) to spend more time with customers; (3) to determine the strategic issues by process reengineering; and (4) to build employee morale in the face of the huge layoffs.

Analysts wondered how Gerstner's strategy would work. They wondered whether Gerstner understood the divisional rivalries that led to IBM's problems and how he expected his new strategy to result in faster product development and the greater sharing of ideas and resources between divisions. Some

critics argued that Gerstner should have aggressively pursued a strategy of breaking up IBM into fully independent operating units and that his new policy of encouraging the sharing of skills and resources between divisions would not work and was no break from the past. Moreover, they claimed he had been slow to reduce IBM's operating costs and the lavish way in which it spent its resources. For example, IBM operated one of the largest fleets of private jets in the corporate world, maintaining three country clubs for its employees, with its own management school complete with skeet shooting and tennis courts.

Had Gerstner, in the first six months of his reign as IBM's CEO, bought into IBM's culture in which the mainframe mindset still controlled the corporation? Gerstner contended that no amount of cost cutting would solve IBM's problems unless IBM could change from the inside out. IBM still spent 10% of its revenues on R&D and had many good ideas continually pouring from its development labs. According to Gerstner, the problem for the company was to use those ideas effectively, and the start of this was to reengineer the company to make better use of its resources. IBM also needed to increase integration among divisions so that they could share skills and resources more effectively. Gerstner believed that continuing Aker's strategy of breaking IBM up into 13 separate companies would do nothing to ensure the survival of the company in the long run.

On September 26, 1993, IBM announced a loss of $46 million for the third quarter, compared to a $40 million loss in 1992, bringing its total loss in 1993 to $8.37 billion. Was Gerstner's strategy working, and when could IBM's investors and employees expect to see the results?

IBM IN 2009

Since he became CEO of IBM in 2003, Sam Palmisano has worked hard to build a new global computer services company, which in 2009 was the largest and one of the most profitable in the world. In 2009, IBM had a market capitalization of more than $119 billion and employed more than 319,000 people worldwide in more than 150 countries. What kind of business model and strategies has Palmisano and his top management team pursued that allowed IBM to regain its position as an industry leader and wiped out memories of its disastrous performance in the 1980s? In addition, what challenges lie ahead if the company is to retain its competitive advantage and leading position in the global business computer services and consulting industry and keep rivals such as HP, Accenture, Dell, and Oracle at bay? That was the question Palmisano was grappling with in the spring of 2009 as the effects of the recession that started in 2008 started to bite into IBM's revenues and profits.

AKERS'S LAST STAND

As discussed in "The Fall of IBM," John Akers' vision of IBM's future was for the corporation to be broken up into 13 different companies that would be spun off to operate independently—essentially dismantling the IBM empire. While IBM's top managers developed a timetable to do this, Akers still faced the problem of how to keep it afloat in the

short run. In his final desperate attempt to keep IBM viable, Akers continued to make drastic cost reductions, and between 1991 and 1993 an additional 80,000 employees were laid off as IBM sought to lower its cost structure. Its workforce was now less than half at its peak. The restructuring charges associated with these layoffs resulted in record losses of more than $15 billion for IBM, and its stock price plunged to record lows as investors decided the future lay not in mainframe computers but in networks of servers and client PCs. Moreover, by this time, its personal systems group that manufactured its PCs and the servers it was developing had become a liability. Competitors such as Dell, Gateway, and Sun had gained a major low-cost advantage over IBM's PCs and servers, and the PC division was losing money.

By 1993, IBM's performance still showed no signs of improvement, so Akers resigned; the board of directors searched for a successor with the strategic skills necessary to find the right business model to turnaround the declining company. They chose Louis Gerstner, an ex-management consultant who had engineered a major turnaround in the performance of American Express and Nabisco, as the new CEO. Gerstner had no background in the computing industry and his appointment was viewed by many analysts—and by many of IBM's powerful top managers—as an enormous mistake. How could an outsider with no knowledge of the way IBM operated, develop a business model to compete against rivals in the rapidly changing computer sector?

For the most recent financial results of the company discussed in this case, go to http://finance.yahoo.com, input the company's stock symbol, and download the latest company report from its homepage.

GERSTNER'S IMMEDIATE MOVES

IBM's board chose Gerstner because they wanted a new CEO who would have a fresh perspective on the company's problems—one who had not been a part of IBM's slow-moving bureaucratic culture characterized by slow, centralized decision-making and power struggles between divisions. Gerstner's task was to build the right business model for IBM— what kinds of products, customers, and distinctive competencies should IBM develop in the future if it was to remain as one company—or should IBM be broken up?

The major argument Akers had made in support of breaking up IBM into 13 different and independent companies was that the managers of each new company would be free to decide what business model to pursue to best compete against rivals in its particular industry. While this was one path to increasing returns to stockholders, before making this decision, Gerstner decided to closely study IBM's different business groups, search out their strengths and weaknesses, and examine the fit between them—what was the rationale for keeping IBM as a whole versus breaking it up into parts? Gerstner had a reputation for "hands-on" management involving frequent visits to talk to managers at all levels and in all divisions. He spent his first months as CEO on a whistle-stop tour interviewing IBM's managers; he also visited many of IBM's largest corporate customers to discover what they wanted from IBM now and in the future.

Gerstner soon announced that he intended to keep IBM as a single united company. His strategic analysis led him to conclude that IBM's ability to provide clients with a complete and comprehensive computing or information technology (IT) solution that could be customized to each client's particular needs was the source of its future competitive advantage. IBM's principal problem was to find a better way to integrate the activities of its hardware, software, and service (HS&S) groups to create more value for customers. In other words, Gerstner decided that IBM needed to work toward offering clients an improved, more comprehensive IT package.

Once he made the decision to keep IBM intact, Gerstner's main challenge was how to speed innovation and decision making both within and across IBM's HS&S groups. He quickly found that IBM's top managers, accustomed to a slow-moving culture based on consensus decision making, could not respond to his demands fast enough. One IBM manager described the old IBM's decision-making process as like "wading through a jar of peanut butter." Gerstner announced IBM's managers "just didn't have what it takes." He began to replace many senior IBM executives with managers from lower down its ranks. To reduce costs, however, he was forced to continue to lay off large numbers of employees in product areas that he felt could not compete successfully in the new advanced competitive IT industry.

GERSTNER'S NEW BUSINESS MODEL

Over the next three years, Gerstner spent his time identifying IBM's core set of distinctive competences and deciding what strategies to develop to build these competences and provide a solid foundation for IBM's new integrated business model. What was Gerstner's vision to rebuild IBM? His business model was that IBM should (1) provide a complete package of state-of-the-art computing solutions HS&S, especially outsourcing and consulting) that could be customized to a particular client's needs and (2) to take advantage of the possibilities created by the Internet to create new markets for IBM's products and services. Gerstner focused on making IBM a customer-driven company, by which he meant that every manager and employee had the responsibility to design, make, or sell those products or services that could best meet the needs of IBM's clients. Given that sales of mainframes were declining and PCs and servers were becoming commodity products with low-profit margins, what IBM had to do was to provide something *unique* so that customers would be willing to pay a premium price for its products and services. The challenge facing IBM was to learn how to customize products to the needs of customers if it was to be able to succeed in the new highly competitive computing environment.

Changes in Computer Hardware

Gerstner instructed his top managers to begin initiatives in all its IT groups to meet clients' changing IT needs. In its traditional hardware business, it faced two major problems. First, because mainframe sales were declining because of the growing popularity of lower-cost network servers and PCs, Gerstner instructed hardware managers to do everything possible to reduce the costs of mainframe computing while increasing the scalability of its computers. Scalability means that a computer can be customized and designed and built to suit the needs of different-sized companies or different-sized computing tasks from managing global databases to operating a small chain of restaurants. IBM began to position its smaller mainframes as "enterprise servers." Sales reps were told to emphasize to clients that computers could be made at a size and price to suit their unique needs, but a large powerful mainframe computer was still needed at the hub of a large company's IT system. In addition, IBM wanted to sell its clients software and services such as maintaining and upgrading their software and managing their databases, so it deliberately set the price of its hardware low, knowing it could make more money later in providing the new software and services.

Changes in Computer Software

The rapid pace of change in computer software resulted in a major challenge for Gerstner and his managers. Before IBM made the mistake of allowing Microsoft to provide the MS-DOS operating system for its own PC, it had been the largest seller of computer software (principally for mainframes and mainframe applications) in the world. Now Microsoft had usurped its position, but there were many other challenges as well from makers of specialized applications software such as Oracle, which is the market leader in database management software, and SAP, the German company whose Enterprise Resource Planning (ERP) software was soaring in popularity. ERP software allows a company to link its value-chain activities and connects mainframes to servers and servers to PCs. It gives a company's managers at all levels extensive real-time information about a company's activities; ERP software has become the backbone of most IT systems in large companies. IBM had little to offer clients in these software applications areas; these companies had gained a first-mover advantage that was difficult for IBM to challenge.

Gerstner instructed the software division to focus its efforts on developing new business applications software that would improve a company's value-chain performance, along with "middleware" software that is designed to link all the different pieces of a company's hardware—mainframes, servers, PCs, and laptops together. To catch up with competitors in these areas, Gerstner acquired software companies that possessed unique solutions to provide clients with valuable new business applications and allow them to make better use of their computer networks. One of the companies IBM acquired at a cost of more than $3 billion in 1995 was Lotus, which had developed the popular Lotus Notes collaborative software. This software created a corporate intranet, an information network inside a company that allows managers at all levels to share information quickly both inside their own department and division and between divisions.

In his push to develop expertise in middleware, Gerstner also bought software companies that had the "middleware" software necessary to link the hardware and software provided by *any* computer company across *all* the levels of computing. In other words, he wanted IBM to control the middleware necessary to provide customers with a "seamless" solution to their computing needs regardless of their legacy system. A *legacy system* is a company's current IT system at any point in time. If IBM had the middleware necessary to link any kind of IT hardware and software, it would be able to upgrade any client that wished to improve its legacy system to take advantage of new and advanced IT applications offered by any company. This revolutionary approach was part of Gerstner's "open standards" strategy designed to make IBM's own services available to *all* kinds of customers.

Changes in Services and Consulting

Gerstner's drive to focus the efforts of all IBM employees on satisfying the needs of clients had been strongly influenced by the continued success of IBM's computer services group, which contributed about 20% to IBM's revenues in 1995. Gerstner recognized that this division possessed the customer-focused business model that IBM needed to grow its revenues in the future, especially if sales of its hardware and software declined. Moreover, Gerstner was familiar with the business model that Jack Welsh, former CEO of General Electric (GE), had developed for his company. GE would sell a product such as a turbine or aircraft or diesel engine at a relatively low price to increase sales because each sale would result in a profitable stream of future income from servicing and maintaining the complex equipment it sold. Gerstner recognized that this model was viable in the new IT environment; he also recognized that in the IT sector, clients need expert help to decide which kind of computer solution best meets their current and future business needs. In IT, companies such as Electronic Data Services (EDS) and Accenture were the leaders and earned huge profits by providing companies with expert help; the market was increasing by double digits each year. For example, SAP could not satisfy the demand of large global clients to install its ERP software in its client's companies. Clients were paying billions of dollars to consulting companies such as Accenture and Cap Gemini for their expert help.

In 1996, Gerstner renamed the services division to Global Services and charged it with the task of spearheading IBM's push into the outsourcing and value-chain management business to go head-to-head with competitors such as EDS and Accenture. Gerstner's business model was now that Global Services would offer clients an outsourcing and business consultancy service based on assessing a customer's current legacy system and its future computing needs. IBM consultants would then design, plan, implement, maintain, and upgrade the client's IT system over time to help reduce the client's cost structure, improve its products, and build its competitive advantage. Gerstner also hoped that providing such expert services would once again build up switching costs and keep IBM's clients loyal on a long-term basis because of its ability to show them how its comprehensive, customized computing solution could help increase their profitability over time. Global services experienced continuing success throughout the 1990s and into the 2000s.

THE NEW GLOBAL SERVICES DIVISION

Gerstner's strategy was now focused on strengthening the global services division, led by Sam Palmisano, because he believed this was the new foundation on which IBM's future success lay. Global services had three main lines of business: (1) strategic outsourcing services that provide customers with competitive cost advantages by outsourcing customers' processes and operations; (2) integrated technology services designs, implements, and maintains customers' technology infrastructures; and (3) business consulting services deliver value to customers through business process innovation, application enablement, and integration services.

Gerstner's business model for IBM was that the company would build such a broad and sophisticated range of computer hardware and software, backed by the best consulting and service competencies in the industry, that it would overwhelm its competitors in the future. EDS and Accenture provide consultancy and service, for example, and HP, Dell, Sun, Oracle, and Microsoft produce computer hardware and software, but none of them had the capability to match the breadth and depth of IBM's growing computer offerings. By the late 1990s, the ability to bundle products together was becoming a major advantage to clients seeking a seamless and cost-effective way of managing their IT systems; it has only become more important since.

In implementing this business model, Gerstner recognized that in many specific computer hardware and software product areas IBM was no longer the industry leader. So he and Palmisano embarked on a strategy of offering IBM's clients the best or "leading-edge" products currently available, such as SAP's ERP software, Peoplesoft's HRM software, Sun's servers, or Dell's PCs when they were either clearly better or lower priced than those supplied by IBM's own divisions. Then, and crucially, IBM's consultants, as a result of its focus on developing expertise in middleware that links any computer products together, were able to guarantee clients that they could install, maintain, and integrate them so that they worked together seamlessly.

In adopting this strategy, IBM was strengthening its commitment to "open standards" in the computer industry by announcing publicly that in the future it would continue to work to make all the *future* software and hardware of all producers— its competitors—compatible by strengthening its expertise in middleware. In doing so, Gerstner and IBM were also assuring clients that when they used IBM's computer consulting services, they would not become locked into IBM's proprietary hardware and software—no switching costs would arise from this source. However, Gerstner hoped at the same time that clients would be impressed by IBM's ability to provide such a complete service that they would become "locked in" because of the high quality of the service that it could provide.

An additional advantage of the open standards approach was that as IBM's consultants went from client to client assessing their needs, they were able to provide detailed feedback to IBM's other divisions about whether their products were adequately meeting clients' needs. So, if a consultant decided that a competitor's software was more appropriate than that offered by IBM, the division making the software could now clearly recognize why its product was not meeting customer needs—and what was necessary to improve its software to make it the "best of breed" or leading-edge product. Thus, Gerstner's strong focus on being close to clients had the additional advantage of spurring innovation throughout the organization; managers had a clear goal to achieve; and they knew Gerstner and his top management team were watching their performance. If a division did not meet customer needs, its managers might lose their jobs, or the division might be sold off or shut down.

E-BUSINESS AT IBM

Another indicator of how well Gerstner was attuned to the changing IT environment was his early recognition that the growth of the Internet and e-commerce would become a dominant force dictating which kinds of IT would be most necessary in the future. IBM coined the term *e-business*, and Gerstner established an Internet division in IBM in 1995 before most other IT companies. IBM's early recognition of the future possibilities of e-business allowed its engineers to adapt its software and hardware to serve Internet-related value-chain transactions before its competitors. Once again, being close to its clients helped IBM understand their changing needs and built its competitive advantage. Also, the acquisition of Lotus helped IBM understand the potential of the Internet. Lotus Notes was a company-specific or internal software collaboration application, while the Internet provided a major channel for collaboration between different companies. It was by chance that IBM's acquisition of Lotus revealed how the power of the Internet could shape supply-chain transactions between companies and their suppliers

and distributors. The Lotus collaborative software provided a model for making IBM's middleware software "Internet compatible."

IBM embarked on its e-business initiative in 1996 with a global marketing campaign aimed at showing companies how value-chain transactions with other companies and clients could be carried out online. Soon companies recognized that its competency in e-business gave it a competitive advantage over companies such as SAP, Oracle, and HP, who now raced to catch up. As a result, it attracted a growing number of e-business clients, which resulted in a major increase in its global computer services revenue. First in line to adopt IBM's e-business software were large corporations that needed to manage transactions with hundreds or even thousands of suppliers and distributors. Companies such as Walmart and Goodyear formed contracts with IBM to use its immense computing resources to manage their huge volume of online transactions.

IBM, however, also recognized that small and medium-sized businesses (SMBs) were another important customer group for its computer services—especially as it had developed scaleable computer hardware and software that could be sold at a price that meets a client's budget. IBM had developed less-expensive software targeted at the needs of SMB clients. It now worked with the thousands of new dot.com start-ups, such as Internet Web-design and Web-hosting companies, to teach these companies how to install and maintain its software in SMBs. IBM hoped that once SMBs had made the connection with IBM, they would start to buy other kinds of its software, for example, to manage their databases and functional, value-chain tasks such as bookkeeping and inventory control.

PALMISANO TAKES OVER

In 2003, Lou Gerstner stepped down, and Sam Palmisano became IBM's new CEO. Since then, IBM has continued to modify its strategies and reorganize the activities of its operating groups to strengthen its business model. Indeed, IBM's growing global strength has forced its major competitors to alter their business models to compete more effectively with IBM. For example, HP merged with

Compaq and took over EDS in 2008 to be able to provide a combination of HS&S to compete with IBM. Oracle has spent more than $50 billion in the 2000s taking over software and consulting companies such as PeopleSoft and BEA Systems for the same reasons. All major IT providers have had to adjust their business models to deal with the threat that IBM's expanding global presence and IT offerings have created.

Nevertheless, after years of growth, by 2005, IBM's performance had started to fall. The problem Palmisano soon realized was that its now dominant global technology services group that had grown like wildfire and provided the largest proportion of IBM's revenues and profits had run into trouble. As discussed following, its global outsourcing business had come under intense competition from low-priced overseas outsourcing companies, particularly Indian companies, at a time when its cost structure was quickly rising because of the rapid growth in the number of its employees, now more than 150,000 people worldwide. With the revenues of global services group plateauing, Palmisano had to search for new strategies to grow IBM's revenues and profits and solve the problems of its global services group.

Palmisano decided to change IBM's business model and strategies in several ways. First, he decided to cut the cost structure of its global services group. Second, to make up for slowing revenues and profits, he accelerated the strategy he had begun in 2003—changing IBM's business model so that all its operating groups focused on investing resources to move into higher profit-margin IT businesses in which the specialized skills of IBM's workforce could be used to develop higher value-added IT services, based on some combination of research, software, and services that would offer its customers greater value. Third, he decided to exit any hardware businesses in which profit margins were thin and focus resources on strengthening and growing its core mainframe business. Finally, he made globalization and the drive to increase IBM's presence in every country in which it operated a major priority across the company. All IBM's business groups were instructed to focus on cooperating to grow global sales of the HS&S package they offered customers, not just in the advanced G7 countries in North America, Europe, and Japan, but across all world regions, especially in the rapidly growing economies of India and China.

To achieve all these strategies, and especially to expand its global customer base quickly, Palmisano also changed IBM's structure. In the early 2000s, IBM's overseas divisions had operated independently on a country-by-country basis; there was little cooperation between them. Palmisano built a more streamlined global structure in which IBM technical experts who specialized in certain business functions or industries were organized into "clusters of business expertise." These clusters might be in any country of the world but are connected to each other and to IBM's HS&S groups through its own proprietary Lotus high-speed communications Intranet. Project managers can search worldwide for the HS&S experts with the right skills for a job located in different countries around the world and form teams of experts quickly to meet the needs of clients in any country. For example, IBM created global and regional teams of skilled experts in particular industries, from airlines to utilities, who travel as needed to consult on projects.

The many changes its new global structure brought about in the operations of its HS&S groups are discussed following, but one of the most important changes was that in 2007 Palmisano decided to split the global services group into two parts: the global technology services (GTS) group that was to specialize in IBM's traditional kinds of IT services such as outsourcing maintenance and database management; and the global business services (GBS) group that was to specialize in developing high-margin business and industry IT solutions customized to the needs of individual clients.

The Global Technology Services Group

Palmisano assigned all of IBM's more traditional "routine" lower-margin IT services to the global technology services (GTS) group. The GTS group handles value-chain infrastructure services and uses IBM's global scale and its expertise in standardizing and automating transactions to manage outsourcing, integrated technology services such as logistics and data center management, and maintenance services for its global clients.

As noted previously, IBM was experiencing increasing low-cost competition in its outsourcing services business that provided it with billions of dollars of revenues from contracts with large global companies to manage their "non-core" business functions such as distribution, logistics, and data center management. This intense competitive pressure was coming from low-cost Indian companies such as Infosys, Tata Consulting Services, and Wipro, which had grown enormously in the 2000s because of their lower labor costs. Indeed, their profit margins were more than 20%, while margins at IBM were half that and shrinking because of the competition. These companies gained such an advantage because labor costs were still about 70% to 80% of the total cost of traditional technology service contracts involving activities such as maintaining and updating software and data centers for corporate clients. They were taking away billions of dollars in revenues from IBM.

IBM had to compete more effectively in this IT services segment, which had been a main source of the increasing revenues that had allowed it to rebuild its competitive advantage. Like most manufacturing companies, IBM was forced to eliminate 20,000 GTS jobs in Europe and the United States and move these jobs to India. Its Indian workforce grew from 30,000 in 2004 to 45,000 in 2006. Then in June 2006, IBM announced it would triple its investment in India to $6 billion over the next three years to take advantage of its growing importance as a market for technology products and a source of high-technology workers. By 2009, it had more than 75,000 Indian employees.

IBM made the investment to establish huge, low-cost service delivery centers for its global clients, improve the software necessary to automate the management of networks and data centers, and develop IT to improve telecommunications, especially Internet services. From India, IBM runs a whole range of IT services for its global customers, including software delivery services such as upgrading and maintaining client software and managing and protecting database centers. For example, in Bangalore, IBM has a command center that monitors the operation of the database server networks of more than 16,000 different clients, including the way thousands of its outsourcing software applications are performing around the world. It is the largest of IBM's three global IT services centers; the other two that are growing in size are in Brazil and China. Palmisano's goal was to expand the scope of IBM's traditional outsourcing operations and attract more and more global clients to compensate for reduced profit margins so it can still increase profits from this group. And IBM has the global reputation necessary to convince customers it will be able to reduce their cost structure and improve their profitability.

However, IBM moved to India not only to take advantage of lower labor costs but also because the country has a huge pool of talented software engineers that IBM recruited to develop new, advanced software that can *automate* the IT jobs currently performed by its Indian employees in logistics and data center management. In other words, IBM's long-term goal is not simply to replace skilled labor with lower-cost skilled labor but to use that skilled labor in combination with advanced automated software. This means that over time, although IBM's Indian workforce will continue to increase in size, engineers will be able to manage a much higher volume of global customer accounts more efficiently, which will significantly increase IBM's profit margins in its traditional services business. IBM has made dozens of acquisitions in the 2000s to help improve its skills in software automation and develop smarter, more customized software that allows it to maintain its clients', value-chain functions at lower cost to compete with its Indian rivals.

Global Business Services Group

If the goal in its GTS group was to increase profit margins and the number of customer accounts by being able to offer global customers lower prices and high-quality customer service, the goal of its global business services (GBS) group is to offer customers state-of-the-art value-creating software services that can be customized to their needs, albeit at a premium price. In other words, in creating the GBS group, Palmisano's goal was accelerate its move into higher-margin service activities, especially consulting and business transformation in which IBM could use the specialized skills of its United States software engineers to offer customers IT services that increase their competitive advantage. Specifically, the GBS group's strategy is to offer its customers professional, innovative services that deliver value by providing them with state-of-the-art solutions that leverage IBM's industry and business process expertise.

Such services include consulting, systems integration, and application management services that tap into IBM's expertise in IT and apply it to fields such as utility grid optimization and energy conservation, genetics-based personalized medicine, fraud detection and prediction, and even traffic management. For example, one of IBM's projects involved working with a Texas utility, CenterPoint Energy, to install computerized electric meters, sensors, and software in a "smart grid" IT project to improve service and conserve energy. Dozens of IBM's industry experts from around the country moved to work on the project to design and build advanced software tailored to the needs of a utility company. Because some of the programming work can be done in India, engineers are on the project team as well.

IBM plans to use the valuable skills learned and software written for the Texas smart-grid project in new projects with utility clients around the world, thus leveraging its skills in a high-profit margin business. In 2008, IBM announced it was entering into a new agreement with CenterPoint to develop the software platform necessary to supply the utilities rural customers with high-speed Internet connections through the power grid. By connecting their PCs to any electrical socket in their homes, they will be able to obtain broadband Internet service. Also, in 2008, IBM announced hundreds of new global services contracts with diverse companies around the world, such as Philippines PSBank, the second-largest savings bank in the country, PTT Chemical Public Company of Thailand, and Skynet in Lithuania to provide Internet protocol television. This was growing evidence of its increasing expertise in specialized IT services.

Building up its repertoire of skills across industries and across business functions is a key way in which IBM intends to grow its revenues and profits over time. And, its competitors recognizing its growing competitive advantage were forced to expand their capabilities to provide customers with a competitive HS&S package. For example, in 2008, HP acquired EDS, the third-largest IT services company in the United States for $14 billion to add its 140,000 employees to the IT services group and improve its repertoire of IT skills and clients to compete better with IBM for global customers. HP, following IBM's lead, has also divided its service activities into those that improve the efficiency of companies' value-chain operations through outsourcing and logistics management and those that involve using its IT expertise to help companies innovate and find new ways to improve their value-creation skills. Of course, IBM continues to emphasize that its combination of vast experience and IT expertise is unmatched on a global scale.

Another competitor that has also been aggressively expanding the breadth of its IT service and software lineup is the database management software leader, Oracle. Oracle has spent more than $50 billion since 2004 to acquire companies such as PeopleSoft and BEA Systems to widen its ERP lineup and better compete with its ERP archrival SAP. At the same time, however, Oracle's new product lineup has resulted in more competition with IBM, especially in the server market. Increasing competition here has prompted IBM to develop closer ties with SAP. In 2009, IBM and SAP announced an agreement with British retailer Marks & Spencer (M&S) to implement a suite of SAP Retail applications. The program aims to provide M&S with accurate business intelligence data and state-of-the-art functional and industry IT solutions that will allow it to discover business improvement initiatives that will increase operating efficiency and responsiveness to customers. IBM will draw on its expertise in organization, process, and technology to provide end-to-end program management, including change management and business process consulting services. SAP will provide its "Industry Solution for Retail," a suite of business applications designed specifically to meet the unique requirements of large and sophisticated retailers. Also in 2009, IBM announced it would be the first global IT company to fully adopt the Run SAP(R) methodology and that it would become a launch partner for SAP(R) Business Suite 7 software, SAP's new flexible and modular software suite. As global partners, SAP and IBM will jointly help customers reduce the total cost of running SAP's ERP software.

Software Group

Clearly, the ability of IBM's two global services groups to provide customers either low-cost traditional IT services or value-creating, customized consulting solutions depends on it having the distinctive competence to develop state-of-the-art software applications across business processes and industries. Since 2005, Palmisano has emphasized the central role advanced software development must play in IBM's future business model to offset the slowing revenues from global services because of low-cost global competition. To spur its efforts in software development, and especially to increase its share of the high-margin services business, IBM began to make many acquisitions. By 2007, had IBM spent $11.8 billion to acquire 36 software and 18 service companies in fields such as security, data management, and Web commerce.

One particularly important acquisition occurred in 2008 when IBM announced it had acquired Cognos, a leading maker of business intelligence software, for $4.9 billion. IBM's acquisition came after SAP's acquisition of Business Objects and Oracle's takeover of Hyperion, the other two leading makers of business intelligence software in 2007. Business intelligence software sifts through huge masses of data and uses sophisticated problem solving procedures to identify and discover crucial events such as changes in the buying habits of a customer group or the "hidden" factors reducing the efficiency of a company's value-chain functions or business processes. Cognos software is used by many retailers, including Home Depot, Amazon .com, American Eagle Outfitters, and 7-Eleven. Recent advances in IT have increased the power of business intelligence software to identify ongoing changes and forecast likely future events, an area in which IBM had no expertise. So, to prevent its competitors from gaining a possible future competitive advantage, IBM decided to make this acquisition, just as it had made the important decision to acquire Lotus Notes over a decade earlier. IBM will be able to incorporate Cognos software into all its software/service packages and hence strengthen its competitive advantage.

In October 2008, IBM unveiled new Express Advantage products aimed at SMBs, including HS&S packages specifically customized to the needs of SMB clients. For example, its new packages help SMB clients improve operational efficiency, increase customer responsiveness, and continuously lower risk. In 2008, in a deal worth as much as $800 million over eight years, Amgen, the biotech company hired IBM to provide a HS&S package that will provide computer networks, software, messaging systems, helpdesk support, and other services.

In 2009, IBM announced a new "virtual world" IT initiative to make it easier for geographically dispersed people to interact and collaborate without the time and expense of in-person meetings. Virtual worlds are interactive, immersive Web sites based on the use of three-dimensional graphics. IBM was using selected clients to test its "Sametime 3D" virtual technology, which allows people inside and between companies to exchange instant messages, chat verbally, share real-time presentations and ideas in private, virtual meeting spaces that exist permanently in real time so people can meet on regular, periodic, or impromptu bases.

In 2009, IBM also announced a new agreement with Amazon Web Services (AWS), a subsidiary of Amazon.com, to deliver IBM's software to clients and developers via cloud computing. The new "pay-as-you-go" model provides clients with access to development and production instances of IBM DB2, Informix Dynamic Server, WebSphere Portal, Lotus Web Content Management, WebSphere sMash, and Novell's SUSE Linux operating system software in the Amazon Elastic Compute Cloud (Amazon EC2) environment, providing a comprehensive portfolio of products available on AWS.

In May 2009, IBM announced it had acquired Exeros, a privately held data discovery software maker and will wrap Exeros' technology into its business intelligence or analytics unit. Exeros software includes Discover X-Profiler, an application that profiles data; Discovery Unified Schema Builder, which allows users to prototype the combination of various data; and the Discovery Transformation Analyzer, which scans business rules and spots anomalies.

Systems and Technology Group

In its hardware division, Palmisano continued his strategy of focusing on high–profit margin products that directly complemented its service and software offerings. As noted earlier, IBM had sold off its PC business to Lenovo for $1.25 billion and its disk drive business Hitachi for $2 billion. In 2007, IBM decided to spin off its printer business, which was suffering from intense competition from HP and Xerox, to Ricoh for $725 million.

Palmisano directed the systems and technology group to put its resources into developing new kinds of mainframes and servers that would appeal to a wider number of customers groups and expand global sales. IBM still receives about 25% of its $100 billion in annual revenue from sales, software, services, and financing related to its mainframes and servers.

Mainframes, the hub of a large company's IT system, crunch the massive amounts of data that are generated, for example, every time someone withdraws money from an automated teller machine, uses a credit card, or buys a product from a large retailer. Since 2005, IBM has been pursuing the strategy of constantly upgrading the performance of its large mainframes to offer its customers a better value prospection, that is, to give them more and more power and flexibility for each IT dollar they spend. And, beginning in 2006, it began to offer customers the option of buying smaller and much-less expensive mainframes to drive sales to medium-sized global customers. In 2007, for example, it introduced its latest generation of mainframes, the powerful z10 Enterprise Class (z10EC) mainframe that retails for about $1 million and the smaller z10 Business Class (z10BC) mainframe that retails for about $100,000. The larger mainframe is twice as powerful as its predecessor; the smaller one is 40% faster, has more than 50% more total systems capacity, and up to four times the maximum main memory compared to the previous "mini-mainframe" IBM introduced in 2005. At a fraction of the cost of its large mainframe, the z10BC is also a way for IBM to offer more machines to more market segments. Priced at $100,000, the machine is not directed at small businesses that would use more inexpensive server rack configurations; it is highly attractive to smaller enterprises and midmarket companies looking to consolidate multiple server racks in many data centers with one large machine.

IBM sells its large mainframes directly to customers through its own salesforce to protect the lucrative software and service revenues that accompany these sales. The smaller mainframe, however, is sold through its 20 global channel partners, who also provide the software and service package customized to each client's needs. IBM pursued this strategy to accelerate the adoption of the machines throughout the world because global customers, particularly those in India and China, are the main targets for these $100,000 machines. Its strategy worked. IBM's mainframe installed base doubled from 2005 to 2009 because of IBM's ability to deliver increasing amounts of processing power to customers at a decreasing cost. In addition, the new mainframes used far less energy, something that is becoming increasingly important throughout the IT hardware industry.

In 2009, IBM was accused of purchasing software maker Platform Solutions to stifle competition in the mainframe market and protect its franchise. Platform Solutions had developed software that turned racks of servers into a linked system that could mimic the performance of IBM's expensive mainframes. IBM announced it would refuse to license its mainframe software to Platform that would allow its software to work. But when its legal attempt to stop Platform from gaining access to its software failed, IBM bought it for $150 million and then shut down work on the software. The Computer and Communications Industry Association, a trade group backed by Google, Oracle, and Microsoft, described the Platform deal as an attempt by IBM to purchase a company solely to foreclose competition in the mainframe marketplace and protect its cash cow at the expense of consumers. IBM contends the continued popularity of its mainframes stems from its continuous efforts to modernize them so that they can run more contemporary business software. Other competitors, such as Sun, HP, and Microsoft, have also attempted to develop software for connected racks of linked servers to enable them to handle the huge number-crunching tasks mainframes can perform, but their efforts have had only limited success.

New software called virtualization technology is currently being developed, however, that may result in linked server racks being able to emulate the power of mainframes. This may be one reason that prompted IBM in 2009 to announce it would acquire Sun, still a leading maker of server HS&S for about $7 billion; the deal would also give IBM control over the key storage systems used for mainframes. In the end, however, the deal fell through when Oracle made a higher offer for Sun to gain control of all its server HS&S assets, including its Java software. It appears that Sun's goal will be to expand the role of servers to also mimic the power of IBM's mainframes, something that will intensify the competition between the two companies.

IBM has always been interested in the idea of hosting its client's data on its own network of mainframes and developed an IT service called "business on demand" to offer them this option. By the mid-2000s, however, the cost of linked racks of servers (which might contain 10,000 powerful individual servers) was falling sharply as Intel and AMD introduced ever-more advanced microprocessors, which when combined with Oracle's database management software, made them low-cost alternatives to renting space on IBM's mainframes. Also in the mid-2000s, the idea of cloud computing had been pioneered by Internet companies such as Google, Yahoo!, and Microsoft, and the concept was gaining in popularity. In the cloud computing business model, Internet and other companies design their own customized data centers to store vast amounts of information that can be accessed and processed from afar using PCs, netbooks, cell phones, or other devices. For example, Google pioneered an online document hosting service in which both individuals and companies can upload documents that are stored in Google's data centers on server racks and then can be accessed using word processing or spread-sheet software programs and so on. Once again, these data centers are composed of tens or even hundreds of thousands of servers linked into racks, which are in turn connected together to provide immense amounts of storage and processing power.

What is unique about the cloud computing model, however, is that, cloud data centers require server racks that have been configured with the right HS&S to meet the needs of each individual company. These data centers are not "off-the-shelf" standardized products, such as IBM's mainframes. Even more unique, the growing number of companies that are competing to offer these integrated server racks have developed a new business model in which these racks are housed in portable storage platforms that are housed in shipping containers similar to those used to deliver products around the world on ships and trucks. These storage platforms are then integrated into a company's physical data center using networking hardware and software. This business is growing fast; it is expected to be a multibillion-dollar business in the future.

Given that its business on demand initiative was not working, IBM was anxious to enter this market. It also is a major maker of server racks, and in 2008, IBM bought the cloud computing platform maker, Platform Systems, to provide new portable computing data centers. IBM calls its new product iDataPlex; it is a self-contained data center housed in different-sized shipping containers that can hold 1,000 to 10,000 server computers powered by Intel or AMD chips. One of its platforms offers customers the option of placing 1,500 server computers into 40-foot semi-trailers that are ready to plug in from parking lots.

Developing hardware platforms that have to be customized to the needs of individual companies is a new strategy for IBM; however, its army of IT services and software experts provide it with the competence necessary to do this. IBM claims its new cloud computer container platform costs only half as much in real estate, set-up, and construction costs than a similar physical data center. In addition, compared to the platform systems offered by competitors such as Dell, HP, and Rackable Systems, IBM claims its trailers have innovative water-cooling mechanisms so that the servers do not heat up the data centers. This eliminates the need for most air-conditioning. As a result, IBM claims its systems consume 40% less power than standard servers and can pack more than twice as many computers into the same space.

Companies trying out its platforms include Yahoo! and other Internet companies; companies in finance and other traditional industries are also testing them. In 2009, Google for the first time publicly showed the design of its own cloud computing data centers, which are also technologically advanced, especially cooling wise. Clearly there is competition ahead.

Finally, in April 2009, IBM announced it was strengthening its strategic alliance with network equipment maker Brocade Communication. IBM sold its own networking equipment business to Cisco Systems in the early 2000s. However, innovations such as its cloud computing data center trailers, as well as the growing need to connect all the different kinds of IT hardware used by its clients seamlessly to the Internet and especially to remote data centers means IBM must have access to state-of-the-art networking products to align perfectly with its own software. In the future, IBM will rebrand Ethernet switching and Internet routing products made by Brocade as IBM products and sell them as a part of its complete IT HS&S package to its global customers. One more reason for this partnership is that rivalry with Cisco increased in 2009 after Cisco announced it was entering the server data center market and planned a "revolutionary" new kind of self-contained rack server that would possess a huge amount of database storage capacity and processing power linked to its own network communication hardware and software. Such a self-contained server would eliminate the need for expensive IT consulting and service; it would offer companies with a low-cost alternative, and, over time, companies could simply order as many of Cisco's server racks as needed to operate or expand their business. Presumably Cisco will also offer a portable container-based platform solution.

IBM'S RECENT PERFORMANCE

By 2006, IBM's performance was recovering as a result of Palmisano's strategic initiatives, especially his decision to split apart the old global services group. Trimming its service workforce had significantly reduced its cost structure, and sales of its new main-frames were up by 25%. Software revenue rose 5%, helped by increasing sales of its popular WebSphere software package that improves the performance of a company's electronic commerce and business applications. In addition, its shift toward higher profit-margin services and automating traditional business processes such as procurement, finance, and human resources was leading to increasing numbers of long-term service contracts. In particular, its higher-profit business transformation outsourcing grew by 45%. Palmisano commented that "the strength of our business model across hardware, software and services is paying off." Geographically, IBM enjoyed solid growth of 5% in the G7 countries, but more rapid growth was occurring in emerging markets. For example, sales in India were up by 50%.

IBM's performance continued to improve through 2007 into 2008. IBM reported profit rising 12% on strong growth in software and services. Due to its success in selling higher-margin software and services, its profit margins were steadily improving. Indeed, by 2008, IBM software's revenue showed the biggest gain and had become the largest contributor to IBM's profits. Palmisano announced that software would be the driving force behind IBM's future growth. Obviously, the ability to develop state-of-the-art business software drives up IBM's service revenues and the sales of mainframes that are optimized to use its new software.

By May 2008, IBM stock was trading near its six-year high level, and it seemed as though Palmisano's new strategies had worked. However, then came the recession in the summer of 2008. Although, as expected, revenues from its hardware group fell sharply as large companies reduced their spending on mainframes and servers, IBM was not hurt as badly as its competitors because of its major push to globalization. In 2007, for example, it had reported that it enjoyed more than 10% percent growth in revenues in more than 50 countries.

In October 2008, analysts were surprised when IBM reported strong third-quarter profits despite the financial services industry meltdown. As IBM's CFO explained, although financial services is IBM's biggest customer segment contributing 28% to its revenues, and the one hit hardest by the economic downturn, 75% of that revenue came from outside the United States. Also, only 15% of those financial institutions that had been severely impacted were IBM clients, so the company was not highly exposed to the meltdown. Moreover, even in the United States, IBM benefitted from many new short-term contracts with financial companies such

as banks and brokers that increased their spending on risk analysis and compliance tools to try to weather the downturn. In fact, globally, IBM had signed more than $12.7 billion in new long-term services contracts in the last quarter of 2008, while short-term contract signings were up 13% to $6.1 billion. This showed IBM was able to generate new business despite tough economic times.

In April 2009, Palmisano expressed more confidence that the company was on track to achieve its projected earnings target for the full year despite uncertain markets worldwide. The company reported solid performance in a period of economic turmoil, helped by cost-cutting and its strategy of moving into higher profit margin software and services businesses. Like most other large companies, in March 2009, IBM announced 5,000 job cuts in the United States, which accounted for more than 4% of its United States workforce—115,000 by the end of 2008. The cuts were mostly in IBM's global services business and, as noted earlier, IBM has greatly expanded its business and employment in fast-growing markets such as India, China, Brazil, and Russia. At the beginning of 2009, IBM had 75,000 workers in India and 13,000 in China.

Similarly, the improving profit margins IBM was enjoying in its expanding services and software businesses were significantly boosted by the 100 acquisitions IBM had made since 2000, which had cost $20 billion, and its moves to aggressively pursue opportunities in faster-growing markets abroad such as India and China. Also, of course, 40% to 60% percent of its profits come from its long-term contracts with customers who pay a fixed yearly fee for its value-chain management software and services. It is difficult to reduce this spending even in a recession. Indeed, the recession had sparked a lot of interest in the cost-saving outsourcing deals offered by its GTS group. One example is a $500 million, seven-year contract IBM signed in March 2009 to manage data centers and software for Kaiser Permanente, a large hospital and managed health care company. In fact, in 2009, the market offering the strongest possibilities for revenue growth was the public sector, with government and state organizations, in which contracts were up 50% as countries around the world announced *$5 trillion* in economic stimulus programs to increase customer demand for technology and other goods to increase spending and boost economic growth.

TiVo 2008

BACKGROUND

With TiVo, TV fits into your busy life, NOT the other way around.

The evolutionary history of television started back in 1939 with an original purpose of providing people with entertainment and enjoyment in life. It was then followed by an invention of the remote control in 1950 known as the "lazy bones." Perhaps television has been one of the biggest breakthroughs and most influential forms of entertainment we have appreciated and enjoyed up until now. However, after the lazy bones was invented, the next generation of TV-watching tools evolved. One of them was TiVo, every couch potato's dream. Two Silicon Valley veterans, with their creative and smart ideas, took the initiative to re-create innovative and advanced technology developments in a radically different approach. TiVo was created not only for entertainment but also for "TV Your Way." Fundamentally designed, "With TiVo, TV fits into your busy life, NOT the other way around."

Now, many people may have heard the name TiVo: it is mentioned on popular TV shows, movies, and many talk shows. Even Oprah wondered in the September 2005 issue of her *O* magazine why life can't be like TiVo. But many people do not know what TiVo is really about.

ONCE UPON A TIVO . . .

Pioneered by Mike Ramsay and Jim Barton, TiVo redefined entertainment in many ways, delivering the promise of technologies that were much hyped. Incorporated in Delaware and originally named "Teleworld," the playback of TiVo started on August 4, 1997. As proposed, the original idea was to create a home network–based multimedia server in which content to clients would be streamed out throughout the homes. To build such a product, a solid software foundation was needed, and the device created needed to operate flawlessly, reliably, and handle power failures gracefully for consumers. At that time, both men were still working at Silicon Graphics (SGI) and were very much involved in the entertainment industry. Jim Barton, though, was involved with on-demand video systems. He was the executive sponsor of an effort to port an open source system called Linux to the SGI Indy workstation. Mike Ramsay was responsible for products that create movies special effects for such companies as ILM and Pixar. With the combination of both worlds, these two SGI veterans thought Linux software would well serve TiVo as the operating system foundation. As for the hardware, it was designed solely by TiVo Inc. and manufactured with the help of various original equipment manufacturers, including Philips, Sony, Hughes,

Written by Alan N. Hoffman, Rendy Halim, Rangki Son, Suzanne Wong, and Bentley University.

The authors would like to thank Audrey Ballara, Will Hoffman, and Ann Hoffman for their research and contributions to this case. Please address all correspondence to Dr. Alan N. Hoffman, MBA Program Director, LAC295D, Bentley University, 175 Forest Street, Waltham, MA 02452-4705, voice 781-891-2287, fax 781-459-0335, ahoffman@bentley.edu. Printed by permission of Dr. Alan N. Hoffman.

Pioneer, Toshiba, and Humax. Combined they created a product that was interactive with real people, delivering a commitment in which people would be able to take charge of their entertainment whenever and wherever they wanted to or needed to.

From the Server Room to the Living Room

Swaying from their original idea to create a home network device, Ramsey and Barton later developed the idea to record digitized video on a hardware storage drive. Inside the Silicon Valley headquarters of TiVo in Alviso, California, both veterans created a "fantasy living room," depicting a room that would be a prototype for 100 million living rooms across North America. At that time, they both knew it would be great to exploit and develop the idea into an actual product with a promising future, a dream of most start-up companies. In the early days, Ramsay said they used to have thoughts like, "Wow, you know, you can pause live television—isn't that a cool thing?" Barton had a computer store with a live TV signal and would play it back. That was the start of TiVo, providing people with more than the original purpose of TV as simply a tube to watch, resulting with an invention to create the world's very first interactive entertainment network in which luxury entertainment and control is in the viewers' own hands. On March 31, 1999, TiVo shipped its first unit. Because that day was a "blue moon," the engineering staff code-named TiVo's first version digital video recorder (DVR) as the "Blue Moon." Both Barton and Ramsay were psyched as the introduction to market a disruptive technology had just begun. Teleworld was renamed to TiVo in July 1999. Now that living rooms are filled only with an oval coffee table and a comfy chair, just like any other living rooms in the households, the only objects that can be distinctively seen and left is what's on the table surface—a telephone and TiVo's distinctive peanut-shaped remote control. The sofa and chairs all face an entertainment center containing a big-screen television that is linked to several TiVo boxes (a few are available; a few are work in progress).

TiVo Acclaimation

Now that the success of on-demand programs and online streaming are flocking to TV networks, many people have found DVR to be an essential part of their digital home entertainment center, catering more to their viewing habits. Consumers went into such big box retailers as Best Buy, Circuit City, Target, and Walmart where salespeople would refer them to TiVo because TiVo has been commonly associated with the DVR. Reminiscing back to the history of DVR, TiVo was actually never the beginner that ReplayTV was. The two early consumer DVRs, ReplayTV and TiVo, both launched their products at the 1999 Consumer Electronics Show in Las Vegas. ReplayTV won the "Best of Show" award in the video category and was later acquired by SONICblue and D&M Holdings. However, it was not ReplayTV, the pioneer of DVRs, that produced a cultlike product like TiVo. TiVo's success includes still being the only standalone DVR company in the industry. According to Forrester, from a scale of 1 to 5, TiVo's brand trust among regular users scores a 4.2, while its brand potential among aspiring users scores an A with 11.1 million potential users.

Spending approximately 13 months for full development of the first TiVo box, the wait was worthwhile as the revolutionary nature of TiVo won an Emmy award in August 19, 2006. This recognition was given to TiVo for providing innovative and interactive services that enhances television viewing to a whole new level. Other finalists for this particular Emmy award included AOL Music on Demand, CNN Enhanced, and DirecTV Interactive Sports. With a cultlike product, TiVo has transformed into a verb. TiVo established a top-notch brand that has become the "it" word among its fervidly loyal customers and even noncustomers. In general, people would say "TiVo it," meaning to record or zap (make something disappear). A working wife, who might have an important business dinner meeting that night and was rushing through the door, could ask her husband "Could you TiVo *Desperate Housewives* for me tonight, dear?" On the other hand, TiVo felt that this verb transformation would jeopardize TiVo and associate its products as a generic brand of DVR when people say, "I want two TiVos." However, with all the TiVo buzz, TiVo became public on September 30, 1999 at a price offering of $16 per share with a total of 5.5 million number of shares listed under the NASDAQ. On its way to the IPO, TiVo established one of the most rapid adoption rates in the history of consumer electronics. Quoted in an April 2007 article by *PC World,* TiVo became the third on the list of

50 best technology products of all time—amazing products that changed our lives forever.

The acknowledgement has well-served the young West Coast company currently available in four countries; the United States, the United Kingdom, Canada, and Taiwan. In addition, although it is not sold yet, TiVo's technology has been modified by end users so it could fit in another four countries: Australia, New Zealand, the Netherlands, and South Africa. Considered to be the best DVR system by a variety of top-notch publications, such as *Business Week, the New York Times,* and *Popular Science,* TiVo hit the 3 million subscriber milestone by February, 18, 2005. Not long after, TiVo finally made its first profitable quarter. TiVo's subscribers include diverse and loyal subscribers, including Oprah Winfrey, Brad Pitt, and entrepreneur Craig Newmark (the owner of Craig's List). The business philosophy of TiVo is relatively simple: TiVo connects consumers to the digital entertainment they want, where and when they want it.

THE BRAIN INSIDE THE BOX

It's not TiVo unless it's a TiVo.

The Surf and Turf

As people's daily lives became busier and demanded more to attain the pleasure of watching TV, DVRs became the tools to satisfy that trend. The trend resulted in audiences wanting to have more direct allegiance with particular programs. TiVo revolutionized a new way to watch TV, with the introduction of the DVR system. Difficult to describe in a sentence or two, the best way to say what TiVo really is, is by the things that it does.

The DVR platform has created massive opportunities for TiVo to continue developing creative and sophisticated applications, features, and services. Unlike a VCR (videocassette recorder), TiVo as a DVR issues only Linux-based software and allows users to capture any TV programming and record them onto internal hard disk storage for later viewing. Its patented feature, "Trick Play" that allows viewers to stop, pause, rewind, and "slo-mo" live shows, is what TiVo was originally best at.

The TiVo device also allows users to watch programs without having to watch the commercials. Users are exposed to promotional messages but are not forced to watch them. While this feature seems very attractive to consumers, understandably, it is not to television networks and advertising agencies. However, unlike ReplayTV that allows users to automatically and completely skip advertisements and was hit by several lawsuits by ad agencies and TV networks, TiVo managed to take a different approach.

With its inventive advertisement feature, TiVo offered to help, turning a difficult situation into a business opportunity, which has become TiVo's hallmark. TiVo surely knows that advertisements are sources of revenue. TiVo then started testing its "pop-up" feature. While recording or watching, some advertisements pop up at the bottom of the TV screen. If a customer is interested in any of these advertisements, he or she has the ability to click to get more information about the product being advertised. People then have the choice to get advertisers' information or not depending on what they have interest in. "Product Watch" allows users to choose the products, services, or even brands that interest them. It will automatically find and deliver the requested/relevant products straight to the customer's list. Surprisingly, during the 2002 Super Bowl, TiVo tracked the viewing patterns of 10,000 subscribers and found that TiVo's instant replay feature was used more on certain commercials, notably the Pepsi ad with Britney Spears, than on the game itself. As of today, TiVo has included 70 "showcase" advertising campaigns in its TiVo platforms for companies such as Acura, Best Buy, BMW, Buick, Cadillac, Charles Schwab, Coca-Cola, Dell, General Motors, New Line Cinema, Nissan, Pioneer, Porsche, and Target.

Beyond the key functions described previously, there is much more for users to surf throughout the integral functionality of a TiVo device. A "Season Pass Manager" avoids conflict resolution such as overlapping recordings; a "Wish List" platform allows viewers to store their searches according to specifics such as actor, keyword, director, etc. So far, no other companies have been able to match these two recording features. In addition, the catchy remote control with its distinctive "Thumbs Up and Down" feature allows users to rate the shows they have watched so that TiVo can assist and provide them with movies similar to what they have rated. The remote itself has won design awards from the Consumer Electronics Association. Jakob Nielsen, a technology consultant of the Nielsen Norman Group, called the oversized yellow pause button in the middle of the remote "the most beautiful pause button I've ever seen." Steve Wozniak, the co-founder of Apple Computer, mentioned, "TiVo adjusts to my tastes, and its remote has been the most ergonomic and easy to use one that I have encountered in many years."

In addition, being portable is now the hottest thing in television. Because many people have yet become more tech savvy, "TiVoToGo," its newest feature launched in January 2005, allows users to connect their TiVo to a computer with Internet or a home network, transferring recorded shows from TiVo boxes to users' personal computers (PCs). Then, through a software program developed with Sonic, customers are able to edit and conserve their TiVo files. In August 2005, TiVo released software that allows customers to transfer MPEG2 video files from their PCs to their TiVo boxes to play the videos on DVRs.

TiVoToGo feature also includes TiVo's "Central Online" that allows users to schedule recordings on its Web site 24/7. "MultiRoom Viewing" allows users to transfer recordings between TiVo units in multiple rooms; download any programs in any format they want to the TiVo box; and transfer them into other devices such as iPods, laptops, or other mobile devices such as cellular phones to view them anytime and anywhere users desire. Additionally, with the partnerships TiVo has established with regard to third-party network content, viewers now can access weather, traffic conditions, purchase a last-minute movie ticket at Fandango.com, and have the pleasure of "Amazon Unbox," allowing users to buy/rent the latest movies and TV shows to be downloaded into the TiVo box.

Behind the Box: The Hardware Anatomy of TiVo 101

Many people have asked how TiVo actually operates. "Even my mother can use TiVo with no problem!" This is the phrase that TiVo wants their customers to say.

Technically speaking, installing TiVo units are self-explanatory because they are designed to be simple enough for everyone to install and operate. Parts that go into the device and its internal architecture are less complex. An online self-installation guide with a step-by-step, pictured instruction, has been the tool to complete the task; however, options come in handy, with a team of door-to-door professional installers from Best Buy or by calling 1-877-Geek-Squad.

In a basic sense, TiVo is simply a cable box with a hard drive that has the ability to record and a fancy user interface. The main idea at the beginning, however, was to free people up from the network schedule. With TiVo, people can watch anytime they want with extra features such as pause, rewind, fast forward, slow motion, and many other great features—including the commercial-free watching experience.

Initially, the box receives the signals coming from cable, antenna, or satellite. Then the signals received by the box are divided into many frequencies and selected with the tuner that is built in the box. The signals with the right selected frequencies are sent and encoded through the encoder, stored on the hard drive, and then decoded again for watchers to view anytime.

TiVo's earlier model Series2 was supported with USB ports that were been integrated into the TiVo system to support network adapters, including wired Ethernet and Wi-Fi. It also provides the possibility to record over the air. The new TiVo Series3 has been built with two internal cable-ready tuners and supports a single external cable or satellite box. As a result, TiVo has the ability to record two shows at once, unlike other DVRs. Moreover, the latest version of the TiVo box has a 10/1000 Ethernet connection port and a SATA port that can support external storage hardware. It also has a HDMI plug that provides an interface between any compatible digital audio/video source, such as a DVD player, a PC, or a video game system. In other words, with the new TiVo box, customers do not even need their cable boxes anymore. Some recent models contain DVD-R/RW drives that transfer recordings from the TiVo box to a DVD.

TiVo hardware can work like a normal digital recorder. People might sometimes want to keep the hardware and cancel their subscriptions with TiVo, which is very damaging for the company's revenue model.

WHAT THE HACK!

Where there is technology involved, there are incentives for hackers to challenge the system. Some people have hacked TiVo boxes to improve the service and expand the recording capacity and/or storage. Others have aimed at making TiVo available in countries where TiVo is not currently available. In the latest version of TiVo, improved encryption of the hardware and software has made it more difficult for people to hack the systems.

THE TIVO OPERATION: BEHIND THE SCENES

. . . . and I never miss an episode. TiVo takes care of the details.

Marketing: Feel the Buzz— Hail Thy TiVo

When it comes to new technology, penetrating consumer markets is usually difficult because customers are slower to embrace new products than forecasters predict and prefer using old and easier technology such as VCRs. Mike Ramsay often became upset in the early days when someone said, "Oh, that's just like a VCR." He would then reply, "No, no, no, no no. It's much more than a VCR, it does this, it does that, let's personalize this and all that stuff." At that point, it would get so difficult to describe what TiVo actually is, leading into a 5–10 minute conversation instead of a 30-second TiVo pitch.

However, this problem has not hindered TiVo from being a great product. Early on, TiVo tried the traditional way of getting the product across with a result of repetitive stumbles in marketing its products. The millions of dollars spent on advertisements did not help consumers understand what TiVo actually does. A customer claimed, "I personally remember seeing TiVo ads on TV before I even knew what a TiVo was, and it took seven years for me to finally see one 'in the flesh.'"

What makes TiVo's DVRs different from other DVRs can be felt and experienced but not seen, even though the feature differences can be seen in Exhibit 1. According to Gartner analyst Van Baker, "For cable and satellite DVRs: The interface stinks. They do a really bad job of it," TiVo rallied people to change

their lives by continuously preaching its brand and products, creating evangelism with many people claiming that TiVo changed their lives. According to a survey on the TiVo Web site, 98% of users said that they could not live without their TiVos.

The one word that explicitly describes the cult-like product is "interactive." When TiVo subscribers feel the buzz, they show and tell, the story goes on and on and on. Between 1999 and 2000, TiVo's subscriptions increased by 86%. In addition to capitalizing on its tens of thousands of customer evangelists to move the product into the mainstream, TiVo's word-of-mouth strategy focuses on celebrity endorsements and television show product placement. The firm began giving its product away to such celebrities as Oprah, Sarah Michelle Gellar, Drew Bledsoe, and many more, turning them into high-profile members of the cult, while Jay Leno and Rosie O'Donnell helped to influence TiVo's consumers in a very positive way.

The Market Research Team The need to create such a unique emotional connection between people and this product is significant to TiVo. Another way for a firm like TiVo to always be a step ahead and develop ways to improve and measure promotions and viewer behavior is to do continuous intensive market research. TiVo's market research team is considered one of its functional units that is driving the company and includes Lieberman Research Worldwide and Nielson Media Research. With Lieberman, the first-ever DVR-based panel was established in August 2002. Internally, TiVo also has built a platform in the system that sends detailed information on its customers watching TV back to TiVo. TiVo also fully embraced the community with its TiVo community and hackers programs, so TiVo's research team knows what people's needs are, when and where they need them.

Financial: Fast Forward or Rewind TiVo's Stock?

TiVo started at a price of $16 during its IPO in 1999. TiVo reached its highest stock price after its IPO at $78.75, with its first eye-catching ad "Hey, if you like us, TiVo us," which became its first milestone. After the rapid growth, TiVo's stock price dropped to a low of $2.25, in 2002. TiVo's stock price started to pick up in 2003 when the FCC Chairman Michael Powell announced that he uses TiVo, claiming it is

Exhibit 1   DVR Features

	TiVo Series2™ Boxes	Leading Cable Service DVR*	Satellite DVR**	DirecTV DVR with TiVo©
Record from multiple sources	Yes, combine satellite, cable, or antenna, depending on product	No, Digital cable only	No, Satellite only	No, DirecTV only
Easy search: Find shows by title, actor, genre, or keyword	Yes	Titles only, browsing only	title, subject, and actor only	Yes
Online scheduling: Schedule recordings from the Internet	Yes	No	No	No
Dual Tuner: Record 2 shows at once[1]	Yes	Yes	Yes	Yes
Movie and TV Downloads: Purchase or rent 1,000 movies and television shows from Amazon Unbox and have them delivered directly to your television.[2]	Yes	No	No	No
Home Movie Sharing: Edit, enhance, and send movies and photo slideshows from your One True Media account to any broadband connected TiVo box.[3]	Yes	No	No	No
Online services: Yahoo! weather, traffic, digital photos, Internet Radio from Live365, podcasts, and movie tickets from Fandango	Yes	Limited	Limited	No
Built-In Ethernet: Broadband-ready right out of the box—connecting to your home network is a snap[4]	Yes	No	No	No
TiVoToGo transfers to mobile devices: Transfer shows to your favorite portable devices or, laptop or burn them to DVD.[3, 5]	Yes	No	No	No
Home media features: Digital photos, digital music, and more	Yes	No	No	No
Transfer shows between boxes: Record shows on one TV and watch them on another.[3]	Yes	No	No	No

Source: http://www.tivo.com/1.0.chart.asp.,

* Leading cable services compared to Time Warner/Cox Communications Explorer® 8000™ DVR and Comcast DVR
** Leading satellite services compared to DISH Network 625 DVR
[1] On the TiVo Series2 DT DVR, you can record two basic cable channels or one basic cable and one digital cable channel, at once.
[2] Requires broadband cable modem or DSL connection.
[3] Requires your TiVo box to be connected to a home network or via Ethernet wirelessly.
[4] Available on the new TiVo Series2 DT DVR and the TiVo Series3 DMR.
[5] In order to burn TiVoToGo transfers to DVD you will need to purchase software from Roxio/Sonic Solutions.

(*continued*)

....

Exhibit 1   DVR Features   *(continued)*

Multiroom Solutions

	Digeo/Moxi	Motorola	Scientific-Atlanta	EchoStar	TiVo	Microsoft
Main DVR	Cable DVR*	Cable DVR†	Cable DVR†	Satelite DVR*	TiVo box	Media Center PC
Set-top box on additional televisions	IP terminal	Cable box◊	Cable box	None	TiVo box	XBox 360
How boxes share content	IP	IP	Digital broadcast	Analog broadcast	IP§	IP
Physical connection	Coax	Coax	Coax	Coax	Home network	Home network
Features available on additional televisions:						
Play back recorded programs	✓	✓	✓	✓	✓	✓
Record programs	✓	✓	☐	✓	✓	✓
Pause programs	✓	✓	☐	✓	✓	✓
View Internet content	✓	✗	☐	☐	✓	✓
View personal digital content	✗	✗	☐	☐	✓	✓

"X" = Available, but operators have not yet deployed

*New product specifically designed for multiroom use
†Standard cable DVR plus modifications for multiroom use
◊Requires additional IP dongle on standard digital set-top box
§Requires transferring files from one TiVo box to the other

Source: Forrester Research Inc., 2006

a "God's machine," and when White House Press Secretary Ari Fleischer was also found to be a loyal user of TiVo. In mid-2003, TiVo hit its first 1 million subscribers, significantly increased its stock price to about $14.00 per share, and then inched back down to $3.50 per share as a result of the resignation of its CEO, Mike Ramsay. With a new CEO in place, TiVo finally reached the 3 million subscribers milestone by mid-2005, reaching a current average stock price of $6 to $7 per share. Now, the question is how to appease investors without killing a feature that helps sell the product.

Deconstructing TiVO   Since it was founded in 1997, TiVo has accumulated more than $400 million in losses. Looking at TiVo's revenues and costs structures in Exhibit 2, TiVo, an enigmatic company, has divided its revenues and costs in a variety of forms, including service, technology, hardware, and shared revenues. Being a company that lives under the great shadow of Wall Street pessimism, the question then becomes what value can TiVo add besides hyping its latest technology developments? For service revenues, for example, TiVo needs to know the actual value of TiVo-owned subscribers, not the number of TiVo's partnership subscribers such as DirecTV and Comcast. Deconstructing the value of this particular matter then leads to larger questions: How long does a TiVo subscriber remain a subscriber? How much does each subscriber pay and is willing to pay? How much advertising revenue do users produce for every tag they click? How long and how can TiVo maintain its subscribers to be TiVo-owned subscribers?

In one way, the chicken and egg problem may have been the bulk of the TiVo's hardware revenues problem when people would say, "What, huh, TiVo, personalizing your own TV network? What the hell are you talking about?" Being able to gain the economies of scale that it desires should be TiVo's point of concern. Even though rebates are being offered, TiVo has not reached the price point that actually attracts people. TiVo offers three types of boxes depending on the hours of programming storage capacity, which range from an 80 hours TiVo Series2 to 300 hours TiVo Series HD. For the basic TiVo Series2 box, there is a one-time fee of $99.99 for 80 hours and $199.99 for 180 hours, while the HD TiVo box costs $799.99 and has a 300-hour storage capacity.

TiVo also has been a heavy user of mail-in rebates, which is one of their forms of revenues shown in Exhibit 2. According to *BusinessWeek,* $5 million in additional revenue was recognized because nearly

Exhibit 2   TiVo Inc.
Condensed Consolidated Statements of Operations (in thousands, except per share and share amounts) (unaudited)

	Three Months Ended October 31,		Nine Months Ended October 31,	
	2006	**2005**	**2006**	**2005**
		Adjusted		**Adjusted**
Revenues				
Service and technology revenues	$ 52,616	$ 43,197	$ 160,605	$ 123,891
Hardware revenues	27,978	24,652	53,666	39,827
Rebates, revenue share, and other payments to channel	(14,934)	(18,234)	(32,932)	(27,860)
Net revenues	65,660	49,615	181,339	135,858
Cost of revenues				
Cost of service and technology revenues (1)	13,826	8,508	44,256	24,832
Cost of hardware revenues	31,925	24,667	68,678	48,006
Total cost of revenues	45,751	33,175	112,934	72,838
Gross margin	19,909	16,440	68,405	63,020
Research and development (1)	12,221	9,712	37,973	30,394
Sales and marketing (1)	10,123	10,006	25,856	24,410
General and administrative (1)	9,811	11,702	35,961	26,249
Total operating expenses	32,155	31,420	99,790	81,053
Loss from operations	(12,246)	(14,980)	(31,385)	(18,033)
Interest income	1,291	826	3,341	2,184
Interest expense and other	(133)	(10)	(165)	(13)
Loss before income taxes	(11,088)	(14,164)	(28,209)	(15,862)
Provision for income taxes	(4)	—	(35)	(51)
Net loss	$ (11,092)	$ (14,164)	$ (28,244)	$ (15,913)
Net loss per common share—basic and diluted	$ (0.12)	$ (0.17)	$ (0.32)	$ (0.19)
Weighted average common shares used to calculate basic and diluted net loss per share	91,930,061	84,200,655	87,680,571	83,362,402

(continued)

Exhibit 2 TiVo Inc. (*continued*)

	Three Months Ended October 31,		Nine Months Ended October 31,	
	2006	**2005**	**2006**	**2005**
		Adjusted		**Adjusted**
(1) Includes stock-based compensation expense (benefit) as follows :				
Cost of service and technology revenues	$ 365	$ —	$ 1,035	$ —
Research and development	1,608	(6)	4,177	(131)
Sales and marketing	474	20	1,264	(20)
General and administrative	1,636	151	4,257	199

The accompanying notes are an integral part of these condensed consolidated statements.

	1999	**2000**	**2001**	**2002**	**2003**	**2004**	**2005**
Consolidated Statement of Operations Data:							
Revenues							
Service revenues	$ 3,782	$ 989	$ 19,297	$ 39,261	$ 61,560	$ 107,166	$ 167,194
Technology revenues	$ —	$ —	$ 100	$ 20,909	$ 15,797	$ 8,310	$ 3,665
Hardware revenues	$ —	$ —	$ —	$ 45,620	$ 72,882	$ 111,275	$ 72,093
Rebates, revenue share, and other payment to the channel	$ (5,029)	$ (630)	$ —	$ (9,780)	$ (9,159)	$ (54,696)	$ (47,027)
Net Revenues	$ (1,247)	$ 359	$ 19,397	$ 96,010	$ 141,080	$ 172,055	$ 195,925
Cost and Expenses							
Cost of service revenues	$ 18,734	$ 1,719	$ 19,852	$ 17,119	$ 17,705	$ 29,360	$ 34,179
Cost of technology revenues	$ —	$ —	$ 62	$ 8,033	$ 13,609	$ 6,575	$ 782
Cost of hardware revenues	$ —	$ —	$ —	$ 44,647	$ 74,836	$ 120,323	$ 84,216
Research and development	$ 25,070	$ 2,544	$ 27,205	$ 20,714	$ 22,167	$ 37,634	$ 41,087
Sales and marketing	$ 151,658	$ 13,946	$ 104,897	$ 48,117	$ 18,947	$ 37,367	$ 35,047
General and administrative	$ 15,537	$ 1,395	$ 18,875	$ 14,465	$ 16,296	$ 16,593	$ 38,018
Total Costs	$ 210,999	$ 19,604	$ 170,891	$ 153,095	$ 163,560	$ 247,852	$ 233,329
% Costs over Revenues	−16921%	5461%	881%	159%	116%	144%	119%
Net Loss from operations	$ (212,246)	$ (19,245)	$ (151,494)	$ (57,085)	$ (22,480)	$ (75,797)	$ (37,404)

(continued)

Exhibit 2   TiVo Inc. (*continued*)

Condensed Consolidated Balance Sheets (in thousands, except share amounts) (unaudited)

	October 31, 2006	January 31, 2006
		Adjusted
ASSETS		
CURRENT ASSETS		
Cash and cash equivalents	$ 78,898	$ 85,298
Short-term investments	28,067	18,915
Accounts receivable, net of allowance for doubtful accounts of $121 and $56	27,300	20,111
Finished goods inventories	34,107	10,939
Prepaid expenses and other, current	4,327	8,744
Total current assets	172,699	144,007
LONG-TERM ASSETS		
Property and equipment, net	10,874	9,448
Purchased technology, capitalized software, and intangible assets, net	17,580	5,206
Prepaid expenses and other, long-term	597	347
Total long-term assets	29,051	15,001
Total assets	$ 201,750	$ 159,008
LIABILITIES AND STOCKHOLDERS' EQUITY/(DEFICIT)		
LIABILITIES		
CURRENT LIABILITIES		
Accounts payable	$ 28,278	$ 24,050
Accrued liabilities	32,553	37,449
Deferred revenue, current	56,596	57,902
Total current liabilities	117,427	119,401
LONG-TERM LIABILITIES		
Deferred revenue, long-term	51,550	67,575
Deferred rent and other	2,208	1,404
Total long-term liabilities	53,758	68,979
Total liabilities	171,185	188,380
COMMITMENTS AND CONTINGENCIES (see Note 10)		

(*continued*)

Exhibit 2 TiVo Inc. (*continued*)

Condensed Consolidated Balance Sheets (in thousands, except share amounts) (unaudited)

	October 31, 2006	January 31, 2006
		Adjusted
STOCKHOLDERS' EQUITY/(DEFICIT)		
Preferred stock, par value $0.001:		
Authorized shares are 10,000,000;		
Issued and outstanding shares = none	—	—
Common stock, par value $0.001:		
Authorized shares are 150,000,000;		
Issued shares are 96,922,295 and 85,376,191, respectively and outstanding shares are 96,841,792 and 85,376,191, respectively	97	85
Additional paid-in capital	753,373	667,055
Deferred compensation	—	(2,421)
Accumulated deficit	(722,335)	(694,091)
Less: Treasury stock, at cost - 80,503 shares	(570)	—
Total stockholders' equity (deficit)	30,565	(29,372)
Total liabilities and stockholders' equity (deficit)	$ 201,750	$ 159,008

half of TiVo's 100,000 new subscribers failed to apply for a $100 rebate. This slippage type of strategy is known to marketers as the "shoebox effect," and this promotional practice has caused a large positive impact for TiVo.

Operations: Research and Development—The "A" Team

Again, the word *interactive* is the buzz word. TiVo's R&D team makes sure that they build TiVo from the user's perspective and viewing habits. TiVo has forums of communication through tivocommunity.com and TiVo hackers. In this forum, criticisms are allowed and even encouraged, as long as they are constructive and help TiVo grow. Users and aspiring users of TiVo are allowed to say what they like

and dislike and voice how they expect to see TiVo in the future. Ideas generated through this forum will help TiVo's R&D team and developers to continuously be hands-on and innovate accordingly to people's ever-changing lifestyles. TiVo is also concerned with how its platform could actually be used the wrong way by children. With this concern, TiVo has collaborated with parents to build a new feature called TiVo Parental Zone, which allows parents to control what their children are actually watching. Privacy concerns have also been an issue in the advanced technology industry. TiVo managed to protect its community regarding privacy concerns by storing such information on a computer behind its "firewall" in a secure location, and often restricts the number of internal employees who can access such data.

Previously TiVo's R&D team consisted of only contract-based engineers; now, TiVo makes sure that its R&D team consists of diverse, creative, and detailed oriented staff of engineers. Its intensive research principle is that benefits must extend existing people's behaviors. The design team has every detail of steps to follow to fit the needs of lifestyles. As an example of TiVo's meticulous product-design process, TiVo created a remote control that combines personalization and interconnectivity. TiVo's remote has a feature of thumbs up and down for users to click on to rate shows so that TiVo will know what to record. In addition, TiVo allows Braille ability on its remote for visually impaired users. Other R&D processes include product testing and development of its software and platforms, product integration of software to satellite systems, and product integration such as the integration of DVD burners and the TiVo recorder. Besides developing its main products, the TiVo R&D team also tries to design platforms and technology that can be used with other products and enhance the demand of TiVo's main products, such as the ability to connect with computers, other home theater technologies, and, especially, cable and satellite systems.

Because intense competition exists in the DVR industry, TiVo found the need to patent its advance software and technology platform. TiVo licensed its TiVoToGo software to chipmaker AMD, digital media software to companies such as Sonic Solutions and Microsoft to enable video playback on pocket PCs and smartphones. As of today, TiVo has 85 patents granted and 117 patent applications pending, which include domestic and foreign patents, further leaving rivals scratching their heads. TiVo licenses its patents through several of its trusted partners, such as Sony, Toshiba, Pioneer, and DirectV. TiVo believes that licensing its technology to third parties has been its best business model.

Executive Team and Management TiVo's top management is always hands-on with its operations and promotions. Former CEO Mike Ramsay often made overseas trips to Japan to conduct meetings and seminars with consumer electronic makers. This effort was an attempt to convince the makers to embed TiVo's software into their products. To make sure everything went well, the ex-CEO focused on maintaining partnerships. He would rarely be in his office; instead, he was on the road talking to companies that could help TiVo build software and subscribers. However, many mistakes were made throughout his history as CEO, including twice laying off employees in 2001. Eighty employees (approx 25% of the workforce) were laid off April 5, 2001, and 40 employees (approx 20% of the workforce) were laid off October 31, 2001. Mike Ramsay was just an engineer on the block. He knew how to be creative and build great machines, but he did not really know the industry very well or how to manage the company and steer TiVo from drowning. As a result, Mike Ramsay resigned in mid-2005, and a change of CEO was implemented. The new CEO is the former president of NBC Cable, Tom Rogers, a strength to TiVo's management.

In addition, TiVo's board of directors consists of individuals from diverse backgrounds and companies; however, this actually is one of TiVo's concerns. TiVo needs more members from TiVo's industry-related background who can influence the future DVR/cable industry; possibly, they could make better decisions.

SLEEPING WITH THE ENEMIES

So Long, TiVo! Hello DVR!

The Industry

The DVR or personal video recorder market is located at the convergence of four established industries: broadcasting and television, software and programming, electronic instruments, and communications equipment.

For TiVo, introducing a disruptive technology into the industry was full of obstacles. When a DVR has the potential to be considered a "disruptive technology," it means that the technology creates something new that usurps existing products, services, and business models. According to Mike Ramsay, the DVR phenomenon established that "people really want to take control of television, and if you give them control, they don't want you to take it back." Though TiVo has innovatively added all the software, platforms, and services that a standalone TiVo DVR has to offer, it must have a connection to a cable network or satellite signals. Therefore, users who want TiVo DVRs need to subscribe to TiVo, pay one-time fees for the TiVo boxes, and subscribe to companies that provide cable or satellite signals such as Comcast and DirecTV. Thus, the TiVo DVR is readily equipped with a built-in cable-ready tuner for use with any external cable box or satellite receiver. TiVo has made many alliances, at the same time competing with cable operators and satellite networks? With cable, satellite, and electronics companies pushing their own DVRs, the DVR industry is expected to grow rapidly.

In terms of market share, TiVo claims to cover the entire United States market.

Friends or Foe?

In 2000, AOL invested $200 million in TiVo and became the largest shareholder of the company and one of its main service partners. The deal allowed TiVo to release a box that provided both TiVo's capabilities and AOL services. Besides AOL, TiVo established other service partnerships. TiVo, Discovery Communication, and NBC agreed on an $8.1 million deal in the form of advertising and promotional services. Later, an additional $5 million was paid to NBC for promotions. NBC also collaborated on (R&D) allowing TiVo to use a portion of its satellite network. AT&T helped TiVo market and sell the service in Boston, Denver, and the Silicon Valley areas. BSkyB was the service partner for TiVo in the United Kingdom. Creative Artists Agency marketed and gave promotional support of the personal video recorder and, in exchange, received 67,122 shares of preferred stock.

Despite all the partnerships that TiVo enjoys TiVo has actually been faced with a difficult challenge: cable and satellite companies who can be either TiVo's friend or foe. They now offer (DVR) equipped set-top boxes of their own. Cable operators such as Time Warner Cable and Cox Communications offer built-in DVR capability in set-top boxes and provide the equipment "free" to subscribers. In late August 2003, Echostar announced a free DVR promotion, which was an unprecedented move in the industry. TiVo's fairly expensive retail-priced unit could possibly jeopardize the company's ability to stay. There are relatively few cable and satellite providers, leaving TiVo with little power over them. These companies

can dictate pricing of the TiVo technology because they can always develop or purchase generic DVR units to market to their subscription base. Although TiVo had to give up a cut of profits to partners, they decided to have strategic relationships with competitors and cable companies for distribution and credit on its sales force.

Previously, DirecTV had been the backbone of TiVo, the service partner that has been fruitfully fueling most of TiVo's growth. In addition, TiVo's current 4.4 million subscribers have mostly come from its deal with DirecTV. As of early 2002, subscribers to TiVo service through DirecTV have increased from 230,000 to 2.1 million, representing more than half of all DVR subscriptions through satellite. Earlier, when DirecTV began talks with TiVo, the satellite provider was already equipped with a DVR service through its partnership with Microsoft's Ultimate TV. For users to watch their shows, subscriptions to DirecTV channels range from $29.99 per month, providing 40 channels, to $65.99 per month, with more than 250 channels.

Since DirecTV developed its own DVR device with the NDS Group, DirecTV stated in 2005 that it would stop marketing and selling TiVo's digital recorders to its satellite TV subscribers. Though DirecTV's DVR costs users a $299 one-time fee, it includes unique features, such as the ability to jump to specific scenes as well as allowing users to pay for any downloaded pay-per-view movies when they are being viewed. In 2006, TiVo and DirecTV reached a commercial extension agreement for three years. The agreement allowed existing DirecTV customers using the TiVo DVR to continue to receive maintenance and support from DirecTV. As part of the agreement, TiVo and DirecTV also said they would not sue each other over patent rights. With the agreement with DirecTV facing expiration, TiVo was rushing to differentiate its product and struggling to strike other distribution deals.

In July 2000, Comcast, a cable operator, agreed to a trial offering of TiVo boxes to its subscribers, hoping that the trial would lead to a bigger deal in which Comcast would integrate TiVo software into Comcast cable boxes. After discussing it, Comcast balked and was unwilling to concede. In April 2001, when another trial failed to lead to a larger deal, TiVo laid off approximately 25% of its staff. In November 2001, AT&T Broadband agreed to offer TiVo DVRs to its customers, but within a few weeks, Comcast killed the deal by acquiring the cable provider and its 14 million customers. In addition, in 2002, cable operators such as Comcast ended up developing their own DVR boxes with makes such as Motorola and Scientific-Atlanta. However, similar to DirecTV, Comcast, the nation's cable company, announced in March 2005, that it would offer customers a video recorder service from TiVo and even allow TiVo to develop its software for Comcast's DVR platform. Comcast and TiVo agreed to work to make TiVo's DVR service and interactive advertising capability (ad management system) available over Comcast's cable network and its set-top DVR boxes. This agreement also included that under the TiVo brand name, the first of their co-developed products would be available in mid- to late 2006.

Monthly subscriptions in 2006 to Comcast's basic or extended basic cable cost users $8.63 or $52.55. To add a DVR feature, Comcast users pay $13.94 in addition to a subscription to TiVo, which ranges from $12.95 to $16.95 per month, depending on the lifetime plan chosen, which varies from one to three years. Due to the agreement with Comcast, TiVo's shares closed up nearly 75%, or $2.87 per share, to $6.70. Investors were positive about the news, some upgrading TiVo's investment rating from a sell to hold. Even though, there are concerns about TiVo's future, especially since DirecTV started using a second company, NDS, to provide DVR service, a deal with Comcast puts to rest some of those concerns by opening up a large, new potential audience for TiVo's service. According to a filing with the SEC, TiVo receives an upfront payment from Comcast for creating a new DVR that works with Comcast's current service. TiVo also receives a recurring monthly fee for each Comcast subscriber who uses TiVo through Comcast.

Both TiVo's deal with Comcast and DirecTV were made merely because of the technological differences that can be tweaked. Rolling out new technologies such as DVRs will be easier for satellite broadcasters because changes can be made in a central location. As for cable operators, technology will have to be deployed gradually as they have different equipment in different areas. With all these deals, could TiVo's opportunities go beyond TV and help it to become a software provider?

In addition, with the hype of being portable, TiVo and BellSouth Fast Access DSL agreed on a variety of co-marketing plans. With strong southeastern presence and renowned customer satisfaction

of BellSouth, TiVo can turn a DSL connection into a pipeline for video content delivered directly to televisions. To expand program recording to cellular phones, its latest TiVo Mobile feature, TiVo struck a deal with Verizon to bring the DVR pioneer's capabilities beyond its set-top boxes and television directly to cell phones for the first time. In terms of content, TiVo also has engaged in new partnerships with CBS Corp., the Reuters Group PLC, and *Forbes* magazine, not to mention the New York Times Company, the National Basketball Association, and other firms. This will make news and entertainment programs available for downloading onto TiVos. International Creative Management will recommend films, television shows, and Internet videos that TiVo users can download onto their boxes. Finally, TiVo has decided to open up to amateur videos through a deal with One True Media Inc., an Internet start-up that operates a Web service designed to help users easily edit their raw footage into slick home movies.

THE TALKATIVO

. . . Bring 'em on! We are talking the HD language now . . . Yeah!.

HD Trend

High-definition electronic sets in the entertainment industry are now the most important new consumer electronic items. HD products focus more toward quality of what is being seen and heard rather than the compactness from a decade ago. These sets include HDTV, HD broadcasting, HD DVD, HD radio, HD photo, and even HD audio.

TiVo is linked particularly to HDTV, first introduced in the United States in the 1990s. It is basically a digital television broadcasting system using a significantly higher resolution than the traditional formats of NTSC, PAL, and SECAM. The technology at that time was very expensive. Today, as prices have decreased, HDTV is going mainstream. A significant number of people have already bought HDTVs; most people are planning to buy HDTVs soon. As of 2007, HDTVs are being used in 24 million United States households. By 2009, HDTV will have replaced the old standard definition TV. With the price of the hard drive becoming lower and lower, and the increasing technology of HDTV, the demand for HD products is also increasing. With HDTV, users are offered a much better picture quality than standard television, with greater on-screen clarity and smoother motion, richer and more natural colors, and surround sound.

HD TiVo

Recently, TiVo issued the TiVo Series3 that will allow customers to record HD television shows and digital cable. As people experience HDTV, TiVo service will be increasingly appealing. Once again, TiVo has established the technological standards in the environment. The TiVo Series3 HD version, allows consumers to do many additional things and delivers both the audio and visual in HD.

TiVo realizes that great quality videos need to be supported by great quality audio; thus, TiVo put a lot of effort into audio development and received the certification of being the first digital media recorder to meet the performance standard in HDTV. THX is well known for having developed the highest standard of audio, mainly the surround systems, in the entertainment as well as the media industry.

TiVo SERIES3

The new TiVo Series3, which is being sold for $799, has the ability to record two HD programs simultaneously while playing back a third previously recorded one. It also has two signal inputs and accepts cable TV and over-the-air signals. It replaces the existing as well as the 30-second commercial skip. The new HD TiVo is different because there is no lifetime membership for the HD TiVo

compared to older DVR products. Is this a shift of the TiVo revenue model? TiVo wants to aim at the subscription-based revenue stream.

Despite that the capability of TiVo being able to record and playback in HD, there are still many considerations for people before buying the TiVo. The downside of the HD TiVo is the price tag, which is overly expensive for most people, especially when there are DVRs offered for free by cable companies.

HD TiVo Enemies

Now that the HD trend is flocking the entertainment industry, TiVo competitors are also offering HD DVRs on their own and not just a DVR.

Comcast allows its subscribers to rent their DVR boxes for $13.94 per month as they do not sell their DVR boxes to their customers. With the HD DVR boxes manufactured by Motorola and Scientific Atlanta, users are able to navigate their own preferences just like using a TiVo, except that TiVo may have better and more features built into the TiVo boxes. Also, with the Comcast DVR boxes, users will be able to watch the variety of cable channels offered by Comcast with an additional monthly subscription fee to cable channels.

DirecTV, once a friend but may soon be a foe, allows subscribers to add an additional DVR subscription service for $4.99 monthly on top of the chosen monthly subscription service package to DirecTV cable channels, which ranges from $29.99 to $65.99. Like Comcast, DirecTV does not allow users to keep their DVR boxes; if a user is in need of an HD DVR box, the user will need to pay an upfront cost of $299 with a $100 rebate. As for the basic DVR, DirecTV charges a $99.99 upfront cost.

References

http://www.tivo.com/
http://en.wikipedia.org/wiki/TiVo
http://en.wikipedia.org/wiki/High-definition_television
http://egotron.com/ptv/ptvintro.htm
http://news.com.com/TiVo,+Comcast+reach+DVR+deal/
    2100-1041_3-5616961.html
http://news.com.com/TiVo+and+DirecTV+extend+contract/
    2100-1038_3-6060475.html
http://www.technologyreview.com
http://www.fastcompany.com/magazine/61/tivo.html

http://iinnovate.blogspot.com/2006/09/mike-ramsay-
    co-founder-of-tivo.html
http://www.acmqueue.org/modules.php?name=Content
    pa=showpagepid=53page=7
http://www.internetnews.com/stats/article.php/3655331
http://thomashawk.com/2006/04/tivo-history-101-how-tivo-
    built-pvr_24.html
http://www.tvpredictions.com/tivohd030807.htm
http://www.tivocommunity.com/tivo-vb/showthread.php?
    threadid=151443

HANSON (A)

INTRODUCTION

Hanson PLC is one of the ten biggest companies in Britain, and its U.S. arm, Hanson Industries, is one of America's sixty largest industrial concerns. A conglomerate with more than 150 different businesses in its portfolio, Hanson PLC has grown primarily by making acquisitions. By the end of 1989, the company had recorded twenty-six years of uninterrupted profit growth, cumulating in 1989 operating income of $1.61 billion on revenues of $11.3 billion and assets of $12.03 billion. The company's shareholders have been major beneficiaries of this growth. Between 1974 and 1989, the price of the company's shares on the London Stock Exchange increased eightyfold, compared with an average increase of fifteenfold for all companies quoted on the London Stock Exchange during this period.[1] Along the way, Hanson has gained a reputation for being one of the most successful takeover machines in the world. Its acquisitions during the 1980s included three American conglomerates (U.S. Industries, SCM Corporation, and Kidde) and three major British companies (London Brick, the Imperial Group, and Consolidated Gold Fields). So high is Hanson's profile that Oliver Stone, in his film *Wall Street*, reportedly used Sir Gordon White, head of Hanson Industries, as the model for the British corporate raider (the one who outmaneuvered the evil Gordon Gekko).

Despite this impressive track record, as Hanson enters the 1990s analysts increasingly wonder about the strategy of the company. There is speculation that the company may be on the verge of breaking itself up and returning the gains to shareholders. The age of the company's founders is fueling this speculation. The two men who built and still run the conglomerate, Lord Hanson and Sir Gordon White, are in their late sixties, and both have promised to consider retiring when they are seventy. As one insider put it, "The guys that started it off will finish it off."[2] Another factor is that Hanson is now so big that it would take some spectacular deals to continue its historic growth rate. According to many, including Harvard Business School strategy guru Michael Porter, there simply are not that many obvious companies for Hanson to buy. Thus, "even Hanson will be faced with poorer and poorer odds of maintaining its record."[3] On the other hand, at the end of 1989 Hanson had $8.5 billion in cash on its balance sheet. That, along with the billions it could borrow if need be (the company reportedly has a borrowing capacity of $20 billion), suggests that if Hanson and White should so wish, they could undertake an acquisition that would rival the RJR-Nabisco deal in size.

Other commentators question the long-term viability of the company. Some claim that Hanson PLC is little more than an asset stripper that in the long run will drive the companies it manages into the ground. According to one investment banker, "I'm not convinced that Hanson runs companies any better than anyone else. But I certainly know it squeezes them for cash, sucking the life from them."[4] Similarly, one former executive noted that "some of the incentive programs that they write for managers actually keep the company from growing. . . . They become so concerned with profit today that they don't re-invest for tomorrow."[5] The company disagrees. Sir Gordon White clearly sees Hanson PLC as reducing inefficiencies in the companies it acquires, not stripping assets. If anything is stripped away from acquisitions, according to White, it is unnecessary corporate bureaucracy, overstaffed head offices, and top-management perks, not assets. He steadfastly maintains that the company treats all acquired businesses as if it were going to keep them.[6]

With these issues in mind, in this case we consider the growth and development of Hanson PLC. We review the administrative systems that the company uses to manage its ongoing businesses, and we look at two acquisitions and their aftermath in depth: the 1987 acquisitions of SCM Corporation and the Imperial Group.

HISTORY

The origins of Hanson PLC go back to the port city of Hull in Yorkshire, England, in the 1950s.[7] At that time, James Hanson was learning his family's transportation business (the family operated a fleet of passenger coaches), and Gordon White was selling advertising for Welbecson Limited, a magazine printing company owned by his father. James Hanson's brother, Bill, was White's closest friend, and when Bill died of cancer at twenty-nine, James and Gordon became close friends. In the late 1950s, Hanson and White decided to team up in business. They formed Hanson White Ltd., a greeting card company. Although the company did well, the two soon became bored with the limited challenges and potential that the greeting card business offered, and in 1963 they sold out and began to look for acquisition opportunities.

Their first buy was Oswald Tillotson Ltd., a vehicle distribution company. This company was subsequently acquired by Wiles Group Ltd., a Yorkshire-based manufacturer of agricultural sacks and fertilizers. As part of the takeover deal, Hanson and White were given a substantial ownership position in the Wiles Group. Hanson and White soon gained management control of the Wiles Group, and in 1969, after deciding that James Hanson's name had a nicer ring to it than Gordon White's,

they changed the name to Hanson Trust. Because of a series of small acquisitions, by the end of 1973 Hanson Trust owned twenty-four companies with combined sales of $120 million.

By 1973, however, the British economy was in deep trouble. The stock market had collapsed; the country was paralyzed by labor disputes; inflation was increasing rapidly, as was unemployment; and Prime Minister Edward Heath of the supposedly probusiness Conservative party had blasted conglomerate companies such as Hanson Trust as representing "the unacceptable face of capitalism." All of this prompted Gordon White to rethink his future. As White put it,

> I was disgusted with England at the time. Disgusted with socialism and unions and excessive, antibusiness government, disgusted with the way initiative was being taxed out of existence. . . . I'd done a lot of thinking. I told James (Hanson) that maybe we should just call it a day. I thought I'd try America.[8]

Hanson replied that there was no need to split up, and they agreed that Hanson would run the British operations while White tried to build operations in America.

White arrived in New York in the fall of 1973 in possession of a round-trip ticket, a one-year work visa, and $3,000 in traveler's checks, which was the most that British currency controls permitted a U.K. citizen to take abroad at that time. Moreover, because of British exchange controls, White could not gain access to Hanson's ample treasury without substantial penalties, and he had to struggle to convince banks that he was creditworthy. Despite this, in 1974 White managed to borrow $32 million from Chemical Bank to finance his first major U.S. acquisition, a friendly takeover of J. Howard Smith Company, a New Jersey-based processor of edible oils and animal feed that was later renamed Seacoast Products. The CEO of J. Howard Smith was David Clarke, whose family business it was. Clarke subsequently became White's right-hand man. He is now president of Hanson Industries and the most senior executive in the United States after White.

Over the next ten years, White made another six major U.S. acquisitions, all of them friendly (see Exhibit 1). Then, in 1984, White was ready for his first hostile takeover, the $532-million purchase of U.S. Industries (USI). USI was a conglomerate that had

....

Exhibit 1   U.S. Acquisitions, 1974–1990

Date	Acquisition	Cost (millions)	Businesses
1974	Seacost	$32	Fish processing, pet food
1975	Carisbrook	36	Textile manufacturing
1976	Hygrade	32	Castings and casing units
1977	Old Salt Seafood	2	Prepared foods
1978	Interstate United	30	Food service management
1978	Templon	7	Textile manufacturing
1981	McDonough	185	Cement, concrete
1984	U.S. Industries	532	33-company conglomerate
1986	SCM	930	22-company conglomerate
1987	Kaiser Cement	250	Cement plants
1988	Kidde	1,700	108-company conglomerate
1990	Peabody	1,230	Coal mining

Source: Adapted from Gordon White, "How I Turned $3,000 into $10 Billion," *Fortune*, November 7, 1988, 80–89; and "Hanson PLC," *Value Line*, July 20, 1990, 832.

grown by acquisitions during the 1960s and 1970s. White became interested in the company when he read in a newspaper that management was putting together a leveraged buyout at $20 a share for a total purchase price of $445 million. He suspected that the company was worth more than that and quickly worked out how big a loan Hanson Industries could handle, using USI's projected cash flow to cover interest charges. To USI's pretax earnings of $67 million he added $40 million generated by depreciation and $24 million in savings that he thought Hanson could effect by removing USI's corporate headquarters. That yielded a total cash flow of $131 million, or more than $70 million after taxes. With interest rates running at 13 percent, white figured that Hanson Industries could afford a loan of $544 million. In what was to become standard White thinking, he also reckoned that even with a worse-case scenario, he could recoup his investment by selling off the disparate pieces of the company.

Hanson Industries began to buy USI shares and by April 1984 held 5 percent of the company. Hanson then made a $19 per share bid for the company, which

was quickly rebuffed by USI management. Three days later White increased Hanson's bid to $22 per share. USI's management, which had yet to raise the financing for its own proposed leveraged buyout, responded by increasing the purchase price to $24 per share. Hanson responded by initiating a tender offer of $23 per share in cash. For stockholders, cash in hand at $23 per share was far more attractive than management's promise of $24 per share if financing could be arranged, and Hanson's bid quickly won the day.

After the acquisition was completed, Hanson Industries President David Clarke spent six months at USI's corporate headquarters reviewing operations. At the end of this period USI's corporate headquarters was closed down, the staff was laid off, and financial control was centralized at Hanson Industries' small headquarters. However, most of the operating managers in charge of USI's constituent companies stayed on, lured by Hanson's incentive pay scheme and the promise that they could run their own shows. In what was also typical Hanson fashion, nine of USI's operating companies were subsequently sold off to outside investors for a price of $225 million.

Exhibit 2   U.K. Acquisitions During the 1980s

Date	Acquisition	Cost (millions)	Businesses
1981	Ever Ready	£95	Dry cell batteries
1983	UDS	£250	Retail operations
1984	London Brick	£247	Brick manufacturer
1984	Powell Duffryn	£150	Engineering, shipping, fuel
1986	Imperial Group	£2,360	Tobacco, brewing, food
1989	Consolidated Gold Fields	£3,610	Gold mining, building aggregates

Source: Various press reports.

The acquisition of USI was followed by three other hostile takeover bids in the United States: for SCM Corporation, Kaiser Cement, and Kidde. Of these, the SCM bid was by far the most acrimonious. SCM took a poison pill and tried to protect its position through the law courts before Hanson finally won control over the company. (The SCM takeover is discussed in detail later in this case.)

While White was making these U.S. acquisitions, Hanson was not sitting idle in Britain. During the 1980s the company made a series of acquisitions in the United Kingdom. These are summarized in Exhibit 2. The most notable were the 1984 acquisition of London Brick, Britain's largest brick manufacturer, against vigorous opposition from London Brick's incumbent management; the £2.36-billion acquisition of Imperial, the largest tobacco company in Britain and the third largest in the world; and the £3.61-billion acquisition of Consolidated Gold Fields, the second largest gold-mining business in the world. The acquisitions of Imperial and Consolidated Gold Fields were the two largest takeovers ever undertaken in Britain. (The Imperial takeover is discussed in detail later in this case.)

ACQUISITIONS PHILOSOPHY

Hanson PLC's acquisitions on both sides of the Atlantic are primarily overseen by Sir Gordon White. Lord Hanson is primarily responsible for the ongoing administration of the company. As Lord Hanson says

of White, "He's the one with the gift for takeovers."[9] In turn, White says of Hanson, "James is a brilliant administrator and really knows how to run a company."[10] White claims that many of his acquisition ideas, including the USI deal, come from the newspapers. Others are suggested to him by contacts in the investment banking community, particularly Bob Pirie, president of the Rothschild investment bank, with whom white has lunch once a week.

Whenever possible, White avoids working at the office, opting instead to work from one of his four houses. Unlike corporate raiders such as Saul Steinberg and Carl Icahn, White rarely reads annual reports or detailed stock reports on a target company, claiming that he can get all of the financial information that he needs from Standard & Poor's two-page summaries. In addition, his three-person takeover staff distills reams of financial data on a target and provides him with a short memo on the target company. Says White, "I'm like Churchill, tell me everything you can tell me. On one page."[11]

Under White's leadership, one of the things that has distinguished Hanson PLC from many other acquisitive conglomerates is its distinctive acquisitions philosophy (which is, in essence, White's philosophy). This philosophy appears to be based on a number of consistent factors that are found to underlie most of Hanson's acquisitions.[12]

1. *Target characteristics.* Hanson looks for companies based in mature, low-technology industries that have a less-than-inspiring record but show potential for improving performance. Normally, the objective has been to identify

a poorly performing target where the incumbent management team has gone some way toward improving the underlying performance but whose efforts have not yet been reflected in either the profit-and-loss account or, more importantly, the target's stock price.

2. *Research*. Although White claims that he does little reading on takeover targets, his takeover staff does undertake detailed research into the potential of target companies before any bid is made. The staff routinely investigates companies undertaking leveraged buyouts.

3. *Risk assessment*. One of White's most often quoted edicts is "watch the downside." What this means is that instead of considering the potential benefits of a deal, give consideration to what can go wrong and the likely consequences of a worst-case scenario. White will purchase a company only if he thinks that in a worst-case scenario he will be able to recover the purchase price by breaking the target up and selling off its constituent parts.

4. *Funding*. White was one of the early pioneers of the highly leveraged takeover deal. All of the U.S. acquisitions have been financed by nonrecourse debt, secured on the assets of the target. This enabled White to engineer substantial acquisitions when Hanson Industries itself had a very small capital base. The British acquisitions have been funded by a mix of cash, equity, convertible securities, and loan stock.

5. *Disposals to reduce debt*. After an acquisition has been completed, Hanson sends some of its own managers along with a group of external accountants to go through and audit the acquired businesses. After a thorough review, Hanson typically sells off the parts of the acquired company that cannot reach Hanson's stringent profitability targets. In the process, Hanson is able to reduce the debt taken on to fund the acquisition. The most outstanding example followed the purchase of SCM for $930 million. After the takeover, Hanson sold off SCM's real estate, pulp and paper, and food holdings for a price of $964 million while holding on to SCM's typewriter and chemicals business, which in effect had been acquired for nothing. Thus, within six months of the takeover's being completed, Hanson was able to eliminate the debt taken on to finance the SCM acquisition. Similar, although

less spectacular, disposals have characterized almost all of Hanson's major acquisitions on both sides of the Atlantic.

6. *Elimination of excess overhead*. Another objective of Hanson's housecleaning of acquired companies is to eliminate any excess overhead. This typically involves closing down the corporate headquarters of the acquired company, eliminating some of the staff, and sending other staff down to the operating level. Before Hanson took over, SCM had 230 people in its corporate office, USI had 180, Kidde had 200, and Hanson itself had 30. Today the total headquarters staff for all four is 120.

Hanson also disposes of any management perks found either at the corporate or the operating level of an acquired company. For example, one of Kidde's operating companies had a collection of art and antiques, a hunting lodge, and three corporate jets. Hanson kept one jet and disposed of the rest, including the man at the top who had spent the money.

7. *The creation of incentives*. Hanson tries to create strong incentives for the management of acquired operating companies to improve performance. This is achieved by (a) decentralization designed to give operating managers full autonomy for the running of their businesses, (b) motivating operating managers by setting profit targets that, if achieved, will result in significant profit enhancements, and (c) motivating managers by giving them large pay bonuses if they hit or exceed Hanson's profit targets.

ORGANIZATION AND MANAGEMENT PHILOSOPHY

In addition to its acquisitions philosophy, Hanson is also renowned for its ongoing management of operating companies, of which there are more than 150 in the corporate portfolio. Although Hanson does have some interests elsewhere, the strategic development of the group has centered on the United States and Britain, where a broad balance has tended to exist in recent years. Hanson PLC looks after the British operations, and Hanson Industries, the U.S. subsidiary, manages the U.S. operations. Each of these two units is operated on an entirely autonomous basis. Only one director sits on the board of both companies. Hanson PLC is headed by Hanson; Hanson Industries is headed by White.[13]

There are two corporate headquarters, one in the United States and one in Britain. At both locations there is a small central staff responsible for monitoring the performance of operating companies, selecting and motivating operating management, the treasury function (including acting as a central bank for the operating units), acquisitions and disposals, and professional services such as legal and taxation.

Below each headquarters are a number of divisions (see Exhibit 3). These are not operating companies. Rather, they are groupings of operating companies. In 1988 there were four U.S. divisions (consumer, building products, industrial, and food) and four British divisions (again, consumer, building products, industrial, and food). There are no personnel at the divisional level with the exception of a divisional CEO. Below the divisions are the operating companies. Each operating company has its own CEO who reports to the divisional CEO. The divisional CEOs in Britain are responsible to Lord Hanson; those in the United States are responsible to David Clarke, White's right-hand man. White himself is primarily concerned with acquisitions and leaves most issues of control to David Clarke. Indeed, White claims that he has never visited Hanson Industries' U.S. corporate headquarters and as a matter of policy never visits operating companies.[14]

The following principles seem to characterize Hanson's management philosophy.

- *Decentralization.* All day-to-day operating decisions are decentralized to operating company managers. The corporate center does not offer suggestions about how to manufacture or market a product. Thus, within the limits set by centrally approved operating budgets and capital expenditures, operating management has unlimited autonomy. As a consequence, operating managers are responsible for the return on capital that they employ.

Exhibit 3   Hanson PLC Organizational Structure

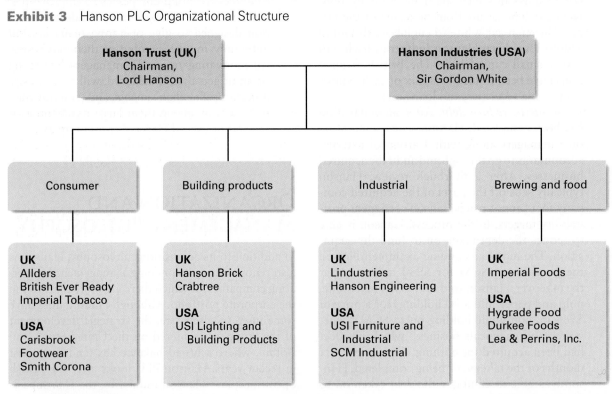

Source: Hanson Industries, Annual Report, 1986.

- *Tight financial control.* Financial control is achieved through two devices: (1) operating budgets and (2) capital expenditure policies. In a bottom-up process, operating budgets are submitted annually to the corporate center by operating company managers. The budgets include detailed performance targets, particularly with regard to return on capital employed (ROK). Corporate staff reviews the budgets and, after consultation with operating management, approves a budget for the coming year. Once agreed upon, the operating budget becomes gospel. The performance of an operating company is compared against budget on a monthly basis, and any variance is investigated by the corporate center. If an operating company betters its projected ROK, the figure used as the base for the next year's budget is the actual ROK, not the budgeted figure.

  Any cash generated by an operating company is viewed as belonging to the corporate center, not to the operating company. Capital expenditures are extremely closely monitored. All cash expenditures in excess of $3,000 (£1,000 in Britain) have to be agreed upon by corporate headquarters. Capital expenditure requests are frequently challenged by headquarters staff. For example, a manager who contends that an investment in more efficient machinery will cut labor costs must even provide the names of the employees that he or she expects to lay off to achieve the savings. According to company insiders, when justifying a request for capital expenditure, a manager must explain every possibility. In general, Hanson looks for a pretax payback on expenditures of three years. The quicker the payback, the more likely it is that an expenditure will be approved.

- *Incentive systems.* A major element of the pay of operating managers is linked directly to operating company performance. A manager can earn up to 60 percent of his or her base salary if the operating company exceeds the ROK target detailed in its annual budget. Bonuses are based strictly on bottom-line performance. As White puts it, "There are no bonuses for being a nice chap."[15] In addition, there is a share option scheme for the most senior operating company and corporate managers. More than 600 managers are members of the option scheme. The options are not exercisable for at least three years after they have been granted.

- *Board structure.* No operating company managers are ever appointed to the board of either Hanson PLC or Hanson Industries. The idea is to eliminate any conflicts of interest that might arise over budgets and capital expenditures.

- *De-emphasizing operating synergy.* In contrast to many diversified companies, Hanson has no interest in trying to realize operating synergy. For example, two of Hanson PLC's subsidiaries, Imperial Tobacco and Elizabeth Shaw (a chocolate firm), are based in Bristol, England, and both deliver goods to news agents and corner shops around Britain. However, Hanson prohibits them from sharing distribution because it reckons that any economies of scale that result would be outweighed by the inefficiencies that would arise if each operating company could blame the other for distribution problems.

THE SCM ACQUISITION

SCM was a diversified manufacturer of consumer and industrial products. SCM had twenty-two operating companies based in five industries: chemicals, coatings and resins, paper and pulp, foods, and typewriters.[16] Among other things, SCM was the world's leading manufacturer of portable typewriters (Smith-Corona typewriters), the world's third largest producer of titanium dioxide (a white inorganic pigment widely used in the manufacture of paint, paper, plastic, and rubber products), the sixth largest paint manufacturer in the world through its Glidden Paints subsidiary, and a major force in the U.S. food industry through its Durkee Famous Foods group (see Exhibit 4).

Attractions to Hanson

The SCM group was first brought to White's attention by Bob Pirie, president of Rothschild Inc. in New York. Pirie thought, and Hanson's research team soon confirmed, that SCM had a number of characteristics that made it a perfect Hanson buy.

1. *Poor financial performance.* Summary financial data for SCM are given in Exhibit 5. Pretax profit had declined from a peak of $83.2 million in 1980 to $54.1 million in 1985. The 1985 return on equity of 7.7 percent was very poor by Hanson's standards, and earnings per share had declined by 19 percent since 1980.

Exhibit 4   SCM Divisional Results for the Year Ended June 1985

Division	Revenues		Profits	
	$m	Percentage of Change from 1984	$m	Percentage of Change from 1984
Chemicals	$539.0	+49%	$73.7	−100%
Coatings and resins	687.0	+5%	49.9	−3%
Paper and pulp	362.0	+3%	23.1	+10%
Foods	422.0	+7%	23.0	+35%
Typewriters	176.0	−11%	(47.4)*	−200%

*Loss after a $35 million charge for restructuring.
Source: Data from Hanson Industries, Annual Report, 1986.

Exhibit 5   Financial Data for SCM

	1980	1981	1982	1983	1984	1985
Net sales ($m)	$1,745.0	$1,761.0	$1,703.0	$1,663.0	$1,963.0	$2,175.0
Pretax profits ($m)	83.2	72.6	35.3	37.8	64.8	54.1
Earnings per share ($)—fully diluted	$4.76	$5.01	$3.20	$2.63	$4.05	$3.85
Return on equity	12.40%	12.00%	5.80%	4.90%	8.00%	7.70%

Source: Data from Hanson Industries, Annual Report, 1986.

2. *Beginnings of a turnaround.* There were signs that incumbent management was coming to grips with SCM's problems, particularly in the troubled typewriter operation, where the 1985 loss was due to a one-time charge of $39 million for restructuring. Financial performance had improved since the low point in 1983, but the benefits of this improvement were not yet reflected in the company's stock price.

3. *Mature businesses.* SCM's presence in mature, proven markets that were technologically stable fit White's preferences.

4. *Low risk.* Some 50 percent of SCM's turnover covered products well known to the U.S. consumer (for example, Smith-Corona typewriters, Glidden paint, Durkee foods). White felt that there would be a ready market for such highly branded businesses if Hanson decided to dispose of any companies that did not meet its stringent ROK requirements.

5. *Titanium dioxide.* Titanium dioxide was dominated by a global oligopoly. Hanson was aware of two favorable trends in the industry that made high returns likely: (a) worldwide demand was forecasted to exceed supply for the next few years, and (b) input costs were declining because of the currency weakness of the major raw material source, Australia.

6. *Corporate overhead.* A corporate staff of 230 indicated to White that SCM was "a lumbering old top-heavy conglomerate with a huge corporate overhead that was draining earnings."[17] He envisioned substantial savings from the elimination of this overhead.

The Takeover Battle

After reviewing the situation, in early August White decided to acquire SCM. He began to buy stock, and on August 21 Hanson Industries formally made a $60 per share tender offer for SCM, valuing the company at $740 million. SCM's top management team responded on August 30 with its own offer to shareholders in the form of a proposed leveraged buyout of SCM. SCM's management had arranged financing from its investment banker Merrill Lynch and offered shareholders $70 per share. On September 4 White responded by raising Hanson's offer to $72 per share.

SCM's management responded to White's second offer by increasing its own offer to $74 per share. To discourage White from making another bid, SCM's management gave Merrill Lynch a "lock-up" option to buy Durkee Famous Foods and SCM Chemicals (the titanium dioxide division) at a substantial discount should Hanson or another outsider gain control. In effect, SCM's management had agreed to give its crown jewels to Merrill Lynch for less than their market value if Hanson won the bidding war.

White's next move was to apparently throw in the towel by announcing withdrawal of Hanson's tender offer. However, in contrast to normal practice on Wall Street, White went into the market and quickly purchased some 25 percent of SCM's stock at a fixed price of $73.5 per share, taking Hanson's stake to 27 percent. Furious at this break with convention, SCM's lawyers drafted a lawsuit against Hanson charging that White's tactics violated tender-offer regulations and demanding a restraining order prohibiting Hanson from making any further market purchases. Hanson quickly filed a countersuit, claiming that Merrill Lynch's lock-up option to buy the two SCM divisions illegally prevented the shareholders from getting the best price.

Hanson lost both suits in federal court in New York. White immediately appealed and on September 30 a U.S. court of appeals ruled in Hanson's favor. This, however, was not to be the end of the matter. On October 7 Hanson spent another $40 million to increase its stake in SCM to 33 percent, thereby effectively stalling the leveraged buyout plan, which needed approval by two-thirds of the shareholders. The following day Hanson revised its tender offer to an all-cash $75 per share offer, subject to SCM's dropping the "lock-up" option because the option had been triggered by Hanson's acquiring 33 percent of SCM.

Hanson's next move, on October 10, was to file a suit to prevent Merrill Lynch from exercising the right to buy SCM's crown jewels. On October 15 it followed this with a second suit against Merrill Lynch for conspiracy. A U.S. district court ruled on November 26 that the lock-up was legal and that Hanson had triggered its exercise by the size of its stake. Once again Hanson appealed to a higher court. On January 6, 1986, a U.S. court of appeals overturned the lower court ruling, granting to Hanson an injunction that prevented SCM from exercising the lock-up option. The following day Hanson Industries won control over SCM after further market purchases. The final purchase price was $930 million, which represented a price/earnings multiple of 11.5.

After the Acquisition

Having gained control of SCM, Hanson immediately set about trying to realize SCM's potential. Within three months, 250 employees were laid off, mostly headquarters staff, and the former SCM headquarters in New York was sold for $36 million in cash. At the same time, White and his team were using their new position as owners to thoroughly audit the affairs of SCM's operating companies. Their objective was to identify those businesses whose returns were adequate or could be improved upon and those businesses for which the outlook was such that they were unlikely to achieve Hanson's stringent ROK requirements.

At the end of this process, four businesses were sold off in as many months for a total amount that recouped for Hanson the original purchase price and left Hanson with the two best businesses in SCM's portfolio: Smith-Corona typewriters and the titanium dioxide business. In May 1986, SCM's paper and pulp operations were sold to Boise Cascade for $160 million in cash, a price that represented a price/earnings multiple of 29 and was 3 times book value. Hanson felt that the outlook for those operations was not good because of a depression in paper and pulp prices. Boise Cascade obviously thought otherwise. Shortly afterward, Sylvachem, part of SCM's chemicals division, was sold for $30 million, representing a price/earnings multiple of 18.5.

In August 1986 Glidden Paints was sold to the British chemical giant and Europe's largest paint manufacturer, Imperial Chemical Industries PLC (ICI) for $580 million. This represented a price/earnings multiple of 17.5 and was 2.5 times book value. The purchase of this operation enabled ICI to become the world's largest paint manufacturer. A few days later Durkee Famous Foods was sold to another British firm, Reckitt & Colman PLC, for $120 million in cash and the assumption of $20 million in debt. This represented a price/earnings multiple of 17 and was 3 times book value. This disposal served to withdraw Hanson from an area that was subject to uncontrollable and volatile commodity price movements. For Reckitt & Colman, however, which was already one of the largest manufacturers of branded food products outside the United States, it represented an important strategic addition.

The four disposals amounted to $926 million and were accomplished at an average price/earnings multiple of 19.5. Having recovered 100 percent of the purchase price paid for SCM within eight months, Hanson had effectively acquired for nothing a number of businesses that were projected to contribute around $140 million to net pretax profit for their first full year under Hanson's control.

Hanson retained the titanium dioxide business for two main reasons. First, with the industry operating at close to 100 percent capacity and with projections indicating an increase in demand through to 1989, prices and margins were expected to increase substantially. Although several companies had plans to expand global capacity, given the three- to four-year time lag in bringing new capacity on stream, this sellers' market was likely to persist for a while. Nor did it look as if the additional capacity would outstrip the projected rise in demand. Second, two-thirds of world production of titanium dioxide is in the hands of global producers. SCM's business is ranked third with 12 percent of world capacity, behind Du Pont and Tioxide PLC. Given this oligopoly, orderly pricing in world markets seemed likely to continue.

Hanson also decided to retain SCM's typewriter business, despite the fact that in recent years it had been the worst-performing unit in SCM's portfolio. Hanson quickly realized that SCM management had in effect just completed a drastic overhaul of the typewriter businesses and that a dramatic turnaround was likely. In the two years prior to Hanson's acquisition, SCM's management had undertaken the following steps:

1. A new line of electronic typewriters had been introduced to match the increasingly sophisticated Japanese models.

2. Capacity had been reduced by 50 percent, and six U.S. production facilities had been consolidated into a single assembly plant and distribution center in New York to manufacture all electronic models.

3. As a result of automation, economies of scale, and labor agreements, productivity at the New York plant had increased fourfold since 1984, and unit labor costs had declined by 60 percent.

4. The manufacture of electric models had been moved offshore to a low-cost facility in Singapore.

5. Smith-Corona had just introduced the first personal word processor for use with a portable electronic typewriter, and it retailed at slightly less than $500.

As a result of these improvements, the Smith-Corona business seemed ready to become a major profit producer. Hanson forecasted profits of $30 million for this business during 1986–1987, compared with an operating loss of $47.4 million in financial year 1985.

THE IMPERIAL ACQUISITION

On December 6, 1985, while still engaged in the SCM acquisition, Hanson opened another takeover battle in Britain by announcing an offer of £1.5 billion for Imperial Group PLC.[18] Imperial Group was one of the ten largest firms in Britain. Imperial was Britain's leading tobacco manufacturer and the third largest tobacco company in the world. Its Courage Brewing subsidiary was one of the "big six" beer companies in Britain. Its leisure operations included 1,371 public houses (taverns), 120-plus restaurants, and more than 750 specialized retail shops. Imperial manufactured more than 1,000 branded food products. (See Exhibit 6 for a breakdown of Imperial's divisional results.) In September 1985 Imperial had sold its fourth business, the U.S. motel chain Howard Johnson, to Marriott. Howard Johnson had been purchased in 1980 and was widely regarded as one of the worst acquisitions ever made by a major British company.

Attractions to Hanson

Hanson's interest in Imperial was prompted by the news on December 2, 1985, of a planned merger between Imperial and United Biscuits PLC, a major

Exhibit 6 Imperial Divisional Results for the Year Ended October 1985

Division	Revenues		Profits	
	£m	Percentage of Change from 1984	£m	Percentage of Change from 1984
Tobacco	£2,641	+7%	£123.1	+11%
Brewing and leisure	974	+8%	97.0	+20%
Foods	719	+4%	33.0	+5%
Howard Johnson	617	+11%	11.1	−40%

Source: Data from Hanson Industries, Annual Report, 1986.

manufacturer of branded food products. The financial press perceived this measure as a defensive move by Imperial. However, despite its well-documented problems with Howard Johnson, Imperial's financial performance was reasonably strong (see Exhibit 7). What factors made Imperial an attractive takeover target to Hanson? The following seem to have been important.

- *Mature business.* Like SCM's businesses, most of Imperial's businesses were based in mature, low-technology industries. There is little prospect of radically changing fashions or technological change in the tobacco, brewing, and food industries.
- *Low risk.* Most of Imperial's products had a high brand recognition within Britain. Thus, Hanson could easily dispose of those that did not stand up to Hanson's demanding ROK targets.
- *Tobacco cash flow.* Imperial's tobacco business was a classic cash cow. The company had 45 percent of the tobacco market and seven of the ten

best-selling brands in 1985. Although tobacco sales are declining in Britain because of a combination of health concerns and punitive taxation, the decline has been gradual, amounting to 29 percent since the peak year of 1973. Given Hanson's emphasis on ROK and cash flow, this made Imperial particularly attractive to Hanson. Imperial had arguably squandered much of this cash flow by using it to underwrite unprofitable growth opportunities, particularly Howard Johnson.

- *Failure of Imperial's diversification strategy.* Imperial's recent track record with respect to diversification was poor. In 1978 it bought a construction company, J. B. Eastward, for £40 million. After four years of trading losses, Eastward was sold in 1982 for a total loss of £54 million. In 1979 Imperial paid $640 million for Howard Johnson, the U.S. motel and restaurant chain. In 1985, after six years of declining profits, this

Exhibit 7 Financial Data for Imperial

	1981	1982	1983	1984	1985
Revenues (£m)	£4,526	£4,614	£4,381	£4,593	£4,918
Pretax profits (£m)	106	154	195	221	236
Earnings per share (pence)	12.8	16.4	18.0	20.3	22.4
Return on capital (%)	12.7%	17.9%	20.4%	21.1%	18.1%

Source: Data from Hanson Industries, Annual Report, 1986.

business was sold for $341 million. These losses suggested a fundamental weakness in Imperial's top management in an area in which Hanson was strong: diversification strategy. Moreover, the failure of Imperial's diversification strategy probably resulted in Imperial's shares being discounted by the stock market.

- *Inadequate returns in brewing and leisure.* Imperial's brewing and leisure operations earned an ROK of 9 percent in 1985. This return was considered very low for the brewing industry, which was characterized by strong demand and was dominated by a mature oligopoly that had engineered high prices and margins. Hanson thought that this return could be significantly improved.

The Takeover Battle

The planned merger between Imperial and United Biscuits PLC (UB), announced on December 2, 1985, gave rise to considerable concern among Imperial's already disgruntled shareholders. Under the terms of the proposed merger, UB, although contributing just 21 percent of net assets, would end up with a 42 percent interest in the enlarged group. The implication was that Imperial's shareholders would experience significant earnings dilution. In addition, it was proposed that the corporate management of the enlarged group would primarily come from UB personnel. These factors prompted a reverse takeover by UB of the much larger Imperial group. See Exhibit 8.

Hanson's interest was sparked by this controversy. Hanson's corporate staff had been tracking Imperial for some time, so when the for-sale sign was raised over Imperial, Hanson was able to move quickly. On December 6, 1985, Hanson made a 250-pence per share offer for Imperial, valuing the group at £1.9 billion. This offer was rejected out of hand by Imperial's management.

The next major development came on February 12, 1986, when the British secretary of state of trade and industry referred the proposed Imperial/UB merger to the Monopolies and Mergers Commission for consideration. Britain's Monopolies and Mergers Commission has the authority to prohibit any merger that might create a monopoly. The referral was due to the recognition that an Imperial/UB group would command more than 40 percent of the British snack-food market.

On February 17, Hanson took advantage of the uncertainty created by the referral to unveil a revised offer 24 percent higher than its original offer, valuing Imperial at £2.35 billion. On the same day, UB announced a bid of £2.5 billion for Imperial and indicated that, if the offer was successful, Imperial's snack-food businesses would be sold, thus eliminating the need for a Monopolies and Mergers Commission investigation. Imperial's board duly recommended the UB offer to shareholders for acceptance.

Many of Imperial's shareholders, however, were in no mood to accept Imperial's recommendation. Under British stock market regulations, once the Imperial board accepted UB's offer, Imperial's shareholders had two months in which to indicate their acceptance or rejection of it. If the offer was rejected, then the shareholders were free to consider the hostile bid from Hanson. What followed was an increasingly acrimonious war of words between Hanson and Imperial. Hanson charged Imperial with mismanagement. Imperial responded by trying to depict Hanson as an asset stripper with no real interest in generating internal growth from the companies it owned. In the words of one Imperial executive during this period, Lord Hanson "buys and sells companies well, but he manages them jolly badly. He buys, squeezes and goes on to the next one. The only way to grow is by bigger and bigger acquisitions. Like all great conglomerate builders of the past, he's over the hill."[19]

Imperial's management failed to win the war of words. By April 17, UB had secured acceptances for only 34 percent of Imperial's shares, including 14.9 percent held by UB associates. The UB offer lapsed, leaving the way clear for Hanson. On April 18 Hanson secured acceptances for more than 50 percent of Imperial's shares, and its offer went unconditional. At £2.5 billion, the takeover was the largest in British history; it implied a price/earnings multiple of 12.3 on Imperial's prospective earnings.

After the Acquisition

After the acquisition Hanson moved quickly to realize potential from Imperial. Of the 300 staff at Imperial's headquarters, 260 were laid off, and most of the remainder were sent back to the operating level. In July Imperial's hotels and restaurants were sold to Trusthouse Forte for £190 million in cash, representing a price/earnings multiple of 24 on prospective earnings and amounting to 1.7 times book value.

Exhibit 8 Hanson PLC—Financial Data

Income Data (million $)*										
Year Ended Sept. 30	Revs.	Oper. Inc.	% Oper. Inc. of Revs.	Cap. Exp.	Depr.	Int. Exp.	Net Bef. Taxes	Eff. Tax Rate	Net† Inc.	% Net Inc. of Revs.
1989§	$11,302	$1,609	14.2%	$2,141	$200	$533	$1,718†	23.6%	1,313	11.6%
1988§	12,507	1,561	12.5%	724	215	485	1,488†	23.2%	1,143	9.1%
1987‖	10,975	1,230	11.2%	522	172	493	1,217†	22.8%	939	8.6%
1986‖	6,196	713	11.5%	848	105	359	667	22.5%	517	8.3%
1985	3,771	477	12.7%	84	74	172	356	23.5%	272	7.2%
1984	2,930	303	10.3%	61	55	119	208	25.7%	154	5.3%
1983	2,226	207	9.3%	59	47	81	137	30.2%	94	4.2%
1982	1,952	NA	NA	NA	NA	NA	NA	NA	72	3.7%
1981	1,549	NA	NA	NA	NA	NA	NA	NA	62	4.0%

Balance Sheet Data (million $)*											
Sept. 30	Cash	Assets	Curr. Liab.	Ratio	Total Assets	% Ret. on Assets	Long-Term Debt	Common Equity	Total Inv. Capital	% LT Debt. of Cap.	% Ret. on Equity
1989	$8,574	$12,038	$5,278	2.3	$17,482	8.5%	$8,028	$1,689	$10,683	75.1%	47.6%
1988	6,527	10,413	4,165	2.5	13,210	9.4%	3,592	3,707	7,878	45.6%	33.5%
1987	5,025	8,236	3,422	2.4	10,471	9.3%	2,837	2,841	6,151	46.1%	37.5%
1986	2,509	7,977	3,572	2.2	9,577	7.6%	2,834	2,068	5,252	54.0%	29.1%
1985	1,659	2,908	1,277	2.3	4,021	7.7%	903	1,376	2,563	35.2%	27.7%
1984	641	1,775	925	1.9	2,638	9.0%	981	505	1,540	63.7%	36.7%

*Data as originally reported; prior to 1986 data as reported in the 1985 Annual Report (prior to 1984, data are from the listing application of November 3, 1986), conversion to U.S. dollars at year-end exchange rates.

†Includes equity in earnings of nonconsolidated subsidiaries.

‡Before specific item(s) in 1989, 1988, 1986.

§Excludes discount operations and reflects merger or acquisition.

‖Reflects merger or acquisition.

Source: Standard & Poor's, *Standard & Poor's NYSE Stock Reports*, Vol. 57, No. 54, Sec. 12, 1096. Reprinted by permission of Standard & Poor's, a division of The McGraw-Hill Companies, Inc.

That sale was followed in September 1986 by the sale of the Courage Brewing operations, along with a wine and spirits wholesaler and an "off-license" chain (liquor stores) to Elders IXL, an Australian brewing company, for £1.4 billion in cash. The price/earnings multiple for that deal amounted to 17.5 times prospective earnings and represented a premium of £150 million over book value. It was quickly followed by the sale of Imperial's Golden Wonder snack-food business to Dalgety PLC, a British food concern, for £87 million in cash, representing a price/earnings multiple of 13.5 over prospective earnings.

As a result of these moves, by the autumn of 1986 Hanson had raised £1.7 billion from the sale of Imperial's businesses. Effectively, Hanson recouped 66 percent of the total cost of its acquisition by selling companies that contributed slightly more than 45 percent of Imperial's net profit forecasted for the year to October 1986. The net cost of Imperial on this basis had fallen to £850 million, with a consequent decline in the price/earnings multiple on prospective earnings from 12.3 to 7.6.

This was followed in 1988 by the sale of Imperial's food businesses for £534 million, along with the sale of various other smaller interests for £56 million. By the end of 1988, therefore, Hanson had raised £2.26 billion from the sale of Imperial's assets. It still retained Imperial Tobacco, by far the largest business in Imperial's portfolio, which it had in effect gained for a net cost of £240 million—this for a business that in 1988 generated £150 million in operating profit.

LATER DEVELOPMENTS

Following the SCM and Imperial acquisitions, in 1987 Hanson acquired Kidde, a 108-company U.S. conglomerate, for $1.7 billion. Kidde seemed set for the "Hanson treatment." Its headquarters was closed within three months of the takeover, and a series of disposals was arranged. These were followed in 1988 by continuing disposals of operations acquired in the Imperial and Kidde acquisitions. In total, they amounted to $1.5 billion.

In mid 1989 Hanson embarked on its biggest takeover ever, the £3.61 billion ($4.8 billion) acquisition of Consolidated Gold Field PLC (CGF). In addition to being the second largest gold-mining operation in the world, CGF also owns a large stone and gravel operation, ARC Ltd., with major holdings in Britain. CGF came to Hanson's attention following an abortive takeover bid for the company from South African-controlled Minorco.

Hanson bought Minorco's 29.9 percent minority stake in CGF and launched its own takeover bid in July 1989. After raising its bid, Hanson won control of CGF in August. CGF also seemed set to be broken up. About half of CGF's value consists of minority stakes in publicly quoted mining companies in the United States, South Africa, and Australia. These stakes range from 38 to 49 percent, enough to hold the key to control in many of the companies. Thus, Hanson should be able to extract a premium price for them. Initial estimates suggest that Hanson should be able to raise $2.5 billion from the sale of CGF's minority holdings.[20] Indeed, by February 1990 Hanson had reportedly recouped about one-third of the purchase price of CGF through disposals and was looking to sell additional operations while gold prices remained high.[21]

The CGF deal led directly to the June 1990 acquisition of Peabody Holdings Co., the largest U.S. coal producer, for a total cost of $1.23 billion in cash. CGF had a 49 percent stake in Newmont Mining Corp., the biggest U.S. gold-mining concern. In turn, Newmont owned 55 percent of Peabody. In April 1990 Hanson purchased the 45 percent of Peabody not owned by Newmont from three minority owners. Then in June it outbid AMAX Corporation for Newmont's stake in Peabody.

The attraction of Peabody to Hanson lies in two factors: (1) the company owns large deposits of low-sulfur coal, which is increasingly in demand because of environmental concerns; (2) the company has recently invested heavily to upgrade its plant. As a result, in the past four years labor productivity has increased 50 percent.[22] In addition, analysts speculate that the deals, by improving Newmont's financial position (Newmont has used the cash to reduce its debt), may make it possible for Hanson to sell off its 49 percent stake in Newmont for a reasonable premium.

Endnotes

1. "The Conglomerate as Antique Dealer," *Economist*, March 11, 1989, 71–73.
2. Quoted in ibid.
3. Quoted in John Byrne and Mark Maremont, "Hanson: The Dangers of Living by Takeover Alone," *Business Week*, August 15, 1988, 62–64.
4. Quoted in Andrew Marton, "The Buccaneer from Britain," *Mergers and Acquisitions* (February 1987), 141–146.
5. Quoted in Byrne and Maremont, "Hanson: The Dangers."
6. Gordon White, "How I Turned $3,000 into $10 Billion," *Fortune*, November 7, 1988, 80–89.

7. The material in this section is based on the following sources: White, "How I Turned," 80–89; Marton, "The Buccaneer from Britain," 141–146; and Hope Lampert, "Britons on the Prowl," *New York Times Magazine*, November 29, 1987, 22–24, 36, 38, 42.

8. White, "How I Turned," 81.

9. Quoted in Lampert, "Britons on the Prowl," 36.

10. Quoted in White, "How I Turned," 81.

11. Quoted in Lampert, "Britons on the Prowl," 24.

12. The material in this section is based on the following sources: White, "How I Turned," 80–89; Lampert, "Britons on the Prowl," 22–24, 36, 38, 42; and Mark Cusack, *Hanson Trust: A Review of the Company and Its Prospects* (London: Hoare Govett Limited, 1987).

13. The material in this section is based on the following sources: Cusack, *Hanson Trust*; "The Conglomerate as Antique Dealer," 71–73; Byrne and Maremont, "Hanson: The Dangers," 62–64; and Gordon White, "Nothing Hurts More Than a Bogus Bonus," *Wall Street Journal*, July 20, 1987, 18.

14. White, "How I Turned," 81.

15. White, "Nothing Hurts More," 18.

16. Most of the detail in this section is drawn from two sources: Cusack, *Hanson Trust*; and Lampert, "Britons on the Prowl," 22–24, 36, 38, 42.

17. White, "How I Turned," 84.

18. The material in this section is based on the following sources: Cusack, *Hanson Trust*; and Lampert, "Britons on the Prowl," 22–24, 36, 38, 42.

19. Quoted in Philip Revzin, "U.K.'s Hanson Trust Aims for Big Leagues in Takeovers," *Wall Street Journal*, February 25, 1986, 30.

20. Mark Maremont and Chuck Hawkins, "Is Consgold Just an Appetizer for Hanson?" *Business Week*, July 10, 1989, 41–42.

21. Joann Lubin, "Hanson to Buy Peabody Stake for $504 Million," *Wall Street Journal*, February 16, 1990, A4.

22. "Hanson PLC," *Value Line*, July 20, 1990, 832.

HANSON (B)

INTRODUCTION

During the 1970s and 1980s, Hanson PLC put together one of the most impressive growth stories of any industrial company in the world. Under the leadership of James Hanson and Gordon White, Hanson PLC made its name by acquiring poorly run conglomerate companies in both Britain and America at prices that were often below their book value. In quick order Hanson would then change the senior management of the acquired company, sell many of the company's assets to other enterprises, typically for a considerable profit, and impose tight financial controls on what remained in order to maximize profitability and cash flow. The locus classicus was Hanson's 1986 acquisition of the Imperial Group, a diversified British tobacco, brewing, and food conglomerate, where some £2.4 billion of the £2.5 billion purchase price was recouped from asset disposals, leaving Hanson with the cash-generating tobacco business intact. The results of this strategy were nothing short of stunning. Between 1973 and 1991, Hanson put together twenty-nine years of uninterrupted profit growth to build a diversified company with revenues of £7.69 billion ($12.3 billion) and operating income of £1.33 billion ($2.13 billion). Hanson's stock price appreciation was also spectacular, increasing more than a hundredfold between 1973 and 1991.

However, 1991 may have been the high-water mark of Hanson's growth story. In 1990 Hanson took a 2.9 percent stake in the British chemical and pharmaceutical company, Imperial Chemical Industries (ICI). Many saw this as a prelude to yet another Hanson acquisition, but ICI was not about to be taken over. After a bitter public relations battle during which ICI characterized Hanson's management as having a   short-term orientation and criticized them for failure to add value to the companies they acquired, Hanson sold its stake in May 1991. While the stake was sold for a profit of £45 million ($70 million), the public relations battle damaged Hanson's image. A year later Hanson was outbid for a British food company, RHM, by a smaller conglomerate run by a former Hanson manager. These two failures raised questions as to whether Hanson's two founders, who were now both in their seventies, were still up to the rough game of hostile takeovers. To compound matters further, for the year ending in September 1993, with many of its cyclical businesses suffering from the effects of a recession in both Britain and America, Hanson reported a 33 percent decline in after-tax profits to $1.5 billion, the first such decline in its history. Reflecting these problems, Hanson's stock price peaked in early 1991 and remained flat over the next few years, while the equity markets in Britain and America boomed.

A NEW DIRECTION?

In 1992 the leadership mantle at Hanson started to pass from the company's charismatic founders, the now ennobled (Lord) Hanson and White, to Derek Bonham and David Clarke, who were then forty-eight and fifty, respectively. Bonham took over as CEO with primary responsibilities for Hanson's British-based operations, while Clarke succeeded White as president of Hanson's substantial American operation. Lord Hanson remained on in the chairman's role, while White continued as the company's senior person in charge of mergers and acquisitions. (White died in 1995.)

Although both long-time Hanson employees, Bonham and Clarke clearly lacked the predatory thirst that had driven Hanson and White. Early in his tenure Bonham admitted that Hanson had become "too much of a mishmash" and stated that he hoped to correct that by focusing management's attention on improving the performance of its core businesses in building materials, chemicals, tobacco, and natural resources (primarily timber and coal). While this might require "bolt on acquisitions," Bonham seemed to be signaling that the swashbuckling days of hostile acquisitions and quick asset disposals to pay down debt were over.[1]

Another signal of a shift in management's philosophy came in May 1994, when Hanson announced that it would lengthen the payback period required of new capital investments from three or four years to five or six years. The company stated that it had lengthened the required payback period to take advantage of low interest rates and continuing low inflation. However, many also saw the shift as an attempt to allay fears in the financial community that Hanson's management style was too focused on the short term. Moreover, the move seemed to be consistent with Bonham's stated goal of increasing internal investments as a way of generating growth.[2] The growth that Bonham was talking about, however, was a far cry from the 20 percent annual rate achieved under the leadership of Hanson and White. According to Bonham, "The reality is that we are living in a low growth, low inflation climate. To suggest that you can continue to grow by 20 percent is out of line."[3]

Both Bonham and Clarke repeatedly stated that they saw Hanson growing at about twice the rate of inflation during the 1990s, which suggested a growth rate of around 6 percent, given British and American inflation rates.

Acquiring Quantum

The first significant strategic move under Bonham occurred on June 31, 1993, when Hanson announced that it had reached an agreement to purchase Quantum Chemical Corp., the largest U.S. producer of polyethylene plastics, in a stock swap that valued Quantum at $20 per share, or $720 million. The purchase price represented a premium of 60 percent over Quantum's closing price of $12.50 on June 30. Hanson also stated that it would assume all of Quantum's $2.5 billion in debt. The acquisition added to Hanson's U.S. chemical operations, which included SCM Chemicals, the world's third largest producer of titanium dioxide.

According to observers, the acquisition represented a strategic bet by Hanson that a protracted cyclical downturn in the polyethylene business was nearing an end. At the peak of the last plastics cycle in 1988, Quantum earned $760 million. However, Quantum had saddled itself with the $2.5 billion debt load in a 1989 restructuring, undertaken while plastics prices were at their previous cyclical peak. Massive debt service requirements and a slump in polyethylene prices had left Quantum with a 1992 loss before accounting charges of $118.4 million, or $3.98 per share. One immediate financial benefit of the acquisition was that Hanson was able to use its superior credit rating to refinance Quantum's debt (much of which was in the form of junk bonds with an average yield of more than 10 percent) at rates closer to Hanson's 5 percent borrowing costs. This move alone cut Quantum's $240 million annual interest bill in half.[4]

In retrospect the Quantum acquisition turned out to be particularly well timed. Prices for low density polyethylene bottomed out in the summer of 1993 at $28 per gallon. By the end of 1994 they had risen to $33 per gallon.[5] Quantum's profits turned out to be highly leveraged to prices. As a result of this leverage and lower interest payments, Quantum's chemical operations earned almost $200 million in fiscal 1994, more than $300 million ahead of its 1992 results. Quantum's results helped Hanson to rebound from its poor showing in 1993. For 1994 it reported a 32 percent rise in pretax profits and a record operating profit of £1.23 billion ($1.92 billion).[6]

1993–1994 Disposals

Throughout 1993 and 1994, Hanson proceeded with a series of relatively minor asset disposals. The objectives of these disposals were twofold: first, to focus the company on its core businesses and, second, to help pay down Hanson's enormous debt load, the legacy of its acquisitions including Quantum. In fiscal 1993 Hanson's long-term debt stood at £7.22 billion ($11.5 billion), and its debt to equity ratio was 1.83 (see Exhibit 1). This debt load was beginning to trouble the financial community, who were starting to question the ability of Hanson to maintain its historically high dividend. In a previous era Hanson had quickly paid down debt from acquisitions by raising cash through asset disposals, but there had been little movement in this direction since the late 1980s.

Between January 1993 and August 1994, Hanson sold more than fifteen companies for a total of £815 million ($1.3 billion). These disposals included its Beazer home building operations in both the United States and the United Kingdom; an office supply business; and Axelson, an oil industry equipment group.[7]

Spinning Off U.S. Industries

The next big strategic move occurred in February 1995, when Hanson announced that it would spin off thirty-four of its smaller American-based companies into a new entity called U.S. Industries under the leadership of David Clarke. Hanson would retain ownership over several of its larger U.S. operations, including Quantum Chemical and Peabody Coal. The new company was to include such well-known brand names as Jacuzzi whirlpools, Farberware cookware, Ames garden tools, Rexair vacuum cleaners, and Tommy Armour golf clubs. In 1994 the thirty-four companies had sales of $3 billion and operating profits of $252 million. The company was to be responsible for $1.4 billion of Hanson's debt. According to one analyst,

> For Hanson, it achieves a one shot divestiture of a number of companies they may have struggled to sell independently, not because the individual assets are unattractive, but because it's messy to sell so many of them. They are able to divest in a tax efficient way and at the same time take a lot of cash out, leaving them with the ability to buy something else.[8]

The spinoff was completed on June 1, 1995. At the time, David Clarke stated that the new company's first objective would be to reduce its debt load, primarily by selling off a number of companies valued at $600 million.[9]

Acquiring Eastern Group

Only July 31, 1995, Hanson announced that it would acquire Eastern Group, one of Britain's major electric utilities, for £2 billion ($3.2 billion). Eastern, which was privatized in 1990, has a customer base of 3 million and is responsible for 15 percent of the electricity produced in Britain, primarily for natural gas-fired generating facilities. Eastern is also the seventh largest natural gas supplier in the country. In the year ending March 31, 1995, Eastern's earnings were up 15 percent to £203 million ($324 billion) on revenues of £2.06 billion ($3.2 billion).[10]

Hanson stated that it was attracted to Eastern by its steady earnings growth. However, critics noted that the deal yet again stretched Hanson's balance sheet, which once more had begun to look solid after the U.S. Industries spinoff. The debt-financed purchase of Eastern caused Hanson's debt-to-equity ratio to shoot up from 37 percent to 130 percent, once more raising concerns that Hanson might not be able to service its historically high dividends. A partial response to these concerns came in December 1995, when the company announced plans to dispose of two additional U.S. subsidiaries—Suburban Propane and Cavenham Forest Industries—for £1.5 billion ($2.4 billion). The proceeds were to be used to pay down Hanson's debt load. Analysts calculated that the cash raised from these spinoffs would reduce Hanson's debt-to-equity ratio to around 90 percent.[11]

THE DEMERGER

By late 1995 it was becoming increasingly clear within Hanson's senior management team that drastic action would be required to boost the company's lagging share price.[12] As the British and American economies continued in their long recovery from recession, Hanson's cyclical business staged a significant performance improvement, with operating profits increasing by 44 percent for the fiscal year that

Exhibit 1   Hanson PLC—Financial Data

Income Data (million £)*												
Year Ended Sept. 30	($) Per pound[†]	Revs.	Oper. Inc.	% Oper. Inc. of Revs.	Cap. Exp.	Depr.	Int. Exp.	Net Bef. Taxes	Eff. Tax Rate	Net Inc.[¶]	% Net Inc. of Revs.	Cash Flow
1994	1.509	11,199	1,633	14.6	293	401	545	1,346	20.9%	1,065	9.5	1,466
1993	1.523	9,760	1,288	13.2	301	310	600	1,016	27.8%	734	7.5	1,044
1992	1.822	8,798	1,322	15.0	279	254	777	1,286	15.3%	1,089	12.4	1,343
1991[‡]	1.820	7,691	1,327	17.3	266	216	741	1,319	21.5%	1,035	13.5	1,251
1990[‡]	1.700	7,153	1,236	17.3	247	180	638	1,285	24.4%	971	13.6	NA
1989[‡]	1.690	6,998	996	14.2	192	124	330	1,064	23.6%	813	11.6	NA
1988[‡]	1.770	7,396	923	12.5	198	127	287	880	23.2%	676	9.1	NA
1987[§]	1.560	6,682	749	11.2	151	105	300	741	22.8%	572	9.6	NA

Balance Sheet Data (million £)*											
			Curr.							% LT	
Sept. 30	($) Per pound[†]	Cash.	Assets	Liab.	Ratio	Total Assets	Ret. on Assets	Long-Term Debt	Common Equity	Total Inv. Cap.	Debt of Cap.	% Ret. on Equity
1994	1.566	6,815	9,933	6,704	1.5	21,536	4.7	5,038	4,598	9,768	51.6	24.9
1993	1.525	8,067	11,636	7,065	1.6	24,057	3.3	7,221	3,953	11,266	64.1	18.0
1992	1.779	8,445	11,204	6,386	1.8	20,541	5.9	5,069	4,224	9,430	53.8	28.9
1991	1.750	7,771	9,955	4,751	2.1	16,583	6.6	4,880	3,325	8,351	58.4	33.6
1990	1.870	6,883	8,993	4,226	2.1	14,754	7.6	4,258	2,834	7,222	59.0	50.1
1989	1.620	5,309	7,454	3,269	2.3	10,825	8.7	4,971	1,046	6,133	81.1	50.1
1988	1.690	3,860	6,158	2,463	2.5	7,812	9.5	2,124	2,192	4,659	45.6	34.1
1987	1.630	3,059	5,014	2,083	2.4	6,375	8.8	1,727	1,730	3,745	46.1	35.5

*Data as originally reported; prior to 1988 as reported in 1987 Annual Report. Based on UK GAAP.

[†]Average exchange rates for income data; fiscal year-end exchange rates for balance sheet.

[‡]Excludes discretionary operations and reflects merger or acquisition.

[§]Reflects merger or acquisition.

[¶]Before special items.

ended in September 1995. Despite this performance, the company's share price had been essentially flat since the early 1990s (see Exhibit 2). Over the same period both the London and New York stock markets had increased substantially. By the end of 1995 the price-to-earnings ratio of Hanson's shares was 30 percent below that of the average stock on the London exchange, while Hanson's dividend yield at over 6.5 percent was among the highest offered by any company. It seemed that nothing could move the stock price, not the strong profit performance, not the spinoff of U.S. Industries, not the Eastern acquisition, and not the recently announced disposals.

It was against this background that Hanson stunned both London and Wall Street with its January 29 announcement that it would divide the company up into four independent businesses, effectively dismantling the conglomerate assembled by Hanson and White. Hanson stated that it would split into a chemicals business, an energy company, a tobacco company, and a building materials enterprise. Imperial Tobacco would be the largest company, with sales of £3.57 billion ($5.37 billion). The energy business, which would include Hanson's coal and electric businesses, would have sales of £3.5 billion ($5.27 billion). The chemicals business would have sales of £2 billion ($3.04 billion), while the building materials group would have sales of £2.3 billion

($3.48 billion).[13] Bonham was to run the energy business, while Hanson was to take over the building materials group until his retirement. The company estimated that the demerger would be completed by early 1997.

Hanson's stock price initially surged 7 percent on the news, but it fell later the same day and ended up less than 0.5 percent. The lack of a sustained positive reaction from the stock markets on both sides of the Atlantic puzzled Hanson's managers. Over the last few years, a number of diversified companies had announced demergers—including ITT, AT&T, and Sears—and their stock prices had almost always responded in a very positive fashion. In Hanson's case, however, this did not occur.

One possible explanation for the lack of a favorable reaction came from Moody's Investor Service, which put Hanson's debt under review for a possible downgrade one day after the breakup was announced. Moody's noted that "this is a highly complex sequence of transactions which are at an early stage and which will require various approvals."[14] Among the concerns expressed were that the demerger might raise Hanson's borrowing costs. The tax consequences of the demerger were also not immediately apparent, although there were some indications that there might be some one-time capital gains tax charges. Moreover, several stock analysts commented that the

Exhibit 2   Hanson PLC

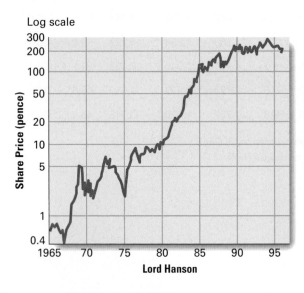

Lord Hanson

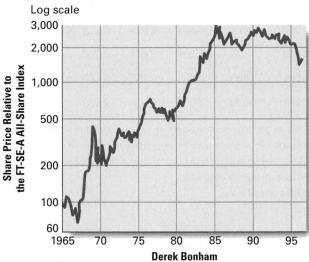

Derek Bonham

demerged Hanson units might not be able or willing to maintain Hanson's historically high level of dividends. One influential London-based stock analyst also noted that unlike most conglomerates that were demerging, there were few if any hidden assets at Hanson. This analyst calculated that Hanson's constituent parts should be valued at 194 pence, which was below the 212 pence price that Hanson's stock closed at on January 30, 1996.[15]

As a further prelude to the demerger, in March 1996 Hanson announced the sale of its remaining U.S. timberland operations to Willamette Industries for $1.59 billion. This sale followed Hanson's disposal of Cavenham Forest Industries in December 1995, and it completed Hanson's exit from the timber business. The cash generated from the sale was to be used to pay down Hanson's debt.[16]

Endnotes

1. R. A. Melcher, "Can This Predator Change Its Stripes?" *Business Week*, June 22, 1992, 38; J. Guyon, "Hanson Crosses the Atlantic to Woo Investors," *Wall Street Journal*, December 6, 1983, 7D.
2. R. Rudd, "Hanson Increases Investment Payback Time," *Financial Times*, May 16, 1994, 15.
3. P. Dwyer and J. Weber, "Hanson Looks for a Hat Trick," *Business Week*, March 14, 1994, 68–69.
4. S. McMurray, "UK's Hanson to Buy Maker of Polyethylene," *Wall Street Journal*, July 1, 1993, A3.
5. D. Wighton, "Conglomerate's $3.2 Billion Gamble Pays Off," *Financial Times*, December 2, 1994, 23.
6. "Hanson Posts 32% Rise in Pre Tax Profits," *Wall Street Journal*, December 2, 1994, B3.
7. P. Taylor, "Hanson Lifted by Quantum Chemical," *Financial Times*, August 17, 1994, 13.
8. R. W. Stevenson, "Hanson Plans to Spin Off 34 U.S. Companies," *New York Times*, February 23, 1995, C1.
9. L. L. Brownless and J. R. Dorfman, "Birth of U.S. Industries Isn't Without Complications," *Wall Street Journal*, May 18, 1995, B4.
10. D. Wighton, "Hanson Plugs into New Current," *Financial Times*, July 31, 1995, 15.
11. D. Wighton, "Hanson Seeks £1.5 Billion from U.S. Disposals," *Financial Times*, December 21, 1995, 13.
12. "Widow Hanson's Children Leave Home," *Economist*, February 3, 1996, 51–52.
13. R. Bonte-Friedheim and J. Guyon, "Hanson to Divide into Four Businesses," *Wall Street Journal*, January 31, 1996, A3.
14. Bonte-Friedheim and Guyon, "Hanson to Divide into Four Businesses."
15. D. Wighton, "Centrifugal Forces That Pulled Hanson Apart," *Financial Times*, January 31, 1996, 18.
16. "Hanson to Sell Mills," *Wall Street Journal: Money & Investing Update*, March 12, 1996.

CHARLES SCHWAB IN 2008

INTRODUCTION

In 1971, Charles Schwab, who was 32 at the time, set up his own stock brokerage concern, First Commander. Later he would change the name to Charles Schwab & Company, Inc. In 1975, when the Securities and Exchange Commission (SEC) abolished mandatory fixed commissions on stock trades, Schwab moved rapidly into the discount brokerage business, offering rates that were as much as 60% below those offered by full commission brokers. Over the next 25 years, the company experienced strong growth, fueled by a customer-centric focus, savvy investments in information technology (IT), and a number of product innovations, including a bold move into online trading in 1996.

By 2000, the company was widely regarded as one of the great success stories of the era. Revenues had grown to $7.1 billion and net income to $803 million, up from $1.1 billion and $124 million, respectively, in 1993. Online trading had grown to account for 84% of all stock trades made through Schwab, up from nothing in 1995. The company's stock price had appreciated by more than that of Microsoft over the prior 10 years. In 1999, the market value of Schwab eclipsed that of Merrill Lynch, the country's largest full-service broker, despite Schwab's revenues being more than 60% lower.

However, 2000 proved to be a high water mark. Between March 2000 and mid-2003, share prices in the United States tumbled, with the technology heavy NASDAQ index losing 80% of its value from peak to trough. The volume of online trading at Schwab slumped from an average of 204,000 trades a day in 2000 to 112,000 trades a day in 2002. In 2003, revenues fell to $4.3 billion, net income fell to $472 million, and the stock price fell from a high of $51.70 a share in 1999 to a low of $6.30 in early 2003. For Schwab, the key strategic question was how to reverse the decline, revitalize growth, and attain the company's goal of 20% a year revenue growth and a profit margin greater than 12%.

THE SECURITIES BROKERAGE INDUSTRY[1]

A security refers to financial instruments, such as stocks, bonds, commodity contracts, stock option contracts, and foreign exchange contracts. The securities brokerage industry is concerned with the issuance and trading of financial securities, as well as a number of related activities. A broker's clients may be individuals, corporations, or government bodies. Brokers undertake one or more of the following functions: assist corporations to raise capital by offering stocks and bonds; help governments raise capital through bond issues; give advice to businesses on their foreign currency needs; assist corporations with mergers and acquisitions; help individuals plan their financial future and trade financial securities; and provide detailed investment research to individuals and institutions so that they can make more informed investment decisions.

This case was prepared by Charles W. L. Hill, University of Washington. Reprinted by permission.

Industry Background

In 2007, there were just over 5,000 broker-dealers registered in the United States, down from 9,515 in 1987. The industry is concentrated with some 195 firms that are members of the New York Stock Exchange (NYSE) accounting for 86% of the assets of all broker-dealers and 75% of the revenue and capital. The 10 largest NYSE firms accounted for 73.6% of the gross revenue in the industry in 2007, up from 48% in 1998. The consolidation of the industry has been driven in part by deregulation, which is discussed in more detail following.

Broker-dealers make their money in a number of ways. They earn commissions (or fees) for executing a customer's order to buy or sell a given security (stocks, bonds, option contracts, etc.). They earn trading income, which is the realized and unrealized gains and losses on securities held and traded by the brokerage firm. They earn money from underwriting fees, which are the fees charged to corporate and government clients for managing an issue of stocks or bonds on their behalf. They earn asset management fees, which represent income from the sale of mutual fund securities, from account supervision fees, or from investment advisory or administrative service fees. They earn margin interest, which is the interest that customers pay to the brokerage when they borrow against the value of their securities to finance purchases. They earn other securities-related revenue from private placement fees (i.e., fees from private equity deals), subscription fees for research services, charges for advisory work on proposed mergers and acquisitions, fees for options done away from an exchange, and so on. Finally, many brokerages earn nonsecurites revenue from other financial services, such as credit card operations or mortgage services.

Exhibit 1 illustrates the breakdown between the various income sources for brokers in 2004 and 2007. Of particular note is the surge in "other securities revenue" in 2007. This reflects the boom in private equity deals, derivatives contracts, and associated fees that were *not* executed through an exchange and therefore were unregulated. The high volume of derivatives, in particular, was a major factor in the 2008 turmoil in global financial markets because many of the derivatives were tied to mortgage-backed securities, the value of which collapsed during 2008.

Exhibit 1 Brokers' Line of Business, as a Percentage of Revenues, 2004 and 2007

Item	2004 (%)	2007 (%)
Commissions	16.5	8.2
Trading Gain	10.9	−2.9
Investment Gain	1.04	0.9
Underwriting	10.5	6.6
Margin Interest	3.9	8.3
Asset Management Fees	8.8	6.1
Commodities	0.6	0.2
Other Securities Revenue	37.2	60.4
Other Revenue	6.8	10

Source: SIFMA.

Industry Groups

Brokerage firms can be segmented into five groups. First, there are national full line firms, which are the largest full-service brokers with extensive branch systems. They provide virtually every financial service and product that a brokerage can offer to both households (retail customers) and institutions (corporations, governments, and other nonprofit organizations such as universities). Examples of such firms include Merrill Lynch, Salomon Smith Barney, and A.G. Edwards. Most of these firms are headquartered in New York. For retail customers, national full-line firms provide access to personal financial consultants; traditional brokerage services; securities research reports; asset management services; financial planning advice; and a range of other services, such as margin loans, mortgage loans, and credit cards. For institutional clients, these firms will also arrange and underwrite the issuance of financial securities, manage their financial assets, provide advice on mergers and acquisitions, and provide more detailed research reports than those normally provided to retail customers, often for a fee.

Large investment banks are a second group. This group includes Lehman Brothers, Bear Stearns, Goldman Sachs, and Morgan Stanley. These banks have a limited branch network and focus primarily on institutional clients, although they also may have a retail business focused on high net worth individuals (typically individuals with more than $1 million to invest). In 2008, Lehman Brothers went bankrupt, a casualty of bad bets on mortgage-backed securities, while the large bank, JP Morgan, acquired Bear Stearns, leaving Goldman Sachs as the sole standalone representative in this class.

A third group are regional brokers, which are full-service brokerage operations with a branch network in certain regions of the country. Regional brokers typically focus on retail customers, although some have an institutional presence.

Fourth, there are a number of New York City-based brokers, who conduct a broad array of financial services, including brokerage, investment banking, traditional money management, and so on.

Finally, there are the discounters, who are primarily involved in the discount brokerage business and focus on executing orders to buy and sell stocks for retail customers. Commissions are their main source of business revenue. They charge lower commissions than full-service brokers but do not offer the same infrastructure such as personal financial consultants and detailed research reports. The discounters provide trading and execution services at deep discounts online via the Web. Many discounters, such as Ameritrade and E*Trade, do not maintain branch offices. Schwab, which was one of the first discounters, and remains the largest, has a network of brick-and-mortar offices, as well as a leading online presence.

Earnings Trends

Industry revenues and earnings are volatile, being driven by variations in the volume of trading activity (and commissions), underwriting, and merger and acquisition activity. All of these tend to be highly correlated with changes in the value of interest rates and the stock market. In general, when interest rates fall, the cost of borrowing declines so corporations and governments tend to issue more securities, which increases underwriting income. Also, low interest rates tend to stimulate economic growth, which leads to higher corporate profits and thus higher stock values. When interest rates decline, individuals typically move some of their money out of low interest-bearing cash accounts or low yielding bonds and into stocks, in an attempt to earn higher returns. This drives up trading volume and hence commissions. Low interest rates, by reducing the cost of borrowing, can also increase merger and acquisition activity. Moreover, in a rising stock market, corporations often use their stock as currency with which to make acquisitions of other companies. This drives up merger and acquisition activity and the fees brokerages earn from such activity.

The 1990s was characterized by one of the strongest stock market advances in history (see Exhibit 2, which shows the value of the Standard and Poor's (S&P) 500 stock market index between January 1990 and October 2008). This was driven by a favorable economic environment, including falling interest rates, new IT advances, productivity gains in American industry, and steady economic expansion,

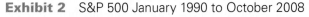

Exhibit 2   S&P 500 January 1990 to October 2008

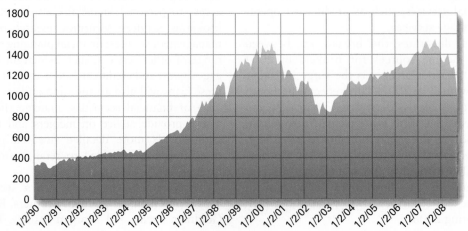

all of which translated into growing corporate profits and rising stock prices.

Also feeding the stock market's advance during the 1990s were favorable demographic trends. During the 1990s, American baby boomers started to save for retirement, pumping significant assets into equity funds. In 1989, some 32.5% of United States households owned equities. By 2002, the figure had risen to 49.5%; by 2005, it stood at 50.3%. In 1975, some 45% of the liquid financial assets of American households were in financial securities, including stocks, bonds, mutual funds, and money market funds. By 2007, this figure had increased to 72%. The total value of household liquid financial assets increased from $1.7 trillion to $21.5 trillion over the same period.[2]

Adding fuel to the fire, by the late 1990s, stock market mania had taken hold. Stock prices rose to speculative highs rarely seen before, as "irrationally exuberant" retail investors who seemed to believe that stock prices could only go up made increasingly risky and speculative "investments" in richly valued equities.[3] The market peaked in late 2000 as the extent of overvaluation became apparent. It fell significantly over the next two years as the economy struggled with a recession. This was followed by a recovery in both the economy and the stock market, with the S&P 500 returning to its old highs by October 2007. However, as the global credit crunch unfolded in 2008, the market crashed, falling precipitously in the second half of 2008 to return to levels not seen since 1998.

The long stock market boom drove an expansion of industry revenues, which, for brokerages that were members of the NYSE, grew from $54 billion in 1990 to $245 billion in 2000. As the bubble burst and the stock market slumped in 2001 and 2002, and brokerage revenues plummeted to $144 billion in 2003, forcing brokerages to cut expenses. By 2007, revenues had recovered again and were at $352 billion, although the sharp decline in the stock market during 2008 clearly depressed revenues for 2008.

The expense structure of the brokerage industry is dominated by two big items: interest expenses and compensation expenses (see Exhibit 3). Together these account for about three quarters of industry expenses. Interest expenses reflect the interest rate paid on cash deposits at brokerages and rise or fall with the size of deposits and interest rates. As such, they are generally not regarded as a controllable expense (since the interest rate is ultimately set by the U.S. Federal Reserve and market forces). Compensation expenses reflect both employee headcount and bonuses. For some brokerage firms, particularly those dealing with institutional clients, bonuses can be enormous, with multimillion dollar bonuses being awarded to productive employees. Compensation expenses and employee headcount tend to grow during bull markets, only to be rapidly curtailed once a bear market sets in.

Exhibit 3 Expense Structure of Brokerages, 1990–2007

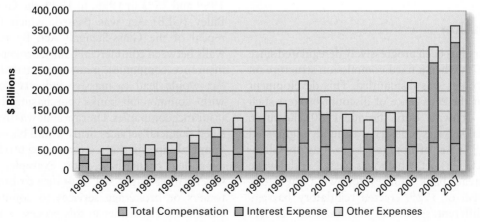

Source: SIFMA.

Exhibit 4   Return on Equity Brokerage (%) Industry, 1990–2007

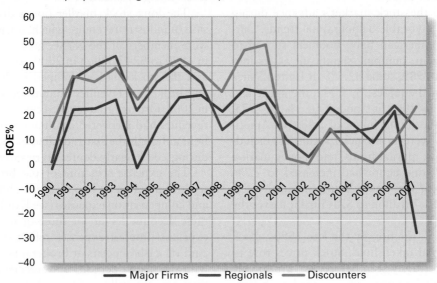

Source: SIFMA.

As shown in Exhibit 4, which graphs the return on equity (ROE) in the brokerage industry between 1990 and 2007, the profitability of the industry is volatile and depends critically on the overall level of stock market activity. Profits were high during the boom years of the 1990s. The bursting of the stock market bubble in 2000–2001 bought a period of low profitability, and although profitability improved after 2002, it did not return to the levels of the 1990s. The financial crisis and stock market crash of 2008 resulted in very low profitability for the industry.

Deregulation

The industry has been progressively deregulated since May 1, 1975, when a fixed commission structure on securities trades was dismantled. This development allowed for the emergence of discount brokers such as Charles Schwab. Until the mid-1980s, however, the financial services industry was highly segmented due to a 1933 Act of Congress known as the Glass-Steagall Act. This act, which was passed in the wake of widespread bank failures following the stock market crash of 1929, erected regulatory barriers between different sectors of the financial services industry, such as commercial banking, insurance,

savings and loans, and investment services (including brokerages). Most significantly, Section 20 of the act erected a wall between commercial banking and investment services, barring commercial banks from investing in shares of stocks, limiting them to buying and selling securities as an agent, prohibiting them from underwriting and dealing in securities and being affiliated with any organization that did so.

In 1987, Section 20 was relaxed to allow banks to earn up to 5% of their revenue from securities underwriting. The limit was raised to 10% in 1989 and 25% in 1996. In 1999, the Gramm-Leach-Bliley (GLB) Act was passed, which finalized the repeal of the Glass-Steagall Act. By removing the walls between commercial banks, broker-dealers, and insurance companies, many predicted that the GLB Act would lead to massive industry consolidation, with commercial banks purchasing brokers and insurance companies. The rationale was that such diversified financial services firms would become one-stop financial supermarkets, cross-selling products to their expanded client base. For example, a financial supermarket might sell insurance to brokerage customers or brokerage services to commercial bank customers. The leader in this process was Citigroup, which was formed in 1998 by a merger between

Citicorp, a commercial bank, and Traveler's, an insurance company. Since Traveler's had already acquired Salomon Smith Barney, a major brokerage firm, the new Citigroup seemed to signal a new wave of consolidation in the industry. The passage of the GLB Act allowed Citigroup to start cross-selling products.

However, industry reports suggest that cross-selling is easier in theory than practice, in part because customers were not ready for the development.[4] In an apparent admission that this was the case, in 2002, Citigroup announced that it would spin off Traveler's Insurance as a separate company. At the same time, the GLB Act made it easier for commercial banks to get into the brokerage business, and there have been several acquisitions to this effect. Most notably, in 2008, Bank of America purchased Merrill Lynch, and JP Morgan Chase purchased Bear Stearns. Both of the acquired enterprises were suffering from serious financial troubles due to their exposure to mortgage-backed securities.

THE GROWTH OF SCHWAB

The son of an assistant district attorney in California, Charles Schwab started to exhibit an entrepreneurial streak from an early age. As a boy, he picked walnuts and bagged them for $5 per 100-pound sack. He raised chickens in his backyard, sold the eggs door to door, killed and plucked the fryers for market, and peddled the manure as fertilizer. Schwab called it "my first fully integrated businesses."[5]

As a child, Schwab had to struggle with a severe case of dyslexia, a disorder that makes it difficult to process written information. To keep up with his classes, he had to resort to Cliffs Notes and Classics Illustrated comic books. Schwab believes, however, that his dyslexia was ultimately a motivator, spurring him on to overcome the disability and excel. Schwab excelled enough to gain admission to Stanford, where he received a degree in economics, which was followed by an MBA from Stanford Business School.

Fresh out of Stanford in the 1960s, Schwab embarked on his first entrepreneurial effort, an investment advisory newsletter, which grew to include a mutual fund with $20 million under management. However, after the stock market fell sharply in 1969, the state of Texas ordered Schwab to stop accepting investments through the mail from its citizens because the fund was not registered to do business in the state. Schwab went to court and lost. Ultimately, he had to close his business, leaving him with $100,000 in debt and a marriage that had collapsed under the emotional strain.

The Early Days

Schwab soon bounced back. Capitalized by $100,000 that he borrowed from his uncle Bill, who had a successful industrial company of his own called Commander Corp., in 1971 Schwab started a new company, First Commander. Based in San Francisco, a world away from Wall Street, First Commander was a conventional brokerage that charged clients fixed commissions for securities trades. The name was changed to Charles Schwab the following year.

In 1974, at the suggestion of a friend, Schwab joined a pilot test of discount brokerages being conducted by the SEC. The discount brokerage idea instantly appealed to Schwab. He personally hated selling, particularly cold calling—the constant calling on actual or prospective customers to encourage them to make a stock trade. Moreover, Schwab was deeply disturbed by the conflict of interest that seemed everywhere in the brokerage world, with stock brokers encouraging customers to make questionable trades to boost commissions. Schwab also questioned the worth of the investment advice brokers gave clients, feeling that it reflected the inherent conflict of interest in the brokerage business and did not empower customers.

Schwab used the pilot test to fine-tune his model for a discount brokerage. When the SEC abolished mandatory fixed commissions the following year, Schwab quickly moved into the business. His basic thrust was to empower investors by giving them the information and tools required to make their own decisions about securities investments, while keeping Schwab's costs low so that this service could be offered at a deep discount to the commissions charged by full-service brokers. Driving down costs meant that unlike full-service brokers, Schwab did not employ financial analysts and researchers who developed proprietary investment research for the firm's clients. Instead, Schwab focused on providing clients with third-party investment research. These "reports" evolved to include a company's financial history, a smattering of comments from securities analysts at other brokerage firms that had appeared in the news, and a tabulation of buy and sell recommendations from full commission brokerage houses. The reports were sold to Schwab's customers at cost (in 1992 this was $9.50 for each report plus $4.75 for each additional report).[6]

A founding principle of the company was a desire to be the most useful and ethical provider of financial services. Underpinning this move was Schwab's own belief in the inherent conflict of interest between brokers at full-service firms and their clients. The desire to avoid a conflict of interest caused Schwab to rethink the traditional commission-based pay structure. As an alternative to commission-based pay, Schwab paid all of its employees, including its brokers, a salary plus a bonus that was tied to attracting and satisfying customers and achieving productivity and efficiency targets. Commissions were taken out of the compensation equation.

The chief promoter of Schwab's approach to business, and marker of the Schwab brand, was none other than Charles Schwab himself. In 1977, Schwab started to use pictures of Charles Schwab in its advertisements, a practice it still follows today.

The customer-centric focus of the company led Schwab to think of ways to make the company accessible to customers. In 1975, Schwab became the first discount broker to open a branch office and offer access 24 hours a day, seven days a week. Interestingly, however, the decision to open a branch was not something that Charles Schwab initially embraced. He wanted to keep costs low and thought it would be better if everything could be managed by way of a telephone. However, Charles Schwab was forced to ask his uncle Bill for more capital to get his nascent discount brokerage off the ground. Bill agreed to invest $300,000 in the company but on one condition, he insisted that Schwab open a branch office in Sacramento and employ Bill's son-in-law as manager![7] Reluctantly, Charles Schwab agreed to Bill's demand for a show of nepotism, hoping that the branch would not be too much of a drain on the company's business.

What happened next was a surprise; there was an immediate and dramatic increase in activity at Schwab, most of it from Sacramento. Customer inquiries, the number of trades per day, and the number of new accounts, all spiked upward. Yet there was also a puzzle here, for the increase was not linked to an increase in foot traffic in the branch. Intrigued, Schwab opened several more branches over the next year, and each time noticed the same pattern. For example, when Schwab opened its first branch in Denver, it had 300 customers. It added another 1,700 new accounts in the months following the opening of the branch, and yet there was a big spike up in foot traffic at the Denver branch.

What Schwab began to realize is that the branches served a powerful psychological purpose; they gave customers a sense of security that Schwab was a real company. Customers were reassured by seeing a branch with people in it. In practice, many clients would rarely visit a branch. They would open an account and execute trades over the telephone (or later, via the Internet). But the branch helped them to make that first commitment. Far from being a drain, Schwab realized that the branches were a marketing tool. People wanted to be "perceptually close to their money," and the branches satisfied that deep psychological need. From one branch in 1975, Schwab grew to 52 branches in 1982, 175 by 1992, and 430 in 2002. The next few years bought retrenchment, however, and Schwab's branches fell to about 300 by 2008.

By the mid-1980s, customers could access Schwab in person at a branch during office hours, by phone day or night, by a telephone voice recognition quote and trading service known as TeleBroker, and by an innovative proprietary online network. To encourage customers to use TeleBroker or its online trading network, Schwab reduced commissions on transactions executed this way by 10%, but it saved much more than that because doing business via computers was cheaper. By 1995, Telebroker was handling 80 million calls and 10 million trades a year, 75% of Schwab's annual volume. To service this system, in the mid-1980s, Schwab invested $20 million in four regional customer call centers, routing all calls to them rather than branches. Today, these call centers have 4,000 employees.

Schwab was the first to establish a computer-based online trading system in 1986, with the introduction of its Equalizer service. The system had 15,000 customers in 1987 and 30,000 by the end of 1988. The online system, which required a PC with a modem, allowed investors to check current stock prices, place orders, and check their portfolios. In addition, an "offline" program for PCs enabled investors to do fundamental and technical analysis on securities. To encourage customers to start using the system, there was no additional charge for using the online system after a $99 sign-up fee. In contrast, other discount brokers with PC-based online systems, such as Quick and Riley's (which had a service known as "Quick Way") or Fidelity's (whose service was called "Fidelity Express"), charged users between 10 cents and 44 cents a minute for online access depending on the time of day.[8]

Schwab's pioneering move into online trading was in many ways just an evolution of the company's early utilization of technology. In 1979, Schwab spent $2 million, an amount equivalent to the company's entire net worth at the time, to purchase a used IBM System 360 computer, plus software, that was left over from CBS's 1976 election coverage. At the time, brokerages generated and had to process massive amounts of paper to execute buy and sell orders. The computer gave Schwab a capability that no other brokerage had at the time; take a buy or sell order that came in over the phone, edit it on a computer screen, and then submit the order for processing without generating paper. Not only did the software provide for instant execution of orders, it also offered what were then sophisticated quality controls, checking a customer's account to see if funds were available before executing a transaction. As a result of this system, Schwab's costs plummeted as it took paper out of the system. Moreover, the cancel and rebill rate—a measure of the accuracy of trade executions—dropped from an average of 4% to 0.1%.[9] Schwab soon found it could handle twice the transaction volume of other brokers, at less cost, and with much greater accuracy. Within two years, every other broker in the nation had developed similar systems, but Schwab's early investment had given it an edge and underpinned the company's belief in the value of technology to reduce costs and empower customers.

By 1982, the technology at Schwab was well ahead of that used by most full-service brokers. It was this commitment to technology that allowed Schwab to offer a product that was similar in conception to Merrill Lynch's revolutionary Cash Management Account (CMA), which was introduced in 1980. The CMA account automatically sweeps idle cash into money market funds and allows customers to draw on their money by check or credit card. Schwab's system, known as the Schwab One Account, was introduced in 1982. It went beyond

Merrill's in that it allowed brokers to execute orders instantly through Schwab's computer link to the exchange floor.

In 1984, Schwab moved into the mutual fund business, not by offering its own mutual funds but by launching a mutual fund marketplace, which allowed customers to invest in some 140 no-load mutual funds (a "no-load" fund has no sales commission). By 1990, the number of funds in the marketplace was 400, and the total assets involved exceeded $2 billion. For the mutual fund companies, the mutual fund marketplace offered distribution to Schwab's growing customer base. For its part, Schwab kept a small portion of the revenue stream that flowed to the fund companies from Schwab clients.

In 1986, Schwab made a gutsy move to eliminate the fees for managing Individual Retirement Accounts (IRAs). IRAs allow customers to deposit money in an account where it accumulates tax free until withdrawal at retirement. The legislation establishing IRAs had been passed by Congress in 1982. At the time, estimates suggest that IRAs could attract as much as $50 billion in assets within 10 years. In actual fact, the figure turned out to be $725 billion.

Initially, Schwab followed industry practice and collected a small fee for each IRA. By 1986, the fees amounted to $9 million a year, not a trivial amount for Schwab in those days. After looking at the issue, Charles Schwab himself made the call to scrap the fee, commenting that "It's a nuisance, and we'll get it back."[10] He was right; Schwab's No-Annual Fee IRA immediately exceeded the company's most optimistic projections.

Despite technological and product innovations, by 1983, Schwab was scrapped for capital to fund expansion. To raise funds, he sold the company to Bank of America for $55 million in stock and a seat on the bank's board of directors. The marriage did not last long. By 1987, the bank was reeling under loan losses, and the entrepreneurially minded Schwab was frustrated by banking regulations that inhibited his desire to introduce new products. Using a mix of loans, his own money, and contributions from other managers, friends, and family, Schwab led a management buyout of the company for $324 million in cash and securities.

Six months later on September 22, 1987, Schwab went public with an IPO that raised some $440 million, enabling the company to pay down debt and leaving it with capital to fund an aggressive expansion. At the time, Schwab had 1.6 million customers, revenues of $308 million, and a pretax profit margin of 21%. Schwab announced plans to increase its branch network by 30% to approximately 120 offices over the next year. Then on Monday, October 19, 1987, the United States stock market crashed, dropping over 22%, the biggest one-day decline in history.

October 1987–1995

After a strong run up over the year, on Friday, October 16, the stock market dropped 4.6%. During the weekend, nervous investors jammed the call centers and branch offices, not just at Schwab but at many other brokerages, as they tried to place sell orders. At Schwab, 99% of the orders taken over the weekend for Monday morning were sell orders. As the market opened on Monday morning, it went into freefall. At Schwab, the computers were overwhelmed by 8 a.m. The toll-free number to the call centers was also totally overwhelmed. All the customers got when they called were busy signals. When the dust had settled, Schwab announced that it had lost $22 million in the fourth quarter of 1987, $15 million of which came from a single customer who had been unable to meet margin calls.

The loss, which amounted to 13% of the company's capital, effectively wiped out the company's profit for the year. Moreover, the inability of customers to execute trades during the crash damaged Schwab's hard-earned reputation for customer service. Schwab responded by posting a two-page ad in the *Wall Street Journal* on October 28, 1987. On one page, there was a message from Charles Schwab thanking customers for their patience, and on the other page was an ad thanking employees for their dedication.

In the aftermath of the October 1987 crash, trading volume fell by 15% as customers, spooked by the volatility of the market, sat on cash balances. The slowdown prompted Schwab to cut back on its expansion plans. Ironically, however, Schwab added a significant number of new accounts in the aftermath of the crash as people looked for cheaper ways to invest.[11]

Beset by week trading volume over the next 18 months and reluctant to lay off employees, Schwab sought ways to boost activity. One strategy started out as a compliance issue within Schwab. A compliance officer in the company noticed a disturbing pattern; a number of people had given other people limited power of attorney over their accounts. This in itself was not unusual—for example, the middle-aged children of elderly individuals might have power of attorney over their accounts—but what the Schwab officer noticed was that some individuals had power of attorney over dozens, if not hundreds, of accounts.

Further investigation turned up the reason—Schwab had been serving an entirely unknown set of customers, independent financial advisors who were managing the financial assets of their clients using Schwab accounts. In early 1989, there were some 500 financial advisors who managed assets totaling $1.5 billion at Schwab, about 8% of all assets at Schwab.

The advisors were attracted to Schwab for a number of reasons, including cost and the company's commitment not to give advice—which was the business of the advisors. When Charles Schwab heard about this, he immediately saw an opportunity. Financial advisors, he reasoned, represented a powerful way to acquire customers. In 1989, the company rolled out a program to aggressively court this group. Schwab hired a marketing team and told them to focus explicitly on financial planners, set apart a dedicated trading desk for them, and gave discounts of as much as 15% on commissions to financial planners with significant assets under management at Schwab accounts. Schwab also established a Financial Advisors Service, which provided its clients with a list of financial planners who were willing to work solely for a fee and had no incentive to push the products of a particular client. At the same time, the company stated that it was not endorsing the planners' advice, which would run contrary to the company's commitment to offer no advice. Within a year, financial advisors had some $3 billion of client's assets under management at Schwab.

Schwab also continued to expand its branch network during this period, at a time when many brokerages, still stunned by the October 1987 debacle, were retrenching. Between 1987 and 1989, Schwab's branch network increased by just five, from 106 to 111, but in 1990, it opened up an additional 29 branches and another 28 in 1991.

By the 1990s, Schwab's positioning in the industry had become clear. Although a discounter, Schwab was by no means the lowest-price discount broker in the country. Its average commission structure

Exhibit 5   Commission Structure in 1990

Type of Broker	Average Commission Price on 20 Trades Averaging $8,975 Each
Deep Discount Brokers	$ 54
Average Discounters	$ 73
Banks	$ 88
Schwab, Fidelity, and Quick & Reilly	$ 92
Full-Service Brokers	$206

Source: E.C. Gottschalk, "Schwab Forges Ahead as Other Brokers Hesitate," *Wall Street Journal*, May 11, 1990, C1.

was similar to that of Fidelity, the Boston-based mutual fund company that had moved into the discount brokerage business, and Quick & Reilly, a major national competitor (see Exhibit 5). While significantly below that of full-service brokers, the fee structure was also above that of deep discount brokers. Schwab differentiated itself from the deep discount brokers, however, by its branch network, technology, and the information (not advice) that it gave to investors.

In 1992 Schwab rolled out another strategy aimed at acquiring assets—OneSource, the first mutual fund "supermarket." OneSource was created to take advantage of America's growing appetite for mutual funds. By the early 1990s, there were more mutual funds than individual equities. On some days, Fidelity, the largest mutual fund company, accounted for 10% of the trading volume on the New York Stock Exchange. As American baby boomers aged, they seemed to have an insatiable appetite for mutual funds. But the process of buying and selling mutual finds had never been easy. As Charles Schwab explained in 1996:

> In the days before the supermarkets, to buy a mutual fund you had to write or call the fund distributor. On Day Six, you'd get a prospectus. On Day Seven or Eight you call up and they say you've got to put your money in. If you're lucky, by Day Ten you've bought it. . . . It was even more cumbersome when you redeemed. You had to send a notarized redemption form.[12]

OneSource took the hassle out of owning funds. With a single visit to a branch office, telephone call, or PC-based computer transaction, a Schwab client could buy and sell mutual funds. Schwab imposed no fee on investors for the service. Rather, in return for shelf space in Schwab's distribution channel and access to the more than 2 million accounts at Schwab, Schwab charged the fund companies a fee amounting to 0.35% of the assets under management. By inserting itself between the fund managers and customers, Schwab changed the balance of power in the mutual fund industry. When Schwab sold a fund through OneSource, it passed along the assets to the fund managers but not the customers' names. Many fund managers did not like this because it limited their ability to build a direct relationship with customers, but they had little choice if they wanted access to Schwab's customer base.

OneSource quickly propelled Schwab to the number-three position in direct mutual fund distribution, behind the fund companies Fidelity and Vanguard. By 1997, Schwab customers could choose from nearly 1,400 funds offered by 200 different fund families, and Schwab customers had nearly $56 billion in assets invested through OneSource.

1996–2000: eSchwab

In 1994, as access to the World Wide Web began to diffuse rapidly throughout America, a two-year-old start-up run by Bill Porter, a physicist and inventor, launched its first dedicated Web site for online trading. The company's name was E*Trade. E*Trade announced a flat $14.95 commission on stock trades, significantly below Schwab's average commission, which at the time $65. It was clear from the outset that E*Trade and other online brokers, such as Ameritrade, offered a direct threat to Schwab. Not only were their commission rates considerably below those of Schwab, but the ease, speed, and flexibility of trading stocks over the Web suddenly made Schwab's proprietary online trading software, Street Smart, seemed limited. (Street Smart was the Windows-based successor to Schwab's DOS-based Equalizer program.) To compound matters, talented people started to leave Schwab for E*Trade and its brethren, which they saw as the wave of the future.

At the time, deep within Schwab, William Pearson, a young software specialist who had worked on the development of Street Smart, quickly saw the transformational power of the Web and believed that it would make proprietary systems like Street Smart obsolete. Pearson believed that Schwab needed to develop its own Web-based software—and quickly. Try as he might, though, Pearson could not get the attention of his supervisor. He tried a number of other executives but found support hard to come by. Eventually he approached Anne Hennegar, a former Schwab manager who now worked as a consultant to the company. Hennegar suggest that Pearson meet with Tom Seip, an executive vice president at Schwab who was known for his ability to think outside of the box. Hennegar approached Seip on Pearson's behalf, and Seip responded positively, asking her to set up a meeting. Hennegar and Pearson turned up expecting to meet just Seip, but to their surprise in walked Charles Schwab, his chief operating officer, David Pottruck, and the vice presidents in charge of strategic planning and the electronic brokerage arena.

As the group watched Pearson's demo of how a Web-based system would look and work, they became increasingly excited. It was clear to those in the room that a Web-based system based on real-time information, personalization, customization, and interactivity all advanced Schwab's commitment to empowering customers. By the end of the meeting, Pearson had received a green light to start work on the project.

It soon transpired that several other groups within Schwab had been working on projects that were similar to Pearson's. These were all pulled together under the control of Dawn Lepore, Schwab's chief information officer, who headed up the effort to develop the Web-based service that would ultimately become eSchwab. Meanwhile, significant strategic issues were now beginning to preoccupy Charles Schwab and David Pottruck. They realized that Schwab's established brokerage and a Web-based brokerage business were based on very different revenue and cost models. The Web-based business would probably cannibalize business from Schwab's established brokerage operations, and that might lead people in Schwab to slow down or even derail the Web-based initiative. As Pottruck later put it:

The new enterprise was going to use a different model for making money than our traditional business, and we didn't want the comparisons to form the basis for a measurement of success or failure. For example, eSchwab's per trade revenue would be less than half that of the mainstream of the company, and that could be seen as a drain on resources rather than a response to what customer would be using in the future.[13]

Pottruck and Schwab understood that unless eSchwab was placed in its own organization, isolated and protected from the established business, it might never get off the ground. They also knew that if they did not cannibalize their own business with eSchwab, someone would do it for them. Thus they decided to set up a separate organization to develop eSchwab. The unit was headed up by Beth Sawi, a highly regarded marketing manager at Schwab who had very good relations with other managers in the company. Sawi set up the development center in a unit physically separated from other Schwab facilities.

eSchwab was launched in May 1996 but without the normal publicity that accompanied most new products at Schwab. Schwab abandoned its sliding scale commission for a flat rate commission of $39 (which was quickly dropped to $29.95) for any stock trade up to 1,000 shares. Within two weeks 25,000 people had opened eSchwab accounts. By the end of 1997, the figure would soar to 1.2 million, bringing in assets of about $81 billion, or 10 times the assets of E*Trade.

Schwab initially kept the two businesses segmented. Schwab's traditional customers were still paying an average of $65 a trade, while eSchwab customers were paying $29.95. While Schwab's traditional customers could make toll-free calls to Schwab brokers, eSchwab clients could not. Moreover, Schwab's regular customers could not access eSchwab at all. The segmentation soon gave rise to problems. Schwab's branch employees were placed in the uncomfortable position of telling customers that they couldn't set up eSchwab accounts. Some eSchwab customers started to set up traditional Schwab accounts with small sums of money so that they could access Schwab's brokers and Schwab's information services while continuing to trade via eSchwab. Clearly the segmentation was not sustainable.

Schwab began to analyze the situation. The company's leaders realized that the cleanest way to deal with the problem would be to give every Schwab customer online access, adopt a commission of $29.95

on trading across all channels, and maintain existing levels of customer service at the branch level and on the phone. However, internal estimates suggested that the cut in commission rates would reduce revenues by $125 million, which would hit Schwab's stock. The problem was compounded by two factors: First, employees owned 40% of Schwab's stock, so they would be hurt by any fall in stock price, and second, employees were worried that going to the Web would result in a decline in business at the branch level and hence a loss of jobs there.

An internal debate ranged within the company for much of 1997, a year when Schwab's revenues surged 24% to $2.3 billion. The online trading business grew by more than 90% during the year, with online trades accounting for 37% of all Schwab trades during 1997, and the trend was up throughout the year.

Looking at these figures, Pottruck knew that Schwab had to bite the bullet and give all Schwab customers access to eSchwab (Pottruck was now running the day-to-day operations of Schwab, leaving Charles Schwab to focus on his corporate marketing and public relations role). His first task was to enroll the support of the company's largest shareholder, Charles Schwab. With 52 million shares, Charles Schwab would take the biggest hit from any share price decline. According to a *Fortune* article, the conversation between Schwab and Pottruck went something like this:[14]

Pottruck: "We don't know exactly what will happen. The budget is shaky. We'll be winging it."

Schwab: "We can always adjust our costs."

Pottruck: "Yes, but we don't have to do this now. The whole year could be lousy. And the stock!"

Schwab: "This isn't that hard a decision because we really have no choice. It's just a question of when, and it will be harder later."

Having the agreement of Schwab's founder, Pottruck formed a task force to look at how best to implement the decision. The plan that emerged was to merge all of the company's electronic services into Schwab.com, which would then coordinate Schwab's online and off-line business. The base commission rate would be $29.95 for whatever channel was used to make a trade—online, branch, or the telephone. The role of the branches would change, and they would start to focus more on customer support.

This required a change in incentive systems. Branch employees had been paid bonuses on the basis of the assets they accrued to their branches, but now they would be paid bonuses on assets that came in via the branch or the Web. They would be rewarded for directing clients to the Web.

Schwab implemented the change of strategy on January 15, 1998. Revenues dropped 3% in the first quarter, as the average commission declined from $63 to $57. Earnings also came in short of expectations by some $6 million. The company's stock had lost 20% of its value by August 1998. However, during much of 1998 new money poured into Schwab. Total accounts surged, with Schwab gaining a million new customers in 1998, a 20% increase, while assets grew by 32%. As the year progressed, trading volume grew, doubling by year end. By the third quarter, Schwab's revenues and earnings were surging past analysts' expectations. The company ultimately achieved record revenues and earnings in 1998. Net income ended up 29% over the prior year, despite falling commission rates, aided by surging trading volume and the lower cost of executing trades over the Web. By the end of the year, 61% of all trades at Schwab were made over the Web. After its summer lows, the stock price recovered, ending the year up 130%, pushing Schwab's market capitalization past that of Merrill Lynch.[15]

2000–2004: After the Boom

In 1998 Charles Schwab appointed his longtime number two, David Pottruck, co-CEO. The appointment signaled the beginning of a leadership transition, with Schwab easing himself out of day-to-day operations. Soon Pottruck had to deal with some major issues. The end of the long stock market boom of the 1990s hit Schwab hard. The average number of trades made per day through Schwab fell from 300 million to 190 million between 2000 and 2002. Reflecting this, revenues slumped from $7.1 billion to $4.14 billion and net income from $803 million to $109 million. To cope with the decline, Schwab was forced to cut back on its employee headcount, which fell from a peak of nearly 26,000 employees in 2000 to just over 16,000 in late 2003.

Schwab's strategic reaction to the sea change in market conditions was already taking form as the market implosion began. In January 2000, Schwab acquired U.S. Trust for $2.7 billion. U.S. Trust was a 149-year old investment advisement business that managed money for high net-worth individuals whose invested assets exceed $2 million. When acquired, U.S. Trust had 7,000 customers and assets of $84 billion, compared to 6.4 million customers and assets of $725 billion at Schwab.[16]

According to Pottruck, widely regarded as the architect of the acquisition, Schwab made the acquisition because it discovered that high-net-worth individuals were starting to defect from Schwab for money managers like U.S. Trust. The main reason: as Schwab's clients got older and richer, they started to need institutions that specialized in services that Schwab did not offer—including personal trusts, estate planning, tax services, and private banking. With baby boomers starting to enter middle to late-middle age, and their average net worth projected to rise, Schwab decided that it needed to get into this business or lose high-net-worth clients.

The decision though, started to bring Schwab into conflict with the network of 6,000 or so independent financial advisors that the company had long fostered through the Schwab Advisers Network and who funneled customers and assets into Schwab accounts. Some advisors felt that Schwab was starting to move in on their turf, and they were not too happy about it.

In May 2002, Schwab made another move in this direction when it announced that it would launch a new service targeted at clients with more than $500,000 in assets. Known as Schwab Private Client and developed with the help of U.S. Trust employees, for a fee of 0.6% of assets, Private Client customers can meet face to face with financial consultants to work out an investment plan and return to the same consultant for further advice. Schwab stressed that the consultant would not tell clients what to buy and sell—that is still left to the client. Nor will clients get the legal, tax, and estate planning advice offered by U.S. Trust and independent financial advisors. Rather, they get financial plans and consultations regarding industry and market conditions.[17]

To add power to this strategy, Schwab also announced that it would start a new stock rating system. The stock rating system is not the result of the work of financial analysts. Rather, it is the product of a computer model, developed at Schwab, that analyzes more than 3,000 stocks on 24 basic measures, such as free cash flow, sales growth, insider trades, and so on, and then assigns grades. The top 10% get

an A, the next 20% a B, the middle 40% a C, the next 20% a D, and the lowest 10% an F. Schwab claims that the new system is "a systematic approach with nothing but objectivity, not influenced by corporate relationships, investment banking, or any of the above."[18]

Critics of this strategy were quick to point out that many of Schwab's branch employees lacked the qualifications and expertise to give financial advice. At the time the service was announced, Schwab had some 150 qualified financial advisers in place and planned to have 300 by early 2003. These elite employees required a higher salary than the traditional Schwab branch employees, who in many respects were little more than order takers and providers of prepackaged information.

The Schwab Private Client service also caused further grumbling among the private financial advisors affiliated with Schwab. In 2002, there were 5,900 of these. In total, their clients amounted to $222 billion of Schwab's $765 billion in client assets. Several stated that they would no longer keep clients' money at Schwab. However, Schwab stated that it would use the Private Client Service as a device for referring people who wanted more sophisticated advice than Schwab could offer to its network of registered financial advisers and particularly an inner circle of 330 advisers who have an average of $500 million in assets under management and 17 years of experience.[19] According to one member of this group, "Schwab is not a threat to us. Most people realize the hand holding it takes to do that kind of work and Schwab wants us to do it. There's just more money behind the Schwab Advisors Network. The dead wood is gone, and firms like ours stand to benefit from even more additional leads."[20]

In 2003, Charles Schwab finally stepped down as co-CEO, leaving Pottruck in charge of the business (Charles Schwab stayed on as chairman). In late 2003, Pottruck announced that Schwab would acquire Soundview Technology Group for $321 million. Soundview was a boutique investment bank with a research arm that covered a couple of hundred companies and offered this research to institutional investors, such as mutual fund managers. Pottruck justified the acquisition by arguing that it would have taken Schwab years to build similar investment research capabilities internally. His plan was to have Soundview's research bundled for Schwab's retail investors.

2004–2008: The Return of Charles Schwab

The Soundview acquisition proved to be Pottruck's undoing. It soon became apparent that the acquisition was a huge mistake. There was little value to be had for Schwab's retail business from Soundview. Moreover, the move had raised Schwab's operating costs. By mid-2004, Pottruck was trying to sell Soundview. The board, which was disturbed at Pottruck's vacillating strategic leadership, expressed their concerns to Charles Schwab. On July 15, 2004, Pottruck was fired, and the 66-year-old Charles Schwab returned as CEO.

Charles Schwab moved quickly to refocus the company. Soundview was sold to the investment bank UBS for $265 million. Schwab reduced the workforce by another 2,400 employees, closed underperforming branches, and removed $600 million in annual cost. This allowed him to reduce commissions on stock trades by 45% and take market share from other discount brokers such as Ameritrade and E*Trade.

Going forward, Charles Schwab reemphasized the traditional mission of Schwab—to empower investors and provide them with ethical financial services. He also reemphasized the importance of the relationships that Schwab had with independent investment advisors. He noted, "Trading has become commoditized. The future is really about competing for client relationships."[21] One major new focus of Charles Schwab was the company's retail banking business. This had been established in 2002, but it had been a low priority for Pottruck. Schwab wanted to make the company a single source for banking, brokerage, and credit card services—one that would give Schwab's customers something of value—a personal relationship they could trust. The goal was to lessen Schwab's dependence on trading income and give it a more reliable earnings stream and a deeper relationship with clients.

In mid-2007, Schwab's reorientation back to its traditional mission reached a logical conclusion when U.S. Trust was sold to Bank of America for $3.3 billion. Unlike in the past, however, Schwab was no longer earning the bulk of its money from trading commissions. As a percentage of net revenues, trading revenues (mostly commissions on stock trades) was down from 36% in 2002 to 17% in 2007. By 2007, asset management fees accounted for 47% of Schwab's net revenue, up from 41% in 2002, while net interest revenue (the difference between earned interest on assets such as loans and interest paid on deposits) was 33%, up from 19% in 2002.[22] Schwab's overall performance had also improved markedly. Net income in 2007 was $1.12 billion, up from a low of $396 million in 2003. Moreover, while many financial service firms suffered sharp profit reversals in 2008, Schwab's earnings were not only stable but projected to hit a record $1.27 billion.

Endnotes

1. Material for this section is drawn from *Securities Industry and Financial Markets Association Fact Book 2008*, SIFMA, New York, 2008.
2. Securities Industry Association. *Key Trends in the Securities Industry*, November 7, 2002.
3. Robert E. Shiller. **Irrational Exuberance,** Princeton University Press, Princeton, NJ, 2002.
4. Anthony O'Donnell, "New Thinking on Convergence," *Wall Street & Technology*, May 2002, 16–18.
5. Terence P. Pare, "How Schwab Wins Investors," *Fortune*, June 1, 1992, 52–59.
6. Ibid.
7. John Kador, *Charles Schwab: How One Company Beat Wall Street and Reinvented the Brokerage Industry*, John Wiley & Sons, New York, 2002.
8. Earl C. Gottschalk, "Computerized Investment Systems Thrive as People Seek Control over Portfolios," *Wall Street Journal*, September 27, 1988, 1.
9. John Kador, *Charles Schwab: How One Company Beat Wall Street and Reinvented the Brokerage Industry*, John Wiley & Sons, New York, 2002.
10. Ibid.
11. G. C. Hill. "Schwab to Curb Expansion, Tighten Belt Because of Post Crash Trading Decline," *Wall Street Journal*, December 7, 1987, 1.
12. John Kador, *Charles Schwab: How One Company Beat Wall Street and Reinvented the Brokerage Industry*, John Wiley & Sons, New York, 2002, 185.
13. John Kador, *Charles Schwab: How One Company Beat Wall Street and Reinvented the Brokerage Industry*, John Wiley & Sons, New York, 2002, 217.
14. Erick Schonfeld, "Schwab Puts It All Online," *Fortune*, December 7, 1998, 94–99.
15. Anonymous, "Schwab's e-Gambit," *Business Week*, January 11, 1999, 61.

16. Amy Kover. "Schwab Makes a Grand Play for the Rich," *Fortune*, February 7, 2000, 32.
17. Louise Lee and Emily Thornton, "Schwab v Wall Street," *Business Week*, June 3, 2002, 64–70.
18. Quoted in Louise Lee and Emily Thornton, "Schwab v Wall Street," *Business Week*, June 3, 2002, 64–70.

19. Erin E. Arvedlund, "Schwab Trades Up," *Barron's*, May 27, 2002, 19–20.
20. Ibid.
21. B. Morris, "Charles Schwab's Big Challenge," *Fortune*, May 30, 2005, 88–98.
22. Charles Schwab, 2007 10K form.

WALT DISNEY COMPANY 1995–2009

"The Walt Disney Company's objective (mission) is to be one of the world's leading producers and providers of entertainment and information, using its portfolio of brands to differentiate its content, services, and consumer products."

(http://home.disney.go.com, **2009**)

In February 2009, Robert Iger CEO of Walt Disney reported that the company's profits had fallen by 32% in what was "likely to be the weakest economy in our lifetime." Just six months earlier, Disney had reported record revenues and profits as the company's performance had recovered under his leadership after he replaced Michael Eisner as CEO in 2005. How did Iger revive Disney's performance, and what was his strategy to respond to the global economic recession that began in 2008? To answer these questions, we need to examine how Iger reworked Disney's strategy and structure to respond to changing conditions in its environment.

DISNEY'S GROWING ENTERTAINMENT EMPIRE

Michael Eisner, Disney's former CEO, continued in the1990s to pursue the same strategy he had pursued with great success in the 1980s: building Disney's core strengths in the three areas of entertainment and recreation, motion pictures, and video and consumer products to take advantage of the value of Disney's franchises and brand name.

Entertainment and Recreation

In the entertainment area, Disney's top managers began by enlarging the size and variety of its theme parks and other entertainment properties. The number of attractions offered at its three Orlando properties—Disney World, EPCOT, and Disney. MGM—was continually expanded during the 1990s, although this significantly increased operating costs. Moreover, three water parks were now in operation, together with the Disney Vacation Club, Discovery Island, and the Disney Boardwalk. These properties extended Disney's hotel, restaurant, and shopping empire.

In 1995, Disney announced it would build a $500 million zoological park as its fourth property in Orlando, but it would be a zoo with a difference. Called Disney's "Wild Animal Kingdom," the 500-acre park is larger than any of Disney's parks worldwide. It has three main areas, showcasing live, extinct, and mythical animals. For example, the live animal section of the park features large herds of African animals, such as elephants and giraffes, in natural settings; the extinct section of the park features Disney's famous moving models (animatronics) of creatures such as dinosaurs and flying lizards; and the mythical section features creatures such as

---

This case was prepared by Gareth R. Jones, Texas A&M University.

For the most up-to-date financial results and analysis of the company in this case, go to http://finance.yahoo.com, click on symbol lookup at top of page, input the company's symbol into the search box, and then follow the appropriate links on the Yahoo page for the information you require (e.g., click profile to find link to company's Web site for its annual financial reports, or click on Yahoo links to the company's SEC filings or financials).

dragons and unicorns. Eisner hoped that the new property would attract both new and repeat visitors to its parks. When these visitors arrive, they have a reason to spend an extra day in the Disney empire, increasing the revenues that Disney receives from its hotels, catering, and shopping businesses.

Another entertainment venture Disney finalized was a revitalization of West 42nd Street in New York. The ambitious venture turned a near red-light district into a huge entertainment complex full of games, theaters, hotels, shops, and restaurants to attract tourists to New York City, which provided $35 million in financing to condemn and clear the buildings so that Disney and other entertainment companies such as Viacom could create a state-of-the-art entertainment complex. (Disney's cost more than $350 million.)

Studio Entertainment

Disney's movie studios also continued to grow throughout the 1990s. Walt Disney Pictures, Touchstone Pictures, Hollywood Pictures, and Buena Vista Pictures divisions continued to increase the number of movies they produced for distribution. Disney also acquired Miramax Pictures, a small company known for its production of high-quality, adult-oriented pictures, for about $60 million. Miramax's critically acclaimed movie output helped propel the revenues of its movie division throughout the next decade, as its films won many Oscars.

An important goal of the studio entertainment division was to take advantage of hit movies to propel the sale of millions of DVDs that contributed greatly to this division's profits. Disney learned the importance of this strategy from the blockbuster movie, *The Lion King,* Disney highest-grossing animated movie ever. The success of this movie extended into the videocassette market, followed by the DVD market, in which it sold more than 60 million copies. It also extended into consumer product areas: *Lion King* games, clothing, books, and so on, generating record profits for Disney—more than $2 billion to date. Disney subsequently opened a *Lion King* attraction at Disneyland to take advantage of the movie's success, and a *Lion King* theatre production has been touring the United States and Europe ever since with great success.

The success of *The Lion King* convinced Disney's executives that they needed to release a new animated movie each year to keep the revenues flowing into the movie division (and eventually into the consumer products division, too). In the 1990s, Disney released movies such as *Pocahontas* and *The Hunchback of Notre Dame*; however, it soon found discovered that these movies did not generate the blockbuster appeal of *The Lion King*. They did not produce the stream of high revenues and profits the studio division expected.

By the late 1990s, Disney's studio division had run into hard times. The Touchstone and Hollywood Pictures units had produced a string of failures, and to reduce high overhead costs, Eisner announced that Disney would close Hollywood Pictures and consolidate movie production in the other divisions. At the same time, making potential blockbuster movies had been fast increasing in cost, leading to higher expenses; Disney found that it had lost its former low-cost strength in movie production with the escalating costs.

So, Disney, as did most other movie companies, announced that it would produce fewer movies per year in the future and focus more on the production of the two successful kinds of movies: (1) expensive blockbuster movies backed by advertising campaigns of $20 million to $40 million that could generate $200 million to $500 million in theater revenues worldwide and (2) inexpensive movies costing about $13 million to $15 million, backed by modest $3 million to $5 million advertising budgets that could find niches and be profitable. It also announced a return to its cost-cutting ways and expressed renewed support for Miramax, which specialized in finding and producing the low-budget, niche movies that often proved highly profitable, because they were relatively inexpensive to make.

Inspired by the incredible profits it had earned releasing its famous films on videocassettes, Disney forged ahead with promoting this business. By 1995, Disney's domestic home video division reached phenomenal sales of $2 billion in revenues; *The Lion King* sold 30 million copies in 1995, and *Snow White* sold 25 million copies. In 1996, the introduction of the new DVD digital movie format opened up a new revenue channel for Disney. Customers had to buy their favorite movies in the new format if they wished to obtain the unsurpassed picture and sound quality that the new DVD players provided. Also, by 1995, the Disney Channel had become the second-most popular pay movie channel in the United States after HBO. Increasingly, Disney used the channel to advertise its new movie, offerings, such as *The Hunchback of Notre Dame,* and all the new happenings at its theme parks.

Consumer Products

Disney's shopping empire also expanded rapidly in the 1990s. By 1995, Disney had opened 429 specialty Disney Stores worldwide (including 26 in Europe and 15 in the Asia-Pacific area). Disney also started a catalog mail-order business to reach customers not served by Disney stores, which tended to be located only in large, prestigious malls in major cities. Disney's publishing interests also increased sharply, publishing more than 500 million books a year worldwide through Mouse Books, Disney Press, and Hyperion Books titles. These books were intended to publicize Disney's new features, attractions, and movies, which extends the popularity of the traditional cast of Disney characters.

THE DISNEY–CAPITAL CITIES/ABC MERGER

In 1995, Michael Eisner astonished the entertainment world when he announced that Disney would acquire Capital Cities/ABC Inc. for $19 billion. He would make it "the world's premier entertainment company, to protect and build on the Disney name and franchise, and to preserve and foster quality, imagination and guest service." Capital Cities/ABC owned one of the three biggest television networks and affiliated television stations in the United States and network of hundreds of radio stations. It also owned a major stake in ESPN and ESPN2, the dominant sports broadcasting channels, the A&E television network, and Lifetime television.

After the acquisition, Disney redefined its three main areas of business as creative content (which includes all its movie and television production operations, all licensing activities involving the Disney name and characters, and consumer products), theme parks and resorts, and media broadcasting. In championing the merger, Eisner spoke enthusiastically about the "synergies" that could be obtained in the future. For example, Disney television programming would be offered primarily through its own

ABC network and then subsequently rerun on the Disney Channel. It could feature its new movies as television specials. Eisner argued that given the high costs of advertising new movies, owning the ABC network would allow it to publicize its movies at much less cost than other studios in the years ahead. Finally, Disney's movie library could be shown at low cost over the years on ABC television, and the resources of the new company could be combined to create new digital cable television channels to strengthen the package of television channels that Disney already owned (such as the Disney Channel, ESPN, and A&E).

Many critics of the merger existed, however. Some industry analysts questioned the price tag of $19 billion that Disney had paid. They pointed out that Capital Cities/ABC was at the peak of its profitability when Disney made its offer; it was enjoying record advertising revenues (which are the main source of profitability of television and radio broadcasting). Other critics also argued that the synergies Eisner claimed would result from the merger could easily have been achieved through a "strategic alliance" between the two companies over such issues as programming content, and advertising revenues. In other words, the two companies could just as easily have entered into a written contract with each other to achieve these gains from cooperation. For example, Disney formed an alliance with Coca-Cola to promote that company's soft drinks in its operations; it had also formed an alliance with McDonald's under which the latter would be given the rights to use new Disney movies and toys to promote foods in its restaurants. Disney did not have to *merge* with these companies to obtain synergies.

Critics even argued that the merger was unnecessary and would lock Disney into an unprofitable situation because the Big Three television networks were attracting less and less of the TV viewing audience (which was 40% in 1995 and about 30% in 2008). The proliferation of new cable television channels and the increasing popularity of the Internet as a media resource were quickly reducing the advantages of owning a major TV network. In any event, in 1995, ABC experienced a steep drop in its share of the viewing audience, and its prime-time ratings plunged. (These ratings are vital because they determine how much the ABC network and its owned and affiliated television stations can charge advertisers.)

ABC's poor performance in the year following the merger brought its top management team under intense scrutiny from Eisner. Although before the merger, it appeared that both organizations had similar cultures (both being managed by strong CEOs who had hands-on approaches), after the merger, it became apparent that the two companies were very different. Eisner had a very centralized management style and expected all his top managers to craft five-year and ten-year plans for their divisions to guide their future growth. He then evaluated them on the success with which they reached their division's performance goals. They were under constant scrutiny—Eisner was the person in charge of Disney's future strategy.

At ABC, however, the situation was very different. In the TV business, events change rapidly, and a network's success depends on how well its shows are received on a week-by-week and month-by-month basis. Because of their shorter time horizon, ABC's executives used one-year plans to guide their choices for the next year's programming. This conflicted with Eisner's desire for longer strategic plans. It became clear that all was not going well between Disney's top management team and the team of managers in charge of ABC. As ABC's performance deteriorated in the fall of 1995, ABC executives came under even closer scrutiny; they were forced to defend their every move to Disney's managers. As a result, several stressed-out senior managers left ABC during this time.

New Problems for Eisner and Disney

Analysts soon publically argued that the merger was a disaster, and Eisner's hands-on management approach had resulted in the conflict with key ABC executives that led to their departure. All of a sudden, things seemed to have gone from bad to worse at Disney and for Eisner. In fact, after his early years of incredible success at Disney, Eisner's final years as CEO were characterized by a major decrease in its performance and a plunging share price. The main reason for this was that Disney's entertainment assets, now organized into four major operating groups—media networks, studio entertainment, consumer products, and parks and resorts—began to perform poorly. This was partly due to poor strategic decision making and partly due to changes in the environment that hurt the company's ability to realize value from its assets.

Problems in Media Networks Disney's problems in its media properties, particularly its ABC network, continued to worsen over time. As analysts had expected, hundreds of new cable channels were being established, and this continued to reduce the size of ABC's viewing audience. Also, the constant screening of Disney programming on the ABC network was no longer attractive—viewers were getting bored. Disney also continued to find it hard to develop hit shows. It was not until 2003 with the introduction of hit shows like *Designing Women* and *Lost* that ABC's fortunes began to look up. In addition, the massive increase in the use of the Internet and growing access to broadband further cut into the time people spent viewing television programming. In particular, men between the ages of 18 and 35, a critical audience for advertisers, had reduced the time they spent watching TV.

In fact, the brightest spot in Disney's media networks was its ESPN sports channels; sports programming was one of the few areas during the 2000s in which the TV viewing audience was increasing; the range of different kinds of televised sports was soaring—as was the price of tickets to sporting events. Disney was able to charge cable TV companies higher fees to carry its ESPN and associated networks. By 2003, ESPN was a major contributor to Disney's profits; its primarily male viewing audience was a major buyer of cars, pickups, home delivered pizza, beer, fast food, and so on. Today, ESPN is broadcast in more than 18 different languages in more than 165 countries; its franchise is booming as the global popularity of many different kinds of sports programming increases.

Problems in Studio Entertainment

Disney also continued to experience major problems in its studio entertainment group, which contains its major movie studios: Walt Disney, Touchstone, and Miramax. The profitability of Disney's movies continued to fall in the 2000s for a variety of reasons. First, in its core animation movie business, Disney Studios found it impossible to create new blockbuster, animated movies that could be released each year to drive up revenues. Its early successes with *The Lion King* and *Pocahontas* were followed by failures such as *Fantasia 2000, 102 Dalmatians,* and *Treasure Planet*. To drive up revenues, Disney turned to releasing regular movies through the studio, such as *Pirates of the Caribbean,* its first PG-13 movie in 2003, a big hit that was followed by sequels that also proved successful, perhaps because of the star, Johnny Depp. However, many other expensive movies such as *Hidalgo* and *Around the World in Eighty Days* were flops that offset the gains from hit movies and lowered the studio entertainment unit's profits.

Second, the shift to produce animated movies using computer-based digital technology accelerated in the 1990s; Pixar and DreamWorks became the leaders in this movie genre. Disney was fortunate to secure its contract to distribute Pixar's films before the obvious advantages of digital technology became apparent. Its revenues from distributing Pixar movies such as *Toy Story* (1995), *Toy Story 2* (1999), *Monsters, Inc.* (2001), *Finding Nemo* (2003), and the hugely successful *The Incredibles* (2004) became the biggest single source of the profits of the studio entertainment operating group. However, the Pixar contract was due to expire in 2005, and Steve Jobs, Pixar's CEO, was reluctant to renew the contract with Disney—one major reason was the hostile relationship that had developed between him and Eisner. Another reason was that Disney announced in 2004 it would make animated movies only using computer-based technology in the future, and the company laid off the animators who had created its past successes. In early 2005, it was still unclear if Jobs, who had been offering the Pixar franchise to other movie distributors, would renew the contract with Disney. Not renewing would be a major blow to Disney, because more than 40% or $1 billion of the operating income of its movie studios had come from its successes with Pixar.

Disney also continued to experience poor success with many of its regular feature film releases. The brightest spot was Miramax Pictures, whose high-quality but relatively low-budget movies continued to enjoy enormous commercial success and reaped many Oscars for the studio. In 2005, however, the Weinstein brothers who had been attributed with producing the successful movies decided to leave the studio they founded after major disputes with Eisner and Disney over increasing studio operating costs.

Problems in Consumer Products Several major developments also led to problems in Disney's consumer products group, which also significantly reduced its profits margins. First, Disney's success with its ESPN sports networks prompted Eisner

to purchase two major sports team franchises, the Mighty Ducks of Anaheim hockey team and the Anaheim Angels baseball team. However, Disney had no experience in operating sports franchises, and both these ventures began to lose money. Eventually, they were both sold off. Second, one of the drivers of Disney's profits had been the decisions to release its classic movies on videotape and DVD. However, because the company was no longer able to re-release these movies in movie theatres, and with millions of Disney videos and DVD's in circulation and movie video piracy rampant, its DVD revenues fell sharply. Finally, Disney's lack of a string of new hit movies in the early 2000s did nothing to help its consumer product revenues at a time when DVD sales were exploding. Consumers attracted by the falling price of DVDs, began to build their own movie collections.

By the early 2000s, it became clear that Eisner's decision to open the Disney Store retail chain to sell Disney merchandise at premium prices was also a disastrous investment decision as these stores began to lose more and more money. Disney's management had not understood the specific competitive problems that exist in the retail store industry, such as intense price competition, high inventory holding, and store maintenance costs that make profit margins thin. Disney searched for a buyer, and in 2004, found one in the Children's Place retail store chain. They agreed to buy Disney's 335 stores and the right to sell Disney's merchandise in these stores. Disney would continue to receive a percentage of revenues from the sale of its products in these stores.

Problems in Theme Parks and Resorts Disney's theme parks also turned in mixed performance during the 2000s. In the early 2000s, to attract new and repeat customers, Disney spent almost five billion dollars to build new rides and modernize its Anaheim and Orlando properties to protect its famous franchise. Only months after it improved its theme parks, however, disasters such as the 9/11 terrorist attacks and the SARS epidemic in Asia occurred.

Disney's attention to improving the quality of its properties while keeping costs in check started to pay off in 2004 as the number of visitors increased sharply and profit margins once again rose. Disney World, with its four theme parks, remains the number one tourist attraction in the world and is its most important asset.

Bob Iger Takes Over

By 2005, analysts claimed that Michael Eisner's micromanagement of the company had reduced the level of innovation in the company, prevented top management from realizing the synergies from the ABC/Capital Cities merger, and was threatening the company's future profitability. Eisner's decision to close down the animation studio in favor of computer animation also brought him into direct conflict with Roy Disney, who had been the head of that division, which he championed because of its links to the past. Roy Disney, with the support of some other disgruntled investors began to publicly challenge Eisner's leadership of the company and began a campaign to oust Eisner as CEO. The dispute between Eisner and his opponents grew bitter as the performance of the company continued to suffer.

In September 2005, Disney announced that Michael Eisner had resigned and Robert Iger had been appointed as Disney's new CEO. Iger immediately began to make overtures to Roy Disney to resolve the conflict that had permeated the company and hurt its strategic decision making. Then, beginning in 2006, he reorganized Disney's decision-making hierarchy to help improve the company's performance.

A New Decentralized Approach

For several years, Iger had noted how slow decision making had become at Disney, and why, as a result, managers had made many mistakes in implementing its strategies. It had fallen behind in the important business of developing new movies that provided it with so many opportunities to develop new attractions in its theme parks and new Disney consumer products such as toys and clothes. Also, although Disney had established several Web sites in the 1990s, its managers were slow to recognize how the fast-growing use of the Internet and the rapid emergence of new digital technologies could transform the media and entertainment industries. Disney's Internet properties were getting relatively few "hits" compared to rapidly growing online companies, such as Yahoo!, YouTube, and social networking sites such as Facebook and MySpace, that were using Disney's media content.

Iger believed one main reason for Disney's declining performance was that under Eisner, it had become too tall and bureaucratic; its top managers were following strict financial rules that did not lead to innovative strategies in creative new media content and new ways to deliver it to customers. Thus, one of his first moves as CEO to turn around the company's performance was to dismantle Disney's centralized corporate-level Strategic Planning Office (SPO). The SPO contained several levels of managers who had become responsible for sifting through all the new ideas and suggestions sent up to corporate headquarters by Disney's different business divisions, such as theme parks, movies, and gaming. SPO managers decided which ones to present to then-CEO Eisner.

Iger regarded the SPO as a bureaucratic bottleneck that actually reduced the number of ideas coming from lower managers. He dissolved the SPO and reassigned its managers back to Disney's different business units. The result of cutting out these unnecessary levels in the hierarchy was that it quickly led the managers of its different business units to generate and implement many new strategies. The pace of innovation increased, because divisional managers were more willing to speak out and champion their ideas when they knew they were dealing directly with Iger and a top management team focused on finding innovative ways to improve performance.

New Initiatives Since 2005   The new initiatives that Iger and the managers of Disney's business units have pioneered since 2005 to increase its business units and the company's revenues and profits are discussed next in order of the size of their contribution to Disney's revenues and profits.

Media Networks

Since it acquired Capital/ABC and its related networks such as ESPN, Disney's media networks have contributed the greatest proportion to Disney's revenues (see Exhibit 1). The main source of these revenues comes from two sources: First, from the advertising revenues it earns from commercials on TV and cable channels, which is why the media network managers must work hard to plan and develop hit shows on all channels, such as ABC, ESPN, and the Disney Channels, which will help boost revenues and profits; second, a major part of media networks' revenues come from distribution agreements with the major cable companies that transmit its content and channels to the final customer. For example, in 2007,

Exhibit 1　Disney's Revenues by Business Unit, 2002–2008

	Studio Entertainment	Consumer Products	Parks and Resorts	Media Networks	Internet Entertainment	Total
2002	6,465	2,440	6,691	9,733	–	**25,329**
2003	7,364	2,344	6,412	10,941	–	**27,061**
2004	8,713	2,511	7,750	11,778	–	**30,752**
2005	7,587	2,127	9,023	13,207	–	**31,944**
2006	7,529	2,193	9,925	14,368	–	**34,285**
2007	7,491	2,347	10,626	15,046	–	**35,510**
2008	7,348	2,415	11,504	15,857	719	**37,843**

Disney announced it had a reached a record revenue-enhancing, multi-year distribution agreement with major cable companies such as Comcast and Time Warner that had agreed to carry all its existing and new channels for the next five years.

At the same time that media network managers strived to find ways to increase revenues by constantly developing unique, differentiated TV shows, the costs of developing these shows was increasing sharply. Disney had multiple production units across its TV channels and movie studios, and its cost structure was rising. So, in 2009, Disney announced it would merge ABC Entertainment and ABC Studios units into the ABC Entertainment Group to streamline the production process and address the need to produce more digital content to stream online.

By 2007, it had become clear that the growth of the Internet was changing the economics of all aspects of the media business. Disney's radio stations were suffering from disappearing advertising revenues that had migrated online; in 2007, Disney announced it would spin off its wholly owned subsidiary, ABC Radio Holdings, which were acquired by Citadel Broadcasting Corporation. Citadel believed it could achieve economies of scale from operating twice as many radio stations and thus offset declining revenues in the future.

As a result of the recession in that started in 2008, Disney was forced to look for more cost savings in its media unit; in January 2009, plans were announced to lay off 200 people at the ABC division and freeze 200 vacant jobs, resulting in a 5% reduction of the Disney-ABC TV group's workforce.

One more major move Disney pursued since 2005 (and intends to take advantage of in the future) is to increasingly target teenagers and young adults, rather than its traditional customer groups of young children and their parents. And, as discussed earlier, to do so, Disney must develop hit programming, including the *High School Musical* mega-hit TV shows and shows starring Hannah Montana and the Jonas brothers. In turn, this has allowed Disney's business units to develop new products from clothing to school supplies to new Web sites for teens of all backgrounds. Iger has explicitly focused on the teen franchise to exploit commonalities between business units.

Studio Entertainment

Disney's studio entertainment unit also faced the need to develop a string of hit movies to keep its revenues rising, especially movies that might spur sales of music albums and Disney merchandise. Its Disney Channel Original Movie studio had a major success in 2006, when it released the first *High School Musical* (HSM) movie, which became the highest-grossing movie the unit had ever made. This was followed by HSM 2 released in 2007 and HSM 3 in 2008. The film's soundtrack was the best-selling album in the United States for 2006; a theatrical version is also planned, and HSM 4 is in production.

Another important development in studio entertainment came in 2006, when Bob Iger, who had worked hard to build a friendly working relationship with Steve Jobs, the principal owner of Pixar Animation Studios, announced that Disney would acquire the company in an all-stock transaction valued at $7.4 billion. For each Pixar share, 2.3 Disney shares were exchanged, which made Steve Jobs Disney's largest shareholder. This was an enormous price to pay, however, given that Disney had closed down its cartoon animation studio. Obtaining Pixar's digital-movie making skills was vitally important to maintain its status as the leader in animated movies. Also, of course, all of Pixar's hit movies could be used to develop new attractions at Disney's theme parks, provide content for its TV channels, and generate sales of Disney's consumer products such as toys and clothing, generating billions of dollars in future revenues across all the company's business units.

Nevertheless, the high cost of this acquisition forced Iger to reexamine the cost structure of studio entertainment, because the cost of making all kinds of movies was soaring. The cost of making a blockbuster movie was well beyond $100 million by 2006, and some movies were costing $150 million. A series of flops would therefore be disastrous and could potentially wipe out the studio unit's profitability. So, in July 2006, Iger announced plans to slash annual movie production by more than half, from 18 films to 8, and eliminate 650 jobs or about 20% of the unit's workforce to reduce the cost structure and improve shareholder returns. The plan was to focus the studio entertainment's resources on the set of movies that had the highest potential to be box office successes. To further cut costs, in 2007, Disney announced it would unify several marketing and production divisions within its TV and film operations and form a new unit, Buena Vista Worldwide Marketing and Distribution, to distribute movies, TV shows, children's programs, and other entertainment around the world.

In February 2009, to boost the studio entertainment unit's revenues without having to incur the major costs of making original movies, Disney announced a major alliance with DreamWorks Studios. Disney obtained the exclusive rights to handle all the distribution and marketing for the approximately six films DreamWorks planned to make each year in the future, in return for a significant percentage of box office revenues.

Nevertheless, by 2009, it was clear that a major determinant of the studio entertainment unit's profitability—sales of DVDs from blockbuster movies that

had been a major contributor to its profitability—were under threat from digital media. Part of the decline in DVD sales was because movies such as *WALL-E* and *The Chronicles of Narnia* had not sold as well as *Pirates of the Caribbean: At World's End* and *Ratatouille*. It was also clear that the 26% drop in studio revenue, to $1.95 billion, outpaced the declines in other businesses, because customers were turning to digital means to access and store movies, many of which were pirated. This could severely impact the film unit's business model and helps explain why Disney has decided to make far fewer major movies each year—it simply cannot recoup the costs of making expensive movies when digital piracy is on the increase.

Parks and Resorts

In its parks and resorts unit, Iger and his managers also worked to find the right strategies to invest the billions of dollars needed to continually upgrade, improve, and expand properties to generate the most potential future revenues. In March 2007, Disney announced two major expansions would be made to its Walt Disney World theme park in Florida to attract new and returning visitors. First, a 900-acre luxury resort with an upscale commercial district outside the entrance to the resort would be built. The new resort would be anchored by a luxury Four Seasons hotel, and Disney would earn a percentage of the profits made by the hotel. The resort would also include a world-class 18-hole golf course and luxury time-share vacation homes. Second, on the western edge of the park, Disney would build a second resort consisting of hotels, stores, and restaurants comparable in size to Disney's Animal Kingdom.

In October 2007, Iger also announced a $1.1 billion, five-year plan to overhaul its California Disneyland park; this was the largest single makeover the company has ever given to one of its theme parks. Disneyland would be given a whole new "modernistic" look, expanded by 12 acres and an increased number of attractions, with a particular focus on attractions based on the Pixar animated movies including *Cars*, *Toy Story*, and *The Incredibles*.

Disney did not forget its sea-operations 'resorts' either. Seeking to realize increased economies of scale in its Disney cruises, in 2007, it announced it would double the size of the cruise line. Each new ship would weigh 122,000 tons and have two more decks than the existing 83,000-ton ships. Then, in October 2008, the parks and resorts unit unveiled a plan for a new $800 million luxury resort on the Hawaiian island of Oahu in 2011. The 21-acre resort would have a 5-star hotel with 350 hotel rooms, and 480 vacation villas that could be used by members of Disney's Vacation Timeshare Club.

Disney has also continued its strategy of opening new theme parks abroad. Its theme park in Hong Kong, opened in 2005 in a joint venture with the Hong Kong government, has had mixed success in appealing to the needs of Asian customers; the number of visitors has not met expectations. In March 2009, Disney announced it was putting its planned expansion of the park on hold and was negotiating hard for the Hong Kong authorities to contribute hundreds of millions more dollars to fund the park's expansion. Analysts were concerned this park might be running into the same kinds of problems as Euro Disney park in France experienced decades earlier. Nevertheless, in January 2009, despite the slowdown in China's economy due to the recession that started in 2008, the Shanghai government and Disney signed an agreement to build a theme park in that booming city that will start operations in 2013.

Consumer Products Division

Disney's ability to develop and market a wide range of consumer products that relate to its classic movies and its new Pixar movies and shows has been a major contributor to its profitability over the years. Not only does Disney license the rights to make toys using its cast of characters to toy companies such as Mattel, it also designs much of the merchandise that it sells at high prices in its theme parks and in the Disney retail stores that it sold to the Children's Place retail chain in 2004. In the growing age of digital media, however, Disney has been making a major push to develop new kinds of toys that appeal to computer- and Internet-savvy children, who have been exposed to the electronic world at a much younger age.

One major initiative in its consumer products unit has been to increase its presence in the highly profitable videogame industry, in which sales of videogames that are played on computers, or specialized consoles such as the PlayStation and Wii, and on handheld devices such as the Game Boy and even the iPhone and other new smartphones and net-

books are booming. The strategy, once again, is to take its hit movies, shows, and the sports content from its ESPN network and turn them into popular videogames that command premium prices. In 2005, Disney announced an agreement between its ESPN sports network and Electronic Arts (EA), the world's leading videogame developer, to create and market EA SPORTS videogames containing ESPN content. The agreement gives EA access to all ESPN programming, personalities, and other assets. The games to be developed will be able to play on EA SPORTS consoles, as well as other handheld, PC, and wireless game consoles.

Beginning in 2005, Disney also began to acquire many small, independent videogame developers and use their expertise to quickly develop new games that take advantage of its brand name media, such as movies and cartoon characters. In 2005, it acquired U.S. videogame-maker Avalanche Software, and Living Mobile, a European mobile game developer and publisher. Disney also announced it had established a start-up game development studio in Vancouver, Canada, staffed by former members of EA to spur the development of Disney-related videogames. In April 2008, Disney agreed to buy a Chinese game developer, Gamestar, to develop games that are customized to the needs of the huge Asian market.

Beyond videogames, its consumer products unit is working in diverse product areas to find profitable new opportunities to take advantage of the Disney name. Clothing has always been one of these. In October 2007, Disney and Hanesbrands Inc. struck a 10-year deal that gives the clothing maker the rights to be the exclusive supplier of basic apparel at Walt Disney resorts and parks, such as T-shirts, sweatshirts, and fleeces. The deal calls for some apparel to be co-labeled, with names such as Disneyland Resort by Hanes, Walt Disney World by Hanes, and ESPN Zone by Champion. In an unusual venture, Disney and Stremick's Heritage Foods announced a new milk beverage line for children and families, sold in supermarkets, that meets Disney's healthy food guidelines, which specify minimal levels of critical vitamins and nutrients. A more usual venture came when the consumer products unit announced its entry into the robotic toy market with a line of programmable robotic toys called Thinkway Toys and WowWe, created in collaboration with Pixar, with USB ports to connect them to desktop and laptop computers.

Then, in a reverse of course, in May 2008, Disney announced that it had acquired the Disney Store chain in North America from the owners of the Children's Place, which had found they could not operate Disney stores profitably; losses had escalated quickly since 2004. Disney took back about 320 stores but continues to operate only 220 of them, closing the 100 that had been making the largest losses. By 2009 the chain was contributing significantly to the consumer product division's revenues and was making some money; and managers are working hard to find the right business model to increase the retail chain's future profitability.

Finally, widespread digital piracy and falling sales of music CDs also led Disney to reexamine the business model of its music album group. To increase profits, Disney's music group decided to eliminate a large proportion of its overhead costs by focusing on only a small number of highly profitable artists, such as Hannah Montana and the Jonas Brothers, and it embraced digital distribution through iTunes and so on to distribute its music products. To further increase profitability, Disney cross-brands its artists, by, for example, signing music contracts with its television actors, and television contracts with its music artists, so that it can then use its control over entertainment channels to increase the popularity of its artists by increasing their exposure through its TV shows, movies, and through nationwide concert tours.

Internet Entertainment

As Exhibit 1 shows, Disney broke out the revenues of its Internet entertainment operations from its other business units for the first time in 2008, and created a new stand-alone Internet entertainment unit. This change signifies Iger's realization that control of digital and electronic media content, and the ways of transmitting it to the final customer, will become a more and more important generator of revenues and profit in the future. Disney, like other media companies Viacom and Time Warner, has been hit hard by digital piracy, which has cost them billions of dollars in lost revenues. In addition, sites like YouTube and MySpace contain tens of thousands of short videos that use Disney's media content, but Disney gets no benefit from this. So Iger set about to change this situation.

In October 2005, Disney and Apple announced a partnership to offer current and past season episodes of ABC and Disney Channel television shows for download on Apple's iTunes Music Store, such as "Desperate Housewives" and "Lost" for $1.99 per episode. Few Internet users like paying fees for accessing digital media on the World Wide Web, so in April 2006 Disney announced plans to generate new revenues from Internet advertising by making these shows available for free over the Internet on its own Web site. Viewers are forced to watch advertising at the beginning of the video, and episodes of the ABC shows contain commercial breaks that viewers cannot skip. Iger's intent was to make the delivery of Disney Internet programming profitable. Ten major advertisers, including Ford, Procter & Gamble, and Unilever, signed up for the initiative.

A major change in strategy occurred in May 2009, when Iger announced that Disney would buy a 30% stake in Hulu.com, whose business model is based on streaming digital media content from the four major U.S. broadcast networks on a Web platform based on generating advertising revenues for these networks. Although millions of Internet users were visiting its ABC Web site, the hundreds of millions of users who surf the content of leading video Web sites like YouTube were not attracted to ABC's Web site. Only CBS had not bought into Hulu.com in May 2009. Disney will get three seats on the 12-member board, the same as News Corp. and NBC Universal. Hulu.com has emerged as one of the most popular online video destinations since it was launched in 2007, although it is still way behind. YouTube is now one of the top three online video sites. However, YouTube is also working to reach an agreement with the major global TV networks and movies studios to show advertising on its Web site when their media content is viewed.

Beyond PC and laptop digital viewing and downloading applications, the number of people downloading media content to smartphones such as the iPhone has soared. So, in January 2009, the media networks unit announced an agreement with Verizon Wireless that would offer Verizon's V CAST video and mobile Web customers a comprehensive portfolio of Disney news, entertainment, and sports programming, including full-length episodes of ABC TV shows, and news, the Disney Channel, and ESPN.

Finally, Disney is in no way abandoning its own Web sites as a way to drive up its push to expand

Internet revenues and profits. It is striving to build social networking capabilities, which is why in 2007 it announced that it has acquired Club Penguin, one of the leading online virtual worlds for kids. To increase the value of this site for users, it is using the skills of its videogame developers to develop interactive games on its Club Penguin and other Web sites to offer users an attractive online experience that will encourage them to return. Indeed, it has been forced to do this because it is battling with Viacom's Nickelodeon, which has, to date, been winning the battle to attract more visitors to its Web site and keep them there longer by providing them with a better interactive experience, including games. It will be interesting to see how the revenues of its Internet entertainment unit increase over the next several years.

In fact, Iger believes that its Internet entertainment unit will enjoy the fastest growth during next five years, as the revenues generated from distributing its media content—movies and TV shows, recorded music, videogames, sports, and business information—over the Internet continues to grow. The tremendous growth of high-speed Internet will allow its users to watch or download increasing amounts of high bandwidth content, and so the company will enjoy increasing online advertising revenues.

DISNEY'S FUTURE PROSPECTS

In 2007, Disney's revenues were a record $35.5 billion, 5% higher than the previous year, and its net income increased to $4.9 billion, which was 26% higher than in 2006, and its stock price soared from $20 to over $35. Bob Iger's new strategic moves had helped the company recover from its creative slump under the last years of Michael Eisner's reign. Even in 2008, Disney seemed well positioned as its revenues for the first nine months of the year were 7% higher than in 2007 although increased operating costs, particularly

because of its expenditures to improve its parks reduced profit by 3%. Even though there was a recession, Disney's stock was down only 19%, whereas the average company's stock was down 36%.

However, when Disney failed to reach analysts' profit estimates in the last quarter of 2008, its stock plunged, and it plunged again in the spring of 2009 when the continuing effects of the recession resulted in sharply lower revenues and profits. Disney's stock price had plummeted from around $35 to $15, and Disney the company found itself in the same situation as other major entertainment media and consumer products companies.

In May 2009, Bob Iger admitted for the first time that the wide scale shift of customers to use the Internet to access digital entertainment was beginning to impact the company's business units in important ways. For example, there had been a broad-based decline in sales of DVDs, a vital component of its studio entertainment unit's profitability, as consumers shifted viewing habits onto the Internet and other wireless formats. Studio entertainment revenue had fallen 26% from the year before. This shift has already cause sharp declines in the stock price of newspapers and recorded music companies. In addition, revenue company-wide fell 8% to $9.60 billion, and net income fell to $845 million. Similarly, revenue at its most popular cable networks, such as the Disney Channel and ESPN, rose 2% to $2.45 billion, but advertising revenues at ABC declined 14% to $1.45 billion, which explains why Iger was anxious to make the deal with Hulu.com in the hope of finding a new online source of advertising revenues to replace those lost on broadcast TV. The recession had also led to a 45% fall in revenues from its parks and resorts unit to $2.67 billion, as attendance at the company's U.S. theme parks and hotel occupancy at its domestic resorts declined by 5%; it would have been much worse had Disney not embarked on a discount price program to offer visitors "four nights for the price of three" and reduced prices for attractions and restaurants.

MICHAEL EISNER'S DISNEY

It was early 1991, and Michael Eisner, chairman and CEO of the Walt Disney Company, was sitting down with Frank Wells, president and COO, and Gary Wilson, executive vice president and CFO, to discuss Disney's prospects for the new year. These men were still basking in the glow generated by another record revenue- and profit-breaking year in Disney's history. Disney's businesses were performing at an unprecedented level, and confidence was high. The problem facing the trio who had engineered Disney's turnaround was how to maintain Disney's explosive growth rate and its return-on-investment goal of increasing earnings per share by 20% over any five-year period to achieve a 20% annual return on equity. Paradoxically, the very success of their strategy, which had originated to protect an underperforming Disney from the rampages of corporate raiders and the threat of takeover, was causing the opposite problem: how to maintain the company's explosive growth in a business environment in which attractive opportunities for expansion were becoming increasingly scarce. The men were reflecting on how to develop a five-year plan that would cement the strategy that had led to their present enviable situation and make the 1990s the "Disney Decade."

DISNEY BEFORE EISNER

When Walt Disney died in 1966, he left a company that was experiencing record revenues and profits. Disney was at its creative peak and forging ahead at full steam on the many ideas generated by Walt Disney's creative genius. However, by the early 1980s, all the drive in the Disney Company had evaporated. Although revenues were increasing somewhat, net income and profit were dropping drastically. Top executives believed they were following what "Walt would have wanted," but the vision that was uniquely Walt Disney's was gone. Exhibit 1 charts the net income of the Walt Disney Company from 1980 to 1990. How did this situation come about? To understand it, we need to look at the way in which Walt Disney built his company and try to find the pattern in his creative endeavors.

Walt Disney's Company

Walt Elias Disney was born in 1901. Raised on a farm, he developed an interest in art and drawing early on in his life, and his ambition was to be a cartoonist. His interest in static cartoons soon waned, however, with the beginning of animated cartoons in movie theaters. At the time, these were extremely crude: the figures bounced rather than moved gracefully around, were silent, and in black and white. He immediately saw the potential for developing high-quality, graphic art cartoons that moved and set about marshaling resources to produce his product.

After a series of early setbacks, Disney had success with a character called Oswald the Rabbit, perhaps the forerunner of Roger the Rabbit. The carefully drawn cartoons were very popular with movie audiences and provided Disney with the money he

For the most recent financial results of the company discussed in this case, go to http://finance.yahoo.com, input the company's stock symbol, and download the latest company report from its homepage.

Exhibit 1 Selected Financial Data (in millions, except per share and other data)

	1989	1988	1987	1986	1985
STATEMENT OF INCOME DATA					
Revenues	$4,594.3	$3,438.2	$2,876.8	$2,165.8	$1,700.1
Operating income	1,229.0	884.8	776.8	527.7	345.7
Interest expense	23.9	5.8	29.1	44.1	54.6
Income from continuing operations	703.3	522.0	392.3	213.2	132.3
Net income	703.3	522.0	444.7	247.3	173.5
BALANCE SHEET DATA					
Total assets	$6,657.2	$5,108.9	$3,806.3	$3,121.0	$2,897.3
Borrowing	860.6	435.5	584.5	547.2	823.1
Stockholders' equity	3,044.0	2,359.3	1,845.4	1,418.7	1,184.9
STATEMENT OF CASH FLOW DATA					
Cash flow	$1,275.6	$1,075.4*	$830.6	$668.4	$518.8
Investments					
Theme parks, resorts, and other property, net	749.6	595.7	280.1	174.1	179.8
Film costs	426.7	225.7	178.3	203.7	149.9
Acquisitions	237.3	221.7			
PER SHARE DATA					
Net income					
Continuing operations	$5.10	$3.80	$2.85	$1.57	$.98
Total	5.10	3.80	3.23	1.82	1.29
Cash dividends	.46	.38	.32	.315	.30
OTHER DATA					
Stockholders at close of year	143,000	124,000	101,000	77,000	58,000
Employees at close of year	47,000	39,000	31,000	30,000	30,000

*Excludes $722.6 million unearned royalty advances.
Source: The Walt Disney Company, Annual Report, 1989.

needed to expand his operations and to hire additional artists and animators. However, after battles about money and profits, Disney lost control of the Oswald character to Charles Mintz, the cartoon's distributor, which taught him an important lesson. From then on, he would retain all the rights to his characters, the films produced using these characters, and the distribution end of the film business. This was the start of Disney's fortune.

With the experience gained from Oswald the Rabbit, Disney set about finding a new character to hang his fortunes to. He came up with the idea of a mouse, and in 1928, he created Mickey Mouse. He was the voice, but the cartoons were drawn by Ubbe (Ub) Iwerks, an artist and animator who had worked closely with Disney from the beginning. The Mickey Mouse cartoons were immensely popular, and their success provided Walt Disney with the resources to expand his repertoire of characters and improve his animation techniques. He and his company then, and now, were always at the forefront of technological developments. The next decade saw the emergence of Disney's now-familiar cast of characters: Donald Duck, Goofy, and the Three Little Pigs, a cartoon for which Disney won an Oscar. At the same time, Disney became involved in making cartoons in color. Using Technicolor's new three-color process, he produced these cartoons in color and won his first Oscar for color in 1932. It was this ability to meld technical developments with his emerging cast of cartoon characters that was the source of Disney's distinctive strength. None of his competitors was able to take this advantage away; although other studios established animation departments, none had the same success.

Full-Length Movies

By the late 1930s, Disney's experience in short cartoons had now developed his studio's skills in the three techniques needed for quality animation and cartoon making: art and drawing, perspective and sound, and color. He had learned the value of using a large number of drawings per second to provide his characters with realistic movements, even though this dramatically increased costs. He had seen the value of color as a way of making his characters more true to life. (One of the virtues of cartoons is that they can extend and amplify reality.) Finally, he had developed a technique that gave depth to previously flat cartoons. This was the famous multi-plane technique, which involved the use of a camera that could focus in and out of three planes of celluloid drawings: the foreground, the characters themselves, and the background. By photographing these planes at an angle, an impression of depth was achieved in the cartoon that gave the characters life. This technique resulted in another Oscar for Disney.

Taking these techniques, Walt Disney set about advancing his long-term dream: a full-length cartoon motion picture. He was careful in his selection of a subject. From the beginning, he believed that his subjects should be characters that were widely accepted

by the public so that little learning by the public was involved. It was with his characteristic genius that he chose Snow White and the Seven Dwarfs as his subject in 1937. *Snow White* cost a fortune to make, but it went on to make animation history as it also grossed a fortune at the box office. It also provided the capital that precipitated Disney into the ranks of the big studios. The money from *Snow White* allowed Disney to build his studio at Burbank and financed the animated films *Pinocchio* and *Bambi*, which were also very successful. Then, in 1940, departing from his own maxim of choosing only "brand-name characters," he made *Fantasia*. Despite being an artistic success, the film was a commercial disaster, which, coinciding with the unpopularity of cartoons during World War II, plunged Walt Disney Productions into debt. When the banks restricted the amount they were willing to provide to fund the company, Walt Disney offered stock to the public for the first time. In 1940, Walt Disney Productions issued 155,000 shares at $25 a share, raising $3,500,000 in working capital.

More Walt Disney Magic

With the end of the war, the public was once again receptive to fun and fantasy. The boom years after the war produced an audience with money in their pockets who were in search of excitement. Walt Disney was determined to provide them with it. He began the search for new projects to exercise the talents of the Disney studios. By 1950, he had come up with new directions for the Disney studios.

Motion Pictures Disney realized that animation was not the only way of bringing the public's favorite fantasy characters to the screen. Many popular heroes, such as Robin Hood, could be depicted in live-action movies. So, Disney took popular fictional characters and turned them into movies. A string of hits resulted as Disney studios came out with *Treasure Island*, *The Swiss Family Robinson*, *The Story of Robin Hood and His Merry Men*, *Kidnapped*, *20,000 Leagues Under the Sea*, and a host of films starring such people as Hayley Mills and Maurice Chevalier. He also decided to create new characters and developed scripts for such projects as *The Shaggy Dog*, *The Absent-Minded Professor*, *Son of Flubber*, and *The Parent Trap*. Side by side with these developments, Disney embarked on a series of nature or wildlife projects. Between 1950 and 1960, films such as *Water Birds*, *The Alaskan Eskimo*, *Bear Country*, and *White Wilderness* were produced for enthusiastic audiences. These films are still popular today.

At the same time, his interest in animation did not lapse and was a major moneymaker for the studio in the 1950s. *Cinderella* was a smash hit, as was *101 Dalmatians*, *Peter Pan*, *Lady and the Tramp*, and *The Jungle Book*. Moreover, by 1960, he was experimenting with combining animation and live action; one result was *Mary Poppins*, an all-time revenue winner for Disney, one of the greatest hits in the history of motion pictures, which also won five Academy Awards.

Television   Another move that helped Disney studios at this time was Walt's decision to take his products to the television screen. While other movie studios were worrying that television would cut into their profits and reduce their audiences, Walt realized the prospective synergies between the television and movie businesses for Disney. Disney was already producing a wide range of family-oriented entertainment: cartoons, full-length animation, live action, and wildlife. What could be more logical than taking its characters and developing its products to fit a television format? Not only would this be the source of additional revenues for Disney and allow it to exploit its resources and people to the full, but it would also provide advertising for the Walt Disney name and its future product offerings. The result was that in 1954 Disney brought *The Wonderful World of Disney* to the screen. In 1955, *The Mickey Mouse Club* was introduced, and the Disney name became part of popular American culture as for the next 20 years. Walt Disney television became a weekly event for the viewing public.

Theme Parks   Walt Disney had another reason for entering the television market. By itself, television was not a great money spinner for Disney. It would provide some free advertising and permit a more efficient utilization of the Disney resources, but animation was expensive compared to live action. What Walt Disney principally saw in television was a way to promote an idea that had been on his mind for years: a permanent amusement park that could exploit the Disney characters' popularity and offer a family a fun-filled day of Disney fantasy. Rather than passively watching a movie, amusement park goers would become a part of the movie; they would become actors in a live Disney entertainment. Television would show viewers how to take part in

this experience; it would also show them what they could expect. Disney realized that the combination of theme park, television, and movies would feed on each other, and each would promote the other. He was right. The theme park idea was wildly successful, and since its opening, Disneyland became the backbone of the Disney empire.

After deliberation, Disney chose Anaheim, California, for the opening of his first theme park. Disneyland opened in July 1955. Anaheim was chosen because of the huge population base in Southern California, and with less than five inches of rain a year, it could be operated all year round with little threat from the weather. Immense planning went into the creation of the Disney experience, and still does. Every ride and attraction was crafted to highlight the Disney theme; all its movies and characters are represented by different kinds of amusements and, of course, by the personal appearances of its characters, too. The number of attractions has grown from 17 in 1955 to 62 in 2009. Exhibits are constantly improved and updated to take advantage of the latest technological developments. Attractions are often connected with a corporate sponsor that buys into a Disney theme and leases an exhibit. For example, AT&T, Sony, and Kodak are some of the many sponsors of Disney's exhibits. The park is divided into seven major areas: Adventureland, Tomorrowland, Fantasyland, Frontierland, Mainstreet, Bearcountry, and New Orleans Square.

Then, in 1965, Walt Disney announced yet another part of his grand plan, the development of Disney World including the EPCOT (Experimental Prototype Community of Tomorrow) Center in Orlando, Florida. As originally imagined by Disney, part of Disney World would include a Magic Kingdom similar to the one already established in Anaheim. However, the EPCOT Center he envisaged was a "living laboratory" where 20,000 to 30,000 people would permanently live, experimenting with advanced technology and literally providing the world with examples of future life on Earth. He did not live to see either dream realized; Walt Disney died in December 1966.

DISNEY AFTER WALT

When Walt Disney died, he left his company at the pinnacle of its success up to that date. There were new films ready to distribute, plans for Disney World, steadily rising attendance at Disneyland, and a secure television audience. However, nothing seemed to go as well as before in the Disney organization. In the years from 1966 to 1984, when Michael Eisner took over, the company seemed to be just spinning its wheels. The problem was that nobody emerged to wear Walt Disney's crown; nobody could provide the creative vision to lead a company whose mission was to provide fun and fantasy. There was a void in the organization, and little was accomplished by the company that did not already have Walt Disney's stamp of approval on it.

Walt's brother Roy took over management of the company and supervised the building of Disney World. Most of the advance planning for Disney World had been carried out by Walt. The first step in that plan had been to purchase a huge tract of land outside Orlando, Florida, to hold Disney World. Walt Disney had never liked the situation that had developed outside Anaheim after the opening of Disneyland. Disney only owns the area on which the theme park and its car park are built. As a result, development around the park proceeded unchecked, and the surrounding area became full of motels and hotels that Walt Disney felt detracted from the Disney image. Moreover, on a financial level, the profits being earned by businesses in the vicinity of the park were vastly more than the revenues Disney received from park attendance. Because Walt Disney was determined that this should not happen in Orlando, he arranged, through subsidiary companies, the purchase of 28,000 acres of undeveloped land, an area the size of 34 square miles, enough to hold any number of hotels and amusements parks. Then, when Disney made the announcement of the park in 1965, the value of the land increased dramatically overnight.

The Magic Kingdom was the first part of Disney World to be built, and it opened in 1971 with 35 attractions; in 2009, there are more than 50. Just as corporate sponsorship was important in financing the development of the Magic Kingdom, it was also very important in providing the financing for the EPCOT Center, with large corporations paying $25 million for the right to sponsor an attraction. Nevertheless, the plans for EPCOT changed dramatically after Walt's death. The company realized that development costs would be enormous, and the venture as devised by Walt was not commercially feasible. Instead, the company changed EPCOT's mission to provide a showcase of modern technology and of international culture. In essence, EPCOT became a kind of permanent World's Fair when it opened in 1982. It is composed of two main areas. The first, World Showcase, consists of pavilions sponsored by many different countries, demonstrating their national culture and products and offering a wide variety of different kinds of national foods. The second area is Future World, which, in the spirit of Walt Disney's original plan, showcases future developments that can be expected in all areas of human commerce and endeavor. Attractions include the Living Seas, sponsored by United Technologies; a future farming exhibit sponsored by Kraft; and, recently, a journey through the human body highlighting advances in medical knowledge. EPCOT was the first Walt Disney exhibit specifically designed to appeal to adults, although Walt Disney always said everything Disney does is designed for the child in everybody.

The development of EPCOT and Disney World was Disney's principal priority during these years, and the opening of EPCOT attracted record crowds. However, despite high attendance, the profit margin of Disney World was lower than that of Disneyland, and both revenues and profits were disappointing, given Disney's huge investment of $1.5 billion. Moreover, by 1984, attendance at Disney World and Disneyland dropped off from its previous record high, further reducing revenues. Clearly, Disney had problems with its theme parks, but management did not know what to do.

Another problem Disney experienced was that while it had developed three large hotels with more than 2,000 rooms at the theme park to exploit the hotel market, they had missed at Anaheim luxury hotels chains such as the Hyatt and Hilton opening at the park's borders. The result was that Disney was losing potential revenues to these hotel chains, and the situation that had happened at Disneyland was in danger of happening again.

The other areas of Disney's business were also not doing well. Planning for the Disney Channel had begun in the late 1970s, and it came online in 1983 with 532,000 subscribers. The channel was a natural complement to Disney's other activities because the vehicle could exploit Disney's skills and characters. However, the start-up costs of the Disney Channel were enormous, and even though it had more than 1 million subscribers by 1984, it was still losing more than $10 million a year. This was another drain on the company's dwindling resources and a threat to its profit margins.

Home Video and Consumer Products

One bright spot for Disney was its entry into the home video market. It began selling videocassettes of some of its movie hits in 1983. Some of these were contemporary hits from its new Touchstone label, such as *Splash*. However, it also began marketing its old classics, first selecting those that, while popular, were not its greatest hits to see customers' reaction and to protect its rerun movie revenues. *Dumbo* and *Alice in Wonderland* were released in 1983 to enthusiastic demand, and Disney, realizing the revenue potential from video sales was enormous, soon orchestrated the gradual release of all its classics on videotape.

The sale of consumer products bearing Disney's logo had long been one of Disney's major lines of business. However, many analysts felt that Disney was not exploiting the potential of this market and that its strategy of franchising rights to the use of Disney's name and characters to other companies was bringing Disney some money, but making far more money for the actual producers and distributors of Disney's products than for the company itself. They felt the potential market for Disney's books, comics, records, clothing, and all kinds of Disney souvenirs had yet to be exploited.

Moviemaking

Since Walt's death, Disney's movie operations suffered, because they failed to find good scripts and projects. The performance of Disney's film business had been lackluster throughout the 1970s, and although the film division accounted for more than 20% of Disney's profits in 1979, by 1982 it was losing money. The situation became so bad that Disney's CEO, E. Cardon (Card) Walker, who had taken over after Roy Disney's death in 1971, was talking about closing it down. The division that had been Disney's core business and the source of its success was now in danger. How had this come about? First, Disney was relying on reruns of its classic movies and living on its past glory rather than on the proceeds of its present activities. Reruns were contributing more than 50% of the revenues of the film division because Disney was having little commercial success with

its new ventures. Although receiving good reviews as animated movies, such as the *Secret of Nimh*, *Watership Down*, and the *Black Hole*, were not big money spinners, and the live-action films Disney had been producing, such as *Something Wicked This Way Comes and Condorman*, lost money; these two movies, for example, lost more than $20 million each.

Moreover, analysts were claiming that Disney was not making the best use of its film library, which contained more than 700 different titles. They felt that Disney could be making a much more creative use of this resource, and, in part as a response to this pressure to exploit this resource, the company drew up plans for the Disney Channel, its pay-TV channel. Meanwhile, industry analysts did not like Card Walker's attitude toward the film division. They felt a turnaround in this division rather than liquidation was the answer; in 1983, Ronald Miller became CEO to implement this turnaround strategy. His answer to the problem was to create a new film division, Touchstone Films, to produce movies that were unsuitable for the family-oriented Disney label. He saw the problem as one of being straight jacketed by Disney's conservative, family image, which had not allowed filmmakers to exploit the opportunities in the market for new kinds of movies. Touchstone brought out *Splash* in 1983; it was a huge hit and the beginning of a turnaround of the film division. Nevertheless, Disney's top management was worried that Walt would not have liked it, and they actively sought to isolate the Touchstone division from the Disney organization. This conflict over Disney's future was the start of infighting between Disney's managers and stockholders over the best way to manage the company.

Roy Disney II, the nephew of Walt Disney, lost confidence in the management team. He felt it lacked the Disney vision and the skills to exploit the Disney resources; in essence, he felt that it was destroying the legacy Walt had left behind. These open conflicts brought Disney to the attention of corporate raiders, and, by 1984, there was an increasing possibility of an unfriendly takeover of the Disney organization. To prevent such a takeover, the Disney family sided with new investors, the Bass family, to oust the old, conservative, management team. The Disney family then set out to recruit someone who could return Disney to a preeminent position in the entertainment industry. They found Michael Eisner, previously vice chairman of Paramount, and widely regarded as the originator of a massive turnaround in the fortunes of that corporation, due to his ability to find and act on new trends in the marketplace. In September 1984, Michael Eisner took control of Disney and a new era began. Finally, someone had emerged who could wear Walt's crown.

MICHAEL EISNER'S WALT DISNEY COMPANY

In December 1984, Michael Eisner sat down with Frank Wells, the person he had recruited to help him turn the Disney Company around, and Roy Disney II, the nephew of the founder, who had been instrumental in Eisner's appointment, to plan Disney's future. They looked over Disney's resources and the activities of its divisions and subsidiaries, and both Eisner and Wells were amazed at the extent and diversity of Disney's resources. Eisner decided that Disney's strengths were in its three principal business segments:

1. *Entertainment and recreation*, which included all its theme parks and hotel businesses, together with shopping centers, conference centers, and golf courses
2. *Motion pictures and home videos*, which included the Disney studios; Buena Vista Productions, which had the Touchstone label; and Buena Vista Distribution, which distributed Disney's films at home and abroad
3. *Consumer products*, which was the licensing arm of Disney and licensed its characters, literary properties, and songs and music to various manufacturers, retailers, printers, and publishers

Why were these businesses underperforming, and what could be done about it? It did not take Eisner and Wells long to realize that the problem was that the potential of these businesses was not being exploited. In none of these business segments was management following any clearly defined strategy to exploit the Disney resources or a vision of what use these resources could be put to in the future. Each division was drifting aimlessly along. For example, despite Disney's raw filmmaking talent, the movie business was losing money. Similarly, due to

inaction, Disney had lost its television presence outside its own movie channel.

Moreover, it was apparent that while Disney was not taking advantage of the opportunities, other people were. For every dollar Disney was collecting in revenues from its characters and theme parks, those manufacturers who were licensing Disney's products or those hotel chains housing and feeding Disney customers at the theme parks, were getting five. Disney was stagnating, and new ways had to be found to exploit its revenue-generating potential and regain "Disney dollars." First, however, they realized the need to recruit some exceptional executives to provide leadership in the financial planning areas of the company to back up the creative end, which they would lead. Eisner had to find the money to finance his expansion plans and develop new business ventures. In 1985, he hired Gary L. Wilson as executive vice president and chief financial officer of Disney and made him a director. Wilson, a project finance specialist, had previously performed the same role for the Marriot Corporation, the hotel chain, and had participated in the enormous growth of that corporation. According to Eisner, his responsibility would be to plan and implement the company's expansion programs, including internal development and acquisitions. With the team set, Eisner began to change Disney.

Entertainment and Recreation

Eisner began to take a long hard look at the theme park business. This was Disney's biggest money spinner, but revenue growth had been slow. How could he revitalize this division's strategy? He started by looking at the customer groups and segments Disney was serving. Was Disney targeting the right segment? What kind of product was Disney really offering? He soon discovered that 70% of theme park attendance was repeat business, and more than anything else, what brought people back time after time was the existence of new attractions and new novelties, not the price of the attractions. However, developing new attractions was expensive; it cost millions to develop a ride, which was why corporate sponsorship was so important. Could he increase the price of attendance to provide the revenue to finance the new attractions and business ventures or would doing so drive customers away? Going against the conventional wisdom that higher prices would reduce attendance, Eisner raised admission prices substantially. The result was only a small falloff in attendance and a huge increase in revenues. Essentially, he had discovered that Disney's theme parks had a captive audience. When he raised the entry price again (prices had now risen 45% in two years), revenues again dramatically increased with little falloff in attendance. In fact, the increase in theme park prices caused a 59% growth in company revenues and accounted for fully 94% of earnings growth in 1986. Pretax profits of Disneyland and Disney World rose by 38% by September 1985 to $266.4 million from $192.7 million a year earlier. This provided some much needed cash for expansion of Disney's attractions and hotel developments and was the source of the turnaround in Disney profits.

Eisner set about revamping the theme park concept to find ways of increasing Disney's revenues and regaining Disney dollars from other firms. On the theme park side, Eisner realized that (1) more kinds of attractions and rides inside existing theme parks, and (2) additional theme parks, or "gates," and new collections of attractions were what was needed. Moreover, competition was developing in Orlando as other entertainment companies opened attractions to capitalize on tourists' presence. For example, a major water park attraction, Wet and Wild, opened, which offered a wide variety of water rides. Also, Sea World opened an Orlando theme park. The popularity of active, physically oriented attractions was accelerating, and Disney, recognizing the possibilities of such attractions, planned Typhoon Lagoon to recapture revenue. This opened in 1989 to major success. It provided one reason to stay an extra day in a Disney hotel.

Disney sought new gate ideas to capture tourists' imagination. In this effort, it was helped by a rival, MCA, who announced that it would build a Universal Studio Tours theme park near Orlando, similar to the one it already operated in Southern California. Eisner, never slow to recognize opportunity, rushed to come out with an alternative. The result was a joint announcement by Disney and MGM that they would build a Disney-MGM Studio theme park on the Orlando site, which would open in 1989. It opened to enthusiastic crowds on time, ahead of Universal's, which was not planned to open until 1990. So popular was the studio tour attraction that Disney announced it would double its size by 1992.

The company began actively searching for a fourth gate at Disney World, and there was speculation that this might take the form of a zoological park. Disney did not ignore shopping and nighttime entertainment at Disney World, in an effort to wrest tourists' dollars from the Orlando competition. At night, many of its guests were leaving Disney World to eat and play in the entertainment district of Church Street Station in Orlando. To keep patrons on the site, Disney built Pleasure Island, a huge complex of shops, bars, restaurant, discos, and nightclubs to attract its guests. This has also been very successful and has provided a new dimension to the Disney experience.

Finally, the company looked at the food concession business. At Disney World and Disneyland, food concessions had previously been licensed to other companies that provided the food and paid Disney a percentage of the proceeds. Eisner realized that this was also a source of revenue loss; as leases and agreements expired, Disney began to take over all the food operations at the theme parks. Not wanting to get into the soft-drink business or photography business, however, Eisner was content to make lucrative deals with Coca-Cola and Kodak that they would be the sole suppliers of soft drinks and film products at Disney's theme parks.

Meanwhile, Eisner was not ignoring either the Magic Kingdom or the EPCOT Center at Orlando. New attractions were being constantly announced. For example, Captain EO, a $17 million 3-D music video starring Michael Jackson, was developed for the EPCOT Center at Disney World. Also, the Living Seas exhibit, sponsored by United Technologies, and the Wonders of Life, sponsored by Metropolitan Life, opened. Similarly, with George Lucas of *Star Wars* fame, a new $32 million spaceship ride, Star Tours, was developed for the Disney-MGM Studios theme park. Production of a ride based on the exploits of Indiana Jones was also planned. At Anaheim, too, attractions were coming thick and fast. In 1985, Eisner announced a collaboration with George Lucas for a Star Wars attraction at Disneyland, and many additional Lucas attractions followed. In 1988, the company announced plans for Splash Mountain at Disneyland, an attraction in which passengers ride replicas of hollowed-out logs down huge slides populated with Disney characters. Moreover, in 1989, the company also bought Henson Associates Inc., the originators of The Muppets characters, and the

Muppet Theater opened at the Disney-MGM Studios to show the exploits of Kermit the Frog and Miss Piggy in glorious 3-D. Under Eisner, the repertoire of Disney's cast of characters constantly increases at its theme parks.

The Imagineering Unit At the source of the new developments in attractions and theme park development is Disney's Imagineering unit. Started by Walt Disney to actualize his ideas, the unit became responsible for all technical advances involving the design and building of Disney's new rides. However, because the company was experiencing problems in the early 1980s, consideration had been given to closing down this unit to save money. Under Eisner, this unit's budget has been increased dramatically, and it is the source of new adventures and attractions at the theme parks. It was this unit that cooperated with George Lucas to develop the Star Wars attractions at the theme parks. It was also this unit that planned EPCOT Center, the Disney-MGM Studio tours attraction, the rides developed for Tokyo Disneyland, and the new Euro Disneyland outside Paris. Disney is selling the skills of this division to other interested parties. For example, Disney agreed to build a $40 million exhibit on the history of space flight for the Johnson Space Center in Houston, Texas.

Hotel Developments In developing new attractions, Eisner and his team had another moneymaking venture in mind. Disney's guests (it calls its visitors guests) would need somewhere to stay; moreover, if there were many attractions to see, they would need to stay for several days. This was an opportunity of which to take advantage. Disney needed to get into the hotel business and build luxury hotels to meet its guests' needs. At Anaheim, but principally in Orlando, this new strategy went into operation. At Disney World, Eisner got his team together to discuss expansion plans for exploiting the vast untapped land and resources in its Orlando site. Eisner realized that Disney was offering far more than eight hours of live entertainment. It could offer a total package of Disney fun whereby its guests could live inside Disney World eating, sleeping, and breathing Disney. In the years since Disney World had been built, several luxury hotels and convention facilities were built on the boundaries of Disney, such as the Grand Hyatt Regency Cypress Hotel and the Hilton Eisner.

Wilson planned to steal back the hotel and food dollars for Disney.

They embarked on an ambitious campaign that involved Disney building not one but many luxury hotels on the Orlando site, each of which would offer a different kind of experience to Disney's guests. Then, each time guests returned, they could stay at a new Disney hotel location and never leave Disney World. In quick succession, they opened hotels such as the Grand Floridian Hotel and the Caribbean Beach Club and Resort, both of which, like the other Disney hotels, enjoyed occupancy rates of more than 90%, well above the industry average of 65%. They also built budget hotels such as Musicland and Sportsland. Moreover, Disney built major convention centers and hotels to reclaim the convention trade it had allowed the Hyatt and Hilton corporations to seize. Near EPCOT Center, Disney opened four new luxury hotels, including the Dolphin Convention Hotel and the Swan Hotel, which together have more than 2,350 rooms and 200,000 square feet of convention space.

Using Wilson's skills, Disney has found the ideal formula for building hotels without putting a financial debt burden on the company. As with its films, Disney arranges limited partnerships to finance its hotel building program and then often brings in the large hotel chains to actually run the hotels themselves. For example, a partnership formed by Tischman Realty and Construction Company, Metropolitan Life Insurance Company, and the Aoki Corporation financed the hotels. The Dolphin was run by the Sheraton Corporation, while the Swan was run by the Westin Company. Disney puts up the land and its name, and continuing this investment strategy it expected to develop 10,000 more hotel rooms by 1992. The proximity of the hotels and convention centers to Disney World and the Magic Kingdom gives the Disney operations a major advantage over its competitors. To get patrons to use Disney's hotels for longer periods, it was logical that Disney should find new ways of entertaining them, and this is just what Eisner did in finding new gates and attractions for his theme parks.

At Disneyland, Eisner's hotel and attraction development strategy was hampered by the fact that Disney did not own much of the land surrounding the park. It owned a small undeveloped tract of land at Disneyland, but this was just barely big enough to contain a new gate or hotel complex. Even if there was no room to build hotels, maybe Disney could acquire some. Under the old management team's operating philosophy, Disney had previously licensed the rights to use the Disney name for a hotel. The result was the Disneyland Hotel owned by the Wrather Corporation, a California entertainment corporation. Disney first acquired a large stake in the Wrather Corporation and took over the whole operation in 1989. It then revamped the hotel to upgrade it to the luxury class, carrying on the Orlando strategy.

As a part of this deal, however, Disney also gained control of the Wrather Corporation's Long Beach entertainment complex, which consisted of the liner Queen Mary, run as a hotel, together with Howard Hughes's Spruce Goose airplane, the largest ever built, and an entertainment village. Disney revamped the liner as a luxury hotel complex, and then Eisner realized that this complex could become Disney's second California gate, one that tourists could stop at on their way to or from Disneyland. Moreover, there was all the revenue currently going to Sea World and Knott's Berry Farm to compete for. In 1990, Disney announced a proposal to develop the Long Beach site as the center for a Disney Sea theme park, which would be a water-based attraction. It would contain the largest aquarium in the world, a glass cage in which tourists could go down among the sharks, and many other water-oriented rides and attractions, such as Captain Nemo's submarine from *20,000 Leagues Under the Sea*, another Imagineering unit project.

Eisner also began to consider ideas for new theme parks abroad. Disney already had participated in the planning of a Disneyland outside Tokyo, Japan. The Tokyo park had opened in April 1983 and had been wildly successful. However, in this venture Disney took no financial stake and, pursuing its old strategy, licensed its name to a group of Japanese investors in return for 10% of the gate receipts and 5% of other proceeds. This cost Disney much loss in profit. Eisner actively considered the idea for a Disney theme park somewhere in Europe to capture the vast European market. After much planning and up-front negotiations with several European countries, in December 1985, Eisner announced the decision to build what became a $2.1 billion Euro Disney theme park and resort complex, modeled on the Disney World concept, about 20 miles east of Paris in a suburb called Marne-La-Vallee. This opened in 1991. Disney owns 49% of the park; the other 51% is held by a company consisting of French and European investors. Disney receives fees for operating the park and royalties on admissions, rides, food, and other operations, but the French company controls the entire project. Plans were for a Disney World kind of complex where, along with the Magic Kingdom, there would be Disney hotels, shopping centers, golf courses, and convention facilities to ensure that Disney captured all the dollars in related entertainment activities, in short, the whole successful Eisner formula.

The result of these developments on Disney theme park revenues can be seen in Exhibit 2. At the same time as Eisner and his team were revamping their theme park strategy, he was working on plans for a turnaround of the motion picture and television business.

Competition in the Theme Park Industry Disney is by far the biggest of the theme park companies and the most profitable. However, as it has been expanding its gates and attractions, it has run into the competition. The new Disney Sea attraction is a prime rival for Sea World, and in California and Florida, Sea World will have to compete against an expanding Disney presence to water-related entertainments. The opening of Typhoon Lagoon hurt Sea World's Orlando operation, for example. In addition, Disney has been battling with MCA, the owner of the Universal Studio Tours. Sidney Sheinberg, the president of MCA, claimed that his company was the originator of the idea of the Orlando studio tours attraction, but Disney took the idea and ran with it. Competition between the Disney-MGM Studio tour and the Universal tour will only heat up in the coming years. Moreover, after announcing that Disney would build a studio tour on its Euro Disney site, MCA announced that it, too, would open one in Paris or London. Other companies in the industry, such as Six Flags and Busch Gardens, and Disney's new Orlando gate might bring it into direct competition with them. Moreover, Disney's huge expansion into hotels brought it up against the major hotel companies, and competition could be expected to be fierce there if ever there was a falloff in demand for hotel rooms.

Motion Pictures and Television

When Eisner took over Disney in 1984, Disney executives were apologizing for the success of their new smash hit movie *Splash*; even though it was produced

Exhibit 2   Consolidated Statement of Income (in millions, except per share data)

Year Ended September 30	1989	1988	1987
REVENUES			
Theme parks and resorts	$2,595.4	$2,042.0	$1,834.2
Filmed entertainment	1,587.6	1,149.2	875.6
Consumer products	411.3	247.0	167.0
	4,594.3	**3,438.2**	**2,876.8**
COSTS AND EXPENSES			
Theme parks and resorts	1,810.0	1,477.2	1,285.3
Filmed entertainment	1,331.1	962.9	745.0
Consumer products	224.2	113.3	69.7
	3,365.3	**2,553.4**	**2,100.0**
OPERATING INCOME			
Theme parks and resorts	785.4	564.8	548.9
Filmed entertainment	256.5	186.3	130.6
Consumer products	187.1	133.7	97.3
	1,229.0	**884.8**	**776.8**
CORPORATE EXPENSES (INCOME)			
General and administrative	119.6	96.0	70.3
Interest expense	23.9	5.8	29.1
Investment and interest income	(67.4)	(58.9)	(49.0)
	76.1	**42.9**	**50.4**
Income from continuing operations	1,152.9	841.9	726.4
Income taxes	449.6	319.9	334.1
Income from continuing operations	**703.3**	**522.0**	**392.3**
Discontinued operations, net			52.4
Net Income	**$703.3**	**$522.0**	**$444.7**
EARNINGS PER SHARE			
Continuing operations	$5.10	$3.80	$2.85
Discontinued operations			.38
	$5.10	**$3.80**	**$3.23**
Average number of common and common equivalent shares outstanding	138.0	137.4	137.8

Source: The Walt Disney Company, Annual Report, 1989.

by their separate Touchstone label, it was not in the tradition of Walt Disney family entertainment. Eisner had no such problems recognizing that times had changed and that the family of 1985 was not the family of 1965. As head of children's entertainment at ABC, he had recognized the changing trends in viewing habits and understood that new definitions of family entertainment were possible in the 1980s. Later, at Paramount, he had been involved in many of that studio's huge successes. It was he who had seen the possibility for projects such as *Raiders of the Lost Ark*, *Airplane*, and *Terms of Endearment*, all of which became blockbust er movies.

At Disney, Eisner used this experience, and, with Jeff Katzenberg, the creative head of Disney's movie division, and began to fashion Disney's new strategy. Katzenberg was also a Paramount veteran, where he was known as the "golden retriever" for his ability to sniff out just the right scripts. He also is a workaholic who makes hundreds of two-minute phone calls a week to producers, directors, and so forth. At Paramount he was attributed with the phrase, "If you don't come in on Saturday, don't bother to come in on Sunday."

By 1984, Disney had only a 4% share of box office revenues for its movies. Its movie division was losing money and had become a drain on the company's resources. The problem facing the two men was how to turn around the division. On the financial side, to lessen the burden on Disney and reduce the fear of failure, Eisner negotiated an agreement to raise money to finance Touchstone's movie productions with Silver Screens Management Inc. The idea was that Silver Screens would sell limited partnerships to outside investors that would put up the money to finance Disney's movies. In return, investors would receive a percentage of the movie's subsequent revenues. By 1985, $193 million had been raised to finance 14 new movies.

With the financing in place, Eisner and Katzenberg moved to change Disney's strategy. Luring talented people away from Paramount, Eisner quickly approved *Down and Out in Beverly Hills*, which grossed an impressive $62 million. He then focused on signing stars who were then not box office draws, such as Bette Midler and Richard Dreyfus, to keep costs low, and he added films to the production schedule that were vehicles for their talents. Disney boasts that while other studios spend $16 million per movie, it spends about $11 million;

low cost is the hallmark of Eisner's strategy. Such films as *Stakeout* and *Outrageous Fortune* were the result. By 1987, Disney had captured 14% of the $4.2 billion movie market; the turnaround was clear, as its film operations became the fastest-growing part of its operations. By 1987, Disney had turned the $10 million loss in 1984 into a huge profit.

He then turned to the next part of his movie strategy that involved deals for the distribution of the movies to television and videocassette sales. Disney had always distributed its own movies to movie theater chains through its distribution company, a subsidiary called Buena Vista Distributions, and had in this way captured the profit rather than give it to distributors. In 1985, the company formed a new television division and hired yet another Paramount executive to orchestrate the sale of movies to television networks and to handle videocassette sales. In 1986, Viacom's Showtime movie channel signed an exclusive agreement to buy cable television rights for movies produced through the Touchstone division through 1990. The deal started with *Down and Out in Beverly Hills* and involved more than 50 movies. Although very expensive for the movie channel, Disney was reported to have received $3 million to $5 million per film when the deal was signed, and both parties have benefited from it. Eisner also went ahead with videocassette sales. He decided to release one classic a year; in 1986, for example, 1 million copies of *Sleeping Beauty* were sold. Small wonder that Disney's stock price increased by five times between 1983 and 1986. Disney is also vigorously expanding foreign sales of videocassettes.

On the television front, Disney also went through a major turnaround. Eisner moved quickly to exploit Disney's resources. He arranged for syndication of the 29 years of *The Wonderful World of Disney* material, cartoons, and feature films on new networks emerging with the advent of cable television. Three packages of material were put up for sale in 1987, which helped to double film revenues. This market had previously been ignored. He also moved to make more products for the small screen. For the adult audience, the hit series *Golden Girls* was developed; he also arranged for a new format for *Siskel & Ebert at the Movies*. Eisner brought back the Disney Sunday Movie, introducing it himself and arranged for the development of *Duck Tales*, *Gummi Bears*, and *The Little Mermaid* new animation series to take advantage of Disney's animation skills. These cartoons shown on afternoon television and then the Disney Channel have proved immensely popular. There were failures, however. For example, two series introduced in 1986, *The Ellen Burstyn Show* and *Sidekicks*, were quickly abandoned. Meanwhile, under new management, the Disney Channel was doing somewhat better. Competition for subscribers is fierce in the pay-TV industry, but Disney made some headway. Its subscriber base grew 27% to almost 3.2 million by 1986 and 4 million by 1988.

In 1989, came another move in the television market. Disney acquired KHU-TV, a Los Angeles television station, and renamed it KCAL-TV. This takeover gave it a wholly owned distribution outlet for the products of its studios, so it could capture some of the value that was currently being earned by its end users. It had previously tried, but failed, to acquire the 360-screen Mann theater chain bought by Gulf & Western and a New York television station that MCA bought. So expansion into the television station market and movie theater market appeared possible. They also approached CBS to buy CBS Records but were spurned by the board, which eventually sold it to the Sony Corporation. As Eisner said, "We are going to be awfully conservative in what we go after, but if there was something out there that could add value to this company, we're going to go for it." The search for new assets was part of Eisner's strategy to reduce its heavy dependence on theme parks and movies for its operating revenues in the future.

By 1987 Walt Disney was number two in the share of box office revenues, with 14% of revenues after Paramount. Twenty-two of the 23 films produced by Disney have made a profit, far higher than the industry ratio of about 3 in 10. Then came such hits as *Three Men and a Baby*, which grossed more than $160 million; *Good Morning Vietnam*, with $110 million; and *Cocktail*, with Tom Cruise. It also introduced two more animation movies, *Who Framed Roger Rabbit?* which cost $38 million, thus departing from the Disney formula of keeping costs low; and *Oliver and Company*. As a result of these films, Disney took the box office lead from Paramount in 1988 with 22% of revenues through Labor Day, the end of the summer film season.

At the beginning of 1989, Disney established a third motion picture company, called Hollywood Pictures, to continue the success story established by Touchstone. It gave charge of this company to Ricardo Mestres, former president of production at Touchstone, and a mega performer in his own right. To finance the intended 24 to 28 movies a year, another silver screen partnership was established, which raised $600 million to fund future Disney films. Clearly, Disney was expecting big things from its three divisions. By the end of 1989, expectations were fulfilled; Disney was the market leader with almost 20% of box office revenues as a result of more successes such as *The Little Mermaid* and *Oliver and Company*. The change in the revenues and profits of the movie division is given in Exhibit 3.

Consumer Products Division

The final area that Eisner turned his attention to was improving revenues from the licensing of the Disney brand name to firms that wished to manufacture and sell products using Disney characters. Eisner's intention might be summed up as saying he would like to see a mouse or duck on every T-shirt, wrist, and toy or piece of baby equipment in every home in every country in the world. He started by developing deals with major manufacturers and retailers, signing an agreement with Mattel, the biggest United States toy manufacturer, to sell Disney-brand infant and preschool toys worldwide. In 1987, Disney signed a 10-year agreement with Sears to develop clothing and toys using certain Disney characters. By 1988, Disney had negotiated more than 3,000 agreements with companies to manufacture more than 14,000 Disney-licensed products.

Meanwhile, in 1987, the company announced plans for a large-scale expansion into retailing stores that would sell nothing but Disney products. The Disney stores market products produced by Disney's manufacturers, so that as in the case of Disney's entry into the television station market, Disney reaped the rewards from selling its own products. These stores sell videotapes of Disney's films, children's clothing, toys, and the whole Disney paraphernalia at premium prices. Given the ability to charge a premium price, each store is proving very profitable, and malls fight to attract a store.

In 1988, Disney paid $52 million to buy Childcraft Education Corporation, which sells educational toys and play equipment through direct mail. This move complemented Disney's mail-order, catalog sales operation, which sends out more than 6 million catalogs

Exhibit 3 Consolidated Balance Sheet (in millions)

September 30	1989	1988
ASSETS		
Cash	$380.8	$428.0
Marketable securities	662.3	668.6
Receivables	908.5	561.5
Merchandise inventories	224.3	159.9
Film costs	443.3	211.0
Theme parks, resorts, and other property, at cost		
Attractions, buildings and equipment	4,143.3	3,322.5
Accumulated depreciation	(1,217.3)	(1,065.2)
	2,926.0	**2,257.3**
Projects in progress	407.4	511.1
Land	63.9	53.3
	3,397.3	**2,821.7**
Other assets	640.7	258.2
	$6,657.2	**$5,108.9**
LIABILITIES AND STOCKHOLDERS' EQUITY		
Accounts payable and other accrued liabilities	$1,011.4	$698.7
Income taxes payable	250.9	204.3
Borrowings	860.6	435.5
Unearned royalty and other advances	912.7	823.3
Deferred income taxes	577.6	587.8
Stockholders' equity		
Common stock, $.10 par value		
Authorized—300.00 million shares		
Outstanding—135.3 million shares and 133.2 million shares	392.8 (135.3 million shares)	349.6
Retained earnings	2,651.2	2,009.7
	3,044.0	**2,359.3**
	$6,657.2	**$5,108.9**

Source: The Walt Disney Company, Annual Report, 1989.

a year and has expanded product offerings by more than 50%. Given its move into mail-order and store operations, it seems as if Disney is looking to become the Sears of the entertainment business. One more benefit to Disney from these store and catalog sales is the intangible brand name loyalty it creates for other Disney ventures. The stores are a marketing vehicle for Disney; they open up the Disney Company to the public and invite attendance at its theme parks and hotels.

International sales of Disney products are extremely important to the company. For example, every year, Japanese consumers buy more than $1 billion worth of Disney-brand products. In Italy, the Mickey Mouse comic book, *Topolino*, sells 700,000 copies a month, and when Disney took over publishing the comic itself, it made an extra $15 million a year in profits. Videocassette sales and records are major revenue earners for Disney Worldwide. In 1989, Eisner pointed to the internationalization of all Disney franchises as the source of the massive gains in the revenues of the consumer products and home video operations.

Another expanding dimension of Disney's business is publishing. While Disney licensed *Mickey Mouse Tales* and *Duck Tales* to Welch Publishing, it planned the publication of *Disney Adventure Digest* to be the official magazine of *Disney Afternoon*, two hours each weekday afternoon of syndicated programming scheduled for the fall of 1990. This had a planned circulation of 100,000. Many more magazine opportunities were also explored, including books to accompany Disney's movies. For example, many books were planned around Disney's successful *Dick Tracy* movie in 1990, and publishing provided new opportunities for Disney to exploit the linkages between its products. This division was geared toward masterminding international publication and sales of Disney's books and magazines, a market that likely grew with the opening of EuroDisney. In 1990, Disney sold more than 500 million books and comics worldwide.

Another venture for Disney involved selling its organizational culture, which is centered on providing high-quality customer service. Disney University in Orlando puts all new recruits through a three-day program designed to bring them into the Disney way of doing things. They learn the history of Disney, its mission, and its emphasis on courtesy to customers to maximize visitors' satisfaction. This is very important

to Disney, given that more than 70% of visitors are repeats. New employees learn the Disney language in which employees are known as cast members, visitors as guests, and employees are said to be onstage when they are working and offstage when they are not. Finally, Disney began to sell its expertise and techniques to major companies. So far, more than 3,000 executives from more than 1,200 companies have attended the two-day seminar Disney offers, called Traditions, to learn Disney's techniques to increase the quality of customer service in their own companies. One of the central features of the Disney approach is to empower employees so that they try to solve problems themselves as and when they occur rather than turn for help. According to Disney, the secret to Disney's success is "pixie dust," a combination of training, communication, and care.

DISNEY'S FUTURE

As a result of these developments, by 1989, sales had jumped from $1.46 billion in 1984 to $4.59 billion. Net profit rose from $97.8 million to $703.3 million, and earnings per share increased more than 10 times during the same period. Everything Disney did was designed to capitalize on the incredible progress that it made. The annual increase in profit was 46% in the 1980s, but Eisner and Wells vowed to increase profits by an average of 20% a year in the 1990s. To do so, they constantly expanded the range and scope of Disney's activities as well as building on the base they established. A new Disneyland theme park somewhere in Asia was in preparation, along with a new studio tours park next to the Euro Disneyland and a new theme park in Southern California. More new attractions based on its more recent successes were planned, including one designed around Dick Tracy. Similarly, Eisner announced that Disney would have 30 hotels with more than 26,000 rooms by 1995.

Industry analysts wondered whether Eisner and his team could maintain the same growth rate and even if the company may be headed for a fall. Because most of Disney's revenue came first from its theme parks and second from its film operations, they wondered whether the pace could be maintained. For example, they pointed out that a recession or an increase in the price of gas could rapidly affect theme park attendance, because the price of airplane seats and auto travel would increase. They also pointed out that historically no movie studio had been able to maintain an unbroken string of successes, and they wondered whether the movie division might be in for a rough ride in the future.

They also wondered about the wisdom of Disney's projects and the direction Michael Eisner's Disney Company was taking. After the incredible successes Eisner and his team achieved, critics claimed that the conceit of Disney executives was huge—people who believed that they could do no wrong. Eisner had been called an egomaniac, albeit by his archcritic Sidney Sheinberg, the president of rival MCA, and was said to be in search of ever-greater opportunities for the expansion of Disney's empire. Already the largest entertainment company in the world, Disney was now exercising its muscle as it sought to enlarge its share of the television station market. However, critics wondered whether such expansion was wise.

Because Disney could already sell its existing film products to the networks, did it need the added burden of owning television stations? In 1990, Eisner was looking around for new acquisitions to add to its Los Angeles station, and CBS was mentioned as a possible takeover target. Critics asked whether this would add value to Disney or to CBS.

In 1990, Disney announced that it would open a new record division, called Hollywood Records, to produce records for the general public, not just the Disney audience. This move would bring it into direct competition with huge record companies such as CBS Records, which Disney bid for but lost in the very competitive record business. The huge expansion into the hotel business was justified if occupancy rates stayed at more than 90% percent, but was the resort market becoming saturated with too many luxury hotels and conference centers being built? Any downturn in the vacation market for whatever cause might put severe pressure on hotel operations. Against opposition from his own team, Eisner also embarked on the concept of a Disney fast-food restaurant. Offering a wide array of food, such restaurants would seek to exploit the Disney cartoon characters in a restaurant format. However, this was a relatively new business for Disney. Although Disney operated restaurants in its own theme parks, it would be entering the highly competitive $65 billion fast-food industry currently dominated by big chains such as McDonald's and Burger King. Did Disney have the core skills to compete in this market?

Moreover, while guests may like to eat, sleep, and breathe Disney on their vacations, did they want to do so 365 days a year? Was there a danger of overexposure as children wear Disney clothes, read Disney books, watch Disney television programs, go to sleep in Disney beds playing with Disney toys, and then eat Disney food, too? Would there be a reaction as people turned from Disney to new forms of excitement and fantasy? However, where would they go? Disney had co-opted George Lucas and his characters; bought The Muppets, and, in films such as *Dick Tracy*, captured more characters. Was there a place for people to run? For the time being, it seemed that Michael Eisner could force the golden goose to keep on laying golden eggs, but if the environment changed, if the film division fell on hard times, or if his new projects failed to meet expectations, the supply of eggs might stop.

NOTES

Chapter 1

[1]"How Big Can It Grow?" *The Economist*, April 17, 2004, 74–78; "Trial by Checkout," *The Economist*, June 26, 2004, 74–76; Walmart Form 10-K, 200; Information at Walmart's Web site (http://www.walmartstores .com); Robert Slater, *The Wal-Mart Triumph* (New York: Portfolio Trade Books, 2004); "The bulldozer from Bentonville Slows; Wal-Mart," *The Economist*, February 17, 2007, 70.

[2]There are several different ratios for measuring profitability, such as return on invested capital, return on assets, and return on equity. Although these different measures are highly correlated with each other, finance theorists argue that the return on invested capital is the most accurate measure of profitability. See T. Copeland, T. Koller, and J. Murrin, *Valuation: Measuring and Managing the Value of Companies* (New York: Wiley, 1996).

[3]Trying to estimate the relative importance of industry effects and firm strategy on firm profitability has been one of the most important areas of research in the strategy literature during the past decade. See Y. E. Spanos and S. Lioukas, "An Examination of the Causal Logic of Rent Generation," *Strategic Management* 22, no. 10 (October 2001): 907–934; and R. P. Rumelt, "How Much Does Industry Matter?" *Strategic Management* 12 (1991): 167–185. See also A. J. Mauri and M. P. Michaels, "Firm and Industry Effects within Strategic Management: An Empirical Examination," *Strategic Management* 19 (1998): 211–219.

[4]This view is known as agency theory. See M. C. Jensen and W. H. Meckling, "Theory of the Firm: Managerial Behavior, Agency Costs and Ownership Structure," *Journal of Financial Economics* 3 (1976): 305–360; and E. F. Fama, "Agency Problems and the Theory of the Firm," *Journal of Political Economy* 88 (1980): 375–390.

[5]K. R. Andrews, *The Concept of Corporate Strategy* (Homewood, Ill.: Dow Jones Irwin, 1971); H. I. Ansoff, *Corporate Strategy* (New York: McGraw-Hill, 1965); C. W. Hofer and D. Schendel, *Strategy Formulation: Analytical Concepts* (St. Paul, Minn.: West, 1978). See also P. J. Brews and M. R. Hunt, "Learning to Plan and Planning to Learn," *Strategic Management* 20 (1999): 889–913; and R. W. Grant, "Planning in a Turbulent Environment," *Strategic Management* 24 (2003): 491–517.

[6]http://ww w.kodak.com/US/en/corp/careers/ why/valuesmission.jhtml.

[7]These three questions were first proposed by P. F. Drucker, *Management: Tasks, Responsibilities, Practices* (New York: Harper & Row, 1974), 74–94.

[8]D. F. Abell, *Defining the Business: The Starting Point of Strategic Planning* (Englewood Cliffs, N.J.: Prentice-Hall, 1980).

[9]P. A. Kidwell and P. E. Ceruzzi, *Landmarks in Digital Computing* (Washington, D.C.: Smithsonian Institute, 1994).

[10]J. C. Collins and J. I. Porras, "Building Your Company's Vision," *Harvard Business Review* (September–October 1996): 65–77.

[11]http://www.nucor.com/.

[12]See J. P. Kotter and J. L. Heskett, *Corporate Culture and Performance* (New York: Free Press, 1992). For similar work, see Collins and Porras, "Building Your Company's Vision."

[13]E. Freeman, *Strategic Management: A Stakeholder Approach* (Boston: Pitman Press, 1984).

[14]M. D. Richards, *Setting Strategic Goals and Objectives* (St. Paul, Minn.: West, 1986).

[15]E. A. Locke, G. P. Latham, and M. Erez, "The Determinants of Goal Commitment," *Academy of Management Review* 13 (1988): 23–39.

[16]R. E. Hoskisson, M. A. Hitt, and C. W. L. Hill, "Managerial Incentives and Investment in R&D in Large Multiproduct Firms," *Organization Science* 3 (1993): 325–341.

[17]Andrews, *Concept of Corporate Strategy*; Ansoff, *Corporate Strategy*; Hofer and Schendel, *Strategy Formulation*.

[18]For details, see R. A. Burgelman, "Intraorganizational Ecology of Strategy Making and Organizational Adaptation: Theory and Field Research," *Organization Science* 2 (1991): 239–262; H. Mintzberg, "Patterns in Strategy Formulation," *Management Science* 24 (1978): 934–948; S. L. Hart, "An Integrative Framework for Strategy Making Processes," *Academy of Management Review* 17 (1992): 327–351; G. Hamel, "Strategy as Revolution," *Harvard Business Review* 74 (July–August 1996): 69–83; and R. W. Grant, "Planning in a Turbulent Environment," *Strategic Management Journal* 24 (2003): 491–517. See also G. Gavetti, D. Levinthal, and J. W. Rivkin, "Strategy Making in Novel and Complex Worlds: The Power of Analogy," *Strategic Management Journal* 26 (2005): 691–712.

[19]This is the premise of those who advocate that complexity and chaos theory should be applied to strategic management. See S. Brown and K. M. Eisenhardt, "The Art of Continuous Change: Linking Complexity Theory and Time Based Evolution in Relentlessly Shifting Organizations," *Administrative Science Quarterly* 29 (1997): 1–34; and R. Stacey and D. Parker, *Chaos, Management and Economics* (London: Institute for Economic Affairs, 1994). See also H. Courtney, J. Kirkland, and P. Viguerie, "Strategy under Uncertainty," *Harvard Business Review* 75 (November–December 1997): 66–79.

[20]Hart, "Integrative Framework"; Hamel, "Strategy as Revolution."

[21]See Burgelman, "Intraorganizational Ecology;" and Mintzberg, "Patterns in Strategy Formulation."

[22]R. A. Burgelman and A. S. Grove, "Strategic Dissonance," *California Management Review* (Winter 1996): 8–28.

[23]C. W. L. Hill and F. T. Rothaermel, "The Performance of Incumbent Firms in the Face of Radical Technological Innovation," *Academy of Management Review* 28 (2003): 257–274.

[24]This story was related to the author by George Rathmann, who at one time was head of 3M's research activities.

[25]R. T. Pascale, "Perspectives on Strategy: The Real Story behind Honda's Success," *California Management Review* 26 (1984): 47–72.

[26]This viewpoint is strongly emphasized by Burgelman and Grove, "Strategic Dissonance."

[27]C. C. Miller and L. B. Cardinal, "Strategic Planning and Firm Performance: A Synthesis of More Than Two Decades of Research," *Academy of Management Journal* 37 (1994): 1649–1665. See also P. R. Rogers, A. Miller, and W. Q. Judge, "Using Information Processing Theory to Understand Planning/Performance Relationships in the Context of Strategy," *Strategic Management* 20 (1999): 567–577.

[28]P. J. Brews and M. R. Hunt, "Learning to Plan and Planning to Learn," *Strategic Management Journal* 20 (1999): 889–913.

[29]P. Cornelius, A. Van de Putte, and M. Romani, "Three Decades of Scenario Planning at Shell," *California Management Review* 48 (2005): 92–110.

[30]H. Courtney, J. Kirkland, and P. Viguerie, "Strategy Under Uncertainty," *Harvard Business Review* 75 (November–December 1997): 66–79.

[31]P. J. H. Schoemaker, "Multiple Scenario Development: Its Conceptual and Behavioral Foundation," *Strategic Management Journal* 14 (1993): 193–213.

[32]P. Schoemaker, P. J. H. van der Heijden, and A. J. M. Cornelius, "Integrating Scenarios into Strategic Planning at Royal Dutch Shell," *Planning Review* 20, no. 3 (1992): 41–47; I. Wylie, "There Is No Alternative to. . . ." *Fast Company* (July 2002): 106–111.

[33]"The Next Big Surprise: Scenario Planning," *The Economist*, October 13, 2001, 71.

[34]See C. R. Schwenk, "Cognitive Simplification Processes in Strategic Decision Making," *Strategic Management* 5 (1984): 111–128; and K. M. Eisenhardt and M. Zbaracki, "Strategic Decision Making," *Strategic Management* 13 (Special Issue, 1992): 17–37.

[35]H. Simon, *Administrative Behavior* (New York: McGraw-Hill, 1957).

[36]The original statement of this phenomenon was made by A. Tversky and D. Kahneman, "Judgment under Uncertainty: Heuristics and Biases," *Science* 185 (1974): 1124–1131. See also D. Lovallo and D. Kahneman, "Delusions of Success: How Optimism Undermines Executives' Decisions," *Harvard Business Review* 81 (July 2003): 56–67; and J. S. Hammond, R. L. Keeny, and H. Raiffa, "The Hidden Traps in Decision Making," *Harvard Business Review* 76 (September–October 1998): 25–34.

[37]Schwenk, *Cognitive Simplification Processes*, 111–128.

[38]B. M. Staw, "The Escalation of Commitment to a Course of Action," *Academy of Management Review* 6 (1981): 577–587.

[39]R. Roll, "The Hubris Hypotheses of Corporate Takeovers," *Journal of Business* 59 (1986): 197–216.

[40]See R. O. Mason, "A Dialectic Approach to Strategic Planning," *Management Science* 13 (1969): 403–414; R. A. Cosier and J. C. Aplin, "A Critical View of Dialectic Inquiry in Strategic Planning," *Strategic Management* 1 (1980): 343–356; and I. I. Mintroff and R. O. Mason, "Structuring III—Structured Policy Issues: Further Explorations in a Methodology for Messy Problems," *Strategic Management* 1 (1980): 331–342.

[41]Mason, *A Dialectic Approach*, 403–414.

[42]Lovallo and Kahneman, "Delusions of Success."

[43]For a summary of research on strategic leadership, see D. C. Hambrick, "Putting Top Managers Back into the Picture," *Strategic Management* 10 (Special Issue, 1989): 5–15. See also D. Goldman, "What Makes a Leader?" *Harvard Business Review* (November–December 1998): 92–105; H. Mintzberg, "Covert Leadership," *Harvard Business Review* (November–December 1998): 140–148; and R. S. Tedlow, "What Titans Can Teach Us," *Harvard Business Review* (December 2001): 70–79.

[44]N. M. Tichy and D. O. Ulrich, "The Leadership Challenge: A Call for the Transformational Leader," *Sloan Management Review* (Fall 1984): 59–68; F. Westley and H. Mintzberg, "Visionary Leadership and Strategic Management," *Strategic Management* 10 (Special Issue, 1989): 17–32.

[45]Comments were made by Jim Donald at a presentation to University of Washington MBA students.

[46]B. McConnell and J. Huba, *Creating Customer Evangelists* (Chicago: Dearborn Trade Publishing, 2003).

[47]E. Wrapp, "Good Managers Don't Make Policy Decisions," *Harvard Business Review* (September–October 1967): 91–99.

[48]J. Pfeffer, *Managing with Power* (Boston: Harvard Business School Press, 1992).

[49]D. Goldman, "What Makes a Leader?" *Harvard Business Review* (November–December 1998): 92–105.

[50]C. Y. Baldwin, Fundamental Enterprise Valuation: Return on Invested Capital, Harvard Business School Note 9-801-125, July 3, 2004; T. Copeland et al., *Valuation: Measuring and Managing the Value of Companies* (New York: Wiley, 2000).

Chapter 2

[1]S. James, "Lofty Steel Prices Could Keep Climbing," *Herald Tribune*, May 19, 2008; "A Changed Game," *The Economist*, July 15, 2006, 61–62; M. Gene, U.S. Steel Is on a Roll, *Business Week*, June 30, 2008, 20.

[2]M. E. Porter, *Competitive Strategy* (New York: Free Press, 1980).

[3]J. E. Bain, *Barriers to New Competition* (Cambridge, Mass.: Harvard University Press, 1956). For a review of the modern literature on barriers to entry, see R. J. Gilbert, "Mobility Barriers and the Value of Incumbency," in R. Schmalensee and R. D. Willig (eds.), *Handbook of Industrial Organization*, vol. 1 (Amsterdam: North-Holland, 1989). See also R. P. McAfee, H. M. Mialon, and M. A. Williams, "What Is a Barrier to Entry?" *American Economic Review* 94 (May 2004): 461–468.

[4]A detailed discussion of switching costs and lock in can be found in C. Shapiro and H. R. Varian, *Information Rules: A Strategic Guide to the Network Economy* (Boston: Harvard Business School Press, 1999).

[5]Most of this information on barriers to entry can be found in the industrial organization economics literature. See especially the following works: Bain, *Barriers to New Competition*; M. Mann, "Seller Concentration, Barriers to Entry and Rates of Return in 30 Industries," *Review of*

Economics and Statistics 48 (1966): 296–307; W. S. Comanor and T. A. Wilson, "Advertising, Market Structure and Performance," *Review of Economics and Statistics* 49 (1967): 423–440; Gilbert, "Mobility Barriers"; and K. Cool, L.-H. Roller, and B. Leleux, "The Relative Impact of Actual and Potential Rivalry on Firm Profitability in the Pharmaceutical Industry," *Strategic Management Journal* 20 (1999): 1–14.

[6]For a discussion of tacit agreements, see T. C. Schelling, *The Strategy of Conflict* (Cambridge, Mass.: Harvard University Press, 1960).

[7]M. Busse, "Firm Financial Condition and Airline Price Wars," *Rand Journal of Economics* 33 (2002): 298–318.

[8]For a review, see F. Karakaya, "Market Exit and Barriers to Exit: Theory and Practice," *Psychology and Marketing* 17 (2000): 651–668.

[9]P. Ghemawat, *Commitment: The Dynamics of Strategy* (Boston: Harvard Business School Press, 1991).

[10]A. S. Grove, *Only the Paranoid Survive* (New York: Doubleday, 1996).

[11]In standard microeconomic theory, the concept used for assessing the strength of substitutes and complements is the cross elasticity of demand.

[12]For details and further references, see C. W. L. Hill, "Establishing a Standard: Competitive Strategy and Technology Standards in Winner Take All Industries," *Academy of Management Executive* 11 (1997): 7–25; and Shapiro and Varian, *Information Rules.*

[13]The development of strategic group theory has been a strong theme in the strategy literature. Important contributions include the following: R. E. Caves and M. E. Porter, "From Entry Barriers to Mobility Barriers," *Quarterly Journal of Economics* (May 1977): 241–262; K. R. Harrigan, "An Application of Clustering for Strategic Group Analysis," *Strategic Management Journal* 6 (1985): 55–73; K. J. Hatten and D. E. Schendel, "Heterogeneity within an Industry: Firm Conduct in the U.S. Brewing Industry, 1952–71," *Journal of Industrial Economics* 26 (1977): 97–113; and M. E. Porter, "The Structure within Industries and Companies' Performance," *Review of Economics and Statistics* 61 (1979): 214–227. See also

K. Cool and D. Schendel, "Performance Differences among Strategic Group Members," *Strategic Management Journal* 9 (1988): 207–233; A. Nair and S. Kotha, "Does Group Membership Matter? Evidence from the Japanese Steel Industry," *Strategic Management Journal* 20 (2001): 221–235; and G. McNamara, D. L. Deephouse, and R. A. Luce, "Competitive Positioning within and across a Strategic Group Structure," *Strategic Management Journal* 24 (2003): 161–180.

[14]For details on the strategic group structure in the pharmaceutical industry, see K. Cool and I. Dierickx, "Rivalry, Strategic Groups, and Firm Profitability," *Strategic Management Journal* 14 (1993): 47–59.

[15]C. W. Hofer argued that life-cycle considerations may be the most important contingency when formulating business strategy. See C. W. Hofer, "Towards a Contingency Theory of Business Strategy," *Academy of Management Journal* 18 (1975): 784–810. There is empirical evidence to support this view. See C. R. Anderson and C. P. Zeithaml, "Stages of the Product Life Cycle, Business Strategy, and Business Performance," *Academy of Management Journal* 27 (1984): 5–24; and D. C. Hambrick and D. Lei, "Towards an Empirical Prioritization of Contingency Variables for Business Strategy," *Academy of Management Journal* 28 (1985): 763–788. See also G. Miles, C. C. Snow, and M. P. Sharfman, "Industry Variety and Performance," *Strategic Management Journal* 14 (1993): 163–177; G. K. Deans, F. Kroeger, and S. Zeisel, "The Consolidation Curve," *Harvard Business Review* 80 (December 2002): 2–3.

[16]The characteristics of declining industries have been summarized by K. R. Harrigan, "Strategy Formulation in Declining Industries," *Academy of Management Review* 5 (1980): 599–604. See also J. Anand and H. Singh, "Asset Redeployment, Acquisitions and Corporate Strategy in Declining Industries," *Strategic Management Journal* 18 (1997): 99–118.

[17]This perspective is associated with the Austrian School of Economics, which goes back to Schumpeter. For a summary of this school and its implications for strategy, see R. Jacobson, "The Austrian School of Strategy," *Academy of Management Review* 17 (1992): 782–807; and C. W. L. Hill and D. Deeds, "The Importance of Industry

Structure for the Determination of Industry Profitability: A Neo-Austrian Approach," *Journal of Management Studies* 33 (1996): 429–451.

[18]"A Tricky Business," *Economist*, June 30, 2001, 55–56.

[19]D. F. Barnett and R. W. Crandall, *Up from the Ashes* (Washington, D.C.: Brookings Institution, 1986).

[20]M. E. Porter, *The Competitive Advantage of Nations* (New York: Free Press, 1990).

[21]The term *punctuated equilibrium* is borrowed from evolutionary biology. For a detailed explanation of the concept, see M. L. Tushman, W. H. Newman, and E. Romanelli, "Convergence and Upheaval: Managing the Unsteady Pace of Organizational Evolution," *California Management Review* 29, no. 1 (1985): 29–44; C. J. G. Gersick, "Revolutionary Change Theories: A Multilevel Exploration of the Punctuated Equilibrium Paradigm," *Academy of Management Review* 16 (1991): 10–36; and R. Adner and D. A. Levinthal, "The Emergence of Emerging Technologies," *California Management Review* 45 (Fall 2002): 50–65.

[22]A. J. Slywotzky, *Value Migration: How to Think Several Moves Ahead of the Competition* (Boston: Harvard Business School Press, 1996).

[23]Hill and Deeds, "Importance of Industry Structure."

[24]R. P. Rumelt, "How Much Does Industry Matter?" *Strategic Management Journal* 12 (1991): 167–185. See also A. J. Mauri and M. P. Michaels, "Firm and Industry Effects within Strategic Management: An Empirical Examination," *Strategic Management Journal* 19 (1998): 211–219.

[25]See R. Schmalensee, "Inter-Industry Studies of Structure and Performance," in R. Schmalensee and R. D. Willig (eds.), *Handbook of Industrial Organization.* Similar results were found by A. N. McGahan and M. E. Porter, "How Much Does Industry Matter, Really?" *Strategic Management Journal* 18 (1997): 15–30.

[26]For example, see K. Cool and D. Schendel, "Strategic Group Formation and Performance: The Case of the U.S. Pharmaceutical Industry, 1932–1992," *Management Science* (September 1987): 1102–1124.

[27]See M. Gort and J. Klepper, "Time Paths in the Diffusion of Product Innovations," *Economic Journal* (September 1982): 630–653. Looking at the history of 46 products, Gort and Klepper found that the length of time before other companies entered the markets created by a few inventive companies declined from an average of 14.4 years for products introduced before 1930 to 4.9 years for those introduced after 1949.

[28]The phrase was originally coined by J. Schumpeter, *Capitalism, Socialism and Democracy* (London: Macmillan, 1950), 68.

[29]For a detailed discussion of the importance of the structure of law as a factor explaining economic change and growth, see D. C. North, *Institutions, Institutional Change, and Economic Performance* (Cambridge: Cambridge University Press, 1990).

[30]S. Theodore, "Brewers Take the Good with the Bad," *Beverage Industry* 97, April 2006: 17–23; V. Tremblay, N. Iwasaki, and C. Tremblay, "The Dynamics of Industry Concentration for U.S. Micro and Macro Brewers," *Review of Industrial Organization* 26 (2005): 307–324; J. P. Nelson, "Beer Advertising and Marketing Update: Structure, Conduct and Social Costs," *Review of Industrial Organization* 26 (2005): 269–306; Beer Institute, *Brewers Almanac, 2008*, (Washington DC: Beer Institute, 2008).

Chapter 3

[1]A. Martin, "McDonald's, the Happiest Meal Is Hot Profits," *New York Times*, January 11, 2009; M. Vella, "A New Look for McDonald's," *Business Week Online*, December 4, 2008; M. Warner, "Salads or No, Cheap Burgers Revive McDonald's," *New York Times*, April 19, 2006.

[2]M. Cusumano, *The Japanese Automobile Industry* (Cambridge, Mass.: Harvard University Press, 1989); S. Spear and H. K. Bowen, "Decoding the DNA of the Toyota Production System," *Harvard Business Review* (September–October 1999): 96–108.

[3]The material in this section relies on the resource-based view of the company. For summaries of this perspective, see J. B. Barney, "Company Resources and Sustained Competitive Advantage," *Journal of Management* 17 (1991): 99–120; J. T. Mahoney

and J. R. Pandian, "The Resource-Based View within the Conversation of Strategic Management," *Strategic Management Journal* 13 (1992): 63–380; R. Amit and P. J. H. Schoemaker, "Strategic Assets and Organizational Rent," *Strategic Management Journal* 14 (1993): 33–46; M. A. Peteraf, "The Cornerstones of Competitive Advantage: A Resource-Based View," *Strategic Management Journal* 14 (1993): 179–191; B. Wernerfelt, "A Resource-Based View of the Company," *Strategic Management Journal* 15 (1994): 171–180; and K. M. Eisenhardt and J. A. Martin, "Dynamic Capabilities: What Are They?" *Strategic Management Journal* 21 (2000): 1105–1121.

[4]J. B. Barney, "Company Resources and Sustained Competitive Advantage," *Journal of Management* 17 (1991): 99–120.

[5]For a discussion of organizational capabilities, see R. R. Nelson and S. Winter, *An Evolutionary Theory of Economic Change* (Cambridge, Mass.: Belknap Press, 1982).

[6]W. C. Kim and R. Mauborgne, "Value Innovation: The Strategic Logic of High Growth," *Harvard Business Review* (January–February 1997): 102–115.

[7]The concept of consumer surplus is an important one in economics. For a more detailed exposition, see D. Besanko, D. Dranove, and M. Shanley, *Economics of Strategy* (New York: Wiley, 1996).

[8]However, $P = U$ only in the special case when the company has a perfect monopoly; it can charge each customer a unique price that reflects the utility of the product to that customer (i.e., where perfect price discrimination is possible). More generally, except in the limiting case of perfect price discrimination, even a monopolist will see most customers capture some of the utility of a product in the form of a consumer surplus.

[9]This point is central to the work of Michael Porter. See M. E. Porter, *Competitive Advantage* (New York: Free Press, 1985). See also P. Ghemawat, *Commitment: The Dynamic of Strategy* (New York: Free Press, 1991), chap. 4.

[10]O. Wyman, *The Harbor Report*, 2008. http://www.oliverwyman.com/ow/automotive.htm.

[11]Porter, *Competitive Advantage*.

[12]Ibid.

[13]This approach goes back to the pioneering work by K. Lancaster: *Consumer Demand: A New Approach* (New York: 1971).

[14]D. Garvin, "Competing on the Eight Dimensions of Quality," *Harvard Business Review* (November–December 1987): 101–119; P. Kotler, *Marketing Management*, Millennium ed. (Upper Saddle River, N.J.: Prentice-Hall, 2000).

[15]"Proton Bomb," *Economist*, May 8, 2004, 77.

[16]C. K. Prahalad and M. S. Krishnan, "The New Meaning of Quality in the Information Age," *Harvard Business Review* (September–October 1999): 109–118.

[17]See D. Garvin, "What Does Product Quality Really Mean?" *Sloan Management Review* 26 (Fall 1984): 25–44; P. B. Crosby, *Quality Is Free* (New York: Mentor, 1980); and A. Gabor, *The Man Who Discovered Quality* (New York: Times Books, 1990).

[18]M. Cusumano, *The Japanese Automobile Industry* (Cambridge, Mass.: Harvard University Press, 1989); S. Spear and H. K. Bowen, "Decoding the DNA of the Toyota Production System," *Harvard Business Review* (September–October 1999): 96–108.

[19]Kim and Mauborgne, "Value Innovation."

[20]G. Stalk and T. M. Hout, *Competing Against Time* (New York: Free Press, 1990).

[21]Ibid.

[22]T. Copeland, T. Koller, and J. Murrin, *Valuation: Measuring and Managing the Value of Companies* (New York: Wiley, 1996). See also S. F. Jablonsky and N. P. Barsky, *The Manager's Guide to Financial Statement Analysis* (New York: Wiley, 2001).

[23]Copeland, Koller, and Murrin, *Valuation*.

[24]This is done as follows. Signifying net profit by π, invested capital by K, and revenues by R, then ROIC = π/K. If we multiply through by revenues, R, this becomes $R \times (\pi/K) = (\pi \times R)/(K \times R)$, which can be rearranged as $\pi/R \times R/K$. π/R is the return on sales and R/K capital turnover.

[25]Note that Figure 3.9 is a simplification and ignores some other important items that enter the calculation, such as depreciation/sales (a determinant of ROS) and other assets/sales (a determinant of capital turnover).

[26]This is the nature of the competitive process. For more detail, see C. W. L. Hill and D. Deeds, "The Importance of Industry Structure for the Determination of Company Profitability: A Neo-Austrian Perspective," *Journal of Management Studies* 33 (1996): 429–451.

[27]As with resources and capabilities, so the concept of barriers to imitation is also grounded in the resource-based view of the company. For details, see R. Reed and R. J. DeFillippi, "Causal Ambiguity, Barriers to Imitation, and Sustainable Competitive Advantage," *Academy of Management Review* 15 (1990): 88–102.

[28]E. Mansfield, "How Economists See R&D," *Harvard Business Review* (November–December 1981): 98–106.

[29]S. L. Berman, J. Down, and C. W. L. Hill, "Tacit Knowledge as a Source of Competitive Advantage in the National Basketball Association," *Academy of Management Journal* 45 (2002): 13–33.

[30]P. Ghemawat, *Commitment: The Dynamic of Strategy* (New York: Free Press, 1991).

[31]W. M. Cohen and D. A. Levinthal, "Absorptive Capacity: A New Perspective on Learning and Innovation," *Administrative Science Quarterly* 35 (1990): 128–152.

[32]M. T. Hannah and J. Freeman, "Structural Inertia and Organizational Change," *American Sociological Review* 49 (1984): 149–164.

[33]See "IBM Corporation," Harvard Business School Case #180-034.

[34]Ghemawat, *Commitment*.

[35]D. Miller, *The Icarus Paradox* (New York: HarperBusiness, 1990).

[36]P. M. Senge, *The Fifth Discipline: The Art and Practice of the Learning Organization* (New York: Doubleday, 1990).

[37]The classic statement of this position was made by A. A. Alchain, "Uncertainty, Evolution, and Economic Theory," *Journal of Political Economy* 84 (1950): 488–500.

[38]M. Brelis, "Simple Strategy Makes Southwest a Model for Success," *Boston Globe*, November 5, 2000, F1; M. Trottman, "At Southwest, New CEO Sits in the Hot Seat," *Wall Street Journal*, July 19, 2004, B1; J. Helyar, "Southwest Finds Trouble in the Air," *Fortune*, August 9, 2004, 38;

Southwest Airlines, Form 10-K, 2007. United Airlines, Form 10-K, 2007; *Bureau of Transportation Statistics*, http://www.transtats.bts.gov/.

Chapter 4

[1]D. Brady, "The Unsung CEO," *Business Week*, October 25, 2004, 74–84; Ernie Cevallos, "Productivity and Leadership Insights from George David," *Ezine Articles*, August 25, 2007; G. G. Marcial, "United Technologies: Going UP?" *Business Week*, November, 21, 2005, 156.

[2]G. J. Miller, *Managerial Dilemmas: The Political Economy of Hierarchy* (Cambridge: Cambridge University Press, 1992).

[3]H. Luft, J. Bunker, and A. Enthoven, "Should Operations Be Regionalized?" *New England Journal of Medicine* 301 (1979): 1364–1369.

[4]S. Chambers and R. Johnston, "Experience Curves in Services," *International Journal of Operations and Production Management* 20 (2000): 842–860.

[5]G. Hall and S. Howell, "The Experience Curve from an Economist's Perspective," *Strategic Management Journal* 6 (1985): 197–212; M. Lieberman, "The Learning Curve and Pricing in the Chemical Processing Industries," *RAND Journal of Economics* 15 (1984): 213–228; R. A. Thornton and P. Thompson, "Learning from Experience and Learning from Others," *American Economic Review* 91 (2001): 1350–1369.

[6]Boston Consulting Group, *Perspectives on Experience* (Boston: Boston Consulting Group, 1972); Hall and Howell, "The Experience Curve," 197–212; W. B. Hirschmann, "Profit from the Learning Curve," *Harvard Business Review* (January–February 1964): 125–139.

[7]A. A. Alchian, "Reliability of Progress Curves in Airframe Production," *Econometrica* 31 (1963): 679–693.

[8]M. Borrus, L. A. Tyson, and J. Zysman, "Creating Advantage: How Government Policies Create Trade in the Semi-Conductor Industry," in P. R. Krugman (ed.), *Strategic Trade Policy and the New International Economics* (Cambridge, Mass.: MIT Press, 1986); S. Ghoshal and C. A. Bartlett, "Matsushita Electrical Industrial (MEI) in 1987," Harvard Business School Case #388-144 (1988).

[9]W. Abernathy and K. Wayne, "Limits of the Learning Curve," *Harvard Business Review* 52 (September–October 1974): Vol 52, 59–69.

[10]D. F. Barnett and R. W. Crandall, *Up from the Ashes: The Rise of the Steel Minimill in the United States* (Washington DC: Brookings Institution, 1986).

[11]See P. Nemetz and L. Fry, "Flexible Manufacturing Organizations: Implications for Strategy Formulation," *Academy of Management Review* 13 (1988): 627–638; N. Greenwood, *Implementing Flexible Manufacturing Systems* (New York: Halstead Press, 1986); J. P. Womack, D. T. Jones, and D. Roos, *The Machine That Changed the World* (New York: Rawson Associates, 1990); and R. Parthasarthy and S. P. Seith, "The Impact of Flexible Automation on Business Strategy and Organizational Structure," *Academy of Management Review* 17 (1992): 86–111.

[12]B. J. Pine, *Mass Customization: The New Frontier in Business Competition* (Boston: Harvard Business School Press, 1993); S. Kotha, "Mass Customization: Implementing the Emerging Paradigm for Competitive Advantage," *Strategic Management Journal* 16 (1995): 21–42; J. H. Gilmore and B. J. Pine II, "The Four Faces of Mass Customization," *Harvard Business Review* (January–February 1997): 91–101.

[13]P. Waurzyniak, "Ford's Flexible Push," *Manufacturing Engineering*, September 2003, 47–50.

[14]F. F. Reichheld and W. E. Sasser, "Zero Defections: Quality Comes to Service," *Harvard Business Review* (September–October 1990): 105–111.

[15]The example comes from ibid.

[16]Ibid.

[17]R. Narasimhan and J. R. Carter, "Organization, Communication and Coordination of International Sourcing," *International Marketing Review* 7 (1990): 6–20.

[18]H. F. Busch, "Integrated Materials Management," *IJDP & MM* 18 (1990): 28–39.

[19]G. Stalk and T. M. Hout, *Competing Against Time* (New York: Free Press, 1990).

[20]See P. Bamberger and I. Meshoulam, *Human Resource Strategy: Formulation, Implementation, and Impact* (Thousand Oaks, Calif.: Sage, 2000); P. M. Wright and

S. Snell, "Towards a Unifying Framework for Exploring Fit and Flexibility in Human Resource Management," *Academy of Management Review* 23 (October 1998): 756–772.

21A. Sorge and M. Warner, "Manpower Training, Manufacturing Organization, and Work Place Relations in Great Britain and West Germany," *British Journal of Industrial Relations* 18 (1980): 318–333; R. Jaikumar, "Postindustrial Manufacturing," *Harvard Business Review* (November–December 1986): 72–83.

22J. Hoerr, "The Payoff from Teamwork," *Business Week*, July 10, 1989, 56–62.

23"The Trouble with Teams," *Economist*, January 14, 1995, 61.

24T. C. Powell and A. Dent-Micallef, "Information Technology as Competitive Advantage: The Role of Human, Business, and Technology Resource," *Strategic Management Journal* 18 (1997): 375–405; B. Gates, *Business @ the Speed of Thought* (New York: Warner Books, 1999).

25 "Cisco@speed," *Economist*, June 26, 1999, 12; S. Tully, "How Cisco Mastered the Net," *Fortune*, August 17, 1997, 207–210; C. Kano, "The Real King of the Internet," *Fortune*, September 7, 1998, 82–93.

26Gates, *Business @ the Speed of Thought.*

27See the articles published in the special issue of the *Academy of Management Review on Total Quality Management* 19, no. 3 (1994). The following article provides a good overview of many of the issues involved from an academic perspective: J. W. Dean and D. E. Bowen, "Management Theory and Total Quality," *Academy of Management Review* 19 (1994): 392–418. See also T. C. Powell, "Total Quality Management as Competitive Advantage," *Strategic Management Journal* 16 (1995): 15–37.

28For general background information, see "How to Build Quality," *Economist*, September 23, 1989, 91–92; A. Gabor, *The Man Who Discovered Quality* (New York: Penguin, 1990); and P. B. Crosby, *Quality Is Free* (New York: Mentor, 1980).

29W. E. Deming, "Improvement of Quality and Productivity through Action by Management," *National Productivity Review* 1 (Winter 1981–1982): 12–22.

30J. Bowles, "Is American Management Really Committed to Quality?" *Management Review* (April 1992): 42–46.

31O. Port and G. Smith, "Quality," *Business Week*, November 30, 1992, 66–75. See also "The Straining of Quality," *Economist*, January 14, 1995, 55–56.

32A. Ries and J. Trout, *Positioning: The Battle for Your Mind* (New York: Warner Books, 1982).

33R. G. Cooper, *Product Leadership* (Reading, Mass.: Perseus Books, 1999).

34R. G. Cooper, *Product Leadership* (Reading, Mass.: Perseus Books, 1999); A. L. Page, "PDMA's New Product Development Practices Survey: Performance and Best Practices," PDMA 15th Annual International Conference, Boston, October 16, 1991; E. Mansfield, "How Economists See R&D," *Harvard Business Review* (November–December 1981): 98–106.

35S. L. Brown and K. M. Eisenhardt, "Product Development: Past Research, Present Findings, and Future Directions," *Academy of Management Review* 20 (1995): 343–378; M. B. Lieberman and D. B. Montgomery, "First Mover Advantages," *Strategic Management Journal* 9 (Special Issue, Summer 1988): 41–58; D. J. Teece, "Profiting from Technological Innovation: Implications for Integration, Collaboration, Licensing and Public Policy," *Research Policy* 15 (1987): 285–305; G. J. Tellis and P. N. Golder, "First to Market, First to Fail?" *Sloan Management Review* (Winter 1996): 65–75; G. A. Stevens, J. Burley, "Piloting the Rocket of Radical Innovation," *Research Technology Management* 46 (2003): 16–26.

36G. Stalk and T. M. Hout, *Competing Against Time* (New York: Free Press, 1990).

37K. B. Clark and S. C. Wheelwright, *Managing New Product and Process Development* (New York: Free Press, 1993); M. A. Schilling and C. W. L. Hill, "Managing the New Product Development Process," *Academy of Management Executive* 12, no. 3 (August 1998): 67–81.

38O. Port, "Moving Past the Assembly Line," *Business Week* (Special Issue, Reinventing America, 1992): 177–180.

39K. B. Clark and T. Fujimoto, "The Power of Product Integrity," *Harvard Business Review* (November–December 1990):

107–118; Clark and Wheelwright, *Managing New Product and Process Development.* Brown and Eisenhardt, "Product Development"; Stalk and Hout, *Competing Against Time.*

40C. Christensen, "Quantum Corporation: Business and Product Teams," Harvard Business School Case, #9-692-023.

41H. Petroski, *Success through Failure: The Paradox of Design* (Princeton, NJ: Princeton University Press, 2006). See also A. C. Edmondson, "Learning from Mistakes Is Easier Said Than Done," *Journal of Applied Behavioral Science* 40 (2004): 66–91.

42S. Caminiti, "A Mail Order Romance: Lands' End Courts Unseen Customers," *Fortune*, March 13, 1989, 43–44.

43Sellers, "Getting Customers to Love You."

44Caminiti, "A Mail Order Romance," 43–44.

45Stalk and Hout, *Competing Against Time.*

46K. Hall, "No One Does Lean Like the Japanese," *Business Week*, July 10, 2006, 40–41; I. Rowley and H. Tashiro, "Lessons from Matsushita's Playbook," *Business Week*, March 21, 2005, 32; K. Hall, "Matsushita's Transformer Steps Down," *Business Week Online*, June 30, 2006.

Chapter 5

1P. Abrahams, "Sony Celebrates the Results of Fine-Tuning," *Financial Times*, April 4, 2001, 5.

2http://www.sony.com, 2009.

3M. Fackler, "Stringer Tries to Rein in Sony," http://global.nytimes.com/?iht. September 23, 2005.

4R. Siklos, and M. Fackler, "Howard Stringer, Sony's Road Warrior," http://nytimes.com, May 28, 2006.

5Ibid.

6D. F. Abell, *Defining the Business: The Starting Point of Strategic Planning* (Englewood Cliffs, N.J.: Prentice-Hall, 1980), 169.

7R. Kotler, *Marketing Management*, 5th ed. (Englewood Cliffs, N.J.: Prentice-Hall, 1984); M. R. Darby and E. Karni, "Free Competition and the Optimal Amount of Fraud," *Journal of Law and Economics* 16 (1973): 67–86.

[8]Abell, *Defining the Business*, 8.

[9]Some of the theoretical underpinnings for this approach can be found in G. R. Jones and J. Butler, "Costs, Revenues, and Business Level Strategy," *Academy of Management Review* 13 (1988): 202–213; and C. W. L. Hill, "Differentiation versus Low Cost or Differentiation and Low Cost: A Contingency Framework," *Academy of Management Review* 13 (1988): 401–412.

[10]This section and material on the business model draw heavily on C. W. L. Hill and G. R. Jones, "The Dynamics of Business-Level Strategy" (unpublished paper, 2002).

[11]Many authors have discussed cost leadership and differentiation as basic competitive approaches—for example, F. Scherer, *Industrial Market Structure and Economic Performance*, 10th ed. (Boston: Houghton Mifflin, 2000). The basic cost-leadership/differentiation dimension has received substantial empirical support; see, for example, D. C. Hambrick, "High Profit Strategies in Mature Capital Goods Industries: A Contingency Approach," *Academy of Management Journal* 26 (1983): 687–707.

[12]C. Campbell-Hunt, "What Have We Learned about Generic Competitive Strategy: A Meta-Analysis," *Strategic Management Journal* 21 (2000): 127–154.

[13]M. E. Porter, *Competitive Advantage: Creating and Sustaining Superior Performance* (New York: Free Press, 1985), 37.

[14]Ibid., 13–14.

[15]http://www.walmart.com, 2009.

[16]M. E. Porter, *Competitive Strategy: Techniques for Analyzing Industries and Competitors* (New York: Free Press, 1980), 46.

[17]W. K. Hall, "Survival Strategies in a Hostile Environment," *Harvard Business Review* 58 (1980): 75–85; Hambrick, "High Profit Strategies," 687–707.

[18]J. Guyon, "Can the Savoy Cut Costs and Be the Savoy?" *Wall Street Journal*, October 25, 1994, B1; http://www.savoy.com, 2007.

[19]The development of strategic-group theory has been a strong theme in the strategy literature. Important contributions include R. E. Caves and M. E. Porter, "From Entry Barriers to Mobility Barriers," *Quarterly Journal of Economics* (May 1977): 241–262; K. R. Harrigan, "An Application of Clustering for Strategic Group Analysis," *Strategic Management Journal* 6 (1985): 55–73; K. J. Hatten and D. E. Schendel, "Heterogeneity Within an Industry: Company Conduct in the U.S. Brewing Industry, 1952–1971," *Journal of Industrial Economics* 26: 97–113; and M. E. Porter, "The Structure within Industries and Companies Performance," *Review of Economics and Statistics* 61 (1979): 214–227.

[20]"The Holiday Inns Trip; A Breeze for Decades, Bumpy Ride in the 1980s," *Wall Street Journal*, February 11, 1987, 1; Holiday Inns, Annual Report (1985); U.S. Bureau of Labor Statistics, U.S. Industrial Output (Washington, D.C.: U.S. Government Printing Office, 1986).

[21]M. Gleason and A. Salomon, "Fallon's Challenge: Make Holiday Inn More 'In,'" *Advertising Age*, September 2, 1996, 14; J. Miller, "Amenities Range from Snacks to Technology," *Hotel and Motel Management*, July 3, 1996, 38–40.

[22]http://www.sixcontinenthotels.com, 2009.

Chapter 6

[1]M. E. Porter, *Competitive Strategy: Techniques for Analyzing Industries and Competitors* (New York: Free Press, 1980), 191–200.

[2]S. A. Shane, "Hybrid Organizational Arrangements and Their Implications for Firm Growth and Survival: A Study of New Franchisors," *Academy of Management Journal* 1 (1996): 216–234.

[3]Microsoft is often accused of not being an innovator, but the fact is that Gates and Allen wrote the first commercial software program for the first commercially available personal computer. Microsoft was the first mover in their industry. See P. Freiberger and M. Swaine, *Fire in the Valley* (New York: McGraw-Hill, 2000).

[4]J. M. Utterback, *Mastering the Dynamics of Innovation* (Boston: Harvard Business School Press, 1994).

[5]See Freiberger and Swaine, *Fire in the Valley*.

[6]G. A. Moore, *Crossing the Chasm* (New York: HarperCollins, 1991).

[7]Utterback, *Mastering the Dynamics of Innovation*.

[8]E. Rogers, *Diffusion of Innovations* (New York: Free Press, 1995).

[9]C. W. Hofer and D. Schendel, *Strategy Formulation: Analytical Concepts* (St. Paul, Minn.: West, 1978).

[10]Ibid.

[11]Ibid.

[12]J. Brander and J. Eaton, "Product Line Rivalry," *American Economic Review* 74 (1985): 323–334.

[13]Ibid.

[14]Porter, *Competitive Strategy*, 76–86.

[15]O. Heil and T. S. Robertson, "Towards a Theory of Competitive Market Signaling: A Research Agenda," *Strategic Management Journal* 12 (1991): 403–418.

[16]R. Axelrod, *The Evolution of Cooperation* (New York: Basic Books, 1984).

[17]F. Scherer, *Industrial Market Structure and Economic Performance*, 10th ed. (Boston: Houghton Mifflin, 2000), chap. 8.

[18]The model differs from Ansoff's model for this reason.

[19]H. I. Ansoff, *Corporate Strategy* (London: Penguin Books, 1984), 97–100.

[20]R. D. Buzzell, B. T. Gale, and R. G. M. Sultan, "Market Share: A Key to Profitability," *Harvard Business Review* (January–February 1975): 97–103; R. Jacobson and D. A. Aaker, "Is Market Share All That It's Cracked Up to Be?" *Journal of Marketing* 49 (1985): 11–22.

[21]Ansoff, *Corporate Strategy*, 98–99.

[22]Figure copyright © Gareth R. Jones, 2004.

[23]The next section draws heavily on Marvin B. Lieberman, "Strategies for Capacity Expansion," *Sloan Management Review* 8 (1987): 19–27; and Porter, *Competitive Strategy*, 324–338.

[24]http://www.mattel.com, 2009.

[25]"Doll Wars," *Business Life*, May 2005, 40–42.

[26]http://www.mattel.com, 2009.

Chapter 7

[1]*The Economist*, "Battle for the Smart-Phone's Soul," November 22, 2008, 76–77; Canalys, "Global SmartPhone Shipments Rise 28%," press release, November 6, 2008, http://www.canalys.com/pr/2008/r2008112.htm; N. Wingfield,

"iPhone Software Sales Take Off," *Wall Street Journal*, August 11, 2008, B1.

[2] Data from Bureau of Economic Analysis, *Survey of United States Current Business, 2006*, http://www.bea.gov/.

[3] J. M. Utterback, *Mastering the Dynamics of Innovation* (Boston: Harvard Business School Press, 1994); C. Shapiro and H. R. Varian, *Information Rules: A Strategic Guide to the Network Economy* (Boston: Harvard Business School Press, 1999).

[4] The layout is not universal, although it is widespread. The French, for example, use a different layout.

[5] For details, see C. W. L. Hill, "Establishing a Standard: Competitive Strategy and Technology Standards in Winner Take All Industries," *Academy of Management Executive* 11 (1997): 7–25; Shapiro and Varian, *Information Rules*; B. Arthur, "Increasing Returns and the New World of Business," *Harvard Business Review* (July–August 1996): 100–109; G. Gowrisankaran and J. Stavins, "Network Externalities and Technology Adoption: Lessons from Electronic Payments," *Rand Journal of Economics* 35 (2004): 260–277; V. Shankar and B. L. Bayus, "Network Effects and Competition: An Empirical Analysis of the Home Video Game Industry," *Strategic Management Journal* 24 (2003): 375–394; and R. Casadesus-Masanell and P. Ghemawat, "Dynamic Mixed Duopoly: A Model Motivated by Linux versus Windows," *Management Science* 52 (2006): 1072–1085.

[6] See Shapiro and Varian, *Information Rules*; Hill, "Establishing a Standard"; and M. A. Shilling, "Technological Lockout: An Integrative Model of the Economic and Strategic Factors Driving Technology Success and Failure," *Academy of Management Review* 23, no 2 (1998): 267–285.

[7] Microsoft does not disclose the per unit licensing fee that it gets from original equipment manufacturers, although media reports speculate it is around $50 a copy.

[8] Much of this section is based on C. W. L. Hill, M. Heeley, and J. Sakson, "Strategies for Profiting from Innovation," in *Advances in Global High Technology Management* (Greenwich, Conn.: JAI Press, 1993), 379–95.

[9] M. Lieberman and D. Montgomery, "First Mover Advantages," *Strategic Management Journal* 9 (Special Issue, Summer 1988): 41–58.

[10] W. Boulding and M. Christen, "Sustainable Pioneering Advantage? Profit Implications of Market Entry Order," *Marketing Science* 22 (2003): 371–386; C. Markides and P. Geroski, "Teaching Elephants to Dance and Other Silly Ideas," *Business Strategy Review* 13 (2003): 49–61.

[11] J. Borzo, "Aging Gracefully," *Wall Street Journal*, October 15, 2001, R22.

[12] The importance of complementary assets was first noted by D. J. Teece. See D. J. Teece, "Profiting from Technological Innovation," in D. J. Teece (ed.), *The Competitive Challenge* (New York: Harper & Row, 1986), 26–54.

[13] M. J. Chen and D. C. Hambrick, "Speed, Stealth, and Selective Attack: How Small Firms Differ from Large Firms in Competitive Behavior," *Academy of Management Journal* 38 (1995): 453–482.

[14] E. Mansfield, M. Schwartz, and S. Wagner, "Imitation Costs and Patents: An Empirical Study," *Economic Journal* 91 (1981): 907–918.

[15] E. Mansfield, "How Rapidly Does New Industrial Technology Leak Out?" *Journal of Industrial Economics* 34 (1985): 217–223.

[16] This argument has been made in the game theory literature. See R. Caves, H. Cookell, and P. J. Killing, "The Imperfect Market for Technology Licenses," *Oxford Bulletin of Economics and Statistics* 45 (1983): 249–267; N. T. Gallini, "Deterrence by Market Sharing: A Strategic Incentive for Licensing," *American Economic Review* 74 (1984): 931–941; and C. Shapiro, "Patent Licensing and R&D Rivalry," *American Economic Review* 75 (1985): 25–30.

[17] C. M. Christensen, *The Innovator's Dilemma* (Boston: Harvard Business School Press, 1997). R. N. Foster, *Innovation: The Attacker's Advantage* (New York: Summit Books, 1986).

[18] Foster, *Innovation*.

[19] R. Kurzweil, *The Age of the Spiritual Machines* (New York: Penguin Books, 1999).

[20] See Christensen, *The Innovator's Dilemma*; and C. M. Christensen and M. Overdorf, "Meeting the Challenge of Disruptive Change," *Harvard Business Review* (March–April 2000): 66–77.

[21] C. W. L. Hill and F. T. Rothaermel, "The Performance of Incumbent Firms in the Face of Radical Technological Innovation," *Academy of Management Review* 28 (2003): 257–274; F. T. Rothaermel and C. W. L. Hill, "Technological Discontinuities and Complementary Assets: A Longitudinal Study of Industry and Firm Performance," *Organization Science* 16, no. 1: 52–70.

[22] *The Economist*, "Singin' the Blus; Standard Wars," November 5, 2005, 87; A. Park, "HD-DVD versus Blu-ray," *Business Week*, October 30, 2006, 110; B. Dipert, "Subpar Wars: High Resolution Disc Formats Fight Each Other, Consumers Push Back," *EDN*, March 2, 2006, 40–48; B. S. Bulik, "Marketing War Looms for Dueling DVD Formats," *Advertising Age*, April 10, 2006, 20; *The Economist*, "Everything's Gone Blu," January 12, 2008, 56.

Chapter 8

[1] "Orange Gold," *The Economist*, March 3, 2007, 68; P. Bettis, "Coke Aims to Give Pepsi a Routing in Cold Coffee War," *Financial Times*, October 17, 2007, 16; P. Ghemawat, *Redefining Global Strategy* (Boston, Mass: Harvard Business School Press, 2007); D. Foust, "Queen of Pop," *Business Week*, August 7, 2006, 44–47.

[2] World Trade Organization, *International Trade Trends and Statistics, 2005* (Geneva: WTO, 2006), and WTO press release, "World Trade for 2005: Prospects for 2006," April 11, 2006, http://www.wto.org.

[3] World Trade Organization, *International Trade Statistics, 2008* (Geneva: WTO, 2008); United Nations, *World Investment Report, 2008*.

[4] P. Dicken, *Global Shift* (New York: Guilford Press, 1992).

[5] D. Pritchard, "Are Federal Tax Laws and State Subsidies for Boeing 7E7 Selling America Short?" *Aviation Week*, April 12, 2004, 74–75.

[6] T. Levitt, "The Globalization of Markets," *Harvard Business Review* (May–June 1983): 92–102.

[7] M. E. Porter, *The Competitive Advantage of Nations* (New York: Free Press, 1990). See also R. Grant, "Porter's Competitive Advantage of Nations: An Assessment," *Strategic Management Journal* 7 (1991): 535–548.

[8]Porter, *Competitive Advantage of Nations.*

[9]Example is disguised. Comes from interviews by Charles Hill.

[10]See J. Birkinshaw and N. Hood, "Multinational Subsidiary Evolution: Capability and Charter Change in Foreign Owned Subsidiary Companies," *Academy of Management Review* 23 (October 1998): 773–795; A. K. Gupta and V. J. Govindarajan, "Knowledge Flows within Multinational Corporations," *Strategic Management Journal* 21 (2000): 473–496; V. J. Govindarajan and A. K. Gupta, *The Quest for Global Dominance* (San Francisco: Jossey-Bass, 2001); T. S. Frost, J. M. Birkinshaw, and P. C. Ensign, "Centers of Excellence in Multinational Corporations," *Strategic Management Journal* 23 (2002): 997–1018; and U. Andersson, M. Forsgren, and U. Holm, "The Strategic Impact of External Networks," *Strategic Management Journal* 23 (2002): 979–996.

[11]S. Leung, "Armchairs, TVs, and Espresso: Is It McDonald's?" *Wall Street Journal,* August 30, 2002, A1, A6.

[12]C. K. Prahalad and Y. L. Doz, *The Multinational Mission: Balancing Local Demands and Global Vision* (New York: Free Press, 1987). See also J. Birkinshaw, A. Morrison, and J. Hulland, "Structural and Competitive Determinants of a Global Integration Strategy," *Strategic Management Journal* 16 (1995): 637–655.

[13]J. E. Garten, "Walmart Gives Globalization a Bad Name," *Business Week,* March 8, 2004, 24.

[14]Prahalad and Doz, *Multinational Mission.* Prahalad and Doz actually talk about local responsiveness rather than local customization.

[15]Levitt, "Globalization of Markets."

[16]C. A. Bartlett and S. Ghoshal, *Managing across Borders* (Boston: Harvard Business School Press, 1989).

[17]W. W. Lewis. *The Power of Productivity* (Chicago: University of Chicago Press, 2004).

[18]C. J. Chipello, "Local Presence Is Key to European Deals," *Wall Street Journal,* June 30, 1998, A15.

[19]Bartlett and Ghoshal, *Managing across Borders.*

[20]Ibid.

[21]T. Hout, M. E. Porter, and E. Rudden, "How Global Companies Win Out," *Harvard Business Review* (September–October 1982): 98–108.

[22]This section draws on numerous studies, including: C. W. L. Hill, P. Hwang, and W. C. Kim, "An Eclectic Theory of the Choice of International Entry Mode," *Strategic Management Journal* 11 (1990): 117–28; C. W. L. Hill and W. C. Kim, "Searching for a Dynamic Theory of the Multinational Enterprise: A Transaction Cost Model," *Strategic Management Journal* 9 (Special Issue on Strategy Content, 1988): 93–104; E. Anderson and H. Gatignon, "Modes of Foreign Entry: A Transaction Cost Analysis and Propositions," *Journal of International Business Studies* 17 (1986): 1–26; F. R. Root, *Entry Strategies for International Markets* (Lexington, MA: D. C. Heath, 1980); A. Madhok, "Cost, Value and Foreign Market Entry: The Transaction and the Firm," *Strategic Management Journal* 18 (1997): 39–61; K. D. Brouthers and L. B. Brouthers, "Acquisition or Greenfield Start-Up?" *Strategic Management Journal* 21, no. 1 (2000): 89–97; X. Martin and R. Salmon, "Knowledge Transfer Capacity and Its Implications for the Theory of the Multinational Enterprise," *Journal of International Business Studies* (July 2003): 356; and A. Verbeke, "The Evolutionary View of the MNE and the Future of Internalization Theory," *Journal of International Business Studies* (November 2003): 498–515.

[23]F. J. Contractor, "The Role of Licensing in International Strategy," *Columbia Journal of World Business* (Winter 1982): 73–83.

[24]O. E. Williamson, *The Economic Institutions of Capitalism* (New York: Free Press, 1985).

[25]A. E. Serwer, "McDonald's Conquers the World," *Fortune,* October 17, 1994, 103–116.

[26]For an excellent review of the basic theoretical literature of joint ventures, see B. Kogut, "Joint Ventures: Theoretical and Empirical Perspectives," *Strategic Management Journal* 9 (1988): 319–32. More recent studies include T. Chi, "Option to Acquire or Divest a Joint Venture," *Strategic Management Journal* 21, no. 6 (2000): 665–88; H. Merchant and D. Schendel, "How Do International Joint Ventures Create Shareholder Value?" *Strategic Management Journal* 21, no. 7 (2000): 723–37; H. K. Steensma and M. A. Lyles, "Explaining

IJV Survival in a Transitional Economy though Social Exchange and Knowledge Based Perspectives," *Strategic Management Journal* 21, no. 8 (2000): 831–51; and J. F. Hennart and M. Zeng, "Cross Cultural Differences and Joint Venture Longevity," *Journal of International Business Studies* (December 2002): 699–717.

[27]J. A. Robins, S. Tallman, and K. Fladmoe-Lindquist, "Autonomy and Dependence of International Cooperative Ventures," *Strategic Management Journal* (October 2002): 881–902.

[28]C. W. L. Hill, "Strategies for Exploiting Technological Innovations," *Organization Science* 3 (1992): 428–441.

[29]See K. Ohmae, "The Global Logic of Strategic Alliances," *Harvard Business Review* (March–April 1989): 143–154; G. Hamel, Y. L. Doz, and C. K. Prahalad, "Collaborate with Your Competitors and Win!" *Harvard Business Review* (January–February 1989): 133–139; W. Burgers, C. W. L. Hill, and W. C. Kim, "Alliances in the Global Auto Industry," *Strategic Management Journal* 14 (1993): 419–432; and P. Kale, H. Singh, and H. Perlmutter, "Learning and Protection of Proprietary Assets in Strategic Alliances: Building Relational Capital," *Strategic Management Journal* 21 (2000): 217–237.

[30]L. T. Chang, "China Eases Foreign Film Rules," *The Wall Street Journal,* October 15, 2004, B2.

[31]B. L. Simonin, "Transfer of Marketing Know-How in International Strategic Alliances," *Journal of International Business Studies* (1999): 463–91, and J. W. Spencer, "Firms' Knowledge Sharing Strategies in the Global Innovation System," *Strategic Management Journal* 24 (2003): 217–33.

[32]C. Souza, "Microsoft Teams with MIPS, Toshiba," *EBN,* February 10, 2003, 4.

[33]M. Frankel, "Now Sony Is Giving Palm a Hand," *BusinessWeek,* November 29, 2000, 50.

[34]Kale, Singh, and Perlmutter, "Learning and Protection of Proprietary Assets."

[35]R. B. Reich and E. D. Mankin, "Joint Ventures with Japan Give Away Our Future," *Harvard Business Review* (March–April 1986): 78–90.

[36]J. Bleeke and D. Ernst, "The Way to Win in Cross-Border Alliances," *Harvard*

Business Review (November–December 1991): 127–135.

[37]E. Booker and C. Krol, "IBM Finds Strength in Alliances," *B to B*, February 10, 2003, 3, 27.

[38]W. Roehl and J. F. Truitt, "Stormy Open Marriages Are Better," *Columbia Journal of World Business* (Summer 1987): 87–95.

[39]See T. Khanna, R. Gulati, and N. Nohria, "The Dynamics of Learning Alliances: Competition, Cooperation, and Relative Scope," *Strategic Management Journal* 19 (1998): 193–210, and P. Kale, H. Singh, H. Perlmutter, "Learning and Protection of Proprietary Assets in Strategic Alliances: Building Relational Capital," *Strategic Management Journal* 21 (2000): 217–37.

[40]Kale, Singh, and Perlmutter, "Learning and Protection of Proprietary Assets."

[41]Hamel, Doz, and Prahalad, "Collaborate with Competitors"; Khanna, Gulati, and Nohria, "The Dynamics of Learning Alliances: Competition, Cooperation, and Relative Scope"; and E. W. K. Tang, "Acquiring Knowledge by Foreign Partners from International Joint Ventures in a Transition Economy: Learning by Doing and Learning Myopia," *Strategic Management Journal* 23 (2002): 835–854.

[42]Hamel, Doz, and Prahalad, "Collaborate with Competitors."

[43]B. Wysocki, "Cross Border Alliances Become Favorite Way to Crack New Markets," *Wall Street Journal*, March 4, 1990, A1.

[44]M. Gunther, "MTV's Passage to India," *Fortune*, August 9, 2004, 117–122; B. Pulley and A. Tanzer, "Sumner's Gemstone," *Forbes*, February 21, 2000, 107–11; K. Hoffman, "Youth TV's Old Hand Prepares for the Digital Challenge," *Financial Times*, February 18, 2000, 8; presentation by Sumner M. Redstone, chairman and CEO, Viacom Inc., delivered to Salomon Smith Barney 11th Annual Global Entertainment Media, Telecommunications Conference, Scottsdale, AZ, January 8, 2001; archived at http://www.viacom.com; and Viacom Form 10-K, 2005.

Chapter 9

[1]http://www.newscorp.com, 2009.

[2]Ibid.

[3]For evidence on acquisitions and performance, see R. E. Caves, "Mergers, Takeovers, and Economic Efficiency," *International Journal of Industrial Organization* 7 (1989): 151–174; M. C. Jensen and R. S. Ruback, "The Market for Corporate Control: The Scientific Evidence," *Journal of Financial Economics* 11 (1983): 5–50; R. Roll, "Empirical Evidence on Takeover Activity and Shareholder Wealth," in J. C. Coffee, L. Lowenstein, and S. Rose (eds.), *Knights, Raiders and Targets* (Oxford: Oxford University Press, 1989); A. Schleifer and R. W. Vishny, "Takeovers in the 60s and 80s: Evidence and Implications," *Strategic Management Journal* 12 (Special Issue, Winter 1991): 51–60; and T. H. Brush, "Predicted Changes in Operational Synergy and Post Acquisition Performance of Acquired Businesses," *Strategic Management Journal* 17 (1996): 1–24.

[4]"Few Takeovers Pay Off for Big Buyers," *Investors Business Daily*, May 25, 2001, 1.

[5]This is the essence of Chandler's argument. See A. D. Chandler, *Strategy and Structure* (Cambridge, Mass.: MIT Press, 1962). The same argument is also made by J. Pfeffer and G. R. Salancik, *The External Control of Organizations* (New York: Harper & Row, 1978). See also K. R. Harrigan, *Strategic Flexibility* (Lexington, Mass.: Lexington Books, 1985); K. R. Harrigan, "Vertical Integration and Corporate Strategy," *Academy of Management Journal* 28 (1985): 397–425; and F. M. Scherer, *Industrial Market Structure and Economic Performance* (Chicago: Rand McNally, 1981).

[6]O. E. Williamson, *The Economic Institutions of Capitalism*. For recent empirical work that uses this framework, see L. Poppo and T. Zenger, "Testing Alternative Theories of the Firm: Transaction Cost, Knowledge Based, and Measurement Explanations for Make or Buy Decisions in Information Services," *Strategic Management Journal* 19 (1998): 853–878.

[7]Williamson, *Economic Institutions of Capitalism*.

[8]A. D. Chandler, *The Visible Hand* (Cambridge, Mass.: Harvard University Press, 1977).

[9]J. Pitta, "Score One for Vertical Integration," *Forbes*, January 18, 1993, 88–89.

[10]Harrigan, *Strategic Flexibility*, 67–87. See also A. Afuah, "Dynamic Boundaries of the Firm: Are Firms Better Off Being Vertically Integrated in the Face of a Technological Change?" *Academy of Management Journal* 44 (2001): 1121–1228.

[11]K. Kelly, Z. Schiller, and J. Treece, "Cut Costs or Else," *Business Week*, March 22, 1993, 28–29.

[12]X. Martin, W. Mitchell, and A. Swaminathan, "Recreating and Extending Japanese Automobile Buyer-Supplier Links in North America," *Strategic Management Journal* 16 (1995): 589–619; C. W. L. Hill, "National Institutional Structures, Transaction Cost Economizing, and Competitive Advantage," *Organization Science* 6 (1995): 119–131.

[13]Williamson, Economic Institutions of Capitalism. See also J. H. Dyer, "Effective Inter-Firm Collaboration: How Firms Minimize Transaction Costs and Maximize Transaction Value," *Strategic Management Journal* 18 (1997): 535–556.

[14]Richardson, "Parallel Sourcing."

[15]W. H. Davidow and M. S. Malone, *The Virtual Corporation* (New York: Harper & Row, 1992).

[16]A. M. Porter, "Outsourcing Gains Popularity," *Purchasing*, March 11, 1999, 22–24.

[17]D. Garr, "Inside Outsourcing," *Fortune* 142, no. 1 (2001): 85–92.

[18]J. Krane, "American Express Hires IBM for $4 Billion," *Columbian*, February 26, 2002, E2; http://www.ibm.com, 2009.

[19]http://www.ibm.com, 2009.

[20]Davidow and Malone, *The Virtual Corporation*.

[21]Ibid; H. W. Chesbrough and D. J. Teece, "When Is Virtual Virtuous? Organizing for Innovation," *Harvard Business Review* (January–February 1996): 65–74; J. B. Quinn, "Strategic Outsourcing: Leveraging Knowledge Capabilities," *Sloan Management Review* (Summer 1999): 9–21.

Chapter 10

[1]This resource-based view of diversification can be traced to Edith Penrose's seminal book, *The Theory of the Growth of the Firm* (Oxford: Oxford University Press, 1959).

[2]D. J. Teece, "Economies of Scope and the Scope of the Enterprise," *Journal of*

Economic Behavior and Organization 3 (1980): 223–247. For recent empirical work on this topic, see C. H. St. John and J. S. Harrison, "Manufacturing Based Relatedness, Synergy and Coordination," *Strategic Management Journal* 20 (1999): 129–145.

[3]Teece, "Economies of Scope." For recent empirical work on this topic, see St. John and Harrison, "Manufacturing Based Relatedness, Synergy and Coordination."

[4]For a detailed discussion, see C. W. L. Hill and R. E. Hoskisson, "Strategy and Structure in the Multiproduct Firm," *Academy of Management Review* 12 (1987): 331–341.

[5]See, for example, G. R. Jones and C. W. L. Hill, "A Transaction Cost Analysis of Strategy Structure Choice," *Strategic Management Journal* (1988): 159–172; and O. E. Williamson, *Markets and Hierarchies, Analysis and Antitrust Implications* (New York: Free Press, 1975), 132–175.

[6]R. Buderi, *Engines of Tomorrow* (New York: Simon & Schuster, 2000).

[7]See, for example, Jones and Hill, "A Transaction Cost Analysis"; Williamson, *Markets and Hierarchies*; and Hill, "The Role of Headquarters in the Multidivisional Firm."

[8]The distinction goes back to R. P. Rumelt, *Strategy, Structure and Economic Performance* (Cambridge, Mass.: Harvard Business School Press, 1974).

[9]For evidence, see C. W. L. Hill, "Conglomerate Performance over the Economic Cycle," *Journal of Industrial Economics* 32 (1983): 197–212; and D. T. C. Mueller, "The Effects of Conglomerate Mergers," *Journal of Banking and Finance* 1 (1977): 315–347.

[10]For reviews of the evidence, see V. Ramanujam and P. Varadarajan, "Research on Corporate Diversification: A Synthesis," *Strategic Management Journal* 10 (1989): 523–551; G. Dess, J. F. Hennart, C. W. L. Hill, and A. Gupta, "Research Issues in Strategic Management," *Journal of Management* 21 (1995): 357–392; and D. C. Hyland and J. D. Diltz, "Why Companies Diversify: An Empirical Examination," *Financial Management* 31 (Spring 2002): 51–81.

[11]M. E. Porter, "From Competitive Advantage to Corporate Strategy," *Harvard Business Review* (May–June 1987): 43–59.

[12]For reviews of the evidence, see Ramanujam and Varadarajan, "Research on Corporate Diversification"; Dess, Hennart, Hill, and Gupta, "Research Issues in Strategic Management"; and Hyland and Diltz, "Why Companies Diversify."

[13]C. R. Christensen et al., *Business Policy Text and Cases* (Homewood, Ill.: Irwin, 1987), 778.

[14]See Booz, Allen, and Hamilton, *New Products Management for the 1980s* (privately published, 1982); A. L. Page, "PDMA's New Product Development Practices Survey: Performance and Best Practices" (presented at the PDMA 15th Annual International Conference, Boston, October 16, 1991); and E. Mansfield, "How Economists See R&D," *Harvard Business Review* (November–December 1981): 98–106.

[15]See R. Biggadike, "The Risky Business of Diversification," *Harvard Business Review* (May–June 1979): 103–111; R. A. Burgelman, "A Process Model of Internal Corporate Venturing in the Diversified Major Firm," *Administrative Science Quarterly* 28 (1983): 223–244; and Z. Block and I. C. MacMillan, *Corporate Venturing* (Boston: Harvard Business School Press, 1993).

[16]Biggadike, "The Risky Business of Diversification"; Block and Macmillan, *Corporate Venturing*.

[17]Buderi, *Engines of Tomorrow*.

[18]I. C. MacMillan and R. George, "Corporate Venturing: Challenges for Senior Managers," *Journal of Business Strategy* 5 (1985): 34–43.

[19]See R. A. Burgelman, M. M. Maidique, and S. C. Wheelwright, *Strategic Management of Technology and Innovation* (Chicago: Irwin, 1996), 493–507. See also Buderi, *Engines of Tomorrow*.

[20]Buderi, *Engines of Tomorrow*.

[21]See Block and Macmillan, Corporate Venturing; and Burgelman, Maidique, and Wheelwright, Strategic Management of Technology and Innovation.

[21]Buderi, *Engines of Tomorrow*.

[21]See Block and Macmillan, *Corporate Venturing*; and Burgelman, Maidique, and Wheelwright, *Strategic Management of Technology and Innovation*.

[22]For evidence on acquisitions and performance, see R. E. Caves, "Mergers, Takeovers, and Economic Efficiency," *International Journal of Industrial Organization* 7 (1989): 151–174; M. C. Jensen and R. S. Ruback, "The Market for Corporate Control: The Scientific Evidence," *Journal of Financial Economics* 11 (1983): 5–50; R. Roll, "Empirical Evidence on Takeover Activity and Shareholder Wealth," in J. C. Coffee, L. Lowenstein, and S. Rose (eds.), *Knights, Raiders and Targets* (Oxford: Oxford University Press, 1989); A. Schleifer and R. W. Vishny, "Takeovers in the 60s and 80s: Evidence and Implications," *Strategic Management Journal* 12 (Special Issue, Winter 1991): 51–60; T. H. Brush, "Predicted Changes in Operational Synergy and Post Acquisition Performance of Acquired Businesses," *Strategic Management Journal* 17 (1996): 1–24; and T. Loughran and A. M. Vijh, "Do Long Term Shareholders Benefit from Corporate Acquisitions?" *Journal of Finance* 5 (1997): 1765–1787.

[23]Ibid.

[24]D. J. Ravenscraft and F. M. Scherer, *Mergers, Sell-offs, and Economic Efficiency* (Washington, D.C.: Brookings Institution, 1987).

[25]See J. P. Walsh, "Top Management Turnover Following Mergers and Acquisitions," *Strategic Management Journal* 9 (1988): 173–183.

[26]See A. A. Cannella and D. C. Hambrick, "Executive Departure and Acquisition Performance," *Strategic Management Journal* 14 (1993): 137–152.

[27]R. Roll, "The Hubris Hypothesis of Corporate Takeovers," *Journal of Business* 59 (1986): 197–216.

[28]"Coca-Cola: A Sobering Lesson from Its Journey into Wine," *Business Week*, June 3, 1985, 96–98.

[29]P. Haspeslagh and D. Jemison, *Managing Acquisitions* (New York: Free Press, 1991).

[30]For views on this issue, see L. L. Fray, D. H. Gaylin, and J. W. Down, "Successful Acquisition Planning," *Journal of Business Strategy* 5 (1984): 46–55; C. W. L. Hill, "Profile of a Conglomerate Takeover: BTR and Thomas Tilling," *Journal of General Management* 10 (1984): 34–50; D. R. Willensky, "Making It Happen: How to Execute an Acquisition," *Business Horizons* (March–April 1985): 38–45; Haspeslagh and Jemison, *Managing Acquisitions*; and P. L. Anslinger and T. E. Copeland, "Growth Through Acquisition: A Fresh Look," *Harvard Business Review* (January–February 1996): 126–135.

[31]M. L. A. Hayward, "When Do Firms Learn from Their Acquisition Experience? Evidence from 1990–1995," *Strategic Management Journal* 23 (2002): 21–39; K. G. Ahuja, "Technological Acquisitions and the Innovation Performance of Acquiring Firms: A Longitudinal Study," *Strategic Management Journal* 23 (2001): 197–220; H. G. Barkema and F. Vermeulen, "International Expansion Through Startup or Acquisition," *Academy of Management Journal* 41 (1998): 7–26.

[32]Hayward, "When Do Firms Learn from Their Acquisition Experience?"

[33]For a review of the evidence and some contrary empirical evidence, see D. E. Hatfield, J. P. Liebskind, and T. C. Opler, "The Effects of Corporate Restructuring on Aggregate Industry Specialization," *Strategic Management Journal* 17 (1996): 55–72.

[34]A. Lamont and C. Polk, "The Diversification Discount: Cash Flows versus Returns," *Journal of Finance* 56 (October 2001): 1693–1721; R. Raju, H. Servaes, and L. Zingales, "The Cost of Diversity: The Diversification Discount and Inefficient Investment," *Journal of Finance* 55 (February 2000): 35–80.

[35]For example, see Schleifer and Vishny, "Takeovers in the '60s and '80s."

[36]J. R. Laing, "Tyco's Titan," *Barron's*, April 12, 1999, 27–32; M. Maremont, "How Is Tyco Accounting or Cash Flow?"; *Wall Street Journal*, March 5, 2002, C1; J. R. Laing, "Doubting Tyco," *Barron's*, January 28, 2002, 19–20.

[37]"Tyco Shares Up on Report Mulling Breakup," http://www.yahoo.com, 2006, January 9.

[38]http://www.tyco.com, 2009.

Chapter 11

[1]D. Fitzpatrick. "Thain Ousted in Clash at Bank of America," *Wall Street Journal*, January 23, 2009; G. Farrell, "BofA Had Role in Merrill Bonuses," *Financial Times*, January 25, 2009; C. Gasparino, "John Thain's $87,000 Rug," *The Daily Beast*, January 22, 2009.

[2]E. Freeman, *Strategic Management: A Stakeholder Approach* (Boston: Pitman Press, 1984).

[3]C. W. L. Hill and T. M. Jones, "Stakeholder-Agency Theory," *Journal of Management*

Studies 29 (1992): 131–154; J. G. March and H. A. Simon, *Organizations* (New York: Wiley, 1958).

[4]Hill and Jones, "Stakeholder-Agency Theory"; C. Eesley and M. J. Lenox, "Firm Responses to Secondary Stakeholder Action," *Strategic Management Journal* 27 (2006): 13–24.

[5]I. C. Macmillan and P. E. Jones, *Strategy Formulation: Power and Politics* (St. Paul, Minn.: West, 1986).

[6]T. Copeland, T. Koller, and J. Murrin, *Valuation: Measuring and Managing the Value of Companies* (New York: Wiley, 1996).

[7]R. S. Kaplan and D. P. Norton, *Strategy Maps* (Boston: Harvard Business School Press, 2004).

[8]A. L. Velocci, D. A. Fulghum, and R. Wall, "Damage Control," *Aviation Week*, December 1, 2003, 26–27.

[9]M. C. Jensen and W. H. Meckling, "Theory of the Firm: Managerial Behavior, Agency Costs and Ownership Structure," *Journal of Financial Economics* 3 (1976): 305–360; E. F. Fama, "Agency Problems and the Theory of the Firm," *Journal of Political Economy* 88 (1980): 375–390.

[10]Hill and Jones, "Stakeholder-Agency Theory."

[11]For example, see R. Marris, *The Economic Theory of Managerial Capitalism* (London: Macmillan, 1964); and J. K. Galbraith, *The New Industrial State* (Boston: Houghton Mifflin, 1970).

[12]Fama, "Agency Problems and the Theory of the Firm."

[13]A. Rappaport, "New Thinking on How to Link Executive Pay with Performance," *Harvard Business Review* (March–April 1999): 91–105.

[14]D Henry and D. Stead, "Worker versus CEO: Room to Run," *Business Week*, October 30, 2006, 13.

[15]For academic studies that look at the determinants of CEO pay, see M. C. Jensen and K. J. Murphy, "Performance Pay and Top Management Incentives," *Journal of Political Economy* 98 (1990): 225–264; C. W. L. Hill and Phillip Phan, "CEO Tenure as a Determinant of CEO Pay," *Academy of Management Journal* 34 (1991): 707–717; H. L. Tosi and L. R. Gomez-

Mejia, "CEO Compensation Monitoring and Firm Performance," *Academy of Management Journal* 37 (1994): 1002–1016; and J. F. Porac, J. B. Wade, and T. G. Pollock, "Industry Categories and the Politics of the Comparable Firm in CEO Compensation," *Administrative Science Quarterly* 44 (1999): 112–144.

[16]A. Ward, "Home Depot Investors Stage a revolt," *Financial Times*, May 26, 2006, 20.

[17]For research on this issue, see P. J. Lane, A. A. Cannella, and M. H. Lubatkin, "Agency Problems as Antecedents to Unrelated Mergers and Diversification: Amihud and Lev Reconsidered," *Strategic Management Journal* 19 (1998): 555–578.

[18]E. T. Penrose, *The Theory of the Growth of the Firm* (London: Macmillan, 1958).

[19]G. Edmondson and L. Cohn, "How Parmalat Went Sour," *Business Week*, January 12, 2004, 46–50; "Another Enron? Royal Dutch Shell," *Economist*, March 13, 2004, 71.

[20]O. E. Williamson, *The Economic Institutions of Capitalism* (New York: Free Press, 1985).

[21]Fama, "Agency Problems and the Theory of the Firm."

[22]S. Finkelstein and R. D'Aveni, "CEO Duality as a Double-Edged Sword," *Academy of Management Journal* 37 (1994): 1079–1108; B. R. Baliga and R. C. Moyer, "CEO Duality and Firm Performance," *Strategic Management Journal* 17 (1996): 41–53; M. L. Mace, *Directors: Myth and Reality* (Cambridge, Mass.: Harvard University Press, 1971); S. C. Vance, *Corporate Leadership: Boards of Directors and Strategy* (New York: McGraw-Hill, 1983).

[23]W. G. Lewellen, C. Eoderer, and A. Rosenfeld, "Merger Decisions and Executive Stock Ownership in Acquiring Firms," *Journal of Accounting and Economics* 7 (1985): 209–231.

[24]C. W. L. Hill and S. A. Snell, "External Control, Corporate Strategy, and Firm Performance," *Strategic Management Journal* 9 (1988): 577–590.

[25]The phenomenon of back dating stock options was uncovered by academic research, and then picked up by the SEC. See E. Lie, "On the Timing of CEO Stock

Option Awards," *Management Science* 51 (2005): 802–812.

26G. Colvin, "A Study in CEO Greed," *Fortune*, June 12, 2006, 53–55.

27J. P. Walsh and R. D. Kosnik, "Corporate Raiders and Their Disciplinary Role in the Market for Corporate Control," *Academy of Management Journal* 36 (1993): 671–700.

28R. S. Kaplan and D. P. Norton, "The Balanced Scorecard—Measures That Drive Performance," *Harvard Business Review* (January–February 1992): 71–79; Kaplan and Norton, *Strategy Maps* (Boston: Harvard Business School Press, 2004).

29R. S. Kaplan and D. P. Norton, "Using the Balanced Scorecard as a Strategic Management System," *Harvard Business Review* (January–February 1996): 75–85; Kaplan and Norton, *Strategy Maps*.

30R. S. Kaplan and D. P. Norton, "Putting the Balanced Scorecard to Work," *Harvard Business Review* (September–October 1993): 134–147; Kaplan and Norton, *Strategy Maps*.

31Kaplan and Norton, "The Balanced Scorecard," 72.

32Timet, "Boeing Settle Lawsuit," *Metal Center News* 41 (June 2001): 38–39.

33J. Kahn, "Ruse in Toyland: Chinese Workers Hidden Woe," *New York Times*, December 7, 2003, A1, A8.

34See N. King, "Halliburton Tells the Pentagon Workers Took Iraq Deal Kickbacks," *Wall Street Journal*, January 23, 2004, A1; Anonymous, "Whistleblowers Say Company Routinely Overcharged," *Reuters*, February 12, 2004; and R. Gold and J. R. Wilke, "Data Sought in Halliburton Inquiry," *Wall Street Journal*, February 5, 2004, A6.

35S. W. Gellerman, "Why Good Managers Make Bad Ethical Choices," *Ethics in Practice: Managing the Moral Corporation*, ed. K. R. Andrews (Harvard Business School Press, 1989).

36Ibid.

37Can be found on Unilever's Web site at http://www.unilever.com/aboutus/purposeandprinciples/.

38Taken from United Technologies Web site.

39Unilever Web site.

40"Money Well Spent: Corporate Parties," *The Economist*, November 1, 2003, 79. "Tyco Pair Sentencing Expected on September 19," *Wall Street Journal*, August 2, 2005, 1. "Off the Jail: Corporate Crime in America," *The Economist*, June 25, 2005, 81. N. Varchaver, "What's Ed Breen Thinking?" *Fortune*, March 20, 2006, 135–139.

Chapter 12

1http://www.lizclaiborne.com, 2009.

2R. Dodes, "Claiborne Seeks to Shed 16 Apparel Brands," http://www.businessweek.com, July 11, 2007.

3http://www.lizclaiborne.com, 2008.

4L. Smircich, "Concepts of Culture and Organizational Analysis," *Administrative Science Quarterly* 28 (1983): 339–358.

5G. R. Jones and J. M. George, "The Experience and Evolution of Trust: Implications for Cooperation and Teamwork," *Academy of Management Review* 3 (1998): 531–546.

6Ibid.

7J. R. Galbraith, *Designing Complex Organizations* (Reading, Mass.: Addison-Wesley, 1973).

8A. D. Chandler, *Strategy and Structure* (Cambridge, Mass.: MIT Press, 1962).

9The discussion draws heavily on Chandler, *Strategy and Structure* and B. R. Scott, *Stages of Corporate Development* (Cambridge, Mass.: Intercollegiate Clearing House, Harvard Business School, 1971).

10R. L. Daft, *Organizational Theory and Design*, 3rd ed. (St. Paul, Minn.: West, 1986), 215.

11J. Child, *Organization 9: A Guide for Managers and Administrators* (New York: Harper & Row, 1977), 52–70.

12G. R. Jones and J. Butler, "Costs, Revenues, and Business Level Strategy," *Academy of Management Review* 13 (1988): 202–213; G. R. Jones and C. W. L. Hill, "Transaction Cost Analysis of Strategy-Structure Choice," *Strategic Management Journal* 9 (1988): 159–172.

13G. R. Jones, *Organizational Theory, Design, and Change: Text and Cases* (Englewood Cliffs, N.J.: Prentice-Hall, 2005).

14P. Blau, "A Formal Theory of Differentiation in Organizations," *American Sociological Review* 35 (1970): 684–695.

15G. R. Jones, "Organization-Client Transactions and Organizational Governance Structures," *Academy of Management Journal* 30 (1987): 197–218.

16S. McCartney, "Airline Industry's Top-Ranked Woman Keeps Southwest's Small-Fry Spirit Alive," *Wall Street Journal* (November 30, 1995): B1; http://www.southwest.com (2005).

17P. R. Lawrence and J. Lorsch, *Organization and Environment* (Boston: Division of Research, Harvard Business School, 1967), 50–55.

18Galbraith, *Designing Complex Organizations*, Chapter 1; J. R. Galbraith and R. K. Kazanjian, *Strategy Implementation: Structure System and Process*, 2nd ed. (St. Paul, Minn.: West, 1986), chap. 7.

19R. Simmons, "Strategic Orientation and Top Management Attention to Control Systems," *Strategic Management Journal* 12 (1991): 49–62.

20R. Simmons, "How New Top Managers Use Control Systems as Levers of Strategic Renewal," *Strategic Management Journal* 15 (1994): 169–189.

21W. G. Ouchi, "The Transmission of Control through Organizational Hierarchy," *Academy of Management Journal* 21 (1978): 173–192; W. H. Newman, *Constructive Control* (Englewood Cliffs, N.J.: Prentice-Hall, 1975).

22E. Flamholtz, "Organizational Control Systems as a Managerial Tool," *California Management Review* (Winter 1979): 50–58.

23O. E. Williamson, *Markets and Hierarchies: Analysis and Antitrust Implications* (New York: Free Press, 1975); W. G. Ouchi, "Markets, Bureaucracies, and Clans," *Administrative Science Quarterly* 25 (1980): 129–141.

24H. Mintzberg, *The Structuring of Organizations* (Englewood Cliffs, N.J.: Prentice-Hall, 1979), 5–9.

25http://www.cypress.com, press release, 1998; http://www.cypress.com, press release, (2009).

26E. E. Lawler III, *Motivation in Work Organizations* (Monterey, Calif.: Brooks/Cole, 1973); Galbraith and Kazanjian, *Strategy Implementation*, chap. 6.

[27]Smircich, "Concepts of Culture and Organizational Analysis."

[28]http://www.microsoft.com, 2009.

[29]Ouchi, "Markets, Bureaucracies, and Clans," 130.

[30]Jones, *Organizational Theory, Design, and Change.*

[31]J. Van Maanen and E. H. Schein, "Towards a Theory of Organizational Socialization," in B. M. Staw (ed.), *Research in Organizational Behavior* (Greenwich, Conn.: JAI Press, 1979), 1, 209–264.

[32]G. R. Jones, "Socialization Tactics, Self-Efficacy, and Newcomers' Adjustments to Organizations," *Academy of Management Journal* 29 (1986): 262–279.

[33]J. P. Kotter and J. L. Heskett, *Corporate Culture and Performance.*

[34]T. J. Peters and R. H. Waterman, *In Search of Excellence: Lessons from America's Best-Run Companies* (New York: Harper & Row, 1982).

[35]G. Hamel and C. K. Prahalad, "Strategic Intent," *Harvard Business Review* (May–June 1989): 64.

[36]Galbraith and Kazanjian, *Strategy Implementation*; Child, *Organization*; R. Duncan, "What Is the Right Organization Structure?" *Organizational Dynamics* (Winter 1979): 59–80.

[37]J. Pettet, "Walmart Yesterday and Today," *Discount Merchandiser* (December 1995): 66–67; M. Reid, "Stores of Value," *Economist* (March 4, 1995): ss5–ss7; M. Troy, "The Culture Remains the Constant," *Discount Store News* (June 8, 1998): 95–98; http://www.walmart.com, 2009.

[38]W. G. Ouchi, "The Relationship between Organizational Structure and Organizational Control," *Administrative Science Quarterly* 22 (1977): 95–113.

[39]R. Bunderi, "Intel Researchers Aim to Think Big While Staying Close to Development," *Research-Technology Management* (March–April 1998): 3–4.

[40]K. M. Eisenhardt, "Control: Organizational and Economic Approaches," *Management Science* 16 (1985): 134–148.

[41]Williamson, *Markets and Hierarchies.*

[42]P. R. Lawrence and J. W. Lorsch, *Organization and Environment.* (Boston: Graduate School of Business Administration, Harvard University, 1967).

[43]M. E. Porter, *Competitive Strategy: Techniques for Analyzing Industries and Competitors* (New York: Free Press, 1980); D. Miller, "Configurations of Strategy and Structure," *Strategic Management Journal* 7 (1986): 233–249.

[44]D. Miller and P. H. Freisen, *Organizations: A Quantum View* (Englewood Cliffs, N.J.: Prentice-Hall, 1984).

[45]J. Woodward, *Industrial Organization: Theory and Practice* (London: Oxford University Press, 1965); Lawrence and Lorsch, *Organization and Environment.*

[46]R. E. White, "Generic Business Strategies, Organizational Context and Performance: An Empirical Investigation," *Strategic Management Journal* 7 (1986): 217–231.

[47]Porter, *Competitive Strategy*; Miller, "Configurations of Strategy and Structure."

[48]E. Deal and A. A. Kennedy, *Corporate Cultures* (Reading, Mass.: Addison-Wesley, 1985); "Corporate Culture," *Business Week*, October 27, 1980, 148–160.

[49]S. M. Davis and R. R. Lawrence, *Matrix* (Reading, Mass.: Addison-Wesley, 1977); J. R. Galbraith, "Matrix Organization Designs: How to Combine Functional and Project Forms," *Business Horizons* 14 (1971): 29–40.

[50]Duncan, "What Is the Right Organizational Structure?"; Davis and Lawrence, *Matrix.*

[51]D. Miller, "Configurations of Strategy and Structure," in R. E. Miles and C. C. Snow (eds.), *Organizational Strategy, Structure, and Process* (New York: McGraw-Hill, 1978).

[52]G. D. Bruton, J. K. Keels, and C. L. Shook, "Downsizing the Firm: Answering the Strategic Questions," *Academy of Management Executive* (May 1996): 38–45.

[53]M. Hammer and J. Champy, *Reengineering the Corporation* (New York: HarperCollins, 1993).

[54]http://www.dell.com, 2009.

[55]G. McWilliams, "Dell Looks for Ways to Rekindle the Fire It Had as an Upstart," *Wall Street Journal* (August 31, 2000): A.1, A.8; "Dell Hopes to Lead Firm out of Desert," *Houston Chronicle* (September 3, 2000): 4D

[56]http://www.dell.com, 2009.

[57]G. Rivlin, "He Naps. He Sings. And He Isn't Michael Dell," *New York Times* (September 11, 2005): 31.

Chapter 13

[1]http://www.avon.com, 2009.

[2]N. Byrnes, "Avon: More Than Just Cosmetic Changes," http://www.businessweek.com, March 12, 2007.

[3]http://www.avon.com, 2009.

[4]A. D. Chandler, *Strategy and Structure* (Cambridge, Mass.: MIT Press, 1962); O. E. Williamson, *Markets and Hierarchies* (New York: Free Press, 1975); L. Wrigley, "Divisional Autonomy and Diversification" (PhD Diss., Harvard Business School, 1970).

[5]R. P. Rumelt, *Strategy, Structure, and Economic Performance* (Boston: Division of Research, Harvard Business School, 1974); B. R. Scott, *Stages of Corporate Development* (Cambridge, Mass.: Intercollegiate Clearing House, Harvard Business School, 1971); Williamson, *Markets and Hierarchies.*

[6]A. P. Sloan, *My Years at General Motors* (Garden City, N.Y.: Doubleday, 1946); A. Taylor III, "Can GM Remodel Itself?" *Fortune*, January 13, 1992, 26–34; W. Hampton and J. Norman, "General Motors: What Went Wrong?" *Business Week*, March 16, 1987, 102–110; http://www.gm.com (2002). The quotations are on 46 and 50 in Sloan, *My Years at General Motors.*

[7]The discussion draws on each of the sources cited in endnotes 20–27 and on G. R. Jones and C. W. L. Hill, "Transaction Cost Analysis of Strategy-Structure Choice," *Strategic Management Journal* 9 (1988): 159–172.

[8]H. O. Armour and D. J. Teece, "Organizational Structure and Economic Performance: A Test of the Multidivisional Hypothesis," *Bell Journal of Economics* 9 (1978): 106–122.

[9]Sloan, *My Years at General Motors.*

[10]Jones and Hill, "Transaction Cost Analysis of Strategy-Structure Choice," *Strategic Management Journal* 9 (1988): 159–172.

[11]Ibid.

[12]R. A. D'Aveni and D. J. Ravenscraft, "Economies of Integration versus Bureaucracy Costs: Does Vertical Integration Improve Performance?" *Academy of Management Journal* 5 (1994): 1167–1206.

[13]P. R. Lawrence and J. Lorsch, *Organization and Environment* (Boston: Division of Research, Harvard Business School, 1967); J. R. Galbraith, *Designing Complex Organizations* (Reading, Mass.: Addison-Wesley, 1973); M. Porter, *Competitive Advantage: Creating and Sustaining Superior Performance* (New York: Free Press, 1985).

[14]P. R. Nayyar, "Performance Effects of Information Asymmetry and Economies of Scope in Diversified Service Firm," *Academy of Management Journal* 36 (1993): 28–57.

[15]L. R. Gomez-Mejia, "Structure and Process of Diversification, Compensation Strategy, and Performance," *Strategic Management Journal* 13 (1992): 381–397.

[16]J. Stopford and L. Wells, *Managing the Multinational Enterprise* (London: Longman, 1972).

[17]R. A. Burgelman, "Managing the New Venture Division: Research Findings and the Implications for Strategic Management," *Strategic Management Journal* 6 (1985): 39–54.

[18]Burgelman, "Managing the New Venture Division."

[19]R. A. Burgelman, "Corporate Entrepreneurship and Strategic Management: Insights from a Process Study," *Management Science* 29 (1983): 1349–1364.

[20]G. R. Jones, "Towards a Positive Interpretation of Transaction Cost Theory: The Central Role of Entrepreneurship and Trust," in M. Hitt, R. E. Freeman, and J. S. Harrison (eds.), *Handbook of Strategic Management* (London: Blackwell, 2001), 208–228.

[21]M. Prendergast, "Is Coke Turning into a Mickey Mouse Outfit?" *Wall Street Journal*, March 5, 2001, A22.

[22]M. S. Salter and W. A. Weinhold, *Diversification through Acquisition* (New York: Free Press, 1979).

[23]F. T. Paine and D. J. Power, "Merger Strategy: An Examination of Drucker's Five Rules for Successful Acquisitions," *Strategic Management Journal* 5 (1984): 99–110.

[24]H. Singh and C. A. Montgomery, "Corporate Acquisitions and Economic Performance" (unpublished manuscript, 1984).

[25]B. Worthen, "Nestlé's ERP Odyssey," *CIO* (May 15, 2002): 1–5.

[26]G. D. Bruton, B. M. Oviatt, and M. A. White, "Performance of Acquisitions of Distressed Firms," *Academy of Management Journal* 4 (1994): 972–989.

[27]T. Dewett and G. R. Jones, "The Role of Information Technology in the Organization: A Review, Model, and Assessment," *Journal of Management* 27 (2001): 313–346.

[28]M. E. Porter, *Competitive Strategy* (New York: Free Press, 1980).

[29]M. Hammer and J. Champy, *Reengineering the Corporation* (New York: Harper Collins, 1993).

[30]G. Hamel and C. K. Prahalad, "*Competing for the Future* (Boston: Harvard Business School Press, 1994).

[31]Ibid.

[32]http://www.accenture.com

[33]B. Koenig, "Ford Reorganizes Executives under New Chief Mulally," http://www.bloomberg.com (accessed December 14, 2006).

[34]http://www.ford.com, 2009.

[35]Ibid.

INDEX